Discovering PSYCHOLOGY

Discovering PSYCHOLOGY

FIFTH EDITION

Don H. Hockenbury
Tulsa Community College

Sandra E. Hockenbury

Worth Publishers

Senior Publisher: Catherine Woods
Executive Editor: Jessica Bayne
Marketing Manager: Amy Shefferd
Development Editor: Marna Miller
Media Editor: Christine Burak
Photo Editor: Christine Buese
Photo Researchers: Donna Ranieri
Art Director: Babs Reingold
Interior Designer: Lissi Sigillo
Layout Designer: Lee McKevitt
Cover Designer: Lyndall Culbertson
Associate Managing Editor: Tracey Kuehn
Project Editors: Mike Ederer, Anthony Calcara
Illustration Coordinator: Bill Page, Eleanor Jaekel
Illustrations: Graphic World, Todd Buck, Kim Martens, Don Stewart
Production Manager: Barbara Seixas
Composition: Graphic World
Printing and Binding: RR Donnelley
Cover Painting: Ken Orvidas

Library of Congress Control Number: 2009940262

ISBN-13: 978-1-4292-1650-0 (paperback)
ISBN-10: 1-4292-1650-6 (paperback)

ISBN-13: 978-1-4292-3202-9 (hardcover)
ISBN-10: 1-4292-3202-1 (hardcover)

Printed in the United States of America

First printing 2010

Worth Publishers
41 Madison Avenue
New York, NY 10010
www.worthpublishers.com

To the loving memories of our mothers,

Fern and **Janet**

ABOUT THE AUTHORS

Don and Sandy Hockenbury are the authors of *Psychology* and *Discovering Psychology*. As an author team, they bring their unique talents and abilities to the teaching of introductory psychology.

Don H. Hockenbury is Associate Professor of Psychology at Tulsa Community College. Don received his B.S. in psychology and his M.A. in clinical psychology from the University of Tulsa. Before he began his teaching career, he worked in psychiatric facilities and in private practice. With over 25 years experience teaching psychology, Don is a recipient of the Tulsa Community College Award for Teaching Excellence. Although he enjoys the unique challenges of teaching online, the classroom setting is still his favorite forum for teaching students about the science and personal relevance of psychology. Before co-authoring *Psychology* and *Discovering Psychology,* Don was a reviewer and supplements author for several psychology textbooks.

Don's favorite research interests include biopsychology, sleep and dreaming, memory, psychological disorders, and the history of psychology. Don belongs to several professional organizations, including the Association of Psychological Science (APS), the American Psychological Association (APA), the Society of Applied Research in Memory and Cognition (SARMAC), and the American Academy of Sleep Medicine (AASM).

Sandra E. Hockenbury is a science writer who specializes in psychology. Sandy received her B.A. from Shimer College and her M.A. from the University of Chicago, where she was also a Research Associate at the Institute of Social and Behavioral Pathology. Prior to co-authoring *Psychology* and *Discovering Psychology,* Sandy worked for several years as a psychology editor in both academic and college textbook publishing. Sandy has also taught as an adjunct faculty member at Tulsa Community College.

Sandy's areas of interest include positive psychology, animal cognition and behavior, cultural psychology, mind-body interaction, and the intersection of Buddhist philosophy, neuroscience, and psychology. She is a member of the Association of Psychological Science (APS) and the American Association for the Advancement of Science (AAAS).

Don and Sandy's daughter, Laura, is a college sophomore who, like her parents, has wide-ranging interests, including geology, psychology, religion, and neuroscience. Laura also plays classical and improvisational piano, performs comedy sketches and improv, and is an enthusiastic ultimate Frisbee player.

BRIEF CONTENTS

CONTENTS

CHAPTER 1
Introduction and Research Methods

CHAPTER 2
Neuroscience and Behavior

CHAPTER 3
Sensation and Perception

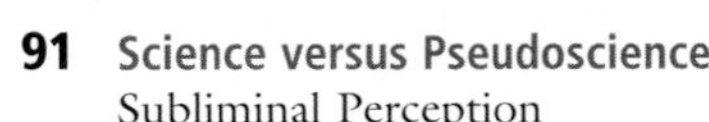

CHAPTER 4
Consciousness and Its Variations

CHAPTER 5
Learning

CHAPTER 6
Memory

CHAPTER 7
Thinking, Language, and Intelligence

CHAPTER 8
Motivation and Emotion

CHAPTER 9
Lifespan Development

CHAPTER 10
Personality

CHAPTER 11
Social Psychology

CHAPTER 12
Stress, Health, and Coping

CHAPTER 13
Psychological Disorders

CHAPTER 14
Therapies

APPENDIX A
Statistics: Understanding Data

APPENDIX B
Industrial/Organizational Psychology

APPENDIX C
APA Goals and Outcomes

TO THE INSTRUCTOR

Welcome to the fifth edition of *Discovering Psychology*! For those of you who are using *Discovering Psychology* for the first time, this faculty preface will help orient you to the many features of our text, its supplements, and its media package. If you want to get the most out of our book and teaching package, reading this preface will be well worth your time. To those of you who used a previous edition of *Discovering Psychology*, thank you for helping make our text a success! Rest assured that, once again, we have taken several steps to help make your transition to the new edition as smooth and easy as possible. As we've done previously, we have assembled a complete, detailed, and page-referenced list of changes in the new edition. You can find that list and other helpful materials in the instructor's section of the *Discovering Psychology*, Fifth Edition, companion Web site.

We've been gratified by the enthusiastic response to the four previous editions of *Discovering Psychology*. We've especially enjoyed the e-mails we've received from students who felt that our book was speaking directly to them. Students and faculty alike told us how much they appreciated *Discovering Psychology's* distinctive voice, its inviting learning environment, the engaging writing style, and the clarity of its explanations—qualities we've maintained in the fifth edition. It's hard to believe, but we've spent the last 20 years of our lives researching and writing five editions of *Discovering Psychology* and its bigger sibling, *Psychology*. Watching the evolution of new research over the past two decades has only further solidified our conviction that psychology is the most exciting science that exists.

Before we wrote the first word of the first edition, we had a clear vision for this book: combine the scientific authority of psychology with a narrative that engages students and relates to their lives. Drawing from decades (yes, it really has been decades) of teaching experience, we wrote a book that weaves cutting-edge psychological science with real-life stories that draw students of all kinds into the narrative.

More so than any other science, psychology speaks to students' lives. It provides a wealth of practical insights about behavior and mental processes. Throughout the text, we strive to communicate the excitement of scientific discovery and the relevance of psychological findings to students. It is a labor of love, not only for the sake of our discipline, but also for those wonderful "aha!" moments when some everyday behavior suddenly makes sense to a student because it's seen in a new light.

This edition of *Discovering Psychology* reflects our continued commitment to the goals that have guided us as teachers and authors. Once again, we invite you to explore every page of the new edition of *Discovering Psychology*, so you can see firsthand how we:

- Communicate both the scientific rigor and personal relevance of psychology
- Clearly explain psychological concepts and how they are linked
- Show how classic psychological studies help set the stage for today's research
- Personalize historical figures in psychology with interesting biographical details
- Encourage and model critical and scientific thinking
- Present controversial topics in an impartial and even-handed fashion
- Expand student awareness of cultural and gender influences
- Create a student-friendly, personal learning environment
- Actively engage diverse students, including adult learners
- Provide an effective pedagogical system that helps students develop more effective learning strategies.

What Do Psychologists Study? Conformity and confrontation, friendliness and fear, assertiveness and aggression. Private thoughts, public behavior. Optimism and hope, pessimism and distress. These are just a few of the wide range of topics studied in *psychology,* the science of behavior and mental processes. But whether psychologists study the behavior of a single brain cell or the behavior of a crowd of people, they rely on the scientific method to guide their investigations.

What's New in the Fifth Edition

We began the revision process with the thoughtful recommendations and feedback we received from hundreds of faculty using the text, from reviewers, and from colleagues. We also had face-to-face dialogues with our own students as well as groups of students across the country. After carefully evaluating the feedback from faculty and students, we worked, fueled at times by too many cups of coffee, to create the book you now have in your hands.

This fifth edition reflects an exhaustive updating with new coverage of the latest research, a stunning new design and artwork, and some exciting new media options. We have pored over dozens of journals and clicked through thousands of Web sites to learn about the latest in psychological science. As a result, this new edition features hundreds of new references, completely revamped sections on research methods (Chapter 1) and sleep and dreaming (Chapter 4), and dramatically revised chapters on neuroscience and behavior (Chapter 2), sensation and perception (Chapter 3), memory (Chapter 6), cognitive psychology (Chapter 7), lifespan development (Chapter 9), and psychological disorders (Chapter 13). In addition, we have significantly updated coverage of neuroscience and expanded our coverage of culture and diversity throughout.

The Latest Psychological Science

Faculty have told us how much they appreciate our efforts to present interesting and current psychology research to students. Keeping up with our incredibly diverse and productive discipline is an ongoing process. Just so you know, we currently subscribe to 19 print and 6 electronic journals, and we regularly monitor multiple psychology, neuroscience, and life science Web sites. And, we both enjoy thumbing through past and current issues of the *New Yorker* in search of just the right cartoon to enliven a new discussion or topic. The stacks of unshelved journals in our home offices can sometimes reach truly frightening heights. But scanning journals, newsletters, and science magazines like *New Scientist* and *Discover* often leads us to fascinating new research studies that ultimately find their way into our text. Examples range from the neuroscience of runner's high, to sleep violence, to controversies about measuring intelligence in autism.

Meditation in Different Cultures Meditation is an important part of many cultures. Tai chi is a form of meditation that involves a structured series of slow, smooth movements. During tai chi, you focus on the present, your movements, and your breathing. Sometimes described as "meditation in motion," tai chi has existed for over 2,000 years. Like this group in Hanoi, Vietnam, many people throughout Asia begin their day with tai chi, often meeting in parks and other public places.

As of our last count, there are over 900 new references in the fifth edition of *Discovering Psychology*, more than half of which are from 2007, 2008, or 2009. These new citations reflect the many new and updated topics and discussions in the fifth edition of *Discovering Psychology*. From positive psychology to the latest discoveries about mirror neurons or the role of sleep in learning, our goal is to present students with understandable explanations of psychological science. Later in this preface, you'll find a list of the updates by chapter.

New Design, New Photos, New Art, and New End-of-Chapter Concept Reviews

Created with today's media-savvy students in mind, the new look of *Discovering Psychology* showcases the book's cutting-edge content and student-friendly style. Carefully chosen photographs—more than 60 percent of them new—apply psychological concepts and research to real-world situations. Accompanied by information-rich captions that expand upon the text, vivid and diverse photographs help make psychology concepts come alive, demonstrating psychology's relevance to today's students.

Award-winning illustrator Todd Buck brings a dynamic, crisp style to the fifth edition's art and graphics. From nerve cells to body processes to experimental models, Todd has created incredibly clear, engaging illustrations that help explain psychology concepts.

The new visual end-of-chapter concept maps show the relationships among concepts and help students consolidate memory of new information. In combination with the new design and chapter-opening artwork, our new photo and art program gives the fifth edition a fresh, contemporary look that will appeal to today's students.

New Connections to the American Psychological Association's Standards and Outcomes

We understand that across the country, more faculty and departments are creating uniform standards for the psychology major and the introductory psychology course. Because we want to support faculty's efforts on this front, the fifth edition offers a new appendix on the APA's Standards and Outcomes. In addition, the revised, fifth edition test bank ties questions directly to the APA Standards.

State-of-the-Art Media Options

There has been a revolution in the educational use of the Web over the past several years. For the fifth edition, our book is accompanied by the latest in educational technology that combines interactive, visually exciting media with high-quality assessment. This edition is accompanied by a *Psychology Portal,* an eBook, a Video Tool Kit, and an Online Study Center. For more information about these supplements, please turn to the heading "The Teaching Package: Media Supplements," or you can get more information by going to our companion Web site at: www.worthpublishers.com/hockenbury.

Major Chapter Revisions

As you page through our new edition, you will encounter new examples, boxes, photos, and illustrations in every chapter. Below are highlights of some of the most significant changes:

Chapter 1, Introduction and Research Methods

- New Prologue, "Miracle Magnets?" on magnet therapy introduces the topics of pseudoscience, placebo effect, and psychology's reliance on empirical evidence
- Coverage added of Francis C. Sumner (now a boldfaced key person) and Kenneth Bancroft Clark as influential figures in the history of psychology
- Charles Darwin and evolution is covered in history of psychology section, stressing Darwin's influence on the development of psychology; expanded coverage of evolutionary psychology
- Positive psychology is boldfaced and discussed as a formal perspective in psychology
- Revised and updated box, "What Is Cross-Cultural Psychology?"
- Forensic psychology, rehabilitation psychology, sports psychology, military psychology, and counseling psychology add to the expanded list of specialties
- New data on specialty areas and employment settings for psychologists
- New Science versus Pseudoscience Box: "What is a Pseudoscience?"
- New section on the experimental method includes expanded discussion of a gingko biloba experiment testing the placebo effect, and features Crum & Langer's 2007 research on exercise and the placebo effect

- New examples throughout the research methods section
- Focus on Neuroscience explaining brain imaging techniques used in psychology research appears in Methods section, emphasizing the increasing importance of brain imaging in many areas of psychology research
- Extended discussion of a natural experiment
- Updated, reorganized section, Enhancing Well-Being with Psychology: "Psychology and the Media: Becoming an Informed Consumer"
- Updated box, "What Is Critical Thinking?" and revised definition of critical thinking

Chapter 2, Neuroscience and Behavior

- Updated discussion of glial cells
- Expanded discussion of neurotransmitters
- New Focus on Neuroscience, "Is Runner's High an Endorphin Rush?," presents 2008 research providing the first direct evidence for an association between "runner's high" and endorphin release in the human brain
- New artwork: Breastfeeding example of interaction among the nervous system, the endocrine system, and behavior
- The newly revised and reorganized section on plasticity and neurogenesis, "The Dynamic Brain," opens the discussion on the brain, emphasizing the importance of the theme of plasticity in understanding brain functioning
- Focus on Neuroscience, "Juggling and Plasticity," updated with 2008 research on the effects of juggling on brain structures in older adults
- Updated research on handedness in non-human primates
- New Critical Thinking box, "'His' and 'Her' Brains?" provides a thoughtful look at contemporary research on gender differences in brain structure and functioning
- Expanded and updated box, "Brain Myths" looks at left-brain/right-brain myths, handedness, and the 10% myth
- Updated and expanded Enhancing Well-Being with Psychology, "Maximizing Your Brain's Potential" presents the latest research on neuroplasticity, and the effects of exercise and enriched environments on brain structure.

Experiencing the World Through Our Senses Imagine biting into a crisp, red apple. All your senses are involved in your experience—vision, smell, taste, hearing, and touch. Although we're accustomed to thinking of our different senses as being quite distinct, all forms of sensation involve the stimulation of specialized cells called sensory receptors.

Chapter 3, Sensation and Perception

- Updated, revised Science versus Pseudoscience box "Subliminal Perception" features new research on the effects of subliminal odors on social judgments and a new Israeli study on the impact of subliminal stimuli on political attitudes
- New section on pitch perception discusses frequency and place theory
- New photos highlighting cross-species comparisons of sensory abilities, including hearing in reptiles and amphibians and olfaction in humans
- New Culture and Human Behavior box, "Ways of Seeing" features new research on cultural differences in perception and how these differences influence brain function
- Added coverage of psychological effects on sensation and perception
- Revised section presenting new research on the human tendency to see faces in ambiguous stimuli
- Streamlined discussion of culture and visual illusions
- Updated coverage of biofeedback and acupuncture as strategies for controlling pain
- Many new visual examples throughout

Chapter 4, Consciousness and Its Variations

- New Prologue, "Even in Good Men," tells the story of Scott Falater, who claimed no memory of murdering his wife during a sleepwalking episode.
- Revised opening discussion on historical interest in consciousness
- Completely rewritten and updated section, "Circadian Rhythms and Sunlight: The 24.2 Hour Day"
- New photo and discussion of the prenatal emergence of circadian rhythms
- Revised and updated In Focus box, "What You Really Want to Know About Sleep," presents the latest research on causes, possible purposes, and contagion effect of yawning; sleep talking; sleep paralysis; and the potential dangers of waking a sleepwalker
- New Focus on Neuroscience, "The Sleep-Deprived Emotional Brain"
- "Changing Patterns of Sleep Over the Lifespan" is completely rewritten with recent research and new figure
- New section, "Do We Need to Sleep?" explores the physical and psychological impact of sleep restriction and sleep deprivation
- Revised and rewritten section, "Dreams and Mental Activity During Sleep," features the latest research on sleep and memory consolidation, common dream themes and imagery, gender differences in dream content, nightmares, and significance of dreams
- New Focus on Neuroscience, "The Dreaming Brain: Turning REM On and Off" discusses brain and neurotransmitter patterns that produce the 90-minute REM cycles
- Reorganized and thoroughly updated sleep disorders section contains new discussions contrasting dyssomnias and parasomnias, and adds new coverage of sleep-related eating disorder and sleepsex
- New photo and caption discussing the role of the popular sleeping medication Ambien in precipitating parasomnia episodes of sleep eating and sleep driving
- Revised and updated discussion of hypnosis includes hypnosis susceptibility, sensory and perceptual changes, using hypnosis for habit control
- Revised and updated Critical Thinking box, "Is Hypnosis a Special State of Consciousness?"
- Updated discussion on the role of racial and genetic differences influencing reduced susceptibility to alcohol abuse
- Revised and updated Focus on Neuroscience box, "The Addicted Brain: Diminishing Rewards"
- New photo discussion using Michael Jackson's death to illustrate that the majority of unintentional drug overdoses are caused by prescription drugs, not illicit drugs
- New section on inhalants
- Updated discussion and research on alcohol, cocaine, caffeine, nicotine, marijuana, and ecstasy (MDMA)
- New photo discussion on the history of medical marijuana and its use in contemporary medicine
- New Enhancing Well-Being with Psychology section describes how to use stimulus control therapy to treat insomnia and specific strategies to prevent sleep problems

Chapter 5, Learning

- New section on higher order conditioning
- New photo illustrations of conditioned emotional reactions, primary and secondary reinforcers, accidental reinforcement, and learned helplessness

- Updated In Focus box, "Evolution, Biological Preparedness, and Conditioned Fears: What Gives You the Creeps?"
- Updated research on learned helplessness in sports
- Added biographical information on Marian and Keller Breland, with historical photo and poster
- New Focus on Neuroscience, "Mirror Neurons: Imitation in the Brain?" presents cutting-edge research on mirror neurons in primates and humans
- Expanded and updated section on observational learning
- New section on observational learning in nonhuman animals
- Completely revised and updated Critical Thinking box, "Does Exposure to Media Violence *Cause* Aggressive Behavior?" introduces 2009 research
- Updated Enhancing Well-Being with Psychology, "Using Learning Principles to Improve Self-Control"

Chapter 6, Memory

- Redrawn figure that more clearly illustrates classic Sperling sensory memory experiment
- New coverage of recent research showing that short-term memory is probably limited to *four plus or minus one* items rather than the classic *seven plus or minus two* items
- Revised discussion of working memory
- Revised and updated Culture and Human Behavior box, "Culture's Effect on Earliest Memories"
- Revised demonstration of retrieval cues
- Updated and rewritten In Focus box, "Déjà Vu Experiences: An Illusion of Memory?"
- New photo and caption discussion of TOT experiences in deaf people
- Expanded discussion of common retrieval glitches
- Discussion of flashbulb memories updated with recent research
- New photo example and discussion of how digitally altered photographs can contribute to source confusion and false memories
- Fully revised section on anterograde amnesia
- New real-world examples of the misinformation effect and eyewitness identification
- Streamlined Focus on Neuroscience, "Assembling Memories"
- New photo of the real H. M. (Henry Molaison) with a discussion of how his life provided numerous scientific insights to memory processes
- Completely revised and updated coverage of dementia and Alzheimer's disease, including discussion of family members providing unpaid care
- Expanded and updated Enhancing Well-Being with Psychology, "Superpower Memory in Minutes per Day!"

Chapter 7, Thinking, Language, and Intelligence

- New Prologue, "The Movie Moment," tells the story of Tom, a bright, self-aware teenager with Asperger Syndrome.
- New photo examples of atypical mammals that are hard to categorize
- New cartoon example of the use of exemplars and concepts in humor
- Updated research on problem-solving, mental set, decision-making, and intuition

- New Critical Thinking box, "Neurodiversity and the Autism Spectrum Disorders," covers the contemporary debate about autism and diversity in brain function and includes new research on intelligence in autism
- New research on the linguistic relativity hypothesis
- Photos illustrating the birth of new sign languages in Nicaragua and a Bedouin village in southern Israel
- Updated research on animal language and cognition
- New photo examples of Howard Gardner's multiple intelligences
- Expanded Culture and Human Behavior box, "Performing with a Threat in the Air" includes many new studies on stereotype threat and introduces its newly defined counterpart, *stereotype lift*
- Updated and revised Enhancing Well-Being with Psychology section, "A Workshop on Creativity"

Chapter 8, Motivation and Emotion

- Section on eating disorders has been moved to Chapter 13, Psychological Disorders
- New cross-cultural research on achievement motivation in Olympic athletes
- The latest on psychological factors that trigger eating
- New introductory section, "Excess Weight and Obesity," includes updated statistics
- New research on the role played by genetics in obesity
- Revised Focus on Neuroscience box, "Dopamine Receptors and Obesity," tracks research suggesting that compulsive eating might compensate for reduced dopamine function by stimulating the brain's reward system
- Reorganized section on human sexuality
- Revised discussion of sexual orientation highlights new studies on the influence of genetic and environmental effects, including the "older brother" effect, and the association of gay, lesbian, and bisexual orientation with cross-gender behavior in childhood
- Updated research on culture and achievement motivation
- New Focus on Neuroscience box, "Do Different Emotions Activate Different Brain Areas?," links emotion to specific brain activity and describes research that shows sensory signals preceding felt emotion
- Revised Critical Thinking box on emotion in nonhuman animals
- Revised material on cognitive theories of emotion introduces the cognitive appraisal theory

Chapter 9, Lifespan Development

- New Prologue, "Future Plans"
- Updated and completely revised section "Genetic Contributions to Your Life Story" includes new material on gene expression, gene-environment interaction, and the new field of epigenetics
- Reorganized discussion of prenatal development includes new coverage of prenatal brain development
- Culture and Human Behavior box, "The Effects of Child Care on Attachment and Development," includes updated research and national standards for quality care
- New section, "The Development of Moral Reasoning," explains Lawrence Kohlberg's classic theory of moral development and critiques Carol Gilligan's approach to moral development; contemporary research on moral development and cross-cultural examples are also included in this new discussion.

- Updated research on adult development and aging, including the latest statistics on the changing structure of U.S. households

Chapter 10, Personality

- Many new photo examples, including super-ego, sublimation, and self-efficacy
- New section on the Myers-Briggs Type Indicator test, its uses and limitations
- New artwork depicting Freud's classic iceberg analogy of personality

Chapter 11, Social Psychology

- New coverage of evolutionary social psychology, social cognitive neuroscience, and implicit attitudes testing
- Revised and updated discussion of person perception
- New photo example using abduction of Shawn Hornbeck to illustrate blaming the victim bias
- New photo example using financial swindler Bernie Madoff to illustrate role of implicit personality theory in deceiving others
- Fully revised section on social categorization now includes implicit and explicit cognition as bolded terms
- Updated and expanded Focus on Neuroscience describes how the brain's rewards system favors physically attractive people
- Revised discussion of attribution adds hindsight bias as new bolded term

Chapter 12, Stress, Health, and Coping

- Updated research documenting the continuing effects of stress following 9/11
- New figure depicting the role of appraisal in stress and coping
- New photo example of how major life events can create daily hassles
- New table listing examples of daily hassles, including specific examples of hassles faced by college students and by children dealing with the stress of adapting to a new culture
- Expanded section on social and cultural sources of stress, with new research on racism as a particularly potent stressor
- New research on the health benefits of diversity in social support
- New photo examples of coping with stress, including a new photo illustration of finding meaning in tragedy and effects of culture on coping
- Enhancing Well-Being with Psychology section, "Minimizing the Effects of Stress," includes a new section on mindfulness meditation and instructions for practicing a simple mindfulness of breathing meditation

Chapter 13, Psychological Disorders

- New data on the prevalence and incidence of psychological disorders in the United States
- Updated coverage of DSM-IV-TR offers a history of the manual, including critiques
- Expanded attention to comorbidity, including updated results from the replication of the National Comorbidity Survey (NCS-R)
- New section on eating disorders, with updated research and new photo examples
- Current research on incidence of post-traumatic stress disorder in U.S. military who have served in Iraq and Afghanistan and on the long-term effects of exposure to terrorist attacks
- Updated information on the personality disorders

- Expanded discussion of borderline personality disorder, with updated statistics and new coverage of Marsha Linehan's biosocial developmental theory
- Updated research on genetic factors in schizophrenia, including 2009 research that identified complex genetic patterns associated with schizophrenia and bipolar disorder
- New photo illustrations of people who have been diagnosed with panic disorder (Jeff Tweedy), post-traumatic stress disorder, obsessive-compulsive disorder (Howard Hughes), major depression (Kurt Cobain, Sheryl Crow), bipolar disorder (Carrie Fisher), anorexia, schizophrenia, dissociative fugue, and multiple personality disorder
- Many new examples throughout chapter

Chapter 14, Therapies

- Added Licensed Professional Counselor to list of mental health professionals
- Updated information on the status of prescription privileges for psychologists, including new photo showing a licensed prescribing psychologist
- Updated research on interpersonal therapy, humanistic therapy, and motivational interviewing
- New extended example of desensitization combined with observational learning to treat flying phobia
- Update on virtual reality therapy and its successful use in treating PTSD in Iraq and Afghanistan war vets; new photo showing its use with current equipment
- Revised and updated discussion of token economies
- Updated research on the use and principles of contingency management therapy
- New photos of Sigmund Freud, Carl Rogers, Albert Ellis, and Aaron Beck
- New discussion of integrative psychotherapy
- Updated research casting doubt on claims that second-generation antipsychotic medications are more effective than the traditional first-generation medications
- New data on the use of antidepressants in the U.S. and research that questions claims for their effectiveness
- Expanded and updated coverage of electroconvulsive therapy, plus new coverage of transcranial magnetic stimulation, vagus nerve stimulation, and deep brain stimulation

Chimpanzee Culture: Observational Learning in the Wild Chimpanzee tribes in the wild develop their own unique "cultures" or behavioral differences in tool use, foraging skills, and even courtship rituals (Hopper & others, 2007). Apparently, these distinct behavior patterns are acquired and transmitted through observational learning (Whiten, 2009). For example, after an individual chimp learned a new food-gathering technique, the rest of its group acquired the new skill within a few days. In turn, the newly acquired skill spread to other chimpanzee groups who could observe the new behavior (Whiten & others, 2007). These chimps in the Edinburgh Zoo are learning how to use a tool to extract food – one of the tasks that Andrew Whiten (2009) has used to study observational learning and the development of unique behavioral traditions among chimpanzee tribes.

Appendix A, Statistics: Understanding Data

- Expanded discussion of inferential statistics includes Type I error and Type II error

Appendix B, Industrial/Organizational Psychology

- Fully revised and updated
- New co-author (Claudia Cochran, El Paso Community College) brings a fresh perspective
- Expanded discussion of theories of leadership, workforce diversity, work-life balance, and job satisfaction
- Two new boxes present high-interest, topical themes

Appendix C, APA Goals and Outcomes

- New to this edition

Features of *Discovering Psychology*

For all that is new in the fifth edition, we were careful to maintain the unique elements that have been so well received in the previous editions. Every feature and element in our text was carefully developed and serves a specific purpose. From comprehensive surveys, reviewers, and our many discussions with faculty and students, we learned what elements people wanted in a text and why they thought those features were important tools that enhanced the learning process. We also surveyed the research literature on text comprehension, student learning, and memory. In the process, we acquired many valuable insights from the work of cognitive and educational psychologists. Described below are the main features of *Discovering Psychology* and how these features enhance the learning process.

The Narrative Approach

Associate the new with the old in some natural and telling way, so that the interest, being shed along from point to point, finally suffuses the entire system of objects. . . . Anecdotes and reminiscences [should] abound in [your] talk; and the shuttle of interest will shoot backward and forward, weaving the new and the old together in a lively and entertaining way.

—WILLIAM JAMES, TALKS TO TEACHERS (1899)

As you'll quickly discover, our book has a very distinctive voice. From the very first page of this text, the reader comes to know us as people and teachers through carefully selected stories and anecdotes. Some of our friends and relatives also graciously allowed us to share stories about their lives. The stories are quite varied—some are funny, others are dramatic, and some are deeply personal. All of them are true.

The stories we tell reflect one of the most effective teaching methods—the *narrative approach*. In addition to engaging the reader, each story serves as a pedagogical springboard to illustrate important concepts and ideas. Every story is used to connect new ideas, terms, and ways of looking at behavior to information with which the student is already familiar.

Prologues

As part of the narrative approach, every chapter begins with a **Prologue**, a true story about ordinary people with whom most students can readily identify. The Prologue stories range from the experiences of a teenager with Asperger's Syndrome, to a young woman struggling with the after-effects of 9/11, to the story of a man who regained his sight after decades of blindness. Each Prologue effectively introduces the chapter's themes and lays the groundwork for explaining why the topics treated by the chapter are important. The Prologue establishes a link between familiar experiences and new information—a key ingredient in facilitating learning. Later in the chapter, we return to the people and stories introduced in the Prologue, further reinforcing the link between familiar experiences and new ways of conceptualizing them.

Logical Organization, Continuity, and Clarity

As you read the chapters in *Discovering Psychology*, you'll see that each chapter tells the story of a major topic in psychology in a logical way that flows continuously from beginning to end. Themes are clearly established in the first pages of the chapter. Throughout the chapter, we come back to those themes as we present subtopics and specific research studies. Chapters are thoughtfully organized so that students can easily see how ideas are connected. The writing is carefully paced to maximize student interest and comprehension. Rather than simply mentioning terms and findings, we explain concepts clearly. And we use concrete analogies and everyday examples, rather than vague or flowery metaphors, to help students grasp abstract concepts and ideas.

Paradoxically, one of the ways that we maintain narrative continuity throughout each chapter is through the use of in-text boxes. The boxes provide an opportunity to explore a particular topic in depth without losing the narrative thread of the chapter. The **In Focus** boxes do just that—they focus on interesting topics in more depth than the chapter's organization would allow. These boxes highlight interesting research, answer questions that students commonly ask, or show students how psychological research can be applied in their own lives. The fifth edition of *Discovering Psychology* includes the following In Focus boxes:

- Questions About the Use of Animals in Psychological Research, p. 36
- Do Pheromones Influence Human Behavior?, p. 107
- What You Really Want to Know About Sleep, p. 144
- What You Really Want to Know About Dreams, p. 149
- Watson, Classical Conditioning, and Advertising, p. 192
- Evolution, Biological Preparedness, and Conditioned Fears: What Gives You the Creeps?, p. 198
- Changing the Behavior of Others: Alternatives to Punishment, p. 206
- Déjà Vu Experiences: An Illusion of Memory?, p. 251
- H.M. and Famous People, p. 266
- Does a High IQ Score Predict Success in Life?, p. 295
- Neurodiversity: Beyond IQ, p. 302
- Explaining Those Amazing Identical-Twin Similarities, p. 444
- Providing Effective Social Support, p. 517
- Gender Differences in Responding to Stress: "Tend-and-Befriend" or "Fight-or-Flight?", p. 521
- Using Virtual Reality to Conquer Phobias, p. 591
- Self-Help Groups: Helping Yourself by Helping Others, p. 599
- Servant Leadership: When It's Not All About You, p. B-10
- Name, Title, Generation, p. B-11

Scientific Emphasis

Many first-time psychology students walk into the classroom operating on the assumption that psychology is nothing more than common sense or a collection of personal opinions. Clearly, students need to come away from an introductory psychology course with a solid understanding of the scientific nature of the discipline. To help you achieve that goal, in every chapter we show students how the scientific method has been applied to help answer different kinds of questions about behavior and mental processes.

Because we carefully guide students through the details of specific experiments and studies, students develop a solid understanding of how scientific evidence is gathered and the interplay between theory and research. And because we rely on original rather than secondary sources, students get an accurate presentation of both classic and contemporary psychological studies.

One unique way that we highlight the scientific method in *Discovering Psychology* is with our trademark **Science versus Pseudoscience** boxes. In these boxes, students see the importance of subjecting various claims to the standards of scientific evidence. These boxes promote and encourage scientific thinking by focusing on topics that students frequently ask about in class. The fifth edition of *Discovering Psychology* includes the following Science versus Pseudoscience boxes:

- What Is a Pseudoscience?, pp. 22–23
- Phrenology: The Bumpy Road to Scientific Progress, p. 63
- Brain Myths, p. 78
- Subliminal Perception, p. 91
- Graphology: The "Write" Way to Assess Personality?, p. 448
- EMDR: Can You Wave Your Fears Away?, p. 604

Critical Thinking Emphasis

Another important goal of *Discovering Psychology* is to encourage the development of critical thinking skills. To that end, we do not present psychology as a series of terms, definitions, and facts to be skimmed and memorized. Rather, we try to give students an understanding of how particular topics evolved. In doing so, we also demonstrate the process of challenging preconceptions, evaluating evidence, and revising theories based on new evidence. In short, every chapter shows the process of psychological research—and the important role played by critical thinking in that enterprise.

Because we do not shrink from discussing the implications of psychological findings, students come to understand that many important issues in contemporary psychology are far from being settled. Even when research results are consistent, how to interpret those results can sometimes be the subject of considerable debate. As the authors of the text, we very deliberately try to be evenhanded and fair in presenting both sides of controversial issues. In encouraging students to join these debates, we often challenge them to be aware of how their own preconceptions and opinions can shape their evaluation of the evidence.

Beyond discussions in the text proper, every chapter includes one or more **Critical Thinking** boxes. These boxes are carefully designed to encourage students to think about the broader implications of psychological research—to strengthen and refine their critical thinking skills by developing their own position on questions and issues that don't always have simple answers. Each Critical Thinking box ends with two or three questions that you can use as a written assignment or for classroom discussions. The fifth edition of *Discovering Psychology* includes the following Critical Thinking boxes:

- What Is Critical Thinking?, p. 17
- "His" and "Her" Brains?, p. 75
- ESP: Can Perception Occur Without Sensation?, p. 116
- Is Hypnosis a Special State of Consciousness?, p. 162
- Is Human Freedom Just an Illusion?, p. 208
- Does Exposure to Media Violence *Cause* Aggressive Behavior?, p. 224
- The Memory Wars: Recovered or False Memories?, pp. 258–259
- The Persistence of Unwarranted Beliefs, p. 288
- Has Evolution Programmed Us to Overeat?, p. 328
- Are Women *Really* More Emotional Than Men?, p. 347
- Emotion in Nonhuman Animals: Laughing Rats, Silly Elephants, and Smiling Dolphins?, pp. 352–353
- The Effects of Child Care on Attachment and Development, pp. 380–381
- Freud Versus Rogers on Human Nature, p. 435
- Abuse at Abu Ghraib: Why Do Ordinary People Commit Evil Acts?, pp. 482–483
- Do Personality Factors Cause Disease?, p. 514
- Are People with a Mental Illness as Violent as the Media Portray Them?, p. 532
- Does Smoking Cause Depression and Other Psychological Disorders?, pp. 550–551

Neuroscience and Behavior Trying to help your friend maintain his balance on a skateboard, laughing and talking as you simultaneously walk and scan the path for obstacles or other people, thinking about how to help him if he falls—even seemingly simple behaviors involve the harmonious integration of multiple internal signals and body processes. What kinds of questions might neuroscientists ask about the common behaviors shown here?

Cultural Coverage

As you can see in Table 1, we weave cultural coverage throughout many discussions in the text. But because students are usually unfamiliar with cross-cultural psychology, we also highlight specific topics in **Culture and Human Behavior** boxes.

Table 1

Integrated Cultural Coverage

In addition to the topics covered in the Culture and Human Behavior boxes, cultural influences are addressed in the following discussions.

Page(s)	Topic
11	Culture, social loafing, and social striving
11–13	Cross-cultural perspective in contemporary psychology
21	Cross-cultural study of "pace of life" as example of naturalistic observation
32	Chronic noise and stress in German elementary schoolchildren
53	Effect of traditional Chinese acupuncture on endorphins
91	Israeli study on the effects of subliminal stimuli on political attitudes
111	Pain experience affected by cultural learning experiences
129	Use of acupuncture in traditional Chinese medicine for pain relief
156	Prevalence of narcolepsy in Japan, Israel, U.S., and Canada
163–164	Meditation in different cultures
164	Research collaboration between Tibetan Buddhist monks and Western neuroscientists
165	Racial and ethnic differences in drug metabolism rate
167	Cultural norms and patterns of drug use
167	Differences in alcohol use by U.S. ethnic groups
171	Tobacco and caffeine use in different cultures
174	Peyote use in religious ceremonies in other cultures
175	Medicinal use of marijuana in ancient China, Egypt, India, and Greece
176	Rave culture and drug use in Great Britain and Europe
208	Clash of B. F. Skinner's philosophy with American cultural ideals and individualistic orientation
222–223	Cross-cultural application of observational learning principles in entertainment-education programming in Mexico, Latin America, Asia, and Africa
245	Cross-cultural research on tip-of-the-tongue phenomenon
289	Spontaneous development of sign languages in Nicaragua and Bedouin village as cross-cultural evidence of innate human predisposition to develop language
294–295	Historical misuse of IQ tests to evaluate immigrants
296	Wechsler's recognition of the importance of culture and ethnicity in developing the WAIS intelligence test
299–301	Role of culture in Gardner's definition and theory of intelligence
301	Role of culture in Sternberg's definition and theory of intelligence
306–307	IQ and cross-cultural comparison of educational differences
307–308	Effect of culture on IQ score comparisons
308–309	Potential effect of culture on intelligence test performance
308–309	Cross-cultural studies of group discrimination and IQ
308	Rapid gains in IQ scores in different nations
310	Role of culture in tests and test-taking behavior
322–323	Culture's effect on food preference and eating behavior
331	Obesity rates in cultures with different levels of economic development
344	Culture and achievement motivation
346	Culturally universal emotions
346, 348	Culture and emotional experience
347	Cross-cultural research on gender and emotional expressiveness
348	Cross-cultural studies of psychological arousal associated with emotions
352–354	Universal facial expressions
354–355	Culture, cultural display rules, and emotional expression
378	Cultural influences on temperament
380	Cross-cultural studies of attachment
382	Native language and infant language development
382	Cross-cultural research on infant-directed speech
382–383	Culture and patterns of language development
388	Influence of culture on cognitive development
399	Cultural influences on timing of adolescent romantic relationships
403	Culture and moral reasoning
408	Culture and images of aging
420–421	Cultural influences on Freud's psychoanalytic theory
428–429	Cultural influences on Jung's personality theory
429	Jung on archetypal images, including mandalas, in different cultures
430	Cultural influences on the development of Horney's personality theory
432	Freud's impact on Western culture
435	Rogers on cultural factors in the development of antisocial behavior
442	Cross-cultural research on the universality of the five-factor model of personality
461–462	Cultural conditioning and the "what is beautiful is good" myth
465–466	Attributional biases in individualistic versus collectivistic cultures
470–472	Stereotypes, prejudice, and group identity
471	Ethnocentrism
476	Influence of cultural norms on conformity
482	Role of cultural differences in abuse at Abu Ghraib prison in Iraq
484	Cross-cultural comparisons of destructive social influence
499	Cross-cultural research on life events and stress
502	Cultural differences as source of stress
510	Cross-cultural research on the benefits of perceived control
522	Effect of culture on coping strategies
531, 533	Role of culture in distinguishing between normal and abnormal behavior
533	Use of DSM categories to compile cross-cultural data on prevalence of psychological disorders
539	Cultural variants of panic disorder and panic attacks
541	*Taijin kyofusho,* a culture-specific disorder related to social phobia
543	PTSD in child soldiers in Uganda and Congo
545	Cultural influences in obsessions and compulsions
555	Western cultural ideals of beauty and prevalence rates of eating disorders
560	Role of culture in dissociative experiences
567	Prevalence of schizophrenia in different cultures
571–572	Findings from the Finnish Adoptive Family Study of Schizophrenia
584	Use of interpersonal therapy to treat depression in Uganda
603	Impact of cultural differences on effectiveness of psychotherapy
607–608	Efficacy of traditional herbal treatment for psychotic symptoms in India

Color-Coded Video Games Little girls and little boys have a lot in common. Both of these children are clearly absorbed in their Nintendo video games. Nevertheless, the little boy's game is silver, and the little girl's game is pink. Why?

These boxes increase student awareness of the importance of culture in many areas of human experience. They are unique in that they go beyond simply describing cultural differences in behavior. They show students how cultural influences shape behavior and attitudes, including the student's own behavior and attitudes. The fifth edition of *Discovering Psychology* includes the following Culture and Human Behavior boxes:

Gender Coverage

Gender influences and gender differences are described in many chapters. Table 2 shows the integrated coverage of gender-related issues and topics in *Discovering Psychology*. To help identify the contributions made by female researchers, the full names of researchers are provided in the References section at the end of the text. When researchers are identified using initials instead of first names (as APA style recommends), many students automatically assume that the researchers are male.

Neuroscience Coverage

Psychology and neuroscience have become intricately intertwined. Especially in the last decade, the scientific understanding of the brain and its relation to human behavior has grown dramatically. The imaging techniques of brain science—PET scans, MRIs, and functional MRIs—have become familiar terminology to many students, even if they don't completely understand the differences between them. To reflect that growing trend, we have increased our neuroscience coverage to show students how understanding the brain can help explain the complete range of human behavior, from the ordinary to the severely disturbed. Each chapter contains one or more **Focus on Neuroscience** discussions that are designed to complement the broader chapter discussion. Here is a complete list of the Focus on Neuroscience features in the fifth edition:

Get some sleep and chill! Whether they are children or adults, people often react with greater emotionality when they're not getting adequate sleep (Zohar & others, 2005). Is this because they're simply tired, or do the brain's emotional centers become more reactive in response to sleep deprivation? To study this question, researcher Seung-Schik Yoo and his colleagues (2007) deprived some participants of sleep for 35 hours while other participants slept normally. Then, all of the participants observed a series of images ranging from emotionally neutral to very unpleasant and disturbing images while undergoing an fMRI brain scan. Compare the two fMRI scans shown here. The orange and yellow areas indicate the degree of activation in the *amygdala*, a key component of the brain's emotional centers. Compared to the adequately rested participants (shown on the left), the amygdala activated 60 percent more strongly when the sleep-deprived participants looked at the aversive images (shown on the right). Yoo's research clearly shows that the sleep-deprived brain is much more prone to strong emotional reactions, especially in response to negative stimuli.

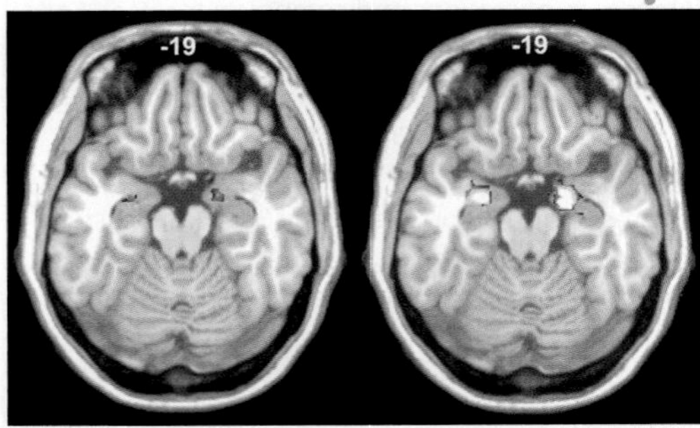

Sleep Control Sleep Deprivation

Table 2

Integrated Gender Coverage

Page(s)	Topic
4	Titchener's inclusion of female graduate students in his psychology program in the late 1800s
6–7	Contributions of Mary Whiton Calkins to psychology
6–7	Contributions of Margaret Floy Washburn to psychology
60–61	Endocrine system and effects of sex hormones
75	Sex differences and the brain
100	Gender differences in incidence of color blindness
107	Gender differences in responses to human chemosignals (pheromones)
111	Gender differences in the perception of pain
150	Gender differences in dream content
150	Gender and nightmare frequency
153	Gender differences in driving while sleepy and traffic accidents related to sleepiness
154–158	Gender differences in incidence of insomnia and other sleep disorders
168	Gender and rate of metabolism of alcohol
168	Gender and binge drinking among college students
176	Gender differences in effects of MDMA (ecstasy) on the brain
186	Women as research assistants in Pavlov's laboratories
224–225	Gender and the long-term effects of viewing media violence
290	How the lack of a gender-neutral pronoun in English influences thinking
310	Test performance and the influence of gender stereotypes
310–311	Language, gender stereotypes, and gender bias
330	Gender differences in caloric intake and sedentary lifestyles
330	Gender differences in rates of overweight and obesity
330	Gender differences in activity level and metabolism
332–333	Sex differences in the pattern of human sexual response
334–335	Sex differences in hormonal influences on sexual motivation
336	Gender differences in mate preferences
337–339	Sexual orientation
347	Gender differences in emotional expression
354	Gender similarities and differences in experience and expression of emotion
355	Gender differences in cultural display rules and emotional expression
371	Sex differences in genetic transmission of recessive characteristics
384	Definitions of gender, gender role, and gender identity
384–385	Gender stereotypes and gender roles
384–385	Sex differences in early childhood behavior
384–386	Development of gender identity and gender roles
386–387	Theories of gender-role development
386–387	Gender identity development in Freud's psychoanalytic theory
394	Gender differences in timing of the development of primary and secondary sex characteristics
395	Gender and accelerated puberty in father-absent homes
396–397	Gender differences in brain maturation
396–398	Gender differences in effects of early and late maturation
403	Gender differences in moral reasoning
404	Gender differences in friendship patterns
405	Average age of first marriage and higher education attainment
406	Gender differences in single parent, head-of-household status
406	Gender and patterns of career development and parenting responsibilities
407	Gender differences in life expectancy
426-427	Freud's contention of gender differences in resolving Oedipus complex
429	Sexual archetypes (anima, animus) in Jung's personality theory
430	Horney's critique of Freud's view of female psychosexual development
432	Critique of sexism in Freud's theory
470	Misleading effect of gender stereotypes
478	Gender similarities in results of Milgram's obedience studies
501	Gender differences in frequency and source of daily hassles
502	Gender differences in the experience and response to traumatic events
516	Gender differences in susceptibility to the stress contagion effect
516–517	Gender differences in providing social support and effects of social support
521	Gender and social networks
521	Gender differences in responding to stress—the "tend-and-befriend" response
537	Gender differences in anxiety disorder
540	Gender differences in prevalence of phobias
540–541	Gender differences in prevalence of social phobia and *taijin kyofusho*
542	Gender differences in prevalence of post-traumatic stress disorder
547–548	Gender differences in prevalence of major depression and seasonal affective disorder
549	Lack of gender differences in prevalence of bipolar disorder
553–555	Gender differences in prevalence of eating disorders
557	Gender differences in incidence of paranoid personality disorder
558	Gender differences in incidence of antisocial personality disorder
559	Gender differences in incidence of borderline personality disorder
568–569	Paternal age and incidence of schizophrenia
573	Gender differences in number of suicide attempts and in number of suicide deaths
617	Gender differences in sexual contact between therapists and clients
B–12	Gender differences in reasons for wanting to telecommute

- Mirror Neurons: Imitation in the Brain?, p. 219
- Assembling Memories: Echoes and Reflections of Perception, p. 262
- Mapping Brain Changes in Alzheimer's Disease, p. 268
- Seeing Faces and Places in the Mind's Eye, p. 279
- Dopamine Receptors and Obesity, p. 331
- Romantic Love and the Brain, p. 334
- Emotions and the Brain, p. 351
- The Adolescent Brain: A Work in Progress, p. 396
- Personality Traits and Patterns of Brain Activity, p. 443
- Brain Reward When Making Eye Contact with Attractive People, p. 462
- The Mysterious Placebo Effect, p. 508
- The Hallucinating Brain, p. 564
- Schizophrenia: A Wildfire in the Brain, p. 570
- Comparing Psychotherapy and Antidepressant Medication, p. 613

Enhancing Well-Being with Psychology

Among all the sciences, psychology is unique in the degree to which it speaks to our daily lives and applies to everyday problems and concerns. The **Enhancing Well-Being with Psychology** feature at the end of each chapter presents the findings from psychological research that address a wide variety of problems and concerns. In each of these features we present research-based information in a form that students can use to enhance everyday functioning. As you can see in the following list, topics range from improving self-control to overcoming insomnia:

- Psychology in the Media: Becoming an Informed Consumer, p. 37
- Maximizing Your Brain's Potential, p. 81
- Strategies to Control Pain, p. 129
- Stimulus Control Therapy for Insomnia, p. 178
- Using Learning Principles to Improve Self-Control, p. 226
- Superpower Memory in Minutes per Day!, p. 270
- A Workshop on Creativity, p. 312
- Turning Your Goals into Reality, p. 361
- Raising Psychologically Healthy Children, p. 411
- Possible Selves: Imagine the Possibilities, p. 451
- The Persuasion Game, p. 489
- Minimizing the Effects of Stress, p. 523
- Understanding and Helping to Prevent Suicide, p. 573
- What to Expect in Psychotherapy, p. 616

Sheryl Crow Grammy award-winning singer Sheryl Crow has struggled with depression since she was a young child. Of her chronic depression, she has said, "I grew up in the presence of melancholy, a feeling of loss. . . . It is a shadow for me. It's part of who I am. It is constantly there. I just know how, at this point, to sort of manage it."

The Pedagogical System

The pedagogical system in *Discovering Psychology* was carefully designed to help students identify important information, test for retention, and learn how to learn. It is easily adaptable to an SQ3R approach, for those instructors who have had success with that technique. As described in the following discussion, the different elements of this text form a pedagogical system that is very student-friendly, straightforward, and effective.

We've found that it appeals to diverse students with varying academic and study skills, enhancing the learning process without being gimmicky or condescending. A special student preface titled **To the Student** on pages xliii to xlvi immediately before Chapter 1 describes the complete pedagogical system and how students can make the most of it.

The pedagogical system has four main components: (1) Advance Organizers, (2) Visual Concept Reviews, (3) Chapter Review, and (4) the Web companion site. Major sections are introduced by an **Advance Organizer** that identifies the section's *Key Theme* followed by a bulleted list of *Key Questions.* Each Advance Organizer mentally primes the student for the important information that is to follow and does so in a way that encourages active learning. Students often struggle with trying to determine what's important to learn in a particular section or chapter. As a pedagogical technique, the Advance Organizer provides a guide that directs the student toward the most important ideas, concepts, and information in the section. It helps students identify main ideas and distinguish them from supporting evidence and examples.

New to this edition, **Concept Maps** are visual reviews that encourage students to review and check their learning at the end of the chapter. The hierarchical layout shows how themes, concepts, and facts are related to one another. Chapter photos are included as visual cues to important chapter information.

Several other in-chapter pedagogical aids support the Advance Organizers and Concept Reviews. A clearly identified **Chapter Outline** provides an overview of topics and organization. Within the chapter, **Key Terms** are set in boldface type and defined in the margin. *Pronunciation guides* are included for difficult or unfamiliar words. Because students often have trouble identifying the most important theorists and researchers, names of **Key People** are set in boldface type within the chapter. We also provide a page-referenced list of Key People and Terms at the end of each chapter.

Beyond the learning aids in the text, every new copy of *Discovering Psychology* comes with a free copy of either the Online Study Center or the print Study Guide written by Cornelius Rea, Douglas College. Supplementing these materials, the **Book Companion Web site** contains multiple review activities. At the companion Web site, each chapter has *two 15-question self-scoring practice quizzes, flashcards for rehearsing key terms,* and *two interactive crossword puzzles.* In addition to the companion Web site, the book is accompanied by some other premium Web materials including **PsychPortal**, which combines all the electronic resources available for the book (including the eBook, interactive activities, and quizzing). The book companion site can be accessed at **www.worthpublishers.com/hockenbury.**

The Teaching Package: Print Supplements

The comprehensive teaching package that accompanies *Discovering Psychology* is designed to help you save time and teach more effectively. Many elements of the supplements package will be particularly helpful to the new, adjunct, or part-time instructor. This superb teaching package, expanded in the fifth edition, includes the following elements:

- **Instructor's Resources and Binder,** prepared by Edna Ross, University of Louisville, with Skip Pollock, Mesa Community College; Claudia Cochran-Miller, El Paso Community College; Beth Finders, St. Charles Community College; Beverly Drinnin, Des Moines Area Community College; Wayne Hall, San Jacinto College-Central Campus; and Nancy Melucci, Los Angeles Community College District. The Instructor's Resources include an abundance of materials to aid instructors in planning their courses, including chapter learning objectives, detailed chapter outlines, lecture guides, classroom demonstrations and activities, student exercises, advice on teaching the nontraditional student, popular video suggestions, and "Psychology in the News" topics. Also included are two **Video Guides,** both written by Don and Sandra Hockenbury. These video guides tie the *Scientific American Teaching Modules* and *The Brain Teaching Modules* directly to the text. **Faculty Guides** tie topics in the text to *Psychology: The Human Experience, The Worth Digital Media Archive, The Mind Teaching Modules, Active Psych,* and the *Video Tool Kit for Introductory Psychology,* which provide the instructor with a rich array of opportunities to teach with media.

- **Test Bank,** written by Don and Sandra Hockenbury with the assistance of Cornelius Rea who taught psychology courses for many years at Simon Fraser University and Douglas College, and currently has a consulting business in West Vancouver, British Columbia, Canada. This revised and enhanced printed Test Bank includes over 6,000 multiple-choice, true-false, and short-answer essay questions, plus Learning Objectives for each chapter that correspond to those in the Instructor's Resources. The Test Bank includes visual questions that you can include when generating and printing your tests. Each question is referenced to the textbook, identified as a factual/definitional or conceptual/analytical question, and keyed to a learning objective and an APA learning outcome.
- ***Diploma* Computerized Test Bank, Online Testing, and Gradebook** This versatile test-generating software allows instructors to edit, add, or scramble questions from the *Discovering Psychology,* Fifth Edition, Test Bank; format tests; and administer exams over a local area network or online. The gradebook software allows you to track student progress and generate grade reports.
- **Study Guide for *Discovering Psychology,*** written by Cornelius Rea who taught psychology courses for many years at Simon Fraser University and Douglas College, and currently has a consulting business in West Vancouver, British Columbia, Canada. The Study Guide is carefully designed to help students understand text information and prepare for exams. Each chapter begins with At a Glance (which provides an overview of the chapter). Each Study Guide section includes a series of Preview Questions followed by fill-ins (some asking for lengthy responses). At the end of each Study Guide section is a Concept Check (application questions) followed by a Review of Key Terms, Concepts, and Names. The Guide also contains Graphic Organizers, which encourage students to complete graphs, charts, and flow diagrams that ultimately provide a visual synopsis of text material. At the end of every Study Guide chapter are Something to Think About questions, which contain thought-provoking questions designed to encourage critical thinking and application of the material, followed by three Progress Tests. All answers are provided at the end of the chapter.
- ***Psychology: The Human Experience* Telecourse Student Guide,** written by Ken Hutchins, Orange Coast College, Costa Mesa, California. The Emmy award– winning Coast Learning Systems telecourse, titled *Psychology: The Human Experience,* is based on *Discovering Psychology,* the designated text to accompany the telecourse. Ken Hutchins, Don Hockenbury, and Sandra Hockenbury were members of the Faculty Advisory Committee and were closely involved in the development of the telecourse. The Telecourse Student Guide by Ken Hutchins draws clear connections between the text and the telecourse, helping students to get the most out of the learning experience.
- **The *Scientific American* Psychology Reader** is a collection of twelve articles selected by Don and Sandra Hockenbury from recent issues of *Scientific American* magazine. Each article is accompanied by an introduction and preview of each article, as well as a series of thoughtful discussion questions to encourage classroom discussions.
- ***Pursuing Human Strengths: A Positive Psychology Guide*** by Martin Bolt, Calvin College. Martin Bolt's new workbook aims to help students build up their strengths. Closely following the research, this book provides a brief

overview of nine positive traits, such as hope, self-respect, commitment, and joy. It also offers self-assessment activities that help students gauge how much of the trait they have developed, and research-based suggestions for how they might work further toward fostering these traits.

- ***Critical Thinking Companion*, Second Edition** by Jane Halonen, University of West Florida, and Cynthia Gray, Alverno College. This engaging and challenging handbook includes exercises in pattern recognition, practical problem-solving, creative problem-solving, scientific problem-solving, psychological reasoning, and perspective-taking.

The Teaching Package: Media Supplements

- **PsychPortal** is a breakthrough online learning space created by psychologists for psychologists. Highlights include:
- **A multimedia-enhanced eBook of *Discovering Psychology*, Fifth Edition—** the eBook fully integrates the text, a rich assortment of media-powered learning opportunities, and a variety of customization features for students and instructors. Worth's acclaimed eBook platform was developed by cognitive psychologist Pepper Williams (Ph.D., Yale University), who taught undergraduate psychology at the University of Massachusetts. The eBook is also available in a standalone version outside the Portal.
- **Concepts in Action.** Embedded throughout the eBook, new Concepts in Action help students solidify their understanding of key concepts as they encounter them in the text. These Flash-based activities, created by award-winning multimedia author Tom Ludwig (Hope College), incorporate video and demonstrations, plus dynamic animations by Terry Bazzett (SUNY College at Geneseo).
- **Diagnostic Quizzing and Personalized Study Plans**—Students can take advantage of PsychPortal's research-based diagnostic quizzing to focus their studying where it is needed most.
- **An Assignment Center**—Where instructors can easily construct and administer tests and quizzes based on the book's Test Bank or their own questions. Quizzes are randomized and timed, and instructors can receive summaries of student results in reports that follow the section order of the chapters.
- **Course Materials**—A convenient location for students to access all interactive media associated with the book, as well as for instructors to find a variety of videos, PowerPoint activities, and animations for classroom and online presentation. Tutorials, animations, and simulations were created by award-winning psychology multimedia author Tom Ludwig from Hope (MI) College. Resources include the popular crossword puzzles and several new activities that came out of the authors' teaching of online courses. PsychPortal contains all of the standard functionality you expect from a site that can serve as an independent online course, but it is the core teaching and learning components (developed with an advisory board of master teachers and learning experts) that make PsychPortal truly unique.
- The **Online Study Center, www.worthstudycenter.com,** (available for free packaged with the book) helps students focus their study and exam prep time. Students can take **Pre-Lecture Quizzes** to assess how well they understand a particular chapter *before* coming to class. Or they can take **Mastery Quizzes** to test their knowledge whenever they choose. Feedback from taking those quizzes is in the form of a **Personalized Study Plan**, which provides direct links to resources that will help them focus on the questions they answered incorrectly. Or students can browse the library of Course Materials to access myriad interactive demonstrations and review materials. Instructors can view reports indicating their students' strengths and weaknesses, allowing them to focus their teaching

efforts accordingly. Student results report to a fully customizable gradebook for easy access and grade assignment.

- **NEW! PsychInvestigator: Laboratory Learning in Introductory Psychology** by Arthur Kohn, Ph.D., Dark Blue Morning Productions. This exciting new Web-based product is a virtual laboratory environment that enables students to participate in real experiments. Students are introduced to psychological experiments in a dynamic environment featuring hosts video-streamed for the most realistic portrayal possible. In **PsychInvestigator,** students participate in classic psychology experiments, generate real data, and analyze their findings. In each experiment, students participate in compelling video tutorials that are displayed before *and* after the actual experiment. PsychInvestigator requires no additional faculty time. Students' quiz scores can be automatically uploaded into an online grade book if instructors wish to monitor students' progress.
- The **Companion Web Site at** www.worthpublishers.com/hockenbury provides students with a free online study guide. Features include Learning Objectives, Crossword puzzles, critical thinking Web activities, online quizzes, Spanish/English glossary, *Scientific American* Podcasts, and interactive Web activities. Instructors access a wealth of teaching materials from PowerPoint slides to iClicker questions.
- The **eBook** for *Discovering Psychology* is a complete online version of the text, equipped with interactive note taking and highlighting capability and fully integrated with all of the media resources available with *Discovering Psychology*.
- **Instructor's CD-ROM.** This CD-ROM includes pre-built PowerPoint presentations for each chapter, a digital library of photographs, figures, and tables from the text, and an electronic version of the Instructor's Resources.

The Teaching Package: Video Supplements

- **Worth Publishers Video Tool Kit for Introductory Psychology.** With its superb collection of 51 brief (1 to 13 minutes) clips and emphasis on the biological basis of behavior, the **Student Video Tool Kit for Introductory Psychology** is available both online and on CD-ROM. This tool kit gives students a fresh way to experience both the classic experiments at the heart of psychological science and cutting-edge research conducted by the field's most influential investigators. The balance of contemporary news footage and classic experiments (both original and re-created) help bring key concepts of the introductory psychology course to life. Each clip is accompanied by multiple-choice questions that focus on the ideas students need to learn. Students can submit their answers online or print their answers and hand them in during class. Fully customizable, the **Online Video Tool Kit** offers instructors the option of incorporating videos into assignments as well as annotating each video with notes or instructions, making the tool kit an integral part of the course. Instructors also have the option of assigning the tool kit to students without instructor involvement. The **Instructor Video Tool Kit** includes a set of more than 72 digitized video clips combining both research and news footage from the BBC Motion Gallery, CBS News, and other sources. The CD version provides the clips in MPEG format, which can be easily incorporated into PowerPoint® or run in a video player application and is accompanied by a faculty guide by Martin Bolt (Calvin College).
- **ActivePsych: Classroom Activities Projects and Video Teaching Modules** offers tools to make class presentations more interactive. This set of instructor presentation CD-ROMs includes interactive flash and PowerPoint demonstrations, and video clips from *Scientific American Frontiers* and various archival sources. *ActivePsych* video clips are available on CD, DVD, and VHS.

- **Worth Digital Media Archive CD-ROM (also available on DVD)** contains a rich collection of 42 digitized video clips of classic experiments and research. Footage includes Albert Bandura's Bobo doll experiment, Harold Takooshian's bystander studies, Piaget's conservation experiment, electrical brain stimulation, Harry Harlow's monkey experiments, Stanley Milgram's obedience study, and Ulric Neisser's selective attention studies.
- ***Psychology: The Human Experience* Teaching Modules (available on DVD or VHS)** This Emmy-award–winning series includes more than three hours of footage from the Introductory Psychology telecourse, *Psychology: The Human Experience,* produced by Coast Learning Systems in collaboration with Worth Publishers. Tied specifically to the Hockenbury text, these brief clips are ideal for lecture. Footage contains noted scholars, the latest research, and beautiful animations. A Faculty Guide is available.
- ***Scientific American Frontiers* Teaching Modules, Second Edition (available on DVD or VHS)** This collection of more than 30 video segments is adapted from the award-winning television series *Scientific American Frontiers.* Hosted by Alan Alda, these 8- to 12-minute teaching modules take your students behind the scenes to see how psychology research is actually conducted. The series features the work of such notable researchers as Steven Pinker, Benjamin Beck, Steve Sumi, Renée Baillargeon, Barry Beyerstein, Ray Hyman, Carl Rosengren, Laura Pettito, Barbara Rothbaum, Robert Stickgold, and Irene Pepperberg. The Faculty Guide written by Don and Sandra Hockenbury links the modules to specific topics in *Discovering Psychology.* These video modules are an excellent resource to stimulate class discussion and interest on a variety of topics.
- ***The Brain* Teaching Modules, Second Edition (available on DVD or VHS)** Along with new modules from the acclaimed PBS series, the second edition of *The Brain* Teaching Modules includes a Faculty Guide written by Don and Sandra Hockenbury that links the modules to specific topics in the fifth edition of *Discovering Psychology.* The second edition contains 10 new and 13 revised modules using added material, new audio, and new graphics. Individual segments range from 4 to 12 minutes in length, providing flexibility in highlighting specific topics.
- ***The Mind* Teaching Modules, Second Edition (available on DVD or VHS)** This revised and rich collection of 35 short clips dramatically enhances and illustrates key topics in the lectures and the text. The second edition contains updated segments on language processing, infant cognitive development, genetic factors in alcoholism, and living without memory (featuring a dramatic interview with Clive Wearing). A Faculty Guide is available.

Acknowledgments

Many talented people contributed to this project. First, we would like to acknowledge the efforts of our supplements team that created materials specifically devoted to our book. Our thanks to:

- **Cornelius Rea** at Douglas College in British Columbia, Canada, for once again writing a very effective Student Study Guide and helping to update the Test Bank and online Web quizzes.
- **Edna Ross** at the University of Louisville for preparing a comprehensive and substantially revised Instructor's Resources.
- **Claudia Cochran-Miller** at El Paso Community College and **Marie Waung** at the University of Michigan at Dearborn for their exceptional appendix on industrial/organizational psychology. **Loren Toussaint** at Luther College and

Andy Pomerantz** from Southern Illinois University at Edwardsville for their comprehensive and thoughtful reviews of the chapters on stress, health, and coping and psychological disorders and therapies.

- **Marie D. Thomas** at California State University, San Marcos, for updating the student-friendly statistics appendix.
- **Angela Ruiz Daudet,** translator of the English/Spanish Glosario/Glossary supplement to this text.

As colleagues who care as much as we do about teaching, they have our gratitude for their hard work and commitment to excellence.

We are indebted to our colleagues who acted as reviewers throughout the development of the fifth edition of *Discovering Psychology.* Their thoughtful suggestions and advice helped us refine and strengthen this edition. To each and every reviewer, thank you for generously sharing your time and candid thoughts with us:

Amber Alliger, *Hunter College*
Steve Barney, *Southern Utah University*
Dave Baskind, *Delta College*
Laura Bittner, *Carroll Community College*
Gena Britt, *John Tyler Community College*
Linda Brunton, *Columbia State Community College*
Emily Cahan, *Wheelock College*
Mary Christina Evans, *Los Angeles Community College District*
Kevin Filter, *Minnesota State University–Mankato*
Robin Franck, *Southwestern College*
Phyllis Freeman, *State University of New York–New Paltz*
Danielle Gagne, *Alfred University*
Erin Goforth, *University of New Hampshire*
Peter Gram, *Pensacola Junior College*
Vicki Hammer, *Cloud County Community College*
Janet King, *Western Nevada College*
Juliana Leding, *University of North Florida*
Paul Macaruso, *Community College of Rhode Island*
Haywood Mason, *Cape Fear Community College*
Timothy May, *Eastern Kentucky University*
Chrystie Meziere, *Tulsa Community College*
Michael Jason McCoy, *Cape Fear Community College*
Robin Musselman, *Lehigh Carbon Community College*
Sundé Nesbit, *California State University–Fresno*
Nancy Schaab, *Delta College*
Patti Simone, *Santa Clara University*
O'Ann Steere, *College of DuPage*
Lisa Stoner, *St. Charles Community College*
Chris Thomas, *Florence Darlington Technical College*
Stephen Tracy, *College of Southern Nevada*
Ayme Turnbull, *Adelphi University*
Lynn David Yankowski, *Maui Community College*
Nancy Zombro, *Cape Cod Community College*

Tulsa Community College

We are also thankful for the support that Don has received from the Tulsa Community College administration and Board of Regents. Dr. Tom McKeon, President of Tulsa Community College, and Dr. Dean VanTrease, President Emeritus of the college, support diverse forms of professional development in both word and deed. From the very beginning, Dr. VanTrease and Dr. McKeon recognized the academic value of Don's role as a coauthor of an introductory psychology text that is used nationally and internationally.

Our colleagues and fellow Tulsa Community College psychology faculty—especially Phoebe Baker, Cathy Furlong, John Hensley, Susan Kamphaus, Fern Marrs, Alicia MacKay, Chrystie Meziere, and Krena White—continue to inspire us with their dedication to excellence in teaching. A special note of appreciation also goes to Sandra Massey, Northeast Campus Provost, Jocelyn Whitney, Liberal Arts Associate Dean, and the outstanding faculty who comprise the TCC Northeast Campus Liberal Arts and Human Services Department.

Worth Publishers

The remarkable people who make up Worth Publishers have a well-earned reputation for producing college textbooks and supplements of the highest quality. Our thanks to our executive editor, Jessica Bayne, for her perceptive, candid, and creative approaches to managing and publishing textbooks. Our developmental editor, Marna Miller, provided thoughtful and well-reasoned editorial suggestions that helped us refine the details and flow of new material. Above and beyond that, Marna's determination, optimism, and unfailing good humor were greatly appreciated. Thanks also go to assistant editor Adam Frese, who expertly kept track of countless details and stacks of paper. The incredible new design for the fifth edition reflects the creative talents of art director and artist Babs Reingold. We never cease to be impressed by designer Lee Ann McKevitt's ability to create the seamless interaction of text, graphics, boxes, and features that you see on every page of *Discovering Psychology*. The text's beautiful layout also owes a great deal to the talented efforts of Lyndall Culbertson. The stunning new art/photo illustrations represent the combined talents of illustrator Todd Buck, Worth photo editor Christine Buese, and photo researcher Donna Ranieri. Along with finding the perfect photos to serve as a base for Todd's astonishing illustrations, Christine and Donna helped us revamp the text's photo program by never giving up in their search for just the right image.

By any standard, associate managing editor Tracey Kuehn is an unbelievably talented and dedicated person. For the last four editions, Tracey's expertise, creativity, and delightful sense of humor have been invaluable to us. With the help of production editor Mike Ederer, Tracey effectively tackled and resolved the inevitable problems that accompany a project of this complexity. Our heartfelt thanks also to Barbara Seixas who coordinated a bewildering array of technical details to bring the book to press on schedule.

Perhaps the greatest unsung heroes in college textbook publishing are the supplements and media editors. At Worth Publishers, those editors work tirelessly to set the standard by which all other publishers are judged. With conscientious attention to a multitude of details, Andrea Musick, Christine Burak, Stacey Alexander, and Betty Probert, have expertly assembled the integrated program of print, video, and Internet supplements that accompanies our text. They are awesome!

Psychology marketing manager Amy Shefferd helped launch the fifth edition with her expertly coordinated advertising, marketing, and sales support efforts. Special thanks to our longtime friend and adopted family member, Steve Patrick, southwest regional manager.

A few personal acknowledgements are in order. Several friends and family members kindly allowed us to share their stories with you. Sandy's mother, Fern, deserves particular thanks and recognition for her constant support and never-ending supply of funny stories. Sadly, our fathers, Ken and Erv, are no longer with us, but they both live on in our memories, as well as in the personal stories that we continue to tell about each of them. We also thank Janeen and Marty, Terry and Jean, Judy and all the other members of our extended family for their support and encouragement. We are grateful to our niece Katie and to our good friends Asha and Paul, Tom and Lynn, and their children, Will, and Lily, and especially Marcia, for allowing us to tell their stories in our book. Had Richard lived to see the publication of *Discovering Psychology*, we know he would have been proud to be part of its pages.

Finally, our daughter Laura has lived with this project since she was born. Now 19 years old, Laura is a sophomore at Carleton College in Northfield, Minnesota. Her wide-ranging interests include neuroscience, the arts, and the outdoors. She has become quite accomplished at classical and improvisational piano, and continues to develop those talents at Carleton. A member of Eclipse, one of Carleton's Ultimate Frisbee teams, Laura is also known for her comedy sketch and improv performances. Thank you for your idealism, your generous spirit, for your drive and self-determination, and for being true to yourself. Wherever you go, Red, go with all your heart!

An Invitation

We hope that you will let us know how you and your students like the fifth edition of *Discovering Psychology*. And, as always, we welcome your thoughts, comments, and suggestions. You can write to us in care of Worth Publishers, 41 Madison Avenue, 35th Floor, New York, NY 10010, or contact us via e-mail at: **DiscoveringPsychology@gmail.com.**

Above all, we hope that your class is an enjoyable and successful one as you introduce your students to the most fascinating and personally relevant science that exists.

With best wishes to you and your students,

TO THE STUDENT

Learning from *Discovering Psychology*

Welcome to psychology! Our names are **Don and Sandy Hockenbury**, and we're the authors of your textbook. Every semester we teach several sections of introductory psychology. We wrote this text to help you succeed in the class you are taking. Every aspect of this book has been carefully designed to help you get the most out of your introductory psychology course. Before you begin reading, you will find it well worth your time to take a few minutes to familiarize yourself with the special features and learning aids in this book.

Learning Aids in the Text

Key Theme

- **You can enhance your chances for success in psychology by using the learning aids that have been built into this textbook.**

Key Questions

- **What are the functions of the Prologue, Advance Organizers, Key Terms, Key People, and Concept Reviews?**
- **What are the functions of the different types of boxes in this text, and why should you read them?**
- **Where can you go to access a virtual study guide at any time of the day or night, and what study aids are provided?**

First, take a look at the **Chapter Outline** at the beginning of each chapter. The Chapter Outline provides an overview of the main topics that will be covered in the chapter. You might also want to flip through the chapter and browse a bit so you have an idea of what's to come.

Next, read the chapter **Prologue.** The Prologue is a true story about real people. Some of the stories are humorous, some dramatic We think you will enjoy this special feature, but it will also help you to understand the material in the chapter that follows and why the topics are important and relevant to your life.

The Prologue will help you relate the new information in this book to experiences that are already familiar to you. In each chapter, we return to the people and stories introduced in the Prologue to illustrate important themes and concepts.

As you begin reading the chapter, you will notice several special elements. **Major Sections** are easy to identify because the heading is in red type. The beginning of each major section also includes an **Advance Organizer**—a short section preview that looks like the one above.

The **Key Theme** provides you with a preview of the material in the section to come. The **Key Questions** will help you focus on some of the most important material in the section. Keep the questions in mind as you read the section. They will help you identify important points in the chapter. After you finish reading each section, look again at the Advance Organizer. Make sure that you can confidently answer each question before you go on to the next section. If you want to maximize your understanding of the material, write out the answer to each question. You can also use the questions in the Advance Organizer to aid you in taking notes or in outlining chapter sections, both of which are effective study strategies.

Notice that some terms in the chapter are printed in **boldface,** or darker, type. Some of these **Key Terms** may already be familiar to you, but most will be new. The dark type signals that the term has a specialized meaning in psychology. Each Key Term is formally defined within a sentence or two of being introduced. The Key Terms are also defined in the margins, usually on the page on which they appear in text. Some Key Terms include a **pronunciation guide** to help you say the word correctly.

Occasionally, we print words in *italic type* to signal either that they are boldfaced terms in another chapter or that they are specialized terms in psychology.

Certain names also appear in boldface type. These are the **Key People**—the researchers or theorists who are especially important within a given area of psychological study. Typically, Key People are the psychologists or other researchers whose names your instructor will expect you to know.

Reviewing for Examinations

The **Chapter Review** at the end of each chapter includes several elements to help you review what you have learned. All the chapter's **Key People** and **Key Terms** are listed, along with the pages on which they appear and are defined. You can check your knowledge of the **Key People** by describing in your own words why each scientist is important. You also want to define each **Key Term** in your own words, then comparing your definition to information on the page where it is discussed. The visual **Concept Maps** at the end of the chapter give you a hierarchical lay-out showing how themes, concepts, and facts are related to one another. The photos in each Concept Map should provide additional visual cues to help you consolidate your memory of important chapter information. Use the visual Concept Maps to review the information in each section.

Special Features in the Text

Each chapter in *Discovering Psychology* has several boxes that focus on different kinds of topics. Take the time to read the boxes because they are an integral part of each chapter. They also present important information that you may be expected to know for class discussion or tests. There are five types of boxes:

- **Critical Thinking** boxes ask you to stretch your mind a bit by presenting issues that are provocative or controversial. They will help you actively question the implications of the material that you are learning.
- **Science Versus Pseudoscience** boxes examine the evidence for various popular pseudosciences—from subliminal persuasion to astrology. These discussions will help teach you how to think scientifically and critically evaluate claims.
- **Culture and Human Behavior** boxes are another special feature of this text. Many students are unaware of the importance of cross-cultural research in contemporary psychology. These boxes highlight cultural differences in thinking and behavior. They will also sensitize you to the ways in which people's behavior, including your own, has been influenced by cultural factors.
- **In Focus** boxes present interesting information or research. Think of them as sidebar discussions. They deal with topics as diverse as human pheromones, whether animals dream, and why snakes give so many people the creeps.
- **Focus on Neuroscience** sections provide clear explanations of intriguing studies that use brain-imaging techniques to study psychological processes. Among the topics that are highlighted: schizophrenic hallucinations, mental images, drug addiction, and romantic love and the brain.

The **Enhancing Well-Being with Psychology** section at the end of each chapter provides specific suggestions to help you deal with real-life concerns. These suggestions are based on psychological research, rather than opinions, anecdotes, or pop psych self-help philosophies. The Enhancing Well-Being sections show you how psychology can be applied to a wide variety of everyday concerns. We hope that these sections make a difference in your life. Because the Enhancing Well-Being sections for Chapters 5, 6, and 8 deal with setting and achieving goals and enhancing motivation and memory, you may want to skip ahead and read them after you finish this student preface.

There are two special appendices at the back of the text. The **Statistics: Understanding Data** appendix discusses how psychologists use statistics to summarize and draw conclusions from the data they have gathered. The **Industrial/Organizational Psychology** appendix describes the branch of psychology that studies human behavior in the workplace. Your instructor may assign one or both of these appendices, or you may want to read them on your own.

Also at the back of this text is a **Glossary** containing the definitions for all **Key Terms** in the book and the pages on which they are discussed in more detail. You can use the **Subject Index** to locate discussions of particular topics and the **Name Index** to locate particular researchers. Finally, interested students can look up the specific studies we cite in the **References** sections.

The *Discovering Psychology* Web Companion Site

The *Discovering Psychology* Web Companion site provides you with a free virtual study guide, available 24 hours a day, 7 days a week. You can access the companion Web site at the following Internet address: **www.worthpublishers.com/hockenbury**

The ***Discovering Psychology*** **Web Companion** has a wealth of helpful study aids for each chapter. Below are some suggestions for how you can use those resources to your advantage.

- Print the **Learning Objectives** to provide a detailed list of the information that you should master for each chapter.
- Take the **Self-Scoring Quizzes** and use the **Flashcards** to test yourself on the Key Terms and Key People. The Web site also offers a Spanish language version of the Flashcards.
- Utilize the **Crossword Puzzles** as a fun way to test your knowledge of Key Terms and Key People. There are two crossword puzzles for each chapter and one for each appendix.
- **Interactive computer simulations**, **demonstrations**, and other activities will help you apply and reinforce your understanding of important chapter concepts.
- **Critical Thinking Exercises** are linked to other Web sites.

If you would like more online quizzes and activities than the free companion Web site offers, follow the links online to the **Online Study Center** or the **Psych2Go** MP3 audio recordings**.** The **Online Study Center** can help you focus your study time. You can take a **Pre-Lecture Quiz** to assess how well you understand a particular chapter *before* coming to class. Or, you can take a **Mastery Quiz** to test your knowledge whenever you choose. Feedback from taking those quizzes is in the form of a **Personalized Study Plan,** which provides direct links to resources that will help you focus on where you need to study most.

The Study Guide

Beyond the learning aids contained in each chapter and on the online resources for *Discovering Psychology*, we also highly recommend the excellent **Study Guide** that accompanies this text. The Study Guide was written by our colleague Cornelius Rea at Douglas College in New Westminster, British Columbia, Canada. If you did not receive a Study Guide, you can order one through your bookstore or online through Worth Publishers.

That's it! We hope you enjoy reading and learning from the fifth edition of *Discovering Psychology*. If you want to share your thoughts or suggestions for the next edition of this book, you can write to us at the following address:

Don and Sandy Hockenbury
c/o Worth Publishers
41 Madison Avenue, 35th Floor
New York, NY 10010

Or you can contact us at our e-mail address:

DiscoveringPsychology@gmail.com

Have a great class!

Discovering PSYCHOLOGY

CHAPTER 1

Introduction and Research Methods

Chapter Outline

Miracle Magnets?

PROLOGUE

You don't need to be a psychologist to notice that every class has its own collective personality. In our 11 o'clock introductory psychology class during this particular semester, multiple personalities emerged as the students quickly segregated themselves by age and life experiences.

The younger students were a hodgepodge of races, ethnic groups, first languages, hair colors and styles, sizes, shapes, tattoos, and piercings. Best described as boisterous bordering on rowdy, this assortment of characters clustered together on the right side of the classroom and regularly asked interesting (and sometimes off-the-wall) questions.

Grouped on the left side of the class were seven middle-aged adult students. Although they occasionally spoke up in class, this group of forty-somethings would probably be best described as reserved. Two of the guys were displaced (and disgruntled) workers training for new jobs. And there were three women who were resuming their educations because their children had reached school age or were grown. Brenda was one of them.

Lingering after class one day, Brenda asked if Don had time to talk. "Do you know anything about magnet therapy for psychological disorders?" she asked.

"I know a little about the research on transcranial magnetic stimulation, if that's what you're asking about," Don responded. Brenda looked puzzled.

"It's abbreviated TMS," Don explained. "It's a procedure that uses powerful electromagnetic fields to stimulate the brain. The device looks kind of like two big, flat donuts side by side on a wand. They set the thing on a person's skull and the magnetic coils inside generate magnetic fields."

"So it's not like a regular magnet?" Brenda asked.

"Oh, no. Not at all. The device is actually an electromagnet. It needs electricity to generate the magnetic field."

"Can it be used for schizophrenia?"

"TMS? From what I've read, TMS is used to treat depression. My understanding is that it's still experimental. I can find out more about it if you want."

"What about magnetic vests? Could something like this be used to treat schizophrenia?" Brenda asked, unfolding a piece of paper and handing it to Don. It was a Web page advertisement for a cloth vest with 48 magnets sewn into the front and back lining. The ad was cluttered with quotes from people who claimed that the vest had improved their athletic ability or relieved pain or other symptoms.

"Wow, forty-eight magnets. These are static magnets. That must be incredibly heavy to wear," Don commented as he studied the ad. "I don't mean to pry,

What Do Psychologists Study? Conformity and confrontation, friendliness and fear, assertiveness and aggression. Private thoughts, public behavior. Optimism and hope, pessimism and distress. These are just a few of the wide range of topics studied in *psychology*, the science of behavior and mental processes. But whether psychologists study the behavior of a single brain cell or the behavior of a crowd of people, they rely on the scientific method to guide their investigations.

Brenda, but can I ask why you're asking about this?"

Brenda glanced around the classroom, checking to make sure no one else was listening to our conversation. "I have a son named Adam. He was diagnosed with schizophrenia about three years ago, just after his thirteenth birthday," she explained. "There's a therapist who works with Adam's psychiatrist who told us to buy this magnetic vest. She said the magnets will help treat Adam's schizophrenia."

"Really? How is it supposed to help?"

"I don't understand it," Brenda admitted. "But my son has been wearing the magnetic vest for the last two weeks, even at school. It cost about $250, and he hates it! It's heavy and hot and it makes his skin itch. The therapist wants us to buy a magnetic mattress that costs about a thousand dollars. That's a lot of money in our household. Do you think it might help?"

"I've never heard of such a thing," Don replied cautiously. "Is the vest helping?"

"It doesn't seem to be," Brenda answered, frowning. "But the therapist said we need to give it time. She said she's seen the magnetic mattress work miracles with some of her patients. And my neighbor swears that his arthritis is much better since he started wearing magnetic bracelets."

"Miracles, huh? Honestly, Brenda, I'm not aware of any research about using regular magnets to treat schizophrenia or any other psychological disorder. Then again, this could be something that slipped by both me and Sandy. Let me scan the research this weekend and we'll talk on Monday," Don said.

Later in the chapter, we'll share what we found out about magnet therapy.

Like Brenda, many of our students respond personally to the topics we cover in our introductory psychology class. As teachers and authors, we've found that building on the many links between psychological knowledge and our students' personal experiences is a very effective way to learn about psychology. Our goal is to build a conceptual bridge between your existing knowledge and new ways of understanding your experiences.

In this introductory chapter, this conceptual bridge will help us establish some important foundations and themes for the rest of the text. You'll see how psychology evolved into a very diverse science that studies many different areas of human and animal experience. The common theme connecting these diverse interests is that psychology rests on a solid foundation of scientific evidence. By the end of the chapter, you'll have a better appreciation of the scientific methods that psychologists use to answer questions, big and small, about behavior and mental processes.

Welcome to psychology!

>> Introduction: The Origins of Psychology

Key Theme

- **Today, psychology is defined as the science of behavior and mental processes, a definition that reflects psychology's origins and history.**

Key Questions

- **What roles did Wundt and James play in establishing psychology?**
- **What were the early schools and approaches in psychology, and how did their views differ?**

We begin this introductory chapter by stepping backward in time to answer several important questions: How did psychology begin? When did psychology begin? Who founded psychology as a science?

It's important to consider these historical issues for several reasons. First, students are often surprised at the wide range of topics studied by contemporary psychologists.

psychology
The scientific study of behavior and mental processes.

Those topics can range from the behavior of a single brain cell to the behavior of people in groups, from prenatal development to old age, and from normal behavior and mental processes to severely maladaptive behavior and mental processes. As you become familiar with how psychology began and developed, you'll have a better appreciation for how it has come to encompass such diverse subjects.

Second, you need to understand how the definition of **psychology** has evolved over the past 130 years to what it is today—*the scientific study of behavior and mental processes.* Indeed, the early history of psychology is the history of a field struggling to define itself as a separate and unique scientific discipline. The early psychologists struggled with such fundamental issues as:

- How should psychology be defined?
- What is the proper subject matter of psychology?
- Which areas of human experience should be studied?
- What methods should be used to investigate psychological issues?
- Should psychology include the study of nonhuman animal behavior?
- Should psychological findings be used to change or enhance human behavior?

These debates helped set the tone of the new science, define its scope, and set its limits. Over the past century, the shifting focus of these debates has influenced the topics studied and the research methods used.

Aristotle (384–322 BCE) The first western thinker to study psychological topics, Aristotle combined the logic of philosophy with empirical observation. His best known psychological work, *De Anima,* is regarded as the first systematic treatise on psychology. Its range of topics include such basic psychological processes as the senses, perception, memory, thinking, and motivation. Aristotle's writings on psychology anticipated topics and theories that would be central to scientific psychology centuries later.

The Influence of Philosophy and Physiology

The earliest origins of psychology can be traced back several centuries to the writings of the great philosophers. More than 2,000 years ago, the Greek philosopher Aristotle wrote extensively about topics like sleep, dreams, the senses, and memory. He also described the traits and dispositions of different animals. Many of Aristotle's ideas remained influential until the beginnings of modern science in the seventeenth century (Kheriaty, 2007).

At that time, the French philosopher René Descartes (1596–1650) proposed a doctrine called *interactive dualism*—the idea that mind and body were separate entities that interact to produce sensations, emotions, and other conscious experiences. Today, psychologists continue to explore the relationship between mental activity and the brain.

Philosophers also laid the groundwork for another issue that would become central to psychology—the *nature–nurture issue.* For centuries, philosophers debated which was more important: the inborn *nature* of the individual or the environmental influences that *nurture* the individual. Today, psychologists acknowledge the importance of both, but they still actively investigate the relative influences of *heredity versus environmental factors* in many aspects of behavior.

Such philosophical discussions influenced the topics that would be considered in psychology. But the early philosophers could advance the understanding of human behavior only to a certain point. Their methods were limited to intuition, observation, and logic.

The eventual emergence of psychology as a science hinged on advances in other sciences, particularly physiology. *Physiology* is a branch of biology that studies the functions and parts of living organisms, including humans. In the 1600s, physiologists were becoming interested in the human brain and its relation to behavior. By the early 1700s, it was discovered that damage to one side of the brain produced a loss of function in the opposite side of the body. By the early 1800s, the idea that different brain areas were related to different behavioral functions was being vigorously debated. Collectively, the early scientific discoveries made by physiologists were establishing the foundation for an idea that was to prove critical to the emergence of psychology—namely, that scientific methods could be applied to answering questions about behavior and mental processes.

Nature or Nurture? Both father and son are clearly enjoying the experience of drawing together. Is the child's interest in art an expression of his natural tendencies, or is it the result of his father's encouragement and teaching? Are such environmental factors more important than the child's inborn abilities? Originally debated by philosophers hundreds of years ago, the relative importance of heredity and environmental factors continues to interest psychologists today.

Wilhelm Wundt (1832–1920) German physiologist Wilhelm Wundt is generally credited as being the founder of psychology as an experimental science. In 1879, he established the first psychology research laboratory in Leipzig, Germany. By the early 1900s, many American students had come to study at Wundt's facilities, which now occupied several floors at the university. By that time, Wundt's research had expanded to include such topics as cultural psychology and developmental psychology.

Wilhelm Wundt

The Founder of Psychology

By the second half of the 1800s, the stage had been set for the emergence of psychology as a distinct scientific discipline. The leading proponent of this idea was a German physiologist named **Wilhelm Wundt.** Wundt used scientific methods to study fundamental psychological processes, such as mental reaction times in response to visual or auditory stimuli. For example, Wundt tried to measure precisely how long it took a person to consciously detect the sight and sound of a bell being struck.

A major turning point in psychology occurred in 1874, when Wundt published his landmark text, *Principles of Physiological Psychology* (Diamond, 2001). In this book, Wundt outlined the connections between physiology and psychology. He also promoted his belief that psychology should be established as a separate scientific discipline that would use experimental methods to study mental processes. A few years later, in 1879, Wundt realized that goal when he opened the first psychology research laboratory at the University of Leipzig. Many regard this event as marking the formal beginning of psychology as an experimental science (Wade & others, 2007).

Wundt defined psychology as the study of consciousness and emphasized the use of experimental methods to study and measure consciousness. Until he died in 1920, Wundt exerted a strong influence on the development of psychology as a science. Two hundred students from around the world, including many from the United States, traveled to Leipzig to earn doctorates in experimental psychology under Wundt's direction. Over the years, some 17,000 students attended Wundt's afternoon lectures on general psychology, which often included demonstrations of devices he had developed to measure mental processes (Blumenthal, 1998).

Edward B. Titchener (1867–1927) Born in England, Titchener studied with Wundt in Germany and then became a psychology professor at Cornell University in 1892. In contrast to the psychology programs at both Harvard and Columbia Universities at the time, Titchener welcomed women into his graduate program at Cornell. In fact, more women completed their psychology doctorates under Titchener's direction than with any other male psychologist of his generation (Evans, 1991).

Edward B. Titchener

Structuralism

One of Wundt's most devoted students was a young Englishman named **Edward B. Titchener.** After earning his psychology doctorate in Wundt's laboratory in 1892, Titchener accepted a position at Cornell University in Ithaca, New York. There he established a psychology laboratory that ultimately spanned 26 rooms.

Titchener eventually departed from Wundt's position and developed his own ideas on the nature of psychology. Titchener's approach, called *structuralism,* became the first major school of thought in psychology. **Structuralism** held that even our most complex conscious experiences could be broken down into elemental *structures,* or component parts, of sensations and feelings. To identify these structures of conscious thought, Titchener trained subjects in a procedure called *introspection*. The subjects would view a simple stimulus, such as a book, and then try to reconstruct their sensations and feelings immediately after viewing it. (In psychology, a *stimulus* is anything perceptible to the senses, such as a sight, sound, smell, touch, or taste.) They might first report on the colors they saw, then the smells, and so on, in the attempt to create a total description of their conscious experience (Tweney, 1997).

In addition to being distinguished as the first school of thought in early psychology, Titchener's structuralism holds the dubious distinction of being the first school to disappear. With Titchener's death in 1927, structuralism as an influential school of thought in psychology essentially ended. But even before Titchener's death, structuralism was often criticized for relying too heavily on the method of introspection.

As noted by Wundt and other scientists, introspection had significant limitations. First, introspection was an unreliable method of investigation. Different subjects often provided very different introspective reports about the same stimulus. Even subjects well trained in introspection varied in their responses to the same stimulus from trial to trial.

Second, introspection could not be used to study children or animals. Third, complex topics, such as learning, development, mental disorders, and personality, could not be investigated using introspection. In the end, the methods and goals of structuralism were simply too limited to accommodate the rapidly expanding interests of the field of psychology.

William James

Functionalism

By the time Titchener arrived at Cornell University, psychology was already well established in the United States. The main proponent of American psychology was one of Harvard's most outstanding teachers—**William James.** James had become intrigued by the emerging science of psychology after reading one of Wundt's articles, "Recent Advances in the Field of Physiological Psychology," in the late 1860s. But there were other influences on the development of James's thinking.

Like many other scientists and philosophers of his generation, James was fascinated by the idea that different species had evolved over time (Menand, 2001). Many nineteenth-century scientists in England, France, and the United States were evolutionists—that is, they believed that species had not been created once and for all, but had changed over time (Caton, 2007).

In the 1850s, British philosopher Herbert Spencer had published several works arguing that modern species, including humans, were the result of gradual evolutionary change. In 1859, **Charles Darwin's** groundbreaking work, *On the Origin of Species,* was published. James and his fellow thinkers actively debated the notion of evolution, which came to have a profound influence on James's ideas (Richardson, 2006). Like Darwin, James stressed the importance of adaptation to environmental challenges.

In the early 1870s, James began teaching a physiology and anatomy class at Harvard University. An intense, enthusiastic teacher, James was prone to changing the subject matter of his classes as his own interests changed (B. Ross, 1991). Gradually, his lectures came to focus more on psychology than on physiology. By the late 1870s, James was teaching classes devoted exclusively to the topic of psychology.

At about the same time, James began writing a comprehensive textbook of psychology, a task that would take him more than a decade. James's *Principles of Psychology* was finally published in two volumes in 1890. Despite its length of more than 1,400 pages, *Principles of Psychology* quickly became the leading psychology textbook. In it, James discussed such diverse topics as brain function, habit, memory, sensation, perception, and emotion. James's views had an enormous impact on the development of psychology in the United States.

James's ideas became the basis for a new school of psychology, called functionalism. **Functionalism** stressed the importance of how behavior *functions* to allow people and animals to adapt to their environments. Unlike structuralists, functionalists did not limit their methods to introspection. They expanded the scope of psychology research to include direct observation of living creatures in natural settings. They also examined how psychology could be applied to areas such as education, child rearing, and the work environment.

Both the structuralists and the functionalists thought that psychology should focus on the study of conscious experiences. But the functionalists had very different ideas about the nature of consciousness and how it should be studied. Rather than trying to identify the essential structures of consciousness at a given moment, James saw consciousness as an ongoing stream of mental activity that shifts and changes.

William James (1842–1910) Harvard professor William James was instrumental in establishing psychology in the United States. In 1890, James published a highly influential text, *Principles of Psychology.* James's ideas became the basis of another early school of psychology, called *functionalism,* which stressed studying the adaptive and practical functions of human behavior.

structuralism
Early school of psychology that emphasized studying the most basic components, or structures, of conscious experiences.

functionalism
Early school of psychology that emphasized studying the purpose, or function, of behavior and mental experiences.

Charles Darwin (1809–1882) Although he was not a psychologist, naturalist Charles Darwin had a profound influence on the early development of psychology. Darwin was not the first scientist to propose that complex organisms evolved from simpler species (Caton, 2007). However, Darwin's book, *On the Origin of Species,* published in 1859, gathered evidence from many different scientific fields to present a readable, compelling account of evolution through the mechanism of natural selection. Darwin's ideas have had a lasting impact on scientific thought (Padian, 2008; Pagel, 2009).

As James wrote in *Talks to Teachers* (1899):

> Now the *immediate* fact which psychology, the science of mind, has to study is also the most general fact. It is the fact that in each of us, when awake (and often when asleep), *some kind of consciousness is always going on.* There is a stream, a succession of states, or waves, or fields (or whatever you please to call them), of knowledge, of feeling, of desire, of deliberation, etc., that constantly pass and repass, and that constitute our inner life. The existence of this is the primal fact, [and] the nature and origin of it form the essential problem, of our science.

Like structuralism, functionalism no longer exists as a distinct school of thought in contemporary psychology. Nevertheless, functionalism's twin themes of the importance of the adaptive role of behavior and the application of psychology to enhance human behavior continue to be evident in modern psychology.

William James and His Students

Like Wundt, James profoundly influenced psychology through his students, many of whom became prominent American psychologists. Two of James's most notable students were G. Stanley Hall and Mary Whiton Calkins.

In 1878, **G. Stanley Hall** received the first Ph.D. in psychology awarded in the United States. Hall founded the first psychology research laboratory in the United States at Johns Hopkins University in 1883. He also began publishing the *American Journal of Psychology,* the first U.S. journal devoted to psychology. Most important, in 1892, Hall founded the American Psychological Association and was elected its first president (Arnett & Cravens, 2006). Today, the American Psychological Association (APA) is the world's largest professional organization of psychologists, with approximately 150,000 members.

G. Stanley Hall (1844–1924) G. Stanley Hall helped organize psychology in the United States. Among his many achievements, Hall established the first psychology research laboratory in the United States and founded the American Psychological Association. In 1888, Hall became the first president of Clark University in Worcester, Massachusetts.

In 1890, **Mary Whiton Calkins** was assigned the task of teaching experimental psychology at a new women's college—Wellesley College. Calkins studied with James at nearby Harvard University. She completed all the requirements for a Ph.D. in psychology. However, Harvard refused to grant her the Ph.D. degree because she was a woman and at the time Harvard was not a coeducational institution (Milar, 2000).

Although never awarded the degree she had earned, Calkins made several notable contributions to psychology (Stevens & Gardner, 1982). She conducted research in many areas, including dreams, memory, and personality. In 1891, she established a psychological laboratory at Wellesley College. At the turn of the twentieth century, she wrote a well-received textbook, titled *Introduction to Psychology.* In 1905, Calkins was elected president of the American Psychological Association—the first woman, but not the last, to hold that position.

Just for the record, the first American woman to earn an official Ph.D. in psychology was **Margaret Floy Washburn.** Washburn was Edward Titchener's first doctoral student at Cornell University. She strongly advocated the scientific study of the mental processes of different animal species. In 1908, she published an influential text, titled *The Animal Mind.* Her book summarized research on sensation, perception, learning, and other "inner experiences" of different animal species. In 1921, Washburn became the second woman elected president of the American Psychological Association (Viney & Burlingame-Lee, 2003).

Finally, one of G. Stanley Hall's notable students was **Francis C. Sumner** (1895–1954). A brilliant student, Sumner was the first black American to receive a Ph.D. in psychology, awarded by Clark University in 1920. After teaching at several southern universities, Sumner moved to Howard University in Washington, D.C. At Howard he published papers on a wide variety of topics and chaired a psychology department that produced more black psychologists than all other American colleges and universities combined (Bayton, 1975; Guthrie, 2000, 2004). One of Sumner's most famous students was Kenneth Bancroft Clark. Clark's research on the negative effects of discrimination was instrumental in the U.S. Supreme Court's 1954 decision to end segregated schools (Sawyer, 2000). In 1970, Clark became the first black president of the American Psychological Association (Belgrave & Allison, 2006).

psychoanalysis
Personality theory and form of psychotherapy that emphasize the role of unconscious factors in personality and behavior.

Mary Whiton Calkins (1863–1930) Under the direction of William James, Mary Whiton Calkins completed all the requirements for a Ph.D. in psychology. Calkins had a distinguished professional career, establishing a psychology laboratory at Wellesley College and becoming the first woman president of the American Psychological Association.

Margaret Floy Washburn (1871–1939) After becoming the first American woman to earn an official Ph.D. in psychology, Washburn went on to a distinguished career. Despite the discrimination against women that was widespread in higher education during the early twentieth century, Washburn made many contributions to psychology. She was the second woman to be elected president of the American Psychological Association.

Francis C. Sumner (1895–1954) Francis Sumner studied under G. Stanley Hall at Clark University. In 1920, he became the first African American to earn a Ph.D. in psychology. Sumner later joined Howard University in Washington, D.C., and became chairman of the psychology department. Over the next 25 years, Sumner helped create a strong psychology program at Howard University that led the country in training black psychologists (Belgrave & Allison, 2006; Guthrie, 2000, 2004).

Sigmund Freud

Psychoanalysis

Wundt, James, and other early psychologists emphasized the study of conscious experiences. But at the turn of the twentieth century, new approaches challenged the principles of both structuralism and functionalism.

In Vienna, Austria, a physician named **Sigmund Freud** was developing an intriguing theory of personality based on uncovering causes of behavior that were *unconscious,* or hidden from the person's conscious awareness. Freud's school of psychological thought, called **psychoanalysis,** emphasized the role of unconscious conflicts in determining behavior and personality.

Freud's psychoanalytic theory of personality and behavior was based largely on his work with his patients and on insights derived from self-analysis. Freud believed that human behavior was motivated by unconscious conflicts that were almost always sexual or aggressive in nature. Past experiences, especially childhood experiences, were thought to be critical in the formation of adult personality and behavior. According to Freud (1904), glimpses of these unconscious impulses are revealed in everyday life in dreams, memory blocks, slips of the tongue, and spontaneous humor. Freud believed that when unconscious conflicts became extreme, psychological disorders could result.

Freud's psychoanalytic theory of personality also provided the basis for a distinct form of psychotherapy. Many of the fundamental ideas of psychoanalysis continue to influence psychologists and other professionals in the mental health field. In Chapter 10, on personality, and Chapter 14, where we cover psychotherapy, we'll explore Freud's views on personality in more detail.

Sigmund Freud (1856–1939) In 1909, Freud (*front left*) and several other psychoanalysts were invited by G. Stanley Hall (*front center*) to participate in Clark University's 20th anniversary celebration in Worcester, Massachusetts (Hogan, 2003). Freud delivered five lectures on psychoanalysis. Listening in the audience was William James, who later wrote to a friend that Freud struck him as "a man obsessed with fixed ideas" (Rosenzweig, 1997). Carl Jung (*front right*), who later developed his own theory of personality, also attended this historic conference. Ernest Jones, Freud's biographer and translator, is standing behind Hall.

behaviorism
School of psychology and theoretical viewpoint that emphasize the study of observable behaviors, especially as they pertain to the process of learning.

humanistic psychology
School of psychology and theoretical viewpoint that emphasize each person's unique potential for psychological growth and self-direction.

John B. Watson

Behaviorism

The course of psychology changed dramatically in the early 1900s when another approach, called **behaviorism,** emerged as a dominating force. Behaviorism rejected the emphasis on consciousness promoted by structuralism and functionalism. It also flatly rejected Freudian notions about unconscious influences. Instead, behaviorism contended that psychology should focus its scientific investigations strictly on *overt behavior*—observable behaviors that could be objectively measured and verified.

Behaviorism is yet another example of the influence of physiology on psychology. Behaviorism grew out of the pioneering work of a Russian physiologist named **Ivan Pavlov.** Pavlov demonstrated that dogs could learn to associate a neutral stimulus, such as the sound of a bell, with an automatic behavior, such as reflexively salivating to food. Once an association between the sound of the bell and the food was formed, the sound of the bell alone would trigger the salivation reflex in the dog. Pavlov enthusiastically believed he had discovered the mechanism by which all behaviors were learned.

In the United States, a young, dynamic psychologist named **John B. Watson** shared Pavlov's enthusiasm. Watson (1913) championed behaviorism as a new school of psychology. Structuralism was still an influential perspective, but Watson strongly objected to both its method of introspection and its focus on conscious mental processes. As Watson (1924) wrote in his classic book, *Behaviorism:*

> Behaviorism, on the contrary, holds that the subject matter of human psychology *is the behavior of the human being*. Behaviorism claims that consciousness is neither a definite nor a usable concept. The behaviorist, who has been trained always as an experimentalist, holds, further, that belief in the existence of consciousness goes back to the ancient days of superstition and magic.

The influence of behaviorism on American psychology was enormous. The goal of the behaviorists was to discover the fundamental principles of *learning*—how behavior is acquired and modified in response to environmental influences. For the most part, the behaviorists studied animal behavior under carefully controlled laboratory conditions.

Although Watson left academic psychology in the early 1920s, behaviorism was later championed by an equally forceful proponent—the famous American psychologist **B. F. Skinner.** Like Watson, Skinner believed that psychology should restrict itself to studying outwardly observable behaviors that could be measured and verified. In compelling experimental demonstrations, Skinner systematically used reinforcement or punishment to shape the behavior of rats and pigeons.

Between Watson and Skinner, behaviorism dominated American psychology for almost half a century. During that time, the study of conscious experiences was largely ignored as a topic in psychology (Baars, 2005). In Chapter 5, on learning, we'll look at the lives and contributions of Pavlov, Watson, and Skinner in greater detail.

Ivan Pavlov (1849–1936)

John B. Watson (1878–1958)

B. F. Skinner (1904–1990)

Three Key Scientists in the Development of Behaviorism Building on the pioneering research of Russian physiologist Ivan Pavlov, American psychologist John B. Watson founded the school of behaviorism. Behaviorism advocated that psychology should study observable behaviors, not mental processes. Following Watson, B. F. Skinner continued to champion the ideas of behaviorism. Skinner became one of the most influential psychologists of the twentieth century. Like Watson, he strongly advocated the study of observable behaviors rather than mental processes.

Carl Rogers

Humanistic Psychology

Carl Rogers (1902–1987)

Abraham Maslow (1908–1970)

Two Leaders in the Development of Humanistic Psychology Carl Rogers and Abraham Maslow were key figures in establishing humanistic psychology. Humanistic psychology emphasized the importance of self-determination, free will, and human potential. The ideas of Carl Rogers have been particularly influential in modern psychotherapy. Abraham Maslow's theory of motivation emphasized the importance of psychological growth.

For several decades, behaviorism and psychoanalysis were the perspectives that most influenced the thinking of American psychologists. In the 1950s, a new school of thought emerged, called **humanistic psychology.** Because humanistic psychology was distinctly different from both psychoanalysis and behaviorism, it was sometimes referred to as the "third force" in American psychology (Cain, 2002).

Humanistic psychology was largely founded by American psychologist **Carl Rogers** (Kirschenbaum, 2004). Like Freud, Rogers was influenced by his experiences with his psychotherapy clients. However, rather than emphasizing unconscious conflicts, Rogers emphasized the *conscious* experiences of his patients, including each person's unique potential for psychological growth and self-direction. In contrast to the behaviorists, who saw human behavior as being shaped and maintained by external causes, Rogers emphasized self-determination, free will, and the importance of choice in human behavior (Bozarth & others, 2002; Kirschenbaum & Jourdan, 2005).

Abraham Maslow was another advocate of humanistic psychology. Maslow developed a theory of motivation that emphasized psychological growth, which we'll discuss in Chapter 8. Like psychoanalysis, humanistic psychology included not only influential theories of personality but also a form of psychotherapy, which we'll discuss in later chapters.

By briefly stepping backward in time, you've seen how the debates among the key thinkers in psychology's history shaped the development of psychology as a whole. Each of the schools that we've described had an impact on the topics and methods of psychological research. As you'll see throughout this textbook, that impact has been a lasting one.

From the founding of Wundt's laboratory in 1879, psychology has evolved to its current status as a dynamic and multidimensional science. In the next section, we'll touch on some of the more recent developments in psychology's evolution. We'll also explore the diversity that characterizes contemporary psychology.

Contemporary Psychology

Key Theme

- **As psychology has developed as a scientific discipline, the topics it investigates have become progressively more diverse.**

Key Questions

- **How do the perspectives in contemporary psychology differ in emphasis and approach?**
- **What are psychology's major specialty areas?**

Since the 1960s, the range of topics in psychology has become progressively more diverse. And, as psychology's knowledge base has increased, psychology itself has become more specialized. Rather than being dominated by a particular approach or school of thought, today's psychologists tend to identify themselves according to (1) the *perspective* they emphasize in investigating psychological topics and (2) the *specialty area* in which they have been trained and practice.

Major Perspectives in Psychology

Any given topic in contemporary psychology can be approached from a variety of perspectives. Each perspective discussed here represents a different emphasis or point of view that can be taken in studying a particular behavior, topic, or issue. As you'll see in this section, the influence of the early schools of psychology is apparent in the first four perspectives that characterize contemporary psychology.

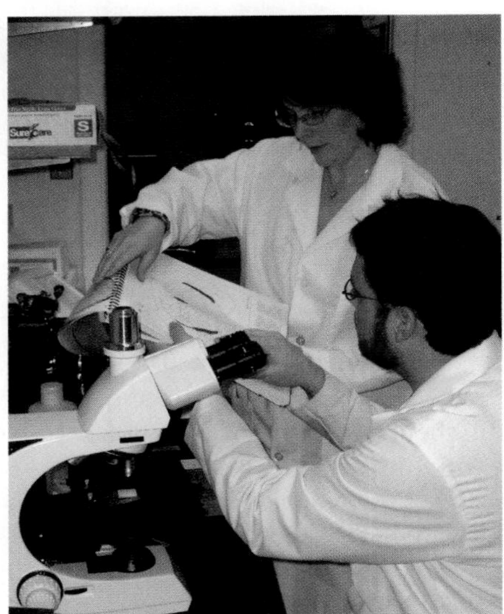

The Biological Perspective The physiological aspects of behavior and mental processes are studied by biological psychologists. Psychologists and other scientists who specialize in the study of the brain and the rest of the nervous system are often called *neuroscientists.* Shown at right is Yale biopsychologist Karyn Frick discussing an experimental design with psychology graduate student Patrick Orr. Frick and her colleagues are studying how aging and sex hormones, especially estrogen and progesterone, alter memory. As Frick (2009) comments, "I find biological psychology fascinating because so much about how the brain creates behavior remains unknown. Nevertheless, modern biopsychologists have an incredible array of tools at their disposal to ask fundamental questions about the neural mechanisms underlying behavioral processes, so this is a particularly exciting time for neuroscience research!" You'll read about Frick's research in more detail in Chapter 6, on memory.

The Biological Perspective

As we've already noted, physiology has played an important role in psychology since it was founded. Today, that influence continues, as is shown by the many psychologists who take the biological perspective. The *biological perspective* emphasizes studying the physical bases of human and animal behavior, including the nervous system, endocrine system, immune system, and genetics. More specifically, **neuroscience** refers to the study of the nervous system, especially the brain.

Interest in the biological perspective has grown in the last few decades, partly because of advances in technology and medicine. For example, in the late 1950s and early 1960s, medications were developed that helped control the symptoms of serious psychological disorders, such as schizophrenia and depression. The relative success of those new drugs sparked new questions about the interaction among biological factors and human behavior, emotions, and thought processes.

Equally important were technological advances that have allowed psychologists and other researchers to explore the human brain as never before. The development of the PET scan, MRI scan, and functional MRI (fMRI) scan has allowed scientists to study the structure and activity of the intact brain. Later in the chapter, we'll describe these brain-imaging techniques and how psychologists use them as research tools.

The Psychodynamic Perspective

The key ideas and themes of Freud's landmark theory of psychoanalysis continue to be important among many psychologists, especially those working in the mental health field. As you'll see in Chapter 10, on personality, and Chapter 14, on therapies, many of Freud's ideas have been expanded or modified by his followers. Today, psychologists who take the *psychodynamic perspective* emphasize the importance of unconscious influences, early life experiences, and interpersonal relationships in explaining the underlying dynamics of behavior or in treating people with psychological problems.

Studying Behavior from Different Psychological Perspectives Psychologists can study a particular behavior, topic, or issue from different perspectives. Consider the heroic efforts of California firefighters in the midst of 2008's massive wildfires. Trained to save people and homes in the face of the devastating heat and destruction of out-of-control fires, these men and women often spent 24-hour days and weeks on the fire line, working against an overwhelming force as well as their own exhaustion.

Taking the *biological perspective,* a psychologist might study whether there are biological differences between the California firefighters and other people, such as the ability to stay calm and focused in the face of dangerous situations. A psychologist taking the *behavioral perspective* might look at how helping behaviors are learned and reinforced. Taking the *cognitive perspective,* another psychologist might investigate the kinds of mental processes that are involved in planning and carrying out the successful evacuation of people from their threatened homes.

The Behavioral Perspective

Watson and Skinner's contention that psychology should focus on observable behaviors and the fundamental laws of learning is evident today in the *behavioral perspective*. Contemporary psychologists who take the behavioral perspective continue to study how behavior is acquired or modified by environmental causes. Many psychologists who work in the area of mental health also emphasize the behavioral perspective in explaining and treating psychological disorders. In Chapter 5, on learning, and Chapter 14, on therapies, we'll discuss different applications of the behavioral perspective.

neuroscience
The study of the nervous system, especially the brain.

positive psychology
The study of positive emotions and psychological states, positive individual traits, and the social institutions that foster positive individuals and communities.

The Humanistic Perspective

The influence of the work of Carl Rogers and Abraham Maslow continues to be seen among contemporary psychologists who take the humanistic perspective. The *humanistic perspective* focuses on the motivation of people to grow psychologically, the influence of interpersonal relationships on a person's self-concept, and the importance of choice and self-direction in striving to reach one's potential. Like the psychodynamic perspective, the humanistic perspective is often emphasized among psychologists working in the mental health field. You'll encounter the humanistic perspective in the chapters on motivation (8), personality (10), and therapies (14).

The Positive Psychology Perspective

The humanistic perspective's emphasis on psychological growth and human potential contributed to the recent emergence of a new perspective. **Positive psychology** is a field of psychological research and theory focusing on the study of positive emotions and psychological states, positive individual traits, and the social institutions that foster those qualities in individuals and communities (Peterson, 2006; Seligman & Csikszentmihalyi, 2000; Seligman & others, 2005). By studying the conditions and processes that contribute to the optimal functioning of people, groups, and institutions, positive psychology seeks to counterbalance psychology's traditional emphasis on psychological problems and disorders (Gable & Haidt, 2005; Seligman & others, 2006).

Topics that fall under the umbrella of positive psychology include personal happiness, optimism, creativity, resilience, character strengths, and wisdom. Positive psychology is also focused on developing therapeutic techniques that increase personal well-being rather than just alleviating the troubling symptoms of psychological disorders (Snyder & Lopez, 2005). Insights from positive psychology research will be evident in many chapters, including the chapters on motivation and emotion (8); lifespan development (9); personality (10); stress, health, and coping (12); and therapies (14).

The Cognitive Perspective

During the 1960s, psychology experienced a return to the study of how mental processes influence behavior. Often referred to as "the cognitive revolution" in psychology, this movement represented a break from traditional behaviorism. Cognitive psychology focused once again on the important role of mental processes in how people process and remember information, develop language, solve problems, and think.

The development of the first computers in the 1950s contributed to the cognitive revolution. Computers gave psychologists a new model for conceptualizing human mental processes—human thinking, memory, and perception could be understood in terms of an information-processing model. We'll consider the cognitive perspective in several chapters, including Chapter 7, on thinking, language, and intelligence.

The Cross-Cultural Perspective

More recently, psychologists have taken a closer look at how cultural factors influence patterns of behavior—the essence of the *cross-cultural perspective.* By the late 1980s, *cross-cultural psychology* had emerged in full force as large numbers of psychologists began studying the diversity of human behavior in different cultural settings and countries (Berry & Triandis, 2006). In the process, psychologists discovered that some well-established psychological findings were not as universal as they had thought.

Influence of Culture on Behavior: Social Loafing Versus Social Striving Cross-cultural psychology highlights the fact that common behaviors are not always universal. On Micronesia's Ifalik Island, these islanders are working together to set a large fishing net. In highly collectivistic cultures like Micronesia, people tend to work harder in a group than when alone. This behavior, called *social striving,* contrasts with *social loafing*, which refers to expending less effort as the size of the group increases (Latané & others, 1979). Although once thought to be universal, social loafing is more common in individualistic cultures (Bond & Smith, 1996).

evolutionary psychology
The application of principles of evolution, including natural selection, to explain psychological processes and phenomena.

culture
The attitudes, values, beliefs, and behaviors shared by a group of people and communicated from one generation to another.

cross-cultural psychology
Branch of psychology that studies the effects of culture on behavior and mental processes.

ethnocentrism
The belief that one's own culture or ethnic group is superior to all others, and the related tendency to use one's own culture as a standard by which to judge other cultures.

individualistic cultures
Cultures that emphasize the needs and goals of the individual over the needs and goals of the group.

collectivistic cultures
Cultures that emphasize the needs and goals of the group over the needs and goals of the individual.

For example, one well-established psychological finding was that people exert more effort on a task when working alone than when working as part of a group, a phenomenon called *social loafing*. First demonstrated in the 1970s, social loafing was a consistent finding in several psychological studies conducted with American and European subjects. But when similar studies were conducted with Chinese participants during the 1980s, the opposite was found to be true (see Moghaddam, 2002). Chinese participants worked harder on a task when they were part of a group than when they were working alone.

Today, psychologists are keenly attuned to the influence of cultural and ethnic factors on behavior (Norenzayan & Heine, 2005). We have included Culture and Human Behavior boxes throughout this textbook to help sensitize you to the influence of culture on behavior—including your own. We describe cross-cultural psychology in more detail in the Culture and Human Behavior box on the next page.

The Evolutionary Perspective

Evolutionary psychology refers to the application of the principles of evolution to explain psychological processes and phenomena (Buss, 2009). The *evolutionary perspective* has grown out of a renewed interest in the work of English naturalist Charles Darwin. As noted previously, Darwin's (1859) first book on evolution, *On the Origin of Species,* played an influential role in the thinking of many early psychologists.

The theory of evolution proposes that the individual members of a species compete for survival. Because of inherited differences, some members of a species are better adapted to their environment than are others. Organisms that inherit characteristics that increase their chances of survival in their particular habitat are more likely to survive, reproduce, and pass on their characteristics to their offspring. Conversely, individuals that inherit less useful characteristics are less likely to survive, reproduce, and pass on their characteristics. This process reflects the principle of *natural selection:* The most adaptive characteristics are "selected" and perpetuated in the next generation.

Psychologists who take the evolutionary perspective assume that psychological processes are also subject to the principle of natural selection. As David Buss (2008) writes, "An evolved psychological mechanism exists in the form that it does because it solved a specific problem of survival or reproduction recurrently over evolutionary history." That is, those psychological processes that helped individuals adapt to their environments also helped them survive, reproduce, and pass those abilities on to their offspring.

As you consider the possible role of evolutionary adaptations in shaping modern psychological processes, keep the time frame of evolutionary changes in perspective. If evolutionary influences helped shaped psychological processes, those influences occurred over hundreds of thousands of years. What we think of as human civilization has existed for only about 10,000 years, since the earliest appearance of agriculture. In contrast, our ancient human ancestors spent more than *2 million years* as primitive hunter-gatherers.

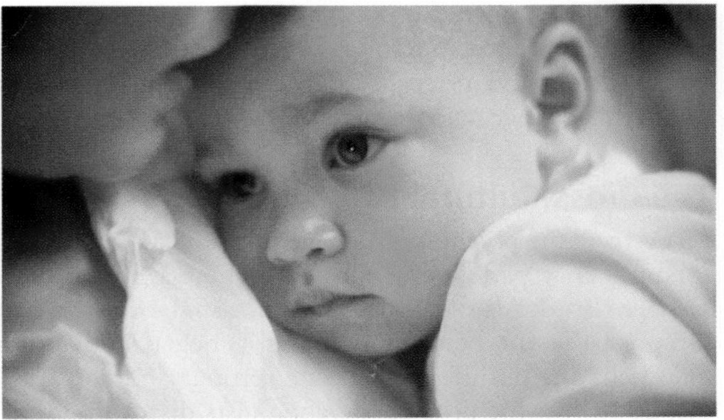

The Evolutionary Perspective The evolutionary perspective analyzes behavior in terms of how it increases a species' chances to survive and reproduce. Comparing behaviors across species can often lead to new insights about the adaptive function of a particular behavior. For example, humans, monkeys, and apes are all members of the primate family. Close bonds with caregivers are essential to the primate infant's survival—whether that infant is a golden monkey at a wildlife preserve in northern China or a human infant at a family picnic in Norway. As you'll see in later chapters, the evolutionary perspective has been applied to many different areas of psychology, including human relationships, mate selection, eating behavior, and emotional responses (Caporael, 2001).

CULTURE AND HUMAN BEHAVIOR

What Is Cross-Cultural Psychology?

> *All cultures are simultaneously very similar and very different.*
>
> HARRY TRIANDIS (2005)

People around the globe share many attributes: We all eat, sleep, form families, seek happiness, and mourn losses. Yet the way in which we express our human qualities can vary considerably among cultures. *What* we eat, *where* we sleep, and *how* we form families, define happiness, and express sadness can differ greatly in different cultures (G. Smith & others, 2006).

Culture is a broad term that refers to the attitudes, values, beliefs, and behaviors shared by a group of people and communicated from one generation to another (Matsumoto, 2000). When this broad definition is applied to people throughout the world, about 4,000 different cultures can be said to exist. Studying the differences among those cultures and examining the influences of culture on behavior are the fundamental goals of **cross-cultural psychology** (Berry & Triandis, 2006).

A person's sense of cultural identity is influenced by such factors as ethnic background, nationality, race, religion, and language. As we grow up within a given culture, we learn our culture's *norms,* or unwritten rules of behavior. Once those cultural norms are understood and internalized, we tend to act in accordance with them without too much thought. For example, according to the dominant cultural norms in the United States, infants and toddlers are not supposed to routinely sleep in the same bed as their parents. In many other cultures around the world, however, it's taken for granted that babies *will* sleep in the same bed as their parents or other adult relatives (Morelli & others, 1992; Welles-Nystrom, 2005). Members of these other cultures are often surprised and even shocked at the U.S. practice of separating infants and toddlers from their parents at night. (In a Culture and Human Behavior box in Chapter 9, we discuss this topic at greater length.)

Whether considering sleeping habits or hairstyles, most people share a natural tendency to accept their *own* cultural rules as defining what's "normal." This tendency to use your own culture as the standard for judging other cultures is called **ethnocentrism.** Although it may be a natural tendency, ethnocentrism can lead to the inability to separate ourselves from our own cultural backgrounds and biases so that we can understand the behaviors of others (Matsumoto, 2000). Ethnocentrism may also prevent us from being aware of how our behavior has been shaped by our own culture.

Some degree of ethnocentrism is probably inevitable, but extreme ethnocentrism can lead to intolerance for other cultures. If we believe that our way of seeing things or behaving is the only proper one, other ways of behaving and thinking may seem not only foreign, but ridiculous, inferior, wrong, or immoral.

In addition to influencing how we behave, culture affects how we define our sense of self (Kitayama & others, 1997; Markus & Kitayama, 1991, 1998). For the most part, the dominant cultures of the United States, Canada, Australia, New Zealand, and Europe can be described as individualistic cultures. **Individualistic cultures** emphasize the needs and goals of the individual over the needs and goals of the group (Triandis, 2005). In individualistic societies, social behavior is more strongly influenced by individual preferences and attitudes than by cultural norms and values. In such cultures, the self is seen as *independent,* autonomous, and distinctive. Personal identity is defined by individual achievements, abilities, and accomplishments.

In contrast, **collectivistic cultures** emphasize the needs and goals of the group over the needs and goals of the individual. Social behavior is more heavily influenced by cultural norms than by individual preferences and attitudes. In a collectivistic culture, the self is seen as being much more *interdependent* with others. Relationships with others and identification with a larger group, such as the family or tribe, are key components of personal identity. The cultures of Asia, Africa, and Central and South America tend to be collectivistic. According to Triandis (2005), about two-thirds of the world's population live in collectivistic cultures.

The distinction between individualistic and collectivistic societies is useful in cross-cultural psychology. Nevertheless, psychologists are careful not to assume that these generalizations are true of *every* member or *every* aspect of a given culture (Matsumoto & Yoo, 2006). Many cultures are neither completely individualistic nor completely collectivistic, but fall somewhere between the two extremes. Equally important, psychologists recognize that there is a great deal of individual variation among the members of every culture (Heine & Norenzayan, 2006). It's important to keep that qualification in mind when cross-cultural findings are discussed, as they will be throughout this book.

The Culture and Human Behavior boxes that we have included in this book will help you learn about human behavior in other cultures. They will also help you understand how culture affects *your* behavior, beliefs, attitudes, and values as well. We hope you will find this feature both interesting and enlightening!

Cultural Differences in Subway Norms Like thousands of commuters in the United States, many commuters in Tokyo take the subway to work each day. In Japan, however, commuters line up politely behind white lines on the subway platform and patiently wait their turn to board the train. White-gloved conductors obligingly "assist" passengers in boarding by shoving them in from behind, cramming as many people into the subway car as possible. Clearly, the norms that govern subway-riding behavior are very different in American and Japanese cultures.

psychiatry
Medical specialty area focused on the diagnosis, treatment, causes, and prevention of mental and behavioral disorders.

The important point here is that a few thousand years are not long enough for sweeping evolutionary changes to take place. Psychological processes that were adaptations to a prehistoric way of life may continue to exist in the human behavioral repertoire today. However, as you'll see in later chapters, some of those processes may not necessarily be adaptive in our modern world (Tooby & Cosmides, 2005).

Specialty Areas in Psychology

The enormous diversity of contemporary psychology as a scientific discipline is reflected in the following thumbnail descriptions of psychology's specialty areas. Figure 1.1 shows the percentage of recent doctoral students who specialized in these areas and, on the right, the primary employment settings of psychologists.

Biological psychology studies the relationship between psychological processes and the body's physical systems, including the brain and the rest of the nervous system, the endocrine system, the immune system, and genetics. Also known as *biopsychology,* this area was formerly called *physiological psychology.*

Clinical psychology studies the causes, diagnosis, treatment, and prevention of different types of behavioral and emotional disorders, such as anxiety, mood, or eating disorders. Clinical psychologists have extensive training in evaluating and diagnosing psychological disorders, psychotherapy techniques, and psychological testing.

Cognitive psychology investigates mental processes, including reasoning and thinking, problem solving, memory, perception, mental imagery, and language.

Counseling psychology helps people of all ages adjust, adapt, and cope with personal and interpersonal problems in such diverse areas as relationships, work, education, marriage, child rearing, and aging.

Educational psychology studies how people of all ages learn. Educational psychologists help develop the instructional methods and materials used to train people in both educational and work settings.

Experimental psychology is the term traditionally used to describe research focused on such basic topics as sensory and perceptual processes, principles of learning, emotion, and motivation. However, note that experiments can be conducted by psychologists in every area of psychology.

Developmental psychology studies the physical, social, and psychological changes that occur at different ages and stages of the lifespan, from conception to old age.

Figure 1.1 Specialty Areas and Employment Settings The left pie chart shows the specialty areas of individuals who recently received their doctorates in psychology. The category "Other areas" includes such specialty areas as health psychology, forensic psychology, and sports psychology. The right pie chart shows psychologists' primary place of employment.

SOURCE: Finno & others (2006).

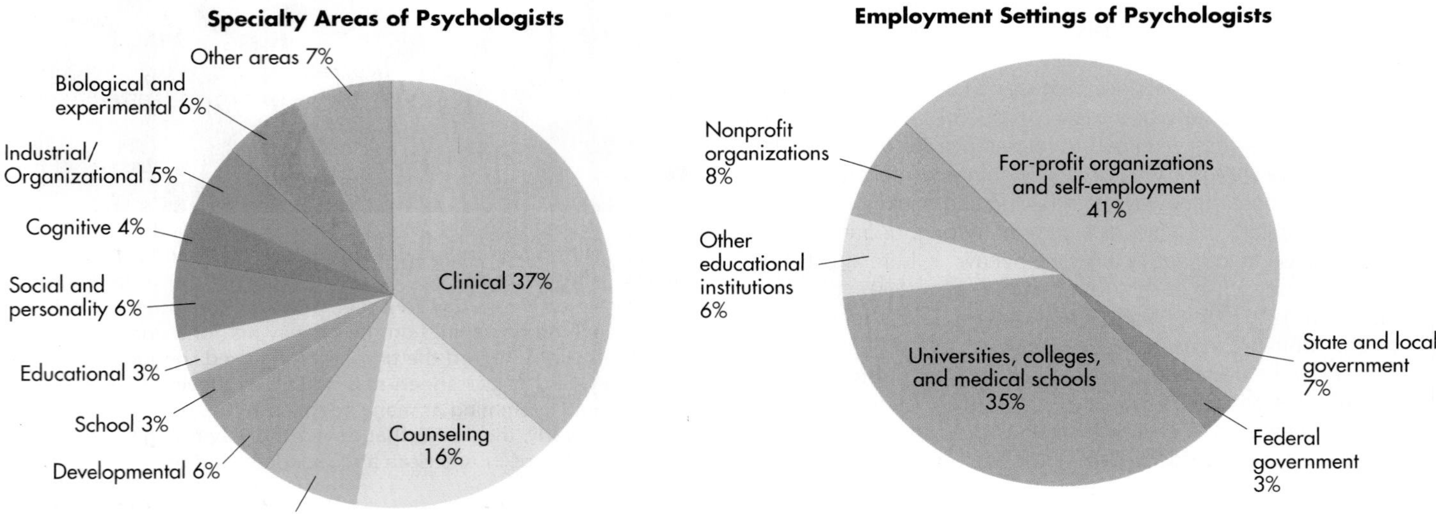

Forensic psychology applies psychological principles and techniques to legal issues, such as assessment and treatment of offenders, mental competency to stand trial, child custody, jury selection, and eyewitness testimony.

Health psychology focuses on the role of psychological factors in the development, prevention, and treatment of illness. Health psychology includes such areas as stress and coping, the relationship between psychological factors and physical health, and ways of promoting health-enhancing behaviors.

Industrial/organizational psychology is concerned with the relationship between people and work. This specialty includes such topics as job analysis, personnel selection and training, worker productivity, job satisfaction, leadership, and group behavior within organizations.

Personality psychology studies the nature of human personality, including individual differences, the characteristics that make each person unique, and how those characteristics originated and developed.

Rehabilitation psychology applies psychological knowledge to helping people with chronic and disabling health conditions, such as accident or stroke victims, adapt to their situation and attain optimal psychological, interpersonal, and physical functioning.

Social psychology explores how people are affected by their social environments, including how people think about and influence others. Topics as varied as conformity, obedience, persuasion, interpersonal attraction, helping behavior, prejudice, aggression, and social beliefs are studied by social psychologists.

Sports psychology uses psychological theory and knowledge to enhance athletic motivation, performance, and consistency.

Military Psychologists: Serving Those Who Serve Shown on duty in Iraq, Army psychologist Captain Jeffrey Bass (left) regularly travels into combat zones with his regiment and supervises a mental health clinic (Munsey, 2008, 2007a). Bass combines on-site counseling with efforts to screen soldiers for the effects of combat stress. There is an increased demand for psychologists in all branches of the military, both in war zones and stateside. At home, military psychologists help returning soldiers and their families deal with the aftereffects of combat stress, readjusting to civilian life, and coping with injuries, especially traumatic brain injuries (Munsey, 2007b; Packard, 2007). Military psychologists also help select and train army personnel for particular roles or assignments, including special operations (Munsey, 2007c).

Many students wonder how clinical psychologists differ from psychiatrists. Both clinical psychologists and psychiatrists are trained in the diagnosis, treatment, causes, and prevention of psychological disorders. However, their training and credentials are different. The training that a *clinical psychologist* receives leads to a doctorate in clinical psychology, either a Ph.D. or Psy.D. Clinical psychologists have extensive training in the different types of psychotherapy, which are described in Chapter 14.

In contrast, **psychiatry** is a medical specialty. Thus, a *psychiatrist* first obtains a medical degree, either an M.D. or D.O., followed by several years of specialized training in the treatment of mental disorders. Psychiatrists are more likely to emphasize the role of biological factors in psychological disorders. As physicians, psychiatrists can hospitalize people and order biomedical therapies, such as *electroconvulsive therapy* (ECT) or *transcranial magnetic stimulation* (TMS). Psychiatrists can also prescribe medications to treat the symptoms of different psychological disorders. These biomedical therapies are described in Chapter 14.

Clinical psychologists are not medical doctors and cannot order medical treatments. In most of the United States, clinical psychologists cannot prescribe medications. However, legislation enacted in New Mexico and Louisiana allows clinical psychologists to prescribe medications after completing additional coursework and supervised clinical training (Munsey, 2008). Especially in rural areas with few mental health professionals, allowing trained psychologists to prescribe medications can help many people who are otherwise unable to gain access to mental health care (LeVine, 2007; Price, 2008).

Despite the diversity of their work settings and interests, psychologists share common methods of investigating human behavior and mental processes. In the next section, we'll look at how psychologists are guided by the *scientific method* in their efforts to understand behavior and mental processes.

School Psychology There are about 25,000 school psychologists in the United States who provide a variety of psychological services to children, adolescents, and families in public and private schools. School psychologists help teachers, school administrators, and parents understand how children learn and develop. Some of the activities that school psychologists perform include counseling and assessing students, consulting with parents and school staff, and working with outside agencies to promote learning and development.

The Scientific Method

Key Theme

- **The scientific method is a set of assumptions, attitudes, and procedures that guide all scientists, including psychologists, in conducting research.**

Key Questions

- **What assumptions and attitudes are held by psychologists?**
- **What characterizes each step of the scientific method?**
- **How does a hypothesis differ from a theory?**

The four basic goals of psychology are to (1) describe, (2) explain, (3) predict, and (4) control or influence behavior and mental processes. To achieve these goals, psychologists rely on the scientific method. The **scientific method** refers to a set of assumptions, attitudes, and procedures that guide researchers in creating questions to investigate, in generating evidence, and in drawing conclusions.

Like all scientists, psychologists are guided by the basic scientific assumption that *events are lawful.* When this scientific assumption is applied to psychology, it means that psychologists assume that behavior and mental processes follow consistent patterns. Psychologists are also guided by the assumption that *events are explainable.* Thus, psychologists assume that behavior and mental processes have a cause or causes that can be understood through careful, systematic study.

In striving to identify and understand consistent patterns of behavior, psychologists are *open-minded.* They are willing to consider new or alternative explanations of behavior and mental processes. However, their open-minded attitude is tempered by a *healthy sense of scientific skepticism.* That is, psychologists critically evaluate the evidence for new findings, especially those that seem contrary to established knowledge. And, in announcing new ideas and findings, psychologists are *cautious* in the claims they make, not wishing to overstate or exaggerate the findings.

Collectively, the assumptions and attitudes that psychologists assume reflect critical thinking. One goal of our text is to help you become a better critical thinker, which we discuss on the next page.

The Steps in the Scientific Method

Systematically Seeking Answers

Like any science, psychology is based on verifiable or **empirical evidence**—evidence that is the result of objective observation, measurement, and experimentation. As part of the overall process of producing empirical evidence, psychologists follow the four basic steps of the scientific method. In a nutshell, these steps are:

- Formulate a specific question that can be tested
- Design a study to collect relevant data
- Analyze the data to arrive at conclusions
- Report the results

Following the basic guidelines of the scientific method does not guarantee that valid conclusions will always be reached. However, these steps help guard against bias and minimize the chances for error and faulty conclusions. Let's look at some of the key concepts associated with each step of the scientific method.

Step 1. Formulate a Testable Hypothesis

Once a researcher has identified a question or an issue to investigate, he or she must formulate a hypothesis that can be tested empirically. Formally, a **hypothesis** is a tentative statement that describes the relationship between two or more variables.

scientific method
A set of assumptions, attitudes, and procedures that guide researchers in creating questions to investigate, in generating evidence, and in drawing conclusions.

empirical evidence
Verifiable evidence that is based upon objective observation, measurement, and/or experimentation.

hypothesis
(high-POTH-eh-sis) A tentative statement about the relationship between two or more variables; a testable prediction or question.

critical thinking
The active process of minimizing preconceptions and biases while evaluating evidence, determining the conclusions that can reasonably be drawn from evidence, and considering alternative explanations for research findings or other phenomena.

variable
A factor that can vary, or change, in ways that can be observed, measured, and verified.

CRITICAL THINKING

What Is Critical Thinking?

As you'll see throughout this text, many issues in contemporary psychology are far from being settled. And although research findings may have been arrived at in a very objective manner, the interpretation of what findings mean and how they should be applied can be a matter of considerable debate. In short, there is a subjective side to any science. But this is especially important in psychology, because psychological research often involves topics and issues that apply directly to people's everyday concerns and behavior.

As you look at the evidence that psychology has to offer on many topics, we want to encourage you to engage in critical thinking. In general, critical thinking refers to *actively questioning* statements rather than blindly accepting them. More precisely, **critical thinking** is the active process of:

- Minimizing the influence of preconceptions and biases while evaluating evidence.
- Determining the conclusions that can reasonably be drawn from the evidence.
- Considering alternative explanations for research findings or other phenomena.

What are the key attitudes and mental skills that characterize critical thinking?

1. The critical thinker is flexible yet maintains an attitude of healthy skepticism.
Critical thinkers are open to new information, ideas, and claims. They genuinely consider alternative explanations and possibilities. However, this open-mindedness is tempered by a healthy sense of skepticism (Hyman, 2007). The critical thinker consistently asks, "What evidence supports this claim?"

2. The critical thinker scrutinizes the evidence before drawing conclusions.
Critical thinkers strive to weigh all the available evidence *before* arriving at conclusions. And, in evaluating evidence, critical thinkers distinguish between *empirical evidence* versus *opinions* based on feelings or personal experience.

3. The critical thinker can assume other perspectives.
Critical thinkers are not imprisoned by their own points of view. Nor are they limited in their capacity to imagine life experiences and perspectives that are fundamentally different from their own. Rather, the critical thinker strives to understand and evaluate issues from many different angles.

4. The critical thinker is aware of biases and assumptions.
In evaluating evidence and ideas, critical thinkers strive to identify the biases and assumptions that are inherent in any argument (Riggio & Halpern, 2006). Critical thinkers also try to identify and minimize the influence of their *own* biases.

5. The critical thinker engages in reflective thinking.
Critical thinkers avoid knee-jerk responses. Instead, critical thinkers are *reflective*. Most complex issues are unlikely to have a simple resolution. Therefore, critical thinkers resist the temptation to sidestep complexity by boiling an issue down to an either/or, yes/no kind of proposition. Instead, the critical thinker expects and *accepts* complexity (Halpern, 2007).

As you can see, critical thinking is not a single skill, but rather a set of attitudes and thinking skills. As is true with any set of skills, you can get better at these skills with practice. That's one reason we've included Critical Thinking boxes in many chapters of this text.

You'll discover that these Critical Thinking boxes do not follow a rigid formula but are very diverse. Some will challenge your preconceptions about certain topics. Others will invite you to take sides in the debates of some of the most important contributors to modern psychology.

We hope you enjoy this feature!

CRITICAL THINKING QUESTIONS

- Why might other people want to discourage you from thinking critically?
- In what situations is it probably most difficult or challenging for you to exercise critical thinking skills? Why?
- What can you do or say to encourage others to use critical thinking in evaluating questionable claims or assertions?

A hypothesis is often stated as a specific prediction that can be empirically tested, such as "psychological stress increases the likelihood of physical illness."

The **variables** contained in any given hypothesis are simply the factors that can vary, or change. These changes must be capable of being observed, measured, and verified. The psychologist must provide an operational definition of each variable to

Formulating a Hypothesis: Do Dogs Look Like Their Owners? Hypotheses are often generated from everyday observations. For example, many people believe that pets resemble their owners (Alpers & Gerdes, 2006). How could this hypothesis be scientifically tested? Psychologists Michael Roy and Nicholas Christenfeld (2004, 2005) found that study participants were able to accurately match photos of dogs with photos of their owners—but only if the dogs were purebred. Other research has come to the same conclusion (Payne & Jaffe, 2005). The explanation? People tend to choose dogs that resemble themselves.

be investigated. An **operational definition** defines the variable in very specific terms as to how it will be measured, manipulated, or changed.

Operational definitions are important because many of the concepts that psychologists investigate—such as memory, happiness, or stress—can be measured in more than one way. In providing operational definitions of the variables in the study, the researcher spells out in very concrete and precise terms how the variables will be manipulated or measured. In this way, other researchers can understand exactly how the variables were measured or manipulated in a particular study.

For example, prior to marrying, some couples attend a premarital education class or workshop designed to help their marriage succeed by exploring such topics as relationship skills, expectations, resolving conflicts, and so on. You could turn that observation into a testable hypothesis: Premarital education enhances marital quality.

To test that specific prediction, you would need to formulate an operational definition of each variable. How could you operationally define *premarital education*? *Marital quality*? What could you observe and measure that would reflect these factors?

In looking at that hypothesis, Scott Stanley and his colleagues (2006) operationally defined *premarital education* as the couple's response to a question asking if they attended a class, workshop, or counseling session designed to help them prepare for marriage. Answering "no" was scored 0, and "yes" was scored 1. *Marital quality* was operationally defined as the person's 1-to-5 rating in response to several questions about their satisfaction with the marriage. Responding with 1 indicated that the person was *not at all satisfied*, and 5 indicated that the person was *completely satisfied*.

Step 2. Design the Study and Collect the Data

This step involves deciding which research method to use for collecting data. There are two basic categories of *methodology* or research methods—*descriptive* and *experimental*. Each research method answers different kinds of questions and provides different kinds of evidence.

Descriptive methods are research strategies for *observing* and *describing* behavior, including identifying the factors that seem to be associated with a particular phenomenon. Descriptive methods answer the who, what, where, and when kinds of questions about behavior. Who engages in a particular behavior? What factors or events seem to be associated with the behavior? Where does the behavior occur? When does the behavior occur? How often? In the next section, we'll discuss commonly used descriptive methods, including *naturalistic observation, surveys, case studies,* and *correlational studies.*

In contrast, the *experimental method* is used to show that one variable causes change in a second variable. In an experiment, the researcher deliberately varies one factor, then measures the changes produced in a second factor. Ideally, all experimental conditions are kept as constant as possible except for the factor that the researcher systematically varies. Then, if changes occur in the second factor, those changes can be attributed to the variations in the first factor.

Step 3. Analyze the Data and Draw Conclusions

Once observations have been made and measurements have been collected, the raw data need to be analyzed and summarized. Researchers use the methods of a branch of mathematics known as **statistics** to analyze, summarize, and draw conclusions about the data they have collected.

Researchers rely on statistics to determine whether their results support their hypotheses. They also use statistics to determine whether their findings are statistically significant. If a finding is **statistically significant,** it means that the results are not very likely to have occurred by chance. As a rule, statistically significant results confirm the hypothesis. Appendix A provides a more detailed discussion of the use of statistics in psychology research.

Keep in mind that *statistical* significance and *practical* significance are not necessarily the same thing. If a study involves a large number of participants, even small differences among groups of subjects may result in a statistically significant finding.

operational definition
A precise description of how the variables in a study will be manipulated or measured.

statistics
A branch of mathematics used by researchers to organize, summarize, and interpret data.

statistically significant
A mathematical indication that research results are not very likely to have occurred by chance.

meta-analysis
A statistical technique that involves combining and analyzing the results of many research studies on a specific topic in order to identify overall trends.

replicate
To repeat or duplicate a scientific study in order to increase confidence in the validity of the original findings.

But the actual average differences may be so small as to have little practical significance or importance.

For example, several significant findings emerged in a study looking at factors that would help predict people who are at risk of attempting suicide (Mann & others, 1999). One statistically significant finding was that suicide attempters had fewer years of education (12.7 years) as compared to nonattempters (14 years). In practical terms, however, the difference was not substantial enough to be clinically meaningful in trying to help identify people who pose a suicide risk. So remember that a statistically significant result is simply one that is not very likely to have occurred by chance. Whether the finding is significant in the everyday sense of being important is another matter altogether.

Using Statistics to Predict College Success How can you draw conclusions when there are many studies investigating the same basic question? Psychologist Steven Robbins and his colleagues (2004) used a statistical technique called *meta-analysis* to pool the results of more than 100 studies investigating the psychological, social, and study skills most strongly associated with success in college. The researchers operationally defined "success in college" as cumulative grade point average (GPA). Beyond high school GPA and standardized test scores, the meta-analysis revealed that the strongest predictors of college success were two psychological factors: academic self-confidence and the desire to achieve. These two factors were more important in predicting college success than socioeconomic status, academic skills, or level of social or financial support.

A statistical technique called meta-analysis is sometimes used in psychology to analyze the results of many research studies on a specific topic. **Meta-analysis** involves pooling the results of several studies into a single analysis. By creating one large pool of data to be analyzed, meta-analysis can help reveal overall trends that may not be evident in individual studies. Meta-analysis is especially useful when a particular issue has generated a large number of studies, some of which have produced weak or contradictory results. When a large number of different factors have been implicated in a particular phenomenon, meta-analysis can help identify the most important factors.

Step 4. Report the Findings

For advances to be made in any scientific discipline, researchers must publish or share their findings with other scientists. In addition to reporting their results, psychologists provide a detailed description of the study itself, including:

- The rationale for testing the hypothesis
- Who participated in the study
- How participants were selected
- How variables were operationally defined
- What procedures or methods were used
- How the data were analyzed
- What the results seem to suggest

Describing the precise details of the study makes it possible for other investigators to **replicate,** or repeat, the study. Replication is an important part of the scientific process. When a study is replicated and the same basic results are obtained again, scientific *confidence* that the results are accurate is increased. Conversely, if the replication of a study fails to produce the same basic findings, confidence in the original findings is reduced.

One way in which psychologists report their findings is by formally presenting their research at a professional conference. A researcher can also write a paper summarizing the study and submit it to one of the many psychology journals for publication. Before accepting papers for publication, most psychology journals send the paper to other

Claude Steele Presenting His Research Along with writing up their research in papers submitted for publication in peer-reviewed journals, psychologists also often discuss their research at national and regional psychology conferences. Here, Stanford University professor Claude Steele discusses his research at the annual meeting of the Association of Psychological Science (APS). Steele's research centers on *stereotype threat,* which refers to the ways that negative stereotypes can affect the performance of people who belong to stigmatized groups. We discuss Steele's influential concept and research in Chapter 7 in the Culture and Human Behavior box.

Figure 1.2 How to Read a Journal Reference Using the References section at the back of this text, you can find the complete source for each citation that appears in a chapter. This figure shows the different components of a typical journal reference. In the chapter itself, the citation for this particular reference would read "(Courtney & Polich, 2009)."

knowledgable psychologists to review. The reviewers critically evaluate different aspects of a study, including how the results were analyzed. If the study conforms to the principles of sound scientific research and contributes to the existing knowledge base, the paper is accepted for publication.

Throughout this text, you'll see citations that look like the following: (Courtney & Polich, 2009). These citations identify the sources of the research and ideas that are being discussed. The citation tells you the author or authors (Courtney & Polich) of the study and the year (2009) in which the study was published. Using this information, you can find the complete reference in the alphabetized References section at the back of this text. The complete reference lists the authors' full names, the article title, and the journal or book in which the article was published. Figure 1.2 shows you how to decipher the different parts of a typical journal reference.

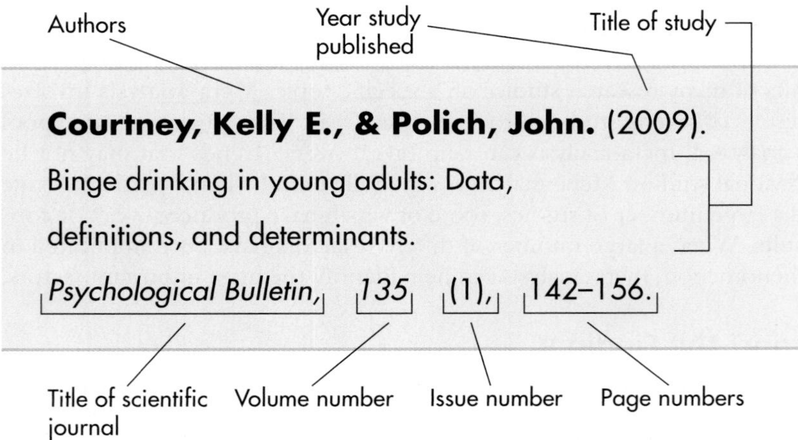

Building Theories

Integrating the Findings from Many Studies

As research findings accumulate from individual studies, eventually theories develop. A **theory**, or *model,* is a tentative explanation that tries to account for diverse findings on the same topic. Note that theories are *not* the same as hypotheses. A hypothesis is a specific question or prediction to be tested. In contrast, a theory integrates and summarizes numerous research findings and observations on a particular topic. Along with explaining existing results, a good theory often generates new predictions and hypotheses that can be tested by further research.

As you encounter different theories, try to remember that theories are *tools* for explaining behavior and mental processes, not statements of absolute fact. Like any tool, the value of a theory is determined by its usefulness. A useful theory is one that furthers the understanding of behavior, allows testable predictions to be made, and stimulates new research. Often, more than one theory proves to be useful in explaining a particular area of behavior or mental processes, such as the development of personality or the experience of emotion.

It's also important to remember that theories often reflect the *self-correcting nature of the scientific enterprise.* In other words, when new research findings challenge established ways of thinking about a phenomenon, theories are expanded, modified, and even replaced. Thus, as the knowledge base of psychology evolves and changes, theories evolve and change to produce more accurate and useful explanations of behavior and mental processes.

While the conclusions of psychology rest on empirical evidence gathered using the scientific method, the same is not true of *pseudoscientific* claims. As you'll read in the Science Versus Pseudoscience box on page 22, pseudosciences often claim to be scientific while ignoring the basic rules of science.

theory
A tentative explanation that tries to integrate and account for the relationship of various findings and observations.

Descriptive Research Methods

descriptive research methods
Scientific procedures that involve systematically observing behavior in order to describe the relationship among behaviors and events.

naturalistic observation
The systematic observation and recording of behaviors as they occur in their natural setting.

Key Theme

- **Descriptive research methods are used to systematically observe and describe behavior.**

Key Questions

- **What are naturalistic observation and case study research, and why and how are they conducted?**
- **What is a survey, and why is random selection important in survey research?**
- **What are the advantages and disadvantages of each descriptive method?**

Descriptive research methods are strategies for observing and describing behavior. Using descriptive methods, researchers can answer important questions, such as when certain behaviors take place, how often they occur, and whether they are related to other factors, such as a person's age, ethnic group, or educational level. As you'll see in this section, descriptive methods can provide a wealth of information about behavior, especially behaviors that would be difficult or impossible to study experimentally.

Naturalistic Observation

The Science of People- and Animal-Watching

When psychologists systematically observe and record behaviors as they occur in their natural settings, they are using the descriptive method called **naturalistic observation.** Usually, researchers engaged in naturalistic observation try to avoid being detected by their subjects, whether people or nonhuman animals. The basic goal of naturalistic observation is to detect the behavior patterns that exist naturally—patterns that might not be apparent in a laboratory or if the subjects knew they were being watched.

As you might expect, psychologists very carefully define the behaviors that they will observe and measure before they begin their research. Often, to increase the accuracy of the observations, two or more observers are used. In some studies, observations are recorded so that the researchers can carefully analyze the details of the behaviors being studied.

One advantage of naturalistic observation is that it allows researchers to study human behaviors that cannot ethically be manipulated in an experiment. For example, suppose that a psychologist wants to study bullying behavior in children. It would not be ethical to deliberately create a situation in which one child is aggressively bullied by another child. However, it *would* be ethical to study bullying by observing aggressive behavior in children on a crowded school playground (see Hawkins & others, 2001).

As a research tool, naturalistic observation can be used wherever patterns of behavior can be openly observed—from the rain forests of the Amazon to fast-food restaurants, shopping malls, and city streets. Because the observations occur in the natural setting, the results of naturalistic observation studies can often be generalized more confidently to real-life situations than can the results of studies using artificially manipulated or staged situations.

Naturalistic Observation: Studying the "Pace of Life" Naturalistic observation can be used to study many different types of behavior. For example, social psychologist Robert Levine (1997) set out to compare the "pace of life" in 31 different countries. How could you operationally define the "pace of life"? One measure that Levine adopted was "the amount of time it took a pedestrian to walk a distance of 60 feet on a downtown city street." To collect the data, observers unobtrusively timed at least 35 male and 35 female pedestrians in each country (Levine & Norenzayan, 1999). The results? The fastest walkers were clocked in Ireland and the slowest in Brazil. Of the 31 countries, walkers in the United States were ranked as the 6th fastest, and Canadian walkers came in at 11th.

SCIENCE VERSUS PSEUDOSCIENCE

What Is a Pseudoscience?

The word *pseudo* means "fake" or "false." Thus, a pseudoscience is a fake science. More specifically, a **pseudoscience** is a theory, method, or practice that promotes claims in ways that appear to be scientific and plausible even though supporting empirical evidence is lacking or nonexistent (Lilienfeld & others, 2001; Shermer, 2002).

Pseudoscientific practices and claims come in all sizes, shapes, and forms (Bausell, 2007; Carroll, 2003). Their unproven claims are often promoted in ways that make them superficially *appear* to be scientifically based. Not surprisingly, surveys have found that pseudoscientific beliefs are common among the general public (National Science Board, 2008).

Remember our Prologue story about Brenda, our student who wanted to know whether a magnetic vest or mattress could help her son? We'll use what we learned about magnet therapy to help illustrate some of the common strategies used to promote pseudosciences.

Magnet Therapy: What's the Attraction?

The practice of applying magnets to the body to supposedly treat various conditions and ailments is called *magnet therapy*. Magnet therapy has been around for centuries. It became popular in the United States in the late 1800s with the sale of magnetic brushes, combs, insoles, and clothing.

Today, Americans spend an estimated $500 million each year on magnetic rings, bracelets, belts, wraps, vests, pillows, and mattresses. Worldwide, the sale of magnetic devices is estimated to be $5 billion per year (Winemiller & others, 2005).

The Internet has been a bonanza for those who market products like magnet therapy. Web sites hail the "scientifically proven healing benefits" of magnet therapy for everything from Alzheimer's disease to schizophrenia (e.g., L. Johnston, 2008; D. Parsons, 2007). Treating pain is the most commonly marketed use of magnet therapy. However, reviews of scientific research on magnet therapy consistently conclude that there is no evidence that magnets can relieve pain (see Finegold & Flamm, 2006; National Standard, 2009). Reviews by the National Center for Complementary and Alternative Medicine (2004, 2009) noted the following:

- Scientific research so far does not firmly support a conclusion that magnets of any type can relieve pain.
- The U.S. Food and Drug Administration (FDA) has not approved the marketing of magnets with claims of benefits to health (such as "relieves arthritis pain").

But proponents of magnet therapy, like those of almost all pseudoscientific claims, use very effective strategies to create the illusion of scientifically validated products or procedures. Each of the ploys below should serve as a warning sign that you need to engage your critical and scientific thinking skills.

Strategy 1: Testimonials rather than scientific evidence

Pseudosciences often use testimonials or personal anecdotes as evidence to support their claims. The testimonials may seem genuine, like the comment by Brenda's son's therapist, who claimed that magnetic vests and mattresses had "worked miracles" for some of her patients. Although they may be sincere and often sound compelling, testimonials are not acceptable scientific evidence. Testimonials lack the basic controls used in scientific research. Many different factors, such as the simple passage of time, could account for a particular individual's response.

Case Studies

Details, Details, Details

A **case study** is an intensive, in-depth investigation of an individual, a family, or some other social unit. Case studies involve compiling a great deal of information from numerous sources to construct a detailed picture of the person. The individual may be extensively interviewed, and his or her friends, family, and co-workers may be interviewed as well. Psychological and biographical records, neurological and medical records, and even school or work records may be examined. Other sources of information can include psychological testing and observations of the person's behavior. Clinical psychologists and other mental health specialists routinely use case studies to develop a complete profile of a psychotherapy client.

pseudoscience
Fake or false science that makes claims based on little or no scientific evidence.

case study
An intensive study of a single individual or small group of individuals.

> *Extraordinary claims require extraordinary evidence.*
> CARL SAGAN

Strategy 2: Scientific jargon without scientific substance
Pseudoscientific claims are littered with scientific jargon to make their claims seem more credible. Vague references are made to "controlled studies," "scientific evidence," "scientists at a leading university," and so on. The ad copy may also be littered with scientific-sounding terms, such as "bio-magnetic balance" or impressive sounding scientific terms that, when examined, turn out to be meaningless.

Strategy 3: Combining established scientific knowledge with unfounded claims
Pseudosciences often mention well-known scientific facts to add credibility to their unsupported claims. For example, the magnet therapy spiel often starts by referring to the properties of the earth's magnetic field, the fact that blood contains minerals and iron, and so on. To further strengthen the illusion of scientific credibility, established scientific procedures are mentioned, such as *magnetic resonance imaging* (MRI). Or, they mention procedures currently being scientifically developed, such as *transcranial magnetic stimulation* (TMS). For the record, MRI and TMS do not use static magnets, which are the type sold at magnet therapy Web sites.

Strategy 4: Irrefutable or nonfalsifiable claims
Consider this claim: Magnet therapy restores the natural magnetic balance required by the body's healing process. How could you test that claim? An *irrefutable* or *nonfalsifiable claim* is one that cannot be disproved or tested in any meaningful way. The irrefutable claims of pseudosciences typically take the form of broad or vague statements that are essentially meaningless.

Strategy 5: Confirmation bias
Scientific conclusions are based on converging evidence from *multiple* studies, not a single study. Pseudosciences ignore this process and instead trumpet the findings of a single study that seems to support their claims. In doing so, they do *not* mention all the other studies that tested the same thing but yielded results that failed to support the claim. This illustrates *confirmation bias*—the tendency to seek out evidence that confirms a claim or belief, while ignoring evidence that contradicts or undermines the claim or belief. When disconfirming evidence is pointed out, it is ignored or explained away.

Strategy 6: Shifting the burden of proof
In science, the responsibility for proving the validity of a claim rests with the person making the claim. Many pseudosciences, however, *shift the burden of proof* to the skeptic. If you express skepticism about a pseudoscientific claim, the pseudoscience advocate will challenge you to *disprove* their claim.

Strategy 7: Multiple outs
What happens when pseudosciences fail to deliver on their promised benefits? Typically, multiple excuses are offered. Brenda's son, for example, did *not* experience any benefits from wearing the magnetic vest. Here are just some of the reasons given when magnet therapy fails to work:

- Magnets act differently on different body parts.
- The magnet was placed in the wrong spot.
- Everyone's body will respond differently to magnet therapy.
- The magnets were the wrong type, size, shape, etc.
- The magnets weren't strong enough.
- The magnets weren't worn long enough.
- The healing effect may not occur until after you stop using the magnets.

One of our goals in this text is to help you develop your scientific thinking skills so you're better able to evaluate claims about behavior or mental processes, especially claims that seem far-fetched or too good to be true. In this chapter, we'll look at the scientific methods used to test hypotheses and claims. And in the Science Versus Pseudoscience boxes in later chapters, you'll see how various pseudoscience claims have stood up to scientific scrutiny. We hope you enjoy this feature!

Case studies are also used in psychological research investigating rare, unusual, or extreme conditions. These kinds of case studies often provide psychologists with information that can be used to help understand normal behavior. For example, the Chapter 3 Prologue features the story of Mike May, who partially regained his sight after being blind since early childhood. You'll read how the information gained from extensive testing of Mike's brain and visual abilities has provided insights into brain and visual development in normally sighted individuals.

The case study method can also be used to study more than one individual. In *case-based research,* information from multiple case studies is systematically combined and analyzed (Edwards & others, 2004). Case-based research can be particularly valuable in clinical psychology, where it can be used to evaluate and improve treatment strategies for people with specific psychological disorders.

"Hi. I'm doing a survey. Do you have a few minutes to answer some questions?"

Surveys

(A) Always (B) Sometimes (C) Never (D) Huh?

A direct way to find out about the behavior, attitudes, and opinions of people is simply to ask them. In a **survey,** people respond to a structured set of questions about their experiences, beliefs, behaviors, or attitudes. One key advantage offered by survey research is that information can be gathered from a much larger group of people than is possible with other research methods.

Typically, surveys involve a carefully designed questionnaire in a paper-and-pencil format that is distributed to a select group of people. Computer-based or Internet-based surveys have become increasingly more common. And, surveys are still often conducted over the telephone or in person, with the interviewer recording the person's responses. As with paper-and-pencil surveys, the interviewer usually asks a structured set of questions in a predetermined order. Such interview-based surveys are typically more expensive and time-consuming than questionnaire-based surveys.

Surveys are seldom administered to everyone within the particular group or population under investigation. Instead, researchers usually select a **sample**—a segment of the larger group or population. Selecting a sample that is representative of the larger group is the key to getting accurate survey results. A **representative sample** very closely parallels, or matches, the larger group on relevant characteristics, such as age, sex, race, marital status, and educational level.

How do researchers select the participants so that they end up with a sample that is representative of the larger group? The most common strategy is to randomly select the sample participants. **Random selection** means that every member of the larger group has an equal chance of being selected for inclusion in the sample.

To illustrate how random selection works, let's look at how the sample was created for the landmark *National Health and Social Life Survey* (*NHSLS*). Conducted by researcher Robert T. Michael and his colleagues (1994) at the University of Chicago, the NHSLS focused on the sexual practices of U.S. adults between the ages of 18 and 59. Here is Michael's description of how his team used random selection to choose the survey participants:

> Essentially, we chose at random geographic areas of the country, using the statistical equivalent of a coin toss to select them. Within these geographic regions, we randomly selected cities, towns, and rural areas. Within those cities and towns we randomly selected neighborhoods. Within those neighborhoods, we randomly selected households. . . . If there were two people living in a household who were in our age range, we flipped a coin to select which one to interview. If there were three people in the household, we did the equivalent of flipping a three-sided coin to select one of them to interview.

Notice that the participants who were interviewed in the NHSLS did *not* volunteer to participate in the survey. A specific individual was randomly selected through the process described. If that person refused to participate, someone else in the household could *not* substitute for that person. Using this random selection process, more than 3,000 people were interviewed for the National Health and Social Life Survey.

How closely did the NHSLS sample match important characteristics of the U.S. population? You can see for yourself by comparing the two columns in Table 1.1. Clearly, the random selection process used in the NHSLS resulted in a sample that very closely approximated the characteristics of the U.S. population as a whole.

Table 1.1

Comparing the NHSLS Sample and the U.S. Population

	NHSLS Sample	U.S. Population
Gender		
Men	44.6%	49.7%
Women	55.4	50.3
	100%	100%
Age		
18–24	15.9%	18.2%
25–29	14.5	14.3
30–39	31.3	29.5
40–49	22.9	22.7
50–59	15.3	15.3
	100%	100%
Education		
Less than high school	13.9%	15.8%
High school or equivalent	62.2	64.0
Any college	16.6	13.9
Advanced	7.3	6.3
	100%	100%
Marital Status		
Never married	28.2%	27.7%
Currently married	53.3	58.3
Divorced, separated	16.2	12.4
Widowed	2.3	1.6
	100%	100%
Race/Ethnicity		
White	76.5%	75.9%
Black	12.7	11.7
Hispanic	5	9.0
Other	3.3	3.3
	100%	100%

SOURCE: Michael & others (1994).

Using random selection, approximately 3,000 people were chosen for the sample used in the National Health and Social Life Survey (NHSLS). In this table, you can see that the overall characteristics of those in the NHSLS sample were very representative of the U.S. population as a whole.

One potential problem with surveys and questionnaires is that people do not always answer honestly. Participants may misrepresent their personal characteristics or lie in their responses. These problems can be addressed in a well-designed survey. One strategy is to rephrase and ask the same basic question at different points in the survey or during the interview. The researchers can then compare the responses to make sure that the participant is responding honestly and consistently.

survey
A questionnaire or interview designed to investigate the opinions, behaviors, or characteristics of a particular group.

sample
A selected segment of the population used to represent the group that is being studied.

representative sample
A selected segment that very closely parallels the larger population being studied on relevant characteristics.

random selection
Process in which subjects are selected randomly from a larger group such that every group member has an equal chance of being included in the study.

correlational study
A research strategy that allows the precise calculation of how strongly related two factors are to each other.

correlation coefficient
A numerical indication of the magnitude and direction of the relationship (the *correlation*) between two variables.

positive correlation
A finding that two factors vary systematically in the same direction, increasing or decreasing together.

Correlational Studies

Looking at Relationships and Making Predictions

Key Theme

- **Correlational studies show how strongly two factors are related.**

Key Questions

- **What is a correlation coefficient?**
- **What is the difference between a positive correlation and a negative correlation?**
- **Why can't correlational studies be used to demonstrate cause-and-effect relationships?**

Along with answering the *who, what, where,* and *when* questions, the data gathered by descriptive research techniques can be analyzed to show how various factors are related. A **correlational study** examines how strongly two variables are related to, or associated with, each other. Correlations can be used to analyze the data gathered by any type of descriptive method.

To illustrate, let's look at a correlational study conducted by psychologists Craig Anderson and Karen Dill (2000). Anderson and Dill were interested in how much time young people spent playing video games. They surveyed more than 200 students taking introductory psychology classes at a large Midwestern university. Figure 1.3 shows some of the survey results. The students also completed some personality tests and a questionnaire on past delinquent behavior. Finally, each student's cumulative grade point average was obtained. Once the data was collected, Anderson and Dill used a statistical procedure to calculate a figure called a *correlation coefficient.*

A **correlation coefficient** is a numerical indicator of the strength of the relationship between two factors. A correlation coefficient always falls in the range from −1.00 to +1.00. The correlation coefficient has two parts—the number and the sign. The number indicates the *strength* of the relationship, and the sign indicates the *direction* of the relationship between the two variables.

More specifically, the closer a correlation coefficient is to 1.00, whether it is positive or negative, the stronger the correlation or association is between the two factors. Hence, a correlation coefficient of +.90 or −.90 represents a very strong association, meaning that the two factors almost always occur together. A correlation coefficient of +.10 or −.10 represents a very weak correlation, meaning that the two factors seldom occur together. (Correlation coefficients are discussed in greater detail in the Statistics Appendix at the back of this book.)

Notice that correlation coefficients do not function like the algebraic number line. A correlation of −.80 represents a stronger relationship than does a correlation of +.10. The plus or minus sign in a correlation coefficient simply tells you the direction of the relationship between the two variables.

A **positive correlation** is one in which the two factors vary in the *same* direction. That is, the two factors increase or decrease together. For example, Anderson and Dill found that there was a positive correlation of +.22 between the amount of time spent playing violent video games and aggressive personality characteristics. That is,

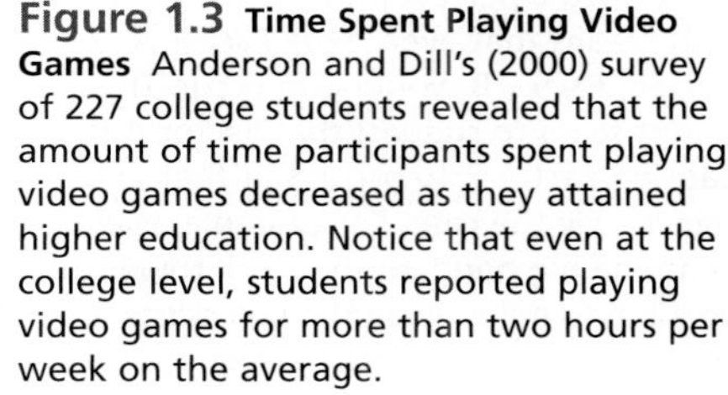

Figure 1.3 Time Spent Playing Video Games Anderson and Dill's (2000) survey of 227 college students revealed that the amount of time participants spent playing video games decreased as they attained higher education. Notice that even at the college level, students reported playing video games for more than two hours per week on the average.

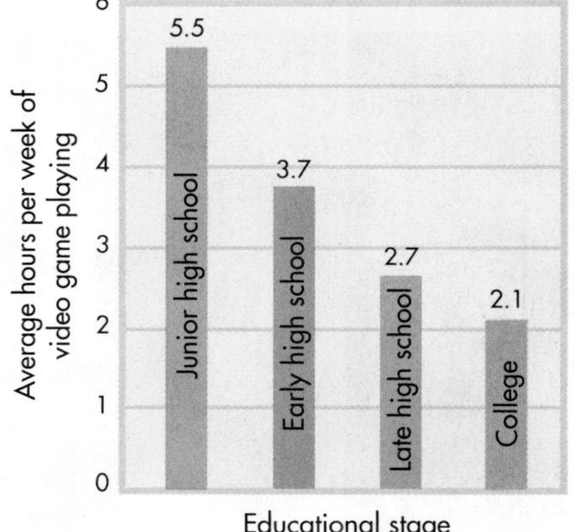

Jazzing Up Your Love Life with Correlation Coefficients Using data from the University of Chicago's ongoing General Social Survey, researchers John Robinson and Geoffrey Godbey (1998) discovered that adult sexual behavior was positively correlated with certain musical preferences. After controlling for age and race, the researchers found that people who have a strong preference for jazz are 30 percent more sexually active than the average American. Liking other types of music, such as rock or rap, was unrelated to sexual activity. Does this mean that listening to jazz *causes* an increase in sexual activity? Not necessarily. Remember, a correlation between two factors does not necessarily indicate causality—only that the two factors co-vary in a systematic way.

as the amount of time spent playing violent video games *increased,* aggression scores on personality tests *increased.*

In contrast, a **negative correlation** is one in which the two variables move in opposite directions: As one factor decreases, the other increases. In analyzing their results, Anderson and Dill found that there was a *negative* correlation of −.20 between the amount of time spent playing video games and academic achievement, as measured by cumulative college grade point average. Thus, as the amount of time spent playing video games *increased,* college grade point average *decreased.*

negative correlation
A finding that two factors vary systematically in opposite directions, one increasing as the other decreases.

Given this basic information about correlation coefficients, what can we conclude about the relationship between the time spent playing video games and academic achievement? Or about exposure to violent video games and aggressive personality characteristics? Does the evidence allow us to conclude that playing video games *causes* a decrease in grade point average? Or that playing violent video games *causes* people to develop more aggressive personalities?

Not necessarily. For example, even if playing video games and getting poor grades were very strongly correlated, it's completely possible that some other factor is involved. For example, it could be that students who lack academic motivation tend to spend their free time playing video games rather than studying. Thus, it might be that a lack of academic motivation, rather than video games, is responsible for lower grades.

Similarly, consider the positive correlation between aggressive personality and amount of time spent playing violent video games. We cannot conclude that playing violent video games *causes* an increase in aggression. It's entirely possible that people who are more aggressive are attracted to violent video games or enjoy playing them. Thus, it could be that people with aggressive personalities are more likely to spend more time playing violent video games than people who are less aggressive.

Here is the critical point: Even if two factors are very strongly correlated, *correlation does not necessarily indicate causality.* A correlation tells you only that two factors seem to be related or that they co-vary in a systematic way. Although two factors may be very strongly correlated, correlational studies cannot be used to demonstrate a true cause-and-effect relationship. As you'll see in the next section, the experimental method is the only scientific strategy that can provide compelling evidence of a cause-and-effect relationship between two variables.

Even though you can't draw conclusions about causality from it, correlational research can be very valuable. First, correlational research can be used to rule out some factors and identify others that merit more intensive study. Second, the results of correlational research can sometimes allow you to make meaningful predictions. For example, when Anderson and Dill (2000) analyzed data from their survey, they discovered that there was a moderately strong correlation of +.46 between the amount of time spent playing violent video games and aggressive delinquent behavior, such as damaging public or private property. That is, the more time that was spent playing violent video games, the higher was the incidence of aggressive delinquent behavior. Looking at the overall results of their survey, Anderson and Dill concluded that there *were* legitimate reasons to be concerned about the potential negative consequences of long-term or excessive exposure to video games, especially violent video games. In Chapter 5, on learning, we'll take a critical look at the relationship between exposure to violent media and aggressive behavior.

A Perfect Positive Correlation: The Clock and the Bell Tower If a +1.00 correlation occurred between two variables, it would be termed a *perfect positive correlation.* This means that every time Factor A occurred, Factor B would also occur. This might seem to suggest that Factor A is causing Factor B to occur, but that's not necessarily the case. For example, every time the big hand on the clock tower gets to 12, two miles away the bell starts ringing. The two events are perfectly correlated yet, in this case, one does not cause the other.

The Experimental Method

Key Theme

- **The experimental method is used to demonstrate a cause-and-effect relationship between two variables.**

Key Questions

- **What roles do the independent variable and dependent variable play in an experiment?**
- **How can experimental controls help minimize the effects of extraneous variables?**
- **How can the placebo effect and practice effect influence experimental results?**

The **experimental method** is a research method used to demonstrate a cause-and-effect relationship between changes in one variable and the effect that is produced on another variable. Conducting an experiment involves deliberately varying one factor, which is called the **independent variable.** The researcher then measures the changes, if any, that are produced in a second factor, called the **dependent variable.** The dependent variable is so named because changes in it depend on variations in the independent variable.

To the greatest degree possible, all other conditions in the experiment are held constant. Thus, when the data are analyzed, any changes that occur in the dependent variable can be attributed to the deliberate manipulation of the independent variable. In this way, an experiment can provide evidence of a cause-and-effect relationship between the independent and dependent variables.

In designing experiments, psychologists try to anticipate and control for **extraneous variables.** Also called *confounding variables,* these factors are not the focus of the experiment. However, extraneous, or confounding, variables might produce inaccurate experimental results by influencing changes in the dependent variable. Depending on the question being investigated, potential extraneous variables in a psychology experiment could include unwanted variability in such factors as the participants' ages, gender, ethnic background, race, health, occupation, personal habits, education, and so on.

Even though researchers try to minimize unwanted influences and variability, it is impossible to control every aspect of an experimental situation. That's why researchers use various *experimental controls.* These are specific strategies and procedures that help minimize the possibility that extraneous variables or some other uncontrolled factor will influence the outcome of the experiment.

The Ginkgo Biloba Experiment

Testing for Effectiveness

The design of an experiment depends on the hypothesis being investigated. For example, some experiments are designed to assess the effectiveness of a therapeutic treatment, such as a medication, a type of psychotherapy, or some other procedure (like wearing a magnetic vest or sleeping on a magnetic mattress). In this type of experiment, participants assigned to the **experimental group** receive the independent variable—the actual medication, therapy, or procedure. The independent variable is also sometimes referred to as the *treatment variable.*

Other participants are assigned to a *placebo control group* and receive a placebo. A **placebo** is a fake substance, treatment, or procedure that has no known direct effects. It *looks* just like the real independent variable—the actual drug or treatment. But despite its convincing appearance, it is a sham, a fake, a sugar pill masquerading as the real deal.

experimental method
A method of investigation used to demonstrate cause-and-effect relationships by purposely manipulating one factor thought to produce change in another factor.

independent variable
The purposely manipulated factor thought to produce change in an experiment; also called the *treatment variable.*

dependent variable
The factor that is observed and measured for change in an experiment; thought to be influenced by the independent variable; also called the *outcome variable.*

extraneous variable
A factor or variable other than the ones being studied that, if not controlled, could affect the outcome of an experiment; also called a *confounding variable.*

experimental group or experimental condition
In an experiment, the group of participants who are exposed to all experimental conditions, including the independent variable.

placebo
A fake substance, treatment, or procedure that has no known direct effects.

Can Ginkgo Biloba Enhance Your Mental Abilities?
The herbal supplement ***ginkgo biloba*** is marketed as a "cognitive enhancer" that supposedly improves memory, alertness, mental focus, and concentration, especially in older adults. However, studies of ginkgo don't support those claims (see DeKosky & others, 2008; Gold & others, 2002; National Standard Research Collaboration, 2008). In reviewing recent placebo-controlled, double-blind studies, researchers Peter Canter and Edzard Ernst (2007) flatly concluded, "We have found no convincing evidence from randomized clinical trials for a robust positive effect of ginkgo biloba upon any aspect of cognitive function in healthy young people." What about normal adults age 75 or older? The large-scale, randomized, double-blind "Ginkgo Evaluation of Memory (GEM) Study" found ginkgo to be ineffective in reducing the development of dementia and Alzheimer's disease in older people (DeKosky & others, 2008).

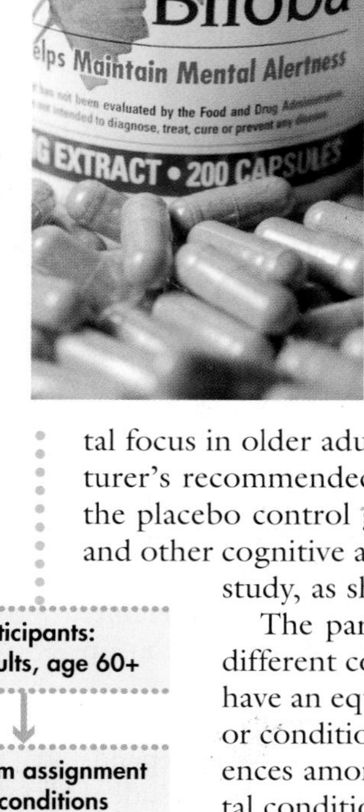

Although it is completely inactive, a placebo can produce very real effects. A **placebo effect** is any change attributed to the person's beliefs and expectations rather than an actual drug, treatment, or procedure. Also called *expectancy effect*, the potential influence of placebo effect should not be underestimated. For example, in one study, participants exposed to placebo poison ivy displayed real and painful responses: outbreaks of skin rashes (see Crum & Langer, 2007).

In a typical therapeutic effectiveness experiment, participants are told that they have a 50–50 chance of receiving the actual versus the placebo treatment. For example, psychologist Paul Solomon and his colleagues (2002) used a placebo control group to test whether an herb called *ginkgo biloba* improves memory, concentration, and mental focus in older adults. Participants in the experimental group took the manufacturer's recommended daily dosage of ginkgo biloba for six weeks, while those in the placebo control group took an identical dosage of placebo capsules. Memory and other cognitive abilities were assessed at the beginning and end of the six-week study, as shown in the experimental design in Figure 1.4.

Figure 1.4 The Ginkgo Biloba Experimental Design

The participants in the ginkgo study were randomly assigned to the different conditions. **Random assignment** means that all the participants have an equal chance of being assigned to any of the experimental groups or conditions. Random assignment helps ensure that any potential differences among the participants are spread out evenly across all experimental conditions. Random assignment also helps minimize the possibility of bias because the same rule or criteria is used to assign all participants to the different experimental groups.

Using a **double-blind technique** is another experimental control in therapeutic effectiveness studies. This means that both the participants and the researchers interacting with them are *blind* or unaware of the treatment or condition to which the participants have been assigned. For example, in the ginkgo biloba study, the researchers who interacted with the participants did not know which participants received the real or fake ginkgo biloba. The researchers who did know the group assignments did *not* interact with or evaluate the participants. In contrast, a *single-blind study* is one in which the researchers, but not the subjects, are aware of critical information.

Using a double-blind technique helps guard against the possibility that the researcher inadvertently becomes an extraneous or confounding variable in the study. This can happen when a researcher, without realizing it, displays **demand characteristics.** These are subtle cues or signals that can bias the outcome of the study by communicating the behavior or response that is expected of the participants. A behavior as subtle as the researcher slightly smiling or frowning when dealing with some participants, but not others, could bias the outcome of a study.

Can you predict the results of the ginkgo biloba experiment? At the end of the six-week study, the test scores of *both* groups rose. However, there were no significant differences between the improvement in the ginkgo biloba and placebo groups. So why did both groups improve? The researchers concluded that it was probably due to **practice effect.** The participants' experience with the tests—the practice they got by simply taking the mental ability tests twice—was the most likely reason that test scores improved in both groups.

The ginkgo biloba experiment illustrates that before any kind of treatment can be claimed as effective, changes caused by placebo effect, practice effect, and other influences must be identified. Only after accounting for changes caused by those effects can you determine the **main effect**—the change that can be directly attributed to the treatment variable.

placebo effect
Any change attributed to a person's beliefs and expectations rather than an actual drug, treatment, or procedure; also called *expectancy effect.*

random assignment
The process of assigning participants to experimental conditions so that all participants have an equal chance of being assigned to any of the conditions or groups in the study.

double-blind technique
An experimental control in which neither the participants nor the researchers interacting with the participants are aware of the group or condition to which the participants have been assigned.

demand characteristics
In a research study, subtle cues or signals expressed by the researcher that communicate the kind of response or behavior that is expected from the participant.

practice effect
Any change in performance that results from mere repetition of a task.

main effect
Any change that can be directly attributed to the independent or treatment variable after controlling for other possible influences.

The Hotel Experiment

Can Perceiving Work as Exercise Produce Health Benefits?

Key Theme

- **Psychological research has found that a person's beliefs and expectations can exert a significant influence on health and well-being.**

Key Questions

- **What were the independent and dependent variables in Crum and Langer's experiment?**
- **What were the results in Crum and Langer's hotel experiment?**
- **What implications are suggested by the results in Crum and Langer's experiment?**

Testing for therapeutic effectiveness represents a classic experimental design involving a placebo control group. Let's look at a different experimental design, which was inspired by this clue from previous research: Elderly people who *believed* that their health was "poor" were six times more likely to die than those who perceived their health as "excellent." This pattern held true regardless of their *actual* state of physical health (Idler & Kasl, 1991).

This association was found in a correlational study. More specifically, the researchers found a positive correlation between "perception of health status" and "length of survival." But as we explained earlier, correlational evidence *cannot* be used to draw conclusions about cause-and-effect relationships. Only an experiment can provide the scientific evidence needed to show that a causal relationship exists between two variables.

So how could you design an experiment to test the notion that a change in belief (the independent variable) produces a change in health (the dependent variable)? Ethically, of course, you could not conduct an experiment in which you deceived people by telling them that their health had suddenly become "poor" or "good," then waiting to see how long the participants survived. Besides, if you told people that their health had changed for better or worse, they might start behaving differently—a potential confounding variable. Instead, the challenge in testing this notion would be to just change a person's beliefs without changing their behavior. Is that even possible? Could it be done experimentally?

The Hypothesis and Participants

That was the challenge faced by Harvard psychologists Alia Crum and Ellen Langer. Crum and Langer (2007) wanted to test the hypothesis that changing a person's beliefs and expectations about the exercise benefits of a particular activity would result in actual health benefits.

The participants in Crum and Langer's experiment were recruited from the housekeeping staff at seven carefully matched hotels. All of the 84 women in the study cleaned an average of 15 hotel rooms per day, spending about 20 to 30 minutes on each room. Although you might not think of room cleaning as healthy physical exercise, vacuuming, making beds, scouring bathrooms, bending, stooping, and pushing heavy supply carts requires a good deal of physical exertion.

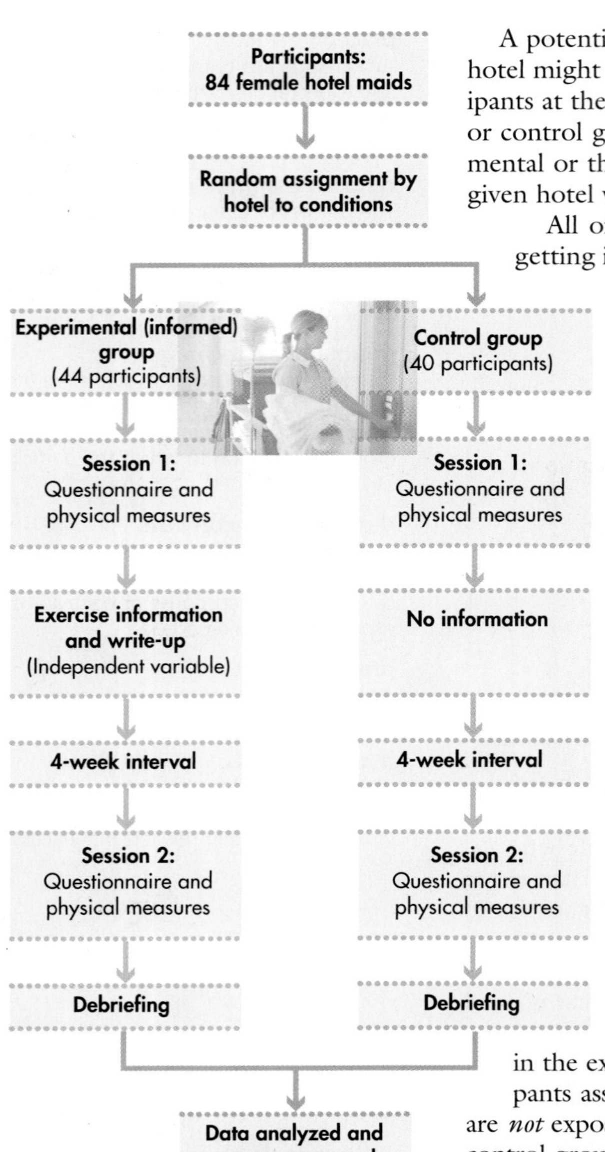

Figure 1.5 The Hotel Experiment Design

A potential confounding variable was that the housekeeping staff at a particular hotel might talk to each other about being in the study. This meant that the participants at the different hotels could not be individually assigned to the experimental or control groups. Instead, each hotel was randomly assigned to either the experimental or the control condition (see Figure 1.5). Thus, all of the participants at a given hotel were assigned to the same group.

All of the participants were told that the experimenters were interested in getting information on their health so that they could study ways to improve it. In return for their help, the participants would receive information about research on health and happiness at the end of the study.

The Independent Variable, Experimental Group, and Control Group

In Crum and Langer's experiment, the independent variable was being informed that housekeeping work was good exercise. Hence, the participants in the experimental group were dubbed "the informed group."

The informed group participants received a write-up discussing the benefits of exercise. It was explained that their daily housekeeping chores satisfied, and even exceeded, government recommendations for healthy daily exercise to burn at least 200 calories. The average calories expended for different housekeeping activities were also detailed. For example, changing bed linens for 15 minutes burns 40 calories, vacuuming a room burns 50 calories, and so forth.

The write-ups were read and explained to the staff. Each informed group participant also received a printed copy. And large posters with the information were displayed on the bulletin boards in the staff lounge. The posters functioned as a daily reminder of how much exercise the staff was getting in performing their housekeeping duties.

In any well-designed experiment, there is at least one control group. The **control group** serves as a baseline against which changes in the experimental group can be compared. In a typical experiment, the participants assigned to the control group go through all the experimental phases but are *not* exposed to the independent variable. In Crum and Langer's experiment, the control group consisted of the participants who were *not* informed that their housekeeping work was beneficial healthy exercise.

The Dependent Variables and Experimental Procedure

Several dependent variables were measured for change. All participants completed a questionnaire about whether they exercised regularly, how much exercise they got, where they got their exercise, and so on. It was noted whether participants already perceived their work-related activities as exercise. The questionnaire responses were used as measures of *self-reported exercise* and to determine if participants *perceived work as exercise.* The questionnaire also asked about their diet during the previous month and personal habits, such as alcohol use and smoking.

Each participant also completed various measures of physical health, including weight, percentage of body fat, body mass index (BMI), waist-to-hip ratio, and blood pressure. After the measurements, the participants in the informed group were given the information and handouts about how their work was good exercise. The participants in the control group were not given this information.

During the month-long study, all other conditions were held constant. The hotel management confirmed that the workload of the housekeeping staff remained constant throughout the study. At the end of four weeks, the questionnaire and measures of physical health were administered again.

control group or control condition
In an experiment, the group of participants who are exposed to all experimental conditions, except the independent variable; the group against which changes in the experimental group are compared.

The Results

Crum and Langer used a variety of statistical measures to analyze the data they collected. Here are the experiment's key findings:

- Participants in both groups reported no changes in exercise outside of work, or in their eating, drinking, or other personal habits.
- The informed group reported higher levels of *perceived exercise* even though their actual exercise activity levels at work and outside of work did *not* change (see Figure 1.6). The informed group also changed their perception of their work-related activities. The physical activities they engaged in at work were now perceived as exercise. In contrast, the work-related perceptions of the control group did not change.
- The informed group participants showed significant improvements over the course of the study in all physical health measures except diastolic blood pressure (see examples in Figure 1.7). In contrast, none of the health measures for the control group participants showed significant changes.

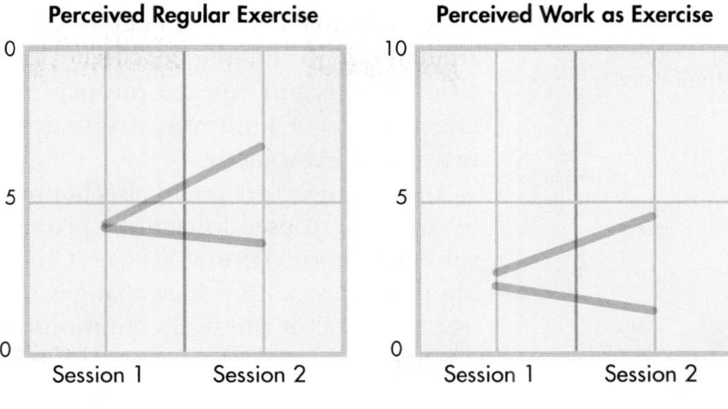

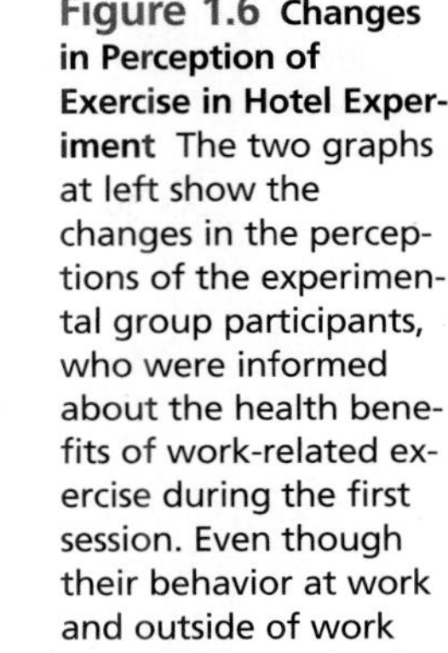

Figure 1.6 Changes in Perception of Exercise in Hotel Experiment The two graphs at left show the changes in the perceptions of the experimental group participants, who were informed about the health benefits of work-related exercise during the first session. Even though their behavior at work and outside of work did not change, the new information increased their perceptions of how much regular exercise they were getting and that work-related tasks were a form of exercise. In comparison, perceptions were unchanged in the control group participants, who did not receive information about the health benefits of work-related exercise.

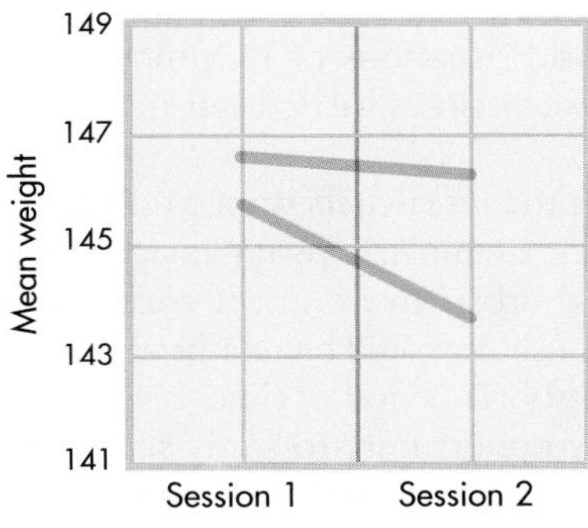

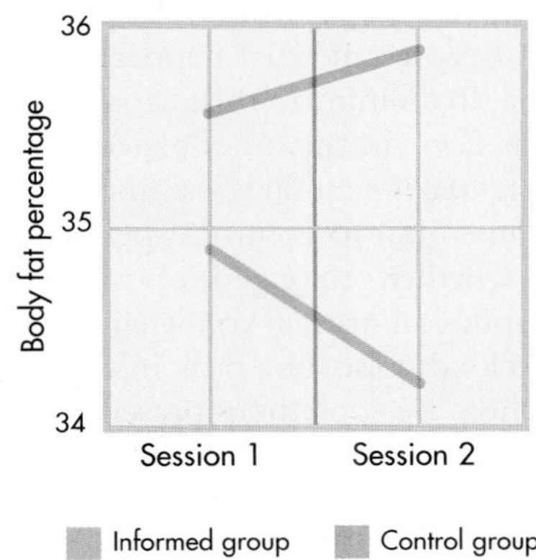

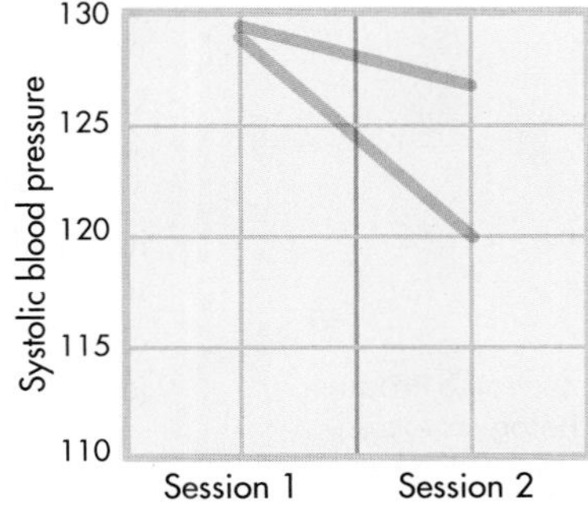

Informed group Control group

Figure 1.7 Changes in Physiological Variables in Hotel Experiment Just four weeks after being told about the health benefits of work-related exercise, the informed group participants showed significant improvements on several health measures, including weight, percentage of body fat, and blood pressure. Control group participants, who were not told about the health benefits of work-related exercise, showed no changes on the same measures.

Crum and Langer (2007) noted that the informed group's change in belief and expectations was accompanied by some remarkable health improvements:

> After only 4 weeks of knowing that their work is good exercise, the subjects in the informed group lost an average of 2 pounds, lowered their systolic blood pressure by 10 points, and were significantly healthier as measured by body-fat percentage, body mass index (BMI), and waist-to-hip ratio (WHR). These results support our hypothesis that increasing perceived exercise independently of actual exercise results in subsequent physiological improvements.

Reporting the Findings

Crum and Langer's study was published in *Psychological Science,* the leading journal of the Association of Psychological Science (APS). The APS news release about their experiment attracted considerable attention from print and online media.

One criticism of the study is that members of the informed group might have behaved differently after being told about the benefits of exercise (Spiegel, 2008). Even though the informed group reported no changes in their behavior or diet, subtle changes may have occurred, such as eating healthier foods, walking more, and so forth. To investigate that possibility, Crum is planning a longer study that would monitor physical activity using pedometers and track food consumption using daily logs.

natural experiment
A study investigating the effects of a naturally occurring event on the research participants.

In combination, the ginkgo biloba experiment and the hotel experiment demonstrate the powerful influence that can be played by people's beliefs and expectations. Could beliefs and expectations play a role in the testimonials of people who hail the effectiveness of unproven magnetic products, such as rings, bracelets, vests, and mattresses? Absolutely.

But other factors could also be involved in the changes that people often report in response to pseudoscientific products or procedures, such as magnet therapy or subliminal motivation CDs (see Chapter 3). For example, the body's natural healing processes can produce changes with the simple passage of time. Further, many psychological or physical conditions cycle up and down, leading to temporary improvements. In later chapters, we'll look at other factors that can contribute to an appearance of effectiveness in unsupported pseudoscientific claims.

Variations and Limitations of Experiments

A well-designed and carefully executed experiment can provide convincing evidence of a cause-and-effect relationship between the independent and dependent variables. But experiments can have their own kinds of limitations or drawbacks, such as difficulties manipulating the variables. Consider trying to test the effectiveness of magnet therapy in an experiment with a placebo control group. Using any metal object, such as a paper clip, participants can (and do) try to determine if they are using the real or sham magnets (Finegold & Flamm, 2006).

Another potential limitation of experiments is that they are often conducted in highly controlled laboratory situations. Because of this, the results may not *generalize* well beyond the people who participated in the experiment. In other words, the results may not represent what happens in real-world situations or to a more general population. To minimize this, experiments are sometimes carried out in natural settings, as was done in the hotel experiment.

Another potential limitation is that the phenomena the researchers want to study are impossible or unethical to control experimentally. For example, a psychologist might want to know whether prolonged exposure to a noisy urban environment creates psychological and physical stress in young children. Obviously, it would be unethical to subject children to loud noise for a prolonged (or even a short) period of time.

But researchers are sometimes presented with the opportunity to study such phenomena by taking advantage of naturally occurring events. In a **natural experiment,** researchers carefully observe and measure the impact of a naturally occurring event on their study participants (Rutter, 2008). Although it is not a true experiment, natural experiments can be used to study the effects of disasters, epidemics, or other events.

Psychologist Gary Evans and his colleagues (1998) used the natural experiment strategy to study the effects of chronic noise exposure on children. They compared stress levels in elementary school children before and after a large international airport was built in their once quiet community near Munich, Germany. The researchers measured both physical and psychological indicators of stress, such as blood pressure, levels of stress hormones, and perceptions of the daily quality of life. They also measured the same indicators over the same time period in a matched control group of children living in a community that remained quiet. The results? The children who were exposed to chronic noise (the independent variable) showed increased psychological and physical stress (the dependent variable). In contrast, the control group children, who were not exposed to constant noise, showed little change in stress. Later research showed that children living near an older airport that was closed after the new airport opened *benefited* from their newly quiet environment: Reading ability and memory improved (Evans & Hygge, 2007; Hygge & others, 2002).

Before leaving the topic of research methods, one contemporary trend deserves special mention: the increasing use of brain-imaging techniques in virtually every area of psychology. To help highlight the importance of neuroscience, every chapter includes a special "Focus on Neuroscience" feature. This chapter's Focus on Neuroscience explores brain-imaging techniques and discusses their increasing use in psychological research (see pp. 34-35).

Does Chronic Exposure to Noise Produce Stress? How could psychologists experimentally determine whether prolonged exposure to noise caused stress or other harmful effects in children? Obviously, psychologists could not ethically expose children to potentially harmful levels of noise for even brief periods of time. In an ingenious study, Gary Evans and his colleagues (1998) used a technique called a *natural experiment* to compare levels of stress in children before and after a noisy airport was built within earshot of their elementary school near Munich, Germany.

Ethics in Psychological Research

Key Theme

- **Psychological research conducted in the United States is subject to ethical guidelines developed by the American Psychological Association.**

Key Questions

- **What are five key provisions of the APA ethics code for research involving humans?**
- **Why do psychologists sometimes conduct research with nonhuman animals?**

What might happen if you were to volunteer to participate in a psychology experiment or study? Are psychologists allowed to manipulate or control you without your knowledge or consent? Could a psychologist force you to reveal your innermost secrets? Could he or she administer electric shocks?

The answer to all these questions is "no." The American Psychological Association (APA) has developed a strict code of ethics for conducting research with both human and animal subjects. This code is contained in a document called *Ethical Principles of Psychologists and Code of Conduct* (APA, 2002). At the Web site www.apa.org/ethics, you can download a copy of the document.

In general, psychologists must respect the dignity and welfare of participants. Psychologists cannot deceptively expose research participants to dangerous or harmful conditions that might cause either physical or emotional harm. At most institutions, any psychological research using human or animal subjects is scrutinized by an institutional review board before approval is granted (Pollick, 2007).

Not surprisingly, the ethical guidelines for research with human and animal subjects are somewhat different. However, the use of animals in psychological research is also governed by specific ethical guidelines (APA, 1996). These guidelines, as well as other issues, are discussed in the In Focus box on page 38.

Here are highlights of five key provisions in the most recent APA ethical principles regulating research with human participants:

- **Informed consent and voluntary participation.** The psychologist must inform the participants of the purpose of the research, including significant factors that might influence a person's willingness to participate in the study, such as potential risks, discomfort, or unpleasant emotional experiences. The psychologist must also explain that participants are free to decline to participate or to withdraw from the research at any time.
- **Students as research participants.** When research participation is a course requirement or an opportunity for extra credit, the student must be given the choice of an alternative activity to fulfill the course requirement or earn extra credit.
- **The use of deception.** Psychologists can use deceptive techniques as part of the study only when two conditions have been met: (1) It is not feasible to use alternatives that do not involve deception, and (2) the potential findings justify the use of deception because of their scientific, educational, or applied value.
- **Confidentiality of information.** In their writing, lectures, or other public forums, psychologists may not disclose personally identifiable information about research participants.
- **Information about the study and debriefing.** All participants must be provided with the opportunity to obtain information about the nature, results, and conclusions of the research. Psychologists are also obligated to *debrief* the participants and to correct any misconceptions that participants may have had about the research.

The Shocking Treatment of Research Participants? Shown above was one of the experimental variations in psychologist Stanley Milgram's landmark—and controversial—study of obedience to an authority figure. Milgram's study was conducted in the early 1960s. In the variation shown, the experimenter directed one subject (the "teacher") to hold another subject's hand (the "learner") down on an electric "shock plate" if he answered incorrectly on a memory task. As you might imagine, Milgram's study generated intense debate about the ethical treatment of research participants in psychology studies. In response to Milgram's experiment and other studies in which participants were pushed to extremes, the American Psychological Association developed stringent guidelines and procedures to help protect human research participants. Some of those guidelines are discussed on this page. Later, in the chapter on social psychology, we will explore Stanley Milgram's famous study, and the implications of his findings, in detail.

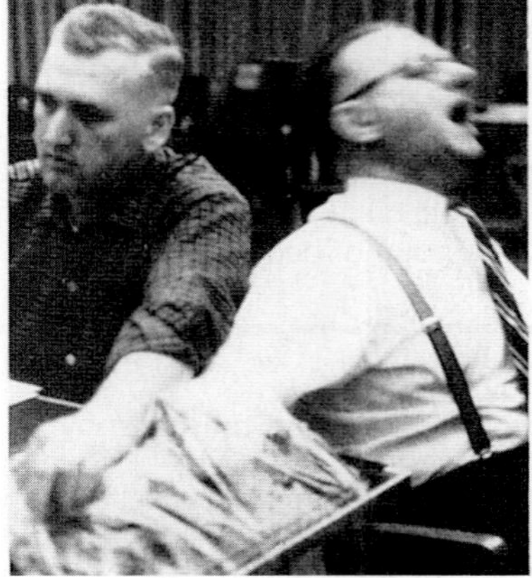

FOCUS ON NEUROSCIENCE

Psychological Research Using Brain Imaging

Brain-scan images have become so commonplace in news articles and popular magazines that it's easy to forget just how revolutionary brain-imaging technology has been to the field of psychology (Cacioppo & others, 2008). Here, we'll look at three commonly used brain-imaging techniques and how they're used in psychological research.

Positron emission tomography, abbreviated **PET,** is based on the fact that increased activity in a particular brain region is associated with increased blood flow and energy consumption. A small amount of radioactively tagged glucose, oxygen, or other substance is injected into the person's bloodstream. Then, the person lies in a PET scanner while performing some mental task. For several minutes, the PET scanner tracks the amounts of radioactive substance used in thousands of different brain regions. A computer analyzes the data, producing color-coded images of the brain's activity.

Magnetic resonance imaging (MRI) does not involve invasive procedures such as injections of radioactive substances. Instead, while the person lies inside a magnetic tube, powerful but harmless magnetic fields bombard the brain. A computer analyzes the electromagnetic signals generated by brain tissue molecules in response to the magnetic fields. The result is a series of digital images, each a detailed "slice" of the brain's structures. MRI scans are routinely used in medicine to produce detailed images of other body parts, such as the joints, spine, or organs.

Functional MRI (fMRI) combines the ability to produce a detailed image of the brain's structures with the capacity to track the brain's activity or functioning. While the person lies in the MRI scanner, a powerful computer tracks the electromagnetic signals that are generated by changes in the brain's metabolic activity, such as increased blood flow to a particular brain region. By measuring the ebb and flow of oxygenated blood in the brain, fMRI produces a series of scans that show detailed moment-by-moment "movies" of the brain's changing activitiy in specific structures or regions.

In the study of brain activity, functional MRI has several advantages over PET scan technology. Because fMRI is a noninvasive procedure and the magnetic waves are harmless, research participants can safely undergo repeated fMRI scans. fMRI produces a much sharper image than PET scans and can detail much smaller brain structures. Another advantage of fMRI is that it provides a picture of brain activity averaged over seconds rather than the several minutes required by PET scans.

How Psychologists Use Brain-Imaging Technology

Brain imaging is used for both descriptive and experimental research. A descriptive study utilizing brain scans might compare the brain structure or functioning of one carefully defined group of people with another.

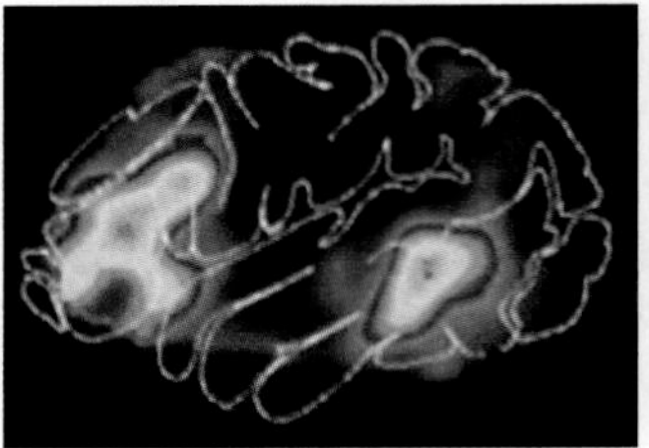

Unpracticed

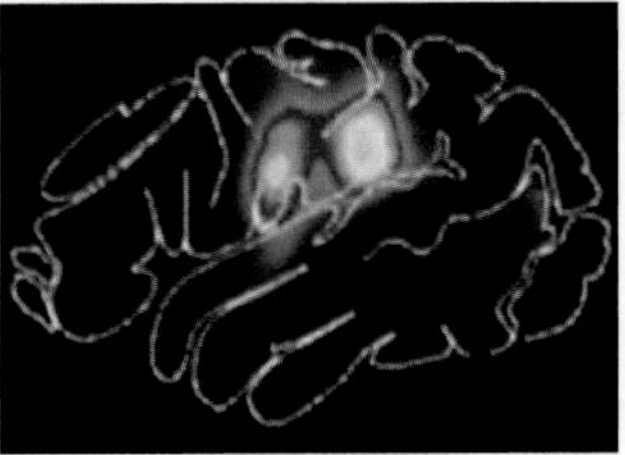

Practiced

Positron Emission Tomography (PET) PET scans provide color-coded images of the brain's activity. This example shows the comparison between subjects learning a new language task (left) and performing the language task after it has been well-learned (right). Red and yellow highlight areas with the highest level of activity while green and blue colors indicate lower levels of brain activity. As you can see, the process of practicing and learning a new language task involves more and different brain areas before becoming established.

For example, MRI scans were used to compare London taxi drivers with matched participants who were not taxi drivers (Maguire & others, 2000, 2006). In order to be licensed, London taxi drivers are required to have an encyclopedic knowledge of the city streets. The MRI scans showed that a brain structure involved in spatial memory, the *hippocampus,* was significantly larger in the experienced taxi drivers than in the control subjects (see MRI scans on the next page). And, the size of the hippocampus was also positively correlated with the length of time the participants had been driving taxis in London: the longer the individual had been driving a taxi, the larger the hippocampus. In Chapter 2, Neuroscience and Behavior, we'll look at how the adult human brain can change in response to learning and environmental influences.

Brain-imaging technology can also be used in experimental research (see fMRI scans on the next page). In a typical experiment, brain scans are taken while research participants are exposed to the experimental treatment or task. These scans are compared to scans taken of control group participants. The differences between the two sets of scans are assumed to be due to the experimental treatment or condition. When multiple participants are compared, researchers combine the results from multiple subjects to produce a composite scan showing the average differences.

Limitations of Brain-Imaging Studies

Images are becoming even more detailed as brain-imaging technology advances. Nevertheless, brain-imaging research has potential limitations (Racine & others, 2005; Vul & others, 2009). When you consider the results of brain-imaging studies, including those presented in this textbook, keep the following points in mind:

positron emission tomography (PET scan)
An invasive imaging technique that provides color-coded images of brain activity by tracking the brain's use of a radioactively tagged compound, such as glucose, oxygen, or a drug.

magnetic resonance imaging (MRI)
A noninvasive imaging technique that produces highly detailed images of the body's structures and tissues using electromagnetic signals generated by the body in response to magnetic fields.

1. ***Brain-imaging studies usually involve a small number of subjects.*** Because of the limited availability and the high cost of the technology, many brain-imaging studies have fewer than a dozen participants. With any research involving a small number of participants, caution must be exercised in generalizing results to a wider population.

2. ***Brain-imaging studies tend to focus on simple aspects of behavior.*** Even seemingly simple tasks involve the smooth coordination of multiple brain regions. As Jerome Kagan (2008) observes, "An event as simple as the unexpected sound of a whistle activates 24 different brain areas." Thus, it's naïve to think that complex psychological or behavioral functions can be mapped to a single brain center.

3. ***Brain imaging may add little to explanations of a psychological process.*** For example, although brain imaging might point to a particular brain structure as being involved in, say, fear or romantic love, knowing this may not advance our understanding of the psychological experience of fear or romantic love.

4. ***Brain imaging is not necessarily a more "scientific" explanation.*** As psychologist Paul Bloom (2006) points out, "Functional MRI seems more like 'real' science than many of the other things that psychologists are up to. It has all the trappings of work with great laboratory credibility: big, expensive, and potentially dangerous machines, hospitals and medical centers, and a lot of people in white coats." To be truly useful, brain activity snapshots of a particular behavior must be accurately interpreted within the context of existing psychological knowledge about the behavior (Cacioppo & Decety, 2009; Henson, 2005).

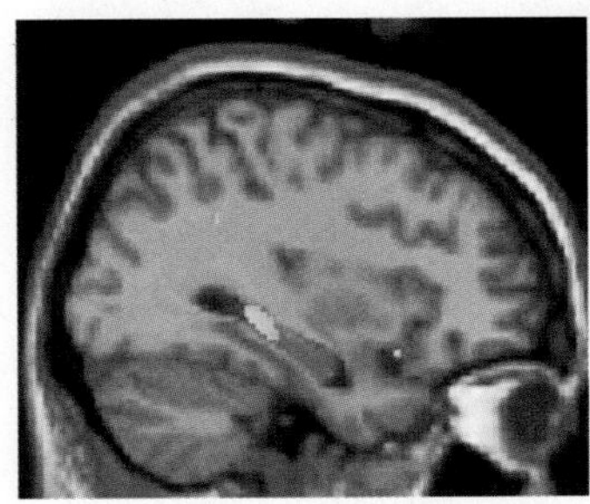

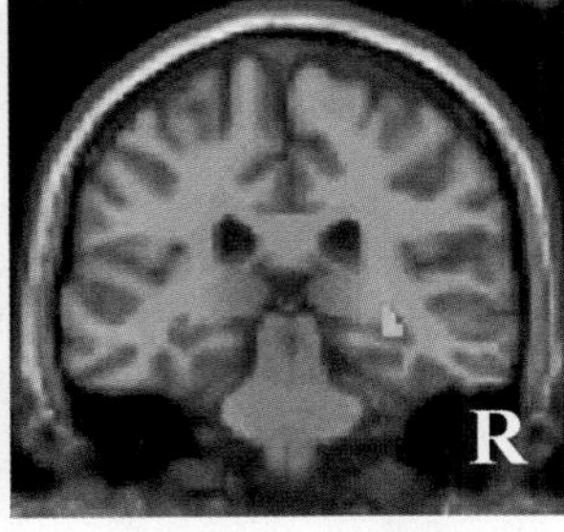

Magnetic Resonance Imaging (MRI) MRI scans can produce a highly detailed image of the brain, showing "slices" of the brain from different angles. The yellow dots highlight the brain region that was significantly larger in experienced London taxi drivers, known for their encyclopedic memory of London streets, as compared to control subjects (Maguire & others, 2000, 2006). This region, called the *hippocampus,* is known to be involved in forming new memories. This landmark study provided solid evidence for the once revolutionary idea that structures in the adult brain change in response to experience and learning.

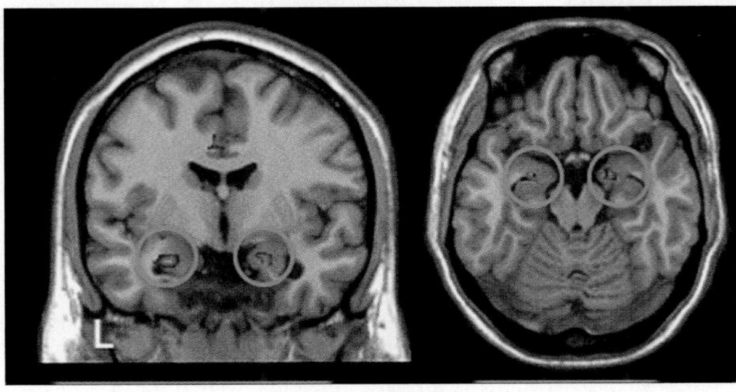

Sleep Rested

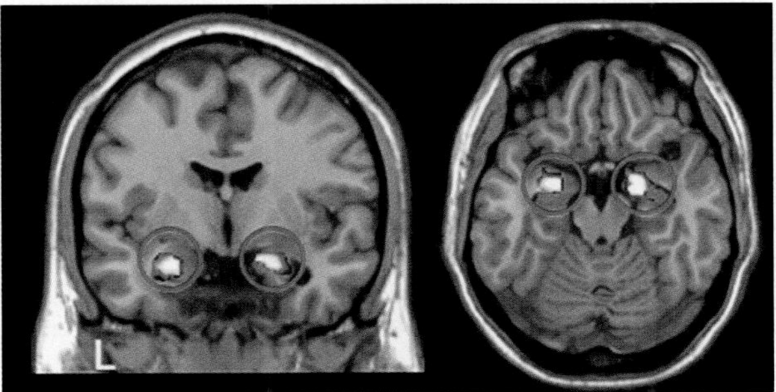

Sleep Deprived

Functional Magnetic Resonance Imaging (fMRI) fMRI combines highly detailed images of brain structures with moment-by-moment tracking of brain activity. In this experiment, fMRI was used to compare emotional responses to disturbing visual images in two groups of participants: participants who had had a normal night's sleep and sleep-deprived participants who had been awake for 35 hours (Yoo & others, 2007). The circled brain region, called the *amygdala,* is known to be involved in emotion. The scans revealed that the amygdala was much more active in sleep-deprived subjects (circled in red) than in participants who were not sleep-deprived (circled in green).

Looking at Brain-Scan Images

What should you notice when you look at the brain-scan images in this text? First, read the text description so you understand the task or condition being measured. Second, read the brain scan caption for specific details or areas to notice. Third, carefully compare the treatment scan with the control scan if both are shown. Fourth, keep the limitations of brain-scan technology in mind. And remember, human experience is much too complex to be captured by a single snapshot of brain activity (Racine & others, 2005).

functional magnetic resonance imaging (fMRI)
A noninvasive imaging technique that uses magnetic fields to map brain activity by measuring changes in the brain's blood flow and oxygen levels.

IN FOCUS

Questions About the Use of Animals in Psychological Research

The use of nonhuman animal subjects in psychological and other research is based on the premise that human life is intrinsically more valuable than animal life. Not everyone agrees with this position (see Herzog, 2005).

The American Psychological Association (1996) condones the use of animals in psychological research under certain conditions. First, research using animal subjects must have an acceptable scientific purpose. Second, there must be a reasonable expectation that the research will (a) increase knowledge about behavior, (b) increase understanding of the species under study, or (c) produce results that benefit the health or welfare of humans or other animals.

What standards must psychologists meet in using animal subjects?

The American Psychological Association publishes the *Guidelines for Ethical Conduct in the Care and Use of Animals,* which you can read at: www.apa.org/science/anguide.html. The APA Guidelines for animal care have been praised as being the most comprehensive set of guidelines of their kind. In addition, psychologists must adhere to federal and state laws governing the use and care of research animals (Garnett, 2005).

How common is the use of animal subjects in psychology research?

Contrary to what many people in the general public believe, the majority of psychology research involves human subjects, not animals. In fact, more than 90 percent of psychology research uses human participants as the subjects. Nonhuman animals are used in only about 7 to 8 percent of psychological studies conducted in a given year. About 90 percent of the animals used in psychological research are rodents and birds, primarily rats, mice, and pigeons. Only about 5 percent of the animals are monkeys and other primates. Use of dogs or cats is rare in psychological studies. The rest of the total includes a wide variety of creatures, from bats to sea snails (APA Committee on Animal Research and Ethics, 2008).

Why are animals used in psychological research?

Here are a few of the key reasons that psychologists might use animal subjects rather than human subjects in research:

1. Many psychologists are interested in the study of animal behavior for its own sake.

The branch of psychology that focuses on the study of the behavior of nonhuman animals is called **comparative psychology.** Some psychologists also do research in *animal cognition,* which is the study of animal learning, memory, thinking, and language (Wasserman & Zentall, 2006).

Animal research is also pursued for its potential benefit to animals themselves. For example, psychological research on animal behavior has been used to improve the quality of life of animals in zoos and to increase the likelihood of survival of endangered species in the wild (Swaisgood, 2007).

2. Animal subjects are sometimes used for research that could not feasibly be conducted on human subjects.

There are many similarities between human and animal behavior, but animal behavior tends to be less complex. Thus, it is sometimes easier to identify basic principles of behavior by studying animals. Psychologists can also observe some animals throughout their entire lifespan. To track such changes in humans would take decades of research. Finally, psychologists can exercise greater control over animal subjects than over human subjects. If necessary, researchers can control every aspect of the animals' environment and even their genetic background (Ator, 2005).

In what areas of psychology has research using animals produced valuable information?

Psychological research with animal subjects has made essential contributions to virtually every area of psychology. Animal research has contributed to psychological knowledge in the areas of neuroscience, learning, memory, cognition, motivation, psychological disorders, therapies, and stress. Research with animals has produced significant gains in the treatment of many conditions, including substance abuse, spinal cord injury, hypertension, and sleep disorders (see Carroll & Overmier, 2001). Significant gains have also been made in helping animals, including the successful breeding and preservation of endangered species, improvements in the care of zoo animals, and the prevention of animal diseases (Swaisgood, 2007).

Comparative psychologist Rebecca Snyder is the curator of giant panda research and management at Zoo Atlanta. Collaborating with scientists at the Chengdu Zoo in the Sichuan province in China, Snyder and her colleagues (2003) have studied topics as diverse as mother-cub interactions, play behavior in cubs, and reproductive behavior in adult pandas. Knowledge gained from such research not only improves the quality of life of pandas in zoos, but also can be applied to conservation efforts in the wild (Maple, 2007, 2006). Many zoos consult comparative psychologists to help design appropriate housing and enrichment activities for all sorts of animals. For more on the giant panda psychological and behavioral research at Zoo Atlanta, visit: www.zooatlanta.org/conservation_giant_panda_research.htm

>> Closing Thoughts

So what happened to Brenda's son, Adam, whose therapist had recommended the use of a magnetic vest and mattress? As it turned out, the magnetic vest produced no beneficial effects, let alone "miracles." Rather than purchase a magnetic mattress, Brenda and her husband took their son to a clinical psychologist who worked at a medical school. A team of specialists that included two clinical psychologists conducted a new diagnostic evaluation of Adam.

The results? Adam did *not* have schizophrenia. He had *Asperger's syndrome,* a developmental disorder that resembles autism. Although people with Asperger's syndrome usually have normal or above-normal intelligence, they also have poor social skills. Other common features of Asperger's syndrome are inappropriate emotional responses, repetitive behaviors or rituals, and odd or peculiar behaviors.

Today, Adam is a senior in high school and his future is much brighter. Brenda's entire family has gone through social skills training to help Adam learn how to interact more successfully with others.

Like Brenda, many of our students come to psychology with questions about personal experiences, seeking explanations for both normal and unusual behaviors. As you'll see in the coming chapters, psychological research has produced many insights into behavior and mental processes. We look forward to sharing those insights with you.

comparative psychology
Branch of psychology that studies the behavior or different animal species.

ENHANCING WELL-BEING WITH PSYCHOLOGY

Psychology in the Media: Becoming an Informed Consumer

Psychologists and psychological findings are often featured in the media. Sometimes it's a researcher, such as Ellen Langer, who is being interviewed about an interesting new study. Or it may be a psychologist who is appearing on a television or radio talk show to discuss the research on a particular topic, such as how violent media or video games influence aggressiveness.

How can you evaluate information about psychology research and psychological topics reported in the mass media? The following guidelines can help.

1. Anecdotes are the essence of talk shows, not scientific evidence.

Psychology-related topics are standard fare on news and talk shows and even the so-called reality TV shows. Although such programs often feature psychologists with research experience and expertise in a particular area, the shows tend to quickly abandon discussions of scientific evidence in favor of anecdotal evidence.

Anecdotal evidence consists of personal stories told to confirm or support a particular claim. The personal stories are often dramatic, funny, or heartrending, making them subjectively interesting and compelling. But as we noted in the chapter, anecdotes are not scientific evidence. By definition, an *anecdote* is one person's subjective experience told from his or her perspective. There's no way to know if the person's experience is representative of the experiences of other people—or if it is exceptional or unusual. There's also no way to determine the story's truthfulness or accuracy. In Chapter 6, on memory, you'll learn about factors that can easily distort the accuracy of a person's memories.

2. Dramatic or sensational headlines are "hooks."

Alia Crum and Ellen Langer's (2007) findings in the hotel experiment were reported in the media with headlines like this: "You Don't Have to Exercise, Just Think You Do" and "Can Your Mind Control Your Weight and Blood Pressure?"(Brain, 2008). Headlines are designed to grab your attention. But if you listen or read further, you'll usually encounter much more cautious statements by the psychologists themselves. As scientists, psychologists tend to be conservative in explaining their research results so as not to exaggerate the findings. Reporters, however, are sometimes more interested in attracting readers or viewers than in accurately portraying scientific results. As media psychologist Rhea Farberman (1999) explains:

> What the researcher sees in his or her research results—one piece of the overall research puzzle that can be applied within the limits of this particular study—is different from what the reporter wants to find in a research study—the all-encompassing headline. The challenge for the psychologist is how to translate the research into a meaningful sound bite.

Given the difficulty of compressing complicated information into a 10-second sound bite, it's common for researchers to be quoted out of context or for important qualifying statements to be left out by a reporter or producer (Farberman, 2003). A 60-minute interview may be edited down to just 20 seconds of air time.

3. Read the actual summary of the study.

Psychological research is usually published in a professional psychology journal before it is shared with the general public. For

> *When journalism and psychology meet, two very different worlds are coming together. The foundation of psychology is the careful analysis of research done over time. The foundation of journalism is the clock, or too often the stopwatch; a continuous rush to meet deadlines and beat the competition.*
>
> RHEA FARBERMAN, 1999

example, it was only *after* Crum and Langer (2007) published their study in the journal *Psychological Science* that they discussed their findings with reporters. If a media report notes the original source of professional publication, you can usually find the study's abstract on the Internet. The *abstract* is a concise summary of the research and its findings. PubMed, at *www.pubmed.gov,* is one excellent source for reading abstracts. Google Scholar, at *scholar.google.com,* is another good source. To try it, go to PubMed and type in the researcher's last name or names (e.g., Crum Langer) and a couple of key words from the study (e.g., exercise hotel). In the list that opens, you should find the study you're looking for in the first few results.

4. Evaluate the design of the study.

Media reports of psychological research usually describe how the study was actually carried out. Look for the elements of good scientific research that we discussed in this chapter, such as operational definitions of variables, random samples, multiple observers in descriptive research, random assignment of participants to experimental conditions, experimental control groups, and so on.

5. Distinguish between correlation and causality.

Remember the correlation we mentioned earlier in the photo caption about the relationship between a preference for jazz and higher levels of sexual activity? As a general rule, when the words *link, tie, connection, association,* or *relationship* are used in the media to describe psychological findings, the research being described is correlational.

Correlational studies are often reported in the mass media with the implication that a cause-and-effect relationship exists. But from our earlier discussion, you understand that even though two factors may be strongly correlated, it is entirely possible that one factor does not actually cause change in the other factor. Instead, a third factor might be responsible for the changes reported. Only the experimental method can provide evidence of a causal relationship between two factors.

6. Embrace an attitude of healthy scientific skepticism.

Basic human nature sometimes leads us to look for easy answers to life's dilemmas, whether that involves increasing your motivation and self-discipline, improving your memory, combating stress, or enhancing relationships. As you'll see in the Application sections at the end of each chapter, psychological research has much to say about these and other practical topics. But achieving these goals is rarely as easy as the popular press portrays it. Although you should always keep your mind open to new possibilities, you must carefully consider the evidence supporting that possibility. Therefore, when evaluating research claims reported in the media, remember one final axiom: If it sounds too good to be true, it probably is!

CHAPTER REVIEW: KEY PEOPLE AND TERMS

Mary Whiton Calkins, p. 7
Charles Darwin, p. 5
Sigmund Freud, p. 7
G. Stanley Hall, p. 6
William James, p. 5
Abraham Maslow, p. 9
Ivan Pavlov, p. 8
Carl Rogers, p. 9
B. F. Skinner, p. 8
Francis C. Sumner, p. 7
Edward B. Titchener, p. 4
Margaret Floy Washburn, p. 7
John B. Watson, p. 8
Wilhelm Wundt, p. 4

psychology, p. 3
structuralism, p. 4
functionalism, p. 5
psychoanalysis, p. 7
behaviorism, p. 8
humanistic psychology, p. 9
neuroscience, p. 10
positive psychology, p. 11
evolutionary psychology, p 12
culture, p. 13
cross-cultural psychology, p. 13
ethnocentrism, p. 13
individualistic cultures, p. 13
collectivistic cultures, p. 13
psychiatry, p. 15
scientific method, p. 16
empirical evidence, p. 16
hypothesis, p. 16
variable, p. 17
critical thinking, p. 17
operational definition, p. 18
statistics, p. 18
statistically significant, p. 18
meta-analysis, p. 19
replicate, p. 19
theory, p. 20
descriptive research methods, p. 21
naturalistic observation, p. 21
pseudoscience, p. 22
case study, p. 22
survey, p. 24
sample, p. 24
representative sample, p. 24
random selection, p. 24
correlational study, p. 25
correlation coefficient, p. 25
positive correlation, p. 25
negative correlation, p. 26
experimental method, p. 27
independent variable, p. 27
dependent variable, p. 27
extraneous variable, p. 27
experimental group (experimental condition), p. 27
placebo, p. 27
placebo effect, p. 28
random assignment, p. 28
double-blind technique, p. 28
demand characteristics, p. 28
practice effect, p. 28
main effect, p. 29
control group (control condition), p. 30
natural experiment, p. 32
positron emission tomography (PET scan), p. 34
magnetic resonance imaging (MRI), p. 34
functional magnetic resonance imaging (fMRI), p. 34
comparative psychology, p. 36

Web Companion Review Activities

You can find additional review activities at **www.worthpublishers.com/discoveringpsych5e.** The *Discovering Psychology* 5th edition Web Companion has self-scoring practice quizzes, flashcards, interactive crossword puzzles, and other activities to help you master the material in this chapter.

CONCEPT MAP

INTRODUCTION AND RESEARCH METHODS

Origins of Psychology

Psychology: The scientific study of behavior and mental processes

The work of early philosophers and psychologists provided a foundation for the birth of psychology as an experimental science.

Wilhelm Wundt (1832–1920)
Founded psychology as experimental science

William James (1842–1910)
Functionalism: Adaptive role of behavior

Edward B. Titchener (1867–1927)
Structuralism: Structures of thought; introspection

Sigmund Freud (1856–1939)
Psychoanalysis: Unconscious influences on behavior

Ivan Pavlov (1849–1936)
John B. Watson (1878–1958)
B. F. Skinner (1904–1990)
Behaviorism: Observable behaviors that can be objectively measured and verified

Carl Rogers (1902–1987)
Abraham Maslow (1908–1970)
Humanistic psychology: Psychological growth, human potential, self-direction

Contemporary Psychology

Perspectives:
Biological
Psychodynamic
Behavioral
Humanistic
Positive psychology
Cognitive
Cross-cultural
Evolutionary psychology

Specialty areas:

Biological	Forensic
Clinical	Health
Cognitive	Industrial/Organizational
Counseling	Personality
Educational	Rehabilitation
Experimental	Social
Developmental	Sports
Comparative	Military

The Scientific Method

Systematic procedure to collect **empirical evidence**. Psychology's goals: To describe, explain, predict, and influence human behavior and mental processes.

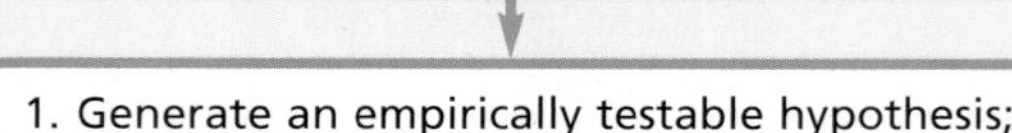

1. Generate an empirically testable hypothesis; **operationally define** all **variables**
2. Design study and collect data
3. Analyze data and draw conclusions
4. Report the findings.

Use **statistics** to analyze findings and determine whether they are **statistically significant**; use **meta-analysis** to combine and analyze data from multiple studies

Publish details of study design so that study can be **replicated**

Develop **theories** to integrate and explain various findings and observations

Research Methods

Must conform to American Psychological Association codes of ethics

Human participants:
- Informed consent
- Voluntary participation
- Deception allowable only when no other alternatives and if justified by study's potential merit
- Confidentiality of personal information
- Debriefed at conclusion of study

Nonhuman subjects:
- Acceptable scientific purpose
- Must increase knowledge about species, behavior, or benefit the health or welfare of humans or nonhuman animals
- Must meet local, state, and federal guidelines regulating care of research animals

Descriptive research methods: Systematically observe and describe behavior

Naturalistic observation

Case studies

Surveys, questionnaires

Correlational studies:
- Determine strength of relationship between two factors; cannot provide evidence of causality
- Relationship is expressed as a numerical correlation coefficient, which can be positive or negative

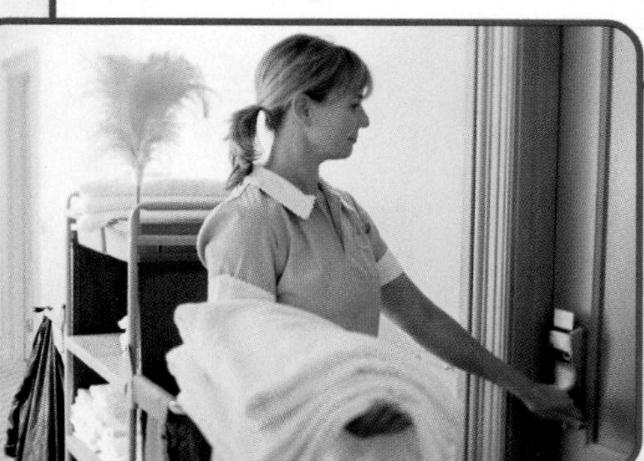

Experimental method: Manipulates **independent variable** and measures the effects on **dependent variable**; used to demonstrate a cause-and-effect relationship

Natural experiments: Investigate effects of naturally occurring events

Experimental controls:
- **Random assignment** of research participants to experimental or control group
- **Double-blind** experimental design to guard against experimenter bias and **demand characteristics**
- Anticipate potential influence of **extraneous variables**

Experimental group: Exposed to independent variable

Control group: Not exposed to independent variable

Placebo control group: (in some experiments): Exposed to fake independent variable

Measure effects, if any, on **dependent variable**

CHAPTER 2

Neuroscience and Behavior

Chapter Outline

Asha's Story

PROLOGUE

The headaches began without warning. A pounding, intense pain just over Asha's left temple. Asha just couldn't seem to shake it—the pain was unrelenting. She was uncharacteristically tired, too.

But our friend Asha, a 32-year-old university professor, chalked up her constant headache and fatigue to stress and exhaustion. After all, the end of her demanding first semester of teaching and research was drawing near. Still, Asha had always been very healthy and usually tolerated stress well. She didn't drink or smoke. And no matter how late she stayed up working on her lectures and research proposals, she still got up at 5:30 every morning to work out at the university gym.

There were other, more subtle signs that something was wrong. Asha's husband, Paul, noticed that she had been behaving rather oddly in recent weeks. For example, at Thanksgiving dinner, Asha had picked up a knife by the wrong end and tried to cut her turkey with the handle instead of the blade. A few hours later, Asha had made the same mistake trying to use scissors: She held the blades and tried to cut with the handle.

Asha laughed these incidents off, and for that matter, so did Paul. They both thought she was simply under too much stress. And when Asha occasionally got her words mixed up, neither Paul nor anyone else was terribly surprised. Asha was born in India, and her first language was Tulu. Although Asha was extremely fluent in English, she often got English phrases slightly wrong—like the time she said that Paul was a "straight dart" instead of a "straight arrow." Or when she said that it was "storming cats and birds" instead of "raining cats and dogs."

There were other odd lapses in language. "I would say something thinking it was correct," Asha recalled, "and people would say to me, 'What are you saying?' I wouldn't realize I was saying something wrong. I would open my mouth and just nonsense would come out. But it made perfect sense to me. At other times, the word was on the tip of my tongue—I knew I knew the word, but I couldn't find it. I would fumble for the word, but it would come out wrong. Sometimes I would slur words, like I'd try to say 'Saturday,' only it would come out 'salad-day.'"

On Christmas morning, Paul and Asha were with Paul's family, opening presents. Asha walked over to Paul's father to look at the pool cue he had received as a gift. As she bent down, she fell forward onto her father-in-law. At first, everyone thought Asha was just joking around. But then she fell to the floor, her body stiff. Seconds later, it was apparent that Asha had lost consciousness and was having a seizure.

Asha remembers nothing of the seizure or of being taken by ambulance to the hospital intensive care unit. She floated in and out of consciousness for the first day and night. A CAT scan showed some sort of blockage in Asha's brain. An MRI scan revealed a large white spot on the left side of her brain. At only 32 years of age, Asha had suffered a stroke—brain damage caused by a disruption of the blood flow to the brain.

She remained in the hospital for 12 days. It was only after Asha was transferred out of intensive care that both she and Paul began to realize just how serious the repercussions of the stroke were. Asha couldn't read or write and had difficulty comprehending what was being said. Although she could speak, she could not name even simple objects, such as a tree, a clock, or her doctor's tie. In this chapter, you will discover why the damage to Asha's brain impaired her ability to perform simple behaviors, like naming common objects.

>> Introduction: Neuroscience and Behavior

As we discussed in Chapter 1, **biological psychology** is the scientific study of the biological bases of behavior and mental processes. This area of research is also called *biopsychology* or *psychobiology.* All three terms emphasize the idea of a biological approach to the study of psychological processes. Biological psychology is one of the scientific disciplines that makes important contributions to **neuroscience**—the scientific study of the nervous system. As *neuroscientists,* biopsychologists bring their expertise in behavior and behavioral research to this scientific endeavor. Some of the other scientific disciplines that contribute to neuroscience include *physiology, pharmacology, biology,* and *neurology.*

Neuroscience and biological psychology are not limited to the study of the brain and the rest of the nervous system. Throughout this textbook, you'll encounter some of the many questions that have been studied by neuroscientists. Here are some examples:

- How do you tell the difference between red and blue, sweet and sour, loud and soft? (Chapter 3)
- What happens in the brain when you sleep, dream, or meditate? (Chapter 4)
- What exactly is a memory, and how are memories stored in the brain? (Chapter 6)
- Why do you get hungry? How do emotions occur? (Chapter 8)
- How do emotions and attitudes affect our vulnerability to infection and disease? (Chapter 12)
- How does heredity influence your development? What role does genetics play in personality traits? (Chapters 9, 10, and 13)
- What role does abnormal brain chemistry play in psychological disorders? How do medications alleviate the symptoms of serious psychological disorders? (Chapters 13 and 14)

This chapter will lay an important foundation for the rest of this book by helping you develop a broad appreciation of the *nervous system*—the body's primary communication network. We'll start by looking at *neurons,* the basic cells of the nervous system. We'll consider the organization of the nervous system and a closely linked communication network, the *endocrine system.* We'll then move on to a guided tour of the brain. We'll look at how certain brain areas are specialized to handle different functions, such as language, vision, and touch. In Enhancing Well-Being with Psychology, at the end of the chapter, we'll describe how the brain responds to environmental stimulation by literally altering its physical structure. And we'll return to Asha's story and tell you how she fared after her stroke.

Neuroscience and Behavior Trying to help your friend maintain his balance on a skateboard, laughing and talking as you simultaneously walk and scan the path for obstacles or other people, thinking about how to help him if he falls—even seemingly simple behaviors involve the harmonious integration of multiple internal signals and body processes. What kinds of questions might neuroscientists ask about the common behaviors shown here?

The Neuron

The Basic Unit of Communication

Key Theme

- **Information in the nervous system is transmitted by specialized cells, called neurons.**

Key Questions

- **What are the basic components of the neuron, and what are their functions?**
- **What are glial cells, and what is their role in the nervous system?**
- **What is an action potential, and how is it produced?**

Communication throughout the nervous system takes place via **neurons**—cells that are highly specialized to receive and transmit information from one part of the body to another. Most neurons, especially those in your brain, are extremely small. A bit of brain tissue no larger than a grain of rice contains about 10,000 neurons! Your entire brain contains an estimated 100 *billion* neurons. Special magnifying equipment, such as an electron microscope, is usually used to study neurons.

Neurons vary greatly in size and shape, reflecting their specialized functions. There are three basic types of neurons, each communicating different kinds of information. **Sensory neurons** convey information about the environment, such as light or sound, from specialized receptor cells in the sense organs to the brain. Sensory neurons also carry information from the skin and internal organs to the brain. **Motor neurons** communicate information to the muscles and glands of the body. Simply blinking your eyes activates thousands of motor neurons. Finally, **interneurons** communicate information *between* neurons. By far, most of the neurons in the human nervous system are interneurons, and many interneurons connect to other interneurons.

Along with neurons, the human nervous system is made up of other specialized cells, called **glial cells** or simply **glia** (see photo). Glial cells outnumber neurons by about 10 to 1 but are much smaller. *Glia* is Greek for "glue," and at one time it was thought that glial cells were the glue that held neurons together. Although they don't actually glue neurons together, glia do provide structural support for neurons throughout the nervous system. They also provide nutrition for neurons and remove waste products. Beyond their support functions, it's now known that some glial cells play an active role in brain development and function (Allen & Barres, 2009).

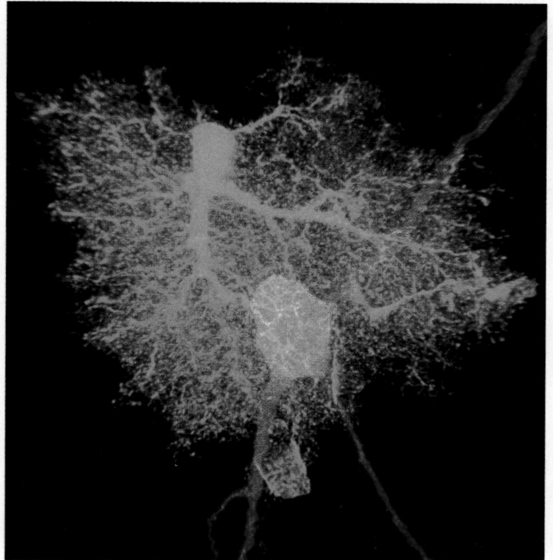

Glial Cells: More than Glue This colored micrograph shows one type of glial cell, an *astrocyte* (green), enveloping a neuron (red). Astrocytes provide connections between neurons and blood vessels in the brain. Other glial cells form the *myelin sheath*, a fatty insulating substance that is wrapped around the parts of some, but not all, neurons. Another type of glial cell removes waste products from the nervous system, including dead and damaged neurons. Beyond those functions, researchers now know that glia are much more actively involved in regulating neuronal communication and activity than previously thought (Allen & Barres, 2009; Gibbs & others, 2008).

biological psychology
Specialized branch of psychology that studies the relationship between behavior and bodily processes and systems; also called *biopsychology* or *psychobiology.*

neuroscience
The study of the nervous system, especially the brain.

neuron
Highly specialized cell that communicates information in electrical and chemical form; a nerve cell.

sensory neuron
Type of neuron that conveys information to the brain from specialized receptor cells in sense organs and internal organs.

motor neuron
Type of neuron that signals muscles to relax or contract.

interneuron
Type of neuron that communicates information from one neuron to the next.

glial cells
(GLEE-ull) Support cells that assist neurons by providing structural support, nutrition, and removal of cell wastes; manufacture myelin.

cell body
Processes nutrients and provides energy for the neuron to function; contains the cell's nucleus; also called the *soma.*

dendrites
Multiple short fibers that extend from the neuron's cell body and receive information from other neurons or from sensory receptor cells.

axon
The long, fluid-filled tube that carries a neuron's messages to other body areas.

Characteristics of the Neuron

Most neurons have three basic components: a *cell body, dendrites,* and an *axon* (see Figure 2.1). The **cell body,** also called the *soma,* contains structures that manufacture proteins and process nutrients, providing the energy the neuron needs to function. The cell body also contains the *nucleus,* which in turn contains the cell's genetic material—twisted strands of DNA called *chromosomes.*

Extending from the cell body are short, branching fibers, called **dendrites.** The term *dendrite* comes from a Greek word meaning "tree." If you have a good imagination, the intricate branching of the dendrites does often resemble the branches of a tree. Dendrites *receive* messages from other neurons or specialized cells. Dendrites with many branches have a greater surface area, which increases the amount of information the neuron can receive. Some neurons have thousands of dendrites.

The **axon** is a single, elongated tube that extends from the cell body in most, though not all, neurons. (Some neurons do not have axons.) Axons carry information *from* the neuron *to* other cells in the body, including other neurons, glands, and muscles. In contrast to the potentially large number of dendrites, a neuron has no more than one axon exiting from the cell body. However, many axons have branches near their tips that allow the neuron to communicate information to more than one target.

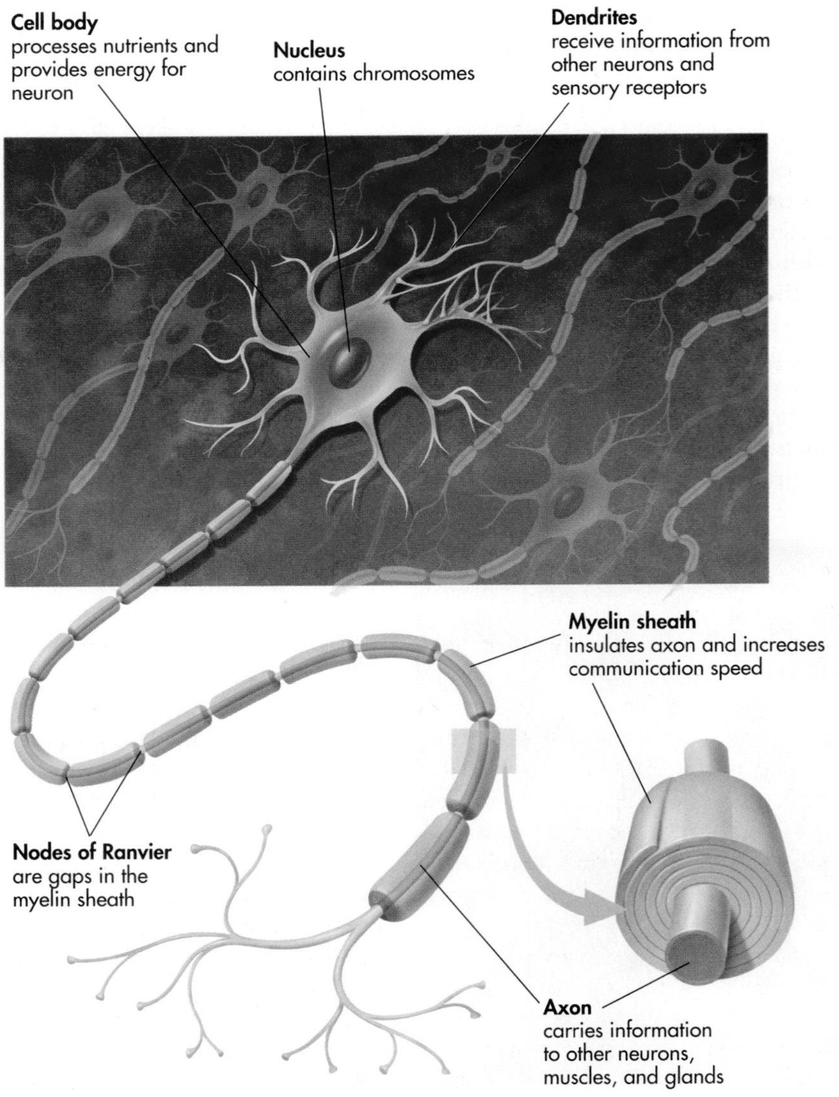

Figure 2.1 The Parts of a Typical Neuron The drawing shows the location and function of key parts of a neuron. The photograph, made with the aid of an electron microscope, reveals actual cell bodies, dendrites, and axons in a cluster of neurons. The green coloring was added to provide contrast in the photograph to make the neurons more visible.

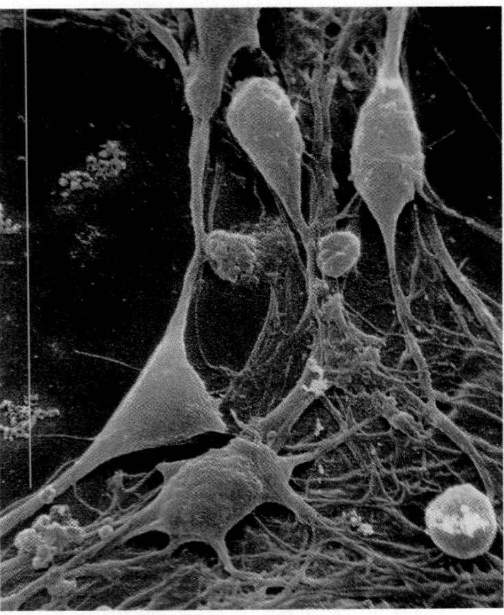

Axons can vary enormously in length. Most axons are very small; some are no more than a few thousandths of an inch long. Other axons are quite long. For example, the longest axon in your body is that of the motor neuron that controls your big toe. This neuron extends from the base of your spine into your foot. If you happen to be a seven-foot-tall basketball player, this axon could be four feet long! For most of us, of course, this axon is closer to three feet long.

The axons of many, though not all, neurons are surrounded by the **myelin sheath.** The myelin sheath is a white, fatty covering formed by special glial cells. In much the same way that you can bundle together electrical wires if they are insulated with plastic, myelin helps insulate one axon from the axons of other neurons. Rather than forming a continuous coating of the axon, the myelin sheath occurs in segments that are separated by small gaps where there is no myelin. The small gaps are called the *nodes of Ranvier,* or simply *nodes* (see Figure 2.1). Neurons wrapped in myelin communicate their messages up to 20 times faster than do unmyelinated neurons.

The importance of myelin becomes readily apparent when it is damaged. For example, *multiple sclerosis* is a disease that involves the degeneration of patches of the myelin sheath. This degeneration causes the transmission of neural messages to be slowed or interrupted, resulting in disturbances in sensation and movement. Muscular weakness, loss of coordination, and speech and visual disturbances are some of the symptoms that characterize multiple sclerosis.

myelin sheath
(MY-eh-lin) A white, fatty covering wrapped around the axons of some neurons that increases their communication speed.

action potential
A brief electrical impulse by which information is transmitted along the axon of a neuron.

stimulus threshold
The minimum level of stimulation required to activate a particular neuron.

resting potential
State in which a neuron is prepared to activate and communicate its message if it receives sufficient stimulation.

Communication Within the Neuron

The All-or-None Action Potential

Essentially, the function of neurons is to transmit information throughout the nervous system. But exactly *how* do neurons transmit information? What form does this information take? In this section, we'll consider the nature of communication *within* a neuron, and in the following section we'll describe communication *between* neurons. As you'll see, communication in and between neurons is an electrochemical process.

In general, messages are gathered by the dendrites and cell body and then transmitted along the axon in the form of a brief electrical impulse called an **action potential.** The action potential is produced by the movement of electrically charged particles, called *ions,* across the membrane of the axon. Some ions are negatively charged, others positively charged.

Think of the axon membrane as a gatekeeper that carefully controls the balance of positive and negative ions on the interior and exterior of the axon. As the gatekeeper, the axon membrane opens and closes *ion channels* that allow ions to flow into and out of the axon.

Each neuron requires a minimum level of stimulation from other neurons or sensory receptors to activate it. This minimum level of stimulation is called the neuron's **stimulus threshold.** While waiting for sufficient stimulation to activate it, the neuron is said to be *polarized.* This means that there is a difference in the electrical charge between the inside and the outside of the axon.

More specifically, there is a greater concentration of negative proteins inside the neuron. Thus, the axon's interior is more negatively charged than is the exterior fluid surrounding the axon. The negative electrical charge is about −70 millivolts (thousandths of a volt) (see Figure 2.3 on page 49). The −70 millivolts is referred to as the neuron's **resting potential.**

In this polarized, negative-inside/positive-outside condition, there are different concentrations of two particular ions: sodium and potassium. While the neuron is in resting potential, the fluid surrounding the axon contains a larger concentration of *sodium* ions than does the fluid within the axon. The fluid within the axon contains a larger concentration of *potassium* ions than is found in the fluid outside the axon.

When sufficiently stimulated by other neurons or sensory receptors, the neuron *depolarizes,* beginning the action potential. At each successive axon segment, sodium ion channels open for a mere thousandth of a second. The sodium ions

The Brain Capturing a Thought In the brain, as in the rest of the nervous system, information is transmitted by electrical impulses (red area) that speed from one neuron to the next.

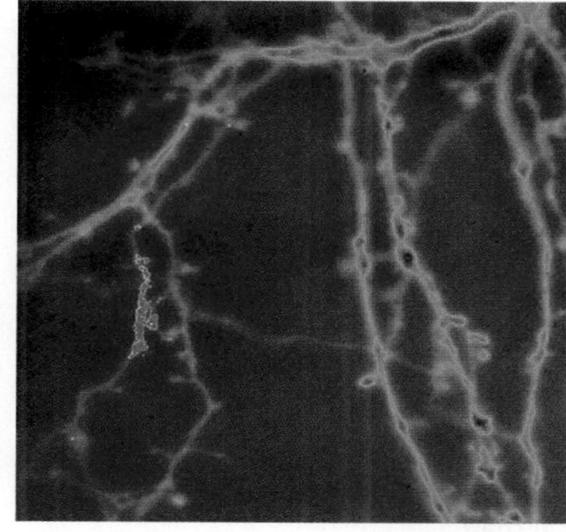

rush to the axon interior from the surrounding fluid, and then the sodium ion channels close. Less than a thousandth of a second later, the potassium ion channels open, allowing potassium to flow out of the axon and into the fluid surrounding it. Then the potassium ion channels close (see Figure 2.2). This sequence of depolarization and ion movement continues in a self-sustaining fashion down the entire length of the axon.

As this ion exchange occurs, the relative balance of positive and negative ions separated by the axon membrane changes. The electrical charge on the inside of the axon momentarily changes to a positive electrical charge of about +30 millivolts. The result is a brief positive electrical impulse that progressively occurs at each segment down the axon—the *action potential.*

Although it's tempting to think of the action potential as being conducted much as electricity is conducted through a wire, that's *not* what takes place in the neuron. The axon is actually a poor conductor of electricity. At each successive segment of the axon, the action potential is *regenerated* in the same way in which it was generated in the previous segment—by depolarization and the movement of ions.

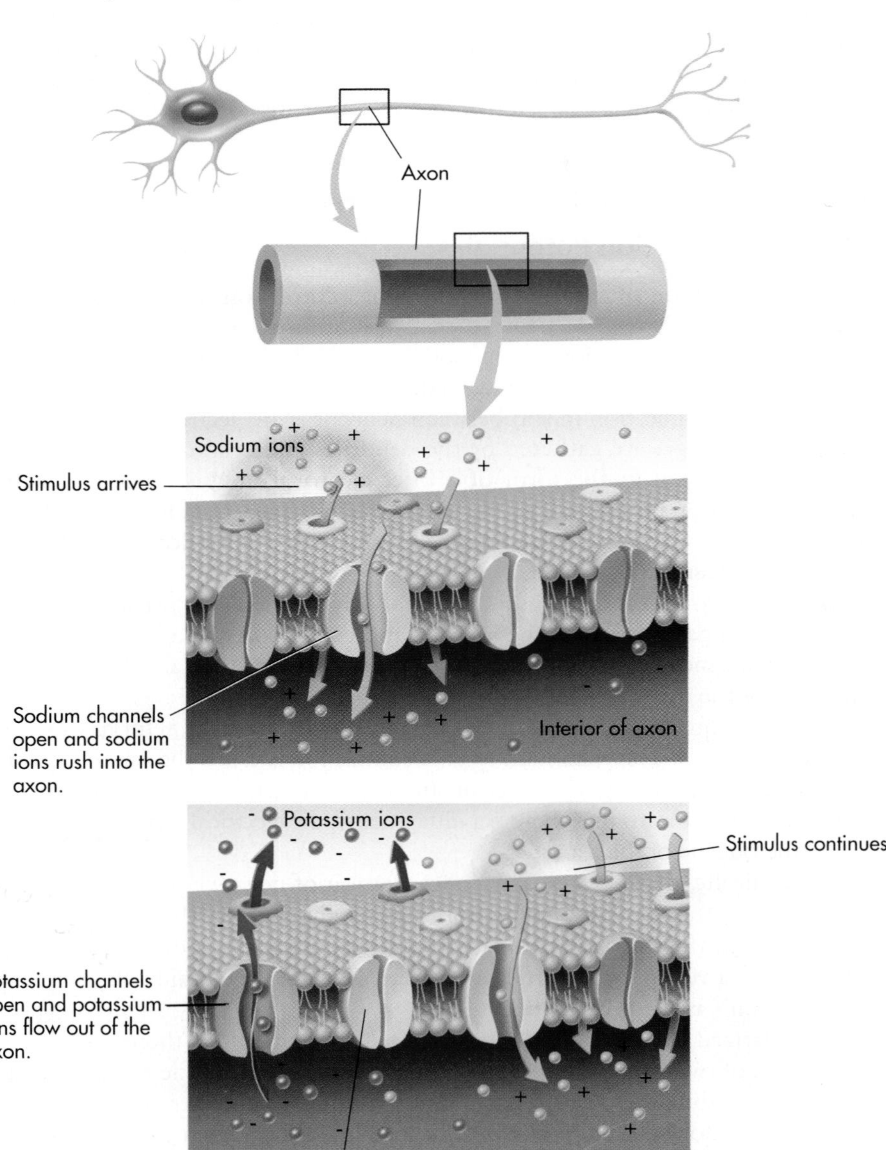

Figure 2.2 Communication Within the Neuron: The Action Potential These drawings depict the ion channels in the membrane of a neuron's axon. When sufficiently stimulated, the neuron depolarizes and an action potential begins. At each progressive segment of the axon's membrane, sodium ion channels open and sodium ions rush into the interior of the axon. A split second later, the sodium ion channels close and potassium channels open, allowing potassium ions to flow out of the axon. As this sequence occurs, there is a change in the relative balance of positive and negative ions separated by the axon membrane. The electrical charge on the interior of the axon briefly changes from negative to positive. Once started, an action potential is self-sustaining and continues to the end of the axon. Following the action potential, the neuron repolarizes and reestablishes its negative electrical charge.

Once the action potential is started, it is *self-sustaining* and continues to the end of the axon. In other words, there is no such thing as a partial action potential. Either the neuron is sufficiently stimulated and an action potential occurs, or the neuron is not sufficiently stimulated and an action potential does not occur. This principle is referred to as the **all-or-none law.**

Following the action potential, a *refractory period* occurs during which the neuron is unable to fire. This period lasts for about a thousandth of a second or less. During the refractory period, the neuron *repolarizes* and reestablishes the negative-inside/positive-outside condition. Like depolarization, repolarization occurs progressively at each segment down the axon. This process reestablishes the *resting potential* conditions so that the neuron is capable of firing again. The graph in Figure 2.3 depicts the complete sequence from resting potential to action potential and back to resting potential.

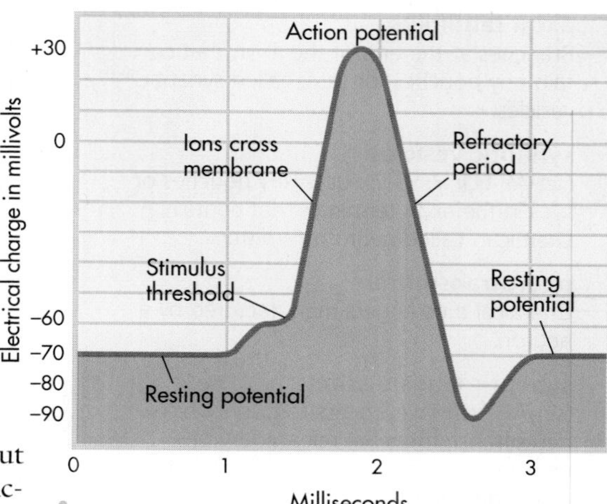

Figure 2.3 Electrical Changes During an Action Potential This graph shows the changing electrical charge of the neuron during an action potential. When the neuron depolarizes and ions cross the axon membrane, the result is a brief positive electrical impulse of +30 millivolts—the action potential. During the refractory period, the neuron reestablishes the resting potential negative charge of −70 millivolts and then is ready to activate again.

For clarity, we've simplified some of the details involved in the action potential, but this is basically how information is communicated *within* the neuron. Remember, action potentials are generated in mere thousandths of a second. Thus, a single neuron can potentially generate hundreds of neural impulses per second. Given these minute increments of time, just how fast do neural impulses zip around your body?

The fastest neurons in your body communicate at speeds of up to 270 miles per hour. In the slowest neurons, messages creep along at about 2 miles per hour. This variation in communication speed is due to two factors: the axon diameter and the myelin sheath. The greater the axon's diameter, the faster the axon conducts action potentials. And, as we said earlier, myelinated neurons communicate faster than unmyelinated neurons. In myelinated neurons, the sodium ion channels are concentrated at each of the nodes of Ranvier where the myelin is missing. So, in myelinated neurons the action potential "jumps" from node to node rather than progressing down the entire length of the axon.

Communication Between Neurons

Bridging the Gap

Key Theme

- **Communication between neurons takes place at the synapse, the junction between two adjoining neurons.**

Key Questions

- **How is information communicated at the synapse?**
- **What is a neurotransmitter, and what is its role in synaptic transmission?**
- **What are five important neurotransmitters, and how do psychoactive drugs affect synaptic transmission?**

The primary function of a neuron is to communicate information to other cells, most notably other neurons. The point of communication between two neurons is called the **synapse.** At this communication junction, the message-*sending* neuron is referred to as the *presynaptic neuron.* The message-*receiving* neuron is called the *postsynaptic neuron.* For cells that are specialized to communicate information, neurons have a surprising characteristic: They don't touch each other. The presynaptic and postsynaptic neurons are separated by a tiny, fluid-filled space, called the **synaptic gap,** which is only about *five-millionths* of an inch wide.

The transmission of information between two neurons occurs in one of two ways: electrically or chemically. When communication is electrical, the synaptic gap is extremely narrow, and special ion channels serve as a bridge between the neurons. Electrical communication between the two neurons is virtually instantaneous. Less than one percent of the synapses in the brain use chemical transmission.

all-or-none law
The principle that either a neuron is sufficiently stimulated and an action potential occurs or a neuron is not sufficiently stimulated and an action potential does not occur.

synapse
(SIN-aps) The point of communication between two neurons.

synaptic gap
(sin-AP-tick) The tiny space between the axon terminal of one neuron and the dendrite of an adjoining neuron.

axon terminals
Branches at the end of the axon that contain tiny pouches, or sacs, called synaptic vesicles.

synaptic vesicles
(sin-AP-tick VESS-ick-ulls) Tiny pouches or sacs in the axon terminals that contain chemicals called neurotransmitters.

neurotransmitters
Chemical messengers manufactured by a neuron.

synaptic transmission
(sin-AP-tick) The process through which neurotransmitters are released by one neuron, cross the synaptic gap, and affect adjoining neurons.

reuptake
The process by which neurotransmitter molecules detach from a postsynaptic neuron and are reabsorbed by a presynaptic neuron so they can be recycled and used again.

In general terms, chemical communication occurs when the presynaptic neuron creates a chemical substance that diffuses across the synaptic gap and is detected by the postsynaptic neuron. This one-way communication process between one neuron and another has many important implications for human behavior.

More specifically, here's how chemical communication takes place between neurons. As you've seen, when the presynaptic neuron is activated, it generates an action potential that travels to the end of the axon. At the end of the axon are several small branches called **axon terminals.** Floating in the interior fluid of the axon terminals are tiny sacs called **synaptic vesicles** (see Figure 2.4). The synaptic vesicles hold special chemical messengers manufactured by the neuron, called **neurotransmitters.**

When the action potential reaches the axon terminals, some of the synaptic vesicles "dock" on the axon terminal membrane, then release their neurotransmitters into the synaptic gap. These chemical messengers cross the synaptic gap and attach to *receptor sites* on the dendrites and other surfaces of the surrounding neurons. This journey across the synaptic gap is slower than electrical transmission but is still extremely rapid; it takes just a few millionths of a second. The entire process of transmitting information at the synapse is called **synaptic transmission.**

What happens to the neurotransmitter molecules after they've attached to the receptor sites of the postsynaptic neuron? Most often, they detach from the receptor and are reabsorbed by the presynaptic neuron so they can be recycled and used again. This process is called **reuptake.** Reuptake also occurs with many of the neurotransmitters that failed to attach to a receptor and are left floating in the synaptic gap.

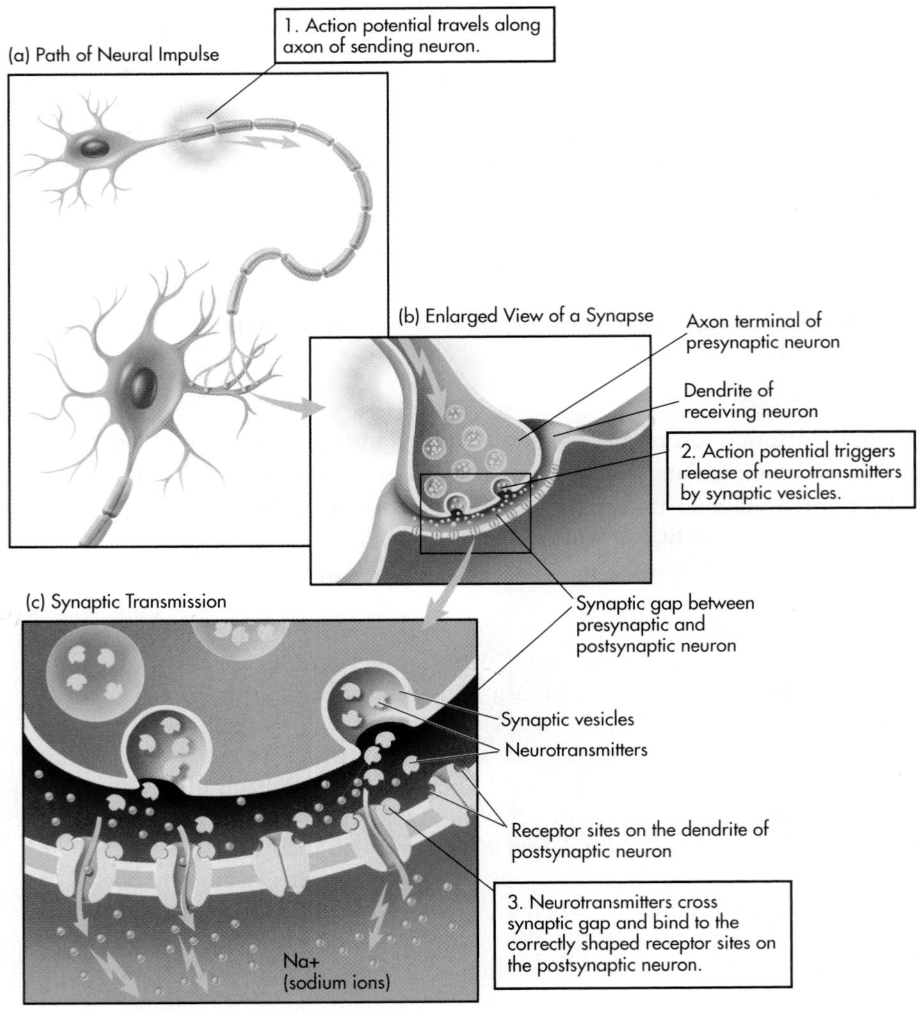

Figure 2.4 Communication Between Neurons: The Process of Synaptic Transmission As you follow the steps in this progressive graphic, you can trace the sequence of synaptic transmission in which neurotransmitters are released by the sending, or presynaptic, neuron, cross the tiny fluid-filled space called the synaptic gap, and attach to receptor sites on the receiving, or postsynaptic, neuron.

Neurotransmitter molecules that are not reabsorbed or that remain attached to the receptor site are broken down or destroyed by enzymes. As you'll see in the next section, certain drugs can interfere with both of these processes, prolonging the presence of the neurotransmitter in the synaptic gap.

The number of neurotransmitters that a neuron can manufacture varies. Some neurons produce only one type of neurotransmitter, whereas others manufacture three or more. Although estimates vary, scientists have identified more than 100 different compounds that function as neurotransmitters in the brain.

Each type of neurotransmitter has a chemically distinct shape. Like a key in a lock, a neurotransmitter's shape must precisely match that of a receptor site on the postsynaptic neuron for the neurotransmitter to affect that neuron. Keep in mind that the postsynaptic neuron can have many differently shaped receptor sites on its dendrites and other surfaces. Thus, a given neuron may be able to receive several different neurotransmitters. The distinctive shapes of neurotransmitters and their receptor sites are shown schematically in Figure 2.5.

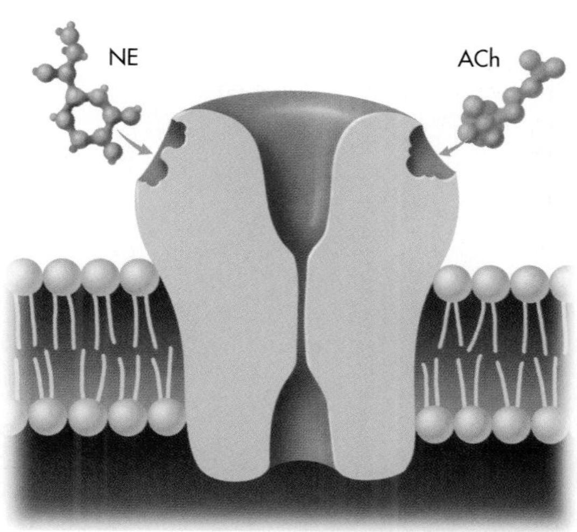

Figure 2.5 Neurotransmitter and Receptor Site Shapes Each neurotransmitter has a chemically distinct shape. Like a key in a lock, a neurotransmitter must perfectly fit the receptor site on the receiving neuron for its message to be communicated. In this figure, NE is the abbreviation for the neurotransmitter norepinephrine and ACh is the abbreviation for acetylcholine.

Excitatory and Inhibitory Messages

A neurotransmitter communicates either an excitatory or an inhibitory message to a postsynaptic neuron. An *excitatory message* increases the likelihood that the postsynaptic neuron will activate and generate an action potential. Conversely, an *inhibitory message* decreases the likelihood that the postsynaptic neuron will activate. If a postsynaptic neuron receives an excitatory and an inhibitory message simultaneously, the two messages cancel each other out.

It's important to note that the effect of any particular neurotransmitter depends on the particular *receptor* to which it binds. So, the same neurotransmitter can have an inhibitory effect on one neuron and an excitatory effect on another.

Depending on the number and kind of neurotransmitter chemicals that are bound to the receptor sites on the adjoining neurons, the postsynaptic neurons are more or less likely to activate. If the net result is a sufficient number of excitatory messages, the postsynaptic neuron depolarizes, generates an action potential, and releases its own neurotransmitters.

When released by a presynaptic neuron, neurotransmitter chemicals cross hundreds, even thousands, of synaptic gaps and affect the intertwined dendrites of adjacent neurons. Because the receiving neuron can have thousands of dendrites that intertwine with the axon terminals of many presynaptic neurons, the number of potential synaptic interconnections between neurons is truly mind-boggling. Each neuron in the brain communicates directly with an average of 1,000 other neurons (Hyman, 2005). However, some specialized neurons have as many as 100,000 connections with other neurons. Thus, in your brain alone, there are up to 100 *trillion* synaptic interconnections.

Neurotransmitters and Their Effects

Your ability to perceive, feel, think, move, act, and react depends on the delicate balance of neurotransmitters in your nervous system. Too much or too little of a given neurotransmitter can have devastating effects. Yet neurotransmitters are present in only minuscule amounts in the human body. If you imagine trying to detect a pinch of salt dissolved in an Olympic-sized swimming pool, you will have some idea of the infinitesimal amounts of neurotransmitters present in brain tissue.

In this section, you'll see that researchers have linked abnormal levels of specific neurotransmitters to various physical and behavioral problems (see Table 2.1 on the next page). Nevertheless, it's important to remember that any connection between a particular neurotransmitter and a particular effect is not a simple one-to-one relationship. Many behaviors are the result of the complex interaction of different neurotransmitters. Further, neurotransmitters sometimes have different effects in different areas of the brain.

Table 2.1

Summary of Important Neurotransmitters

Neurotransmitter	Primary Roles	Associated Disorders
Acetylcholine	Learning, memory Muscle contractions	Alzheimer's disease
Dopamine	Movement Thought processes Rewarding sensations	Parkinson's disease Schizophrenia Drug addiction
Serotonin	Emotional states Sleep Sensory perception	Depression
Norepinephrine	Physical arousal Learning, memory Regulation of sleep	Depression, stress
GABA	Inhibition of brain activity	Anxiety disorders
Endorphins	Pain perception Positive emotions	Opiate addiction

Important Neurotransmitters

Acetylcholine, the first neurotransmitter discovered, is found in all motor neurons. It stimulates muscles to contract, including the heart and stomach muscles. Whether it is as simple as the flick of an eyelash or as complex as a back flip, all movement involves acetylcholine.

Acetylcholine is also found in many neurons in the brain, and it is important in memory, learning, and general intellectual functioning. People with *Alzheimer's disease,* which is characterized by progressive loss of memory and deterioration of intellectual functioning, have a severe depletion of several neurotransmitters in the brain, most notably acetylcholine.

The neurotransmitter **dopamine** is involved in movement, attention, learning, and pleasurable or rewarding sensations. Evidence suggests that the addictiveness of many drugs, including cocaine and nicotine, is related to their ability to increase dopamine activity in the brain (Koob & Volkow, 2009; Volkow & others, 2007).

The degeneration of the neurons that produce dopamine in one brain area causes *Parkinson's disease,* which is characterized by rigidity, muscle tremors, poor balance, and difficulty in initiating movements. Symptoms can be alleviated by a drug called *L-dopa,* which converts to dopamine in the brain.

Excessive brain levels of dopamine are sometimes involved in the hallucinations and perceptual distortions that characterize the severe mental disorder called *schizophrenia.* Some antipsychotic drugs that relieve schizophrenic symptoms work by blocking dopamine receptors and reducing dopamine activity in the brain. Unfortunately, these antipsychotic drugs can also produce undesirable side effects. Because the drugs reduce dopamine in several different areas of the brain, long-term use sometimes produces symptoms that are very similar to those of Parkinson's disease. In the chapters on psychological disorders (Chapter 13) and therapies (Chapter 14), we'll discuss schizophrenia, dopamine, and antipsychotic drugs in more detail.

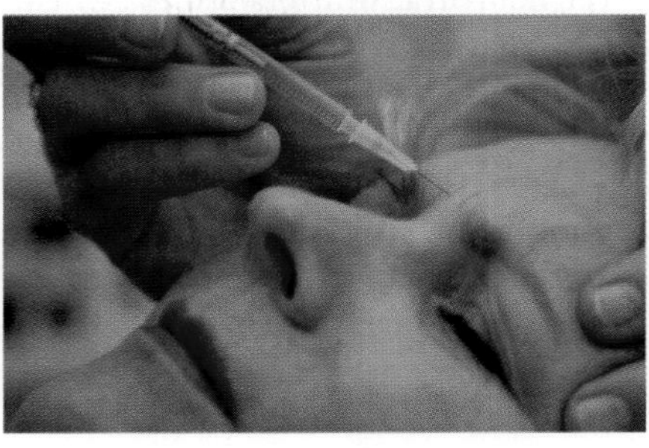

Botulism: Blocking Acetylcholine for Cosmetic Reasons How does Botox eliminate facial wrinkles? Botox injections contain very minute amounts of *botulinum*, a toxin that causes muscle paralysis around the injection site by blocking the release of acetylcholine from motor neurons. Because the muscles can't contract, the skin smoothes out, and facial wrinkles are diminished or eliminated. Produced by bacteria, botulinum toxin is extremely lethal, and can produce death if ingested in food, if inhaled, or if the toxin enters the bloodstream through broken skin (Arnon & others, 2001). But when purified and properly administered in infinitesimal amounts, botulinum toxin can safely be used for cosmetic purposes and to help treat a variety of conditions, including migraine headaches and severe muscle spasms (Montecucco & Molgó, 2005).

The neurotransmitters **serotonin** and **norepinephrine** are found in many different brain areas. Serotonin is involved in the sleep, sensory perceptions, moods, and emotional states, including depression. Antidepressant drugs such as *Prozac* increase the availability of serotonin in certain brain regions. Norepinephrine is

Dopamine and Parkinson's Disease Boxing legend Muhammad Ali fakes a swing at actor Michael J. Fox before they both testified at a Congressional hearing on Parkinson's disease. Parkinson's disease affects approximately 1.5 million Americans, with an estimated 60,000 new cases diagnosed each year. Parkinson's disease usually affects older adults, but Fox was diagnosed with Parkinson's at the age of 30. Muhammad Ali has Parkinson's syndrome, a related disease thought to be caused by brain damage he suffered from years of professional boxing. Caused by the degeneration of dopamine-producing neurons, Parkinson's symptoms include uncontrollable trembling, rigid or stiff muscles, impaired balance, and movement and speech difficulties. To help ease their symptoms, both Ali and Fox take medications containing L-dopa, which temporarily increases brain levels of dopamine. Fox's foundation has raised over $50 million for Parkinson's research. Intel founder Andy Grove has joined this effort, donating millions of his personal fortune to support Parkinson's research after he too was diagnosed with the disease (Dolan, 2008).

implicated in the activation of neurons throughout the brain and helps the body gear up in the face of danger or threat. Norepinephrine also plays a key role in the regulation of sleep, learning, and memory retrieval (McCarley, 2007). Like serotonin and dopamine, norepinephrine dysfunction in implicated in some mental disorders, especially depression (Robinson, 2007).

GABA is the abbreviation for **gamma-aminobutyric acid,** a neurotransmitter found primarily in the brain. GABA usually communicates an inhibitory message to other neurons, helping to balance and offset excitatory messages. For normal functioning, GABA must be finely balanced. Like a dimmer switch, GABA regulates excitation in the brain. Too much GABA impairs learning, motivation, and movement, but too little GABA can lead to seizures (McCarthy, 2007). Alcohol makes people feel relaxed and less inhibited partly by increasing GABA activity, which reduces brain activity. Antianxiety medications, such as Valium and Xanax, also work by increasing GABA activity, which inhibits action potentials.

Endorphins: Regulating the Perception of Pain

In 1973, researchers Candace Pert and Solomon Snyder of Johns Hopkins University made the startling discovery that the brain contains receptor sites that are specific for the group of painkilling drugs called *opiates* (Pert & Snyder, 1973). Opiates include morphine, heroin, and codeine, all derived from the opium poppy. In addition to alleviating pain, opiates often produce a state of euphoria. Why would the brain have receptor sites for specific drugs like morphine? Pert, Snyder, and other researchers concluded that the brain must manufacture its own painkillers, morphinelike chemicals that act as neurotransmitters.

Within a few years, researchers identified a number of such chemicals manufactured by the brain (Snyder, 1984). Collectively, they are called **endorphins,** a term derived from the phrase *endogenous morphines.* (The word *endogenous* means "produced internally in the body.") Although chemically similar to morphine, endorphins are 100 times more potent. Today, it is known that endorphins are released in response to stress or trauma and that they reduce the perception of pain.

Researchers have found that endorphins are implicated in the pain-reducing effects of *acupuncture,* an ancient Chinese medical technique that involves inserting needles at various locations in the body (Ulett & Han, 2002; Kemmer, 2007). Endorphins are also associated with positive mood. For example, the "runner's high" associated with aerobic exercise has been attributed to endorphins, a topic that is examined in the Focus on Neuroscience, "Is 'Runner's High' an Endorphin Rush?" on the next page.

acetylcholine
(uh-*seet*-ull-KO-leen) Neurotransmitter that causes muscle contractions and is involved learning and memory.

dopamine
(DOPE-uh-meen) Neurotransmitter involved in the regulation of bodily movement, thought processes, and rewarding sensations.

serotonin
(ser-ah-TONE-in) Neurotransmitter involved in sensory perceptions, sleep, and emotions.

norepinephrine
(nor-ep-in-EF-rin) Neurotransmitter involved in learning, memory, and regulation of sleep; also a hormone manufactured by adrenal glands.

GABA (gamma-aminobutyric acid)
Neurotransmitter that usually communicates an inhibitory message.

endorphins
(en-DORF-ins) Neurotransmitters that regulate pain perceptions.

FOCUS ON NEUROSCIENCE

Is "Runner's High" an Endorphin Rush?

"Runner's high" is the rush of euphoria that many people experience after sustained aerobic exercise, especially running or cycling. It's thought to be caused by endorphins, which are associated with positive moods and reduced feelings of pain.

Although blood levels of one type of endorphins, called *beta-endorphins,* do increase during intense exercise, it seems unlikely that beta-endorphins cause runner's high. Why? Because the beta-endorphins circulating in the blood do *not* affect the brain. When you add the fact that it's impossible to directly measure endorphin levels in the intact human brain, the "endorphin hypothesis" of runner's high has lacked solid evidence to support it (Dietrich & McDaniel, 2004).

But an ingenious experiment by German neuroscientist Henning Boecker and his colleagues (2008) found a way to directly test the endorphin hypothesis. Boecker recruited 10 highly conditioned male runners who trained an average of eight or more hours per week. The runners completed mood questionnaires and underwent a baseline PET scan after 24 hours with no physical exertion.

To indirectly measure endogenous opioid (endorphin) activity in the brain, the runners were injected with a radioactively tagged chemical that binds to opioid receptors. A PET scan detects the radioactively tagged chemical. The reasoning was that if endorphins were released in the brain during exercise, the radioactive substance would be unable to bind to the opioid receptors because the receptors would already be occupied by the brain's own natural opioids—the endorphins. Thus, the number of opioid receptors that did *not* take up the radioactive chemical would provide an accurate measure of endorphin activity caused by the long-distance running.

On the day of the second PET scan, each participant returned to the lab after a two-hour run. After a 30-minute cool down, each athlete again completed the mood questionnaire, followed by a second PET scan.

The post-run PET scans showed high levels of endorphins binding to opioid receptors in several brain regions, especially frontal regions known to be involved in positive emotions (see figure). The analysis also showed that the greater the subjective feelings of euphoria experienced by each individual runner, the *higher* the brain level of endorphin activity.

After decades of speculation, Boecker and his colleagues (2008) have provided the first human evidence that runner's high is at least partially due to the release of endorphins in the brain. The involvement of the brain's opioid system in runner's high suggests one possible explanation for why some people can become addicted to excessive exercise, continuing to train despite illness or injuries. But endorphins do not provide a complete explanation. As the researchers point out, other neurotransmitters, such as dopamine, are probably also involved in runner's high.

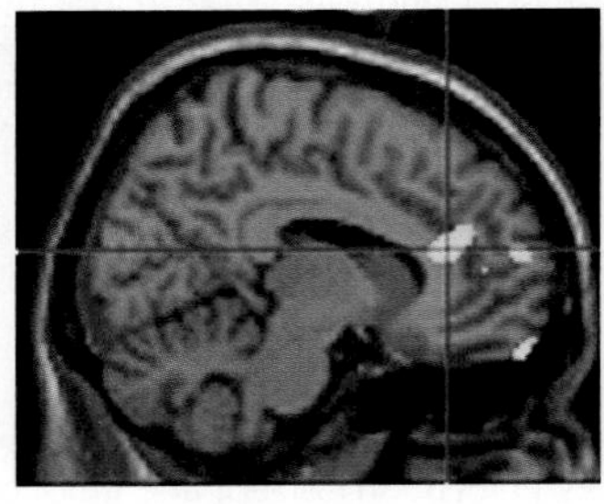

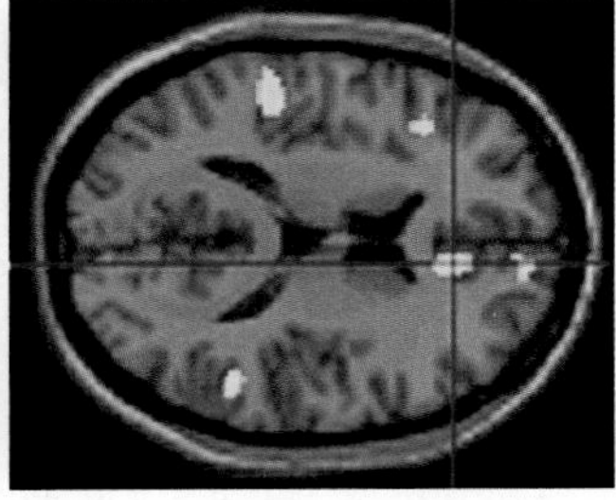

Endorphins and Runner's High After two hours of endurance running, highly conditioned athletes underwent PET scans. Yellow and orange highlight regions in which opioid receptors were blocked by the athlete's naturally produced endorphins. Endorphin activity was highest in regions known to be involved in positive emotion and mood, including the frontal cortex. The scans also showed that endorphin activity was positively correlated with subjective experience: The more intense the euphoria experienced by the individual runner, the higher the level of endorphin activity in his brain.

How Drugs Affect Synaptic Transmission

Much of what is known about different neurotransmitters has been learned from observing the effects of drugs and other substances. Many drugs, especially those that affect moods or behavior, work by interfering with the normal functioning of neurotransmitters in the synapse (Self, 2005; Volkow & others, 2007).

As Figure 2.6 illustrates, some drugs increase or decrease the amount of neurotransmitter released by neurons. For example, the venom of a black widow spider bite causes acetylcholine to be released continuously by motor neurons, causing severe muscle spasms. Drugs may also affect the length of time the neurotransmitter remains in the synaptic gap, either increasing or decreasing the amount available to the postsynaptic receptor.

One way in which drugs can prolong the effects of the neurotransmitter is by blocking the reuptake of the neurotransmitter by the sending neuron. For example, there is a category of antidepressant medications that are referred to as SSRIs, which stands for *selective seroatonin reuptake inhibitors.* SSRIs include such trade name medications as Prozac, Zoloft, and Paxil. Each of these medications inhibits the reuptake of serotonin in certain neurons, increasing the availability of serotonin in the brain. Similarly, the illegal drug cocaine produces its exhilarating rush by interfering with the reuptake of dopamine (Volkow & others, 2007).

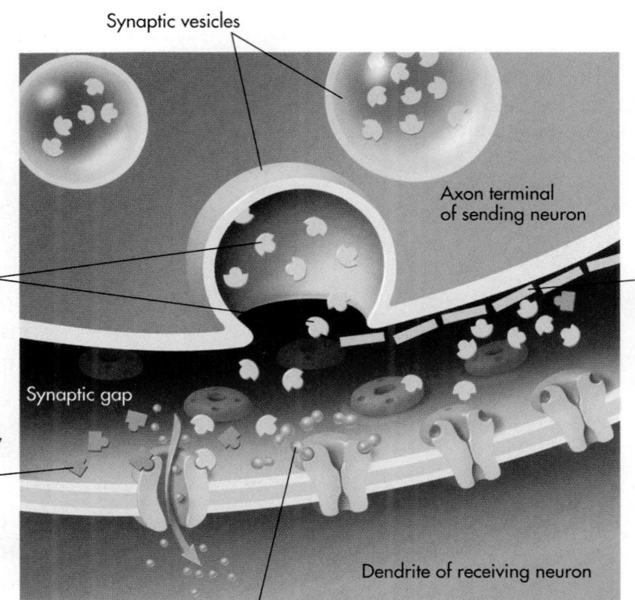

Figure 2.6 How Drugs Affect Synaptic Transmission Drugs affect brain activity by interfering with neurotransmitter functioning in the synapse. Drugs may also affect synaptic transmission by increasing or decreasing the amount of a particular neurotransmitter that is produced.

Drugs can also mimic specific neurotransmitters. When a drug is chemically similar to a specific neurotransmitter, it may produce the same effect as that neurotransmitter. It is partly through this mechanism that nicotine works as a stimulant. Nicotine is chemically similar to acetylcholine and can occupy acetylcholine receptor sites, stimulating skeletal muscles and causing the heart to beat more rapidly.

Alternatively, a drug can block the effect of a neurotransmitter by fitting into receptor sites and preventing the neurotransmitter from acting. For example, the drug *curare* blocks acetylcholine receptor sites, causing almost instantaneous paralysis. The brain sends signals to the motor neurons, but the muscles can't respond because the motor neuron receptor sites are blocked by the curare. Similarly, a drug called *naloxone* eliminates the effects of both endorphins and opiates by blocking opiate receptor sites.

The Nervous System and the Endocrine System
Communication Throughout the Body

Key Theme

- **Two major communication systems in the body are the nervous system and the endocrine system.**

Key Questions

- **What are the divisions of the nervous system and their functions?**
- **How is information transmitted in the endocrine system, and what are its major structures?**
- **How do the nervous and endocrine systems interact to produce the fight-or-flight response?**

Specialized for communication, up to 1 *trillion* neurons are linked throughout your body in a complex, organized communication network called the **nervous system.** The human nervous system is divided into two main divisions: the *central nervous*

nervous system
The primary internal communication network of the body; divided into the central nervous system and the peripheral nervous system.

Figure 2.7 The Nervous System The nervous system is a complex, organized communication network that is divided into two main divisions: the central nervous system (shown in blue) and the peripheral nervous system (shown in yellow).

system and the *peripheral nervous system* (see Figure 2.7). In order for even simple behaviors to occur, such as curling your toes or scratching your nose, these two divisions must function as a single, integrated unit. Yet each of these divisions is highly specialized and performs different tasks.

The neuron is the most important transmitter of messages in the central nervous system. In the peripheral nervous system, communication occurs along **nerves.** Nerves and neurons are not the same thing. Nerves are made up of large bundles of neuron axons. Unlike neurons, many nerves are large enough to be seen easily with the unaided eye.

The Central Nervous System

The **central nervous system (CNS)** includes the brain and the spinal cord. The central nervous system is so critical to your ability to function that it is entirely protected by bone—the brain by your skull and the spinal cord by your spinal column. Surrounding and protecting the brain and the spinal cord are three layers of membranous tissues, called the *meninges.* As an added measure of protection, the brain and spinal cord are suspended in *cerebrospinal fluid* to protect them from being jarred. There are four hollow cavities in the brain, called *ventricles,* which are also filled with cerebrospinal fluid. The inner surfaces of the ventricles are lined with *neural stem cells,* specialized cells that produce neurons in the developing brain.

The central nervous system is aptly named. It is central to all your behaviors and mental processes. And it is the central processing center—every action, thought, feeling, and sensation you experience is processed through the central nervous system. The most important element of the central nervous system is, of course, the brain, which acts as the command center. We'll take a tour of the human brain in a later section.

nerves
Bundles of neuron axons that carry information in the peripheral nervous system.

central nervous system (CNS)
Division of the nervous system that consists of the brain and spinal cord.

spinal reflexes
Simple, automatic behaviors that are processed in the spinal cord.

The spinal cord handles both incoming and outgoing messages. Sensory receptors send messages along sensory nerves to the spinal cord, then up to the brain. To activate muscles, the brain sends signals down the spinal cord, which are relayed out along motor nerves to the muscles.

Most behaviors are controlled by your brain. However, the spinal cord can produce **spinal reflexes**—simple, automatic behaviors that occur without any brain involvement. For example, the *withdrawal reflex* occurs when you touch a painful stimulus, such as something hot, electrified, or sharp. As you can see in Figure 2.8, this simple reflex involves a loop of rapid communication among *sensory neurons,* which communicate sensation to the spinal cord; *interneurons,* which relay information within the spinal cord; and *motor neurons,* which signal the muscles to react.

Spinal reflexes are crucial to your survival. The additional few seconds that it would take you to consciously process sensations and decide how to react could result in serious injury. Spinal reflexes are also important as indicators that the neural pathways in your spinal cord are working correctly. That's why physicians test spinal reflexes during neurological examinations by tapping just below your kneecap for the knee-jerk spinal reflex or scratching the sole of your foot for the toe-curl spinal reflex.

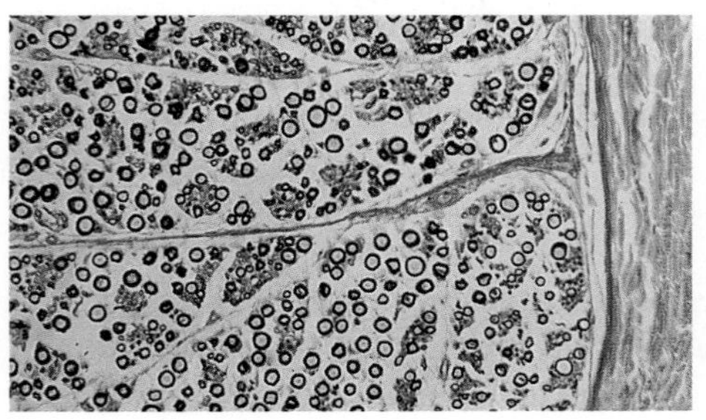

Nerves and Neurons Are Not the Same A cross section of a peripheral nerve is shown in this electron micrograph. Each black circle represents the end of one axon. As you can see, a nerve is actually composed of bundles of neuron axons.

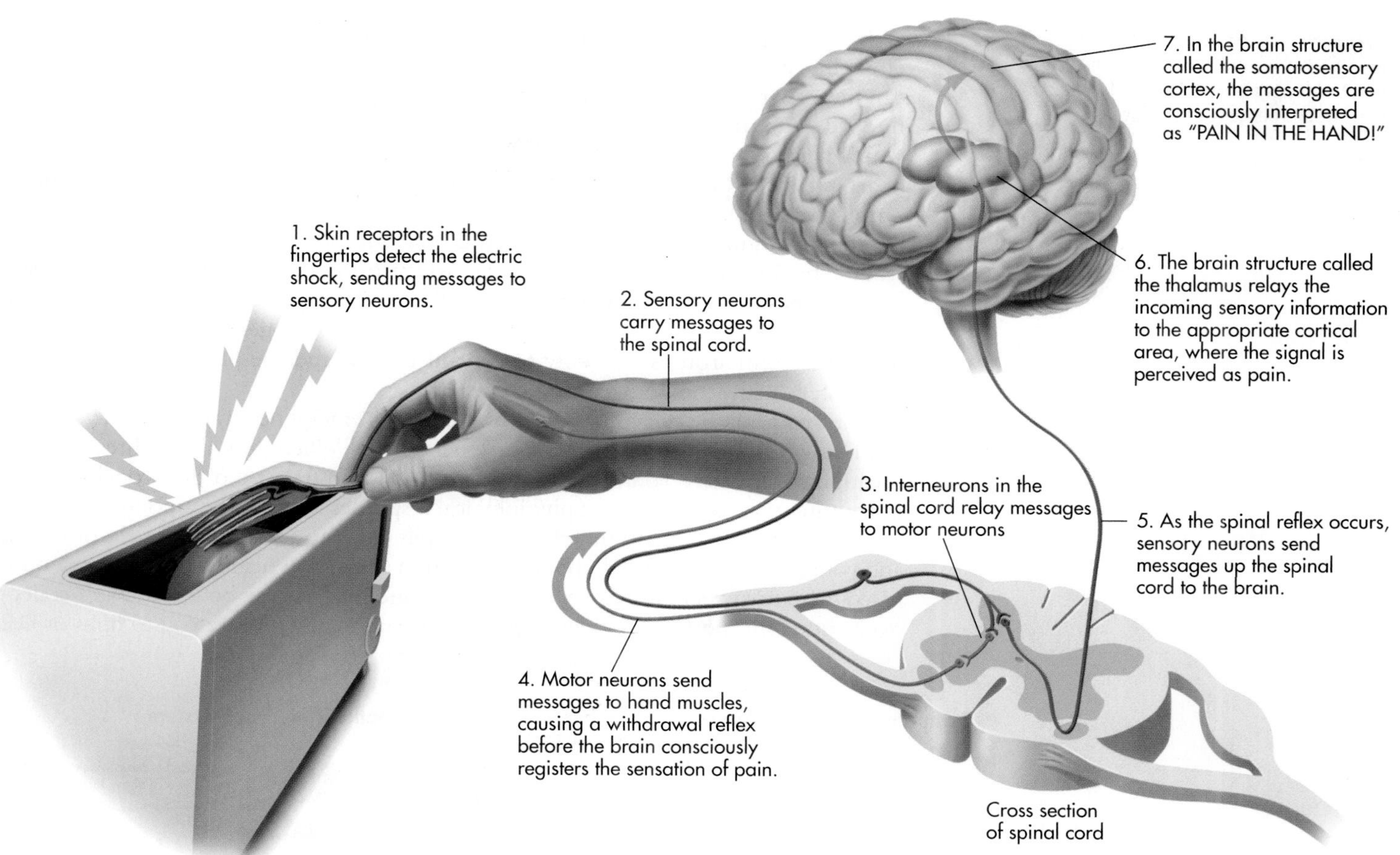

Figure 2.8 A Spinal Reflex A spinal reflex is a simple, involuntary behavior that is processed in the spinal cord without brain involvement. If you accidentally shock yourself by using a metal fork to pry a bagel out of a plugged-in toaster, you'll instantly pull your hand away from the painful stimulus—an example of the withdrawal reflex. The sequence shown below illustrates how the withdrawal reflex can occur before the brain processes the conscious perception of pain.

The Peripheral Nervous System

The **peripheral nervous system** is the other major division of your nervous system. The word *peripheral* means "lying at the outer edges." Thus, the peripheral nervous system comprises all the nerves outside the central nervous system that extend to the outermost borders of your body, including your skin. The communication functions of the peripheral nervous system are handled by its two subdivisions: the *somatic nervous system* and the *autonomic nervous system.*

The **somatic nervous system** takes its name from the Greek word *soma,* which means "body." It plays a key role in communication throughout the entire body. First, the somatic nervous system communicates sensory information received by sensory receptors along sensory nerves *to* the central nervous system. Second, it carries messages *from* the central nervous system along motor nerves to perform voluntary muscle movements. All the different sensations that you're experiencing right now are being communicated by your somatic nervous system to your spinal cord and on to your brain. When you perform a voluntary action, such as turning a page of this book, messages from the brain are communicated down the spinal cord, then out to the muscles via the somatic nervous system.

The other subdivision of the peripheral nervous system is the **autonomic nervous system.** The word *autonomic* means "self-governing." Thus, the autonomic nervous system regulates *involuntary* functions, such as heartbeat, blood pressure, breathing, and digestion. These processes occur with little or no conscious involvement. This is fortunate, because if you had to mentally command your heart to beat or your stomach to digest the food you had for lunch, it would be difficult to focus your attention on anything else.

peripheral nervous system
(per-IF-er-ull) Division of the nervous system that includes all the nerves lying outside the central nervous system.

somatic nervous system
Subdivision of the peripheral nervous system that communicates sensory information to the central nervous system and carries motor messages from the central nervous system to the muscles.

autonomic nervous system
(aw-toe-NOM-ick) Subdivision of the peripheral nervous system that regulates involuntary functions.

sympathetic nervous system
Branch of the autonomic nervous system that produces rapid physical arousal in response to perceived emergencies or threats.

However, the autonomic nervous system is not completely self-regulating. By engaging in physical activity or purposely tensing or relaxing your muscles, you can increase or decrease autonomic activity. Emotions and mental imagery also influence your autonomic nervous system. Vividly imagining a situation that makes you feel angry, frightened, or even sexually aroused can dramatically increase your heart rate and blood pressure. A peaceful mental image can lower many autonomic functions.

The involuntary functions regulated by the autonomic nervous system are controlled by two different branches: the *sympathetic* and *parasympathetic nervous systems*. These two systems control many of the same organs in your body but cause them to respond in opposite ways (see Figure 2.9). In general, the sympathetic nervous system arouses the body to expend energy, and the parasympathetic nervous system helps the body conserve energy.

The **sympathetic nervous system** is the body's emergency system, rapidly activating bodily systems to meet threats or emergencies. When you are frightened, your breathing accelerates, your heart beats faster, digestion stops, and the bronchial tubes in your lungs expand. All these physiological responses increase the amount of oxygen available to your brain and muscles. Your pupils dilate to increase your field of vision, and your mouth becomes dry, because salivation stops. You begin to sweat in response to your body's expenditure of greater energy and heat. These bodily changes collectively represent the *fight-or-flight response*—they physically prepare you to fight or flee

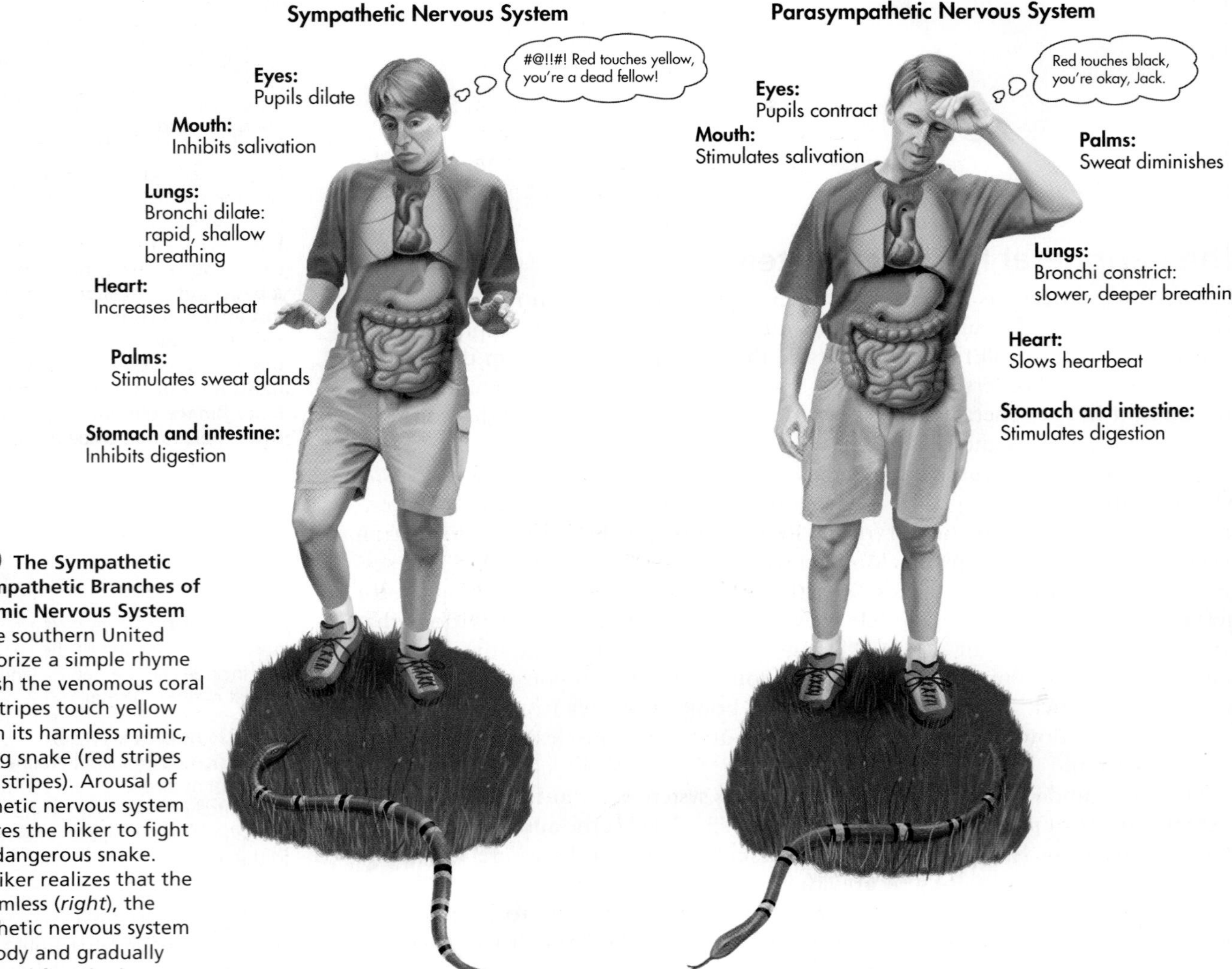

Figure 2.9 The Sympathetic and Parasympathetic Branches of the Autonomic Nervous System Hikers in the southern United States memorize a simple rhyme to distinguish the venomous coral snake (red stripes touch yellow stripes) from its harmless mimic, a scarlet king snake (red stripes touch black stripes). Arousal of the sympathetic nervous system (*left*) prepares the hiker to fight or flee the dangerous snake. When the hiker realizes that the snake is harmless (*right*), the parasympathetic nervous system calms the body and gradually restores normal functioning.

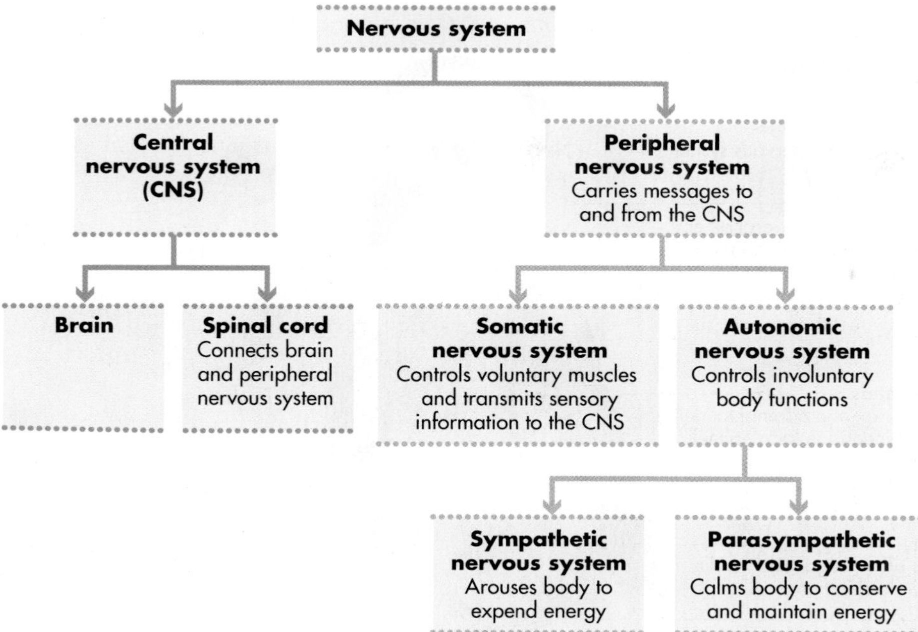

Figure 2.10 Organization of the Nervous System

from a perceived danger. We'll discuss the fight-or-flight response in greater detail in Chapter 8, on emotion, and Chapter 12, on stress.

Whereas the sympathetic nervous system mobilizes your body's physical resources, the **parasympathetic nervous system** conserves and maintains your physical resources. It calms you down after an emergency. Acting much more slowly than the sympathetic nervous system, the parasympathetic nervous system gradually returns your body's systems to normal. Heart rate, breathing, and blood pressure level out. Pupils constrict back to their normal size. Saliva returns, and the digestive system begins operating again.

Although the sympathetic and parasympathetic nervous systems produce opposite effects, they act together, keeping the nervous system in balance (see Figure 2.10). Each division handles different functions, yet the whole nervous system works in unison so that both automatic and voluntary behaviors are carried out smoothly.

Activating the Sympathetic Nervous System When the sympathetic nervous system activates in humans, tiny muscles in the skin contract, which elevates your hair follicles, producing the familiar sensation of "goose bumps" and making your hair stand on end. A similar process takes place in many mammals, making the fur or hair bristle, with rather spectacular results in this long-haired cat.

The Endocrine System

As you can see in Figure 2.11 on the next page, the **endocrine system** is made up of glands that are located throughout the body. Like the nervous system, the endocrine system involves the use of chemical messengers to transmit information from one part of the body to another. Although the endocrine system is not part of the nervous system, it interacts with the nervous system in some important ways.

Endocrine glands communicate information from one part of the body to another by secreting messenger chemicals called **hormones** into the bloodstream. The hormones circulate throughout the bloodstream until they reach specific hormone receptors on target organs or tissue. Hormones regulate physical processes and influence behavior in a variety of ways. Metabolism, growth rate, digestion, blood pressure, and sexual development and reproduction are just some of the processes that are regulated by the endocrine hormones. Hormones are also involved in emotional response and your response to stress.

Endocrine hormones are closely linked to the workings of the nervous system. For example, the release of hormones may be stimulated or inhibited by certain parts of the nervous system. In turn, hormones can promote or inhibit the generation of

parasympathetic nervous system
Branch of the autonomic nervous system that maintains normal bodily functions and conserves the body's physical resources.

endocrine system
(EN-doe-krin) System of glands located throughout the body that secrete hormones into the bloodstream.

hormones
Chemical messengers secreted into the bloodstream primarily by endocrine glands.

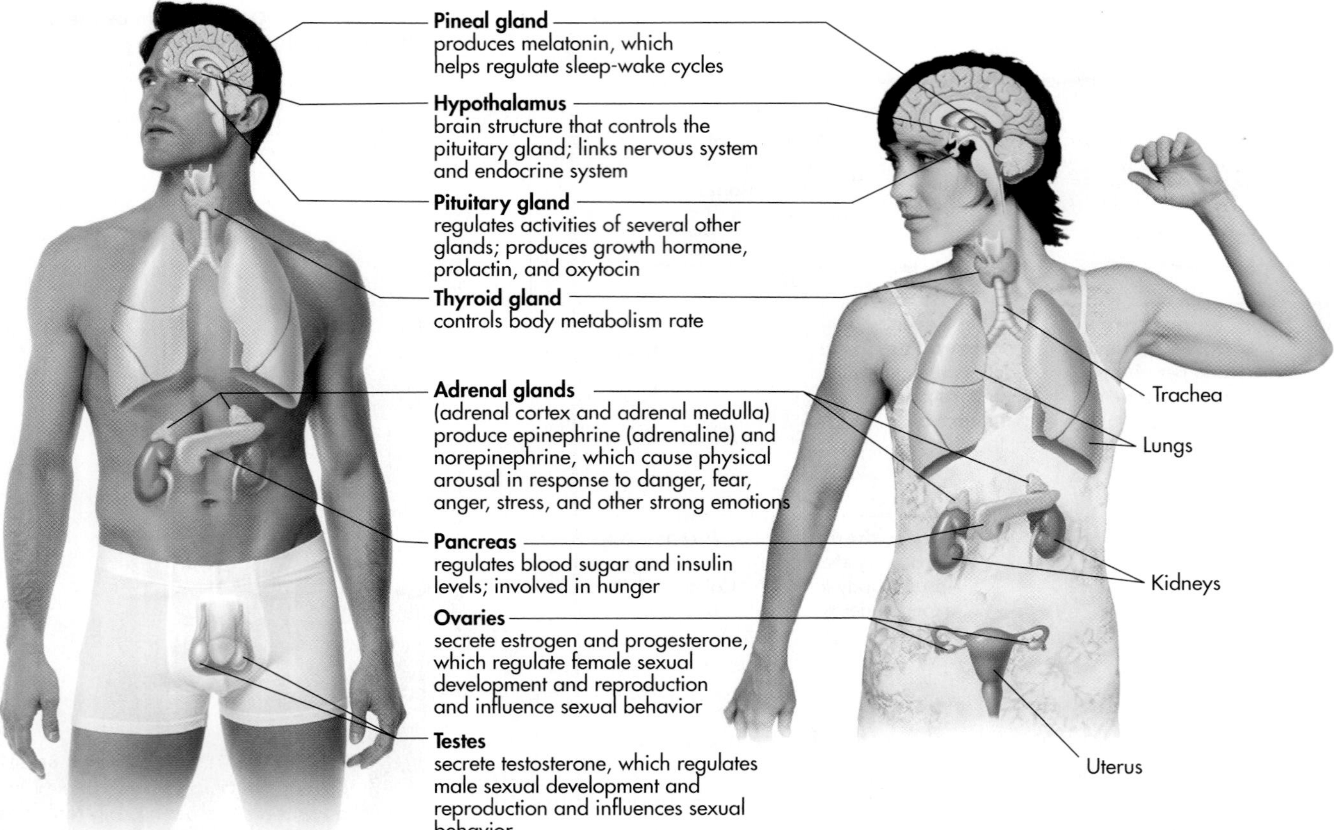

Figure 2.11 The Endocrine System The endocrine system and the nervous system are directly linked by the hypothalamus in the brain, which controls the pituitary gland. In turn, the pituitary releases hormones that affect the hormone production of several other endocrine glands. In the male and female figures shown here, you can see the location and main functions of several important endocrine glands.

nerve impulses. Finally, some hormones and neurotransmitters are chemically identical. The same molecule can act as a hormone in the endocrine system and as a neurotransmitter in the nervous system.

In contrast to the rapid speed of information transmission in the nervous system, communication in the endocrine system takes place much more slowly. Hormones rely on the circulation of the blood to deliver their chemical messages to target organs, so it may take a few seconds or longer for the hormone to reach its target organ after it has been secreted by the originating gland.

The signals that trigger the secretion of hormones are regulated by the brain, primarily by a brain structure called the *hypothalamus.* (You'll learn more about the hypothalamus later in the chapter.) The hypothalamus serves as the main link between the endocrine system and the nervous system. The hypothalamus directly regulates the release of hormones by the **pituitary gland,** a pea-sized gland just under the brain. The pituitary's hormones, in turn, regulate the production of other hormones by many of the glands in the endocrine system. This is why the pituitary gland is often referred to as the body's master gland. Under the direction of the hypothalamus, the pituitary gland controls hormone production in other endocrine glands.

The pituitary gland also produces some hormones that act directly. For example, the pituitary produces *growth hormone,* which stimulates normal skeletal growth during childhood. The pituitary gland can also secrete endorphins to reduce the perception of pain. In nursing mothers, the pituitary produces both *prolactin,* the hormone that stimulates milk production, and *oxytocin,* the hormone that produces the let-down reflex, in which stored milk is "let down" into the nipple. Breastfeeding is a good example of the complex interaction among behavior, the nervous system, and the endocrine system (see Figure 2.12).

Another set of glands, called the **adrenal glands,** is of particular interest to psychologists. The adrenal glands consist of the **adrenal cortex,** which is the outer

pituitary gland
(pih-TOO-ih-tare-ee) Endocrine gland attached to the base of the brain that secretes hormones that affect the function of other glands as well as hormones that act directly on physical processes.

adrenal glands
Pair of endocrine glands that are involved in the human stress response.

adrenal cortex
The outer portion of the adrenal glands.

gland, and the **adrenal medulla,** which is the inner gland. Both the adrenal cortex and the adrenal medulla produce hormones that are involved in the human stress response. As you'll see in Chapter 12, on stress, hormones secreted by the adrenal cortex also interact with the *immune system,* the body's defense against invading viruses or bacteria.

The adrenal medulla plays a key role in the fight-or-flight response, described earlier. When aroused, the sympathetic nervous system stimulates the adrenal medulla. In turn, the adrenal medulla produces *epinephrine* and *norepinephrine.* (You may be more familiar with the word *adrenaline,* which is another name for epinephrine.)

As they circulate through the bloodstream to the heart and other target organs, epinephrine and norepinephrine complement and enhance the effects of the sympathetic nervous system. These hormones also act as neurotransmitters, stimulating activity at the synapses in the sympathetic nervous system. The action of epinephrine and norepinephrine is a good illustration of the long-lasting effects of hormones. If you've noticed that it takes a while for you to calm down after a particularly upsetting or stressful experience, it's because of the lingering effects of epinephrine and norepinephrine in your body.

Also important are the **gonads,** or sex organs—the *ovaries* in women and the *testes* in men. In women, the ovaries secrete the hormones *estrogen* and *progesterone.* In men, the testes secrete male sex hormones called *androgens,* the most important of which is *testosterone.* Testosterone is also secreted by the adrenal glands in both males and females. In both males and females, the sex hormones influence sexual development, sexual behavior, and reproduction.

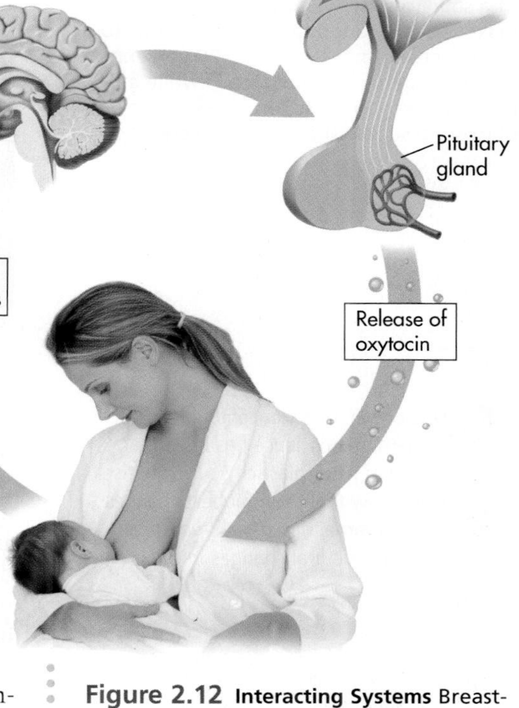

Figure 2.12 Interacting Systems Breastfeeding is an example of the complex interaction among the nervous system, the endocrine system, and behavior. Nerve impulses from sensory receptors in the mother's skin are sent to the brain. The hypothalamus signals the production of oxytocin by the pituitary gland, which causes the mother's milk to let down and begin flowing.

A Guided Tour of the Brain

Key Theme

- **The brain is a highly complex, integrated, and dynamic system of interconnected neurons.**

Key Questions

- **What are neural pathways and why are they important?**
- **What are functional and structural plasticity?**
- **What is neurogenesis, and what is the evidence for its occurrence in the adult human brain?**

Think about it: the most complex mass of matter in the universe sits right behind your eyes and between your two ears—your brain. Not even the Internet can match the human brain for speed and sophistication of information transmission.

In this part of the chapter, we'll take you on a guided tour of the human brain. As your tour guides, our goal here is not to tell you everything that is known or suspected about the human brain. Such an endeavor would take stacks of books rather than a single chapter in a college textbook. Instead, our first goal is to familiarize you with the basic organization and structures of the brain. Our second goal is to give you a general sense of how the brain works. In later chapters, we'll add to your knowledge of the brain as we discuss the brain's involvement in specific psychological processes.

At the beginning of this tour, it's important to note that the brain generally does not lend itself to simple explanations. One early simplistic approach to mapping the

adrenal medulla
The inner portion of the adrenal glands; secretes epinephrine and norepinephrine.

gonads
The endocrine glands that secrete hormones that regulate sexual characteristics and reproductive processes; *ovaries* in females and *testes* in males.

The Human Brain Weighing roughly three pounds, the human brain is about the size of a small cauliflower. Although your brain makes up only about 2 percent of your total body weight, it uses some 20 percent of the oxygen your body needs while at rest. The oxygen is used in breaking down glucose to supply the brain with energy.

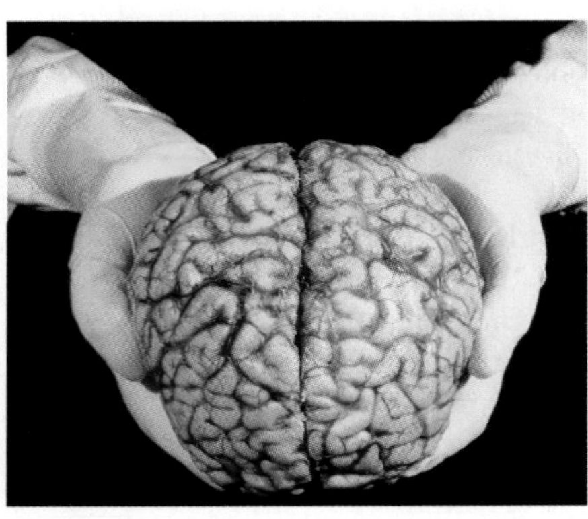

brain is discussed in Science Versus Pseudoscience, "Phrenology: The Bumpy Road to Scientific Progress." Although we will identify the functions that seem to be associated with particular brain regions, it's important to remember that specific functions seldom correspond neatly to a single, specific brain site. Many psychological processes, particularly complex ones, involve *multiple* brain structures and regions. Even seemingly simple tasks—such as carrying on a conversation, catching a ball, or watching a movie—involve the smoothly coordinated synthesis of information among many different areas of your brain.

> One of the great conceptual leaps of modern neuroscience has been the notion of neuroplasticity. . . . Scientists now know that even modest changes in the internal or external world can lead to structural changes in the brain.
>
> BARRY L. JACOBS (2004)

How is information communicated and shared among these multiple brain regions? Many brain functions involve the activation of neural pathways that link different brain structures (Knight, 2007). *Neural pathways* are formed by groups of neuron cell bodies in one area of the brain that project their axons to other brain areas. These neural pathways form communication networks and circuits that link different brain areas. Thus, even though we'll talk about brain centers and structures that are involved in different aspects of behavior, the best way to think of the brain is as an *integrated system.*

The Dynamic Brain: Plasticity and Neurogenesis

Before embarking on our tour, we need to describe one last important characteristic of the brain: its remarkable capacity to change in response to experience. Until the mid-1960s, neuroscientists believed—and taught—that by early adulthood the brain's physical structure was *hard-wired* or fixed for life (Raisman, 2004). But today it's known that the brain's physical structure is literally sculpted by experience (Pascual-Leone & others, 2005). The brain's ability to change function and structure is referred to as *neuroplasticity,* or simply *plasticity* (Lledo & others, 2006). (The word *plastic* originally comes from a Greek word, *plastikos,* that meant the quality of being easily shaped or molded.)

One form of plasticity is **functional plasticity,** which refers to the brain's ability to shift functions from damaged to undamaged brain areas. Depending on the location and degree of brain damage, stroke or accident victims often need to "relearn" once-routine tasks like speaking, walking, or reading. If the rehabilitation is successful, undamaged brain areas gradually assume the ability to process and execute the tasks (Pascual-Leone & others, 2005).

But the brain can do more than just shift functions from one area to another. **Structural plasticity** refers to the brain's ability to physically change its structure in response to learning, active practice, or environmental stimulation. It is now known that even subtle changes in your circumstances can lead to structural changes in the brain (Jacobs, 2004). In the Focus on Neuroscience, "Juggling and Brain Plasticity" on page 64, we describe an ingenious experiment that dramatically demonstrated structural plasticity in the human brain.

Neurogenesis

For many years, scientists believed that people and most animals did not experience **neurogenesis**—the development of new neurons—after birth (Gross, 2000; Kaplan, 2001). With the exception of birds, tree shrews, and some rodents, it was thought that the mature brain could lose neurons but could not grow new ones. But new studies offered compelling evidence that challenged that dogma (see Gould, 2007).

functional plasticity
The brain's ability to shift functions from damaged to undamaged brain areas.

structural plasticity
The brain's ability to change its physical structure in response to learning, active practice, or environmental influences.

neurogenesis
The development of new neurons.

phrenology
(freh-NOL-uh-gee) A pseudoscientific theory of the brain that claimed that personality characteristics, moral character, and intelligence could be determined by examining the bumps on a person's skull.

cortical localization
The notion that different functions are located or localized in different areas of the brain; also called *localization of function.*

SCIENCE VERSUS PSEUDOSCIENCE

Phrenology: The Bumpy Road to Scientific Progress

Are people with large foreheads smarter than people with small foreheads? Does the shape of your head provide clues to your abilities, character, and personality characteristics? Such notions were at the core of **phrenology,** a popular pseudoscience founded by Franz Gall, a German physician and brain anatomist.

In the early 1800s, Gall made several important contributions to the understanding of brain anatomy. He correctly noted, for example, that the cortex of animals was smaller and less developed than the cortex of intellectually superior humans. Eventually, he became convinced that the size and shape of the cortex were reflected in the size and shape of the skull. Taking this notion a step further, he suspected that variations in the size and shape of the human skull might reflect individual differences in abilities, character, and personality.

To gather evidence, Gall went to hospitals, prisons, asylums, and schools to examine people with oddly shaped heads. Gall noted the association between a particular person's characteristics and any distinctive bulges and bumps on the person's skull. On the basis of these observations, he identified 27 personality characteristics, or "faculties," that he believed could be diagnosed by examining specific areas of the head. Gall devised elaborate maps showing the skull location of various personality characteristics and abilities. For instance, Gall believed that a thick neck was associated with increased sexual motivation and that a prominent forehead was associated with greater intellectual ability (McCoy, 1996).

When Gall's theory of phrenology was ridiculed by other scientists for lack of adequate evidence, Gall took his ideas to the general public by presenting lectures and demonstrations. He lectured widely and gave "readings" in which he provided a personality description based on measuring the bumps on a person's head. Phrenology continued to be popular with the general public well into the 1900s.

Is phrenology merely a historical curiosity? Actually, phrenology played a significant role in advancing the scientific study of the human mind and brain (Zola-Morgan, 1995). As it became popular in the early 1800s, phrenology triggered scientific interest in the possibility of **cortical localization,** or *localization of function*—the idea that specific psychological and mental functions are located (or localized) in specific brain areas (Livianos-Aldano & others, 2007; van Wyhe, 2000). Although phrenology was eventually dismissed as pseudoscience, scientists began debating the more general notion of cortical localization. By the mid-1800s, solid scientific evidence for cortical localization began to emerge (Damasio & others, 1994). Later in the chapter, we'll look at how the work of Broca and Wernicke provided that initial evidence.

Today, sophisticated imaging techniques that reveal the brain's activity, such as PET and functional MRI scans, are providing numerous insights about the cortical localization of cognitive and perceptual abilities. So although Franz Gall and the phrenologists were wrong about the significance of bumps on the skull, they were on target about the idea that different psychological functions are localized in different brain areas.

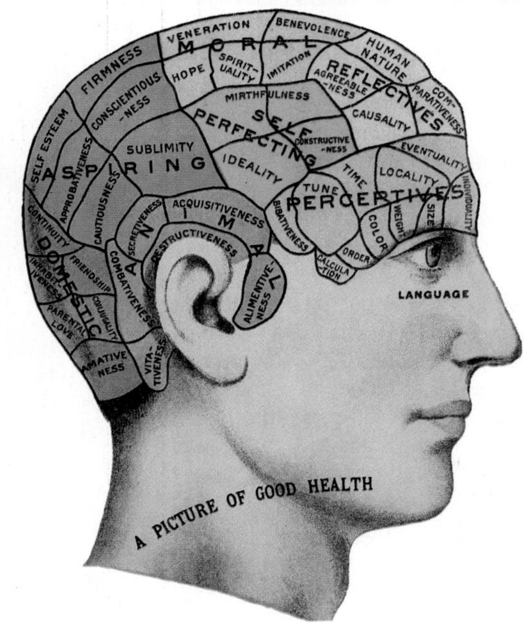

Mapping the Brain? Phrenology was a popular pseudoscience throughout the nineteenth century. As shown on this 1870 phrenological map, different "faculties" or psychological traits were thought to be located in different brain areas or "organs." Bumps on the skull were thought to be associated with greater development of particular brain regions and the traits that corresponded with them. At the height of phrenology's popularity, some physicians even used leeches to drain blood from areas of the head that were believed to correspond to overdeveloped characteristics, such as "Combativeness" or "Amativeness" (McCoy, 2000).

The Psycograph Henry Lavery invented the psycograph in the early 1900s to improve the accuracy of phrenology measurements. More than 30 probes in the helmetlike headpiece made contact with the skull. The machines stamped out brief summaries of the different "faculties" measured, such as: "You are fairly secretive but can improve. You tell things to your friends. Don't do it." Forty of the machines were built, and they were popular attractions in department stores and theater lobbies throughout the United States (McCoy, 1996, 2000).

FOCUS ON NEUROSCIENCE

Juggling and Brain Plasticity

What happens to the brain when you learn a new, challenging skill? Does learning affect the brain's physical structure?

German researcher Bogdan Draganski and his colleagues (2004) have compelling experimental evidence showing that learning a new skill produces structural changes in the human brain. In their study, 24 young adults—21 women and 3 men—were assigned to either the "jugglers" or "nonjugglers" group. A baseline MRI scan indicated that there were no significant regional brain differences between the two groups at the beginning of the study.

Then the juggling group members were given three months to master and practice a basic juggling routine called the three-ball cascade. When the participants were able to show that they could juggle the three balls for at least 60 seconds, a second brain scan was performed.The nonjugglers were also scanned at the same point.

The researchers used a sophisticated whole-brain imaging technique to detect regional changes in gray and white matter. Compared to their baseline brain scans, the jugglers showed a 3 to 4 percent increase in the size of gray matter in two brain regions involved in perceiving, remembering, and anticipating complex visual motions. These two regions are shown in yellow in the composite MRI scans shown below. In comparison, there were *no* brain changes in the scans of the nonjugglers over the same three-month period.

After the second brain scan, the participants in the juggling group were told to stop practicing their newly acquired skills. Three months later, the third and final round of brain scans was taken of both groups. Now, the same regions that had grown while the jugglers were practicing their skills every day had *decreased* in size. While still larger than before the participants had learned to juggle, the regions were 1 to 2 percent smaller than when the participants were juggling every day. In comparison, the same regions in the nonjuggling control group remained unchanged.

Because they couldn't take direct tissue samples of the affected brain areas, Draganski and his colleagues (2004) could not definitively identify the nature of the changes in the gray matter. However, it seems likely that the number and shape of neuronal dendrites and axon terminals probably increased, enhancing the communication ability of neurons (Grutzendler & others, 2002; Trachtenberg & others, 2002). It's also likely that the number of glial cells increased (Haydon, 2001).

In a later study, novice jugglers showed changes in brain regions within just seven days after learning to juggle (Driemeyer & others, 2008). And, demonstrating the plasticity of even the aging brain, similar changes were found in a group of senior citizens after they learned to juggle (Boyke & others, 2008).

As co-researcher Arne May (Draganski & others, 2004) noted, their results challenged prevailing views of the human central nervous system. "Human brains," he observed, "must

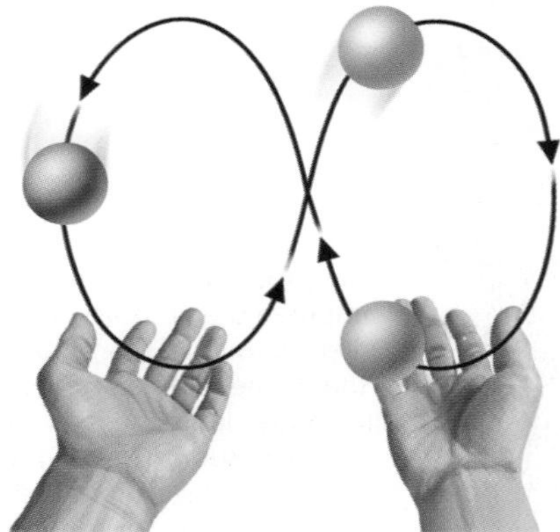

Three-Ball Cascade

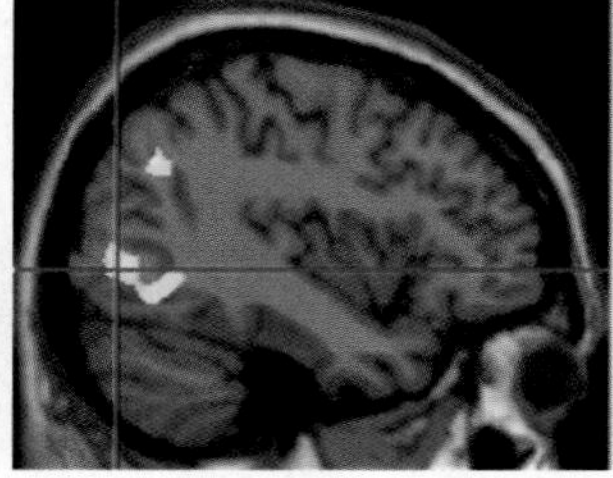

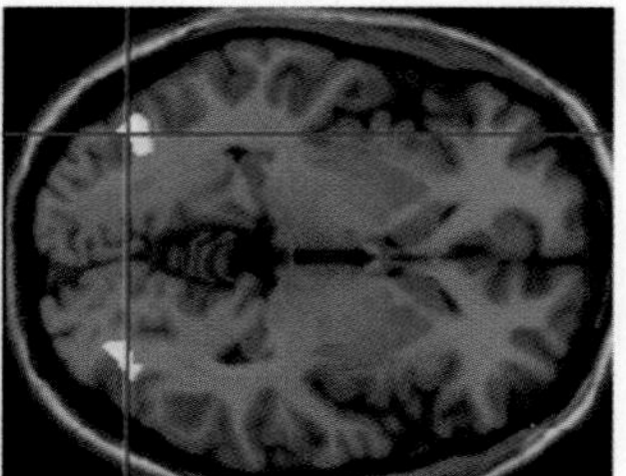

Learning a New Skill Makes Its Mark on the Brain The yellow in these MRIs shows the brain areas that temporarily increased by 3 to 4 percent in size in those participants who learned to juggle. These brain regions are involved in the ability to perceive, remember, and anticipate complex visual motions.

First, research by psychologist Elizabeth Gould and her colleagues (1998) showed that adult marmoset monkeys were generating a significant number of new neurons every day in the *hippocampus,* a brain structure that plays a critical role in the ability to form new memories. Gould's groundbreaking research provided the first demonstration that new neurons could develop in an adult primate brain. Could it be that the human brain also has the capacity to generate new neurons in adulthood?

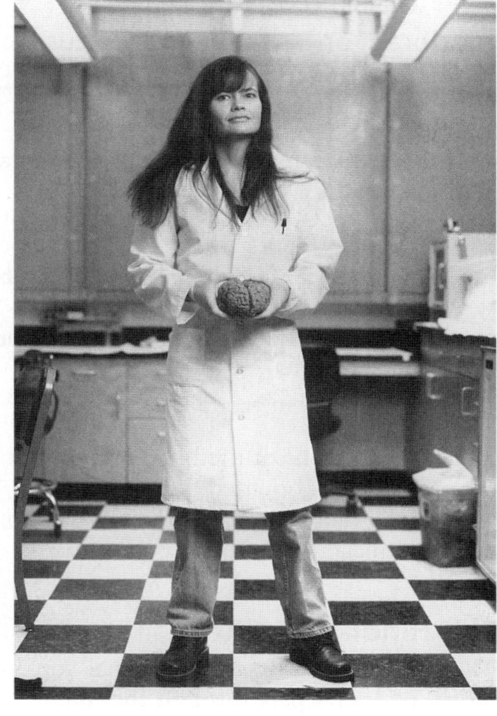

Elizabeth Gould: Challenging Scientific Dogma After earning her psychology doctorate at UCLA, Gould investigated the effect of stress hormones on rats. In the process, she found evidence of the development of new neurons in the rats' brains, a discovery that, if true, contradicted scientific understandings at that time. Her research eventually showed that neurogenesis takes place in the adult brains of many species, from rats to primates. Today, Gould's research in her Princeton University lab focuses on the effects of environmental deprivation and enrichment on the mammalian brain (Lehrer, 2006). You can visit Gould's Princeton lab at: http://www.princeton.edu/~goulde/index.html

Researchers Peter Eriksson, Fred Gage, and their colleagues (1998) provided the first evidence that it does. The subjects were five adult cancer patients, whose ages ranged from the late fifties to the early seventies. These patients were all being given a drug used in cancer treatments to determine whether tumor cells are multiplying. The drug is incorporated into newly dividing cells, coloring them. Using fluorescent lights, this chemical tracer can be detected in the newly created cells. Eriksson and Gage reasoned that if new neurons were being generated, the drug would be present in their genetic material.

Within hours after each patient died, an autopsy was performed and the hippocampus was removed and examined. The results were unequivocal. In each patient, *hundreds* of new neurons had been generated since the drug had been administered, even though all the patients were over 50 years old (see accompanying photo). The conclusion? Contrary to the traditional scientific view, the human brain has the capacity to generate new neurons throughout the lifespan (Eriksson & others, 1998; Kempermann & Gage, 1999).

As new research on neurogenesis has exploded, new findings—and new questions—have arisen (Sahay & Hen, 2007). For example, Gould and her colleagues have found that new neurons develop and migrate to *multiple* brain regions in adult macaque monkeys (see Gould, 2007). Stress, exercise, environmental complexity, and even social status have been shown to affect the rate of neurogenesis in rodents, birds, and monkeys (see Gage & others, 2008). It is now generally accepted that newborn neurons develop into mature functioning neurons in at least two regions of the human brain—the hippocampus, involved in learning and memory, and the *olfactory bulb,* responsible for odor perception. And, it appears that these new neurons are incorporated into the existing neural networks in the adult human brain (Gage, 2003; Lledo & others, 2006).

In the next section, we'll begin our guided tour of the brain. Following the general sequence of the brain's development, we'll start with the structures at the base of the brain and work our way up to more complicated brain regions, which are responsible for complex mental activity.

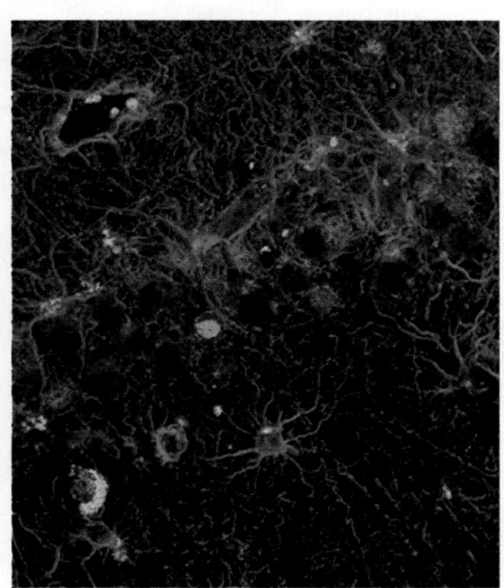

Neurogenesis in the Adult Human Brain Using laser microscopes to examine sections of the adult hippocampus, researchers Peter Eriksson and Fred Gage (1998) documented the presence of new neurons, shown in green, amid already established neurons, shown in red. In the area of the hippocampus studied, each cubic centimeter of brain tissue contained from 100 to 300 new neurons. Research on adult mice has shown that the newly generated neurons develop into fully functional neurons that form synaptic connections with existing cells in the hippocampus (van Praag & others, 2002).

"We've always known that our brains control our behavior, but not that our behavior could control and change the structure of our brains."
FRED GAGE (2007)

The Brainstem
Hindbrain and Midbrain Structures

Key Theme

- **The brainstem includes the hindbrain and midbrain, located at the base of the brain.**

Key Questions

- **Why does damage to one side of the brain affect the opposite side of the body?**
- **What are the key structures of the hindbrain and midbrain, and what are their functions?**

brainstem
A region of the brain made up of the hindbrain and the midbrain.

hindbrain
A region at the base of the brain that contains several structures that regulate basic life functions.

The major regions of the brain are illustrated in Figure 2.13, which can serve as a map to keep you oriented during our tour. At the base of the brain lie the hindbrain and, directly above it, the midbrain. Combined, the structures of the hindbrain and midbrain make up the brain region that is also called the **brainstem.**

The Hindbrain

The **hindbrain** connects the spinal cord with the rest of the brain. Sensory and motor pathways pass through the hindbrain to and from regions that are situated higher up in the brain. Sensory information coming in from one side of the body crosses over at the hindbrain level, projecting to the opposite side of the brain. And outgoing motor messages from one side of the brain also cross over at the hindbrain level, controlling movement and other motor functions on the opposite side of the body. This is referred to as *contralateral organization.*

Contralateral organization accounts for why people who suffer strokes on one side of their brain experience muscle weakness or paralysis on the opposite side of

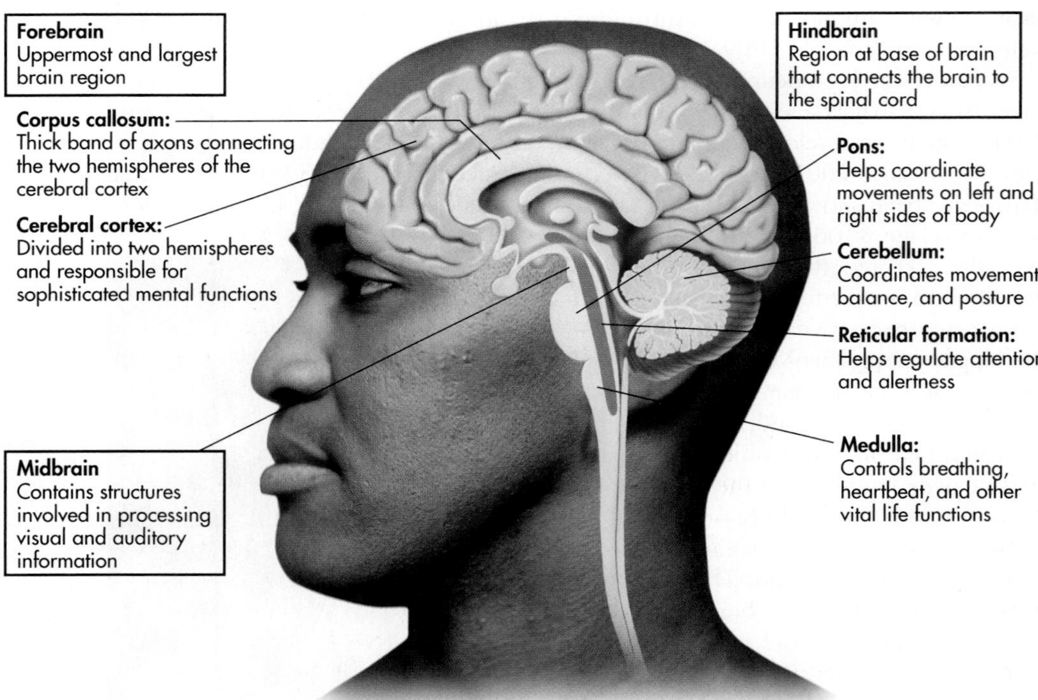

Figure 2.13 Major Regions of the Brain Situated at the base of the brain, the hindbrain's functions include coordinating movement and posture, regulating alertness, and maintaining vital life functions. The midbrain helps process sensory information. In combination, the hindbrain and the midbrain comprise the brainstem. The forebrain is the largest brain region and is involved in more sophisticated behaviors and mental processes.

their body. Our friend Asha, for example, suffered only minor damage to motor control areas in her brain. However, because the stroke occurred on the *left* side of her brain, what muscle weakness she did experience was localized on the *right* side of her body, primarily in her right hand.

Three structures make up the hindbrain—the medulla, the pons, and the cerebellum. The **medulla** is situated at the base of the brain directly above the spinal cord. It is at the level of the medulla that ascending sensory pathways and descending motor pathways crisscross to the contralateral side of the body.

The medulla plays a critical role in basic life-sustaining functions. It contains centers that control such vital autonomic functions as breathing, heart rate, and blood pressure. The medulla also controls a number of vital reflexes, including swallowing, coughing, vomiting, and sneezing. Because the medulla is involved in such critical life functions, damage to this brain region can rapidly prove fatal.

Above the medulla is a swelling of tissue called the **pons,** which represents the uppermost level of the hindbrain. Bulging out behind the pons is the large **cerebellum.** On each side of the pons, a large bundle of axons connects it to the cerebellum. The word *pons* means "bridge," and the pons is a bridge of sorts: Information from various other brain regions located higher up in the brain is relayed to the cerebellum via the pons. The pons also contains centers that play an important role in regulating breathing.

The cerebellum functions in the control of balance, muscle tone, and coordinated muscle movements. It is also involved in the learning of habitual or automatic movements and motor skills, such as typing, writing, or backhanding a tennis ball.

Jerky, uncoordinated movements can result from damage to the cerebellum. Simple movements, such as walking or standing upright, may become difficult or impossible. The cerebellum is also one of the brain areas affected by alcohol consumption, which is why a person who is intoxicated may stagger and have difficulty walking a straight line or standing on one foot. (This is also why a police officer will ask a suspected drunk driver to execute these normally effortless movements.)

At the core of the medulla and the pons is a network of neurons called the **reticular formation,** or the *reticular activating system,* which is composed of many groups of specialized neurons that project up to higher brain regions and down to the spinal cord. The reticular formation plays an important role in regulating attention and sleep.

The Midbrain

The **midbrain** is an important relay station that contains centers involved in the processing of auditory and visual sensory information. Auditory sensations from the left and right ears are processed through the midbrain, helping you orient toward the direction of a sound. The midbrain is also involved in processing visual information, including eye movements, helping you visually locate objects and track their movements. After passing through the midbrain level, auditory and visual information is relayed to sensory processing centers farther up in the forebrain region, which will be discussed shortly.

A midbrain area called the **substantia nigra** is involved in motor control and contains a large concentration of dopamine-producing neurons. *Substantia nigra* means "dark substance," and as the name suggests, this area is darkly pigmented. The substantia nigra is part of a larger neural pathway that helps prepare other brain regions to initiate organized movements or actions. In the section on neurotransmitters, we noted that Parkinson's disease involves symptoms of abnormal movement, including difficulty initiating or starting a particular movement. Many of those movement-related symptoms are associated with the degeneration of dopamine-producing neurons in the substantia nigra.

medulla
(meh-DOOL-uh) A hindbrain structure that controls vital life functions such as breathing and circulation.

pons
A hindbrain structure that connects the medulla to the two sides of the cerebellum; helps coordinate and integrate movements on each side of the body.

cerebellum
(sare-uh-BELL-um) A large, two-sided hindbrain structure at the back of the brain; responsible for muscle coordination and maintaining posture and equilibrium.

reticular formation
(reh-TICK-you-ler) A network of nerve fibers located in the center of the medulla that helps regulate attention, arousal, and sleep; also called the *reticular activating system.*

midbrain
The middle and smallest brain region, involved in processing auditory and visual sensory information.

substantia nigra
(sub-STAN-she-uh NYE-gruh) An area of the midbrain that is involved in motor control and contains a large concentration of dopamine-producing neurons.

The Forebrain

Key Theme

- **The forebrain includes the cerebral cortex and the limbic system structures.**

Key Questions

- **What are the four lobes of the cerebral cortex and their functions?**
- **What is the limbic system?**
- **What functions are associated with the thalamus, hypothalamus, hippocampus, and amygdala?**

Situated above the midbrain is the largest region of the brain: the **forebrain.** In humans, the forebrain represents about 90 percent of the brain. In Figure 2.14, you can see how the size of the forebrain has increased during evolution, although the general structure of the human brain is similar to that of other species (Clark & others, 2001). Many important structures are found in the forebrain region, but we'll begin by describing the most prominent—the cerebral cortex.

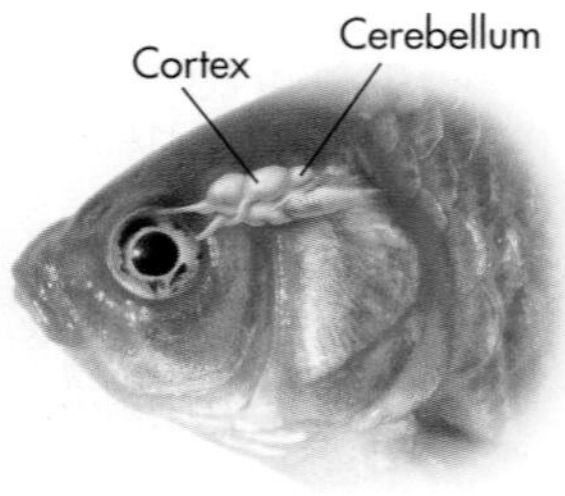

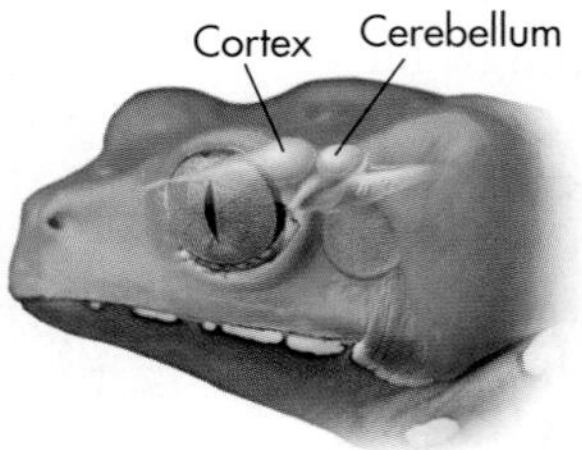

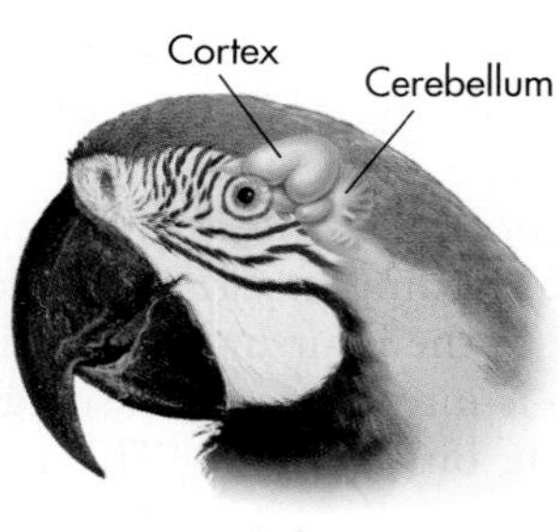

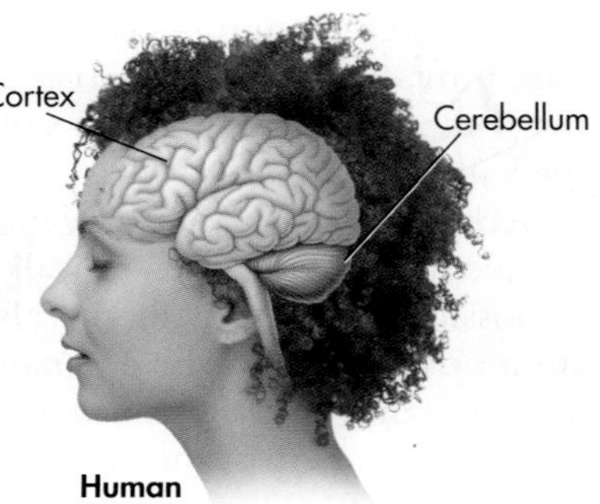

Figure 2.14 Evolution and the Cerebral Cortex The brains of these different animal species have many structures in common, including a cerebellum and cortex. However, the proportion devoted to the cortex is much higher in mammals than in species that evolved earlier, such as fish and amphibians. The relative size of the different structures reflects their functional importance (Kaas & Collins, 2001).

forebrain
The largest and most complex brain region, which contains centers for complex behaviors and mental processes; also called the *cerebrum.*

cerebral cortex
(suh-REE-brull or SARE-uh-brull) The wrinkled outer portion of the forebrain, which contains the most sophisticated brain centers.

cerebral hemispheres
The nearly symmetrical left and right halves of the cerebral cortex.

corpus callosum
A thick band of axons that connects the two cerebral hemispheres and acts as a communication link between them.

The Cerebral Cortex

The outer portion of the forebrain, the **cerebral cortex,** is divided into two **cerebral hemispheres.** The word *cortex* means "bark," and much like the bark of a tree, the cerebral cortex is the outer covering of the forebrain. A thick bundle of axons, called the **corpus callosum,** connects the two cerebral hemispheres, as shown in Figure 2.15. The corpus callosum serves as the primary communication link between the left and right cerebral hemispheres.

The cerebral cortex is only about a quarter of an inch thick. It is mainly composed of glial cells and neuron cell bodies and axons, giving it a grayish appearance—which is why the cerebral cortex is sometimes described as being composed of *gray matter.* Extending inward from the cerebral cortex are white myelinated axons that are sometimes referred to as *white matter.* These myelinated axons connect the cerebral cortex to other brain regions.

Cerebral hemispheres
Cerebral hemispheres
Corpus callosum

Figure 2.15 The Cerebral Hemispheres and the Corpus Callosum The two hemispheres of the cerebral cortex can be clearly seen in this side-to-side cross-sectional view jof the brain. The main communications link connecting the two cerebral hemispheres is the corpus callosum, a thick, broad bundle of some 300 million myelinated neuron axons. The corpus callosum is often described as a C-shaped brain structure, which is depicted more clearly in Figure 2.13.

Numerous folds, grooves, and bulges characterize the human cerebral cortex. The purpose of these ridges and valleys is easy to illustrate. Imagine a flat, three-foot by three-foot piece of paper. You can compact the surface area of this piece of paper by scrunching it up into a wad. In much the same way, the grooves and bulges of the cerebral cortex allow about three square feet of surface area to be packed into the small space of the human skull.

Look again at Figure 2.13 on page 66. The drawing of the human brain is cut through the center to show how the cerebral cortex folds above and around the rest of the brain. In contrast to the numerous folds and wrinkles of the human cerebral cortex, notice the smooth appearance of the cortex in fish, amphibians, and birds in Figure 2.14. Mammals with large brains—such as cats, dogs, and nonhuman primates—also have wrinkles and folds in the cerebral cortex, but to a lesser extent than humans (Jarvis & others, 2005).

Each cerebral hemisphere can be roughly divided into four regions, or *lobes:* the *temporal, occipital, parietal,* and *frontal* lobes (see Figure 2.16). Each lobe is associated with distinct functions. Located near your temples, the **temporal lobe** contains the *primary auditory cortex,* which receives auditory information. At the very back of the brain is the **occipital lobe.** The occipital lobe includes the *primary visual cortex,* where visual information is received.

The **parietal lobe** is involved in processing bodily, or *somatosensory,* information, including touch, temperature, pressure, and information from receptors in the muscles and joints. A band of tissue on the parietal lobe, called the *somatosensory cortex,* receives information from touch receptors in different parts of the body.

Each part of the body is represented on the somatosensory cortex, but this representation is not equally distributed (see Figure 2.17 on the next page). Instead, body parts are represented in proportion to their sensitivity to somatic sensations. For example, on the left side of Figure 2.17 you can see that your hands and face, which are very responsive to touch, have much greater representation on the somatosensory cortex than do the backs of your legs, which are far less sensitive to touch.

The largest lobe of the cerebral cortex, the **frontal lobe,** is involved in planning, initiating, and executing voluntary movements. The movements of different body parts are represented in a band of tissue on the frontal lobe called the *primary motor cortex.* The degree of representation on the primary motor cortex for a particular body part reflects the diversity and precision of its potential movements, as

temporal lobe
An area on each hemisphere of the cerebral cortex near the temples that is the primary receiving area for auditory information.

occipital lobe
(ock-SIP-it-ull) An area at the back of each cerebral hemisphere that is the primary receiving area for visual information.

parietal lobe
(puh-RYE-et-ull) An area on each hemisphere of the cerebral cortex located above the temporal lobe that processes somatic sensations.

frontal lobe
The largest lobe of each cerebral hemisphere; processes voluntary muscle movements and is involved in thinking, planning, and emotional control.

Figure 2.16 Lobes of the Cerebral Cortex Each hemisphere of the cerebral cortex can be divided into four regions, or *lobes.* Each lobe is associated with distinct functions. The association areas, shaded in purple, make up most of the cerebral cortex.

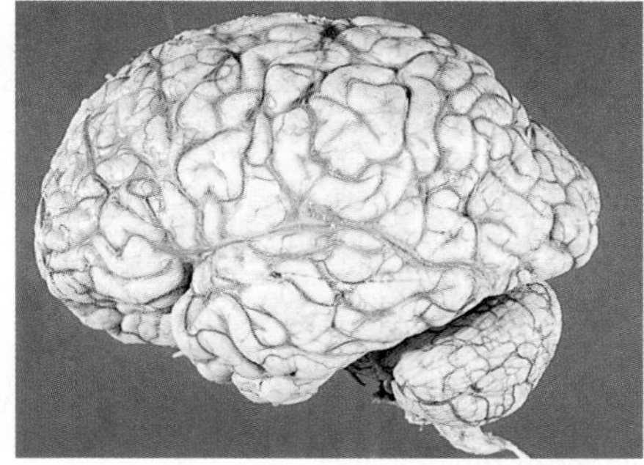

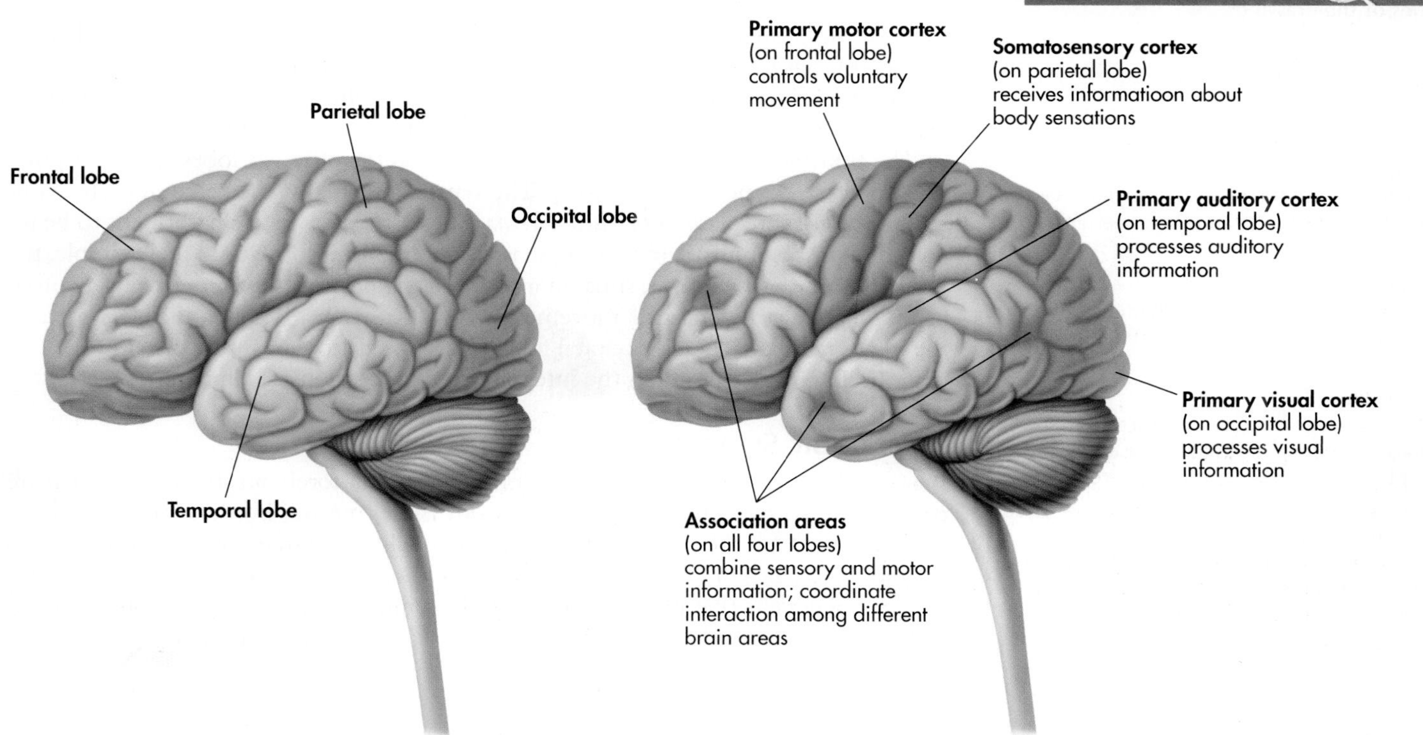

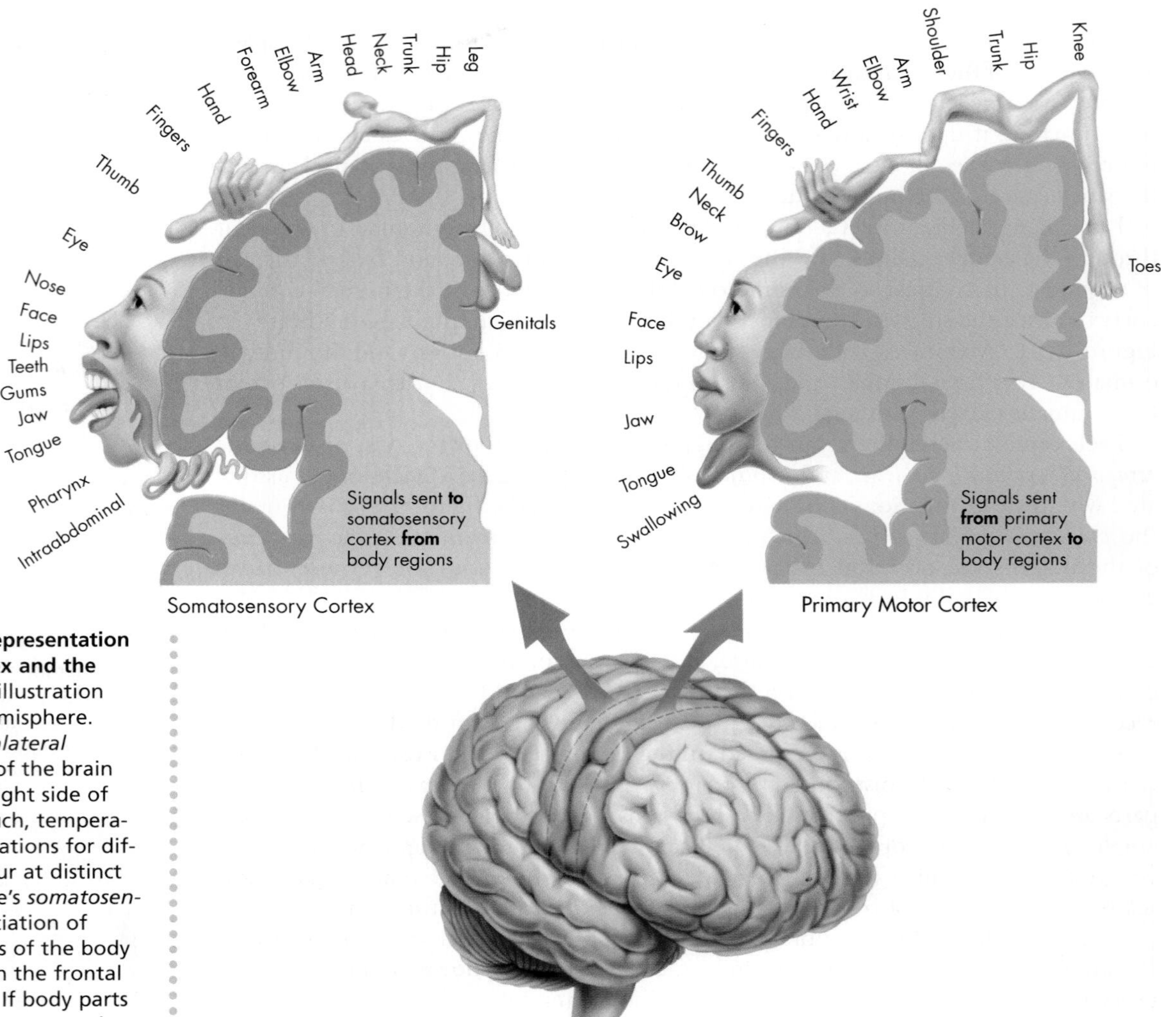

Figure 2.17 The Body's Representation on the Somatosensory Cortex and the Primary Motor Cortex This illustration depicts the right cerebral hemisphere. Because of the brain's *contralateral organization,* the right side of the brain processes functions for the right side of the body, and vice versa. Touch, temperature, pressure, and pain sensations for different areas of the body occur at distinct locations on the parietal lobe's *somatosensory cortex.* Similarly, the initiation of movement for different parts of the body occurs at distinct locations on the frontal lobe's *primary motor cortex.* If body parts were proportional to their representation on the somatosensory cortex and primary motor cortex, they would look like the misshapen human figures on the outer edges of the drawings.

shown on the right side of Figure 2.17. Thus, it's not surprising that almost one-third of the primary motor cortex is devoted to the hands and another third is devoted to facial muscles. The disproportionate representation of these two body areas on the primary motor cortex is reflected in the human capacity to produce an extremely wide range of hand movements and facial expressions.

The primary sensory and motor areas found on the different lobes represent just a small portion of the cerebral cortex. The remaining bulk of the cerebral cortex consists mostly of three large *association areas.* These areas are generally thought to be involved in processing and integrating sensory and motor information. For example, the *prefrontal association cortex,* situated in front of the primary motor cortex, is involved in the planning of voluntary movements. Another association area includes parts of the temporal, parietal, and occipital lobes. This association area is involved in the formation of perceptions and in the integration of perceptions and memories.

The Limbic System

Beneath the cerebral cortex are several other important forebrain structures, which are components of the **limbic system.** The word *limbic* means "border," and as you can see in Figure 2.18, the structures that make up the limbic system form a border of sorts around the brainstem. In various combinations, the limbic system structures form complex neural circuits that play critical roles in learning, memory, and emotional control.

Let's briefly consider some of the key limbic system structures and the roles they play in behavior.

limbic system
A group of forebrain structures that form a border around the brainstem and are involved in emotion, motivation, learning, and memory.

hippocampus
A curved forebrain structure that is part of the limbic system and is involved in learning and forming new memories.

thalamus
(THAL-uh-muss) A forebrain structure that processes sensory information for all senses, except smell, and relays it to the cerebral cortex.

hypothalamus
(hi-poe-THAL-uh-muss) A peanut-sized forebrain structure that is part of the limbic system and regulates behaviors related to survival, such as eating, drinking, and sexual activity.

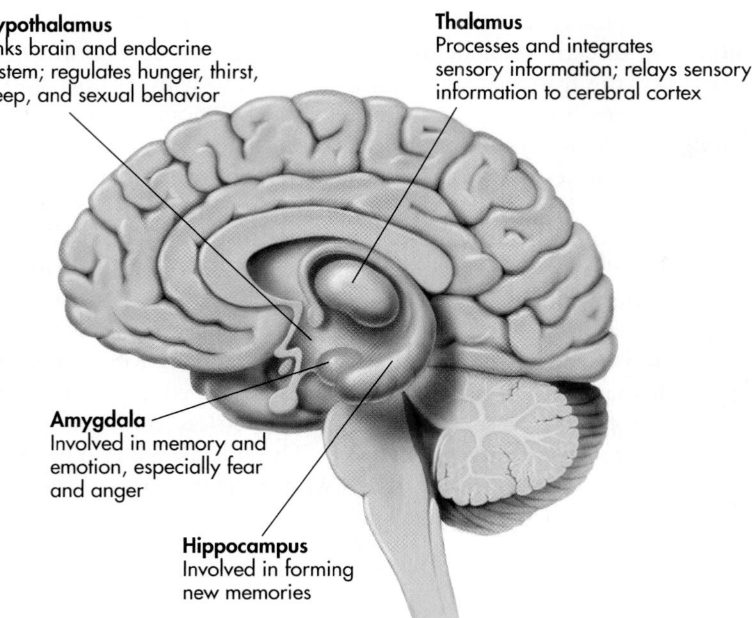

Figure 2.18 Key Structures of the Forebrain and Limbic System In the cross-sectional view shown here, you can see the locations and functions of four important subcortical brain structures. In combination, these structures make up the *limbic system,* which regulates emotional control, learning, and memory.

The Hippocampus The **hippocampus** is a large structure embedded in the temporal lobe in each cerebral hemisphere (see Figure 2.18). The word *hippocampus* comes from a Latin word meaning "sea horse." If you have a vivid imagination, the hippocampus does look a bit like the curved tail of a sea horse. The hippocampus plays an important role in your ability to form new memories of events and information. As noted earlier, neurogenesis takes place in the adult hippocampus. The possible role of new neurons in memory formation is an active area of neuroscience research (see Gould, 2007; Lledo & others, 2006). In Chapter 6, we'll take a closer look at the role of the hippocampus and other brain structures in memory.

The Thalamus The word *thalamus* comes from a Greek word meaning "inner chamber." And indeed, the **thalamus** is a rounded mass of cell bodies located within each cerebral hemisphere. The thalamus processes and distributes motor information and sensory information (except for smell) going to and from the cerebral cortex. Figure 2.19 depicts some of the neural pathways going from the thalamus to the different lobes of the cerebral cortex. However, the thalamus is more than just a sensory relay station. The thalamus is also thought to be involved in regulating levels of awareness, attention, motivation, and emotional aspects of sensations.

Figure 2.19 The Thalamus Almost all sensory and motor information going to and from the cerebral cortex is processed through the thalamus. This figure depicts some of the neural pathways from different regions of the thalamus to specific lobes of the cerebral cortex.

The Hypothalamus *Hypo* means "beneath" or "below." As its name implies, the **hypothalamus** is located below the thalamus. Although it is only about the size of a peanut, the hypothalamus contains more than 40 neural pathways. These neural pathways ascend to other forebrain areas and descend to the midbrain, hindbrain, and spinal cord. The hypothalamus is involved in so many different functions, it is sometimes referred to as "the brain within the brain."

The hypothalamus regulates both divisions of the autonomic nervous system, increasing and decreasing such functions as heart rate and blood pressure. It also helps regulate a variety of behaviors related to survival, such as eating, drinking, frequency of sexual activity, fear, and aggression.

One area of the hypothalamus, called the *suprachiasmatic nucleus* (SCN), plays a key role in regulating daily sleep–wake cycles and other rhythms of the body. We'll take a closer look at the SCN in Chapter 4.

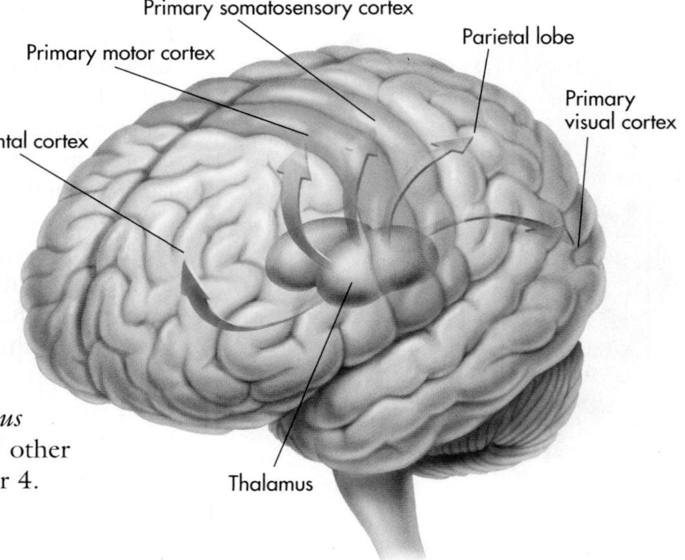

amygdala
(uh-MIG-dull-uh) Almond-shaped cluster of neurons in the brain's temporal lobe, involved in memory and emotional responses, especially fear.

cortical localization
The notion that different functions are located or localized in different areas of the brain; also called *localization of function.*

lateralization of function
The notion that specific psychological or cognitive functions are processed primarily on one side of the brain.

aphasia
(uh-FAZE-yuh) The partial or complete inability to articulate ideas or understand spoken or written language because of brain injury or damage.

The hypothalamus exerts considerable control over the secretion of endocrine hormones by directly influencing the pituitary gland. The *pituitary gland* is situated just below the hypothalamus and is attached to it by a short stalk. The hypothalamus produces both neurotransmitters and hormones that directly affect the pituitary gland. As we noted in the section on the endocrine system, the pituitary gland releases hormones that influence the activity of other glands.

The Amygdala The **amygdala** is an almond-shaped clump of neuron cell bodies at the base of the temporal lobe. The amygdala is involved in a variety of emotional response patterns, including fear, anger, and disgust. Studies with animals have shown that electrical stimulation of the amygdala can produce these emotions. In contrast, destruction of the amygdala reduces or disrupts behaviors that are linked to fear and rage. For example, when their amygdala is destroyed, monkeys lose their fear of natural predators, such as snakes. In humans, electrical stimulation of the amygdala produces feelings of fear and apprehension. The amygdala is also involved in learning and forming memories, especially those with a strong emotional component (Phelps, 2006). In Chapters 6 and 8, we'll take a closer look at the amygdala's role in emotion.

Specialization in the Cerebral Hemispheres

Key Theme

- **Although they have many functions in common, the two hemispheres of the cerebral cortex are specialized for different tasks.**

Key Questions

- **How did Broca, Wernicke, and Sperry contribute to our knowledge of the brain?**
- **Why would the corpus callosum be surgically severed and what effects would that produce?**
- **How do the functions of the right and left cerebral hemispheres differ?**

The Corpus Callosum Brain tissue from the top of the brain has been cut away to expose the thick fibers of the corpus callosum, the structure that connects the left and right hemispheres of the brain. As you'll read in this section, cutting the corpus callosum eliminates the transfer of information between the two hemispheres, with some surprising consequences.

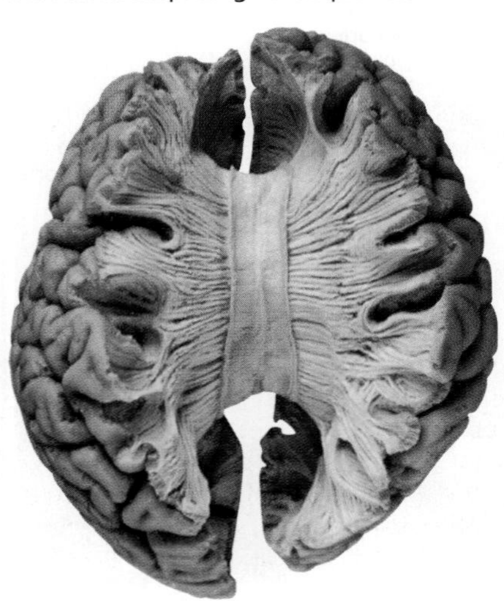

If you hold a human brain in your hand, the two cerebral hemispheres would appear to be symmetrical. Although the left and right hemispheres are very similar in appearance, they are not identical. Anatomically, one hemisphere may be slightly larger than the other. There are also subtle differences in the sizes of particular structures, in the distribution of gray matter and white matter, and in the patterns of folds, bulges, and grooves that make up the surface of the cerebral cortex.

What about differences in the functions of the two hemispheres? In many cases, the functioning of the left and right hemispheres is symmetrical, meaning that the same functions are located in roughly the same places on each hemisphere. Examples of such functional symmetry include the primary motor cortex and the somatosensory cortex, which we discussed in the previous section. With regard to other important processes, however, the left and right cerebral hemispheres do differ—each cerebral hemisphere is specialized for particular abilities.

Here's a rough analogy. Imagine two computers that are linked through a network. One computer is optimized for handling word processing, the other for handling graphic design. Although specialized for different functions, the two computers actively share information and can communicate with each other across the network. In this analogy, the two computers correspond to the left and right cerebral hemispheres, and the network that links them is the corpus callosum.

As you'll see in this section, the first discoveries about the differing abilities of the two brain hemispheres were made more than a hundred years ago by two important pioneers in brain research, Pierre Broca and Karl Wernicke.

Language and the Left Hemisphere

The Early Work of Broca and Wernicke

Paul Broca (1824–1880): Evidence for the Localization of Speech Paul Broca was already a famous scientist and surgeon when he announced in 1861 that he had discovered solid evidence for the localization of language functions in the human brain. His patient was an unpleasant middle-aged man universally known as Tan because that was the only word he could speak—aside from a single swear word when angered. Of normal intelligence, Tan could comprehend the speech of others but could not produce language himself. After Tan's death, an autopsy revealed a distinct lesion on the lower left frontal lobe. This area is still known as *Broca's area.*

By the end of the 1700s it had already been well established that injury to one side of the brain could produce muscle paralysis or loss of sensation on the opposite side of the body. By the early 1800s, animal experiments had shown that specific functions would be lost if particular brain areas were destroyed. And, as discussed in the Science Versus Pseudoscience box on page 63, phrenology triggered scientific debates about **cortical localization,** or *localization of function*—the idea that particular brain areas are associated with specific functions.

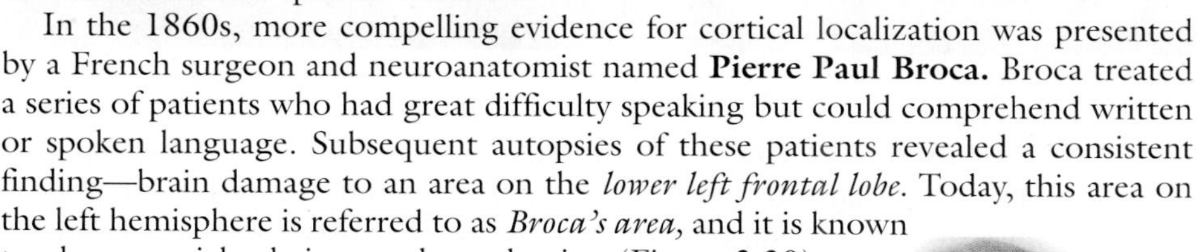

In the 1860s, more compelling evidence for cortical localization was presented by a French surgeon and neuroanatomist named **Pierre Paul Broca.** Broca treated a series of patients who had great difficulty speaking but could comprehend written or spoken language. Subsequent autopsies of these patients revealed a consistent finding—brain damage to an area on the *lower left frontal lobe.* Today, this area on the left hemisphere is referred to as *Broca's area,* and it is known to play a crucial role in speech production (Figure 2.20).

Karl Wernicke (1848–1905): Evidence for the Localization of Language Comprehension Born in Poland but educated in Germany, psychiatrist and neurologist Karl Wernicke was only 26 when he published his findings on a type of aphasia that differed from that identified by Paul Broca. Wernicke's patients were unable to comprehend written or spoken language, although they could produce speech. Well-known for his research in clinical neurology, Wernicke published many articles and books, including a comprehensive textbook on psychiatry.

About a decade after Broca's discovery, a young German neurologist named **Karl Wernicke** discovered another area in the left hemisphere that, when damaged, produced a different type of language disturbance. Unlike Broca's patients, Wernicke's patients had great difficulty understanding spoken or written communications. They could speak quickly and easily, but their speech sometimes made no sense. They sometimes used meaningless words or even nonsense syllables, though their sentences seemed to be grammatical. In response to the question "How are you feeling?" a patient might say something like, "Don't glow glover. Yes, uh, ummm, bick, bo chipickers the dallydoe mick more work mittle." Autopsies of these patients' brains revealed consistent damage to an area on the *left temporal lobe* that today is called *Wernicke's area* (see Figure 2.20).

The discoveries of Broca and Wernicke provided the first compelling clinical evidence that language and speech functions are performed primarily by the left cerebral hemisphere. If similar brain damage occurs in the exact same locations on the *right* hemisphere, these severe disruptions in language and speech are usually *not* seen.

The notion that one hemisphere exerts more control over or is more involved in the processing of a particular psychological function is termed **lateralization of function.** Speech and language functions are *lateralized* on the left hemisphere. Generally, the left hemisphere exerts greater control over speech and language abilities in virtually all right-handed and the majority of left-handed people.

The language disruptions demonstrated by Broca's and Wernicke's patients represent different types of aphasia. **Aphasia** refers to the partial or complete inability to articulate ideas or understand spoken or written language because of brain injury or damage. There are many different types of aphasia.

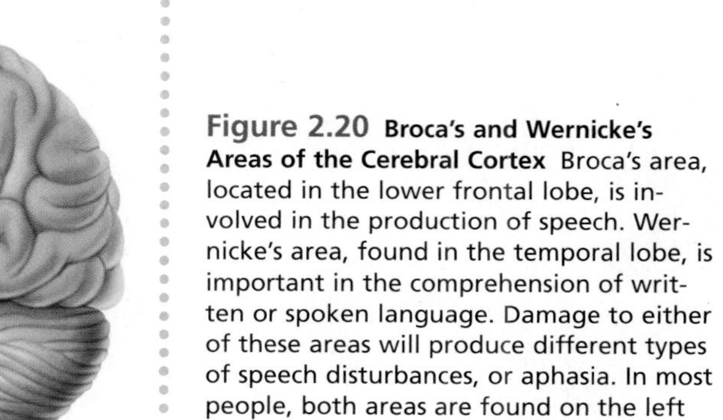

Figure 2.20 **Broca's and Wernicke's Areas of the Cerebral Cortex** Broca's area, located in the lower frontal lobe, is involved in the production of speech. Wernicke's area, found in the temporal lobe, is important in the comprehension of written or spoken language. Damage to either of these areas will produce different types of speech disturbances, or aphasia. In most people, both areas are found on the left hemisphere.

Left-Handed Orangutans and Right-Handed Chimpanzees Like humans, many animals also display a preference for one hand or paw. Even fish display a preference for a right eye or left eye to look at novel objects (Brown & others, 2007). Unlike humans, who are predominantly right-handed, animals tend to vary by species, population, and task (Hopkins & Cantalupo, 2005). For example, bonobos tend to be right-handed, and orangutans, like the one shown in the top photo, tend to be left-handed (Hopkins, 2006). Chimpanzees are more likely to be right-handed, especially when raised in captivity. One recent study found that chimpanzees who are strongly right-handed tend to have more asymmetrical brain hemispheres than chimpanzees who use both hands for tools and simple reaching tasks (Hopkins & others, 2007).

People with *Broca's aphasia* find it difficult or impossible to produce speech, which is why it is often referred to as *expressive aphasia*. Despite their impairments in speaking, their comprehension of verbal or written words is relatively unaffected.

People with *Wernicke's aphasia* have great difficulty comprehending written or spoken communication, which is why it is often referred to as *receptive aphasia*. Although they can speak, they often have trouble finding the correct words.

At the beginning of this chapter, we described the symptoms experienced by our friend Asha in the weeks before and the months following her stroke. Asha, who is right-handed, experienced the stroke in her left hemisphere. About three days after her stroke, an MRI brain scan showed where the damage had occurred: the left temporal lobe.

Asha experienced many symptoms of Wernicke's aphasia. Talking was difficult, not because Asha couldn't speak, but because she had to stop frequently to search for the right words. Asha was unable to name even simple objects, like the cup on her hospital dinner tray or her doctor's necktie. She recognized the objects but was unable to say what they were. She had great difficulty following a normal conversation and understanding speech, both in English and in her native language, Tulu.

Asha also discovered that she had lost the ability to read. She could see the words on the page, but they seemed to have no meaning. Paul brought some of their Christmas cards to the hospital. Asha recalls, "When I realized I couldn't read the Christmas cards, I thought my life was over. I just lost it. I remember crying and telling the nurse, 'I have a doctorate and I can't read, write, or talk!' "

When we visited Asha in the hospital, we brought her a Christmas present: a portable music player with headphones and some albums of relaxing instrumental music. Little did we realize how helpful the music would be for her. One album was a recording of Native American flute music called *Sky of Dreams*. The music was beautiful and rather unusual, with intricate melodies and unexpected, complex harmonies. Although it was very difficult for Asha to follow normal speech, listening to *Sky of Dreams* was an entirely different experience. As Asha explained:

> I tried cranking up the music very high and it soothed me. I could sleep. At the time, the flute music seemed to be just perfectly timed with the way my brain was working. It was tuning out all the other noises so I could focus on just one thing and sleep. So I would play the music over and over again at a very high level. I did that for a long time because my mind was so active and jumbled that I couldn't think.

Asha's language functions were severely disrupted, yet she was able to listen to and appreciate instrumental music—even very complex music. Why? At the end of the next section, we'll offer a possible explanation for what seems to have been a disparity in Asha's cognitive abilities following her stroke.

CRITICAL THINKING

"His" and "Her" Brains?

Sex Differences and the Brain Subtle gender differences in brain function and structure make headlines. This headline implies that new discoveries about the brain will explain "why men and women think differently." How valid is this conclusion?

Do the brains of men and women differ? And if so, do those differences cause them to "think differently," as headlines sometimes claim?

Media reports often refer to physiological sex differences as "innate," "biological," or "hard-wired." But even differences that are biological in origin are not necessarily fixed, permanent, or inevitable (Hyde, 2007). For example, brain development and function are affected by the sex hormones both before birth and throughout life (Morris & others, 2004). However, hormone levels themselves are strongly influenced by environmental factors, ranging from the food we eat to the stressful circumstances we experience. As we've emphasized throughout this chapter, brain function and structure are highly responsive to environmental influences (Fiavell & Greenberg, 2008).

Neuroscientists have identified a number of differences between male and female brains, such as structures that on the average tend to be slightly larger in one sex (Cahill, 2006). The following are the best-substantiated differences:

1. *Men's brains tend to be larger than women's brains.* Even at birth, the male newborn has a larger brain, primarily because their skulls are also larger. (Gilmore & others, 2007).

2. *Women and men have different proportions of gray to white matter.* Adult men and women have roughly the same amount of gray matter. However, women have a much higher proportion of gray matter in their brains, and the neuron cell bodies and dendrites that make up gray matter are much more closely packed (Gur & others, 1999, 2002). Women also display greater *cortical complexity,* meaning that they have more folds, fissures, and wrinkles in their cerebral cortex (Luders & others, 2004).

Gray matter is also distributed differently in male and female brains. Males have a higher percentage of gray matter in their left hemisphere than in their right hemisphere. But in females, the distribution of gray and white matter is roughly equivalent in the left and right hemispheres. This observation leads to the next difference.

3. *In general, the male brain is more asymmetrical and functions are more lateralized than in the female brain.* For example, women tend to rely on brain structures in both hemispheres for language tasks, while men are more reliant on one brain hemisphere, usually the left, for language tasks (Shaywitz & others, 1995; Cahill, 2006). Some brain-imaging studies have found that when it comes to solving complex arithmetic problems, spatial tasks, or mental rotation problems, males are more likely to rely on focused activation of specific brain regions in the right hemisphere. Females are more likely to draw upon multiple regions in *both* hemispheres to solve the same problems (Kucian & others, 2005; Grön & others, 2000).

So what does this mean? After an extensive review of research, Diane Halpern and her colleagues (2007) summarized the major anatomical and functional differences in this way: Male brains appear to be optimized for network connections *within* each hemisphere. Female brains appear to have better connections *between* the two hemispheres. The better communication between the left and right hemispheres gives females an advantage in language. Females also have a greater ability to integrate the left hemisphere's verbal-analytical processing with the right hemisphere's spatial and holistic mode of information processing.

However, not all structural differences lead to differences in measurable behaviors or abilities. In a series of studies, neuroscientist Jill Goldstein found that for several brain regions, the average size is slightly different in men and women (Goldstein, 2007; Goldstein & others, 2005). For example, the female hippocampus tends to be larger than the male hippocampus. But, when tested, memory skills were the *same.* As neuroscientist Geert J. De Vries (2004) points out, "Despite decades of research, we still do not know the functional significance of most sex differences in the brain."

Thinking Critically About Brain Differences

So do such findings support the belief that "men and women think differently"? Do they explain gender differences in cognitive abilities or personality traits? All the findings we've discussed need to be examined in the context of what is known—and, more importantly, what is *not* known—about the brain.

First, brain studies are typically based on small samples. Those samples may or may not be representative of the wider population of men and women. And while scientists are careful to qualify their conclusions and describe the limitations of their research, media reports rarely mention these qualifications.

Second, many sex differences amount to minor variations in a particular brain region. When differences are found, they are typically statistically significant differences in the amount or kind of tissue, such as the gender differences in gray matter distribution noted earlier. Even so, the basic brain structures are still the *same* in men and women.

Third, *every brain is different* to some degree (Gernsbacher, 2007a). Regardless of gender, no two brains are identical.

Finally, every brain is a "work in progress." Experience affects the brain, including the size of brain structures. Thus, sex differences in structures or function might well be the *result* of the different life experiences of men and women, rather than the *cause* (Halpern & others, 2007).

CRITICAL THINKING QUESTIONS

- Why are sweeping claims about fundamental sex differences in the human brain misleading?
- What is wrong with the statement that certain behaviors or personality traits are "hard-wired" in the male or female brain?
- Why is the notion that sex differences might be due to brain differences so appealing to many people?

Roger Sperry (1913–1994) For his pioneering research using split-brain patients to investigate the relationship between brain and behavior, Sperry received the 1981 Nobel Prize in Physiology or Medicine.

Cutting the Corpus Callosum

The Split Brain

Since the discoveries by Broca and Wernicke, the most dramatic evidence illustrating the independent functions of the two cerebral hemispheres has come from a surgical procedure called the **split-brain operation.** This operation is used to stop or reduce recurring seizures in severe cases of epilepsy that can't be treated in any other fashion. The procedure involves surgically cutting the corpus callosum, the thick band of axons that connects the two hemispheres.

split-brain operation
A surgical procedure that involves cutting the corpus callosum.

What was the logic behind cutting the corpus callosum? An epileptic seizure typically occurs when neurons begin firing in a disorganized fashion in one region of the brain. The disorganized neuronal firing quickly spreads from one hemisphere to the other via the corpus callosum. If the corpus callosum is cut, seizures should be contained in just one hemisphere, reducing their severity or eliminating them altogether. This is exactly what happened when the split-brain operation was first tried in this country in the 1940s (Springer & Deutsch, 1998).

Surprisingly, cutting the corpus callosum initially seemed to produce no noticeable effect on the patients, other than reducing their epileptic seizures. Their ability to engage in routine conversations and tasks seemed to be unaffected. On the basis of these early observations, some brain researchers speculated that the corpus callosum served no function whatsoever (Gazzaniga, 1995). One famous psychologist, Karl Lashley, joked that the primary function of the corpus callosum seemed to be to keep the two hemispheres from sagging (Hoptman & Davidson, 1994).

In the 1960s, however, psychologist and neuroscientist **Roger Sperry** and his colleagues began unraveling the puzzle of the left and right hemispheres. Sperry and his colleagues used the apparatus shown in Figure 2.21 to test the abilities of split-brain patients. They would direct a split-brain subject to focus on a point in the middle of a screen, while briefly flashing a word or picture to the left or right of the midpoint.

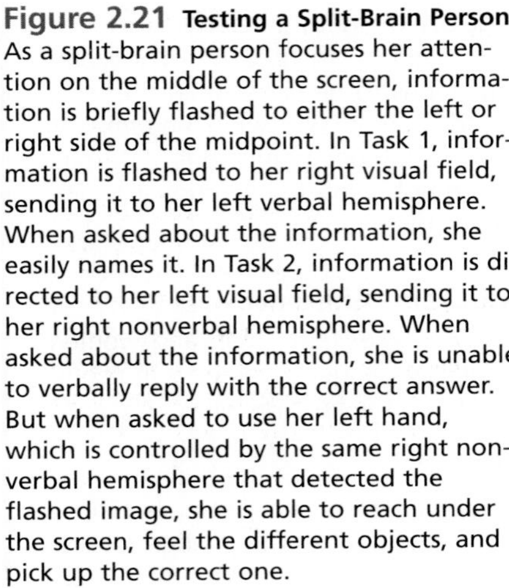

Figure 2.21 Testing a Split-Brain Person As a split-brain person focuses her attention on the middle of the screen, information is briefly flashed to either the left or right side of the midpoint. In Task 1, information is flashed to her right visual field, sending it to her left verbal hemisphere. When asked about the information, she easily names it. In Task 2, information is directed to her left visual field, sending it to her right nonverbal hemisphere. When asked about the information, she is unable to verbally reply with the correct answer. But when asked to use her left hand, which is controlled by the same right nonverbal hemisphere that detected the flashed image, she is able to reach under the screen, feel the different objects, and pick up the correct one.

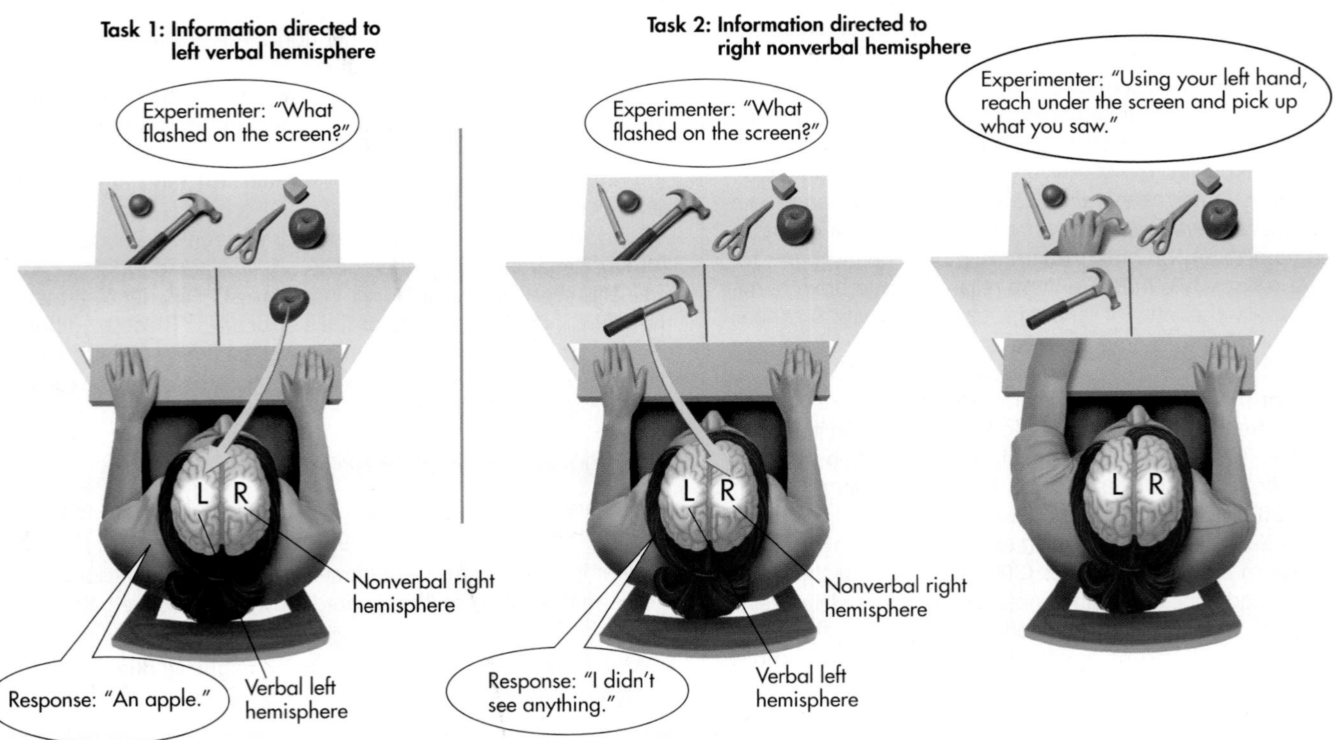

In this procedure, visual information to the right of the midpoint is projected to the person's *left* hemisphere, and visual information to the left of the midpoint is projected to the *right* hemisphere. Behind the screen several objects were hidden from the split-brain subject. The subject could reach under a partition below the screen to pick up the concealed objects but could not see them (Sperry, 1982).

In a typical experiment, Sperry projected the image of an object concealed behind the screen, such as a hammer, to the left of the midpoint. This is shown in Task 2, Figure 2.21. Thus, the image of the hammer was sent to the right, nonverbal hemisphere. If a split-brain subject was asked to *verbally* identify the image flashed on the screen, he could not do so and often denied that anything had appeared on the screen. Why? Because his verbal left hemisphere had no way of knowing the information that had been sent to his right hemisphere. However, if a split-brain subject was asked to use his left hand to reach under the partition for the object that had been displayed, he would correctly pick up the hammer. This was because his left hand was controlled by the same right hemisphere that saw the image of the hammer.

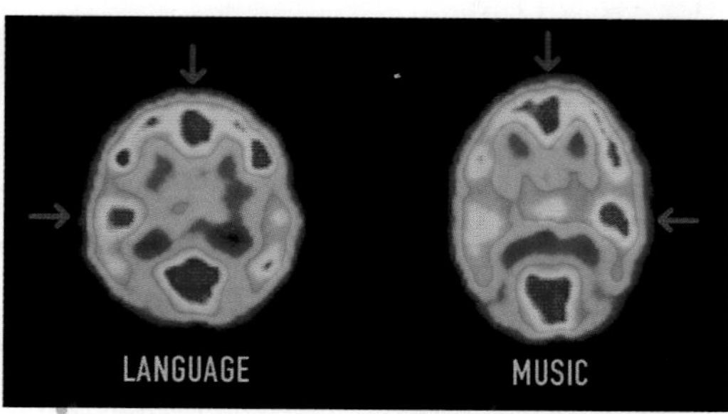

Specialization in the Left and Right Hemispheres The red arrow at the top of each PET scan points to the front of the brain. The red and yellow colors indicate the areas of greatest brain activity. Listening to speech involves a greater degree of activation of the language areas of the left hemisphere. Listening to music involves more activation in right-hemisphere areas. Notice, however, that there is some degree of activity in both hemispheres during these tasks.

Sperry's experiments reconfirmed the specialized language abilities of the left hemisphere that Broca and Wernicke had discovered more than a hundred years earlier. But notice, even though the split-brain subject's right hemisphere could not express itself verbally, it still processed information and expressed itself *nonverbally:* The subject was able to pick up the correct object.

Over the last four decades, researchers have gained numerous insights about the brain's lateralization of functions by studying split-brain patients, using brain-imaging techniques with normal subjects, and other techniques (Gazzaniga, 2005). On the basis of this evidence, researchers have concluded that—in most people—the left hemisphere is superior in language abilities, speech, reading, and writing.

In contrast, the right hemisphere is more involved in nonverbal emotional expression and visual-spatial tasks (Corballis & others, 2002). Deciphering complex visual cues, such as completing a puzzle or manipulating blocks to match a particular design, also relies on right-hemisphere processing (Gazzaniga, 1995, 2005). And the right hemisphere excels in recognizing faces and emotional facial cues, reading maps, copying designs, and drawing. Finally, the right hemisphere shows a higher degree of specialization for musical appreciation or responsiveness—but not necessarily for musical ability, which involves the use of the left hemisphere as well (Springer & Deutsch, 2001).

Figure 2.22 summarizes the research findings for the different specialized abilities of the two hemispheres for right-handed people. As you look at the figure, it's important to keep two points in mind. First, the differences between the left and right hemispheres are almost always relative differences, *not* absolute differences. In other words, *both* hemispheres of your brain are activated to some extent as you perform virtually any task (Toga & Thompson, 2003). In the normal brain, the left and right hemispheres function in an integrated fashion, constantly exchanging information (Banich, 1998; Allen & others, 2007). Thus, Figure 2.22 indicates the hemisphere that typically displays greater activation or exerts greater control over a particular function. Misconceptions about the roles played by the left and right hemispheres are common in the popular media. The Science Versus Pseudoscience box, "Brain Myths" on the next page, explores some of the most common misperceptions about the brain. Second, many functions of the cerebral hemispheres, such as those involving the primary sensory and

Figure 2.22 Specialized Abilities of the Two Hemispheres Most people are left-hemisphere dominant for speech and language tasks and right-hemisphere dominant for visual-spatial tasks. Although the hemispheres display some specialized abilities, many functions are symmetrical and performed the same way on both hemispheres.

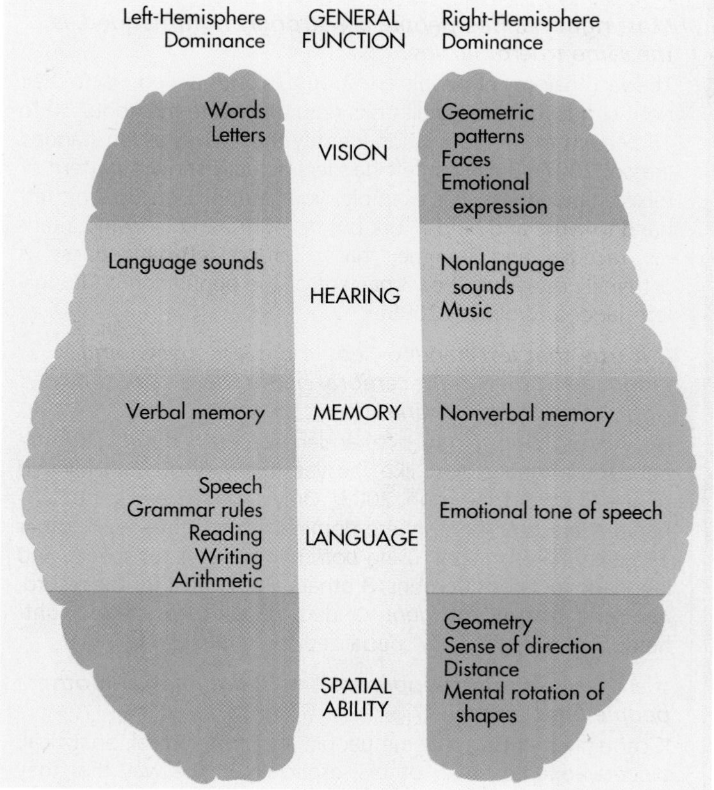

SCIENCE VERSUS PSEUDOSCIENCE

Brain Myths

Is it true that we only use 10 percent of our brain?

Sorry, but this popular notion simply isn't true. Think about the information presented in this chapter. As brain-imaging techniques clearly show, multiple brain areas are activated in response to even simple tasks, such as speaking or listening to music. Further, if we used only 10 percent of our brain, then people who have a stroke or brain injury would probably not experience any obvious consequences. Of course, that's not what happens. There is *no* area of the brain that can be damaged without some kind of consequences. Finally, how well do you think you would function if a brain injury destroyed a "mere" 25 percent of your brain?

So where did the 10 percent myth come from?

The famous psychologist William James may have inadvertently contributed to the 10 percent myth when he wrote in 1908, "We are making use of only a small part of our possible mental and physical resources." Whether James contributed to the myth or not, the myth has been around since at least the early 1900s (Beyerstein, 1999). Some of those who perpetuate the 10 percent myth probably mean well, like teachers, coaches, and motivational speakers. Their basic message is that each of us should strive to reach our full potential. Others, however, are hawking a product that they promise will enhance your creativity, psychic powers, intelligence, or other hidden potential. But you will *never* hear a neuroscientist make the 10 percent claim. In fact, you'll hear just the opposite. As neuroscientist Barry Gordon (2008) comments, "It turns out that we use virtually every part of the brain, and that the brain is active almost all the time. Let's put it this way: the brain represents three percent of the body's weight and uses 20 percent of the body's energy."

Most right-handed people are strongly right-handed. Is the same true of lefties?

The vast majority of people are strongly right-handed, using their right hands for virtually all tasks requiring dexterity. About 10 to 13 percent of the population identify themselves as left-handed (Basso, 2007). But most left-handers actually show a pattern of mixed-handedness. For example, your author Don uses his left hand to write and hold a fork but his right hand to swing a tennis racquet and hammer nails. Strong left-handedness is extremely rare: only 2 or 3 percent of the population is strongly left-handed (Wolman, 2005).

Is it true that left-handed people process speech and language in their right cerebral hemisphere? Are they right-hemisphere dominant?

No. About 70 percent of left-handers are *left-hemisphere* dominant for language, just like the vast majority of right-handed people (Toga & Thompson, 2003). Only about 15 percent of left-handers are right-hemisphere dominant for language. Another 15 percent are bilateral, using *both* hemispheres for speech and language functions (Jörgens & others, 2007). Just for the record, about 3 percent of *right*-handed people are either right-hemisphere or bilaterally specialized for language.

Is it true that some people are "right-brained" and other people "left-brained"?

It certainly seems as if some people are more logical, analytical, or detail-oriented than others, especially in the way that they make decisions or tackle problems. However, in the normal, intact human brain, left and right hemispheres are highly interconnected. So, unless their corpus callosum has been surgically sliced, *all* humans rely on the smooth integrated functioning of *both* their left and right hemispheres to speak, learn, and generally navigate everyday life. In fact, the more complex the task, the greater the likelihood that *both* hemispheres will be involved in performing it (Allen & others, 2007; Weissman & Banich, 2000; Yoshizaki & others, 2007). So, in that sense, the simple answer to this question is "No."

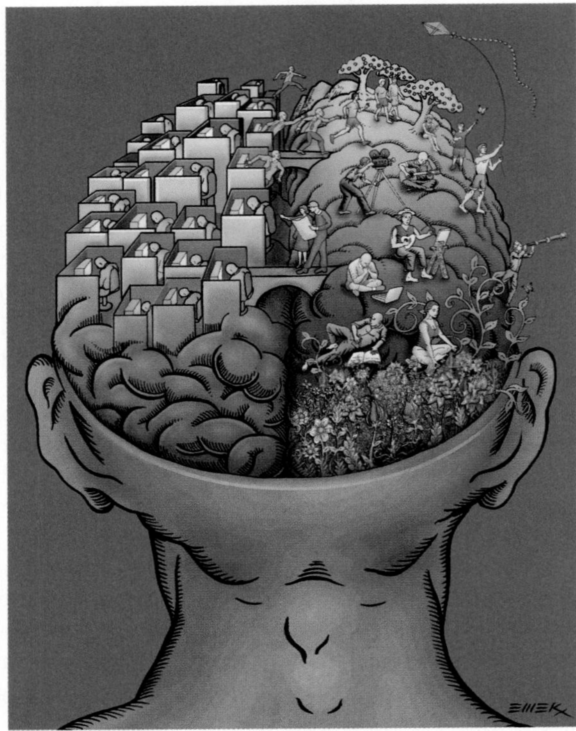

Left Brain, Right Brain? As this image rather playfully suggests, many people see the two hemispheres as representing diametrically opposed ways of thinking and behaving: the left brain is cold, rational, and analytical; the right brain is emotional, artistic, and free-spirited. But how much truth is there to this myth?

Is the right brain responsible for creativity and intuition? Can you train your right brain?

Although the right hemisphere is specialized for holistic processing, there is no evidence that the right hemisphere is any more "intuitive" or "creative" than the left hemisphere (Gazzaniga, 2005). Nor is there evidence that any teacher, however skilled, could somehow selectively "educate" one side of your brain in isolation from the other (Goswami, 2006). While it is true that each hemisphere is specialized for different abilities, you rely on the smooth, integrated functioning of *both* hemispheres to accomplish most tasks. This is especially true for such cognitively demanding tasks as artistic creativity, musical performance, or finding innovative solutions to complex problems.

motor areas, *are* symmetrical. They are located in the same place and are performed in the same way on both the left and the right hemisphere.

Given the basic findings on the laterality of different functions in the two hemispheres, can you speculate about why Asha was unable to read or follow a simple conversation but could easily concentrate on a complex piece of music? Why were her language abilities so disrupted, while her ability to focus on and appreciate music remained intact after her stroke?

A plausible explanation has to do with the location of the stroke's damage on Asha's left temporal lobe. Because language functions are usually localized on the left hemisphere, the stroke produced serious disruptions in Asha's language abilities. However, her *right* cerebral hemisphere sustained no detectable damage. Because one of the right hemisphere's abilities is the appreciation of musical sounds, Asha retained the ability to concentrate on and appreciate music.

>> Closing Thoughts

In our exploration of neuroscience and behavior, we've traveled from the activities of individual neurons to the complex interaction of the billions of neurons that make up the human nervous system, most notably the brain. In the course of those travels, we presented four themes that are crucial to a scientific understanding of brain function: *localization, lateralization, integration,* and *plasticity.*

More than just a historical scientific oddity, phrenology's incorrect interpretation of bumps on the skull helped focus scientific debate on the notion of *localization*—the idea that different functions are localized in different brain areas. Although rejected in the early 1800s when Franz Gall was in his heyday, localization of brain functioning is well established today. The early clinical evidence provided by Broca and Wernicke, and the later split-brain evidence provided by Sperry and his colleagues, confirmed the idea of *lateralization*—that some functions are performed primarily by one cerebral hemisphere.

The ideas of localization and lateralization are complemented by another theme evident in this chapter—*integration*. Although the nervous system is highly specialized, even simple behaviors involve the highly integrated interaction of trillions of synapses. Your ability to process new information and experiences, your memories of previous experiences, your sense of who you are and what you know, your actions and reactions—all depend upon the harmony of the nervous system.

The story of Asha's stroke illustrated what can happen when that harmony is disrupted. Asha survived her stroke, but many people who suffer strokes do not. Of those who do survive a stroke, about one-third are left with severe impairments in their ability to function.

What happened to Asha? Fortunately, her story has a happy ending. Asha was luckier than many stroke victims—she was young, strong, and otherwise healthy. Asha's recovery was also aided by her high level of motivation, willingness to work hard, and sheer will to recover. After being discharged from the hospital, Asha began months of intensive speech therapy. Her speech therapist assigned a great deal of homework that consisted of repeatedly pairing pictures with words, objects with words, and words with objects. Asha was literally rewiring her brain by relearning the correct associations between words and their meanings.

Asha set a very high goal for herself: to return to teaching at the university the following fall semester. With the help of her husband, Paul, and her mother, Nalini, who traveled from India to help coach her back to full recovery, Asha made progressive and significant gains. With remarkable determination, Asha reached the goal she had set for herself. Eight months after her stroke, Asha returned to the classroom and her research lab.

Asha's Recovery After leaving the hospital, Asha began retraining her brain with speech therapy. Asha's husband, Paul, and her mother, Nalini, helped her with the speech drills. Day after day, Asha repeatedly paired words with objects or identified numbers, weekdays, or months. As Asha recalls, "My mom was a Montessori teacher for many years and she was incredibly patient with me, like she was with her own students and with us as children." As Asha gradually made progress, Nalini began taking her to stores. "She'd tell the clerk I was from India and that my English wasn't very good and ask them to please be patient with me. She basically forced me to talk to the sales clerks." Today, more than five years after the stroke, Asha has completely recovered and resumed teaching.

Today, more than five years after her stroke, the average person would never know that Asha had sustained significant brain damage. Other than an occasional tendency to "block" on familiar words—especially when she's very tired—Asha seems to have made a complete recovery.

Thus, Asha's story illustrates the final theme—the brain's remarkable *plasticity*. Next, we take a closer look at how the brain responds to different types of environments. You will also learn how you can use the research to enhance your own dendritic potential!

ENHANCING WELL-BEING WITH PSYCHOLOGY

Maximizing Your Brain's Potential

It was 1962 when a group of neuroscientists led by psychologist Mark Rosenzweig published the unexpected finding that the brains of rats raised in *enriched environments* were significantly different from the brains of rats raised in *impoverished environments.*

For lab rats, an *enriched environment* is spacious, houses several rats, and has assorted wheels, ladders, tunnels, and objects to explore. The environment is also regularly changed for further variety. Some enriched environments have been designed to mimic an animal's natural environment (see Heyman, 2003). In the *impoverished environment*, a solitary rat lives in a small, bare laboratory cage with only a water bottle and food tray to keep it company.

Decades of research have shown that enrichment increases the number and length of dendrites and dendritic branches, increases the number of glial cells, and enlarges the size of neurons (Cohen, 2003). Enrichment produces more synaptic connections between brain neurons, while impoverishment decreases synaptic connections. With more synapses, the brain has a greater capacity to integrate and process information and to do so more quickly. In young rats, enrichment increases the number of synapses in the cortex by as much as 20 percent. But even the brains of extremely old rats respond to enriched environments. In fact, no matter what the age of the rats studied, environmental enrichment or impoverishment had a significant impact on brain structure (Kempermann & others, 1998).

Enrichment has also been shown to increase the rate of neurogenesis in many different species, from rodents to monkeys (Fan & others, 2007; Nithianantharajah & Hannan, 2006). Both the number and the survival time of new neurons increase in response to enrichment (Gould & Gross, 2002; van Praag & others, 2000). Interestingly, while enriched environments can increase neurogenesis, social isolation and a stressful environment *decrease* neurogenesis (Ming & Song, 2005).

Collectively, these changes result in increased processing and communication capacity in the brain. Behaviorally, enrichment has been shown to enhance performance on tasks designed to measure learning and memory, such as performance in different types of mazes (van Praag & others, 2000).

Who Moved My Exercise Wheel?

Neuroscientists have identified an additional factor that improves brain function, even in aging mammals: exercise (see Hillman & others, 2008). In one study, just a month of daily exercise helped reverse cognitive declines associated with aging in previously sedentary, elderly mice (van Praag & others, 2005). After having access to an exercise wheel for 30 days, mice that were the rodent equivalent of 70 years old learned to navigate a maze much faster than mice of the same age that did not exercise. They also had better memories of maze locations. Finally, the physically active elderly mice had a greatly increased rate of neurogenesis, and the new neurons functioned as well as new neurons generated in the brains of young mice. As study co-author Henriette van Praag (2005) points out, "Our findings show that it is never too late in life to start to exercise, and that doing so will likely delay the onset of aging-associated memory loss."

An Enriched Environment Primates in the wild live in complex, challenging, and ever-changing environments. At psychologist Elizabeth Gould's Princeton lab, marmosets are housed in large enclosures with natural vegetation and novel objects that are changed frequently. To encourage naturalistic foraging, branches with holes are filled with dried fruit and live worms. In one experiment, synaptic and dendritic connections increased dramatically in marmosets who lived in the enriched environment for just four weeks after being raised in standard laboratory cages (Kozorovitskiy & others, 2004).

From Animal Studies to Humans

Enrichment studies have been carried out with many other species, including monkeys, cats, birds, honeybees, and even fruit flies. In all cases, enriched environments are associated with striking changes in the brain, however primitive.

Can the conclusions drawn from studies on rats, monkeys, and other animals be applied to human brains? Obviously, researchers cannot directly study the effects of enriched or impoverished environments on human brain tissue as they can with rats.

Consider a study conducted by Ana Pereira and her colleagues (2007). Male and female participants, aged 21 to 45, were assessed for their overall level of fitness. Using MRI scans, each participant's brain was also mapped for amount of blood flowing into the hippocampus. Over the next three months, the participants worked out for one hour four times a week. Finally, the same physical and brain measurements were taken again.

As you probably anticipated, all of the participants had significantly improved their overall level of aerobic fitness. More importantly, they had also substantially increased the blood flow to their hippocampuses, in some cases doubling the blood flow as measured prior to the exercise program. In general, the greater the increase in a participant's aerobic fitness, the greater the increase in blood flow to the hippocampus.

Now for the key finding of the study: Along with the human subjects, a group of mice followed a comparable exercise program. In the mice, the exercise program resulted in increased blood flow in the *same* hippocampus regions as the humans. However, the researchers were able to directly examine brain changes in the mice. They found that the increased blood flow to the hippocampus in the mice was *directly* correlated to the birth of new neurons in the same region of the hippocampus. Although neuroscientists tend to be cautious in drawing conclusions, the implication of Pereira's study is obvious: Exercise promotes neurogenesis in the adult human brain just as it does in other mammals. A footnote: The participants in Pereira's study *also* improved their scores on several tests of mental abilities.

Neuroscientists have also amassed an impressive array of correlational evidence showing the human benefits from enriched, stimulating environments. For example, several studies have compared symptoms of Alzheimer's disease in elderly individuals with different levels of education (Bennett & others, 2003; Stern & others, 1992, 1994). Autopsies showed that the more educated individuals had just as much damage to their brain cells as did the poorly educated individuals. However, because the better-educated people had more synaptic connections, their symptoms were much less severe than those experienced by the less educated people (Melton, 2005).

The results of this study echo earlier research on intellectual enrichment: A mentally stimulating, intellectually challenging environment is associated with enhanced cognitive functioning. Just as physical activity strengthens the heart and muscles, mental activity strengthens the brain. Even in late adulthood, remaining mentally and physically active can help prevent or lessen mental decline (Hillman & others, 2008; Kramer & Erickson, 2007).

Pumping Neurons: Exercising Your Brain

So, here's the critical question: Are you a mental athlete—or a cerebral couch potato? Whatever your age, there seems to be a simple prescription for keeping your brain fit. Along with regular physical activity, engaging in any kind of intellectually challenging pursuits will keep those dendrites developing. Enrichment need not involve exotic or expensive pursuits. Novelty and complexity can be as close as your college campus or library. Here are just a few suggestions:

- Don't hide in your room or apartment—seek out social interaction (except when it interferes with studying). Remember, the brain thrives on social stimulation.

Cranial Calisthenics? Brain training is available in many forms today. These British women are trying out Nintendo's *Brain Age* game, a video game that claims to enhance the aging brain (Fuyuno, 2006). Web sites offer a slew of games, puzzles, and quizzes that promise to provide a mental workout. Whether such cranial calisthenics offer lasting results is yet unproven. However, research suggests that staying mentally active can help keep the aging brain healthy and alert, especially if mental workouts are accompanied by physical ones (Willis & others, 2006).

- Learn to play a musical instrument. If you can't afford music lessons, join a singing group or choir. If you already play a musical instrument, experiment with a new style or musical genre.
- Take a class in a field outside your college major or in a new area. Experiment by learning something in a field completely new to you.
- Read, and read widely. Buy magazines or check out library books in fields that are new to you.
- Try puzzles of all kinds—word, number, maze, or matching.
- Get regular aerobic exercise, even if it's no more than a brisk daily walk. If possible, vary your routes and try to notice something new about your surroundings on each walk.
- Unplug your television set for two weeks—or longer.

Better yet, take a few minutes and generate your own list of mind-expanding opportunities!

CHAPTER REVIEW: KEY PEOPLE AND TERMS

Pierre Paul Broca, p. 73
Roger Sperry, p. 76
Karl Wernicke, p. 73

biological psychology, p. 44
neuroscience, p. 44
neuron, p. 45
sensory neuron, p. 45
motor neuron, p. 45
interneuron, p. 45
glial cells, p. 45
cell body, p. 46
dendrites, p. 46
axon, p. 46
myelin sheath, p. 47
action potential, p. 47
stimulus threshold, p. 47
resting potential, p. 47
all-or-none law, p. 49
synapse, p. 49
synaptic gap, p. 49
axon terminals, p. 50
synaptic vesicles, p. 50
neurotransmitters, p. 50
synaptic transmission, p. 50

acetylcholine, p. 52
dopamine, p. 52
serotonin, p. 52
norepinephrine, p. 52
GABA (gamma-aminobutyric acid), p. 53
endorphins, p. 53
nervous system, p. 55
nerves, p. 56
central nervous system (CNS), p. 56
spinal reflexes, p. 56
peripheral nervous system, p. 57
somatic nervous system, p. 57
autonomic nervous system, p. 57
sympathetic nervous system, p. 58
parasympathetic nervous system, p. 59

endocrine system, p. 59
hormones, p. 59
pituitary gland, p. 60
adrenal glands, p. 60
adrenal cortex, p. 60
adrenal medulla, p. 61
gonads, p. 61
functional plasticity, p. 62
structural plasticity, p. 62
neurogenesis, p. 62
phrenology, p. 63
cortical localization, p. 63
brainstem, p. 66
hindbrain, p. 66
medulla, p. 67
pons, p. 67
cerebellum, p. 67
reticular formation, p. 67
midbrain, p. 67

substantia nigra, p. 67
forebrain, p. 68
cerebral cortex, p. 68
cerebral hemispheres, p. 68
corpus callosum, p. 68
temporal lobe, p. 69
occipital lobe, p. 69
parietal lobe, p. 69
frontal lobe, p. 69
limbic system, p. 70
hippocampus, p. 71
thalamus, p. 71
hypothalamus, p. 71
amygdala, p. 72
cortical localization, p. 73
lateralization of function, p. 73
aphasia, p. 73
split-brain operation, p. 76

Web Companion Review Activities

You can find additional review activities at **www.worthpublishers.com/discoveringpsych5e.** The *Discovering Psychology* 5th edition Web Companion has self-scoring practice quizzes, flashcards, interactive crossword puzzles, and other activities to help you master the material in this chapter.

CONCEPT MAP

NEUROSCIENCE AND BEHAVIOR

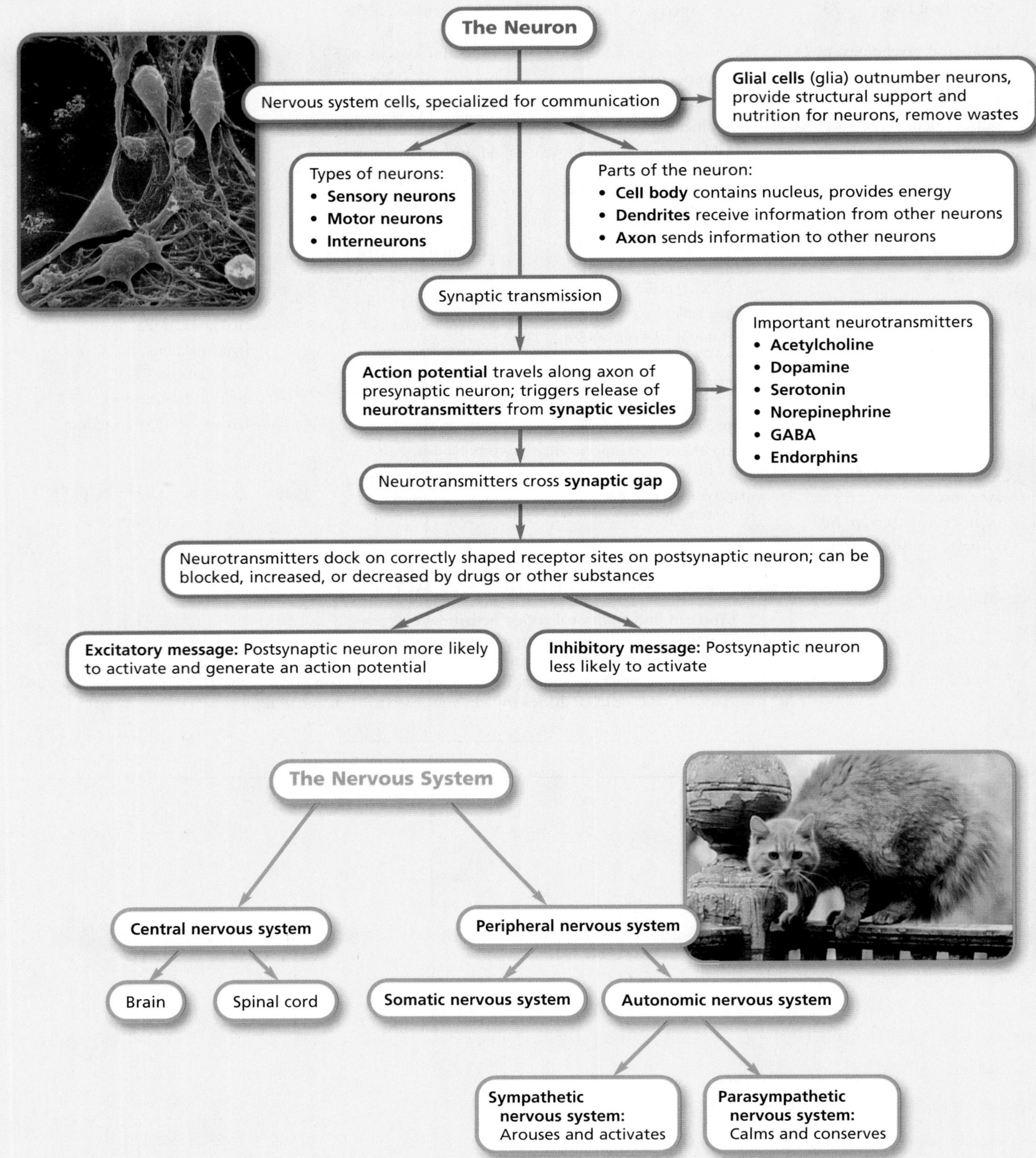

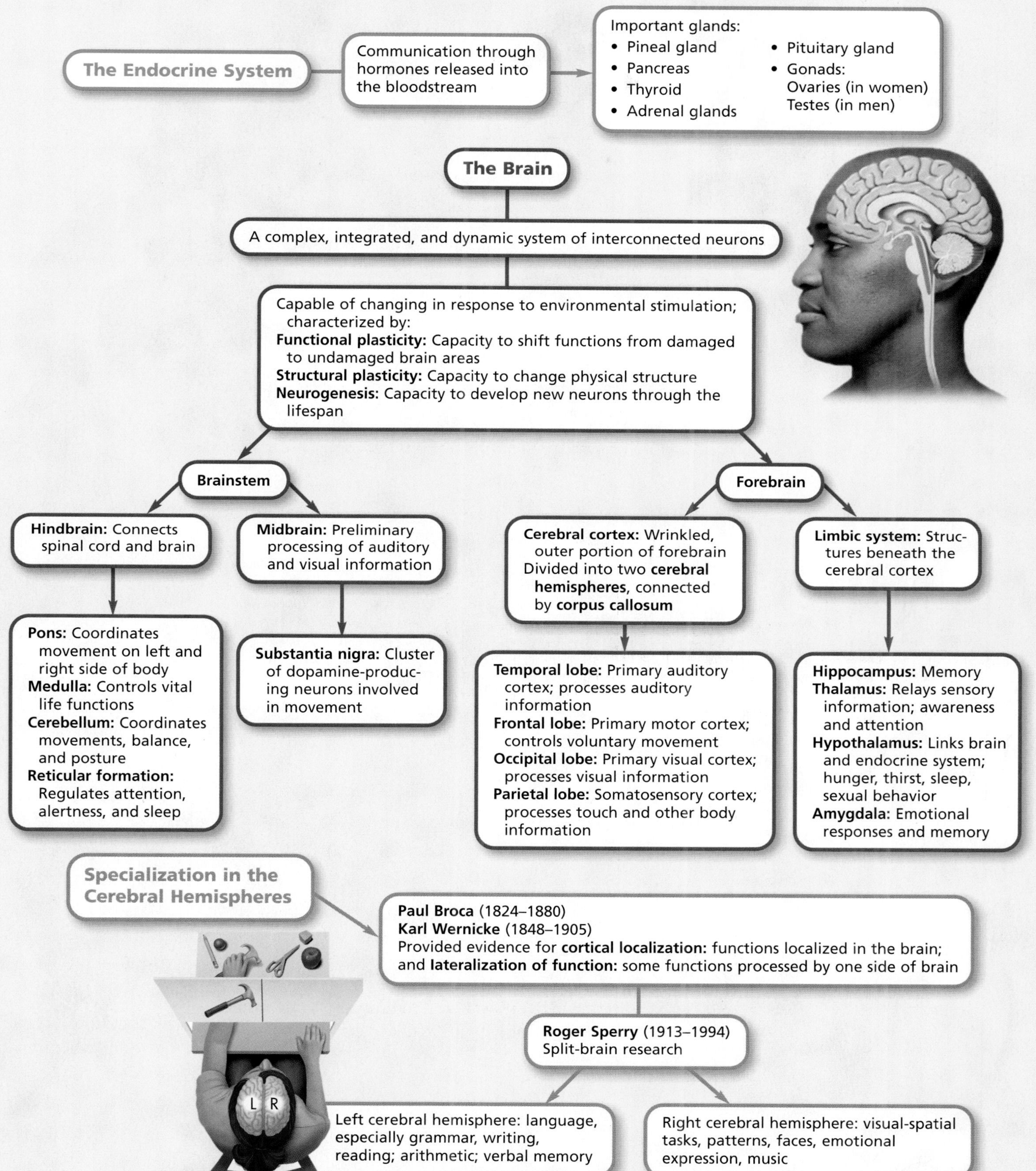
The Endocrine System
Communication through hormones released into the bloodstream
Important glands:
• Pineal gland
• Pancreas
• Thyroid
• Adrenal glands
• Pituitary gland
• Gonads: Ovaries (in women) Testes (in men)
The Brain
A complex, integrated, and dynamic system of interconnected neurons
Capable of changing in response to environmental stimulation; characterized by:
Functional plasticity: Capacity to shift functions from damaged to undamaged brain areas
Structural plasticity: Capacity to change physical structure
Neurogenesis: Capacity to develop new neurons through the lifespan
Brainstem
Hindbrain: Connects spinal cord and brain
Midbrain: Preliminary processing of auditory and visual information
Pons: Coordinates movement on left and right side of body
Medulla: Controls vital life functions
Cerebellum: Coordinates movements, balance, and posture
Reticular formation: Regulates attention, alertness, and sleep
Substantia nigra: Cluster of dopamine-producing neurons involved in movement
Forebrain
Cerebral cortex: Wrinkled, outer portion of forebrain
Divided into two cerebral hemispheres, connected by corpus callosum
Limbic system: Structures beneath the cerebral cortex
Temporal lobe: Primary auditory cortex; processes auditory information
Frontal lobe: Primary motor cortex; controls voluntary movement
Occipital lobe: Primary visual cortex; processes visual information
Parietal lobe: Somatosensory cortex; processes touch and other body information
Hippocampus: Memory
Thalamus: Relays sensory information; awareness and attention
Hypothalamus: Links brain and endocrine system; hunger, thirst, sleep, sexual behavior
Amygdala: Emotional responses and memory
Specialization in the Cerebral Hemispheres
Paul Broca (1824–1880)
Karl Wernicke (1848–1905)
Provided evidence for cortical localization: functions localized in the brain; and lateralization of function: some functions processed by one side of brain
Roger Sperry (1913–1994)
Split-brain research
L
R
Left cerebral hemisphere: language, especially grammar, writing, reading; arithmetic; verbal memory
Right cerebral hemisphere: visual-spatial tasks, patterns, faces, emotional expression, music

CHAPTER

3

Sensation and Perception

Chapter Outline

PROLOGUE

Learning to See

MIKE WAS JUST 3 YEARS OLD when a jar of chemicals left in an old storage shed exploded in his face. The blast destroyed his left eye, and severely damaged his right eye. For more than four decades, Mike May was completely blind (Kurson, 2007).

But despite his blindness, Mike experienced—and accomplished—much more than most people ever dream of achieving. Always athletic, Mike played flag football in elementary school and wrestled and played soccer in high school and college. As an adult, he earned a master's degree in international affairs from Johns Hopkins University, went to work for the CIA, and then became a successful businessman.

He also learned to skydive, windsurf, water-ski, and snow-ski. How does a blind person ski down mountains? If you answered, "very carefully," you'd be wrong—at least in Mike's case. With a guide skiing in front of him shouting "left" or "right" to identify obstacles, Mike hurtled down the most difficult black diamond slopes at speeds up to 65 miles per hour. In fact, Mike has won several medals in national and international championships for blind downhill speed skiing.

It was through skiing that Mike met his wife, Jennifer. An accomplished skier herself, she volunteered to be his guide at a ski slope. Today, Mike and Jennifer and their two sons are all avid skiers (Abrams, 2002).

In the 1990s, Mike started a successful company that develops global positioning devices, along with other mobility devices, for the blind. The portable navigation system gives visually impaired people information about their location, landmarks, streets, and so forth wherever they travel. With his white cane and guide dog, Josh, Mike traveled the world, both as a businessman and a tourist, ever optimistic and open to adventure (Kurson, 2007). His personal motto: "There is always a way."

But in 1999, Mike's keen sensory world of touch, sounds, and aroma was on the verge of expanding. A new surgical technique became available that offered the chance that Mike's vision might be restored in his right eye. On March 7, 2000, Jennifer held her breath as the bandages were removed. "It was so unexpected—there was just a whoosh! of light blasting into my eye," Mike later recalled (May, 2002b). For the first time since he was 3 years old, Mike May could see.

And what was it like when Mike could see Jennifer for the first time? "It was incredible," he explained, "but the truth is, I knew exactly what she looked like, so it wasn't all that dramatic to see her. The same with my kids. Now, seeing other people that I can't touch, well, that's interesting because I couldn't see them before."

A Little Bit of Vision . . . Although Mike could "see" from the moment the bandages were removed from his eye *(left),* he still had trouble identifying objects, especially stationary ones. Mike tells this story of a walk down an unfamiliar street in Barcelona, Spain: "I picked my way through some street construction. I saw a fluorescent green object in my path and tapped it with my cane. It wasn't hard like a sign so I tapped it a bit harder as I still couldn't figure out visually what it was. I was startled as a burst of Spanish profanity came from the workman bent over digging out a hole in the sidewalk. He didn't take too kindly to me poking him in the behind with my cane. A little bit of vision can be dangerous sometimes" (May, 2004).

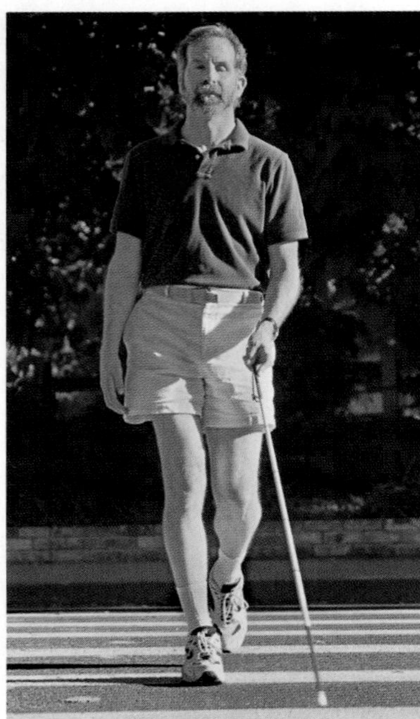

But what did Mike see? Anatomically, his right eye was now normal. But rather than being 20/20, his vision was closer to 20/1,000. What that means is his view of the world was very blurry. He could see colors, shapes, lines, shadows, light and dark patches. So why wasn't the world crystal clear?

Although the structures of his eye were working, his brain did not know how to interpret the signals it was receiving. As neuropsychologist Ione Fine (2002) explained, "Most people learn the language of vision between the age of birth and two years old. Mike has had to learn it as an adult." Indeed, there is much more to *seeing* than meets the eye.

Faces posed a particular challenge for Mike. During conversations, he found it very distracting to look at people's faces. As Mike wrote in his journal, "I can see their lips moving, eyelashes flickering, head nodding, and hands gesturing. It was easiest to close my eyes or tune out the visual input. This was often necessary in order to pay attention to what they were saying" (May, 2004).

And what was it like the first time he went skiing, just weeks after his surgery? Mike was dazzled by the sight of the tall, dark green trees, the snow, and the distant peaks against the blue sky (May, 2004). But although you might think that vision, even blurry vision, would be a distinct advantage to an expert skier, this was not the case. Mike found it easier to ski with his eyes closed, with Jennifer skiing ahead and shouting out directions. With his eyes open, he was overwhelmed by all the visual stimuli and the frightening sense that objects were rushing toward him. "By the time I thought about and guessed at what the shadows on the snow meant, I would miss the turn or fall on my face. It was best to close my eyes," he explained.

Throughout this chapter, we will come back to Mike's story. We'll also tell you what neuropsychologists Ione Fine and Don MacLeod learned after conducting fMRI scans of Mike's brain. And, later in the chapter, we'll see how well you do at deciphering some visual illusions as compared to Mike.

>> Introduction: What Are Sensation and Perception?

Glance around you. Notice the incredible variety of colors, shades, shadows, and images. Listen carefully to the diversity of sounds, loud and soft, near and far. Focus on everything that's touching you—your clothes, your shoes, the chair you're sitting on. Now, inhale deeply through your nose and identify the aromas in the air.

With these simple observations you have exercised four of your senses: vision, hearing, touch, and smell. As we saw in Chapter 2, the primary function of the nervous system is communication—the transmission of information from one part of the body to the other. Where does that information come from? Put simply, your senses are the gateway through which your brain receives all its information about the environment. It's a process that is so natural and automatic that we typically take it for granted until it is disrupted by illness or injury. Nevertheless, as Mike's story demonstrates, people with one nonfunctional sense are amazingly adaptive. Often, they learn to compensate for the missing environmental information by relying on their other senses.

In this chapter, we will explore the overlapping processes of *sensation* and *perception*. **Sensation** refers to the detection and basic sensory experience of environmental stimuli, such as sounds, images, and odors. **Perception** occurs when we integrate, organize, and interpret sensory information in a way that is meaningful. Here's a simple example to contrast the two terms. Your eyes' physical response to light, splotches of color, and lines reflects *sensation*. Integrating and organizing those sensations so that you interpret the light, splotches of color, and lines as a painting, a flag, or some other object reflects *perception*. Mike's visual world reflects this distinction. Although his eye was accurately transmitting visual information from his environment (*sensation*), his brain was unable to make sense out of the information (*perception*).

Where does the process of sensation leave off and the process of perception begin? There is no clear boundary line between the two processes as we actually experience them. In fact, many researchers in this area of psychology regard sensation and perception as a single process.

Although the two processes overlap, we will present sensation and perception as separate discussions. In the first half of the chapter, we'll discuss the basics of *sensation*—how our sensory receptors respond to stimulation and transmit that information in usable form to the brain. In the second half of the chapter, we'll explore *perception*—how the brain actively organizes and interprets the signals sent from our *sensory receptors*.

Experiencing the World Through Our Senses Imagine biting into a crisp, red apple. All your senses are involved in your experience—vision, smell, taste, hearing, and touch. Although we're accustomed to thinking of our different senses as being quite distinct, all forms of sensation involve the stimulation of specialized cells called sensory receptors.

Basic Principles of Sensation

Key Theme

- **Sensation is the result of neural impulses transmitted to the brain from sensory receptors that have been stimulated by physical energy from the external environment.**

Key Questions

- **What is the process of transduction?**
- **What is a sensory threshold, and what are two main types of sensory thresholds?**
- **How do sensory adaptation and Weber's law demonstrate that sensation is relative rather than absolute?**

We're accustomed to thinking of the senses as being quite different from one another. However, all our senses involve some common processes. All sensation is a result of the stimulation of specialized cells, called **sensory receptors,** by some form of *energy*.

Imagine biting into a crisp, red apple. Your experience of hearing the apple crunch is a response to the physical energy of vibrations in the air, or *sound waves*. The sweet taste of the apple is a response to the physical energy of *dissolvable chemicals* in your mouth, just as the distinctive sharp aroma of the apple is a response to *airborne chemical molecules* that you inhale through your nose. The smooth feel of the apple's skin is a response to the *pressure* of the apple against your hand. And the mellow red color of the apple is a response to the physical energy of *light waves* reflecting from the irregularly shaped object into which you've just bitten.

Sensory receptors convert these different forms of physical energy into electrical impulses that are transmitted via neurons to the brain. The process by which a form of physical energy is converted into a coded neural signal that can be processed by the nervous system is called **transduction.** These neural signals are sent to the brain, where the perceptual processes of organizing and interpreting the coded messages occur. Figure 3.1 on the next page illustrates the basic steps involved in sensation and perception.

We are constantly being bombarded by many different forms of energy. For instance, at this very moment radio and television waves are bouncing around the

sensation
The process of detecting a physical stimulus, such as light, sound, heat, or pressure.

perception
The process of integrating, organizing, and interpreting sensations.

sensory receptors
Specialized cells unique to each sense organ that respond to a particular form of sensory stimulation.

transduction
The process by which a form of physical energy is converted into a coded neural signal that can be processed by the nervous system.

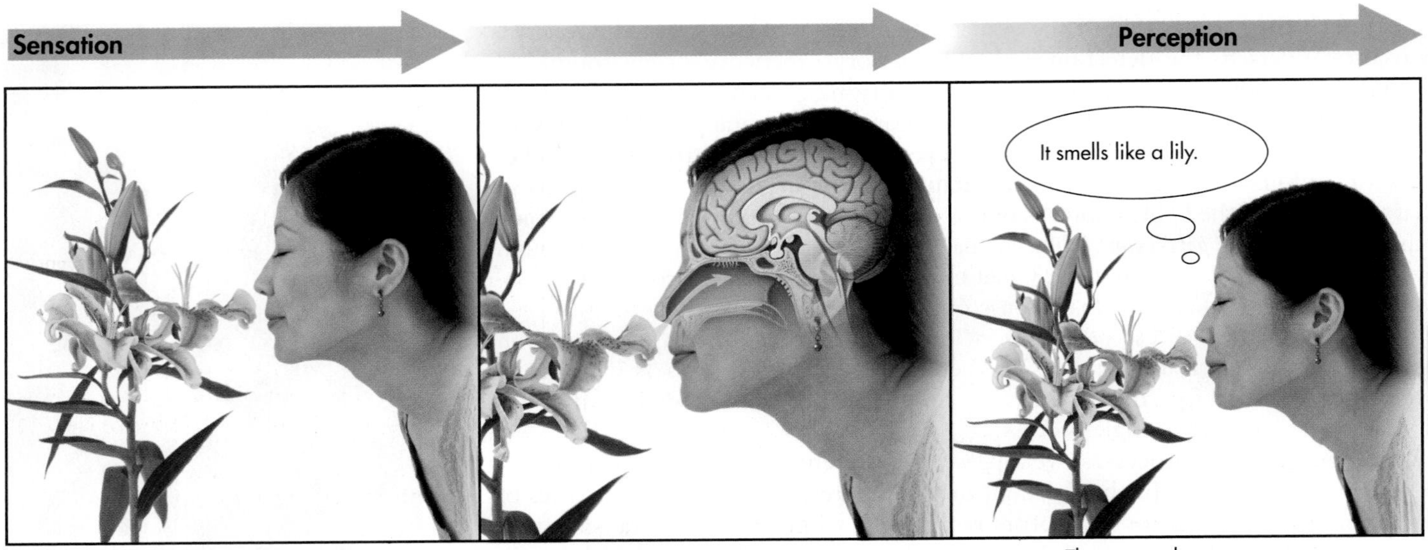

Energy from an environmental stimulus activates specialized receptor cells in the sense organ.

Coded neural messages are sent along a specific sensory pathway to the brain.

These neural messages are decoded and interpreted in the brain as a meaningful perception.

Figure 3.1 The Basic Steps of Sensation and Perception

atmosphere and passing through your body. However, sensory receptors are so highly specialized that they are sensitive only to very specific types of energy (which is lucky, or you might be seeing *Gilligan's Island* reruns in your brain right now). So, for any type of stimulation to be sensed, the stimulus energy must first be in a form that can be detected by our sensory receptor cells. Otherwise, transduction cannot occur.

Sensory Thresholds

Along with being specialized as to the types of energy that can be detected, our senses are specialized in other ways as well. We do not have an infinite capacity to detect all levels of energy. To be sensed, a stimulus must first be strong enough to be detected—loud enough to be heard, concentrated enough to be smelled, bright enough to be seen. The point at which a stimulus is strong enough to be detected because it activates a sensory receptor cell is called a *threshold*. There are two general kinds of sensory thresholds for each sense—the absolute threshold and the difference threshold.

The **absolute threshold** refers to the smallest possible strength of a stimulus that can be detected half the time. Why just half the time? It turns out that the minimum level of stimulation that can be detected varies from person to person and from trial to trial. Because of this human variability, researchers have arbitrarily set the limit as the minimum level of stimulation that can be detected half the time. Under ideal conditions (which rarely occur in normal daily life), our sensory abilities are far more sensitive than you might think (see Table 3.1). Can stimuli that are below the absolute threshold affect us? We discuss this question in the Science Versus Pseudoscience box, "Subliminal Perception."

Table 3.1

Absolute Thresholds

Sense	Absolute Threshold
Vision	A candle flame seen from 30 miles away on a clear, dark night
Hearing	The tick of a watch at 20 feet
Taste	One teaspoon of sugar in two gallons of water
Smell	One drop of perfume throughout a three-room apartment
Touch	A bee's wing falling on your cheek from a height of about half an inch

Psychologist Eugene Galanter (1962) provided these classic examples of the absolute thresholds for our senses. In each case, people are able to sense these faint stimuli at least half the time.

absolute threshold
The smallest possible strength of a stimulus that can be detected half the time.

subliminal perception
The detection of stimuli that are below the threshold of conscious awareness; nonconscious perception.

mere exposure effect
The finding that repeated exposure to a stimulus increases a person's preference for that stimulus.

SCIENCE VERSUS PSEUDOSCIENCE

Subliminal Perception

What are subliminal messages? Can they influence people to quit smoking, lose weight, or change their personalities? **Subliminal perception** refers to the detection of stimuli that are below the threshold of conscious perception or awareness. Such stimuli might be rapidly flashed visual images, sounds, or odors that are too faint to be consciously detected. Although not consciously perceived, subliminal stimuli can evoke a brain response (Bahrami & others, 2007).

The notion that people's behavior could be manipulated by subliminal messages first attracted public attention in 1957. James Vicary, a marketing executive, claimed to have increased concession sales at a New Jersey movie theater by subliminally flashing the words "Eat popcorn" and "Drink Coke" during the movie.

Controlled tests, however, failed to replicate Vicary's claims, and Vicary later admitted that his boast was a hoax to drum up customers for his failing marketing business (Dijksterhuis & others, 2005). Nevertheless, to this day, many people still believe—and some advertisements claim—that subliminal messages can exert an irresistible, lasting influence.

Can your behavior be profoundly influenced by subliminal self-help CDs, audio tapes, or computer programs? Or by vague images or words embedded in advertisements? *No.* Numerous studies have shown that subliminal self-help products do *not* produce the changes they claim to produce (Strahan & others, 2005). Likewise, numerous studies on subliminal messages in advertising have shown that they do *not* influence actual consumer decisions (Simons & others, 2007).

But do subliminal stimuli have *any* effect? Surprisingly, the answer is a qualified *yes.* For example, consider the **mere exposure effect,** which refers to the well-documented finding that repeated exposure to a particular stimulus leads to increased liking for that stimulus (Zajonc, 2001). The mere exposure effect also holds for subliminally presented stimuli. For example, when people are exposed to subliminal images of a particular geometric shape and, minutes later, are asked to pick the shape they prefer from a group of shapes, they are much more likely to choose the subliminally presented shape.

Beyond preferences, attitudes and emotions can also be influenced by subliminal stimuli (Smith & others, 2008; Westen & others, 2007). In a classic study, subliminally flashing a pleasant image (cute kittens) versus an unpleasant image (a skull) influenced how participants judged the personality traits of a stranger shown in a neutral situation (Krosnick & others, 1992).

Can other sensory cues affect us without our awareness? One intriguing study investigated the effect of subliminal odors (Li & others, 2007). Participants rated pictures of faces for "likeability" after sniffing either a pleasant, lemony scent; an unpleasant scent (think high school locker room); a neutral scent; or no scent at all (air). The catch was that 75% of the time, the odors were so faint that they could not be consciously detected. Did the subliminal odors affect the likeability ratings?

Yes—but *only* when participants were unaware of which scent they were sniffing. Faces paired with the subliminal pleasant odor received the highest ratings, while faces paired with the subliminal unpleasant odor received the lowest ratings (see graph). However, when participants were aware of an odor, the correlation between likeability and odor pleasantness disappeared.

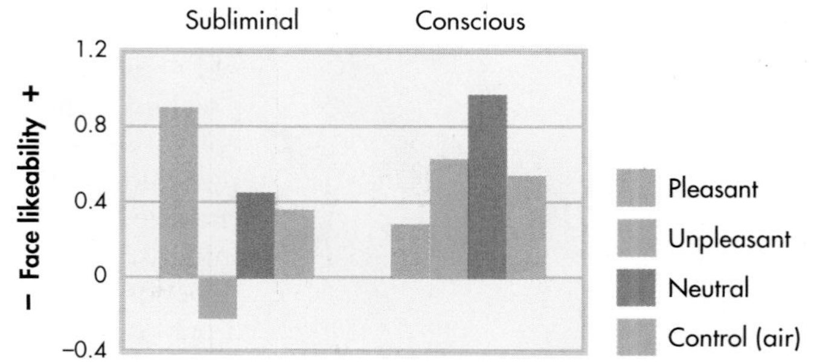

Effects of Subliminal Odors After smelling pleasant, unpleasant, or neutral odors, participants rated photographs of faces on a scale ranging from "extremely unlikeable" to "extremely likeable." Participants' judgments were affected by subliminal odors—but not odors that they could consciously perceive.

Why? According to lead researcher Wen Li (2007), "People who were conscious of the barely noticeable scents were able to discount that sensory information and just evaluate the faces." But participants who were *not* conscious of the odors attributed their response to the "pleasantness" or "unpleasantness" of the face they were rating, rather than to the smell that they could not consciously perceive.

Studies on subliminal effects usually involve expressing preferences about contrived stimuli, such as geometric figures or photographs of strangers. But an Israeli study demonstrated that subliminal stimuli can also briefly influence real-world attitudes (Hassin & others, 2007). Participants with known political views were exposed to subliminal images of either the Israeli flag or, as a control, a scrambled flag image, before answering a series of questions about controversial political issues.

Did subliminal exposure to the Israeli flag have any effect on political attitudes? *Yes.* Participants who were exposed to the Israeli flag expressed more moderate responses to the political questions than would have been predicted from their previous political positions. But the control group participants, who saw only a scrambled image, did not change their views.

Why did subliminal exposure to the national flag shift attitudes toward a more middle-of-the-road stance? Israeli psychologist Ran Hassin and his colleagues (2007) speculated that subliminal images of the Israeli flag evoked a sense of national unity, drawing people closer to the political center, at least temporarily.

The bottom line? Subliminal stimuli can briefly influence attitudes, thoughts, preferences, and emotions (Dijksterhuis & Nordgren, 2006). But the key word here is *briefly.* These transient influences are a far cry from the pseudoscientific claims of some subliminal self-help products that promise easy and sweeping changes in behavior, personality, or motivation.

Experimental Stimulus

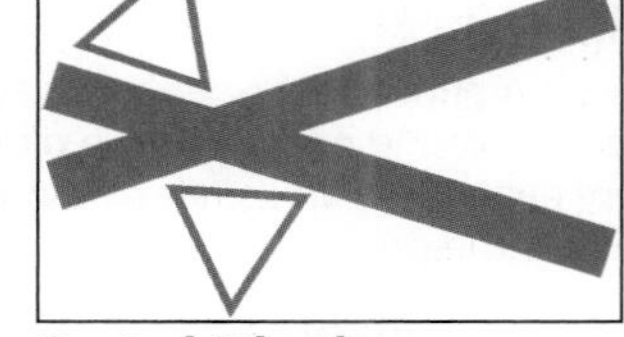

Control Stimulus

Subliminal stimuli used in Hassin & others, 2007 study.

The other important threshold involves detecting the *difference* between two stimuli. The **difference threshold** is the smallest possible difference between two stimuli that can be detected half the time. Another term for the difference threshold is *just noticeable difference,* which is abbreviated *jnd.*

The just noticeable difference will *vary* depending on its relation to the original stimulus. This principle of sensation is called *Weber's law,* after the German physiologist Ernst Weber (1795–1878). **Weber's law** holds that for each sense, the size of a just noticeable difference is a constant proportion of the size of the initial stimulus. So, whether we can detect a change in the strength of a stimulus depends on the intensity of the *original* stimulus. For example, if you are holding a pebble (the original stimulus), you will notice an increase in weight if a second pebble is placed in your hand. But if you start off holding a very heavy rock (the original stimulus), you probably won't detect an increase in weight when the same pebble is balanced on it.

What Weber's law underscores is that our psychological experience of sensation is *relative.* That is, there is no simple, one-to-one correspondence between the objective characteristics of a physical stimulus, such as the weight of a pebble, and our psychological experience of it.

Sensory Adaptation

Suppose your best friend has invited you over for a spaghetti dinner. As you walk in the front door, you're almost overwhelmed by the odor of onions and garlic cooking on the stove. However, after just a few moments, you no longer notice the smell. Why? Because your sensory receptor cells become less responsive to a constant stimulus. This gradual decline in sensitivity to a constant stimulus is called **sensory adaptation.** Once again, we see that our experience of sensation is relative—in this case, relative to the *duration of exposure.*

Because of sensory adaptation, we become accustomed to constant stimuli, which allows us to quickly notice new or changing stimuli. This makes sense. If we were continually aware of all incoming stimuli, we'd be so overwhelmed with sensory information that we wouldn't be able to focus our attention. So, for example, once you manage to land your posterior on the sofa, you don't need to be constantly reminded that the sofa is beneath you.

Vision

From Light to Sight

Key Theme

- **The receptor cells for vision respond to the physical energy of light waves and are located in the retina of the eye.**

Key Questions

- **What is the visible spectrum?**
- **What are the key structures of the eye and their functions?**
- **What are rods and cones, and how do their functions differ?**

A lone caterpillar on the screen door, the pile of dirty laundry in the corner of the closet, a spectacular autumn sunset, the intricate play of color, light, and texture in a painting by Monet. The sense organ for vision is the eye, which contains receptor cells that are sensitive to the physical energy of *light.* Before we can talk about how the eye functions, we need to briefly discuss some characteristics of light as the visual stimulus.

difference threshold
The smallest possible difference between two stimuli that can be detected half the time; also called *just noticeable difference.*

Weber's law
(VAY-berz) A principle of sensation that holds that the size of the just noticeable difference will vary depending on its relation to the strength of the original stimulus.

sensory adaptation
The decline in sensitivity to a constant stimulus.

Visible light

Invisible long waves

Invisible short waves

AC circuits | Radio | TV | Cell phones | Microwaves | Infrared | Ultra-violet rays | X-rays | Gamma rays | Cosmic rays

Amplitude

Wavelength

750 | 700 Red | 600 Yellow | 500 Green | 400 Blue-violet | 350

Wavelengths in nanometers (billionths of a meter)

Figure 3.2 The Electromagnetic Spectrum We are surrounded by different kinds of electromagnetic energy waves, yet we are able to see only a tiny portion of the entire spectrum of electromagnetic energy. Some electronic instruments, like radio and television, are specialized receivers that detect a specific wavelength range. Similarly, the human eye is sensitive to a specific and very narrow range of wavelengths.

What We See

The Nature of Light

Light is just one of many different kinds of electromagnetic energy that travel in the form of waves. Other forms of electromagnetic energy include X-rays, the microwaves you use to pop popcorn, and the infrared signals or radio waves transmitted by your TV's remote control. The various types of electromagnetic energy differ in **wavelength,** which is the distance from one wave peak to another.

Humans are capable of seeing only a minuscule portion of the electromagnetic energy range. In Figure 3.2, notice that the visible portion of the electromagnetic energy spectrum can be further divided into different wavelengths. As we'll discuss in more detail later, the different wavelengths of visible light correspond to our psychological perception of different colors.

How a Pit Viper Sees a Mouse at Night Does the world look different to other species? In many cases, yes. Each species has evolved a unique set of sensory capabilities. Pit vipers see infrared light, which we sense only as warmth. The mouse here has been photographed through an infrared viewer. The image shows how a pit viper uses its infrared "vision" to detect warm-blooded prey at night (Safer & Grace, 2004). Similarly, many insect and bird species can detect ultraviolet light, which is invisible to humans.

wavelength
The distance from one wave peak to another.

cornea
(CORE-nee-uh) A clear membrane covering the visible part of the eye that helps gather and direct incoming light.

pupil
The opening in the middle of the iris that changes size to let in different amounts of light.

iris
(EYE-riss) The colored part of the eye, which is the muscle that controls the size of the pupil.

lens
A transparent structure located behind the pupil that actively focuses, or bends, light as it enters the eye.

accommodation
The process by which the lens changes shape to focus incoming light so that it falls on the retina.

How We See

The Human Visual System

Suppose you're watching your neighbor's yellow and white tabby cat sunning himself on the front steps. How do you see the cat? Simply seeing a yellow tabby cat involves a complex chain of events. We'll describe the process of vision from the object to the brain. You can trace the path of light waves through the eye in Figure 3.3.

First, light waves reflected from the cat enter your eye, passing through the *cornea, pupil,* and *lens.* The **cornea,** a clear membrane that covers the front of the eye, helps gather and direct incoming light. The *sclera,* or white portion of the eye, is a tough, fibrous tissue that covers the eyeball except for the cornea. The **pupil** is the black opening in the eye's center. The pupil is surrounded by the **iris,** the colored structure that we refer to when we say that someone has brown eyes. The iris is actually a ring of muscular tissue that contracts or expands to precisely control the size of the pupil and thus the amount of light entering the eye. In dim light, the iris widens the pupil to let light in; in bright light, the iris narrows the pupil.

Behind the pupil is the **lens,** another transparent structure. In a process called **accommodation,** the lens thins or thickens to bend or focus the incoming light so that the light falls on the retina. If the eyeball is abnormally shaped, the lens may not properly focus the incoming light on the retina, resulting in a visual disorder. In

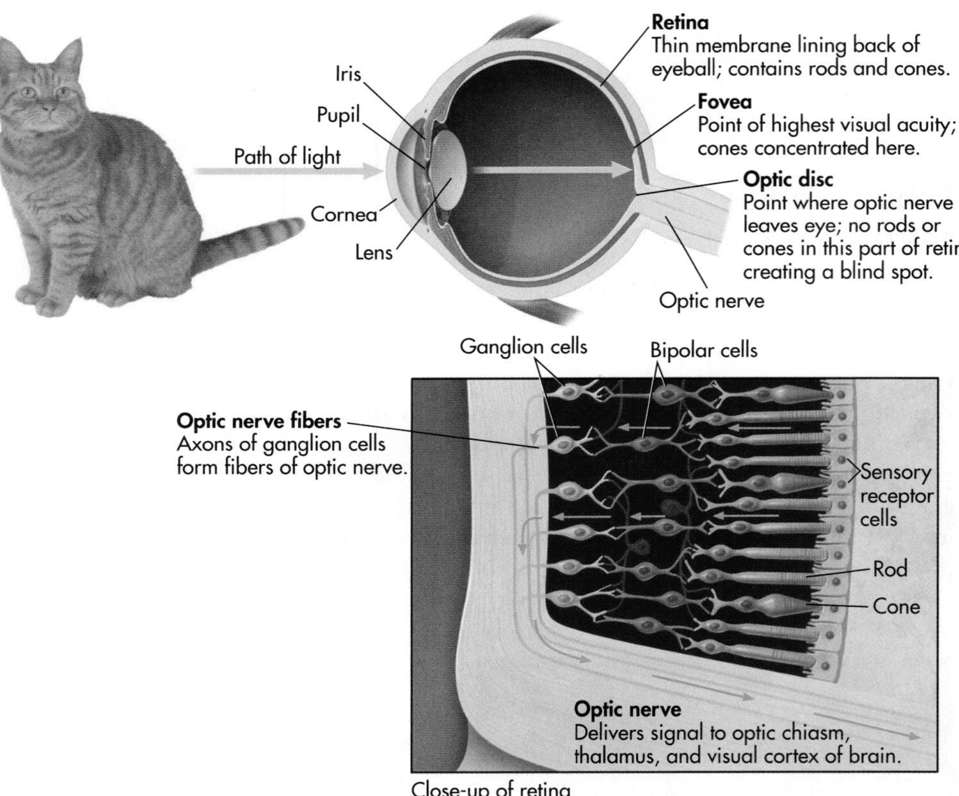

Figure 3.3 Path of Light in a Human Eye Light waves pass through the cornea, pupil, and lens. The iris controls the amount of light entering the eye by controlling the size of the pupil. The lens changes shape to focus the incoming light onto the retina. As the light strikes the retina, the light energy activates the rods and cones. Signals from the rods and cones are collected by the bipolar cells, which transmit the information to the ganglion cells. The ganglion cell axons are bundled together to form the optic nerve, which transmits the information to the brain. The optic nerve leaves the eye at the optic disk, creating a blind spot in our visual field. (For a demonstration of the blind spot, see Figure 3.4 on page 96.)

nearsightedness, or *myopia,* distant objects appear blurry because the light reflected off the objects focuses in front of the retina. In farsightedness, or *hyperopia,* objects near the eyes appear blurry because light reflected off the objects is focused behind the retina. During middle age, another form of farsightedness often occurs, called *presbyopia*. Presbyopia is caused when the lens becomes brittle and inflexible. In *astigmatism,* an abnormally curved eyeball results in blurry vision for lines in a particular direction. Corrective glasses remedy these conditions by intercepting and bending the light so that the image falls properly on the retina. New surgical techniques, such as LASIK, correct visual disorders by reshaping the cornea so that light rays focus more directly on the retina.

The Retina

Rods and Cones

Slim Rods and Fat Cones
The rods and cones in the retina are the sensory receptors for vision. They convert light into electrical impulses that are ultimately transmitted to the brain. Color has been added to this scanning electro micrograph to clearly distinguish the rods and cones. The rods, colored green, are long, thin, and more numerous than the cones, colored blue, which are tapered at one end and shorter and fatter than the rods. As the photo shows, the rods and cones are densely packed in the retina, with many rods surrounding a few cones.

The **retina** is a thin, light-sensitive membrane that lies at the back of the eye, covering most of its inner surface (see Figure 3.3). Contained in the retina are the **rods** and **cones.** Because these sensory receptor cells respond to light, they are often called *photoreceptors.* When exposed to light, the rods and cones undergo a chemical reaction that results in a neural signal.

Rods and cones differ in many ways. First, as their names imply, rods and cones are shaped differently. Rods are long and thin, with blunt ends. Cones are shorter and fatter, with one end that tapers to a point. The eye contains far more rods than cones. It is estimated that each eye contains about 7 million cones and about 125 million rods!

Rods and cones are also specialized for different visual functions. Although both are light receptors, rods are much more sensitive to light than are cones. Once the rods are fully adapted to the dark, they are about a thousand times better than cones at detecting weak visual stimuli (Masland, 2001). We therefore rely primarily on rods for our vision in dim light and at night.

Rods and cones also react differently to *changes* in the amount of light. Rods adapt relatively slowly, reaching maximum sensitivity to light in about 30 minutes. In contrast, cones adapt quickly to bright light, reaching maximum sensitivity in about 5 minutes. That's why it takes several minutes for your eyes to adapt to the dim light of a darkened room but only a few moments to adapt to the brightness when you switch on the lights.

You may have noticed that it is difficult or impossible to distinguish colors in very dim light. This difficulty occurs because only the cones are sensitive to the different wavelengths that produce the sensation of color, and cones require much more light than rods do to function effectively. Cones are also specialized for seeing fine details and for vision in bright light.

Most of the cones are concentrated in the **fovea,** which is a region in the very center of the retina. Cones are scattered throughout the rest of the retina, but they become progressively less common toward the periphery of the retina. There are no rods in the fovea. Images that do not fall on the fovea tend to be perceived as blurry or indistinct. For example, focus your eyes on the word *For* at the beginning of this sentence. In contrast to the sharpness of the letters in *For,* the words to the left and right are somewhat blurry. The image of the outlying words is striking the peripheral areas of the retina, where rods are more prevalent and there are very few cones.

retina
(RET-in-uh) A thin, light-sensitive membrane located at the back of the eye that contains the sensory receptors for vision.

rods
The long, thin, blunt sensory receptors of the eye that are highly sensitive to light, but not to color, and that are primarily responsible for peripheral vision and night vision.

cones
The short, thick, pointed sensory receptors of the eye that detect color and are responsible for color vision and visual acuity.

fovea
(FO-vee-uh) A small area in the center of the retina, composed entirely of cones, where visual information is most sharply focused.

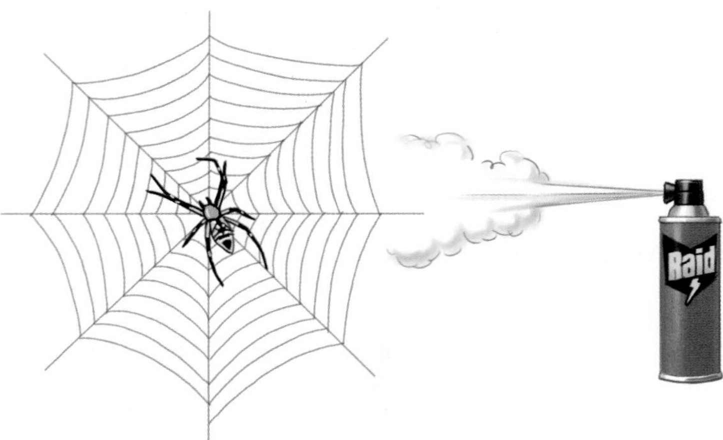

Figure 3.4 Demonstration of the Blind Spot Hold the book a few feet in front of you. Close your right eye and stare at the insect spray can with your left eye. Slowly bring the book toward your face. At some point the spider will disappear because you have focused it onto the part of your retina where the blind spot is located. Notice, however, that you still perceive the spider web. That's because your brain has filled in information from the surrounding area (Komatsu, 2006).

The Blind Spot

One part of the retina lacks rods and cones altogether. This area, called the **optic disk,** is the point at which the fibers that make up the optic nerve leave the back of the eye and project to the brain. Because there are no photoreceptors in the optic disk, we have a tiny hole, or **blind spot,** in our field of vision. To experience the blind spot, try the demonstration in Figure 3.4.

Why don't we notice this hole in our visual field? The most compelling explanation is that the brain actually fills in the missing background information (Ramachandran, 1992a, 1992b). In effect, signals from neighboring neurons fill in the blind spot with the color and texture of the surrounding visual information (Komatsu, 2006; Spillmann & others, 2006).

Processing Visual Information

Key Theme

- **Signals from the rods and cones undergo preliminary processing in the retina before they are transmitted to the brain.**

Key Questions

- **What are the bipolar and ganglion cells, and how do their functions differ?**
- **How is visual information transmitted from the retina to the brain?**
- **What properties of light correspond to color perceptions, and how is color vision explained?**

Visual information is processed primarily in the brain. However, before visual information is sent to the brain, it undergoes some preliminary processing in the retina by specialized neurons called **ganglion cells.** This preliminary processing of visual data in the cells of the retina is possible because the retina develops from a bit of brain tissue that "migrates" to the eye during fetal development (see Hubel, 1995).

When the numbers of rods and cones are combined, there are over 130 million receptor cells in each retina. However, there are only about 1 million ganglion cells. How do just 1 million ganglion cells transmit messages from 130 million visual receptor cells?

Visual Processing in the Retina

Information from the sensory receptors, the rods and cones, is first collected by specialized neurons, called **bipolar cells** (see the lower part of Figure 3.3). The bipolar cells then funnel the collection of raw data to the ganglion cells. Each ganglion cell

optic disk
Area of the retina without rods or cones, where the optic nerve exits the back of the eye.

blind spot
The point at which the optic nerve leaves the eye, producing a small gap in the field of vision.

ganglion cells
In the retina, the specialized neurons that connect to the bipolar cells; the bundled axons of the ganglion cells form the optic nerve.

bipolar cells
In the retina, the specialized neurons that connect the rods and cones with the ganglion cells.

receives information from the photoreceptors that are located in its *receptive field* in a particular area of the retina. In this early stage of visual processing, each ganglion cell combines, analyzes, and encodes the information from the photoreceptors in its receptive field before transmitting the information to the brain (Masland, 2001).

Signals from rods and signals from cones are processed differently in the ganglion cells. For the most part, a single ganglion cell receives information from only one or two cones but might well receive information from a hundred or more rods. The messages from these many different rods are combined in the retina before they are sent to the brain. Thus, the brain receives less specific visual information from the rods and messages of much greater visual detail from the cones.

As an analogy to how rod information is processed, imagine listening to a hundred people trying to talk at once over the same telephone line. You would hear the sound of many people talking, but individual voices would be blurred. Now imagine listening to the voice of a single individual being transmitted across the same telephone line. Every syllable and sound would be clear and distinct. In much the same way, cones use the ganglion cells to provide the brain with more specific visual information than is received from rods.

Because of this difference in how information is processed, cones are especially important in *visual acuity*—the ability to see fine details. Visual acuity is strongest when images are focused on the fovea because of the high concentration of cones there.

From Eye to Brain

How is information transmitted from the ganglion cells of the retina to the brain? The 1 million axons of the ganglion cells are bundled together to form the **optic nerve,** a thick nerve that exits from the back of the eye at the optic disk and extends to the brain (see Figure 3.5). The optic nerve has about the same diameter as a pencil. After exiting the eyes, the left and right optic nerves meet at the **optic chiasm.** Then the fibers of the left and right optic nerves split in two. One set of axons crosses over and projects to the opposite side of the brain. The other set of axons forms a pathway that continues along the same side of the brain (see Figure 3.5).

From the optic chiasm, most of the optic nerve axons project to the brain structure called the *thalamus.* This primary pathway seems to be responsible for processing information about form, color, brightness, and depth. A smaller number of axons follow a detour to areas in the *midbrain* before they make their way to the

optic nerve
The thick nerve that exits from the back of the eye and carries visual information to the visual cortex in the brain.

optic chiasm
(KI-az-em) Point in the brain where the optic nerve fibers from each eye meet and partly cross over to the opposite side of the brain.

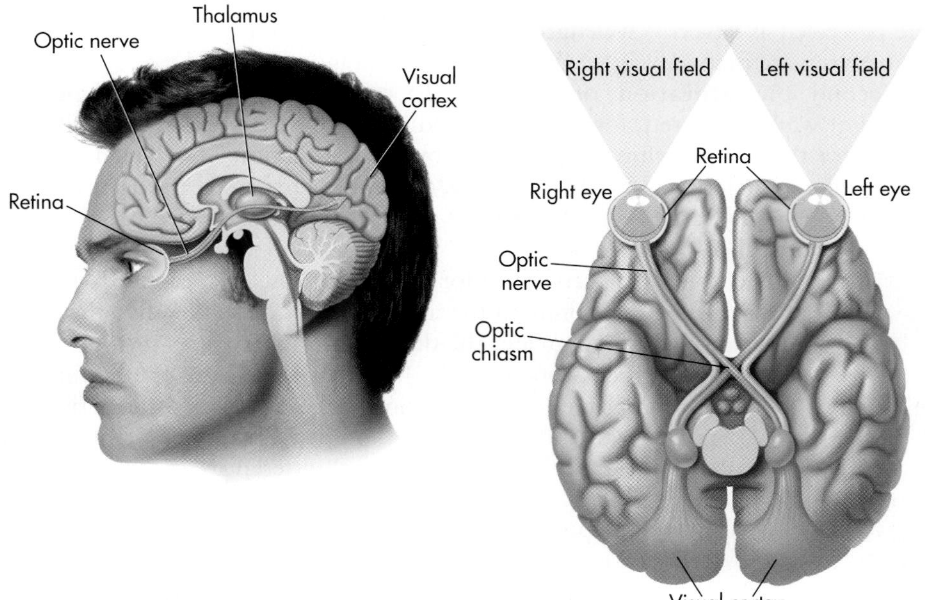

Figure 3.5 Neural Pathways from Eye to Brain The bundled axons of the ganglion cells form the optic nerve, which exits the retina at the optic disk. The optic nerves from the left and right eyes meet at the optic chiasm, then split apart. One set of nerve fibers crosses over and projects to the opposite side of the brain, and another set of nerve fibers continues along the same side of the brain. Most of the nerve fibers travel to the thalamus and then on to the visual cortex of the occipital lobe.

thalamus. This secondary pathway seems to be involved in processing information about the location of an object.

Neuroscientists now know that there are several distinct neural pathways in the visual system, each responsible for handling a different aspect of vision (Zeki, 2001). Although specialized, the separate pathways are highly interconnected. From the thalamus, the signals are sent to the *visual cortex,* where they are decoded and interpreted.

Most of the receiving neurons in the visual cortex of the brain are highly specialized. Each responds to a particular type of visual stimulation, such as angles, edges, lines, and other forms, and even to the movement and distance of objects (Hubel & Wiesel, 2005; Livingstone & Hubel, 1988). These neurons are sometimes called *feature detectors* because they detect, or respond to, particular features or aspects of more complex visual stimuli. Reassembling the features into a recognizable image involves additional levels of processing in the visual cortex and other regions of the brain, including the *frontal lobes.*

Understanding exactly how neural responses of individual feature detection cells become integrated into the visual perceptions of faces and objects is a major goal in contemporary neuroscience (Martin, 2007; Peissig & Tarr, 2007). As the Focus on Neuroscience illustrates, experience plays a key role in perception.

Color Vision

We see images of an apple, a banana, and an orange because these objects reflect light waves. But why do we perceive that the apple is red and the banana yellow? What makes an orange orange?

The Experience of Color

What Makes an Orange Orange?

Color is *not* a property of an object, but a sensation perceived in the brain (Werner & others, 2007). To explain how we perceive color, we must return to the original visual stimulus—light.

Our experience of **color** involves three properties of the light wave. First, what we usually refer to as color is a property more accurately termed **hue.** Hue varies with the wavelength of light. Look again at Figure 3.2. *Different wavelengths correspond to our subjective experience of different colors.* Wavelengths of about 400 nanometers are perceived as violet. Wavelengths of about 700 nanometers are perceived as red. In between are orange, yellow, green, blue, and indigo.

Second, the **saturation,** or *purity,* of the color corresponds to the purity of the light wave. Pure red, for example, produced by a single wavelength, is more *saturated* than pink, which is produced by a combination of wavelengths (red plus white light). In everyday language, saturation refers to the richness of a color. A highly saturated color is vivid and rich; a less saturated color is faded and washed out.

The third property of color is **brightness,** or perceived intensity. Brightness corresponds to the amplitude of the light wave: the higher the amplitude, the greater the degree of brightness.

These three properties of color—hue, saturation, and brightness—are responsible for the amazing range of colors we experience. A person with normal color vision can discriminate from 120 to 150 color differences based on differences in hue, or wavelength, alone. When saturation and brightness are also factored in, we can potentially perceive millions of different colors (Bornstein & Marks, 1982).

Many people mistakenly believe that white light contains no color. White light actually contains all wavelengths, and thus all

When Red + Blue + Green = White When light waves of different wavelengths are combined, the wavelengths are added together, producing the perception of a different color. Thus, when green light is combined with red light, yellow light is produced. When the wavelengths of red, green, and blue light are added together, we perceive the blended light as white. If you're wondering why mixing paints together produces a muddy mess rather than pure white, it's because the wavelengths are *subtracted* rather than added. Each color of pigment absorbs a different part of the color spectrum, and each time a color is added, less light is reflected. Thus, the mixed color appears darker. If you mix all three primary colors together, they absorb the entire spectrum—so we perceive the splotch as black.

FOCUS ON NEUROSCIENCE

Vision, Experience, and the Brain

After Mike's surgery, his retina and optic nerve were completely normal. Formal testing showed that Mike had excellent color perception and that he could easily identify simple shapes and lines that were oriented in different directions. These abilities correspond to visual pathways that develop very early. Mike's motion perception was also very good. When thrown a ball, he could catch it more than 80 percent of the time.

Perceiving and identifying common objects, however, was difficult. Although Mike could "see" an object, he had to consciously use visual cues to work out its identity. For example, when shown the simple drawing above right, called a "Necker cube," Mike described it as "a square with lines." But when shown the same image as a rotating image on a computer screen, Mike immediately identified it as a cube. Functional MRI scans showed that Mike's brain activity was nearly normal when shown a *moving* object.

What about more complex objects, like faces? Even three years after his surgery, Mike recognizes his wife and sons by their hair color, gait, and other clues, *not* by their faces. He can't tell whether a face is male or female, or whether its expression is happy or sad. Functional MRI scans revealed that when Mike is shown faces or objects, the part of the brain that is normally activated is silent (see brain scans).

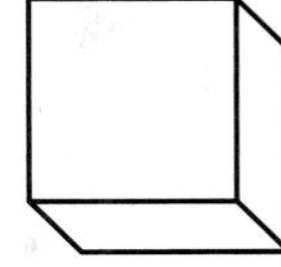

Necker Cube

Necker Cube Shown a stationary image of a Necker cube, Mike described it as "a square with lines." Only when the image began to rotate did Mike perceive it as a drawing of a cube.

For people with normal vision, recognizing complex three-dimensional objects—like tables, shoes, trees, or pencils—is automatic. But as Mike's story shows, these perceptual conclusions are actually based on experience and built up over time.

Neuroscientist Ione Fine and her colleagues (2003), who have studied Mike's visual abilities, believe that Mike's case indicates that some visual pathways develop earlier than others. Color and motion perception, they point out, develop early in infancy. But because people will continue to encounter new objects and faces throughout life, areas of the brain that are specialized to process faces and objects show plasticity. In Mike's case, these brain centers never developed.

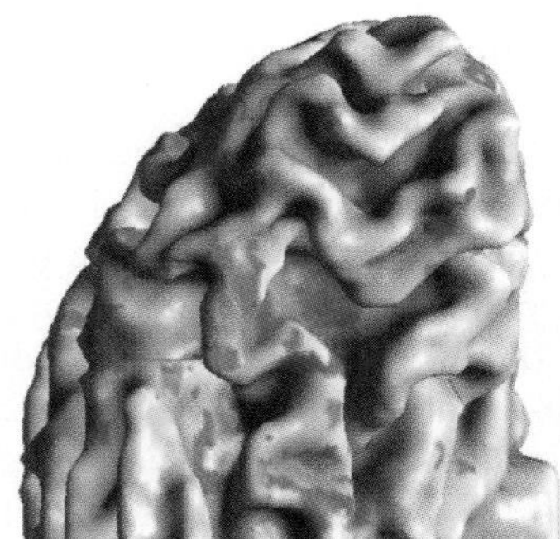

Normal Control

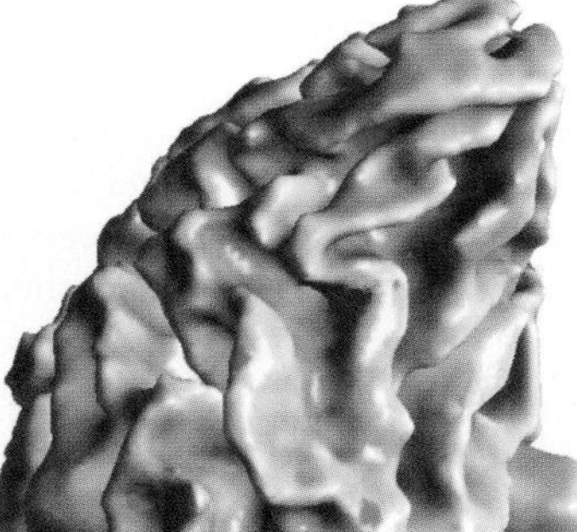

Mike May

Scanning Mike's Brain The red, orange, and yellow colors in the left fMRI scan show the areas of the occipital lobe that are normally activated in response to faces. Blue and purple indicate the typical pattern of brain activity in response to objects. In contrast to a normal sighted individual, Mike's fMRI scan on the right shows virtually no response to faces and only slight brain activation in response to objects.

colors, of the visible part of the electromagnetic spectrum. A glass prism placed in sunlight creates a rainbow because it separates sunlight into all the colors of the visible light spectrum.

So we're back to the question: Why is an orange orange? Intuitively, it seems obvious that the color of any object is an inseparable property of the object—unless we spill paint or spaghetti sauce on it. In reality, *color is a sensation perceived in the brain* (Werner & others, 2007).

Our perception of color is primarily determined by the wavelength of light that an object reflects. If your T-shirt is red, it's red because the cloth is *reflecting* only the wavelength of light that corresponds to the red portion of the spectrum. The T-shirt is *absorbing* the wavelengths that correspond to all other colors. An object appears white because it *reflects* all the wavelengths of visible light and absorbs none. An object appears black when it *absorbs* all the wavelengths of visible light and reflects none. Of course, in everyday life, our perceptions of color are also strongly affected by the amount or type of light falling on an object or the textures and colors that surround it (Shevell & Kingdom, 2008).

color
The perceptual experience of different wavelengths of light, involving hue, saturation (purity), and brightness (intensity).

hue
The property of wavelengths of light known as color; different wavelengths correspond to our subjective experience of different colors.

saturation
The property of color that corresponds to the purity of the light wave.

brightness
The perceived intensity of a color, which corresponds to the amplitude of the light wave.

The Most Common Form of Color Blindness To someone with the most common form of red–green color blindness, these two photographs look almost exactly the same. People with this type of color blindness have normal blue-sensitive cones, but their other cones are sensitive to either red *or* green. Because of the way red–green color blindness is genetically transmitted, it is much more common in men than in women. About 8 percent of the male population is born with red–green color deficiency, and about a quarter of these males experience only the colors coded by the blue/yellow cones. People who are completely color blind and see the world only in shades of black, white, and gray are extremely rare (Shevell & Kingdom, 2008).

How We See Color

Color vision has interested scientists for hundreds of years. The first scientific theory of color vision, proposed by Hermann von Helmholtz (1821–1894) in the mid-1800s, was called the *trichromatic theory.* A rival theory, the *opponent-process theory,* was proposed in the late 1800s. Each theory was capable of explaining some aspects of color vision, but neither theory could explain all aspects of color vision. Technological advances in the last few decades have allowed researchers to gather direct physiological evidence to test both theories. The resulting evidence indicates that *both* theories of color vision are accurate. Each theory describes color vision at a different stage of visual processing (Hubel, 1995).

The Trichromatic Theory As you'll recall, only the cones are involved in color vision. According to the **trichromatic theory of color vision,** there are three varieties of cones. Each type of cone is especially sensitive to certain wavelengths—red light (long wavelengths), green light (medium wavelengths), and blue light (short wavelengths). For the sake of simplicity, we will refer to red-sensitive, green-sensitive, and blue-sensitive cones, but keep in mind that there is some overlap in the wavelengths to which a cone is sensitive (Abramov & Gordon, 1994). A given cone will be *very* sensitive to one of the three colors and only slightly responsive to the other two.

When a color other than red, green, or blue strikes the retina, it stimulates a *combination* of cones. For example, if yellow light strikes the retina, both the red-sensitive and green-sensitive cones are stimulated; purple light evokes strong reactions from red-sensitive and blue-sensitive cones. The trichromatic theory of color vision received compelling research support in 1964, when George Wald showed that different cones were indeed activated by red, blue, and green light.

The trichromatic theory provides a good explanation for the most common form of **color blindness:** red–green color blindness. People with red–green color blindness cannot discriminate between red and green. That's because they have normal blue-sensitive cones, but their other cones are *either* red-sensitive or green-sensitive. Thus, red and green look the same to them. Because red–green color blindness is so common, stoplights are designed so that the location of the light as well as its color provides information to drivers. In vertical stoplights the red light is always on top, and in horizontal stoplights the red light is always on the far left.

The Opponent-Process Theory The trichromatic theory cannot account for all aspects of color vision. One important phenomenon that the theory does not explain is the afterimage. An **afterimage** is a visual experience that occurs after the original source of stimulation is no longer present. To experience an afterimage firsthand, follow the instructions in Figure 3.6 on the next page. What do you see?

Afterimages can be explained by the opponent-process theory of color vision, which proposes a different mechanism of color detection from the one set forth in the trichromatic theory. According to the **opponent-process theory of color vision,** there are four basic colors, which are divided into two pairs of color-sensitive neurons: red–green and blue–yellow. The members of each pair *oppose* each other. If red is stimulated, green is inhibited; if green is stimulated, red is inhibited. Green and red cannot both be stimulated simultaneously. The same is true for the blue–yellow pair. In addition, black and white act as an opposing pair. Color, then, is sensed and encoded in terms of its proportion of red OR green, and blue OR yellow.

For example, red light evokes a response of RED-YES–GREEN-NO in the red–green opponent pair. Yellow light evokes a response of BLUE-NO–YELLOW-YES. Colors other than red, green, blue, and yellow activate one member of each of these pairs to differing degrees. Purple stimulates the *red* of the red–green pair plus the *blue* of the blue–yellow pair. Orange activates *red* in the red–green pair and *yellow* in the blue–yellow pair.

trichromatic theory of color vision
The theory that the sensation of color results because cones in the retina are especially sensitive to red light (long wavelengths), green light (medium wavelengths), or blue light (short wavelengths).

color blindness
One of several inherited forms of color deficiency or weakness in which an individual cannot distinguish between certain colors.

afterimage
A visual experience that occurs after the original source of stimulation is no longer present.

opponent-process theory of color vision
The theory that color vision is the product of opposing pairs of color receptors, red–green, blue–yellow, and black–white; when one member of a color pair is stimulated, the other member is inhibited.

Afterimages can be explained when the opponent-process theory is combined with the general principle of sensory adaptation (Jameson & Hurvich, 1989). If you stare continuously at one color, sensory adaptation eventually occurs and your visual receptors become less sensitive to that color. What happens when you subsequently stare at a white surface?

If you remember that white light is made up of the wavelengths for *all* colors, you may be able to predict the result. The receptors for the original color have adapted to the constant stimulation and are temporarily "off duty." Thus they do not respond to that color. Instead, only the receptors for the opposing color will be activated, and you perceive the wavelength of only the *opposing* color. For example, if you stare at a patch of green, your green receptors eventually become "tired." The wavelengths for both green and red light are reflected by the white surface, but since the green receptors are "off," only the red receptors are activated. Staring at the green, black, and yellow flag in Figure 3.6 should have produced an afterimage of opposing colors: a red, white, and blue American flag.

Figure 3.6 Experiencing an Afterimage Stare at the white dot in the center of this oddly colored flag for about 30 seconds, and then look at a white wall or white sheet of paper. What do you see?

An Integrated Explanation of Color Vision At the beginning of this section we said that current research has shown that *both* the trichromatic theory and the opponent-process theory of color vision are accurate. How can both theories be right? It turns out that each theory correctly describes color vision at a *different level* of visual processing.

As described by the *trichromatic theory,* the cones of the retina do indeed respond to and encode color in terms of red, green, and blue. But recall that signals from the cones and rods are partially processed in the ganglion cells before being transmitted along the optic nerve to the brain. Researchers now believe that an additional level of color processing takes place in the ganglion cells.

As described by the *opponent-process theory,* the ganglion cells respond to and encode color in terms of opposing pairs (DeValois & DeValois, 1975). In the brain, the thalamus and visual cortex also encode color in terms of opponent pairs. Consequently, both theories contribute to our understanding of the process of color vision. Each theory simply describes color vision at a different stage of visual processing (Hubel, 1995; Werner & others, 2007).

Hearing

From Vibration to Sound

Key Theme

- **Auditory sensation, or hearing, results when sound waves are collected in the outer ear, amplified in the middle ear, and converted to neural messages in the inner ear.**

Key Questions

- **How do sound waves produce different auditory sensations?**
- **What are the key structures of the ear and their functions?**
- **How do place theory and frequency theory explain pitch perception?**

We have hiked in a desert area that was so quiet we could hear the whir of a single grasshopper's wings in the distance. And we have waited on a subway platform where the screech of metal wheels against metal rails forced us to cover our ears.

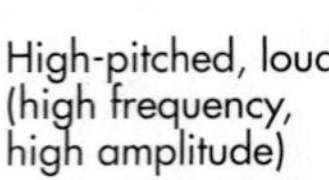

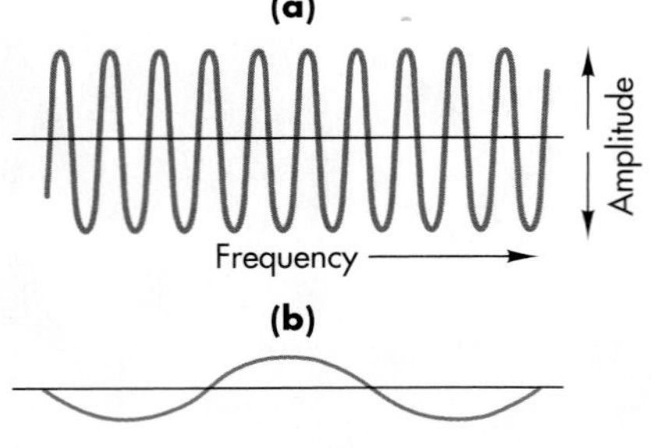

Low-pitched, soft
(low frequency,
low amplitude)

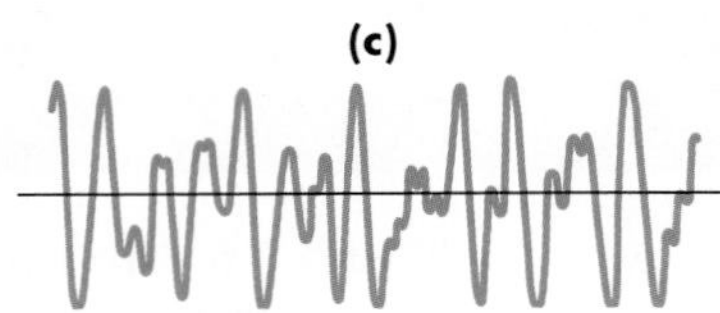

(c)

Complex
(high and low
frequency,
high and low
amplitude)

Figure 3.7 Characteristics of Sound Waves The length of a wave, its height, and its complexity determine the loudness, pitch, and timbre that we hear. The sound produced by **(a)** would be high-pitched and loud. The sound produced by **(b)** would be soft and low. The sound in **(c)** is complex, like the sounds we usually experience in the natural world.

The sense of hearing, or **audition,** is capable of responding to a wide range of sounds, from faint to blaring, simple to complex, harmonious to discordant. The ability to sense and perceive very subtle differences in sound is important to physical survival, social interactions, and language development. Most of the time, all of us are bathed in sound—so much so that moments of near-silence, like our experience in the desert, can seem almost eerie.

What We Hear

The Nature of Sound

Whether it's the ear-splitting screech of metal on metal or the subtle whir of a grasshopper's wings, *sound waves* are the physical stimuli that produce our sensory experience of sound. Usually, sound waves are produced by the rhythmic vibration of air molecules, but sound waves can be transmitted through other media, too, such as water. Our perception of sound is directly related to the physical properties of sound waves (see Figure 3.7).

One of the first things that we notice about a sound is how loud it is. **Loudness** is determined by the intensity, or **amplitude,** of a sound wave and is measured in units called **decibels.** Zero decibels represents the loudness of the softest sound that humans can hear, or the absolute threshold for hearing. As decibels increase, perceived loudness increases.

Pitch refers to the relative "highness" or "lowness" of a sound. Pitch is determined by the frequency of a sound wave. **Frequency** refers to the rate of vibration, or number of waves per second, and is measured in units called *hertz.* Hertz simply refers to the number of wave peaks per second. The faster the vibration, the higher the frequency, the closer together the waves are—and the higher the tone produced. If you pluck the high E and the low E strings on a guitar, you'll notice that the low E vibrates far fewer times per second than does the high E.

Most of the sounds we experience do not consist of a single frequency but are *complex,* consisting of several sound-wave frequencies. This combination of frequencies produces the distinctive quality, or **timbre,** of a sound, which enables us to distinguish easily between the same note played on a saxophone and on a piano. Every human voice has its own distinctive timbre, which is why you can immediately identify a friend's voice on the telephone from just a few words, even if you haven't talked to each other for years.

How We Hear

The Path of Sound

The ear is made up of the outer ear, the middle ear, and the inner ear. Sound waves are *collected* in the outer ear, *amplified* in the middle ear, and *transduced,* or *transformed into neural messages,* in the inner ear (see Figure 3.8).

The **outer ear** includes the *pinna,* the *ear canal,* and the *eardrum.* The pinna is that oddly shaped flap of skin and cartilage that's attached to each side of your head. The pinna helps us pinpoint the location of a sound. But the pinna's primary role is to catch sound waves and funnel them into the ear canal. The sound wave travels down the ear canal, then bounces into the **eardrum,** a tightly stretched membrane. When the sound wave hits the eardrum, the eardrum vibrates, matching the vibrations of the sound wave in intensity and frequency.

The eardrum separates the outer ear from the **middle ear.** The eardrum's vibration is transferred to three tiny bones in the middle ear—the *hammer,* the *anvil,* and the *stirrup.* Each bone sets the next bone in motion. The joint action of these three bones almost doubles the amplification of the sound. The innermost bone,

audition
The technical term for the sense of hearing.

loudness
The intensity (or amplitude) of a sound wave, measured in decibels.

amplitude
The intensity or amount of energy of a wave, reflected in the height of the wave; the amplitude of a sound wave determines a sound's loudness.

decibel
(DESS-uh-bell) The unit of measurement for loudness.

pitch
The relative highness or lowness of a sound, determined by the frequency of a sound wave.

frequency
The rate of vibration, or the number of sound waves per second.

timbre
(TAM-ber) The distinctive quality of a sound, determined by the complexity of the sound wave.

outer ear
The part of the ear that collects sound waves; consists of the pinna, the ear canal, and the eardrum.

eardrum
A tightly stretched membrane at the end of the ear canal that vibrates when hit by sound waves.

middle ear
The part of the ear that amplifies sound waves; consists of three small bones: the hammer, the anvil, and the stirrup.

the stirrup, transmits the amplified vibration to the *oval window.* If the tiny bones of the middle ear are damaged or become brittle, as they sometimes do in old age, *conduction deafness* may result. Conduction deafness can be helped by a hearing aid, which amplifies sounds.

Like the eardrum, the oval window is a membrane, but it is many times smaller than the eardrum. The oval window separates the middle ear from the **inner ear.** As the oval window vibrates, the vibration is next relayed to an inner structure called the **cochlea,** a fluid-filled tube that's coiled in a spiral. The word *cochlea* comes from the Greek word for "snail," and the spiral shape of the cochlea does resemble a snail's shell. Although the cochlea is a very complex structure, it is quite tiny—no larger than a pea.

As the fluid in the cochlea ripples, the vibration in turn is transmitted to the **basilar membrane,** which runs the length of the coiled cochlea. Embedded in the basilar membrane are the sensory receptors for sound, called **hair cells,** which have tiny, projecting fibers that look like hairs. Damage to the hair cells or auditory nerve can result in *nerve deafness,* which cannot be helped by a hearing aid. Exposure to loud noise can cause nerve deafness (see Table 3.2 on the next page).

inner ear
The part of the ear where sound is transduced into neural impulses; consists of the cochlea and semicircular canals.

cochlea
(COCK-lee-uh) The coiled, fluid-filled inner-ear structure that contains the basilar membrane and hair cells.

basilar membrane
(BAZ-uh-ler or BAZE-uh-ler) The membrane within the cochlea of the ear that contains the hair cells.

hair cells
The hairlike sensory receptors for sound, which are embedded in the basilar membrane of the cochlea.

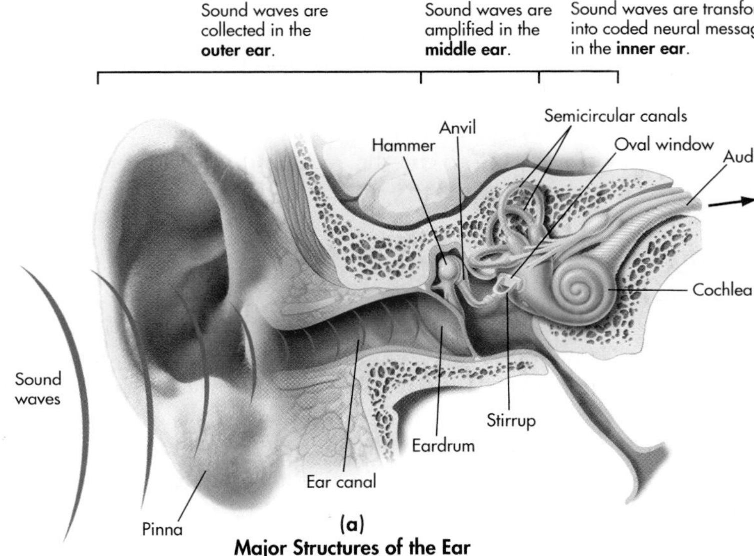

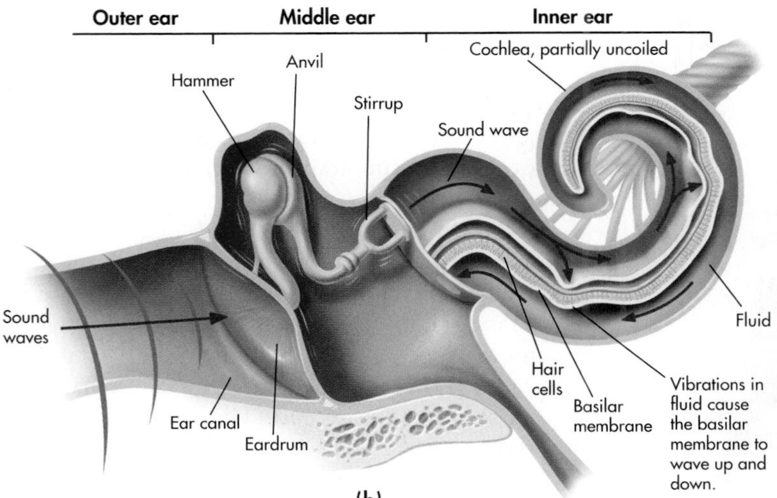

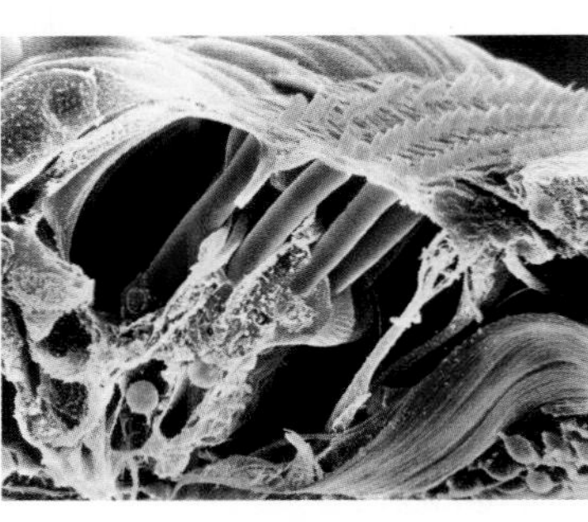
(c)

Figure 3.8 The Path of Sound Through the Human Ear The path that sound waves take through the major structures of the human ear is shown in **(a).** After being caught by the outer ear, sound waves are funneled down the ear canal to the eardrum, which transfers the vibrations to the structures of the middle ear. In the middle ear, the vibrations are amplified and transferred in turn to the oval window and on to the fluid-filled cochlea in the inner ear **(b).** As the fluid in the cochlea vibrates, the basilar membrane ripples, bending the hair cells, which appear as rows of yellow tips in the top right section of the color-enhanced scanning electro micrograph **(c).** The bending of the hair cells stimulates the auditory nerve, which ultimately transmits the neural messages to the auditory cortex in the brain.

frequency theory
The view that the basilar membrane vibrates at the same frequency as the sound wave.

place theory
The view that different frequencies cause larger vibrations at different locations along the basilar membrane.

olfaction
Technical name for the sense of smell.

gustation
Technical name for the sense of taste.

Table 3.2

Decibel Level of Some Common Sounds

Decibels	Examples	Exposure Danger
180	Rocket launching pad	Hearing loss inevitable
140	Shotgun blast, jet plane	Any exposure is dangerous
120	Speakers at rock concert, sandblasting, thunderclap	Immediate danger
100	Chain saw, pneumatic drill	2 hours
90	Truck traffic, noisy home appliances, lawn mower	Less than 8 hours
80	Subway, heavy city traffic, alarm clock at 2 feet	More than 8 hours
70	Busy traffic, noisy restaurant	Critical level begins with constant exposure
60	Air conditioner at 20 feet, conversation, sewing machine	
50	Light traffic at a distance, refrigerator	
40	Quiet office, living room	
30	Quiet library, soft whisper	
0	Lowest sound audible to human ear	

The hair cells bend as the basilar membrane ripples. It is here that transduction finally takes place: The physical vibration of the sound waves is converted into neural impulses. As the hair cells bend, they stimulate the cells of the auditory nerve, which carries the neural information to the thalamus and the auditory cortex in the brain (Recanzone & Sutter, 2008).

Distinguishing Pitch

How do we distinguish between the low-pitched throb of a bass guitar and the high-pitched tones of a piccolo? Remember, pitch is determined by the *frequency* of a sound wave. The basilar membrane is a key structure involved in our discrimination of pitch. Two complementary theories describe the role of the basilar membrane in the transmission of differently pitched sounds.

According to **frequency theory,** the basilar membrane vibrates at the *same* frequency as the sound wave. Thus, a sound wave of about 100 hertz would excite each hair cell along the basilar membrane to vibrate 100 times per second, and neural impulses would be sent to the brain at the same rate. However, there's a limit to how fast neurons can fire. Individual neurons cannot fire faster than about 1,000 times per second. But we can sense sounds with frequencies that are many times higher than 1,000 hertz. A child, for example, can typically hear pitches ranging from about 20 to 20,000 hertz. Frequency theory explains how low-frequency sounds are transmitted to the brain, but it cannot explain the transmission of higher-frequency sounds.

So how do we distinguish higher-pitched sounds? According to **place theory,** different frequencies cause larger vibrations at different *locations* along the basilar membrane. High-frequency sounds, for example, cause maximum vibration near the stirrup end of the basilar membrane. Lower-frequency sounds cause maximum vibration at the opposite end. Thus, different pitches excite different hair cells along the basilar membrane. Higher-pitched sounds are interpreted according to the place where the hair cells are most active.

Can Snakes Hear? Snakes have functional inner ears, but they don't have outer ears. So how do snakes hear? With their jaws. When a desert viper rests its head on the ground, a bone in its jaw picks up minute vibrations in the sand. From the jaw, these vibrations are transmitted along a chain of tiny bones to the cochlea in the inner ear, allowing the snake to "hear" the faint footsteps of a mouse or other prey (Freidel & others, 2008). Similarly, in some species of salamanders, frogs, toads, and lizards, vibrations in the air are picked up by the lungs and transmitted to functional inner ears.

Both frequency theory and place theory are involved in explaining our discrimination of pitch. Frequency theory helps explain our discrimination of frequencies lower than 500 hertz. Place theory helps explain our discrimination of higher-pitched sounds. For intermediate frequencies or midrange pitches, both place and frequency are involved.

The Chemical and Body Senses

Smell, Taste, Touch, and Position

Key Theme

- **Chemical stimuli produce the sensations of smell and taste, while pressure and other stimuli are involved in touch, pain, position, and balance sensations.**

Key Questions

- **How do airborne molecules result in the sensation of an odor?**
- **What are the primary tastes, and how does the sensation of taste arise?**
- **How do fast and slow pain systems differ, and what is the gate-control theory of pain?**
- **How are body sensations of movement, position, and balance produced?**

The senses of smell and taste are closely linked. If you've ever temporarily lost your sense of smell because of a bad cold, you've probably noticed that your sense of taste was also disrupted. Even a hot fudge sundae tastes bland.

Smell and taste are linked in other ways, too. Unlike vision and hearing, which involve sensitivity to different forms of energy, the sensory receptors for taste and smell are specialized to respond to different types of *chemical* substances. That's why smell, or **olfaction,** and taste, or **gustation,** are sometimes called the "chemical senses" (Mombaerts, 2004).

People can get along quite well without a sense of smell. A surprisingly large number of people are unable to smell specific odors or lack a sense of smell completely, a condition called *anosmia*. Fortunately, humans gather most of their information about the world through vision and hearing. However, many animal species depend on chemical signals as their primary source of information.

Even for humans, smell and taste can provide important information about the environment. Tastes help us determine whether a particular substance is to be savored or spat out. Smells, such as the odor of a smoldering fire, leaking gas, or spoiled food, alert us to potential dangers.

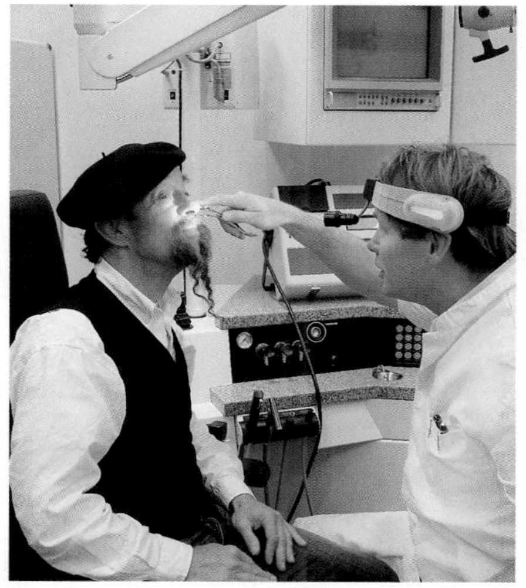

Smell, Taste, and the Eight Million Dollar Nose According to Dutch winemaker Ilja Gort, "Tasting wine is something you do with your nose, not your mouth." Wine connoisseurs are keenly aware of the fact that the senses of smell and taste are closely intertwined. Specialized receptors in the nasal passages are able to detect the subtle aromas that differentiate among fine wines (Simons & Noble, 2003). After hearing about a man who lost his sense of smell in an auto accident, Dutch winemaker Ilja Gort approached Lloyd's of London about insuring his nose—for $8 million. After a thorough examination, Lloyd's agreed, but with a few conditions. Gort is not allowed to box, ride a motorcycle, or have his moustache trimmed by anyone other than an experienced barber.

olfactory bulb
(ole-FACK-toe-ree) The enlarged ending of the olfactory cortex at the front of the brain where the sensation of smell is registered.

How We Smell (Don't Answer That!)

The sensory stimuli that produce our sensation of an odor are *molecules in the air.* These airborne molecules are emitted by the substance we are smelling. We inhale them through the nose and through the opening in the palate at the back of the throat. In the nose, the molecules encounter millions of *olfactory receptor cells* located high in the nasal cavity.

Unlike the sensory receptors for hearing and vision, the olfactory receptors are constantly being replaced. Each cell lasts for only about 30 to 60 days. Neuroscientists Linda Buck and Richard Axel won the 2004 Nobel Prize for their identification of the odor receptors that are present on the hairlike fibers of the olfactory neurons. Like synaptic receptors, each odor receptor seems to be specialized to respond to molecules of a different chemical structure. When these olfactory receptor cells are stimulated by the airborne molecules, the stimulation is converted into neural messages that pass along their axons, bundles of which make up the *olfactory nerve.*

So far, hundreds of different odor receptors have been identified (Mombaerts, 2004). We don't have a separate receptor for each of the estimated 10,000 different odors that we can detect, however. Rather, each receptor is like a letter in an olfactory alphabet. Just as different combinations of letters in the alphabet are used to produce recognizable words, different combinations of olfactory receptors produce the sensation of distinct odors. Thus, the airborne molecules activate specific combinations of receptors. In turn, the brain identifies an odor by interpreting the *pattern* of olfactory receptors that are stimulated (Shepherd, 2006).

As shown in Figure 3.9, the olfactory nerves directly connect to the **olfactory bulb** in the brain, which is actually the enlarged ending of the *olfactory cortex* at the front of the brain. Axons from the olfactory bulb form the *olfactory tract.* These neural pathways project to different brain areas, including the temporal lobe and structures in the limbic system (Shepherd, 2006). The projections to the *temporal lobe* are thought to be part of the neural pathway involved in our conscious recognition of smells. The projections to the *limbic system* are thought to regulate our emotional response to odors.

The direct connection of olfactory receptor cells to areas of the cortex and limbic system is unique to our sense of smell. As discussed in Chapter 2, all other bodily

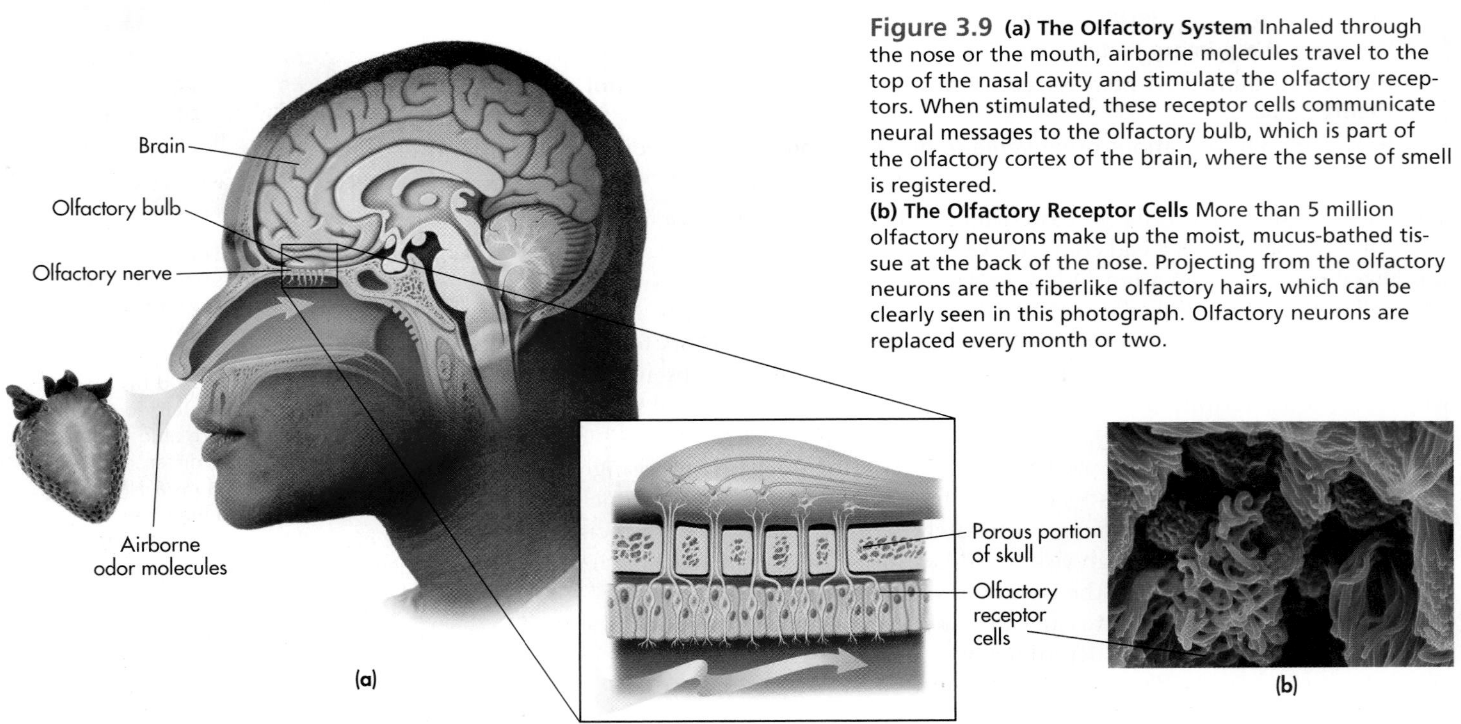

Figure 3.9 **(a) The Olfactory System** Inhaled through the nose or the mouth, airborne molecules travel to the top of the nasal cavity and stimulate the olfactory receptors. When stimulated, these receptor cells communicate neural messages to the olfactory bulb, which is part of the olfactory cortex of the brain, where the sense of smell is registered.
(b) The Olfactory Receptor Cells More than 5 million olfactory neurons make up the moist, mucus-bathed tissue at the back of the nose. Projecting from the olfactory neurons are the fiberlike olfactory hairs, which can be clearly seen in this photograph. Olfactory neurons are replaced every month or two.

IN FOCUS

Do Pheromones Influence Human Behavior?

Many animals communicate by releasing **pheromones,** chemical signals that provide information about social and sexual status to other members of the same species (Dulac & Torello, 2003). Pheromones may mark territories and serve as warning signals to other members of the same species. Ants use pheromones to mark trails for other ants, as do snakes and snails. Pheromones are also extremely important in regulating sexual attraction, mating, and reproductive behavior in many animals (Wyatt, 2009). A lusty male cabbage moth, for example, can detect pheromones released from a sexually receptive female cabbage moth that is several miles away.

Do humans produce pheromones as other animals do? The best evidence for the existence of human pheromones comes from studies of the female menstrual cycle by University of Chicago biopsychologist Martha McClintock (1992). While still a college student, McClintock (1971) set out to scientifically investigate the folk notion that women who live in the same dorm eventually develop synchronized menstrual periods. McClintock was able to show that the more time women spent together, the more likely their cycles were to be in sync.

Later research showed that smelling an unknown chemical substance in underarm sweat from female donors synchronized the recipients' menstrual cycles with the donors' cycles (Preti & others, 1986; Stern & McClintock, 1998).

Since this finding, McClintock and her co-researchers have made a number of discoveries in their quest to identify human pheromones, which they prefer to call *human chemosignals.* Their search has narrowed to chemicals found in steroid compounds that are naturally produced by the human body and found in sweat, armpit hair, blood, and semen. In one study, Suma Jacob and McClintock (2000) found that exposure to the male or the female steroid helped women maintain a positive mood after spending two hours filling out a tedious, frustrating questionnaire. Men's moods, however, tended to deteriorate after exposure to either steroid. PET scans of the women showed that exposure to the steroid increased activity in several key brain areas involved in emotion and attention, including the prefrontal cortex, amygdala, and cerebellum (Jacob & others, 2001).

The Scent of Attraction Some perfume manufacturers claim that their products contain human pheromones that will make you "irresistible" to members of the opposite sex. But is there any evidence that pheromones affect human sexual attraction?

No study as yet has shown that human chemosignals can function as an irresistible sexual signal (Brennan & Zufall, 2006). Rather than producing sexual attraction, McClintock (2001) believes, it's more likely that human chemosignals affect mood and emotional states.

Confirming this view, a later study by McClintock's lab showed that exposure to a chemical compound in the perspiration of breast-feeding mothers significantly increased sexual motivation in other, non-breast-feeding women (Spencer & others, 2004). The study's authors speculate that the presence of breast-feeding women acts as a social signal—an indicator that the social and physical environment is one in which pregnancy and breast-feeding will be supported.

Thus, rather than triggering specific behaviors, including sexual behavior, human chemosignals may be social signals, subliminally affecting social interactions and relationships in ways that we don't consciously recognize.

sensations are first processed in the thalamus before being relayed to the higher brain centers in the cortex. Olfactory neurons are unique in another way, too. They are the only neurons that *directly* link the brain and the outside world. The axons of the sensory neurons that are located in your nose extend directly into your brain!

As with the other senses, we experience sensory adaptation to odors when exposed to them for a period of time. In general, we reach maximum adaptation to an odor in less than a minute. We continue to smell the odor, but we have become about 70 percent less sensitive to it.

Olfactory function tends to decline with age. About half of those aged 65 to 80 have a significant loss of olfactory function, a number that increases to two-thirds of people aged 80 and above (Rawson, 2006). At any age, air pollution, smoking, and exposure to some industrial chemicals can decrease the ability to smell. Loss of olfactory function is also associated with several diseases—including Parkinson's disease, schizophrenia, and multiple sclerosis—and may be an early marker of Alzheimer's disease (Devanand & others, 2000).

pheromones
Chemical signals released by an animal that communicate information and affect the behavior of other animals of the same species.

Can Humans Track a Scent? Dogs are famous for their ability to track a scent. Humans? Not so much. However, it turns out that people are better trackers than you might think. Berkeley scientist Jess Porter and colleagues (2007) embedded a long line of chocolate-scented twine into the ground and then tested whether human undergraduates could find and track the scent using their olfactory sense alone. To block all other sensory cues, the college students wore opaque eye masks, earmuffs, and thick knee pads, elbow pads, and work gloves. Although the human trackers were able to locate and follow the trail, their average speed was only about one inch per second. However, after only a few days of practice, the trackers' speed doubled, improving to two inches per second.

Although humans are highly sensitive to odors, many animals display even greater sensitivity. Dogs, for example, have about 200 million olfactory receptor cells, compared with the approximately 10 million receptors that humans have. However, humans are more sensitive to smell than most people realize (Shepherd, 2004).

In fact, people can train their sense of smell (see photo). In a fascinating study, Wen Li and her colleagues (2006) showed that with repeated exposure to a particular class of odors (floral or minty), participants improved in their ability to distinguish subtle differences among the different scents. They also became more sensitive to the odors. These behavioral changes were accompanied by changes in the brain: fMRI scans showed increased activation in the olfactory cortex. The moral? Stop and smell the flowers often enough, and you will improve your ability to discriminate a geranium from a marigold.

Taste

Our sense of taste, or *gustation*, results from the stimulation of special receptors in the mouth. The stimuli that produce the sensation of taste are chemical substances in whatever you eat or drink. These substances are dissolved by saliva, allowing the chemicals to activate the **taste buds.** Each taste bud contains about 50 receptor cells that are specialized for taste.

The surface of the tongue is covered with thousands of little bumps with grooves in between (see Figure 3.10). These grooves are lined with the taste buds. Taste

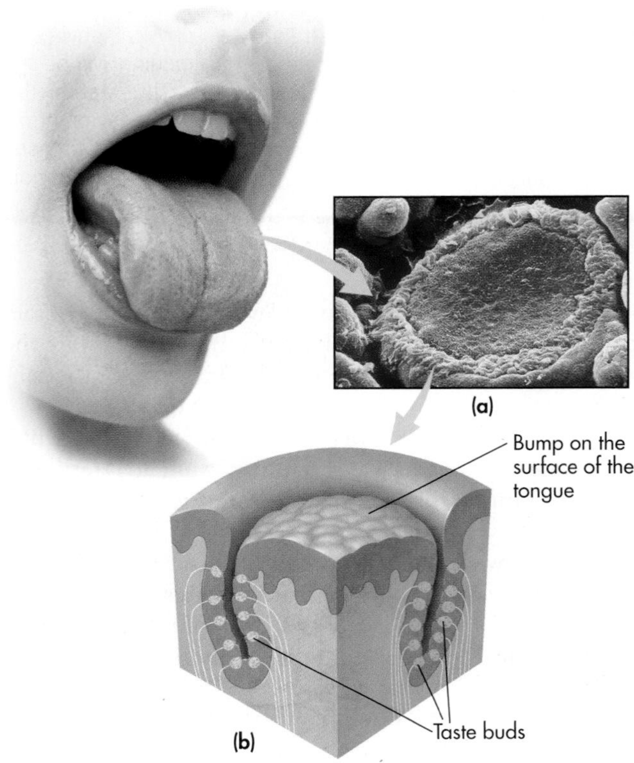

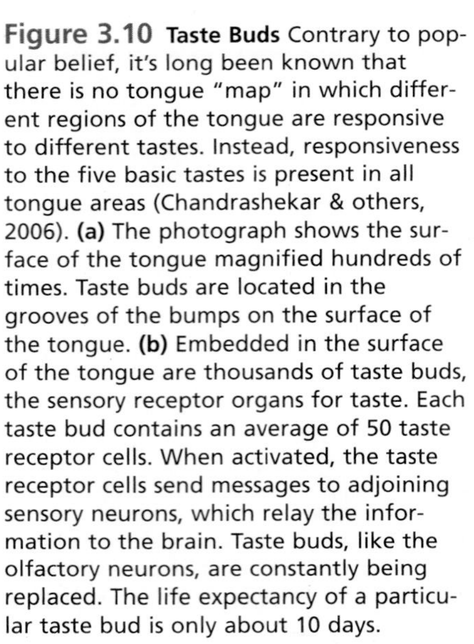

Figure 3.10 Taste Buds Contrary to popular belief, it's long been known that there is no tongue "map" in which different regions of the tongue are responsive to different tastes. Instead, responsiveness to the five basic tastes is present in all tongue areas (Chandrashekar & others, 2006). **(a)** The photograph shows the surface of the tongue magnified hundreds of times. Taste buds are located in the grooves of the bumps on the surface of the tongue. **(b)** Embedded in the surface of the tongue are thousands of taste buds, the sensory receptor organs for taste. Each taste bud contains an average of 50 taste receptor cells. When activated, the taste receptor cells send messages to adjoining sensory neurons, which relay the information to the brain. Taste buds, like the olfactory neurons, are constantly being replaced. The life expectancy of a particular taste bud is only about 10 days.

buds are also located on the insides of your cheeks, on the roof of your mouth, and in your throat. Each taste bud shows maximum sensitivity to one particular taste and lesser sensitivity to other tastes (Chandrashekar & others, 2006). When activated, special receptor cells in the taste buds send neural messages along pathways to the thalamus in the brain. In turn, the thalamus directs the information to several regions in the cortex (Shepherd, 2006).

There were long thought to be four basic taste categories: sweet, salty, sour, and bitter. However, scientists identified the receptor cells for a fifth basic taste, *umami* (Chaudhari & others, 2000). Loosely translated, *umami* means "yummy" or "delicious" in Japanese. *Umami* is the distinctive taste of monosodium glutamate and is associated with meat and other protein-rich foods. It's also responsible for the savory flavor of Parmesan and other aged cheeses, mushrooms, and seaweed.

Expensive Taste Nominated for several Oscars, *Sideways* told the story of a wine connoisseur and his friend on a road trip through California wine country, tasting different vintages as they traveled from one vineyard to another. Although wine experts may be able to discern subtle differences among wines, amateurs may not be as objective. To determine the effect of *price* on perceived quality, Hilke Plassmann and her colleagues (2008) asked participants to decide which tasted better: wine poured from a bottle labeled as costing $90 or from a bottle that cost $10. Although the wine in the two bottles was identical, participants overwhelmingly thought the $90 bottle tasted better. Their subjective, verbal rating was confirmed by brain scans: Activity in a brain region associated with pleasant sensations was much higher when they sipped the wine that they thought cost $90 a bottle than when they sipped the same wine from a bottle that supposedly cost $10. The moral: Many different factors affect taste, not the least of which is your expectation of just how good something is likely to taste.

From an evolutionary view, these five basic tastes supply the information we need to seek out nutrient-rich foods and avoid potentially hazardous substances (Chandrashekar & others, 2006). Sweet tastes attract us to energy-rich foods, *umami* to protein-rich nutrients. Bitter or sour tastes warn us to avoid many toxic or poisonous substances. Sensitivity to salty-tasting substances helps us regulate the balance of electrolytes in our diets.

Most tastes are complex and result from the activation of different combinations of basic taste receptors. Taste is just one aspect of *flavor,* which involves several sensations, including the aroma, temperature, texture, and appearance of food (Shepherd, 2006).

The Skin and Body Senses

While vision, hearing, smell, and taste provide you with important information about your environment, another group of senses provides you with information that comes from a source much closer to home: your own body. In this section, we'll first consider the *skin senses,* which provide essential information about your physical status and your physical interaction with objects in your environment. We'll next consider the *body senses,* which keep you informed as to your position and orientation in space.

Touch

We usually don't think of our skin as a sense organ. But the skin is in fact the largest and heaviest sense organ. The skin of an average adult covers about 20 square feet of surface area and weighs about six pounds.

There are many different kinds of sensory receptors in the skin. Some of these sensory receptors are specialized to respond to just one kind of stimulus, such as pressure, warmth, or cold. Other skin receptors respond to more than one type of stimulus (Patapoutian & others, 2003).

One important receptor involved with the sense of touch, called the *Pacinian corpuscle,* is located beneath the skin. When stimulated by pressure, the Pacinian corpuscle converts the stimulation into a neural message that is relayed to the brain. If a pressure is constant, sensory adaptation takes place. The Pacinian corpuscle either reduces the number of signals sent or quits responding altogether (which is fortunate, or you'd be unable to forget the fact that you're wearing underwear).

Sensory receptors are distributed unevenly among different areas of the body, which is why sensitivity to touch and temperature varies from one area of the body to another. Your hands, face, and lips, for example, are much more sensitive to touch than are your back, arms, and legs. That's because your hands, face, and lips are much more densely packed with sensory receptors.

taste buds
The specialized sensory receptors for taste that are located on the tongue and inside the mouth and throat.

Pain

From the sharp sting of a paper cut to the dull ache of a throbbing headache, a wide variety of stimuli can trigger pain. **Pain** can be defined as an unpleasant sensory and emotional experience associated with actual or potential tissue damage. As unpleasant as it can be, pain helps you survive. Pain warns you about potential or actual injury, prompting you to pay attention and stop what you are doing. Sudden pain can trigger the withdrawal reflex—you jerk back from the object or stimulus that is injuring you. (We discussed the withdrawal reflex and other spinal reflexes in Chapter 2.)

Your body's pain receptors are called **nociceptors.** Nociceptors are actually small sensory fibers, called *free nerve endings,* in the skin, muscles, or internal organs. You have millions of nociceptors throughout your body, mostly in your skin (see Table 3.3). For example, your fingertips may have as many as 1,200 nociceptors per square inch. Your muscles and joints have fewer nociceptors, and your internal organs have the smallest number of nociceptors.

Table 3.3

Sensitivity of Different Body Areas to Pain

Most Sensitive	Least Sensitive
Back of the knee	Tip of the nose
Neck region	Sole of the foot
Bend of the elbow	Ball of the thumb

Source: Geldard (1972).

Fast and Slow Pain Systems To help illustrate pain pathways, imagine this scene: Don was trying to close a stuck window in our old house. As he wrapped his left hand on the top of the window and used his right hand to push down the lower edge, it suddenly came free and slammed shut, jamming his left fingertips between the upper and lower windows. As pain shot through him, he jerked the window back up to dislodge his mangled fingers, then headed to the kitchen for ice.

Don took little comfort in knowing that his injury had triggered two types of nociceptors: *A-delta fibers* and *C fibers.* The myelinated *A-delta fibers* represent the fast pain system. A-delta fibers transmit the sharp, intense, but short-lived pain of the immediate injury. The smaller, unmyelinated *C fibers* represent the slow pain system. As the sharp pain subsides, C fibers transmit the longer-lasting throbbing, burning pain of the injury (Hunt & Mantyh, 2001). The throbbing pain carried by the C fibers gradually diminishes as a wound heals over a period of days or weeks.

As shown in Figure 3.11, both the fast A-delta fibers and the slow C fibers transmit their messages to the spinal cord. Several neurotransmitters are involved in processing pain signals, but most C fibers produce a pain enhancer called substance P. **Substance P** stimulates free nerve endings at the site of the injury and also increases pain messages within the spinal cord (Rosenkranz, 2007).

Most of these messages from C fibers and A-delta fibers cross to the other side of the spinal cord, then to the brain. The fast pain messages travel to the thalamus, then to the somatosensory cortex, where the sensory aspects of the pain message are interpreted, such as the location and intensity of the pain. Interestingly, morphine and other opiates have virtually no effect on the fast pain system.

In contrast, slow pain messages follow a different route in the brain. From the spinal cord, the slow pain messages travel first to the hypothalamus and thalamus, and then to limbic system structures, such as the amygdala. Its connections to the limbic system suggest that the slow pain system is more involved in the emotional aspects of pain. Morphine and other opiates very effectively block painful sensations in the slow pain system (Lu & others, 2004).

Factors That Influence Pain "Gates" There is considerable individual variation in the experience of pain. When sensory pain signals reach the brain, the sensory information is integrated with psychological and situational information. According to the **gate-control theory of pain,** depending on how the brain interprets the pain experience, it regulates pain by sending signals down the spinal cord that either open or close pain "gates," or pathways (Melzack & Wall, 1965, 1996). If, because of psychological, social, or situational factors, the brain signals the gates to open, pain is experienced or intensified. If for any of the same reasons the brain signals the gates to close, pain is reduced.

Anxiety, fear, and a sense of helplessness are just a few of the psychological factors that can intensify the experience of pain. Positive emotions, laughter, distraction, and a sense of control can reduce the perception of pain. As one example, consider the athlete who has conditioned himself to minimize pain during competition. The experience of pain is also influenced by genetic factors, social and situational

pain
The unpleasant sensation of physical discomfort or suffering that can occur in varying degrees of intensity.

nociceptors
Specialized sensory receptors for pain that are found in the skin, muscles, and internal organs.

substance P
A neurotransmitter that is involved in the transmission of pain messages to the brain.

gate-control theory of pain
The theory that pain is a product of both physiological and psychological factors that cause spinal gates to open and relay patterns of intense stimulation to the brain, which perceives them as pain.

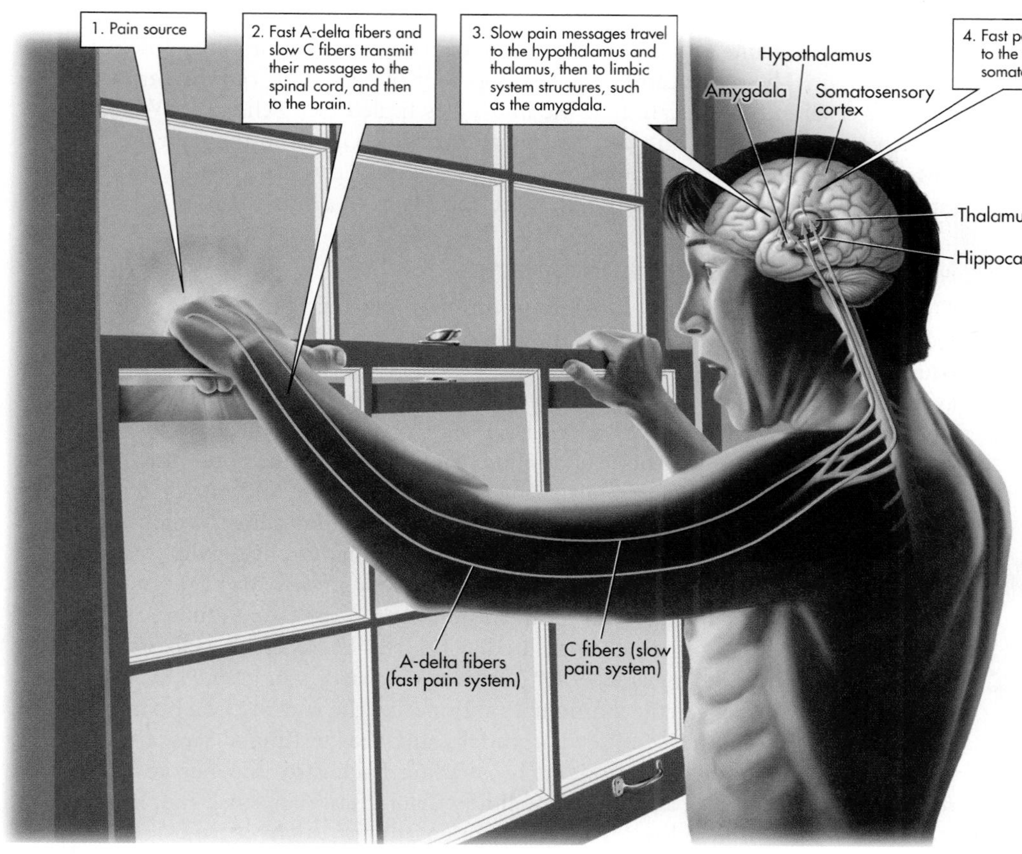

Figure 3.11 Fast and Slow Pain Pathways The fast pain pathway consists of myelinated A-delta fibers, shown in red, which project first to the thalamus and then on to the somatosensory cortex. Signals carried along this pathway produce the sensory aspects of pain—the sharp but short-lived pain of an immediate injury. In contrast, the slow pain pathway consists of unmyelinated C fibers, shown in blue. The slow pain pathway is much more involved with the emotional aspects of pain. The C fibers project to the thalamus and hypothalamus, then to limbic system structures, including the amygdala.

factors, and cultural learning experiences about the meaning of pain and how people should react to it (Gatchel & others, 2007; Raichle & others, 2007). In the chapter section on Enhancing Well-Being with Psychology, we discuss some helpful strategies that you can use to minimize pain.

Psychological factors also influence the release of *endorphins* and *enkephalins,* the body's natural painkillers (see Chapter 2). Endorphins and enkephalins are produced in the brain and spinal cord. They are released as part of the body's overall response to physical pain or stress. In the brain and spinal cord, endorphins and enkephalins inhibit the transmission of pain signals, including the release of substance P.

Red-Headed Women and Pain Gender differences in pain have been extensively researched (see Fillingim, 2000). In general, women are more sensitive to pain than men. Studies also show that women respond better than men to some morphine-like pain medications called "kappa opioids" (Gear & others, 1996). Psychologist Jeffrey Mogil and his colleagues (2003) found that a gene associated with red hair and fair skin was implicated in the response to these pain medications. Women with two copies of this gene, like the three sisters in the photo here, experience much greater pain relief from kappa opioids than men or other women.

Sensitization: Unwarranted Pain One of the most frustrating aspects of pain management is that it can continue even after an injury has healed, such as after recovering from a spinal cord injury or severe burns. A striking example of this phenomenon is *phantom limb pain,* in which a person continues to experience intense painful sensations in a limb that has been amputated (Flor & others, 2006).

How can phantom limb pain be explained? Basically, the neurons involved in processing the pain signals undergo *sensitization*. Earlier in the chapter, we discussed *sensory adaptation,* in which sensory receptors become gradually less responsive to steady stimulation over time. Sensitization is the opposite of adaptation. In sensitization, pain pathways in the brain become increasingly *more* responsive over time. It's like a broken volume control knob on your stereo that you can turn up, but not down or off.

kinesthetic sense
(kin-ess-THET-ick) The technical name for the sense of location and position of body parts in relation to one another.

proprioceptors
(pro-pree-oh-SEP-ters) Sensory receptors, located in the muscles and joints, that provide information about body position and movement.

vestibular sense
(vess-TIB-you-ler) The technical name for the sense of balance, or equilibrium.

bottom-up processing
Information processing that emphasizes the importance of the sensory receptors in detecting the basic features of a stimulus in the process of recognizing a whole pattern; analysis that moves from the parts to the whole; also called *data-driven processing.*

top-down processing
Information processing that emphasizes the importance of the observer's knowledge, expectations, and other cognitive processes in arriving at meaningful perceptions; analysis that moves from the whole to the parts; also called *conceptually driven processing.*

As the pain circuits undergo sensitization, pain begins to occur in the absence of any sensory input. The result can be the development of persistent, *chronic pain* that continues after all indications are that the injury has healed (see Scholz & Woolf, 2002). In the case of phantom limb pain, sensitization has occurred in the pain transmission pathways from the site of the amputation. The sensitized pathways produce painful sensations that mentally feel as though they are coming from a limb that is no longer there.

Movement, Position, and Balance

The phone rings. Without looking up from your textbook, you reach for the receiver, pick it up, and guide it to the side of your head. You have just demonstrated your **kinesthetic sense**—the sense that involves the location and position of body parts in relation to one another. (The word *kinesthetics* literally means "feelings of motion.") The kinesthetic sense involves specialized sensory neurons, called **proprioceptors,** which are located in the muscles and joints. The proprioceptors constantly communicate information to the brain about changes in body position and muscle tension.

Closely related to the kinesthetic sense is the **vestibular sense,** which provides a sense of balance, or equilibrium, by responding to changes in gravity, motion, and body position. The two sources of vestibular sensory information, the *semicircular canals* and the *vestibular sacs,* are both located in the ear (see Figure 3.12). These structures are filled with fluid and lined with hairlike receptor cells that shift in response to motion, changes in body position, or changes in gravity.

When you experience environmental motion, like the rocking of a boat in choppy water, the fluids in the semicircular canals and the vestibular sacs are affected. Changes in your body's position, such as falling backward in a heroic attempt to return a volleyball serve, also affect the fluids. Your vestibular sense supplies the critical information that allows you to compensate for such changes and quickly reestablish your sense of balance.

Maintaining equilibrium also involves information from other senses, particularly vision. Under normal circumstances, this works to our advantage. However, when information from the eyes conflicts with information from the vestibular system, the result can be dizziness, disorientation, and nausea. These are the symptoms commonly experienced in motion sickness, the bane of many travelers in cars, on planes, on boats, and even in space. One strategy that can be used to combat motion sickness is to minimize sensory conflicts by focusing on a distant point or an object that is fixed, such as the horizon.

In the first part of this chapter, we've described how the body's senses respond to stimuli in the environment. Table 3.4 summarizes these different sensory systems. To make use of this raw sensory data, the brain must organize and interpret the data and relate them to existing knowledge. Next, we'll look at the process of perception—how we make sense out of the information that we receive from our environment.

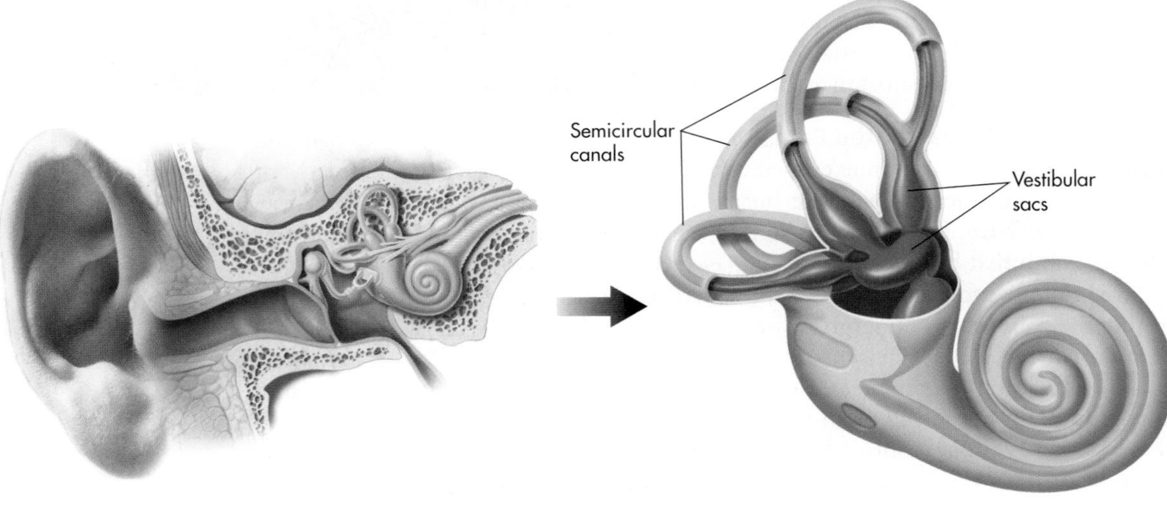

Figure 3.12 The Vestibular Sense The vestibular sense provides our sense of balance, or equilibrium. Shown here are the two sources of vestibular sensory information, both located in the ear: the semicircular canals and the vestibular sacs. Both structures are filled with fluids that shift in response to changes in body position, gravity, or motion.

Table 3.4

Summary Table of the Senses

Sense	Stimulus	Sense Organ	Sensory Receptor Cells
Hearing (audition)	Sound waves	Ear	Hair cells in cochlea
Vision	Light waves	Eye	Rods and cones in retina
Color vision	Different wavelengths of light	Eye	Cones in retina
Smell (olfaction)	Airborne odor molecules	Nose	Hairlike receptor cells at top of nasal cavity
Taste (gustation)	Chemicals dissolved in saliva	Mouth	Taste buds
Touch	Pressure	Skin	Pacinian corpuscle
Pain	Tissue injury or damage; varied	Skin, muscles, and organs	Nociceptors
Movement (kinesthetic sense)	Movement of the body	None; muscle and joint tissue	Proprioceptors in muscle and joint tissue
Balance (vestibular sense)	Changes in position, gravity	Semicircular canals and vestibular sacs	Hairlike receptor cells in semicircular canals and vestibular sacs

Perception

Key Theme

- **Perception refers to the process of integrating, organizing, and interpreting sensory information into meaningful representations.**

Key Questions

- **What are bottom-up and top-down processing, and how do they differ?**
- **What is Gestalt psychology?**
- **What Gestalt principles explain how we recieve objects and their relationship to their surroundings?**

As we've seen, our senses are constantly registering a diverse range of stimuli from the environment and transmitting that information to the brain. But to make use of this raw sensory data, we must organize, interpret, and relate the data to existing knowledge.

Psychologists sometimes refer to this flow of sensory data from the sensory receptors to the brain as **bottom-up processing.** Also called *data-driven processing,* bottom-up processing is often at work when we're confronted with an ambiguous stimulus. For example, imagine trying to assemble a jigsaw puzzle one piece at a time, without knowing what the final picture will be. To accomplish this task, you would work with the individual puzzle pieces to build the image from the "bottom up," that is, from its constituent parts.

But as we interact with our environment, many of our perceptions are shaped by **top-down processing,** which is also referred to as *conceptually driven processing.* Top-down processing occurs when we draw on our knowledge, experiences, expectations, and other cognitive processes to arrive at meaningful perceptions, such as people or objects in a particular context.

Both top-down and bottom-up processing are involved in our everyday perceptions. As a simple illustration, look at the photograph (right), which sits on Don's desk. Top-down processing was involved as you reached a number of perceptual conclusions about the image. You quickly perceived a little girl holding a black cat—our daughter Laura when she was three, holding her cat, Nubbin. You also perceived a child as a whole object even though the cat is actually blocking a good portion of the view of Laura.

But now look at the background in the photograph, which is more ambiguous. Deciphering these images involves both bottom-up and top-down processing. Bottom-up processes help you determine that behind the little girl looms a large, irregularly shaped, dark green object with brightly colored splotches on it. But what is it?

Organizing Sensations into Meaningful Perceptions With virtually no conscious effort, the psychological process of perception allows you to integrate, organize, and interpret the lines, colors, and contours in this image as meaningful objects—a laughing child holding a panicky black cat in front of a Christmas tree. How did you reach those perceptual conclusions?

CULTURE AND HUMAN BEHAVIOR

Ways of Seeing

Do people in different cultures perceive the world differently? In Chapter 1, we described two types of cultures. Unlike people in *individualistic* cultures, who tend to emphasize independence, people in *collectivistic* cultures see humans as being enmeshed in complex relationships. This social perspective is especially pronounced in the East Asian cultures of Korea, Japan, and China, where a person's sense of self is highly dependent upon his or her social context (Nisbett & Masuda, 2003). Consequently, East Asians pay much closer attention to the social context in which their own actions, and the actions of others, occur (Chua & others, 2005).

The Cultural Eye of the Beholder

Researcher Hannah Faye Chua and her colleagues (2005) have shown that these cultural differences in social perspective influence visual perception and memory. Study the photo on the right for a few seconds. Was most of your attention focused on the tiger? Or was it focused on the tiger's surroundings?

Which do you notice—the tiger or its rocky surroundings?

Using sophisticated eye-tracking equipment, Chua and her colleagues monitored the eye movements of U.S. and Chinese students while they looked at similar photographs that showed a single focal object against a realistic, complex background. The results showed that their eye movements differed: The U.S. students looked sooner and longer at the focal object in the foreground than the Chinese students. In contrast, the Chinese students spent more time looking at the background than the U. S. students. And, the Chinese were also less likely to recognize the foreground objects when they were placed in front of a new background.

According to Chua and her colleagues (2005), the results reflect the more "holistic" perceptual style that characterizes collectivistic cultures. Rather than separating the object from its background, the Chinese students tended to see—and remember—object and background as a single perceptual image. Other research has produced similar findings (Miyamoto & others, 2006; Nisbett & Masuda, 2003).

Cultural Comfort Zones and Brain Functioning

Do these cultural differences in social and perceptual style influence brain function? Psychologist Trey Hedden and his colleagues (2008) compared brain functioning in East Asian and U.S. participants while they made rapid perceptual judgments comparing two images of a square with an embedded line as shown in this image at right.

The *relative* task involved determining if the lines in the two images were in the same proportion to the surrounding squares. The *absolute* task involved determining whether the two lines were the same absolute length, regardless of the size of the squares (see figure). Each participant made these judgments while their brain activity was tracked by an fMRI scanner.

Both groups were equally proficient at the task and used the same brain regions in making the simple perceptual judgments. However, the *pattern* of brain activation differed.

The individualistic U. S. participants showed greater brain activation while making relative judgments, meaning they had to exert more mental effort. The collectivistic East Asians showed the opposite pattern. The East Asians devoted greater brain effort to making absolute judgments that required them to ignore the context. Essentially, all participants had to work harder at making perceptual judgments that were outside their cultural comfort zones.

The bottom line? People from different cultures use the same neural processes to make perceptual judgments. But, as John Gabrieli (2008) points out, "they are trained to use them in different ways, and it's the culture that does the training. The way in which the brain responds to these simple drawings reflects, in a predictable way, how the individual thinks about independent or interdependent social relationships." People from different cultures may not literally see the world differently—but they notice different things and think differently about what they *do* see.

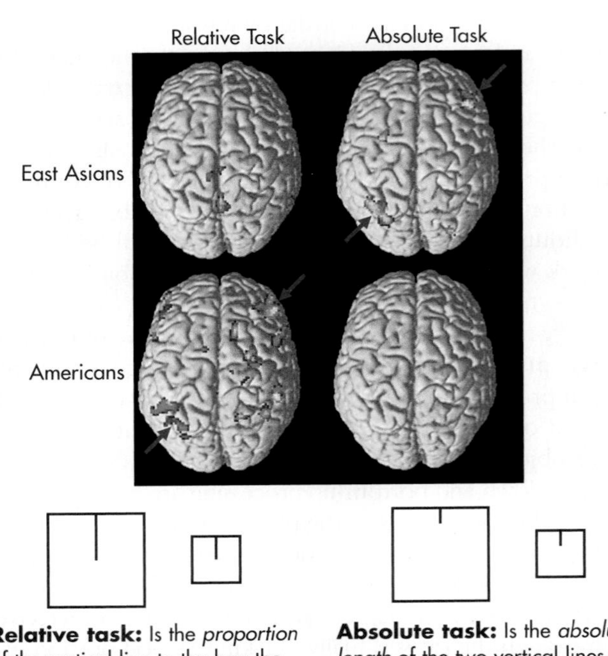

Relative task: Is the *proportion* of the vertical line to the box the same in both images?

Absolute task: Is the *absolute length* of the two vertical lines the same?

To identify the mysterious object, you must interpret the sensory data. Top-down processes help you identify the large green blotch as a Christmas tree—a conclusion that you probably would *not* reach if you had no familiarity with the way many Americans celebrate the Christmas holiday. The Christmas tree branches, ornaments, and lights are just fuzzy images, but other images work as clues—a happy child, a stuffed bear with a red-and-white stocking cap. Learning experiences create a conceptual knowledge base from which we can identify and interpret many objects, including kids, cats, and Christmas trees.

Clearly, bottom-up and top-down processing are both necessary to explain how we arrive at perceptual conclusions. But whether we are using bottom-up or top-down processing, a useful way to think about perception is to consider the basic perceptual questions we must answer in order to survive. We exist in an ever-changing environment that is filled with objects that may be standing still or moving, just like ourselves. Whether it's a bulldozer or a bowling ball, we need to be able to identify objects, locate objects in space, and, if they are moving, track their motion. Thus, our perceptual processes must help us organize our sensations to answer three basic, important questions: (1) What is it? (2) How far away is it? and (3) Where is it going?

In the next few sections, we will look at what psychologists have learned about the principles we use to answer these perceptual questions. Much of our discussion reflects the work of an early school of psychology called **Gestalt psychology,** which was founded by German psychologist **Max Wertheimer** in the early 1900s. The Gestalt psychologists emphasized that we perceive whole objects or figures *(gestalts)* rather than isolated bits and pieces of sensory information. Roughly translated, the German word *Gestalt* means a unified whole, form, or shape. Although the Gestalt school of psychology no longer formally exists, the pioneering work of the Gestalt psychologists established many basic perceptual principles (S. Palmer, 2002).

Max Wertheimer (1880–1943) Arguing that the whole is always greater than the sum of its parts, Wertheimer founded Gestalt psychology. Wertheimer and other Gestalt psychologists began by studying the principles of perception but later extended their approach to other areas of psychology.

Gestalt psychology
(geh-SHTALT) A school of psychology founded in Germany in the early 1900s that maintained that our sensations are actively processed according to consistent perceptual rules that result in meaningful whole perceptions, or *gestalts.*

figure–ground relationship
A Gestalt principle of perceptual organization that states that we automatically separate the elements of a perception into the feature that clearly stands out (the figure) and its less distinct background (the ground).

The Perception of Shape

What Is It?

When you look around your world, you don't see random edges, curves, colors, or splotches of light and dark. Rather, you see countless distinct objects against a variety of backgrounds. Although to some degree we rely on size, color, and texture to determine what an object might be, we rely primarily on an object's *shape* to identify it.

Figure–Ground Relationship

How do we organize our perceptions so that we see an object as separate from other objects? The early Gestalt psychologists identified an important perceptual principle called the **figure–ground relationship,** which describes how this works. When we view a scene, we automatically separate the elements of that scene into the *figure,* which is the main element of the scene, and the *ground,* which is its background.

You can experience the figure–ground relationship by looking at a coffee cup on a table. The coffee cup is the figure, and the table is the ground. Notice that usually the figure has a definite shape, tends to stand out clearly, and is perceptually meaningful in some way. In contrast, the ground tends to be less clearly defined, even fuzzy, and usually appears to be behind and farther away than the figure.

Survival and Figure–Ground Relationships The natural camouflage that protects some animals, like this Brazilian moth, from predators illustrates the importance of figure–ground relationships in survival. When an animal's coloring and markings blend with its background, a predator cannot distinguish the animal (the *figure*) from its surroundings (the *ground*). In much the same way, military personnel and equipment are often concealed from enemy forces by clothing or tarps that are designed to blend in with the terrain, whether it be jungle, desert, forest, or snowy mountain range.

CRITICAL THINKING

ESP: Can Perception Occur Without Sensation?

ESP, or **extrasensory perception,** means the detection of information by some means other than through the normal processes of sensation.

Do you believe in ESP? If you do, you're not alone. Recent surveys conducted by the Associated Press and the Gallup Poll have found that close to 50 percent of American adults believe in ESP, including telepathy and clairvoyance (Fram, 2007; Moore, 2005). Forms of ESP include:

- *Telepathy*—direct communication between the minds of two individuals
- *Clairvoyance*—the perception of a remote object or event, such as sensing that a friend has been injured in a car accident
- *Psychokinesis*—the ability to influence a physical object, process, or event, such as bending a key or stopping a clock, without touching it
- *Precognition*—the ability to predict future events

The general term for such unusual abilities is *paranormal phenomena. Paranormal* means "outside the range of normal experience." Thus, these phenomena cannot be explained by known laws of science and nature. **Parapsychology** refers to the scientific investigation of claims of various paranormal phenomena. Contrary to what many people think, very few psychologists conduct any kind of parapsychological research.

Have you ever felt as if you had just experienced ESP? Consider the following two examples:

- Your sister was supposed to stop by around 7:00. It's now 7:15, and you "sense" that something has happened to her. Shortly after 8:00 she calls, informing you that she's been involved in a fender bender. Did you experience clairvoyance?
- Some years ago, Sandy had a vivid dream that our cat Nubbin got lost. The next morning, Nubbin sneaked out the back door, went for an unauthorized stroll in the woods, and was gone for three days. Did Sandy have a precognitive dream?

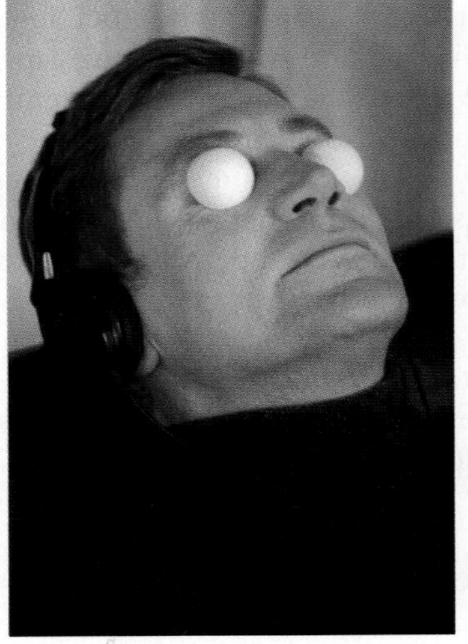

The Ganzfeld Technique Clairvoyance and telepathy experiments often involve use of the *ganzfeld* technique. The research subject lies in a quiet room, with his eyes covered by ping-pong balls cut in half. White noise plays through the headphones covering his ears. Along with blocking extraneous sensory stimuli, this technique can induce mild hallucinations in some subjects (Wackerman & others, 2008).

Such common experiences may be used to "prove" that ESP exists. However, two less extraordinary concepts can explain both occurrences: coincidence and the fallacy of positive instances.

Coincidence describes an event that occurs simply by chance. For example, you have over a thousand dreams per year, most of which are about familiar people and situations. By mere chance, *some* aspect of *some* dream will occasionally correspond with reality.

The *fallacy of positive instances* is the tendency to remember coincidental events that seem to confirm our belief about unusual phenomena and to forget all the instances that do not. For example, think of the number of times you've thought something happened to someone but nothing did. Such situations are far more common than their opposites, but we quickly forget about the hunches that are not confirmed.

Why do people attribute chance events to ESP? Research has shown that believers in ESP are less likely to accurately estimate the

ESP (extrasensory perception) Perception of information by some means other than through the normal processes of sensation.

The early Gestalt psychologists noted that figure and ground have vastly different perceptual qualities (N. Rubin, 2001). As Gestalt psychologist Edgar Rubin (1921) observed, "In a certain sense, the ground has no shape." We notice the shape of the figure but *not* the shape of the background, even when that ground is used as a well-defined frame (see Figure 3.13). It turns out that brain neurons *also* respond differently to a stimulus that is perceived as a figure versus a stimulus that is part of the ground (Baylis & Driver, 2001). Particular neurons in the cortex that responded to a specific shape when it was the shape of the figure did *not* respond when the same shape was presented as part of the background.

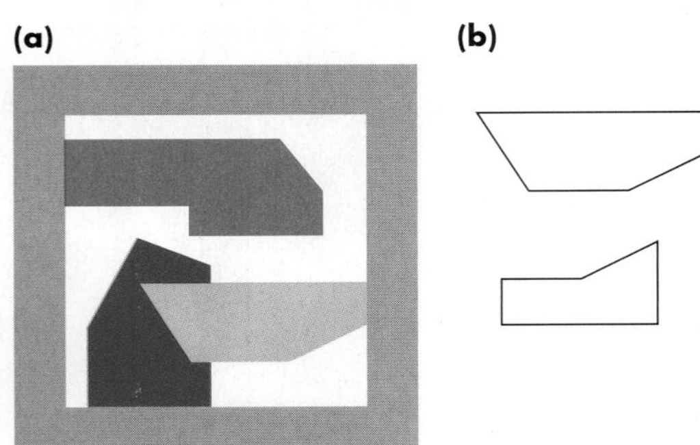

Figure 3.13 Figures Have Shape, but Ground Doesn't Which shape in **(b)** can also be found in **(a)?** The answer is that both shapes are in **(a)**. It's easy to spot the top shape because it corresponds to one of the shapes perceived as a *figure* in **(a)**. The bottom shape is harder to find because it is part of the *ground* or background of the total scene. Because we place more importance on figures, we're more likely to notice their shape while ignoring the shape of background regions.

Source: Rubin (2001).

probability of an event occurring by chance alone. Nonbelievers tend to be more realistic about the probability of events being the result of simple coincidence or chance (Blackmore, 1985).

Parapsychologists attempt to study ESP in the laboratory under controlled conditions. Many initially convincing demonstrations of ESP are later shown to be the result of research design problems or of the researcher's unintentional cuing of the subject. Occasionally, outright fraud is involved on the part of either the subject or experimenter.

Another problem involves *replication*. To be considered valid, experimental results must be able to be replicated, or repeated, by other scientists under identical laboratory conditions. To date, no parapsychology experiment claiming to show evidence of the existence of ESP has been successfully replicated (Hyman, 1994; Milton & Wiseman, 2001).

One active area of parapsychological research is the study of clairvoyance using an experimental procedure called the *ganzfeld procedure* (J. Palmer, 2003). (*Ganzfeld* is a German word that means "total field.") In a ganzfeld study, a "sender" in one room attempts to communicate the content of pictures or short video clips to a receiver in a separate room. Isolated from all contact and wearing goggles and headphones to block external sensory stimuli, the "receiver" attempts to detect the image that is being sent.

One set of carefully controlled ganzfeld studies showed a "hit" rate that was well above chance, implying that some sort of transfer of information had taken place between sender and receiver (Bem & Honorton, 1994). These results, published in a well-respected psychology journal, *Psychological Bulletin,* led some psychologists to speculate that there might be something to extrasensory perception after all—and that the ganzfeld procedure might be the way to detect it. But other psychologists, like Ray Hyman (1994), argued that the study did *not* offer conclusive proof that ESP had been demonstrated.

Many ganzfeld studies have been published, some showing positive results, some negative. Psychologists have used meta-analysis to try to determine whether the so-called ganzfeld effect has been successfully replicated. The verdict? British psychologists Julie Milton and Richard Wiseman (1999, 2001) concluded that the ganzfeld effect has *not* produced replicable evidence of an ESP effect in the laboratory. Other psychologists, however, dispute *that* conclusion with their own meta-analyses (Storm & Ertel, 2001). Most psychologists agree with Milton and Wiseman's (2001) bottom line: "The final verdict on [ESP] depends upon replication of an effect across experimenters under methodologically stringent conditions." To date, that bottom-line requirement has not been met (J. Palmer, 2003).

Of course, the history of science is filled with examples of phenomena that were initially scoffed at and later found to be real. For example, the pain-relieving effects of acupuncture were initially dismissed by Western scientists as mere superstition or the power of suggestion. However, controlled studies have shown that acupuncture does effectively relieve pain and may be helpful in treating other conditions (Ulett & Han, 2002; National Center for Complementary and Alternative Medicine, 2002).

So keep an open mind about ESP, but also maintain a healthy sense of scientific skepticism. It is entirely possible that some day convincing experimental evidence will demonstrate the existence of ESP abilities (see Schlitz & others, 2006). In the final analysis, all psychologists, including those who accept the possibility of ESP, recognize the need for evidence that meets the requirements of the scientific method.

CRITICAL THINKING QUESTIONS

- Why do you think that people who believe in ESP are less likely to attribute events to chance than people who don't think ESP is a real phenomenon?
- Can you think of any reasons why replication might be particularly elusive in research on extrasensory perception?
- Why is replication important in all psychological research, but particularly so in studies attempting to prove extraordinary claims, like the existence of ESP?

The separation of a scene into figure and ground is not a property of the actual elements of the scene at which you're looking. Rather, your ability to separate a scene into figure and ground is a psychological accomplishment. To illustrate, look at the classic example shown in Figure 3.14. This perception of a single image in two different ways is called a *figure–ground reversal.*

parapsychology
The scientific investigation of claims of paranormal phenomena and abilities.

Perceptual Grouping

Many of the forms we perceive are composed of a number of different elements that seem to go together (Prinzmetal, 1995). It would be more accurate to say that we actively organize the elements to try to produce the stable perception of well-defined, whole objects. This is what perceptual psychologists refer to as "the urge to organize." What principles do we follow when we attempt to organize visual elements?

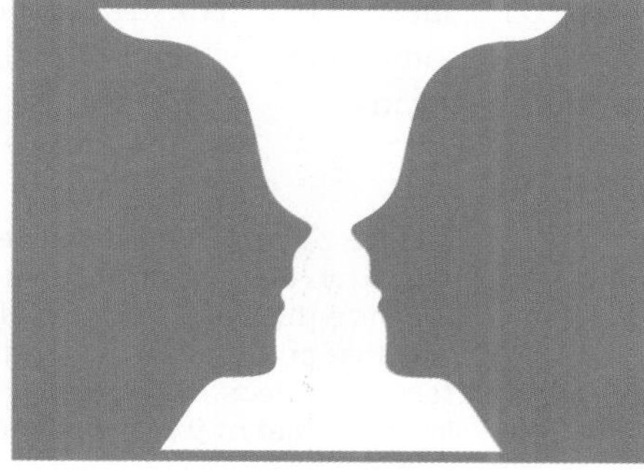

Figure 3.14 A Classic Example of Figure–Ground Reversal Figure–ground reversals illustrate the psychological nature of our ability to perceptually sort a scene into the main element and the background. If you perceive the white area as the figure and the dark area as the ground, you'll perceive a vase. If you perceive the dark area as the figure, you'll perceive two faces.

(a) The Law of Similarity

(b) The Law of Closure

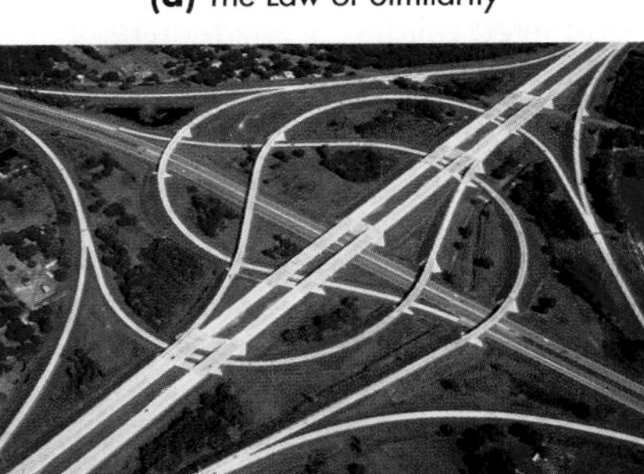

(c) The Law of Good Continuation

(d) The Law of Proximity

Figure 3.15
The Gestalt Principles of Organization
(a) *The law of similarity* is the tendency to perceive objects of a similar size, shape, or color as a unit or figure. Thus, you perceive four horizontal rows rather than six vertical columns of holiday cookies.
(b) The *law of closure* is the tendency to fill in the gaps in an incomplete image. Thus, you perceive the curved lines on the clock as smooth, continuous circles, even though they are interrupted by workers and the clock's hands.
(c) The *law of good continuation* is the tendency to group elements that appear to follow in the same direction as a single unit or figure. Thus, you tend to see the curved sections of the highways as continuous units.
(d) The *law of proximity* is the tendency to perceive objects that are close to one another as a single unit. Thus, you perceive these five people as one group of two people and one group of three people.

The Gestalt psychologists studied how the perception of visual elements becomes organized into patterns, shapes, and forms. They identified several laws, or principles, that we tend to follow in grouping elements together to arrive at the perception of forms, shapes, and figures. These principles include *similarity, closure, good continuation,* and *proximity.* Examples and descriptions of these perceptual laws are shown in Figure 3.15.

The Gestalt psychologists also formulated a general principle called the *law of Prägnanz,* or the *law of simplicity.* This law states that when several perceptual organizations of an assortment of visual elements are possible, the perceptual interpretation that occurs will be the one that produces the "best, simplest, and most stable shape" (Koffka, 1935). To illustrate, look at Figure 3.16. Do you perceive the image as two six-sided objects and one four-sided object? If you are following the law of Prägnanz, you don't. Instead, you perceptually organize the elements in the most cognitively efficient and simple way, perceiving them as three overlapping squares.

According to the Gestalt psychologists, the law of Prägnanz encompasses all the other Gestalt principles, including the figure–ground relationship. The implication of the law of Prägnanz is that our perceptual system works in an economical way to promote the interpretation of stable and consistent forms (van der Helm, 2000). The ability to efficiently organize elements into stable objects helps us perceive the world accurately. In effect, we actively and automatically construct a perception that reveals "the essence of something," which is roughly what the German word *Prägnanz* means.

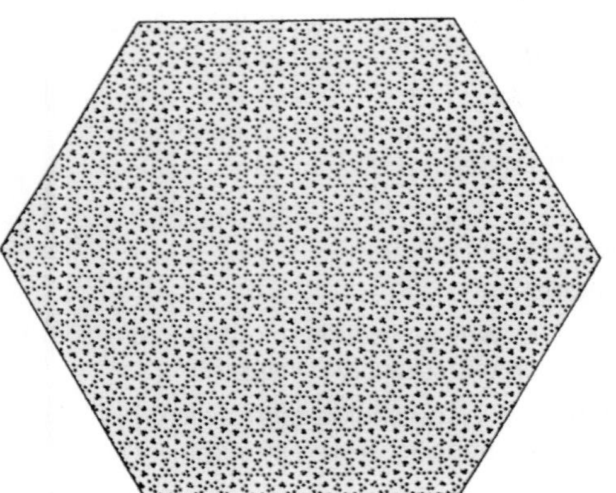

The Perceptual Urge to Organize As you scan this image, you'll experience firsthand the strong psychological tendency to organize visual elements to arrive at the perception of whole figures, forms, and shapes. Notice that as you shift your gaze across the pattern, you momentarily perceive circles, squares, and other geometric forms.

Figure 3.16 What Do You See? The law of simplicity refers to our tendency to efficiently organize the visual elements of a scene in a way that produces the simplest and most stable forms or objects. You probably perceived this image as that of three overlapping squares rather than as two six-sided objects and one four-sided object.

Depth Perception

How Far Away Is It?

Key Theme

- **Perception of distance and motion helps us gauge the position of stationary objects and predict the path of moving objects.**

Key Questions

- **What are the monocular and binocular cues for distance or depth perception, and how does binocular disparity explain our ability to see three-dimensional forms in two-dimensional images?**
- **What visual cues help us perceive distance and motion?**
- **Why do we perceive the size and shape of objects as unchanging despite changes in sensory input?**

Being able to perceive the distance of an object has obvious survival value, especially regarding potential threats, such as snarling dogs or oncoming trains. But simply walking through your house or apartment also requires that you accurately judge the distance of furniture, walls, other people, and so forth. Otherwise, you'd be constantly bumping into doors, walls, and tables. The ability to perceive the distance of an object as well as the three-dimensional characteristics of an object is called **depth perception.**

depth perception
The use of visual cues to perceive the distance or three-dimensional characteristics of objects.

Monocular Cues

We use a variety of cues to judge the distance of objects. **Monocular cues** require the use of only one eye (*mono* means "one"). When monocular cues are used by artists to create the perception of distance or depth in paintings or drawings, they are called *pictorial cues.* After familiarizing yourself with these cues, look at the photographs on the next page. Try to identify the monocular cues you used to determine the distance of the objects in each photograph.

monocular cues
(moe-NOCK-you-ler) Distance or depth cues that can be processed by either eye alone.

1. *Relative size.* If two or more objects are assumed to be similar in size, the object that appears larger is perceived as being closer.
2. *Overlap.* When one object partially blocks or obscures the view of another object, the partially blocked object is perceived as being farther away. This cue is also called *interposition.*
3. *Aerial perspective.* Faraway objects often appear hazy or slightly blurred by the atmosphere.
4. *Texture gradient.* As a surface with a distinct texture extends into the distance, the details of the surface texture gradually become less clearly defined. The texture of the surface seems to undergo a gradient, or continuous pattern of change, from crisp and distinct when close to fuzzy and blended when farther away.
5. *Linear perspective.* Parallel lines seem to meet in the distance. For example, if you stand in the middle of a railroad track and look down the rails, you'll notice that the parallel rails seem to meet in the distance. The closer together the lines appear to be, the greater the perception of distance.
6. *Motion parallax.* When you are moving, you use the speed of passing objects to estimate the distance of the objects. Nearby objects seem to zip by faster than do distant objects. When you are riding on a commuter train, for example, houses and parked cars along the tracks seem to whiz by, while the distant downtown skyline seems to move very slowly.

Depth Perception in Photographs Several monocular cues combine to produce the illusion of depth in this photgraph of the Ginza, a major shopping and entertainment district in Tokyo. See if you can identify examples of relative size, overlap, aerial perspective, texture gradient, and linear perspective.

Another monocular cue is *accommodation.* Unlike pictorial cues, accommodation utilizes information about changes in the shape of the lens of the

Texture Gradient, Overlap, and Aerial Perspective Monocular cues are used to gauge distance of objects in a photograph. The tall grass appears crisp in the foreground and fuzzy in the background, an example of texture gradient. Similarly, haze blurs the foothills, creating the impression of even greater distance. The bushes are perceived as being closer than the house they overlap. Linear perspective is also evident in the parallel wheel tracks in the grass that seem to converge.

Relative Size, Linear Perspective, and Aerial Perspective Several monocular depth cues are operating in this photograph. Relative size is particularly influential: The very small image of the jogger and the decreasing size of the street lamps contribute to the perception of distance. Linear perspective is evident in the apparent convergence of the walkway railings. Aerial perspective contributes to the perception of depth from the hazy background.

Motion Parallax This photograph of waiters in India passing a tray from one train car to the next captures the visual flavor of motion parallax. Objects that whiz by faster are perceptually judged as being closer, as in the case here of the blurred ground and bushes. Objects that pass by more slowly are judged as being farther away, as conveyed by the clearer details of buildings and more distant objects.

eye to help us estimate distance. When you focus on a distant object, the lens is flat, but focusing on a nearby object causes the lens to thicken. Thus, to some degree, we use information provided by the muscles controlling the shape of the lens to judge depth. In general, however, we rely more on pictorial cues than on accommodation for depth perception.

Binocular Cues

Binocular cues for distance or depth perception require information from both eyes. One binocular cue is *convergence*—the degree to which muscles rotate your eyes to focus on an object. The more the eyes converge, or rotate inward, to focus on an object, the greater the strength of the muscle signals and the closer the object is perceived to be. For example, if you hold a dime about six inches in front of your nose, you'll notice the slight strain on your eye muscles as your eyes converge to focus on the coin. If you hold the dime at arm's length, less convergence is needed. Perceptually, the information provided by these signals from your eye muscles is used to judge the distance of an object.

Another binocular distance cue is *binocular disparity.* Because our eyes are set a couple of inches apart, a slightly different image of an object is cast on the retina of each eye. When the two retinal images are very different, we interpret the object as being close by. When the two retinal images are more nearly identical, the object is perceived as being farther away (Parker, 2007).

Here's a simple example that illustrates how you use binocular disparity to perceive distance. Hold a pencil just in front of your nose. Close your left eye, then your right.

binocular cues
(by-NOCK-you-ler) Distance or depth cues that require the use of both eyes.

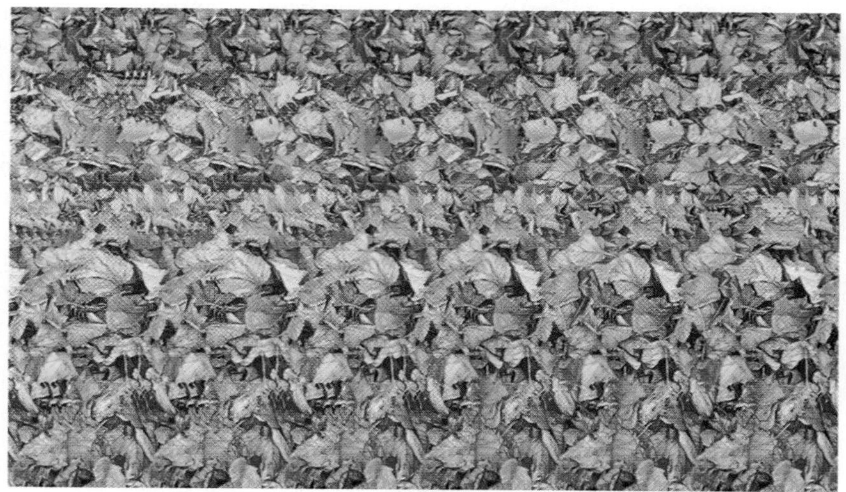

Binocular Disparity and the Perception of Depth in Stereograms This stereogram, *Rustling Hares,* was created by artist Hiroshi Kunoh (Kunoh & Takaoki, 1994). To see the three-dimensional images, first hold the picture close to your face. Focus your eyes as though you are looking at an object that is beyond the book and farther away. Without changing your focus, slowly extend your arms and move the picture away from you. The image of the leaves will initially be blurry, then details will come into focus and you should see three rabbits. The three-dimensional images that can be perceived in stereograms occur because of binocular disparity—each eye is presented with slightly different visual information.

These images are quite different—that is, there is a great deal of binocular disparity between them. Thus you perceive the pencil as being very close. Now focus on another object across the room and look at it first with one eye closed, then the other. These images are much more similar. Because there is less binocular disparity between the two images, the object is perceived as being farther away. Finally, notice that with both eyes open, the two images are fused into one.

A *stereogram* is a picture that uses the principle of binocular disparity to create the perception of a three-dimensional image (Kunoh & Takaoki, 1994). Look at the stereogram shown above. When you first look at it, you perceive a two-dimensional picture of leaves. Although the pictorial cues of overlap and texture gradient provide some sense of depth to the image, the elements in the picture appear to be roughly the same distance from you.

However, a stereogram is actually composed of repeating columns of carefully arranged visual information. If you focus as if you are looking at some object that is farther away than the stereogram, the repeating columns of information will present a slightly different image to each eye. This disparate visual information then fuses into a single image, enabling you to perceive a three-dimensional image—three rabbits! To see the rabbits, follow the directions in the caption.

The Perception of Motion

Where Is It Going?

In addition to the ability to perceive the distance of stationary objects, we need the ability to gauge the path of moving objects, whether it's a baseball whizzing through the air, a falling tree branch, or an egg about to roll off the kitchen counter. How do we perceive movement?

As we follow a moving object with our gaze, the image of the object moves across the retina. Our eye muscles make microfine movements to keep the object in focus. We also compare the moving object to the background, which is usually stationary. When the retinal image of an object enlarges, we perceive the object as moving toward us. Our perception of the speed of the object's approach is based on our estimate of the object's rate of enlargement (Schrater & others, 2001). Neural pathways in the brain combine information about eye-muscle activity, the changing retinal image, and the contrast of the moving object with its stationary background. The end result? We perceive the object as moving.

Neuroscientists do not completely understand how the brain's visual system processes movement. It's known that some neurons are highly specialized to detect motion in one direction but not in the opposite direction. Other neurons are

Mike and Motion Perception Catching a ball involves calculating an array of rapidly changing bits of visual information, including the ball's location, speed, and trajectory. Mike was especially appreciative of his newly regained motion perception. As Mike wrote in his journal, "Top on my list is being able to catch a ball in the air. This is pretty hard to do if you are totally blind, and now I can play ball with my boys and catch the ball 80 percent of the time it is thrown to me. I have spent half my life chasing a ball around in one way or another, so this is a big deal."

specialized to detect motion at one particular speed. Research also shows that different neural pathways in the cerebral cortex process information about the depth of objects, movement, form, and color (Zeki, 2001).

Psychologically, we tend to make certain assumptions when we perceive movement. For example, we typically assume that the *object,* or figure, moves while the background, or frame, remains stationary (Rock, 1995). Thus, as you visually follow a bowling ball down the alley, you perceive the bowling ball as moving and not the alley, which serves as the background.

Because we have a strong tendency to assume that the background is stationary, we sometimes experience an illusion of motion called *induced motion.* Induced motion was first studied by Gestalt psychologist **Karl Duncker** in the 1920s (King & others, 1998). Duncker (1929) had subjects sit in a darkened room and look at a luminous dot that was surrounded by a larger luminous rectangular frame. When the *frame* slowly moved to the right, the subjects perceived the *dot* as moving to the left.

Why did subjects perceive the dot as moving? Part of the explanation has to do with top-down processing. Perceptually, Duncker's subjects *expected* to see the smaller dot move within the larger rectangular frame, not the other way around. If you've ever looked up at a full moon on a windy night when the clouds were moving quickly across its face, you've probably experienced the induced motion effect. The combination of these environmental elements makes the moon appear to be racing across the sky.

Another illusion of apparent motion is called *stroboscopic motion.* First studied by Gestalt psychologist Max Wertheimer in the early 1900s, stroboscopic motion creates an illusion of movement with two carefully timed flashing lights (Wertheimer, 1912). A light briefly flashes at one location, followed about a tenth of a second later by another light briefly flashing at a second location. If the time interval and distance between the two flashing lights are just right, a very compelling illusion of movement is created.

What causes the perception of stroboscopic motion? Although different theories have been proposed, researchers aren't completely sure. The perception of motion typically involves the movement of an image across the retina. However, during stroboscopic motion the image does *not* move across the surface of the retina. Rather, the two different flashing lights are detected at two different points on the

Stroboscopic Motion and Movies The perception of smooth movements in a movie is due to stroboscopic motion. Much like this series of still photographs of an athlete performing a long jump, a motion picture is actually a series of static photographs that are projected onto the screen at the rate of 24 frames per second, producing the illusion of smooth motion.

surface of the retina. Somehow the brain's visual system combines this rapid sequence of visual information to arrive at the perceptual conclusion of motion, even though no movement has occurred. The perception of smooth motion in a movie is also due to stroboscopic motion.

Perceptual Constancies

Consider this scenario. As you're driving on a flat stretch of highway, a red SUV zips past you and speeds far ahead. As the distance between you and the SUV grows, its image becomes progressively smaller until it is no more than a dot on the horizon. Yet, even though the image of the SUV on your retinas has become progressively smaller, you don't perceive the vehicle as shrinking. Instead, you perceive its shape, size, and brightness as unchanged.

This tendency to perceive objects, especially familiar objects, as constant and unchanging despite changes in sensory input is called **perceptual constancy.** Without this perceptual ability, our perception of reality would be in a continual state of flux. If we simply responded to retinal images, our perceptions of objects would change as lighting, viewing angle, and distance from the object changed from one moment to the next. Instead, the various forms of perceptual constancy promote a stable view of the world.

perceptual constancy
The tendency to perceive objects, especially familiar objects, as constant and unchanging despite changes in sensory input.

size constancy
The perception of an object as maintaining the same size despite changing images on the retina.

shape constancy
The perception of a familiar object as maintaining the same shape regardless of the image produced on the retina.

Size and Shape Constancy

Size constancy is the perception that an object remains the same size despite its changing image on the retina. When our distance from an object changes, the image of the object that is cast on the retinas of our eyes also changes, yet we still perceive it to be the same size. The example of the red SUV illustrates the perception of size constancy. As the distance between you and the red SUV increased, you could eventually block out the retinal image of the vehicle with your hand, but you don't believe that your hand has suddenly become larger than the SUV. Instead, your brain automatically adjusts your perception of the vehicle's size by combining information about retinal image size and distance.

The Doors of Perception Each door in the photograph is positioned at a different angle and thus produces a differently shaped image on your retinas. Nevertheless, because of the perceptual principle of shape constancy, you easily identify all five shapes as rectangular doors.

An important aspect of size constancy is that if the retinal image of an object does *not* change but the perception of its distance *increases,* the object is perceived as larger. To illustrate, try this: Stare at a 75-watt lightbulb for about 10 seconds. Then focus on a bright, distant wall. You should see an afterimage of the lightbulb on the wall that will look several times larger than the original lightbulb. Why? When you looked at the wall, the lingering afterimage of the lightbulb on your retina remained constant, but your perception of distance increased. When your brain combined and interpreted this information, your perception of the lightbulb's size increased. Remember this demonstration. We'll mention it again when we explain how some perceptual illusions occur.

Shape constancy is the tendency to perceive familiar objects as having a fixed shape regardless of the image they cast on our retinas. Try looking at a familiar object, such as a door, from different angles, as in the photograph above. Your perception of the door's rectangular shape remains constant despite changes in its retinal image. Shape constancy has a greater influence on your perceptions than you probably realize (see Figure 3.17).

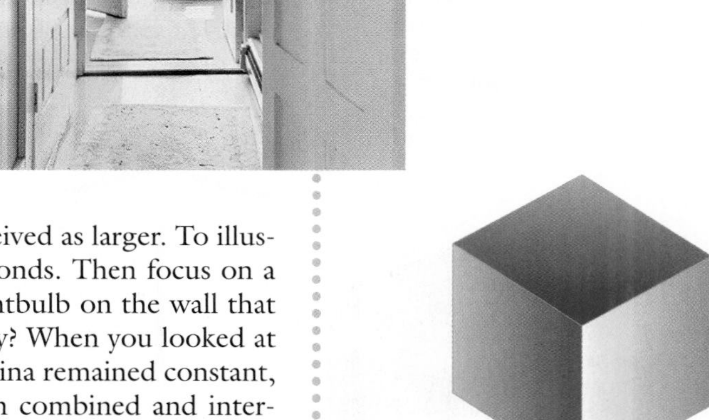

Figure 3.17 How many right angles do you see? Most people find 12 right angles in this drawing of a slightly tilted cube. But look again. There are *no* right angles in the drawing. Shape constancy leads you to perceive an image of a cube with right angles, despite the lack of sensory data to support that perception.

Figure 3.18 Illusory Contours: How Many Triangles Do You See? The Gestalt principles of perceptual organization contribute to the illusion of triangular contours in this image. The second you look at this ambiguous image, you instantly reverse figure and ground so that the black circular regions become the ground, while the white region is visually favored as the figure. In organizing these visual fragments, which are lined up very precisely, the Gestalt principles of closure and good continuation contribute to the perceptual construction of a solid white triangle covering three black disks and an inverted triangle. The images produce a second intriguing illusion: The pure white illusory triangle seems brighter than the surrounding white paper.

Perceptual Illusions

Key Theme

- **Perceptual illusions underscore the idea that we actively construct our perceptual representations of the world according to psychological principles.**

Key Questions

- **How can the Müller-Lyer and moon illusions be explained?**
- **What do perceptual illusions reveal about perceptual processes?**
- **What roles do perceptual sets, learning experiences, and culture play in perception?**

Our perceptual processes are largely automatic and unconscious. On the one hand, this arrangement is mentally efficient. With a minimum of cognitive effort, we decipher our surroundings, answering important perceptual questions and making sense of the environment. On the other hand, because perceptual processing is largely automatic, we can inadvertently arrive at the wrong perceptual conclusion. When we misperceive the true characteristics of an object or an image, we experience a **perceptual illusion.**

During the past century, well over 200 perceptual illusions have been discovered. One famous perceptual illusion is shown in Figure 3.18. The perceptual contradictions of illusions are not only fascinating but can also shed light on how the normal processes of perception guide us to perceptual conclusions. Given the basics of perception that we've covered thus far, you're in a good position to understand how and why some famous illusions seem to occur.

The Müller-Lyer Illusion

Look at the center line made by the corners of the glass walls in photographs (a) and (c) in Figure 3.19. Which line is longer? If you said photograph (c), then you've just experienced the **Müller-Lyer illusion.** In fact, the two center lines are the same length, even though they *appear* to have different lengths. You can confirm that they are the same length by measuring them. The same illusion occurs when you look at a simple line drawing of the Müller-Lyer illusion, shown in parts (b) and (d) of Figure 3.19.

Figure 3.19 The Müller-Lyer Illusion Compare the two photographs. Which *corner* line is longer? Now compare the two line drawings. Which center line is longer? In reality, the center lines in the photographs and the line drawings are all exactly the same length, which you can prove to yourself with a ruler.

(a)

(b)

(c)

(d)

The Müller-Lyer illusion is caused in part by visual depth cues that promote the perception that the center line in photograph (c) is *farther* from you (Gregory, 1968; Rock, 1995). When you look at photograph (c), the center line is that of a wall jutting away from you. When you look at drawing (d), the outward-pointing arrows create much the same visual effect—a corner jutting away from you. In Figure 3.19(a) and (b), visual depth cues promote the perception of *lesser* distance—a corner that is jutting toward you.

Size constancy also seems to play an important role in the Müller-Lyer illusion. Because they are the same length, the two center lines in the photographs and the line drawings produce retinal images that are the same size. However, as we noted in our earlier discussion of size constancy, if the retinal size of an object stays the same but the perception of its distance increases, we will perceive the object as being larger. Previously, we demonstrated this with the afterimage of a lightbulb that seemed much larger when viewed against a distant wall.

The same basic principle seems to apply to the Müller-Lyer illusion. Although all four center lines produce retinal images that are the same size, the center lines in images (c) and (d) are embedded in visual depth cues that make you perceive them as farther away. Hence, you perceive the center lines in these images as being longer, just as you perceived the afterimage of the lightbulb as being larger when viewed on a distant wall.

Keep in mind that the arrows pointing inward or outward are responsible for creating the illusion in the Müller-Lyer illusion. Take away those potent depth cues and the Müller-Lyer illusion evaporates. You perceive the two lines just as they are—the same length.

perceptual illusion
The misperception of the true characteristics of an object or an image.

Müller-Lyer illusion
A famous visual illusion involving the misperception of the identical length of two lines, one with arrows pointed inward, one with arrows pointed outward.

moon illusion
A visual illusion involving the misperception that the moon is larger when it is on the horizon than when it is directly overhead.

The Moon Illusion

Another famous illusion is one you've probably experienced firsthand—the **moon illusion.** When a full moon is rising on a clear, dark night, it appears much larger when viewed on the horizon against buildings and trees than it does when viewed in the clear sky overhead. But the moon, of course, doesn't shrink as it rises. In fact, *the retinal size of the full moon is the same in all positions.* Still, if you've ever watched the moon rise from the horizon to the night sky, it does *appear* to shrink in size. What causes this illusion?

Part of the explanation has to do with our perception of the distance of objects at different locations in the sky (Kaufman & others, 2007). Researchers have found that people perceive objects on the horizon as farther away than objects that are directly overhead in the sky. The horizon contains many familiar distance cues, such as buildings, trees, and the smoothing of the texture of the landscape as it fades into the distance. The moon on the horizon is perceived as being *behind* these depth cues, so the depth perception cue of overlap adds to the perception that the moon on the horizon is farther away.

The moon illusion also involves the misapplication of the principle of size constancy. Like the afterimage of the glowing lightbulb, which looked larger on a distant wall, the moon looks larger when the perception of its distance increases. Remember, the retinal image of the moon is the *same* in all locations, as was the afterimage of the lightbulb. Thus, even though the retinal image of the moon remains constant, we perceive the moon as being larger because it seems farther away on the horizon (Kaufman & others, 2007).

The Moon Illusion Dispelled The *moon illusion* is subjectively very compelling. When viewed on the horizon, the moon appears to be much larger than when it is viewed higher in the sky. But as this time-lapse sequence of the moon rising over the Seattle skyline shows, the size of the moon remains the same as it ascends in the sky.

An Impossible Figure: Escher's *Waterfall* (1961) Impossible figures are visual riddles that capitalize on our urge to organize visual elements into a meaningful whole. Though not illusions in the true sense, these figures baffle our natural tendency to perceptually organize a scene (Ramachandran & Rogers-Ramachandran, 2007). Dutch artist M. C. Escher (1898–1972) became famous for creating elaborate impossible figures, using perceptual principles to create complex visual puzzles. In most paintings, depth and distance cues are used to produce realistic scenes. But in Escher's work, the depth cues are often incompatible, producing a perceptual paradox. As you try to integrate the various perceptual cues in the drawing into a stable, integrated whole, you confront perceptual contradictions—such as the conclusion that water is running uphill. Escher was fascinated by the "psychological tension" created by such images (Schattschneider, 1990).

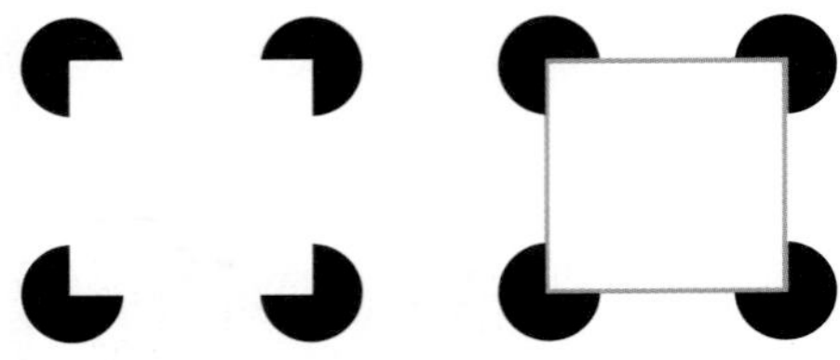

What Is The Hidden Shape?

If you look at a full moon on the horizon through a cardboard tube, you'll remove the distance cues provided by the horizon. The moon on the horizon shrinks immediately—and looks the same size as it does when directly overhead.

Mike and Perceptual Illusions

Perceptual illusions underscore the fact that what we see is *not* merely a simple reflection of the world, but our subjective perceptual interpretation of it. We've been developing and refining our perceptual interpretations from infancy onward. But what about Mike, who regained low vision after more than four decades of blindness?

Psychologist Ione Fine and her colleagues (2003) assessed Mike's perceptual processing with a couple of perceptual illusions. For example, Mike was presented with an image containing illusory contours, shown above left. It's much like the more complex image we discussed in Figure 3.18. When asked, "What is the 'hidden' shape outlined by the black apertures?" Mike had no response. However, when the form was outlined in red, Mike immediately perceived the red square.

Now look at Figure 3.20 shown in the margin. Which tabletop is longer? If you used your keen perceptual skills and confidently said (a), you're wrong. If you responded as Mike did and said that the two tabletops are of identical size and shape, you'd be correct. You can use a ruler or tracing paper to verify this. This illusion is referred as the *Shepard Tables,* named after its creator, psychologist Roger Shepard (1990).

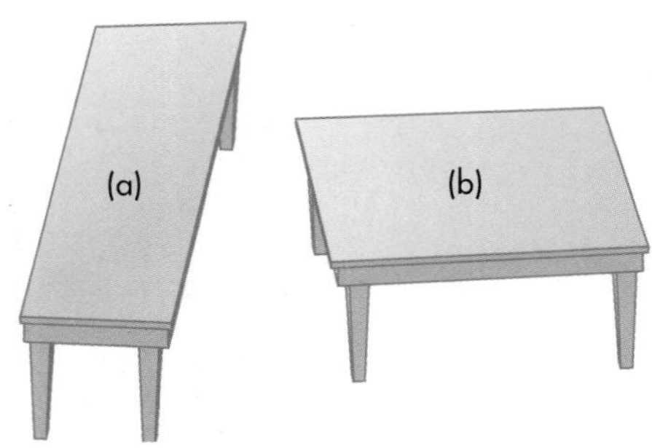

Figure 3.20 Which Tabletop Is Longer? The *Shepard Tables* illusion consists of two tables that are oriented in different directions. It capitalizes on our automatic use of depth perception cues to perceive what is really a two-dimensional drawing as three-dimensional objects. By relying on these well-learned depth perception cues, most people pick (a) as being the longer tabletop. In contrast, Mike May was oblivious to the perceptual illusion. He correctly responded that the two tabletops were the same size and shape (Fine & others, 2003). You can verify this with a ruler.

Source: Illusion adapted from Shepard (1990).

Why wasn't Mike susceptible to this compelling visual illusion? Partly, it's because he does not automatically use many of the depth perception cues we discussed earlier (Gregory, 2003). As psychologist Donald MacLeod explained, "Mike is impressively free from some illusions that beset normal vision, illusions that reflect the constructive processes involved in the perception of three-dimensional objects" (Abrams, 2002).

Although seeing is said to be believing, in the case of illusions, believing can lead to seeing something that isn't really there. As Mike gets more perceptual practice with the world, it will be interesting to see if he learns to fall for the same illusions that most of us do.

Like any psychological process, perception can be influenced by many factors, including our expectations. In the final section of this chapter, we'll consider how prior experiences and cultural factors can influence our perceptions of reality.

The Effects of Experience on Perceptual Interpretations

Our educational, cultural, and life experiences shape what we perceive. As a simple example, consider airplane cockpits. If your knowledge of the instruments contained in an airplane cockpit is limited, as is the case with your author Sandy, an airplane cockpit looks like a meaningless jumble of dials. But your author Don, who is a pilot, has a very different perception of an airplane cockpit. Rather than a blur of dials, he sees altimeters, VORs, airspeed and RPM indicators, and other instruments, each with a specific function. Our different perceptions of an airplane cockpit are shaped by our prior learning experiences.

Learning experiences can vary not just from person to person but also from culture to culture. The Culture and Human Behavior box, "Culture and the Müller-Lyer Illusion," discusses the important role that unique cultural experiences can play in perception.

Perception can also be influenced by an individual's expectations, motives, and interests. The term **perceptual set** refers to the tendency to perceive objects or situations from a particular frame of reference. Perceptual sets usually lead us

perceptual set
The tendency to perceive objects or situations from a particular frame of reference.

CULTURE AND HUMAN BEHAVIOR

Culture and the Müller-Lyer Illusion: The Carpentered-World Hypothesis

Since the early 1900s, it has been known that people in industrialized societies are far more susceptible to the Müller-Lyer illusion than are people in some nonindustrialized societies (see Matsumoto & Juang, 2008). How can this difference be explained?

Cross-cultural psychologist Marshall Segall and his colleagues (1963, 1966) proposed the *carpentered-world hypothesis.* They suggested that people living in urban, industrialized environments have a great deal of perceptual experience in judging lines, corners, edges, and other rectangular, manufactured objects. Thus, people in carpentered cultures would be more susceptible to the Müller-Lyer illusion, which involves arrows mimicking a corner that is jutting toward or away from the perceiver.

In contrast, people who live in noncarpentered cultures more frequently encounter natural objects. In these cultures, perceptual experiences with straight lines and right angles are relatively rare. Segall predicted that people from these cultures would be less susceptible to the Müller-Lyer illusion.

To test this idea, Segall and his colleagues (1963, 1966) compared the responses of people living in carpentered societies, such as Evanston, Illinois, with those of people living in noncarpentered societies, such as remote areas of Africa. The results confirmed their hypothesis. The Müller-Lyer illusion was stronger for those living in carpentered societies. Could the difference in illusion susceptibility be due to some sort of biological difference rather than a cultural difference? To address this issue, psychologist V. Mary Stewart (1973) compared groups of white and African American schoolchildren living in Evanston, Illinois. Regardless of race, all of the children living in the city were equally susceptible to the Müller-Lyer illusion. Stewart also compared groups of black African children in five different areas of Zambia—ranging from the very carpentered capital city of Lusaka to rural, noncarpentered areas of the country. Once again, the African children living in the carpentered society of Lusaka were just as susceptible to the illusion as the Evanston children, but the African children living in the noncarpentered countryside were not.

These findings provided some of the first evidence for the idea that culture could shape perception. As Segall (1994) later concluded, "Every perception is the result of an interaction between a stimulus and a perceiver shaped by prior experience." Thus, people who grow up in very different cultures might well perceive aspects of their physical environment differently.

A Noncarpentered Environment People who live in urban, industrialized environments have a great deal of perceptual experience with straight lines, edges, and right angles. In contrast, people who live in a noncarpentered environment, like the village shown here, have little experience with right angles and perfectly straight lines. Are people who grow up in a noncarpentered environment equally susceptible to the Müller-Lyer illusion?

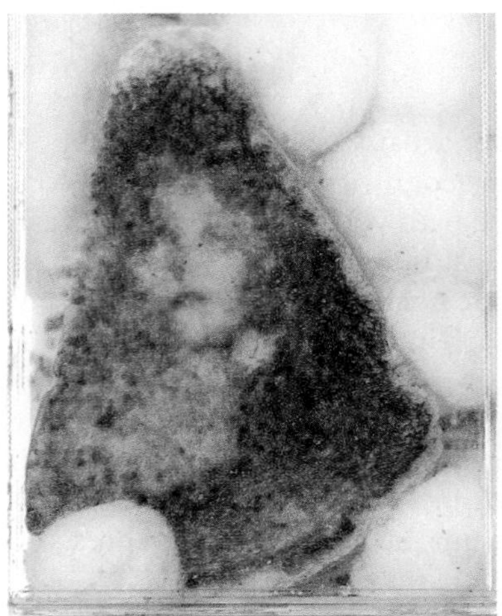

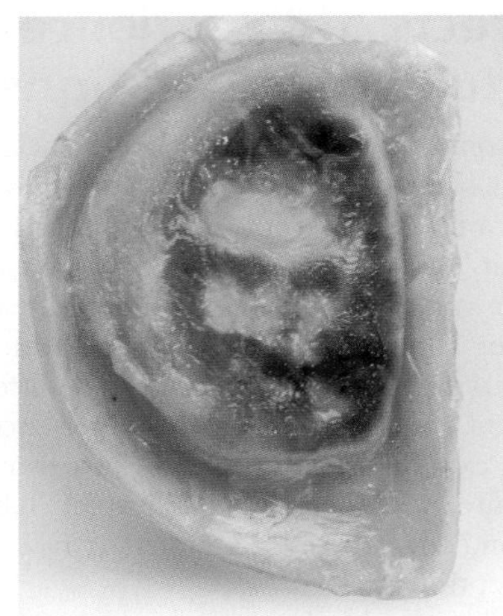

The $28,000 Grilled Cheese Sandwich: What Do You See? Is that Marlene Dietrich on that grilled cheese sandwich? Ten years after she first noticed what she thought was the face of the Virgin Mary on her grilled cheese sandwich (left), Diana Duyser auctioned it off on eBay. The winning bid? Duyser got $28,000 for her carefully preserved (and partially eaten) relic. Donna Lee, however, only made a paltry $1,775 for her pirogi, a type of Polish dumpling, which she believes bears the face of Jesus. (We think it looks like Al Pacino . . . or Abraham Lincoln.) Why are we so quick to perceive human faces in ambiguous stimuli?

to reasonably accurate conclusions. If they didn't, we would develop new perceptual sets that were more accurate. But sometimes a perceptual set can lead us astray. For example, someone with an avid interest in UFOs might readily interpret unusual cloud formations as a fleet of alien spacecraft. Sightings of Bigfoot, mermaids, and the Loch Ness monster that turn out to be brown bears, manatees, or floating logs are all examples of perceptual set.

People are especially prone to seeing *faces* in ambiguous stimuli, as in the photos shown above. Why? One reason is that the brain is wired to be uniquely responsive to faces or face-like stimuli. Research by Doris Tsao (2006a, 2006b) showed that the primate brain contains individual brain neurons that respond exclusively to faces or face-like images. This specialized face recognition system allows us to identify an individual face out of the thousands that we can recognize (Kanwisher, 2006).

But this extraordinary neural sensitivity also makes us more liable to false positives, seeing faces that aren't there. Vague or ambiguous images with face-like blotches and shadows can also trigger the brain's face recognition system. Thus, we see faces where they don't exist at all—except in our own minds.

>> Closing Thoughts

From reflections of light waves to perceptual illusions, the world you perceive is the result of a complex interaction among distinctly dissimilar elements—environmental stimuli, sensory receptor cells, neural pathways, and brain mechanisms. Equally important are the psychological and cultural factors that help shape your perception of the world. As Mike's story illustrated, the world we experience relies not only on the functioning of our different sensory systems but also on neural pathways sculpted by years of learning experiences from infancy onward.

"By getting some sight, I gained some new elements of my personality and lifestyle without rejecting the blindness. I am not a blind person or a sighted person. I am not even simply a visually impaired person. I am Mike May with his quirky sense of humor, graying hair, passion for life, and rather unusual combination of sensory skills."

Although he spent more than four decades totally blind, Mike never seemed to lack vision. With conviction, humor, and curiosity, he sought out a life of change and adventure. And he found it. Rather than expecting his surgery to fundamentally change his life, he simply welcomed the opportunity for new experiences. Throughout his life, Mike wrote, "I have sought change and thrive on it. I expected new and interesting experiences from getting vision as an adult but not that it would change my life" (May, 2004). As Mike points out, "My life was incredibly good before I had my operation. I've been very fortunate and had incredible opportunities, and so I can say that life was incredible. It was fantastic as a non-seeing person, and life is still amazing now that I have vision. That's been consistent between not seeing and seeing. Experiencing life to its fullest doesn't depend on having sight" (May, 2002b).

We hope that learning about Mike's experiences has provided you with some insights as to how your own life experiences have helped shape your perceptions of the world. In the next section, we'll provide you with some tips that we think you'll find useful in influencing your perceptions of painful stimuli.

ENHANCING WELL-BEING WITH PSYCHOLOGY

Strategies to Control Pain

Pain specialists use a variety of techniques to control pain, including ***hypnosis*** and ***painkilling drugs.*** We'll discuss both of these topics in the next chapter. Two other pain-relieving strategies are **biofeedback** and **acupuncture.**

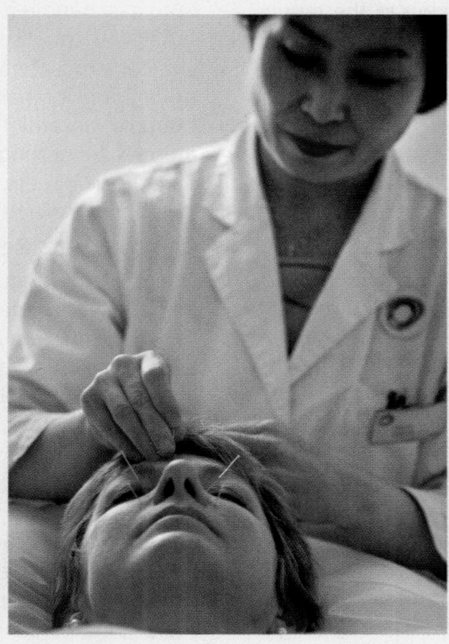

Biofeedback is a process of learning voluntary control over largely automatic body functions, such as heart rate, blood pressure, blood flow, and muscle tension. Using sensitive equipment that signals subtle changes in a specific bodily function, people can learn to become more keenly aware of their body's internal state. With the auditory or visual feedback provided by the biofeedback instrument, the person learns how to exercise conscious control over a particular bodily process.

For example, an individual who experiences chronic tension headaches might use biofeedback to learn to relax shoulder, neck, and facial muscles. Numerous studies have shown that biofeedback is effective in helping people who experience tension headaches, migraine headaches, jaw pain, and back pain (Astin, 2004; Nestoriuc & Martin, 2007).

Acupuncture is a pain-relieving technique that has been used in traditional Chinese medicine for thousands of years. In the United States, acupuncture has been practiced for about 200 years. Currently, about 3 million Americans each year seek acupuncture treatment for various types of pain (National Center for Complementary and Alternative Medicine, 2009).

Acupuncture involves inserting tiny, sterile needles at specific points in the body. The needles are then twirled, heated, or stimulated with a mild electrical current. Exactly how this stimulation diminishes pain signals or the perception of pain has yet to be completely explained (Moffet, 2006). Some research has shown that acupuncture stimulates the release of endorphins in the brain and may also inhibit the production of substance P (Field, 2009; Lee & others, 2009). However, evidence suggests that psychological factors also play a significant role in the pain-relieving effects of acupuncture. Reviews of clinical studies involving patients who received true acupuncture, placebo acupuncture, or no acupuncture found that true acupuncture was only slightly more effective than placebo acupuncture in diminishing pain (Madsen & others, 2009; Moffet, 2009).

Relief from back pain is the most commonly reported reason for seeking acupuncture treatment, followed by joint pain, neck pain, and headache (National Center for Complementary and Alternative Medicine, 2007, 2009). Acupuncture is also being scientifically evaluated as a treatment for other conditions, including menstrual pain, osteoarthritis of the knee, nausea associated with cancer chemotherapy, and infertility (e.g., Domar & others, 2009; Huang & others, 2009; National Cancer Institute, 2008; Streitberger & others, 2006).

But what about everyday pain, such as the pain that accompanies a sprained ankle or a trip to the dentist? There are several simple techniques that you can use to help cope with minor pain.

biofeedback
Technique that involves using auditory or visual feedback to learn to exert voluntary control over involuntary body functions, such as heart rate, blood pressure, blood flow, and muscle tension.

acupuncture
Ancient Chinese medical procedure involving the insertion and manipulation of fine needles into specific locations on the body to alleviate pain and treat illness; modern acupuncture may involve sending electrical current through the needles rather than manipulating them.

Of course, the techniques described here are not a substitute for seeking appropriate medical attention, especially when pain is severe, recurring, or of unknown origin.

Self-Administered Strategies

1. Distraction

By actively focusing your attention on some nonpainful stimulus, you can often reduce pain (Cohen, 2002). For example, you can mentally count backward by sevens from 901, multiply pairs of two-digit numbers, draw different geometric figures in your mind, or count ceiling tiles. You can also focus on the details of a picture or other object.

Or, try our favorite technique, which we'll dub the "iPod pain relief strategy." Intently listening to music, especially calming music, can reduce discomfort (Mitchell & McDonald, 2006).

2. Imagery

Creating a vivid mental image can help control pain (Ball & others, 2003). Usually people create a pleasant and progressive scenario, such as walking along the beach or hiking in the mountains. Try to imagine all the different sensations involved, including the sights, sounds, aromas, touches, and tastes. The goal is to become so absorbed in your fantasy that you distract yourself from sensations of pain (Astin, 2004).

3. Relaxation

Deep relaxation can be a very effective strategy for deterring pain sensations (Turk & Winter, 2006). One simple relaxation strategy is deep breathing: Inhale deeply, then exhale very slowly and completely, releasing tension throughout your body. As you exhale, consciously note the feelings of relaxation and warmth you've produced in your body.

4. Counterirritation

The technique of counterirritation has been used for centuries. Counterirritation decreases pain by creating a strong, competing sensation that's mildly stimulating or irritating. People often do this naturally, as when they vigorously rub an injury or bite their lip during an injection.

How does rubbing the area where an injury has occurred reduce pain? The intense sensations of pain and the normal sensations of touch are processed through different nerve fibers going to the spinal cord. Increasing normal sensations of touch interferes with the transmission of high-intensity pain signals.

While undergoing a painful procedure, you can create and control a competing discomfort by pressing your thumbnail into your index finger. Focusing your attention on the competing discomfort may lessen your overall experience of pain.

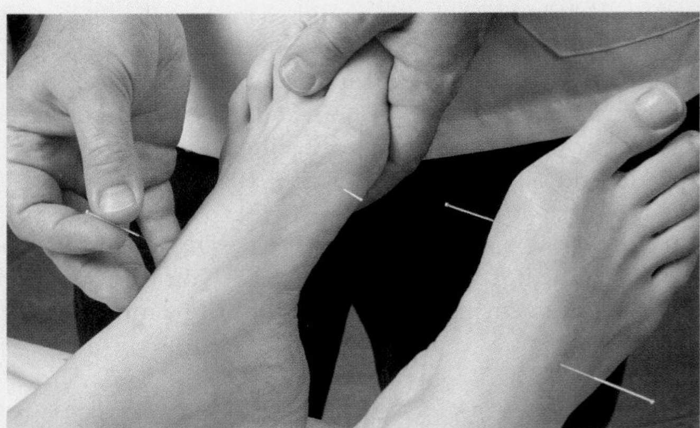

5. Positive self-talk

This strategy involves making positive coping statements, either silently or out loud, during a painful episode or procedure. Examples of positive self-talk include statements such as, "It hurts, but I'm okay, I'm in control" and "I'm uncomfortable, but I can handle it."

Self-talk can also include redefining the pain. By using realistic and constructive thoughts about the pain experience in place of threatening or harmful thoughts, you can minimize pain. For example, an athlete in training might say, "The pain means my muscles are getting stronger." Or, consider the Marine Corps slogan: "Pain is weakness leaving the body."

Can Magnets Relieve Pain?

Our students frequently ask us about different *complementary and alternative medicines (CAM)*. Complementary and alternative medicines are a diverse group of health care systems, practices, or products that are *not* presently considered to be part of conventional medicine. Scientific evidence exists for some CAM therapies, such as the benefits of massage (Moyer & others, 2004). Therapies that are scientifically proven to be safe and effective usually become adopted by the mainstream health care system. However, the effectiveness and safety of many CAMs have not been proven by well-designed scientific studies.

Magnets are one popular CAM that have been used for many centuries to treat pain. But can magnets relieve pain? To date, there is no evidence supporting the idea that magnets relieve pain (National Standard Monograph, 2009). As discussed in Chapter 1 (see page 3), the pain relief that some people experience could be due to a placebo effect and expectations that pain will decrease. Or the relief could come from whatever holds the magnet in place, such as a warm bandage or the cushioned insole (Weintraub & others, 2003).

CHAPTER REVIEW: KEY PEOPLE AND TERMS

Karl Duncker, p. 122

Max Wertheimer, p. 115

sensation, p. 89
perception, p. 89
sensory receptors, p. 89
transduction, p. 89
absolute threshold, p. 90
subliminal perception, p. 91
mere exposure effect, p. 91
difference threshold, p. 92
Weber's law, p. 92
sensory adaptation, p. 92
wavelength, p. 93
cornea, p. 94
pupil, p. 94
iris, p. 94
lens, p. 94
accommodation, p. 94
retina, p. 95
rods, p. 95
cones, p. 95
fovea, p. 95
optic disk, p. 96
blind spot, p. 96

ganglion cells, p. 96
bipolar cells, p. 96
optic nerve, p. 97
optic chiasm, p. 97
color, p. 98
hue, p. 98
saturation, p. 98
brightness, p. 98
trichromatic theory of color vision, p. 100
color blindness, p. 100
afterimage, p. 100
opponent-process theory of color vision, p. 100
audition, p. 102
loudness, p. 102
amplitude, p. 102
decibel, p. 102
pitch, p. 102
frequency, p. 102
timbre, p. 102

outer ear, p. 102
eardrum, p. 102
middle ear, p. 102
inner ear, p. 103
cochlea, p. 103
basilar membrane, p. 103
hair cells, p. 103
frequency theory, p. 104
place theory, p. 104
olfaction, p. 105
gustation, p. 105
olfactory bulb, p. 106
pheromones, p. 107
taste buds, p. 108
pain, p. 110
nociceptors, p. 110
substance P, p. 110
gate-control theory of pain, p. 110
kinesthetic sense, p. 112
proprioceptors, p. 112

vestibular sense, p. 112
bottom-up processing, p. 113
top-down processing, p. 113
Gestalt psychology, p. 115
figure–ground relationship, p. 115
ESP (extrasensory perception), p. 116
parapsychology, p. 116
depth perception, p. 119
monocular cues, p. 119
binocular cues, p. 120
perceptual constancy, p. 123
size constancy, p. 123
shape constancy, p. 123
perceptual illusion, p. 124
Müller-Lyer illusion, p. 124
moon illusion, p. 125
perceptual set, p. 127
biofeedback, p. 129
acupuncture, p. 129

Web Companion Review Activities

You can find additional review activities at **www.worthpublishers.com/discoveringpsych5e.** The *Discovering Psychology* 5th edition Web Companion has self-scoring practice quizzes, flashcards, interactive crossword puzzles, and other activities to help you master the material in this chapter.

CONCEPT MAP

SENSATION AND PERCEPTION

Sensation → Stimulation of **sensory receptors** by some form of energy

To be detected, must exceed **sensory threshold**. Sensory thresholds include:
- **Absolute threshold**
- **Difference threshold** (just noticeable difference) as defined by **Weber's law**
- **Sensory adaptation**

Transduction: Energy is converted into neural signals and transmitted to the brain

Perception: Signals are interpreted in the brain

Vision

Color vision: Psychological experience of different wavelengths

Hue: Light wavelength
Saturation: Purity of light wavelength
Brightness: Amplitude of light wave

Trichromatic theory: Explains color processing in cones
Opponent-process theory: Explains color processing in ganglion cells and brain

Rods:
- Dim light
- Peripheral vision
- Black/white vision

Cones:
- Bright light
- Concentrated in **fovea**
- Fine details (visual acuity)
- Color vision

Send information to:
- **Bipolar cells**
- **Ganglion cells**
- **Optic nerve**
- Thalamus
- Visual cortex

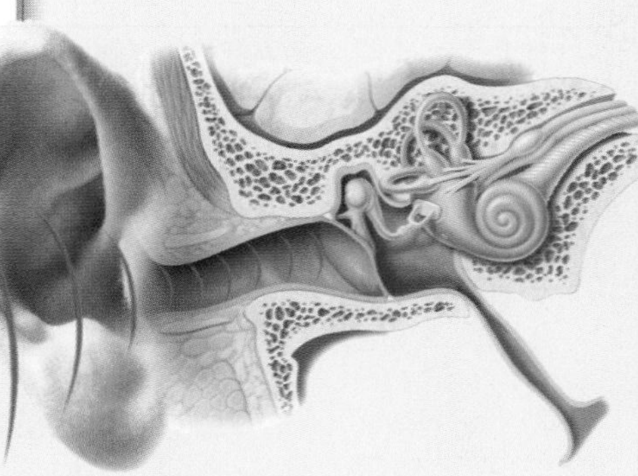

Hearing

Sound wave **amplitude** determines **loudness**
Sound wave **frequency** determines **pitch**
Sound wave **complexity** determines **timbre**

Pitch perception explained by
- **Frequency theory**
- **Place theory**

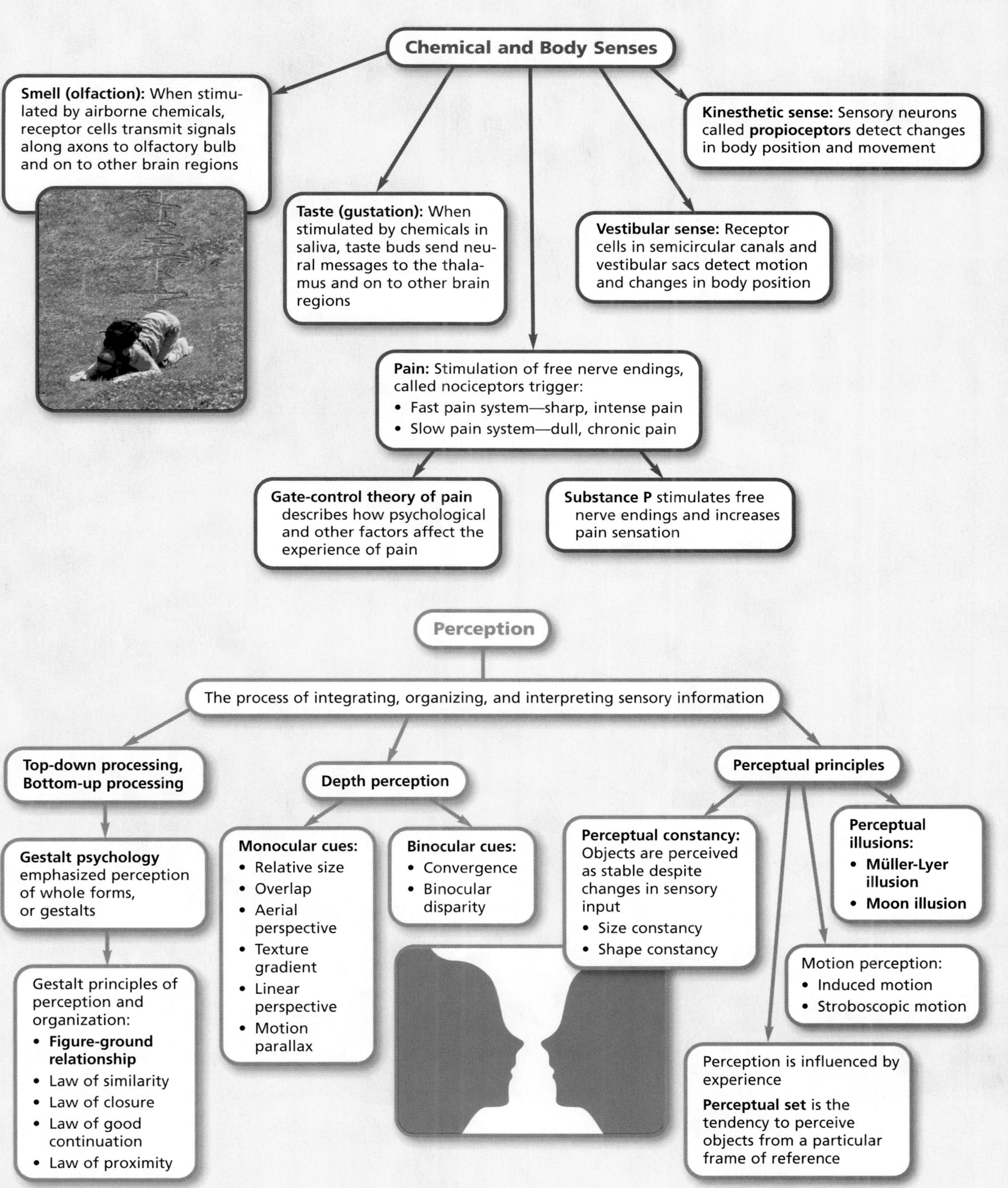

Chemical and Body Senses
Smell (olfaction): When stimulated by airborne chemicals, receptor cells transmit signals along axons to olfactory bulb and on to other brain regions
Taste (gustation): When stimulated by chemicals in saliva, taste buds send neural messages to the thalamus and on to other brain regions
Kinesthetic sense: Sensory neurons called **propioceptors** detect changes in body position and movement
Vestibular sense: Receptor cells in semicircular canals and vestibular sacs detect motion and changes in body position
Pain: Stimulation of free nerve endings, called nociceptors trigger:
• Fast pain system—sharp, intense pain
• Slow pain system—dull, chronic pain
Gate-control theory of pain describes how psychological and other factors affect the experience of pain
Substance P stimulates free nerve endings and increases pain sensation
Perception
The process of integrating, organizing, and interpreting sensory information
Top-down processing, Bottom-up processing
Gestalt psychology emphasized perception of whole forms, or gestalts
Gestalt principles of perception and organization:
• **Figure-ground relationship**
• Law of similarity
• Law of closure
• Law of good continuation
• Law of proximity
Depth perception
Monocular cues:
• Relative size
• Overlap
• Aerial perspective
• Texture gradient
• Linear perspective
• Motion parallax
Binocular cues:
• Convergence
• Binocular disparity
Perceptual principles
Perceptual constancy: Objects are perceived as stable despite changes in sensory input
• Size constancy
• Shape constancy
Perceptual illusions:
• **Müller-Lyer illusion**
• **Moon illusion**
Motion perception:
• Induced motion
• Stroboscopic motion
Perception is influenced by experience
Perceptual set is the tendency to perceive objects from a particular frame of reference

CHAPTER

4

Consciousness and Its Variations

Even in Good Men
PROLOGUE

SCOTT HAD SOME SLEEPWALKING episodes as he was growing up, but his parents weren't overly concerned about them. Sleepwalking is pretty common among kids. "I remember Scott getting dressed at midnight, glassy-eyed, saying he had to go to school," Scott's mother recalled. "Once as a big boy—twelve or so—he walked into the living room stark naked. He said, 'I'm going to school.' His dad put his hands on Scott's shoulders, and Scott resisted him. But nobody thought it was a big deal." Besides, Scott wasn't the only sleepwalker in the family. Two of his younger siblings were also sleepwalkers.

Scott's sister, Laura, remembers another sleepwalking incident. At the time, she was 15 and Scott was five years older. "Scott was getting ready to get married that June and he was coming up on college finals, and he was stressing," Laura recalled. The incident happened in the kitchen as she was eating a late-night snack. Scott wandered into the kitchen with a glazed facial expression. As he reached the back door and began fumbling with the doorknob, Laura realized that her older brother was sleepwalking. She quickly leaned around him to lock the deadbolt. That's when Scott grabbed her. "He kind of lifted me up and tossed me," Laura recalls. "His face looked almost demonic when he reacted to me. It really scared the hell out of me."

Scott eventually married his high school sweetheart, Yarmila. Both of them graduated from college and Scott went on to obtain an M.B.A. During the 1980s, Scott and Yarmila had two children. In the early 1990s, the family settled in Phoenix and Scott worked as a managing engineer for a technology company. By all accounts, Scott and Yarmila's marriage was happy, revolving around their children and Scott's involvement with a teen ministry program at their church.

During most of 1996, Scott was under tremendous pressure at work. A new product line that Scott's team had been developing—a hard drive chip—was not living up to its promise. "I smelled failure for months. I had basically come to the conclusion that the company should discontinue our product line," Scott recalled. "But I would have essentially ended my co-workers' jobs if the bosses followed through on my suggestion." It was a no-win situation.

As the work pressures carried over into 1997, Scott often went for night after night with three hours of sleep or less. To stay alert and focused at work, he resorted to taking caffeine tablets, 200 milligrams a pop. After several nights in a row with very little sleep, Scott would "crash" early to catch up on his sleep.

It was at work on January 16 when Scott got into a heated exchange with one of his bosses. It was decided that the following day Scott would meet with his workgroup team and explain that their project would probably be cancelled.

At dinner that night, Scott discussed the troubling work situation with his family. After dinner, he worked on a software game he had been developing for his youth

Chapter Outline

ministry group. Around 9:00 P.M., after the kids were in bed, Scott went out to the backyard to work on the broken swimming pool pump. But after trying to repair the pump by flashlight, he eventually gave up. He would deal with the pump later, he decided.

Back in the house, Yarmila had fallen asleep on the couch in the family room, the television still on. It was close to 10:00 P.M. Scott kissed her good night, went upstairs, changed into his pajama bottoms, and "crashed."

In all of us, even in good men, there is a lawless wild-beast nature, which peers out in sleep.

PLATO (360 BCE)

Less than an hour later, Scott was startled awake by the sound of their two dogs barking wildly. Disoriented and confused, he rushed downstairs. Two police officers, guns drawn and pointing at him, confronted him, yelling at him to get facedown on the floor.

"What's wrong? What's going on?" Scott asked as he complied.

"How many people are in the house?"

"Four," Scott answered, his heart racing.

Scott was wrong. Not counting the police officers, there were only three people in the house—himself and his two children. Yarmila was *not* in the house.

For almost an hour, Scott sat handcuffed in the back of a police car. He caught bits and pieces of the comments being made by the police officers and emergency personnel. At first he thought that Yarmila had been seriously hurt and that the police were searching for the person who had done it. But then he realized he was wrong. Yarmila was dead.

It was almost 2:00 A.M. when a Phoenix Police Department detective began interrogating Scott. "What set this thing off, got it going?" the detective asked.

As he sat huddled in the corner of the interrogation room, Scott replied, "Obviously, you think I did it. I don't know what makes you think that."

"Because I have a neighbor staring at you, watching you do it, that's why."

"I'm sorry. I don't remember doing it," Scott answered, then paused. "How did she die?"

"Well, the neighbor says you stabbed her and dragged her over to the pool and held her under the water. From what people are telling me about you guys, you spend a lot of time in the church. A quiet family, so this is really out of character. I want to know what went on, what would lead to something like this? What did she do to set you off like that?"

"Nothing."

"Okay, then what did *you* do to set yourself off like that? Something set you off, Scott."

"I'm sorry, I just don't know."

"Nothing went wrong?"

"I love my wife. I love my kids."

Although he had no memory of his actions, Scott had stabbed Yarmila 44 times, then left her floating facedown in the swimming pool.

Could Scott Falater have unknowingly committed such violent acts while he was sleepwalking? Is it even possible for someone to carry out complex actions, such as driving a car, while asleep?

In this chapter, we'll tackle those questions and many others as we explore variations in our experience of consciousness. As you'll see, psychologists have learned a great deal about our daily fluctuations of consciousness. Psychologists have also gained insight into the different ways that alterations in consciousness can be induced, such as through the use of hypnosis, meditation, or psychoactive drugs. Scott's story will help illustrate some of these concepts, so we'll come back to it before long.

>> Introduction: Consciousness

Experiencing the "Private I"

Key Theme

- **Consciousness refers to your immediate awareness of internal and external stimuli.**

Key Questions

- **What did William James mean by the phrase *stream of consciousness*?**
- **How has research on consciousness evolved over the past century?**

consciousness
Personal awareness of mental activities, internal sensations, and the external environment.

Your immediate awareness of thoughts, sensations, memories, and the world around you represents the experience of **consciousness.** That the experience of consciousness can vary enormously from moment to moment is easy to illustrate. Imagine that we could hook you up to a mental video camera during your psychology class.

At random times as your instructor is teaching, the video camera would record one-minute segments of the conscious mental activities occurring. What might those recordings of your consciousness reveal? Here are just a few possibilities:

- Focused concentration on your instructor's words and gestures
- Drifting from one fleeting thought, memory, or image to another
- Awareness of physical sensations, such as the beginnings of a headache or the lingering sting of a paper cut
- Replaying an emotionally charged conversation and thinking about what you wish you had said
- Romantic or sexual fantasies
- Mentally rehearsing what you'll say and how you'll act when you meet a friend later in the day
- Wishful, grandiose daydreams about yourself in the future

Capturing the Stream of Consciousness One thought, memory, or fantasy seems to blend seamlessly into another. It was this characteristic of conscious experience that led William James to describe our mental life as being like a "river" or "stream."

Most likely, the mental video clips would reveal very different scenes, dialogues, and content as the focus of your consciousness shifted from one moment to the next. Yet even though your conscious experience is constantly changing, you don't experience your personal consciousness as disjointed. Rather, the subjective experience of consciousness has a sense of continuity. One stream of conscious mental activity seems to blend into another, effortlessly and seamlessly.

This characteristic of consciousness led the influential American psychologist **William James** (1892) to describe consciousness as a "stream" or "river." Although always changing, consciousness is perceived as unified and unbroken, much like a stream. Despite the changing focus of our awareness, our experience of consciousness as unbroken helps provide us with a sense of personal identity that has continuity from one day to the next.

The nature of human consciousness was one of the first topics to be tackled by the fledgling science of psychology in the late 1800s. In Chapter 1, we discussed how the first psychologists tried to determine the nature of the human mind through *introspection*—verbal self-reports that tried to capture the "structure" of conscious experiences. But because such self-reports were not objectively verifiable, many of the leading psychologists at the turn of the twentieth century rejected the study of consciousness. Instead, they emphasized the scientific study of *overt behavior,* which could be directly observed, measured, and verified.

Beginning in the late 1950s, many psychologists once again turned their attention to the study of consciousness. This shift occurred for two main reasons. First, it was becoming clear that a complete understanding of behavior would *not* be possible unless psychologists considered the role of conscious mental processes in behavior.

Second, although the experience of consciousness is personal and subjective, psychologists had devised more objective ways to study conscious experiences. For example, psychologists could often *infer* the conscious experience that seemed to be occurring by carefully observing behavior. Technological advances in studying brain activity were also producing intriguing correlations between brain activity and different states of consciousness.

Today, the scientific study of consciousness is incredibly diverse. Working from a variety of perspectives, psychologists and other neuroscientists are piecing together a picture of consciousness that takes into account the role of psychological, physiological, social, and cultural influences.

Consciousness, then, does not appear to itself chopped up in bits. . . . It is nothing jointed; it flows. A "river" or a "stream" are the metaphors by which it is most naturally described. In talking of it hereafter, let us call it the stream of thought, or consciousness, of subjective life.

WILLIAM JAMES (1892)

Biological and Environmental "Clocks" That Regulate Consciousness

Key Theme

- **Many body functions, including mental alertness, are regulated by circadian rhythms, which systematically vary over a 24-hour period.**

Key Questions

- **How do sunlight, the suprachiasmatic nucleus, and melatonin regulate the sleep–wake cycle?**
- **How do free-running conditions affect circadian rhythms?**
- **What is jet lag, and how is it produced?**

Throughout the course of each day, there is a natural ebb and flow to consciousness. The most obvious variation of consciousness that we experience is the daily sleep–wake cycle. However, researchers have identified more than 100 other physical and psychological processes that rhythmically peak and dip at consistent times each day, including blood pressure, the secretion of different hormones, mental alertness, and pain sensitivity.

Each of those examples represents a specific **circadian rhythm.** The word *circadian* combines the Latin words for "about" and "day." So, the term *circadian rhythm* refers to a biological or psychological process that systematically varies over the course of each day.

Normally, your different circadian rhythms are closely synchronized. For example, the circadian rhythm for the release of growth hormone is synchronized with the sleep–wake circadian rhythm so that growth hormone is released only during sleep. Table 4.1 lists other examples of circadian rhythms.

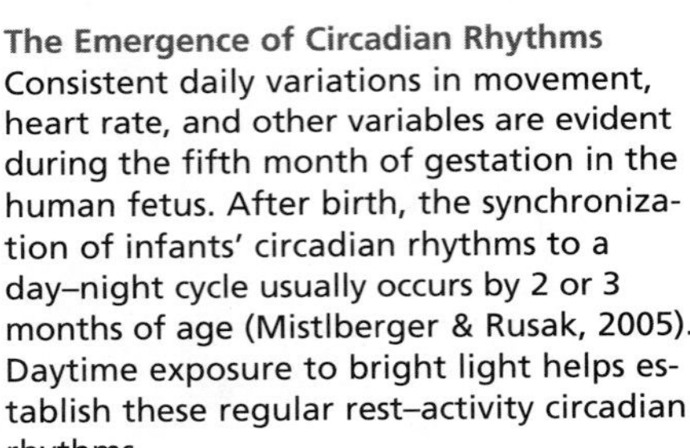

The Emergence of Circadian Rhythms Consistent daily variations in movement, heart rate, and other variables are evident during the fifth month of gestation in the human fetus. After birth, the synchronization of infants' circadian rhythms to a day–night cycle usually occurs by 2 or 3 months of age (Mistlberger & Rusak, 2005). Daytime exposure to bright light helps establish these regular rest–activity circadian rhythms.

Table 4.1

Examples of Human Circadian Rhythms

Function	Typical Circadian Rhythm
Peak mental alertness and memory	Two daily peaks: around 9:00 A.M. and 9:00 P.M.
Lowest body temperature	About 97°F around 4:00 A.M.
Highest body temperature	About 99°F around 4:00 P.M.
Peak hearing, visual, taste, and smell sensitivity	Two daily peaks: around 3:00 A.M. and 6:00 P.M.
Lowest sensitivity to pain	Around 4:00 P.M.
Peak sensitivity to pain	Around 4:00 A.M.
Peak degree of sleepiness	Two daily peaks: around 3:00 A.M. and 3:00 P.M.
Peak melatonin hormone in blood	Between 1:00 A.M. and 3:00 A.M.

Sources: Campbell (1997); Czeisler & Dijk (2001); Refinetti (2000); M. Young (2000).

circadian rhythm
(ser-KADE-ee-en) A cycle or rhythm that is roughly 24 hours long; the cyclical daily fluctuations in biological and psychological processes.

suprachiasmatic nucleus (SCN)
(soup-rah-*kye*-az-MAT-ick) A cluster of neurons in the hypothalamus in the brain that governs the timing of circadian rhythms.

melatonin
(mel-ah-TONE-in) A hormone manufactured by the pineal gland that produces sleepiness.

The Suprachiasmatic Nucleus
The Body's Clock

Your many circadian rhythms are controlled by a master biological clock—a tiny cluster of neurons in the *hypothalamus* in the brain. As shown in Figure 4.1, this cluster of neurons is called the **suprachiasmatic nucleus,** abbreviated **SCN.** The SCN is the internal pacemaker that governs the timing of circadian rhythms, including the sleep–wake cycle (R. Moore, 2007).

Keeping the circadian rhythms synchronized with one another and on a 24-hour schedule also involves environmental time cues. The most important of these cues is bright light, especially sunlight. In people, light detected by special photoreceptors in the eye is communicated via the visual system to the SCN in the hypothalamus (Berson & others, 2002; Drouyer & others, 2007).

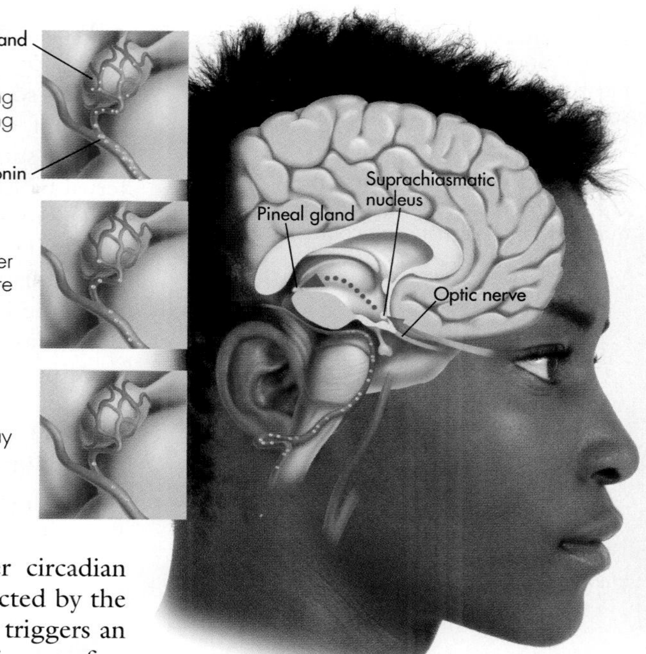

Figure 4.1 The Biological Clock Special photoreceptors in the retina regulate the effects of light on the body's circadian rhythms (Menaker, 2003). In response to morning light, signals from these special photoreceptors are relayed via the optic nerve to the suprachiasmatic nucleus. In turn, the suprachiasmatic nucleus reduces the pineal gland's production of melatonin, a hormone that causes sleepiness. As blood levels of melatonin decrease, mental alertness increases. Daily exposure to bright light, especially sunlight, helps keep the body's circadian rhythms synchronized and operating on a 24-hour schedule.

How does sunlight help regulate the sleep–wake cycle and other circadian rhythms? As the sun sets each day, the decrease in available light is detected by the SCN through its connections with the visual system. In turn, the SCN triggers an increase in the production of a hormone called **melatonin.** Melatonin is manufactured by the *pineal gland,* an endocrine gland located in the brain.

Increased blood levels of melatonin help make you sleepy and reduce activity levels. At night, blood levels of melatonin rise, peaking between 1:00 and 3:00 A.M. Shortly before sunrise, the pineal gland all but stops producing melatonin, and you soon wake up. As the sun rises, exposure to sunlight and other bright light suppresses melatonin levels, and they remain very low throughout the day. In this way, sunlight regulates, or *entrains,* the SCN so that it keeps your circadian cycles synchronized and operating on a 24-hour schedule.

Circadian Rhythms and Sunlight: The 24.2-hour Day

Sunlight plays a critical role in regulating your internal clock. So what would happen if you were deprived of all environmental time cues, like sunlight/darkness cues, clocks, and schedules? In the absence of all external time cues, researchers have found that our internal body clock drifts to its natural—or *intrinsic*—rhythm. Interestingly, our intrinsic circadian rhythm is about 24.2 hours, or slightly *longer* than a day (Czeisler & others, 1999). And our normally coordinated circadian rhythms become desynchronized (Dijk & Lockley, 2002). For example, your sleep–wake, body temperature, and melatonin cycles are usually very closely coordinated. At about 3:00 A.M., your body temperature dips to its lowest point just as melatonin is reaching its highest level and you are at your sleepiest. But when deprived of all environmental time cues, the sleep–wake, body temperature, and melatonin circadian rhythms become desynchronized so that they are no longer properly coordinated with one another.

Circadian Rhythms and the Blind Many blind people have desynchronized circadian rhythms because they're unable to detect the sunlight that normally sets the body's internal biological clock, the SCN. Like sighted people deprived of all environmental time cues, blind people can experience melatonin, body temperature, and sleep–wake circadian cycles that operate independently. Consequently, about 60 percent of blind people suffer from recurring bouts of insomnia and other sleep problems (Arendt & others, 2005; Mistlberger & Skene, 2005).

electroencephalograph
(e-lec-tro-en-SEFF-uh-low-graph) An instrument that uses electrodes placed on the scalp to measure and record the brain's electrical activity.

EEG (electroencephalogram)
The graphic record of brain activity produced by an electroencephalograph.

What this means is that exposure to environmental time signals is necessary for us to stay precisely synchronized, or *entrained,* to a 24-hour day. Practically speaking, this has some important applications. For example, imagine that you leave Denver at 2:00 P.M. on a 10-hour flight to London. When you arrive in London, it's 7:00 A.M. and the sun is shining. However, your body is still on Denver time. As far as your internal biological clock is concerned, it's midnight.

The result? Your circadian rhythms are drastically out of synchronization with daylight and darkness cues. The psychological and physiological effects of this disruption in circadian rhythms can be severe. Thinking, concentration, and memory get fuzzy. You experience physical and mental fatigue, depression or irritability, and disrupted sleep (Eastman & others, 2005). Collectively, these symptoms are called *jet lag.*

Although numerous physiological variables are involved in jet lag, the circadian cycle of the hormone melatonin plays a key role. When it's 10:00 A.M. in London, it's 3:00 A.M. in Denver. Since your body is still operating on Denver time, your melatonin production is peaking. Rather than feeling awake, you feel very sleepy, sluggish, and groggy. For many people, it can take a week or longer to fully adjust to such an extreme time change.

Sleep

Key Theme

- **Modern sleep research began with the invention of the EEG and the discovery that sleep is marked by distinct physiological processes and stages.**

Key Questions

- **What characterizes sleep onset, the NREM sleep stages, and REM sleep?**
- **What is the typical progression of sleep cycles? How do sleep patterns change over the lifespan?**
- **What evidence suggests that we have a biological need for sleep?**

From Aristotle to Shakespeare to Freud, history is filled with examples of scholars, writers, and scientists who have been fascinated by sleep and dreams. But prior to the twentieth century, there was no objective way to study the internal processes that might be occurring during sleep. Instead, sleep was largely viewed as a period of restful inactivity in which dreams sometimes occurred.

Wired for Sleep Three main measurements are recorded throughout the night in a sleep lab or clinic. Using electrodes pasted to the scalp, the *electroencephalogram* (EEG) detects changes in the brain's electrical activity. The *electromyogram* (EMG) uses electrodes taped to the chin to record changes in muscle tone and chin movements. The *electrooculogram* (EOG) records eyeball movements using electrodes positioned near each eye. This young woman's upper and lower limb movements, respirations, heart rate, and airflow are also being measured. Although it may look uncomfortable, most people involved in sleep studies become oblivious to the electrodes and wires as they drift into sleep (Carskadon & Rechtschaffen, 2005).

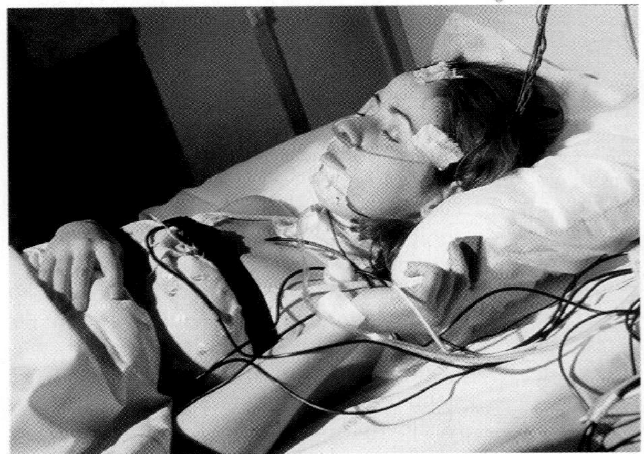

The Dawn of Modern Sleep Research

The invention of the **electroencephalograph** by German psychiatrist Hans Berger in the 1920s gave sleep researchers an important tool for measuring the rhythmic electrical activity of the brain (Stern, 2001). These rhythmical patterns of electrical activity are referred to as *brain waves.* The electroencephalograph produces a graphic record called an **EEG, or electroencephalogram.** By studying EEGs, sleep researchers firmly established that brain-wave activity systematically changes throughout sleep.

Along with brain activity, today's sleep researchers monitor a variety of other physical functions during sleep. Eye movements, muscle movements, breathing rate, airflow, pulse, blood pressure, amount of exhaled carbon dioxide, body temperature, and breathing sounds are just some of the body's functions that are measured in contemporary sleep research (Carskadon & Dement, 2005).

Today, sleep researchers distinguish between two basic types of sleep. **REM sleep** is often called *active sleep* or *paradoxical sleep* because it is associated with heightened body and brain activity during which dreaming consistently occurs. **NREM sleep,** or *non-rapid-eye-movement sleep,* is often referred to as *quiet sleep* because the body's physiological functions and brain activity slow down during this period of slumber. Usually pronounced as "Non-REM sleep," it is further divided into four stages, as we'll describe shortly.

The Onset of Sleep and Hypnagogic Hallucinations

Awake and reasonably alert as you prepare for bed, your brain generates small, fast brain waves, called **beta brain waves.** After your head hits the pillow and you close your eyes, your muscles relax. Your brain's electrical activity gradually gears down, generating slightly larger and slower **alpha brain waves.** As drowsiness sets in, your thoughts may wander and become less logical.

During this drowsy, presleep phase, you may experience odd but vividly realistic sensations. You may hear your name called or a loud crash, feel as if you're falling, floating, or flying, or see kaleidoscopic patterns or an unfolding landscape. These brief, vivid sensory phenomena that occasionally occur during the transition to light sleep are called **hypnagogic hallucinations.** Some hypnagogic hallucinations can be so vivid or startling that they cause a sudden awakening (Vaughn & D'Cruz, 2005).

GARFIELD

Jim Davis

Probably the most common hypnagogic hallucination is the vivid sensation of falling. The sensation of falling is often accompanied by a *myoclonic jerk*—an involuntary muscle spasm of the whole body that jolts the person completely awake (Cooper, 1994). Also known as *sleep starts,* these experiences can seem really weird (or embarrassing) when they occur. But you can rest assured because hypnagogic hallucinations and sleep starts are normal—if not completely understood—events that sometimes occur during sleep onset (Mahowald, 2005).

The First 90 Minutes of Sleep and Beyond

The course of a normal night's sleep follows a relatively consistent cyclical pattern. As you drift off to sleep, you enter NREM sleep and begin a progression through the four NREM sleep stages (see Figure 4.2 on the next page). Each progressive NREM sleep stage is characterized by corresponding decreases in brain and body activity. On average, the progression through the first four stages of NREM sleep occupies the first 50 to 70 minutes of sleep.

Stage 1 NREM

As the alpha brain waves of drowsiness are replaced by even slower *theta brain waves,* you enter the first stage of sleep. Lasting only a few minutes, stage 1 is a transitional stage during which you gradually disengage from the sensations of the surrounding world. Familiar sounds, such as the hum of the refrigerator or the sound of traffic, gradually fade from conscious awareness. During stage 1 NREM, you can quickly regain conscious alertness if needed. Although hypnagogic experiences can occur in stage 1, less vivid mental imagery is common, such as imagining yourself engaged in some everyday activity. These imaginations lack the unfolding, storylike details of a true dream.

REM sleep
Type of sleep during which rapid eye movements (REM) and dreaming usually occur and voluntary muscle activity is suppressed; also called *active sleep* or *paradoxical sleep.*

NREM sleep
Quiet, typically dreamless sleep in which rapid eye movements are absent; divided into four stages; also called *quiet sleep.*

beta brain waves
Brain-wave pattern associated with alert wakefulness.

alpha brain waves
Brain-wave pattern associated with relaxed wakefulness and drowsiness.

hypnagogic hallucinations
(hip-na-GAH-jick) Vivid sensory phenomena that occur during the onset of sleep.

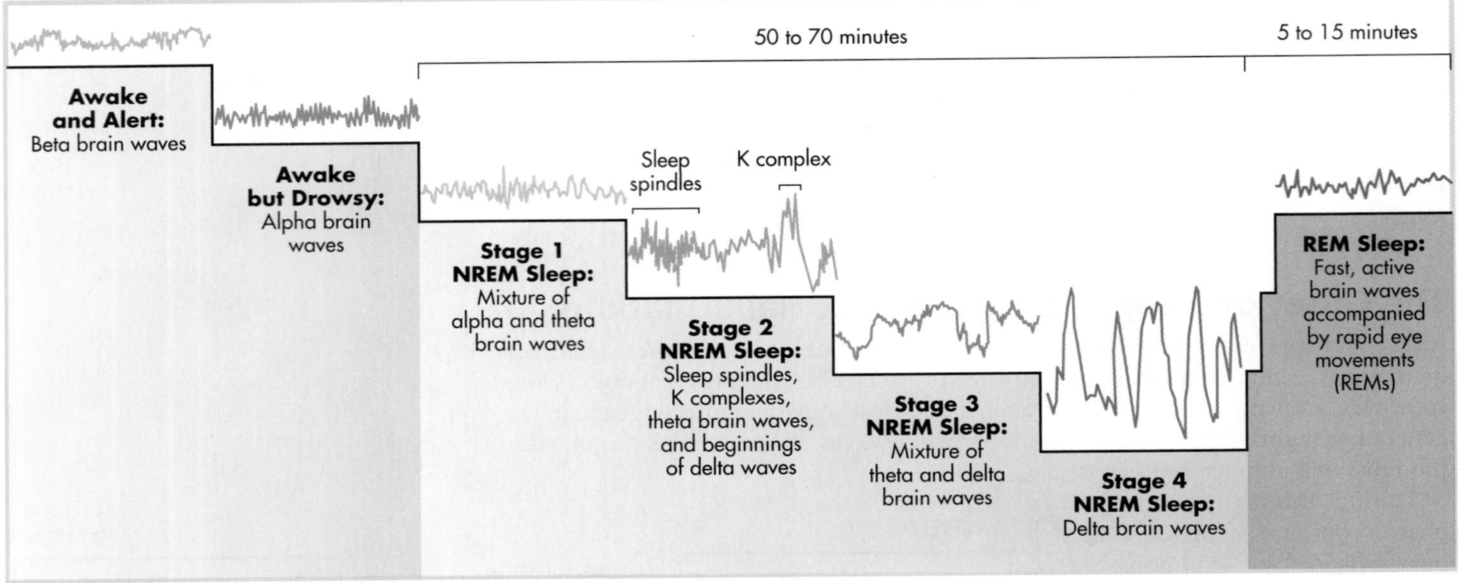

Figure 4.2 The First 90 Minutes of Sleep From wakefulness to the deepest sleep of stage 4 NREM, the brain's activity, measured by EEG recordings, progressively diminishes, as demonstrated by larger and slower brain waves. The four NREM stages occupy the first 50 to 70 minutes of sleep. Then, in a matter of minutes, the brain cycles back to smaller, faster brain waves, and the sleeper experiences the night's first episode of dreaming REM sleep, which lasts 5 to 15 minutes. During the rest of the night, the sleeper continues to experience 90-minute cycles of alternating NREM and REM sleep.

Source: Based on Carskadon & Dement (2005).

Stage 2 NREM

Stage 2 represents the onset of true sleep. Stage 2 sleep is defined by the appearance of **sleep spindles,** brief bursts of brain activity that last a second or two, and **K complexes,** single high-voltage spikes of brain activity (see Figure 4.2). Other than these occasional sleep spindles and K complexes, brain activity continues to slow down considerably. Breathing becomes rhythmical. Slight muscle twitches may occur. Theta waves are predominant in stage 2, but larger, slower brain waves, called *delta brain waves,* also begin to emerge. During the 15 to 20 minutes initially spent in stage 2, delta brain-wave activity gradually increases.

Stage 3 and Stage 4 NREM

In combination, stages 3 and 4 are often referred to as *slow-wave sleep* (SWS). Both stages are defined by the amount of delta brain-wave activity. When delta brain waves represent more than 20 percent of total brain activity, the sleeper is said to be in stage 3 NREM. When delta brain waves exceed 50 percent of total brain activity, the sleeper is said to be in stage 4 NREM.

During the 20 to 40 minutes spent in the night's first episode of stage 4 NREM, delta waves eventually come to represent 100 percent of brain activity. At that point, heart rate, blood pressure, and breathing rate drop to their lowest levels. Not surprisingly, the sleeper is almost completely oblivious to the world. Noises as loud as 90 decibels may fail to wake him. However, his muscles are still capable of movement. For example, if sleepwalking occurs, it typically happens during stage 4 NREM sleep.

Synchronized Sleepers As these time-lapse photographs show, couples who regularly sleep in the same bed tend to have synchronized sleep cycles. Since bed partners fall asleep at about the same time, they are likely to have similarly timed NREM–REM sleep cycles. The movements of this couple are also synchronized. Both sleepers shift position just before and after episodes of REM sleep.

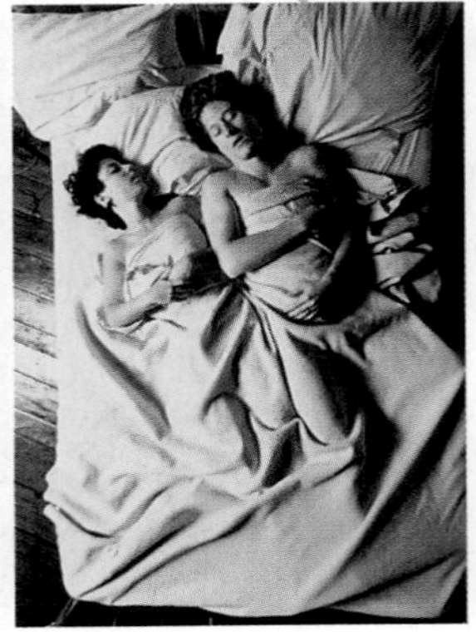

It can easily take 15 minutes or longer to regain full waking consciousness from stage 4. It's even possible to answer your cell phone or respond to a text message, carry on a conversation for several minutes, and hang up without ever leaving stage 4 sleep—and without remembering having done so the next day. When people are briefly awakened by sleep researchers during stage 4 NREM and asked to perform some simple task, they often don't remember it the next morning.

Thus far, the sleeper is approximately 70 minutes into a typical night's sleep and immersed in deeply relaxed stage 4 NREM sleep. At this point, the sequence reverses. In a matter of minutes, the sleeper cycles back from stage 4 to stage 3 to stage 2 and enters a dramatic new phase: the night's first episode of REM sleep.

sleep spindles
Short bursts of brain activity that characterize stage 2 NREM sleep.

K complex
Single but large high-voltage spike of brain activity that characterizes stage 2 NREM sleep.

REM Sleep

During REM sleep, the brain becomes more active, generating smaller and faster brain waves. Visual and motor neurons in the brain activate repeatedly, just as they do during wakefulness. Dreams usually occur during REM sleep. Although the brain is very active, voluntary muscle activity is suppressed, which prevents the dreaming sleeper from acting out his or her dreams.

REM sleep is accompanied by considerable physiological arousal. The sleeper's eyes dart back and forth behind closed eyelids—the rapid eye movements. Heart rate, blood pressure, and respirations can fluctuate up and down, sometimes extremely. Muscle twitches occur. In both sexes, sexual arousal may occur, which is not necessarily related to dream content.

This first REM episode tends to be brief, about 5 to 15 minutes. From the beginning of stage 1 NREM sleep through the completion of the first episode of REM sleep, about 90 minutes have elapsed.

Beyond the First 90 Minutes

Throughout the rest of the night, the sleeper cycles between NREM and REM sleep. Each sleep cycle lasts about 90 minutes on average, but the duration of cycles may vary from 70 to 120 minutes. Usually, four more 90-minute cycles of NREM and REM sleep occur during the night. Just before and after REM periods, the sleeper typically shifts position.

The progression of a typical night's sleep cycles is depicted in Figure 4.3. Stages 3 and 4 NREM, slow-wave sleep, usually occur only during the first two 90-minute cycles. As the night progresses, REM sleep episodes become increasingly longer and less time is spent in NREM. During the last two 90-minute sleep cycles before awakening, NREM sleep is composed primarily of stage 2 sleep and periods of REM sleep that can last as long as 40 minutes. In a later section, we'll look at dreaming and REM sleep in more detail.

Changing Sleep Patterns over the Lifespan

The different elements of sleep first emerge during prenatal development. During the last trimester of prenatal development, active (REM) and quiet (NREM) sleep cycles emerge. In the final weeks, REM and NREM sleep are clearly distinguishable in the fetus (Mirmiran & others, 2003).

IN FOCUS

What You Really Want to Know About Sleep

Why do I yawn?

Researchers aren't certain. But the notion that too little oxygen or too much carbon dioxide causes yawning is not supported by research. Some evidence suggests that yawning regulates and increases your level of arousal. Yawning is typically followed by an *increase* in activity level. Hence, you frequently yawn after waking up in the morning, while attempting to stay awake in the late evening, or when you're bored.

Is yawning contagious?

Seeing, hearing, or thinking about yawning can trigger a yawn. More than half of adults will yawn when they're shown videos of other people yawning. Blind people will yawn more frequently in response to audio recordings of yawning. (Have you yawned yet?) Some psychologists believe that contagious yawning is related to our ability to feel empathy for others. Interestingly, chimpanzees and macaques, both highly social animals, display contagious yawning. And so do domestic dogs, which in a recent study were shown to "catch" yawns from human strangers. From an evolutionary perspective, such observations lend support to the idea that contagious yawning may have evolved as an adaptive social cue, allowing groups to signal and coordinate times of activity and rest.

Why do I get sleepy?

A naturally occurring compound in the body called *adenosine* may be the culprit. In studies with cats, prolonged wakefulness sharply increases adenosine levels, which reflect energy used for brain and body activity. As adenosine levels shoot up, so does the need for sleep. Slow-wave NREM sleep reduces adenosine levels. In humans, the common stimulant drug caffeine blocks adenosine receptors, promoting wakefulness.

Sometimes in the morning when I first wake up, I can't move. I'm literally paralyzed! Is this normal?

REM sleep is characterized by paralysis of the voluntary muscles, which keeps you from acting out your dreams. In a relatively common phenomenon called **sleep paralysis,** the paralysis of REM sleep carries over to the waking state for up to 10 minutes. If preceded by an unpleasant dream or hypnagogic experience, this sensation can be frightening. Sleep paralysis can also occur as you're falling asleep. In either case, the sleep paralysis lasts for only a few minutes. So, if this happens to you, relax—voluntary muscle control will soon return.

Do deaf people who use sign language sometimes "sleep sign" during sleep?

Yes.

Do the things people say when they talk in their sleep make any sense?

Sleeptalking typically occurs during NREM stages 3 and 4. There are many anecdotes of spouses who have supposedly engaged their sleeptalking mates in extended conversations, but sleep researchers have been unsuccessful in having extended dialogues with people who chronically talk in their sleep. As for the truthfulness of the sleeptalker's utterances, they're reasonably accurate insofar as they reflect whatever the person is responding to while asleep. By the way, not only do people talk in their sleep, but they can also sing or laugh in their sleep. In one case we know of, a little boy sleepsang "Frosty the Snowman."

Is it dangerous to wake a sleepwalker?

As a general rule, no, it's not dangerous to wake a sleepwalker. Sleepwalking tends to occur during the first third of the night when the deep, slow-wave sleep of stages 3 and 4 NREM is occurring. Consequently, it's difficult to rouse the person from deep sleep and, even if you do, the sleepwalker may be confused and have no memory of sleepwalking. Although their judgment is impaired, most sleepwalkers usually respond to verbal suggestions and can be guided back to bed.

However, without realizing what they are doing, some sleepwalkers can respond aggressively, even violently, if touched. In the Prologue, this occurred on a couple of occasions to Scott as he was growing up. A little later, we'll take a more detailed look at sleepwalking and violent sleep behavior.

Sources: J. R. Anderson & Meno (2003); J. R. Anderson & others (2004); Campbell & others (2009); Cartwright (2004); Empson (2002); Gallup & Gallup (2007); Landolt (2008); J. E. Moore (1942); Platek & others (2003); Platek & others (2005); Pressman (2007); Porkka-Heiskanen & others (1997); Provine (1989); Rétey & others (2005); Roenneberg & others (2003); Saper & others (2005); Spanos, McNulty, & others (1995a); Stickgold (2005); Takeuchi & others (2002).

The newborn sleeps about 16 hours a day, though not all at once. Up to 8 hours—or 50 percent—of the newborn's sleep time is spent in REM sleep. The rest is spent in quiet sleep that is very similar to NREM stages 1 and 2. It's not until about the third month of life that the deep, slow-wave sleep of NREM stages 3 and 4 appears.

The typical 90-minute sleep cycles gradually emerge over the first few years of life. The infant's sleep during the first months of life is characterized by shorter 60-minute sleep cycles, producing up to 13 sleep cycles per day. By age 2, the toddler is experiencing 75-minute sleep cycles. By age 5, the typical 90-minute sleep cycles of alternating REM and NREM sleep are established (Grigg-Damberger & others, 2007; Jenni & others, 2004).

sleep paralysis
A temporary condition in which a person is unable to move upon awakening in the morning or during the night.

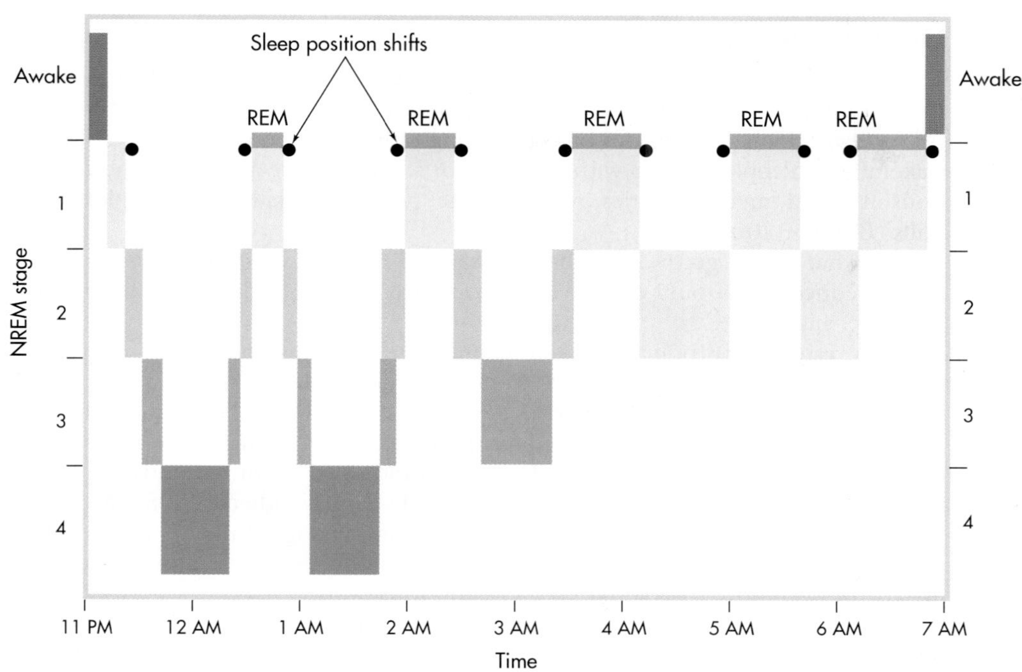

Figure 4.3 The 90-Minute Cycles of Sleep During a typical night, you experience five 90-minute cycles of alternating NREM and REM sleep. The deepest stages of NREM sleep, stages 3 and 4, occur during the first two 90-minute cycles. Dreaming REM sleep episodes become progressively longer as the night goes on. Sleep position shifts, indicated by the dots, usually occur immediately before and after REM episodes.

Source: Based on Hobson (2004).

From childhood through late adulthood, the pattern of a typical night's sleep evolves and changes (see Figure 4.4). Total sleep time and the percentage of a night's sleep spent in deeper slow-wave sleep decrease. This is offset by gradual increases in the percentage of time spent each night in lighter NREM stages 1 and 2. The percentage of a night's sleep devoted to REM sleep increases during childhood and adolescence, remains stable throughout adulthood, and then decreases during late adulthood (Ohayon & others, 2004).

Sleep-Deprived Adolescents Teenagers require about 8.5 to 9 hours of sleep each night to be fully rested. However, only 1 out of 7 U.S. teens actually gets that much sleep. Most adolescents report getting around 7 to 7.5 hours of sleep on school nights, which is probably why they sleep about 2 hours longer on weekends. Consequences of regular sleep loss include poor school performance, increased risk of accidents and injuries, and depressed mood (National Sleep Foundation, 2000).

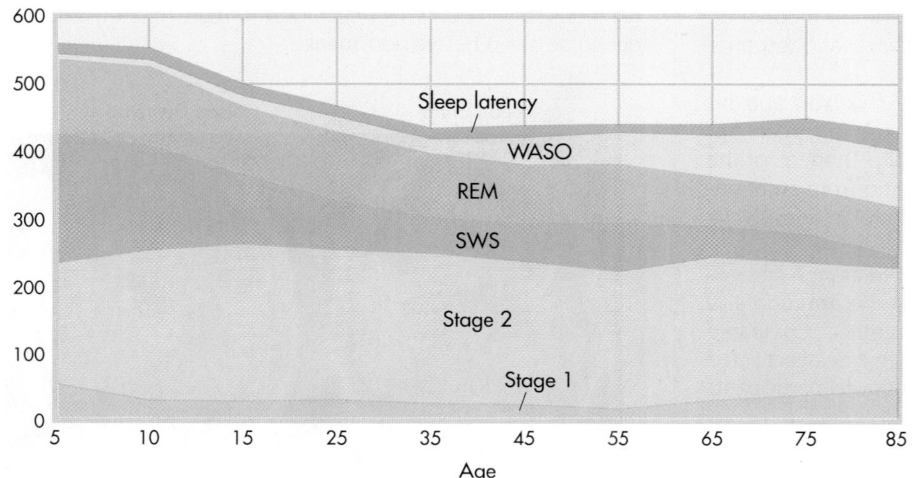

Figure 4.4 Sleep over the Lifespan Sleep quality changes significantly over the lifespan. In particular, notice that slow-wave sleep decreases over the lifespan, as does total sleep time. By middle adulthood, people are more likely to experience *wakefulness after sleep onset,* abbreviated *WASO.* Senior adults aged 55 and older often take longer to fall asleep, which is technically called *sleep latency.* Many senior adults spend an hour or more each night simply dozing or resting quietly in bed.

REM rebound
A phenomenon in which a person who is deprived of REM sleep greatly increases the amount of time spent in REM sleep at the first opportunity to sleep uninterrupted.

Do We Need to Sleep?

That we have a biological need for sleep is clearly demonstrated by *sleep deprivation studies.* After being deprived of sleep for just one night, research subjects develop *microsleeps,* which are episodes of sleep lasting only a few seconds that occur during wakefulness. People who go without sleep for a day or more also experience disruptions in mood, mental abilities, reaction time, perceptual skills, and complex motor skills (Bonnet, 2005).

But what about getting *less* than your usual amount of sleep? *Sleep restriction studies* reduce the amount of time that people are allowed to sleep to as little as four hours per night.

Sleep restriction produces numerous impairments and changes, not the least of which is an increased urge to sleep. Concentration, vigilance, reaction time, memory skills, and the ability to gauge risks are diminished. Motor skills—including driving skills—decrease, producing a greater risk of accidents. As discussed in the Focus on Neuroscience titled "The Sleep-Deprived Emotional Brain," moods, especially negative moods, become much more volatile (Dinges & others, 2005). Metabolic and hormonal disruptions occur, including harmful changes in levels of stress hormones (Van Cauter, 2005). The immune system's effectiveness is diminished, making the person more susceptible to colds and infections.

As sleep restriction continues for night after night, all of these changes become more pronounced. The problem is that most people are *not* good at judging the extent to which their performance is impaired by inadequate sleep. People tend to think they are performing adequately, but in fact, their abilities and reaction time are greatly diminished (Walker, 2008).

Sleep researchers have also selectively deprived people of different components of normal sleep. To study the effects of *REM deprivation,* researchers wake sleepers whenever the monitoring instruments indicate that they are entering REM sleep. After several nights of being selectively deprived of REM sleep, the subjects are allowed to sleep uninterrupted. What happens? They experience **REM rebound**—the amount of time spent in REM sleep increases by as much as 50 percent. Similarly, when people are selectively deprived of NREM stages 3 and 4, they experience *NREM rebound,* spending more time in NREM sleep (Borbély & Achermann, 2005; Tobler, 2005). Thus, it seems that the brain needs to experience the full range of sleep states, making up for missing sleep components when given the chance.

FOCUS ON NEUROSCIENCE

The Sleep-Deprived Emotional Brain

Whether they are children or adults, people often react with greater emotionality when they're not getting adequate sleep (Zohar & others, 2005). Is this because they're simply tired, or do the brain's emotional centers become more reactive in response to sleep deprivation?

To study this question, researcher Seung-Schik Yoo and his colleagues (2007) deprived some participants of sleep for 35 hours while other participants slept normally. Then, all of the participants observed a series of images ranging from emotionally neutral to very unpleasant and disturbing images while undergoing an fMRI brain scan.

Compare the two fMRI scans shown here. The orange and yellow areas indicate the degree of activation in the ***amygdala,*** a key component of the brain's emotional centers. Compared to the adequately rested participants, the amygdala activated 60 percent more strongly when the sleep-deprived participants looked at the aversive images.

Yoo's research clearly shows that the sleep-deprived brain is much more prone to strong emotional reactions, especially in response to negative stimuli. So when you're consistently operating on too little sleep, monitor and gauge your emotional reactions so you don't overreact, only to regret it later. Better yet, get some sleep before you speak.

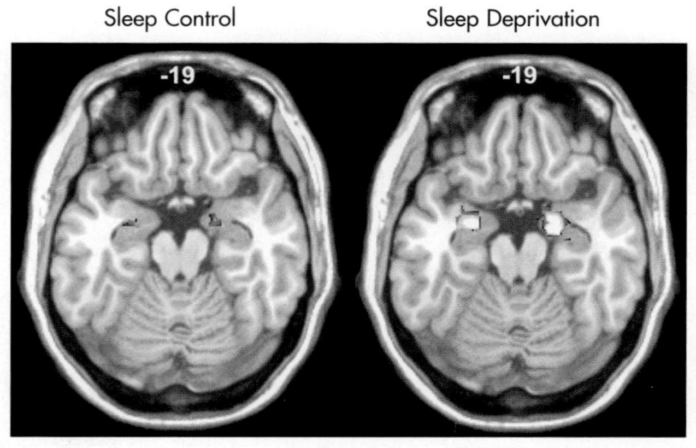

Dreams and Mental Activity During Sleep

Key Theme

- **A dream is an unfolding sequence of perceptions, thoughts, and emotions during sleep that is experienced as a series of actual events.**

Key Questions

- **How does brain activity change during dreaming sleep, and how are those changes related to dream content?**
- **What role do the different stages of sleep play in forming new memories?**
- **What do people dream about, and why don't we remember many of our dreams?**

sleep thinking
Vague, bland, thoughtlike ruminations about real-life events that typically occur during NREM sleep; also called *sleep mentation.*

dream
An unfolding sequence of thoughts, perceptions, and emotions that typically occurs during REM sleep and is experienced as a series of real-life events.

Dreams have fascinated people since the beginning of time. By adulthood, about 25 percent of a night's sleep, or almost two hours every night, is spent dreaming. So, assuming you live to a ripe old age, you'll devote more than 50,000 hours, or about six years of your life, to dreaming.

Although dreams may be the most interesting brain productions during sleep, they are not the most common. More prevalent is **sleep thinking,** also called *sleep mentation.* Sleep thinking usually occurs during NREM slow-wave sleep and consists of vague, bland, thoughtlike ruminations about real-life events (McCarley, 2007). Sleep thinking probably contributes to those times when you wake up with a solution to some vexing problem. But at other times, the ruminating thoughts of sleep thinking can interfere with your sleep. For example, on the night before an important exam, anxious students will sometimes toss and turn their way through the night as they mentally review terms and concepts during NREM sleep thinking.

In contrast to sleep thinking, a **dream** is an unfolding sequence of perceptions, thoughts, and emotions during sleep that is experienced as a series of real-life events (Domhoff, 2005). Granted, the storyline and details of those dream events may be illogical, even bizarre. But in the unique mental landscape of our own internally generated reality, the bizarre and illogical are readily accepted as disbelief is suspended.

Although dreams can occur in NREM sleep, most dreams happen during REM sleep. When awakened during active REM sleep, people report a dream about 95 percent of the time, even people who claim that they never dream. The dreamer is usually the main participant in these events, and at least one other person is involved in the dream story. But sometimes the dreamer is simply the observer of the unfolding dream story.

People usually have four or five dreaming episodes each night. The first REM episode of the night is the shortest, lasting only about 10 minutes. Subsequent REM episodes average around 30 minutes and tend to get longer as the night continues. Early morning dreams, which can last 40 minutes or longer, are the dreams most likely to be recalled.

PET and fMRI scans have revealed that the brain's activity during REM sleep is distinctly different from its activity during either wakefulness or NREM slow-wave sleep (Fuller & others, 2006; Nofzinger, 2006). These differences and the role they play in dream content are explored in the Focus on Neuroscience box titled "The Dreaming Brain: Turning REM On and Off."

Dream Images Although people tend to emphasize visual imagery when describing their dreams, sounds and physical sensations are also commonly present. Sensations of falling, flying, spinning, or trying to run may be experienced. We tend to dream of familiar people and places, but the juxtapositions of characters, objects, and events are typically illogical, even bizarre (Nielsen & Stenstrom, 2005). Nevertheless, the dreamer rarely questions a dream's details—until he or she wakes up!

FOCUS ON NEUROSCIENCE

The Dreaming Brain: Turning REM On and Off

Neuroscientists are making sense out of the fact that our dreams often don't make sense. Compared to the awake brain, or even the brain in NREM sleep, the dreaming brain undergoes distinct changes. About every 90 minutes, key brain areas are ramped up, scaled back, or blocked from sending or receiving input during REM sleep. Levels of certain neurotransmitters surge while other neurotransmitters recede. As the internal dynamics of the brain fluctuate, they are reflected in the psychological and emotional aspects of the dream itself (Fuller & others, 2006; Nofzinger, 2006; Pace-Schott, 2005).

REM-off and REM-on Neurons

Earlier on page 145, Figure 4.3 depicted the 90-minute cycles of NREM and REM sleep over a typical night. Although the figure gives the impression of distinct shifts from one NREM stage to another, and from NREM to REM sleep, it's not quite like shifting gears. Instead, each 90-minute cycle of NREM and REM sleep reflects the gradually changing balance of REM-off and REM-on neuronal activity.

REM-off neurons produce the neurotransmitters *norepinephrine* and *serotonin,* which suppress REM sleep. In contrast, REM-on neurons produce the neurotransmitter *acetylcholine,* which promotes REM sleep. When the activity of REM-on neurons and acetylcholine levels reach a certain threshold, the characteristic signs of REM sleep emerge—increased brain activity, rapid eye movements, and suppressed voluntary muscle movements. As acetylcholine levels continue to rise, these REM-related characteristics intensify. When acetylcholine and REM activity peaks, REM-off neuronal activity picks up, increasing serotonin and norepinephrine levels. Eventually, REM sleep is suppressed and the characteristic features of slow-wave NREM sleep reemerge—reduced brain and physiological activity, movement capabilities, and the vague, ruminating thoughts of sleep thinking (McCarley, 2007).

Adjusting the Brain for REM Sleep

PET scan and other neuroimaging studies have revealed how the brain's activity during REM sleep is distinctly different from its activity as compared to wakefulness (PET scan *a*) and NREM slow-wave sleep (PET scan *b*). To help orient you, the top of each PET scan corresponds to the front of the brain and the bottom to the back of the brain. The PET scans are color-coded: Bluish-purple indicates areas of decreased brain activity and yellow-red indicates areas of increased brain activity.

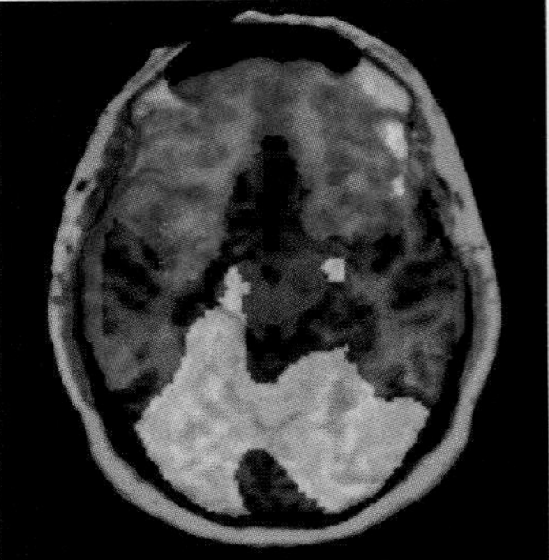

(a) REM sleep compared to wakefulness

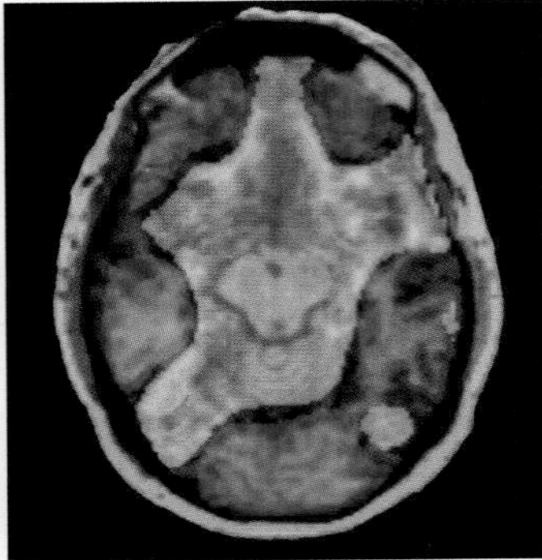

(b) REM sleep compared to slow-wave sleep

Compared to wakefulness, PET scan (*a*) reveals that REM sleep involves decreased activity in the frontal lobes, which are involved in rational thinking. Also decreased is the activity of the primary visual cortex, which normally processes external visual stimuli. In effect, the dreamer is cut off from the reality-testing functions of the frontal lobes—a fact that no doubt contributes to the weirdness of some dreams. The yellow-red areas in PET scan (*a*) indicate increased activity in association areas of the visual cortex. This brain activation gives rise to the visual images occurring in a dream.

Compared to slow-wave sleep, the yellow-red areas in PET scan (*b*) indicate that REM sleep is characterized by a sharp increase in limbic system brain areas associated with emotion, motivation, and memory. The activation of limbic system brain areas reflects the dream's emotional qualities, which can sometimes be intense (Braun & others, 1998; Nofzinger, 2005b).

Sleep and Memory Formation: Let Me Sleep on It!

Sleep plays a critical role in strengthening new memories and in integrating new memories with existing memories (Ellenbogen & others, 2007; Walker, 2005). Interestingly, different sleep states and stages seem to contribute to forming different kinds of memories. For example, research suggests that NREM slow-wave sleep contributes to forming new *episodic memories,* which are memories of personally experienced events (Rasch & Born, 2008). In contrast, REM sleep and NREM stage 2 sleep seem to help consolidate new *procedural memories,* which involve learning a new skill or task until it can be performed automatically (Stickgold & Walker, 2007; Walker & Stickgold, 2006).

Sleep researchers are finding that the strengthening and enhancement of new memories during sleep is a very active process. That active process seems to work like this: New memories formed during the day are *reactivated* during the 90-minute cycles of sleep that occur throughout the night. This process of repeatedly reactivating these newly encoded memories during sleep strengthens the neuronal connections that contribute to forming long-term memories. But along with helping solidify new memories, sleep is also critical to integrating the new memories into existing networks of memories (Rasch & Born, 2008; Stickgold & Walker, 2007).

Dream Themes and Imagery

The Golden Horse in the Clouds

"Look, don't try to weasel out of this. It was my dream, but you had the affair in it."

The popular stereotype is that very weird and highly emotional dreams are the norm. Granted, almost everyone can remember having had a really bizarre, rapidly shifting dream at some time or another. But research on dream content shows that bizarre dream stories tend to be the exception, not the rule. As psychologist William Domhoff (2007) explains:

> A wide range of studies in both laboratory and non-laboratory settings shows that dreams are far more coherent, patterned, and thoughtful than is suggested by the usual image of them. Rather than bizarre, dreams are, by and large, a realistic simulation of waking life. At the same time, there are aspects of dream content that are unusual and perhaps nonsensical. Nevertheless, controlled laboratory studies reveal that dreams are overwhelmingly about everyday settings, people, activities, and events, with only a relatively small amount of bizarreness.

So if dreams are reasonable reflections of the dreamer's waking world, what about unlikely or impossible events that are supposedly very common themes, such as dreaming that you are naked in a public place, flying through the air under your own power, wandering around lost, or tumbling through space? Common student dream themes supposedly include failing an exam or being completely unprepared in class. Are such dream themes really that common?

Apparently not. In reviewing studies of dream content, Domhoff (2005) has concluded that so-called common dream themes are actually quite rare in dream reports. Although dream story details may be original in that the events have never

IN FOCUS

What You Really Want to Know About Dreams

If I fall off a cliff in my dreams and don't wake up before I hit the bottom, will I die?

The first obvious problem with this bit of folklore is that if you did die before you woke up, how would anyone know what you'd been dreaming about? Beyond this basic contradiction, studies have shown that about a third of dreamers can recall a dream in which they died or were killed.

Do animals dream?

Virtually all mammals experience sleep cycles in which REM sleep alternates with slow-wave NREM sleep. Animals clearly demonstrate perception and memory. They also communicate using vocalizations, facial expressions, posture, and gestures to show territoriality and sexual receptiveness. Thus, it's quite reasonable to conclude that the brain and other physiological changes that occur during animal REM sleep are coupled with mental images.

What do blind people "see" when they dream?

People who become totally blind before the age of 5 typically do not have visual dreams as adults. Even so, their dreams are just as complex and vivid as sighted people's dreams; they just involve other sensations—of sound, taste, smell, and touch.

Is it possible to control your dreams?

Yes, if you have lucid dreams. A *lucid dream* is one in which you become aware that you are dreaming while you are still asleep. About half of all people can recall at least one lucid dream, and some people frequently have lucid dreams. The dreamer can often consciously guide the course of a lucid dream, including backing it up and making it go in a different direction.

Can you predict the future with your dreams?

History is filled with stories of dream prophecies. Over the course of your life, you will have over 100,000 dreams. Simply by chance, it's not surprising that every now and then a dream contains elements that coincide with future events.

Are dreams in color or black and white?

Up to 80 percent of our dreams contain color. When dreamers are awakened and asked to match dream colors to standard color charts, soft pastel colors are frequently chosen.

Sources: Anch & others (1988); Blackmore (1998); Empson (2002); Halliday (1995); Hobson (2004); Hurovitz & others (1999); Schatzman & Fenwick (1994); Weinstein & others (1991).

actually happened, the details usually aren't fantastic (e.g., being naked in public) or completely off the wall (e.g., flying through the air). And rather than wildly fluctuating emotions, when emotions are experienced in dreams, they are usually appropriate in the context of the dream story.

So what patterns and themes are typical? Here are some of the well-substantiated findings on common dream content (Domhoff, 2007, 2003):

- Women report males and females in equal proportion as other dream story characters.
- Men are more likely to report other males as the dream story characters.
- Negative feelings and events are more common than positive ones.
- Instances of aggression are more common than are instances of friendliness.
- Dreamers are more likely to be victims of aggression than aggressors in their dreams.
- Men are much more likely than women to report dreams involving physical aggression.
- Women are more likely than men to report emotions in their dreams.
- Sex or sexual behaviors seldom occur as elements of the dream story.
- Apprehension or fear is the most frequently reported dream emotion for both sexes, followed by happiness and confusion.

"Off with his head! Off with his head!"

If apprehensive or fearful emotions become progressively more intense as a dream story unfolds, the person may experience a nightmare. A **nightmare** is a vivid and disturbing dream that often awakens the sleeper. The typical nightmare storyline is that of being helpless or powerless in the face of being aggressively attacked or pursued. Although fear, anxiety, and even terror are the most commonly experienced emotions, some nightmares involve intense feelings of sadness, anger, disgust, or embarrassment (Nielsen & Zadra, 2005).

During a nightmare, the disturbing and emotionally charged dream imagery rapidly accelerates, often causing the person to awaken. Upon jolting awake, the person is alert and can immediately recall the exact, frightening dream details.

The frequency of nightmares is closely related to age. Nightmares occur most commonly during middle and late childhood, then decrease in frequency during adolescence and young adulthood. Although estimates vary, approximately 25 percent of kids in the 5–11 age group report having at least one nightmare per week (Mindell & Barrett, 2002).

Among adults, nightmares are much more common than generally believed. Approximately 5 percent to 10 percent of adults experience nightmares on a weekly basis. Family and twin studies strongly suggest that some people may be genetically predisposed to regular nightmares.

Gender also plays a role in nightmare frequency. Compared to men, women at all ages report more frequent nightmares. Daytime stress, anxiety, and emotional difficulties are often associated with nightmares. As a general rule, nightmares are not indicative of a psychological or sleep disorder unless they occur frequently, cause difficulties returning to sleep, or cause daytime distress (Levin & Nielsen, 2007; Nielsen & others, 2006).

nightmare
A vivid and frightening or unpleasant anxiety dream that occurs during REM sleep.

The Significance of Dreams

Key Theme

- **The notion that dream images contain symbolic messages has been challenged by contemporary neuroscience studies of the dreaming brain.**

Key Questions

- **How did Freud explain dreams?**
- **How does the activation–synthesis model explain dreams?**
- **What general conclusions can be drawn about the nature of dreams?**

For thousands of years and throughout many cultures, dreams have been thought to contain highly significant, cryptic messages. Do dreams mean anything? Do they contain symbolic or hidden messages? In this section, we will look at two theories that try to account for the purpose of dreaming, starting with the most famous one.

Sigmund Freud

Dreams as Fulfilled Wishes

Freud on the Meaning of Dreams Dream intrepretation played an important role in Sigmund Freud's famous form of psychotherapy, called *psychoanalysis.* Freud believed that because psychological defenses are reduced during sleep, frustrated sexual and aggressive wishes are expressed symbolically in dreams. "In every dream an instinctual wish has to be represented as fulfilled," Freud (1933) wrote. According to Freud, we consciously remember the *manifest content,* or actual dream images. Hidden is what Freud called the *latent content*—the true, unconscious meaning of the dream, which is disguised by the dream symbols.

In the chapters on personality and therapies (Chapters 10 and 14), we'll look in detail at the ideas of **Sigmund Freud,** the founder of psychoanalysis. As we discussed in Chapter 1, Freud believed that sexual and aggressive instincts are the motivating forces that dictate human behavior. Because these instinctual urges are so consciously unacceptable, sexual and aggressive thoughts, feelings, and wishes are pushed into the unconscious, or *repressed.* However, Freud believed that these repressed urges and wishes could surface in dream imagery.

In his landmark work, *The Interpretation of Dreams* (1900), Freud wrote that dreams are the "disguised fulfillments of repressed wishes" and provide "the royal road to a knowledge of the unconscious mind." In fact, he contended that "wish-fulfillment is the meaning of each and every dream." According to Freud, then, dreams function as a sort of psychological "safety valve" for the release of unconscious and unacceptable urges.

Freud (1904) believed that dreams have two components: the **manifest content,** or the dream images themselves, and the **latent content,** the disguised psychological meaning of the dream. For example, Freud (1911) believed that dream images of sticks, swords, brooms, and other elongated objects were *phallic symbols,* representing the penis. Dream images of cupboards, boxes, and ovens supposedly symbolized the vagina.

In some types of psychotherapy today, especially those that follow Freud's ideas, dreams are still seen as an important source of information about psychological conflicts (Auld & others, 2005; Pesant & Zadra, 2004). However, Freud's belief that dreams represent the fulfillment of repressed wishes has not been substantiated by psychological research (Fisher & Greenberg, 1996; Schatzman & Fenwick, 1994). Furthermore, research does not support Freud's belief that the dream images themselves—the manifest content of dreams—are symbols that disguise the dream's true psychological meaning (Domhoff, 2003). According to psychologist William Domhoff (2004):

manifest content
In Freud's psychoanalytic theory, the elements of a dream that are consciously experienced and remembered by the dreamer.

latent content
In Freud's psychoanalytic theory, the unconscious wishes, thoughts, and urges that are concealed in the manifest content of a dream.

Many different kinds of studies refute Freudian dream theory on every point where it has proved to be testable. Beyond the general idea that the brain becomes "activated" or "aroused" during dreaming, an idea that is now accepted by all theorists, there is nothing else to salvage from Freudian dream theory. It is time to abandon Freud's theory and use [contemporary] findings in the development of a new theory of dreams.

Dream Researcher J. Allan Hobson Neuroscientist J. Allan Hobson developed the activation–synthesis model of dreaming with his colleague Robert McCarley. Although Hobson believes that dreams are the by-products of physiological processes in the brain, he does not believe that dreams are meaningless. Hobson (1999) observed, "Dreaming may be our most creative conscious state, one in which the chaotic, spontaneous recombination of cognitive elements produces novel configurations of information: new ideas. While many or even most of these ideas may be nonsensical, if even a few of its fanciful products are truly useful, our dream time will not have been wasted."

The Activation–Synthesis Model of Dreaming

Researchers **J. Allan Hobson** and **Robert McCarley** first proposed a new model of dreaming in 1977. Called the **activation–synthesis model of dreaming,** this model maintains that dreaming is our subjective awareness of the brain's internally generated signals during sleep. Since it was first proposed, the model has evolved as new findings have been reported (see McCarley, 2007; Pace-Schott, 2005).

Specifically, the activation–synthesis model maintains that the experience of dreaming sleep is due to the automatic activation of brainstem circuits at the base of the brain (see Figure 4.5). These circuits arouse more sophisticated brain areas, including visual, auditory, and motor pathways. As noted earlier in the Focus on Neuroscience box "The Dreaming Brain," limbic system structures involved in emotion, such as the amygdala and hippocampus, are activated during REM sleep. When we're awake, these brain structures and pathways are involved in registering stimuli from the external world. But rather than responding to stimulation from the external environment, the dreaming brain is responding to its own internally generated signals (Hobson, 2005).

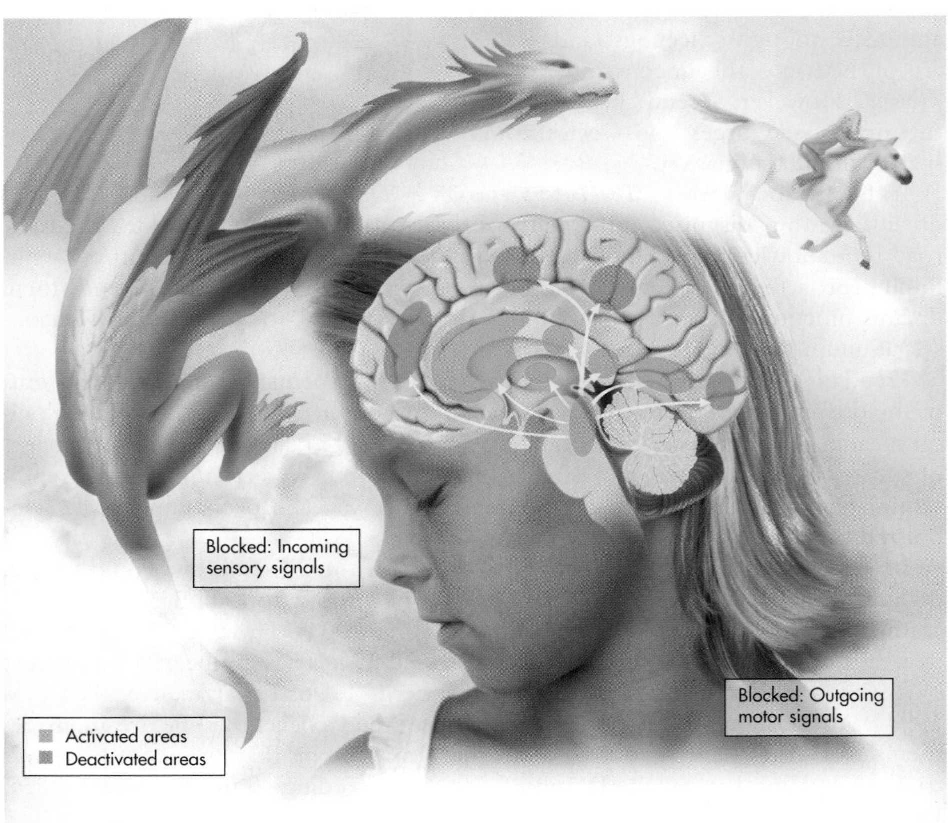

Figure 4.5 The Activation–Synthesis Model of Dreaming According to the activation–synthesis model of dreaming, dreaming is our subjective awareness of the brain's internally generated signals during sleep. Dreaming is initiated when brainstem circuits arouse brain areas involved in emotions, memories, movements, and sensations. These activated brain areas, shown in green, give rise to dreaming consciousness and the dream imaginations of sensations, perceptions, movements, and feelings. The activated brain synthesizes, or combines, these elements, drawing on previous experiences and memories to impose a personal meaning on the dream story (Hobson, 2005; McCarley, 2007).

Other brain areas, highlighted in purple, are deactivated or blocked during dreaming. Outgoing motor signals and incoming sensory signals are blocked, keeping the dreamer from acting out the dream or responding to external stimuli (Pace-Schott, 2005). The logical, rational, and planning functions of the prefrontal cortex are suspended. Hence, dream stories can evolve in ways that seem disjointed or illogical. And because the prefrontal cortex is involved in processing memories, most nightly dream productions evaporate with no lingering memories of having had these experiences (Muzur & others, 2002).

Sources: Adapted from Hobson (2005); Pace-Schott (2005).

In the absence of external sensory input, the activated brain combines, or synthesizes, these internally generated sensory signals and imposes meaning on them. The dream story itself is derived from a hodgepodge of memories, emotions, and sensations that are triggered by the brain's activation and chemical changes during sleep. According to this model, then, dreaming is essentially the brain synthesizing and integrating memory fragments, emotions, and sensations that are internally triggered (Hobson & others, 1998).

The activation–synthesis theory does *not* contend that dreams are completely meaningless. But if there is a meaning to dreams, that meaning lies in the deeply personal way in which the images are organized, or synthesized. In other words, the meaning is to be found not by decoding the dream symbols, but by analyzing the way the dreamer makes sense of the progression of chaotic dream images. As Hobson (2005) explains:

> For activation–synthesis, both emotional salience and the cognitive mishmash of dreams are the undisguised read-out of the dreaming brain's unique chemistry and physiology. This doesn't mean that dreams make no psychological sense. On the contrary, dreams are dripping with emotional salience. Dreams can and should be discussed for their informative messages about the emotional concerns of the dreamer.

activation–synthesis model of dreaming
The theory that brain activity during sleep produces dream images (*activation*), which are combined by the brain into a dream story (*synthesis*).

sleep disorders
Serious and consistent sleep disturbances that interfere with daytime functioning and cause subjective distress.

dyssomnias
(dis-SOM-nee-uz) A category of sleep disorders involving disruptions in the amount, quality, or timing of sleep; includes insomnia, obstructive sleep apnea, and narcolepsy.

parasomnias
(pare-uh-SOM-nee-uz) A category of sleep disorders characterized by arousal or activation during sleep or sleep transitions; includes *sleepwalking, sleep terrors, sleepsex, sleep-related eating disorder,* and *REM sleep behavior disorder.*

insomnia
A condition in which a person regularly experiences an inability to fall asleep, to stay asleep, or to feel adequately rested by sleep.

Sleep Disorders

Key Theme

- **Sleep disorders are surprisingly common, take many different forms, and interfere with a person's daytime functioning.**

Key Questions

- **How do the two broad categories of sleep disorders differ?**
- **Which sleep disorders are characterized by excessive daytime sleepiness?**
- **What kinds of behavior are displayed in the different parasomnias?**

Data from the National Sleep Foundation's annual polls indicate that about 7 out of 10 people experience regular sleep disruptions. Such disruptions become a **sleep disorder** when (a) abnormal sleep patterns consistently occur, (b) they cause subjective distress, and (c) they interfere with a person's daytime functioning (Thorpy, 2005a).

In this section, you'll see how those complaints are magnified in different sleep disorders, which fall into two broad categories. First, we'll consider **dyssomnias**, which are sleep disorders involving disruptions in the amount, quality, or timing of sleep. Insomnia, obstructive sleep apnea, and narcolepsy are examples of dyssomnias. Then we'll consider the **parasomnias**, which are sleep disorders involving undesirable physical arousal, behaviors, or events during sleep or sleep transitions.

The Perils of Driving While Drowsy
According to studies reported by the National Highway Traffic Safety Administration (2003), drowsiness is blamed for at least 100,000 traffic accidents each year, causing more than 70,000 injuries—and 1,500 deaths. While many people in the United States get by with too little sleep, one group is especially prone to the effects of sleepiness behind the wheel—adult males age 25 or younger. Young male drivers have the highest number of traffic accidents that can be attributed to drowsiness (National Sleep Foundation, 2000).

Insomnia

Fragmented, Dissatisfying Sleep

Insomnia is not defined solely based on how long a person sleeps because people vary in how much sleep they need to feel refreshed. Rather, people are said to experience **insomnia** when they repeatedly (a) complain about the quality or duration of their sleep, (b) have difficulty going to sleep or staying asleep, or (c) wake before it is time to get up. In terms of going to sleep, regularly taking 30 minutes or longer to fall asleep is considered a symptom of insomnia. These disruptions produce daytime sleepiness, fatigue, impaired social or occupational performance, or mood disturbances (Edinger & Means, 2005).

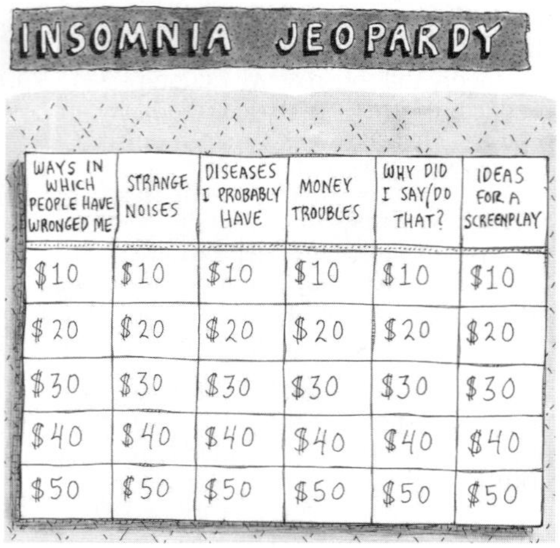

INSOMNIA JEOPARDY

WAYS IN WHICH PEOPLE HAVE WRONGED ME	STRANGE NOISES	DISEASES I PROBABLY HAVE	MONEY TROUBLES	WHY DID I SAY/DO THAT?	IDEAS FOR A SCREENPLAY
$10	$10	$10	$10	$10	$10
$20	$20	$20	$20	$20	$20
$30	$30	$30	$30	$30	$30
$40	$40	$40	$40	$40	$40
$50	$50	$50	$50	$50	$50

Insomnia is the most common sleep complaint among adults. Estimates of the prevalence of insomnia vary widely depending on the criteria used. Using conservative estimates, about 1 out of 3 people occasionally experience *transient insomnia* lasting from one or two nights to a couple of weeks. About 1 out of 10 adults experience *chronic insomnia* with symptoms at least three nights each week that persist for a month or longer (Mahowald & Schenck, 2005; National Sleep Foundation, 2005).

The risk of insomnia is influenced by gender and age. Women are twice as likely to suffer from insomnia as men. Certain social factors, such as being unemployed or divorced, are related to poor sleep and increase the risk of insomnia in women. Pregnancy can also disrupt how well a woman sleeps (see Table 4.2). Insomnia also tends to increase with age. In older women who are approaching menopause, hot flashes and night sweats can often disturb sleep (Edinger & Means, 2005; National Sleep Foundation, 2006).

The sleep-related disruptions of insomnia are often a matter of *hyperarousal*—the person's level of arousal interferes with his or her ability to go to sleep or stay asleep. The source of the arousal can be physical, psychological, or behavioral. For example, insomnia can be caused by excitement or anticipation of an event, physical pain or discomfort, psychological distress or depression, or medications, such as antihistamines. Use of common stimulants, such as caffeine or nicotine, or poor sleep habits can also disrupt sleep. Noise, excessive heat or cold, unfamiliar surroundings, and other environmental factors can also contribute to sleep-related problems.

Most commonly, insomnia can be traced to anxiety over stressful life events, such as job or school difficulties, troubled relationships, the illness or death of a loved one, or financial problems. As the person worries and ruminates over the matter, anxiety intensifies, disrupting the ability to go to sleep or stay asleep. After a few nights of fragmented sleep, concerns about sleeping get added to whatever waking anxieties the person may already be experiencing. As the person becomes hypersensitive to their sleeping difficulties, a self-perpetuating *vicious circle* can develop—concerns about the inability to sleep make disrupted sleep even more likely, further intensifying anxiety and worry over personal difficulties, producing more sleep difficulties, and so on (Perlis & others, 2005).

Although numerous causes can initially trigger insomnia, psychological and behavioral factors are almost always involved in perpetuating the problem. Fortunately, there are effective evidence-based psychological and behavioral treatments. In Enhancing Well-Being with Psychology, at the end of the chapter, we'll describe one effective behavioral treatment for insomnia and give you several suggestions to improve the quality of your sleep.

Table 4.2

Sleep by the Numbers: America's Women

72%	Working mothers who experience symptoms of insomnia a few nights each week
74%	Stay-at-home mothers who experience insomnia symptoms a few nights each week
84%	Pregnant women who report insomnia symptoms a few nights each week
54%	Single, working women who wake up feeling unrefreshed at least a few days each week
3.1	Cups or cans of caffeinated beverages consumed daily by single, working women
27%	Women who have driven while drowsy at least 1 or 2 times in the past month

Source: National Sleep Foundation (2007).

Obstructive Sleep Apnea

Blocked Breathing During Sleep

Excessive daytime sleepiness is also a key symptom of the second most common sleep disorder. In **obstructive sleep apnea (OSA),** the sleeper's airway becomes narrowed or blocked, causing very shallow breathing or repeated pauses in breathing. Over the course of a night, 300 or more sleep apnea episodes can occur (Schwab & others, 2005).

Each time breathing stops, oxygen blood levels decrease and carbon dioxide blood levels increase. In response to these internal warning signals, the brain triggers a momentary awakening. As breathing resumes and the sleeper gulps in air, snorting or choking sounds typically occur. Often the sleeper has no recollection of these repeated brief awakenings. Not surprisingly, these symptoms are usually first noticed by the sleeper's bed partner or another family member.

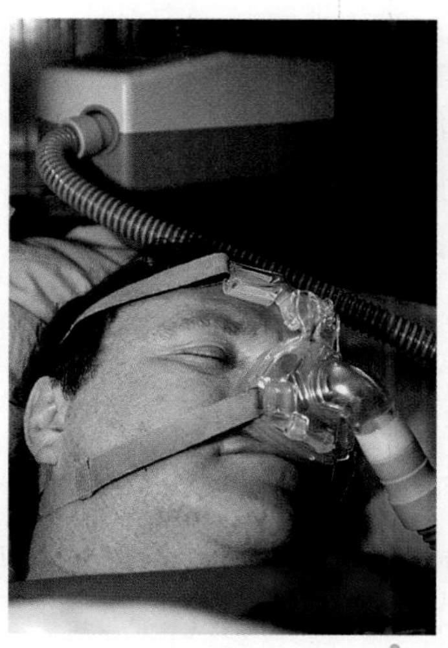

Treating Sleep Apnea: CPAP The most common treatment for sleep apnea is CPAP, which stands for *continuous positive airway pressure.* The sleeping person wears a mask that covers the nose and sometimes the mouth. A flexible tube connects the mask to the CPAP machine, which gently blows air through the airway passage at a pressure that is high enough to keep the airway open. For people with moderate to severe sleep apnea, CPAP treatment often produces rapid improvements, including reduced daytime sleepiness, greater alertness, and reduced blood pressure (Lindberg & others, 2006; Lüthje & Andreas, 2008).

Obstructive sleep apnea disrupts the quality and quantity of a person's sleep, causing daytime grogginess, poor concentration, memory and learning problems, and irritability (Weaver & George, 2005). It also increases other serious health risks, such as high blood pressure, heart attack, and stroke.

Family and twin studies indicate that obstructive sleep apnea tends to run in families (Redline, 2005). Although OSA can occur in any age group, including small children, it becomes more common as people age. It is also more common in men than women. Among middle-aged adults, about 1 out of 25 men and 1 out of 50 women have sleep apnea. Among senior adults, approximately 1 in 10 has sleep apnea.

Sleep apnea can often be treated with lifestyle changes, such as avoiding alcohol or losing weight (Hoffstein, 2005; Powell & others, 2005). For people who experience sleep apnea only when they sleep on their backs, treatment can be as simple as sewing a tennis ball to the back of their pajama tops, forcing the person to sleep on his or her side. Moderate to severe cases of sleep apnea are usually treated with *continuous positive airway pressure* (CPAP), which is described in the photo caption (Grunstein, 2005).

Narcolepsy

Blurring the Boundaries Between Sleep and Wakefulness

Even with adequate nighttime sleep, people with **narcolepsy** experience overwhelming bouts of excessive daytime sleepiness and brief, uncontrollable episodes of sleep. These involuntary sleep episodes, called *sleep attacks* or *microsleeps*, typically last from a few seconds to several minutes. After the brief sleep episode, the person usually feels refreshed. And, for the next hour or two, grogginess and drowsiness diminish.

During a microsleep, people with narcolepsy can display *automatic behavior* and continue performing a routine behavior, such as writing or text messaging. But as you might suspect, task performance is impaired. Handwriting becomes illegible. Mistyped letters occur. This automatic behavior is very similar to the movement capabilities that can occur during normal NREM sleep at night.

Most people with narcolepsy—about 70 percent—experience regular episodes of cataplexy. Much like the suppression of voluntary muscle movements that occurs during normal REM sleep, **cataplexy** is the sudden loss of voluntary muscle strength and control, lasting from several seconds to several minutes. Usually triggered by a sudden, intense emotion, such as laughter, anger, fear, or surprise, mild cataplectic episodes might not even be noticed by others. The narcoleptic person's eyelids or head droops. His or her grip of an object loosens. Facial muscles momentarily sag.

obstructive sleep apnea
(APP-nee-uh) A sleep disorder in which the person repeatedly stops breathing during sleep.

narcolepsy
(NAR-ko-lep-see) A sleep disorder characterized by excessive daytime sleepiness and brief lapses into sleep throughout the day.

cataplexy
A sudden loss of voluntary muscle strength and control that is usually triggered by an intense emotion.

But in more severe episodes of cataplexy, the person may completely lose muscle control, knees buckling as he or she collapses. Although unable to move or speak, the person is conscious and aware of what is happening.

Narcolepsy is a dyssomnia that occurs in every culture and ethnic group, and it affects males and females equally. Although nowhere near as common as insomnia or sleep apnea, narcolepsy affects about 1 person in every 2,000 in the United States and Canada. Interestingly, prevalence rates vary by culture. For example, narcolepsy is much more common—about 1 in every 600 people—in Japan. Compare that with Israel, where a prevalence rate of less than 1 out of every 500,000 people makes narcolepsy rare (Longstreth & others, 2007; Silber & others, 2002).

Narcolepsy is considered a lifelong, chronic condition. The onset of narcolepsy can occur at any age, including very young children. Onset usually occurs during adolescence or young adulthood, but the condition often goes undiagnosed or is misdiagnosed for years. Although genetics may play a role—about 10 percent of people with narcolepsy have a relative with the same symptoms—most people with the disorder have no family history of narcolepsy.

Research points to multiple factors in the development of narcolepsy, including chromosomal, brain, neurotransmitter, and immune system abnormalities. Of note is the recent scientific discovery of a special class of neurotransmitters called **hypocretins.** Also called *orexins*, hypocretins are produced exclusively by neurons in the *hypothalamus*. These hypothalamus neurons actively produce hypocretins during the daytime to maintain a steady state of wakefulness. When measured in spinal fluid, people with narcolepsy have very low or nonexistent hypocretin levels. Autopsies of people who had narcolepsy have revealed greatly reduced numbers of hypocretin-producing neurons in their brains (Datta & MacLean, 2007; Ohno & Sakurai, 2008).

Although narcolepsy cannot yet be cured, various medications can help minimize symptoms. For example, *modafinil* (Provigil®) and *sodium oxybate* (Xyrem®) are medications that reduce the excessive daytime sleepiness experienced by people with narcolepsy (Kim & others, 2007). Antidepressant medications can help reduce episodes of cataplexy, sleep paralysis, and unpleasant hallucinations associated with sleep onset or awakening from sleep. Although they can be helpful, these medications are far from being a panacea and, in fact, have potentially serious side effects (Thorpy, 2007).

An Episode of Cataplexy in Narcolepsy In this sequence of images, a man with narcolepsy experiences one of its most dramatic symptoms—cataplexy. Cataplexy involves the sudden and complete loss of muscle tone, and it is typically triggered by laughter, embarrassment, or some other type of emotional arousal. Although unable to move, the person remains conscious and aware of what is going on around him.

The Parasomnias

Undesired Arousal or Actions During Sleep

The parasomnias are a diverse collection of sleep disorders involving undesirable physical arousal, behaviors, or events during sleep or sleep transitions (Mahowald & Schenck, 2005; Schenck, 2007). In the past, people were reluctant to discuss these sleep disturbances, hence the parasomnias were long thought to be rare. But as you'll see in this section, collectively, the parasomnias are very common.

Ranging from simple to very complex behaviors, each of the parasomnias involves some degree of waking arousal mixed with sleep. The person's brain is just awake enough to carry out the actions yet is still so immersed in sleep that he or she has no conscious awareness or subsequent memory of having performed the actions. Along with amnesia for the behaviors or events, other features tend to characterize the parasomnias. As a general rule, parasomnias:

- Arise during the NREM stages 3 and 4 slow-wave sleep that occurs in the first half of the night.
- Are more common in children and decrease with age.

hypocretins
A special class of neurotransmitters produced during the daytime to maintain a steady state of wakefulness.

- Occur in multiple family or extended family members, suggesting a genetic predisposition or susceptibility.
- Can be triggered by wide-ranging stimuli, including sleep deprivation, stress, erratic sleep schedules, sleeping medications, stimulants, pregnancy, and tranquilizers.
- Are not fully understood as sleep researchers try to disentangle the roles of brain, neurotransmitter, genetic, and environmental mechanisms in these disturbances.

Sleep Terrors

Also called *night terrors,* **sleep terrors** typically occur in the first few hours of sleep during stage 3 or 4 NREM sleep. Physiologically, the first sign of a sleep terror is sharply increased physiological arousal—restlessness, sweating, and a racing heart. The person abruptly sits up in bed and may let out a panic-stricken scream or cry for help. To anyone who investigates, the person appears to be awake, thrashing in bed, terrified, and disoriented.

Whereas a *nightmare* involves a progressive unpleasant dream story, a sleep terror is usually accompanied by a single but terrifying sensation, such as being crushed or falling. Often, the person imagines that he or she is choking or being smothered or that a threatening figure is present, such as an animal or a monster. Despite the appearance of being awake, it is impossible to calm down the person. In fact, such efforts may actually produce the opposite effect, increasing the person's confusion (Mahowald & Schenck, 2005).

Sleep terrors are dramatic but tend to be brief, usually lasting for a minute or less. As the episode passes, the person drops back to quiet sleep and wakes in the morning with no recollection of the incident.

Sleep terrors are more common in children than adults. For most children who experience sleep terrors, the episodes subside and stop during adolescence. Nonetheless, approximately 4 to 5 percent of adults experience sleep terrors (Mahowald & Bornemann, 2005).

Sleepsex

Also called *sexsomnia,* **sleepsex** involves abnormal sexual behaviors and experiences during sleep. Without realizing what he or she is doing, the sleeper initiates some kind of sexual behavior, such as masturbation, sleepsex-talking, groping or fondling their bed partner's genitals, or sexual intercourse. Although sometimes described as loving or playful, more often sleepsex behavior is characterized as "robotic," aggressive, and impersonal. Whether affectionate or forceful, the person's sleepsex behavior is usually depicted as being out of character with the individual's sexual behavior when awake (Schenck & others, 2007). As is the case in other parasomnias, the person typically has no memory of his or her actions the next day (Schenck, 2007).

Repeated episodes of sleep masturbation, fending off one's bed partner in the middle of the night, or rough sex can strain or destroy a relationship. Feelings of embarrassment, shame, or guilt about the unremembered behaviors are common. The thought of sleeping away from home is anxiety provoking.

Sleepwalking

The Prologue story about Scott described several key features of another parasomnia—**sleepwalking,** or *somnambulism.* Although the behavior of most sleepwalkers is pretty benign, some can react aggressively if touched or interrupted (Cartwright, 2004; Pressman, 2007). Equally important, a sleepwalker can engage in elaborate and complicated behaviors, such as unlocking locks, opening windows, dismantling equipment, using tools, and even driving.

Approximately 15 percent of all children have had at least one sleepwalking episode. A commonly believed notion is that sleepwalking disappears by adulthood. Although the prevalence does decrease, about 4 percent of adults are sleepwalkers, making it much more common in adulthood than is generally believed.

sleep terrors
A sleep disturbance characterized by an episode of increased physiological arousal, intense fear and panic, frightening hallucinations, and no recall of the episode the next morning; typically occurs during stage 3 or stage 4 NREM sleep; also called *night terrors.*

sleepsex
A sleep disorder invoving abnormal sexual behaviors and experiences during sleep; also called *sexsomnia.*

sleepwalking
A sleep disturbance characterized by an episode of walking or performing other actions during stage 3 or stage 4 NREM sleep; also called *somnambulism.*

Sleepwalking Sleepwalking is fairly common in children. Approximately 1 percent of preschoolers and 2 percent of school-aged children walk in their sleep at least a few nights per week (National Sleep Foundation, 2004). More generally, about 15 percent of all children have had at least one sleepwalking episode. Researchers used to believe that children outgrew their tendency to sleepwalk by late adolescence. However, sleepwalking in adulthood is much more common than once thought. It's now known that about 4 percent of adults are sleepwalkers (Hughes, 2007).

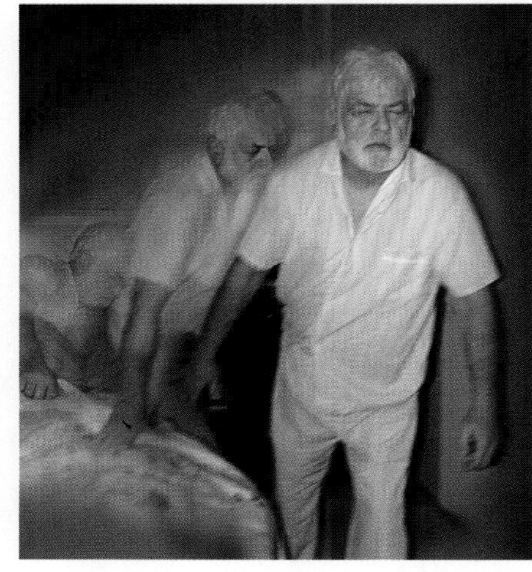

Warning: May Cause Sleep-Driving and Sleep-Eating As the most widely prescribed sleeping pill in the United States, *Ambien®* was originally marketed as being safer, less addictive, and having fewer side effects than previous sleeping medications. But growing numbers of patient complaints, published case studies, and news reports underscore that Ambien and similar sleeping pills can produce their own unique problems (Najjar, 2007; Sansone, 2008). Ambien users, in particular, have reported waking up to find the oven turned on and food strewn around the kitchen and in their bed. Other Ambien users have reported driving while asleep, waking up only after being arrested on the side of the road (Saul, 2007a, 2007b). Amnesia for performing these behaviors while asleep is common. Because of these risks, the U.S. Food and Drug Administration now requires more stringent warnings about using Ambien and similar sleeping medications (FDA News, 2007; Sanofi-Aventis, 2008).

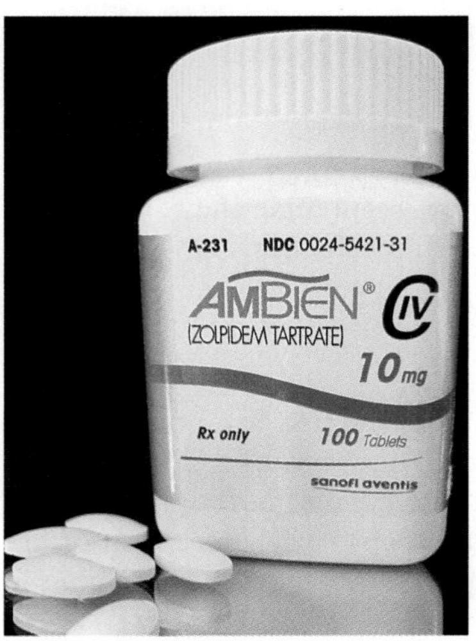

Sleep-Related Eating Disorder (SRED)

Sleepwalking nightly to the kitchen, eating compulsively, and then awakening the next morning with no memory of having done so are the hallmarks of **sleep-related eating disorder.** SRED affects at least 1 percent of Americans, or about 3 to 4 million people. Females are more than twice as likely as males to sleep-eat. Onset of the sleep-eating behavior typically occurs during young adulthood and is usually preceded by a history of sleepwalking as a child. Contrary to what you might expect, SRED is usually not associated with a daytime eating disorder (Howell & others, 2009; Winkelman, 2006).

Although sweet-tasting foods like candy or cake are most commonly consumed, the sleepwalker can also voraciously eat bizarre items, like raw bacon, dry pancake mix, salt sandwiches, coffee grounds, or cat food sandwiches. Interestingly, alcoholic beverages are hardly ever consumed during an episode.

SRED poses potential dangers to the sleepwalker, including burns and injuries from cooking utensils. However, the sleepwalker can become irritable, agitated, and even aggressive if someone tries to intervene. Reports of consuming nonfood items include hand cream, buttered cigarettes, and soap slices. Even toxic substances, such as cleaning solutions, can be ingested. Along with being sickened by eating such things, the person may eat foods to which they are allergic, or they may choke if eating while lying down (Schenck, 2007).

REM Sleep Behavior Disorder (RBD)

The parasomnias described thus far emerge during NREM stages 3 and 4 slow-wave sleep. In contrast, **REM sleep behavior disorder (RBD)** represents a failure of the brain mechanisms that normally suppress voluntary actions during REM sleep. As a result, the person verbally and physically responds to the unfolding dream story, which they remember in vivid detail upon awakening.

The enacted dream story usually revolves around intense fear in response to being threatened or attacked by unfamiliar people or animals. In the dream, the person defensively fights back or tries to escape (Schenck & Mahowald, 2002). Because the brain fails to suppress voluntary actions, the person may punch, kick, yell, swear, gesture, jump out of bed, crouch, crawl on the floor, or run. In the process, they may pummel, grab, or choke their bed partner, charge full force into bedroom furniture, or crash through a window. Serious physical injuries to the dreamer or his or her bed partner may require medical attention, which is often how RBD is first diagnosed (Mahowald & Schenck, 2005).

Although it can occur at any age, REM sleep behavior disorder typically occurs in males over the age of 60. Approximately 1 out of 200 senior males are affected by it. Once it emerges, RBD is a chronic condition that gets progressively worse. Onset is usually preceded by a longer history of sleeptalking and twitching or jerking during sleep. Chronic REM sleep behavior disorder may be an early symptom of an underlying neurological disorder, such as Parkinson's disease or Alzheimer's disease (Abad & Guilleminault, 2004; Mahowald & Schenck, 2005). Temporary episodes of RBD can be triggered by antidepressant medications, excessive caffeine use, or alcohol withdrawal.

Interested students can find more information about sleep disorders by visiting the American Academy of Sleep Medicine's Web site, www.SleepEducation.com, or the National Sleep Foundation's Web site at www.SleepFoundation.org.

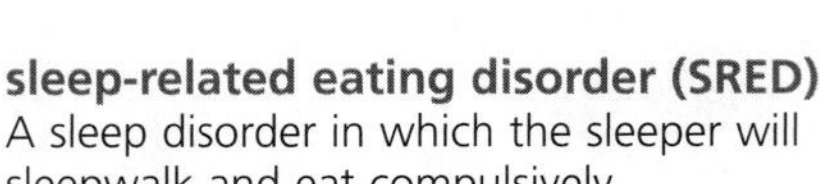

sleep-related eating disorder (SRED) A sleep disorder in which the sleeper will sleepwalk and eat compulsively.

REM sleep behavior disorder (RBD) A sleep disorder characterized by the brain's failure to suppress voluntary actions during REM sleep resulting in the sleeper verbally and physically responding to the dream story.

Hypnosis

Key Theme

- **During hypnosis, people respond to suggestions with changes in perception, memory, and behavior.**

Key Questions

- **What characteristics are associated with responsiveness to hypnotic suggestions?**
- **What are some important effects of hypnosis?**
- **How has hypnosis been explained?**

What is hypnosis? Definitions vary, but **hypnosis** can be defined as a cooperative social interaction in which the hypnotic participant responds to suggestions made by the hypnotist. These suggestions for imaginative experiences can produce changes in perception, memory, thoughts, and behavior (American Psychological Association, 2005).

For many people the word *hypnosis* conjures up the classic but sinister image of a hypnotist inducing hypnosis by slowly swinging a pocket watch back and forth. But, as psychologist John Kihlstrom (2001) explains, "The hypnotist does not hypnotize the individual. Rather, the hypnotist serves as a sort of coach or tutor whose job is to help the person become hypnotized." After experiencing hypnosis, some people are able to self-induce hypnosis.

The word *hypnosis* is derived from the Greek *hypnos,* meaning "sleep." The idea that the hypnotized person is in a sleeplike trance is still very popular among the general public. However, the phrase *hypnotic trance* is misleading and rarely used by researchers today (Wagstaff, 1999). When hypnotized, people do *not* lose control of their behavior. Instead, they typically remain aware of where they are, who they are, and what is transpiring.

Rather than being a sleeplike trance, hypnosis is characterized by highly focused attention, increased responsiveness to suggestions, vivid images and fantasies, and a willingness to accept distortions of logic or reality. During hypnosis, the person temporarily suspends her sense of initiative and voluntarily accepts and follows the hypnotist's instructions (Hilgard, 1986a).

Although most adults are moderately hypnotizable, people vary in their responsiveness to hypnotic suggestions (see Kihlstrom, 2007). About 15 percent of adults are highly susceptible to hypnosis, and 10 percent are difficult or impossible to hypnotize. Children tend to be more responsive to hypnosis than are adults, and children as young as 5 years old can be hypnotized (Kuttner & Catchpole, 2007). Evidence suggests that the degree of susceptibility to hypnosis tends to run in families. For example, identical twins are more similar in their susceptibility to hypnosis than are fraternal twins (Nash, 2001).

The best candidates for hypnosis are individuals who approach the experience with positive, receptive attitudes. The expectation that you will be responsive to hypnosis also plays an important role (Kirsch & others, 1995; Silva & others, 2005). People who are highly susceptible to hypnosis have the ability to become deeply absorbed in fantasy and imaginary experience. For instance, they easily become absorbed in reading fiction, watching movies, and listening to music (Kihlstrom, 2007).

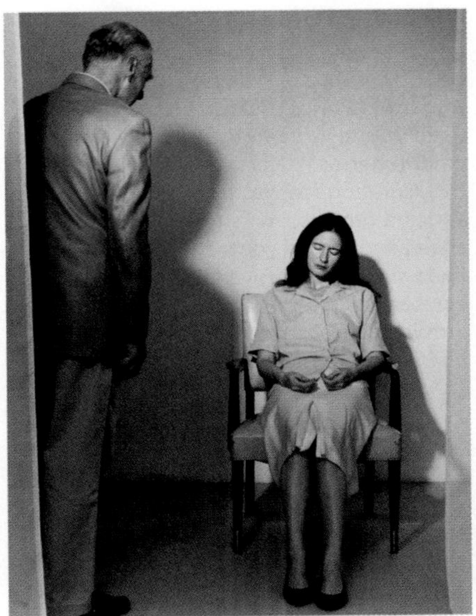

How Is the Hypnotic State Produced? In a willing volunteer, hypnosis can be induced in a variety of ways, but swinging a pocket watch is usually not one of them. Instead, as psychologist Michael Nash demonstrates, hypnosis is more commonly induced by speaking in a calm, monotonous voice, suggesting that the person is becoming drowsy, sleepy, and progressively more relaxed. To help the volunteer focus her attention, the hypnotist may also ask her to concentrate on a simple visual stimulus, such as a spot on the wall.

Effects of Hypnosis

Deeply hypnotized subjects sometimes experience profound changes in their subjective experience of consciousness. They may report feelings of detachment from their bodies, profound relaxation, or sensations of timelessness. More commonly, hypnotized people converse normally and remain fully aware of their surroundings. Often, they will later report that carrying out the hypnotist's suggestions seemed to happen by itself. The action seems to take place outside the hypnotized person's will or volition.

hypnosis
(hip-NO-sis) A cooperative social interaction in which the hypnotized person responds to the hypnotist's suggestions with changes in perception, memory, and behavior.

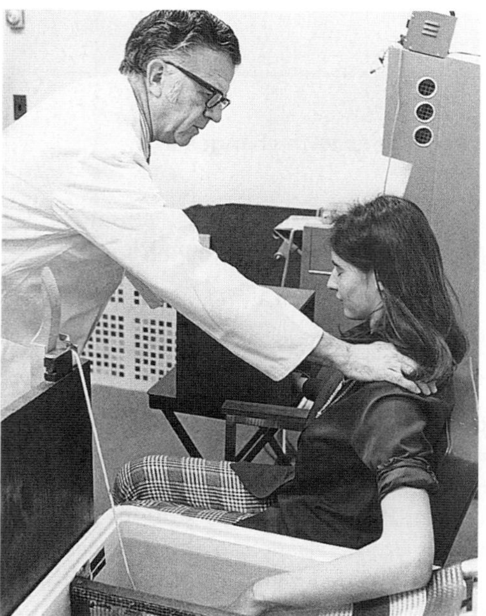

Hypnotic Suppression of Pain In this classic photo taken at the Stanford Laboratory of Hypnosis Research, psychologist Ernest Hilgard (1904–2001) instructs this hypnotized young woman that she will feel no pain in her arm. Her arm is then immersed in circulating ice water for several minutes, and she reports that she does not experience any pain. In contrast, a nonhypnotized subject perceives the same experience as extremely painful and can keep his arm in the ice water for no more than a few seconds.

Sensory and Perceptual Changes

Some of the most dramatic effects that can be produced with hypnosis are alterations in sensation and perception. Sensory changes that can be induced through hypnosis include temporary blindness, deafness, or a complete loss of sensation in some part of the body (Kihlstrom, 2007). For example, when the suggestion is made to a highly responsive subject that her arm is numb and cannot feel pain, she will not consciously experience the pain of a pinprick or of having her arm immersed in ice water. This property of hypnosis has led to its use as a technique in pain control (Martinez-Salazer & others, 2008). Painful dental and medical procedures, including surgery, have been successfully performed with hypnosis as the only anesthesia (Hilgard & others, 1994).

People can experience hallucinations under hypnosis. If a highly responsive hypnotic subject is told that a close friend is sitting in a chair on the other side of the room, she will not only report seeing the friend in vivid detail but can walk over and "touch" the other person. Under hypnosis, people can also *not* perceive something that *is* there. For example, if the suggestion is made that a jar of rotten eggs has no smell, a highly suggestible person will not consciously perceive any odor.

Hypnosis can also influence behavior outside the hypnotic state. When a **posthypnotic suggestion** is given, the person will carry out that specific suggestion after the hypnotic session is over. For example, under hypnosis, a student was given the posthypnotic suggestion that the number 5 no longer existed. He was brought out of hypnosis and then asked to count his fingers. He counted 11 fingers! Counting again, the baffled young man was at a loss to explain his results.

Some posthypnotic suggestions have been reported to last for months, but most last only a few hours or days (Barnier & McConkey, 1999). So, even if the hypnotist does not include some posthypnotic signal to cancel the posthypnotic suggestion, the suggestion will eventually wear off.

Hypnosis and Memory

Memory can be significantly affected by hypnosis (see Kihlstrom, 2007). In **posthypnotic amnesia,** a subject is unable to recall specific information or events that occurred before or during hypnosis. Posthypnotic amnesia is produced by a hypnotic suggestion that suppresses the memory of specific information, such as the subject's street address. The effects of posthypnotic amnesia are usually temporary, disappearing either spontaneously or when a posthypnotic signal is suggested by the hypnotist. When the signal is given, the information floods back into the subject's mind.

The opposite effect is called **hypermnesia,** which is enhancement of memory for past events through hypnotic suggestion. Police investigators sometimes use hypnosis in an attempt to enhance the memories of crime victims and witnesses. Despite the common belief that you can "zoom in" on briefly seen crime details under hypnosis, such claims are extremely exaggerated. Compared with regular police interview methods, hypnosis does *not* significantly enhance memory or improve the accuracy of memories (Mazzoni & Lynn, 2006).

posthypnotic suggestion
A suggestion made during hypnosis that the person should carry out a specific instruction following the hypnotic session.

posthypnotic amnesia
The inability to recall specific information because of a hypnotic suggestion.

hypermnesia
(high-perm-NEE-zha) The supposed enhancement of a person's memory for past events through a hypnotic suggestion.

Age Regression Through Hypnosis? Some people believe that hypnosis can allow you to re-experience an earlier stage of your life—a phenomenon called *age regression* (J. Green, 1999b). Under hypnosis, some adults *do* appear to relive experiences from their childhood, confidently displaying childlike speech patterns and behaviors. However, when attempts are made to verify specific details of the experiences, the details are usually inaccurate (Spanos, 1987–1988). Just as actual deafness and blindness are not produced by hypnotic suggestion, neither is a true return to childhood. Instead, hypnotic subjects combine fragments of actual memories with fantasies and ideas about how children of a particular age should behave.

Many studies have shown that efforts to enhance memories hypnotically can lead to distortions and inaccuracies. In fact, hypnosis can greatly increase confidence in memories that are actually incorrect. False memories, also called *pseudomemories*, can be inadvertently created when hypnosis is used to aid recall (Mazzoni & Scoboria, 2007; Lynn & others, 2003).

Explaining Hypnosis

Consciousness Divided?

How can hypnosis be explained? Psychologist **Ernest R. Hilgard** (1986a, 1991, 1992) believed that the hypnotized person experiences **dissociation**—the splitting of consciousness into two or more simultaneous streams of mental activity. According to Hilgard's **neodissociation theory of hypnosis,** a hypnotized person consciously experiences one stream of mental activity that is responding to the hypnotist's suggestions. But a second, dissociated stream of mental activity is also operating, processing information that is unavailable to the consciousness of the hypnotized subject. Hilgard (1986a, 1992) referred to this second, dissociated stream of mental activity as the **hidden observer.** (The phrase *hidden observer* does *not* mean that the hypnotized person has multiple personalities.)

Hilgard accidentally discovered the "hidden observer" while conducting a classroom demonstration. Hilgard hypnotized a student and induced hypnotic deafness. The student was completely unresponsive to very loud, sudden sounds, such as the sound of a starter pistol firing or of wooden blocks being banged together.

Another student, observing the demonstration, asked Hilgard if "some part" of the hypnotized person was actually aware of the sounds. Hilgard instructed the hypnotized student to raise his right index finger if some part of him could still hear. To Hilgard's surprise, the hypnotized student's right index finger rose! When brought out of hypnosis, the student had no recall of any sounds during the hypnotically induced deafness, including Hilgard's suggestion to raise his index finger. Hypnosis, it seems, had produced a split in consciousness. A conscious segment complied with the hypnotic suggestion of deafness, but a separate, dissociated segment unavailable to consciousness—the hidden observer—continued to process information.

Not all psychologists agree that hypnotic phenomena are due to dissociation, divided consciousness, or a hidden observer. In the Critical Thinking box on the next page, we examine this controversy more fully.

dissociation
The splitting of consciousness into two or more simultaneous streams of mental activity.

neodissociation theory of hypnosis
Theory proposed by Ernest Hilgard that explains hypnotic effects as being due to the splitting of consciousness into two simultaneous streams of mental activity, only one of which the hypnotic participant is consciously aware of during hypnosis.

hidden observer
Hilgard's term for the hidden, or dissociated, stream of mental activity that continues during hypnosis.

CRITICAL THINKING

Is Hypnosis a Special State of Consciousness?

Are the changes in perception, thinking, and behaviors that occur during hypnosis the result of a "special" or "altered" state of consciousness? Here, we'll consider the evidence for three competing points of view on this issue.

The State View: Hypnosis Involves a Special State

Considered the traditional viewpoint, the "state" explanation contends that hypnosis is a unique state of consciousness, distinctly different from normal waking consciousness (Kosslyn & others, 2000). The state view is perhaps best represented by Hilgard's *neodissociation theory of hypnosis*. According to this view, consciousness is split into two simultaneous streams of mental activity during hypnosis. One stream of mental activity remains conscious, but a second stream of mental activity—the one responding to the hypnotist's suggestions—is "dissociated" from awareness. So according to the neodissociation theory, the hypnotized young woman shown on page 160 reported no pain because the painful sensations were dissociated from awareness.

The Non-State View: Ordinary Psychological Processes

Some psychologists flatly reject the notion that hypnotically induced changes involve a "special" state of consciousness. According to the *social-cognitive view of hypnosis*, subjects are responding to the *social demands* of the hypnosis situation. They act the way they think good hypnotic subjects are supposed to act, conforming to the expectations of the hypnotist, their own expectations, and situational cues. In this view, the "hypnotized" young woman on page 160 reported no pain because that's what she expected to happen during the hypnosis session.

To back up the social-cognitive theory of hypnosis, Nicholas Spanos (1991, 1994, 2005) and his colleagues amassed an impressive array of evidence showing that highly motivated people often perform just as well as hypnotized subjects in demonstrating pain reduction, amnesia, age regression, and hallucinations. Studies of people who simply *pretended* to be hypnotized have shown similar results. On the basis of such findings, non-state theorists contend that hypnosis can be explained in terms of rather ordinary psychological processes, including imagination, situational expectations, role enactment, compliance, and conformity (Wagstaff, 1999; Wagstaff & Cole, 2005).

PET Scans During Hypnosis: Does the Brain Respond Differently?

Researcher Stephen Kosslyn and his colleagues (2000) conducted a brain-imaging study. Highly hypnotizable volunteers viewed two images of rectangles, one in bright colors and one in shades of gray, while lying in a PET scanner. The researchers measured

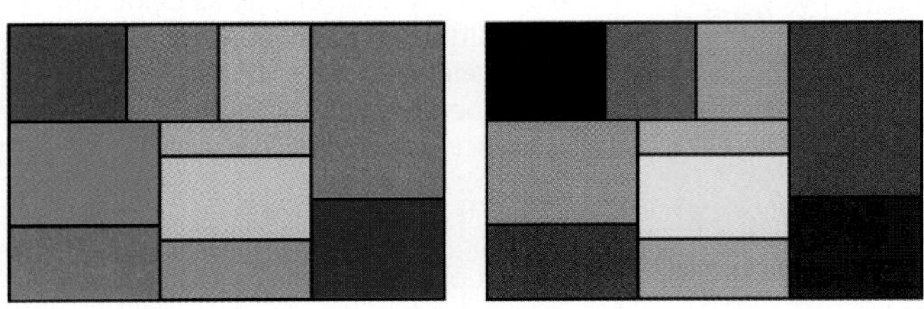

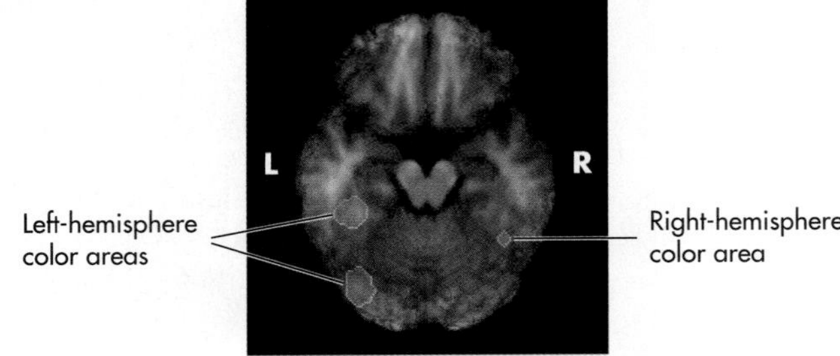

activity in brain regions involved in color perception. While hypnotized, the participants were instructed to perform three tasks: (a) to see the images as they were; (b) to mentally "drain" color from the colored rectangles in order to see them in shades of gray; and (c) to mentally "add" color to the gray rectangles. These last two tasks were hypnosis-induced hallucinations.

What did the PET scans reveal? When the hypnotized participants were instructed to perceive colored rectangles, color regions in the brain activated, *regardless* of whether the participants were shown colored or gray rectangles. When participants were instructed to perceive gray rectangles, color regions in the brain deactivated, *regardless* of whether the participants were shown colored or gray rectangles. In other words, brain activity reflected the hypnosis-induced hallucinations—not the actual images that were shown to the participants. On the basis of these findings, Kosslyn (2001) concluded, "Hypnosis is not simply 'role playing,' but does in fact reflect the existence of a distinct mental brain state."

The Imaginative Suggestibility View: Imagination

Psychologists Irving Kirsch and Wayne Braffman (2001) dismiss the idea that hypnotic subjects are merely acting. But they also contend that brain-imaging studies don't necessarily prove that hypnosis is a unique state. Rather, Kirsch and Braffman maintain that such studies emphasize individual differences in *imaginative suggestibility*—the degree to which a person is able to experience an imaginary state of affairs as if it were real.

Braffman and Kirsch (1999) have shown that many highly suggestible participants were just as responsive to suggestions when they had *not* been hypnotized as when they had been hypnotized. "Hypnotic responses reveal an astounding capacity that some people have to alter their experience in profound ways," Kirsch and Braffman (2001) write. "Hypnosis is only one of the ways in which this capacity is revealed. It can also be evoked—and almost to the same extent—without inducing hypnosis."

Despite the controversy over how best to explain hypnotic effects, psychologists do agree that hypnosis can be a highly effective therapeutic technique (Lynn & Kirsch, 2006; Kihlstrom, 2007).

CRITICAL THINKING QUESTIONS

- Does the fact that highly motivated subjects can "fake" hypnotic effects invalidate the notion of hypnosis as a unique state of consciousness? Why or why not?
- What kinds of evidence could prove or disprove the notion that hypnosis is a unique state of consciousness?

Limits and Applications of Hypnosis

Although the effects of hypnosis can be dramatic, there are limits to the behaviors that can be influenced by hypnosis. First, contrary to popular belief, you cannot be hypnotized against your will. Second, hypnosis cannot make you perform behaviors that are contrary to your morals and values. Thus, you're very unlikely to commit criminal or immoral acts under the influence of hypnosis—unless, of course, you find such actions acceptable (Hilgard, 1986b).

Third, hypnosis cannot make you stronger than your physical capabilities or bestow new talents. However, hypnosis *can* enhance physical skills or athletic ability by increasing self-confidence and concentration (Barker & Jones, 2006; Morgan, 2002). Table 4.3 provides additional examples of how hypnosis can be used to help people.

Can hypnosis be used to help you lose weight, stop smoking, or stop biting your nails? Hypnosis is not a magic bullet. However, research *has* shown that hypnosis can be helpful in modifying problematic behaviors, especially when used as part of a structured treatment program (Bonshtein & others, 2005). For example, when combined with cognitive-behavioral therapy or other supportive treatments, hypnosis has been shown to help motivated people quit smoking (Green & others, 2006; Elkins & others, 2006; Lynn & Kirsch, 2006). In children and adolescents, hypnosis can be an effective treatment for such habits as thumb-sucking, nail-biting, and compulsive hair-pulling (Wester, 2007).

Table 4.3

Help Through Hypnosis

Research has demonstrated that hypnosis can effectively:

- Reduce pain and discomfort associated with cancer, rheumatoid arthritis, burn wounds, and other chronic conditions
- Reduce pain and discomfort associated with childbirth
- Reduce the use of narcotics to relieve postoperative pain
- Improve the concentration, motivation, and performance of athletes
- Lessen the severity and frequency of asthma attacks
- Eliminate recurring nightmares
- Enhance the effectiveness of psychotherapy in the treatment of obesity, hypertension, and anxiety
- Remove warts
- Eliminate or reduce stuttering
- Suppress the gag reflex during dental procedures

Meditation

Key Theme

- **Meditation involves using one of various techniques to deliberately change conscious experience, inducing a state of focused attention and awareness.**

Key Questions

- **What are two general types of meditation?**
- **What are the effects of meditation?**

Meditation refers to a group of techniques that induce an altered state of focused attention and heightened awareness. Meditation takes many forms and has been used for thousands of years as part of religious practices throughout the world. Virtually every major religion—Hinduism, Taoism, Buddhism, Judaism, Christianity, and Islam—has a rich tradition of meditative practices (Nelson, 2001). However, many people practice meditation independently of any religious tradition or spiritual context. Some forms of psychotherapy also include meditative practice as a component of the overall therapy (Epstein, 1995; Segal & others, 2002).

meditation
Any one of a number of sustained concentration techniques that focus attention and heighten awareness.

Meditation in Different Cultures Meditation is an important part of many cultures. Tai chi is a form of meditation that involves a structured series of slow, smooth movements. During tai chi, you focus on the present, your movements, and your breathing. Sometimes described as "meditation in motion," tai chi has existed for over 2,000 years. Like this group in Hanoi, Vietnam, many people throughout Asia begin their day with tai chi, often meeting in parks and other public places.

Common to all forms of meditation is the goal of controlling or retraining attention. Although meditation techniques vary a great deal, they can be divided into two general categories. *Concentration techniques* involve focusing awareness on a visual image, your breathing, a word, or a phrase. When a sound is used, it is typically a short word or a religious phrase, called a *mantra,* that is repeated mentally. In contrast, *opening-up techniques* involve a present-centered awareness of the passing moment, without mental judgment (Tart, 1994). Rather than concentrating on an object, sound, or activity, the meditator engages in quiet awareness of the "here and now" without distracting thoughts. The *zazen,* or "just sitting," technique of Zen Buddhism is a form of opening-up meditation (Austin, 1998).

Some meditative traditions, such as Zen Buddhism and mindfulness techniques, also stress the attainment of emotional control. This aspect of meditation has led to investigations of its effectiveness in programs to relieve anxiety and improve physical health and psychological well-being (Baer, 2003; Davidson & others, 2003).

Effects of Meditation

If you want to learn how to meditate, you can find the instructions for a simple but effective meditation technique in Chapter 12.

Much of the early research on meditation focused on its use as a relaxation technique that relieved stress and improved cardiovascular health. The meditation technique that was most widely used in this research was a form of concentrative meditation called *transcendental meditation* or *TM.* From a research standpoint, TM had many advantages. It can be quickly mastered and does not require any changes in lifestyle or beliefs. Practitioners follow a standardized, simple format. Meditators sit quietly with eyes closed and mentally repeat the mantra they have been given. Rather than struggling to clear the mind of thoughts, meditators are taught to allow distracting thoughts to simply "fall away" while they focus their attention on their mantra.

Numerous studies showed that even beginning meditators practicing TM experience a state of lowered physiological arousal, including a decrease in heart rate, lowered blood pressure, and changes in brain waves (C. N. Alexander & others, 1994; Dillbeck & Orme-Johnson, 1987). Advocates of TM claimed that such physical changes produce a unique state of consciousness with a wide variety of benefits, including stress reduction.

While much of the early research on meditation focused on short-term effects and meditation's health benefits, contemporary research on meditation is much more wide-ranging. One approach involves using sophisticated brain-imaging technology to study how the brain changes during meditation (Newberg & Iversen, 2003). Another approach involves the ongoing research collaboration among neuroscientists, psychologists, and a group of Tibetan Buddhist monks who have devoted decades to intensive study and meditative practice (Barinaga, 2003; Davidson, 2002). Because Tibetan Buddhism represents a rigorous system of mental training, researchers hope to learn more about conscious experience as well as meditation's effects on attention, emotional control, personality, and the brain (Houshmand & others, 2002; Lutz & others, 2004).

Studying the Well-Trained Mind Psychologist Richard Davidson talks with Buddhist monk Matthieu Ricard after a brain-imaging study. Tenzin Gyatso, the 14th Dalai Lama, has been instrumental in encouraging such collaborations between Western scientists and Tibetan Buddhists. As the Dalai Lama wrote, "Buddhists have a 2,500-year history of investigating the workings of the mind. . . . Using imaging devices that show what occurs in the brain during meditation, Dr. Davidson has been able to study the effects of Buddhist practice for cultivating compassion, equanimity, or mindfulness" (Gyatso, 2003).

Many studies have shown that regular meditation can enhance physical and psychological functioning beyond that provided by relaxation alone (Andresen, 2000; Austin, 1998, 2003). Meditation and hypnosis are similar in that both involve the deliberate use of mental techniques to change the experience of consciousness. In the final section of this chapter, we'll consider one of the oldest strategies for deliberately altering conscious awareness—psychoactive drugs.

Psychoactive Drugs

Key Theme

- **Psychoactive drugs alter consciousness by changing arousal, mood, thinking, sensations, and perceptions.**

Key Questions

- **What are four broad categories of psychoactive drugs?**
- **What are some common properties of psychoactive drugs?**
- **What factors influence the effects, use, and abuse of drugs?**

Psychoactive drugs are chemical substances that can alter arousal, mood, thinking, sensation, and perception. In this section, we will look at the characteristics of four broad categories of psychoactive drugs:

1. *Depressants*—drugs that depress, or inhibit, brain activity
2. *Opiates*—drugs that are chemically similar to morphine and that relieve pain and produce euphoria
3. *Stimulants*—drugs that stimulate, or excite, brain activity
4. *Psychedelic drugs*—drugs that distort sensory perceptions

psychoactive drug
A drug that alters consciousness, perception, mood, and behavior.

physical dependence
A condition in which a person has physically adapted to a drug so that he or she must take the drug regularly in order to avoid withdrawal symptoms.

drug tolerance
A condition in which increasing amounts of a physically addictive drug are needed to produce the original, desired effect.

withdrawal symptoms
Unpleasant physical reactions, combined with intense drug cravings, that occur when a person abstains from a drug on which he or she is physically dependent.

drug rebound effect
Withdrawal symptoms that are the opposite of a physically addictive drug's action.

Common Properties of Psychoactive Drugs

Addiction is a broad term that refers to a condition in which a person feels psychologically and physically compelled to take a specific drug. People experience **physical dependence** when their body and brain chemistry have physically adapted to a drug. Many physically addictive drugs gradually produce **drug tolerance,** which means that increasing amounts of the drug are needed to gain the original, desired effect.

When a person becomes physically dependent on a drug, abstaining from the drug produces withdrawal symptoms. **Withdrawal symptoms** are unpleasant physical reactions to the lack of the drug, plus an intense craving for it. Withdrawal symptoms are alleviated by taking the drug again. Often, the withdrawal symptoms are opposite to the drug's action, a phenomenon called the **drug rebound effect.** For example, withdrawing from stimulating drugs, like the caffeine in coffee, may produce depression and fatigue. Withdrawal from depressant drugs, such as alcohol, may produce excitability.

Each psychoactive drug has a distinct biological effect. Psychoactive drugs may influence many different bodily systems, but their consciousness-altering effects are primarily due to their effect on the brain. Typically, these drugs influence brain activity by altering synaptic transmission among neurons. As we discussed in Chapter 2, drugs affect synaptic transmission by increasing or decreasing neurotransmitter amounts or by blocking, mimicking, or influencing a particular neurotransmitter's effects (see Figure 2.6). Chronic drug use can also produce long-term changes in brain structures and functions, as discussed in the Focus on Neuroscience on the next page.

The biological effects of a drug can vary considerably from person to person. An individual's race, gender, age, and weight may influence the intensity of a particular drug's effects. For example, many Asians and Asian Americans have a specific genetic variation that makes them much more responsive to alcohol's effects. In turn, this heightened sensitivity to alcohol is associated with significantly lower rates of alcohol dependence seen among people of Asian heritage as compared to other races (Cook & others, 2005; Kufahl & others, 2008).

Psychological and environmental factors can also influence a drug's effects. An individual's response to a drug can be greatly affected by his or her personality characteristics, mood, expectations, experience with the drug, and the setting in which the drug is taken (Blume & others, 2003; Kufahl & others, 2008).

"At this point, we know it's addictive."

FOCUS ON NEUROSCIENCE

The Addicted Brain: Diminishing Rewards

Addictive drugs include alcohol, cocaine, heroin, nicotine, and the amphetamines. Although their effects are diverse, these addictive drugs share one thing in common: They all activate dopamine-producing neurons in the brain's reward system (Li & others, 2007; Volkow & others, 2009). The initial dopamine surge in response to an addictive drug is a powerful brain reward, one that prompts the person to repeat the drug-taking behavior (Self, 2005).

The brain's reward system evolved to reinforce behaviors that promote survival, such as eating and sexuality. A wide range of pleasurable activities can cause a temporary increase in dopamine levels, including exercising, listening to music, eating a delicious dessert, and even looking at an attractive person.

But in contrast to such naturally rewarding activities and substances, addictive drugs hijack the brain's reward system. Initially, the drug produces the intense dopamine-induced feelings of euphoria. But with repeated drug use, the brain's reward pathways *adapt* to the high dopamine levels. One result is that the availability of dopamine receptors is down-regulated or greatly reduced (Volkow & others, 2007). Along with decreased dopamine activity, other biochemical changes dampen or inhibit the brain's reward circuits, reducing the pleasurable effects of the abused substance. These adaptations create the conditions for *drug tolerance*—more of the substance is now needed to produce a response that is similar to the drug's original effect (Nestler & Malenka, 2004).

As the brain's reward circuits down-regulate to counter the dopamine surge, another change occurs. The normally reinforcing experiences of everyday life are no longer satisfying or pleasurable. Emotionally, the addict experiences depression, boredom, and apathy (Little & others, 2003).

While lying in a PET scanner and viewing images of a beautiful sunset, laughing children, or other pleasurable scenes, the cocaine addict's brain shows little or no dopamine response. But when shown even brief flashes of images associated with cocaine use—a coke spoon, a syringe, the neighborhood where the drugs were bought—the brain's reward circuit "lights up like a Christmas tree" (Hoffman & Froemke, 2007). Thus, because everyday experiences are no longer enjoyable, the addict is even more motivated to seek out the reinforcing effects of the drug. At this point, the addicted person needs the substance not to get high but just to feel "normal."

When the addictive drug is not taken, withdrawal symptoms occur, accompanied by intense craving for the abused substance. What causes the craving? One explanation is that the neurons in the brain's reward circuits have become hypersensitive to the abused substance. Because the neurons physically change, this sensitization can be long-lasting, persisting for months and even years after drug use has ended. This is also why relapse can occur long after someone has stopped abusing drugs. Simply being exposed to drug-related stimuli or stressful life events can trigger craving—and relapse (Volkow & others, 2006).

With advanced imaging techniques, researchers are pinpointing the structural and functional changes in the brain's reward system in response to drug abuse (Fowler & others, 2007). By identifying the common biochemical and physical changes that occur, scientists may one day be able to create more effective treatments to counteract the destructive effects of addictive drugs.

Comparison Subject | Drug Abuser

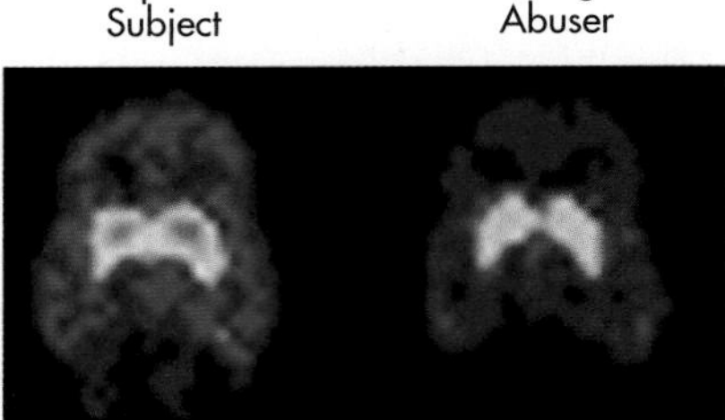
Cocaine

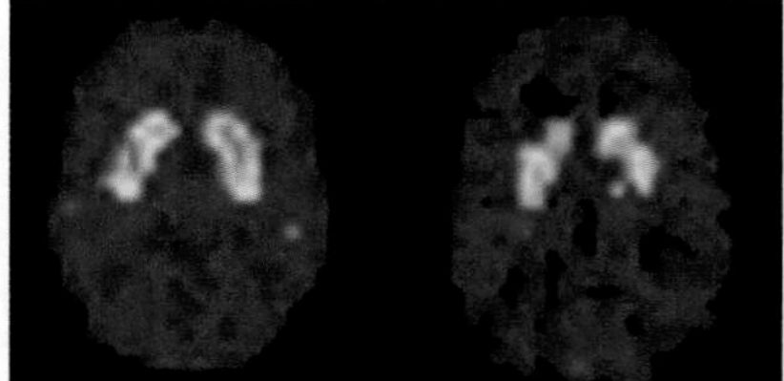
Methamphetamine

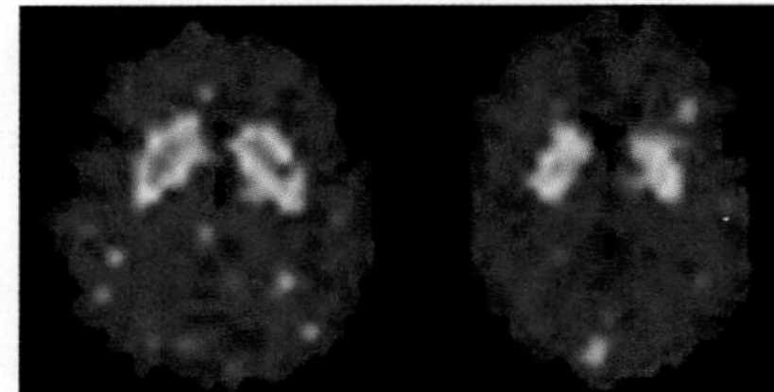
Alcohol

Common Effects of Abused Drugs Different abused drugs initially produce their intoxicating effects in the same way—by increasing dopamine levels in the brain's reward system (Volkow & others, 2009). But as the brain adjusts to the effects of drug abuse, long-term changes occur in the brain's reward circuitry. In the brain scans shown here, orange and yellow areas indicate the greatest number of dopamine receptors. As you compare the scans, you can see that regardless of the specific drug, drug abuse sharply reduces the number of dopamine receptors in the brain's reward system.

drug abuse
Recurrent drug use that results in disruptions in academic, social, or occupational functioning or in legal or psychological problems.

depressants
A category of psychoactive drugs that depress or inhibit brain activity.

In contrast to drug use, **drug abuse** refers to recurrent drug use that results in the disruption of academic, social, or occupational functioning or in legal or psychological problems (American Psychiatric Association, 2000a). In the United States, rather than illicit drugs, alcohol is, by far, the most widely abused substance (Substance Abuse and Mental Health Services Administration, 2009).

How Pervasive Is the Use of Psychoactive Drugs? The Contemporary Art Centre Café in Vilnius, Lithuania, is a popular hangout for young people to discuss their interests in art—with the help of coffee, cigarettes, and alcohol. Although not used in every culture, caffeine, nicotine, and alcohol are three of the most widely used psychoactive substances in the world.

Many factors influence what is considered drug abuse. For example, determining what level of alcohol use constitutes "abuse" varies from one culture to another (Tanaka-Matsumi & Draguns, 1997). Even in the United States, different ethnic groups have very different norms regarding the use of alcohol. Jewish-, Italian-, Greek-, and Chinese-Americans have a tradition of moderate drinking. Drinking alcohol may be restricted to particular social occasions, such as weddings and other formal celebrations. Some U.S. religious groups, such as Mormons, Amish, and Muslims, forbid drinking alcohol under any circumstances. Asian-Americans and African-Americans have the lowest rates of alcohol use (Substance Abuse and Mental Health Services Administration, 2009).

The Depressants

Alcohol, Barbiturates, Inhalants, and Tranquilizers

Key Theme

- **Depressants inhibit central nervous system activity, while opiates are addictive drugs that relieve pain and produce euphoria.**

Key Questions

- **What are the physical and psychological effects of alcohol?**
- **How do barbiturates, inhalants, and tranquilizers affect the body?**
- **What are the effects of opiates, and how do they affect the brain?**

The **depressants** are a class of drugs that depress or inhibit central nervous system activity. In general, depressants produce drowsiness, sedation, or sleep. Depressants also relieve anxiety and lower inhibitions. All depressant drugs are potentially physically addictive. Further, the effects of depressant drugs are *additive,* meaning that the sedative effects are increased when depressants are combined.

Deadly Additive Drug Effects Having already been nominated for an Academy Award for the 2005 movie *Brokeback Mountain,* actor Heath Ledger was receiving advance critical acclaim for his portrayal of "The Joker" in the 2008 movie *The Dark Knight.* But in January of 2008, Ledger died from an accidental overdose in his New York apartment. In the weeks before his death, Ledger had complained about severe sleeping difficulties. The medical examination found multiple prescription drugs in his body, including two kinds of narcotic painkillers, two kinds of anti-anxiety drugs, and two kinds of sleeping medications. None of the legally prescribed medications had been taken in excess. Even so, the combination produced a lethal additive drug effect, depressing his brain's vital life functions to the point that respiratory failure occurred. Heath Ledger was 28.

Alcohol

Weddings, parties, and other social gatherings often include alcohol, a tribute to its relaxing and social lubricating properties. Used in small amounts, alcohol reduces tension and anxiety. But even though it is legal for adults and readily available, alcohol also has a high potential for abuse. Partly because of its ready availability, many drug experts consider alcohol to have the highest social cost of all the addictions. Consider these points:

- Excessive alcohol consumption accounts for an estimated 75,000 deaths annually in the United States, and is a factor in the deaths of over 1,400 college students each year (Nelson & others, 2005).

- Alcohol is involved in more than half of all assaults, homicides, and motor vehicle accidents (Julien, 2008).
- Alcohol intoxication is often a factor in domestic and partner violence, child abuse, and public violent behavior (Shepherd, 2007; Easton & others, 2007).
- Drinking during pregnancy is a leading cause of birth defects. It is the most common cause of mental retardation—and the only preventable one (Niccols, 2007).

Although the majority of adults drink on an occasional basis, an estimated 17 million Americans are either dependent upon alcohol or have serious alcohol problems. They drink heavily on a regular basis and suffer social, occupational, and health problems as a result (Substance Abuse and Mental Health Services Administration, 2009).

However, the numerous adverse health and social consequences associated with excessive drinking—health problems, injuries, accidents, violence—are not limited to those who are alcohol dependent. In fact, most of those who periodically drink heavily or drive while intoxicated do *not* meet the formal criteria for alcohol dependence (Woerle & others, 2007).

What Are Alcohol's Psychological Effects? People are often surprised that alcohol is classified as a depressant. Initially, alcohol produces a mild euphoria, talkativeness, and feelings of good humor and friendliness, leading many people to think of alcohol as a stimulant. But these subjective experiences occur because alcohol *lessens inhibitions* by depressing the brain centers responsible for judgment and self-control. Reduced inhibitions and self-control contribute to the aggressive and violent behavior sometimes associated with alcohol abuse. But the loss of inhibitions affects individuals differently, depending on their environment and expectations regarding alcohol's effects.

The Dangers of Driving Under the Influence Intoxicated drivers have impaired perceptual ability and psychomotor functions, delayed reaction time, and poor coordination. They are also likely to display impaired judgment, poor impulse control, and an inflated self-image. This deadly combination results in more than 17,000 U.S. traffic deaths each year.

How Does Alcohol Affect the Body? As a general rule, it takes about one hour to metabolize the alcohol in one drink, which is defined as 1 ounce of 80-proof whiskey, 4 ounces of wine, or 12 ounces of beer. All three drinks contain the same amount of alcohol; the alcohol is simply more diluted in beer than in hard liquor.

Factors such as body weight, gender, food consumption, and the rate of alcohol consumption also affect blood alcohol levels. A slender person who quickly consumes three drinks on an empty stomach will become more than twice as intoxicated as a heavier person who consumes three drinks with food. Women metabolize alcohol more slowly than do men. If a man and a woman of equal weight consume the same number of drinks, the woman will become more intoxicated. Table 4.4 shows the behavioral effects and impairments associated with different blood alcohol levels.

Binge drinking is a particularly risky practice. *Binge drinking* is defined as five or more drinks in a row for men, or four or more drinks in a row for women. Every year, several college students die of alcohol poisoning after ingesting large amounts of liquor in a short amount of time. Less well publicized are the other negative effects associated with binge drinking, including aggression, sexual assaults, accidents, and property damage (Hingson & others, 2002; Wechsler & others, 2002).

A national survey of college students at 119 colleges found that close to 50 percent of all male students and 40 percent of all female students had engaged in binge drinking (Wechsler & others, 2002). White students were most likely to binge-drink, while African-American students were least likely.

In a person who is addicted to alcohol, withdrawal causes rebound hyperexcitability in the brain. The severity of the withdrawal symptoms depends on the level of physical dependence. With a low level of dependence, withdrawal may involve disrupted sleep, anxiety, and mild tremors ("the shakes"). At higher levels of physical dependence on alcohol, withdrawal may involve confusion, hallucinations, and severe tremors or seizures. Collectively, these severe symptoms are called *delirium tremens,* or the *DTs.* In cases of extreme physical dependence, alcohol withdrawal can cause seizures, convulsions, and even death in the absence of medical supervision.

Table 4.4

Behavioral Effects of Blood Alcohol Levels

Blood Alcohol Level	Behavioral Effects
0.05%	Lowered alertness; release of inhibitions; impaired judgment
0.10%	Slowed reaction times; impaired motor function; less caution
0.15%	Large, consistent increases in reaction time
0.20%	Marked depression in sensory and motor capability; obvious intoxication
0.25%	Severe motor disturbance; staggering; sensory perceptions greatly impaired
0.30%	Stuporous but conscious; no comprehension of the world around them
0.35%	Surgical anesthesia; minimal level causing death
0.40%	About half of those at this level die

This Is Fun? According to a national survey of college students, more than half "drank to get drunk" in the previous year (Wechsler & others, 2002). Despite the deaths from alcohol poisoning of several college students each year, binge drinking and public drunkenness remain common at spring break celebrations. College students currently spend $5.5 billion a year on alcohol, more than they spend on textbooks, soft drinks, tea, milk, juice, and coffee combined (Nelson & others, 2005).

Inhalants

Inhalants are chemical substances that are inhaled to produce an alteration in consciousness. Paint solvents, model airplane glue, spray paint and paint thinner, gasoline, nitrous oxide, and aerosol sprays are just a few of the substances that are abused in this way. Inhalants are inexpensive and readily available. Inhalant abuse is most prevalent among adolescent and young adult males.

Although psychoactive inhalants do not have a common chemical structure, they generally act as central nervous system depressants. At low doses, they may cause relaxation, giddiness, and reduced inhibition. At higher doses, inhalants can lead to hallucinations and a loss of consciousness. Because the effects usually last only a few minutes, abusers may try to prolong the high by repeatedly inhaling, a practice that increases the risk of serious damage to the brain, heart, and other organs.

Inhalants are very dangerous. Suffocation is one hazard, but many inhaled substances are also toxic to the liver and other organs. Chronic abuse also leads to neurological and brain damage. One study compared cognitive functioning in cocaine and inhalant abusers. Both groups scored well below the normal population, but inhalant users scored even below the cocaine abusers on problem-solving and memory tests. MRI scans showed that the inhalant users also had more extensive brain damage than the cocaine users (Mathias, 2002; Rosenberg & others, 2002).

Barbiturates and Tranquilizers

Barbiturates are powerful depressant drugs that reduce anxiety and promote sleep, which is why they are sometimes called "downers." Barbiturates depress activity in the brain centers that control arousal, wakefulness, and alertness. They also depress the brain's respiratory centers.

Like alcohol, barbiturates at low doses cause relaxation, mild euphoria, and reduced inhibitions. Larger doses produce a loss of coordination, impaired mental functioning, and depression. High doses can produce unconsciousness, coma, and death. Barbiturates produce a very deep but abnormal sleep in which REM sleep is greatly reduced. Because of the additive effect of depressants, barbiturates combined with alcohol are particularly dangerous.

Common barbiturates include the prescription sedatives *Seconal* and *Nembutal.* The illegal drug *methaqualone* (street name *quaalude*) is almost identical chemically to barbiturates and has similar effects.

inhalants
Chemical substances that are inhaled to produce an alteration in consciousness.

barbiturates
(barb-ITCH-yer-ets) A category of depressant drugs that reduce anxiety and produce sleepiness.

Prescription Depressant Drugs—and Unintentional Overdoses Michael Jackson's sudden death from cardiac arrest made headlines around the world on June 25, 2009. During rehearsals for his sold-out "This is It!" concert series, Jackson had appeared healthy and fit. An autopsy revealed that his unexpected death was caused by a lethal combination of depressant drugs: the antianxiety drugs Ativan, Valium, and Medved, plus the powerful anesthetic drug, propofol. Propofol is normally used to sedate patients before surgery. The propofol and other drugs had been intravenously administered by Jackson's personal physician to help Jackson sleep (Moore, 2009). In combination, these powerful but legally prescribed depressants had stopped Jackson's heart. Jackson's death is emblematic of a disturbing trend. At one time, most fatal drug overdoses were caused by illegal narcotics. Today, however, most of the 20,000 unintentional overdose deaths that occur each year are caused by prescription drugs, including painkillers, antianxiety medications, and antidepressant medications. Contrary to what most people think, illicit drugs like cocaine, heroin, and methamphetamines account for just over a third (39%) of fatal overdoses (Paulozzi & Annest, 2007; Paulozzi, 2008).

Barbiturates produce both physical and psychological dependence. Withdrawal from low doses of barbiturates produces irritability and REM rebound nightmares. Withdrawal from high doses of barbiturates can produce hallucinations, disorientation, restlessness, and life-threatening convulsions.

Tranquilizers are depressants that relieve anxiety. Commonly prescribed tranquilizers include *Xanax, Valium, Librium,* and *Ativan.* Chemically different from barbiturates, tranquilizers produce similar, although less powerful, effects. We will discuss these drugs in more detail in Chapter 14, on therapies.

The Opiates

From Poppies to Demerol

Often called *narcotics,* the **opiates** are a group of addictive drugs that relieve pain and produce feelings of euphoria. Natural opiates include *opium,* which is derived from the opium poppy; *morphine,* the active ingredient in opium; and *codeine,* which can be derived from either opium or morphine. Synthetic and semisynthetic opiates include *heroin, methadone, oxycodone,* and the prescription painkillers *OxyContin, Vicodin, Percodan, Demerol,* and *Fentanyl.*

Opiates produce their powerful effects by mimicking the brain's own natural painkillers, called *endorphins.* Opiates occupy endorphin receptor sites in the brain. As you may recall from Chapter 2, the word *endorphin* literally means "the morphine within."

When used medically, opiates alter an individual's reaction to pain not by acting at the pain site but by reducing the brain's perception of pain. Many people recovering from surgery experience a wave of pain relief after receiving narcotics such as morphine, Demerol, or Percodan. It was once believed that people who took medically prescribed opiates or synthetic opioids rarely developed drug tolerance or addiction. Today, physicians and researchers are more aware of the addictive potential of these drugs. However, it's important to note that most patients do *not* abuse prescription pain pills or develop physical dependence or addiction, especially when their condition is carefully monitored and when no underlying substance abuse problems are present (Noble & others, 2008).

Among the most dangerous opiates is *heroin.* When injected into a vein, heroin reaches the brain in seconds, creating an intense rush of euphoria that is followed by feelings of contentment, peacefulness, and warmth. For the person addicted to heroin, withdrawal is not life threatening, but it does produce unpleasant drug rebound symptoms. Withdrawal symptoms include an intense craving for heroin, fever, chills, muscle cramps, and gastrointestinal problems.

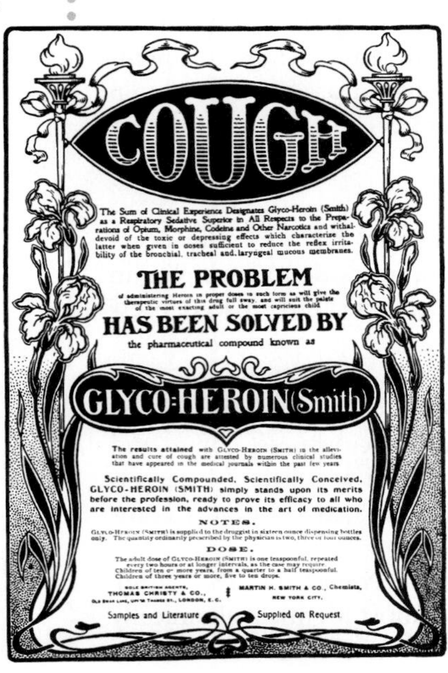

Heroin Cough Syrup Opium and its derivatives, including heroin, morphine, and codeine, were legal in the United States until 1914. In the late nineteenth and early twentieth centuries, opiates were commonly used in over-the-counter medications for a variety of ailments, from sleeplessness to "female problems" (Musto, 1991). This ad for "Glyco-Heroin" cough syrup appeared in 1904. Codeine is still used in some prescription cough syrups.

Heroin is not the most commonly abused opiate. That distinction belongs to the prescription pain pills, especially *OxyContin,* which combines the synthetic opioid *oxycodone* with a time-release mechanism. Street users discovered that crushing the OxyContin tablets easily destroyed the time-release mechanism. The resulting powder could be snorted, smoked, or diluted in water and injected—resulting in a rapid, intense high.

Abuse of OxyContin and similar prescription pain pills has skyrocketed in recent years (Fischer & Rehm, 2007). In fact, in terms of frequency of illicit use, prescription pain pills are second only to marijuana (Savage, 2005). As with any of the opiates, prescription pain pills are especially dangerous when mixed with other drugs, such as alcohol or barbiturates. Many occasional abusers of prescription medications are not aware the substance they are ingesting is a powerful—and potentially deadly—narcotic.

The Stimulants

Caffeine, Nicotine, Amphetamines, and Cocaine

Key Theme

- **Stimulant drugs increase brain activity, while the psychedelic drugs create perceptual distortions, alter mood, and affect thinking.**

Key Questions

- **What are the general effects of stimulants and the specific effects of caffeine, nicotine, amphetamines, and cocaine?**
- **What are the effects of mescaline, LSD, and marijuana?**
- **What are the "club drugs," and what are their effects?**

tranquilizers
Depressant drugs that relieve anxiety.

opiates
(OH-pee-ets) A category of psychoactive drugs that are chemically similar to morphine and have strong pain-relieving properties.

stimulants
A category of psychoactive drugs that increase brain activity, arouse behavior, and increase mental alertness.

caffeine
(kaff-EEN) A stimulant drug found in coffee, tea, cola drinks, chocolate, and many over-the-counter medications.

Stimulants vary in the strength of their effects, legal status, and the manner in which they are taken. All stimulant drugs, however, are at least mildly addicting, and all tend to increase brain activity. We'll first look at the most widely used and legal stimulants, caffeine and nicotine. Then we'll examine much more potent stimulants, cocaine and the amphetamines.

Caffeine and Nicotine

Caffeine is the most widely used psychoactive drug in the world and is found in such common sources as coffee, tea, cola drinks, chocolate, and certain over-the-counter medications (see Table 4.5). Caffeine promotes wakefulness, mental alertness, vigilance, and faster thought processes by stimulating the release of dopamine in the brain's prefrontal cortex.

Caffeine also produces its mentally stimulating effects by blocking *adenosine* receptors in the brain. *Adenosine* is a naturally occurring compound in your body that influences the release of several neurotransmitters in the central nervous system. As noted earlier, adenosine levels gradually increase the longer a person is awake. When adenosine levels reach a certain level in your body, the urge to sleep greatly intensifies. Caffeine staves off the urge and promotes alertness by blocking adenosine's sleep-inducing effects (Roehrs & Roth, 2008). Caffeine's adenosine-blocking ability has another effect—it stimulates *indirect* and mild dopamine release in the brain's reward system.

Caffeine and Conversation People enjoy a cup of coffee or an espresso at the Cafe Artigiano in Vancouver. In all its different forms, caffeine is the most widely used psychoactive drug in the world (Juliano & Griffiths, 2004).

Table 4.5

Common Sources of Caffeine

Item	Milligrams Caffeine
Coffee (short, 8 ounces)	85–250
Coffee (grande, 16 ounces)	220–550
Tea (8 ounces)	16–60
Chocolate (semisweet, baking; 1 ounce)	25
Soft drinks (12 ounces)	35–70
Energy drinks (8 ounces, Red Bull, Jolt)	40–80
Caffeinated waters (8 ounces, Water Joe, Java Water)	25–60
Over-the-counter stimulants (NoDoz, Vivarin)	200
Over-the-counter analgesics (Anacin, Midol)	25–130
Over-the-counter cold remedies (Triaminicin, Coryban-D)	30

Source: National Sleep Foundation (2004).

Yes, coffee drinkers, there is ample scientific evidence that caffeine is physically addictive. However, because the brain reward effects of caffeine are mild, coffee junkies are not likely to rampage the nearest Starbucks and take hostages if deprived of their favorite espresso. However, they will experience withdrawal symptoms if they abruptly stop their caffeine intake. Headaches, irritability, drowsiness, and fatigue can last a week or longer (Juliano & Griffiths, 2004; Reissig & others, 2009).

Taken to excess, caffeine can produce anxiety, restlessness, and increased heart rate and can disrupt normal sleep patterns. Excessive caffeine use can also contribute to the incidence of sleep disorders, including the NREM parasomnias, like sleepwalking (Cartwright, 2004). Recall that Scott, whose story we told in the Prologue, had been taking caffeine pills for several weeks before his sleepwalking episode. Because Scott never drank coffee or other caffeinated beverages, his caffeine tolerance would have been low. Especially when combined with sleep deprivation, irregular sleep schedules, and high levels of stress—all of which Scott experienced—excessive caffeine intake can trigger sleepwalking and other NREM parasomnias. At least one sleep expert believes that Scott's high caffeine use may have contributed to his outburst of sleep violence (Cartwright, 2007).

For many people, a cup of coffee and a cigarette go hand in hand. Cigarettes contain **nicotine,** another potent and addictive stimulant. Nicotine is found in all tobacco products, including pipe tobacco, cigars, cigarettes, and smokeless tobacco. About 25 percent of American adults are cigarette smokers, and another 5 percent use other tobacco products (SAMHSA, 2007). The proportion of smokers is much higher in Japan, many European countries, and developing countries.

Like coffee, nicotine increases mental alertness and reduces fatigue or drowsiness. Brain-imaging studies show that nicotine increases neural activity in many brain areas, including the frontal lobes, thalamus, hippocampus, and amygdala (Rose & others, 2003). Thus, it's not surprising that smokers report that tobacco enhances mood, attention, arousal, and vigilance.

When cigarette smoke is inhaled, nicotine reaches the brain in seconds. But over the next hour or two, nicotine's desired effects diminish. For the addicted person, smoking becomes a finely tuned and regulated behavior so that steady brain levels of nicotine are maintained. At regular intervals ranging from about 30 to 90 minutes, the smoker lights up, avoiding the withdrawal effects that are starting to occur. For the pack-a-day smoker, that averages out to some 70,000 "hits" of nicotine every year.

Nicotine is highly addictive, both physically and psychologically (Laviolette & van der Kooy, 2004). People who start smoking for nicotine's stimulating properties often continue smoking to avoid the withdrawal symptoms. Along with an intense craving for cigarettes, withdrawal symptoms include jumpiness, irritability, tremors, headaches, drowsiness, "brain fog," and light-headedness.

Amphetamines and Cocaine

Like caffeine and nicotine, amphetamines and cocaine are addictive substances that stimulate brain activity, increasing mental alertness and reducing fatigue. However, amphetamines and cocaine also elevate mood and produce a sense of euphoria. When abused, both drugs can produce severe psychological and physical problems.

Sometimes called "speed" or "uppers," **amphetamines** suppress appetite and were once widely prescribed as diet pills. Tolerance to the appetite-suppressant effects occurs quickly, so progressive increases in amphetamine dosage are required to maintain the effect. Consequently, amphetamines are rarely prescribed today for weight control.

nicotine
A stimulant drug found in tobacco products.

amphetamines
(am-FET-uh-meens) A class of stimulant drugs that arouse the central nervous system and suppress appetite.

cocaine
A stimulant drug derived from the coca tree.

Using any type of amphetamines for an extended period of time is followed by "crashing"—withdrawal symptoms of fatigue, deep sleep, intense mental depression, and increased appetite. This is another example of a drug rebound effect. Users also become psychologically dependent on the drug for the euphoric state, or "rush," that it produces, especially when injected.

Benzedrine and *dexedrine* are prescription amphetamines. *Methamphetamine,* also known as *meth,* is an illegal drug that can be easily manufactured in home or street laboratories. Providing an intense high that is longer-lasting and less expensive than that of cocaine, methamphetamine use has spread from the western United States to the rest of the country, including small towns in the rural Midwest and South.

Methamphetamine is highly addictive and can cause extensive brain damage and tissue loss, as discussed in the Focus on Neuroscience titled "How Methamphetamines Erode the Brain." Even after months of abstinence, PET scans of former meth users showed significant reductions in the number of dopamine receptors and dopamine transporters (Volkow & others, 2001a). *Dopamine transporters* play a critical role in removing dopamine from the synaptic gap between neurons, then transporting it back to the dopamine-producing neurons.

What are the behavioral effects of losing dopamine receptors and transporters? Memory and motor skill problems are common in former abusers. Numerous studies have shown that the most severe deficits occurred in those with the greatest loss of dopamine transporters (Chang & others, 2008; Tomasi & others, 2007a, 2007b; Volkow & others, 2001b). Extensive neurological damage, especially to the frontal lobes, adds to the cognitive and social skill deficits that are evident in heavy methamphetamine users (Homer & others, 2008). Depression, emotional instability, and impulsive and violent behavior are also common. Finally, recent research suggests that it may take years for the brain to recover from damage caused by methamphetamine abuse (Bamford & others, 2008).

Cocaine is an illegal stimulant derived from the leaves of the coca plant, which is found in South America. (The coca plant is not the source of cocoa or chocolate, which is made from the beans of the *cacao* tree.) Psychologically, cocaine produces intense euphoria, mental alertness, and self-confidence. These psychological responses occur because cocaine blocks the reuptake of three different neurotransmitters—dopamine, serotonin, and norepinephrine. Blocking reuptake *potentiates* or increases the effects of these neurotransmitters.

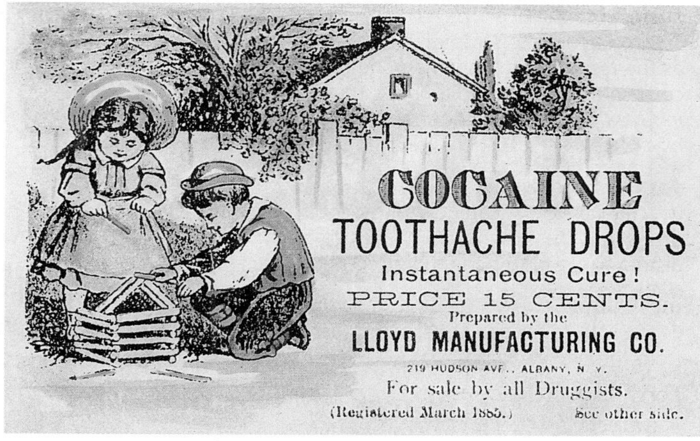

Cocaine Toothache Drops? Prior to 1914, cocaine was legal in the United States and, like the opiates, was widely used as an ingredient in over-the-counter medicines (Jonnes, 1999). From this 1885 advertisement for Cocaine Toothache Drops, it's clear that cocaine was used to treat children as well as adults. Cocaine derivatives, such as novocaine and lidocaine, are still used medically as anesthetics. Cocaine was also part of Coca-Cola's original formula in 1888. It was replaced in 1903 with another stimulant, caffeine. Coca leaves, with the cocaine extracted for medical purposes, are still used for flavoring cola drinks.

FOCUS ON NEUROSCIENCE

How Methamphetamines Erode the Brain

Researcher Paul Thompson and his colleagues (2004) used MRI scans to compare the brains of chronic methamphetamine users to those of healthy adults. In the composite scan shown here, red indicates areas with tissue loss from 5 to 10 percent. Green indicates 3 to 5 percent tissue loss, and blue indicates relatively intact brain regions. Thompson found that meth abusers experienced up to 10 percent tissue loss in limbic system areas involved in emotion and reward. Significant tissue loss also occurred in hippocampal regions involved in learning and memory. "We expected some brain changes, but we didn't expect so much brain tissue to be destroyed," Thompson said. Not surprisingly, methamphetamine abusers performed more poorly on memory tests as compared to healthy people the same age (Thompson & others, 2004).

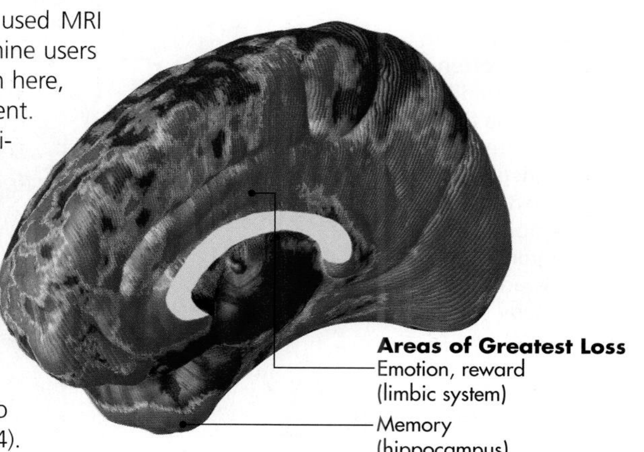

stimulant-induced psychosis
Schizophrenia-like symptoms that can occur as the result of prolonged amphetamine or cocaine use; also called *amphetamine-induced psychosis* or *cocaine-induced psychosis*.

psychedelic drugs
(*sy*-kuh-DEL-ick) A category of psychoactive drugs that create sensory and perceptual distortions, alter mood, and affect thinking.

mescaline
(MESS-kuh-*lin*) A psychedelic drug derived from the peyote cactus.

LSD
A synthetic psychedelic drug.

How quickly cocaine's psychological effects occur, and how long they last, depends on whether cocaine is snorted, swallowed, smoked, or injected. *Crack cocaine,* a more concentrated form of cocaine, is smoked. (The name crack refers to the sound of the cocaine crystals popping and cracking when smoked.) When smoked or injected, cocaine reaches the brain in seconds and its effects peak in about 5 minutes. When snorted, the nasal membranes absorb cocaine more slowly, with peak blood levels occurring some 30 to 60 minutes later.

Chronic cocaine use produces a wide range of psychological disorders. Of particular note, the prolonged use of amphetamines or cocaine can result in **stimulant-induced psychosis,** also called *amphetamine-induced psychosis* or *cocaine-induced psychosis.* Schizophrenia-like symptoms develop, including auditory hallucinations of voices and bizarrely paranoid ideas. In response to imagined threats, the psychotic person can become highly aggressive and dangerous.

Psychedelic Drugs

Mescaline, LSD, and Marijuana

The term **psychedelic drug** was coined in the 1950s to describe a group of drugs that create profound perceptual distortions, alter mood, and affect thinking. *Psychedelic* literally means "mind manifesting."

Mescaline and LSD

Naturally occurring psychedelic drugs have been used for thousands of years. **Mescaline,** which is derived from the peyote cactus, has been used for centuries in the religious ceremonies of Mexican Indians. Another psychedelic drug, called *psilocybin,* is derived from *Psilocybe* mushrooms, which are sometimes referred to as "magic mushrooms" or "shrooms." Psilocybin has been used since 500 B.C. in religious rites in Mexico and Central America.

In contrast to these naturally occurring psychedelics, **LSD** (*lysergic acid diethylamide*) is a powerful psychedelic drug that was first synthesized in the late 1930s. LSD is far more potent than mescaline or psilocybin. Just 25 micrograms, or one-millionth of an ounce, of LSD can produce profound psychological effects with relatively few physiological changes.

LSD and psilocybin are very similar chemically to the neurotransmitter *serotonin,* which is involved in regulating moods and sensations (see Chapter 2). LSD and psilocybin mimic serotonin in the brain, stimulating serotonin receptor sites in the somatosensory cortex (González-Maeso & others, 2007).

The effects of a psychedelic experience vary greatly, depending on an individual's personality, current emotional state, surroundings, and the other people present. A "bad trip" can produce extreme anxiety, panic, and even psychotic episodes. Tolerance to psychedelic drugs may occur after heavy use. However, even heavy users of LSD do not develop physical dependence, nor do they experience withdrawal symptoms if the drug is not taken.

Peyote-Inspired Visions The Huichol Indians of Mexico have used peyote in religious ceremonies for hundreds of years. Huichol yarn paintings, like the one shown here, often depict imagery and scenes inspired by traditional peyote visions. These visions resemble the geometric shapes and radiating patterns of hallucinations induced by psychedelic drugs. Today, peyote continues to be used as a sacrament in the religious ceremonies of the Native American Church, a religion with more than 300,000 members (Swan & Big Bow, 1995). According to one study, the use of peyote as a sacrament in the context of church ritual was not associated with either psychological or cognitive problems in Navajo members of the Native American Church (Halpern & others, 2005).

Adverse reactions to LSD include flashbacks (recurrences of the drug's effects), depression, long-term psychological instability, and prolonged psychotic reactions (Smith & Seymour, 1994). In a psychologically unstable or susceptible person, even a single dose of LSD can precipitate a psychotic reaction.

Marijuana

The common hemp plant, *Cannabis sativa,* is used to make rope and cloth. But when its leaves, stems, flowers, and seeds are dried and crushed, the mixture is called **marijuana,** one of the most widely used illegal drugs. Marijuana's active ingredient is the chemical *tetrahydrocannabinol,* abbreviated *THC.* When marijuana is smoked, THC reaches the brain in less than 30 seconds. One potent form of marijuana, *hashish,* is made from the resin of the hemp plant. Hashish is sometimes eaten.

To lump marijuana with the highly psychedelic drugs mescaline and LSD is somewhat misleading. At high doses, marijuana can sometimes produce sensory distortions that resemble a mild psychedelic experience. Low to moderate doses of THC typically produce a sense of well-being, mild euphoria, and a dreamy state of relaxation. Senses become more focused and sensations more vivid. Taste, touch, and smell may be enhanced; time perception may be altered.

Medical Marijuana The medical use of marijuana can be traced back for thousands of years to ancient China, Egypt, India, and Greece, among other countries. Its use was legal in the United States until 1937, when marijuana was outlawed, despite protests from the American Medical Association (Aggarwal & others, 2009). Research into the possible medical benefits of marijuana continued, however, and in 1996 California became the first state to legalize the medical use of marijuana. Now, people with a physician's referral and a state-issued ID card can legally purchase medical-grade marijuana at one of hundreds of California dispensaries, like the San Francisco dispensary shown here. Marijuana can relieve certain types of chronic pain, inflammation, muscle spasms, nausea, vomiting, and other symptoms caused by such illnesses as multiple sclerosis, cancer, and AIDS (see Pisanti & others, 2009; Rahn & Hohmann, 2009). Twelve other states have legalized medical marijuana; similar legislation is pending in several other states.

In the early 1990s, researchers discovered receptor sites in the brain that are specific for THC. They also discovered a naturally occurring brain chemical, called *anandamide,* that is structurally similar to THC and that binds to the THC receptors in the brain (Devane & others, 1992). Anandamide appears to be involved in regulating the transmission of pain signals and may reduce painful sensations. Researchers also suspect that anandamide may be involved in mood and memory.

Marijuana and its active ingredient, THC, have been shown to be helpful in the treatment of pain, epilepsy, hypertension, nausea, glaucoma, and asthma (Piomelli, 2003). In cancer patients, THC can prevent the nausea and vomiting caused by chemotherapy. However, the medical use of marijuana is limited and politically controversial.

On the negative side, marijuana interferes with muscle coordination and perception and may impair driving ability. When marijuana and alcohol use are combined, marijuana's effects are intensified—a dangerous combination for drivers. Marijuana has also been shown to interfere with learning, memory, and cognitive functioning (Harvey & others, 2007).

There are very few THC receptors in the brainstem, the part of the brain that controls such life-support functions as breathing and heartbeat. Thus, high doses of THC do not interfere with respiratory and cardiac functions as depressants and opiates do (Piomelli, 2003).

Most marijuana users do not develop tolerance or physical dependence. Chronic users of high doses can develop some tolerance to THC and may experience withdrawal symptoms when its use is discontinued (Budney & others, 2007; Nocon & others, 2006). Such symptoms include irritability, restlessness, insomnia, tremors, and decreased appetite.

Designer "Club" Drugs

Ecstasy and the Dissociative Anesthetic Drugs

Some drugs don't fit into neat categories. The "club drugs" are a loose collection of psychoactive drugs that are popular at dance clubs, parties, and the all-night dance parties called "raves." Many of these drugs are *designer drugs,* meaning that they were synthesized in a laboratory rather than derived from naturally occurring compounds. In this section, we'll take a look at three of the most popular club drugs—*ecstasy, ketamine,* and *PCP.*

The initials **MDMA** stand for the long chemical name of the quintessential club drug better known as **ecstasy.** Other street names are *X, XTC, Adam,* and the "love drug." Ecstasy was developed by a German pharmaceutical company in 1912 for possible use as an appetite suppressant, but it was not tested on humans until the 1970s. Structurally similar to both mescaline and amphetamine, MDMA has stimulant and psychedelic effects.

marijuana
A psychoactive drug derived from the hemp plant.

MDMA or ecstasy
Synthetic club drug that combines stimulant and mild psychedelic effects.

Rave Culture All-night dance parties, called raves, originated in Great Britain and quickly spread to other European countries and to the United States. Raves may draw anywhere from a few hundred to a few thousand people or more. Highly caffeinated "energy drinks," amphetamines, methamphetamine, and other stimulants may be consumed to maintain the energy needed to dance all night. Rave culture helped popularize the use of ecstasy, a synthetic drug. Ecstasy users may suck on baby pacifiers to cope with the drug's side effects, which include jaw clenching and tooth grinding.

At low doses, MDMA acts as a stimulant, but at high doses it has mild psychedelic effects. Its popularity, however, results from its emotional effects: Feelings of euphoria and increased well-being are common. People who have taken ecstasy also say that the drug makes them feel loving, open, and closer to others—effects that led to its use in psychotherapy for a brief time until its adverse effects became apparent (Braun, 2001). Ecstasy's side effects hint at the problems that can be associated with its use: dehydration, rapid heartbeat, tremors, muscle tension and involuntary teeth-clenching, and hyperthermia (abnormally high body temperature). Rave partygoers who take MDMA in crowded, hot surroundings are particularly at risk for collapse or death from dehydration and hyperthermia.

The "love drug" effects of ecstasy may result from its unique effect on serotonin in the brain. Along with causing neurons to release serotonin, MDMA also blocks serotonin reuptake, amplifying and prolonging serotonin effects (Braun, 2001). While flooding the brain with serotonin may temporarily enhance feelings of emotional well-being, there are adverse trade-offs.

First, the "high" of ecstasy is often followed by depression when the drug wears off. More ominously, animal studies have shown that moderate or heavy use of ecstasy can damage serotonin nerve endings in the brain (Ricaurte & McCann, 2001). Several studies have shown similar damage to serotonin neurons in the human brain (Croft & others, 2001; Reneman & others, 2006). Evidence suggests that female users are more susceptible to brain damage than male users (see Figure 4.6).

Other studies have shown that serotonin levels become severely depleted after long-term use, possibly causing the depression that follows when the drug wears off (Kuhn & Wilson, 2001). Equally troubling are cognitive effects: In one study, memory and verbal reasoning problems persisted up to a year after the last dose was taken (Reneman & others, 2001b). Some research suggests that even occasional

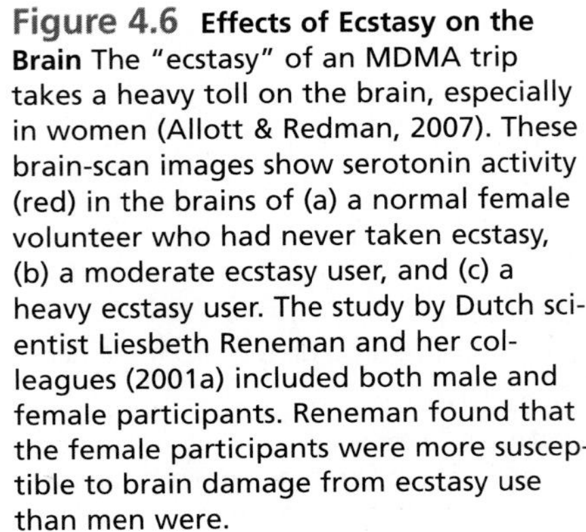

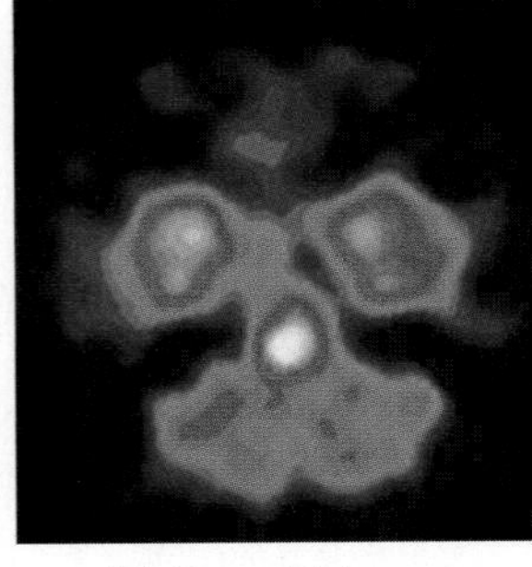

(a) Control, Non-use

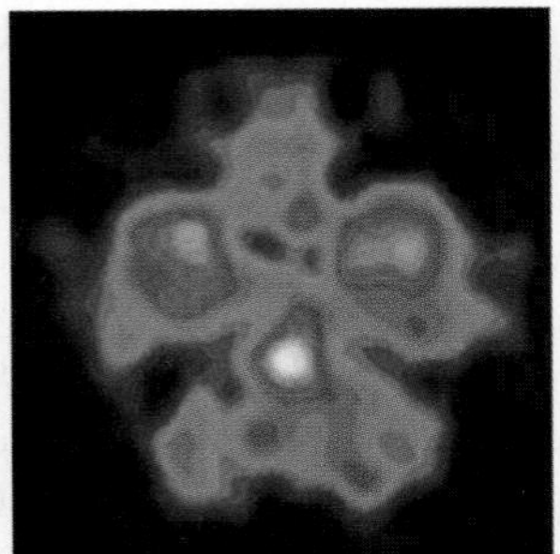

(b) Moderate MDMA use

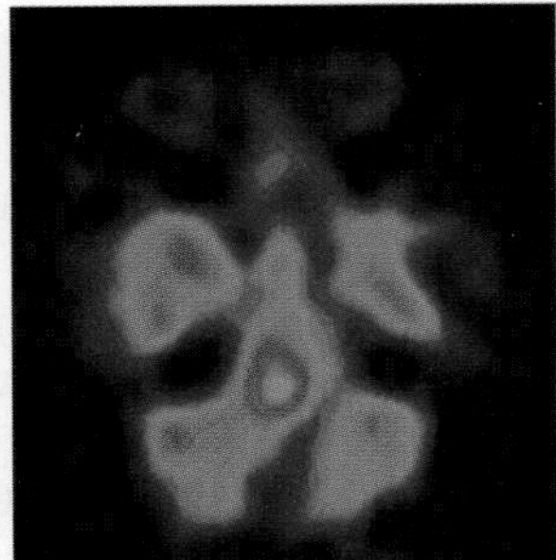

(c) Heavy MDMA use

Figure 4.6 Effects of Ecstasy on the Brain The "ecstasy" of an MDMA trip takes a heavy toll on the brain, especially in women (Allott & Redman, 2007). These brain-scan images show serotonin activity (red) in the brains of (a) a normal female volunteer who had never taken ecstasy, (b) a moderate ecstasy user, and (c) a heavy ecstasy user. The study by Dutch scientist Liesbeth Reneman and her colleagues (2001a) included both male and female participants. Reneman found that the female participants were more susceptible to brain damage from ecstasy use than men were.

use of ecstasy may produce memory problems (Schilt & others, 2007). Several studies have shown that frequent ecstasy users suffer a broad range of cognitive problems, such as impaired memory and decision making (Kalechstein & others, 2007; Montgomery & Fisk, 2008).

Another class of drugs found at dance clubs and raves are the **dissociative anesthetics,** including phencyclidine, better known as *PCP* or *angel dust,* and *ketamine* (street name *Special K*). Originally developed as anesthetics for surgery in the late 1950s, both PCP and ketamine deaden pain and, at high doses, can induce a stupor or coma. Because of their psychological effects, these drugs were largely abandoned for surgical use in humans.

Rather than producing actual hallucinations, PCP and ketamine produce marked feelings of dissociation and depersonalization. Feelings of detachment from reality—including distortions of space, time, and body image—are common. Generally, PCP has more intense and longer effects than ketamine does.

PCP can be eaten, snorted, or injected, but it is most often smoked or sprinkled on tobacco or marijuana. The effects are unpredictable, and a PCP trip can last for several days. Some users of PCP report feelings of invulnerability and exaggerated strength. PCP users can become severely disoriented, violent, aggressive, or suicidal. High doses of PCP can cause hyperthermia, convulsions, and death. PCP affects levels of the neurotransmitter *glutamate,* indirectly stimulating the release of dopamine in the brain. Thus, PCP is highly addictive. Memory problems and depression are common effects of long-term use.

dissociative anesthetics
Class of drugs that reduce sensitivity to pain and produce feelings of detachment and dissociation; includes the club drugs phencyclidine (PCP) and ketamine.

>> Closing Thoughts

Internal biological rhythms and external environmental factors influence the natural ebb and flow of your consciousness over the course of any given day. Beyond those natural oscillations, hypnosis and meditation are techniques that can profoundly alter your experience of consciousness. Meditation, in particular, produces numerous benefits that can help us cope more effectively with life's demands. Some psychoactive drugs, including widely available substances like caffeine, can also influence our experience of consciousness in beneficial ways. But other psychoactive substances, while producing dramatic alterations in consciousness, do so with the potential risk of damaging the finely tuned balance of the brain's neurotransmitters and reward system.

Both natural and deliberate factors seem to have played a role in the extreme breach of consciousness that Scott Falater claimed to experience. Severe disruptions in his normal sleep patterns, his out-of-character use of caffeine, and intense work-related stresses combined to trigger sleepwalking, a parasomnia that Scott had demonstrated when he was younger. And that Scott reacted violently when his wife tried to guide him back to bed also had precedent; Scott had reacted aggressively earlier in his life when family members tried to intervene during one of his sleepwalking episodes.

Scott Falater's trial for murdering his wife drew international attention. In the end, the Arizona jury convicted Falater of first-degree, premeditated murder. Falater was sentenced to life in prison with no possibility of parole. Today, Scott Falater is incarcerated in the Arizona State Prison Complex at Yuma, where he works as an educational aide and library clerk.

Life in Prison Scott Falater could have received the death penalty after being convicted by a Phoenix jury of first-degree murder in the death of his wife, Yarmila. But during the presentencing investigation, Falater's two children, and even Yarmila's mother, pleaded to spare his life. The sentencing judge agreed, and sentenced Falater to life in prison with no possibility for parole.

ENHANCING WELL-BEING WITH PSYCHOLOGY

Stimulus Control Therapy for Insomnia

In this section, we'll provide some simple tips to help you minimize sleep problems. If you frequently suffer from insomnia, we'll also describe a very effective treatment that you can implement on your own—**stimulus control therapy.**

Preventing Sleep Problems

You may not realize the degree to which your daily habits can contribute to or even create sleeping difficulties. The following four strategies can help you consistently get a good night's sleep.

1. Monitor your intake of stimulants.

Many people don't realize how much caffeine they're ingesting. Coffee, tea, soft drinks, chocolate, and many over-the-counter medications contain significant amounts of caffeine (see Table 4.5). Monitor your caffeine intake, and avoid caffeine products for at least 4 hours before going to bed. Some people are very sensitive to caffeine's stimulating effects and may need to avoid caffeine for up to 10 hours before bedtime. Beyond caffeine, some herbal teas and supplements contain ginseng, ephedrine, or other stimulants that can keep you awake.

2. Establish a quiet bedtime routine.

Avoid stimulating mental or physical activity for at least an hour before your bedtime. That means no suspenseful television shows, violent videos, exciting video games, or loud arguments right before bedtime. Ditto for strenuous exercise. Although regular exercise is an excellent way to improve your sleep, exercising within 3 hours of bedtime may keep you awake. Finally, soaking in a very warm bath shortly before bed promotes deep sleep by raising your core body temperature.

3. Create the conditions for restful sleep.

Your bedroom should be quiet, cool, and dark. If you live in a noisy environment, invest in a pair of earplugs or some sort of "white noise" source, such as a fan, for your bedroom. Turn off or mute all devices that can potentially disrupt your sleep, including cell phones and computers.

4. Establish a consistent sleep–wake schedule.

While this is probably the single most effective strategy to achieve quality sleep, it's also the most challenging for a lot of college students. Try to go to bed at about the same time each night and get up at approximately the same time every morning so that your circadian rhythms stay in sync. Exposure to bright lights or sunlight shortly after awakening in the morning helps keep your internal clock set.

Many students try to "catch up" on their sleep by sleeping in on the weekends. Unfortunately, this strategy can work against you by producing a case of the "Monday morning blues," which is a self-induced case of jet lag caused by resetting your circadian rhythms to the later weekend schedule.

If you've tried all these suggestions and are still troubled by frequent insomnia, you may need to take a more systematic approach, as outlined in the next section.

Stimulus Control Therapy

Without realizing it, you can sabotage your ability to sleep by associating mentally arousing activities and stimuli with your bedroom, such as watching TV, text messaging, reading, surfing the Internet, eating, listening to music, doing homework or paperwork, and so on. Over time, your bed and bedroom become stimuli that trigger arousal rather than drowsiness and the rapid onset of sleep. In turn, this increases the amount of time that you're lying in bed awake, thrashing around, and trying to force yourself to sleep.

"It's only insomnia if there's nothing good on."

Stimulus control therapy is designed to help you (a) establish a consistent sleep–wake schedule and (b) associate your bedroom and bedtime with falling asleep rather than other activities (Morin & others, 2006). To realize improved sleep, you must commit to the following rules with *no* exceptions for at least two weeks:

- Only sleep and sex are allowed in your bedroom. None of the sleep-incompatible activities mentioned above are allowed in your bed or bedroom.
- Only go to bed when you are sleepy, not tired or wiped out, but *sleepy.*
- Once in bed, if you're still awake after 15 minutes, don't try to force yourself to go to sleep. Instead, get out of bed and go sit in another room. Only go back to bed when you get sleepy.
- Get up at the *same* time *every* morning, including weekends, regardless of how much sleep you got the night before.
- No daytime napping. None. Zip. Nada. Zilch.

Strictly adhering to these rules can be challenging given the realities of work, family, school, and other personal commitments. However, those situations are much easier to manage when you are adequately rested.

Keeping a *sleep diary* can help you track your sleep and sleep-related behaviors. It will also increase your awareness of your sleep habits and the factors that interfere with restorative sleep. The National Sleep Foundation has a diary available as a downloadable PDF. Other sleep diaries can easily be found with an Internet search. Sleep well!

stimulus control therapy
Insomnia treatment involving specific guidelines to create a strict association between the bedroom and rapid sleep onset.

CHAPTER REVIEW: KEY PEOPLE AND TERMS

Sigmund Freud, p. 151
Ernest R. Hilgard, p. 161
J. Alan Hobson, p. 152
William James, p. 137
Robert W. McCarley, p. 152

consciousness, p. 136
circadian rhythm, p. 138
suprachiasmatic nucleus (SCN), p. 139
melatonin, p. 139
electroencephalograph, p. 140
EEG (electroencephalogram), p. 140
REM sleep, p. 141
NREM sleep, p. 141
beta brain waves, p. 141
alpha brain waves, p. 141
hypnagogic hallucinations, p. 141
sleep spindles, p. 142
K complex, p. 142
sleep paralysis, p. 144
REM rebound, p. 146
sleep thinking, p. 147
dream, p. 147
nightmare, p. 150
manifest content, p. 151
latent content, p. 151
activation–synthesis model of dreaming, p. 152
sleep disorders, p. 153
dyssomnias, p. 153
parasomnias, p. 153
insomnia, p. 153
obstructive sleep apnea (OSA), p. 155
narcolepsy, p. 155
cataplexy, p. 155
hypocretins, p. 156
sleep terrors, p. 157
sleepsex, p. 157
sleepwalking, p. 157
sleep-related eating disorder, p. 158
REM sleep behavior disorder, p. 158
hypnosis, p. 159
posthypnotic suggestion, p. 160
posthypnotic amnesia, p. 160
hypermnesia, p. 160
dissociation, p. 161
neodissociation theory of hypnosis, p. 161
hidden observer, p. 161
meditation, p. 163
psychoactive drug, p. 165
physical dependence, p. 165
drug tolerance, p. 165
withdrawal symptoms, p. 165
drug rebound effect, p. 165
drug abuse, p. 166
depressants, p. 167
inhalants, p. 169
barbiturates, p. 169
tranquilizers, p. 170
opiates, p. 170
stimulants, p. 171
caffeine, p. 171
nicotine, p. 172
amphetamines, p. 172
cocaine, p. 173
stimulant-induced psychosis, p. 174
psychedelic drugs, p. 174
mescaline, p. 174
LSD, p. 174
marijuana, p. 175
MDMA (ecstasy), p. 175
dissociative anesthetics, p. 177
stimulus control therapy, p. 178

Web Companion Review Activities

You can find additional review activities at **www.worthpublishers.com/discoveringpsych5e.** The *Discovering Psychology* 5th edition Web Companion has self-scoring practice quizzes, flashcards, interactive crossword puzzles, and other activities to help you master the material in this chapter.

CONCEPT MAP

CONSCIOUSNESS AND ITS VARIATIONS

Consciousness:
The immediate awareness of internal and external stimuli

William James (1842–1910)
Described subjective experience of consciousness as an ongoing stream of mental activity

Circadian rhythms:
- Daily cycles of psychological and biological processes
- Regulated by **suprachiasmatic nucleus,** which responds to light and triggers pineal gland to decrease **melatonin**

Wakefulness:
Beta brain waves

Sleep

REM sleep:
Dreaming sleep
- Voluntary muscle activity is suppressed
- Fast brain wave activity
- Physiological arousal
- Rapid eye movements

NREM sleep:
Quiet sleep

Stage 1 NREM:
- Transition from wakefulness to light sleep
- **Alpha and theta brain waves**

Stage 2 NREM:
- **Sleep spindles**
- **K complexes**

Stage 3 NREM:
Slow-wave sleep (SWS)
- Theta and delta brain waves

Stage 4 NREM:
Slow-wave sleep
- Delta brain waves
- Deep, sound sleep
- Difficult to awaken

Sleep patterns

Over the night:
- Five 90-minute NREM/REM sleep cycles
- Slow-wave sleep during first half of night
- REM episodes get longer as sleep progresses

Over the lifespan:
- Infant has shorter 60-minute sleep cycles
- Typical 90-minute cycles emerge by age 5
- From childhood to late adulthood, total sleep time and SWS decrease; percentage of NREM Stages 1 & 2 increases
- REM sleep decreases during late adulthood

Dreams and Mental Activity During Sleep

Sleep thinking

Dreams
Nightmares

Sleep and memory formation:
- NREM slow-wave sleep helps form new *episodic memories*
- REM sleep and NREM stage 2 sleep help form new *procedural memories*

Significance of dreams:

Sigmund Freud (1856–1939)
Psychoanalytic theory of dreams
- Dream images symbolize repressed wishes and urges; include **manifest content** and **latent content**

J. Allan Hobson (b. 1933) and
Robert McCarley (b. 1937)
Activation-synthesis model of dreaming
- Dreams are subjective awareness of internally generated signals during sleep

Sleep Disorders

Dyssomnias: Disruptions in amount, quality, or timing of sleep
- **Insomnia**
- **Obstructive sleep apnea**
- **Narcolepsy**

Parasomnias: Undesirable physical arousal, behaviors, or events during sleep
- **Sleep terrors**
- **Sleepsex**
- **Sleep-related eating disorder**
- **Sleepwalking**
- **REM sleep behavior disorder**

Hypnosis

A cooperative social interaction in which the participant responds to suggestions made by the hypnotist

Effects of hypnosis:
- Sensory, perceptual changes
- **Posthypnotic suggestions**
- Memory changes, including **posthypnotic amnesia,** but not **hypermnesia**

Explaining hypnosis:
- Hypnosis as a special state of consciousness: **Ernest Hilgard** (1904–2001) proposed **neodissociation theory of hypnosis**
- Hypnosis due to ordinary psychological processes; the *social-cognitive view of hypnosis*
- The *imaginative suggestibility view*; hypnosis due to capacity to imagine and heightened suggestibility

Limitations of hypnosis:
- Not all people capable of being hypnotized
- Cannot hypnotize a person against his or her will
- Cannot hypnotically induce immoral or criminal acts

Meditation

Sustained concentration techniques that focus attention and heighten awareness

Forms of meditation:
- Concentration techniques
- Opening-up techniques

Effects of meditation:
- Lowers physiological arousal
- Reduces stress
- Enhances physical and psychological functioning

Psychoactive Drugs

Alter synaptic transmission in the brain and induce changes in arousal, mood, thinking, sensation, and perception
Can be addictive, producing:
- **Physical dependence**
- **Drug tolerance**
- **Withdrawal symptoms**
- **Drug rebound effect**

Depressants: Addictive drugs that inhibit central nervous system activity
- Alcohol
- **Barbiturates**
- **Inhalants**
- **Tranquilizers**

"Club" drugs: Synthetic drugs used at dance clubs, parties, and "raves"
- **MDMA (ecstasy)**
- **Dissociative anesthetics** include PCP and ketamine

Opiates: Addictive drugs that relieve pain and produce feelings of euphoria
- Opium
- Morphine
- Codeine
- Heroin
- Methadone
- Prescription painkillers

Stimulants: Addictive drugs that increase brain activity
- **Caffeine**
- **Nicotine**
- **Amphetamines**
- Methamphetamines
- **Cocaine**

Psychedelic drugs: Create perceptual distortions, alter mood and thinking
- **Mescaline**
- **LSD**
- **Marijuana**

CHAPTER 5

Learning

The Killer Attic

PROLOGUE

SANDY'S PARENTS, ERV AND FERN, were married for more than 50 years. Sometimes it seems truly amazing that they managed to stay together for so long, as you'll see from this true story.

It was a warm summer morning in Chicago. Erv and Fern drank their coffee and made plans for the day. The lawn needed mowing, the garage needed cleaning, and someone had to go to the post office to buy stamps. Fern, who didn't like driving, said that she would mow the lawn if Erv would go to the post office. Erv, who didn't like yard work, readily agreed to the deal.

As Erv left for the post office, Fern started cutting the grass in the backyard. When Erv returned, he parked the car around the corner under some large shade trees so that it would stay cool while he puttered around in the garage. Walking through the front door to drop off the stamps, he noticed that the attic fan was squeaking loudly. Switching it off, Erv decided to oil the fan before he tackled the garage. He retrieved the stepladder and oil from the basement, propped the ladder under the attic's trapdoor, and gingerly crawled up into the attic, leaving the trapdoor open.

Meanwhile, Fern was getting thirsty. As she walked past the garage on the way into the house, she noticed the car was still gone. "Why isn't Erv back yet? He must have stopped somewhere on the way back from the post office," she thought. As she got a glass of water, she noticed the stepladder and the open attic door. Muttering that Erv never put anything away, Fern latched the trapdoor shut and dragged the ladder back down to the basement.

Erv, who had crawled to the other side of the attic to oil the fan, never heard the attic trapdoor shut. It was very hot in the well-insulated, airless attic, so he tried to work fast. After oiling the fan, he crawled back to the trapdoor—only to discover that it was latched shut from the outside! "Fern," he hollered, "open the door!" But Fern was already back outside, mowing away, and couldn't hear Erv over the noise of the lawn mower. Erv, dripping with sweat, kept yelling and pounding on the trapdoor.

Outside, Fern was getting hot, too. She stopped to talk to a neighbor, leaving the lawn mower idling. He offered Fern a cold beer, and the two of them leaned over the fence, laughing and talking. From a small, sealed attic window, Erv watched the whole scene. Jealousy was now added to his list of discomforts. He was also seriously beginning to think that he might sweat to death in the attic heat. He could already see the tabloid headlines in the supermarket checkout line: LAUGHING WIFE DRINKS BEER WHILE HUSBAND COOKS IN ATTIC!

Finally, Fern went back to mowing, wondering what in the world had happened to Erv. Meanwhile, up in the attic, Erv was drenched with sweat and his heart was racing. He promised God he'd never complain about Chicago winters again. At last, Fern finished the lawn and walked back to the house. Hearing the back door

Chapter Outline

open, Erv began to yell and pound on the trapdoor again.

"Hey, Fern! Fern!"

Fern froze in her tracks.

"Fern, let me out! I'm going to suffocate up here!"

"Erv! Is that you? Where are you?" she called, looking around.

"I'm in the attic! Let me out!"

"What are you doing in the attic? I thought you were at the store!"

"What do you *think* I'm doing? Let me out of here! Hurry!"

Once Fern was reassured that Erv had suffered no ill effects from being trapped in the attic, she burst out laughing. Later that day, still grumbling about Fern's harebrained sense of humor, Erv removed the latch from the attic door. Ever since, whenever Erv went up into the attic, he posted a sign on the ladder that read MAN IN THE ATTIC! In fact, for years afterward, Erv got nervous whenever he had to go up into attic.

For her part, Fern began carefully checking on Erv's whereabouts before closing the attic door. But she still laughs when she tells the story of the "killer attic"—which she does frequently, as it never fails to crack up her listeners. Luckily, Erv was a good sport and was used to Fern's sense of humor.

Erv and Fern both learned from their experience, as is reflected in the changes in their behavior. Learning new behaviors can occur in many ways, but it almost always helps us adapt to changing circumstances, as you'll see in this chapter.

>> Introduction: What Is Learning?

Key Theme

- **Learning refers to a relatively enduring change in behavior or knowledge as a result of experience.**

Key Questions

- **What is conditioning?**
- **What are three basic types of learning?**

What do we mean when we say that Fern and Erv have "learned" from their experience with the killer attic? In the everyday sense, *learning* often refers to formal methods of acquiring new knowledge or skills, such as learning in the classroom or learning to play the flute.

In psychology, however, the topic of learning is much broader. Psychologists formally define **learning** as a process that produces a relatively enduring change in behavior or knowledge as a result of an individual's experience. For example, Erv has learned to feel anxious and uncomfortable whenever he needs to enter the attic. He's also learned to take simple precautions, such as posting his MAN IN THE ATTIC! sign, to avoid getting locked in the attic again. As Erv's behavior demonstrates, the learning of new behaviors often reflects adapting to your environment. As the result of experience, you acquire new behaviors or modify old behaviors so as to better cope with your surroundings.

In this broad sense of the word, learning occurs in every setting, not just in classrooms. And learning takes place at every age. Further, the psychological study of learning is not limited to humans. From alligators to zebras, learning is an important aspect of the behavior of virtually all animals.

Psychologists have often studied learning by observing and recording the learning experiences of animals in carefully controlled laboratory situations. Using animal subjects, researchers can precisely control the conditions under which a particular behavior is learned. The goal of much of this research has been to identify the general principles of learning that apply across a wide range of species, including humans.

learning
A process that produces a relatively enduring change in behavior or knowledge as a result of past experience.

conditioning
The process of learning associations between environmental events and behavioral responses.

Much of this chapter will focus on a very basic form of learning, called *conditioning*. **Conditioning** is the process of learning associations between environmental events and behavioral responses. This description may make you think conditioning has only a limited application to your life. In fact, however, conditioning is reflected in most of your everyday behavior, from simple habits to emotional reactions and complex skills.

In this chapter, we'll look at basic types of conditioning—classical conditioning and operant conditioning. As you'll see in the next section, *classical conditioning* explains how certain stimuli can trigger an automatic response, as the attic now triggers mild anxiety in Erv. And, as you'll see in a later section, *operant conditioning* is useful in understanding how we acquire new, voluntary actions, such as Erv's posting his sign whenever he climbs into the attic. Finally, toward the end of the chapter, we'll consider the process of *observational learning*, or how we acquire new behaviors by observing the actions of others.

Conditioning, Learning, and Behavior Through different kinds of experiences, people and animals acquire enduring changes in their behaviors. Psychologists have identified general principles of learning that explain how we acquire new behaviors. These principles apply to simple responses, but they can also help explain how we learn complex skills, like the traditional style of drumming that these children are learning in an after-school class in Bungwe, Rwanda.

Classical Conditioning
Associating Stimuli

Key Theme

- **Classical conditioning is a process of learning associations between stimuli.**

Key Questions

- **How did Pavlov discover and investigate classical conditioning?**
- **How does classical conditioning occur?**
- **What factors can affect the strength of a classically conditioned response?**

One of the major contributors to the study of learning was not a psychologist but a Russian physiologist who was awarded a Nobel Prize for his work on digestion. **Ivan Pavlov** was a brilliant scientist who directed several research laboratories in St. Petersburg, Russia, at the turn of the twentieth century. Pavlov's involvement with psychology began as a result of an observation he made while investigating the role of saliva in digestion, using dogs as his experimental subjects.

In order to get a dog to produce saliva, Pavlov (1904) put food on the dog's tongue. After he had worked with the same dog for several days in a row, Pavlov noticed something curious. The dog began salivating *before* Pavlov put the food on its tongue. In fact, the dog began salivating when Pavlov entered the room or even at the sound of his approaching footsteps. But salivating is a *reflex*—a largely involuntary, automatic response to an external stimulus. (As we've noted in previous chapters, a *stimulus* is anything perceptible to the senses, such as a sight, sound, smell, touch, or taste.) The dog should salivate only *after* the food is presented, not before. Why would the reflex occur before the stimulus was presented? What was causing this unexpected behavior?

If you own a dog, you've probably observed the same basic phenomenon. Your dog gets excited and begins to slobber when you shake a box of dog biscuits, even before you've given him a doggie treat. In everyday language, your pet has learned to anticipate food in association with some signal—namely, the sound of dog biscuits rattling in a box.

Ivan Pavlov (1849–1936) In his laboratory, Pavlov was known for his meticulous organization, keen memory, and attention to details (Windholz, 1990). But outside his lab, Pavlov was absentminded, forgetful, and impractical, especially regarding money. He often forgot to pick up his paycheck, and he sometimes lent money to people with hard luck stories who couldn't possibly pay him back (Fancher, 1996). On a trip to New York City, Pavlov carried his money so carelessly that he had his pocket picked in the subway, and his American hosts had to take up a collection to pay his expenses (Skinner, 1966).

classical conditioning
The basic learning process that involves repeatedly pairing a neutral stimulus with a response-producing stimulus until the neutral stimulus elicits the same response.

unconditioned stimulus (UCS)
The natural stimulus that reflexively elicits a response without the need for prior learning.

unconditioned response (UCR)
The unlearned, reflexive response that is elicited by an unconditioned stimulus.

conditioned stimulus (CS)
A formerly neutral stimulus that acquires the capacity to elicit a reflexive response.

conditioned response (CR)
The learned, reflexive response to a conditioned stimulus.

Pavlov's extraordinary gifts as a researcher enabled him to recognize the important implications of what had at first seemed a problem—a reflex (salivation) that occurred *before* the appropriate stimulus (food) was presented. He also had the discipline to systematically study how such associations are formed. In fact, Pavlov abandoned his research on digestion and devoted the remaining 30 years of his life to investigating different aspects of this phenomenon. Let's look at what he discovered in more detail.

Principles of Classical Conditioning

The process of conditioning that Pavlov discovered was the first to be extensively studied in psychology. Thus, it's called *classical conditioning* (Hilgard & Marquis, 1940). **Classical conditioning** deals with behaviors that are elicited automatically by some stimulus. *Elicit* means "draw out" or "bring forth." That is, the stimulus doesn't produce a new behavior but rather *causes an existing behavior to occur.*

Classical conditioning always involves some kind of reflexive behavior. Remember, a reflex is a relatively simple, unlearned behavior, governed by the nervous system, that occurs *automatically* when the appropriate stimulus is presented. In Pavlov's (1904) original studies of digestion, the dogs salivated reflexively when food was placed on their tongues. But when the dogs began salivating in response to the sight of Pavlov or to the sound of his footsteps, a new, *learned* stimulus elicited the salivary response. Thus, in classical conditioning, a *new* stimulus–response sequence is learned.

How does this kind of learning take place? Essentially, classical conditioning is a process of learning an *association between two stimuli*. Classical conditioning involves pairing a *neutral* stimulus (e.g., the sight of Pavlov) with an *unlearned, natural* stimulus (food in the mouth) that automatically elicits a reflexive response (the dog salivates). If the two stimuli (Pavlov + food) are repeatedly paired, eventually the neutral stimulus (Pavlov) elicits the same basic reflexive response as the natural stimulus (food)—even in the absence of the natural stimulus. So, when the dog in the laboratory started salivating at the sight of Pavlov *before* the food was placed on its tongue, it was because the dog had formed a new, *learned association* between the sight of Pavlov and the food.

Pavlov used special terms to describe each element of the classical conditioning process. The natural stimulus that reflexively produces a response without prior learning is called the **unconditioned stimulus** (abbreviated **UCS**). In this example, the unconditioned stimulus is the food in the dog's mouth. The unlearned, reflexive response is called the **unconditioned response** (or **UCR**). The unconditioned response is the dog's salivation.

To learn more about his discovery, Pavlov (1927) controlled the stimuli that preceded the presentation of food. For example, in one set of experiments, he used a

Life in Pavlov's Laboratories During Pavlov's four decades of research, more than 140 scientists and students worked in the two laboratories under his direction. Twenty of his co-researchers were women, including his daughter, V. I. Pavlova. Pavlov, who had an extraordinary memory for details, carefully supervised the procedures of dozens of ongoing research projects. Nevertheless, he acknowledged that the scholarly achievements produced by his laboratories represented the collective effort of himself and his co-workers (Windholz, 1990).

bell as a neutral stimulus—neutral because dogs don't normally salivate to the sound of a ringing bell. Pavlov first rang the bell and then gave the dog food. After this procedure was repeated several times, the dog began to salivate when the bell was rung, before the food was put in its mouth. At that point, the dog was *classically conditioned* to salivate to the sound of a bell alone. That is, the dog had *learned a new association* between the sound of the bell and the presentation of food.

Pavlov called the sound of the bell the *conditioned stimulus*. The **conditioned stimulus** (or **CS**) is the stimulus that is originally neutral but comes to elicit a reflexive response. He called the dog's salivation to the sound of the bell the **conditioned response** (or **CR**), which is the *learned* reflexive response to a previously neutral stimulus. The steps of Pavlov's conditioning process are outlined in Figure 5.1.

Classical conditioning terminology can be confusing. You may find it helpful to think of the word *conditioned* as having the same meaning as "learned." Thus, the "conditioned stimulus" refers to the "learned stimulus," the "unconditioned response" refers to the "unlearned response," and so forth.

It's also important to note that in this case the unconditioned response and the conditioned response describe essentially the same behavior—the dog's salivating. Which label is applied depends on which stimulus elicits the response. If the dog is salivating in response to a *natural* stimulus that was not acquired through learning, the salivation is an *unconditioned* response. If, however, the dog has learned to salivate to a *neutral* stimulus that doesn't normally produce the automatic response, the salivation is a *conditioned* response.

Before Conditioning:

Prior to conditioning, the dog notices the bell ringing, but does not salivate. Here, the bell is a neutral stimulus. Food placed in the dog's mouth (the **UCS**) naturally produces the salivation reflex (the **UCR**).

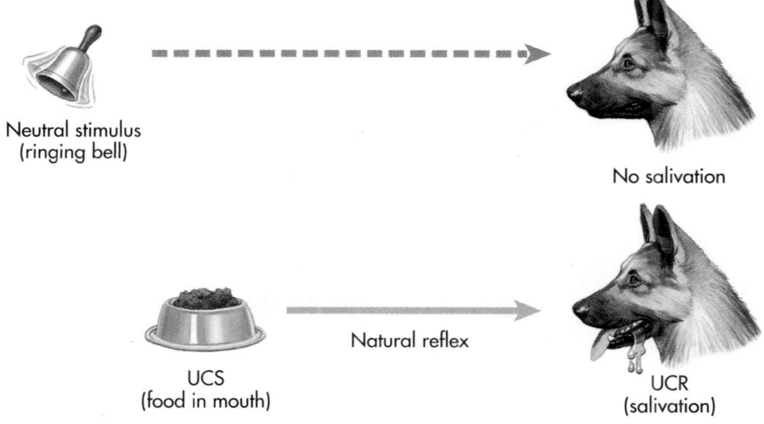

During Conditioning:

In the conditioning phase, the neutral stimulus (the ringing bell) is repeatedly sounded immediately before food is placed in the dog's mouth (the **UCS**), which produces the natural reflex of salivation (the **UCR**).

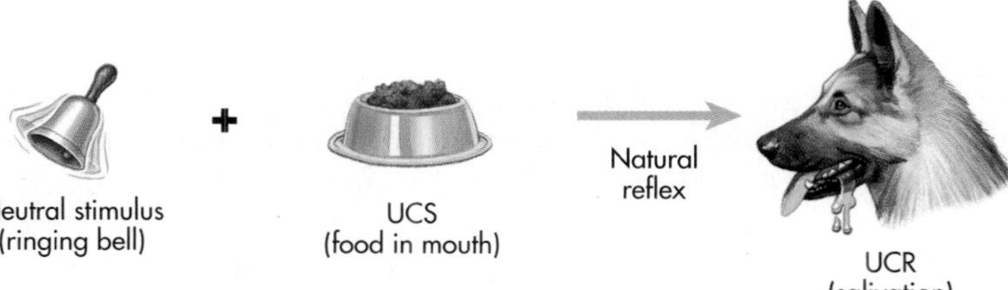

After Conditioning:

The ringing bell is no longer neutral. It is now called a **CS** because, when the bell is rung, the dog reacts with a conditioned reflex: It salivates even though no food is present. The salivation response is called a **CR**.

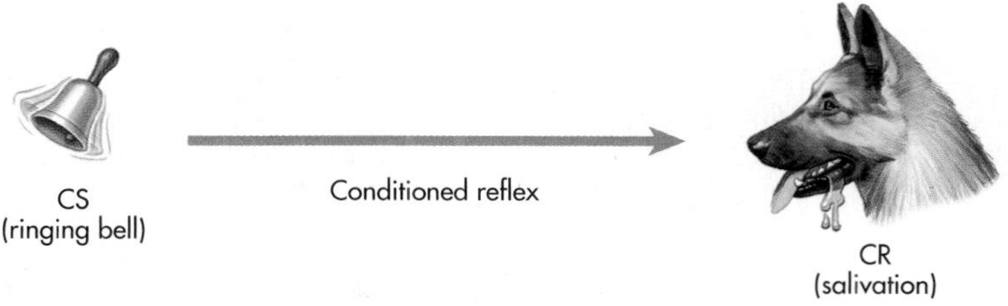

Figure 5.1 The Process of Classical Conditioning The diagram shows Pavlov's classical conditioning procedure. As you can see, classical conditioning involves the learning of an association between a neutral stimulus (the ringing bell) and a natural stimulus (food).

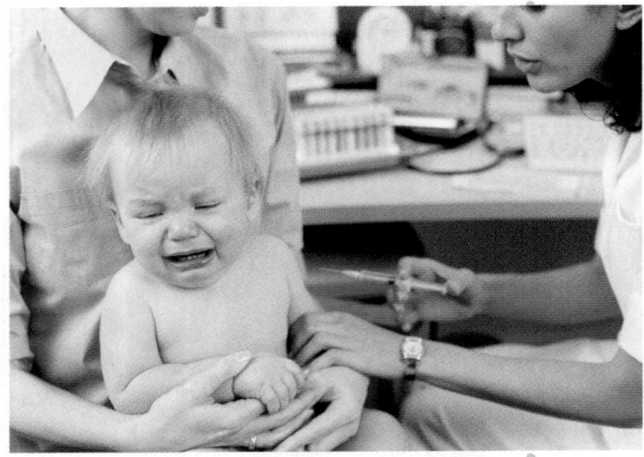

Classical Conditioning in Early Life: White Coats and Doctor Visits Most infants receive several vaccinations in their first few years of life. The painful injection (a UCS) elicits fear and distress (a UCR). After a few office visits, the clinic, nurse, or even the medical staff's white lab coats can become a conditioned stimulus (CS) that elicits fear and distress—even in the absence of a painful injection.

Factors That Affect Conditioning

Over the three decades that Pavlov (1928) spent studying classical conditioning, he discovered many factors that could affect the strength of the conditioned response (Bitterman, 2006). For example, he discovered that the more frequently the conditioned stimulus and the unconditioned stimulus were paired, the stronger was the association between the two.

Pavlov also discovered that the *timing* of stimulus presentations affected the strength of the conditioned response. He found that conditioning was most effective when the conditioned stimulus was presented immediately *before* the unconditioned stimulus. In his early studies, Pavlov found that a half-second was the optimal time interval between the onset of the conditioned stimulus and the beginning of the unconditioned stimulus. Later, Pavlov and other researchers found that the optimal time interval could vary in different conditioning situations but was rarely more than a few seconds.

Stimulus Generalization and Discrimination

Pavlov (1927) noticed that once a dog was conditioned to salivate to a particular stimulus, new stimuli that were similar to the original conditioned stimulus could also elicit the conditioned salivary response. For example, Pavlov conditioned a dog to salivate to a low-pitched tone. When he sounded a slightly higher-pitched tone, the conditioned salivary response would also be elicited. Pavlov called this phenomenon *stimulus generalization*. **Stimulus generalization** occurs when stimuli that are similar to the original conditioned stimulus also elicit the conditioned response, even though they have never been paired with the unconditioned stimulus.

Just as a dog can learn to respond to similar stimuli, so it can learn the opposite—to *distinguish* between similar stimuli. For example, Pavlov repeatedly gave a dog some food following a high-pitched tone but did not give the dog any food following a low-pitched tone. The dog learned to distinguish between the two tones, salivating to the high-pitched tone but not to the low-pitched tone. This phenomenon, **stimulus discrimination,** occurs when a particular conditioned response is made to one stimulus but not to other, similar stimuli.

Higher Order Conditioning

In further studies of his classical conditioning procedure, Pavlov (1927) found that a conditioned stimulus could itself function as an unconditioned stimulus in a new conditioning trial. This phenomenon is called **higher order conditioning** or *second-order conditioning*. Pavlov paired a ticking metronome with food until the sound of the ticking metronome became established as a conditioned stimulus. Then Pavlov repeatedly paired a new unconditioned stimulus, a black square, with the ticking metronome—but no food. After several pairings, would the black square alone produce salivation? It did, even though the black square had never been directly paired with food. The black square had become a *new* conditioned stimulus, simply by being repeatedly paired with the first conditioned stimulus: the ticking metronome. Like the first conditioned stimulus, the black square produced the conditioned response: salivation.

It is important to note that in higher order conditioning, the new conditioned stimulus has *never* been paired with the unconditioned stimulus. The new conditioned stimulus acquires its ability to produce the conditioned response by virtue of being paired with the first conditioned stimulus (Gewirtz & Davis, 2000; Jara & others, 2006).

Consider this example: Like most children, our daughter Laura received several rounds of immunizations when she was an infant. Each painful injection (the UCS) elicited distress and made her cry (the UCR). After only the *second* vaccination, Laura developed a strong classically conditioned response—just the sight of a nurse's white uniform (the CS) triggered an emotional

outburst of fear and crying (the CR). Interestingly, Laura's conditioned fear generalized to a wide range of white uniforms, including a pharmacist's white smock, a veterinarian's white lab coat, and even the white jacket of a cosmetics saleswoman in a department store.

To illustrate higher order conditioning, imagine that baby Laura reacted fearfully when she saw a white-jacketed cosmetics saleswoman in a department store. Imagine further that the saleswoman compounded Laura's reaction by spraying her mother Sandy with a new perfume fragrance and handing Sandy a free perfume sample to take home. If Laura responded with fear the next time she smelled the fragrance, higher order conditioning would have taken place. The perfume scent had never been paired with the original UCS, the painful injection. The scent became a new CS by virtue of being paired with the first CS, the white jacket.

Extinction and Spontaneous Recovery

Once learned, can conditioned responses be eliminated? Pavlov (1927) found that conditioned responses could be gradually weakened. If the conditioned stimulus (the ringing bell) was repeatedly presented *without* being paired with the unconditioned stimulus (the food), the conditioned response seemed to gradually disappear. Pavlov called this process of decline and eventual disappearance of the conditioned response **extinction.**

Pavlov also found that the dog did not simply return to its unconditioned state following extinction (see Figure 5.2). If the animal was allowed a period of rest (such as a few hours) after the response was extinguished, the conditioned response would reappear when the conditioned stimulus was again presented. This reappearance of a previously extinguished conditioned response after a period of time without exposure to the conditioned stimulus is called **spontaneous recovery.** The phenomenon of spontaneous recovery demonstrates that extinction is not unlearning. That is, the learned response may seem to disappear, but it is *not* eliminated or erased (Bouton, 2007; Rescorla, 2001).

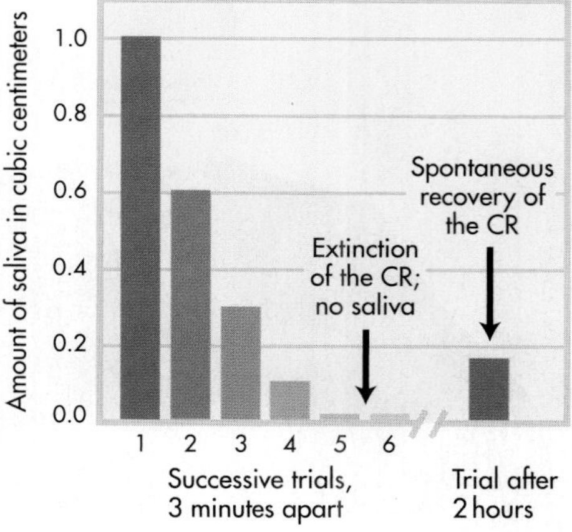

Figure 5.2 Extinction and Spontaneous Recovery in Pavlov's Laboratory This demonstration involved a dog that had already been conditioned to salivate (the CR) to just the sight of the meat powder (the CS). During the extinction phase, the CS was repeatedly presented at three-minute intervals and held just out of the dog's reach. As you can see in the graph, over the course of six trials the amount of saliva secreted by the dog quickly decreased to zero. This indicates that *extinction* had occurred. After a two-hour rest period, the CS was presented again. At the sight of the meat powder, the dog secreted saliva once more, evidence for the *spontaneous recovery* of the conditioned response.

Source: Data adapted from Pavlov (1927).

From Pavlov to Watson

The Founding of Behaviorism

Key Theme

- **Behaviorism was founded by John Watson, who redefined psychology as the scientific study of behavior.**

Key Questions

- **What were the fundamental assumptions of behaviorism?**
- **How did Watson use classical conditioning to explain and produce conditioned emotional responses?**
- **How did Watson apply classical conditioning techniques to advertising?**

Over the course of three decades, Pavlov systematically investigated different aspects of classical conditioning. Throughout this process, he used dogs almost exclusively as his experimental subjects. Since Pavlov believed he had discovered the mechanism by which all learning occurs, it seems ironic that he had very little to say about applications of classical conditioning to human behavior. This irony is less puzzling when you understand that Pavlov wanted nothing to do with the newly established science of psychology. Why?

At the beginning of the twentieth century, psychology's early founders had defined the field as *the scientific study of the mind* (see Chapter 1). They advocated the use of introspective self-reports to achieve two fundamental goals: describing and explaining conscious thought and perceptions. Because the early psychologists wanted to study subjective states of consciousness, Pavlov did not see psychology as

stimulus generalization
The occurrence of a learned response not only to the original stimulus but to other, similar stimuli as well.

stimulus discrimination
The occurrence of a learned response to a specific stimulus but not to other, similar stimuli.

higher order conditioning (also called *second-order conditioning*)
A procedure in which a conditioned stimulus from one learning trial functions as the unconditioned stimulus in a new conditioning trial; the second conditioned stimulus comes to elicit the conditioned response, even though it has never been directly paired with the unconditioned stimulus.

extinction (in classical conditioning)
The gradual weakening and apparent disappearance of conditioned behavior. In classical conditioning, extinction occurs when the conditioned stimulus is repeatedly presented without the unconditioned stimulus.

spontaneous recovery
The reappearance of a previously extinguished conditioned response after a period of time without exposure to the conditioned stimulus.

an exact or precise science, like physiology or chemistry. As Pavlov (1927) wrote, "It is still open to discussion whether psychology is a natural science, or whether it can be regarded as a science at all."

At about the same time Pavlov was conducting his systematic studies of classical conditioning in the early 1900s, a young psychologist named **John B. Watson** was attracting attention in the United States. Watson, like Pavlov, believed that psychology was following the wrong path by focusing on the study of subjective mental processes (Berman & Lyons, 2007). In 1913, Watson directly challenged the early founders of psychology in his landmark article titled "Psychology as the Behaviorist Views It." Watson's famous article opened with these sentences:

John Broadus Watson (1878–1958) Watson founded behaviorism in the early 1900s, emphasizing the scientific study of observable behaviors rather than the study of subjective mental processes. His influence spread far beyond the academic world. He wrote many books and articles for the general public on child rearing and other topics, popularizing the findings of the "new" science of psychology (Rilling, 2000).

> Psychology as the behaviorist views it is a purely objective experimental branch of natural science. Its theoretical goal is the prediction and control of behavior. Introspection forms no essential part of its methods, nor is the scientific value of its data dependent upon the readiness with which they lend themselves to interpretation in terms of consciousness.

With the publication of this article, Watson founded a new school, or approach, in psychology, called **behaviorism.** Watson strongly advocated that psychology should be redefined as *the scientific study of behavior.* As he later (1924) wrote, "Let us limit ourselves to things that can be observed, and formulate laws concerning only those things. Now what can we observe? We can observe *behavior—what the organism does or says.*"

But having soundly rejected the methods of introspection and the study of consciousness, the young Watson was somewhat at a loss for a new method to replace them (Fancher, 1996). By 1915, when Watson was elected president of the American Psychological Association, he had learned of Pavlov's research. Watson (1916) embraced the idea of the conditioned reflex as the model he had been seeking to investigate and explain human behavior (Evans & Rilling, 2000).

Watson believed that virtually *all* human behavior is a result of conditioning and learning—that is, due to past experience and environmental influences. In championing behaviorism, Watson took these views to an extreme, claiming that neither talent, personality, nor intelligence was inherited. In a characteristically bold statement, Watson (1924) proclaimed:

> I should like to go one step further now and say, "Give me a dozen healthy infants, well-formed, and my own specified world to bring them up in and I'll guarantee to take any one at random and train him to become any type of specialist I might select—doctor, lawyer, artist, merchant-chief and yes, even beggar-man and thief, regardless of his talents, penchants, tendencies, abilities, vocations, and race of his ancestors." I am going beyond my facts and I admit it, but so have the advocates of the contrary and they have been doing it for many thousands of years.

Needless to say, Watson never actually carried out such an experiment, and his boast clearly exaggerated the role of the environment to make his point. Nevertheless, Watson's influence on psychology cannot be overemphasized. Behaviorism was to dominate psychology in the United States for more than 50 years. And, as you'll see in the next section, Watson did carry out a famous and controversial experiment to demonstrate how human behavior could be classically conditioned.

Conditioned Emotional Reactions

Watson believed that, much as Pavlov's dogs reflexively salivated to food, human emotions could be thought of as reflexive responses involving the muscles and glands. In studies with infants, Watson (1919) identified three emotions that he believed represented inborn and natural unconditioned reflexes—fear, rage, and love. According to Watson, each of these innate emotions could be reflexively triggered by a small number of specific stimuli. For example, he found two stimuli that could trigger the reflexive fear response in infants: a sudden loud noise and a sudden dropping motion.

behaviorism
School of psychology and theoretical viewpoint that emphasize the scientific study of observable behaviors, especially as they pertain to the process of learning.

The Famous Case of Little Albert

Watson's interest in the role of classical conditioning in emotions set the stage for one of the most famous and controversial experiments in the history of psychology. In 1920, Watson and a graduate student named Rosalie Rayner set out to demonstrate that classical conditioning could be used to deliberately establish a conditioned emotional response in a human subject. Their subject was a baby, whom they called "Albert B.," but who is now more popularly known as "Little Albert." Little Albert lived with his mother in the Harriet Lane Hospital in Baltimore, where his mother was employed.

Watson and Rayner (1920) first assessed Little Albert when he was only 9 months old. Little Albert was a healthy, unusually calm baby who showed no fear when presented with a tame white rat, a rabbit, a dog, and a monkey. He was also unafraid of cotton, masks, and even burning newspapers! But, as with other infants whom Watson had studied, fear could be triggered in Little Albert by a sudden loud sound—clanging a steel bar behind his head. In this case, the sudden clanging noise is the unconditioned stimulus, and the unconditioned response is fear.

Two months after their initial assessment, Watson and Rayner attempted to condition Little Albert to fear the tame white rat (the conditioned stimulus). Watson stood behind Little Albert. Whenever Little Albert reached toward the rat, Watson clanged the steel bar with a hammer. Just as before, of course, the unexpected loud CLANG! (the unconditioned stimulus) startled and scared the daylights out of Little Albert (the unconditioned response).

During the first conditioning session, Little Albert experienced two pairings of the white rat with the loud clanging sound. A week later, he experienced five more pairings of the two stimuli. After only these seven pairings of the loud noise and the white rat, the white rat alone triggered the conditioned response—extreme fear—in Little Albert (see Figure 5.3). As Watson and Rayner (1920) described:

> The instant the rat was shown, the baby began to cry. Almost instantly he turned sharply to the left, fell over on [his] left side, raised himself on all fours and began to crawl away so rapidly that he was caught with difficulty before reaching the edge of the table.

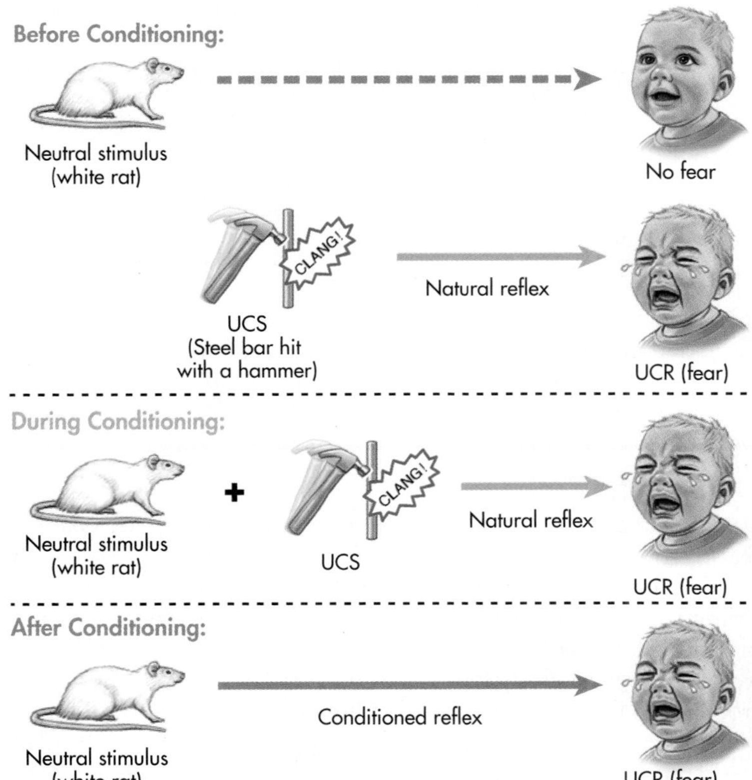

Figure 5.3 A Classically Conditioned Fear Response In the photograph below, Rosalie Rayner holds Little Albert as John Watson looks on. Little Albert is petting the tame white rat, clearly not afraid of it. But, after being repeatedly paired with the UCS (a sudden, loud noise), the white rat becomes a CS. After conditioning, Little Albert is terrified of the tame rat. His fear generalized to other furry objects, including rabbits, cotton, Rayner's fur coat, and Watson in a Santa Claus beard.

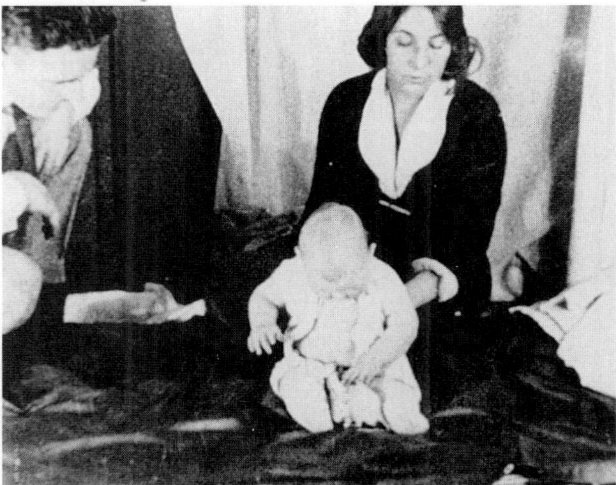

IN FOCUS

Watson, Classical Conditioning, and Advertising

From shampoos to soft drinks, advertising campaigns often use sexy models to promote their products. Today, we take this advertising tactic for granted. But it's actually yet another example of Watson's influence.

Shortly after the Little Albert experiment, Watson's wife discovered that he was having an affair with his graduate student Rosalie Rayner. Following a scandalous and highly publicized divorce, Watson was fired from his academic position. Despite his international fame as a scientist, no other university would hire him (Benjamin & others, 2007). Banned from academia, Watson married Rayner and joined the J. Walter Thompson advertising agency (Buckley, 1989).

Watson was a pioneer in the application of classical conditioning principles to advertising. "To make your consumer react," Watson told his colleagues at the ad agency, "tell him something that will tie him up with fear, something that will stir up a mild rage, that will call out an affectionate or love response, or strike at a deep psychological or habit need" (quoted in Buckley, 1982).

Watson applied this technique to ad campaigns for Johnson & Johnson Baby Powder and Pebeco toothpaste in the 1920s. For the baby powder ad, Watson intentionally tried to stimulate an anxiety response in young mothers by creating doubts about their ability to care for their infants.

The Pebeco toothpaste campaign targeted the newly independent young woman who smoked. The ad raised the fear that attractiveness might be diminished by the effects of smoking—and Pebeco toothpaste was promoted as a way of increasing sexual attractiveness. One ad read, "Girls! Don't worry any more about smoke-stained teeth or tobacco-tainted breath. You can smoke and still be lovely if you'll just use Pebeco twice a day." Watson also developed ad campaigns for Pond's cold cream, Maxwell House coffee, and Camel cigarettes.

While Watson may have pioneered the strategy of associating products with "sex appeal," modern advertising has taken this technique to an extreme. Similarly, some ad campaigns pair products with images of adorable babies, cuddly kittens, happy families, or other "natural" stimuli that elicit warm, emotional responses. If classical conditioning occurs, the product by itself will also elicit a warm, emotional response.

Are such procedures effective? In a word, yes. Attitudes toward a product or a particular brand can be influenced by advertising and marketing campaigns that use classical conditioning methods (see Grossman & Till, 1998; Olson & Fazio, 2001).

Watson and Rayner also found that stimulus generalization had taken place. Along with fearing the rat, Little Albert was now afraid of other furry animals, including a dog and a rabbit. He had even developed a classically conditioned fear response to a variety of fuzzy objects—a sealskin coat, cotton, Watson's hair, and a white-bearded Santa Claus mask!

Although the Little Albert study has achieved legendary status in psychology, it had several problems (Harris, 1979; Paul & Blumenthal, 1989). One criticism is that the experiment was not carefully designed or conducted. For example, Albert's fear and distress were not objectively measured but were subjectively evaluated by Watson and Rayner.

The experiment is also open to criticism on ethical grounds. Watson and Rayner (1920) did not extinguish Little Albert's fear of furry animals and objects, even though they believed that such conditioned emotional responses would "persist and modify personality throughout life." Whether they had originally intended to extinguish the fear is not completely clear (see Paul & Blumenthal, 1989). Little Albert left the hospital shortly after the completion of the experiment. Watson (1930) later wrote that he and Rayner could not try to eliminate Albert's fear response because the infant had been adopted by a family in another city shortly after the experiment had concluded. Today, conducting such an experiment would be considered unethical.

Classically Conditioned Emotional Reactions After being involved in a serious auto accident, many people develop a conditioned emotional response to the scene of the accident. Your author Don is no exception. He still shudders when he drives through the intersection of 10th and Cincinnati streets near the downtown campus of Tulsa Community College. His car (shown here) was crumpled by an SUV that sped up through a red light and smashed into the driver's side, spinning the car almost 180 degrees. (Fortunately, the entire sequence of events was witnessed by the Tulsa police officer in the car directly behind Don.) Although Don wasn't seriously hurt, just looking at the photo of the intersection (and his totaled car) makes his neck tighten up and his heart race. In this example, can you identify the UCS, UCR, CS, and CR?

You can probably think of situations, objects, or people that evoke a strong classically conditioned emotional reaction in you, such as fear or anger. One example that many of our students can relate to is that of becoming classically conditioned to cues associated with a person whom you strongly dislike, such as a demeaning boss or a hateful ex-lover. After repeated negative experiences (the UCS) with the person eliciting anger or fear (the UCR), a wide range of cues can become conditioned stimuli (CSs)—the person's name, the sight of the person, locations associated with the person, and so forth—and elicit a strong negative emotional reaction (the CR) in you. Just mentioning the person's name can make your heart pound and send your blood pressure soaring. Other emotional responses, such as feelings of happiness or sadness, can also be classically conditioned.

In this chapter's Prologue, we saw that Erv became classically conditioned to feel anxious whenever he entered the attic. The attic (the original neutral stimulus) was coupled with being trapped in extreme heat (the UCS), which produced fear (the UCR). Following the episode, Erv found that going into the attic (now a CS) triggered mild fear and anxiety (the CR). Like Erv, many people experience a conditioned fear response to objects, situations, or locations that are associated with some kind of traumatic experience or event. In fact, despite their knowledge of classical conditioning, your authors are not immune to this effect (see photo).

Other Classically Conditioned Responses

Under the right conditions, virtually any automatic response can become classically conditioned. For example, some aspects of sexual responses can become classically conditioned, sometimes inadvertently. To illustrate, suppose that a neutral stimulus, such as the scent of a particular cologne, is regularly paired with the person with whom you are romantically involved. In other words, your romantic partner almost always wears his or her "signature" cologne. You, of course, are most aware of the scent when you are physically close to your partner in sexually arousing situations. After repeated pairings, the initially neutral stimulus—the particular cologne scent—can become a conditioned stimulus. Now, the scent of the cologne evokes feelings of romantic excitement or mild sexual arousal even in the absence of your lover or, in some cases, long after the relationship has ended. And, in fact, a wide variety of stimuli can become "sexual turn-ons" through classical conditioning.

CATHY Cathy Guisewite

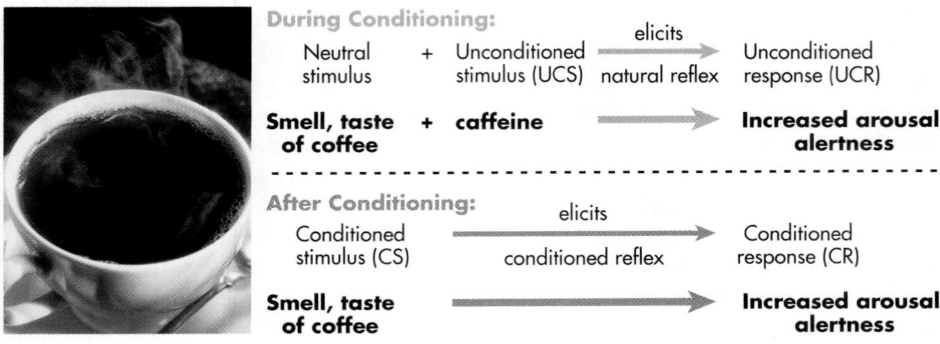

Figure 5.4 Classically Conditioned Drug Effects: Does Just the Smell of a Starbucks Espresso Perk You Up? If it does, classical conditioning is at work! Pavlov (1927) suggested that administering a drug could be viewed as a conditioning trial. Just like pairing the sound of a bell with the presentation of food, if specific environmental cues are repeatedly paired with a drug's administration, they can become conditioned stimuli that eventually elicit the drug's effect. For a regular coffee drinker, the sight, smell, and taste of freshly brewed coffee are the original neutral stimuli that, after being repeatedly paired with caffeine (the UCS), eventually become conditioned stimuli, producing the CS: increased arousal and alertness.

Classical conditioning can also influence drug responses. For example, if you are a regular coffee drinker like both of your authors, you may have noticed that you begin to feel more awake and alert after just a few groggy sips of your first cup of coffee in the morning. However, it takes at least 20 minutes for the caffeine from the coffee to reach significant levels in your bloodstream. If you're feeling more awake *before* blood levels of caffeine rise, it's probably because you've developed a classically conditioned response to the sight, smell, and taste of coffee (see Figure 5.4). Confirming that everyday experience, such conditioned responses to caffeine-associated stimuli have also been demonstrated experimentally (e.g., Flaten & Blumenthal, 1999; Mikalsen & others, 2001).

Once this classically conditioned drug effect becomes well established, the smell or taste of coffee—even decaffeinated coffee—can trigger the conditioned response of increased arousal and alertness (A. W. Smith & others, 1997).

Conditioned drug effects seem to be involved in at least some instances of placebo response (Stewart-Williams & Podd, 2004). Also called *placebo effect,* a **placebo response** occurs when an individual has a psychological and physiological reaction to what is actually a fake treatment or drug. We'll discuss this phenomenon in more detail in Chapter 12.

placebo response
An individual's psychological and physiological response to what is actually a fake treatment or drug; also called *placebo effect.*

Contemporary Views of Classical Conditioning

Key Theme

- **Contemporary learning researchers acknowledge the importance of both cognitive factors and evolutionary influences in classical conditioning.**

Key Questions

- **How has the involvement of cognitive processes in classical conditioning been demonstrated experimentally?**
- **What is meant by the phrase "the animal behaves like a scientist" in classical conditioning?**
- **How do taste aversions challenge the basic conditioning principles, and what is biological preparedness?**

The traditional behavioral perspective holds that classical conditioning results from a simple association of the conditioned stimulus and the unconditioned stimulus. According to the behaviorists, mental or cognitive processes such as thinking, anticipating, or deciding were not needed to explain the conditioning process.

However, not all psychologists were convinced that mental processes were so uninvolved in learning. Some wondered whether conditioning procedures did more than simply change how an organism responded. Could conditioning procedures change what the organism *knows* as well as what it *does*? According to the *cognitive perspective* (see Chapter 1), mental processes as well as external events are an important component in the learning of new behaviors. In the next section, we'll look at the role cognitive processes seem to play in classical conditioning. As you'll see, today's psychologists view the classical conditioning process very differently than Pavlov or Watson did (see Bouton, 2007).

Pavlovian conditioning is a sophisticated and sensible mechanism by which organisms represent the world. Our current understanding of Pavlovian conditioning leads to its characterization as a mechanism by which the organism encodes relationships between events in the world. The conditioned stimulus and the unconditioned stimulus are simply two events and the organism can be seen as trying to determine the relationship between them.

—ROBERT A. RESCORLA (1997)

Cognitive Aspects of Classical Conditioning

Reliable Signals

According to Pavlov, classical conditioning occurs simply because two stimuli are associated closely in time. The conditioned stimulus (the bell) precedes the unconditioned stimulus (the food) usually by no more than a few seconds. But is it possible that Pavlov's dogs were learning more than the mere association of two stimuli that occurred very close together in time?

To answer that question, let's begin with an analogy. Suppose that on your way to class you have to go through a railroad crossing. Every time a train approaches the crossing, warning lights flash. Being rather intelligent for your species, after a few weeks you conclude that the flashing lights will be quickly followed by a freight train barreling down the railroad tracks. You've learned an association between the flashing lights and an oncoming train, because the lights are a *reliable signal* that predict the presence of the train.

Now imagine that a friend of yours also has to cross train tracks but at a different location. The railroad has had nothing but problems with the warning lights at that crossing. Sometimes the warning lights flash before a train roars through, but sometimes they don't. And sometimes they flash when no train is coming. Does your friend learn an association between the flashing lights and oncoming trains? No, because here the flashing lights are an *unreliable signal*—they seem to have no relationship to a train's arrival.

Psychologist **Robert A. Rescorla** demonstrated that classically conditioned rats also assess the reliability of signals, much like you and your friend did at the different railroad crossings. In Rescorla's 1968 experiment, one group of rats heard a tone (the conditioned stimulus) that was paired 20 times with a brief electric shock (the unconditioned stimulus). A second group of rats experienced the *same* number of tone–shock pairings, but this group also experienced an *additional* 20 shocks with *no* tone (see Figure 5.5).

Then Rescorla tested for the conditioned fear response by presenting the tone alone to each group of rats. According to the traditional classical conditioning model, both groups of rats should have displayed the same levels of conditioned fear. After all, each group had received 20 tone–shock pairings. However, this is not what Rescorla found. The rats in the first group displayed a much stronger fear response to the tone than did the rats in the second group. Why?

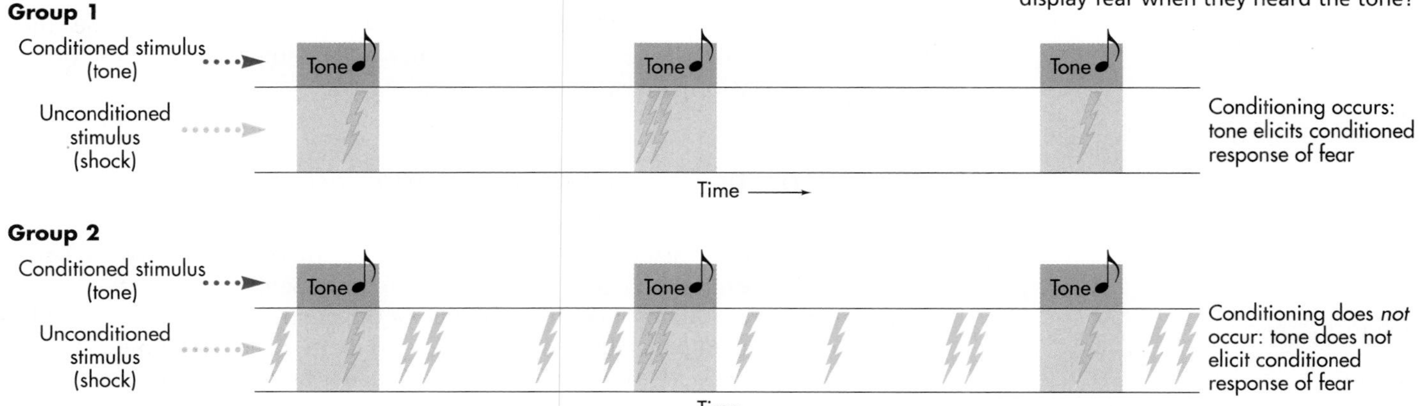

Figure 5.5 Reliable and Unreliable Signals In Rescorla's experiment, both groups of rats experienced the same number of tone–shock pairings. However, the rats in group 1 received a shock only when the tone was sounded, while the rats in group 2 experienced additional shocks that were not paired with the tone. Subsequently, the rats in group 1 displayed a conditioned fear response to the tone and the rats in group 2 did not. Why did only the rats in group 1 become conditioned to display fear when they heard the tone?

Classical Conditioning and Survival Animals quickly learn the signals that predict the approach of a predator. In classical conditioning terms, they learn to associate the approach of a predator (the unconditioned stimuli) with particular sounds, smells, or sights (the originally neutral stimuli that become conditioned stimuli). To survive, animals that are vulnerable to predators, such as this frightened deer, must be able to use environmental signals to predict events in their environment. A rustle in the underbrush, the faint whiff of a mountain lion, or a glimpse of a human tells the animal that it's time to flee.

According to Rescorla (1988), classical conditioning depends on the *information* the conditioned stimulus provides about the unconditioned stimulus. For learning to occur, the conditioned stimulus must be a *reliable signal* that predicts the presentations of the unconditioned stimulus. For the first group of rats, that was certainly the situation. Every time the tone sounded, a shock followed. But for the second group, the tone was an unreliable signal. Sometimes the tone preceded the shock, and sometimes the shock occurred without warning.

Rescorla concluded that the rats in both groups were *actively processing information* about the reliability of the signals they encountered. Rather than merely associating two closely paired stimuli, as Pavlov suggested, the animals assess the *predictive value* of stimuli. Applying this interpretation to classical conditioning, we can conclude that Pavlov's dogs learned that the bell was a signal that *reliably predicted* that food would follow.

According to this view, animals use cognitive processes to draw inferences about the signals they encounter in their environments. To Rescorla (1988), classical conditioning "is not a stupid process by which the organism willy-nilly forms associations between any two stimuli that happen to co-occur." Rather, his research suggests that "the animal behaves like a scientist, detecting causal relations among events and using a range of information about those events to make the relevant inferences" (Rescorla, 1980).

Because of studies by Rescorla and other researchers, today's understanding of how learning occurs in classical conditioning is very different from the explanations offered by Pavlov and Watson (Kirsch & others, 2004). Simply pairing events in time may not be enough for classical conditioning to occur. Instead, a conditioned stimulus must *reliably signal* that the unconditioned stimulus will follow. Put simply, classical conditioning seems to involve *learning the relationships between events* (Rescorla, 1988).

Evolutionary Aspects of Classical Conditioning

Biological Predispositions to Learn

According to Darwin's *theory of evolution by natural selection,* both the physical characteristics and the natural behavior patterns of any species have been shaped by evolution to maximize adaptation to the environment. Thus, just as physical characteristics vary from one species to another, so do natural behavior patterns. Some psychologists wondered whether an animal's natural behavior patterns, as shaped by evolution, would also affect how it learned new behaviors, especially behaviors important to its survival.

According to traditional behaviorists, the general principles of learning applied to virtually all animal species and all learning situations. Thus, they argued that the general learning principles of classical conditioning would be the same regardless of the species or the response being conditioned. However, in the 1960s, some researchers began to report "exceptions" to the well-established principles of classical conditioning (Lockard, 1971; Seligman, 1970). As you'll see in this section, one important exception involved a phenomenon known as a *taste aversion.* The study of taste aversions contributed to a new awareness of the importance of the organism's natural behavior patterns in classical conditioning.

Taste Aversions and Classical Conditioning: Spaghetti? No, Thank You!

A few years ago, Sandy made a pot of super spaghetti, with lots of mushrooms, herbs, spices, and some extra-spicy sausage. Being very fond of Sandy's spaghetti, Don ate two platefuls. Several hours later, in the middle of the night, Don came down with a nasty stomach virus. Predictably, Sandy's super spaghetti came back up—a colorful spectacle, to say the least. As a result, Don developed a **taste aversion**—he avoided eating spaghetti and felt queasy whenever he smelled spaghetti sauce. Don's taste aversion to spaghetti persisted for more than a year.

Such learned taste aversions are relatively common. Our students have told us about episodes of motion sickness, morning sickness, or illness that resulted in taste aversions to foods as varied as cotton candy, strawberries, and chicken soup. In some cases, a taste aversion can persist for years.

At first glance, it seems as if taste aversions can be explained by classical conditioning. In Don's case, a neutral stimulus (spaghetti) was paired with an unconditioned stimulus (a stomach virus), which produced an unconditioned response (nausea). Now a conditioned stimulus, the spaghetti sauce by itself elicited the conditioned response of nausea.

But notice that this explanation seems to violate two basic principles of classical conditioning. First, the conditioning did not require repeated pairings. Conditioning occurred in a *single pairing* of the conditioned stimulus and the unconditioned stimulus. Second, the time span between these two stimuli was *several hours,* not a matter of seconds. Is this possible? The anecdotal reports of people who develop specific taste aversions seem to suggest it is. But such reports lack the objectivity and systematic control that a scientific explanation of behavior requires.

Enter psychologist **John Garcia,** who demonstrated that taste aversions could be produced in laboratory rats under controlled conditions (Garcia & others, 1966). Garcia's procedure was straightforward. Rats first drank saccharin-flavored water (the neutral stimulus). Hours later, the rats were injected with a drug (the unconditioned stimulus) that produced gastrointestinal distress (the unconditioned response). After the rats recovered from their illness, they refused to drink the flavored water again. The rats had developed a taste aversion to the saccharin-flavored water, which had become a conditioned stimulus.

At first, many psychologists were skeptical of Garcia's findings because they seemed to violate the basic principles of classical conditioning. Several leading psychological journals refused to publish Garcia's research, saying the results were unconvincing or downright impossible (Garcia, 1981, 2003). But Garcia's results have been replicated many times. In fact, later research showed that taste aversions could develop even when a full 24 hours separated the presentation of the flavored water and the drug that produced illness (Etscorn & Stephens, 1973).

Conditioned taste aversions also challenged the notion that virtually any stimulus can become a conditioned stimulus. As Pavlov (1928) wrote, "Any natural phenomenon chosen at will may be converted into a conditioned stimulus . . . any visual stimulus, any desired sound, any odor, and the stimulation of any part of the skin." After all, Pavlov had demonstrated that dogs could be classically conditioned to salivate to a ringing bell, a ticking metronome, and even the sight of geometric figures.

But if this were the case, then why didn't Don develop an aversion to other stimuli he encountered between the time he ate the spaghetti and when he got sick? Why was it that only the spaghetti sauce became a conditioned stimulus that triggered nausea, not the dinner table, the silverware—or even Sandy, for that matter?

Contrary to what Pavlov suggested, Garcia and his colleagues demonstrated that the particular conditioned stimulus that is used *does* make a difference in classical conditioning (Garcia & Koelling, 1966). In another series of experiments, Garcia found that rats did *not* learn to associate a taste with a painful event, such as a shock. Nor did they learn to associate a flashing light and noise with illness. Instead, rats were much more likely to associate a *painful stimulus,* such as a shock, with *external stimuli,* such as flashing lights and noise. And rats were much more likely to associate a *taste stimulus* with *internal stimuli*—the physical discomfort of illness. Garcia and Koelling (1966) humorously suggested that a sick rat, like a sick person, speculates, "It must have been something I ate."

Why is it that certain stimuli are more easy to associate than others? One factor that helps explain Garcia's results is **biological preparedness**—the idea that an organism is innately predisposed to form associations between certain stimuli and responses. If the particular stimulus and response combination is *not* one that an animal is biologically prepared to associate, then the association may not occur or may occur only with great difficulty (see the In Focus box, "Evolution, Biological Preparedness, and Conditioned Fears: What Gives You the Creeps?").

taste aversion
A classically conditioned dislike for and avoidance of a particular food that develops when an organism becomes ill after eating the food.

biological preparedness
In learning theory, the idea that an organism is innately predisposed to form associations between certain stimuli and responses.

John Garcia (b. 1917) John Garcia grew up working on farms in northern California. In his late 20s, Garcia enrolled at a community college. At the age of 48, Garcia earned his Ph.D. in psychology from the University of California, Berkeley (Garcia, 1997). Garcia was one of the first researchers to experimentally demonstrate the existence of taste aversions and other "exceptions" to the general laws of classical conditioning. His research emphasized the importance of the evolutionary forces that shape the learning process.

IN FOCUS

Evolution, Biological Preparedness, and Conditioned Fears: What Gives You the Creeps?

Do these photographs make you somewhat uncomfortable?

A *phobia* is an extreme, irrational fear of a specific object, animal, or situation. It was once believed that all phobias were acquired through classical conditioning, as was Little Albert's fear of the rat and other furry objects. But many people develop phobias without having experienced a traumatic event in association with the object of their fear (Merckelbach & others, 1992). Obviously, other forms of learning, such as observational learning, are involved in the development of some fears (Olsson & Phelps, 2007).

When people do develop conditioned fears as a result of traumatic events, they are more likely to associate fear with certain stimuli rather than others. Erv, not surprisingly, has acquired a conditioned fear response to the "killer attic." But why doesn't Erv shudder every time he hears a lawn mower or sees a ladder, the clothes he was wearing when he got trapped, or his can of oil?

Psychologist **Martin Seligman** (1971) noticed that phobias seem to be quite selective. Extreme, irrational fears of snakes, spiders, heights, and small enclosed places (like Erv and Fern's attic) are relatively common. But very few people have phobias of stairs, ladders, electrical outlets or appliances, or sharp objects, even though these things are far more likely to be associated with accidents or traumatic experiences.

Seligman proposed that humans are biologically prepared to develop fears of objects or situations—such as snakes, spiders, and heights—that may once have posed a threat to humans' evolutionary ancestors. As Seligman (1971) put it, "The great majority of phobias are about objects of natural importance to the survival of the species." According to this view, people don't commonly develop phobias of knives, stoves, or cars because they're not biologically prepared to do so.

Support for this view is provided by early studies that tried to replicate Watson's Little Albert research. Elsie Bregman (1934) was unable to produce a conditioned fear response to wooden blocks and curtains, although she followed Watson's procedure carefully. And Horace English (1929) was unable to produce a conditioned fear of a wooden duck. Perhaps we're more biologically prepared to learn a fear of furry animals than of wooden ducks, blocks, or curtains!

More recently, psychologists Arne Öhman and Susan Mineka (2001, 2003) have accumulated experimental evidence that supports an evolutionary explanation for the most common phobias, especially fear of snakes. For example, people seem to be biologically prepared to rapidly detect snakes. One study involved having people look at groups of photographs of natural stimuli like flowers or snakes. Participants were faster at spotting a single snake image among photos of flowers than they were at detecting a flower image among photos of snakes. Other research has shown that people more readily acquire conditioned fear responses to pictures of snakes that have been paired with electric shock than to pictures of mushrooms and flowers that have been paired with electric shock. These results suggest that people are biologically prepared to easily acquire fears of snakes.

However, these studies have been conducted in adults, raising the question that the response to snake images might be due to accumulated knowledge about snakes. But Vanessa LoBue and Judy S. DeLoache (2008) showed that 3- to 5-year-olds were *also* faster at spotting a lone snake image among photos of flowers, frogs, or caterpillars than they were at spotting a lone flower, frog, or caterpillar among photos of snakes. This finding lends support to the idea that humans have an innate evolved ability to detect threatening stimuli more quickly than nonthreatening stimuli.

Öhman and Mineka (2003) suggest that because poisonous snakes, reptiles, and insects have been associated with danger throughout the evolution of mammals, there is an evolved "fear module" in the brain that is highly sensitized to such evolutionarily relevant stimuli. According to this explanation, individuals who more rapidly detected such dangerous animals would have been more likely to learn to avoid them and survive to reproduce and pass on their genes to future generations (Öhman & others, 2007). For more on how evolved brain mechanisms might be involved in fearful responses, see Chapter 8.

When this concept is applied to taste aversions, rats (and people) seem to be biologically prepared to associate an illness with a taste rather than with a location, a person, or an object. Hence, Don developed an aversion to the spaghetti sauce and not to the fork he had used to eat it. Apparently, both humans and rats are biologically prepared to learn taste aversions relatively easily. Thus, taste aversions can be classically conditioned more readily than can more arbitrary associations, such as that between a ringing bell and a plate of food.

Conditioning Taste Aversions in Coyotes The fact that coyotes readily form taste aversions has been used to prevent them from preying on livestock (Bower, 1997; Garcia & Gustavson, 1997). To stop coyotes from killing lambs on sheep ranches, sheep carcasses are injected with lithium chloride, a drug that produces extreme nausea. In the left photo, the coyote has discovered the carcass and is eating it. In the right photo, the nauseous coyote is writhing on the ground. In one study, captive coyotes were fed lithium-tainted rabbit and sheep carcasses. When later placed in a pen with live rabbits and sheep, the coyotes avoided them rather than attack them. In fact, some of the coyotes threw up at the sight of a live rabbit (Gustavson & others, 1976).

Associations that are easily learned may reflect the evolutionary history and survival mechanisms of the particular animal species. For example, rats in the wild eat a wide variety of foods. If a rat eats a new food and gets sick several hours later, it's likely to survive longer if it learns from this experience to avoid that food in the future (Kalat, 1985; Seligman, 1970).

That different species form some associations more easily than others also probably reflects the unique sensory capabilities and feeding habits that have evolved as a matter of environmental adaptation. Bobwhite quail, for instance, rely primarily on vision for identifying potential meals. In contrast, rats have relatively poor eyesight and rely primarily on taste and odor cues to identify food. Given these species differences, it shouldn't surprise you that quail, but not rats, can easily be conditioned to develop an aversion to blue-colored water—a *visual* stimulus. On the other hand, rats learn more readily than quail to associate illness with sour water—a *taste* stimulus (Wilcoxon & others, 1971). In effect, quail are biologically prepared to associate visual cues with illness, while rats are biologically prepared to associate taste cues with illness.

Taste aversion research emphasizes that the study of learning must consider the unique behavior patterns and capabilities of different species. As the result of evolution, animals have developed unique forms of behavior to adapt to their natural environments (Bolles, 1985). These natural behavior patterns and unique characteristics ultimately influence what an animal is capable of learning—and how easily it can be conditioned to learn a new behavior.

Operant Conditioning

Associating Behaviors and Consequences

Key Theme

- **Operant conditioning deals with the learning of active, voluntary behaviors that are shaped and maintained by their consequences.**

Key Questions

- **How did Edward Thorndike study the acquisition of new behaviors, and what conclusions did he reach?**
- **What were B. F. Skinner's key assumptions?**
- **How are positive and negative reinforcement similar, and how are they different?**

Classical conditioning can help explain the acquisition of many learned behaviors, including emotional and physiological responses. However, recall that classical conditioning involves reflexive behaviors that are automatically elicited by a specific stimulus. Most everyday behaviors don't fall into this category. Instead, they involve nonreflexive, or *voluntary,* actions that can't be explained with classical conditioning.

Edward Lee Thorndike (1874–1949) As a graduate student, Thorndike became fascinated by psychology after taking a class taught by William James at Harvard University. Interested in the study of animal behavior, Thorndike conducted his first experiments with baby chicks. When his landlady protested about the chickens in his room, Thorndike moved his experiments, chicks and all, to the cellar of William James's home—much to the delight of the James children. Following these initial experiments, Thorndike constructed his famous "puzzle boxes" to study learning in cats. Later in life, Thorndike focused his attention on improving educational materials. Among his contributions was the Thorndike Barnhart Student Dictionary for children, which is still published today (R. L. Thorndike, 1991).

Thorndike's Puzzle Box Shown here is one of Thorndike's puzzle boxes, which were made mostly out of wood slats and wire mesh. Thorndike constructed a total of 15 different puzzle boxes, which varied in how difficult they were for a cat to escape from. In a simple box like this one, a cat merely had to pull on a loop of string at the back of the cage to escape. More complex boxes required the cat to perform a chain of three responses—step on a treadle, pull on a string, and push a bar up or down (Chance, 1999).

The investigation of how voluntary behaviors are acquired began with a young American psychology student named Edward L. Thorndike. A few years before Pavlov began his extensive studies of classical conditioning, Thorndike was using cats, chicks, and dogs to investigate how voluntary behaviors are acquired. Thorndike's pioneering studies helped set the stage for the later work of another American psychologist named B. F. Skinner. It was Skinner who developed *operant conditioning,* another form of conditioning that explains how we acquire and maintain voluntary behaviors.

Thorndike and the Law of Effect

Edward L. Thorndike was the first psychologist to systematically investigate animal learning and how voluntary behaviors are influenced by their consequences. At the time, Thorndike was only in his early 20s and a psychology graduate student. He conducted his pioneering studies to complete his dissertation and earn his doctorate in psychology. Published in 1898, Thorndike's dissertation, titled *Animal Intelligence: An Experimental Study of the Associative Processes in Animals,* is the most famous dissertation ever published in psychology (Chance, 1999). When Pavlov later learned of Thorndike's studies, he expressed admiration and credited Thorndike with having started objective animal research well before his own studies of classical conditioning (Hearst, 1999).

Thorndike's dissertation focused on the issue of whether animals, like humans, use reasoning to solve problems (Dewsbury, 1998). In an important series of experiments, Thorndike (1898) put hungry cats in specially constructed cages that he called "puzzle boxes." A cat could escape the cage by a simple act, such as pulling a loop or pressing a lever that would unlatch the cage door. A plate of food was placed just outside the cage, where the hungry cat could see and smell it.

Thorndike found that when the cat was first put into the puzzle box, it would engage in many different, seemingly random behaviors to escape. For example, the cat would scratch at the cage door, claw at the ceiling, and try to squeeze through the wooden slats (not to mention complain at the top of its lungs). Eventually, however, the cat would accidentally pull on the loop or step on the lever, opening the door latch and escaping the box. After several trials in the same puzzle box, a cat could get the cage door open very quickly.

Thorndike (1898) concluded that the cats did *not* display any humanlike insight or reasoning in unlatching the puzzle box door. Instead, he explained the cats' learning as a process of *trial and error* (Chance, 1999). The cats gradually learned to associate certain responses with successfully escaping the box and gaining the food reward. According to Thorndike, these successful behaviors became "stamped in," so that a cat was more likely to repeat these behaviors when placed in the puzzle box again. Unsuccessful behaviors were gradually eliminated.

Thorndike's observations led him to formulate the **law of effect:** Responses followed by a "satisfying state of affairs" are "strengthened" and more likely to occur again in the same situation. Conversely, responses followed by an unpleasant or "annoying state of affairs" are "weakened" and less likely to occur again.

Thorndike's description of the law of effect was an important first step in understanding how active, voluntary behaviors can be modified by their consequences. Thorndike, however, never developed his ideas on learning into a formal model or system (Hearst, 1999). Instead, he applied his findings to education, publishing many books on educational psychology (Beatty, 1998). Some 30 years after Thorndike's famous puzzle-box studies, the task of further investigating how voluntary behaviors are acquired and maintained would be taken up by another American psychologist, B. F. Skinner.

B. F. Skinner and the Search for "Order in Behavior"

From the time he was a graduate student in psychology until his death, the famous American psychologist **B. F. Skinner** searched for the "lawful processes" that would explain "order in behavior" (Skinner, 1956, 1967). Skinner was a staunch behaviorist. Like John Watson, Skinner strongly believed that psychology should restrict itself to studying only phenomena that could be objectively measured and verified—outwardly observable behavior and environmental events.

Skinner (1974) acknowledged the existence of what he called "internal factors," such as thoughts, expectations, and perceptions (Moore, 2005a). However, Skinner believed that internal thoughts, beliefs, emotions, or motives could *not* be used to explain behavior. These fell into the category of "private events" that defy direct scientific observation and should not be included in an objective, scientific explanation of behavior (Baum & Heath, 1992).

Along with being influenced by Watson's writings, Skinner greatly admired Ivan Pavlov's work. Prominently displayed in Skinner's university office was one of his most prized possessions—an autographed photo of Pavlov (Catania & Laties, 1999). Skinner acknowledged that Pavlov's classical conditioning could explain the learned association of stimuli in certain reflexive responses (Iversen, 1992). But classical conditioning was limited to existing behaviors that were reflexively elicited. Skinner (1979) was convinced that he had "found a process of conditioning that was different from Pavlov's and much more like most learning in daily life." To Skinner, the most important form of learning was demonstrated by *new* behaviors that were *actively emitted* by the organism, such as the active behaviors produced by Thorndike's cats in trying to escape the puzzle boxes.

Skinner (1953) coined the term **operant** to describe any "active behavior that operates upon the environment to generate consequences." In everyday language, Skinner's principles of operant conditioning explain how we acquire the wide range of *voluntary* behaviors that we perform in daily life. But as a behaviorist who rejected mentalistic explanations, Skinner avoided the term *voluntary* because it would imply that behavior was due to a conscious choice or intention.

Skinner defined operant conditioning concepts in very objective terms and he avoided explanations based on subjective mental states (Moore, 2005b). We'll closely follow Skinner's original terminology and definitions.

Burrhus Frederick Skinner (1904–1990) As a young adult, Skinner had hoped to become a writer. When he graduated from college, he set up a study in the attic of his parents' home and waited for inspiration to strike. After a year of "frittering" away his time, he decided that there were better ways to learn about human nature (Moore, 2005a). As Skinner (1967) later wrote, "A writer might portray human behavior accurately, but he did not understand it. I was to remain interested in human behavior, but the literary method had failed me; I would turn to the scientific. . . . The relevant science appeared to be psychology, though I had only the vaguest idea of what that meant."

Reinforcement

Increasing Future Behavior

In a nutshell, Skinner's **operant conditioning** explains learning as a process in which behavior is shaped and maintained by its consequences. One possible consequence of a behavior is reinforcement. **Reinforcement** is said to occur when a stimulus or an event follows an operant and increases the likelihood of the operant being repeated. Notice that reinforcement is defined by the effect it produces—increasing or strengthening the occurrence of a behavior in the future.

Let's look at reinforcement in action. Suppose you put your money into a soft-drink vending machine and push the button. Nothing happens. You push the button again. Nothing. You try the coin-return lever. Still nothing. Frustrated, you slam the machine with your hand. Yes! Your can of soda rolls down the chute. In the future, if another vending machine swallows your money without giving you what you want, what are you likely to do? Hit the machine, right?

In this example, slamming the vending machine with your hand is the *operant*—the active response you emitted. The soft drink is the *reinforcing stimulus,* or *reinforcer*—the stimulus or event that is sought in a particular situation. In everyday language, a reinforcing stimulus is typically something desirable, satisfying, or pleasant. Skinner, of course, avoided such terms because they reflected subjective emotional states.

law of effect
Learning principle, proposed by Thorndike, that responses followed by a satisfying effect become strengthened and are more likely to recur in a particular situation, while responses followed by a dissatisfying effect are weakened and less likely to recur in a particular situation.

operant
Skinner's term for an actively emitted (or voluntary) behavior that operates on the environment to produce consequences.

operant conditioning
The basic learning process that involves changing the probability that a response will be repeated by manipulating the consequences of that response.

reinforcement
The occurrence of a stimulus or event following a response that increases the likelihood of that response being repeated.

positive reinforcement
A situation in which a response is followed by the addition of a reinforcing stimulus, increasing the likelihood that the response will be repeated in similar situations.

negative reinforcement
A situation in which a response results in the removal of, avoidance of, or escape from a punishing stimulus, increasing the likelihood that the response will be repeated in similar situations.

primary reinforcer
A stimulus or event that is naturally or inherently reinforcing for a given species, such as food, water, or other biological necessities.

conditioned reinforcer
A stimulus or event that has acquired reinforcing value by being associated with a primary reinforcer; also called a *secondary reinforcer.*

Positive and Negative Reinforcement

There are two forms of reinforcement: *positive reinforcement* and *negative reinforcement.* Both affect future behavior, but they do so in different ways (see Table 5.1). It's easier to understand these differences if you note at the outset that Skinner did not use the terms *positive* and *negative* in their everyday sense of meaning "good" and "bad" or "desirable" and "undesirable." Instead, think of the words *positive* and *negative* in terms of their mathematical meanings. *Positive* is the equivalent of a plus sign (+), meaning that something is added. *Negative* is the equivalent of a minus sign (−), meaning that something is subtracted or removed. If you keep that distinction in mind, the principles of positive and negative reinforcement should be easier to understand.

Positive reinforcement involves following an operant with the addition of a reinforcing stimulus. In positive reinforcement situations, a response is strengthened because something is *added* or presented. Everyday examples of positive reinforcement in action are easy to identify. Here are some examples:

- Your backhand return of the tennis ball (the operant) is low and fast, and your tennis coach yells "Excellent!" (the reinforcing stimulus).
- You watch a student production of *Hamlet* and write a short paper about it (the operant) for 10 bonus points (the reinforcing stimulus) in your literature class.
- You reach your sales quota at work (the operant) and you get a bonus check (the reinforcing stimulus).

In each example, if the addition of the reinforcing stimulus has the effect of making you more likely to repeat the operant in similar situations in the future, then positive reinforcement has occurred.

It's important to point out that what constitutes a *reinforcing stimulus* can vary from person to person, species to species, and situation to situation. While gold stars and stickers may be reinforcing to a third-grader, they would probably have little reinforcing value to your average high school student. As Skinner (1953) explained, "The only way to tell whether or not a given event or stimulus is reinforcing to a given organism under given conditions is to make a direct test."

It's also important to note that the reinforcing stimulus is not necessarily something we usually consider positive or desirable. For example, most teachers would not think of a scolding as being a reinforcing stimulus to children. But to children, adult attention can be a powerful reinforcing stimulus. If a child receives attention from the teacher only when he misbehaves, then the teacher may unwittingly be reinforcing misbehavior. The child may actually increase disruptive behavior in order to get the sought-after reinforcing stimulus—adult attention—even if it's in the form of being scolded. To reduce the child's disruptive behavior, the teacher would do better to reinforce the child's appropriate behavior by paying attention to him when he's *not* being disruptive, such as when he is working quietly.

Negative reinforcement involves an operant that is followed by the removal of an aversive stimulus. In negative reinforcement situations, a response is strengthened because something is being *subtracted* or removed. Remember that the word *negative* in the phrase *negative reinforcement* is used like a mathematical minus sign (−).

Both positive and negative reinforcement increase the likelihood of a behavior being repeated. Positive reinforcement involves a behavior that leads to a reinforcing or rewarding event. In contrast, negative reinforcement involves behavior that leads to the avoidance of or escape from an aversive or punishing event. Ultimately, both positive and negative reinforcement involve outcomes that strengthen future behavior.

Table 5.1

Comparing Positive and Negative Reinforcement

Process	Operant	Consequence	Effect on Behavior
Positive reinforcement	Studying to make dean's list	Make dean's list	Increase studying in the future
Negative reinforcement	Studying to avoid losing academic scholarship	Avoid loss of academic scholarship	Increase studying in the future

For example, you take two aspirin (the operant) to remove a headache (the aversive stimulus). Thirty minutes later, the headache is gone. Are you now more likely to take aspirin to deal with bodily aches and pain in the future? If you are, then negative reinforcement has occurred.

Negative Reinforcement What behavior is being negatively reinforced? If you're having trouble answering this question, first identify the aversive stimulus.

Aversive stimuli typically involve physical or psychological discomfort that an organism seeks to escape or avoid. Consequently, behaviors are said to be negatively reinforced when they let you either (1) *escape* aversive stimuli that are already present or (2) *avoid* aversive stimuli before they occur. That is, we're more likely to repeat the same escape or avoidance behaviors in similar situations in the future. The headache example illustrates the negative reinforcement of *escape behavior*. By taking two aspirin, you "escaped" the headache. Paying your electric bill on time to avoid a late charge illustrates the negative reinforcement of *avoidance behavior*. Here are some more examples of negative reinforcement involving escape or avoidance behavior:

- You make backup copies of important computer files (the operant) to avoid losing the data if the computer's hard drive should fail (the aversive stimulus).
- You dab some hydrocortisone cream on an insect bite (the operant) to escape the itching (the aversive stimulus).
- You get a flu shot (the operant) in November to avoid catching the flu (the aversive stimulus).

In each example, if escaping or avoiding the aversive event has the effect of making you more likely to repeat the operant in similar situations in the future, then negative reinforcement has taken place.

Primary and Conditioned Reinforcers

Skinner also distinguished two kinds of reinforcing stimuli: primary and conditioned. A **primary reinforcer** is one that is *naturally* reinforcing for a given species. That is, even if an individual has not had prior experience with the particular stimulus, the stimulus or event still has reinforcing properties. For example, food, water, adequate warmth, and sexual contact are primary reinforcers for most animals, including humans.

A **conditioned reinforcer,** also called a *secondary reinforcer*, is one that has acquired reinforcing value by being associated with a primary reinforcer. The classic example of a conditioned reinforcer is money. Money is reinforcing not because those flimsy bits of paper and little pieces of metal have value in and of themselves, but because we've learned that we can use them to acquire primary reinforcers and other conditioned reinforcers. Awards, frequent-flyer points, and college degrees are just a few other examples of conditioned reinforcers.

Conditioned reinforcers need not be as tangible as money or college degrees. The respect of your peers and the approval of your instructors or managers can be

Types of Reinforcers Primary reinforcers, like water when you're thirsty, are naturally reinforcing—you don't have to learn their value. In contrast, the value of conditioned reinforcers, like grades and awards, has to be learned through their association with primary reinforcers. But conditioned reinforcers can be just as reinforcing as primary reinforcers. As proof, a beaming Michael Phelps displays one of the eight gold medals he earned for the United States at the 2008 summer Olympics in Beijing, China.

punishment
The presentation of a stimulus or event following a behavior that acts to decrease the likelihood of the behavior's being repeated.

punishment by application
A situation in which an operant is followed by the presentation or addition of an aversive stimulus; also called *positive punishment.*

punishment by removal
A situation in which an operant is followed by the removal or subtraction of a reinforcing stimulus; also called *negative punishment.*

powerful conditioned reinforcers. Conditioned reinforcers can be as subtle as a smile, a touch, or a nod of recognition. Looking back at the Prologue, for example, Fern was reinforced by the laughter of her friends and relatives each time she told "the killer attic" tale—so she keeps telling the story!

Punishment

Using Aversive Consequences to Decrease Behavior

Key Theme

- **Punishment is a process that decreases the future occurrence of a behavior.**

Key Questions

- **What factors influence the effectiveness of punishment?**
- **What effects are associated with the use of punishment to control behavior, and what are some alternative ways to change behavior?**
- **What are discriminative stimuli?**

Positive and negative reinforcement are processes that *increase* the frequency of a particular behavior. The opposite effect is produced by punishment. **Punishment** is a process in which a behavior is followed by an aversive consequence that *decreases* the likelihood of the behavior's being repeated. Many people tend to confuse punishment and negative reinforcement, but these two processes produce entirely different effects on behavior (see Table 5.2). Negative reinforcement *always increases* the likelihood that an operant will be repeated in the future. Punishment *always decreases* the future performance of an operant.

Skinner (1953) identified two types of aversive events that can act as punishment. **Punishment by application,** also called *positive punishment,* involves a response being followed by the presentation of an aversive stimulus. The word *positive* in the phrase *positive punishment* signifies that something is added or presented in the situation. In this case, it's an aversive stimulus. Here are some everyday examples of punishment by application:

- An employee wears jeans to work (the operant) and is reprimanded by his supervisor for dressing inappropriately (the punishing stimulus).
- You make a comment (the operant) in your workgroup meetings, and a co-worker responds with a sarcastic remark (the punishing stimulus).

In each of these examples, if the presentation of the punishing stimulus has the effect of decreasing the behavior it follows, then punishment has occurred. Although the punishing stimuli in these examples were administered by other people, punishing stimuli also occur as natural consequences for some behaviors. Inadvertently touching a hot iron, a live electrical wire, or a sharp object (the operant) can result in a painful injury (the punishing stimulus).

Table 5.2

Comparing Punishment and Negative Reinforcement

Process	Operant	Consequence	Effect on Behavior
Punishment	Using radar detector	Receive speeding ticket and fine for illegal use of radar detector	Decrease use of radar detector in the future
Negative reinforcement	Using radar detector	Avoid speeding ticket and fine	Increase use of radar detector in the future

Punishment and negative reinforcement are two different processes that produce *opposite* effects on a given behavior. Punishment *decreases* the future performance of the behavior, while negative reinforcement *increases* it.

Table 5.3

Types of Reinforcement and Punishment

	Reinforcing stimulus	Aversive stimulus
Stimulus presented	Positive reinforcement	Positive punishment
Stimulus removed	Negative punishment	Negative reinforcement

This table provides a simple way of identifying the type of reinforcement or punishment based on whether a reinforcing or an aversive stimulus is presented or removed following an operant.

The second type of punishment is **punishment by removal,** also called *negative punishment.* The word *negative* indicates that some stimulus is subtracted or removed from the situation (see Table 5.3). In this case, it is the loss or withdrawal of a reinforcing stimulus following a behavior. That is, the behavior's consequence is the loss of some privilege, possession, or other desirable object or activity. Here are some everyday examples of punishment by removal:

- After she buys stock (the operant) in a "hot" new start-up company, the company fails and the investor loses all of her money (loss of reinforcing stimulus).
- Because he was flirting with another woman (the operant), a guy gets dumped by his girlfriend (loss of reinforcing stimulus).

In each example, if the behavior decreases in response to the removal of the reinforcing stimulus, then punishment has occurred. It's important to stress that, like reinforcement, punishment is defined by the effect it produces. In everyday usage, people often refer to a particular consequence as a punishment when, strictly speaking, it's not. Why? Because the consequence has *not* reduced future occurrences of the behavior. Hence, many consequences commonly thought of as punishments—being sent to prison, fined, reprimanded, ridiculed, or fired from a job—fail to reduce a particular behavior.

Why is it that aversive consequences don't always function as effective punishments? Skinner (1953) as well as other researchers have noted that several factors influence the effectiveness of punishment (see Axelrod & Apsche, 1983; Kazdin, 2001). For example, punishment is more effective if it immediately follows a response than if it is delayed. Punishment is also more effective if it consistently, rather than occasionally, follows a response. Though speeding tickets and prison sentences are commonly referred to as punishments, these aversive consequences are inconsistently applied and often administered only after a long delay. Thus, they don't always effectively decrease specific behaviors.

Even when punishment works, its use has several drawbacks. First, punishment may decrease a specific response, but it doesn't necessarily teach or promote a more appropriate response to take its place. Second, punishment that is intense may produce undesirable results, such as complete passivity, fear, anxiety, or hostility (Skinner, 1974). Finally, the effects of punishment are likely to be temporary (Estes & Skinner, 1941; Skinner, 1938). A child who is sent to her room for teasing her little brother may well repeat the behavior when her mother's back is turned. As Skinner (1971) noted, "Punished behavior is likely to reappear after the punitive consequences are withdrawn." For some suggestions on how to change behavior without using a punishing stimulus, see the In Focus box, "Changing the Behavior of Others: Alternatives to Punishment."

The Effects of Spanking Defined as hitting a child on the buttocks with an open hand without causing a bruise or physical harm, *spanking* is a common form of discipline in the United States (Kazdin & Benjet, 2003). Some researchers believe that mild and occasional spanking is not necessarily harmful, especially when used as a backup for other forms of discipline (Baumrind & others, 2002).

However, in a wide-ranging meta-analysis, psychologist Elizabeth Gershoff (2002) concluded that physical punishment is associated with increased aggressiveness, delinquency, and antisocial behavior in the child. Other negative effects include poor parent–child relationships and an increased risk that parental disciplinary tactics might escalate into physical abuse. As Skinner (1974) cautioned, gaining immediate compliance through punishment must be weighed against punishment's negative long-term effects.

IN FOCUS

Changing the Behavior of Others: Alternatives to Punishment

Although punishment may temporarily decrease the occurrence of a problem behavior, it doesn't promote more desirable or appropriate behaviors in its place. Throughout his life, Skinner remained strongly opposed to the use of punishment. Instead, he advocated the greater use of positive reinforcement to strengthen desirable behaviors (Dinsmoor, 1992; Skinner, 1971). Here are four strategies that can be used to reduce undesirable behaviors without resorting to punishment.

Strategy 1: Reinforce an Incompatible Behavior

The best method to reduce a problem behavior is to reinforce an *alternative* behavior that is both constructive and incompatible with the problem behavior. For example, if you're trying to decrease a child's whining, respond to her requests (the reinforcer) only when she talks in a normal tone of voice.

Strategy 2: Stop Reinforcing the Problem Behavior

Technically, this strategy is called *extinction.* The first step in effectively applying extinction is to observe the behavior carefully and identify the reinforcer that is maintaining the problem behavior. Then eliminate the reinforcer.

Suppose a co-worker is wasting your time with gossip. You want to extinguish his behavior of interrupting your work with needless chitchat. In the past, trying to be polite, you've responded to his behavior by acting interested (a reinforcer). You could eliminate the reinforcer by acting uninterested and continuing to work while he talks.

It's important to note that when the extinction process is initiated, the problem behavior often *temporarily* increases. This situation is more likely to occur if the problem behavior has only occasionally been reinforced in the past. Thus, once you begin, be consistent in nonreinforcement of the problem behavior.

Strategy 3: Reinforce the Non-occurrence of the Problem Behavior

This strategy involves setting a specific time period after which the individual is reinforced if the unwanted behavior has *not* occurred. For example, if you're trying to reduce bickering between your children, set an appropriate time limit, and then provide positive reinforcement if they have *not* squabbled during that interval.

Strategy 4: Remove the Opportunity to Obtain Positive Reinforcement

It's not always possible to identify and eliminate all the reinforcers that maintain a behavior. For example, a child's obnoxious behavior might be reinforced by the social attention of siblings or classmates.

In a procedure called *time-out from positive reinforcement,* the child is removed from the reinforcing situation for a short time, so that the access to reinforcers is eliminated. When the undesirable behavior occurs, the child is immediately sent to a time-out area that is free of distractions and social contact. The time-out period begins as soon as the child's behavior is under control. For children, a good rule of thumb is one minute of time-out per year of age.

Using Reinforcement in the Classroom Teachers at all levels use positive reinforcement to increase desired behaviors. Often, conditioned reinforcers, like stickers or gold stars, can be exchanged for other, more tangible rewards, like a new pencil.

Enhancing the Effectiveness of Positive Reinforcement

Often, these four strategies are used in combination. However, remember the most important behavioral principle: *Positively reinforce the behaviors that you want to increase.* There are several ways in which you can enhance the effectiveness of positive reinforcement:

- Make sure that the reinforcer is *strongly* reinforcing to the individual whose behavior you're trying to modify.
- The positive reinforcer should be delivered *immediately* after the preferred behavior occurs.
- The positive reinforcer should initially be given *every* time the preferred behavior occurs. When the desired behavior is well established, *gradually reduce the frequency of reinforcement.*
- Use a *variety* of positive reinforcers, such as tangible items, praise, special privileges, recognition, and so on. Minimize the use of food as a positive reinforcer.
- Capitalize on what is known as the *Premack principle*— a more preferred activity (e.g., painting) can be used to reinforce a less preferred activity (e.g., picking up toys).
- Encourage the individual to engage in *self-reinforcement* in the form of pride, a sense of accomplishment, and feelings of self-control.

Discriminative Stimuli

Setting the Occasion for Responding

Another component of operant conditioning is the **discriminative stimulus**—the specific stimulus in the presence of which a particular operant is more likely to be reinforced. For example, a ringing phone is a discriminative stimulus that sets the occasion for a particular response—picking up the telephone and speaking.

This example illustrates how we've learned from experience to associate certain environmental cues or signals with particular operant responses. We've learned that we're more likely to be reinforced for performing a particular operant response when we do so in the presence of the appropriate discriminative stimulus. Thus, you've learned that you're more likely to be reinforced for screaming at the top of your lungs at a football game (one discriminative stimulus) than in the middle of class (a different discriminative stimulus).

In this way, according to Skinner (1974), behavior is determined and controlled by the stimuli that are present in a given situation. In Skinner's view, an individual's behavior is *not* determined by a personal choice or a conscious decision. Instead, individual behavior is determined by environmental stimuli and the person's reinforcement history in that environment. Skinner's views on this point have some very controversial implications, which are discussed in the Critical Thinking box, "Is Human Freedom Just an Illusion?"

We have now discussed all three fundamental components of operant conditioning (see Table 5.4). In the presence of a specific environmental stimulus (the *discriminative stimulus*), we emit a particular behavior (the *operant*), which is followed by a consequence (*reinforcement* or *punishment*). If the consequence is either positive or negative reinforcement, we are *more* likely to repeat the operant when we encounter the same or similar discriminative stimuli in the future. If the consequence is some form of punishment, we are *less* likely to repeat the operant when we encounter the same or similar discriminative stimuli in the future.

Next, we'll build on the basics of operant conditioning by considering how Skinner explained the acquisition of complex behaviors.

discriminative stimulus
A specific stimulus in the presence of which a particular response is more likely to be reinforced, and in the absence of which a particular response is not reinforced.

Table 5.4

Components of Operant Conditioning

The examples given here illustrate the three key components involved in operant conditioning. The basic operant conditioning process works like this: In the presence of a specific discriminative stimulus, an operant response is emitted, which is followed by a consequence. Depending on the consequence, we are either more or less likely to repeat the operant when we encounter the same or a similar discriminative stimulus in the future.

	Discriminative Stimulus	Operant Response	Consequence	Effect on Future Behavior
Definition	The environmental stimulus that precedes an operant response	The actively emitted or voluntary behavior	The environmental stimulus or event that follows the operant response	Reinforcement increases the likelihood of operant being repeated; punishment or lack of reinforcement decreases the likelihood of operant being repeated.
Examples	Wallet on college sidewalk	Give wallet to security	$50 reward from wallet's owner	Positive reinforcement: More likely to turn in lost items to authorities
	Gas gauge almost on "empty"	Fill car with gas	Avoid running out of gas	Negative reinforcement: More likely to fill car when gas gauge shows empty
	Informal social situation at work	Tell an off-color, sexist joke	Formally reprimanded for sexism and inappropriate workplace behavior	Positive punishment: Less likely to tell off-color, sexist jokes in workplace
	Soft-drink vending machine	Put in quarters	Get no soft drink and lose money	Negative punishment: Less likely to use that vending machine

CRITICAL THINKING

Is Human Freedom Just an Illusion?

Skinner's most famous invention was the *operant chamber,* more popularly known as a *Skinner box*, in which rats or pigeons were conditioned to perform simple behaviors, such as pressing a lever or pecking at a disk, to receive a food reward (see page 209). Had Skinner been content to confine his observations to the behavior of rats or pigeons in a Skinner box, his career might have been relatively uncontroversial. But Skinner was intensely interested in human behavior and social problems (Bjork, 1997a). He believed that operant conditioning principles could, and *should,* be applied on a broad scale to help solve society's problems.

Skinner's most radical—and controversial—belief was that such ideas as free will, self-determination, and individual choice are just illusions. Skinner (1971) argued that behavior is not simply influenced by the environment but is *determined* by it. Control the environment, he said, and you will control human behavior. As he bluntly asserted in his controversial best-seller, *Beyond Freedom and Dignity* (1971), "A person does not act upon the world, the world acts upon him."

Such views did not sit well with the American public (Rutherford, 2003). Following the publication of *Beyond Freedom and Dignity,* one member of Congress denounced Skinner for "advancing ideas which threaten the future of our system of government by denigrating the American tradition of individualism, human dignity, and self-reliance" (quoted in Rutherford, 2000). Why the uproar?

Skinner's ideas clashed with the traditional American ideals of personal responsibility, individual freedom, and self-determination. Such ideals are based on the assumption that behavior arises from causes that are *within* the individual. All individuals are held responsible for their conduct and given credit for their achievements. Skinner labeled such notions the "traditional prescientific view" of human behavior.

According to Skinner, "A scientific analysis [of behavior] shifts both the responsibility and the achievement to the environment." Applying his ideas to social problems, such as alcoholism and crime, Skinner (1971) wrote, "It is the environment which is 'responsible' for objectionable behavior, and it is the environment, not some attribute of the individual, which must be changed."

To understand Skinner's point of view, it helps to think of society as a massive, sophisticated Skinner box. From the moment of birth, the environment shapes and determines your behavior through reinforcing or punishing consequences. Taking this view, you are no more personally responsible for your behavior than is a rat in a Skinner box pressing a lever to obtain a food pellet. Just like the rat's behavior, your behavior is simply a response to the unique patterns of environmental consequences to which you have been exposed.

Time for Skinner's Ideas? The impact of the publication of *Beyond Freedom and Dignity* can be measured by Skinner's appearance on the cover of *Time* on September 20, 1971, shortly after the book was published. Skinner is shown in the middle of some of his most famous creations. Clockwise from upper left: pigeons trained to peck at a ping-pong ball; a rat pressing a lever in an operant chamber; an idealized rural scene representing the fictional utopia described in Skinner's novel *Walden Two* (1948a); and a teaching machine, an early mechanical device for programmed instruction based on operant conditioning principles.

Skinner (1971) proposed that "a technology of behavior" be developed, one based on a scientific analysis of behavior. He believed that society could be redesigned using operant conditioning principles to produce more socially desirable behaviors—and happier citizens. He described such an ideal, utopian society in *Walden Two,* a novel he published in 1948. Critics charged Skinner with advocating a totalitarian state. They asked who would determine which behaviors were shaped and maintained (Rutherford, 2000; Todd & Morris, 1992).

As Skinner pointed out, however, human behavior is *already* controlled by various authorities: parents, teachers, politicians, religious leaders, employers, and so forth. Such authorities regularly use reinforcing and punishing consequences to shape and control the behavior of others. Skinner insisted that it is better to control behavior in a rational, humane fashion than to leave the control of behavior to the whims and often selfish aims of those in power. Skinner himself was adamantly opposed to the use of punishment and other aversive stimuli to control behavior. Instead, he repeatedly advocated the greater use of positive reinforcement (Dinsmoor, 1992).

On the one hand, it may seem convenient to blame your history of environmental consequences for your failures and misdeeds. On the other hand, that means you can't take any credit for your accomplishments and good deeds, either!

CRITICAL THINKING QUESTIONS

- If Skinner's vision of a socially engineered society using operant conditioning principles were implemented, would such changes be good or bad for society?
- Are human freedom and personal responsibility illusions? Or is human behavior fundamentally different from a rat's behavior in a Skinner box? If so, how?
- Is your behavior almost entirely the product of environmental conditioning? Think about your answer carefully. After all, exactly *why* are you reading this box?

Shaping and Maintaining Behavior

operant chamber or **Skinner box** The experimental apparatus invented by B. F. Skinner to study the relationship between environmental events and active behaviors.

shaping The operant conditioning procedure of selectively reinforcing successively closer approximations of a goal behavior until the goal behavior is displayed.

Key Theme

- **New behaviors are acquired through shaping and can be maintained through different patterns of reinforcement.**

Key Questions

- **How does shaping work?**
- **What is the partial reinforcement effect, and how do the four schedules of reinforcement differ in their effects?**
- **What is behavior modification?**

To scientifically study the relationship between behavior and its consequences in the laboratory, Skinner invented the **operant chamber,** more popularly known as the **Skinner box.** An operant chamber is a small cage with a food dispenser. Attached to the cage is a device that automatically records the number of operants made by an experimental animal, usually a rat or pigeon. For a rat, the typical operant is pressing a bar; for a pigeon, it is pecking at a small disk. Food pellets are usually used for positive reinforcement. Often, a light in the cage functions as a discriminative stimulus. When the light is on, pressing the bar or pecking the disk is reinforced with a food pellet. When the light is off, these responses do not result in reinforcement.

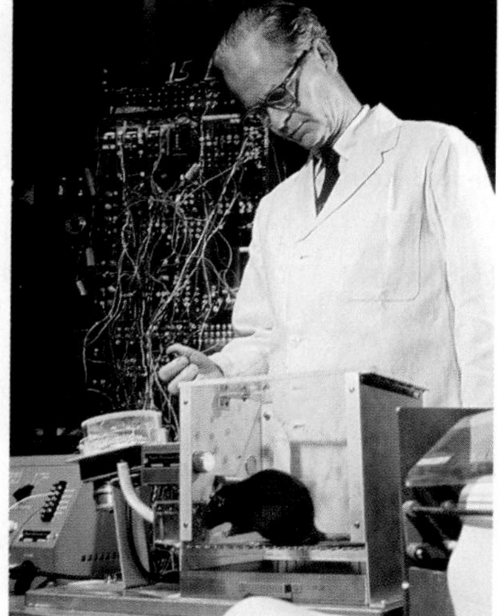

The Skinner Box Popularly called a Skinner box after its inventor, an operant chamber is used to experimentally study operant conditioning in laboratory animals.

When a rat is first placed in a Skinner box, it typically explores its new environment, occasionally nudging or pressing the bar in the process. The researcher can accelerate the rat's bar-pressing behavior through a process called shaping. **Shaping** involves reinforcing successively closer approximations of a behavior until the correct behavior is displayed. For example, the researcher might first reinforce the rat with a food pellet whenever it moves to the half of the Skinner box in which the bar is located. Other responses would be ignored. Once that response has been learned, reinforcement is withheld until the rat moves even closer to the bar. Then the rat might be reinforced only when it touches the bar. Step by step, the rat is reinforced for behaviors that correspond ever more closely to the final goal behavior—pressing the bar.

Skinner believed that shaping could explain how people acquire a wide variety of abilities and skills—everything from tying shoes to operating sophisticated computer programs. Athletic coaches, teachers, parents, and child-care workers all use shaping techniques.

(a)

(b)

(c)

Operant Conditioning at Sea-World This sequence shows a Sea-World trainer using operant conditioning principles with a dolphin that has already been shaped to perform somersaults. **(a)** The trainer gives the dolphin two discriminative stimuli—a distinct vocal sound and a specific hand gesture. **(b)** The dolphin quickly responds with the correct operant—a perfect somersault in the air. **(c)** The operant is positively reinforced with a piece of fish. The same basic techniques are also used to teach seals, sea lions, walruses, and killer whales to perform different tricks on cue.

Superstitious Rituals: Behaviors Shaped by Accidental Reinforcement Many professional athletes develop quirky superstitious rituals (Wargo, 2008). Pittsburgh Steelers quarterback Ben Roethlisberger was so depressed after losing an important game that he didn't bother to shave. But after an unshaven Roethlisberger won the next game, he decided that the beard was a good luck charm. After five months of winning games, a still-unshaven Roethlisberger led the Steelers to a Super Bowl victory. One night later, an elated Roethlisberger celebrated by publicly shaving his beard on David Letterman's *Late Show*.

Skinner (1948b) pointed out that superstitions may result when a behavior is accidentally reinforced—that is, when reinforcement is just a coincidence. So although it was really just a fluke that wearing your "lucky" shirt or playing your "lucky" number was followed by a win, the illusion of reinforcement can shape and strengthen behavior.

The Partial Reinforcement Effect

Building Resistance to Extinction

Once a rat had acquired a bar-pressing behavior, Skinner found that the most efficient way to strengthen the response was to immediately reinforce *every* occurrence of bar pressing. This pattern of reinforcement is called **continuous reinforcement.** In everyday life, of course, it's common for responses to be reinforced only sometimes—a pattern called **partial reinforcement.** For example, practicing your basketball skills isn't followed by putting the ball through the hoop on every shot. Sometimes you're reinforced by making a basket, and sometimes you're not.

Now suppose that despite all your hard work, your basketball skills are dismal. If practicing free throws was *never* reinforced by making a basket, what would you do? You'd probably eventually quit playing basketball. This is an example of **extinction.** In operant conditioning, when a learned response no longer results in reinforcement, the likelihood of the behavior's being repeated gradually declines.

Skinner (1956) first noticed the effects of partial reinforcement when he began running low on food pellets one day. Rather than reinforcing every bar press, Skinner tried to stretch out his supply of pellets by rewarding responses only periodically. He found that the rats not only continued to respond, but actually increased their rate of bar pressing.

One important consequence of partially reinforcing behavior is that partially reinforced behaviors tend to be more resistant to extinction than are behaviors conditioned using continuous reinforcement. This phenomenon is called the **partial reinforcement effect.** For example, when Skinner shut off the food-dispensing mechanism, a pigeon conditioned using continuous reinforcement would continue pecking at the disk 100 times or so before the behavior decreased significantly, indicating extinction. In contrast, a pigeon conditioned with partial reinforcement continued to peck at the disk thousands of times! If you think about it, this is not surprising. When pigeons, rats, or humans have experienced partial reinforcement, they've learned that reinforcement may yet occur, despite delays and nonreinforced responses, if persistent responses are made.

In everyday life, the partial reinforcement effect is reflected in behaviors that persist despite the lack of reinforcement. Gamblers may persist despite a string of losses, writers will persevere in the face of repeated rejection slips, and the family dog will continue begging for the scraps of food that it has only occasionally received at the dinner table in the past.

The Schedules of Reinforcement

Skinner (1956) found that specific preset arrangements of partial reinforcement produced different patterns and rates of responding. Collectively, these different reinforcement arrangements are called **schedules of reinforcement.** As we describe the four basic schedules of reinforcement, it will be helpful to refer to Figure 5.6, which shows the typical pattern of responses produced by each schedule.

With a **fixed-ratio (FR) schedule,** reinforcement occurs after a fixed number of responses. A rat on a 10-to-1 fixed-ratio schedule (abbreviated FR-10) would have to press the bar 10 times in order to receive one food pellet. Fixed-ratio schedules typically produce a high rate of responding that follows a burst–pause–burst pattern. In everyday life, the fixed-ratio schedule is reflected

continuous reinforcement
A schedule of reinforcement in which every occurrence of a particular response is reinforced.

partial reinforcement
A situation in which the occurrence of a particular response is only sometimes followed by a reinforcer.

extinction (in operant conditioning)
The gradual weakening and disappearance of conditioned behavior. In operant conditioning, extinction occurs when an emitted behavior is no longer followed by a reinforcer.

partial reinforcement effect
The phenomenon in which behaviors that are conditioned using partial reinforcement are more resistant to extinction than behaviors that are conditioned using continuous reinforcement.

schedule of reinforcement
The delivery of a reinforcer according to a preset pattern based on the number of responses or the time interval between responses.

fixed-ratio (FR) schedule
A reinforcement schedule in which a reinforcer is delivered after a fixed number of responses has occurred.

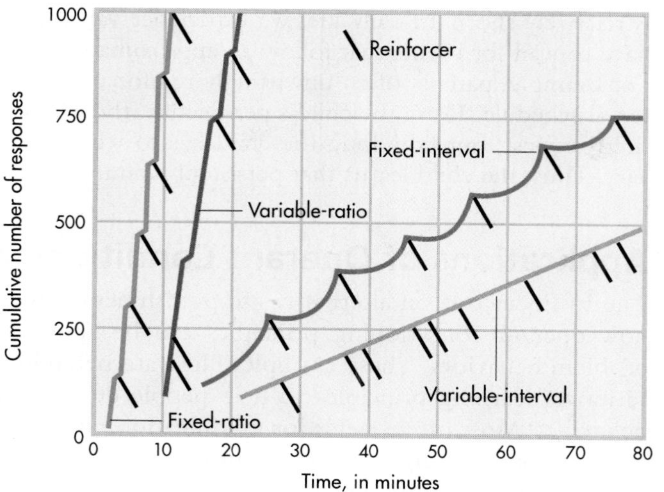

Figure 5.6 Schedules of Reinforcement and Response Patterns Different patterns of responding are produced by the four basic schedules of reinforcement. The predictable nature of a *fixed-ratio schedule* (the blue line at far left) produces a high rate of responding, with a pause after the reinforcer is delivered. The unpredictable nature of *variable-ratio schedules* (red) also produces high, steady rates of responding, but with hardly any pausing between reinforcers. *Fixed-interval schedules* (purple) produce a scallop-shaped pattern of responding. The unpredictable nature of *variable-interval schedules* (orange) produces a moderate but steady rate of responding. (Based on Skinner, 1961.)

in any activity that requires a precise number of responses in order to obtain reinforcement. Piecework—work for which you are paid for producing a specific number of items, such as being paid $1 for every 100 envelopes you stuff—is an example of an FR-100 schedule.

With a **variable-ratio (VR) schedule,** reinforcement occurs after an *average* number of responses, which *varies* from trial to trial. A rat on a variable-ratio-20 schedule (abbreviated VR-20) might have to press the bar 25 times on the first trial before being reinforced and only 15 times on the second trial before reinforcement. Although the number of responses required on any specific trial is *unpredictable,* over repeated trials the ratio of responses to reinforcers works out to the predetermined average.

Variable-ratio schedules of reinforcement produce high, steady rates of responding with hardly any pausing between trials or after reinforcement. Gambling is the classic example of a variable-ratio schedule in real life. Each spin of the roulette wheel, toss of the dice, or purchase of a lottery ticket could be the big one, and the more often you gamble, the more opportunities you have to win (and lose, as casino owners are well aware).

On a **fixed-interval (FI) schedule,** a reinforcer is delivered for the first response emitted *after* the preset time interval has elapsed. A rat on a two-minute fixed-interval schedule (abbreviated FI-2 minutes) would receive no food pellets for any bar presses made during the first two minutes. But the first bar press *after* the two-minute interval had elapsed would be reinforced.

Fixed-interval schedules typically produce a scallop-shaped pattern of responding in which the number of responses tends to increase as the time for the next reinforcer draws near. For example, if your instructor gives you a test every four weeks, your studying behavior would probably follow the same scallop-shaped pattern of responding as the rat's bar-pressing behavior. As the end of the four-week interval draws near, studying behavior increases. After the test, studying behavior drops off until the end of the next four-week interval approaches.

On a **variable-interval (VI) schedule,** reinforcement occurs for the first response emitted after an *average* amount of time has elapsed, but the interval varies from trial to trial. Hence, a rat on a VI-30 seconds schedule might be reinforced for the first bar press after only 10 seconds have elapsed on the first trial, for the first bar press after 50 seconds have elapsed on the second trial, and for the first bar press after 30 seconds have elapsed on the third trial. This works out to an average of one reinforcer every 30 seconds.

Generally, the unpredictable nature of variable-interval schedules tends to produce moderate but steady rates of responding, especially when the average interval

variable-ratio (VR) schedule
A reinforcement schedule in which a reinforcer is delivered after an average number of responses, which varies unpredictably from trial to trial.

fixed-interval (FI) schedule
A reinforcement schedule in which a reinforcer is delivered for the first response that occurs after a preset time interval has elapsed.

variable-interval (VI) schedule
A reinforcement schedule in which a reinforcer is delivered for the first response that occurs after an average time interval, which varies unpredictably from trial to trial.

is relatively short. In daily life, we experience variable-interval schedules when we have to wait for events that follow an approximate, rather than a precise, schedule. For example, parents often unwittingly reinforce a whining child on a variable interval schedule. From the child's perspective, the whining usually results in the desired request, but how long the child has to whine before getting reinforced can vary. Thus, the child learns that persistent whining will eventually pay off.

Applications of Operant Conditioning

behavior modification The application of learning principles to help people develop more effective or adaptive behaviors.

The In Focus box on alternatives to punishment earlier in the chapter described how operant conditioning principles can be applied to reduce and eliminate problem behaviors. These examples illustrate **behavior modification,** the application of learning principles to help people develop more effective or adaptive behaviors. Most often, behavior modification involves applying the principles of operant conditioning to bring about changes in behavior.

Behavior modification techniques have been successfully applied in many different settings (see Kazdin, 2008). Coaches, parents, teachers, and employers all routinely use operant conditioning. For example, behavior modification has been used to reduce public smoking by teenagers (Jason & others, 2006), improve student behavior in school cafeterias (Fabiano & others, 2008), reduce tantrums in preschool children (Wilder & others, 2006), and improve social skills and reduce self-destructive behaviors in people with autism and related disorders (Matson & others, 2007; Matson & LoVullo, 2008).

Businesses also use behavior modification. For example, one large retailer increased productivity by allowing employees to choose their own reinforcers. A casual dress code and flexible work hours proved to be more effective reinforcers than money (Raj & others, 2006). In each of these examples, the systematic use of reinforcement, shaping, and extinction increased the occurrence of desirable behaviors and decreased the incidence of undesirable behaviors. In Chapter 14, on therapies, we'll look at behavior modification techniques in more detail.

The principles of operant conditioning have also been used in the specialized training of animals, such as the capuchin monkey in the photo below, to help people who are physically challenged. Other examples are Seeing Eye dogs and dogs who assist people who are hearing-impaired.

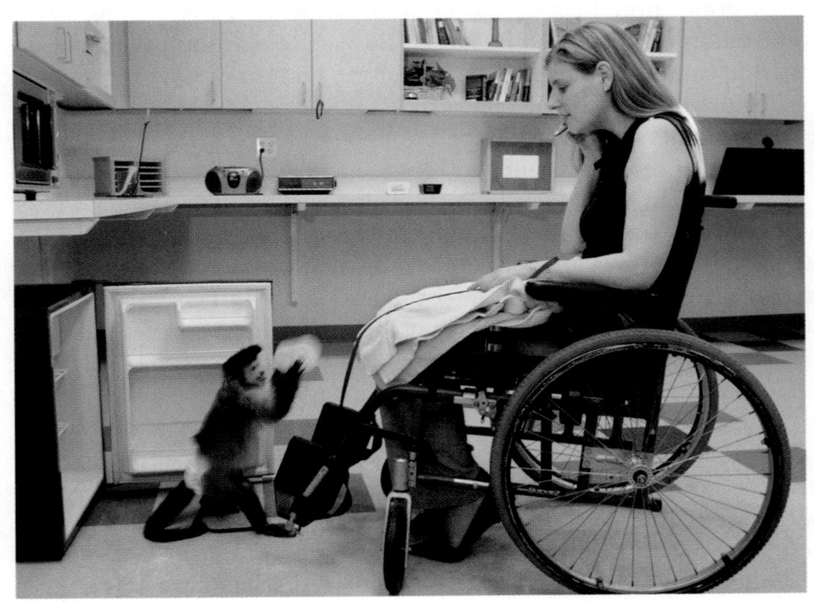

Creating "Helping Hands" with Operant Conditioning Founded by behavioral psychologist Mary Joan Willard, "Helping Hands" is a nonprofit organization that uses operant conditioning to train capuchin monkeys to provide live-in help to people who are paralyzed or otherwise severely disabled. Capuchins are used because of their high intelligence, dexterity, and ability to form a close bond with their human companions. At the Helping Hands "monkey college" near Boston, capuchins are trained to perform a wide range of helping behaviors, such as turning on lights, combing a person's hair, and loading a CD or DVD. Training can take up to two years. Shown is Toby, a 10-year-old capuchin monkey, as he retrieves a bottle from inside a closed refrigerator for his trainer.

Contemporary Views of Operant Conditioning

Key Theme

- **In contrast to Skinner, today's psychologists acknowledge the importance of both cognitive and evolutionary factors in operant conditioning.**

Key Questions

- **How did Tolman's research demonstrate the involvement of cognitive processes in learning?**
- **What are cognitive maps, latent learning, and learned helplessness?**
- **How do an animal's natural behavior patterns affect the conditioning of operant behaviors?**

In our discussion of classical conditioning, we noted that contemporary psychologists acknowledge the important roles played by cognitive factors and biological predispositions in classical conditioning. The situation is much the same with operant conditioning. The basic principles of operant conditioning have been confirmed in thousands of studies. However, our understanding of operant conditioning has been broadened by the consideration of cognitive factors and the recognition of the importance of natural behavior patterns.

Cognitive Aspects of Operant Conditioning

Rats! I Thought *You* Had the Map!

In Skinner's view, operant conditioning did not need to invoke cognitive factors to explain the acquisition of operant behaviors. Words such as *expect, prefer, choose,* and *decide* could not be used to explain how behaviors were acquired, maintained, or extinguished. Similarly, Thorndike and other early behaviorists believed that complex, active behaviors were no more than a chain of stimulus–response connections that had been "stamped in" by their effects.

However, not all learning researchers agreed with Skinner and Thorndike. **Edward C. Tolman** firmly believed that cognitive processes played an important role in the learning of complex behaviors—even in the lowly laboratory rat. According to Tolman, although such cognitive processes could not be observed directly, they could still be experimentally verified and inferred by careful observation of outward behavior (Tolman, 1932).

Much of Tolman's research involved rats in mazes. When Tolman began his research in the 1920s, many studies of rats in mazes had been done. In a typical experiment, a rat would be placed in the "start" box. A food reward would be put in the "goal" box at the end of the maze. The rat would initially make many mistakes in running the maze. After several trials, it would eventually learn to run the maze quickly and with very few errors.

But what had the rats learned? According to traditional behaviorists, the rats had learned a *sequence of responses,* such as "first corner—turn left; second corner—turn left; third corner—turn right," and so on. Each response was associated with the "stimulus" of the rat's position in the maze. And the entire sequence of responses was "stamped in" by the food reward at the end of the maze.

Tolman (1948) disagreed with that view. He noted that several investigators had reported as incidental findings that their maze-running rats had occasionally taken their own shortcuts to the food box. In one case, an enterprising rat had knocked the cover off the maze, climbed over the maze wall and out of the maze, and scampered directly to the food box (Lashley, 1929; Tolman & others, 1946). To Tolman, such reports indicated that the rats had learned more than simply the sequence

Edward Chace Tolman (1898–1956) Although he looks rather solemn in this photo, Tolman was known for his openness to new ideas, energetic teaching style, and playful sense of humor. During an important speech, he showed a film of a rat in a maze with a short clip from a Mickey Mouse cartoon spliced in at the end (Gleitman, 1991). Tolman's research demonstrated that cognitive processes are an important part of learning, even in the rat.

cognitive map
Tolman's term for the mental representation of the layout of a familiar environment.

latent learning
Tolman's term for learning that occurs in the absence of reinforcement but is not behaviorally demonstrated until a reinforcer becomes available.

of responses required to get to the food. Tolman believed instead that the rats eventually built up, through experience, a **cognitive map** of the maze—a mental representation of its layout.

As an analogy, think of the route you typically take to get to your psychology classroom. If a hallway along the way were blocked off for repairs, you would use your cognitive map of the building to come up with an alternative route to class. Tolman showed experimentally that rats, like people, seem to form cognitive maps (Tolman, 1948). And, like us, rats can use their cognitive maps to come up with an alternative route to a goal when the customary route is blocked (Tolman & Honzik, 1930a).

Tolman challenged the prevailing behaviorist model on another important point. According to Thorndike, for example, learning would not occur unless the behavior was "strengthened," or "stamped in," by a rewarding consequence. But Tolman showed that this was not necessarily the case. In a classic experiment, three groups of rats were put in the same maze once a day for several days (Tolman & Honzik, 1930b). For group 1, a food reward awaited the rats at the end of the maze. Their performance in the maze steadily improved; the number of errors and the time it took the rats to reach the goal box showed a steady decline with each trial. The rats in group 2 were placed in the maze each day with *no* food reward. They consistently made many errors, and their performance showed only slight improvement. The performance of the rats in groups 1 and 2 was exactly what the traditional behaviorist model would have predicted.

Now consider the behavior of the rats in group 3. These rats were placed in the maze with no food reward for the first 10 days of the experiment. Like the rats in group 2, they made many errors as they wandered about the maze. But, beginning on day 11, they received a food reward at the end of the maze. As you can see in Figure 5.7, there was a dramatic improvement in group 3's performance from day 11 to day 12. Once the rats had discovered that food awaited them at the end of the maze, they made a beeline for the goal. On day 12, the rats in group 3 ran the maze with very few errors, improving their performance to the level of the rats in group 1 that had been rewarded on every trial!

Tolman concluded that *reward*—or reinforcement—is *not necessary* for learning to take place (Tolman & Honzik, 1930b). The rats in group 3 had learned the layout of the maze and formed a cognitive map of the maze simply by exploring it for 10 days. However, they had not been motivated to *demonstrate* that learning until a reward was introduced. Rewards, then, seem to affect the *performance* of what has

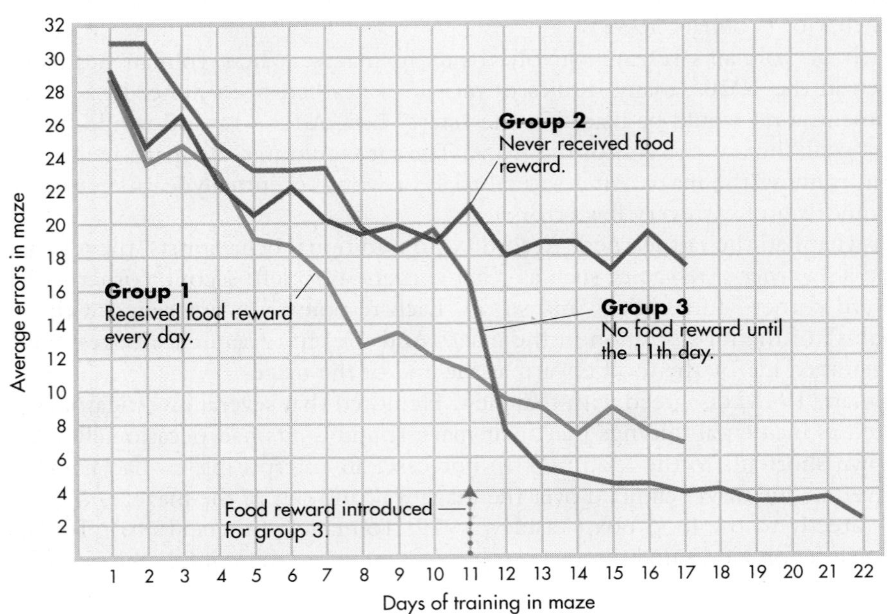

Figure 5.7 Latent Learning Beginning with day 1, the rats in group 1 received a food reward at the end of the maze, and the number of errors they made steadily decreased each day. The rats in group 2 never received a food reward; they made many errors as they wandered about in the maze. The rats in group 3 did not receive a food reward on days 1 through 10. Beginning on day 11, they received a food reward at the end of the maze. Notice the sharp decrease in errors on day 12 and thereafter. According to Tolman, the rats in group 3 had formed a cognitive map of the maze during the first 11 days of the experiment. Learning had taken place, but this learning was not demonstrated until reinforcement was present—a phenomenon that Tolman called latent learning.

Source: Tolman & Honzik (1930b).

been learned rather than learning itself. To describe learning that is not immediately demonstrated in overt behavior, Tolman used the term **latent learning.**

From these and other experiments, Tolman concluded that learning involves the acquisition of knowledge rather than simply changes in outward behavior. According to Tolman (1932), an organism essentially learns "what leads to what." It learns to "expect" that a certain behavior will lead to a particular outcome in a specific situation.

Tolman is now recognized as an important forerunner of modern cognitive learning theorists (Gleitman, 1991; Olton, 1992). Many contemporary cognitive learning theorists follow Tolman in their belief that operant conditioning involves the *cognitive representation* of the relationship between a behavior and its consequence. Today, operant conditioning is seen as involving the cognitive *expectancy* that a given consequence will follow a given behavior (Bouton, 2007; Dickinson & Balleine, 2000).

"Well, you don't look like an experimental psychologist to me."

Learned Helplessness

Expectations of Failure and Learning to Quit

Cognitive factors, particularly the role of expectation, are involved in another learning phenomenon, called *learned helplessness.* Learned helplessness was discovered by accident. Psychologists were trying to find out if classically conditioned responses would affect the process of operant conditioning in dogs. The dogs were strapped into harnesses and then exposed to a tone (the neutral stimulus) paired with an unpleasant but harmless electric shock (the UCS), which elicited fear (the UCR). After conditioning, the tone alone—now a CS—elicited the conditioned response of fear.

In the classical conditioning setup, the dogs were unable to escape or avoid the shock. But the next part of the experiment involved an operant conditioning procedure in which the dogs *could* escape the shock. The dogs were transferred to a special kind of operant chamber called a *shuttlebox,* which has a low barrier in the middle that divides the chamber in half. In the operant conditioning setup, the floor on one side of the cage became electrified. To escape the shock, all the dogs had to do was learn a simple escape behavior: Jump over the barrier when the floor was electrified. Normally, dogs learn this simple operant very quickly.

However, when the classically conditioned dogs were placed in the shuttlebox and one side became electrified, the dogs did *not* try to jump over the barrier. Rather than perform the operant to escape the shock, they just lay down and whined. Why?

To Steven F. Maier and **Martin Seligman**, two young psychology graduate students at the time, the explanation of the dogs' passive behavior seemed obvious. During the tone–shock pairings in the classical conditioning setup, the dogs *had learned that shocks were inescapable.* No active behavior that they engaged in—whether whining, barking, or struggling in the harness—would allow them to avoid or escape the shock. In other words, the dogs had "learned" to be helpless: They had developed the *cognitive expectation* that their behavior would have no effect on the environment.

Martin E. P. Seligman: From Learned Helplessness to Positive Psychology Seligman (b. 1942) began his research career by studying learned helplessness in dogs, and later, in humans. He applied his findings to psychological problems in humans, including depression. He also investigated why some people succumb to learned helplessness while others persist in the face of obstacles. Seligman (1991, 2005) eventually developed a program to teach "learned optimism" as a way of overcoming feelings of helplessness, habitual pessimism, and depression. Elected president of the American Psychological Association in 1996, Seligman launched a new movement called positive psychology, which would emphasize research on human strengths, rather than human problems. As Seligman (2004) explained, "It became my mission in life to help create a positive psychology whose mission would be the understanding and building of positive emotion, of strength and virtue, and of positive institutions."

learned helplessness
A phenomenon in which exposure to inescapable and uncontrollable aversive events produces passive behavior.

To test this idea, Seligman and Maier (1967) designed a simple experiment. Dogs were arranged in groups of three. The first dog received shocks that it could escape by pushing a panel with its nose. The second dog was "yoked" to the first and received the same number of shocks. However, nothing the second dog did could stop the shock—they stopped only if the first dog pushed the panel. The third dog was the control and got no shocks at all.

After this initial training, the dogs were transferred to the shuttlebox. As Seligman and Maier had predicted, the first and third dogs quickly learned to jump over the barrier when the floor became electrified. But the second dog, the one that had learned that nothing it did would stop the shock, made no effort to jump over the barrier. Because the dog had developed the cognitive expectation that its behavior would have no effect on the environment, it had become passive (Seligman & Maier, 1967). The name of this phenomenon is **learned helplessness**—a phenomenon in which exposure to inescapable and uncontrollable aversive events produces passive behavior (Maier & others, 1969).

Since these early experiments, learned helplessness has been demonstrated in many different species, including primates, cats, rats, and fish (LoLordo, 2001). Even cockroaches demonstrate learned helplessness in a cockroach-sized shuttlebox after being exposed to inescapable shock (G. E. Brown & others, 1999).

In humans, numerous studies have found that exposure to uncontrollable, aversive events can produce passivity and learned helplessness. For example, college students who have experienced failure in previous academic settings may feel that academic tasks and setbacks are beyond their control. Thus, when faced with the demands of exams, papers, and studying, rather than rising to the challenge, they may experience feelings of learned helplessness (McKean, 1994). If a student believes that academic tasks are unpleasant, unavoidable, and beyond her control, even the slightest setback can trigger a sense of helpless passivity. Such students may be prone to engage in self-defeating responses, such as procrastinating or giving up prematurely.

How can learned helplessness be overcome? In their early experiments, Seligman and Maier discovered that if they forcibly dragged the dogs over the shuttlebox barrier when the floor on one side became electrified, the dogs would eventually overcome their passivity and begin to jump over the barrier on their own (LoLordo, 2001; Seligman, 1992). For students who experience academic learned helplessness, establishing a sense of control over their schoolwork is the first step. Seeking knowledge about course requirements and assignments and setting goals, however modest, that can be successfully met can help students begin to acquire a sense of mastery over environmental challenges (McKean, 1994).

Learned Helplessness on the Field In humans, learned helplessness can be produced when negative events are perceived as uncontrollable. Even highly trained athletes can succumb to feelings of learned helplessness in the face of persistent defeats. Athletes who believe that they have no control over the factors that led to their loss or poor performance are less likely to believe that they can succeed in the future (Coffee & others, 2009). They're also less likely to persist in the face of failure (LeFoll & others, 2008).

Since the early demonstrations of learned helplessness in dogs, the notion of learned helplessness has undergone several revisions and refinements (Abramson & others, 1978; Gillham & others, 2001). Learned helplessness has been shown to play a role in psychological disorders, particularly depression, and in the ways that people respond to stressful events. Learned helplessness has also been applied in such diverse fields as management, sales, and health psychology (Wise & Rosqvist, 2006). In Chapter 12, on stress, health, and coping, we will take up the topic of learned helplessness again.

Operant Conditioning and Biological Predispositions

Misbehaving Chickens

Skinner and other behaviorists firmly believed that the general laws of operant conditioning applied to all animal species—whether they were pecking pigeons or bar-pressing rats. As Skinner (1956) wrote:

> Pigeon, rat, monkey, which is which? It doesn't matter. Of course, these species have behavioral repertoires which are as different as their anatomies. But once you have allowed for differences in the ways in which they make contact with the environment, and in the ways in which they act upon the environment, what remains of their behavior shows astonishingly similar properties.

However, psychologists studying operant conditioning, like those studying classical conditioning, found that an animal's natural behavior patterns *could* influence the learning of new behaviors. Consider the experiences of Keller and Marian Breland, two of Skinner's students at the University of Minnesota. The Brelands established a successful business training animals for television commercials, trade shows, fairs, and even displays in department stores (Bailey & Bailey, 1993; Breland & Breland, 1961). Using operant conditioning, the Brelands trained thousands of animals of many different species to perform all sorts of complex tricks.

But the Brelands weren't always successful in training the animals. For example, they tried to train a chicken to play baseball. The chicken learned to pull a loop that activated a swinging bat. After hitting the ball, the chicken was supposed to run to first base. The chicken had little trouble learning to pull the loop, but instead of running to first base, the chicken would chase the ball.

The Brelands also tried to train a raccoon to pick up two coins and deposit them into a metal box. The raccoon easily learned to pick up the coins but seemed to resist putting them into the box. Like a furry little miser, it would rub the coins together. And rather than dropping the coins in the box, it would dip the coins in the box and take them out again. As time went on, this behavior became more persistent, even though the raccoon was not being reinforced for it. In fact, the raccoon's "misbehavior" was actually *preventing* it from getting reinforced for correct behavior.

The Brelands noted that such nonreinforced behaviors seemed to reflect innate, instinctive responses. The chicken chasing the ball was behaving like a chicken chasing a bug. Raccoons in the wild instinctively clean and moisten their food by dipping it in streams or rubbing it between their forepaws. These natural behaviors interfered with the operant behaviors the Brelands were attempting to condition—a phenomenon called **instinctive drift.**

instinctive drift
The tendency of an animal to revert to instinctive behaviors that can interfere with the performance of an operantly conditioned response.

Keller and Marian Breland's "IQ Zoo"
B. F. Skinner's former students Keller and Marian Breland moved their animal training business from Minnesota to the warmer climate of Hot Springs, Arkansas in 1951. By the 1960s, the Brelands' "IQ Zoo" was one of the most popular roadside attractions in the U.S. Among its nonhuman stars were basketball-playing raccoons, reindeer who operated a printing press, ducks who played the piano, and chickens who danced, walked a tightrope, and played tic-tac-toe. Beyond entertainment, the Brelands were pioneers in the development of animal training and behavior modification techniques. Marian Breland was one of the first psychologists to use positive reinforcement to teach basic self-help skills to people with developmental disabilities and also helped train marine mammals for the U.S. Navy (Bihm & Gillaspy, 2007; Bailey & Gillaspy, 2005).

Table 5.5

Comparing Classical and Operant Conditioning

	Classical Conditioning	Operant Conditioning
Type of behavior	Reflexive, involuntary behaviors	Nonreflexive, voluntary behaviors
Source of behavior	Elicited by stimulus	Emitted by organism
Basis of learning	Associating two stimuli: CS + UCS	Associating a response and the consequence that follows it
Responses conditioned	Physiological and emotional responses	Active behaviors that operate on the environment
Extinction process	Conditioned response decreases when conditioned stimulus is repeatedly presented alone	Responding decreases with elimination of reinforcing consequences
Cognitive aspects	Expectation that CS reliably predicts the UCS	Performance of behavior influenced by the expectation of reinforcement or punishment
Evolutionary influences	Innate predispositions influence how easily an association is formed between a particular stimulus and response	Behaviors similar to natural or instinctive behaviors are more readily conditioned

The biological predisposition to perform such natural behaviors was strong enough to overcome the lack of reinforcement. These instinctual behaviors also prevented the animals from engaging in the learned behaviors that would result in reinforcement. Clearly, reinforcement is not the sole determinant of behavior. And, inborn or instinctive behavior patterns can interfere with the operant conditioning of arbitrary responses.

Before you go on to the next section, take a few minutes to review Table 5.5 and make sure you understand the differences between classical and operant conditioning.

Observational Learning

Imitating the Actions of Others

Key Theme

- **In observational learning, we learn through watching and imitating the behaviors of others.**

Key Questions

- **How did Albert Bandura demonstrate the principles of observational learning?**
- **What four mental processes are involved in observational learning?**
- **How has observational learning been shown in nonhuman animals?**

Classical conditioning and operant conditioning emphasize the role of direct experiences in learning, such as directly experiencing a reinforcing or punishing stimulus following a particular behavior. But much human learning occurs *indirectly*, by watching what others do, then imitating it. In **observational learning**, learning takes place through observing the actions of others.

Humans develop the capacity to learn through observation at a very early age. Studies of 21-day-old infants have shown that they will imitate a variety of actions, including opening their mouths, sticking out their tongues, and making other facial expressions (Field & others, 1982; Meltzoff & Moore, 1977, 1983). In fact, even newborn infants can imitate adult expressions when they are less than an hour old (Meltzoff & Moore, 1989; Meltzoff, 2007). Clearly, the human brain is wired for imitation. The Focus on Neuroscience describes a fascinating new discovery that may shed some light on the brain mechanisms that support our ability to learn through observation.

observational learning
Learning that occurs through observing the actions of others.

mirror neurons
A type of neuron that activates both when an action is performed and when the same action is perceived.

FOCUS ON NEUROSCIENCE

Mirror Neurons: Imitation in the Brain?

Psychologists have only recently begun to understand the neural underpinnings of the human ability to imitate behavior. The first clue emerged from an accidental discovery in a lab in Palermo, Italy, in the mid-1990s. Neuroscientist Giacomo Rizzolatti and his colleagues were studying neurons in the premotor cortex of macaque monkeys. Using tiny electrodes to record the activity of individual neurons, Rizzolatti's team had painstakingly identified the specific motor neurons involved in simple behaviors, such as picking up a peanut or grabbing a toy (see Rizzolatti & Sinigaglia, 2008).

Then Rizzolatti noticed something odd. As one of the wired-up monkeys watched a lab assistant pick up a peanut, a neuron fired in the monkey's brain—the *same* neuron that fired when the monkey itself picked up a peanut. At first, the researchers thought that the monkey must be making tiny muscle movements, and that these movements were responsible for the motor neuron activity. But the monkey was sitting perfectly still. The researchers were baffled, because a motor neuron was thought to fire only if a motor behavior was occurring.

The explanation? Rizzolatti's team had discovered a new class of specialized neurons, which they dubbed **mirror neurons.** Mirror neurons are neurons that fire both when an action is performed and when the action is simply perceived (Iacoboni, 2009). In effect, these neurons imitate or "mirror" the observed action as though the observer were actually carrying out the action.

It's important to note that mirror neurons are *not* a new physical type of neurons. A mirror neuron is defined by its *function,* rather than its physical structure.

Do mirror neurons simply reflect visual stimuli, or are they somehow involved in providing a mental representation of an action? Rizzolatti's team conducted a series of experiments to find out (see Rizzolatti & Sinigaglia, 2008; Rizzolatti & others, 2006). First, Evelyne Kohler and her colleagues (2002) showed that the same neurons that activated when a monkey cracked open a peanut shell also activated when a monkey simply *heard* a peanut shell breaking.

Another study extended the idea that mirror neurons are involved in the mental representation of an action. M. Alessandra Umiltà and her colleagues (2001) identified the motor mirror neurons that fired when a monkey saw the researcher's hand reaching for and grasping food. Then a screen was placed in front of the food. Now the monkey could see the researcher's hand moving towards the screen but could *not* actually see the hand touching the food. Would the motor mirror neurons fire if the monkey could only imagine the action of grasping the food? Yes. Even when the action was hidden from view and could only be inferred, the mirror neurons associated with that action fired.

Following their discovery in the motor cortex, mirror neurons have since been identified in many other brain regions (see Iacoboni, 2009; Oberman & Ramachandran, 2007). Today, many psychologists use the term *mirror neuron system* to describe mirroring in the brain. That's because even simple behaviors and sensations often involve groups of mirror neurons firing together rather than single neurons (Rizzolatti & Craighero, 2004).

Evidence of Human Mirror Neurons

Brain-imaging studies like the one illustrated below have provided *indirect* evidence of mirror neurons in the human brain (see Oberman & Ramachandran, 2007; Slack, 2007). A recent study provided the first direct evidence for the existence of mirror neurons in humans. Electrodes were temporarily implanted in the brains of epileptic patients as part of their preparation for surgery. A team led by Marco Iacoboni (2009) recorded the activity of individual neurons as the patients performed simple actions, such as grasping a cup and making facial expressions. Then the researchers recorded neuron activity while the patients simply viewed short video clips and photographs of others executing the same actions. The result? The researchers identified 34 neurons that were activated by both the performance and observation of a behavior—the first direct evidence of individual mirror neurons in the human brain (Slack, 2007).

Many neuroscientists and psychologists believe that mirror neurons play an important role in imitation and observational learning (Rizzolatti, 2005; Iacoboni & Depretto, 2006). Research has also implicated the mirror neuron system in highly complex human behavior, ranging from empathy to language (Rizzolatti & Sinigaglia, 2008; Iacoboni, 2008, 2009). Some scientists think that dysfunctions in the mirror system may be involved in autism and other disorders that are associated with impaired social functioning (Oberman & Ramachandran, 2007). Although such speculations are intriguing, more scientific evidence is needed before such conclusions can be drawn (Dinstein & others, 2008).

(a) Trained-Music

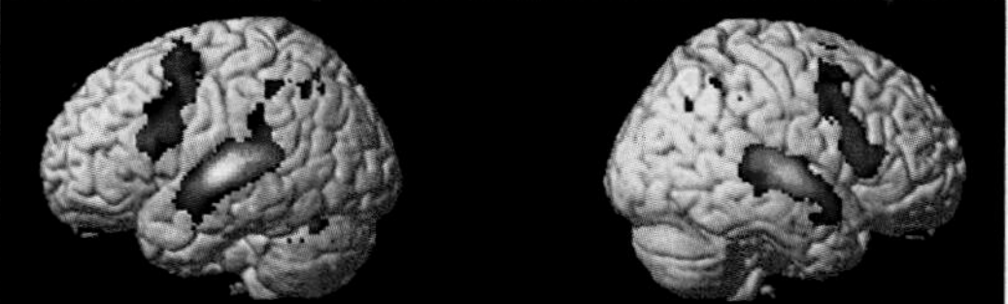

(b) Untrained-Different-Notes-Music

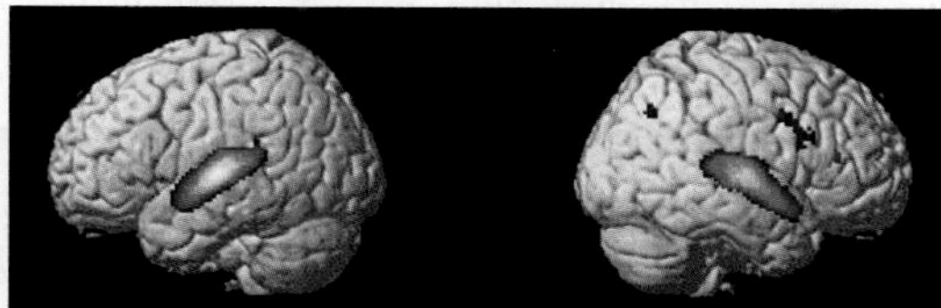

Musical Mirror Neurons Non-musicians were trained to play a piece of music by ear on a piano keyboard, then underwent a series of fMRI scans (Lahav & others, 2007). Panel (a) shows the participants' brain activity as they listened to the same music they had already learned to play. Even though they were not moving as they laid in the scanner, motor areas of the brain were activated (dark red). The brighter red/yellow color indicates activation in the brain's auditory areas. Panel (b) shows participants' brain activity while they listened to unfamiliar music utilizing the same musical notes but in a different sequence.

As you compare the scans in (a) and (b), notice the extensive activation in motor-related brain regions when the participants listened to the music that they had already learned to play (a) but *not* when they listened to the unfamiliar music that they had never played (b).

Albert Bandura (b. 1925) Bandura contends that most human behavior is acquired through observational learning rather than through trial and error or direct experience of the consequences of our actions. Watching and processing information about the actions of others, including the consequences that occur, influence the likelihood that behavior will be imitated.

Albert Bandura is the psychologist most strongly identified with observational learning. Bandura (1974) believes that observational learning is the result of cognitive processes that are "actively judgmental and constructive," not merely "mechanical copying." To illustrate his theory, let's consider his famous experiment involving the imitation of aggressive behaviors (Bandura, 1965). In the experiment, 4-year-old children separately watched a short film showing an adult playing aggressively with a Bobo doll—a large, inflated balloon doll that stands upright because the bottom is weighted with sand. All the children saw the adult hit, kick, and punch the Bobo doll in the film.

However, there were three different versions of the film, each with a different ending. Some children saw the adult *reinforced* with soft drinks, candy, and snacks after performing the aggressive actions. Other children saw a version in which the aggressive adult was *punished* for the actions with a scolding and a spanking by another adult. Finally, some children watched a version of the film in which the aggressive adult experienced *no consequences.*

After seeing the film, each child was allowed to play alone in a room with several toys, including a Bobo doll. The playroom was equipped with a one-way window so that the child's behavior could be observed. Bandura found that the consequences the children observed in the film made a difference. Children who watched the film in which the adult was punished were much less likely to imitate the aggressive behaviors than were children who watched either of the other two film endings.

Then Bandura added an interesting twist to the experiment. Each child was asked to show the experimenter what the adult did in the film. For every behavior they could imitate, the child was rewarded with snacks and stickers. Virtually all the children imitated the adult's behaviors they had observed in the film, including the aggressive behaviors. The particular version of the film the children had seen made no difference.

Bandura (1965) explained these results much as Tolman explained latent learning. Reinforcement is *not* essential for learning to occur. Rather, the *expectation of reinforcement* affects the *performance* of what has been learned.

The Classic Bobo Doll Experiment Bandura demonstrated the powerful influence of observational learning in a series of experiments conducted in the early 1960s. Children watched a film showing an adult playing aggressively with an inflated Bobo doll. If they saw the adult rewarded with candy for the aggressive behavior or experience no consequences, the children were much more likely to imitate the behavior than if they saw the adult punished for the aggressive behavior (Bandura, 1965; Bandura & others, 1963).

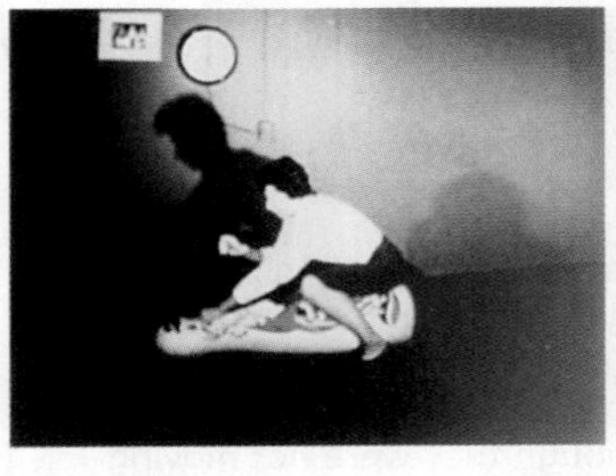

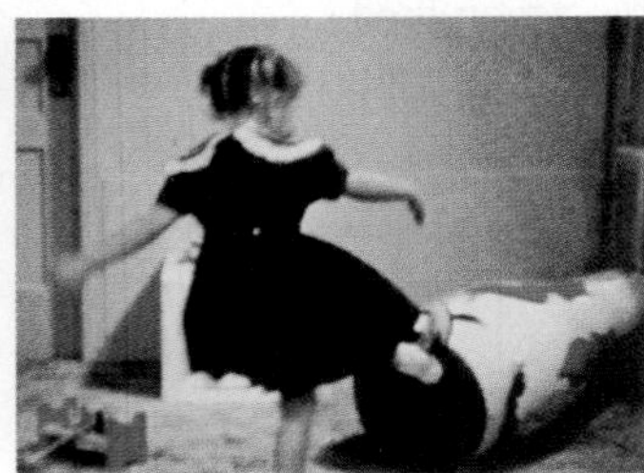

Bandura (1986) suggests that four cognitive processes interact to determine whether imitation will occur. First, you must pay *attention* to the other person's behavior. Second, you must *remember* the other person's behavior so that you can perform it at a later time. That is, you must form and store a mental representation of the behavior to be imitated. Third, you must be able to transform this mental representation into *actions that you are capable of reproducing*. These three factors—attention, memory, and motor skills—are necessary for learning to take place through observation.

Fourth, there must be some *motivation* for you to imitate the behavior. This factor is crucial to the actual performance of the learned behavior. You are more likely to imitate a behavior if there is some expectation that doing so will produce reinforcement or reward. Thus, all the children were capable of imitating the adult's aggressive behavior. But the children who saw the aggressive adult being rewarded were much more likely to imitate the aggressive behavior than were the children who saw the adult punished. Table 5.6 summarizes other factors that increase the likelihood of imitation.

Table 5.6

Factors That Increase Imitation

You're more likely to imitate:

- People who are rewarded for their behavior
- Warm, nurturing people
- People who have control over you or have the power to influence your life
- People who are similar to you in terms of age, sex, and interests
- People you perceive as having higher social status
- When the task to be imitated is not extremely easy or difficult
- If you lack confidence in your own abilities in a particular situation
- If the situation is unfamiliar or ambiguous
- If you've been rewarded for imitating the same behavior in the past

Source: Based on research summarized in Bandura (1977, 1986, 1997).

Observational Learning in Animals

Many nonhuman animals have been shown to learn new behaviors through observation and imitation. One study involved German shepherd puppies whose mothers were specially trained to locate and retrieve hidden drugs (Slabbert & Rasa, 1997). Puppies who had observed their mothers locate and retrieve the packets of narcotics were significantly better at performing the same task three months later than were puppies who had not seen adult dogs perform this behavior.

The ability to learn a novel behavior through observation has been demonstrated in animals as diverse as golden hamsters (Previde & Poli, 1996), starlings (Templeton, 1998), and Japanese quail (Zentall, 2003). Even guppies can learn foraging behavior and escape routes from other guppies (Reader & others, 2003). Along with learning new behaviors, animals learn to modify existing behaviors by observing others of their species. For example, young rats that observed the eating preferences of older rats mimicked the food choices of the older rats (Galef & Whiskin, 1995).

Chimpanzees, apes, and other primates are quite adept at learning through observation, sometimes in sophisticated ways (Brosnan & de Waal, 2004). For example, macaque monkeys are capable of learning a cognitive rule for ordering lists of photographs simply from watching another macaque successfully complete the task (Subiaul & others, 2004).

Just as with humans, motivational factors seem to play a role in observational learning by primates. One study involved imitative behavior of free-ranging orangutans in a preserve located in central Indonesia (Russon & Galdikas, 1995). The orangutans imitated the behavior of both humans and other orangutans, but they were more likely to imitate high-status or dominant models than low-status models. The orangutans were also more likely to imitate models with whom they had close relationships, such as biological parents, siblings, or their human caregivers. Human strangers were virtually never imitated.

Chimpanzee Culture: Observational Learning in the Wild Chimpanzee tribes in the wild develop their own unique "cultures" or behavioral differences in tool use, foraging skills, and even courtship rituals (Hopper & others, 2007). Apparently, these distinct behavior patterns are acquired and transmitted through observational learning (Whiten, 2009). For example, after an individual chimp learned a new food-gathering technique, the rest of its group acquired the new skill within a few days. In turn, the newly acquired skill spread to other chimpanzee groups who could observe the new behavior (Whiten & others, 2007). These chimps in the Edinburgh Zoo are learning how to use a tool to extract food – one of the tasks that Andrew Whiten (2009) has used to study observational learning and the development of unique behavioral traditions among chimpanzee tribes.

Television and Teen Pregnancy? Shown here is a still from the hit TV series *Gossip Girl*. Anita Chandra and her colleagues (2008) found that teen pregnancies were positively correlated with exposure to sexual content on television. Compared to teens who watched low levels, teenagers who watched high levels of sexual content on television were twice as likely to get pregnant or get a partner pregnant. Mainstream television shows such as *Sex and the City*, *That '70s Show*, and *Friends* were classified as having high sexual content. According to Chandra and her colleagues, the findings of their correlational study suggest that such television shows emphasize only the positive aspects of sexual behavior—while ignoring the risks.

Applications of Observational Learning

Bandura's finding that children will imitate film footage of aggressive behavior has more than just theoretical importance. One obvious implication has to do with the effects of negative behaviors that are depicted in films and television shows. Is there any evidence that television and other media can increase negative or destructive behaviors in viewers?

One recent study conducted by psychologist Rebecca Collins and her colleagues (2004) examined the impact of television portrayals of sexual activity on the behavior of U.S. adolescents between the ages of 12 and 17. Over the two-year period of the study, researchers found that adolescents who watched large amounts of television containing sexual content were twice as likely to begin engaging in sexual intercourse in the following year as adolescents who were the same age but watched the least amount of sexually oriented programming.

Are we talking about X-rated cable programs or sexually suggestive music videos? No. Among the programs that the researchers rated as high in sexual content were such popular network programs as *Friends* and *That '70s Show*. In fact, researchers found that exposure to TV shows that simply *talked* about sex was associated with the same risks as exposure to TV that depicted sexual behavior. Although other factors contributed to the likelihood that adolescents would become sexually active, the impact of TV programming was substantial. "The 12-year-olds who watched a lot of television with sexual content behaved like the 14- or 15-year-olds who watched the least amount of sexual television," Collins (2004) pointed out.

Another important implication of Bandura's research relates to the effects of media depictions of violence on behavior. In the Critical Thinking box on page 224, we take an in-depth look at the relationship between media portrayals of violence and aggressive behavior.

Given the potential impact of negative media images, let's look at the flip side. Is there any evidence that television and other media can encourage socially desirable behavior?

A remarkably effective application of observational learning has been the use of television and radio dramas to promote social change and healthy behaviors in Asia, Latin America, and Africa (Population Communications International, 2004). Pioneered by Mexican television executive Miguel Sabido, the first such attempt was a long-running serial drama that used observational learning principles to promote literacy among adults. The main storyline centered on the experiences of a group of people in a literacy self-instruction group. Millions of viewers faithfully watched the series. In the year before the televised series, about 90,000 people were enrolled in such literacy groups. In the year during the series, enrollment jumped to 840,000 people (Bandura, 1997).

> The serials dramatize the everyday problems people struggle with, and model functional strategies and solutions to them. This approach succeeds because it informs, enables, motivates and guides people for personal and social changes that improve their lives.
>
> —ALBERT BANDURA (2004a)

Since the success of this program, the nonprofit group Population Communications International (2004) has developed many such "entertainment-education programs" based on Bandura's observational learning paradigm. Each series is developed with the input of local advisers and is written, produced, and performed

"Ordinary People" Population Communications International is a nonprofit group that develops television and radio dramatic series that are based on the principles of observational learning. This scene is from the Chinese television series *Bai Xing,* which means "Ordinary People." Set in a small village on the banks of the Yellow River in China, this award-winning dramatic series centers on the experiences of Lüye, a young woman who struggles against the rigidity of traditional beliefs and customs. Among the series' goals are to show the importance of economic independence for women and the need to overcome the traditional Chinese preference for sons over daughters. In this scene, Lüye is distraught over her impending marriage to a man she does not love, and is being comforted by her mother.

by creative talent in the country of the intended audience. These serial dramas motivate individuals to adopt new attitudes and behavior by modeling behaviors that promote family health, stable communities, and a sustainable environment. Among the most popular radio and television serial dramas:

- Culturally sensitive programs encouraging family planning and reproductive health in India, Brazil, and Tanzania
- Radio serials aimed at preventing the transmission of HIV/AIDS in Kenya and Peru
- An award-winning dramatic series set in a rural Chinese village, starring a young female protagonist, that emphasized the value of female children and economic independence for women

One popular series in India focused on motivating villagers to improve sanitation, adopt fuel-conservation practices to reduce pollution, and launch a tree-planting campaign (Papa & others, 2000).

These long-running programs feature characters with whom the average viewer can easily identify. While the storylines are dramatic, they also reflect everyday challenges. As Bandura (2002) notes, "Seeing people similar to themselves change their lives for the better not only conveys strategies for how to do it but raises viewers' sense of efficacy that they too can succeed. Viewers come to admire and are inspired by characters in their likenesses who struggle with difficult obstacles and eventually overcome them."

Education-entertainment programs are designed to fulfill the optimal conditions for observational learning to occur (Bandura, 2002). The dramatic intensity, highly involving plot lines, and engaging characters ensure that viewers will become involved in the dramas and pay *attention*. To ensure that the modeled messages are *remembered,* an epilogue at the conclusion of each episode summarizes the key points and issues of the episode. To enhance the viewers' *ability* to carry out the modeled behaviors, a variety of support programs and groups are put in place when the series airs. And *motivating* people to change their behaviors in line with the modeled behaviors is accomplished by depicting the benefits of doing so. Research studies have confirmed the highly successful impact of these extremely popular dramas (see Singhal & others, 2004; Sood & others, 2004).

Beyond the effects of media depictions on behavior, observational learning has been applied in a wide variety of settings. The fields of education, vocational and job training, psychotherapy, and counseling use observational learning to help teach appropriate behaviors.

CRITICAL THINKING

Does Exposure to Media Violence *Cause* Aggressive Behavior?

Bandura's early observational learning studies showed preschoolers enthusiastically mimicking the movie actions of an adult pummeling a Bobo doll. His research provided a powerful paradigm to study the effects of "entertainment" violence. Bandura found that observed actions were most likely to be imitated when:

- They were performed by a model who is attractive and who has high status or is a dominant member of the viewer's social group.
- The model is rewarded for his or her behavior.
- The model is not punished for his or her actions.

Over the past four decades, more than 1,000 studies have investigated the relationship between media depictions of violence and increases in aggressive behavior in the real world (see Bushman & Anderson, 2007). We'll highlight some key findings here.

How Prevalent Is Violence on Television in the United States?

The amount of violence depicted on American television is truly staggering. One major research project, the National Television Violence Study (NTVS) (1996, 1997, 1998), systematically analyzed depictions of violence in more than 8,000 hours of cable and network programming.

The study found that more than 60 percent of television programs contained depictions of violence. More troubling, much of the violent behavior was depicted in ways that are known to *increase* the likelihood of imitation. For example, violent behavior was not punished and was often perpetrated by the heroes or other "good guys." In 80 percent of the violent shows, the violence did not result in any long-term consequences. Since that study, television and film depictions of violence have become more graphic, not less—and more readily available (Signorielli, 2005).

Is Exposure to Media Violence Linked to Aggressive Behavior?

Numerous research studies show that exposure to media violence produces short-term increases in laboratory measures of aggressive thoughts and behavior. And, hundreds of correlational studies demonstrate a link between exposure to violent media and aggressive behavior both in and out of the classroom (see Bushman & Anderson, 2007; Huesmann & Taylor, 2006; Murray, 2008).

The American Psychological Association, the American Academy of Pediatrics, and four other public health organizations issued a joint statement on the impact of entertainment violence on children (Congressional Public Health Summit, 2000). Based on a review of more than 30 years of research, they concluded that "viewing entertainment violence can lead to increases in aggressive attitudes, values, and behavior, particularly in children."

Does Exposure to Media Violence Have Long-Term, Real-World Effects?

According to several longitudinal studies, the answer is "yes" (C. A. Anderson & others, 2003; Huesmann & Taylor, 2006). For example, psychologist L. Rowell Huesmann and his colleagues (2003) conducted a 15-year longitudinal study that began with more than 500 boys and girls, ages 6 to 10, growing up in the Chicago area. When these individuals reached their early 20s, the researchers were able track down and resurvey 329 of them. The researchers also interviewed the participants' spouses or friends, and they obtained court records of criminal convictions.

The results showed that men who watched the most television violence as children were significantly more likely to have pushed, grabbed, or shoved their spouses and to have shoved another person in response to an insult. They were also three times more likely to have been convicted of a crime. A similar

>> Closing Thoughts

One theme throughout this chapter has been the quest to discover general laws of learning that would apply across virtually all species and situations. Watson was convinced that these laws were contained in the principles of classical conditioning. Skinner contended that they were to be found in the principles of operant conditioning. In a sense, they were both right. Thousands of experiments have shown that behavior can be reliably and predictably influenced by classical and operant conditioning procedures. By and large, the general principles of classical and operant conditioning hold up quite well across a wide range of species and situations.

But you've also seen that the general principles of classical and operant conditioning are just that—general, not absolute. Such researchers as John Garcia and Marian and Keller Breland recognized the importance of a species' evolutionary and biological heritage in acquiring new behaviors. Other researchers, such as Edward Tolman and Robert Rescorla, drew attention to the important role played by cognitive processes in learning. And Albert Bandura's investigations of obser-

pattern emerged with women. In another study, Paul Boxer and his colleagues (2009) compared the childhood and current media preferences of teenagers in juvenile justice facilities with a matched group of adolescents. The teenagers with a history of antisocial behavior were much more likely to have preferred violent media throughout their childhood and adolescence than the matched controls. According to the researchers, violent media may "enhance" violent tendencies in susceptible youth.

But Does Media Violence *Cause* Aggressive or Violent Behavior?

It's important to note that violent behavior is a complex phenomenon that is unlikely to have a single cause. Can exposure to violent media contribute to aggressive behavior? In some people, the answer is apparently "yes." But not everyone is affected in the same way. For example, in a longitudinal study of the effects of television viewing on elementary school children, Seymour Feshbach and June Tangney (2008) came up with a very unexpected finding. Hours spent viewing violent television programming was associated with lower cognitive performance and negative social behavior in white males, African-American females, and white females—but *not* in African-American males.

Consequently, some psychologists are cautious in their conclusions about the effects of media violence, pointing out that the vast majority of studies are *correlational* (Ferguson & Kilbourn, 2009; Savage & Yancey, 2008). As you learned in Chapter 1, correlation does not necessarily imply causation. Even if two factors are strongly correlated, some other variable could be responsible for the association between the two factors. Experimental studies, on the other hand, *are* designed to demonstrate causality. However, most experimental studies involve artificial measures of aggressive behavior, which may *not* accurately measure the likelihood that a participant will act aggressively in real life.

Psychologists generally agree that some viewers *are* highly susceptible to the negative effects of media violence (see Grimes & others, 2008). Some researchers think that the time has come to go beyond the question of *whether* media violence causes aggressive behavior and focus instead on investigating the factors that are most likely to be associated with its harmful effects (Feshbach & Tangney, 2008).

CRITICAL THINKING QUESTIONS

- Given the evidence summarized here, what conclusions can you draw about the effect of violent media images on aggressive behavior?
- Why is it so difficult to design an experimental study that would conclusively demonstrate that violent media *causes* aggressive behavior?
- Given the general conclusion that some, but not all, viewers are likely to become more aggressive after viewing violent media, what should be done about media violence?

vational learning underscored that classical and operant conditioning principles could not account for all learning.

Another prominent theme has been the adaptive nature of learning. Faced with an ever-changing environment, an organism's capacity to learn is critical to adaptation and survival. Clearly, there are survival advantages in being able to learn that a neutral stimulus can signal an important upcoming event, as in classical conditioning. An organism also enhances its odds of survival by being responsive to the consequences of its actions, as in operant conditioning. And, by observing the actions and consequences experienced by others, behaviors can be acquired through imitation. Thus, it is probably because these abilities are so useful in so many environments that the basic principles of learning are demonstrated with such consistency across so many species.

In the final analysis, it's probably safe to say that the most important consequence of learning is that it promotes the adaptation of many species, including humans, to their unique environments. Were it not for the adaptive nature of learning, Erv would probably have gotten trapped in the attic again!

ENHANCING WELL-BEING WITH PSYCHOLOGY

Using Learning Principles to Improve Self-Control

Self-control often involves choosing between two reinforcers: (1) a *long-term reinforcer* that will provide gratification at some point in the future or (2) a *short-term reinforcer* that provides immediate gratification but gets in the way of obtaining a long-term reinforcer. Objectively, the benefits of the long-term reinforcer far outweigh the benefits associated with the short-term, immediate reinforcer. Yet despite our commitment to the long-term goal, sometimes we choose a short-term reinforcer that conflicts with it. Why?

The Shifting Value of Reinforcers

The key is that *the relative value of reinforcers can shift over time* (Ainslie, 1975, 1992; Rachlin, 1974, 2000). Let's use an example to illustrate this principle. Suppose you sign up for an 8:00 A.M. class that meets every Tuesday morning. On Monday night, the short-term reinforcer (getting extra sleep on Tuesday morning) and the long-term reinforcer (getting a good course grade at the end of the semester) are both potential future reinforcers. Neither reinforcer is immediately available. So, when you compare these two future reinforcers, the value of making a good grade easily outweighs the value of getting extra sleep on Tuesday morning. That's why you duly set the alarm clock for 6:00 A.M. so you will get to class on time.

However, as the availability of a reinforcer gets closer, the subjective value of the reinforcer increases. Consequently, when your alarm goes off on Tuesday morning, the situation is fundamentally different. The short-term reinforcer is now immediately available: staying in that warm, comfy bed. Compared with Monday night when you set the alarm, the subjective value of extra sleep has increased significantly. Although making a good grade in the course is still important to you, its subjective value has not increased on Tuesday morning. After all, that long-term reinforcer is still in the distant future.

At the moment you make your decision, you choose whichever reinforcer has the greatest apparent value to you. At that moment, if the subjective value of the short-term reinforcer outweighs that of the long-term reinforcer, you're very likely to choose the short-term reinforcer (Rachlin, 1995, 2000). In other words, you'll probably stay in bed.

When you understand how the subjective values of reinforcers shift over time, the tendency to impulsively cave in to available short-term reinforcers starts to make more sense. The availability of an immediate, short-term reinforcer can temporarily outweigh the subjective value of a long-term reinforcer in the distant future (Steel, 2007). How can you counteract these momentary surges in the subjective value of short-term reinforcers? Fortunately, there are several strategies that can help you overcome the temptation of short-term reinforcers and improve self-control (Trope & Fishbach, 2000).

Strategy 1: Precommitment

Precommitment involves making an advance commitment to your long-term goal, one that will be difficult to change when a conflicting reinforcer becomes available (Ariely & Wertenbroch, 2002). In the case of getting to class on time, a precommitment could involve setting multiple alarms and putting them far enough away that you will be forced to get out of bed to shut each of them off. Or you could ask an early-rising friend to call you on the phone and make sure you're awake.

Strategy 2: Self-Reinforcement

Sometimes long-term goals seem so far away that your sense of potential future reinforcement seems weak compared with immediate reinforcers. One strategy to increase the subjective value of the long-term reinforcer is to use self-reinforcement for current behaviors related to your long-term goal. For example, promise yourself that if you spend two hours studying in the library, you'll reward yourself by watching a movie.

It's important, however, to reward yourself only *after* you perform the desired behavior. If you say to yourself, "Rather than study tonight, I'll go to this party and make up for it by studying tomorrow," you've blown it. You've just reinforced yourself for *not* studying! This would be akin to trying to increase bar-pressing behavior in a rat by giving the rat a pellet of food *before* it pressed the bar. Obviously, this contradicts the basic principle of positive reinforcement in which behavior is *followed* by the reinforcing stimulus.

Strategy 3: Stimulus Control

Remember, environmental stimuli can act as discriminative stimuli that "set the occasion" for a particular response. In effect, the environmental cues that precede a behavior can acquire some control over future occurrences of that behavior. So be aware of the environmental cues that are likely to trigger unwanted behaviors, such as studying in the kitchen (a cue for eating) or in an easy chair in the living room (a cue for watching television). Then replace those cues with others that will help you achieve your long-term goals.

For example, always study in a specific location, whether it's the library, in an empty classroom, or at a table or desk in a certain corner of your apartment. Over time, these environmental cues will become associated with the behavior of studying.

Strategy 4: Focus on the Delayed Reinforcer

The cognitive aspects of learning also play a role in choosing behaviors associated with long-term reinforcers (Metcalfe & Mischel, 1999; Mischel, 1996). When faced with a choice between an immediate and a delayed reinforcer, focus your attention on the delayed reinforcer. You'll be less likely to impulsively choose the short-term reinforcer (Ainslie, 1975).

Practically speaking, this means that if your goal is to save money for school, don't fantasize about a new stereo system or expensive running shoes. Focus instead on the delayed reinforcement of achieving your long-term goal (see Mischel & others, 1989). Imagine yourself proudly walking across the stage and receiving your college degree. Visualize yourself fulfilling your long-term career goals. The idea in selectively focusing on the delayed reinforcer is to mentally bridge the gap between the present and the ultimate attainment of your future goal. One of our students, a biology major, put a picture of a famous woman biologist next to her desk to help inspire her to study.

Strategy 5: Observe Good Role Models

Observational learning is another strategy you can use to improve self-control. Psychologist Walter Mischel (1966) found that children who observed others choose a delayed reinforcer over an immediate reinforcer were more likely to choose the delayed reinforcer themselves. So look for good role models. Observing others who are currently behaving in ways that will ultimately help them realize their long-term goals can make it easier for you to do the same.

CHAPTER REVIEW: KEY PEOPLE AND TERMS

Albert Bandura, p. 220
John Garcia, p. 197
Ivan Pavlov, p. 185
Robert A. Rescorla, p. 195
Martin Seligman, p. 215
B. F. Skinner, p. 201
Edward L. Thorndike, p. 200
Edward C. Tolman, p. 213
John B. Watson, p. 190

learning, p. 184
conditioning, p. 185
classical conditioning, p. 186
unconditioned stimulus (UCS), p. 186
unconditioned response (UCR), p. 186
conditioned stimulus (CS), p. 187
conditioned response (CR), p. 187
stimulus generalization, p. 188
stimulus discrimination, p. 188
higher order conditioning, p. 188
extinction (in classical conditioning), p. 189
spontaneous recovery, p. 189
behaviorism, p. 190
placebo response, p. 194
taste aversion, p. 196
biological preparedness, p. 197
law of effect, p. 200
operant, p. 201
operant conditioning, p. 201
reinforcement, p. 201
positive reinforcement, p. 202
negative reinforcement, p. 202
primary reinforcer, p. 203
conditioned reinforcer, p. 203
punishment, p. 204
punishment by application, p. 204
punishment by removal, p. 205
discriminative stimulus, p. 207
operant chamber (Skinner box), p. 209
shaping, p. 209
continuous reinforcement, p. 210
partial reinforcement, p. 210
extinction (in operant conditioning), p. 210
partial reinforcement effect, p. 210
schedule of reinforcement, p. 210
fixed-ratio (FR) schedule, p. 210
variable-ratio (VR) schedule, p. 211
fixed-interval (FI) schedule, p. 211
variable-interval (VI) schedule, p. 211
behavior modification, p. 212
cognitive map, p. 214
latent learning, p. 215
learned helplessness, p. 216
instinctive drift, p. 217
observational learning, p. 218
mirror neurons, p. 219

Web Companion Review Activities

You can find additional review activities at **www.worthpublishers.com/discoveringpsych5e.** The *Discovering Psychology* 5th edition Web Companion has self-scoring practice quizzes, flashcards, interactive crossword puzzles, and other activities to help you master the material in this chapter.

CONCEPT MAP: LEARNING

Learning: A relatively enduring change in behavior or knowledge as a result of experience

Conditioning: Process of learning associations between environmental events and behavioral responses

- **Classical conditioning:** Learning associations between stimuli
  - Reflexive behaviors
  - **Ivan Pavlov** (1849–1936)
    John B. Watson (1878–1958)
- **Operant conditioning:** Learning associations between behavior and environmental consequence
  - Nonreflexive ("voluntary") behaviors
  - **Edward L. Thorndike** (1874–1949)
    B. F. Skinner (1904–1990)
- **Observational learning:** Learning through observing behavior of others
  - Observed behaviors
  - **Albert Bandura** (b. 1925)

Classical Conditioning

Learning associations between stimuli

- **Ivan Pavlov** (1849–1936) Discovered principles of classical conditioning
- **John B. Watson** (1878–1958) Founded behaviorism

Process

Neutral stimulus + (repeatedly paired) **Unconditioned stimulus (UCS):** — elicits (natural reflex) → **Unconditioned response (UCR)**

Conditioned stimulus (CS) — elicits (conditioned reflex) → **Conditioned response (CR)**

Factors affecting classical conditioning

- **Stimulus generalization:** Occurs when a new stimulus that is similar to the CS also produces the CR
  Stimulus discrimination: Occurs when one stimulus elicits the CR, but another, similar stimulus does not
  Higher order conditioning: Occurs when an established CS functions as UCS in a new conditioning trial
- **Extinction:** CR will gradually weaken and disappear if the CS is repeatedly presented without the UCS
  Spontaneous recovery: After extinction and following a rest, the CR may reappear if the CS is presented

Contemporary Views Of Classical Conditioning

- Role of cognitive factors
  - **Robert Rescorla** (b. 1940) Classical conditioning involves learning the relationships between events; CS must reliably predict UCS
- Role of evolutionary factors
  - **John Garcia** (b. 1917) Classical conditioning occurs more readily when associations are **biologically prepared;** examples include taste aversions and phobias

Learning associations between behaviors and their consequences

Process

Discriminative stimulus sets the occasion → **Operant** is emitted → Consequence

Primary reinforcer: Naturally reinforcing
Conditioned reinforcer: Becomes reinforcing by being associated with a primary reinforcer

Reinforcement: Increases the likelihood that a behavior will be repeated

Punishment: Decreases the likelihood that a behavior will be repeated

Types of Reinforcement:
Positive reinforcement: Addition of a reinforcing stimulus strengthens an operant response
Negative reinforcement: Removal or subtraction of an aversive stimulus strengthens an operant response

Types of Punishment:
Punishment by application: Addition of a punishing stimulus weakens an operant response
Punishment by removal: Removal of a reinforcing stimulus weakens an operant response

New behaviors can be acquired through **shaping,** which involves reinforcing progressively closer approximations of a goal behavior

Behaviors on a **partial reinforcement** schedule are more resistant to **extinction.**
Schedules of reinforcement:
- **Fixed ratio (FR)**
- **Variable-ratio (VR)**
- **Fixed-interval (FI)**
- **Variable-interval (VI)**

Contemporary Views of Operant Conditioning

Role of cognitive factors

Edward C. Tolman (1898–1956)
Discovery of **cognitive maps** and **latent learning** provided evidence that learning involves the cognitive representation of the relationship between a behavior and its consequence

Martin Seligman (b. 1942)
Discovery of **learned helplessness** provided evidence for the role of cognitive expectations in learning

Role of evolutionary factors

Instinctive drift provided evidence for the importance of natural behavior patterns in learning

Observational Learning

Learning that occurs through observing the actions of others and the consequences of those actions

Albert Bandura (b. 1925)
Bobo doll experiment demonstrated that reinforcement is not necessary for learning to occur; expectation of reinforcement affects the performance of what has been learned

Processes necessary for imitation to occur:
1. Attention: pay attention to the model's behavior
2. Memory: remember the behavior so that it can be performed later
3. Motor skill: ability to transform the mental representation into action
4. Motivation: expectation that the behavior will be reinforced

CHAPTER 6

Memory

The Drowning PROLOGUE

ELIZABETH WAS ONLY 14 YEARS OLD when her mother drowned. Although Elizabeth remembered many things about visiting her Uncle Joe's home in Pennsylvania that summer, her memory of the details surrounding her mother's death had always been hazy. As she explained:

> *In my mind I've returned to that scene many times, and each time the memory gains weight and substance. I can see the cool pine trees, smell their fresh tarry breath, feel the lake's algae-green water on my skin, taste Uncle Joe's iced tea with fresh-squeezed lemon. But the death itself was always vague and unfocused. I never saw my mother's body, and I could not imagine her dead. The last memory I have of my mother was her tiptoed visit the evening before her death, the quick hug, the whispered, "I love you."*

Some 30 years later, at her Uncle Joe's 90th birthday party, Elizabeth learned from a relative that she had been the one to discover her mother's body in Uncle Joe's swimming pool. With this realization, memories that had eluded Elizabeth for decades began to come back.

> *The memories began to drift back, slow and unpredictable, like the crisp piney smoke from the evening campfires. I could see myself, a thin, dark-haired girl, looking into the flickering blue-and-white pool. My mother, dressed in her nightgown, is floating facedown. "Mom? Mom?" I ask the question several times, my voice rising in terror. I start screaming. I remember the police cars, their lights flashing, and the stretcher with the clean, white blanket tucked in around the edges of the body. The memory had been there all along, but I just couldn't reach it.*

As the memory crystallized, it suddenly made sense to Elizabeth why she had always felt haunted by her vague memories of the circumstances surrounding her mother's death. And it also seemed to explain, in part, why she had always been so fascinated by the topic of memory.

However, several days later, Elizabeth learned that the relative had been wrong—it was *not* Elizabeth who discovered her mother's body, but her Aunt Pearl. Other relatives confirmed that Aunt Pearl had been the one who found Elizabeth's mother in the swimming pool. Yet Elizabeth's memory had seemed so real.

The Elizabeth in this true story is Elizabeth Loftus, a psychologist who is nationally recognized as the leading expert on the distortions that can occur in the memories of eyewitnesses. Loftus shares this personal story in her book *The Myth of Repressed Memory: False Memories and Allegations of Sexual Abuse.*

In this chapter, we'll consider the psychological and biological processes that underlie how memories are formed and forgotten. As you'll see, memory distortions such as the one Elizabeth Loftus experienced are relatively common. By the end of this chapter, you'll have a much better understanding of the memory process, including the reason that Elizabeth's "memory" of finding her mother's body seemed so real.

Chapter Outline

memory
The mental processes that enable you to retain and retrieve information over time.

encoding
The process of transforming information into a form that can be entered into and retained by the memory system.

storage
The process of retaining information in memory so that it can be used at a later time.

retrieval
The process of recovering information stored in memory so that we are consciously aware of it.

stage model of memory
A model describing memory as consisting of three distinct stages: sensory memory, short-term memory, and long-term memory.

>> Introduction: What Is Memory?

Key Theme

- **Memory is a group of related mental processes that are involved in acquiring, storing, and retrieving information.**

Key Questions

- **What are encoding, storage, and retrieval?**
- **What is the stage model of memory?**
- **What are the nature and function of sensory memory?**

Like Elizabeth's memories of her uncle's home, memories can be vivid and evoke intense emotions. We can conjure up distinct memories that involve all our senses, including smells, sounds, and even tactile sensations. For example, close your eyes and try to recall the feeling of rain-soaked clothes against your skin, the smell of popcorn, and the sound of the half-time buzzer during a high school basketball game.

Memory refers to the mental processes that enable us to acquire, retain, and retrieve information. Rather than being a single process, memory involves three fundamental processes: *encoding, storage,* and *retrieval.*

Encoding refers to the process of transforming information into a form that can be entered and retained by the memory system. For example, to memorize the definition of a key term that appears on a text page, you would visually *encode* the patterns of lines and dots on the page as meaningful words that could be retained by your memory. **Storage** is the process of retaining information in memory so that it can be used at a later time. **Retrieval** involves recovering the stored information so that we are consciously aware of it.

Memories Can Involve All Your Senses Think back to a particularly memorable experience from your high school years. Can you conjure up vivid memories of smells, tastes, sounds, or emotions associated with that experience? In the years to come, these teenagers may remember many sensory details associated with this summer gathering at the lake.

The Stage Model of Memory

No single model has been shown to capture all aspects of human memory (Tulving, 2007). However, one very influential model, the **stage model of memory,** is useful in explaining the basic workings of memory. In this model, shown in Figure 6.1, memory involves three distinct stages: *sensory memory, short-term memory,* and *long-term memory* (Atkinson & Shiffrin, 1968; Shiffrin & Atkinson, 1969). The stage model is based on the idea that information is *transferred* from one memory stage to another.

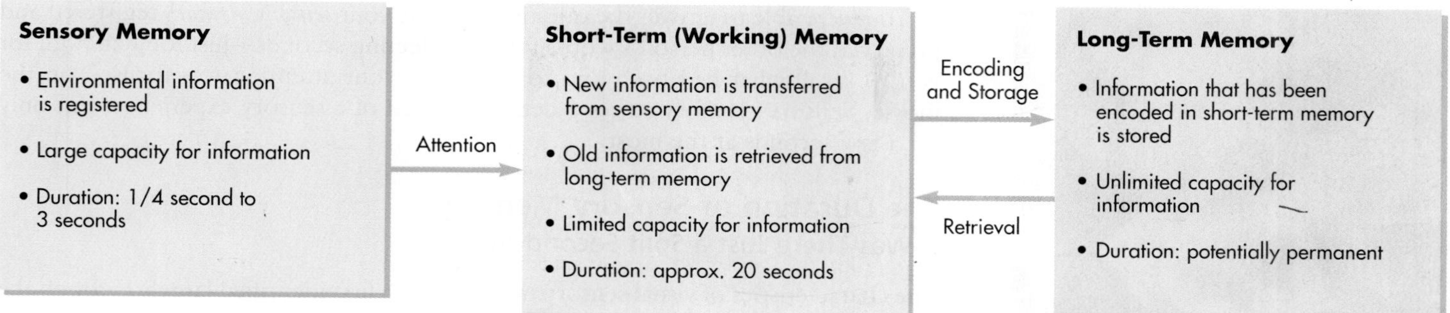

Figure 6.1 **Overview of the Stage Model of Memory**

The first stage of memory is called *sensory memory.* **Sensory memory** registers a great deal of information from the environment and holds it for a very brief period of time. After three seconds or less, the information fades. Think of your sensory memory as an internal camera that continuously takes "snapshots" of your surroundings. With each snapshot, you momentarily focus your attention on specific details. Almost instantly, the snapshot fades, only to be replaced by another.

During the very brief time the information is held in sensory memory, you "select," or pay *attention* to, just a few aspects of all the environmental information that's being registered. While studying, for example, you focus your attention on one page of your textbook, ignoring other environmental stimuli. The information you select from sensory memory is important, because this information is transferred to the second stage of memory, *short-term memory.*

Short-term memory refers to the active, working memory system. Your short-term memory temporarily holds all the information you are currently thinking about or consciously aware of. That information is stored briefly in short-term memory—for up to about 20 seconds. Because you use your short-term memory to actively process conscious information in a variety of ways, short-term memory is often referred to as *working memory* (Baddeley, 1995, 2007). Imagining, remembering, and problem solving all take place in short-term memory.

Over the course of any given day, vast amounts of information flow through your short-term memory. Most of this information quickly fades and is forgotten in a matter of seconds. However, some of the information that is actively processed in short-term memory may be encoded for storage in long-term memory.

Long-term memory, the third memory stage, represents what most people typically think of as memory—the long-term storage of information, potentially for a lifetime. It's important to note that the transfer of information between short-term and long-term memory goes two ways. Not only does information flow from short-term memory to long-term memory, but much information also flows in the other direction, from long-term memory to short-term memory.

If you think about it, this makes a great deal of sense. Consider a routine cognitive task, such as carrying on a conversation. Such tasks involve processing current sensory data and retrieving relevant stored information, such as the meaning of individual words. In the next few sections, we'll describe each of the stages of memory in more detail.

The Interaction of Memory Stages in Everyday Life Imagine driving on a busy street in pouring rain. How might each of your memory stages be involved in successfully navigating the wet streets? What kinds of information would be transferred from sensory memory and retrieved from long-term memory?

Sensory Memory

Fleeting Impressions of the World

Has something like this ever happened to you? You're engrossed in watching a suspenseful movie. From another room, a family member calls out, "Where'd you put the phone book?" You respond with, "What?" Then, a split second later, the question registers in your mind. Before the other person can repeat the question, you reply, "Oh. It's on the kitchen counter."

sensory memory
The stage of memory that registers information from the environment and holds it for a very brief period of time.

short-term memory
The active stage of memory in which information is stored for up to about 20 seconds.

long-term memory
The stage of memory that represents the long-term storage of information.

George Sperling Sperling carried out his research on the duration of sensory memory while still a graduate student at Harvard. Now at the University of California–Irvine, he continues to study perception, attention, and cognition.

You were able to answer the question because your *sensory memory* registered and preserved the other person's words for a few fleeting seconds—just long enough for you to recall what had been said to you while your attention was focused on the movie. Sensory memory stores a detailed record of a sensory experience, but only for a few seconds at the most.

The Duration of Sensory Memory

It Was There Just a Split Second Ago!

The characteristics of visual sensory memory were first identified largely through the research of psychologist **George Sperling** in 1960. In his experiment, Sperling flashed the images of 12 letters on a screen for one-twentieth of a second. The letters were arranged in four rows of 3 letters each. Subjects focused their attention on the screen and, immediately after the screen went blank, reported as many letters as they could remember.

On average, subjects could report only 4 or 5 of the 12 letters. However, several subjects claimed that they had actually seen *all* the letters but that the complete image had faded from their memory as they spoke, disappearing before they could verbally report more than 4 or 5 letters.

On the basis of this information, Sperling tried a simple variation on the original experiment (see Figure 6.2). He arranged the 12 letters in three rows of 4 letters each. Then, immediately *after* the screen went blank, he sounded a high-pitched, medium-pitched, or low-pitched tone. If the subjects heard the high-pitched tone, they were to report the letters in the top row; the medium-pitched tone signaled the middle row; and the low-pitched tone signaled the bottom row. If the subjects actually did see all the letters, Sperling reasoned, then they should be able to report the letters in a given row by focusing their attention on the indicated row *before* their visual sensory memory faded.

This is exactly what happened. If the tone followed the letter display in under one-third of a second, subjects could accurately report about 3 of the 4 letters in whichever row was indicated by the tone. However, if the interval between the screen going blank and the sound of the tone was more than one-third of a second, the accuracy of the reports decreased dramatically. By the time one second had elapsed, the image in the subject's visual sensory memory had already faded beyond recall.

Sperling's classic experiment demonstrated that our visual sensory memory holds a great deal of information very briefly, for about half a second. This information is available just long enough for us to pay attention to specific elements that are significant to us at that moment. This meaningful information is then transferred from the very brief storage of sensory memory to the somewhat longer storage of short-term memory.

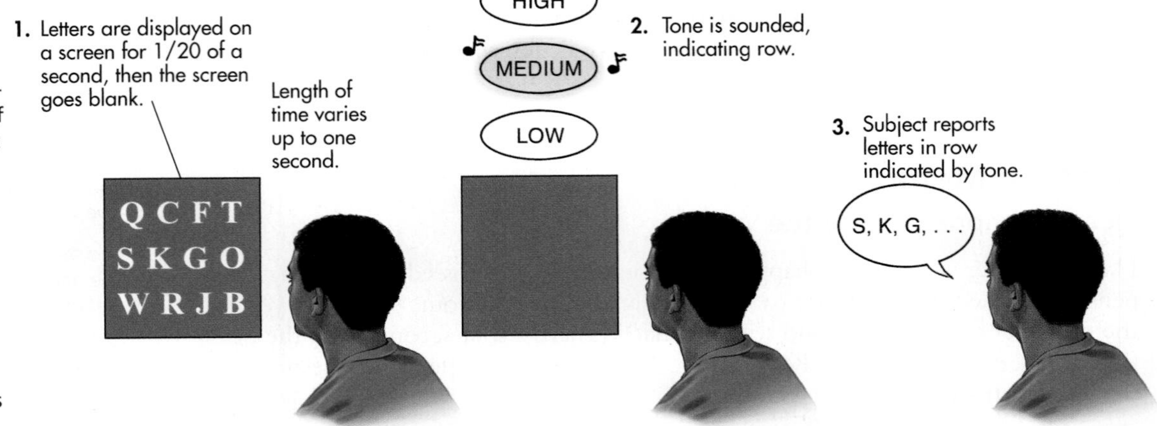

Figure 6.2 Sperling's Experiment Demonstrating the Duration of Sensory Memory In George Sperling's (1960) classic experiment, (1) subjects stared at a screen on which rows of letters were projected for just one-twentieth of a second, then the screen went blank. (2) After intervals varying up to one second, a tone was sounded that indicated the row of letters the subject should report. (3) If the tone was sounded within about one-third of a second, subjects were able to report the letters in the indicated row because the image of *all* the letters was still in sensory memory.

Types of Sensory Memory
Pick a Sense, Any Sense!

Perception and Sensory Memory Traces Because your visual sensory memory holds information for a fraction of a second before it fades, rapidly presented stimuli overlap and appear continuous. Thus, you perceive the separate blades of a rapidly spinning windmill as a smooth blur of motion. Similarly, you perceive a lightning bolt streaking across the sky as continuous even though it is actually three or more separate bolts of electricity.

Memory researchers believe there is a separate sensory memory for each sense—vision, hearing, touch, smell, and so on. Of the different senses, however, visual and auditory sensory memories have been the most thoroughly studied. *Visual sensory memory* is sometimes referred to as *iconic memory,* because it is the brief memory of an image, or *icon. Auditory sensory memory* is sometimes referred to as *echoic memory,* meaning a brief memory that is like an *echo.*

Researchers have found slight differences in the duration of sensory memory for visual and auditory information. Your visual sensory memory typically holds an image of your environment for about one-quarter to one-half second before it is replaced by yet another overlapping "snapshot." This is easy to demonstrate. Quickly wave a pencil back and forth in front of your face. Do you see the fading image of the pencil trailing behind it? That's your visual sensory memory at work. It momentarily holds the snapshot of the environmental image you see before it is almost instantly replaced by another overlapping image.

Your auditory sensory memory holds sound information a little longer, up to three or four seconds. This brief auditory sensory trace for sound allows you to hear speech as continuous words, or a series of musical notes as a melody, rather than as disjointed sounds. It also explains why you are able to "remember" something that you momentarily don't "hear," as in the example of the family member asking you where the phone book is.

An important function of sensory memory is to very briefly store sensory impressions so that they overlap slightly with one another. Thus, we perceive the world around us as continuous, rather than as a series of disconnected visual images or disjointed sounds.

Short-Term, Working Memory
The Workshop of Consciousness

Key Theme

- **Short-term memory provides temporary storage for information transferred from sensory and long-term memory.**

Key Questions

- **What are the duration and capacity of short-term memory?**
- **How can you overcome the limitations of short-term memory?**
- **What are the main components of Baddeley's model of working memory?**

You can think of *short-term memory,* or *working memory,* as the "workshop" of consciousness. It is the stage of memory in which information transferred from sensory memory *and* information retrieved from long-term memory become conscious. When you recall a past event or mentally add two numbers, the information is temporarily held and processed in your short-term memory. Your short-term memory also allows you to make sense out of this sentence by holding the beginning of the sentence in active memory while you read the rest of the sentence. Thus, short-term, working memory provides temporary storage for information that is currently being used in some conscious cognitive activity.

maintenance rehearsal
The mental or verbal repetition of information in order to maintain it beyond the usual 20-second duration of short-term memory.

chunking
Increasing the amount of information that can be held in short-term memory by grouping related items together into a single unit, or *chunk*.

The Duration of Short-Term Memory

Going, Going, Gone!

Information in short-term memory lasts longer than information in sensory memory, but its duration is still very short. Estimates vary, but generally you can hold most types of information in short-term memory up to about 20 seconds before it's forgotten (Peterson & Peterson, 1959). However, information can be maintained in short-term memory if it is *rehearsed,* or repeated, over and over. Because consciously rehearsing information will maintain it in short-term memory, this process is called **maintenance rehearsal.** For example, suppose that you decide to order a pizza for yourself and some friends. You look up the number in the phone book and mentally rehearse it until you can dial the phone.

Information that is *not* actively rehearsed is rapidly lost. Why? One possible explanation is that information that is not maintained by rehearsal simply fades away, or *decays,* with the passage of time. Another potential cause of forgetting in short-term memory is *interference* from new or competing information (Baddeley, 2002; Nairne, 2002). For example, if you are distracted by one of your friends asking you a question before you dial the pizza place, your memory of the phone number will quickly evaporate. Interference may also explain the irritating experience of forgetting someone's name just moments after you're introduced to him or her. If you engage the new acquaintance in conversation without rehearsing his or her name, the conversation may "bump" the person's name out of your short-term memory.

The Capacity of Short-Term Memory

So That's Why There Were Seven Dwarfs!

Demonstration of Short-Term Memory Capacity

Row 1 — 8 7 4 6
Row 2 — 3 4 9 6 2
Row 3 — 4 2 7 7 1 6
Row 4 — 5 1 4 0 8 1 3
Row 5 — 1 8 3 9 5 5 2 1
Row 6 — 2 1 4 9 7 5 2 4 8
Row 7 — 9 3 7 1 0 4 2 8 9 7
Row 8 — 7 1 9 0 4 2 6 0 4 1 8

Along with having a relatively short duration, short-term memory also has a relatively limited capacity. This is easy to demonstrate. Take a look at the numbers in the margin. If you've got a friend handy who's willing to serve as your research subject, simply read the numbers out loud, one row at a time, and ask your friend to repeat them back to you in the same order. Try to read the numbers at a steady rate, about one per second. Note each row that he correctly remembers.

How many numbers could your friend repeat accurately? Most likely, he could correctly repeat between five and nine numbers. That's what psychologist George Miller (1956) described as the limits of short-term memory in a classic paper titled "The Magical Number Seven, Plus or Minus Two." Miller believed that the capacity of short-term memory is limited to about seven items, or bits of information, at one time. It's no accident that local telephone numbers are seven digits long (Cowan & others, 2004).

So what happens when your short-term memory store is filled to capacity? New information *displaces,* or bumps out, currently held information. Maintenance rehearsal is one way to avoid the loss of information from short-term memory. By consciously repeating the information you want to remember, you keep it active in short-term memory and prevent it from being displaced by new information.

U A V F C I D B D S A I

Although the capacity of your short-term memory is limited, there are ways to increase the amount of information you can hold in short-term memory at any given moment. To illustrate this point, let's try another short-term memory demonstration. Read the sequence of letters in the margin, then close your eyes and try to repeat the letters out loud in the same order.

How many letters were you able to remember? Unless you have an exceptional short-term memory, you probably could not repeat the whole sequence correctly. Now try this sequence of letters: D V D F B I U S A C I A.

You probably managed the second sequence with no trouble at all, even though it is made up of exactly the same letters as the first sequence. The ease with which you handled the second sequence demonstrates **chunking**—the grouping of related items together into a single unit. The first letter sequence was perceived as 12 separate items and probably exceeded your short-term memory's capacity. But the second letter sequence was perceived as only four "chunks" of information, which you easily remembered: DVD, FBI, USA, and CIA. Thus, chunking can increase the amount of information held in short-term memory. But to do so, chunking also often involves the retrieval of meaningful information from *long-term memory,* such as the meaning of the initials FBI (Ericsson & Kintsch, 1995).

The basic principle of chunking is incorporated into many numbers that we need to remember. Long strings of identification numbers, such as Social Security numbers or credit card numbers, are usually broken up by hyphens so that you can chunk them easily.

Not every memory researcher accepts that short-term memory is limited to exactly seven items, plus or minus two. Over the half-century since the publication of Miller's classic article, researchers have challenged the seven-item limit (Jonides & others, 2008; Cowan & others, 2007). Current research suggests that the true "magical number" is more likely to be *four plus or minus one* than *seven plus or minus two* (Cowan & others, 2007; Saults & Cowan, 2007).

Cognitive psychologist Nelson Cowan (2001, 2005) believes that the type of stimuli used in many short-term memory tests has led researchers to overestimate its capacity. Typically, such memory tests use lists of letters, numbers, or words. According to Cowan, many people *automatically* chunk such stimuli to help them remember them. For example, even seemingly random numbers may be easily associated with a date, an address, or another familiar number sequence.

To overcome this tendency, Jeffrey Rouder and his colleagues (2008) used a simple visual stimulus instead of a sequence of numbers, letters, or words. The memory task? Remembering the position of colored squares on a computer screen. In this and similar studies, participants were able to hold only three or four items in their short-term memory at a time. Thus, many researchers today believe that the capacity of working memory is no more than about three to four items at a time when chunking is not an option (Saults & Cowan, 2007).

Whether the "magic number" is four or seven, the point remains: Short-term memory has a limited number of mental "slots" for information. Chunking can increase the amount of information held in each slot, but the number of slots is still limited.

working memory
The temporary storage and active, conscious manipulation of information needed for complex cognitive tasks, such as reasoning, learning, and problem solving.

From Short-Term Memory to Working Memory

Our discussion of the short-term memory store has so far focused on just one type of information—verbal or acoustic codes, that is, speechlike stimuli that we can mentally recite. Lists of numbers, letters, words, or other items fall into this category. However, if you think about it, we also use our short-term memory to temporarily store and manipulate other types of stimuli, such as visual images. For example, suppose you're out shopping with a close friend who asks you whether you think a particular chair will match her living room furniture. Before you respond, you need to call up and hold a mental image of her living room. You are surely using your short-term memory as you consider her question, but how?

In this example, you are actively processing information in a short-term memory system that is often referred to as working memory. Although the terms *working memory* and *short-term memory* are sometimes used interchangeably, **working memory** refers to the active, conscious manipulation of temporarily stored information. Working memory is what you're using when you engage in problem solving, reasoning, language comprehension, and mental comparisons. In contrast, short-term memory is more likely to be used when the focus is on simpler memory processes, such as rehearsing lists of syllables, words, or numbers.

The best-known model of working memory was developed by British psychologist Alan Baddeley. In Baddeley's (1992, 2007) model of working memory, there are three main components, each of which can function independently (see Figure 6.3 on the next page). One component, called the phonological loop, is specialized for verbal material, such as lists of numbers or words. This is the aspect of

"Did you ever start to do something and then forget what the heck it was?"

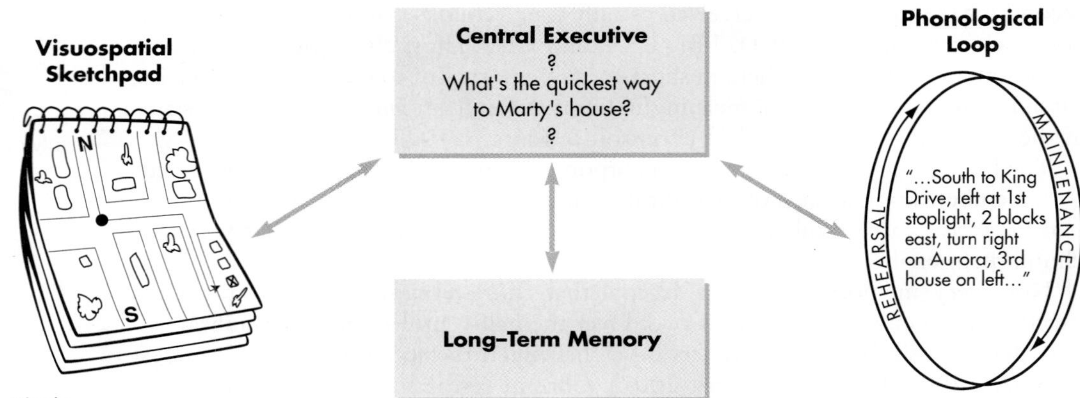

Figure 6.3 Baddeley's Model of Working Memory: How Do I Get to Marty's House? Suppose you are trying to figure out the fastest way to get to a friend's house. In Baddeley's model of working memory, you would use the *phonological loop* to verbally recite the directions. Maintenance rehearsal helps keep the information active in the phonological loop. You would use the *visuospatial sketchpad* to imagine your route and any landmarks along the way. The *central executive* is the conscious part of your mind, which actively processes and integrates information from the phonological loop, the visuospatial sketchpad, and long-term memory.

working memory that is often tested by standard memory tasks (Mueller & others, 2003). The second component, called the visuospatial sketchpad, is specialized for spatial or visual material, such as remembering the layout of a room or city.

The third component is what Baddeley calls the central executive, which controls attention, integrates information, and manages the activities of the phonological loop and the visuospatial sketchpad. The central executive also initiates retrieval and decision processes as necessary and integrates information coming into the system.

Long-Term Memory

Key Theme

- **Once encoded, an unlimited amount of information can be stored in long-term memory, which has different memory systems.**

Key Questions

- **What are ways to improve the effectiveness of encoding?**
- **How do procedural, episodic, and semantic memories differ, and what are implicit and explicit memory?**
- **How does the semantic network model explain the organization of long-term memory?**

Long-term memory refers to the storage of information over extended periods of time. Technically, any information stored longer than the roughly 20-second duration of short-term memory is considered to be stored in long-term memory. In terms of maximum duration, some long-term memories last a lifetime.

In contrast to the limited capacities of sensory and short-term memory, the amount of information that can be held in long-term memory is limitless. Granted, it doesn't always feel limitless, but consider this: Every day, you remember the directions to your college; the names of hundreds of friends, relatives, and acquaintances; and how to start your car. Retrieving information from long-term memory happens quickly and with little effort—most of the time.

Encoding Long-Term Memories

How does information get "into" long-term memory? One very important function that takes place in short-term memory is *encoding*, or transforming the new information into a form that can be retrieved later (see Figure 6.4). As a student, you may have tried to memorize dates, facts, or definitions by simply repeating them to yourself over and over. This strategy reflects an attempt to use maintenance rehearsal to encode material into long-term memory. However, maintenance rehearsal is *not* a very effective strategy for encoding information into long-term memory.

elaborative rehearsal
Rehearsal that involves focusing on the meaning of information to help encode and transfer it to long-term memory.

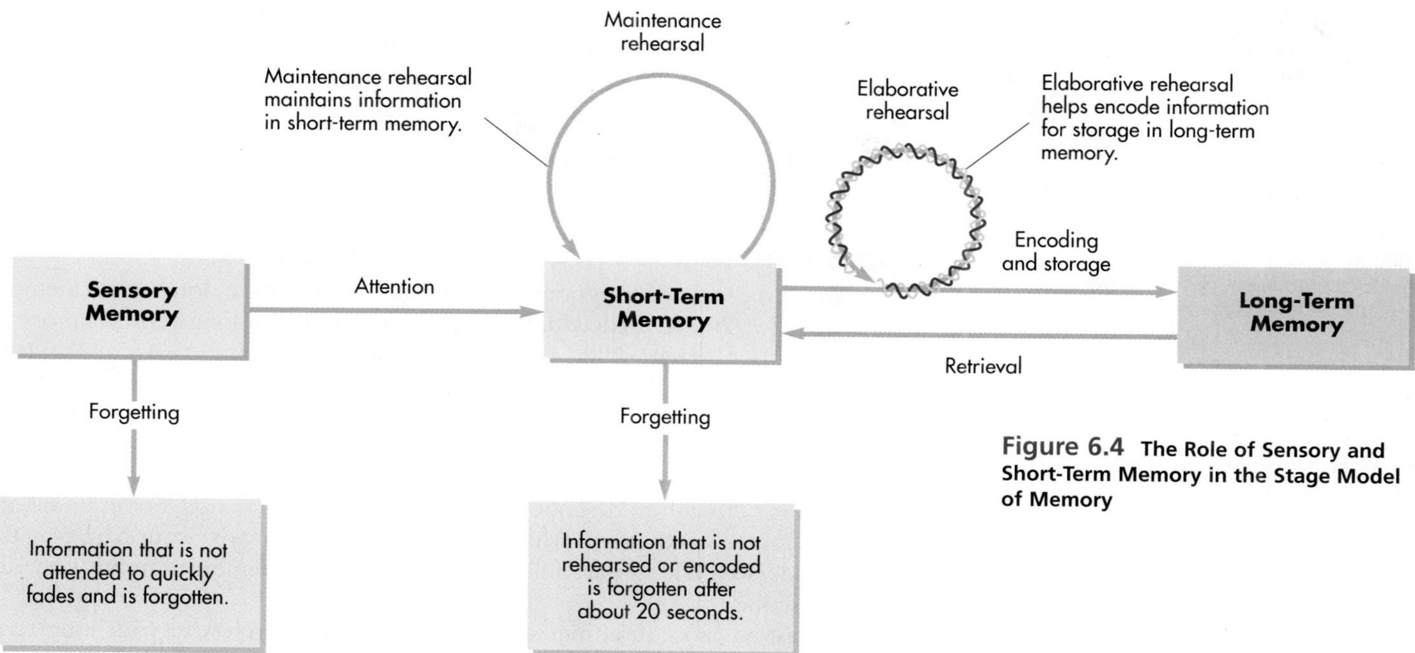

Figure 6.4 The Role of Sensory and Short-Term Memory in the Stage Model of Memory

A much more effective encoding strategy is **elaborative rehearsal,** which involves focusing on the *meaning* of information to help encode and transfer it to long-term memory. With elaborative rehearsal, you relate the information to other information you already know. That is, rather than simply repeating the information, you *elaborate* on the new information in some meaningful way.

Elaborative rehearsal significantly improves memory for new material. This point is especially important for students, because elaborative rehearsal is a helpful study strategy. Here's an example of how you might use elaborative rehearsal to improve your memory for new information. In Chapter 2 we discussed three brain structures that are part of the limbic system: the *hypothalamus,* the *hippocampus,* and the *amygdala.* If you tried to memorize the definitions of these structures by reciting them over and over to yourself, you engaged in the not-so-effective memory strategy of maintenance rehearsal.

But if you elaborated on the information in some meaningful way, you would be more likely to recall it. For example, you could think about the limbic system's involvement in emotions, memory, and motivation by constructing a simple story. "I knew it was lunchtime because my hypothalamus told me I was *h*ungry, *th*irsty, and cold. My hippocampus helped me remember a new restaurant that opened on *campus,* but when I got there I had to wait in line and my amygdala reacted with *a*nger." The story may be a bit silly, but many studies have shown that elaborative rehearsal leads to better retention (Lockhart & Craik, 1990).

Creating this simple story to help you remember the limbic system illustrates two additional factors that enhance encoding. First, applying information to yourself, called the *self-reference effect,* improves your memory for information. Second, the use of *visual imagery,* especially vivid images, also enhances encoding (Czienskowski & Giljohann, 2002; Paivio, 1995).

The fact that elaborative rehearsal results in more effective encoding and better memory of new information has many practical applications for students. As you study:

- Make sure you understand the new information by restating it in your own words.
- Actively question new information.
- Think about the potential applications and implications of the material.

"The matters about which I'm being questioned, Your Honor, are all things I should have included in my long-term memory but which I mistakenly inserted in my short-term memory."

procedural memory
Category of long-term memory that includes memories of different skills, operations, and actions.

episodic memory
Category of long-term memory that includes memories of particular events.

semantic memory
Category of long-term memory that includes memories of general knowledge, concepts, facts, and names.

- Relate the new material to information you already know, searching for connections that make the new information more meaningful.
- Generate your own examples of the concept, especially examples from your own experiences.

At the end of the chapter, in Enhancing Well-Being with Psychology, we'll give you more suggestions for strategies you can use to improve your memory.

Types of Information in Long-Term Memory

There are three major categories of information stored in long-term memory (Tulving, 1985, 2002). **Procedural memory** refers to the long-term memory of how to perform different skills, operations, and actions. Typing, riding a bike, running, and making scrambled eggs are all examples of procedural information stored in long-term memory. We begin forming procedural memories early in life when we learn to walk, talk, feed ourselves, and so on.

Often, we can't recall exactly when or how we learned procedural information. And usually it's difficult to describe procedural memories in words. For example, try to describe *precisely* and *exactly* what you do when you blow-dry your hair, play the guitar, or ride a bicycle. A particular skill may be easy to demonstrate but very difficult to describe.

In contrast to procedural memory, **episodic memory** refers to your long-term memory of specific events or episodes, including the time and place that they occurred (Tulving, 2002). Your memory of attending a friend's wedding or your first day at college would both be examples of episodic memories. Closely related to episodic memory is *autobiographical memory,* which refers to the events of your life—your personal life history (Nelson & Fivush, 2004). Autobiographical memory plays a key role in your sense of self. Does culture affect autobiographical memory? In the Culture and Human Behavior box, we examine the impact of culture on people's earliest memories.

Types of Information Stored in Long-Term Memory A memorable skateboard ride involves all three types of long-term memory. Remembering how to steer and balance on a skateboard are examples of *procedural memory.* Knowing the names of the different parts of a skateboard and the different kinds of skateboards available would be examples of *semantic memory.* And, if this young man forms a vivid memory of the day he rode his skateboard in a huge drainpipe, it will be an example of an *episodic memory.*

The third category of long-term memory is **semantic memory**—general knowledge that includes facts, names, definitions, concepts, and ideas. Semantic memory represents your personal encyclopedia of accumulated data and trivia stored in your long-term memory. Typically, you store semantic memories in long-term memory *without* remembering when or where you originally acquired the information. For example, can you remember when or where you learned that there are different time zones across the United States? Or when you learned that there are nine innings in a baseball game?

Implicit and Explicit Memory
Two Dimensions of Long-Term Memory

Studies with patients who have suffered different types of amnesia as a result of damage to particular brain areas have led memory researchers to recognize that long-term memory is *not* a simple, unitary system. Instead, long-term memory appears to be composed of separate but interacting subsystems and abilities (Slotnick & Schacter, 2007).

CULTURE AND HUMAN BEHAVIOR

Culture's Effects on Early Memories

For most adults, earliest memories are for events that occurred between the ages of 2 and 4. These early memories mark the beginning of autobiographical memory, which provides the basis for the development of an enduring sense of self (Howe, 2003). Do cultural differences in the sense of self influence the content of our earliest memories?

Comparing the earliest memories of European American college students and Taiwanese and Chinese college students, developmental psychologist Qi (pronounced "chee") Wang (2001, 2006) found a number of significant differences. First, the average age for earliest memory was much earlier for the U.S.-born students than for the Taiwanese and Chinese students.

Wang also found that the Americans' memories were more likely to be discrete, one-point-in-time events reflecting individual experiences or feelings, such as "I remember getting stung by a bee when I was 3 years old. I was scared and started crying." In contrast, the earliest memories of both the Chinese and Taiwanese students were of general, routine activities with family, schoolmates, or community members, such as playing in the park or eating with family members.

For Americans, Wang notes, the past is like a drama in which the self plays the lead role. Themes of self-awareness and individual autonomy were more common in the American students' memories, which tended to focus on their own experiences, emotions, and thoughts.

In contrast, Chinese students were more likely to include other people in their memories. Rather than focusing exclusively on their own behavior and thoughts, their earliest memories were typically brief accounts that centered on collective activities. For the Chinese students, the self is not easily separated from its social context.

Wang (2007, 2008) believes that cultural differences in autobiographical memory are formed in very early childhood, through interaction with family members. For example, *shared reminiscing*—the way that mothers talk to their children about their past experiences—differs in Eastern and Western cultures (Fivush & Nelson, 2004). When Asian mothers reminisce with their children, they tend to talk about group settings or situations, and to de-emphasize emotions, such as anger, that might separate the child from the group. In comparison, Western mothers tend to focus more on the child's individual activities, accomplishments, and emotional reactions. As Katherine Nelson and Robyn Fivush (2004) observe, such conversations about the personal past "provide children with information about how to be a 'self' in their culture."

Culture and Earliest Memories Psychologist Qi Wang (2001, 2006) found that the earliest memories of Chinese and Taiwanese adults tended to focus on routine activities that they shared with other members of their family or social group rather than individual events. Perhaps years from now, these children will remember walking with their preschool friends to play in the park.

What are these subsystems? One basic distinction that has been made is between *explicit memory* versus *implicit memory*. **Explicit memory** is *memory with awareness*—information or knowledge that can be consciously recollected, including episodic and semantic information. Thus, remembering what you did last New Year's Day or the topics discussed in your last psychology class are both examples of explicit memory. Explicit memories are also called *declarative memories,* because, if asked, you can "declare" the information.

In contrast, **implicit memory** is *memory without awareness*. Implicit memories cannot be consciously recollected, but they still affect your behavior, knowledge, or performance of some task. For example, let's assume that you are a pretty good typist. Imagine that we asked you to type the following phrase with your eyes closed: "most zebras cannot be extravagant." Easy, right? Now, without looking at a typewriter or computer keyboard, try reciting, from left to right, the seven letters of the alphabet that appear on the bottom row of a keyboard. Can you do it? Your authors are both expert typists, and neither one of us could do this. Chances are, you can't either. (In case you're wondering, the letters are *ZXCVBNM*.)

explicit memory
Information or knowledge that can be consciously recollected; also called *declarative memory.*

implicit memory
Information or knowledge that affects behavior or task performance but cannot be consciously recollected; also called *nondeclarative memory.*

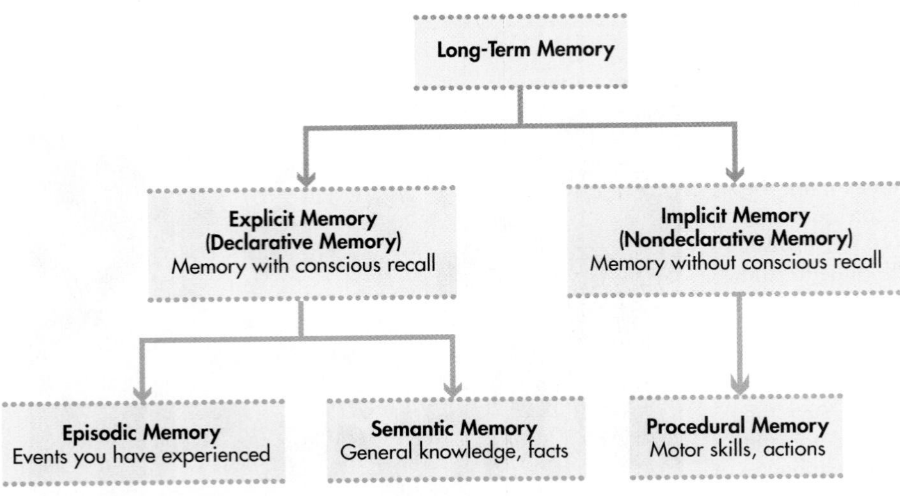

Figure 6.5 **Types of Long-Term Memory**

Here's the point: Your ability to type the phrase "most zebras cannot be extravagant" without looking demonstrates that you *do* know the location of the letters *Z, X, C, V, B, N,* and *M.* But your inability to recite that knowledge demonstrates that your memory of each key's location cannot be consciously recollected. Even though you're not consciously aware of the memory, it still affects your behavior. Implicit memories are also called *nondeclarative memories,* because you're unable to "declare" the information. Procedural memories, including skills and habits, typically reflect implicit memory processes. Figure 6.5 summarizes the different types of long-term memory.

Although much of the memory research covered in this chapter centers on explicit memory, psychologists and neuroscientists have become increasingly interested in implicit memory. As we'll see in a later section, there is growing evidence that implicit memory and explicit memory involve different brain regions (Thompson, 2005). Some memory theorists believe that implicit memory and explicit memory are two distinct memory systems (Kihlstrom & others, 2007; Tulving, 2002).

The Organization of Information in Long-Term Memory

Exactly how information is organized in long-term memory is not completely understood by memory researchers. Nonetheless, memory researchers know that information in long-term memory is *clustered* and *associated.*

Clustering means organizing items into related groups, or *clusters,* during recall. Before reading further, try the demonstration in Figure 6.6. Even though the words are presented in random order, you probably recalled groups of vehicles, fruits, and furniture. In other words, you organized the bits of information by clustering them into related categories.

chair	apple
boat	car
footstool	airplane
orange	lamp
pear	banana
peach	dresser
bed	sofa
bus	bookcase
train	truck
plum	table
grapes	strawberry
motorcycle	bicycle

Figure 6.6 **Clustering Demonstration** Study the words on this list for one minute. Then count backward by threes from 108 to 0. When you've completed that task, write down as many of the words from the list as you can remember.

Different bits and pieces of information in long-term memory are also logically linked, or associated. For example, what's the first word that comes to your mind in response to the word *red*? When we asked our students that same question, their top five responses were "blue," "apple," "color," "green," and "rose." Even if you didn't answer with one of the same associations, your response was based on some kind of logical association that you could explain if asked.

Memory researchers have developed several models to show how information is organized in long-term memory. One of the best-known models is called the **semantic network model** (Collins & Loftus, 1975). When one concept is activated in the semantic network, it can *spread* in any number of directions, *activating* other associations in the semantic network. For example, the word *red* might activate "blue" (another color), "apple" or "fire truck" (objects that are red), or "alert" (as in the phrase, "red alert"). In turn, these associations can activate other concepts in the network.

The semantic network model is a useful way of conceptualizing how information is organized in long-term memory. However, keep in mind that it is just a metaphor, not a physical structure in the brain. Nevertheless, the fact that information *is* organized in long-term memory has important implications for the retrieval process, as you'll see in the next section.

clustering
Organizing items into related groups during recall from long-term memory.

semantic network model
A model that describes units of information in long-term memory as being organized in a complex network of associations.

Retrieval

Getting Information from Long-Term Memory

Key Theme

- **Retrieval refers to the process of accessing and retrieving stored information in long-term memory.**

Key Questions

- **What are retrieval cues and how do they work?**
- **What do tip-of-the-tongue experiences tell us about the nature of memory?**
- **How is retrieval tested, and what is the serial position effect?**

So far, we've discussed some of the important factors that affect encoding and storing information in memory. In this section, we will consider factors that influence the retrieval process. Before you read any further, try the demonstration in Figure 6.7. After completing part (a) on this page, turn the page and try part (b). We'll refer to this demonstration throughout this section, so please take a shot at it. After you've completed both parts of the demonstration, continue reading.

Instructions: Spend 3 to 5 seconds reading each of the following sentences, and read through the list only once. As soon as you are finished, cover the list and write down as many of the sentences as you can remember (you need not write "can be used" each time). Please begin now.

A brick can be used as a doorstop.
A ladder can be used as a bookshelf.
A wine bottle can be used as a candleholder.
A pan can be used as a drum.
A fork can be used to comb hair.
A guitar can be used as a canoe paddle.
A leaf can be used as a bookmark.
An orange can be used to play catch.
A newspaper can be used to swat flies.
A T-shirt can be used as a coffee filter.
A sheet can be used as a sail.
A boat can be used as a shelter.
A bathtub can be used as a punch bowl.
A flashlight can be used to hold water.
A rock can be used as a paperweight.
A knife can be used to stir paint.
A pen can be used as an arrow.
A barrel can be used as a chair.
A rug can be used as a bedspread.
A CD can be used as a mirror.
A scissors can be used to cut grass.
A board can be used as a ruler.
A balloon can be used as a pillow.
A shoe can be used to pound nails.
A dime can be used as a screwdriver.
A lampshade can be used as a hat.

Now that you've recalled as many sentences as you can, turn to Figure 6.7(b) on the next page.

Figure 6.7(a) **Demonstration of Retrieval Cues**

Source: Adapted from Bransford & Stein (1993).

The Importance of Retrieval Cues

Retrieval refers to the process of accessing, or *retrieving,* stored information. There's a vast difference between what is stored in our long-term memory and what we can actually access. In many instances, our ability to retrieve stored memories hinges on having an appropriate retrieval cue. A **retrieval cue** is a clue, prompt, or hint that can help trigger recall of a stored memory. If your performance on the demonstration experiment in Figure 6.7 was like ours, the importance of retrieval cues should have been vividly illustrated.

Let's compare results. How did you do on the first part of the demonstration, in Figure 6.7(a)? Don initially remembered 12 pairs of items. Sandy blew Don out of the water on the first part—she remembered 19 pairs of items. Like us, you undoubtedly reached a point at which you were unable to remember any more pairs. At that point, you experienced **retrieval cue failure,** which refers to the inability to recall long-term memories because of inadequate or missing retrieval cues.

retrieval
The process of accessing stored information.

retrieval cue
A clue, prompt, or hint that helps trigger recall of a given piece of information stored in long-term memory.

retrieval cue failure
The inability to recall long-term memories because of inadequate or missing retrieval cues.

Figure 6.7(b) Demonstration of Retrieval Cues

Source: Adapted from Bransford & Stein (1993).

Instructions: *Do not* look back at the list of sentences in Figure 6.7(a). Use the following list as retrieval cues, and now write as many sentences as you can. Be sure to keep track of how many you can write down.

flashlight	lampshade
sheet	shoe
rock	guitar
CD	scissors
boat	leaf
dime	brick
wine bottle	knife
board	newspaper
pen	pan
balloon	barrel
ladder	rug
T-shirt	orange
fork	bathtub

Your authors both did much better on the demonstration in Figure 6.7(b), and you probably did, too. (Sandy got 24 of 26, and Don got 26 of 26 words, except that he remembered bedspread as blanket.) Why the improvement? In part (b) you were presented with retrieval cues that helped you access your stored memories.

This exercise demonstrates the difference between information that is *stored* in long-term memory versus the information that you can *access*. Many of the items on the list that you could not recall in part (a) were not forgotten. They were simply inaccessible—until you had a retrieval cue to help jog your memory. This exercise illustrates that many memories only *appear* to be forgotten. With the right retrieval cue, you can often access stored information that seemed to be completely unavailable.

Common Retrieval Glitches

The Tip-of-the-Tongue Experience

Quick—what was the name of the substance that could kill Superman? What was the name of Spiderman's uncle, who was killed in a robbery? If comic books aren't your thing, how about this question: Who wrote the words to "The Star-Spangled Banner"?

Did any of these questions leave you feeling as if you knew the answer but just couldn't quite recall it? If so, you experienced a common, and frustrating, form of retrieval failure, called the **tip-of-the-tongue (TOT) experience.** The TOT experience refers to the inability to get at a bit of information that you're absolutely certain is stored in your memory. Subjectively, it feels as though the information is very close, but just out of reach—or on the tip of your tongue (Schwartz, 2002).

A "Tip-of-the-Fingers" Experience American Sign Language (ASL) users sometimes have a "tip-of-the-fingers" experience when they are sure they know a sign but can't retrieve it. During a TOT experience, people are often able to remember the first letter or sound of the word they're struggling to remember. Similarly, ASL users tend to remember the hand shape, which appears as the signer begins to make the sign, rather than later parts of the sign, like the hand movement. For words that are finger-spelled, ASL users were more likely to recall the first letters than later letters (Thompson & others, 2005).

TOT experiences appear to be universal, and the "tongue" metaphor is used to describe the experience in many cultures (Schwartz, 1999). On average, people have about one TOT experience per week. Although people of all ages experience such word-finding memory glitches, TOT experiences tend to be more common among older adults than younger adults (Burke & Shafto, 2004; James & Burke, 2000).

When experiencing this sort of retrieval failure, people can almost always dredge up partial responses or related bits of information from their memory. About half the time, people can accurately identify the first letter of the target word and the number of syllables in it. They can also often produce words with similar meanings or sounds. While momentarily frustrating, about 90 percent of TOT experiences are eventually resolved, often within a few minutes.

Tip-of-the-tongue experiences illustrate that retrieving information is not an all-or-nothing process. Often, we remember bits and pieces of what we want to remember. In many instances, information is stored in memory, but not accessible without the right retrieval cues. TOT experiences also emphasize that information stored in memory is *organized* and connected in relatively logical ways. As you mentally struggle to retrieve the blocked information, logically connected bits of information are frequently triggered. In many instances, these related tidbits of information act as additional retrieval cues, helping you access the desired memory.

tip-of-the-tongue (TOT) experience
A memory phenomenon that involves the sensation of knowing that specific information is stored in long-term memory, but being temporarily unable to retrieve it.

recall
A test of long-term memory that involves retrieving information without the aid of retrieval cues; also called *free recall*.

cued recall
A test of long-term memory that involves remembering an item of information in response to a retrieval cue.

recognition
A test of long-term memory that involves identifying correct information out of several possible choices.

serial position effect
The tendency to remember items at the beginning and end of a list better than items in the middle.

Testing Retrieval

Recall, Cued Recall, and Recognition

The first part of the demonstration in Figure 6.7 illustrated the use of recall as a strategy to measure memory. **Recall,** also called *free recall,* involves producing information using no retrieval cues. This is the memory measure that's used on essay tests. Other than the essay questions themselves, an essay test provides no additional retrieval cues to help jog your memory.

The second part of the demonstration used a different memory measurement, called **cued recall.** Cued recall involves remembering an item of information in response to a retrieval cue. Fill-in-the-blank and matching questions are examples of cued-recall tests.

A third memory measurement is **recognition,** which involves identifying the correct information from several possible choices. Multiple-choice tests involve recognition as a measure of long-term memory. The multiple-choice question provides you with one correct answer and several wrong answers. If you have stored the information in your long-term memory, you should be able to recognize the correct answer.

Cued-recall and recognition tests are clearly to the student's advantage. Because these kinds of tests provide retrieval cues, the likelihood that you will be able to access stored information is increased.

The Serial Position Effect

Notice that the first part of the demonstration in Figure 6.7 did not ask you to recall the sentences in any particular order. Instead, the demonstration tested *free recall*—you could recall the items in any order. Take another look at your answers to Figure 6.7(a). Do you notice any sort of pattern to the items that you did recall?

Both your authors were least likely to recall items from the middle of the list. This pattern of responses is called the **serial position effect,** which refers to the tendency to retrieve information more easily from the beginning and the end of a list rather than from the middle. There are two parts to the serial position effect. The tendency to recall the first items in a list is called the *primacy effect,* and the tendency to recall the final items in a list is called the *recency effect.*

The primacy effect is especially prominent when you have to engage in *serial recall,* that is, when you need to remember a list of items in their original order. Remembering speeches, telephone numbers, and directions are a few examples of serial recall.

A Demonstration of the Serial Position Effect Without singing them, try to recite the words of "The Star-Spangled Banner." If you're like most people, you'll correctly remember the words at the beginning and the end of "The Star-Spangled Banner" but have difficulty recalling the words and phrases in the middle—the essence of the serial position effect.

encoding specificity principle
The principle that when the conditions of information retrieval are similar to the conditions of information encoding, retrieval is more likely to be successful.

context effect
The tendency to recover information more easily when the retrieval occurs in the same setting as the original learning of the information.

mood congruence
An encoding specificity phenomenon in which a given mood tends to evoke memories that are consistent with that mood.

flashbulb memory
The recall of very specific images or details surrounding a vivid, rare, or significant personal event; details may or may not be accurate.

The Encoding Specificity Principle

Key Theme

- **According to the encoding specificity principle, re-creating the original learning conditions makes retrieval easier.**

Key Questions

- **How can context and mood affect retrieval?**
- **What role does distinctiveness play in retrieval, and how accurate are flashbulb memories?**

One of the best ways to increase access to information in memory is to re-create the original learning conditions. This simple idea is formally called the **encoding specificity principle** (Tulving, 1983). As a general rule, the more closely retrieval cues match the original learning conditions, the more likely it is that retrieval will occur.

For example, have you ever had trouble remembering some bit of information during a test but immediately recalled it as you entered the library where you normally study? When you intentionally try to remember some bit of information, such as the definition of a term, you often encode much more into memory than just that isolated bit of information. As you study in the library, at some level you're aware of all kinds of environmental cues. These cues might include the sights, sounds, and aromas within that particular situation. *The environmental cues in a particular context can become encoded as part of the unique memories you form while in that context.* These same environmental cues can act as retrieval cues to help you access the memories formed in that context.

This particular form of encoding specificity is called the context effect. The **context effect** is the tendency to remember information more easily when the retrieval occurs in the same setting in which you originally learned the information. Thus, the environmental cues in the library where you normally study act as additional retrieval cues that help jog your memory. Of course, it's too late to help your test score, but the memory *was* there.

A different form of encoding specificity is called **mood congruence**—the idea that a given mood tends to evoke memories that are consistent with that mood. In other words, a specific emotional state can act as a retrieval cue that evokes memories of events involving the same emotion. So, when you're in a positive mood, you're more likely to recall positive memories. When you're feeling blue, you're more likely to recall negative or unpleasant memories.

Flashbulb Memories? Can you remember where you were when you heard about the terrorist attacks on the World Trade Center and the Pentagon? The Oklahoma City bombing? Shocking national events can supposedly trigger highly accurate, long-term flashbulb memories. Meaningful personal events, such as your high school graduation or wedding day, can also produce vivid flashbulb memories.

Flashbulb Memories

Vivid Events, Accurate Memories?

If you rummage around your own memories, you'll quickly discover that highly unusual, surprising, or even bizarre experiences are easier to retrieve from memory than are routine events (Pillemer, 1998). Such memories are said to be characterized by a high degree of *distinctiveness.* That is, the encoded information represents a unique, different, or unusual memory.

Various events can create vivid, distinctive, and long-lasting memories that are sometimes referred to as *flashbulb memories* (Brown & Kulik, 1982). Just as a camera flash captures the specific details of a scene, a **flashbulb memory** is thought to involve the recall of very specific details or images surrounding a significant, rare, or vivid event.

Do flashbulb memories literally capture specific details, like the details of a photograph, that are unaffected by the passage of time? Emotionally charged national events have provided a unique opportunity to study flashbulb memories. On September 12, 2001, psychologists Jennifer Talarico and David Rubin (2003, 2007) had Duke University students complete questionnaires about the terrorist attacks on the United States that had occurred the previous day. The students were asked such questions as: "Where were you when you first heard the news?" "Were there others present, and if so, who?" "What were you doing immediately before you first heard the news?" For comparison, the students also described some ordinary, everyday event that had occurred in their lives at about the same time, such as attending a sporting event or party.

Students were randomly assigned to a follow-up session either 1 week, 6 weeks, or 32 weeks later. At the follow-up sessions, they were asked to describe their memories of the ordinary event as well as their memory of the 9/11 attacks. They were also asked to evaluate the accuracy and vividness of their memories. Then, the researchers compared these accounts to their reports on September 12, 2001. All of the students were tested again in late August 2002—almost a full year after the attacks.

How did the flashbulb memories compare to the ordinary memories? Were the flashbulb memories more likely to be preserved unchanged over time? Not at all. Both the flashbulb and everyday memories gradually decayed over time: The number of consistent details *decreased* and the number of inconsistent details *increased*. However, when the students rated the memory's vividness, their ability to recall the memory, and their belief in the memory's accuracy, only the ratings for the ordinary memory declined. In other words, despite having the same level of inconsistencies as the ordinary memories, the students *perceived* their flashbulb memories of 9/11 as being vivid and accurate.

Although flashbulb memories can seem incredibly vivid, they appear to function just as normal, everyday memories do. We remember some details, forget some details, and think we remember some details (Curci & others, 2001; Squire & others, 2001). What does seem to distinguish flashbulb memories from ordinary memories is the high degree of confidence the person has in the accuracy of these memories. But clearly, confidence in a memory is *no* guarantee of accuracy. We'll come back to that important point shortly.

Flashbulb memories are not immune to forgetting, nor are they uncommonly consistent over time. Instead, exaggerated belief in memory's accuracy at long delays is what may have led to the conviction that flashbulb memories are more accurate than everyday memories.

JENNIFER TALARICO AND DAVID RUBIN (2003)

Memories of Traumatic Events If you are like most Americans, you have vivid memories of watching media coverage of the terrorist attacks on September 11, 2001. Although such "flashbulb" memories are emotionally charged, they are not necessarily more accurate than memories of more common events (Talarico & Rubin, 2007).

Forgetting

When Retrieval Fails

Key Theme

- **Forgetting is the inability to retrieve information that was once available.**

Key Questions

- **What discoveries were made by Hermann Ebbinghaus?**
- **How do encoding failure, interference, and decay contribute to forgetting, and how can prospective memory be improved?**
- **What is repression and why is the topic controversial?**

Forgetting is so common that life is filled with reminders to safeguard against forgetting important information. Cars are equipped with beeping tones so you don't forget to fasten your seatbelt or turn off your headlights. Dentists thoughtfully send brightly colored postcards and call you the day before so that your scheduled appointment doesn't slip your mind.

Although forgetting can be annoying, it does have adaptive value. Our minds would be cluttered with mountains of useless information if we remembered the name of every person we'd ever met, or every word of every conversation we'd ever had (Kuhl & others, 2007).

Psychologists define **forgetting** as the inability to remember information that was previously available. Note that this definition does not refer to the "loss" or "absence" of once-remembered information. While it's tempting to think of forgetting as simply the gradual loss of information from long-term memory over time, you'll see that this intuitively compelling view of forgetting is much too simplistic. And although psychologists have identified several factors that are involved in forgetting, exactly how—and why—forgetting occurs is still being actively researched (Dudai, 2004; Wixted, 2004).

Hermann Ebbinghaus (1850–1909) After earning his Ph.D. in philosophy in 1873, Ebbinghaus worked as a private tutor for several years. It was during this time that he conducted his famous research on the memory of nonsense syllables. In 1885, he published his results in *Memory: A Contribution to Experimental Psychology.* In that text, Ebbinghaus observed, "Left to itself, every mental content gradually loses its capacity for being revived. Facts crammed at examination time soon vanish, if they were not sufficiently grounded by other study and later subjected to a sufficient review." Among his other notable contributions, he developed an early intelligence test, called the *Ebbinghaus Completion Test* (Lander, 1997).

Hermann Ebbinghaus

The Forgetting Curve

German psychologist **Hermann Ebbinghaus** began the scientific study of forgetting in the 1870s. Because there was a seven-year gap between obtaining his doctorate and his first university teaching position, Ebbinghaus couldn't use university students for experimental subjects (Fancher, 1996). So to study forgetting, Ebbinghaus had to rely on the only available research subject: himself.

Ebbinghaus's goal was to determine how much information was forgotten after different lengths of time. But he wanted to make sure that he was studying the memory and forgetting of completely new material, rather than information that had preexisting associations in his memory. To solve this problem, Ebbinghaus (1885) created new material to memorize: thousands of nonsense syllables. A ***nonsense syllable*** is a three-letter combination, made up of two consonants and a vowel, such as WIB or MEP. It almost sounds like a word, but it is meaningless.

Ebbinghaus carefully noted how many times he had to repeat a list of 13 nonsense syllables before he could recall the list perfectly. To give you a feeling for this task, here's a typical list:

ROH, LEZ, SUW, QOV, XAR, KUF, WEP,
BIW, CUL, TIX, QAP, WEJ, ZOD

Once he had learned the nonsense syllables, Ebbinghaus tested his recall of them after varying amounts of time, ranging from 20 minutes to 31 days. He plotted his results in the now-famous Ebbinghaus *forgetting curve,* shown in Figure 6.8.

The Ebbinghaus forgetting curve reveals two distinct patterns in the relationship between forgetting and the passage of time. First, much of what we forget is lost relatively soon after we originally learned it. How quickly we forget material depends on several factors, such as how well the material was encoded in the first place, how meaningful the material was, and how often it was rehearsed.

In general, if you learn something in a matter of minutes on just one occasion, most forgetting will occur very soon after the original learning—also in a matter of minutes. However, if you spend many sessions over days or weeks encoding new information into memory, the period of most rapid forgetting will be the first several weeks or months after such learning.

Second, the Ebbinghaus forgetting curve shows that the amount of forgetting eventually levels off. As you can see in Figure 6.8, there's very little difference between how much Ebbinghaus forgot eight hours later and a month later. The information that is *not* quickly forgotten seems to be remarkably stable in memory over long periods of time.

forgetting
The inability to recall information that was previously available.

encoding failure
The inability to recall specific information because of insufficient encoding of the information for storage in long-term memory.

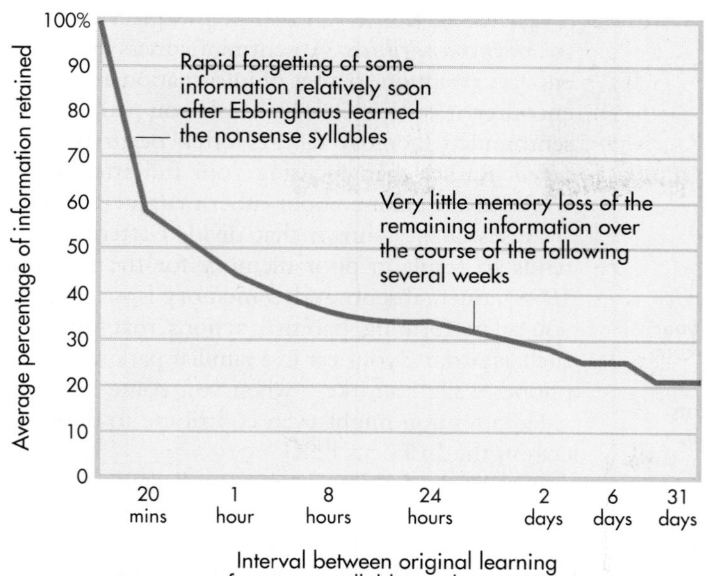

Figure 6.8 **The Ebbinghaus Forgetting Curve** Ebbinghaus's research demonstrated the basic pattern of forgetting: relatively rapid loss of some information, followed by stable memories of the remaining information.

Source: Adapted from Ebbinghaus (1885).

Why Do We Forget?

Ebbinghaus was a pioneer in the study of memory. His major contribution was to identify the basic pattern of forgetting: rapid forgetting of some information relatively soon after the original learning, followed by stability of the memories that remain. But what causes forgetting? Psychologists have identified several factors that contribute to forgetting, including encoding failure, decay, interference, and motivated forgetting.

Encoding Failure

It Never Got to Long-Term Memory

Without rummaging through your loose change, take a look at Figure 6.9. Circle the drawing that accurately depicts the face of a U.S. penny. Now, check your answer against a real penny. Were you correct?

When this task was presented to participants in one study, fewer than half of them picked the correct drawing (Nickerson & Adams, 1982). The explanation? Unless you're a coin collector, you've probably never looked carefully at a penny. Even though you may have handled thousands of pennies, chances are that you've encoded only the most superficial characteristics of a penny—its size, color, and texture—into your long-term memory.

In a follow-up study, William Marmie and Alice Healy (2004) allowed participants to study an unfamiliar coin for short periods of time, ranging from 15 seconds to 60 seconds. Even with only 15 seconds devoted to focusing on the coin's appearance, participants were better able to remember the details of the *unfamiliar* coin than the all-too-familiar penny. In effect, Marmie and Healy (2004) confirmed that lack of attention at the time of encoding was responsible for the failure to accurately remember the appearance of a penny.

As these simple demonstrations illustrate, one of the most common reasons for forgetting is called **encoding failure**—we never encoded the information into long-term memory in the first place. Encoding failure explains why you forget a person's name two minutes after being introduced to her: The information was momentarily present in your short-term memory, but was never encoded into long-term memory.

Figure 6.9 **Test for Memory of Details of a Common Object** Which of these drawings is an accurate picture of a real penny?

Table 6.1

Eight Suggestions for Avoiding Prospective Memory Failure

1. Be proactive! Create a reminder the instant you realize that you need to do something in the future.
2. Make reminder cues DISTINCTIVE and make sure that they tell you *what* you are supposed to remember to do.
3. Make reminder cues **obvious** by posting them where you will definitely see them, such as on your mirror, front or back door, rearview car mirror, computer monitor, and so on.
4. Put a notepad or Post-it notes and a pencil in lots of convenient places (e.g., your dresser, your car, the kitchen counter, etc.).
5. For things you need to remember to do in the next few hours, buy small battery-operated kitchen timers. (Yes, it's true. We have seven timers scattered throughout our home offices.)
6. Leave yourself a voicemail message with the reminder at home or at work.
7. Use the calendar reminder and follow-up features on your computer or use a free Internet reminder service (e.g., www.memotome.com).
8. iPhone fans, check out reminder apps. Mac people, check out reminder widgets. PC people, download free reminder software, such as the classic 3M Post-it Notes Lite software.

Encoding failure can also help explain everyday memory failures due to *absentmindedness*. Absentmindedness occurs because you don't pay enough attention to a bit of information at the time when you should be encoding it, such as in which aisle you parked your car at the airport. Absentminded memory failures often occur because your attention is *divided*. Rather than focusing your full attention on what you're doing, you're also thinking about other matters (Schacter, 2001).

Research has shown that divided attention at the time of encoding tends to result in poor memory for the information (Craik & others, 1996). Such absentminded memory lapses are especially common when you're performing habitual actions that don't require much thought, such as parking your car in a familiar parking lot or setting down your cell phone, wallet, and keys when you come home. In some situations, divided attention might even contribute to déjà vu experiences, as we discuss in the In Focus box.

Absentmindedness is also implicated in another annoying memory problem—forgetting to do something in the future, such as returning a library book or taking a medication on schedule. Remembering to do something in the future is called **prospective memory.** In contrast to other types of memories, the crucial component of a prospective memory is *when* something needs to be remembered, rather than *what*.

Rather than encoding failure, prospective memory failures are due to *retrieval cue failure*—the inability to recall a memory because of missing or inadequate retrieval cues. For example, you forget to mail your credit card payment on time and incur a late fee. The problem with this sort of scenario is that there is no strong, distinctive retrieval cue embedded in the situation. This is why ovens are equipped with timers that buzz and why your authors' kitchen calendar looks like a multicolored Post-it notes decoupage. Such strategies provide distinctive retrieval cues that will (hopefully) trigger those prospective memories at the appropriate moment. Table 6.1 lists additional suggestions to help minimize prospective memory failures.

Decay Theory
Fading with the Passage of Time

According to **decay theory** we forget memories because we don't use them and they fade away over time as a matter of normal brain processes. The idea is that when a new memory is formed, it creates a *memory trace*—a distinct structural or chemical change in the brain. Over time, the normal metabolic processes of the brain are thought to erode the memory trace, especially if it is not "refreshed" by frequent rehearsal. The gradual fading of memories, then, would be similar to the fading of letters on billboards or newsprint exposed to environmental elements, such as sunlight.

Although decay theory makes sense intuitively, too much evidence contradicts it (Jonides & others, 2008). Look again at the Ebbinghaus forgetting curve on page 249. If memories simply faded over time, you would expect to see a steady decline in the amount of information remembered with the passage of time. Instead, once the information held in memory stabilizes, it changes very little over time. In other words, the rate of forgetting actually *decreases* over time (Wixted, 2004).

Beyond that point, many studies have shown that information can be remembered decades after it was originally learned, even though it has not been rehearsed or recalled since the original memory was formed (Bahrick & Hall, 1991; Bahrick & Phelps, 1987). As we discussed earlier, the ability to access memories is strongly influenced by the kinds of retrieval cues provided when memory is tested. If the memory trace simply decayed over time, the presentation of potent retrieval cues should have no effect on the retrieval of information or events experienced long ago—but they do!

prospective memory
Remembering to do something in the future.

decay theory
The view that forgetting is due to normal metabolic processes that occur in the brain over time.

IN FOCUS

Déjà Vu Experiences: An Illusion of Memory?

The term *déjà vu* is French for "already seen." A **déjà vu experience** involves brief but intense feelings of familiarity in a situation that has not been previously experienced. Or, in some instances, you have this intense, even eerie, feeling of having experienced the exact situation before as it is happening to you but you're not able to recall precisely when or where. Psychology's interest in déjà vu extends back to the late 1800s when the famous American psychologist William James (1890, 1902) wrote about these experiences.

Déjà Vu Characteristics

Déjà vu experiences are common. Psychologist Alan Brown (2004) analyzed the results of more than 30 surveys and found that about two-thirds of individuals (68 percent) reported having had one or more déjà vu experiences in their life. He also found that the incidence of déjà vu experiences changes over the lifespan. Young adults in the 20–24 age range tend to have the most frequent occurrences, averaging three déjà vu experiences per year. For about 1 out of 6 people (16 percent), déjà vu experiences happen about once a month. But by the time people reach the threshold of middle adulthood in their early 40s, déjà vu experiences have dwindled to less than one per year.

Although typically triggered by a visual scene, déjà vu experiences can involve all of the senses. For example, blind people can also experience déjà vu (O'Connor & Moulin, 2006). The experiences are most common when people are feeling fatigued or emotionally distressed. They usually occur in the evening hours and in the company of other people. Interestingly, there is a higher incidence of déjà vu experiences in people who are well-educated, travel frequently, often watch movies, and regularly remember their dreams (Brown, 2003; Cleary, 2008). We'll come back to that last point shortly.

Because déjà vu experiences are often described as being a weird sensation, some people immediately assume that the experience must have been an instance of clairvoyance, telepathy, or some other paranormal experience. But rather than paranormal explanations, contemporary psychologists believe that déjà vu can provide insights about basic memory processes (see Cleary, 2008; Cleary & Specker, 2007).

Explaining Déjà Vu

The déjà vu experience typically involves the brief, intense, and eerie feeling of familiarity in a situation you're certain you've *never* experienced before. For example, let's suppose that you have an intense déjà vu experience as you arrive to stand in line to enter Chicago's Shedd Aquarium. You *know* you've never visited the Shedd Aquarium before, so there is *no* memory source you can identify for the intense feeling of recognition.

Psychologist Anne Cleary (2008) believes this sense of familiarity suddenly arises when enough features in the current situation trigger the sensation of matching features already contained in a previous memory. But even though you intuitively sense and recognize the memory as familiar, you can't pinpoint a *source* for that familiarity. This is what memory researchers refer to as a disruption in **source memory** or **source monitoring**—your ability to remember the original details or features of a memory, including when, where, and how you acquired the information or had the experience.

Most likely, your déjà vu experience was due to *source amnesia:* You have *indirectly* experienced this scene or situation before but you've forgotten the memory's source. And what might that indirect but forgotten memory source be? Earlier we noted that people who are well-educated, travel a lot, often watch movies, and remember their dreams are more prone to déjà vu experiences (see Brown, 2004; Cleary, 2008). Any one of those factors is a potential gold mine of memory retrieval clue fragments that can match elements of the current scene, triggering a sense of familiarity. Other sources might be magazine photos, Web sites, or travel brochures. Of course, had you immediately recalled the previous source from a little over two years ago—a Discovery Channel show you watched that featured lots of scenes at Chicago's Shedd Aquarium—you probably wouldn't have had a déjà vu experience.

Another memory explanation for déjà vu involves a form of *encoding failure* called *inattentional blindness*. According to the inattentional blindness explanation, déjà vu can be produced when you're not really paying attention to your surroundings (Brown, 2005). So, suppose you're oblivious (or blind) to your surroundings while chatting on your cell phone as you wait in line to enter the Shedd Aquarium. As the call ends and you're still thinking about the conversation, you glance up at the entrance to the Shedd Aquarium and bang! A *déjà vu experience!*

In this case, the feeling that you have been there before is due to the fact that you really *have* been there before—a split second ago. While talking on your cell phone, you were nonconsciously processing information about your surroundings. But when you ended the call, and, a split second later, you shifted your attention, your surroundings were suddenly—and inexplicably—consciously perceived as familiar.

A different possible explanation comes from the brain itself. Neurological evidence suggests that at least some instances of déjà vu are related to brain dysfunction. In particular, it has long been known that déjà vu experiences can be triggered by temporal lobe disruptions (see Milner, 1954; Zeman, 2005). For many people with epilepsy, the seizures often originate in the temporal lobe. In these people, a déjà vu experience sometimes occurs just prior to a seizure (Lytton, 2008).

For most people, however, déjà vu experiences probably involve the common memory processes of *source amnesia* and *inattentional blindness*. To learn about other scientific explanations for déjà vu, check out Alan Brown's (2004) scholarly compilation of the research in his book *The Déjà Vu Experience*.

déjà vu experience
A memory illusion characterized by brief but intense feelings of familiarity in a situation that has never been experienced before.

source memory or **source monitoring**
Memory for when, where, and how a particular experience or piece of information was acquired.

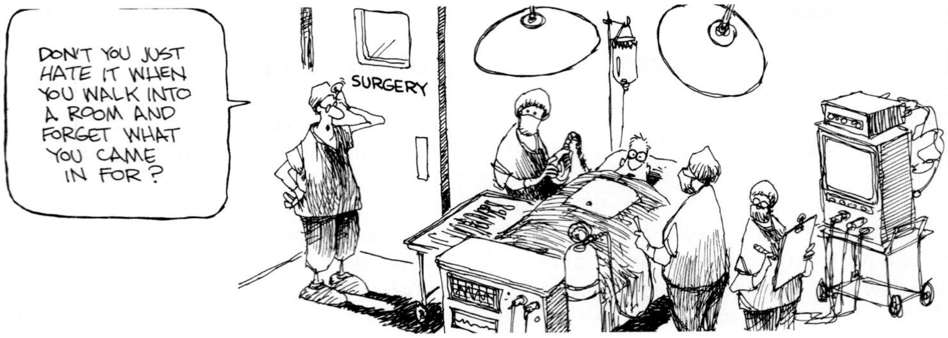

So have contemporary memory researchers abandoned decay theory as an explanation of forgetting? Not completely. Although decay is not regarded as the primary cause of forgetting, many of today's memory researchers believe that it contributes to forgetting (Altmann & Gray, 2002; Portrat & others, 2008; Schacter, 2001).

Interference Theory

Memories Interfering with Memories

According to the **interference theory** of forgetting, forgetting is caused by one memory competing with or replacing another memory. The most critical factor is the similarity of the information. The more similar the information is in two memories, the more likely it is that interference will be produced.

There are two basic types of interference. **Retroactive interference** is backward-acting memory interference. It occurs when a *new* memory (the combination for the new lock you just bought for your bicycle) interferes with remembering an *old* memory (the combination for the lock you've been using at the gym).

Proactive interference is forward-acting memory interference. It occurs when an *old* memory (your previous zip code) interferes with remembering a *new* memory (your new zip code). A rather embarrassing example of proactive interference occurs when someone uses the name of his or her previous partner in referring to a current partner. Such spontaneous memory glitches can occur in the rapid-fire verbal exchange of a heated argument or in the thralls of passion (hopefully not both).

Motivated Forgetting

Forgetting Unpleasant Memories

Motivated forgetting refers to the idea that we forget because we are motivated to forget, usually because a memory is unpleasant or disturbing. One form of motivated forgetting, called **suppression,** involves the deliberate, conscious effort to forget information. For example, after seeing a disturbing report of a horrendous crime or massacre on the evening news, you consciously avoid thinking about it, turning your attention to other matters. According to some researchers, over time and with repeated effort, pushing an unwanted memory out of awareness may make the memory less accessible (M.C. Anderson & others, 2004; Levy & Anderson, 2002).

Another form of motivated forgetting is fundamentally different and much more controversial. **Repression** is motivated forgetting that occurs unconsciously (Wilson & Dunn, 2004). With repression, all memory of a distressing event or experience is blocked from conscious awareness.

As we'll discuss in greater detail in Chapters 10 (Personality) and 14 (Therapies), the idea of repression is a cornerstone of *psychoanalysis,* Sigmund Freud's famous theory of personality and psychotherapy. Freud (1904) believed that psychologically threatening emotions, feelings, conflicts, and urges, especially those that originated in early childhood, become repressed. Even though they are blocked and unavailable to consciousness, the repressed conflicts continue to unconsciously influence the person's behavior, thoughts, and personality, often in maladaptive or unhealthy ways.

interference theory
The theory that forgetting is caused by one memory competing with or replacing another.

retroactive interference
Forgetting in which a new memory interferes with remembering an old memory; backward-acting memory interference.

proactive interference
Forgetting in which an old memory interferes with remembering a new memory; forward-acting memory interference.

suppression
Motivated forgetting that occurs consciously; a deliberate attempt to not think about and remember specific information.

repression
Motivated forgetting that occurs unconsciously; a memory that is blocked and unavailable to consciousness.

Among clinical psychologists who work with psychologically troubled people, the notion that behavior can be influenced by repressed memories is widely, but certainly not universally, accepted (Gleaves & others, 2004). Among the general public, many people believe that we are capable of repressing memories of unpleasant events (Loftus & others, 1994). However, trying to scientifically confirm and study the influence of memories that a person does not remember is tricky, if not impossible.

One obvious problem is determining whether a memory has been "repressed" or simply forgotten. For example, several studies have found that people are better able to remember positive life experiences than negative life experiences (Lindsay & others, 2004). Is that because unhappy experiences have been "repressed"? Or is it simply that people are less likely to think about, talk about, dwell on, or rehearse unhappy memories?

Among psychologists, repression is an extremely controversial topic (Kihlstrom, 2004; McNally, 2004). At one extreme are those who believe that true repression *never* occurs (Holmes, 1990). At the other extreme are those who are convinced that repressed memories are at the root of many psychological problems, particularly repressed memories of childhood sexual abuse (Briere & Conte, 1993; Gleaves & others, 2004). This latter contention gave rise to a form of psychotherapy involving the recovery of repressed memories. Later in the chapter, we'll explore this controversy in the Critical Thinking box, "The Memory Wars: Recovered or False Memories?"

Imperfect Memories

Errors, Distortions, and False Memories

Key Theme

- **Memories can be easily distorted so that they contain inaccuracies. Confidence in a memory is no guarantee that the memory is accurate.**

Key Questions

- **What is the misinformation effect?**
- **What is source confusion, and how can it distort memories?**
- **What are schemas and scripts, and how can they contribute to memory distortions?**

Although people usually remember the general gist of what they experience, the fallibility of human memory is disturbing. Human memory does *not* function like a camera or digital recorder that captures a perfect copy of visual or auditory information. Instead, memory details can change over time. Without your awareness, details can be added, subtracted, exaggerated, or downplayed (Clifasefi & others, 2007). In fact, each of us has the potential to confidently and vividly remember the details of some event—and be completely *wrong*. Confidence in a memory is no guarantee that the memory is accurate.

How do errors and distortions creep into memories? A new memory is not simply recorded, but *actively constructed*. To form a new memory, you actively organize and encode different types of information—visual, auditory, tactile, and so on. When you later attempt to retrieve those details, you actively *reconstruct*, or rebuild, the details of the memory (Bartlett, 1932; Schacter & others, 1998). In the process of actively constructing or reconstructing a memory, various factors can contribute to errors and distortions in what you remember. Or, more accurately, what you *think* you remember.

misinformation effect
A memory-distortion phenomenon in which a person's existing memories can be altered if the person is exposed to misleading information.

source confusion
A memory distortion that occurs when the true source of the memory is forgotten.

At the forefront of research on memory distortions is **Elizabeth Loftus,** whose story we told in the Prologue. Loftus is one of the most widely recognized authorities on eyewitness memory and the different ways it can go awry. She has not only conducted extensive research on this topic but also testified as an expert witness in many high-profile cases (see Garry & Hayne, 2007; Loftus, 2007).

The Misinformation Effect

The Influence of Postevent Information on Misremembering

Let's start by considering a Loftus study that has become a classic piece of research. Loftus and co-researcher John C. Palmer (1974) had subjects watch a film of an automobile accident, write a description of what they saw, and then answer a series of questions. There was one critical question in the series: "About how fast were the cars going when they contacted each other?" Different subjects were given different versions of that question. For some subjects, the word *contacted* was replaced with *hit.* Other subjects were given the words *bumped, collided,* or *smashed.*

Depending on the specific word used in the question, subjects gave very different speed estimates. As shown in Table 6.2, the subjects who gave the highest speed estimates got *smashed* (so to speak). Clearly, how a question is worded can influence what is remembered.

A week after seeing the film, the subjects were asked another series of questions. This time, the critical question was "Did you see any broken glass?" Although *no* broken glass was shown in the film, the majority of the subjects whose question had used the word *smashed* a week earlier said "yes." Notice what happened: Following the initial memory (the film of the automobile accident), new information (the word *smashed*) distorted the reconstruction of the memory (remembering broken glass that wasn't really there).

Table 6.2

Estimated Speeds

Word Used in Question	Average Speed Estimate
smashed	41 m.p.h.
collided	39 m.p.h.
bumped	38 m.p.h.
hit	34 m.p.h.
contacted	32 m.p.h.

Source: After Loftus & Palmer (1974).

The use of suggestive questions is but one example of how the information a person gets *after* an event can change what the person later remembers about the event. Literally hundreds of studies have demonstrated the different ways that the **misinformation effect** can be produced (Loftus, 1996; Wells & Loftus, 2003). Basically, the research procedure involves three steps. First, participants are exposed to a simulated event, such as an automobile accident or a crime. Next, after a delay, half of the participants receive misinformation, while the other half receive no misinformation. In the final step, all of the participants try to remember the details of the original event.

In study after study, Loftus as well as other researchers have confirmed that postevent exposure to misinformation can distort the recollection of the original

The Misinformation Effect in Action In October 2002, the Washington, D.C., area was terrorized by a series of random sniper attacks. Early on, the police issued an alert that an eyewitness reported a white van speeding from the scene of a shooting. Later attacks brought more eyewitness reports of a white van or truck. Hundreds of white vans were pulled over and searched by the police. In reality, the killers, John Allen Muhammad and Lee Boyd Malvo, were traveling in a dark blue Chevrolet Caprice. Ironically, several people had reported seeing a blue Caprice near different shooting scenes, but these reports were largely ignored because of the misinformed fixation on a white van.

event by eyewitnesses (see Davis & Loftus, 2007). People have recalled stop signs as yield signs, normal headlights as broken, barns along empty country roads, a blue vehicle as being white, and Minnie Mouse when they really saw Mickey Mouse! Whether it is in the form of suggestive questions, misinformation, or other exposure to conflicting details, such postevent experiences can distort eyewitness memories.

Source Confusion
Misremembering the Source of a Memory

Have you ever confidently remembered hearing something on television only to discover that it was really a friend who told you the information? Or mistakenly remembered doing something that you actually only *imagined* doing? Or confidently remembered that an event happened at one time and place only to learn later that it really happened at a *different* time and place?

If so, you can blame your faulty memories on a phenomenon called source confusion. **Source confusion** arises when the true source of the memory is forgotten or when a memory is attributed to the wrong source (Johnson & others, 1993; Leichtman & Ceci, 1995). The notion of source confusion can help explain the misinformation effect: False details provided *after* the event become confused with the details of the original memory. For example, in one classic study, participants viewed images showing the use of a screwdriver in a burglary (Loftus & others, 1989). Later, they read a written account of the break-in, but this account featured a hammer instead of a screwdriver. When tested for their memory of the images, 60 percent said that a hammer (the postevent information), rather than a screwdriver (the original information), had been used in the burglary. And they were just as confident of their *false* memories as they were when recalling their *accurate* memories of other details of the original event.

More recently, photographs have been used to demonstrate how false details presented after an original event can become confused with the authentic details of the original memory (Garry & Gerrie, 2005; Garry & others, 2007). For example, shown digitally doctored photos of famous news events, such as the violent 1989 Tiananmen Square protests in Beijing, China, details from the *fake* photos were incorporated into participants' memories of the actual news event (Sacchi & others, 2007).

Elizabeth's story in the Prologue also demonstrated how confusion about the source of a memory can give rise to an extremely vivid, but inaccurate, recollection. Vivid and accurate memories of her uncle's home, such as the smell of the pine trees and the feel of the lake water, became blended with Elizabeth's fantasy of finding

Psychological studies have shown that it is virtually impossible to tell the difference between a real memory and one that is a product of imagination or some other process. Our job as researchers in this area is to understand how it is that pieces of experience are combined to produce what we experience as "memory."

ELIZABETH LOFTUS (2002)

Which is the Real Photo? The photograph of an unknown young man bravely defying oncoming tanks in an antigovernment protest in China's Tiananmen Square has become an iconic image of individual courage and the global struggle for human rights. But after people who remembered the original image correctly were shown the doctored image on the right, their memories changed to incorporate the crowds of onlookers in the fake photo (Sacchi & others, 2007).

false memory
A distorted or fabricated recollection of something that did not actually occur.

schema
(SKEE-muh) An organized cluster of information about a particular topic.

script
A schema for the typical sequence of an everyday event.

her mother's body. The result was a **false memory,** which is a distorted or fabricated recollection of something that did not actually happen. Nonetheless, the false memory subjectively feels authentic and is often accompanied by all the emotional impact of a real memory.

Schemas, Scripts, and Memory Distortions

The Influence of Existing Knowledge on What Is Remembered

Given that information presented after a memory is formed can change the contents of that memory, let's consider the opposite effect: Can the knowledge you had *before* an event occurred influence your later memory of the event? If so, how?

Since you were a child, you have been actively forming mental representations called **schemas**—organized clusters of knowledge and information about particular topics. The topic can be almost anything—an object (e.g., a wind chime), a setting (e.g., a movie theater), or a concept (e.g., freedom). One kind of schema, called a **script,** involves the typical sequence of actions and behaviors at a common event, such as eating in a restaurant or taking a plane trip.

Schemas are useful in organizing and forming new memories. Using the schemas you already have stored in long-term memory allows you to quickly integrate new experiences into your knowledge base. For example, consider your schema for "phone." No longer just a utilitarian communication device, phones can be used to play games, flirt, or make a fashion statement. As the capabilities and functions of phones have expanded, your schema has changed to incorporate these new attributes. Your schema for "phone" includes cordless, wireless, and cellular phones, including devices that can transmit photos and text messages. So now, when you hear about a new cell phone that can handle your e-mail, cruise the Internet, act as an onboard GPS unit, and that has hundreds of other applications, you can quickly integrate that information into your existing schema for "phone."

Although useful, schemas can also contribute to memory distortions. In the classic "psychology professor's office" study described in the photo caption on the left, students erroneously remembered objects that were not actually present but were consistent with their schema of a professor's office (Brewer & Treyens, 1981). The schemas we have developed can promote memory errors by prompting us to fill in missing details with schema-consistent information.

But what if a situation contains elements that are *inconsistent* with our schemas or scripts for that situation? Are inconsistent items more likely to stand out in our minds and be better remembered? In a word, yes. Numerous studies have demonstrated that items that are inconsistent with our expectations tend to be better recalled and recognized than items that are consistent with our expectations (e.g., Kleider & others, 2008; Lampinen & others, 2001).

For example, University of Arkansas psychologist James Lampinen and his colleagues (2000) had participants listen to a story about a guy named Jack who performed some everyday activities, like washing his car and taking his dog to the veterinarian for shots. In each scene, Jack performed some actions that would have been consistent with the script (e.g., filling a bucket with soapy water, filling out forms at the vet's office) and some behaviors that were *not* part of a typical script for the activity (e.g., spraying the neighbor's kid with the hose, flirting with the vet's receptionist). When tested for details of the story, participants were more likely to recognize and remember the atypical actions than the consistent actions.

Much like the subjects in the professor's office study, participants in Lampinen's study also experienced compelling *false memories.* Almost always, the false memories were for actions that would have been consistent with the script—if they had actually happened in the story. For

False Memories of a Psychology Professor's Office After briefly waiting in the psychology professor's office shown below, participants were taken to another room and asked to recall details of the office—the real purpose of the study. Many participants falsely remembered objects that were not actually in the office, such as books, a filing cabinet, a telephone, a lamp, pens, pencils, and a coffee cup. Why? The details that the participants erroneously remembered were all items that would be consistent with a typical professor's office (Brewer & Treyens, 1981). Schemas can cause memory errors by prompting us to fill in missing details with schema-consistent information (Kleider & others, 2008).

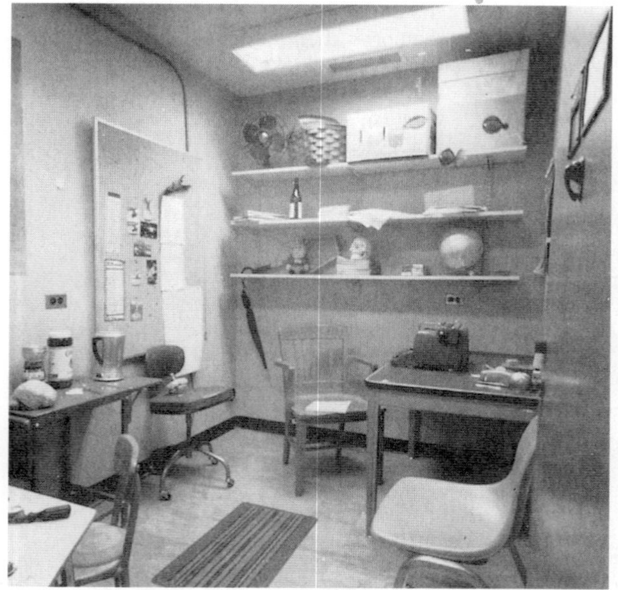

example, some participants vividly remembered that Jack rinsed the car off with a hose or that he put a leash on the dog before taking him to the vet's office. Neither of those actions occurred in the story.

Forming False Memories
From the Plausible to the Impossible

Key Theme

- **A variety of techniques can create false memories for events that never happened.**

Key Questions

- **What is the *lost-in-the-mall* technique, and how does it produce false memories?**
- **What is imagination inflation, and how has it been demonstrated?**
- **What factors contribute to the formation of false memories?**

Up to this point, we've talked about how misinformation, source confusion, and the mental schemas and scripts we've developed can change or add details to a memory that already exists. However, memory researchers have gone beyond changing a few details here and there. Since the mid-1990s, an impressive body of research has accumulated showing how false memories can be created for events that *never* happened (Loftus & Cahill, 2007). We'll begin with another Loftus study that has become famous—the *lost-in-the-mall* study.

Imagination Inflation
Remembering Being Lost in the Mall

Loftus and Jacqueline Pickrell (1995) gave each of 24 participants written descriptions of four childhood events that had been provided by a parent or other older relative. Three of the events had really happened, but the fourth was a *pseudoevent*—a false story about the participant getting lost in a shopping mall. Here's the gist of the story: At about the age of 5 or 6, the person got lost for an extended period of time in a shopping mall, became very upset and cried, was rescued by an elderly person, and ultimately was reunited with the family. (Family members verified that the participant had never actually been lost in a shopping mall or department store as a child.)

After reading the four event descriptions, the participants wrote down as many details as they could remember about each event. About two weeks later, participants were interviewed and asked to recall as many details as they could about each of the four events. Approximately one to two weeks after that, participants were interviewed a second time and asked once again what they could remember about the four events.

By the final interview, 6 of the 24 participants had created either full or partial memories of being lost in the shopping mall. How entrenched were the false memories for those who experienced them? Even after being debriefed at the end of the

Can Real Photos Create False Memories? Psychologist Stephen Lindsay and his colleagues (2004a, 2004b) had participants look at their first-grade class photo and read a description of a prank that they were led to believe had occurred in the first grade—putting slime in their teacher's desk. After a week of trying to remember the prank, 65 percent of the participants reported vivid, detailed memories of the prank. In contrast, only about a quarter (23 percent) of participants who tried to remember the prank but did *not* view a school photo developed false memories of the pseudoevent. Viewing an actual school photo, Lindsay believes, added to the legitimacy of the pseudoevent, making it seem more probable. It also provided vivid sensory details that blended with the imagined details to create elaborate and subjectively compelling false memories. Real photos can lend credibility to imaginary events (Garry & Gerrie, 2005).

study, some of the participants continued to struggle with the vividness of the false memory. "I totally remember walking around in those dressing rooms and my mom not being in the section she said she'd be in," one participant said (Loftus & Pickrell, 1995).

The research strategy of using information from family members to help create or induce false memories of childhood experiences has been dubbed the *lost-in-the-mall technique* (Loftus, 2003). By having participants remember real events along with imagining pseudoevents, researchers have created false memories for a wide variety of events. For example, participants have been led to believe that as a child they had been saved by a lifeguard from nearly drowning (Heaps & Nash, 2001). Or that they had knocked over a punch bowl on the bride's parents at a wedding reception (Hyman & Pentland, 1996).

Clearly, then, research has demonstrated that people can develop beliefs and memories for events that definitely did not happen to them. One key factor in the creation of false memories is the power of imagination. Put simply, *imagining the past as different from what it was can change the way you remember it.* Several studies have shown that vividly imagining an event markedly increases confidence that the event actually occurred in childhood, an effect called **imagination inflation** (Garry & Polaschek, 2000; Thomas & others, 2003).

CRITICAL THINKING

The Memory Wars: Recovered or False Memories?

Repressed memory therapy, recovery therapy, recovered memory therapy, trauma therapy—these are some of the names of a therapy introduced in the 1990s and embraced by many psychotherapists, counselors, social workers, and other mental health workers. Proponents of the therapy claimed they had identified the root cause of a wide assortment of psychological problems: repressed memories of sexual abuse that had occurred during childhood.

This therapeutic approach assumed that incidents of sexual and physical abuse experienced in childhood, especially when perpetrated by a trusted caregiver, were so psychologically threatening that the victims repressed all memories of the experience (Gleaves & others, 2004). Despite being repressed, these unconscious memories of unspeakable traumas continued to cause psychological and physical problems, ranging from low self-esteem to eating disorders, substance abuse, and depression.

The goal of repressed memory therapy was to help adult incest survivors "recover" their repressed memories of childhood sexual abuse. Reliving these painful experiences would help them begin "the healing process" of working through their anger and other intense emotions (Bass & Davis, 1994). Survivors were encouraged to confront their abusers and, if necessary, break all ties with their abusive families.

The Controversy: The "Recovery" Methods

The validity of the memories recovered in therapy became the center of a highly charged public controversy that has been dubbed "the memory wars" (Loftus, 2004; Mazzoni & Scoboria, 2007). A key issue was the methods used to help people unblock, or recover, repressed memories. Some recovered memory therapists used hypnosis, dream analysis, guided imagery, intensive group therapy, and other highly suggestive techniques to recover the long-repressed memories (Thayer & Lynn, 2006).

Many patients supposedly recovered memories of repeated incidents of physical and sexual abuse, sometimes beginning in early infancy, ongoing for years, and involving multiple victimizers (Pendergrast, 1996). Even more disturbing, some patients recovered vivid memories of years of alleged ritual satanic abuse involving secret cults practicing cannibalism, torture, and ritual murder (Loftus & Davis, 2006; Sakheim & Devine, 1992).

The Critical Issue: Recovered or False Memories?

Are traumatic memories likely to be repressed? It is well established that in documented cases of trauma, most survivors are troubled by the *opposite* problem—they cannot forget their traumatic memories (Kihlstrom, 2004; McNally, 2004). Rather than being unable to remember the experience, trauma survivors suffer from recurring flashbacks, intrusive thoughts and memories of the trauma, and nightmares. This pattern is a key symptom of posttraumatic stress disorder (PTSD), which we'll discuss in Chapter 13.

> *In more than twenty-five years of doing several hundred studies involving perhaps 20,000 people, we had distorted a significant portion of the subjects' memories. And the mechanism by which we can convince people they were lost, frightened, and crying in a mall is not so different than the mechanism by which therapists might unwittingly encourage memories of sexual abuse.*
>
> ELIZABETH LOFTUS (2003)

How does imagining an event—even one that never took place—help create a memory that is so subjectively compelling? Several factors seem to be involved. First, repeatedly imagining an event makes the event seem increasingly *familiar*. People then misinterpret the sense of familiarity as an indication that the event really happened (Sharman & others, 2004).

Second, coupled with the sense of increased familiarity, people experience *source confusion*. That is, subtle confusion can occur as to whether a retrieved "memory" has a real event—or an imagined event—as its source. Over time people may misattribute their memory of *imagining* the pseudoevent as being a memory of the *actual* event.

Third, the more vivid and detailed the imaginative experience, the more likely it is that people will confuse the imagined event with a real occurrence (Thomas & others, 2003). Vivid sensory and perceptual details can make the imagined events "feel" more like "real" events.

Simple manipulations, such as suggestions and imagination exercises, can increase the incidence and realism of false memories. So can vivid memory cues and family photos. The ease with which false memories can be implanted is more than just an academic question. It also has some powerful real-world implications. In the Critical Thinking box, we explore the highly charged controversy that has been dubbed "the memory wars."

imagination inflation
A memory phenomenon in which vividly imagining an event markedly increases confidence that the event actually occurred.

While it is relatively common for a person to be unable to remember *some* of the specific details of a traumatic event or to be troubled by memory problems after the traumatic event, such memory problems do *not* typically include difficulty in remembering the trauma itself (McNally, 2007). Memory researchers agree that a person might experience amnesia for a single traumatic incident but are skeptical that anyone could repress *all* memories of *repeated* incidents of abuse, especially when those incidents occurred over a period of several years (Loftus, 2001; Schacter, 1995).

Critics of repressed memory therapy contend that many of the supposedly "recovered" memories are actually *false memories* that were produced by the well-intentioned but misguided use of suggestive therapeutic techniques (de Rivera, 2000). Memory experts object to the use of hypnosis and other highly suggestive techniques to recover repressed memories (Ceci & Loftus, 1994; Gerrie & others, 2004; Lindsay & Read, 1994; Lynn & others, 1997). Understandably so. As you've seen in this chapter, compelling research shows the ease with which misinformation, suggestion, and imagination can create vivid—but completely *false*—memories.

What Conclusions Can Be Drawn?

After years of debate, some areas of consensus have emerged (Knapp & VandeCreek, 2000). First, there is no question that physical and sexual abuse in childhood is a serious social problem that also contributes to psychological problems in adulthood (Kendler, Bulik, & others, 2000; Nelson & others, 2002).

Second, some psychologists contend it is *possible* for memories of childhood abuse to be completely forgotten, only to surface many years later in adulthood (Brenneis, 2000; Schooler, 2001). Nevertheless, it's clear that repressed memories that have been recovered in psychotherapy need to be regarded with caution (Bowers & Favolden, 1996; Cloitre, 2004).

Third, the details of memories can be distorted with disturbing ease. Consequently, the use of highly suggestive techniques to recover memories of abuse raises serious concerns about the accuracy of such memories. As we have noted repeatedly in this chapter, a person's confidence in a memory is no guarantee that the memory is indeed accurate. False or fabricated memories can seem just as detailed, vivid, and real as accurate ones (Gerrie & others, 2004; Lampinen & others, 2005).

Fourth, keep in mind that every act of remembering involves reconstructing a memory. Remembering an experience is not like replaying a movie captured with your cell phone. Memories can change over time. Without our awareness, memories can grow and evolve, sometimes in unexpected ways.

Finally, psychologists and other therapists have become more aware of the possibility of inadvertently creating false memories in therapy (Palm & Gibson, 1998). Guidelines have been developed to help mental health professionals avoid unintentionally creating false memories in clients (American Psychological Association Working Group, 1998; Colangelo, 2007).

CRITICAL THINKING QUESTIONS

- Why is it difficult to determine the accuracy of a "memory" that is recovered in therapy?
- How could the phenomenon of source confusion be used to explain the production of false memories?

Table 6.3

Factors Contributing to False Memories

Factor	Description
Misinformation effect	When erroneous information received after an event leads to distorted or false memories of the event
Source confusion	Forgetting or misremembering the true source of a memory
Schema distortion	False or distorted memories caused by the tendency to fill in missing memory details with information that is consistent with existing knowledge about a topic
Imagination inflation	Unfounded confidence in a false or distorted memory caused by vividly imagining the pseudoevent
False familiarity	Increased feelings of familiarity due to repeatedly imagining an event
Blending fact and fiction	Using vivid, authentic details to add to the legitimacy and believability of a pseudoevent
Suggestion	Hypnosis, guided imagery, or other highly suggestive techniques that can inadvertently or intentionally create vivid false memories

Finally, we don't want to leave you with the impression that it's astonishing that anybody remembers *anything* accurately. In reality, people's memories tend to be quite accurate for the gist of what occurred. When memory distortions occur spontaneously in everyday life, they usually involve limited bits of information.

Still, the surprising ease with which memory details can become distorted is unnerving. Distorted memories can ring true and feel just as real as accurate memories (Clifasefi & others, 2007). In the chapter Prologue, you saw how easily Elizabeth Loftus created a false memory. You also saw how quickly she became convinced of the false memory's authenticity and the strong emotional impact it had on her. Rather than being set in stone, human memories are more like clay: They can change shape with just a little bit of pressure.

The Search for the Biological Basis of Memory

Key Theme

- **Early researchers believed that memory was associated with physical changes in the brain, but these changes were discovered only in the past few decades.**

Key Questions

- **How are memories both localized and distributed in the brain?**
- **How do neurons change when a memory is formed?**

"And here I am at two years of age. Remember? Mom? Pop? No? Or how about this one. My first day of school. Anyone?"

Does the name *Ivan Pavlov* ring a bell? We hope so. As you should recall from Chapter 5, Pavlov was the Russian physiologist who classically conditioned dogs to salivate to the sound of a bell and other neutral stimuli. Without question, learning and memory are intimately connected. Learning an adaptive response depends on our ability to form new memories in which we associate environmental stimuli, behaviors, and consequences.

Pavlov (1927) believed that the memory involved in learning a classically conditioned response would ultimately be explained as a matter of changes in the brain. However, Pavlov only speculated about the kinds of brain changes that would produce the memories needed for classical conditioning to occur. Other researchers

memory trace or **engram** The hypothetical brain changes associated with a particular stored memory.

would take up the search for the physical changes associated with learning and memory. In this section, we look at some of the key discoveries that have been made in trying to understand the biological basis of memory.

Karl S. Lashley (1890–1958) Lashley was trained as a zoologist but turned to psychology after he became friends with John B. Watson, the founder of behaviorism. Interested in discovering the physical basis of the conditioned reflex, Lashley focused his research on how learning and memory were represented in the brain. After years of frustrating research, Lashley (1950) humorously concluded, "This series of experiments has yielded a good bit of information about what and where memory is not. It has discovered nothing directly of the real nature of the engram. I sometimes feel in reviewing the evidence on the localization of the memory trace, that the necessary conclusion is that learning just is not possible."

The Search for the Elusive Memory Trace

An American physiological psychologist named **Karl Lashley** set out to find evidence for Pavlov's speculations. In the 1920s, Lashley began the search for the **memory trace,** or **engram**—the brain changes that were presumed to occur in forming a long-term memory (see photo caption). Guiding Lashley's research was his belief that memory was *localized,* meaning that a particular memory was stored in a specific brain area.

Lashley searched for the specific location of the memory trace that a rat forms for running a maze. Lashley (1929) suspected that the specific memory was localized at a specific site in the *cerebral cortex,* the outermost covering of the brain that contains the most sophisticated brain areas. Once a rat had learned to run the maze, Lashley surgically removed tiny portions of the rat's cortex. After the rat recovered, Lashley tested the rat in the maze again. Obviously, if the rat could still run the maze, then the portion of the brain removed did not contain the memory.

Over the course of 30 years, Lashley systematically removed different sections of the cortex in trained rats. The result of Lashley's painstaking research? No matter which part of the cortex he removed, the rats were still able to run the maze (Lashley, 1929, 1950). At the end of his professional career, Karl Lashley concluded that memories are not localized in specific locations but instead are *distributed,* or stored, throughout the brain.

Lashley was wrong, but not completely wrong. Some memories *do* seem to be localized at specific spots in the brain. Some 20 years after Lashley's death, psychologist **Richard F. Thompson** and his colleagues resumed the search for the location of the memory trace that would confirm Pavlov's speculations.

Thompson classically conditioned rabbits to perform a very simple behavior—an eye blink. By repeatedly pairing a tone with a puff of air administered to the rabbit's eye, he classically conditioned rabbits to blink reflexively in response to the tone alone (Thompson, 1994, 2005).

Thompson discovered that after a rabbit had learned this simple behavior, there was a change in the brain activity in a small area of the rabbit's *cerebellum,* a lower brain structure involved in physical movements. When this tiny area of the cerebellum was removed, the rabbit's memory of the learned response disappeared. It no longer blinked at the sound of the tone. However, the puff of air still caused the rabbit to blink reflexively, so the reflex itself had not been destroyed.

Thompson and his colleagues had confirmed Pavlov's speculations. The long-term memory trace of the classically conditioned eye blink was formed and stored in a very localized region of the cerebellum.

So why had Karl Lashley failed? Unlike Thompson, Lashley was working with a relatively complex behavior. Running a maze involves the use of several senses, including vision, smell, and touch. In contrast, Thompson's rabbits had learned a very simple reflexive behavior—a classically conditioned eye blink.

Thus, part of the reason Lashley failed to find a specific location for a rat's memory of a maze was that the memory was not a single memory. Instead, the rat had developed a complex set of *interrelated memories* involving information from multiple senses. These interrelated memories were processed and stored in different brain areas. As a result, the rat's memories were *distributed* and stored across multiple brain locations. Hence, no matter which small brain area Lashley removed, the rat could still run the maze. So Lashley was right in suggesting that some memories are distributed throughout the brain.

Richard F. Thompson (b. 1930) Like Karl Lashley, Richard Thompson (1994, 2005), sought to discover the neurobiological basis for learning and memory. But, unlike Lashley, Thompson (2005) decided to use a very simple behavior—a classically conditioned eye blink—as a model system to locate a memory trace in the brain. He succeeded, identifying the critical region in the cerebellum where the memory of the learned behavior was stored.

long-term potentiation
A long-lasting increase in synaptic strength between two neurons.

Combined, the findings of Lashley and Thompson indicate that memories have the potential to be *both localized and distributed*. Very simple memories may be localized in a specific area, whereas more complex memories are distributed throughout the brain. A complex memory involves clusters of information, and each part of the memory may be stored in the brain area that originally processed the information (Greenberg & Rubin, 2003).

Adding support to Lashley's and Thompson's findings, brain imaging technology has confirmed that many kinds of memories are distributed in the human brain. When we are performing a relatively complex memory task, multiple brain regions are activated—evidence of the distribution of memories involved in complex tasks (Frankland & Bontempi, 2005).

The Focus on Neuroscience on page 262 describes a clever study that looked at how memories involving different sensory experiences are assembled when they are retrieved.

The Role of Neurons in Long-Term Memory

What exactly is it that is localized or distributed? The notion of a memory trace suggests that some change must occur in the workings of the brain when a new long-term memory is stored. Logically, two possible changes could occur. First, the *functioning* of the brain's neurons could change. Second, the *structure* of the neurons could change.

FOCUS ON NEUROSCIENCE

Assembling Memories: Echoes and Reflections of Perception

If we asked you to remember the theme from *Sesame Street*, you would "hear" the song in your head. Conjure up a memory of your high school cafeteria, and you "see" it in your mind. Memories can include a great deal of sensory information—sounds, sights, and even odors, textures, and tastes. How are such rich sensory aspects of an experience incorporated into a memory that is retrieved?

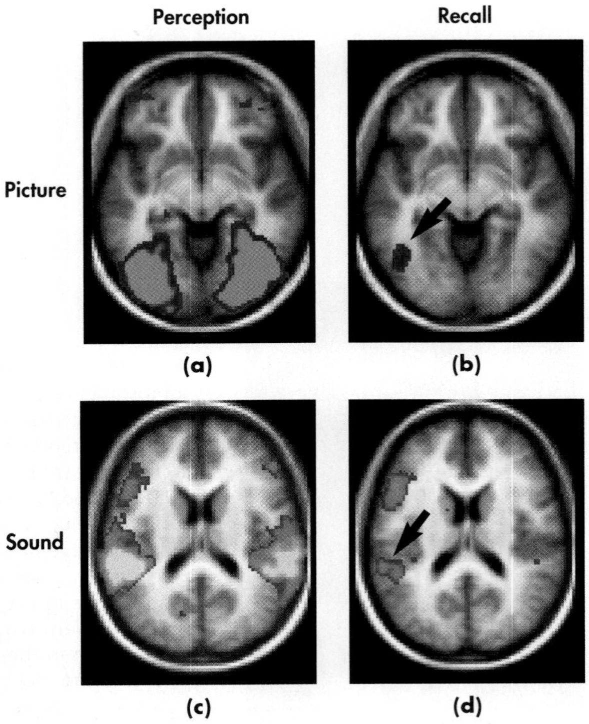

Perception | Recall

Picture

(a) (b)

Sound

(c) (d)

Researchers set out to investigate this question using a simple memory task and fMRI (Wheeler & others, 2000). Participants studied names for common objects that were either paired with a picture or a sound associated with the word. For example, the word "dog" was either paired with a picture of a dog or the sound of a dog barking. The researchers then used fMRI to measure brain activity when the volunteers were instructed to recall the words they'd memorized.

The results? Retrieving the memory activated a subset of the same brain areas that were involved in perceiving the sensory stimulus. Participants who had memorized the word *dog* with a *picture* of a dog showed a high level of activation in the *visual cortex* when they retrieved the memory. And participants who had memorized the word *dog* with the *sound* of a barking dog showed a high level of activation in the *auditory cortex* when they retrieved the memory.

Of course, many of our memories are highly complex, involving not just sensations but also thoughts and emotions. Neuroscientists assume that such complex memories involve traces that are widely distributed throughout the brain. However, they still don't understand how all these neural records are bound together and interrelated to form a single, highly elaborate memory.

Retrieving the Memory of a Sensory Experience
Top row: (a) Perceiving a picture activates areas of the visual cortex. (b) When the memory of the picture is recalled, it reactivates some of the same areas of the visual cortex *(arrow)* that were involved in the initial perception of the picture. Bottom row: (c) Perceiving a sound activates areas of the auditory cortex. (d) When the memory of the sound is recalled, it reactivates some of the same areas of the auditory cortex *(arrow)* that were involved in the initial perception of the sound.

Source: Wheeler & others (2000).

Given those two possibilities, the challenge for memory researchers has been to identify the specific neurons involved in a given memory, a task that is virtually impossible with the human brain because of its enormous complexity. What this task required was a creature with a limited number of neurons that is also capable of learning new memories.

Enter *Aplysia,* a gentle, seaweed-munching sea snail that resides off the California coast. The study of *Aplysia* over the past 30 years has given memory researchers important insights to the brain changes involved in memory. Why *Aplysia?* Because *Aplysia* has only about 20,000 good-sized neurons. That was a key reason why memory researcher **Eric Kandel** (2001, 2006) chose this unassuming creature to study the neuronal changes that occur when a new memory is formed for a simple classically conditioned response.

If you give *Aplysia* a gentle squirt with a WaterPik, followed by a mild electric shock to its tail, the snail reflexively withdraws its gill flap. When the process is repeated several times, *Aplysia* wises up and acquires a new memory of a classically conditioned response—it withdraws its gill when squirted with the WaterPik alone. This learned gill-withdrawal reflex seems to involve a circuit of just three neurons: one that detects the water squirt, one that detects the tail shock, and one that signals the gill-withdrawal reflex (see Figure 6.10).

When *Aplysia* acquires this new memory through repeated training trials, significant changes occur in the three-neuron circuit (Kandel, 2001). First, the *function* of the neurons is altered: There is an increase in the amount of the neurotransmitters produced by the neurons. Second, the *structure* of the snail's neurons changes: The number of interconnecting branches between the neurons increases, as does the number of synapses, or communication points, on each branch. These changes allow the neurons involved in the particular memory circuit to communicate more easily. Collectively, these changes are called **long-term potentiation,** which refers to a long-lasting increase in synaptic strength (Fedulov & others, 2007; Malenka, 2003).

The same kinds of brain changes have been observed in more sophisticated mammals. Chicks, rats, and rabbits also show structural and functional neuron changes associated with new learning experiences and memories. And, as you may recall from Enhancing Well-Being with Psychology in Chapter 2, there is evidence that the same kinds of changes occur in the human brain (e.g., Draganski & others, 2004).

***Aplysia,* the Supersnail of Memory Research** Eric Kandel holds *Aplysia,* the sea snail that is used to study how neurons change when simple behaviors are learned and remembered. Kandel was awarded the Nobel Prize in 2000 for his discoveries on the neural basis of memory.

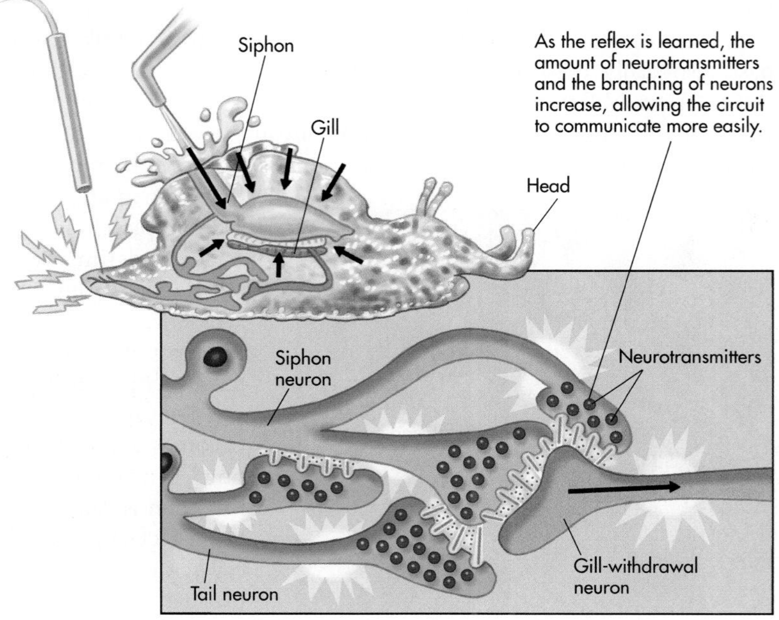

Figure 6.10 How Neurons Change as *Aplysia* Forms a New Memory When *Aplysia* is repeatedly squirted with water, and each squirt is followed by a mild shock to its tail, the snail learns to withdraw its gill flap if squirted with the water alone. Conditioning leads to structural and functional changes in the three neurons involved in the memory circuit.

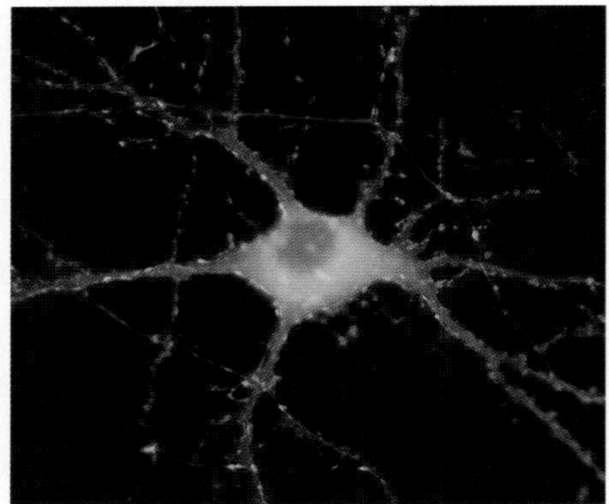

Creating New Synaptic Connections Forming new memories involves strengthening existing synaptic connections and creating new synaptic connections between neurons in the brain. Neuroscientist Michael Colicos and his colleagues at the University of California–San Diego (2001) photographed structural changes in a single hippocampus neuron that occurred in response to repeated electrical stimulation. The spidery blue lines in the photo are physical changes in the neuron's structure that represent the first steps toward the formation of new synaptic connections with other neurons.

In terms of our understanding of the memory trace, what do these findings suggest? Although there are vast differences between the nervous system of a simple creature such as *Aplysia* and the enormously complex human brain, some tentative generalizations are possible. Forming a memory seems to produce distinct functional and structural changes in specific neurons. These changes create a memory circuit. Each time the memory is recalled, the neurons in this circuit are activated. As the structural and functional changes in the neurons strengthen the communication links in this circuit, the memory becomes established as a long-term memory (Kandel, 2006).

Processing Memories in the Brain
Clues from Amnesia

Key Theme

- **Important insights into the brain structures involved in normal memory have been provided by case studies of people with amnesia caused by damaged brain tissue.**

Key Questions

- **Who was H.M. and what did his case reveal about normal memory processes?**
- **What brain structures are involved in normal memory?**
- **What are dementia and Alzheimer's disease?**

Prior to the advent of today's sophisticated brain-imaging technology, researchers studied individuals who had sustained a brain injury or had part of their brain surgically removed for medical reasons. Often, such individuals experienced **amnesia,** or severe memory loss. By relating the type and extent of amnesia to the specific damaged brain areas, researchers uncovered clues as to how the human brain processes memories.

amnesia
(am-NEE-zha) Severe memory loss.

retrograde amnesia
Loss of memory, especially for episodic information; backward-acting amnesia.

memory consolidation
The gradual, physical process of converting new long-term memories to stable, enduring memory codes.

anterograde amnesia
Loss of memory caused by the inability to store new memories; forward-acting amnesia.

Retrograde Amnesia
Disrupting Memory Consolidation

One type of amnesia is retrograde amnesia. *Retrograde* means "backward moving." People who have **retrograde amnesia** are unable to remember some or all of their past, especially episodic memories for recent events. Retrograde amnesia often results from a blow to the head. Boxers sometimes suffer such memory losses after years of fighting. Head injuries from automobile and motorcycle accidents are another common cause of retrograde amnesia. Typically, memories of the events that immediately preceded the injury are completely lost, as in the case of accident victims who cannot remember details about what led up to the accident.

Disrupting the Consolidation of Memories Head injuries are common in football and many other sports. In one study, football players who were questioned immediately after a concussion or other head injury could remember how they were injured and the name of the play just performed. But if questioned 30 minutes later for the same information, they could not. Because the head injury had disrupted the memory consolidation process, the memories were permanently lost (Yarnell & Lynch, 1970).

Apparently, establishing a long-term memory is like creating a Jell-O mold—it needs time to "set" before it becomes solid. This process of "setting" a new memory permanently in the brain is called memory consolidation (McGaugh, 2000). More specifically, **memory consolidation** is the gradual, physical process of converting new long-term memories to stable, enduring memory codes (Medina & others, 2008). If memory consolidation is disrupted before the process is complete, the vulnerable memory may be lost (Dudai, 2004).

In humans, memory consolidation can be disrupted by brain trauma, such as a sudden blow, concussion, electric shock, or encephalitis (Riccio & others, 2003). Similarly, many drugs, such as alcohol and the benzodiazepines, interfere with memory consolidation. In contrast, stimulants and the stress hormones that are released during emotional arousal tend to *enhance* memory consolidation (McGaugh, 2000).

Henry Gustav Molaison: The Real H.M. (1926–2008) At the age of 9, Henry was hit hard by a bicyclist and jarred his head badly. Not long after, Henry began experiencing seizures. By early adulthood, Henry's seizures had increased in both severity and frequency. In an effort to control the seizures, Dr. William Beecher Scoville performed an experimental surgery, removing the hippocampus and amygdala on each side of Henry's brain. It was the first—and last—time that the surgical procedure would be performed.

Because of the profound anterograde amnesia caused by the surgery, Henry became one of the most intensive case studies in psychology and neuroscience. Over the next half century, Henry participated in hundreds of studies that fundamentally altered the scientific understanding of memory.

Henry died on December 2, 2008, but his contributions to science continue. Neuroscientists at the Brain Observatory at the University of California–San Diego continue to study Henry's brain, which was removed shortly after his death. Eventually, a complete atlas of Henry's brain will be available online.

Anterograde Amnesia

Disrupting the Formation of Explicit Memories

Another form of amnesia is **anterograde amnesia**—the inability to form *new* memories. *Anterograde* means "forward moving." The most famous case study of anterograde amnesia lasted over 50 years. It was of a man who for years was known only by his initials—H.M. But the need to protect H.M.'s privacy ended when Henry Molaison died at the age of 82 on December 2, 2008.

In 1953, Henry was 27 years old and had a 10-year history of severe, untreatable epileptic seizures. Henry's doctors located the brain area where the seizures seemed to originate. With no other options available at the time, the decision was made to surgically remove portions of the *medial* (inner) *temporal lobe* on each side of Henry's brain, including the brain structure called the *hippocampus* (Scoville & Milner, 1957).

After the experimental surgery, the frequency and severity of Henry's seizures were greatly reduced. However, it was quickly discovered that Henry's ability to form new memories of events and information had been destroyed. Although the experimental surgery had treated H.M.'s seizures, it also dramatically revealed the role of the hippocampus in forming new explicit memories for episodic and semantic information.

Psychologists **Brenda Milner** and **Suzanne Corkin** studied Henry extensively over the past 50 years (Corkin, 1984; Milner, 1970; Scoville & Milner, 1957). If you had had the chance to meet Henry, he would have appeared normal enough. He had a good vocabulary and social skills, normal intelligence, and a delightful sense of humor. And he was well aware of his memory problem. When Suzanne Corkin (2002) once asked him, "What do you do to try to remember?" Henry quipped, "Well, that I don't know because I don't remember (chuckle) what I tried."

Despite superficially appearing normal, Henry lived in the eternal present. Had you talked with Henry for 15 minutes, then left the room for 2 or 3 minutes before coming back, he wouldn't remember having met you before. Although some of the psychologists and doctors had treated Henry for years, even decades, Henry was meeting them for the first time on each occasion he interacted with them (Ogden & Corkin, 1991; Corkin, 2002).

For the most part, Henry's short-term memory worked just fine. In fact, he could fool you. If Henry actively repeated or rehearsed information, he could hold it in short-term memory for an hour or more (Nader & Wang, 2006). Yet just moments after he switched his attention to something else and stopped rehearsing the information, it was gone forever. However, Henry's long-term memory was partially intact. He could retrieve long-term memories from *before* the time he was 16 years old, when the severe epileptic seizures began.

Suzanne Corkin Since the mid-1960s, MIT neuropsychologist Suzanne Corkin has evaluated different aspects of Henry's memory abilities. In looking back on Henry's life, Corkin (2002) commented, "We all understand the rare opportunity we have had to work with him, and we are grateful for his dedication to research. He has taught us a great deal about the cognitive and neural organization of memory. We are in his debt."

In general, Henry was unable to acquire new long-term memories of events (episodic information) or general knowledge (semantic information). Still, every now and then, Henry surprised his doctors and visitors with some bit of knowledge that he acquired after the surgery (see the In Focus box "H.M. and Famous People").

Henry's case suggests that the hippocampus is not involved in most short-term memory tasks, nor is it the storage site for already established long-term memories. Instead, the critical role played by the hippocampus seems to be the *encoding* of new memories for events and information and the *transfer* of those new memories from short-term to long-term memory.

Implicit and Explicit Memory in Anterograde Amnesia Henry's case and those of other patients with anterograde amnesia have contributed greatly to our understanding of implicit versus explicit memories. To refresh your memory, *implicit memories* are memories without conscious awareness. In contrast, *explicit memories* are memories with conscious awareness.

Henry could not form new episodic or semantic memories, which reflects the explicit memory system. But he *could* form new procedural memories, which reflects the implicit memory system. For example, when given the same logical puzzle to solve several days in a row, Henry was able to solve it more quickly each day. This improvement showed that he *implicitly* "remembered" the procedure involved

IN FOCUS

H.M. and Famous People

When his hippocampus was removed, Henry Molaison lost the ability to quickly encode new semantic and episodic memories. For example, he was unable to learn new vocabulary words or remember people he had met. But is the hippocampus necessary for *all* semantic learning? Or is it possible that other brain areas might support some limited learning of new knowledge?

To test this idea, psychologists Gail O'Kane, Elizabeth Kensinger, and Suzanne Corkin (2004) evaluated Henry for his knowledge of people who became famous after his surgery in 1953. On the first day, Henry was given the famous person's first name as a cue and asked to say the last name that came to his mind. Examples were "Elvis_____ (Presley)" and "Fidel _____ (Castro)," who first became famous during the 1950s; "Lyndon _____ (Johnson)" and "Ray _____ (Charles)" from the 1960s; "Sophia _____ (Loren)" from the 1970s; and "Ronald _____ (Reagan)" from the 1980s. Henry was able to correctly supply the last name of 12 out of 35 famous people including Martin Luther King, Sophia Loren, and Ronald Reagan.

In a second test on the next day, Henry was able to generate the last names for an additional 11 famous people after being given background information about them. For example, provided with the details "famous artist, born in Spain, formulated Cubism, works include *Guernica,*" Henry responded "Picasso" to the cue "first name is Pablo."

Henry's ability to generate the last names of well-known people indicated that he had acquired some declarative semantic knowledge. O'Kane and her colleagues (2004) wondered whether Henry could go beyond this superficial knowledge and provide specific details. In a different test, Henry was able to provide two or more pieces of information about 12 people who had become prominent after the onset of his amnesia.

For example, after correctly identifying John F. Kennedy as a famous person, Henry indicated that Kennedy was Catholic, had become president, that somebody shot him, and that he didn't survive. Henry was also able to provide details about John Glenn, Ray Charles, Woody Allen, Liza Minnelli, and Sophia Loren.

According to O'Kane and her colleagues (2004), "These results provide robust, unambiguous evidence that at least some semantic learning can be supported by structures beyond the hippocampus." However, the limitations of Henry's semantic learning must also be stressed. Henry was still unable to quickly acquire new semantic or episodic memories. It was only after years of extended repetitions of information that Henry acquired some limited bits and pieces of new knowledge about a few famous people.

in solving the puzzle. But if you asked Henry if he had ever seen the puzzle before, he would answer "no" because he could not consciously (or *explicitly*) remember having learned how to solve the puzzle. This suggests that the hippocampus is less crucial to the formation of new implicit memories, such as procedural memories, than it is to the formation of new explicit memories.

Were Henry's memory anomalies an exception? Not at all. Studies conducted with other people who have sustained damage to the hippocampus and related brain structures showed the same anterograde amnesia (e.g., Bayley & Squire, 2002). Like Henry, these patients are unable to form new explicit memories, but their performances on implicit memory tasks, which do not require conscious recollection of the new information, are much closer to normal. Such findings indicate that implicit and explicit memory processes involve different brain structures and pathways.

Brain Structures Involved in Memory

Along with the hippocampus, several other brain regions involved in memory include the cerebellum, the amygdala, and the frontal cortex (see Figure 6.11). As you saw earlier, the *cerebellum* is involved in classically conditioning simple reflexes, such as the eye-blink reflex. The cerebellum is also involved in procedural memories and other motor skill memories.

The *amygdala,* which is situated very close to the hippocampus, is involved in encoding and storing the emotional qualities associated with particular memories, such as fear or anger (McGaugh, 2004). For example, normal monkeys are afraid of snakes. But if the amygdala is damaged, a monkey loses its fear of snakes and other natural predators.

The *frontal lobes* are involved in retrieving and organizing information that is associated with autobiographical and episodic memories (Greenberg & Rubin, 2003). The *prefrontal cortex* seems to play an important role in working memory (McNab & Klingberg, 2008).

The *medial temporal lobes,* like the frontal lobes, do not actually store the information that comprises our autobiographical memories. Rather, they are involved in encoding complex memories, by forming links among the information stored in multiple brain regions (Greenberg & Rubin, 2003). As we described in the Focus on Neuroscience, "Assembling Memories," on page 262, retrieving a memory activates the same brain regions that were involved in initially encoding the memory.

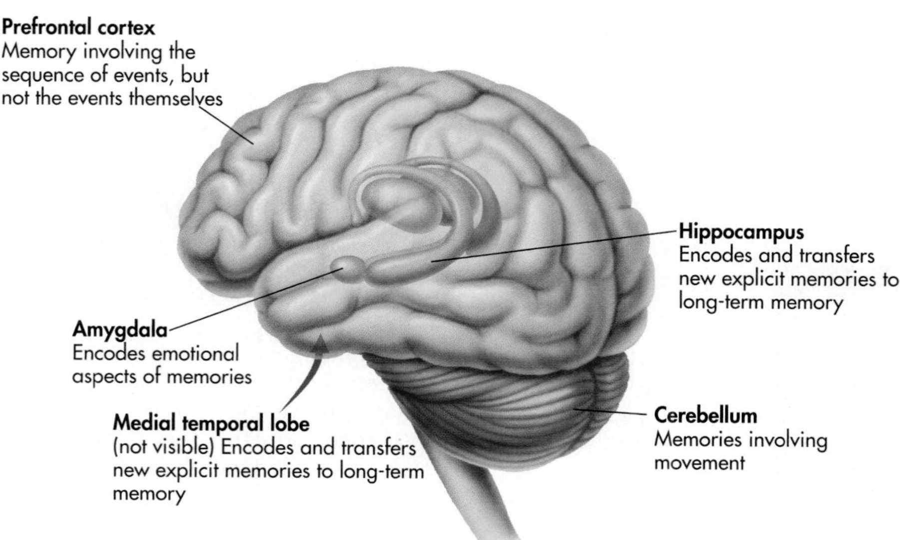

Figure 6.11 Brain Structures Involved in Human Memory Shown here are some of the key brain structures involved in encoding and storing memories.

dementia
Progressive deterioration and impairment of memory, reasoning, and other cognitive functions occurring as the result of a disease or a condition.

Alzheimer's disease (AD)
A progressive disease that destroys the brain's neurons, gradually impairing memory, thinking, language, and other cognitive functions, resulting in the complete inability to care for oneself; the most common cause of *dementia*.

Alzheimer's Disease

Gradually Losing the Ability to Remember

Understanding how the brain processes and stores memories has important implications. **Dementia** is a broad term that refers to the decline and impairment of memory, reasoning, language, and other cognitive functions. These cognitive disruptions occur to such an extent that they interfere with the person's ability to carry out daily activities. Dementia is not a disease itself. Rather, it describes a group of symptoms that often accompanies a disease or a condition.

The most common cause of dementia is **Alzheimer's disease (AD).** It is estimated that about 5.3 million Americans suffer from AD. That number is expected to dramatically escalate as the first of the "baby boomers" are just now reaching age 65. The disease usually doesn't begin until after age 60, but the risk goes up with age. About 5 percent of men and women in the 65–74 age group have AD. Among adults age 85 and older, about half may have Alzheimer's disease (Alzheimer's Association, 2009).

Although the cause or causes of Alzheimer's disease are still unknown, it is known that the brains of AD patients develop an abundance of two abnormal structures—*beta-amyloid plaques* and *neurofibrillary tangles* (Masliah, 2008; Meyer-Luehmann & others, 2008). The *plaques* are dense deposits of protein and other cell materials

FOCUS ON NEUROSCIENCE

Mapping Brain Changes in Alzheimer's Disease

The hallmark of Alzheimer's disease is its relentless, progressive destruction of neurons in the brain, turning once-healthy tissue into a tangled, atrophied mass. This progressive loss of brain tissue is dramatically revealed in the MRI images shown below. Created by neuroscientist Paul Thompson and his colleagues (2003), these high-resolution "brain maps" represent composite images of the progressive effects of Alzheimer's disease (AD) in 12 patients over the course of two years. In these color-coded images, blue corresponds to normal tissue (no loss), red indicates up to 10 percent tissue loss, and white indicates up to 20 percent tissue loss.

Thompson likens the progression of AD to that of molten lava flowing around rocks—the disease leaves islands of brain tissue unscathed. The disease first attacks the temporal lobes, affecting areas involved in memory, especially short-term memory. Next affected are the frontal areas, which are involved in thinking, reasoning, self-control, and planning ahead. You can also see significant internal loss in limbic areas, which are involved in regulating emotion. At this point in the progression of AD, there is very little loss in sensory and visual brain areas. Eventually the disease engulfs the entire brain. The photo to the right contrasts cross sections of a normal brain (top) and the brain of a person who died of Alzheimer's disease (bottom). In the normal brain, the temporal lobes are intact. The ventricles, which hold the cerebral spinal fluid, are slender. In the brain ravaged by Alzheimer's, the gaping ventricles extend into the space left by the death of brain cells in the temporal lobes.

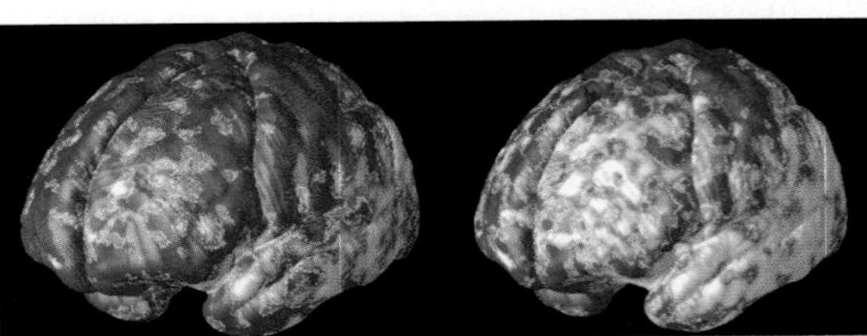

Initital diagnosis 18 months later

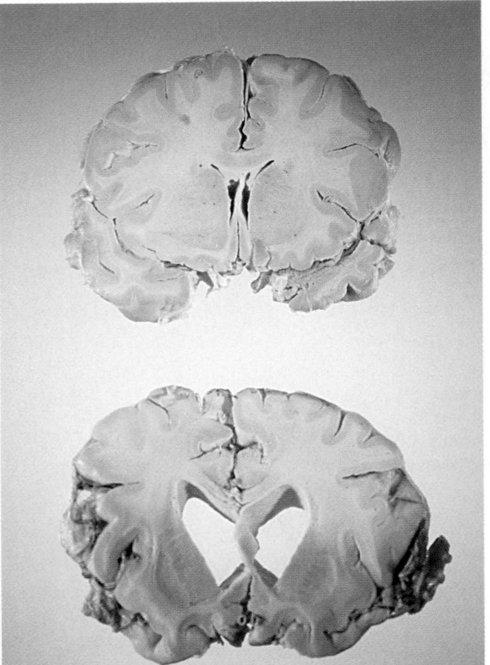

outside and around neurons. The plaques interfere with the ability of neurons to communicate, damaging the neurons to the point that they die. The *tangles* are twisted fibers that build up inside the neuron and interrupt the flow of nourishment to the neuron, ultimately causing the neuron to die. Although most older people develop some plaques and tangles in their brains, the brains of AD patients have them to a much greater extent (Petersen, 2002). In the Focus on Neuroscience, you can vividly see the progressive loss of neurons that is the root cause of Alzheimer's disease.

In the early stages of AD, the symptoms of memory impairment are often mild, such as forgetting the names of familiar people, forgetting the location of familiar places, or forgetting to do things. But as the disease progresses, memory loss and confusion become more pervasive. The person becomes unable to remember what month it is or the names of family members. Frustrated and disoriented by the inability to retrieve even simple information, the person can become agitated and moody. In the last stage of AD, internal brain damage has become widespread. The person no longer recognizes loved ones and is unable to communicate in any meaningful way. All sense of self and identity has vanished. At the closing stages, the person becomes completely incapacitated. Ultimately, Alzheimer's disease is fatal (Alzheimer's Association, 2009).

Some 10 million Americans provide unpaid care for a person with Alzheimer's disease or other dementia. These unpaid caregivers are primarily family members but also include friends and neighbors. In 2008, these caregivers provided 8.5 billion hours of unpaid care (Alzheimer's Association, 2009). Not only is there a financial toll, but families and caregivers struggle with great physical and emotional stress as they try to cope with the mental and physical changes occurring in their loved one. The average number of hours of unpaid care provided for a relative or friend with Alzheimer's increases as the person's condition worsens.

Numerous resources are available to help support families and other caregivers, such as the Alzheimer's Disease Education & Referral Center (www.alzheimers.org) and the Alzheimer's Association (www.alz.org).

>> Closing Thoughts

Human memory is at once both perfectly ordinary and quite extraordinary. With next to no mental effort, you form and recall countless memories as you go through daily life. Psychologists have made enormous progress in explaining how those memories are encoded, stored, retrieved, and forgotten.

Perhaps the most fascinating aspect of human memory is its fallibility. Memory is surprisingly susceptible to errors and distortions. Under some conditions, completely false memories can be experienced, such as Elizabeth Loftus's memory of discovering her mother's body in the swimming pool. Such false memories can be so subjectively compelling that they feel like authentic memories, yet confidence in a memory is not proof of the memory's truth.

Many mysteries of human memory remain, including exactly how memories are stored in and retrieved from the brain. Nevertheless, reliable ways of improving memory in everyday life have been discovered. In the Enhancing Well-Being with Psychology feature, we provide several suggestions to enhance your memory for new information.

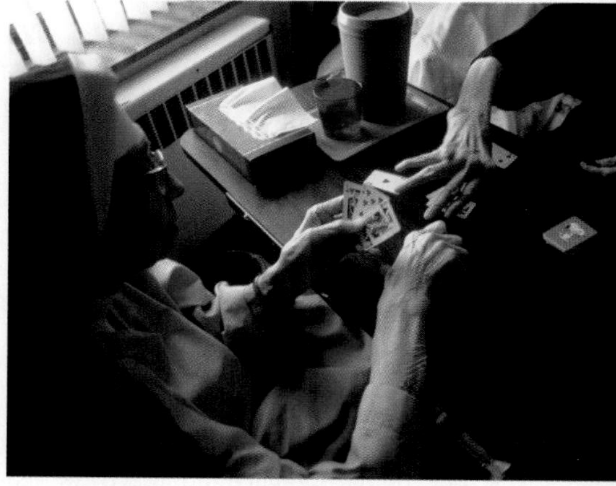

The Nun Study of Aging and Alzheimer's Disease Since 1986 David Snowdon (2002, 2003) has been studying 678 elderly Roman Catholic nuns. From a scientific perspective, the nuns are an ideal group to study because their lifestyles and environment are so similar. Although the study is ongoing, several findings have already emerged (see Riley & others, 2005; Tyas & others, 2007a, 2007b).

For example, the outward signs of Alzheimer's disease (AD) and the degree of brain damage evident at death are not perfectly correlated. Although some nuns had clear brain evidence of AD, they did not display observable cognitive and behavior declines prior to their deaths. Other nuns had only mild brain evidence of AD but showed severe cognitive and behavioral declines.

Interestingly, the sisters who displayed better language abilities when they were young women were less likely to display AD symptoms. This held true regardless of how much brain damage was evident at the time of their death (Iacono & others, 2009). As researcher Diego Iacono (2009) commented, "It's the first time that we're shown that a complex cognitive activity, like language ability, is connected with a neurodegenerative disease."

ENHANCING WELL-BEING WITH PSYCHOLOGY

Superpower Memory in Minutes per Day!

Yes, that's what many memory self-help programs promise you. But after you cut through all the hype, what are you left with? Mostly what we're going to give you in this section—some well-established and effective but less-than-magical strategies to help boost your memory for important information.

1. Space your study sessions.
Distributed practice means that you learn information over several sessions, which gives you time to mentally process and incorporate the information (Son, 2004). Students who take the distributed-practice approach to learning retain significantly more information than students who use cramming, or *massed practice* (Rohrer & Taylor, 2006).

2. Sleep on it to help consolidate those memories.
As we discussed in Chapter 4 on page 148, sleep helps you consolidate new memories. (Don't try this as an excuse in class.) Non-REM sleep (nondreaming) seems to help consolidate declarative memories, while dreaming REM sleep seems to help consolidate procedural memories (Marshall & Born, 2007; Wixted, 2004). All-night cram sessions just before an exam are one of the *least* effective ways to learn new material.

3. Focus your attention.
Problems in absorbing new information arise when distracting thoughts, background noise, and other interruptions sidetrack your attention. Television and cell phones are common culprits. Rather than studying in front of the tube or responding to text messages, locate a quiet study space that's free from distractions so you can focus your attention. If distracting thoughts are competing for your attention, start your study session by reading aloud part of what you need to study.

4. Commit the necessary time.
The more time you spend learning material, the better you will understand it and the longer you will remember it. Budget enough time to read the assigned material carefully. If you read material faster than you can comprehend it, you not only won't understand the material, you also won't remember it.

5. Organize the information.
We have a strong natural tendency to organize information in long-term memory into categories. You can capitalize on this tendency by actively organizing information you want to remember. One way to accomplish this is by outlining chapters or your lecture notes. Use the chapter headings and subheadings as categories, or, better yet, create your own categories. Under each category, list and describe the relevant terms, concepts, and ideas. This strategy can double the amount of information you can recall.

6. Elaborate on the material.
You've probably noticed that virtually every term or concept in this text is formally defined in just a sentence or two. But we also spend a paragraph or more explaining what the concept means. To remember the information you read, you have to do the same thing—engage in *elaborative rehearsal* and actively process the information for meaning (see page 239). Actively question new information and think about its implications. Form memory associations by relating the material to what you already know. Try to come up with examples that relate to your own life.

7. Use visual imagery.
Two memory codes are better than one (Paivio, 1986). Rather than merely encoding the information verbally, use mental imagery (Carretti & others, 2007; Sadoski, 2005). Much of the information in this text easily lends itself to visual imagery. Use the photographs and other illustrations to help form visual memories of the information. A simple way to make text information visually distinct is to highlight different concepts in different colors.

8. Explain it to a friend.
After you read a section of material, stop and summarize what you have read in your own words. When you think you understand it, try explaining the information to a friend or family member. As you'll quickly discover, it's hard to explain material that you don't really understand! Memory research has shown that explaining new material in your own words forces you to integrate the new information into your existing knowledge base—an excellent way to solidify new information in your memory (Kornell, 2008).

9. Reduce interference within a topic.
If you occasionally confuse related terms and concepts, it may be because you're experiencing *interference* in your memories for similar information. To minimize memory interference for related information, first break the chapter into manageable sections, then learn the key information one section at a time. As you encounter new concepts, compare them with previously learned concepts, looking for differences and similarities. By building distinct memories for important information as you progress through a topic, you're more likely to distinguish between concepts so they don't get confused in your memory.

10. Counteract the serial position effect.
The *serial position effect* is the tendency to have better recall of information at the beginning and end of a sequence. To counteract this effect, spend extra time learning the information that falls in the middle. Once you've mastered a sequence of material, start at a different point each time you review or practice the information.

11. Use contextual cues to jog memories.
Ideally, study in the setting in which you're going to be tested. If that's not possible, when you're taking a test and a specific memory gets blocked, imagine that your books and notes are in front of you and that you're sitting where you normally study. Simply imagining the surroundings where you learned the material can help jog those memories.

12. Use a mnemonic device for remembering lists.
A *mnemonic device* is a method or strategy to aid memory. Some of the most effective mnemonic devices use visual imagery. For example, the *method of loci* is a mnemonic device in which you remember items by visualizing them at specific locations in a familiar setting, such as the different rooms in your house or at specific locations on your way to work or school. To recall the items, mentally revisit the locations and imagine the specific item at that location.

Another mnemonic that involves creating visual associations is the *peg-word method*. First, you learn an easily remembered list containing the peg words, such as: 1 is bun, 2 is shoe, 3 is tree, 4 is door, 5 is hive, 6 is sticks, 7 is heaven, 8 is gate, 9 is vine, 10 is a hen, and you can keep going as needed. Then, you create a vivid mental image associating the first item you want to remember with the first peg word, the next item with the next peg word, and so on. To recall the list, use each successive peg word to help retrieve the mental image.

13. Forget the ginkgo biloba.

Think you can supercharge your memory banks by taking the herb *ginkgo biloba*? If only it were that easy! Researcher Paul R. Solomon and his colleagues (2002) pitted ginkgo against a placebo in a randomized, double-blind study for six weeks involving over 200 participants who were mentally healthy. The bottom line? No effect. The ginkgo biloba did not improve performance on tests of learning, memory, attention, or concentration. Other studies have come to the same conclusion (see Canter & Ernst, 2007)..

CHAPTER REVIEW: KEY PEOPLE AND TERMS

Suzanne Corkin, p. 265
Hermann Ebbinghaus, p. 248
Eric Kandel, p. 263
Karl Lashley, p. 261
Elizabeth F. Loftus, p. 254
Brenda Milner, p. 265
George Sperling, p. 234
Richard F. Thompson, p. 261

memory, p. 232
encoding, p. 232
storage, p. 232
retrieval, p. 232
stage model of memory, p. 232
sensory memory, p. 233
short-term memory, p. 233
long-term memory, p. 233
maintenance rehearsal, p. 236
chunking, p. 236
working memory, p. 238
elaborative rehearsal, p. 239
procedural memory, p. 240
episodic memory, p. 240
semantic memory, p. 240
explicit memory, p. 241
implicit memory, p. 241
clustering, p. 242
semantic network model, p. 242
retrieval, p. 243
retrieval cue, p. 243
retrieval cue failure, p. 243
tip-of-the-tongue (TOT) experience, p. 244
recall, p. 245
cued recall, p. 245
recognition, p. 245
serial position effect, p. 245
encoding specificity principle, p. 246
context effect, p. 246
mood congruence, p. 246
flashbulb memory, p. 246
forgetting, p. 248
encoding failure, p. 249
prospective memory, p. 250
decay theory, p. 250
déjà vu experience, p. 251
source memory (source monitoring), p. 251
interference theory, p. 252
retroactive interference, p. 252
proactive interference, p.252
suppression, p. 252
repression, p. 252
misinformation effect, p. 254
source confusion, p. 255
false memory, p. 256
schema, p. 256
script, p. 256
imagination inflation, p. 258
memory trace, p. 261
long-term potentiation, p. 263
amnesia, p. 264
retrograde amnesia, p. 264
memory consolidation, p. 264
anterograde amnesia, p. 265
dementia, p. 268
Alzheimer's disease (AD), p. 268

CONCEPT MAP — MEMORY

Memory

Key processes:
- **Encoding**
- **Storage**
- **Retrieval**

The Stage Model of Memory

Memory is the process of transferring information from one memory stage to another

Sensory memory:
- Briefly stores sensory information about the environment
- Each sense thought to have own sensory memory
- **George Sperling** (b. 1934) demonstrated that visual sensory memory holds information for about half a second before fading

Short-term memory (STM):
- Temporarily stores information transferred from sensory memory and information retrieved from long-term memory
- Capacity is limited to a few "slots," or units of information
- **Maintenance rehearsal** keeps information active and in STM
- If not actively rehearsed, information is lost within 20 seconds

Long-term memory (LTM):
- Stores a potentially unlimited amount of information for up to a lifetime
- **Elaborative rehearsal** involves focusing on the meaning of information encoded into LTM
- Information in LTM is clustered and associated with related groups during recall
- **Semantic network model** describes the organization of LTM as a complex network of associations

Working memory: The active, conscious manipulation of verbal or spatial information temporarily held in STM; thought to consist of:
- Phonological loop
- Visuospatial sketchpad
- Central executive

Explicit memory (declarative memory): Memory with conscious recall
- **Episodic memory:** Events you have experienced
- **Semantic memory:** General facts, knowledge

Implicit memory (nondeclarative memory): Memory without conscious recall
- **Procedural memory:** Motor skills, actions

Retrieval

Process of accessing information stored in long-term memory

Retrieval cues: Hints or prompts that help trigger recall of stored memories
Retrieval cue failure: Recall failure due to inadequate or missing retrieval cues; common example is a **tip-of-the-tongue experience**
Recall, cued recall, and **recognition** are strategies to test retrieval of information
Serial position effect: Tendency to have better recall of first and last items in a series
Encoding specificity principle forms include the **context effect** and **mood congruence**
Flashbulb memories: Vivid memories perceived as accurate but actually no more accurate than ordinary memories

Forgetting

Inability to recall information that was previously available

Hermann Ebbinghaus (1850–1909)
Identified basic pattern of forgetting: rapid loss of some information, then stable memories of the remaining information

Factors contributing to forgetting:
- **Encoding failure**
- **Retrieval cue failure** contributes to **prospective memory** failures
- **Decay theory**
- **Retroactive interference** and **proactive interference**
- **Suppression** and **repression**

Imperfect Memories

Factors that contribute to **false memories:**

- **Elizabeth Loftus** (b. 1944) studies showed how **misinformation effect** can distort memories
- **Source confusion**
- Schema distortion can occur because of previously learned information about a topic **(schemas)** or a sequence of actions **(scripts)**
- **Imagination inflation** can produce a sense of false familiarity
- Blending fact and fiction
- Suggestion

The Search for the Biological Basis of Memory

Karl S. Lashley (1890–1958)

- Concluded memories are *distributed* rather than *localized* as a memory trace in the brain

Richard F. Thompson (b. 1930)

- Showed that memory for a simple conditioned reflex is *localized* in the brain
- Memories can be both distributed and localized

Eric Kandel (b. 1929)

- Showed that forming a new memory produces functional and structural changes in neurons
- As memory becomes established, **long-term potentiation** occurs

Insights about how memory is processed in the brain have come from studying people with **amnesia,** which can be caused by injury or brain surgery.

Retrograde amnesia: Backward-acting amnesia that disrupts process of **memory consolidation**

Anterograde amnesia: Forward-acting amnesia

Most famous case of anterograde amnesia was that of Henry Molaison (1926–2008), known for years only by his initials H.M.

Brenda Milner (b. 1918) and **Suzanne Corkin** (b. 1937)
Studies of H.M. showed that **explicit memory** and **implicit memory** involve different brain regions.

Brain structures involved in memory:

- Hippocampus
- Cerebellum
- Amygdala
- Frontal lobes, including the prefrontal cortex
- Medial temporal lobes

Dementia is the progressive deterioration of cognitive functions, especially memory and reasoning; occurs as a result of a disease or other physical condition.

Most common form of dementia is **Alzheimer's disease (AD),** which is characterized by beta-amyloid plaques and neurofibrillary tangles in the brain.

CHAPTER 7

Thinking, Language, and Intelligence

The Movie Moment

PROLOGUE

Mount Magazine State Park in Arkansas is an easy three-hour drive from Tulsa. So when my friend Lynn and her family invited me to join them for the evening in the hilltop cabin they rented, I jumped at the chance. They were lined up to greet me as I pulled up to their cabin in my trusty, now dusty, red Subaru. Lynn and Will, relaxed and smiling, were happy to be on vacation with their two teenagers in such a beautiful location. Lily, laughing and talkative, was excited about starting college in the fall. And Tom, Lily's younger brother, was standing off to one side, looking away.

"Tom," Lynn prompted, "Tom, say hello to Sandy."

Ducking his head, Tom looked out from beneath the bill of his baseball cap. "Hell-oooooooo," he said with an odd, singsongy cadence in his voice, then quickly turned away.

"Good to see you, Tom!" I replied. If you didn't know Tom, you might think he was being rude. But I was well aware of Tom's social reticence and other "oddball habits," as he called them, which were most noticeable when he interacted with other people.

On the back deck of their cabin we savored the incredible view of the river valley below. Sheer cliffs dropped hundreds of feet. Far in the distance, a river curled its way through miles of fields and woodlands.

Later, as we hiked to the top of Mount Magazine, Tom pushed ahead while Lynn and Will stopped often to identify the butterflies and wildflowers along the path. I thought of some of the conversations that Lynn and I had had over the years about Tom. When Tom was 3, a preschool teacher had recommended that he be screened for vague "developmental delays." She wrote, "Tom doesn't interact with the other children." Sometimes, she said, he was "unresponsive," and seemed "lost in his own world." But Lynn and Will thought that Tom was just shy. At home, he was affectionate with his family and especially close to his older sister.

Tom was unusual in other ways. He was smart—very smart. At the age of 4, Tom had the reading and writing abilities of a child twice his age. Although he seldom talked, when Tom *did* talk, you couldn't help but do a double-take in response to his large vocabulary. And like lots of little boys, Tom would become obsessed with a particular topic. On one of my yearly visits it was volcanoes; on another, construction equipment. But *unlike* lots of other little boys, Tom learned everything he could about his obsession and had little interest in anything else.

As Tom got older, it became harder to minimize the differences between Tom and his peers. In middle school, while other kids were joining teams, clubs, and expanding their social circles, Tom's only friends were online chat room acquaintances. Lynn and Will signed Tom up for Scouts, tennis lessons, and other group activities. But rather than participate, Tom would simply withdraw and sit on the sidelines.

It was when Tom was in the eighth grade that Will experienced what he later called "the movie moment." He was reading a magazine article about some famous artists who shared several unusual personality

Chapter Outline

characteristics. An obsessive interest in a single topic or object. High intelligence. Unusual speech or vocal patterns. An inability to "read" other people's emotions or facial expressions. Poor social skills.

"Wow," Will exclaimed. "This sounds like Tom!"

The article explained that these characteristics reflected a condition called *Asperger's syndrome,* named after the Austrian pediatrician who first described it. Although related to autism, it was far less disabling, and sometimes called the "geek syndrome" because it seemed to be more common among engineers and computer experts—people who were technically brilliant but socially inept.

Will and Tom read up on Asperger's syndrome. Eventually, Tom was evaluated by a pediatric neurologist, who formally diagnosed Tom with Asperger's syndrome. Tom was an "Aspie," as he and others with the condition sometimes refer to themselves.

When I asked Tom if he would share his experiences for this Prologue, I already knew that conversations with him could be difficult. Tom often doesn't pick up on the verbal and nonverbal "signals" that most people use to regulate their interactions with others. Talking to Tom can involve long unexpected pauses when he gazes off to one side or at the floor. You don't know whether he is thinking about what you've said, waiting for you to ask another question, or thinking about something else entirely. So Tom and I agreed that I would interview him using instant text messaging. All clips below are exactly as they were typed during our interview.

Sandy: Tell me how you felt when you were given the diagnosis of Asperger's.
Tom: I felt that I finally had something to pin my weirdness on
S: What do you mean? How did you feel weird?
T: Because I wasn't "normal" and making friends like the rest of my peers.
T: I mean, I'm not schizoid. . . I get lonely like anyone else

For most people, sensing when a person is angry or happy is an intuitive, almost instinctual process. But while Aspies experience emotions like anyone else, they lack the ability to read those emotions in other people. For an Aspie, decoding another person's emotions is a puzzle to be solved, one piece at a time.

Tom: I don't have an easy time communicating.
T: If people are talking out of politeness, I get horribly confused.
Sandy: What is it about Asperger's that makes social interaction so difficult?
T: Well, I suppose it's because of a lack of understanding on the part of the person with Asperger's we don't understand some aspects of politeness, for example.
T: I don't think they're necessary.
S: But what about when honesty might hurt someone's feelings?
T: Sometimes I pick up on that, sometimes not.
T: Sometimes I don't understand why people would be hurt by something.

It's hard for an Aspie to be tactful because they have trouble interpreting other people's emotional state. They don't intend to be rude; they are simply being honest. For example, consider this exchange:

Sandy: I have one more question if that's ok?
Tom: okay. just one?
Sandy: I'm afraid you might be getting bored. See, that's me being polite ☺
Tom: Well, it's not like I have anything better to do.

As is true for many with Asperger's, Tom's intellectual gifts have helped him compensate for his social deficits. By the end of his freshman year of high school, Tom ranked first in his class of over 800 students. He also scored so highly on the SAT that he was admitted to a special school for gifted students.

Although some of his fellow students envy his intellectual abilities, Tom is well aware of the special challenges he faces. For example, like many with Asperger's syndrome, Tom can get "stuck" on a math problem or writing assignment, unable to complete his homework because it doesn't meet his own standards for perfection.

Sandy: Ok, so here's the last question: you can tell thousands of college students whatever you want to say about Asperger's. What would you say?
Tom: hmm, that's a tough question.
T: well, I could try being a smart aleck and say "We're not as smart as the shrinks say we are. Be thankful you're normal."
S: what's to be thankful for?
T: You can turn in work that's less than perfect. You can make friends.

We'll come back to Tom's story as we discuss the different mental abilities involved in thinking, language, and intelligence. We'll also provide more information about autism and Asperger's syndrome. As you'll see, there is more to "intelligence" than just academic ability. Other types of mental abilities—such as the ability to "read" faces, voices, emotions, and social cues—are also important in successfully navigating everyday life.

>> Introduction: Thinking, Language, and Intelligence

Key Theme

- ***Thinking* is a broad term that refers to how we use knowledge to analyze situations, solve problems, and make decisions.**

Key Questions

- **What are some of the basic characteristics of mental images?**
- **How do we manipulate mental images?**
- **What are concepts, and how are they formed?**

cognition
The mental activities involved in acquiring, retaining, and using knowledge.

thinking
The manipulation of mental representations of information in order to draw inferences and conclusions.

mental image
A mental representation of objects or events that are not physically present.

Cognition is a general term that refers to the mental activities involved in acquiring, retaining, and using knowledge. In previous chapters, we've looked at fundamental cognitive processes such as perception, learning, and memory. These processes are critical in order for us to acquire and retain new knowledge.

In this chapter, we will focus on how we *use* that knowledge to analyze situations, solve problems, make decisions, and use language. As you'll see, such cognitive abilities are widely regarded as key dimensions of *intelligence*—a concept that we will also explore.

The Building Blocks of Thought

Mental Imagery and Concepts

In the most general sense, *thinking* is involved in all conscious mental activity, whether it is acquiring new knowledge, remembering, planning ahead, or daydreaming. More narrowly, we can say that **thinking** involves manipulating mental representations of information in order to draw inferences and conclusions. Thinking, then, involves active mental processes and is often directed toward some goal, purpose, or conclusion.

What exactly is it that we think *with?* Thinking often involves the manipulation of two forms of mental representations: *mental images* and *concepts*. We'll look first at mental images.

Mental Images

When you read the Prologue, did you form a mental image of the view from the deck of a cabin perched above a river valley? Or of a steep hiking trail, lined with wildflowers and butterflies? Or Sandy and Tom sitting in front of their computers and exchanging instant messages? The stories we tell in our prologues typically lend themselves to the creation of mental images. Formally, a **mental image** is a mental representation of objects or events that are not physically present.

We often rely on mental images to accomplish some cognitive task. For example, try reciting the letters of the alphabet that consist of only curved lines. To accomplish this task, you have to mentally visualize and then inspect an image of each letter of the alphabet.

Note that mental imagery is not strictly limited to visual "pictures." Most people are able to form images that involve senses other than vision (Cattaneo & Vecchi, 2008; Djordjevic & others, 2004). For example, you can probably easily create a mental representation for the taste of a chocolate milk shake, the smell of freshly popped popcorn, or the feel of wet clothing sticking to your skin. Nonetheless, most research on mental images has looked at how we manipulate visual images, and we'll focus on visual images in our discussion here.

Thinking What types of cognitive activities might be required in planning and implementing a complex bridge repair? Drawing on existing knowledge, analyzing new information, and making decisions about how best to proceed would all be involved. Success would involve the ability to form mental images, effectively solve problems, and make good decisions.

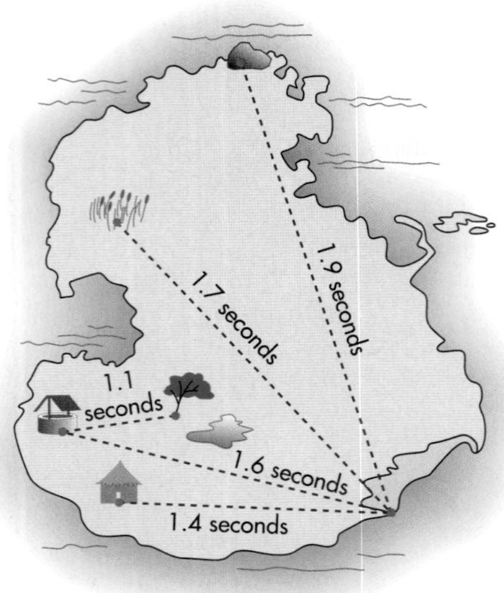

Figure 7.1 Mentally Scanning Images This is a reduced version of the map used by Stephen Kosslyn and his colleagues (1978) to study the scanning of mental images. After subjects memorized the map, the map was removed. Subjects then mentally visualized the map and scanned from one location to another. As you can see by the average scanning times, it took subjects longer to scan greater distances on their mental images of the map, just as it takes longer to scan greater distances on an actual map.

Do people manipulate mental images in the same way that they manipulate their visual images of actual objects? Suppose we gave you a map of the United States and asked you to visually locate San Francisco. Then suppose we asked you to fix your gaze on another city. If the other city was far away from San Francisco (like New York), it would take you longer to visually locate it than if it was close by (like Los Angeles). If you were scanning a *mental* image rather than an actual map, would it also take you longer to scan across a greater distance?

In a classic study by Stephen Kosslyn and his colleagues (1978), participants first viewed and memorized a map of a fictitious island with distinct locations, such as a lake, a hut, and grass (see Figure 7.1). After the map was removed, participants were asked to imagine a specific location on the island, such as the sandy beach. Then a second location, such as the rock, was named. The participants mentally scanned across their mental image of the map and pushed a button when they reached the rock.

The researchers found that the amount of time it took to mentally scan to the new location was directly related to the distance between the two points. The greater the distance between the two points, the longer it took to scan the mental image of the map (Kosslyn & others, 1978). It seems, then, that we tend to scan a mental image in much the same way that we visually scan an actual image (Kosslyn & Thompson, 2000).

However, we don't simply look at mental images in our minds. Sometimes thinking involves the *manipulation* of mental images. For example, try the problem in Figure 7.2 at the bottom of the page, and then continue reading.

It probably took you longer to determine that the 3 in the middle was backward than to determine that the 3 on the far left was backward. Determining which 3s were backward required you to mentally *rotate* each one to an upright position. Just as it takes time to rotate a physical object, it takes time to mentally rotate an image. Furthermore, the greater the degree of rotation required, the longer it takes you to rotate the image mentally (Wohlschläger & Wohlschläger, 1998). Thus, it probably took you longer to mentally rotate the 3 in the middle, which you had to rotate 180 degrees, than it did to mentally rotate the 3 on the far left, which you had to rotate only 60 degrees.

Collectively, research seems to indicate that we manipulate mental images much as we manipulate the actual objects they represent (Rosenbaum & others, 2001). However, mental images are not perfect duplicates of our actual sensory experience. The mental images we use in thinking have some features in common with actual visual images, but they are not like photographs. Instead, they are *memories* of visual images. And, like memories, visual images are actively constructed and potentially subject to error (Cattaneo & Vecchi, 2008).

Concepts

Along with mental images, thinking also involves the use of concepts. A **concept** is a mental category we have formed to group objects, events, or situations that share similar features or characteristics. Concepts provide a kind of mental shorthand, economizing the cognitive effort required for thinking and communication.

Using concepts makes it easier to communicate with others, remember information, and learn new information. For example, the concept "food" might include anything from a sardine to a rutabaga. Although very different, we can still group rutabagas and sardines together because they share the central feature of being edible. If someone introduces us to a new delicacy and tells us it is *food*, we immediately know that it is something to eat—even if it is something we've never seen before.

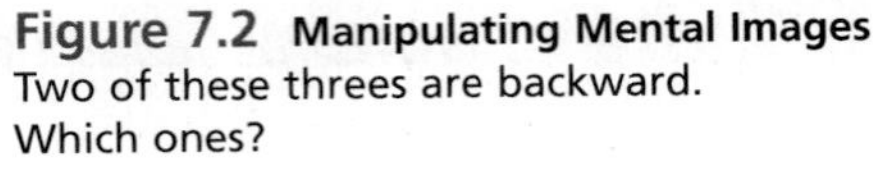

Figure 7.2 Manipulating Mental Images Two of these threes are backward. Which ones?

FOCUS ON NEUROSCIENCE

Seeing Faces and Places in the Mind's Eye

Until the advent of sophisticated brain-scanning techniques, studying mental imagery relied on cognitive tasks, such as measuring how long participants reported it took to scan a mental image (see Kosslyn & others, 2001). Today, however, psychologists are using brain-imaging techniques to study mental imagery. One important issue is whether mental images activate the same brain areas that are involved in perception. Remember, perception takes place when the brain registers information that is received directly from sensory organs.

Previously, researchers have found that perceiving certain types of scenes or objects activates specific brain areas. For example, when we look at *faces,* a brain area dubbed the *fusiform facial area (FFA)* is activated. When we look at pictures of *places,* a different brain area, called the *parahippocampal place area,* or *PPA,* is activated (Epstein & Kanwisher, 1998; Kanwisher, 2001). Given these findings, the critical question is this: If we simply *imagine* faces or places, will the same brain areas be activated?

To answer that question, psychologists Kathleen O'Craven and Nancy Kanwisher (2000) used functional magnetic resonance imaging (fMRI) to compare brain activity during perception and imagery. Study participants underwent fMRI scans while they looked at photographs of familiar faces and places (scenes from their college campus). Next, the participants were asked to close their eyes and form a vivid mental image of each of the photographs they had just viewed.

Three key findings emerged from the study. First, as you can see from the fMRI scans of two participants shown here, *imagining* a face or place activated the same brain region that is activated when *perceiving* a face or a place. More specifically, forming a mental image of a place activated the parahippocampal place area. And, forming a mental image of a face activated the fusiform facial area.

Second, compared to imagining a face or place, actually perceiving a face or place evoked a stronger brain response, as indicated by the slightly larger red and yellow areas in the perception fMRIs (upper row). Third, because the brain responses between the two conditions were so distinctive, O'Craven and Kanwisher could determine what the participants were imagining—faces or places—simply from looking at the fMRI scans.

Other neuroscientists have confirmed that there is considerable overlap in the brain areas involved in visual perception and mental images (Ganis & others, 2004). Clearly, perception and imagination share common brain mechanisms. So, at least as far as the brain is concerned, "the next best thing to being there" might just be closing your eyes . . . and going there in your mind's eye.

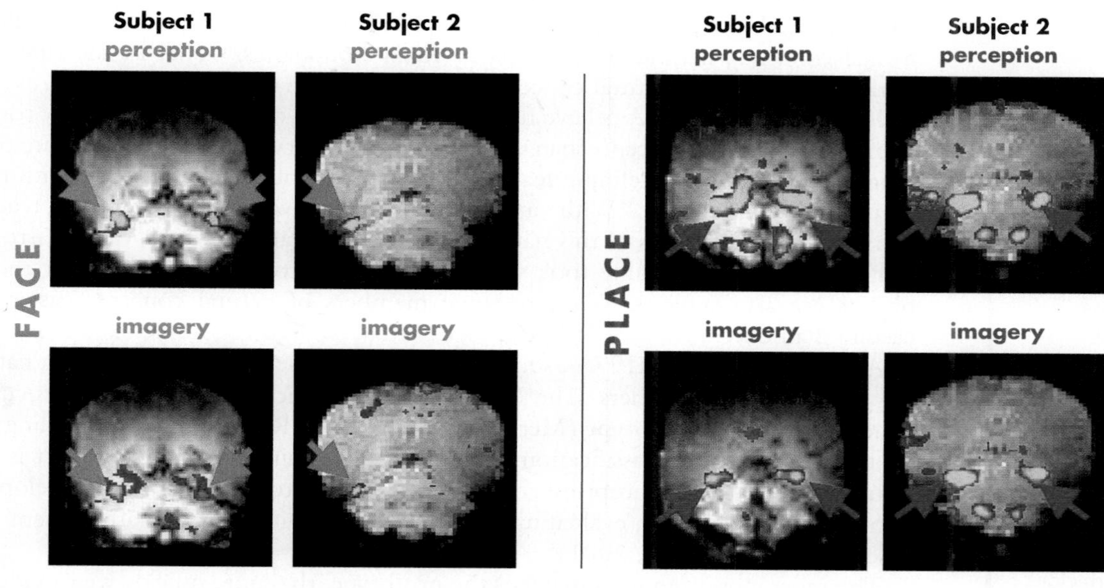

Brain Activation During Perception and Mental Imagery Shown here are the fMRIs of two participants in O'Craven and Kanwisher's (2000) study. Notice that the same brain areas are activated while perceiving or imagining a familiar face. Likewise, the same brain areas are activated while perceiving or imagining a familiar place. Also notice that the brain activation is slightly stronger in the perception condition than in the mental imagery condition.

Adding to the efficiency of our thinking is our tendency to organize the concepts we hold into orderly hierarchies composed of main categories and subcategories (Markman & Gentner, 2001). Thus, a very general concept, such as "furniture," can be mentally divided into a variety of subcategories: tables, chairs, lamps, and so forth. As we learn the key properties that define general concepts, we also learn how members of the concept are related to one another.

How are concepts formed? When we form a concept by learning the *rules* or *features* that define the particular concept, it is called a **formal concept.** Children are taught the specific rules or features that define many simple formal concepts,

concept
A mental category of objects or ideas based on properties they share.

formal concept
A mental category that is formed by learning the rules or features that define it.

Are These Mammals? The more closely an item matches the prototype of a concept, the more quickly we can identify the item as being an example of that concept. Because bats, walruses, and the rather peculiar-looking African long-tailed pangolin (center) don't fit our prototype for a mammal, it takes us longer to decide whether they belong to the category "mammal" than it does to classify animals that are closer to the prototype.

such as geometric shapes. These defining rules or features can be simple or complex. In either case, the rules are logical but rigid. If the defining features, or *attributes,* are present, then the object is included as a member or example of that concept. For some formal concepts, this rigid all-or-nothing categorization procedure works well. For example, a substance can be categorized as a solid, liquid, or gas. The rules defining these formal concepts are very clear-cut.

However, as psychologist Eleanor Rosch (1973) pointed out, the features that define categories of natural objects and events in everyday life are seldom as clear-cut as the features that define formal concepts. A **natural concept** is a concept formed as a result of everyday experience rather than by logically determining whether an object or event fits a specific set of rules. Rosch suggested that, unlike formal concepts, natural concepts have "fuzzy boundaries." That is, the rules or attributes that define natural concepts are not always sharply defined.

Because natural concepts have fuzzy boundaries, it's often easier to classify some members of natural concepts than others (Rosch & Mervis, 1975). To illustrate this point, think about the defining features or rules that you usually associate with the natural concept "vehicle." With virtually no hesitation, you can say that a car, truck, and bus are all examples of this natural concept. How about a sled? Wheelbarrow? Raft? Elevator? It probably took you a few seconds to determine whether these objects are also vehicles. Why are some members of natural concepts easier to classify than others?

According to Rosch (1978), some members are better representatives of a natural concept than are others. The "best," or most typical, instance of a particular concept is called a **prototype** (Mervis & Rosch, 1981; Rosch, 1978). According to prototype theories of classification, we tend to determine whether an object is an instance of a natural concept by comparing it to the prototype we have developed rather than by logically evaluating whether the defining features are present or absent (Minda & Smith, 2001).

The more closely an item matches the prototype, the more quickly we can identify it as being an example of that concept (Rosch & Mervis, 1975). For example, it usually takes us longer to identify an olive or a coconut as being a fruit because they are so dissimilar from our prototype of a typical fruit, like an apple or an orange (see Table 7.1).

Some researchers believe that we don't classify a new instance by comparing it to a single "best example" or prototype. Instead, they believe that we store memories of individual instances, called **exemplars,** of a concept (Nosofsky & Zaki, 2002; Voorspoels & others, 2008). Then, when we encounter a new object, we compare it to the exemplars that we have stored in memory to determine whether it belongs to that category. So, if you're trying to decide whether a coconut is a fruit, you compare it to your memories of other items that you know to be fruits. Is it like an apple? An orange? How about a peach? Or a cantaloupe?

Table 7.1

From Prototypes to Atypical Examples

Vehicles	Fruit
car	orange
truck	apple
bus	banana
motorcycle	peach
train	pear
trolley car	apricot
bicycle	plum
airplane	grape
boat	strawberry
tractor	grapefruit
cart	pineapple
wheelchair	blueberry
tank	lemon
raft	watermelon
sled	honeydew
horse	pomegranate
blimp	date
skates	coconut
wheelbarrow	tomato
elevator	olive

Source: Rosch & Mervis (1975).

The first items listed under each general concept are the ones most people tend to think of as the prototype examples of that concept. As you move down the list, the items become progressively less similar to the prototype examples.

Concepts, Exemplars, and Humor What makes this cartoon funny? One source of humor is *incongruity*—the juxtaposition of two concepts, especially when an unexpected similarity between the concepts is revealed (Martin, 2007). Here, the joke relies on the juxtaposition of cats and the familiar exemplar for a barbershop—the striped pole outside the door, plate glass window, and chairs and magazines for clients waiting their turn. Exemplars are often used in cartoons to communicate a situation or concept to the audience. If you didn't share the exemplar for *barbershop,* you probably wouldn't find the joke to be very funny.

As the two building blocks of thinking, mental images and concepts help us impose order on the phenomena we encounter and think about. We often rely on this knowledge when we engage in complex cognitive tasks, such as solving problems and making decisions, which we'll consider next.

Solving Problems and Making Decisions

Key Theme

- ***Problem solving* refers to thinking and behavior directed toward attaining a goal that is not readily available.**

Key Questions

- **What are some advantages and disadvantages of each problem-solving strategy?**
- **What is insight, and how does intuition work?**
- **How can functional fixedness and mental set interfere with problem solving?**

natural concept
A mental category that is formed as a result of everyday experience.

prototype
The most typical instance of a particular concept.

exemplars
Individual instances of a concept or category, held in memory.

problem solving
Thinking and behavior directed toward attaining a goal that is not readily available.

trial and error
A problem-solving strategy that involves attempting different solutions and eliminating those that do not work.

From fixing flat tires to figuring out how to pay for college classes, we engage in the cognitive task of problem solving so routinely that we often don't even notice the processes we follow. Formally, **problem solving** refers to thinking and behavior directed toward attaining a goal that is not readily available (Novick & Bassok, 2005).

Before you can solve a problem, you must develop an accurate understanding of the problem. Correctly identifying the problem is a key step in successful problem solving (Bransford & Stein, 1993). If your representation of the problem is flawed, your attempts to solve it will also be flawed.

Problem-Solving Strategies

As a general rule, people tend to attack a problem in an organized or systematic way. Usually, the strategy you select is influenced by the nature of the problem and your degree of experience, familiarity, and knowledge about the problem you are confronting (Chrysikou, 2006). In this section, we'll look at some of the common strategies used in problem solving.

Trial and Error

A Process of Elimination

The strategy of **trial and error** involves actually trying a variety of solutions and eliminating those that don't work. When there is a limited range of possible solutions, trial and error can be a useful problem-solving strategy. If you were trying to develop a new spaghetti sauce recipe, for example, you might use trial and error to fine-tune the seasonings.

Trial and Error Even an expert chef needs to "adjust the seasonings"—tasting the food before serving to make sure that the flavors are just right. Many new recipes are developed through a process of trial and error.

algorithm
A problem-solving strategy that involves following a specific rule, procedure, or method that inevitably produces the correct solution.

heuristic
A problem-solving strategy that involves following a general rule of thumb to reduce the number of possible solutions.

insight
The sudden realization of how a problem can be solved.

intuition
Coming to a conclusion or making a judgment without conscious awareness of the thought processes involved.

"Yup, I'm guessing here's your problem."

When the range of possible answers or solutions is large, however, trial and error can be very time-consuming. For example, our friend Robert typically learns new computer programs by trial and error. Rather than taking 20 minutes to look through the manual, he'll spend hours trying different menu commands to see if he can make the software do what it's supposed to do.

Algorithms
Guaranteed to Work

Unlike trial and error, an **algorithm** is a procedure or method that, when followed step by step, always produces the correct solution. Mathematical formulas are examples of algorithms. For instance, the formula used to convert temperatures from Celsius to Fahrenheit (multiply C by 9/5, then add 32) is an algorithm.

Even though an algorithm may be guaranteed to eventually produce a solution, using an algorithm is not always practical. For example, imagine that while rummaging in a closet you find a combination lock with no combination attached. Using an algorithm will eventually produce the correct combination. You can start with 0–0–0, then try 0–0–1, followed by 0–0–2, and so forth, and systematically work your way through combinations to 36–36–36. But this solution would take a while, because there are 46,656 potential combinations to try. So, although using an algorithm to generate the correct combination for the combination lock is guaranteed to work eventually, it's not a very practical approach to solving this particular problem.

Heuristics
Rules of Thumb

In contrast to an algorithm, a **heuristic** is a general rule-of-thumb strategy that may or may not work. Although heuristic strategies are not guaranteed to solve a given problem, they tend to simplify problem solving because they let you reduce the number of possible solutions. With a more limited range of solutions, you can use trial and error to eventually arrive at the correct one. In this way, heuristics may serve an adaptive purpose by allowing us to use patterns of information to solve problems quickly and accurately (Goldstein & Gigerenzer, 2002).

Here's an example. Creating footnotes is described somewhere in the onscreen "Help" documentation for a word-processing software program. If you use the algorithm of scrolling through every page of the Help program, you're guaranteed to solve the problem eventually. But you can greatly simplify your task by using the heuristic of entering "footnotes" in the Help program's search box. This strategy does not guarantee success, because the search term may not be indexed.

One common heuristic is to break a problem into a series of *subgoals.* This strategy is often used in writing a term paper. Choosing a topic, locating information about the topic, organizing the information, and so on become a series of subproblems. As you solve each subproblem, you move closer to solving the larger problem.

Another useful heuristic involves *working backward* from the goal. Starting with the end point, you determine the steps necessary to reach your final goal. For example, when making a budget, people often start off with the goal of spending no more than a certain total each month, then work backward to determine how much of the target amount they will allot for each category of expenses.

Perhaps the key to successful problem solving is *flexibility.* A good problem solver is able to recognize that a particular strategy is unlikely to yield a solution—and knows to switch to a different approach (Bilalić & others, 2008). And, sometimes, the reality is that a problem may not have a single "best" solution.

Remember Tom, whose story we told in the Prologue? One characteristic of Asperger's syndrome is cognitive rigidity and inflexible thinking (Kleinhans & others, 2005; Toth & King, 2008). Like Tom, many people can become frustrated when they are "stuck" on a problem. Unlike Tom, most people are able to sense when it's time to switch to a new strategy, take a break for a few hours, seek assistance from experts or others who may be more knowledgeable—or accept defeat and give up. In Tom's case, rather than give up on a problem or seek a different approach to solving it, Tom will persevere in his attempt to solve it. For example, faced with a difficult homework problem in an advanced mathematics class, Tom often stayed up until 2:00 or 3:00 A.M., struggling to solve a single problem until he literally fell asleep at his desk.

"Sometimes it's easier if you break the work up into little chunks."

Similarly, successful problem solving sometimes involves accepting a less-than-perfect solution to a particular problem—knowing when a solution is "good enough" even if not perfect. But to many with Asperger's syndrome, things are either right or wrong—there is no middle ground (Toth & King, 2008). So when Tom got a 98 rather than 100 on a difficult math test, he was inconsolable. When he ranked in the top five in his class, he was upset because he wasn't first. Tom would sometimes be unable to write an essay because he couldn't think of a perfect opening sentence, or turn in an incomplete essay because he couldn't think of the perfect closing sentence.

Insight and Intuition

Finally, the solution to some problems seems to arrive in a sudden realization, or flash of **insight,** that happens after you mull a problem over (Chronicle & others, 2004; Öllinger & others, 2008). Sometimes an insight will occur when you recognize how the problem is similar to a previously solved problem. Or an insight can involve the sudden realization that an object can be used in a novel way. Try your hand at the two problems in Figure 7.3 at the bottom of the page. The solution to each of those problems is often achieved by insight.

Insights rarely occur through the conscious manipulation of concepts or information. In fact, you're usually not aware of the thought processes that led to an insight. Increasingly, cognitive psychologists and neuroscientists are investigating nonconscious processes, including unconscious problem solving, insight, and intuition (Hodgkinson & others, 2008). **Intuition** means coming to a conclusion or making a judgment without conscious awareness of the thought processes involved.

One influential model of intuition is the two-stage model (Bowers & others, 1990). In the first stage, called the *guiding stage,* you perceive a pattern in the information you're considering, but not consciously. The perception of such patterns is based on your expertise in a given area and your memories of related information.

In the second stage, the *integrative stage,* a representation of the pattern becomes conscious, usually in the form of a hunch or hypothesis. At this point, conscious analytic thought processes take over. You systematically attempt to prove or disprove the hypothesis. For example, an experienced doctor might integrate both obvious and subtle cues to recognize a pattern in a patient's symptoms, a pattern that takes the form of a hunch or an educated guess. Once the hunch is consciously formulated, she might order lab tests to confirm or disprove her tentative diagnosis.

"Actually, I got some pretty good ideas when I was in the box."

An intuitive hunch, then, is a new idea that integrates new information with existing knowledge stored in long-term memory. Such hunches are likely to be accurate only in contexts in which you already have a broad base of knowledge and experience (M. Lieberman, 2000; Jones, 2003).

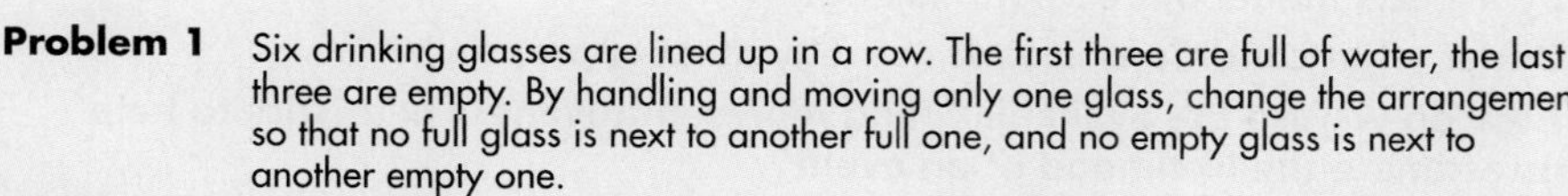

Problem 1 Six drinking glasses are lined up in a row. The first three are full of water, the last three are empty. By handling and moving only one glass, change the arrangement so that no full glass is next to another full one, and no empty glass is next to another empty one.

Problem 2 A man who lived in a small town married 20 different women in that same town. All of them are still living, and he never divorced any of them. Yet he broke no laws. How could he do this?

Figure 7.3 A Demonstration of Insightful Solutions The solutions to these problems are often characterized by sudden flashes of insight. See if you have the "That's it!" experience in solving these problems without looking at the solutions on page 285.

Source: Adapted from Ashcraft (1994); problem 2 adapted from Sternberg (1986).

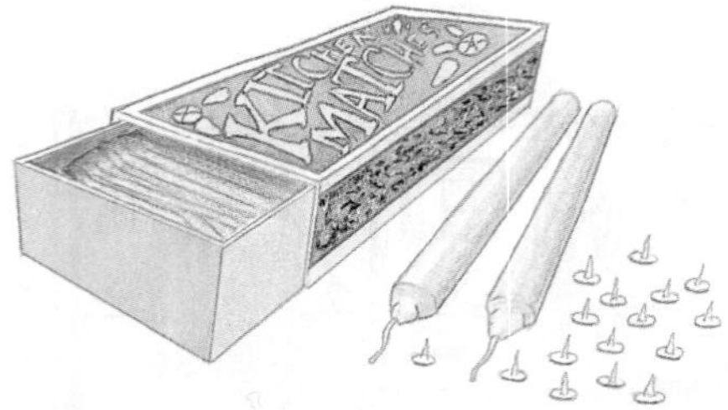

Figure 7.4 Overcoming Functional Fixedness Here's a classic problem for you to solve. You have two candles, some thumbtacks, and a box of matches. Using just these objects, try to figure out how to mount the candles on a wall. (The solution is on page 287.)

Source: Adapted from Duncker (1945).

Obstacles to Solving Problems

Thinking Outside the Box

When we view objects as functioning only in the usual or customary way, we're engaging in a tendency called **functional fixedness.** Functional fixedness often prevents us from seeing the full range of ways in which an object can be used. To get a feel for how functional fixedness can interfere with your ability to find a solution, try the problem in Figure 7.4.

Here's an example of functional fixedness. When pilots fly through clouds, they watch an instrument called an artificial horizon, which shows an outline of an airplane against a horizontal line that represents the horizon. By watching the movement of the outline, they can tell if the aircraft is tilting up or down, or banking to the left or right.

When Don was first learning to fly, he was publicly chastised by a salty old flight instructor for failing to wear a St. Christopher's medal around his neck when flying. Since St. Christopher is the patron saint of travelers, Don assumed that the flight instructor was a bit superstitious. Don's functional fixedness kept him from thinking of any other reason for a pilot to wear a St. Christopher's medal. Finally, Don asked the instructor.

It turned out that a St. Christopher's medal or any other object on a chain can be used to create a makeshift artificial horizon if the flight instrument should fail. You simply drape the chain over the throttle stick. If the aircraft starts pointing down, the medal swings forward; if the aircraft starts pointing upward, the medal swings back. When the aircraft banks, the medal swings to one side or the other. This novel use of an object on a chain could potentially help save the lives of the people in the plane.

Another common obstacle to problem solving is **mental set**—the tendency to persist in solving problems with solutions that have worked in the past (Öllinger & others, 2008). Obviously, if a solution has worked in the past, there's good reason to consider using it again. However, if we approach a problem with a rigid mental set, we may not see other possible solutions (Kershaw & Ohlsson, 2004).

Ironically, mental set is sometimes most likely to block insight in areas in which you are already knowledgeable or well trained. Before you read any further, try solving the simple arithmetic problems in Figure 7.5. If you're having trouble coming up with the answer, it's probably because your existing training in solving arithmetic problems is preventing you from seeing the equations from a different perspective than what you have been taught (Knoblich & Öllinger, 2006; Öllinger & others, 2008).

Mental sets can sometimes suggest a useful heuristic. But they can also prevent us from coming up with new, and possibly more effective, solutions. If we try to be flexible in our thinking and overcome the tendency toward mental sets, we can often identify simpler solutions to many common problems.

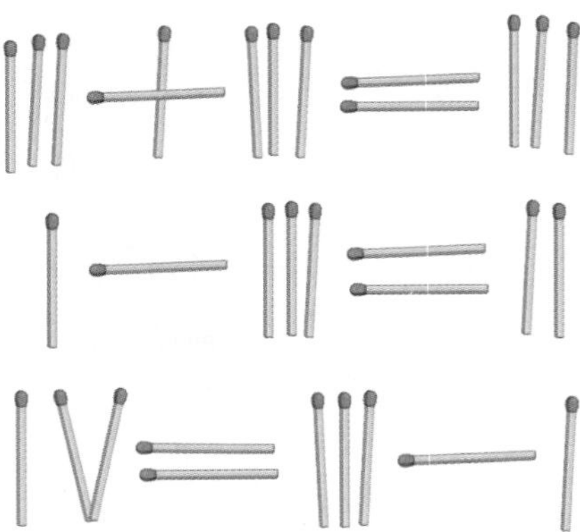

Figure 7.5 Mental Set The equations above, expressed in Roman numerals, are obviously incorrect. Your task is to transform each incorrect equation into a correct equation by moving ONE matchstick in each equation. The matchstick can only be moved once. Only Roman numerals and the three arithmetic operators +, –, or = are allowed. Take your best shot at solving the equations before looking at the solutions on page 287. Remember, in the Roman numeral system, I = 1; II = 2; III = 3; IV = 4; V = 5.

Decision-Making Strategies

Key Theme

- **Different cognitive strategies are used when making decisions, depending on the type and number of options available to us.**

Key Questions

- **What are the single-feature model, the additive model, and the elimination by aspects model of decision making?**
- **Under what conditions is each strategy most appropriate?**
- **How do we use the availability and representativeness heuristics to help us estimate the likelihood of an event?**

Who hasn't felt like flipping a coin when faced with an important or complicated decision? Fortunately, most of the decisions we make in everyday life are relatively minor. But every now and then we have to make a decision where much more is at stake. When a decision is important or complex, we're more likely to invest time, effort, and other resources in considering different options.

The decision-making process becomes complicated when each option involves the consideration of several features. It's rare that one alternative is superior in every category. So, what do you do when each alternative has pros and cons? In this section, we'll describe three common decision-making strategies.

The Single-Feature Model

One decision-making strategy is called the *single-feature model*. In order to simplify the choice among many alternatives, you base your decision on a single feature. When the decision is a minor one, the single-feature model can be a good decision-making strategy. For example, faced with an entire supermarket aisle of laundry detergents, you could simplify your decision by deciding to buy the cheapest brand. When a decision is important or complex, however, making decisions on the basis of a single feature can increase the riskiness of the decision.

The Additive Model

A better strategy for complex decisions is to systematically evaluate the important features of each alternative. One such decision-making model is called the *additive model*.

In this model, you first generate a list of the factors that are most important to you. Then, you rate each alternative on each factor using an arbitrary scale, such as −5 to +5. If a particular factor has strong advantages or appeal, you give it the maximum rating (+5). If a particular factor has strong drawbacks or disadvantages, you give it the minimum rating (−5). Finally, you add up the ratings for each alternative. This strategy can often reveal the best overall choice. If the decision involves a situation in which some factors are more important than others, you can emphasize the more important factors by multiplying the rating.

Taking the time to apply the additive model to important decisions can greatly improve your decision making. By allowing you to evaluate the features of one alternative at a time, then comparing the alternatives, the additive model provides a logical strategy for identifying the most acceptable choice from a range of possible decisions. Although we seldom formally calculate the subjective value of individual features for different options, we often informally use the additive model by comparing two choices feature by feature. The alternative with the "best" collection of features is then selected.

Problem 1	Pour the water in glass number 2 into glass number 5.
Problem 2	The man is a minister.

Solutions to the Problems in Figure 7.3

The Elimination by Aspects Model

Psychologist Amos Tversky (1972) proposed another decision-making model called the *elimination by aspects model*. Using this model, you evaluate all the alternatives one characteristic at a time, typically starting with the feature you consider most important. If a particular alternative fails to meet that criterion, you scratch it off your list of possible choices, even if it possesses other desirable attributes. As the range of possible choices is narrowed down, you continue to compare the remaining alternatives, one feature at a time, until just one alternative is left.

For example, suppose you want to buy a new computer. You might initially eliminate all the models that aren't powerful enough to run the software you need to use, then the models outside your budget, and so forth. Continuing in this fashion, you would progressively narrow down the range of possible choices to the one choice that satisfies all your criteria.

Good decision makers adapt their strategy to the demands of the specific situation. If there are just a few choices and features to compare, people tend to use the additive method, at least informally. However, when the decision is complex, involving the comparison of many choices that have multiple features, people often use *both* strategies. That is, we usually begin by focusing on the critical features, using the elimination by aspects strategy to quickly narrow down the range of acceptable choices. Once we have narrowed the list of choices down to a more manageable short list, we tend to use the additive model to make a final decision.

functional fixedness
The tendency to view objects as functioning only in their usual or customary way.

mental set
The tendency to persist in solving problems with solutions that have worked in the past.

availability heuristic
A strategy in which the likelihood of an event is estimated on the basis of how readily available other instances of the event are in memory.

representativeness heuristic
A strategy in which the likelihood of an event is estimated by comparing how similar it is to the prototype of the event.

language
A system for combining arbitrary symbols to produce an infinite number of meaningful statements.

Decisions Involving Uncertainty

Estimating the Probability of Events

Some decisions involve a high degree of uncertainty. In these cases, you need to make a decision, but you are unable to predict with certainty that a given event will occur. Instead, you have to estimate the probability of an event occurring. But how do you actually make that estimation?

For example, imagine that you're running late for a very important appointment. You may be faced with this decision: "Should I risk a speeding ticket to get to the appointment on time?" In this case, you would have to estimate the probability of a particular event occurring—getting pulled over for speeding.

In such instances, we often estimate the likelihood that certain events will occur, then gamble. In deciding what the odds are that a particular gamble will go our way, we tend to rely on two rule-of-thumb strategies to help us estimate the likelihood of events: the *availability heuristic* and the *representativeness heuristic* (Tversky & Kahneman, 1982; Kahneman, 2003).

Vivid Images and the Availability Heuristic After the terrorist attacks of September 11, 2001, vivid scenes of the devastation at the Pentagon in Washington, D.C., and at the site of the World Trade Center were highly publicized. Fears of another terrorist hijacking caused sales of airline tickets to plunge, and many Americans turned to automobiles for long-distance travel. But as the number of miles driven on interstate highways surged, so did traffic deaths. In fact, there were 353 more traffic deaths during the last three months of 2001 than there were for the same months during the previous three years. As German psychologist Gerd Gigerenzer (2004) points out, "The number of Americans who lost their lives on the road by avoiding the risk of flying was higher than the total number of passengers—266—killed on the four fatal flights." How does the availability heuristic explain the fact that so many people are unwilling to fly on a commercial airliner after highly publicized plane crashes?

The Availability Heuristic

When we use the **availability heuristic,** we estimate the likelihood of an event on the basis of how readily available other instances of the event are in our memory. When instances of an event are easily recalled, we tend to consider the event as being more likely to occur. So, we're less likely to exceed the speed limit if we can readily recall that a friend recently got a speeding ticket.

However, when a rare event makes a vivid impression on us, we may overestimate its likelihood (Tversky & Kahneman, 1982). State lottery commissions capitalize on this cognitive tendency by running many TV commercials showing that lucky person who won the $100 million Powerball. A vivid memory is created, which leads viewers to an inaccurate estimate of the likelihood that the event will happen to them.

The key point here is that the less accurately our memory of an event reflects the actual frequency of the event, the less accurate our estimate of the event's likelihood will be. That's why the lottery commercials don't show the other 50 million people staring dejectedly at their TV screens because they did *not* win the $100 million.

The Representativeness Heuristic

The other heuristic we often use to make estimates is called the **representativeness heuristic** (Kahneman & Tversky, 1982; Kahneman, 2003). Here, we estimate an event's likelihood by comparing how similar its essential features are to our prototype of the event. Remember, a *prototype* is the most typical example of an object or an event.

To go back to our example of deciding whether to speed, we are more likely to risk speeding if we think that we're somehow significantly different from the prototype of the driver who gets a speeding ticket. If our prototype of a speeder is a teenager driving a flashy, high-performance car, and we're an adult driving a minivan with a baby seat, then we will probably estimate the likelihood of our getting a speeding ticket as low.

Like the availability heuristic, the representativeness heuristic can lead to inaccurate judgments. Consider the following description:

> Maria is a perceptive, sensitive, introspective woman. She is very articulate, but measures her words carefully. Once she's certain she knows what she wants to say, she expresses herself easily and confidently. She has a strong preference to work alone.

On the basis of this description, is it more likely that Maria is a successful fiction writer or that Maria is a registered nurse? Most people guess that she is a successful fiction writer. Why? Because the description seems to mesh with what many people think of as the typical characteristics of a writer.

However, when you compare the number of registered nurses (which is very large) to the number of successful female fiction writers (which is very small), it's actually much more likely that Maria is a nurse. Thus, the representativeness heuristic can produce faulty estimates if (1) we fail to consider possible variations from the prototype or (2) we fail to consider the approximate number of prototypes that actually exist.

What determines which heuristic is most likely to be used? Research suggests that the availability heuristic is most likely to be used when people rely on information held in their long-term memory to determine the likelihood of events occurring. On the other hand, the representativeness heuristic is more likely to be used when people compare different variables to make predictions (Harvey, 2007).

The Critical Thinking box "The Persistence of Unwarranted Beliefs" on the next page discusses some of the other psychological factors that can influence the way in which we evaluate evidence, make decisions, and draw conclusions.

Language and Thought

Key Theme

- **Language is a system for combining arbitrary symbols to produce an infinite number of meaningful statements.**

Key Questions

- **What are the characteristics of language?**
- **How does language affect thinking?**
- **How have nonhuman animals been shown to use language?**

The human capacity for language is surely one of the most remarkable of all our cognitive abilities. With little effort, you produce hundreds of new sentences every day. And you're able to understand the vast majority of the thousands of words contained in this chapter without consulting a dictionary.

Human language has many special qualities—qualities that make it flexible, versatile, and complex. **Language** can be formally defined as a system for combining arbitrary symbols to produce an infinite number of meaningful statements. We'll begin our discussion of the relationship between language and thought by describing these special characteristics of language. In Chapter 9, we'll discuss language development in children.

The Characteristics of Language

The purpose of language is to communicate—to express meaningful information in a way that can be understood by others. To do so, language requires the use of *symbols.* These symbols may be sounds, written words, or, as in American Sign Language, formalized gestures.

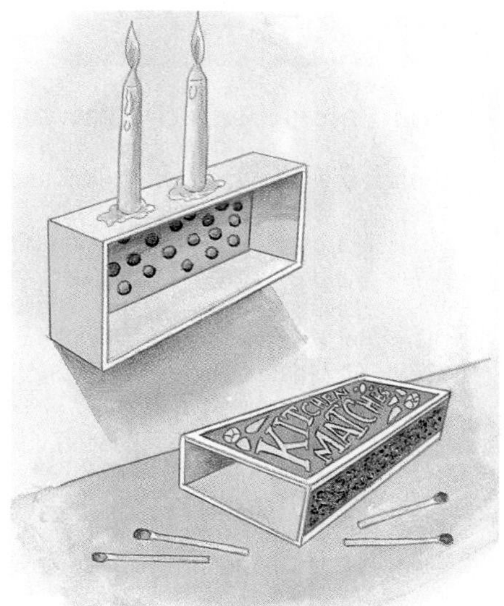

Solution to Figure 7.4

Solution to Figure 7.5 Most people try to correct the equations in Figure 7.5 by moving a matchstick that changes one of the numbers. Why? Because solving the math problems that we are assigned in school almost always involves manipulating the numbers, not the arithmetic signs. While this assumption is a useful one in solving the vast majority of math problems—especially the ones that you are assigned as homework—it is an example of a mental set that can block you from arriving at new, creative solutions to problems.

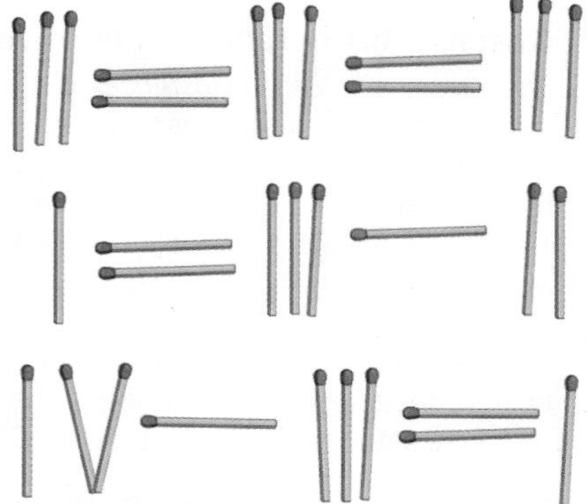

CRITICAL THINKING

The Persistence of Unwarranted Beliefs

Throughout this text, we show how many pseudoscientific claims fail when subjected to scientific scrutiny. However, once a belief in a pseudoscience or paranormal phenomenon is established, the presentation of contradictory evidence often has little impact (Lester, 2000). Ironically, contradictory evidence can actually *strengthen* a person's established beliefs (Lord & others, 1979). How do psychologists account for this?

Several psychological studies have explored how people deal with evidence, especially evidence that contradicts their beliefs (see Ross & Anderson, 1982; Zusne & Jones, 1989). The four obstacles to logical thinking described here can account for much of the persistence of unwarranted beliefs in pseudosciences or other areas (Risen & Gilovich, 2007).

Obstacle 1: The Belief-Bias Effect

The *belief-bias effect* occurs when people accept only the evidence that conforms to their belief, rejecting or ignoring any evidence that does not. For example, in a classic study conducted by Warren Jones and Dan Russell (1980), ESP believers and ESP disbelievers watched two attempts at telepathic communication. In each attempt, a "receiver" tried to indicate what card the "sender" was holding.

In reality, both attempts were rigged. One attempt was designed to appear to be a successful demonstration of telepathy, with a significant number of accurate responses. The other attempt was designed to convincingly demonstrate failure. In this case, the number of accurate guesses was no more than chance and could be produced by simple random guessing.

Following the demonstration, the participants were asked what they believed had taken place. Both believers and disbelievers indicated that ESP had occurred in the successful attempt. But only the believers said that ESP had also taken place in the clearly *unsuccessful* attempt. In other words, the ESP believers ignored or discounted the evidence in the failed attempt. This is the essence of the belief-bias effect.

Obstacle 2: Confirmation Bias

Confirmation bias is the strong tendency to search for information or evidence that confirms a belief, while making little or no effort to search for information that might disprove the belief (Gilovich, 1997). For example, we tend to read the newspaper and magazine columns of editorial writers who interpret events from our perspective and to avoid the columns of writers who don't see things our way (Ruscio, 1998).

Obstacle 3: The Fallacy of Positive Instances

The *fallacy of positive instances* is the tendency to remember uncommon events that seem to confirm our beliefs and to forget events that disconfirm our beliefs. Often, the occurrence is really nothing more than coincidence. For example, you find yourself thinking of an old friend. A few moments later, the phone rings and it's him. You remember this seemingly telepathic event, but forget all the times that you've thought of your old friend and he did not call. In other words, you remember the positive instance but fail to notice the negative instances when the anticipated event did not occur (Gilovich, 1997).

"What's nice about working in this place is we don't have to finish any of our experiments."

Obstacle 4: The Overestimation Effect

The tendency to overestimate the rarity of events is referred to as the *overestimation effect.* Suppose a "psychic" comes to your class of 23 students. Using his psychic abilities, the visitor "senses" that two people in the class were born on the same day. A quick survey finds that, indeed, two people share the same month and day of birth. This is pretty impressive evidence of clairvoyance, right? After all, what are the odds that two people in a class of 23 would have the same birthday?

When we perform this "psychic" demonstration in class, our students usually estimate that it is very unlikely that 2 people in a class of 23 will share a birthday. In reality, the odds are *1 in 2,* or 50–50 (Martin, 1998). Our students' overestimation of the rarity of this event is an example of the *overestimation effect.*

Thinking Critically About the Evidence

On the one hand, it is important to keep an open mind. Simply dismissing an idea as impossible shuts out the consideration of evidence for new and potentially promising ideas or phenomena. At one time, for example, scientists thought it impossible that rocks could fall from the sky (Hines, 2003).

On the other hand, the obstacles described here underscore the importance of choosing ways to gather and think about evidence that will help us avoid unwarranted beliefs and self-deception.

The critical thinking skills we described in Chapter 1 are especially useful in this respect. Boxes "What Is Critical Thinking?" and "What Is a Pseudoscience?" provided guidelines that can be used to evaluate all claims, including pseudoscientific or paranormal claims. In particular, it's important to stress again that good critical thinkers strive to evaluate *all* the available evidence before reaching a conclusion, not just the evidence that supports what they want to believe.

CRITICAL THINKING QUESTIONS

- How can using critical thinking skills help you avoid these obstacles to logical thinking?
- Beyond the logical fallacies described here, what might motivate people to maintain beliefs in the face of contradictory evidence?

A few symbols may be similar in form to the meaning they signify, such as the English words *boom* and *pop*. However, for most words, the connection between the symbol and the meaning is completely *arbitrary* (Pinker, 1995). For example, *ton* is a small word that stands for a vast quantity, whereas *nanogram* is a large word that stands for a very small quantity. Because the relationship between the symbol and its meaning is arbitrary, language is tremendously flexible (Pinker, 1994). New words can be invented, such as *podcast, metrosexual,* and *bling*. And the meanings of words can change and evolve, such as *gay, stock market,* and *union*.

American Sign Language American Sign Language, used by hearing-impaired people, meets all the formal requirements for language, including syntax, displacement, and generativity. The similarities between spoken language and sign language have been confirmed by brain-imaging studies. The same brain regions are activated in hearing people when they speak as in deaf people when they use sign language (Hickok & others, 2001; Lubbadeh, 2005).

The meaning of these symbols is *shared* by others who speak the same language. That is, speakers of the same language agree on the connection between the sound and what it symbolizes. Consequently, a foreign language sounds like a stream of meaningless sounds because we do not share the memory of the connection between the arbitrary sounds and the concrete meanings they symbolize.

> The word *duck* does not look like a duck, walk like a duck, or quack like a duck, but refers to a duck all the same, because the members of a language community, as children, all memorized the pairing [between a sound and a meaning].
>
> STEVEN PINKER (1995)

Further, language is a highly structured system that follows specific rules. Every language has its own unique *syntax,* or set of rules for combining words. Although you're usually unaware of these rules as you're speaking or writing, you immediately notice when a rule has been violated.

The rules of language help determine the meaning that is being communicated. For example, word-order rules are very important in determining the meaning of an English phrase. "The boy ate the giant pumpkin" has an entirely different meaning from "The giant pumpkin ate the boy." In other languages, meaning may be conveyed by different rule-based distinctions, such as specific pronouns, the class or category of word, or word endings.

Another important characteristic of language is that it is creative, or *generative*. That is, you can generate an infinite number of new and different phrases and sentences.

A final important characteristic of human language is called *displacement*. You can communicate meaningfully about ideas, objects, and activities that are not physically present. You can refer to activities that will take place in the future, that took place in the past, or that will take place only if certain conditions are met ("If you get that promotion, maybe we can afford a new car"). You can also carry on a vivid conversation about abstract ideas ("What is justice?") or strictly imaginary topics ("If you were going to spend a year in a space station orbiting Neptune, what would you bring along?").

Giving Birth to a New Language In 1977, a special school for deaf children opened in Managua, Nicaragua. The children quickly developed a system of gestures for communicating with one another. Over the past 30 years, the system of gestures has evolved into a unique new language with its own grammar and syntax—*Idioma de Signos Nicaragense* (Senghas & othe-- 2004; Siegal, 2004). The birth of Nica aguan Sign Language is not a unique even. Recently, linguists Wendy Sandler and her colleagues (2006) at the University of Haifa documented the spontaneous development of another unique sign language, this one in a remote Bedouin village where a large number of villagers share a form of hereditary deafness (Fox, 2008). Like Nicaraguan Sign Language, *Al-Sayyid Bedouin Sign Language* has its own syntax and grammatical rules, which differ from other languages in the region. The spontaneous evolution of these two unique sign languages vividly demonstrates the human predisposition to develop rule-based systems of communication (Fox, 2008).

CULTURE AND HUMAN BEHAVIOR

The Effect of Language on Perception

Professionally, Benjamin Whorf (1897–1941) was an insurance company inspector. But his passion was the study of languages, particularly Native American languages. In the 1950s, Whorf proposed an intriguing theory that became known as the *Whorfian hypothesis.*

Whorf (1956) believed that a person's language determines the very structure of his or her thought and perception. Your language, he claimed, determines how you perceive and "carve up" the phenomena of your world. He argued that people who speak very different languages have completely different worldviews. More formally, the Whorfian hypothesis is called the **linguistic relativity hypothesis**—the notion that differences among languages cause differences in the thoughts of their speakers.

To illustrate his hypothesis, Whorf contended that the Eskimos had many different words for "snow." But English, he pointed out, has only the word *snow.* According to Whorf (1956):

> We have the same word for falling snow, snow on the ground, snow packed hard like ice, slushy snow, wind-driven flying snow—whatever the situation may be. To an Eskimo, this all-inclusive word would be almost unthinkable; he would say that falling snow, slushy snow, and so on are sensuously and operationally different, different things to contend with; he uses different words for them and for other kinds of snow.

Whorf's example would be compelling except for one problem: The Eskimos do *not* have dozens of different words for "snow." Rather, they have just a few words for "snow" (Martin, 1986; Pullum, 1991). Beyond that minor sticking point, think carefully about Whorf's example. Is it really true that English-speaking people have a limited capacity to describe snow? Or do not discriminate between different types of snow? The English language includes *snowflake, snowfall, slush, sleet, flurry, blizzard,* and *avalanche.* Avid skiers have many additional words to describe snow, from *powder* to *mogul* to *hardpack.*

More generally, people with expertise in a particular area tend to perceive and make finer distinctions than nonexperts do. Experts are also more likely to know the specialized terms that reflect those distinctions (Pinker, 1994). To the knowledgeable bird-watcher, for example, there are distinct differences between a cedar waxwing and a bohemian waxwing. To the nonexpert, they're just two brownish birds with yellow tail feathers.

Despite expert/nonexpert differences in noticing and naming details, we don't claim that the expert "sees" a different reality than a nonexpert. In other words, our perceptions and thought processes influence the language we use to describe those perceptions (Rosch, 1987). Notice that this conclusion is the exact *opposite* of the linguistic relativity hypothesis.

Whorf also pointed out that many languages have different color-naming systems. English has names for 11 basic colors: *black, white, red, green, yellow, blue, brown, purple, pink, orange,* and *gray*. However, some languages have only a few color terms. Navajo, for example, has only one word to describe both blue and green, but two different words for black (Fishman, 1960). Would people who had just a few words for colors "carve up" and perceive the electromagnetic spectrum differently?

Eleanor Rosch set out to answer this question (Heider & Olivier, 1972). The Dani-speaking people of New Guinea have words for only two colors. *Mili* is used for the dark, cool colors of black, green, and blue. *Mola* is used for light, warm colors, such as white, red, and yellow. According to the Whorfian hypothesis, the people of New Guinea, with names for only two

How Language Influences Thinking

All your cognitive abilities are involved in understanding and producing language. Using learning and memory, you acquire and remember the meaning of words. You interpret the words you hear or read (or see, in the case of American Sign Language) through the use of perception. You use language to help you reason, represent and solve problems, and make decisions (Polk & Newell, 1995).

Language can influence thinking in several ways. For example, when you hear about a course titled "Man and His Environment," what image comes to mind? Do you visualize a group of men tromping through the forest, or do you imagine a mixed group of men and women?

The word *man* or the pronouns *he* and *his* can refer to either a male or a female in English, because English has no gender-neutral pronoun. So, according to the rules of the English language, the course title "Man and His Environment" technically refers to both men and women.

However, several studies have shown that using the masculine pronoun tends to produce images of males and exclude females (Beasley, 2007; Crawford, 2001). In a classic study by Nancy Henley (1989), participants were given identical sentence fragments to complete. Examples included "If a writer expects to get a book published . . ." and "If an employee wants a raise . . ." Participants in the first group were given the masculine generic *he* to use in finishing the sentences. Participants in the second group were given either *they* or *he or she* to use in completing the sentences.

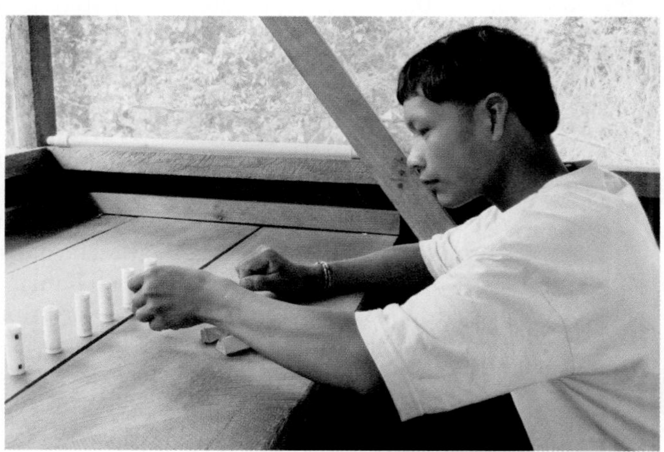

Can You Count Without Number Words? Cognitive neuroscientist Edward Gibson traveled to a remote Amazon village to confirm previous research by anthropologist and linguist David Everett (2008, 2005) that showed the Pirahã people lacked the ability to count and had no comprehension of numbers. Gibson found that rather than identifying quantities by exact numbers, the Pirahã research participants used only relative terms like "few," "some," and "many." According to Gibson, the Pirahã are capable of learning to count, but did not develop a number system because numbers are simply not useful in their culture (Frank & others, 2008).

classes of colors, should perceive color differently than English-speaking people, with names for 11 basic colors.

Rosch showed Dani speakers a brightly colored chip and then, 30 seconds later, asked them to pick out the color they had seen from an array of other colors. Despite their lack of specific words for the colors they had seen, the Dani did as well as English speakers on the test. The Dani people used the same word to label red and yellow, but they still distinguished between the two. Rosch concluded that the Dani people perceived colors in much the same way as English-speaking people.

Other research on color-naming in different languages has arrived at similar conclusions: Although color *names* may vary, color *perception* does not appear to depend on the language used (Lindsey & Brown, 2004; Delgado, 2004; Kay & Regier, 2007).

The bottom line? Whorf's strong contention that language *determines* perception and the structure of thought has not been supported. However, cultural and cognitive psychologists today are actively investigating the ways in which language can *influence* perception and thought (Frank & others, 2008; Majid & others, 2004).

A striking demonstration of the influence of language comes from recent studies of remote indigenous peoples living in the Amazon region of Brazil (Everett, 2005, 2008). The language of the Pirahã people, an isolated tribe of fewer than 200 members, has no words for specific numbers (Frank & others, 2008). Their number words appear to be restricted to words that stand for "few," "more," and "many" rather than exact quantities such as "three," "five," or "twenty." Similarly, the Mundurukú language, spoken by another small Amazon tribe, has words only for quantities one through five (Pica & others, 2004). Above that number, they used such expressions as "some," "many," or "a small quantity." In both cases, individuals were unable to complete simple arithmetical tasks (Gordon, 2004).

Such findings do not, by any means, confirm Whorf's belief that language *determines* thinking or perception (Gelman & Gallistel, 2004). Rather, they demonstrate how language categories can affect *how* individuals think about particular concepts.

After completing the sentences, the subjects were asked to describe their mental imagery for each sentence and to provide a first name for the person they visualized. When the word *he* was used, subjects were much more likely to produce a male image and name than a female image and name. When the phrase *he or she* was used, subjects were only slightly more likely to use a male rather than a female image and name.

Using the masculine generic pronoun influences people to visualize a male, even when they "know" that *he* supposedly includes both men and women (Hamilton, 1988, 1991). Thus, using *he* to refer to both men and women in speech and writing tends to increase male bias.

Animal Communication

Can Animals Learn Language?

Without question, animals communicate. Chimpanzees "chutter" to warn of snakes, "rraup" to warn of an eagle, and "chirp" to let the others know that a leopard is nearby (Marler, 1967). Each of the warning calls of the vervet monkey of East Africa triggers specific behaviors for a particular danger, such as scurrying for cover in the bushes when the warning for an airborne predator is sounded (Cheney & Seyfarth, 1990). Even insects have complex communication systems. For example, honeybees perform a "dance" to report information about the distance, location, and quality of a pollen source to their hive mates (Riley & others, 2005).

linguistic relativity hypothesis
The hypothesis that differences among languages cause differences in the thoughts of their speakers.

Vervet Monkeys Vervet monkeys sound different alarm calls for different kinds of predators. The "leopard" call sends the troop into the trees to avoid leopards and other ground predators. In response to the "eagle" call, the monkeys look up and take cover in bushes to hide from aerial predators.

Clearly, animals communicate with one another, but are they capable of mastering language? Some of the most promising results have come from the research of psychologists Sue Savage-Rumbaugh and Duane Rumbaugh (Lyn & others, 2006). These researchers are working with a rare chimpanzee species called the *bonobo*. In the mid-1980s, they taught a female bonobo, named Matata, to press symbols on a computer keyboard. Although Matata did not learn many symbols, her infant son, Kanzi, appeared to learn how to use the keyboard simply from watching his mother and her caretakers (Savage-Rumbaugh & Lewin, 1994).

Along with learning symbols, Kanzi also comprehends spoken English. Altogether, Kanzi understands more than 500 spoken English words. And, Kanzi can respond to new, complex spoken commands, such as "Put the ball on the pine needles," and "Can you go scare Matata with the mask?" (Segerdahl & others, 2006). Because these spoken commands are made by an assistant out of Kanzi's view, he cannot be responding to nonverbal cues.

Kanzi also seems to demonstrate an elementary understanding of syntax. He is able to respond correctly to commands whose meaning is determined by word order. For example, using a toy dog and toy snake, he responds appropriately to such commands as "Make the dog bite the snake" and "Make the snake bite the dog." Kanzi seems to demonstrate a level of language comprehension that is roughly equivalent to that of a 2½-year-old human child (Lyn & others, 2006).

Research evidence suggests that nonprimates also can acquire limited aspects of language. For example, Louis Herman and his coworkers (1993, 2002) have trained bottle-nosed dolphins to respond to sounds and gestures, each of which stands for a word. This artificial language incorporates syntax rules, such as those that govern word order.

Finally, consider Alex, an African gray parrot. Trained by Irene Pepperberg (1993, 2000), Alex could answer spoken questions with spoken words. By the time of his death in 2007, Alex could identify 50 different objects, 7 colors, 5 shapes, and quantities up to 7. He could accurately answer questions about the color and number of objects, and could categorize objects by color, shape, and material, which suggested that he comprehended simple concepts (Pepperberg, 2007). Alex also used many simple phrases, such as "Come here" and "How many?" He could even indicate where he wanted to be taken by saying, "Want to go knee" (to sit on a knee) or "Want to go back."

Sue Savage-Rumbaugh with Kanzi Kanzi, a bonobo, communicates by pressing symbols on a computer keyboard. Kanzi uses the symbols to communicate requests and intentions—and even, when alone, to "talk" to himself. Kanzi now resides at the Great Ape Trust in Des Moines, Iowa, in a colony with seven other bonobos, where study of primate cognition continues in a natural environment (Segerdahl & others, 2006). To learn more about the Great Ape Trust sanctuary and the orangutans, bonobos, and research psychologists—including Savage-Rumbaugh—who live and work there, visit the Web site at www.GreatApeTrust.org.

When animal language research began in the 1960s and 1970s, some critics contended that primates were simply producing learned responses to their trainers' nonverbal cues rather than demonstrating true language skills (Terrace, 1985). Over the last two decades, however, studies conducted under more carefully controlled conditions have produced some compelling demonstrations of animal language learning. Nevertheless, even the performance of primate superstars such as Kanzi pales in comparison with the language learning demonstrated by a 3-year-old child (Pinker, 1994).

Collectively, animal language research reflects an active area of psychological research that is referred to as **animal cognition** or *comparative cognition* (Papini, 2002; Wasserman & Zentall, 2006). Although the results of these studies are fascinating, a great deal remains to be discovered about the potential of different species of animals to communicate, produce language, and solve problems—and their limitations in doing so. Many psychologists caution against jumping to the conclusion that animals can "think" or that they possess self-awareness, because such conclusions are far from proven (Premack, 2007).

Irene Pepperberg with Alex When Alex died suddenly in September 2007, the story was reported in newspapers around the world, including the *New York Times* (Carey, 2007; Talbot, 2008). Over 30 years of research, Pepperberg and Alex revolutionized ideas about avian intelligence and animal communication. Along with his remarkable language abilities, Alex also displayed an understanding of simple concepts, including an understanding of bigger and smaller, similarity and difference. Shown a green block and a green ball and asked "What's the same?" Alex responds, "Color." Alex could even accurately label quantities up to the number six (Pepperberg, 2007). To learn more about Pepperberg's ongoing research with gray parrots Griffin and Arthur, visit www.alexfoundation.org.

Measuring Intelligence

Key Theme

- ***Intelligence* is defined as the global capacity to think rationally, act purposefully, and deal effectively with the environment.**

Key Questions

- **What roles did Binet, Terman, and Wechsler play in the development of intelligence tests?**
- **How did Binet, Terman, and Wechsler differ in their beliefs about intelligence and its measurement?**
- **Why are standardization, validity, and reliability important components of psychological tests?**

Up to this point, we have talked about a broad range of cognitive abilities—the use of mental images and concepts, problem solving and decision making, and the use of language. All these mental abilities are aspects of what we commonly call *intelligence*.

What exactly is intelligence? We will rely on a formal definition developed by psychologist David Wechsler. Wechsler (1944, 1977) defined **intelligence** as the global capacity to think rationally, act purposefully, and deal effectively with the environment. Although many people commonly equate intelligence with "book smarts," notice that Wechsler's definition is much broader. To Wechsler, intelligence is reflected in effective, rational, and goal-directed behavior.

The Development of Intelligence Tests

Can intelligence be measured? If so, how? Intelligence tests attempt to measure general mental abilities, rather than accumulated knowledge or aptitude for a specific subject or area. In the next several sections, we will describe the evolution of intelligence tests, including the qualities that make any psychological test scientifically acceptable.

Alfred Binet
Identifying Students Who Needed Special Help

In the early 1900s, the French government passed a law requiring all children to attend school. Faced with the need to educate children from a wide variety of backgrounds, the French government commissioned psychologist **Alfred Binet** to develop procedures to identify students who might require special help.

animal cognition
The study of animal learning, memory, thinking, and language; also called *comparative cognition.*

intelligence
The global capacity to think rationally, act purposefully, and deal effectively with the environment.

Alfred Binet French psychologist Alfred Binet (1857–1911) is shown here with an unidentified child and an instrument from his laboratory that was used to measure his young subjects' breathing rates while they performed different tasks (Cunningham, 1997). Although Binet developed the first systematic intelligence tests, he did not believe that he was measuring innate ability. Instead, he believed that his tests could identify schoolchildren who could benefit from special help.

With the help of French psychiatrist Théodore Simon, Binet devised a series of tests to measure different mental abilities. Binet deliberately did not test abilities, such as reading or mathematics, that the students might have been taught. Instead, he focused on elementary mental abilities, such as memory, attention, and the ability to understand similarities and differences.

Binet arranged the questions on his test in order of difficulty, with the simplest tasks first. He found that brighter children performed like older children. That is, a bright 7-year-old might be able to answer the same number of questions as an average 9-year-old, while a less capable 7-year-old might only do as well as an average 5-year-old.

This observation led Binet to the idea of a mental level, or **mental age,** that was different from a child's chronological age. An "advanced" 7-year-old might have a mental age of 9, while a "slow" 7-year-old might demonstrate a mental age of 5.

It is somewhat ironic that Binet's early tests became the basis for modern intelligence tests. First, Binet did *not* believe that he was measuring an inborn or permanent level of intelligence (Foschi & Cicciola, 2006; Kamin, 1995). Rather, he believed that his tests could help identify "slow" children who could benefit from special help.

Second, Binet believed that intelligence was too complex a quality to describe with a single number (Siegler, 1992). He steadfastly refused to rank "normal" children on the basis of their scores, believing that such rankings would be unfair. He recognized that many individual factors, such as a child's level of motivation, might affect the child's score. Finally, Binet noted that an individual's score could vary from time to time (Fancher, 1996; Gould, 1993).

> To judge well, to comprehend well, to reason well, these are the essential activities of intelligence.
>
> ALFRED BINET AND THÉODORE SIMON (1905)

Lewis Terman and the Stanford-Binet Intelligence Test

There was enormous interest in Binet's test in the United States. The test was translated and adapted by Stanford University psychologist **Lewis Terman.** Terman's revision was called the *Stanford-Binet Intelligence Scale*. First published in 1916, the Stanford-Binet was for many years the standard for intelligence tests in the United States.

Terman adopted the suggestion of a German psychologist that scores on the Stanford-Binet test be expressed in terms of a single number, called the **intelligence quotient,** or **IQ.** This number was derived by dividing the individual's mental age by the chronological age and multiplying the result by 100. Thus, a child of average intelligence, whose mental age and chronological age were the same, would have an IQ score of 100. A "bright" 10-year-old child with a mental age of 13 would have an IQ of 130 ($^{13}/_{10} \times 100$). A "slow" child with a chronological age of 10 and a mental age of 7 would have an IQ of 70 ($^{7}/_{10} \times 100$). It was Terman's use of the intelligence quotient that resulted in the popularization of the phrase "IQ test."

World War I and Group Intelligence Testing

When the United States entered World War I in 1917, the U.S. military was faced with the need to rapidly screen 2 million army recruits. Using a group intelligence test designed by one of Terman's students, army psychologists developed the Army Alpha and Beta tests. The *Army Alpha* test was administered in writing, and the *Army Beta* test was administered orally to recruits and draftees who could not read.

After World War I ended, the Army Alpha and Army Beta group intelligence tests were adapted for civilian use. The result was a tremendous surge in the intelligence-testing movement. Group intelligence tests were designed to test virtually all ages and types of people, including preschool children, prisoners, and newly arriving immigrants (Anastasi, 1988; Kamin, 1995). However, the indiscriminate use of the tests also resulted in skepticism and hostility.

For example, immigrants were screened as they arrived at Ellis Island. The result was sweeping generalizations about the intelligence of different nationalities and races. During the 1920s, a few intelligence testing experts even urged the U.S. Congress to limit the immigration of certain nationalities to keep the country from

mental age
A measurement of intelligence in which an individual's mental level is expressed in terms of the average abilities of a given age group.

intelligence quotient (IQ)
A measure of general intelligence derived by comparing an individual's score with the scores of others in the same age group.

being "overrun with a horde of the unfit" (see Kamin, 1995).

Despite concerns about the misuse of the so-called IQ tests, the tests quickly became very popular. Lost was Binet's belief that intelligence tests were useful only to identify those who might benefit from special educational help. Contrary to Binet's contention, it soon came to be believed that the IQ score was a fixed, inborn characteristic that was resistant to change (Gould, 1993).

Testing Immigrants at Ellis Island This photograph, taken in 1917, shows an examiner administering a mental test to a newly arrived immigrant at the U.S. immigration center on Ellis Island. According to one intelligence "expert" of the time, 80 percent of the Hungarians, 79 percent of the Italians, and 87 percent of the Russians were "feeble-minded" (see Kamin, 1995). The new science of "mental testing" was used to argue for restrictions on immigration.

Terman and other American psychologists also believed that a high IQ predicted more than success in school. To investigate the relationship between IQ and success in life, Terman (1926) identified 1,500 California schoolchildren with "genius" IQ scores. He set up a longitudinal research study to follow their careers throughout their lives. Some of the findings of this landmark study are described in the In Focus box "Does a High IQ Score Predict Success in Life?"

IN FOCUS

Does a High IQ Score Predict Success in Life?

In 1921, Lewis M. Terman identified 1,500 California children between the ages of 8 and 12 who had IQs above 140, the minimum IQ score for genius-level intelligence. Terman's goal was to track these children by conducting periodic surveys and interviews to see how genius-level intelligence would affect the course of their lives.

Within a few years, Terman (1926) showed that the highly intelligent children tended to be socially well-adjusted, as well as taller, stronger, and healthier than average children, with fewer illnesses and accidents. Not surprisingly, those children performed exceptionally well in school.

But how did Terman's "gifted" children fare in the real world as adults? As a group, they showed an astonishing range of accomplishments (Terman & Oden, 1947, 1959). In 1955, when average income was $5,000 a year, the average income for the group was $33,000. Two-thirds had graduated from college, and a sizable proportion had earned advanced academic or professional degrees.

However, not all of Terman's subjects were so successful. To find out why, Terman's colleague Melita Oden compared the 100 most successful men (the "A" group) and the 100 least successful men (the "C" group) in Terman's sample. Despite their high IQ scores, only a handful of the C group were professionals, and, unlike the A group, the Cs were earning only slightly above the national average income. In terms of their personal lives, the Cs were less healthy, had higher rates of alcoholism, and were three times more likely to be divorced than the As (Terman & Oden, 1959).

Given that the IQ scores of the A and C groups were essentially the same, what accounted for the difference in their levels of accomplishment? Terman noted that, as children, the As were much more likely to display "prudence and forethought, will power, perseverance, and the desire to excel." As adults, the As were rated differently from the Cs on only three traits: They were more goal oriented, had greater perseverance, and had greater self-confidence. Overall, the As seemed to have greater ambition and a greater drive to achieve. In other words, *personality factors* seemed to account for the differences in level of accomplishment between the A group and the C group (Terman & Oden, 1959).

With the exception of moral character, there is nothing as significant for a child's future as his grade of intelligence.

LEWIS M. TERMAN (1916)

As the general success of Terman's gifted children demonstrates, high intelligence can certainly contribute to success in life. But intelligence alone is not enough. Although IQ scores do reliably predict academic success, success in school is no guarantee of success beyond school. Many different personality factors are involved in achieving success, such as motivation, emotional maturity, commitment to goals, creativity, and—perhaps most important—a willingness to work hard (Duckworth & others, 2007; Furnham, 2008). None of these attributes are measured by traditional IQ tests.

David Wechsler Born in Romania, David Wechsler (1896–1981) emigrated with his family to New York when he was 6 years old. Like Binet, Wechsler believed that intelligence involved a variety of mental abilities. He also strongly believed that IQ scores could be influenced by personality, motivation, and cultural factors (Matarazzo, 1981).

David Wechsler and the Wechsler Intelligence Scales

The next major advance in intelligence testing came as a result of a young psychologist's dissatisfaction with the Stanford-Binet and other intelligence tests in widespread use. **David Wechsler** was in charge of testing adults of widely varying cultural and socioeconomic backgrounds and ages at a large hospital in New York City. He designed a new intelligence test, called the *Wechsler Adult Intelligence Scale (WAIS),* which was first published in 1955.

The WAIS had two advantages over the Stanford-Binet. First, the WAIS was specifically designed for adults, rather than for children. Second, Wechsler's test provided scores on 11 subtests measuring different abilities. The subtest scores were grouped to provide an overall verbal score and performance score. The *verbal score* represented scores on subtests of vocabulary, comprehension, knowledge of general information, and other verbal tasks. The *performance score* reflected scores on largely nonverbal subtests, such as identifying the missing part in incomplete pictures, arranging pictures to tell a story, or arranging blocks to match a given pattern.

The design of the WAIS reflected Wechsler's belief that intelligence involves a variety of mental abilities. Because the WAIS provided an individualized profile of the subject's strengths and weaknesses on specific tasks, it marked a return to the attitudes and goals of Alfred Binet (Fancher, 1996; Sternberg, 1990).

The subtest scores on the WAIS also proved to have practical and clinical value. For example, a pattern of low scores on some subtests combined with high scores on other subtests might indicate a specific learning disability (Kaufman, 1990). Or someone who did well on the performance subtests but poorly on the verbal subtests might be unfamiliar with the culture rather than deficient in these skills (Aiken, 1997). That's because many items included on the verbal subtests draw on cultural knowledge.

Wechsler's test also provided an overall, global IQ score, but he changed the way that the IQ score was calculated. On the Stanford-Binet and other early tests, the IQ represented the mental age divided by chronological age. But this approach makes little sense when applied to adult subjects. Although a 12-year-old is typically able to answer more questions than an 8-year-old because of developmental differences, such year-by-year age differences lose their meaning in adulthood.

Instead, Wechsler calculated the IQ by comparing an individual's score with the scores of others in the same general age group, such as young adults. The average score for a particular age group was statistically fixed at 100. The range of scores is statistically defined so that two-thirds of all scores fall between 85 and 115—the range considered to indicate "normal" or "average" intelligence. This procedure proved so successful that it was adopted by the administrators of other tests, including the current version of the Stanford-Binet. Today, IQ scores continue to be calculated by this method.

The Wechsler Intelligence Scale for Children (WISC) Revised and updated in 2003, the WISC-IV is designed to assess the intelligence of children ages 6 to 16. This psychologist is administering the WISC-IV block design subtest to a 6-year-old girl. Other WISC-IV subtests include vocabulary, arithmetic, and arranging pictures so that they logically tell a story.

The WAIS was revised in 1981, 1997, and most recently, in 2008. The fourth edition of the WAIS is known as WAIS-IV. Since the 1960s, the WAIS has remained the most commonly administered intelligence test. Wechsler also developed two tests for children: the *Wechsler Intelligence Scale for Children (WISC)* and the *Wechsler Preschool and Primary Scale of Intelligence (WPPSI)*.

achievement test
A test designed to measure a person's level of knowledge, skill, or accomplishment in a particular area.

aptitude test
A test designed to assess a person's capacity to benefit from education or training.

standardization
The administration of a test to a large, representative sample of people under uniform conditions for the purpose of establishing norms.

normal curve or **normal distribution**
A bell-shaped distribution of individual differences in a normal population in which most scores cluster around the average score.

reliability
The ability of a test to produce consistent results when administered on repeated occasions under similar conditions.

Principles of Test Construction

What Makes a Good Test?

Many kinds of psychological tests measure various aspects of intelligence or mental ability. **Achievement tests** are designed to measure a person's level of knowledge, skill, or accomplishment in a particular area, such as mathematics or a foreign language. In contrast, **aptitude tests** are designed to assess a person's capacity to benefit from education or training. The overall goal of an aptitude test is to predict your ability to learn certain types of information or perform certain skills.

Any psychological test must fulfill certain requirements to be considered scientifically acceptable. The three basic requirements of good test design are standardization, reliability, and validity. Let's briefly look at what each of those requirements entails.

Standardization

If you answer 75 of 100 questions correctly, what does that score mean? Is it high, low, or average? For an individual's test score to be interpreted, it has to be compared against some sort of standard of performance.

Standardization means that the test is given to a large number of subjects who are representative of the group of people for whom the test is designed. All the subjects take the same version of the test under uniform conditions. The scores of this group establish the *norms,* or the standards against which an individual score is compared and interpreted.

For IQ tests, such norms closely follow a pattern of individual differences called the **normal curve,** or **normal distribution.** In this bell-shaped pattern, most scores cluster around the average score. As scores become more extreme, fewer instances of the scores occur. In Figure 7.6, you can see the normal distribution of IQ scores on the WAIS-III. About 68 percent of subjects taking the WAIS-III will score between 85 and 115, the IQ range for "normal" intelligence. Less than one-tenth of 1 percent of the population have extreme scores that are above 145 or below 55.

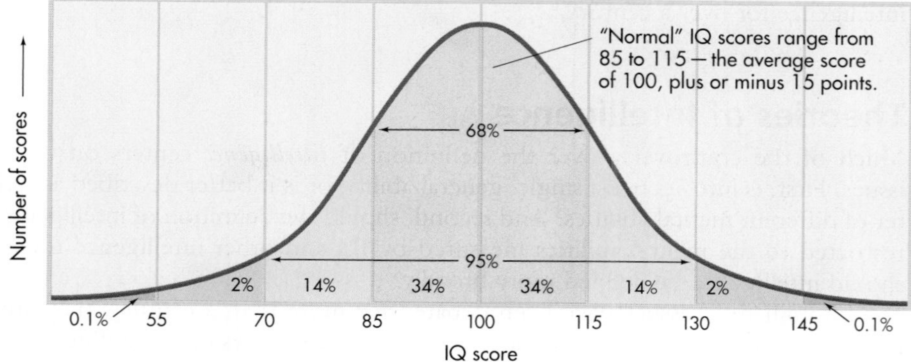

Figure 7.6 The Normal Curve of Distribution of IQ Scores The distribution of IQ scores on the WAIS-III in the general population tends to follow a bell-shaped normal curve, with the average score defined as 100. Notice that 68 percent of the scores fall within the "normal" IQ range of 85 to 115. Ninety-five percent of the general population score between 70 and 130, while only one-tenth of 1 percent score lower than 55 or higher than 145.

Reliability

A good test must also have **reliability.** That is, it must consistently produce similar scores on different occasions. How do psychologists determine whether a psychological test is reliable? One method is to administer two similar, but not identical, versions of the test at different times. Another procedure is to compare the scores on one half of the test with the scores on the other half of the test. A test is considered reliable if the test and retest scores are highly similar when such strategies are used.

validity
The ability of a test to measure what it is intended to measure.

***g* factor** or **general intelligence**
The notion of a general intelligence factor that is responsible for a person's overall performance on tests of mental ability.

Validity

Finally, a good test must demonstrate **validity,** which means that the test measures what it is supposed to measure. One way to establish the validity of a test is by demonstrating its predictive value. For example, if a test is designed to measure mechanical aptitude, people who received high scores should ultimately prove more successful in mechanical jobs than people who received low scores.

The Nature of Intelligence

Key Theme

- **Psychologists do not agree about the basic nature of intelligence, including whether it is a single, general ability and whether it includes skills and talents as well as mental aptitude.**

Key Questions

- **What is *g*, and how did Spearman and Thurstone view intelligence?**
- **What is Gardner's theory of multiple intelligences?**
- **What is Sternberg's triarchic theory of intelligence?**

The Wechsler Adult Intelligence Scale and the Stanford-Binet Intelligence Scale are standardized, reliable, and valid. But do they adequately measure intelligence? The question is not as simple as it sounds. There is considerable disagreement among psychologists about the nature of intelligence, including how intelligence should best be defined and measured (Neisser & others, 1996; Shavinina, 2001).

Take another look at the chapter Prologue about Tom and his family. In terms of the type of intelligence that is measured by IQ and other standardized tests, Tom is extremely intelligent. But despite his high IQ, Tom can find it extremely difficult to carry out many activities that those with a more "normal" or average intelligence can perform almost effortlessly. Applying for an after-school job, joining a conversation that is already in progress, or even knowing why—or whether—a particular joke is funny are very difficult, if not impossible, tasks for Tom. As you'll see in the next section, psychologists have struggled with the challenge of how to define intelligence for over a century.

Theories of Intelligence

Much of the controversy over the definition of *intelligence* centers on two key issues. First, is intelligence a single, general ability, or is it better described as a cluster of different mental abilities? And second, should the definition of intelligence be restricted to the mental abilities measured by IQ and other intelligence tests? Or should intelligence be defined more broadly?

Although these issues have been debated for more than a century, they are far from being resolved. In this section, we'll describe the views of four influential psychologists on both issues.

Charles Spearman

Intelligence Is a General Ability

Some psychologists believe that a common factor, or general mental capacity, is at the core of different mental abilities. This approach originated with British psychologist **Charles Spearman.** Although Spearman agreed that an individual's scores could vary on tests of different mental abilities, he found that the scores on different tests tended to be similar. That is, people who did well or poorly on a test of one mental ability, such as verbal ability, tended also to do well or poorly on the other tests.

Spearman recognized that particular individuals might excel in specific areas. However, Spearman (1904) believed that a factor he called **general intelligence,** or the ***g* factor,** was responsible for their overall performance on tests of mental ability. Psychologists who follow this approach today think that intelligence can be described as a single measure of general cognitive ability, or *g* factor (Gottfredson, 1998). Thus, general mental ability could accurately be expressed by a single number, such as the IQ score. Lewis Terman's approach to measuring and defining intelligence as a single, overall IQ score was in the tradition of Charles Spearman. In terms of Spearman's model, Tom would undoubtedly score very highly on any test that measured *g* factor or general intelligence. For example, when he took the SAT as a high school junior, he scored in the top 3 percent in math and received a perfect score on the writing section.

Charles Spearman (1863–1945) British psychologist Charles Spearman (1904) believed that a single factor, which he called the *g* factor, underlies many different kinds of mental abilities. To Spearman, a person's level of general intelligence was equivalent to his or her level of "mental energy."

Louis L. Thurstone

Intelligence Is a Cluster of Abilities

Psychologist **Louis L. Thurstone** disagreed with Spearman's notion that intelligence is a single, general mental capacity. Instead, Thurstone believed that there were seven different "primary mental abilities," each a relatively independent element of intelligence. Abilities such as verbal comprehension, numerical ability, reasoning, and perceptual speed are examples Thurstone gave of independent "primary mental abilities."

To Thurstone, the so-called *g* factor was simply an overall average score of such independent abilities and consequently was less important than an individual's specific *pattern* of mental abilities (Thurstone, 1937). David Wechsler's approach to measuring and defining intelligence as a pattern of different abilities was very similar to Thurstone's approach.

Louis L. Thurstone (1887–1955) American psychologist Louis Thurstone studied electrical engineering and was an assistant to Thomas Edison before he became interested in the psychology of learning. Thurstone was especially interested in the measurements of people's attitudes and intelligence, and was an early critic of the idea of "mental age," believing that intelligence was too diverse to be quantified in a single number or IQ score.

Howard Gardner

"Multiple Intelligences"

More recently, **Howard Gardner** has expanded Thurstone's basic notion of intelligence as different mental abilities that operate independently. However, Gardner has stretched the definition of intelligence (Gardner & Taub, 1999). Rather than analyzing intelligence test results, Gardner (1985, 1993) looked at the kinds of skills and products that are valued in different cultures. He also studied brain-damaged individuals, noting that some mental abilities are spared when others are lost. To Gardner, this phenomenon implies that different mental abilities are biologically distinct and controlled by different parts of the brain.

Like Thurstone, Gardner has suggested that such mental abilities are independent of each other and cannot be accurately reflected in a single measure of intelligence. Rather than one intelligence, Gardner (1993, 1998a) believes, there are "multiple intelligences." To Gardner, "an intelligence" is the ability to solve problems, or to create products, that are valued within one or more cultural settings. Thus, he believes that intelligence must be defined within the context of a particular culture. Gardner (1998b) has proposed eight distinct, independent intelligences, which are summarized in Figure 7.7 on the next page.

Figure 7.7 **Gardner's Multiple Intelligences**

Linguistic intelligence	Adept use of language: poet, writer, public speaker, native storyteller
Logical-mathematical intelligence	Logical, mathematical, and scientific ability: scientist, mathematician, navigator, surveyor
Musical intelligence	Ability to create, synthesize, or perform music: musician, composer, singer
Spatial intelligence	Ability to mentally visualize the relationships of objects or movements: sculptor, painter, expert chess player, architect
Bodily-kinesthetic intelligence	Control of bodily motions and capacity to handle objects skillfully: athlete, dancer, craftsperson
Interpersonal intelligence	Understanding of other people's emotions, motives, intentions: politician, salesperson, clinical psychologist
Intrapersonal intelligence	Understanding of one's own emotions, motives, and intentions: essayist, philosopher
Naturalist intelligence	Ability to discern patterns in nature: ecologist, zoologist, botanist

According to Gardner's model of intelligence, everyone has a different pattern of strengths and weaknesses. How would Tom rate? In terms of linguistic, logical-mathematical, and spatial intelligence, Tom would measure very highly. What about an "intelligence" that wouldn't be measured by a standard IQ test, such as musical intelligence? When I asked Tom what type of music he liked, he couldn't tell me.

If I like a song, I like it.
If I don't, I stop listening.
I really can't categorize it.
It's not within my power.

Although lacking musical intelligence probably doesn't affect your ability to function in our culture, other "intelligences" are much more crucial. Without question, Tom's biggest shortcoming falls in the realm of interpersonal intelligence. Understanding and relating to other people is extremely difficult for him.

In most cultures, the ability to effectively navigate social situations is crucial to at least one aspect of Wechsler's definition of intelligence: "the ability to deal effectively with the environment." Although people with Asperger's are neither physically nor intellectually disabled, their inability to understand and successfully

Howard Gardner and His Theory of Multiple Intelligences According to Howard Gardner, many mental abilities are not adequately measured by traditional intelligence tests. As Gardner (2003) explains, "Different tasks call on different intelligences or combinations of intelligence. To perform music intelligently involves a different set of intelligences than preparing a meal, planning a course, or resolving a quarrel." Examples might include the spatial intelligence shown by the complex designs of a Navajo weaver, the extraordinary bodily-kinesthetic intelligence of tennis player Roger Federer, and the musical intelligence of singer Ricky Martin.

interact with others contributes to Asperger's syndrome being categorized as a disability. However, not everyone considers Asperger's to be a true disorder. Are the autism spectrum disorders disabilities—or are they differences? We consider this topic in the In Focus box, "Neurodiversity: Beyond IQ," on the next page.

Some of the abilities emphasized by Gardner, such as logical-mathematical intelligence, might be tapped by a standard intelligence test. However, other abilities, such as bodily-kinesthetic intelligence or musical intelligence, do not seem to be reflected on standard intelligence tests. Yet, as Gardner points out, such abilities are recognized and highly valued in many different cultures, including our own.

Robert Sternberg

Three Forms of Intelligence

Robert Sternberg agrees with Gardner that intelligence is a much broader quality than is reflected in the narrow range of mental abilities measured by a conventional IQ test. However, Sternberg (1988, 1995) disagrees with Gardner's notion of multiple, independent intelligences. He believes that some of Gardner's intelligences are more accurately described as specialized talents, whereas intelligence is a more general quality. Sternberg (1988) points out that you would be able to manage just fine if you were tone-deaf and lacked "musical intelligence" in most societies. However, if you didn't have the ability to reason and plan ahead, you would be unable to function in any culture.

Robert Sternberg (b. 1949) first became interested in studying intelligence after he did poorly on a sixth grade intelligence test. Sternberg soon came to realize that test anxiety had interfered with his performance. Throughout his college years, Sternberg did poorly in courses that required rote learning—including his first psychology course at Yale. However, Sternberg persevered. He went on win many awards for his research and, in 2003, was elected president of the American Psychological Association. Much of Sternberg's career has been devoted to studying nontraditional types of intelligence, such as creativity and wisdom, and developing new ways to measure these qualities (Kaufman & others, 2009).

Sternberg's **triarchic theory of intelligence** emphasizes both the universal aspects of intelligent behavior and the importance of adapting to a particular social and cultural environment. More specifically, Sternberg (1997) has proposed a different conception of intelligence, which he calls *successful intelligence*. Successful intelligence involves three distinct types of mental abilities: analytic, creative, and practical.

Analytic intelligence refers to the mental processes used in learning how to solve problems, such as picking a problem-solving strategy and applying it. Although conventional intelligence tests measure mental abilities, they do not evaluate the strategies used to solve problems, which Sternberg considers important in determining analytic intelligence. In the Prologue, Tom's ability to solve complex mathematical equations reflects analytical intelligence.

Creative intelligence is the ability to deal with novel situations by drawing on existing skills and knowledge. The intelligent person effectively draws on past experiences to cope with new situations, which often involves finding an unusual way to relate old information to new. We'll explore the topic of creativity in more detail in the Enhancing Well-Being with Psychology section at the end of the chapter.

Practical intelligence involves the ability to adapt to the environment and often reflects what is commonly called "street smarts." Sternberg notes that what is required to adapt successfully in one particular situation or culture may be very different from what is needed in another situation or culture. He stresses that the behaviors that reflect practical intelligence can vary depending on the particular situation, environment, or culture.

How would Tom fare by Sternberg's criteria? Although high in most measures of analytic intelligence, Tom would probably not rank very highly in creative or practical intelligence. Successful adaptation involves the flexibility to choose the best problem-solving strategy or to know when to change strategies.

triarchic theory of intelligence
Robert Sternberg's theory that there are three distinct forms of intelligence: analytic, creative, and practical.

IN FOCUS

Neurodiversity: Beyond IQ

Can intelligence be summarized by an IQ score? Do standard intelligence tests adequately measure intelligence? Although the questions seem very abstract, their answers can have very real consequences. To give these questions a human face, consider the case of people with autistic symptoms.

Tom, whose story you read in the Prologue, has a very high IQ as measured on standard intelligence tests. However, his inability to navigate social situations makes him less competent in many everyday activities than people with lower IQ scores.

Such difficulties are the hallmark of the *autism spectrum disorders,* whose common feature is problems with communication and social interaction. **Autism** is the most severe of these disorders. Along with severely impaired communication, autistic individuals may be unresponsive to social interaction, engage in repetitive or odd motor behaviors, and have highly restricted routines and interests (Toth & King, 2008).

Unlike children with autism, children with **Asperger's syndrome** show normal, even advanced, language development. They may exhibit unusually narrow interests and inflexible behavior, but to a much lesser degree than people with autism. And by definition, people with Asperger's have an IQ in the normal to genius range.

What about the cognitive abilities of people with autism? Many people believe that most autistics are *autistic savants,* like the character "Raymond" played by Dustin Hoffman in the movie *Rainman.* Autistic savants have some extraordinary talent or ability, usually in a very limited area such as math, music, or art. In reality, only about 1 in 10 autistic people are savants (see Dawson & others, 2008; Treffert & Wallace, 2003). However, fewer than 1 in 2,000 non-autistic people have such exceptional abilities.

Another common assumption is that most people with autism are mentally retarded (e.g., Brown & others, 2008). **Mental retardation** is a condition in which IQ is 70 or below. However, surveying decades of research, psychologist Meredyth Edelson (2006) found that there was little empirical research to support the claim that the majority of autistic people are mentally retarded. In fact, because their symptoms vary so much, it's very difficult to generalize about the cognitive abilities of people with autistic spectrum disorders (Sigman & others, 2006).

It is also hard to accurately *measure* intelligence in people who lack the ability to communicate or who are not good at social interaction. In children, for example, intelligence is most commonly measured by Wechsler-based tests, like the WISC-III. But is the WISC-III, which relies heavily on verbal instruction and oral

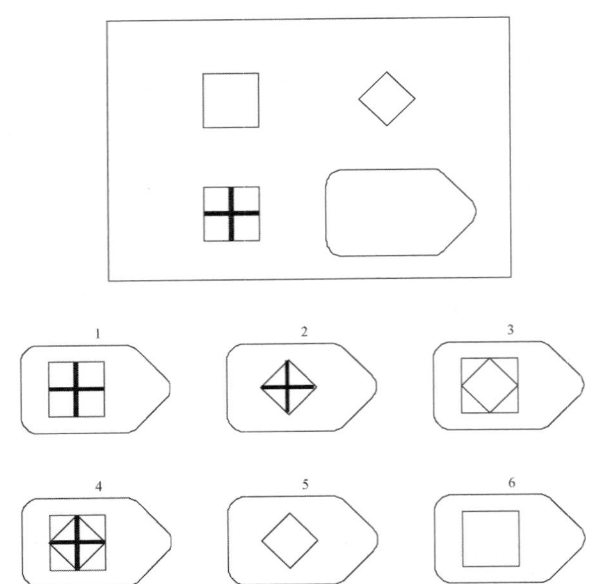

Sample Items from the Raven's Progressive Matrices Test The Raven's test consists of matrix problems that become progressively more difficult. The instructions are simple: Choose the item that best completes the pattern. The test was developed to test general mental ability and is thought to be the "purest" measure of Charles Spearman's *g* factor (Holyoak, 2005).

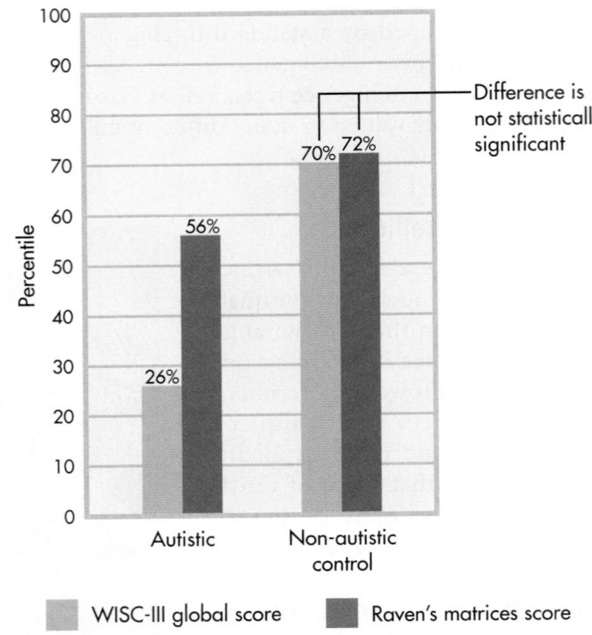

Source: Dawson & others (2007).

Measuring Intelligence On the average, autistic children scored fully 30 percentile points higher on the nonverbal Raven's Progressive Matrices Test than they did on the WISC-III, which depends heavily on oral instruction and responses. In contrast, a matched control group of non-autistic children received scores that were essentially identical. Adult participants showed a similar pattern. Although a small-scale study, such results suggest that traditional intelligence tests may underestimate intelligence in autistic children and adults. In fact, one-third of the autistic children scored above the 90th percentile on the Raven's, but none did so on the WISC-III. One child raised his score 70 percentile points from 24 to 94 percent—putting him in the "highly intelligent" range rather than the "low-functioning" range.

communication, an appropriate instrument for measuring intelligence in autistic children?

To address this question, Michelle Dawson and her colleagues (2007) used the *Raven's Progressive Matrices Test* to measure intelligence in autistic children and adults (see sample items). A *nonverbal* test of logic and higher-level abstract thinking, the test was developed by John Raven, one of Spearman's students. Because the test does not rely upon previously learned information, many cognitive psychologists regard it as an especially pure test of Spearman's *g* factor (Holyoak, 2005).

In Dawson's study, children and adults with autism took both the Wechsler and the Raven's tests. How did they do? On average, the autistic children scored at the 26th percentile on the Wechsler—a score that would label them as mentally retarded or low-functioning and well below an average score of 50 percent. In contrast, their average score on the Raven's was 56 percent, *fully 30 percentile points higher,* a difference that moved many children from the low-functioning or mentally retarded range to the normal range. A similar pattern was found in autistic adults.

Did non-autistic subjects also show a big difference in scores on the Wechsler versus the Raven's? No. Members of the non-autistic control groups received very similar scores on the Wechsler and Raven's tests (see graph).

> *Many autistics affirm that it would be impossible to segregate the part of them that is autistic. To take away their autism is to take away their personhood . . . Like their predecessors in human rights, many autistics don't want to be cured; they want to be accepted. And like other predecessors in civil rights, many autistics don't want to be required to imitate the majority just to earn their rightful place in society.*
>
> MORTON ANN GERNSBACHER, 2004

There's an interesting twist to this story. The lead author, Michelle Dawson, who planned the study, handled the data collection, supervised the statistical analysis, and wrote the first draft, is herself autistic. Dawson can't cook, drive, take public transportation, or handle many other everyday tasks. However, Dawson has a phenomenal memory and a razor-sharp logical mind. According to her co-researcher, University of Montreal psychiatrist Laurent Mottron (2008), Dawson also has a remarkable gift for scientific analysis.

It was Dawson who came up with the idea for the study (Gernsbacher, 2007, April). As Dawson (2007) observes, testing autistic kids' intelligence in a way that requires them to verbally interact with a stranger "is like giving a blind person an intelligence test that requires him to process visual information." On intelligence tests, the assumption has always been that when someone doesn't answer a question, it's because they don't know the answer. But there is another possibility: Perhaps they simply can't express what they know (Gernsbacher, 2004; Gernsbacher & others, 2007).

Why are such findings so important? Well, what happens to children who are labeled as "mentally retarded," "low-functioning," or "uneducable"? As Laurent Mottron (2006) points out, "If we classify children as intellectually deficient, then that is how they will be treated. They will be denied a host of opportunities."

Today, many researchers, parents, and people "on the spectrum" are embracing a new approach to spectrum disorders. Called *neurodiversity,* it is the recognition that people with autistic spectrum symptoms process information, communicate, and experience their social and physical environment differently than *neurotypical* people who don't have autistic symptoms. Rather than viewing autism as a *disorder* or *disease,* advocates of this viewpoint believe that it should be viewed as a *disability,* like deafness, or a *difference,* like left-handedness (see Trivedi, 2005).

Neurodiversity advocates do *not* deny that autistic people need special training and support (Baron-Cohen, 2000, 2005). Autism rights activists Amy Roberts and Gareth Nelson (2005) suggest that rather than trying to "cure" autistics and make them more like non-autistic people, researchers should emphasize giving autistic children and adults the tools that they need to survive in a world that is designed for non-autistic people.

Disorder, disease, disability, or difference? We'll give noted autism researcher Simon Baron-Cohen (2007) the last word:

> Autism is both a disability and a difference. We need to find ways of alleviating the disability while respecting and valuing the difference.

Michelle Dawson Michelle Dawson readily admits that coping with many everyday challenges is beyond her. Yet, according to her colleague Laurent Mottron (2008), "Michelle is someone who will change the way an entire sector of humanity is considered." Dawson met neuroscientist and autism researcher Mottron when they both appeared on a documentary about autism. Recognizing Dawson's intelligence, Mottron asked her to read some of his scientific papers. When she responded with an insightful critique of his methodology, Mottron took her on as a research collaborator. Since that time, Dawson has co-authored several papers with Mottron and other scientists, including Morton Ann Gernsbacher, former president of the Association for Psychological Science.

"I don't have to be smart, because someday I'll just hire lots of smart people to work for me."

What about practical intelligence? As shown in the Prologue, dealing with the social and academic environment of high school is not easy for Tom. However, many people with Asperger's find a compatible niche in workplaces in which their ability to focus their attention on a particular technical problem, their preoccupation with details, and other unusual abilities are highly valued, such as in computer programming or engineering firms. In such an environment, their lack of social skills might actually be advantageous (Mayor, 2008). As Sternberg's theory would predict, behaviors that are deemed "intelligent" in one environment—such as a software development firm—might well be maladaptive in another environment—like a high school cafeteria (Sternberg, 2008).

The exact nature of intelligence will no doubt be debated for some time. However, the intensity of this debate pales in comparison with the next issue we consider: the origins of intelligence.

The Roles of Genetics and Environment in Determining Intelligence

Key Theme

- **Both genes and environment contribute to intelligence, but the relationship is complex.**

Key Questions

- **How are twin studies used to measure genetic and environmental influences on intelligence?**
- **What is a heritability estimate, and why can't it be used to explain differences between groups?**
- **What social and cultural factors affect performance on intelligence tests?**

> The nature-versus-nurture debate is now informed by current research on molecular biology that moves the question from which factor is more important to how and when expression of the human genome is triggered and maintained. The basic behavior genetics issue has become how environment influences gene expression.
>
> BERNARD BROWN (1999)

Given that psychologists do not agree on the definition or nature of intelligence, it probably won't surprise you to learn that psychologists also do not agree on the *origin of intelligence*. On the surface, the debate comes down to this: Do we essentially *inherit* our intellectual potential from our parents, grandparents, and great-grandparents? Or is our intellectual potential primarily determined by our *environment* and upbringing?

Virtually all psychologists agree that *both* heredity and environment are important in determining intelligence level. Where psychologists disagree is in identifying how much of intelligence is determined by heredity, how much by environment. The implications of this debate have provoked some of the most heated arguments in the history of psychology.

Let's start with some basic points about the relationship between genes and the environment. At one time, it was commonly believed that genes provided an unchanging, permanent blueprint for human potential and development. Today, the "genes as blueprint" metaphor has been replaced by a "genes as data bank" metaphor (Brown, 1999; Marcus, 2004). It's now known that environmental factors influence *which* of the many genes we inherit are actually switched on, or activated. As psychologist Bernard Brown (1999) writes, "Genes are not destiny. There are many places along the gene–behavior pathway where genetic expression can be regulated."

Take the example of height. You inherit a potential *range* for height, rather than an absolute number of inches. Environmental factors influence how close you come to realizing that genetic potential. If you are healthy and well-nourished, you may reach the maximum of your genetic height potential. But if you are poorly nourished and not healthy, you probably won't.

To underscore the interplay between heredity and environment, consider the fact that the average height of Americans increased by several inches in the past half-century. The explanation for this increase is that nutritional and health standards have steadily improved, not that the genetic heritage of Americans has fundamentally changed. However, heredity does play a role in establishing *limits* on height. If you're born with "short" genes (like your authors), you're unlikely to reach six foot four, no matter how good your nutrition. (For more on genetics see Chapter 9.)

The roles of heredity and environment in determining intelligence and personality factors are much more complex than the simple examples of height or eye color (Plomin, 2003). However narrowly intelligence is defined, the genetic range of intellectual potential is influenced by *many* genes, not by one single gene (Plomin & Spinath, 2004). No one knows how many genes might be involved. Given the complexity of genetic and environmental influences, how do scientists estimate how much of intelligence is due to genetics, how much to environment?

autism
Behavioral syndrome associated with differences in brain functioning and sensory responses, and characterized by impaired social interaction, impaired verbal and nonverbal communication skills, repetitive or odd motor behaviors, and highly restricted interests and routines.

Asperger's syndrome
Behavioral syndrome characterized by varying degrees of difficulty in social and conversational skills but normal-to-above-average intelligence and language development; often accompanied by obsessive preoccupation with particular topics or routines.

mental retardation
Disorder characterized by intellectual function that is significantly below average, usually defined as a measured IQ of 70 or below, and that is caused by brain injury, disease, or a genetic disorder.

heritability
The percentage of variation within a given population that is due to heredity.

Twin Studies

Sorting Out the Influence of Genetics Versus Environment

One way this issue has been explored is by comparing the IQ scores of individuals who are genetically related to different degrees. *Identical twins* share exactly the same genes, because they developed from a single fertilized egg that split into two. Hence, any dissimilarities between them must be due to environmental factors rather than hereditary differences. *Fraternal twins* are like any other pair of siblings, because they develop from two different fertilized eggs.

As you can see in Figure 7.8 on the next page, comparing IQ scores in this way shows the effects of both heredity and environment. Identical twins raised together have very similar IQ scores, whereas fraternal twins raised together have IQs that are less similar (Plomin & Spinath, 2004).

However, notice that identical twins raised in separate homes have IQs that are slightly less similar, indicating the effect of different environments. And, although fraternal twins raised together have less similar IQ scores than do identical twins, they show more similarity in IQs than do nontwin siblings. Recall that the degree of genetic relatedness between fraternal twins and nontwin siblings is essentially the same. But because fraternal twins are the same age, their environmental experiences are likely to be more similar than are those of siblings who are of different ages.

Thus, *both* genetic *and* environmental influences are important. Genetic influence is shown by the fact that the closer the genetic relationship, the more similar the IQ scores. Environmental influences are demonstrated by two findings: First, two people who are genetically identical but are raised in different homes have different IQ scores. And second, two people who are genetically unrelated but are raised in the same home have IQs that are much more similar than are those of two unrelated people from randomly selected homes.

Using studies based on degree of genetic relatedness and using sophisticated statistical techniques to analyze the data, researchers have scientifically estimated **heritability**—the percentage of variation within a given population that is due to heredity. The currently accepted *heritability estimate* is about 50 percent for the general population (see Plomin, 2003; Plomin & Spinath, 2004).

Genetics or Environment? These identical twins have a lot in common—including a beautiful smile. Twins are often used in studies of the relative contributions that heredity and environment make to personality and other characteristics.

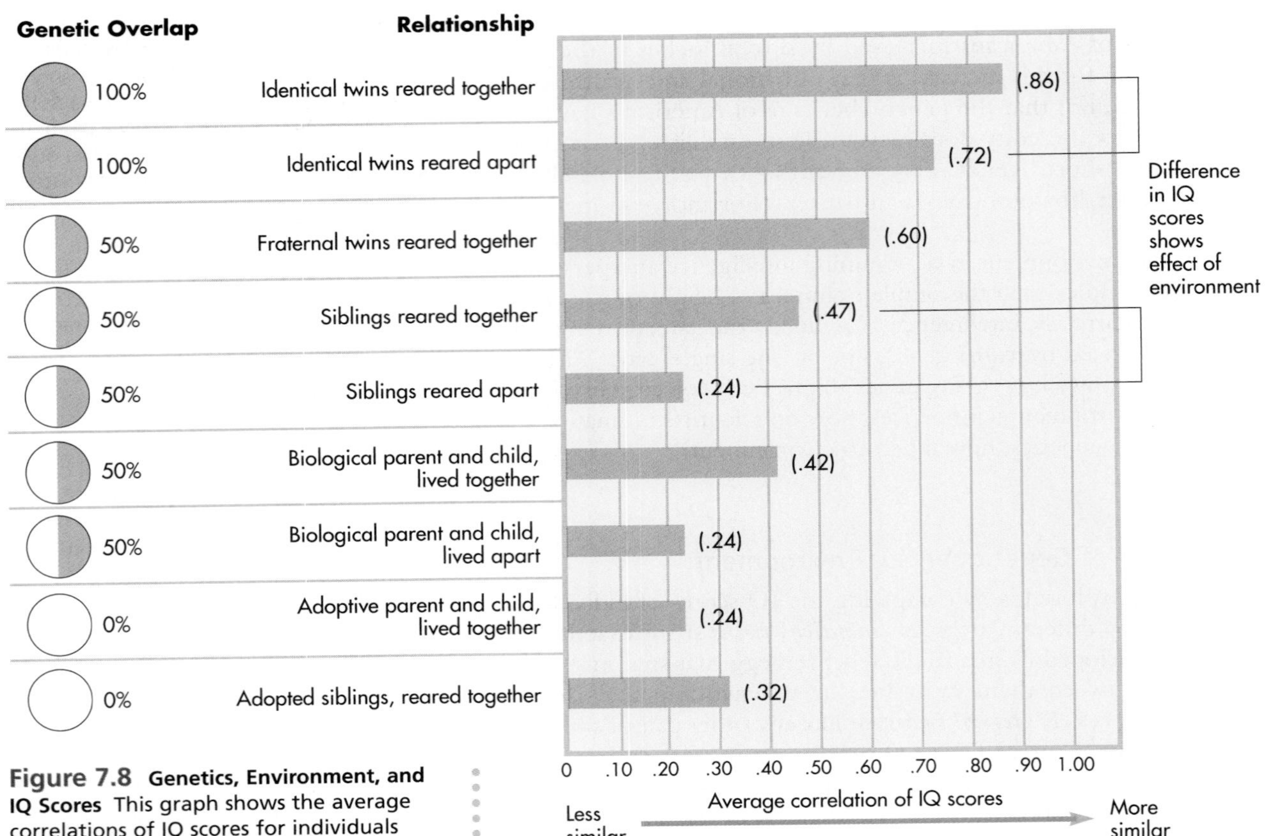

Figure 7.8 Genetics, Environment, and IQ Scores This graph shows the average correlations of IQ scores for individuals who are genetically related to different degrees. The graph is based on research by psychologists Thomas Bouchard and Matt McGue, who summarized the results from more than 100 separate studies on over 100,000 pairs of relatives (McGue & others, 1993). The data show that both genetics and environment have an effect on IQ scores. The more closely two individuals are related genetically, the more similar their IQ scores: Identical twins reared together are more alike than are fraternal twins reared together. However, the same data also show the importance of environmental influences: Identical twins reared together are more alike than are identical twins reared apart, and siblings who are reared together are more alike than are siblings reared in different homes.

In other words, approximately 50 percent of the difference in IQ scores *within* a given population is due to genetic factors. But there is disagreement even over this figure, depending on the statistical techniques and data sources used (Turkheimer & others, 2003).

It is important to stress that the 50 percent figure does *not* apply to a single individual's IQ score. If Mike's IQ is 120, it does not mean that 60 IQ points are due to Mike's environment and 60 points are genetically inherited. Instead, the 50 percent heritability estimate means that approximately 50 percent of the difference in IQ scores *within a specific group of people* is due to differences in their genetic makeup. More on this key point shortly.

Group Differences in IQ Scores

If the contributions of heredity and environment are roughly equal, why all the fuss? Much of the controversy over the role of heredity in intelligence is due to attempts to explain the differences in average IQ scores for different racial groups.

In comparing the *average IQ* for various racial groups, several studies have shown differences. For example, Japanese and Chinese schoolchildren tend to score above European American children on intelligence and achievement tests, especially in math (Lynn, 1987; Stevenson & Lee, 1990). Are Japanese and Chinese children genetically more intelligent than European American children?

Consider this finding: In early childhood, there are *no* significant differences in IQ among European American, Japanese, and Chinese schoolchildren. The scores of the three groups are essentially the same (Stevenson & Stigler, 1992). The gap begins to appear only after the children start school, and it increases with every year of school attended. By middle school, Asian students tend to score much higher than American students on both math and reading tests.

Culture and Educational Achievement These little girls attend kindergarten in Tokyo, Japan. Children in Japan attend school six days a week. Along with spending more time in school each year than American children, Japanese children grow up in a culture that places a strong emphasis on academic success as the key to occupational success.

Why the increasing gap once children enter school? Japanese and Chinese students spend more time in school, spend more time doing homework, and experience more pressure and support from their parents to achieve academically. In addition, the Japanese and Chinese cultures place a high value on academic achievement (Gardner, 1995; Li, 2005). Clearly, the difference between American and Asian students is due not to genetics but to the educational system.

Differences *Within* Groups Versus Differences *Between* Groups

Some group differences in average IQ scores do exist (Ceci & Williams, 2009). In many societies, the average IQ scores of minority groups are lower than the average IQ scores of the dominant or majority groups. The question is how to explain such differences. But heritability cannot be used to explain group differences. Although it is possible to estimate the degree of difference *within* a specific group that is due to genetics, it makes no sense to apply this estimate to the differences *between* groups (Rose, 2009). Why? A classic analogy provided by geneticist Richard Lewontin (1970) may help you understand this important point (see Ceci & Williams, 2009).

Suppose you have a 50-pound bag of corn seeds and two pots. A handful of seeds is scooped out and planted in pot A, which has rich, well-fertilized soil. A second handful is scooped out and planted in pot B, which has poor soil with few nutrients (see Figure 7.9 on the next page).

Because the seeds are not genetically identical, the plants *within group A* will vary in height. So will the plants *within group B.* Given that the environment (the soil) is the same for all the plants in one particular pot, this variation within each group of seeds is *completely* due to heredity—nothing differs but the plants' genes.

However, when we compare the average height of the corn plants in the two pots, pot A's plants have a higher average height than pot B's. Can the difference in these average heights be explained in terms of overall genetic differences between the seeds in each pot? No. The overall differences can be attributed to the two different environments, the good soil and the poor soil. In fact, because the environments are so different, it is impossible to estimate what the overall genetic differences are between the two groups of seeds.

Note also that even though, on the average, the plants in pot A are taller than the plants in pot B, some of the plants in pot B are taller than some of the plants in

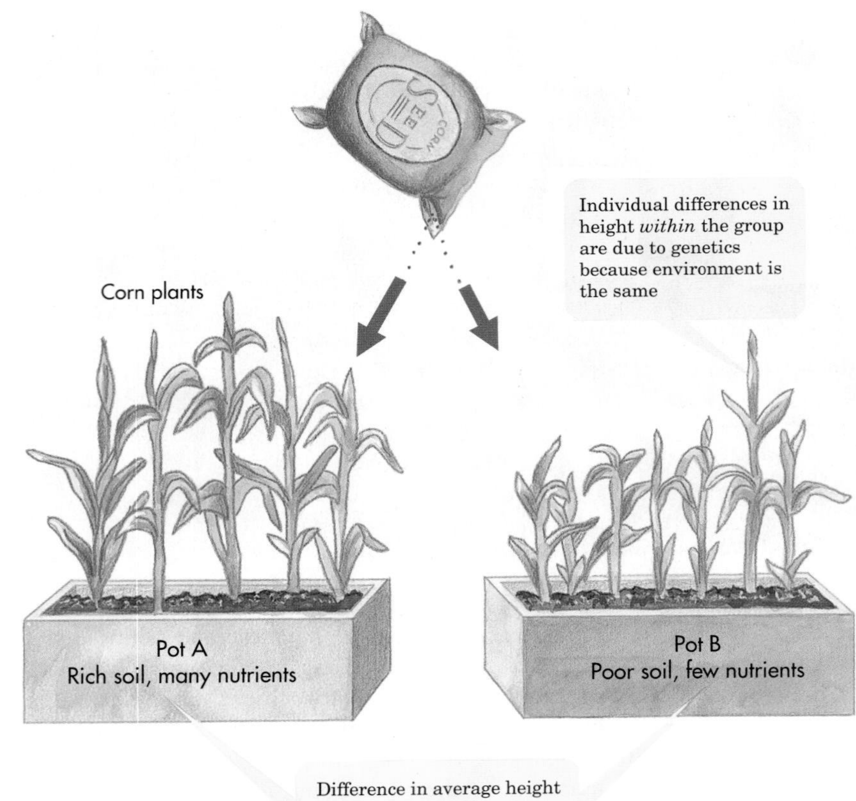

Figure 7.9 The Two Pots Analogy Because the two environments are very different, no conclusions can be drawn about possible overall genetic differences between the plants in pot A and the plants in pot B.

pot A. In other words, the average differences *within a group* of plants tell us nothing about whether an *individual* member of that group is likely to be tall or short.

The same point can be extended to the issue of average IQ differences between racial groups. Unless the environmental conditions of two racial groups are virtually identical, it is impossible to estimate the overall genetic differences between the two groups. Even if intelligence were *primarily* determined by heredity, which is not the case, IQ differences between groups could still be due entirely to the environment.

Other evidence for the importance of the environment in determining IQ scores derives from the improvement in average IQ scores that has occurred in several cultures and countries during the past few generations (Flynn, 2007a, 2007b; Neisser & others, 1996).

In a survey of intelligence test scores around the world, 14 nations were found to have shown significant gains in average IQ scores in just one generation (Flynn, 1994, 1999). The average IQ score in the United States has also steadily increased over the past century (Flynn, 2007a, 2007b). Such changes in a population can be accounted for only by environmental changes, because the amount of time involved is far too short for genetically influenced changes to have occurred.

We need to appreciate that all human behavior is based on biology and, hence, will involve some degree of genetic influence. But, equally, all social behavior is bound to be affected by social context and, hence, will involve an important environmental influence.

MICHAEL RUTTER (1997)

Cross-Cultural Studies of Group Discrimination and IQ Differences

The effect of social discrimination on intelligence test scores has been shown in numerous cross-cultural studies (see Ogbu, 1986, 2008). In many different societies, average IQ is lower for members of a discriminated-against minority group, even when that group is not racially different from the dominant group. The Culture and Human Behavior box on page 310 explains how belonging to a stigmatized group can affect performance on tests of many different abilities.

Take the case of the Burakumin people of Japan. Americans typically think of Japan as relatively homogeneous, and indeed the Burakumin are not racially different from other Japanese. They look the same and speak the same language. However, the Burakumin are the descendants of an outcast group that for generations worked as tanners and butchers. Because they handled dead bodies and killed animals, the Burakumin were long considered unclean and unfit for social contact. For centuries, they were forced to live in isolated enclaves, apart from the rest of Japanese society (DeVos, 1992; DeVos & Wagatsuma, 1967).

Today, there are about 3 million Burakumin in Japan. Although the Burakumin were legally emancipated from their outcast status many years ago, substantial social discrimination against them persists (Payton, 1992). Because there is no way to tell if a Japanese citizen is of Burakumin descent, there are dozens of private detective agencies in Tokyo and other Japanese cities that openly specialize in tracking Burakumin who are trying to "pass" and hide their background. Until fairly recently, corporations in Japan openly consulted computer databanks to identify Burakumin who applied for jobs, as did individuals who wished to investigate the ancestral background of prospective marriage partners.

The Burakumin are the poorest people in Japan. They are only half as likely as other Japanese to graduate from high school or attend college. Although there are no racial differences between the Burakumin and other Japanese, the average IQ scores of the Burakumin in Japan are well below those of other Japanese. As shown in Table 7.2, their average IQ scores are about 10 to 15 points below those of mainstream Japanese. But, when Burakumin families immigrate to the United States, they are treated like any other Japanese. The children do just as well in school—and on IQ tests—as any other Japanese Americans (Ogbu, 1986).

Of course, Japan is not the only society that discriminates against a particular social group. Many societies discriminate against specific minority groups, such as the Harijans in India (formerly called the untouchables), West Indians in Great Britain, Maoris in New Zealand, and Jews of non-European descent in Israel.

Children belonging to these minority groups score 10 to 15 points lower on intelligence tests than do children belonging to the dominant group in their societies. Children of the minority groups are often one or two years behind dominant-group children in basic reading skills and mathematical skills. Minority-group children are overrepresented in remedial programs and in school dropout rates. They are also underrepresented in higher education. The impact of discrimination on group differences in IQ remains even when the minority-group and dominant-group members are of similar socioeconomic backgrounds (Ogbu, 1986, 2008). In many ways, the educational experiences of these minority groups seem to parallel those of minority groups around the world, providing a cross-cultural perspective on the consistent effects of discrimination in many different societies.

Table 7.2

The Effects of Discrimination on IQ Scores in Japan

Range of IQ Scores	Percentage of Children Scoring in a Given Range: Non-Burakumin	Burakumin
Above 125	23.3	2.6
124–109	31.8	19.5
108–93	23.3	22.1
92–77	11.7	18.2
Below 76	9.9	37.6

Source: Adapted from DeVos & Wagatsuma (1967), Table 2, p. 261.

The Burakumin of Japan are not racially different from other Japanese, but they have suffered from generations of discrimination. Their average IQ scores are about 10 to 15 points below those of mainstream Japanese (Ogbu, 1986). In many other cultures, a similar gap in IQ scores exists between the discriminated-against minority and the dominant group.

Defying Centuries of Discrimination Members of the Buraku Liberation League sing a traditional Buraku lullaby on a rooftop in Japan. They chose a lullaby, the group's leader said, "to sing this as a song for protecting children while reflecting our suffering, sadness and wishes, all of which are conveyed in the song." Overt discrimination against the estimated 1 million Buraku people is technically illegal in Japan, yet they remain the poorest group in Japan and discrimination persists in employment, marriage, and other areas (Ikeda, 2001).

CULTURE AND HUMAN BEHAVIOR

Performing with a Threat in the Air: How Stereotypes Undermine Performance

Your anxiety intensifies as you walk into the testing center. You know how much you've prepared for this test. You should feel confident, but you can't ignore the nagging awareness that not everyone expects you to do well. Can your performance be influenced by your awareness of those expectations?

Standardized testing situations are designed so that everyone is treated as uniformly as possible. Nevertheless, some factors, such as the attitudes and feelings that individuals bring to the testing situation, can't be standardized. Among the most powerful of these factors are the expectations that you think other people might hold about your performance.

As psychologist **Claude Steele** (1997) discovered, if those expectations are negative, being aware of that fact can cause you to perform below your actual ability level. Steele coined the term **stereotype threat** to describe this phenomenon. It's a response that occurs when members of a group are aware of a negative stereotype about their group and fear they will be judged in terms of that stereotype. Even more unsettling is the fear that you might somehow confirm the stereotype, even when you know that the negative beliefs are false.

For example, one common stereotype is that women perform poorly in math, especially advanced mathematics. Multiple studies have shown that when women are reminded of their gender identity before taking an advanced mathematics test, their scores are lower than would be expected (see Steele & others, 2007). Even mathematically gifted women show a drop in scores when they are made aware of gender stereotypes (Good & others, 2008; Kiefer & Sekaquaptewa, 2007).

What about positive stereotypes, such as the racial stereotype that Asians are good at advanced mathematics? In a related phenomenon, called *stereotype lift,* awareness of *positive* expectations can actually improve performance on tasks (Walton & Cohen, 2003).

Psychologist Margaret Shih and her colleagues (1999, 2006) showed how easily gender and racial stereotypes can be manipulated to affect test performance. In one study, mathematically gifted Asian-American female college students were randomly assigned to three groups. Group 1 filled out a questionnaire about their Asian background, designed to remind them of their Asian identity. Group 2 filled out a questionnaire designed to remind them of their female identity. Group 3 was the control group and filled out a neutral questionnaire.

The results? The students who were reminded of their racial identity as Asians scored significantly higher on the exam than the students who were reminded of their gender identity as women. The control group of female students who filled out the neutral questionnaire scored in the middle of the other two groups.

In another study, Shih and her colleagues (2006) assessed the performance of Asian-American women on a test of *verbal* ability, an area in which women are stereotypically expected to excel but Asians are not. In this study, the women scored *higher* on the verbal test when reminded of the *gender* identity, but scored *lower* on the test when reminded of their *racial* identity.

Members of virtually any group can experience a decline in performance due to stereotype threat (Schmader & others, 2008). For example:

- When a test was described as measuring "problem-solving skills," African-American students did just as well as white students. But when told that the *same* test measured "intellectual ability," African-American students scored lower than white students (Aronson & others, 2002; Steele & Aronson, 1995).

Are IQ Tests Culturally Biased?

Another approach to explaining group differences in IQ scores has been to look at cultural bias in the tests themselves. If standardized intelligence tests reflect white, middle-class cultural knowledge and values, minority-group members might do poorly on the tests not because of lower intelligence but because of unfamiliarity with the white, middle-class culture.

Researchers have attempted to create tests that are "culture-fair" or "culture-free." However, it is now generally recognized that it is virtually impossible to design a test that is completely culture-free. As cross-cultural psychologist Patricia Greenfield (1997) argues, ability tests "reflect the values, knowledge, and communication strategies of their culture of origin." Within that culture, the intelligence test may be a valid measure. Thus, a test will tend to favor the people from the culture in which it was developed.

Testing, Testing, Testing . . . Virtually all college students will be evaluated with standardized tests at some point in their college careers. Although great pains are taken to make tests as unbiased and objective as possible, many factors, both personal and situational, can affect performance on tests. Cultural factors, familiarity with the testing process, and anxiety or nervousness are just a few of the factors that can skew test results. So perhaps the best way to view standardized tests is as just one of many possible indicators of a student's level of knowledge—and of his or her potential to learn.

Cultural differences may also be involved in *test-taking behavior* (Sternberg, 1995). People from different cultural backgrounds may use strategies in solving problems or organizing information that are different from those required on standard intelligence tests (Miller-Jones, 1989). In addition, such cultural factors as motivation, attitudes toward test taking, and previous experiences with tests can affect performance and scores on tests.

- When reminded of their racial identity, white males did worse on a math test when they thought they were competing with Asian males (Aronson & others, 1999). And, when reminded of their gender identity, men performed worse than women on a test that was described as measuring "social sensitivity," but not when the test was described as measuring "complex information processing" (Koenig & Eagly, 2005).
- When tests were described as measuring intelligence, Hispanic students performed more poorly than white students (Gonzales & others, 2002); children from a low socioeconomic background performed more poorly than students from higher socioeconomic backgrounds (Croizet & Claire, 1998); and social science majors scored lower than natural science majors (Croizet & others, 2004).
- When reminded of the stereotype of the "elderly as forgetful," older adults scored lower on a memory test than a matched group not given that reminder. Conversely, when reminded of the "elderly as wise" stereotype, senior adults scored *higher* on the same test than those who were not reminded of that positive stereotype (Levy, 1996).
- Women who were reminded of the stereotype that females are bad drivers were *more than twice as likely* to run over pedestrians than women who were *not* reminded of the stereotype (Yeung & Von Hippel, 2008). (Note from your authors: No actual pedestrians were harmed in this study, which was conducted in a driving simulator, not a real car.)

How does being reminded of a negative stereotype undermine a person's performance? First, there's the fear that you might confirm the stereotype, which creates psychological stress, self-doubt, and anxiety (Ben-Zeev & others, 2005; Beilock & others, 2007; Osborne, 2007). In turn, physiological arousal and distracting thoughts interfere with concentration, memory, and problem-solving abilities (Schmader & others, 2008). And, ironically, those individuals who are most highly motivated to perform well are the ones most likely to be affected by stereotype threat (Good & others, 2008).

Hundreds of psychological studies have demonstrated that individual performance on tests—even tests that are carefully designed to be fair and objective—is surprisingly susceptible to stereotype threat (Good & others, 2008; Kiefer & Sekaquaptewa, 2007; Walton & Spencer, 2009). However, research also shows that simply being aware of how stereotype threat can affect your performance helps minimize its negative effects (Johns & others, 2005, 2008).

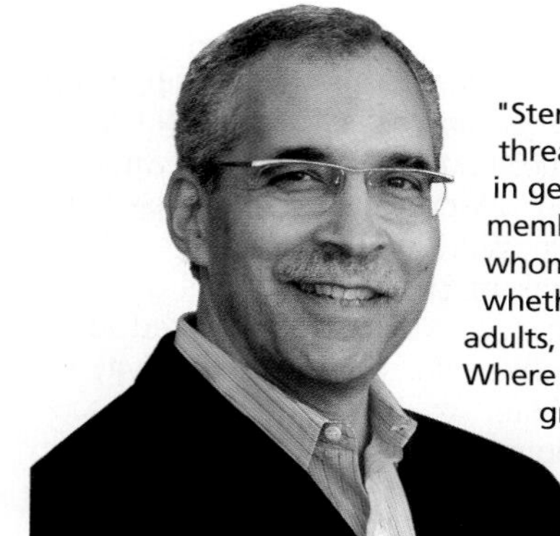

"Stereotype threat is a situational threat—a threat in the air—that, in general form, can affect the members of any group about whom a negative stereotype exists, whether it's skateboarders, older adults, white men, or gang members. Where bad stereotypes about these groups apply, members of these groups can fear being reduced to that stereotype."

Claude Steele (1997)

>> Closing Thoughts

So what conclusions can we draw about the debates surrounding intelligence, including the role of heredity in mental ability?

First, it's clear that the IQ score of any individual—regardless of his or her racial, social, or economic group—is the result of a complex interaction among genetic and environmental factors. Second, environmental factors are much more likely than genetic factors to account for average IQ differences among distinct groups of people (Ceci & Williams, 2009). Third, within *any* given group of people, IQ differences among people are due at least as much to environmental influences as they are to genetic influences (Plomin & Spinath, 2004). And finally, IQ scores reflect what IQ tests are designed to measure—a particular group of mental abilities.

As we've seen throughout this chapter, we draw on *many* different types of mental abilities to solve problems, adapt to our environment, and communicate with others. Our culture tends to define "intelligence" in terms of intellectual ability. However, as Tom's story in the Prologue illustrates, social intelligence is an important ingredient in everyday life. Cognitive flexibility and creative thinking also contribute to our ability to successfully adapt to our particular environment. Can you learn to be more creative? We invite you to attend a Workshop on Creativity in the Enhancing Well-Being with Psychology section at the end of this chapter.

stereotype threat
A psychological predicament in which fear that you will be evaluated in terms of a negative stereotype about a group to which you belong creates anxiety and self-doubt, lowering performance in a particular domain that is important to you.

ENHANCING WELL-BEING WITH PSYCHOLOGY

A Workshop on Creativity

Creativity can be defined as a group of cognitive processes used to generate useful, original, and novel ideas or solutions to problems (Runco, 2007). Notice that usefulness, along with originality, is involved in judging creativity. An idea can be highly original, but if it lacks usefulness it is not regarded as creative.

Although we typically think of creativity in terms of artistic expression, the act of creativity is almost always linked to the process of solving some problem. In that sense, creativity can occur in virtually any area of life.

Can you learn to be more creative? In general, creativity experts agree that you can. Although there is no simple formula that guarantees creative success, a few basic ingredients are central to the process of creative thinking. Here are several suggestions that can enhance your ability to think creatively.

1. Choose the goal of creativity.

Psychologists have found that virtually everyone possesses the intelligence and cognitive processes needed to be creative (Weisberg, 1988, 1993). But the creative individual values creativity as a personal goal. Without the personal goal of creativity, the likelihood of doing something creative is slim.

2. Reinforce creative behavior.

People are most creative when motivated by their own interest, the enjoyment of a challenge, and a personal sense of satisfaction and fulfillment (Amabile, 1996, 2001). This is called *intrinsic motivation.* In contrast, when people are motivated by external rewards, such as money or grades, they are displaying *extrinsic motivation.*

Researchers used to believe that extrinsic rewards made creative behavior much less likely. New research, however, seems to demonstrate that rewards can increase creative behavior in a person who has some training in generating creative solutions to problems (Eisenberger & others, 1998). When people know that creative behavior will be rewarded, they are more likely to behave in a creative way (Eisenberger & Cameron, 1996).

3. Engage in problem finding.

In many cases, the real creative leap involves recognizing that a problem exists. This is referred to as *problem finding.* We often overlook creative opportunities by dismissing trivial annoyances rather than recognizing them as potential problems to be solved.

For example, consider the minor annoyance experienced by a man named Art Fry. Fry, a researcher for 3M Corporation, regularly sang in his church choir. To locate the hymns quickly during the Sunday service, Fry used little scraps of paper to mark their places. But the scraps of paper would sometimes fall out when Fry stood up to sing, and he'd have to fumble to find the right page (Kaplan, 1990).

While sitting in church, Fry recognized the "problem" and came up with a relatively simple solution. If you put a substance that is sticky, but not *too* sticky, on the scraps of paper, they'll stay on the page and you can take them off when they are not needed anymore.

If you haven't already guessed, Art Fry invented Post-it notes. The formula for the adhesive had been discovered years earlier at 3M, but nobody could imagine a use for a glue that did not bond permanently. The mental set of the 3M researchers was to find *stronger* glues, not weaker ones. Fry's story demonstrates the creative value of recognizing problems instead of simply dismissing them.

A technique called *bug listing* is one useful strategy to identify potential problems. Bug listing involves creating a list of things that annoy, irritate, or bug you. Such everyday annoyances are problems in need of creative solutions.

4. Acquire relevant knowledge.

Creativity requires a good deal of preparation (Weisberg, 1993). Acquiring a solid knowledge base increases your potential for recognizing how to creatively extend your knowledge or apply it in a new way. As the famous French chemist Louis Pasteur said, "Chance favors the prepared mind."

5. Try different approaches.

Creative people are flexible in their thinking. They step back from problems, turn them over, and mentally play with possibilities. By being flexible and imaginative, people seeking creative solutions generate many different responses. This is called *divergent thinking,* because it involves moving away (or diverging) from the problem and considering it from a variety of perspectives (Baer, 1993).

Looking for analogies is one technique to encourage divergent thinking. In problem solving, an *analogy* is the recognition of some similarity or parallel between two objects or events that are not usually compared. Similarities can be drawn in terms of the objects' operation, function, purpose, materials, or other characteristics.

For example, consider inventor Dean Kamen's ingenious "self-balancing human transporter," the *Segway,* which is modeled on the human body. As Kamen (2001) explains, "There's a gyroscope that acts like your inner ear, a computer that acts like your brain, motors that act like your muscles, and wheels that act like your feet." Rather than brakes, engine, or steering wheel, sophisticated sensors detect subtle shifts in body weight to maintain direction, speed, and balance. Designed for riding on sidewalks, the Segway can move at speeds up to 17 mph and can carry the average rider for a full day.

"Never, ever, think outside the box."

The Segway Mexico City police use Segways to patrol city streets—and give directions. Police in dozens of cities have adopted Dean Kamen's invention because it is so easy to maneuver on city streets, on crowded sidewalks, in parks, and in other public areas.

6. Exert effort and expect setbacks.

Flashes of insight or inspiration can play a role in creativity, but they usually occur only after a great deal of work. Whether you're trying to write a brilliant term paper or design the next Beanie Baby, creativity requires effort and persistence.

Finally, the creative process is typically filled with obstacles and setbacks. The best-selling novelist Stephen King endured years of rejection of his manuscripts before his first book was published. Thomas Edison tried thousands of filaments before he created the first working lightbulb. In the face of obstacles and setbacks, the creative person perseveres.

To summarize our workshop on creativity, we'll use the letters of the word *create* as an acronym. Thus, the basic ingredients of creativity are:

- **C**hoose the goal of creativity.
- **R**einforce creative behavior.
- **E**ngage in problem finding.
- **A**cquire relevant knowledge.
- **T**ry different approaches.
- **E**xert effort and expect setbacks.

CHAPTER REVIEW: KEY PEOPLE AND TERMS

Alfred Binet, p. 293
Howard Gardner, p. 299
Charles Spearman, p. 298
Claude Steele, p. 310
Robert Sternberg, p. 301
Lewis Terman, p. 294
Louis L. Thurstone, p. 299
David Wechsler, p. 296

cognition, p. 277
thinking, p. 277
mental image, p. 277
concept, p. 278
formal concept, p. 279
natural concept, p. 280
prototype, p. 280
exemplars, p. 280
problem solving, p. 281
trial and error, p. 281
algorithm, p. 282
heuristic, p. 282
insight, p. 283
intuition, p. 283
functional fixedness, p. 284
mental set, p. 284
availability heuristic, p. 286
representativeness heuristic, p. 286
language, p. 287
linguistic relativity hypothesis, p. 290
animal cognition, p. 293
intelligence, p. 293
mental age, p. 294
intelligence quotient (IQ), p. 294
achievement test, p. 297
aptitude test, p. 297
standardization, p. 297
normal curve (normal distribution), p. 297
reliability, p. 297
validity, p. 298
g factor (general intelligence), p. 299
triarchic theory of intelligence, p. 301
autism, p. 302
Asperger's syndrome, p. 302
mental retardation, p. 302
heritability, p. 305
stereotype threat, p. 310
creativity, p. 312

Web Companion Review Activities

You can find additional review activities at **www.worthpublishers.com/discoveringpsych5e.** The *Discovering Psychology* 5th edition Web Companion has self-scoring practice quizzes, flashcards, interactive crossword puzzles, and other activities to help you master the material in this chapter.

CONCEPT MAP

THINKING, LANGUAGE, AND INTELLIGENCE

Cognition:
The mental activities involved in acquiring, retaining, and using knowledge

Thinking:
The manipulation of mental representations of information in order to draw inferences and conclusions

Mental images:
Are manipulated in the same way as actual objects

Concepts:
Mental categories of objects or ideas based on shared properties

Formal concepts:
Defined by strict rules or specific features

Natural concepts:
- Have "fuzzy boundaries"
- Develop out of everyday experience
- New instances are classified by comparing them to **prototypes** or **exemplars**

Solving Problems and Making Decisions

Problem-solving strategies:
- **Trial and error:** Try different solutions, eliminate those that don't work
- **Algorithm:** Follow a specific rule or procedure that always produces the correct solution
- **Heuristics:** Follow a rule of thumb to reduce number of potential solutions
- **Insight:** Reach solutions through sudden realization of correct answer
- **Intuition:** Reach conclusion or judgment without conscious awareness of the thought processes involved

Decision-making models:
- Single-feature model
- Additive model
- Elimination by aspects model

When events are uncertain, decision-making strategies that involve estimating the likelihood of an event:
- **Availability heuristic:** How easily can you remember similar instances?
- **Representativeness heuristic:** How similar is the current situation to your prototype for an event?

Language and Thought

Language characteristics:
- Meaning is conveyed by arbitrary symbols whose meaning is shared by speakers of the same language
- Rule-based system
- Generative
- Involves displacement

Effect of language on thinking:
- Language can alter our perceptions of others.
- **Linguistic relativity hypothesis:** Do differences among languages cause differences in the thoughts of their speakers?

Animal cognition, or *comparative cognition,* is the study of animal learning, memory, thinking, and language.

Measuring Intelligence

Intelligence: The global capacity to think rationally, act purposefully, and deal effectively with the environment.

History of intelligence tests

Alfred Binet (1857–1911)
- Developed the first widely accepted intelligence test
- Originated idea of **mental age** as different from chronological age

Lewis Terman (1877–1956)
- Translated and adapted Binet's test for U.S.
- Defined **intelligence quotient (IQ),** a measure of general intelligence derived by comparing an individual's score with the scores of others in the same age group

David Wechsler (1896–1981)
- Developed the **Wechsler Adult Intelligence Scale (WAIS)**

Psychological tests include **achievement tests** and **aptitude tests.**

Requirements:
- **Standardization:** Norms are established by administering test to a large, representative sample of people under uniform conditions; norms usually reflect **normal curve** or **normal distribution** of scores.
- **Reliability:** Test produces consistent results when administered on repeated occasions under similar conditions.
- **Validity:** Test measures what it is purported to measure.

The Nature of Intelligence

Is intelligence a single factor or a cluster of different abilities? How narrowly should intelligence be defined?

Charles Spearman (1863–1945)
- Intelligence can be described as a single factor called **general intelligence,** or the ***g* factor.**

Louis L. Thurstone (1887–1955)
- Seven primary mental abilities

Howard Gardner (b. 1943)
- Multiple intelligences

Robert Sternberg (b. 1949)
- Triarchic theory of intelligence: Successful intelligence involves analytic, creative, and practical mental abilities.

- Intelligence, as measured by IQ, is the result of a complex interaction between heredity and the environment.
- **Hereditability:** the percentage of variation within a given population that is due to heredity.
- There is more variation within groups than between groups.

Effects of culture on measurements of intelligence:
- Average IQ scores of the dominant social group tend to be higher than the average IQ scores of other groups.
- Intelligence tests can be culturally biased.
- **Stereotype threat** can lower test scores in people who are aware that they belong to negatively viewed groups.

JAPAN
Sydney 2000

CHAPTER

8

Motivation and Emotion

Chapter Outline

Soaring with Angels

PROLOGUE

RICHARD AND I HAD BEEN BEST FRIENDS since our paths first crossed at Central High School in Sioux City, Iowa. Even then, Richard was extraordinary. He was good-looking and liked by everyone. He maintained almost a straight-A average in his classes. In our senior year, he was elected student body president. (To be perfectly honest, he beat me in the race for student body president.) And his talent as a diver had attracted the attention of college swimming coaches. Coming from a family of very modest means, Richard hoped for an athletic scholarship to attend college. He got one: The University of Arkansas awarded him a four-year athletic scholarship.

Richard met Becky when they were freshmen at the University of Arkansas. They seemed like a good match. Becky was smart, pretty, athletic, and had a wonderful sense of humor. They were also both Catholic, which greatly pleased Becky's parents. So it came as no surprise when Richard and Becky announced their plans to marry after graduating. But, in retrospect, I can't help thinking that Richard's timing was deliberate when he asked me, in front of Becky, to be his best man.

"You're *sure* you want to marry this guy?" I half-jokingly asked Becky.

"Only if he takes nationals on the three-meter board," Becky quipped. As it turned out, Richard did place third on the three-meter board the following spring at the national collegiate swimming competition.

Three months before their wedding, Richard and I had the only argument we've ever had. At the time we had the argument, the word *gay* meant lighthearted and cheerful, so the word never came up in our heated exchange.

"What do you mean, you haven't told her!?"

"I don't need to tell her about the past," Richard insisted.

"That's bull, Richard," I shouted. "This woman loves you and if you don't tell her about your homosexual urges, then you are marrying her under false pretenses."

"I do *not* have those feelings anymore!" Richard yelled back.

"If that's true, then tell her!" I demanded.

But it wasn't true, of course. Although Richard would not admit it to himself, he had only become adept at suppressing his sexual attraction to other men. At the time we had that argument, I was still the only person who knew that Richard harbored what he called "homosexual urges." Richard had first told me when we were juniors in high school. I was stunned. But Richard was also adamant that he did not want to feel the way he did. In fact, he felt ashamed and guilty. Back then, being homosexual carried a much greater social stigma than it does today.

So when Richard and I were still in high school, we scraped up enough money to secretly send him to a psychologist for a few sessions. Despite our naive hopes for a quick "cure," Richard's troubling feelings remained. When he got to the University of Arkansas, Richard saw a counselor on a regular basis. After months of counseling,

Richard believed he was capable of leading a heterosexual life.

Richard and Becky's wedding was magnificent. And, yes, I was the best man. After the wedding, they decided to stay in Fayetteville so that Richard could start graduate school. The inevitable happened less than a year later. Becky called me.

"I'm driving to Tulsa tonight. Don, you've *got* to tell me what's going on," she said, her voice strained, shaking. And I did, as gently as I could.

Richard and Becky's marriage was annulled. In time, Becky recovered psychologically, remarried, and had two children. Her bitterness toward Richard softened over the years. The last time we talked, she seemed genuinely forgiving of Richard.

For his part, Richard gave up trying to be something he was not. Instead, he came to grips with his sexual orientation, moved to San Francisco, and became a co-owner of two health clubs. True to form, Richard quickly became a respected and well-liked member of San Francisco's large gay community. He eventually met John, an accountant, with whom he formed a long-term relationship. But after Richard's move to San Francisco, our friendship faded.

It was our 20-year high school reunion that triggered Richard's unexpected call. When I told him I simply did not have the time to attend, he suggested stopping in Tulsa on his way to the reunion to meet Sandy and our daughter, Laura.

So on a warm May evening, Richard, Sandy, and I drank some margaritas, ate Chinese carryout, and talked until midnight. Just as I had expected, Sandy was quite taken with Richard. Indeed, Richard *was* a wonderful man—smart, funny, thoughtful, and sensitive. Laura, who was not quite 2 years old, was also enchanted by Richard. My only regret about that evening is that I did not take a picture of Richard sitting on our back deck as Laura brought him first one toy, then another, then another. As it turned out, it would be the last time I saw Richard.

About a year after he visited us in Tulsa, Richard was killed in a hang-gliding accident. As he was soaring over the rocky California coast, Richard swerved to miss an inexperienced flyer who crossed his path in the air. Richard lost control of his hang glider and was killed on impact when he plummeted into the rocky coastline.

A week later, more than 300 people crowded into St. Mary's Catholic Church in Sioux City, where Richard had been an altar boy in his youth. The outpouring of love and respect for Richard at the memorial service was a testament to the remarkable man he was.

What Richard's story illustrates is that who we are in this life—our identity—is not determined by any single characteristic or quality. Yes, Richard was gay, but that's not all Richard was, just as your sexual orientation is not the only characteristic that defines you or motivates your behavior. In this chapter, we'll look at a wide variety of factors that motivate our behavior, including sexuality, striving to achieve, and the emotions we experience. In the process, we'll come back to Richard's story.

>> Introduction: **Motivation and Emotion**

Key Theme

- **Motivation refers to the forces acting on or within an organism to initiate and direct behavior.**

Key Questions

- **What three characteristics are associated with motivation?**
- **How is emotion related to the topic of motivation?**

"Something" energized Richard's behavior, moving him not just to become an accomplished diver and hang glider, but also to marry, attend college, divorce, and move to San Francisco. For that matter, "something" inspired you to pick up this text, so that you are reading these words right now. And, going a step further, "something" moved us to write these words.

That "something" is what the topic of **motivation** is about—the biological, emotional, cognitive, or social forces that act on or within you, initiating and directing your behavior. Typically, psychologists don't measure motivation directly. Instead, some type of motivation is *inferred* when an organism performs a particular behavior, such as curiosity motivating exploratory behavior or hunger motivating eating behavior. Indeed, the forces that activate your behavior can take many different forms, including biological, psychological, or social forces.

As an explanatory concept, motivation is very useful in both the scientific sense and the everyday sense. In conversations, people routinely use the word *motivation* to understand or explain the "why" behind the behavior of others. "And what motivated you to take up hang gliding?" "She is so motivated to get her pilot's license that she started going to the library every night to study for the written exam." Such statements reflect three basic characteristics commonly associated with motivation: activation, persistence, and intensity.

Activation is demonstrated by the initiation or production of behavior, such as Richard's decision to pursue competitive diving in high school. *Persistence* is demonstrated by continued efforts or the determination to achieve a particular goal, often in the face of obstacles. Day after day, Richard spent hours at the swimming pool honing the precision of his dives. Finally, *intensity* is seen in the greater vigor of responding that usually accompanies motivated behavior.

Motivation is closely tied to emotional processes, and vice versa. Often we are motivated to experience a particular emotion, such as feeling proud. In turn, the experience of an emotion—such as love, fear, or dissatisfaction—can motivate us to take action. Many forms of motivation have an emotional component, which is involved in the initiation and persistence of behavior. One reflection of the emotional intensity of Richard's motivation was the exhilaration he experienced when he placed third at a national collegiate swimming competition.

In the second half of the chapter, we'll take a detailed look at emotion. As you'll see, *emotion* is a psychological state involving three distinct components: subjective experience, a physiological response, and a behavioral or expressive component.

"Could you give me a little push?"

Motivational Concepts and Theories

Key Theme

- **Over the past century, instinct, drive, incentive, arousal, and humanistic theories were proposed to explain the general principles of motivation.**

Key Questions

- **How does each theory explain motivation?**
- **What were the limitations of each theory?**
- **What lasting ideas did each theory contribute to the study of motivation?**

During the twentieth century, several broad theories of motivation were proposed. Each model eventually proved to be limited, explaining only certain aspects of motivation. However, key ideas and concepts from each model became essential to a complete understanding of motivation and were incorporated into newer theories (Fiske, 2008). As you'll see in this section, the concepts used to explain motivation have become progressively more diverse over the years.

Instinct Theories

Inborn Behaviors as Motivators

In the late 1800s, the fledgling science of psychology initially embraced instinct theories to explain motivation. According to **instinct theories,** people are motivated to engage in certain behaviors because of evolutionary programming. Just as animals

motivation
The biological, emotional, cognitive, or social forces that activate and direct behavior.

instinct theories
The view that certain human behaviors are innate and due to evolutionary programming.

Table 8.1

James's List of Human Instincts

Attachment	Resentment
Fear	Curiosity
Disgust	Shyness
Rivalry	Sociability
Greediness	Bashfulness
Suspicion	Secretiveness
Hunting	Cleanliness
Play	Modesty
Shame	Love
Anger	Parental Love

In his famous text, *Principles of Psychology,* William James (1890) devoted a lengthy chapter to the topic of instinct. With an air of superiority, James noted that "no other mammal, not even the monkey, shows so large an array of instincts" as humans. The table shows some of the human instincts identified by James.

display automatic and innate instinctual behavior patterns called *fixed action patterns,* such as migration or mating rituals, human behavior was also thought to be motivated by inborn instinctual behavior patterns.

Inspired by Charles Darwin's (1859, 1871) landmark theory of evolution, early psychologists like William James and William McDougall (1908) devised lists of human instincts. Table 8.1 lists some of the human instincts that William James (1890) included in his famous text, *Principles of Psychology.*

By the early 1900s, thousands of instincts had been proposed in one expert's list or another to account for just about every conceivable human behavior (Bernard, 1924). (The early instinct theorists were, no doubt, motivated by a "listing instinct.") But what does it mean to say that an assertive person has a "self-assertion instinct"? Or to say that our friend Richard had a "diving instinct"? The obvious problem with the early instinct theories was that merely describing and labeling behaviors did not explain them.

By the 1920s, instinct theories had fallen out of favor as an explanation of human motivation, primarily because of their lack of explanatory power. But the more general idea that some human behaviors are innate and genetically influenced remained an important element in the overall understanding of motivation. Today, psychologists taking the *evolutionary perspective* consider how our evolutionary heritage may influence patterns of human behaviors, such as eating behaviors or the expression of emotions. We'll consider what the evolutionary perspective has to say about both of those examples later in the chapter.

Drive Theories

Biological Needs as Motivators

Beginning in the 1920s, instinct theories were replaced by drive theories. In general, **drive theories** asserted that behavior is motivated by the desire to reduce internal tension caused by unmet biological needs, such as hunger or thirst. The basic idea was that these unmet biological needs "drive" or "push" us to behave in certain ways that will lead to a reduction in the drive. When a particular behavior successfully reduces a drive, the behavior becomes more likely to be repeated when the same need state arises again.

Leading drive theorists, including psychologists Robert S. Woodworth (1918, 1921) and Clark L. Hull (1943, 1952), believed that drives are triggered by the internal mechanisms of homeostasis. The principle of **homeostasis** states that the body monitors and maintains relatively constant levels of internal states, such as body temperature, fluid levels, and energy supplies. If any of these internal conditions deviates very far from the optimal level, the body initiates processes to bring the condition back to the normal or optimal range. Thus, the body automatically tries to maintain a "steady state," which is what *homeostasis* means.

Motivation and Drive Theories According to drive theories of motivation, behavior is motivated by biological drives to maintain *homeostasis,* or an optimal internal balance. After a long soccer practice on a hot day, these high school students are motivated to rest, cool off, and drink water. Drive theories of motivation are useful in explaining biological motives like hunger, thirst, and fatigue, but are less useful in explaining psychological motives. For example, how could we explain their motivation to play competitive soccer? To practice long and hard on a hot summer day?

According to drive theorists, when an internal imbalance is detected by homeostatic mechanisms, a **drive** to restore balance is produced. The drive activates behavior to reduce the need and to reestablish the balance of internal conditions. For example, after you have not eaten anything for several hours, this unmet biological need creates a *drive state*—hunger—that motivates or energizes your behavior. And how might the drive of hunger energize you to behave? You might make your way to the kitchen and forage in the refrigerator for some leftover guacamole dip or chocolate cake.

Today, the drive concept remains useful in explaining motivated behaviors that clearly have biological components, such as hunger, thirst, and sexuality. However, drive theories also have limitations. Let's consider hunger again. Is the motivation of eating behavior strictly a matter of physiological need? Obviously not. People often eat when they're not hungry and don't eat when they are hungry. And how could drive theories account for the motivation to buy a lottery ticket or run a marathon?

Incentive Motivation

Goal Objects as Motivators

Building on the base established by drive theories, incentive theories emerged in the 1940s and 1950s. **Incentive theories** proposed that behavior is motivated by the "pull" of external goals, such as rewards, money, or recognition. It's easy to think of many situations in which a particular goal, such as a promotion at work, can serve as an external incentive that helps activate particular behaviors.

Incentive theories drew heavily from well-established learning principles, such as *reinforcement,* and the work of influential learning theorists, such as Pavlov, Watson, Skinner, and Tolman (see Chapter 5). Edward Tolman (1932) also stressed the importance of cognitive factors in learning and motivation, especially the *expectation* that a particular behavior will lead to a particular goal.

When combined, drive and incentive theories account for a broad range of the "pushes" and "pulls" motivating many of our behaviors. But even in combination, drive and incentive explanations of motivation still had limitations. In some situations, such as playing a rapid-response video game, our behavior seems to be directed toward *increasing* tension and physiological arousal. If you think about it, our friend Richard's decision to take up hang gliding was not motivated by either an internal, biological drive or an external incentive.

Arousal Theory

Optimal Stimulation as a Motivator

Racing your car along a barren stretch of highway, watching a suspenseful movie, shooting down the Super Slide at a water park—none of these activities seem to involve tension reduction, the satisfaction of some biological need, or the lure of some reward. Rather, performing the activity itself seems to motivate us. Why?

Arousal theory is based on the observation that people experience both very high levels of arousal and very low levels of arousal as being quite unpleasant. When arousal is too low, we experience boredom and become motivated to *increase* arousal by seeking out stimulating experiences (Berlyne, 1960, 1971). But when arousal is too high, we seek to *reduce* arousal in a less stimulating environment. Thus, people are motivated to maintain an *optimal* level of arousal, one that is neither too high nor too low (Hebb, 1955). This optimal level of arousal varies from person to person, from time to time, and from one situation to another.

That the optimal level of arousal varies from person to person is especially evident in people dubbed *sensation seekers.* Sensation seekers find the heightened arousal of novel experiences very pleasurable. According to psychologist Marvin Zuckerman (1979, 2007), people who rank high on the dimension of **sensation seeking** have a need for varied, complex, and unique sensory experiences. No doubt Don ranks high on this dimension, since he has tried skydiving, aerobatic flying, and white-water rafting. (He also once ate a handful of biodegradable packing peanuts, much to the horror of a college secretary.) Although such experiences can sometimes involve physical or social risks, sensation seekers aren't necessarily drawn to danger—but rather to the novel

Ice-Climbing in Keene Valley, New York Aptly called "extreme sports," they include such diverse activities as hang gliding, ice climbing, white-water kayaking, bungee jumping, and parachuting from mountain cliffs and radio towers. People who enjoy such high-risk activities are usually sensation seekers. For them, the rush of adrenaline they feel when they push the outer limit is an exhilarating and rewarding experience.

drive theories
The view that behavior is motivated by the desire to reduce internal tension caused by unmet biological needs.

homeostasis
(home-ee-oh-STAY-sis) The idea that the body monitors and maintains internal states, such as body temperature and energy supplies, at relatively constant levels; in general, the tendency to reach or maintain equilibrium.

drive
A need or internal motivational state that activates behavior to reduce the need and restore homeostasis.

incentive theories
The view that behavior is motivated by the pull of external goals, such as rewards.

arousal theory
The view that people are motivated to maintain a level of arousal that is optimal—neither too high nor too low.

sensation seeking
The degree to which an individual is motivated to experience high levels of sensory and physical arousal associated with varied and novel activities.

experience itself. For example, college students who study abroad score significantly higher on sensation seeking than college students who stay in their country of origin (Schroth & McCormack, 2000).

Like people, animals also seem to seek out novel environmental stimulation. Rats, cats, dogs, and other animals actively explore a new environment. In a series of classic studies, psychologist Harry Harlow (1953a, 1953b) showed that a monkey will spend hours trying to open a complicated lock, even when there is no incentive or reward for doing so. And, when kept in a boring cage, a monkey will "work" for the opportunity to open a window to peek into another monkey's cage or to watch an electric train run (Butler & Harlow, 1954).

Seeking Stimulation Like humans, animals are also motivated to seek out stimulation and explore novel environments. In his research with monkeys, Harry Harlow (1953c) found that arousal was a powerful motive. These young monkeys are trying to open a complicated lock, despite the lack of an incentive or reward for their behavior.

Humanistic Theory

Human Potential as a Motivator

In the late 1950s, **humanistic theories of motivation** were championed by psychologists Carl Rogers and Abraham Maslow. Although not discounting the role of biological and external motivators, humanistic theories emphasized psychological and cognitive components in human motivation (Sheldon, 2008). Motivation was thought to be affected by how we perceive the world, how we think about ourselves and others, and our beliefs about our abilities and skills (Rogers, 1961, 1977).

According to the humanistic perspective, people are motivated to realize their highest personal potential. Although the motivation to strive for a positive self-concept and personal potential was thought to be inborn, humanistic theories also recognized the importance of the environment (Maslow, 1970). Without a supportive and encouraging environment—personal, social, and cultural—the motivation to strive toward one's highest potential could be jeopardized (King, 2008). Later in the chapter, we'll consider the most famous humanistic model of motivation, Maslow's *hierarchy of needs.*

In the next several sections, we'll look at several basic motives, starting with the fundamentally biological motive of hunger and eating. Later, we'll consider psychological motives, including competence and achievement motivation. As you'll see, the motivation concepts of drive, homeostasis, incentive, and arousal all come into play in understanding many different human behaviors.

Biological Motivation

Hunger and Eating

Key Theme

- **Hunger is a biological motive, but eating behavior is motivated by a complex interaction of biological, social, and psychological factors.**

Key Questions

- **What is energy homeostasis, and how does it relate to energy balance?**
- **What are the short-term signals that regulate eating behavior?**
- **What chemical signals are involved in the long-term regulation of a stable body weight?**
- **How do set-point and settling-point theories differ?**

It seems simple: You're hungry, so you eat. But even a moment's reflection will tell you that eating behavior is not that straightforward. When, what, how much, and how often you eat is influenced by an array of psychological, biological, social, and cultural factors.

humanistic theories of motivation The view that emphasizes the importance of psychological and cognitive factors in motivation, especially the notion that people are motivated to realize their personal potential.

For example, think about what you ate yesterday. Now contrast your choices with food preferences in other cultures. A typical diet for the Dusan of northern Borneo in Southeast Asia includes anteater, gibbon (a small ape), snake, mouse, and rat meat. After these meats have spoiled to the point of being liquefied, the Dusan consume them with rice. South American Indians eat head lice, bees, iguanas, and monkeys. The Guianese of South America eat pebbles as a regular part of their diet, while the Vedda of Sri Lanka like rotted wood (see Fieldhouse, 1986). Clearly, cultural experience shapes our food choices (Rozin, 2006, 2007).

Delicious or Disgusting? The need to eat is a universal human motive. However, culture influences *what* we eat, *when* we eat, and *how* we eat (Rozin, 1996, 2007). At a Cambodian marketplace, this young boy is carrying a platter of cooked spiders, a local delicacy. While not a feature at your typical U.S. restaurant, insects are standard fare in many countries. For example, grasshoppers, ant and fly larvae, and worms can be purchased as snacks in traditional markets in Mexico, where they have been a staple of the diet for thousands of years.

Themes of food and eating permeate many different dimensions of our lives. Psychologically, eating can be related to emotional states, such as depression, anxiety, or stress (Macht, 2008). Interpersonally, eating is often used to foster relationships, as when you have friends over for dinner or take a potential customer to lunch. We often rely on food-related adjectives to describe other people, as when we say that someone has a *sweet disposition* or a *sour outlook* on life. And, interestingly, our judgments about others may be influenced by what they eat (Vartanian & others, 2007).

In the next several sections, we look at what researchers have learned about the motivational factors that trigger hunger and eating behavior. As you'll see, these research efforts have focused on answering several key questions:

- What signals regulate the motivation to start and stop eating?
- How do people maintain a stable body weight over time?
- Why do people become overweight or obese?
- What causes eating disorders?

Energy Homeostasis

Calories Consumed = Calories Expended

In order to explain the regulation of hunger and eating behavior, we need to begin with some basics on how food is converted to energy in the body. The food that you eat is broken down by enzymes and gradually absorbed in your intestines. As part of this process, food is converted into amino acids, fatty acids, and simple sugars, providing "fuel" for your body. The simple sugar **glucose,** commonly called *blood sugar,* provides the main source of energy for all mammals, including humans. In the liver, glucose is converted to and stored as *glycogen,* which can be easily converted back to glucose for energy. The hormone **insulin,** secreted by the pancreas, helps control blood levels of glucose and promotes the uptake of glucose by the muscles and other body tissues. Insulin also helps in regulating eating behavior and maintaining a stable body weight.

Not one man in a billion, when taking his dinner, ever thinks of utility. He eats because the food tastes good and makes him want more.

—WILLIAM JAMES *Principles of Psychology* (1890)

About one-third of your body's energy is expended for the routine physical activities of daily life, such as walking, lifting objects, brushing your teeth, and digesting the food you eat. The remaining two-thirds of your body's energy is used for continuous bodily functions that are essential to life, such as generating body heat, heartbeat, respiration, and brain activity. When you are lying down and resting, the rate at which your body uses energy for vital body functions is referred to as your **basal metabolic rate (BMR).**

Obviously, you have to eat in order to have sufficient immediate energy for vital body functions and to survive. But another reason you eat is to maintain a reserve of stored energy. **Adipose tissue,** or body fat, is the main source of stored calories. Your liver, which monitors glucose levels in your bloodstream, can utilize this stored energy if necessary.

glucose
Simple sugar that provides energy and is primarily produced by the conversion of carbohydrates and fats; commonly called *blood sugar.*

insulin
Hormone produced by the pancreas that regulates blood levels of glucose and signals the hypothalamus, regulating hunger and eating behavior.

basal metabolic rate (BMR)
When the body is at rest, the rate at which it uses energy for vital functions, such as heartbeat and respiration.

adipose tissue
Body fat that is the main source of stored, or reserve, energy.

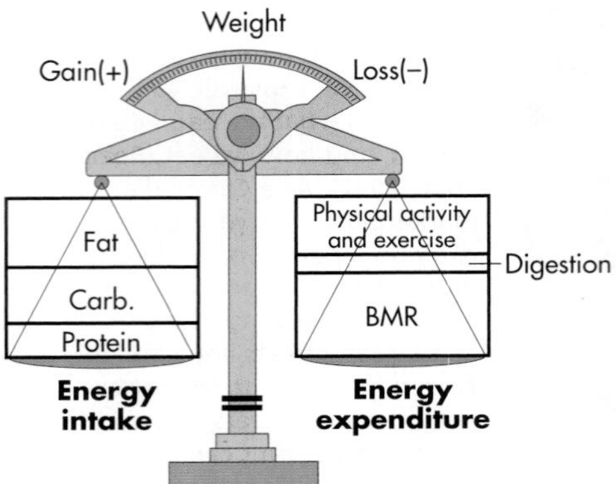

Figure 8.1 **Energy Balance** The tendency of our bodies to maintain a stable body weight is well documented (Schwartz & others, 2000). Maintaining a stable body weight occurs when you experience *energy balance*—that is, when the calories you take in almost exactly match the calories you expend for physical activity and metabolism.

Source: Adapted from Ravussin & Danforth (1999).

Positive Versus Negative Energy Balance

For most of us, there is considerable daily variation in what, when, how often, and how much we eat (de Castro & others, 2000; Marcelino & others, 2001). Yet despite this day-to-day variability in eating behavior, our body weight, including our stores of body fat, tends to stay relatively constant over the course of weeks, months, and even years (Keesey & Hirvonen, 1997). Your typical or average body weight is called your *baseline body weight*.

A regulatory process called **energy homeostasis** helps you maintain your baseline body weight. Over time, most people experience *energy balance* (see Figure 8.1). This means that the number of calories you consume almost exactly matches the number of calories you expend for energy. The result is that your body weight, including body fat stores, tends to remain stable.

However, energy balance can become disrupted if you eat more or less food than you need. If your caloric intake exceeds the amount of calories expended for energy, you experience *positive energy balance*. When there is more glucose than your body needs for its energy requirements, the excess glucose is converted into reserve energy—fat. If positive energy balance persists over time, the size and number of the body fat cells that make up the adipose tissue increase. Conversely, if you diet or fast, *negative energy balance* occurs: Caloric intake falls short of the calories expended for energy. If this imbalance continues, body fat stores shrink as the reserve energy in fat cells is used for physical activity and metabolic functions.

These findings imply that energy homeostasis and a stable body weight are actively regulated by internal signals and mechanisms that influence eating behavior. But what exactly are these signals or mechanisms?

Short-Term Signals That Regulate Eating

Consuming food is so routine in our lives that most of us don't really think about what motivates us to stop what we're doing and begin eating. Psychologists and other researchers, however, are very motivated to answer that question. In the past few years, they've made important new discoveries about the physiological and psychological factors involved in the motivation to eat (Strubbe & Woods, 2004).

Physiological Changes That Predict Eating

The idea that some internal, biochemical factor triggers our desire to eat makes intuitive sense. But what? Many people believe that eating is triggered by a drastic drop in blood glucose levels, which are rapidly restored by food consumption. This popular belief is *not* accurate. Actually, your blood levels of glucose and fats fluctuate very little over the course of a typical day. However, about 30 minutes before you eat, you experience a *slight* increase in blood levels of insulin and a *slight* decrease in blood levels of glucose. In experimental studies with both humans and rats, these small changes reliably predict the initiation of eating (Melanson & others, 1999).

Figure 8.2 **Blood Glucose and the Motivation to Eat** In this graph, the red dots depict the effects of insulin triggering a small decline in blood glucose over the course of about 30 minutes. As blood glucose decreases, the person's subjective desire to eat increases sharply, depicted by the blue line. Notice that although this person did not eat, his blood glucose level returned to normal within the hour and his desire to eat diminished. In daily life, a small decline in blood glucose level is one of the factors that reliably predict our motivation to eat (Campfield & others, 1996).

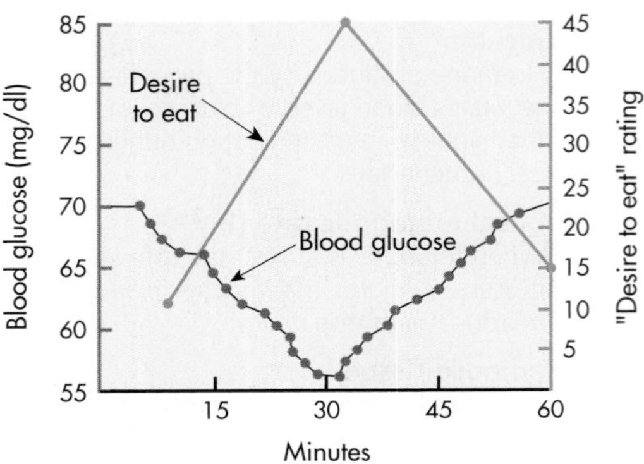

Once the meal is begun, blood glucose levels return to their baseline level. Interestingly, glucose returns to its baseline level well *before* the food is actually digested and absorbed. And, in fact, glucose will return to its baseline level even if you do *not* eat (see Figure 8.2).

A more important internal signal is a new hormone discovered by Japanese researcher Masayasu Kojima and his colleagues in 1999. **Ghrelin** (pronounced GRELL-in) is primarily manufactured by cells lining the stomach. It stimulates the secretion of growth hormone by the pituitary gland in the brain (Kojima & others, 1999; Olszweski & others, 2008).

Ghrelin was quickly dubbed "the hunger hormone" when research showed that it strongly stimulates appetite. When rats were deprived of food, ghrelin levels increased sharply (see Inui, 2001). More directly, rats whose brains were continuously infused with ghrelin ate voraciously and gained weight. When ghrelin receptors were blocked, their eating behavior subsided (Nakazato & others, 2001; Tschöp & others, 2000).

What about people? Researcher Donald Cummings and his colleagues (2002, 2006) showed that ghrelin is involved in the short-term regulation of eating behavior. As you can see in Figure 8.3, blood levels of ghrelin rise sharply before and fall abruptly after meals. Cummings also found that ghrelin seems to be involved in the long-term regulation of energy balance and weight. When participants in one of his studies lost weight by dieting, their overall plasma levels of ghrelin—and feelings of hunger—increased.

Two other internal factors are correlated with meal onset—body temperature and metabolism rate. Prior to eating, body temperature increases and metabolism decreases. As the meal is consumed, this internal physiological pattern reverses: Body temperature decreases and metabolism increases (De Vries & others, 1993; LeBlanc, 2000). This slight post-eating decrease in body temperature might explain why some people, including about a third of our students, occasionally feel cold after eating a meal.

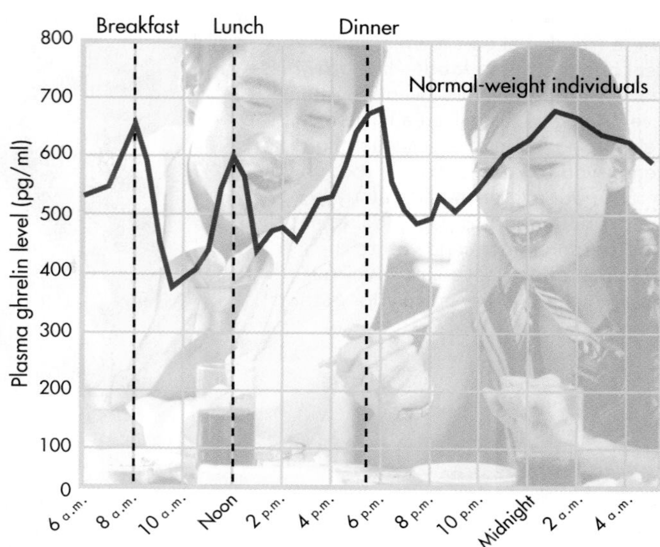

Figure 8.3 Ghrelin: The Hunger Hormone The recently discovered hormone named *ghrelin* is manufactured primarily by the stomach and stimulates appetite (Nakazato & others, 2001). The graph shows the average plasma levels of ghrelin for 10 normal-weight individuals over the course of 24 hours. Ghrelin levels rise shortly before eating, precipitating feelings of hunger. During and shortly after the meal, ghrelin levels, and feelings of hunger, fall (Cummings & others, 2002). So, if your stomach is ghrelin, you must be hungry!

Psychological Factors That Trigger Eating

In Chapter 5, we described *classical conditioning* and *operant conditioning*. Both forms of conditioning can affect your eating behavior. For example, much as Pavlov's dogs were conditioned to salivate at the sound of a bell, your eating behavior has probably been influenced by years of classical conditioning. The time of day at which you normally eat (the *conditioned stimulus)* elicits reflexive internal physiological changes (the *conditioned response)*, such as the changes in blood levels of insulin, glucose, and ghrelin, increased body temperature, and decreased metabolism. In turn, these internal physiological changes increase your sense of hunger. Other stimuli, such as the setting in which you normally eat or just the sight of food utensils, can also become associated with the anticipation of eating (Davidson, 2000; Nederkoorn & others, 2000).

Operant conditioning and *positive reinforcement* play a role in eating, too. Voluntary eating behaviors are followed by a *reinforcing stimulus*—the taste of food. Granted, not all foods are equally reinforcing. Because of prior reinforcement experiences, people develop preferences for certain tastes, especially sweet, salty, and fatty tastes. In other words, foods with one of these tastes hold greater **positive incentive value** for some people. Hence, your motivation to eat is influenced by prior learning experiences that have shaped your expectations, especially the anticipated pleasure of eating certain foods.

Satiation Signals

Sensing When to Stop Eating

The feeling of fullness and diminished desire to eat that accompanies eating a meal is termed **satiation.** Several signals combine to help trigger satiation. One satiation signal involves *stretch receptors* in the stomach that communicate sensory information to the brainstem. The sensitivity of the stomach stretch receptors is increased by a hormone called **cholecystokinin,** thankfully abbreviated **CCK.** During meals, cholecystokinin is secreted by the small intestines and enters the bloodstream. In the brain, CCK acts as a neurotransmitter. Many studies have shown that CCK promotes satiation and reduces or stops eating (Smith & Gibbs, 1998). CCK also magnifies the satiety-producing effects of food in the stomach by slowing the rate at which the stomach empties.

Psychological factors play a role in satiation, too. As you eat a meal, there is a decline in the positive incentive value of any available food, but especially the specific

energy homeostasis
The long-term matching of food intake to energy expenditure.

ghrelin
(GRELL-in) Hormone manufactured primarily by the stomach that stimulates appetite and the secretion of growth hormone by the pituitary gland.

positive incentive value
In eating behavior, the anticipated pleasure of consuming a particular food; in general, the expectation of pleasure or satisfaction in performing a particular behavior.

satiation
(say-she-AY-shun) In eating behavior, the feeling of fullness and diminished desire to eat that accompanies eating a meal; in general, the sensation of having an appetite or desire fully or excessively satisfied.

cholecystokinin (CCK)
(kola-sis-tow-KINE-in) Hormone secreted primarily by the small intestine that promotes satiation; also found in the brain.

Is Your Mouth Watering? Does the sight of these freshly baked brownies make you feel hungry? Some foods—like brownies—have a strong positive incentive value. Even if you've just eaten a large meal, the reinforcing value of a brownie might tempt you to keep eating. Although you might not have been particularly hungry before you read this page, looking at this photograph might send you to the kitchen in search of a sweet snack—which is exactly what happened to your authors!

foods you are eating. So, after you have wolfed down four slices of pizza, the pizza's appeal begins to diminish. This phenomenon is termed **sensory-specific satiety** (Maier & others, 2007). Of course, if a *different* appealing food becomes available, your willingness to eat might return. Restaurants are well aware of this, which is why servers will bring a tempting platter of scrumptious desserts to your table after you've finished a large and otherwise satisfying dinner.

Long-Term Signals That Regulate Body Weight

In the past decade, researchers have discovered more than 20 different chemical messengers that monitor and help us maintain a stable body weight over time (see Schwartz & others, 2000; Woods & others, 2000). Three of the best-documented internal signals are *leptin, insulin,* and *neuropeptide Y.*

Leptin is a hormone secreted by the body's adipose tissue into the bloodstream. The amount of leptin that is secreted is directly correlated with the amount of body fat. The brain receptor sites for leptin are located in several areas of the hypothalamus. Neurons in the stomach and the gut also have leptin receptor sites.

Leptin is a key element in the feedback loop that regulates energy homeostasis. Under conditions of positive energy balance, the body's fat stores increase, and so do blood levels of leptin. When the leptin level in the brain increases, food intake is reduced and the body's fat stores shrink over time (Ahima & Osei, 2004). Increased leptin levels also intensify the satiety-producing effects of CCK, further decreasing the amount of food consumed (Matson & others, 2000). Should negative energy balance occur, fat stores shrink and there is a corresponding decrease in leptin blood levels, which triggers eating behavior.

The hormone *insulin* is also involved in brain mechanisms controlling food intake and body weight. Like leptin, the amount of insulin secreted by the pancreas is directly proportional to the amount of body fat. In the brain, insulin receptors are located in the same hypothalamus areas as leptin receptors (Brüning & others, 2000). Increased brain levels of insulin are also associated with a reduction in food intake and body weight. So in much the same way as leptin, insulin levels vary in response to positive or negative energy balance, triggering an increase or decrease in eating.

***Ob/ob* Mice, Before and After Leptin** Leptin is a hormone produced by body fat. Because of a genetic mutation, these mice, dubbed *ob/ob* mice, lack the ability to produce leptin. Consequently, *ob/ob* mice behave as though their brains were telling them that their body fat reserves are completely depleted and that they are starving. *Ob/ob* mice have voracious appetites and five times as much body fat as normal-weight mice. Yet they display the characteristics of starving animals, including decreased immune system functioning, low body temperatures, and lack of energy. When the *ob/ob* mouse on the right was given supplemental leptin, it lost the excess fat and began eating normally. Its body temperature, immune system, and metabolism also became normal (Friedman & Halaas, 1998). Unfortunately, what worked for obese mice has not worked as easily for obese people, although researchers remain hopeful (Morrison, 2008).

Abbreviated **NPY, neuropeptide Y** is a neurotransmitter manufactured throughout the brain, including the hypothalamus. During periods of negative energy balance and weight loss, decreased leptin and insulin levels promote the secretion of NPY by the hypothalamus. In turn, increased brain levels of neuropeptide Y trigger eating behavior, reduce body metabolism, and promote fat storage. Conversely, if positive energy balance and weight gain occur, neuropeptide Y activity decreases.

In combination, the long-term and short-term eating-related signals we've discussed provide a feedback loop that is monitored by the hypothalamus (see Figure 8.4). As the hypothalamus detects changes in leptin, insulin, neuropeptide Y, ghrelin, CCK, and other internal signals, food intake and BMR are adjusted to promote or reduce weight gain. The end result? Over the course of time, energy balance is achieved. Your average body weight stays stable because the number of calories you consume closely matches the number of calories you expend for energy. Or, at least, that's how it's supposed to work.

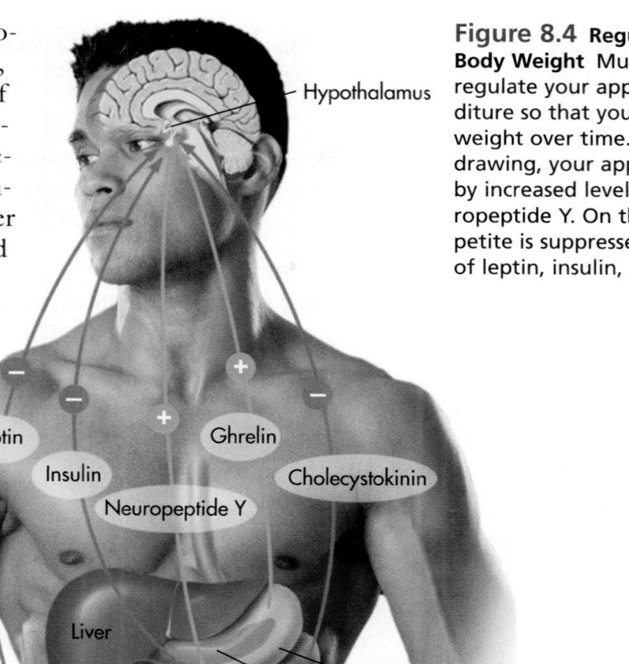

Figure 8.4 Regulating Appetite and Body Weight Multiple signals interact to regulate your appetite and energy expenditure so that you maintain a stable body weight over time. As summarized in this drawing, your appetite is stimulated (+) by increased levels of ghrelin and neuropeptide Y. On the other hand, your appetite is suppressed (–) by increased levels of leptin, insulin, and CCK.

Eating and Body Weight over the Lifespan

Set Point or Settling Point?

So far we've discussed the regulation of eating in terms of the energy balance model, which is the essence of a popular theory called *set-point theory.* According to **set-point theory,** the body has a natural or optimal weight, called the *set-point weight,* that it is set to maintain. Much like a thermostat set to a particular temperature, your body vigorously defends this set-point weight from becoming lower or higher by regulating feelings of hunger and body metabolism (Major & others, 2007).

Set-point theory helps explain why body weight tends to be stable for extended periods of time. However, it's obvious that baseline body weight doesn't always remain fixed at an optimal level throughout the lifespan. Instead, many, if not most, people tend to drift to a heavier average body weight as they get older. But why? According to set-point theory, if food intake increases, metabolic rate and hunger should change to compensate for the increased calories so as to maintain a consistent body weight. But obviously, this is not always the case.

Settling-point models of weight regulation provide an alternate view that seems to better explain this tendency (see Pinel & others, 2000). According to settling-point models of weight regulation, your body weight tends to "settle" around the point at which equilibrium is achieved between energy expenditure and food consumption. Your *settling-point weight* will stay relatively stable as long as the factors influencing food consumption and energy expenditure don't change. However, if these factors do change, creating positive or negative energy balance, you will drift to a higher or lower settling-point body weight. In the next few sections, we'll consider some of the factors that contribute to the upward drift of body weight.

sensory-specific satiety
(sah-TIE-it-tee) The reduced desire to continue consuming a particular food.

leptin
Hormone produced by fat cells that signals the hypothalamus, regulating hunger and eating behavior.

neuropeptide Y (NPY)
Neurotransmitter found in several brain areas, most notably the hypothalamus, that stimulates eating behavior and reduces metabolism, promoting positive energy balance and weight gain.

set-point theory
Theory that proposes that humans and other animals have a natural or optimal body weight, called the *set-point weight,* that the body defends from becoming higher or lower by regulating feelings of hunger and body metabolism.

settling-point models of weight regulation
General model of weight regulation suggesting that body weight settles, or stabilizes, around the point at which there is balance between the factors influencing energy intake and energy expenditure.

Excess Weight and Obesity

Key Theme

- **Many different factors contribute to the high rates of overweight and obesity in the United States and other countries.**

Key Questions

- **What is BMI?**
- **What factors contribute to excess weight and obesity?**

From buses to billboards, movies and magazines to MTV, images of beautiful people are everywhere. They come in a vast variety of ethnicities, wardrobes, and poses, but the beautiful people have one thing in common: They are *thin*. Without question, the "thin ideal" is pervasive in American culture. In fact, over the past decades, actresses, models, Miss America Pageant winners, *Playboy* centerfolds, and even cartoon characters have become progressively thinner (Grabe & others, 2008).

But there is an enormous gap between the cultural *ideal* of a slender body and the cultural *reality* of the expanding American waistline. Far from conforming to the "thin ideal," more than two-thirds of American adults are above their healthy weight (Ogden & others, 2007).

CRITICAL THINKING

Has Evolution Programmed Us to Overeat?

Could eating less help you live longer? Numerous correlational studies of humans and experiments with rodents and Rhesus monkeys have consistently come to the same conclusion: Eating a restricted but balanced diet produces a variety of health benefits and promotes longevity (e.g., Barzilai & Gupta, 1999; Cefalu & others, 1997; Weindruch, 1996). So if eating a calorically restricted but balanced diet confers numerous health benefits and promotes longevity, *why* do so many people overeat?

University of British Columbia psychologists John P. J. Pinel, Sunaina Assanand, and Darrin R. Lehman (2000) believe that the evolutionary perspective provides several insights. For animals in the wild, food sources are often sporadic and unpredictable. When animals do find food, competition for it can be fierce, even deadly. If an animal waited to eat until it was hungry and its energy reserves were significantly diminished, it would run the risk of starving or falling prey to another animal.

Thus, the eating patterns of many animals have evolved so that they readily eat even if not hungry (Berthoud, 2007). Overeating when food is available ensures ample energy reserves to survive times when food is *not* available.

For most people living in food-abundant Western societies, foraging for your next meal is usually about as life-threatening as waiting your turn in the Taco Bell drive-through lane. According to Pinel and his colleagues, people in food-rich societies do *not* eat because they are hungry or because their bodies are suffering from depleted energy resources. Rather, we are enticed by the anticipated pleasure of devouring that supersize burrito or calzone. In other words, we are motivated to eat by the *positive incentive value* of highly palatable foods.

When a food with a high positive incentive value is readily available, we eat, and often overeat, until we are satiated by that specific taste, which is termed *sensory-specific satiety*. Should another food with high positive incentive value become available, we continue eating and overconsume (Raynor & Epstein, 2001). As noted in the text, this is referred to as the *cafeteria diet effect*. From the evolutionary perspective, there is adaptive pressure to consume a variety of foods. Why? Because consuming a varied diet helps promote survival by ensuring that essential nutrients, vitamins, and minerals are obtained.

But unlike our ancient ancestors scrounging through the woods for seeds, fruits, and vegetables to survive, today's humans are confronted with foraging for burgers, cheese fries, and Oreo McFlurries. Therein lies the crux of the problem. As Pinel and his colleagues (2000) explain, "The increases in the availability of high positive-incentive value foods that have occurred over the past few decades in industrialized nations—increases that have been much too rapid to produce adaptive evolutionary change—have promoted levels of ad libitum consumption that are far higher than those that are compatible with optimal health and long life."

CRITICAL THINKING QUESTIONS

- Look back at the section on motivation theories. How might each theory (instinct, drive, incentive, arousal, and humanistic) explain the behavior of overeating?
- How might the insights provided by the evolutionary explanation be used to resist the temptation to overeat?

How is healthy weight determined? For statistical purposes, the most widely used measure of weight status is **body mass index,** abbreviated **BMI.** For adults, the body mass index provides a single numerical value that reflects your weight in relation to your height (see Figure 8.5). A healthy BMI falls between 18 and 25. Generally, people with a BMI between 25 and 29.9 are considered *overweight,* unless their high BMI is due to muscle or bone rather than fat. Thus, it is possible to have a high BMI and still be very healthy, as are many athletes or bodybuilders. In contrast, people who are **obese** have a BMI of 30 or greater *and* an abnormally high proportion of body fat.

Let's break down the statistics on obesity and overweight. More than one-third of the adult U.S. population are considered to be overweight. But another third of adults—over 72 million people—are considered medically obese, weighing in with a BMI of 30 or above (Ogden & others, 2006, 2007). Beyond the United States, rapidly increasing rates of obesity have become a global health problem. More than one billion adults are overweight, and at least 300 million of these are clinically obese (World Health Organization, 2009).

As people age, they tend to gain excess weight. The percentage of overweight people increases throughout adulthood, peaking in the fifth and sixth decades of life. However, excess weight is also a problem in early life. Over 17 percent of U.S. children and adolescents are overweight. Even more unsettling, almost 14 percent of 2- to 5-year-olds—that's one out of every eight preschoolers—is overweight (Ogden & others, 2006).

The **body mass index**, or **BMI**, is one measure of weight status. The BMI provides a single numerical value that represents your height in relation to your weight. To determine your BMI, grab a calculator and follow these steps:

Step 1. Multiply your weight in pounds by 703 ________

Step 2. Square your height in inches ________

Step 3. Divide step 1 by step 2 ________ This is your BMI.

If your BMI is:	You are:
18.4 or below	Underweight
18.5 to 24.9	Healthy weight
25.0 to 29.9	Overweight
30.0 and above	Obese

Source: Centers for Disease Control and Prevention (2009).

Figure 8.5 **Calculating Your BMI: Where Do You Weigh In?**

Factors Involved in Becoming Overweight

At the simplest level, the only way you can become overweight is if your caloric intake consistently exceeds your energy expenditure—the essence of *positive energy balance.* So the critical question is this: What kinds of factors are creating positive energy balance for so many people?

Too Little Sleep: Disrupting Hunger Hormones Multiple studies have shown that going without adequate sleep disrupts the hunger-related hormones leptin and ghrelin (Taheri & others, 2004). In one study, the sleep of healthy young men was restricted to just four hours a night for two nights. In response, blood levels of the appetite-suppressing hormone leptin fell by 18 percent and the appetite-increasing hormone ghrelin soared by 24 percent. This significantly increased feelings of hunger, especially for foods with high carbohydrate content (Spiegel & others, 2004). Other research has shown that adults who sleep only about five hours a night are 50 percent more likely to be obese (Gangwisch, 2004).

Positive Incentive Value: Highly Palatable Foods Rather than being motivated by hunger, we are often enticed to eat by the *positive incentive value* of the available foods and the anticipated pleasures of consuming those highly palatable foods (Epstein & others, 2007). Did someone say Ben and Jerry's ice cream?

body mass index (BMI)
A numerical scale indicating adult height in relation to weight; calculated as (703 × weight in pounds)/(height in inches)².

obese
Condition characterized by excessive body fat and a body mass index equal to or greater than 30.0.

cafeteria diet effect
The tendency to eat more when a wide variety of palatable foods is available.

leptin resistance
A condition in which higher-than-normal blood levels of the hormone leptin do not produce the expected physiological response.

weight cycling
Repeated cycles of dieting, weight loss, and weight regain; also called *yo-yo dieting*.

The "Supersize It" Syndrome: Overeating In the past two decades, average daily caloric intake has increased nearly 10 percent for men and 7 percent for women (Koplan & Dietz, 1999). Every day, we are faced with the opportunity to overeat at all-you-can-eat buffets and fast-food restaurants that offer to supersize your portions for only a few cents more.

The Cafeteria Diet Effect: Variety = More Consumed If variety is the spice of life, it's also a surefire formula to pack on the pounds. Offered just one choice or the same old choice for a meal, we consume less. But when offered a variety of highly palatable foods, such as at a cafeteria or an all-you-can-eat buffet, we consume more (Zandstra & others, 2000). This is sometimes called the **cafeteria diet effect** (Raynor & Epstein, 2001).

Sedentary Lifestyles Four out of 10 American adults report that they ***never*** exercise, play sports, or engage in physically active hobbies like gardening or walking the dog. Both men and women tend to become more sedentary with age. When the averages are broken down by gender, more women (43 percent) than men (37 percent) lead sedentary lifestyles (National Center for Health Statistics, 2000b).

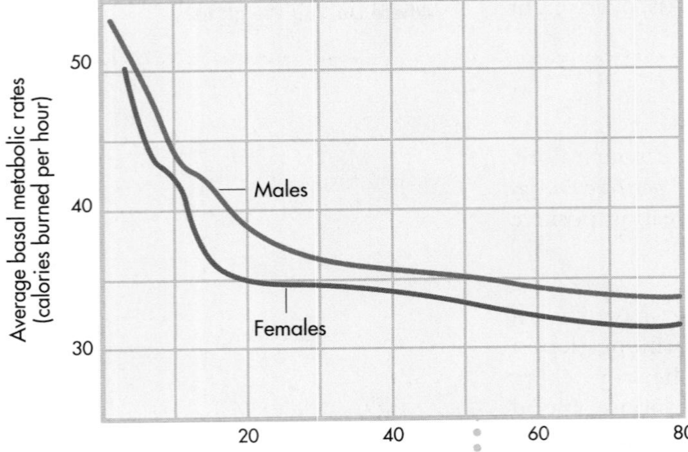

Figure 8.6 Age and Gender Differences in Metabolism From infancy through adolescence, there is a steep decline in the rate at which your body uses energy for vital functions, such as heartbeat, breathing, and body heat. Your BMR continues to decrease by about 2 to 3 percent during each decade of adulthood. At all points in the lifespan, women's metabolic rate is 3 to 5 percent lower than men's.

Source: Stuart & Davis (1972).

BMR: Individual Differences and Lifespan Changes Not everyone who overeats gains excess weight. One reason is that people vary greatly in their basal metabolic rate, which accounts for about two-thirds of your energy expenditure. On average, women have a metabolic rate that is 3 to 5 percent lower than men's. Metabolism also decreases with age. Body metabolism is highest during growth periods early in the lifespan (see Figure 8.6). After declining sharply between infancy and early adulthood, BMR decreases more slowly, by about 2 to 3 percent per decade of life. As your BMR decreases with age, less food is required to meet your basic energy needs. Consequently, it's not surprising that many people, upon reaching early adulthood, must begin to watch how much they eat.

Of the six factors we've covered here, you can exert control over five of them—all except BMR—to counteract becoming or remaining overweight. The bad news is that if people don't exercise control, all six factors can contribute to becoming obese.

Factors Involved in Obesity

Especially in the past decade, there has been intensive research investigating the causes of obesity—and for good reason. Health care costs directly attributable to obesity exceed $60 ***billion*** a year (Friedman, 2009). Regardless of how it develops, a BMI of 30 or above has life-threatening consequences (Kopelman, 2000). Annually, about 300,000 adult deaths in the United States are ***directly*** attributable to obesity. Several variables derail the normal mechanisms of energy homeostasis in obesity (see Friedman, 2000). In this section, we'll summarize some of those factors.

The Interaction of Genetics and Environment Current research suggests that multiple genes on multiple chromosomes are involved in creating susceptibility to obesity (Barsh & others, 2000; Friedman, 2009). People with a family history of obesity are two to three times more likely than people with no such family history to become obese. And, the more closely related two people are genetically, the more likely they are to have similar body mass indexes.

But genetics is ***not*** necessarily destiny. About 30 percent of the time, obese children have obese parents. However, obesity also occurs about 30 percent of the time among children with parents who are of normal weight (Bouchard, 1997).

FOCUS ON NEUROSCIENCE

Dopamine Receptors and Obesity

Eating to Stimulate Brain Reward? In Chapter 2, we noted that dopamine brain pathways are involved in the reinforcing feelings of pleasure and satisfaction. In Chapter 4, we also noted that many addictive drugs produce their pleasurable effects by increasing brain dopamine levels. These pleasurable effects are most reinforcing in people who have a low level of dopamine brain receptors (Volkow & others, 1999b, 2007). Given that eating can be highly reinforcing and produces pleasurable sensations, could the same mechanisms also play a role in obesity?

In a landmark study, researchers injected obese and normal-weight individuals with a slightly radioactive chemical "tag" that binds to brain dopamine receptors. Positron emission tomography (PET) scans detected where the chemical tag bound with dopamine receptors, shown in red. The two PET scans reveal significantly fewer dopamine receptors for obese individuals (left) as compared to the normal-weight control subjects (right). And, among the obese people in the study, the number of dopamine receptors decreased as BMI increased (Wang & others, 2001, 2004).

Researchers don't know yet whether the reduced number of dopamine receptors is a cause or a consequence of obesity. One clue may come from a new study that compared genetically obese, leptin-deficient rats with normal, lean rats (Thanos & others, 2008). The genetically obese rats had significantly lower levels of dopamine receptors than normal, lean rats. Taken together, such findings suggest that compulsive or binge eating might compensate for reduced dopamine function by stimulating the brain's reward system (Volkow & Wise, 2005).

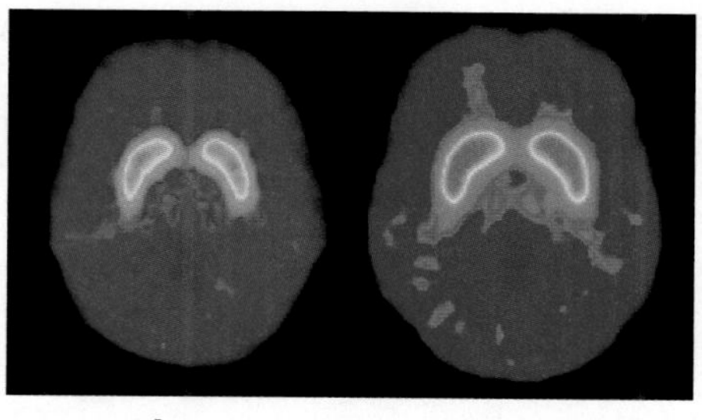

Obese **Normal**

The key phrase here is *susceptibility to obesity.* Even though someone may be genetically predisposed to obesity, environmental factors still play a role. If an individual is genetically susceptible and lives in a high-risk environment, obesity is more likely to occur. And what constitutes a high-risk environment for obesity? An environment characterized by ample and easily obtainable high-fat, high-calorie, palatable foods. A real-world example of this interaction is shown in Figure 8.7. As countries develop stable economies and food supplies, the prevalence of obesity rapidly escalates.

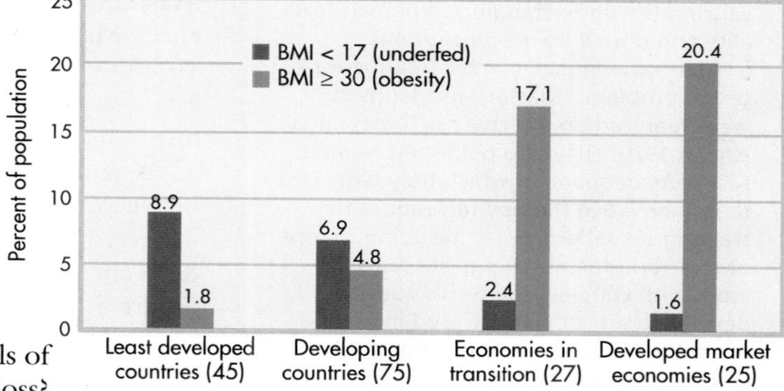

Figure 8.7 Genetic Susceptibility and Environmental Conditions If different populations have similar percentages of people who are genetically susceptible to obesity, then the critical factor becomes environmental conditions. In a low-risk environment, the availability of food, especially high-calorie foods, is limited. In countries with poorly developed economies and food supplies, the prevalence of underfed people (BMI < 17) is higher than the prevalence of obesity (BMI > 30). But in countries with established or well-developed economies, such as most Western countries, food is plentiful and easily attainable, creating high-risk conditions for obesity. In highly developed market economies, obesity rates have soared.

Sources: Barsh & others (2000); World Health Organization (2001).

Leptin Resistance Having greater fat stores, most obese people have high blood levels of leptin. So why don't these high blood levels of the leptin hormone reduce eating behavior and induce weight loss? Many obese people experience **leptin resistance,** in which the normal mechanisms through which leptin regulates body weight and energy balance are disrupted (Enriori & others, 2006; Morrison, 2008). Although leptin levels are high in the blood, they are often low in the obese person's cerebrospinal fluid. This suggests that leptin is not sufficiently transported from the blood to the brain. One possibility is that the obese person's high blood levels of leptin are overwhelming the transport system to the brain (Schwartz & others, 2000).

Dieting: BMR Resistance to Maintaining Weight Loss Any diet that reduces caloric intake will result in weight loss. The difficult challenge is to maintain the weight loss. Many overweight or obese dieters experience **weight cycling,** or *yo-yo dieting*—the weight lost through dieting is regained in weeks or months and maintained until the next attempt at dieting.

One reason this occurs is because the human body is much more effective at vigorously defending against weight *loss* than it is at protecting against weight *gain* (Keel & others, 2007). As caloric intake is reduced and fat cells begin to shrink, the body actively defends against weight loss by decreasing metabolism rate and energy level. With energy expenditure reduced, far fewer calories are needed to maintain the excess weight. In effect, the body is using energy much more efficiently. If dieters continue to restrict caloric intake, weight loss will plateau in a matter of weeks. When they go off the diet, their now more energy-efficient bodies quickly utilize the additional calories, and they regain the weight they lost.

Human Sexuality

Key Theme

- **Multiple factors are involved in understanding human sexuality.**

Key Questions

- **What are the four stages of human sexual response?**
- **How does sexual motivation differ among animal species?**
- **What biological factors are involved in sexual motivation?**

Psychologists consider the drive to have sex a basic human motive. But what exactly motivates that drive? Obviously, there are differences between sex and other basic motives, such as hunger. Engaging in sexual intercourse is essential to the survival of the human species, but it is not essential to the survival of any specific person. In other words, you'll die if you don't eat, but you won't die if you don't have sex (you just may *think* you will).

Pioneers of Sex Research: William Masters (1915–2001) and Virginia Johnson (b. 1925) In 1966 Masters and Johnson broke new ground in the scientific study of sexual behavior when they published *Human Sexual Response*. Their book provided the first extensive laboratory data on the anatomy and physiology of the male and female sexual response. Although intended for clinicians, the book became a best seller that was translated into over thirty languages. Some critics felt the Masters and Johnson research had violated "sacred ground" and dehumanized sexuality. But others applauded *Human Sexual Response* for advancing the understanding of human sexuality and dispelling misconceptions.

After opening a clinic for treatment of sexual problems, Masters and Johnson were featured on the cover of *Time* magazine in 1970. They also published *Human Sexual Inadequacy,* in which they described their innovative therapy techniques for treating sexual problems, including the use of male and female therapist teams to work with couples. The techniques they developed are still widely used in sex therapy today. Ultimately, Masters and Johnson promoted a view of human sexuality as a healthy and natural activity, one that could be a meaningful source of intimacy and fulfillment.

First Things First

The Stages of Human Sexual Response

The human sexual response cycle was first mapped by sex research pioneers **William Masters** and **Virginia Johnson** during the 1950s and 1960s. In the name of science, Masters and Johnson observed hundreds of people engage in more than 10,000 episodes of sexual activity in their laboratory. Their findings, published in 1966, indicated that the human sexual response could be described as a cycle with four stages.

As you read the descriptions of these stages, keep in mind that the transitions between stages are not as precise or abrupt as the descriptions might lead you to believe. Moreover, the duration of time spent in any particular stage can vary on different occasions of sexual interaction. Although it is simplified somewhat, Figure 8.8 depicts the basic patterns of sexual response for men and women.

Stage 1: Excitement

The *excitement phase* marks the beginning of sexual arousal. Sexual arousal can occur in response to sexual fantasies or other sexually arousing stimuli, physical contact with another person, or masturbation. In both sexes, the excitement stage is accompanied by a variety of bodily changes in anticipation of sexual interaction. There is a rapid rise in pulse rate and blood pressure. The rate of breathing increases. Blood shifts to the genitals, producing an erect penis in the male and swelling of the clitoris in the female. The female's vaginal lips expand and open up, and her vagina becomes lubricated in preparation for intercourse. Her nipples and breasts may also become enlarged, and the nipples become erect and more sensitive.

Stage 2: Plateau

In the second phase, the *plateau phase,* physical arousal builds as pulse and breathing rates continue to increase. The penis becomes fully erect and sometimes secretes a few drops of fluid, which may contain active sperm. The testes increase in size. The clitoris withdraws under the clitoral hood but remains very sensitive to stimulation. The vaginal entrance tightens, putting pressure on the penis during intercourse. Vaginal lubrication continues. During the excitement and plateau stages, the degree of arousal may fluctuate up and down (Masters & others, 1995). During the plateau stage, the firmness of the male's erection may increase and decrease, and so may the female's degree of vaginal lubrication.

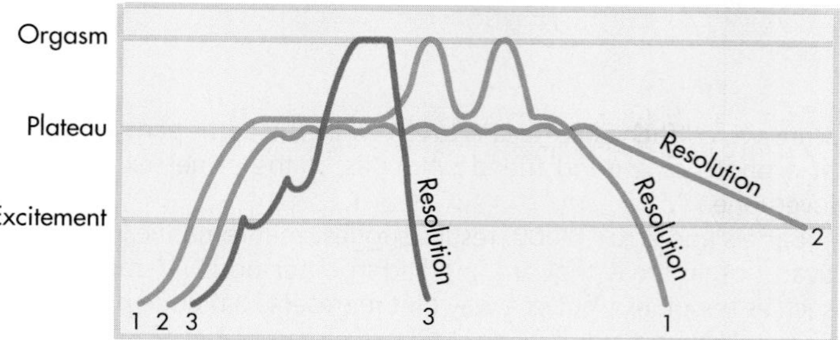

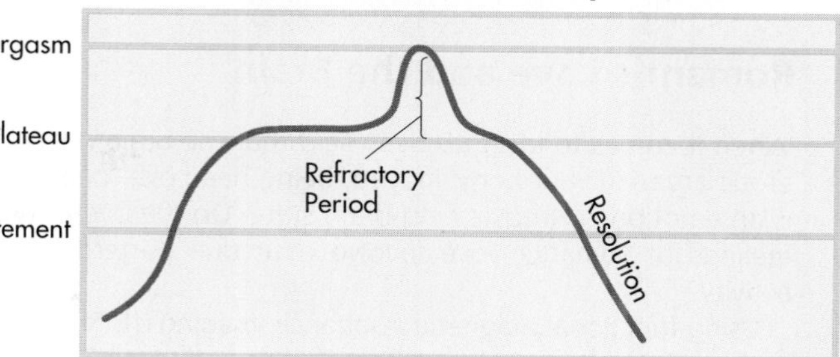

Figure 8.8 The Male and Female Sexual Response Cycles The figure on the left depicts the three basic variations of the female sexual response. Pattern 1 shows multiple orgasms. Pattern 2 shows sexual arousal that reaches the plateau stage but not orgasm, followed by a slow resolution. Pattern 3 depicts brief reductions in arousal during the excitement stage, followed by rapid orgasm and resolution. The figure on the right depicts the most typical male sexual response, in which orgasm is followed by a refractory period.

Source: Masters & Johnson (1966).

Stage 3: Orgasm

Orgasm is the third and shortest phase of the sexual response cycle. During orgasm, blood pressure and heart rate reach their peak. The muscles in the vaginal walls and the uterus contract rhythmically, as do the muscles in and around the penis as the male ejaculates. Other muscles may contract as well, such as those in the face, arms, and legs. Both men and women describe the subjective experience of orgasm in similar—and very positive—terms.

The vast majority of men experience one intense orgasm. But many women are capable of experiencing multiple orgasms. If sexual stimulation continues following orgasm, women may experience additional orgasms within a short period of time.

Stage 4: Resolution

Following orgasm, both sexes tend to experience a warm physical "glow" and a sense of well-being. Arousal slowly subsides and returns to normal levels in the *resolution phase.* The male experiences a *refractory period,* during which he is incapable of having another erection or orgasm. The duration of the male's refractory period varies. For one man it may last a matter of minutes, for another several hours. As men age, the duration of the refractory period tends to increase.

What Motivates Sexual Behavior?

In most animals, sexual behavior is biologically determined and triggered by hormonal changes in the female. During the cyclical period known as *estrus,* a female animal is fertile and receptive to male sexual advances. Roughly translated, the Greek word *estrus* means "frantic desire." Indeed, the female animal will often actively signal her willingness to engage in sexual activity—as any owner of an unneutered female cat or dog that's "in heat" can testify. In many, but not all, species, sexual activity takes place only when the female is in estrus.

As you go up the evolutionary scale, moving from relatively simple to more sophisticated animals, sexual behavior becomes less biologically determined and more subject to learning and environmental influences. Sexual behavior also becomes less limited to the goal of reproduction (Buss, 2007a, 2007b). For example, in some primate species, such as monkeys and apes, sexual activity can occur at any time, not just when the female is fertile. In these species, sexual interaction serves important social functions, defining and cementing relationships among the members of the primate group.

One rare species of chimplike apes, the bonobos of the Democratic Republic of the Congo, exhibits a surprising variety of sexual behaviors (de Waal, 2007; Parish & de Waal, 2000). Although most animals *copulate,* or have sex, with the male mounting the female from behind, bonobos often copulate face to face. Bonobos also engage in oral sex and intense tongue kissing. And bonobos seem to like variety. Along with having frequent heterosexual activity, whether the female is fertile or not, bonobos also engage in homosexual and group sex.

The Bonobos of the Congo Bonobos demonstrate a wide variety of sexual interactions, including face-to-face copulation, kissing, and sexual interaction among same-sex pairs (Fruth & Hohmann, 2006; Parish & de Waal, 2000). Sexual behavior is not limited to reproduction; it seems to play an important role in maintaining peaceful relations among members of the bonobo group. As Frans de Waal (1995) wrote, "For these animals, sexual behavior is indistinguishable from social behavior."

FOCUS ON NEUROSCIENCE

Romantic Love and the Brain

When it comes to love, it's been said that the brain is the most erotic organ in your body. Indeed, being head over heels in love is an emotionally intoxicating brain state. Do the overpowering feelings of romantic love involve a unique pattern of brain activity?

Using functional magnetic resonance imaging (fMRI) to detect brain activity, researchers Andreas Bartels and Semir Zeki (2000) investigated that idea with 17 love-struck young adults, all professing to be "truly, deeply, madly in love" with their romantic partner. Each participant was scanned several times while gazing at a photo of the romantic partner. Alternating with the "love" scans were "friendship" scans taken while the participant looked at a photo of a good friend who was of the same sex as the loved one.

Bartels and Zeki's (2000) results suggest that romantic love activates brain areas that are involved in other positive emotions, such as happiness, but in a way that represents a unique pattern. Shown here is a side-to-side fMRI brain scan depicting some of the brain areas activated by romantic love. Compared to looking at a photo of a close friend, looking at a photo of one's romantic partner produced heightened activity in four brain areas associated with emotion, including the *anterior cingulate cortex* (not shown), *caudate nucleus* (C), *putamen* (P), and *insula* (I).

Given the complexity of the sentiment of romantic love, the researchers were surprised that the brain areas activated were so small and limited to so few regions. (Perhaps this lack of extensive brain activation explains why love-struck individuals are sometimes oblivious to everything except the object of their infatuation.) Nonetheless, the four activated brain areas offer some insight into the intoxicating effects of romantic love. Why? Because these are the same brain areas that are activated in response to euphoria-producing drugs, such as opiates and cocaine. Clearly, there seem to be some close neural links between romantic love and euphoric states.

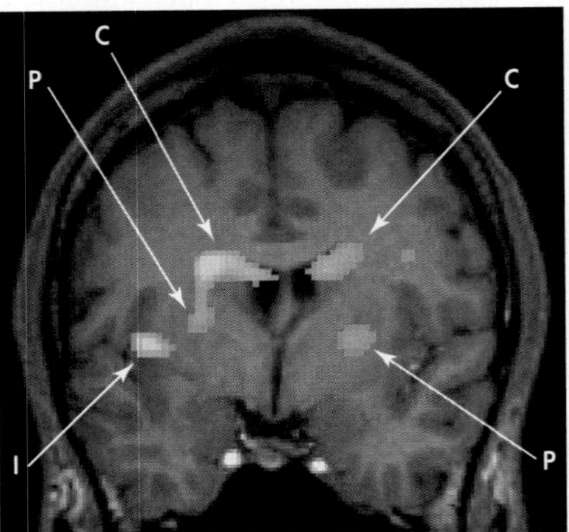

Feelings of euphoria are just one of the many sensations, thoughts, and emotions that accompany moments of impassioned, romantic love. As is shown in the fMRI scan, romantic love also produces a unique pattern of activation in the brain.

Emory University psychology professor Frans de Waal (1995, 2007), who has extensively studied bonobos, observes that their frequent and varied sexual behavior seems to serve important social functions. Sexual behavior is not limited to fulfilling the purpose of reproduction. Among the bonobos, sexual interaction is used to increase group cohesion, avoid conflict, and decrease tension that might be caused by competition for food. According to de Waal (1995), the bonobos' motto seems to be "Make love, not war."

In humans, of course, sexual behavior is not limited to a female's fertile period (Buss, 2007). Nor is the motivational goal of sex limited to reproduction. A woman's fertility is regulated by monthly hormonal cycles. Some, but not all, women also experience monthly fluctuations in sexual interest and motivation. However, these changes are highly influenced by social and psychological factors, such as relationship quality (Thornhill, 2007; Gangestad & others, 2007). Even when a woman's ovaries, which produce the female sex hormone *estrogen,* are surgically removed or stop functioning during menopause, there is little or no drop in sexual interest. In many nonhuman female mammals, however, removal of the ovaries results in a complete loss of interest in sexual activity. If injections of estrogen and other female sex hormones are given, the female animals' sexual interest returns.

In male animals, removal of the testes (castration) typically causes a steep drop in sexual activity and interest, although the decline is more gradual in sexually experienced animals. Castration causes a significant decrease in levels of *testosterone,* the hormone responsible for male sexual development. When human males experience lowered levels of testosterone because of illness or castration, a similar drop in sexual interest tends to occur, although the effects vary among individuals. Some men continue to lead a normal sex life for years, but others quickly lose all interest in sexual activity. In castrated men who experience a loss of sexual interest, injections of testosterone restore the sexual drive.

Testosterone is also involved in female sexual motivation (Davis, 2000). Most of the testosterone in a woman's body is produced by her adrenal glands. If these glands are removed or malfunction, causing testosterone levels to become abnormally low, sexual interest often wanes. When supplemental testosterone is administered, the woman's sex drive returns. Thus, in *both* men and women, sexual motivation is biologically influenced by the levels of the hormone testosterone in the body.

Of course, sexual behavior is greatly influenced by many cultural and social factors. We consider one aspect of sexual behavior in the Culture and Human Behavior box, "Evolution and Mate Preferences," on the next page.

sexual orientation
The direction of a person's emotional and erotic attraction toward members of the opposite sex, the same sex, or both sexes.

Sexual Orientation
The Elusive Search for an Explanation

Key Theme

- **Sexual orientation refers to whether a person is attracted to members of the opposite sex, the same sex, or both sexes.**

Key Questions

- **Why is sexual orientation sometimes difficult to identify?**
- **What factors have been associated with sexual orientation?**

Given that biological factors seem to play an important role in motivating sexual desire, it seems only reasonable to ask whether biological factors also play a role in sexual orientation. **Sexual orientation** refers to whether a person is sexually aroused by members of the same sex, the opposite sex, or both sexes. A *heterosexual* person is sexually attracted to individuals of the other sex, a *homosexual* person to individuals of the same sex, and a *bisexual* person to individuals of both sexes. Technically, the term *homosexual* can be applied to either males or females. However, female homosexuals are usually called *lesbians.* Male homosexuals typically use the term *gay* to describe their sexual orientation.

Sexual orientation is not nearly as cut and dried as many people believe. Some people *are* exclusively heterosexual or homosexual, but others are less easy to categorize.

Famous Gay Couples Legendary singer, songwriter, and musician Elton John spent years claiming to be bisexual, even marrying German sound engineer Renata Blauel in 1984. But when that marriage ended four years later, Elton admitted publicly what he said he had known privately for years—that he was homosexual. Since 1993, John's companion has been Canadian film producer David Furnish. In the photo, John and Furnish are shown leaving Guildhall in Windsor, England, after their civil partnership ceremony on December 21, 2005. "We love each other just as much as any other two human beings love each other," John (2005) explained. "In the twenty-first century, tolerance should be something that we promote a little more."

Comedian and popular talk show host Ellen DeGeneres struggled for many years to come to grips with her sexual orientation before publicly coming out as a lesbian. As DeGeneres (2005) recalled, "To be 37 years old and be feeling this sense of shame, that nobody would like me if they found out I was gay, it was a pretty emotional thing to expose yourself to." In 1997, she made television history when she "outed" herself and her character in her television series *Ellen.* Ellen's first public relationship with Anne Heche created something of a media frenzy. However, her marriage to long-time companion Portia deRossi in August, 2008, a few months after same-sex marriage became legal in California, was covered like any other celebrity wedding ceremony.

CULTURE AND HUMAN BEHAVIOR

Evolution and Mate Preferences

BIZARRO

Did the cartoon make you laugh—or at least smile? If it did, it's because you recognized a cultural pattern—the belief that men seek a beautiful, youthful partner, while women are more likely to value financial security and wealth. Cartoons and jokes aside, is there any merit to this observation? *Do* men and women differ in what they look for in a mate?

To investigate mate preferences, psychologist David Buss (1994, 2009) coordinated a large-scale survey of more than 10,000 people in 37 different cultures.

Across all cultures, Buss found, men were more likely than women to value youth and physical attractiveness in a potential mate. In contrast, women were more likely than men to value financial security, access to material resources, high status and education, and good financial prospects. Buss, an evolutionary psychologist, interprets these gender differences as reflecting the different "mating strategies" of men and women.

According to evolutionary psychology, mating behavior is adaptive to the degree that it furthers the reproductive success of transmitting one's genes to the next generation and beyond. And when it comes to reproductive success, Buss (1995a, 2009) contends that men and women face very different "adaptive problems" in selecting a mate.

According to Buss (1995b, 1996), the adaptive problem for men is to identify and mate with women who are fertile and likely to be successful at bearing their children. Thus, men are more likely to place a high value on youth, because it is associated with fertility and because younger women have a greater number of childbearing years ahead of them than older women. And, men value physical attractiveness because it signals that the woman is probably physically healthy and has high-quality genes.

Buss sees the adaptive problem for women as very different. Women also seek "good" genes, and thus they value men who are healthy and attractive. But they have a more pressing need: making sure that the children they do bear survive to carry their genes into future generations. Pregnancy, lactation, and caring for infants, says Buss, leave women unable to acquire the resources needed to protect and feed themselves and their children. Thus, women look for a mate who will be a "good provider." They seek men who possess the resources that the women and their offspring will need to survive.

In most cultures, Buss (1995a) points out, men of high status and wealth are more able to marry younger and more attractive women than poor, low-status men are. In other words, older successful men, whether they are tribal chiefs, corporate CEOs, or aging rock superstars, have the greatest access to young, attractive women—the so-called "trophy wife." On the flip side, physically attractive women can, and often do, marry men with more resources and higher status than do unattractive women.

Not surprisingly, this evolutionary explanation of sex differences is controversial. Some psychologists argue that it is overly deterministic and does not sufficiently acknowledge the role of culture, gender-role socialization, and other social factors (Eagly & Wood, 2006; Gangestad & others, 2006; Schmitt, 2006).

Other psychologists interpret Buss's data in a different way. Tim Kasser and Yadika Sharma (1999) analyzed the mate preference data in terms of women's reproductive freedom and educational opportunity in each culture. They found that women who live in cultures that are low in both female reproductive freedom and educational equality between the sexes placed a higher value on a prospective mate's resources.

According to Kasser and Sharma (1999), "When a female is provided with opportunities to fend for herself, she can become less concerned with finding a mate who will provide resources for her, but when she has few opportunities to educate herself or control her own fertility, she will be more concerned with finding a mate who can provide her with the resources needed to support her and her children."

For his part, Buss (1996, 2007a, 2007b) is careful to point out that this theory does *not* claim that personal preferences have no effect on mate preferences. In fact, his extensive survey also found that men and women in all 37 cultures agreed that the *most* important factor in choosing a mate was mutual attraction and love. And, here's a finding that will probably be reassuring to those singles who have neither fabulous wealth nor heart-stopping beauty: Both sexes rated kindness, intelligence, emotional stability, health, and a pleasing personality as more important than a prospective mate's financial resources or good looks.

Finally, Buss and other evolutionary psychologists reject the idea that people, cultures, or societies are powerless to overcome tendencies that evolved over hundreds of thousands of years. Buss also flatly states that explaining some of the reasons that might underlie sexual inequality does *not* mean that sexual inequality is natural, correct, or justified. Rather, evolutionary psychologists believe that we must understand the conditions that foster sexual inequality in order to overcome or change those conditions (Smuts, 1996).

Many people who consider themselves heterosexual have had a homosexual experience at some point in their lives. In the same vein, many homosexuals have had heterosexual experiences (Rieger & others, 2005). Other people, like our friend Richard in the chapter Prologue, consider themselves to be homosexual but have had heterosexual relationships. The key point is that there is not always a perfect correspondence between a particular person's sexual identity, sexual desires, and sexual behaviors.

Determining the number of people who are homosexual or heterosexual is problematic for several reasons (see Savin-Williams, 2008). First, survey results vary depending on how the researchers define the terms *homosexual, heterosexual,* and *bisexual.* Second, gays and lesbians are not distributed evenly throughout the population. In rural areas and small towns, gays, lesbians, and bisexuals make up about 1 percent of the population. But in the largest U.S. cities, approximately 1 of 8 people (or 12 percent) consider themselves gay, lesbian, or bisexual (Michael & others, 1994). Estimates of the size of the gay and lesbian population can vary, depending on:

- How researchers structure survey questions
- How they define the criteria for inclusion in gay, lesbian, or bisexual categories
- Where the survey is conducted
- How survey participants are selected

Depending upon how sexual orientation is defined, estimates of the prevalance rate of homosexuality in the general population ranges from 1 percent to 21 percent (Savin-Williams, 2006). More important than the exact number of gays and lesbians is the recognition that gays and lesbians constitute a significant segment of the adult population in the United States. According to the most reasonable estimates, it's safe to say that between 7 million and 15 million American men and women are gay or lesbian.

What Determines Sexual Orientation?

Despite considerable research on this question, psychologists and other researchers cannot say with certainty why people become homosexual or bisexual. For that matter, psychologists don't know exactly why people become *heterosexual* either. Still, research on sexual orientation has pointed toward several general conclusions, especially with regard to homosexuality.

Evidence from multiple studies shows that genetics plays a role in determining sexual orientation (Bailey & others, 2000). For example, psychologists Michael Bailey and Richard Pillard (1991) compared the incidence of male homosexuality among pairs of identical twins (who have identical genes), fraternal twins (who are genetically as similar as any two non-twin siblings), and adoptive brothers (who have no common genetic heritage but share the same upbringing). The researchers found that the closer the degree of genetic relationship, the more likely it was that when one brother was homosexual, the other brother would also be homosexual. Specifically, both brothers were homosexual in 52 percent of the identical twins, 22 percent of the fraternal twins, and 11 percent of the adoptive brothers.

Bailey and his colleagues (1993) discovered very similar results in twin studies of lesbians. In 48 percent of identical twins and 16 percent of fraternal twins, when one sister was lesbian, so was the other sister, compared with only 6 percent of adoptive sisters. However, since the identical twins were both homosexual in only half of the twin pairs, it's clear that genetic predisposition alone cannot explain sexual orientation.

In the largest twin study to date, Swedish researchers showed that *both* genetic and nonshared environmental factors were involved in sexual orientation (Långström & others, 2008). What are "nonshared" environmental factors? Influences that are experienced by one, but not both, twins. More specifically, these are social and biological factors, rather than upbringing or family environment.

These studies and others support the notion that sexual orientation is at least partly influenced by genetics (Hyde, 2005). However, that genetic influence is likely to be complex, involving the interaction of multiple genes, not a single "gay gene"

U.S. Congressman Barney Frank: "You Can't Make Yourself a Different Person." One of the first openly gay politicians, Frank has been a member of the U.S. Congress since 1981. Frank first realized he was gay in his early teenage years. When asked if heterosexuality was ever an option for him, Frank (1996) responded, "I wished it was. But it wasn't. I can't imagine that anybody believes that a 13-year-old in 1953 thinks, 'Boy, it would really be great to be part of this minority that everybody hates and to have a really restricted life.' You can't make yourself a different person. I am who I am. I have no idea why."

I heard this on the news: "For every older brother a man has, the chances of him being gay increase by one-third." I got a few problems with this theory. Specifically, Jimmy, Eddie, Billy, Tommy, Jay, Paul, and Peter. Those are my older brothers—seven brothers. By their math, I should be 233 percent gay. That's getting up there.

STEPHEN COLBERT—*THE COLBERT REPORT*

(see Vilain, 2008). Beyond heredity, there is also evidence that sexual orientation may be influenced by other biological factors, such as prenatal exposure to sex hormones or other aspects of the prenatal environment.

For example, one intriguing finding is that the more older brothers a man has, the more likely he is to be homosexual (Blanchard & Bogaert, 1996; Bogaert, 2005b, 2003). Could a homosexual orientation be due to psychological factors, such as younger brothers being bullied or indulged by older male siblings? Or being treated differently by their parents, or some other family dynamics? No. Collecting data on men who grew up in adoptive or blended families, Anthony Bogaert (2006) found that only the number of biologically related older brothers predicted homosexual orientation. Living with older brothers who were *not* biologically related had no effect at all. As Anthony Bogaert (2007) explains, "It's not the brothers you lived with; it's the environment within the same womb—sharing the same mom." Researchers don't have an explanation for the effect, which has been replicated in multiple studies (see Bogaert, 2007). One suggestion is that carrying successive male children might trigger some sort of immune response in the mother that, in turn, influences brain development in the male fetus.

Finally, a number of researchers have discovered differences in brain function or structure among gay, lesbian, and heterosexual men and women (e.g., LeVay, 2007; Savic & Lindström, 2008). However, most of these studies have proved small or inconclusive. It's also important to note that there is no way of knowing whether brain differences are the *cause* or the *effect* of different patterns of sexual behavior.

In general, the only conclusion we can draw from these studies is that some biological factors are *correlated* with a homosexual orientation (Mustanski & others, 2002). As we've stressed, correlation does not necessarily indicate causality, only that two factors *seem* to occur together. So stronger conclusions about the role of genetic and biological factors in determining sexual orientation await more definitive research findings.

In an early study involving in-depth interviews with over 1,000 gay men and lesbians, Alan Bell and his colleagues (1981) found that homosexuality was *not* the result of disturbed or abnormal family relationships. They also found that sexual orientation was determined before adolescence and long before the beginning of sexual activity. Gay men and lesbians typically became aware of homosexual feelings about three years before they engaged in any such sexual activity. In this regard, the pattern was very similar to that of heterosexual children, in whom heterosexual feelings are aroused long before the child expresses them in some form of sexual behavior.

Several researchers now believe that sexual orientation is established as early as age 6 (Strickland, 1995). Do children who later grow up to be homosexuals differ from children who later grow up to be heterosexuals? In at least one respect, there seems to be a difference.

Same-Sex Couples and Their Children Research on same-sex couples in committed, long-term relationships shows that their relationships are quite similar to those of heterosexual couples in most ways (Balsam & others, 2008). One exception: Lesbian couples were better than heterosexual or gay couples at harmonious problem-solving (Roisman & others, 2008). What about their children? Research consistently has shown that the children of same-sex parents are very similar to the children of heterosexual parents (Patterson, 2006, 2008). And, contrary to popular belief, teenagers with same-sex parents have peer relationships and friendships that are very similar to those of teenagers with heterosexual or single parents (Wainwright & Patterson, 2008; Rivers & others, 2008).

Typically, boys and girls differ in their choice of toys, playmates, and activities from early childhood. However, evidence suggests that male and female homosexuals are less likely to have followed the typical pattern of gender-specific behaviors in childhood (Bailey & others, 2000; Rieger & others, 2008). Compared to heterosexual men, gay men recall engaging in more cross-sex-typed behavior during childhood. For example, they remembered playing more with girls than with other boys, preferring girls' toys over boys' toys, and disliking rough-and-tumble play. Lesbians are also more likely to recall cross-gender behavior in childhood, but to a lesser degree than gay men.

A potential problem with such *retrospective studies* is that the participants may be biased in their recall of childhood events. One way to avoid that problem is by conducting a prospective study. A *prospective study* involves systematically observing a group of people over time to discover what factors are associated with the development of a particular trait, characteristic, or behavior.

One influential prospective study was conducted by Richard Green (1985, 1987). Green followed the development of sexual orientation in two groups of boys. The first group of boys had been referred to a mental health clinic because of their "feminine" behavior. He compared the development of these boys to a matched control group of boys who displayed typically "masculine" behavior in childhood. When all the boys were in their late teens, Green compared the two groups. He found that approximately 75 percent of the previously feminine boys were either bisexual or homosexual, as compared to only 4 percent of the control group.

Less is known about girls who are referred to clinics because of cross-gender behavior, partly because girls are less likely to be referred to clinics for "tomboy" behavior (Zucker & Cohen-Kettenis, 2008). However, Kelley Drummond and her colleagues (2008) found that cross-gender behavior in girls was also associated with the later development of bisexual or homosexual orientation, although at a lower rate than was true for boys. As researchers J. Michael Bailey and Kenneth J. Zucker (1995) summarized, "There is clear evidence of a relation between patterns of childhood sex-typed behavior and later sexual orientation."

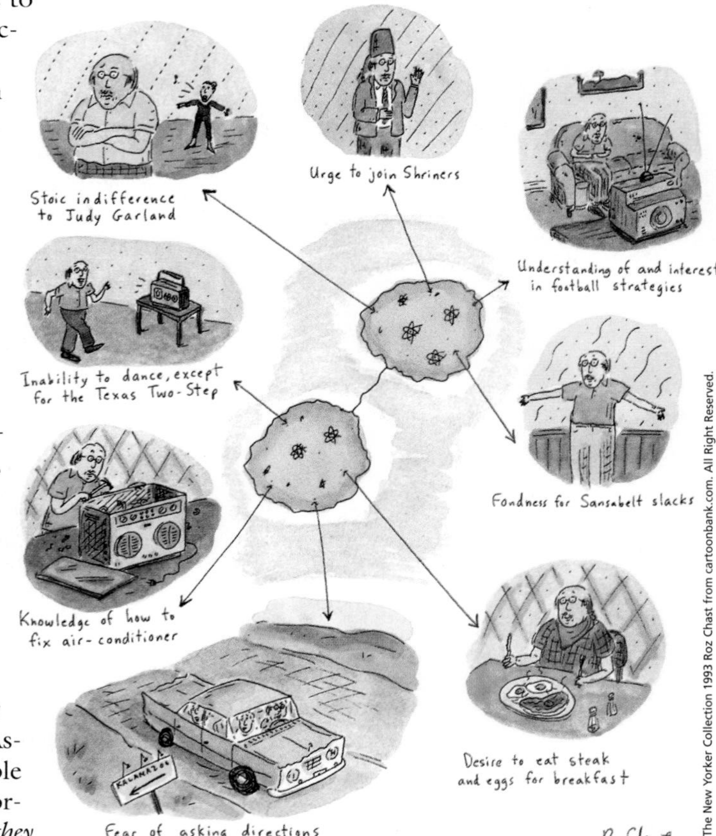

Once sexual orientation is established, whether heterosexual or homosexual, it is highly resistant to change (American Psychiatric Association, 1994). The vast majority of homosexuals would be unable to change their orientation even if they wished to, just as the majority of heterosexuals would be unable to change their orientation if *they* wished to. Thus, it's a mistake to assume that homosexuals have deliberately chosen their sexual orientation any more than heterosexuals have. Indeed, when Richard was in high school, he would gladly have "chosen" to be heterosexual if the matter had been that simple.

It seems clear that no single factor determines whether people identify themselves as homosexual, heterosexual, or bisexual (Patterson, 2008). Psychological, biological, social, and cultural factors are undoubtedly involved in determining sexual orientation. However, researchers are still unable to pinpoint exactly what those factors are and how they interact. As psychologist Bonnie Strickland (1995) has pointed out, "Sexual identity and orientation appear to be shaped by a complexity of biological, psychological, and social events. Gender identity and sexual orientation, at least for most people, especially gay men, occur early, are relatively fixed, and are difficult to change." As Richard learned, changing his sexual orientation was simply not possible.

Homosexuality is no longer considered a sexual disorder by clinical psychologists or psychiatrists (American Psychiatric Association, 1994). Many research studies have also found that homosexuals who are comfortable with their sexual orientation are just as well adjusted as are heterosexuals (see Strickland, 1995).

Like heterosexuals, gays and lesbians can be found in every occupation and at every socioeconomic level in our society. And, like heterosexuals, many gays and lesbians are involved in long-term, committed, and caring relationships (Roisman & others, 2008). Children who are raised by gay or lesbian parents are as well adjusted as children who are raised by heterosexual parents (Patterson, 2006; Wainwright & Patterson, 2008). Finally, children who are raised by gay or lesbian parents are no more likely to be gay or lesbian in adulthood than are children who are raised by heterosexual parents (Bailey & others, 1995; Golombok & Tasker, 1996).

Psychological Needs as Motivators

Key Theme

- **According to the motivation theories of Maslow and of Deci and Ryan, psychological needs must be fulfilled for optimal human functioning.**

Key Questions

- **How does Maslow's hierarchy of needs explain human motivation?**
- **What are some important criticisms of Maslow's theory?**
- **What are the basic premises of self-determination theory?**

In studying the idea that we are motivated to satisfy fundamental psychological needs, psychologists have grappled with several key questions:

- Are there universal psychological needs?
- Are we internally or externally motivated to satisfy psychological needs?
- What psychological needs must be satisfied for optimal human functioning?

In this section, we'll first consider two theories that have tried to answer those questions: Abraham Maslow's famous *hierarchy of needs* and the more recently developed *self-determination theory* of Edward L. Deci and Richard M. Ryan.

Maslow's Hierarchy of Needs

A major turning point in the discussion of human needs occurred when humanistic psychologist **Abraham Maslow** developed his model of human motivation in the 1940s and 1950s. Maslow acknowledged the importance of biological needs as motivators. But once basic biological needs are satisfied, he believed, "higher" psychological needs emerge to motivate human behavior.

The centerpiece of Maslow's (1954, 1968) model of motivation was his famous **hierarchy of needs,** summarized in Figure 8.9. Maslow believed that people are motivated to satisfy the needs at each level of the hierarchy before moving up to the next level. As people progressively move up the hierarchy, they are ultimately motivated by the desire to achieve self-actualization. The lowest levels of Maslow's hierarchy emphasize fundamental biological and safety needs. At the higher levels, the needs become more social and psychologically growth-oriented, culminating in the need to achieve *self-actualization.*

What exactly is self-actualization? Maslow (1970) himself had trouble defining the term, saying that self-actualization is "a difficult syndrome to describe accurately." Nonetheless, Maslow defined **self-actualization** in the following way:

> It may be loosely described as the full use and exploitation of talents, capacities, potentialities, etc. Such people seem to be fulfilling themselves and to be doing the best that they are capable of doing. . . . They are people who have developed or are developing to the full stature of which they are capable.

Beyond that general description, Maslow's research identified several characteristics of self-actualized people, which are summarized in Table 8.2 on page 341.

Maslow's model of motivation generated considerable research, especially during the 1970s and 1980s. Some researchers found support for Maslow's ideas (e.g., Graham & Balloun, 1973). Others, however, criticized his model on several points

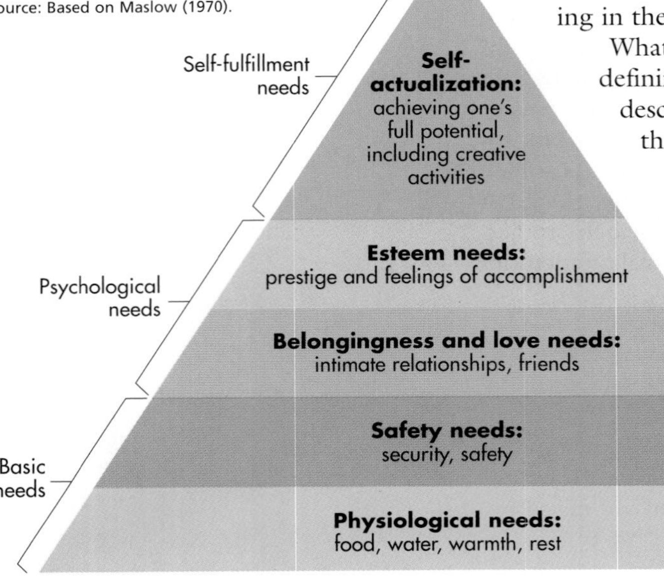

Figure 8.9 Maslow's Hierarchy of Needs Abraham Maslow believed that people are innately motivated to satisfy a progression of needs, beginning with the most basic physiological needs. Once the needs at a particular level are satisfied, the individual is motivated to satisfy the needs at the next level, steadily progressing upward. The ultimate goal is self-actualization, the realization of personal potential.

Source: Based on Maslow (1970).

Table 8.2

Maslow's Characteristics of Self-Actualized People

Realism and acceptance	Self-actualized people have accurate perceptions of themselves, others, and external reality.
Spontaneity	Self-actualized people are spontaneous, natural, and open in their behavior and thoughts. However, they can easily conform to conventional rules and expectations when necessary.
Problem centering	Self-actualized people focus on problems outside themselves. They often dedicate themselves to a larger purpose in life.
Autonomy	Although they accept and enjoy other people, self-actualized individuals have a strong need for privacy and independence.
Continued freshness of appreciation	Self-actualized people continue to appreciate the simple pleasures of life with awe and wonder.
Peak experiences	Self-actualized people commonly have *peak experiences,* or moments of intense ecstasy, wonder, and awe during which their sense of self is lost or transcended.

Source: Based on Maslow (1970).

(e.g., Fox, 1982; Neher, 1991; Wahba & Bridwell, 1976). Maslow's concept of self-actualization is very vague and almost impossible to define in a way that would allow it to be tested scientifically. And Maslow's initial studies on self-actualization were based on limited samples with questionable reliability. For example, Maslow (1970) often relied on the life stories of acquaintances whose identities were never revealed. He also studied the biographies and autobiographies of famous historical figures he believed had achieved self-actualization, such as Eleanor Roosevelt, Abraham Lincoln, and Albert Einstein.

There is a more important criticism. Despite the claim that self-actualization is an inborn motivational goal toward which all people supposedly strive, most people do *not* experience or achieve self-actualization. Maslow (1970) himself wrote that self-actualization "can seem like a miracle, so improbable an event as to be awe-inspiring." Maslow explained this basic contradiction in a number of different ways. For instance, he suggested that few people experience the supportive environment that is required to achieve self-actualization.

Although interest in Maslow's theory has waned, it continues to generate occasional research (e.g., Koltko-Rivera, 2006; Pfaffenberger, 2007). But in general, Maslow's notion that we must satisfy needs at one level before moving to the next level has not stood up (Sheldon & others, 2001). Perhaps Maslow's most important contribution was to encourage psychology to focus on the motivation and development of psychologically healthy people (King, 2008). In advocating that idea, he helped focus attention on psychological needs as motivators.

It is quite true that man lives by bread alone—where there is no bread. But what happens to man's desires when there is plenty of bread and when his belly is chronically filled? At once other (and "higher") needs emerge and these, rather than physiological hungers, dominate the organism. And when these in turn are satisfied, again new (and still "higher") needs emerge, and so on. That is what we mean by saying that the basic human needs are organized into a hierarchy of relative prepotency.

—ABRAHAM MASLOW (1943)

Deci and Ryan's Self-Determination Theory

University of Rochester psychologists **Edward L. Deci** and **Richard M. Ryan** (2000, 2008a, 2008b) have developed **self-determination theory,** abbreviated **SDT.** Much like Maslow's theory, SDT's premise is that people are actively growth oriented and that they move toward a unified sense of self and integration with others. To realize optimal psychological functioning and growth throughout the lifespan, Ryan and Deci contend that three innate and universal psychological needs must be satisfied:

- *Autonomy*—the need to determine, control, and organize one's own behavior and goals so that they are in harmony with one's own interests and values.
- *Competence*—the need to learn and master appropriately challenging tasks.
- *Relatedness*—the need to feel attached to others and experience a sense of belongingness, security, and intimacy.

hierarchy of needs
Maslow's hierarchical division of motivation into levels that progress from basic physical needs to psychological needs to self-fulfillment needs.

self-actualization
Defined by Maslow as a person's "full use and exploitation of talents, capacities, and potentialities."

self-determination theory (SDT)
Edward Deci and Richard Ryan's theory that optimal human functioning can occur only if the psychological needs for autonomy, competence, and relatedness are satisfied.

Like Maslow, Deci and Ryan view the need for social relationships as a fundamental psychological motive. The benefits of having strong, positive social relationships are well documented (Baumeister & Leary, 1995; Leary & Cox, 2008). Another well-established psychological need is having a sense of competence or mastery (Bandura, 1997; White, 1959).

One subtle difference in Maslow's views compared to those of Deci and Ryan has to do with the definition of *autonomy.* Deci and Ryan's definition of *autonomy* emphasizes the need to feel that your activities are self-chosen and self-endorsed. This reflects the importance of self-determination in Deci and Ryan's theory. In contrast, Maslow's view of *autonomy* stressed the need to feel independent and focused on your own potential (see Table 8.2 on page 341).

How does a person satisfy the needs for autonomy, competence, and relatedness? In a supportive social, psychological, and physical environment, an individual will pursue interests, goals, and relationships that tend to satisfy these psychological needs. In turn, this enhances the person's psychological growth and intrinsic motivation. **Intrinsic motivation** is the desire to engage in tasks that the person finds inherently satisfying and enjoyable, novel, or optimally challenging.

Of course, much of our behavior in daily life is driven by extrinsic motivation (Ryan & La Guardia, 2000). **Extrinsic motivation** consists of external influences on behavior, such as rewards, social evaluations, rules, and responsibilities. According to Ryan and Deci, the person who has satisfied the needs for competence, autonomy, and relatedness actively *internalizes* and *integrates* different external motivators as part of his or her identity and values. In effect, the person incorporates societal expectations, rules, and regulations as values or rules that he or she personally endorses.

What if one or more of the psychological needs are thwarted by an unfavorable environment, one that is overly challenging, controlling, rejecting, punishing, or even abusive? According to SDT, the person may compensate with substitute needs, defensive behaviors, or maladaptive behaviors. For example, if someone is frustrated in satisfying the need for relatedness, he or she may compensate by chronically seeking the approval of others or by pursuing substitute goals, such as accumulating money or material possessions.

In support of self-determination theory, Deci and Ryan have compiled an impressive array of studies, including cross-cultural studies (Deci & Ryan, 2000, 2008a, 2008b; Ryan & Deci, 2000, 2001). Taking the evolutionary perspective, they also argue that the needs for autonomy, competence, and relatedness have adaptive advantages. For example, the need for relatedness promotes resource sharing, mutual protection, and the division of work, increasing the likelihood that both the individual and the group will survive.

Competence and Achievement Motivation

Key Theme

- **Competence and achievement motivation are important psychological motives.**

Key Questions

- **How does competence motivation differ from achievement motivation, and how is achievement motivation measured?**
- **What characteristics are associated with a high level of achievement motivation, and how does culture affect achievement motivation?**

In self-determination theory, Deci and Ryan identified *competence* as a universal motive. You are displaying **competence motivation** when you strive to use your cognitive, social, and behavioral skills to be capable and exercise control in a situation

intrinsic motivation
The desire to engage in tasks that are inherently satisfying and enjoyable, novel, or optimally challenging; the desire to do something for its own sake.

extrinsic motivation
External factors or influences on behavior, such as rewards, consequences, or social expectations.

Extraordinary Achievement Motivation Regional winners of the Siemens Competition in Math, Science, and Technology display their awards. More than a thousand high school science and math students compete every year to earn scholarships in the annual competition, which attracts talented students from across the country. Hundreds of hours of hard work go into these student projects, which are evaluated in terms of originality, scientific importance, and clarity of presentation.

(White, 1959). Competence motivation provides much of the motivational "push" to prove to yourself that you can successfully tackle new challenges, such as striving to do well in this class.

A step beyond competence motivation is **achievement motivation**—the drive to excel, succeed, or outperform others at some task. In the chapter Prologue, Richard clearly displayed a high level of achievement motivation. Running for student body president, competing as a diver at the national level of collegiate competition, and striving to maintain a straight-A average are all examples of Richard's drive to achieve.

In the 1930s, Henry Murray identified 20 fundamental human needs or motives, including achievement motivation. Murray (1938) defined the "need to achieve" as the tendency "to overcome obstacles, to exercise power, [and] to strive to do something difficult as well and as quickly as possible." Also in the 1930s, Christiana Morgan and Henry Murray (1935) developed a test to measure human motives called the **Thematic Apperception Test (TAT).** The TAT consists of a series of ambiguous pictures. The person being tested is asked to make up a story about each picture, and the story is then coded for different motivational themes, including achievement. In Chapter 10, on personality, we'll look at the TAT in more detail.

In the 1950s, David McClelland, John Atkinson, and their colleagues (1953) developed a specific TAT scoring system to measure the *need for achievement,* often abbreviated *nAch.* Other researchers developed questionnaire measures of achievement motivation (Spangler, 1992). Over the next four decades, McClelland and his associates investigated many different aspects of achievement motivation, especially its application in work settings. In cross-cultural studies, McClelland explored how differences in achievement motivation at the national level have influenced economic development (McClelland, 1961, 1976; McClelland & Winter, 1971). He also studied organizational leadership and *power motivation*—the urge to control or influence the behavior of other people or groups (McClelland, 1975, 1989).

Hundreds of studies have shown that measures of achievement motivation generally correlate well with various areas of success, such as school grades, job performance, and worker output (Senko & others, 2008). This is understandable, since people who score high in achievement motivation expend their greatest efforts when faced with moderately challenging tasks. In striving to achieve the task, they often choose to work long hours and have the capacity to delay gratification and focus on the goal. They also tend to display original thinking, seek expert advice, and value feedback about their performance (McClelland, 1985b).

Although people high in achievement motivation prefer to work independently, the most successful people also have the ability to work well with others (McClelland, 1985a, 1987). And in assessing their own performance, high achievers tend to attribute their successes to their own abilities and efforts, and to explain their failures as being due to external factors or bad luck (Weiner, 1985).

competence motivation
The desire to direct your behavior toward demonstrating competence and exercising control in a situation.

achievement motivation
The desire to direct your behavior toward excelling, succeeding, or outperforming others at some task.

Thematic Apperception Test (TAT)
A projective test developed by Henry Murray and his colleagues that involves creating stories about ambiguous scenes that can be interpreted in a variety of ways.

Celebrating Achievement in a Collectivistic Culture When Japanese marathoner Naoko Takahashi won an Olympic gold medal, she credited "the best coach in the world, the best manager in the world, and all the people who supported me. I didn't [win] it alone, not by myself." Comparing statements by Japanese and American athletes during the Olympics, Hazel Rose Markus found that Japanese emphasized the importance of their supportive relationships, but Americans tended to see their wins as an individual achievement (Markus & others, 2006).

Achievement Motivation and Culture

When it is broadly defined as "the desire for excellence," achievement motivation is found in many, if not all, cultures. In individualistic cultures, like those that characterize North American and European countries, the need to achieve emphasizes personal, individual success rather than the success of the group. In these cultures, achievement motivation is also closely linked with succeeding in competitive tasks (Markus & others, 2006; Morling & Kitayama, 2008).

In collectivistic cultures, like those of many Asian countries, achievement motivation tends to have a different focus. Instead of being oriented toward the individual, achievement orientation is more *socially* oriented (Bond, 1986; Kitayama & Park, 2007). For example, students in China felt that it was unacceptable to express pride for personal achievements but that it was acceptable to feel proud of achievements that benefited others (Stipek, 1998). The person strives to achieve not to promote himself or herself but to promote the status or well-being of other members of the relevant social group, such as family members (Matsumoto & Juang, 2008).

Individuals in collectivistic cultures may persevere or aspire to do well in order to fulfill the expectations of family members and to fit into the larger group. For example, the Japanese student who strives to do well academically is typically not motivated by the desire for personal recognition. Rather, the student's behavior is more likely to be motivated by the desire to enhance the social standing of his or her family by gaining admission to a top university (Kitayama & Park, 2007).

Emotion

Key Theme

- **Emotions are complex psychological states that serve many functions in human behavior and relationships.**

Key Questions

- **What are the three components of emotion, and what functions do emotions serve?**
- **How do evolutionary psychologists view emotion?**
- **What are the basic emotions?**

The Many Functions of Emotion Emotions play an important role in relationships and social communication. If a friend tells you that she is thrilled, happy, or excited, you immediately understand her internal emotional state.

With a final score of 25 to 23, our daughter Laura's freshman high school basketball team had just won its first game of the season. After lining up for the ceremonial "high fives" with the defeated team, Laura's team erupted in shouts of joy, leaping into the air, hugging, and slapping more high fives. In contrast, the girls on the defeated team maintained polite but resigned smiles. One seemed to fight back tears. Another was downright angry. The girls, their coaches, and many of the spectators were clearly having an emotional experience—one that is familiar to everyone. But what, exactly, is emotion?

Emotion is a complex psychological state that involves three distinct components: a *subjective experience*, a *physiological response*, and a *behavioral* or *expressive response*. How are emotions different from moods? Generally, emotions are intense but rather short-lived. Emotions are also more likely to have a specific cause, to be directed toward some particular object, and to motivate a person to take some sort of action. In contrast, a *mood* involves a milder emotional state that is more general and pervasive, such as gloominess or contentment. Moods may last for a few hours or even days (Gendolla, 2000).

The Functions of Emotion

Emotional Intelligence on the Job Have you ever known people who were very intelligent but couldn't hold down a job because they constantly alienated supervisors and co-workers? Success in any field is at least partly dependent on your ability to manage your own emotions and understand the emotions of others—key aspects of *emotional intelligence.* Resolving conflicts in a constructive way, getting along with other workers, and functioning well as part of a team are the kinds of abilities that require a high degree of emotional intelligence (Mayer & others, 2008).

Emotional processes are closely tied to motivational processes. Like the word *motivation,* the root of the word *emotion* is the Latin word *movere,* which means "to move." And indeed, emotions can move us to act, triggering motivated behavior. In the Prologue, Becky's frustration and unhappiness motivated her to end her marriage with Richard. Similarly, anger might motivate you to seek another job when you feel you've been treated unfairly.

Emotions help us to set goals, but emotional states can also be goals in themselves. We ride a roller coaster to achieve emotional excitement or practice every day to relish the satisfaction of eventually winning a piano competition. And most of us direct our lives so as to maximize the experience of positive emotions and minimize the experience of negative emotions (Gendolla, 2000).

At one time, psychologists considered emotions to be disruptive forces that interfered with rational behavior (Cacioppo & Gardner, 1999). Emotions were thought of as primitive impulses that needed to be suppressed or controlled.

Today, psychologists are much more attuned to the importance of emotions in many different areas of behavior, *including* rational decision making, purposeful behavior, and setting appropriate goals (Loewenstein & others, 2001; Mellers, 2000). Most of our choices are guided by our feelings, sometimes without our awareness (Bechara & others, 1997; Kihlstrom & others, 2000). But consider the fate of people who have lost the capacity to feel emotion because of damage to specific brain areas. Despite having an intact ability to reason, such people tend to make disastrous decisions (Damasio, 2004; Koenigs & Tranel, 2007).

Similarly, people who are low in what is termed **emotional intelligence** may have superior reasoning powers, but they sometimes experience one failure in life after another (Mayer & others, 2004; Van Heck & den Oudsten, 2008). Why? Because they lack the ability to manage their own emotions, comprehend the emotional responses of others, and respond appropriately to the emotions of other people. In contrast, people who are high in emotional intelligence possess these abilities, and they are able to understand and use their emotions (Mayer & others, 2008; Zeidner & others, 2008).

emotion
A complex psychological state that involves subjective experience, a physiological response, and a behavioral or expressive response.

emotional intelligence
The capacity to understand and manage your own emotional experiences and to perceive, comprehend, and respond appropriately to the emotional responses of others.

Evolutionary Explanations of Emotion

One of the earliest scientists to systematically study emotions was **Charles Darwin.** Darwin published *The Expression of the Emotions in Man and Animals* in 1872, 13 years after he had laid out his general theory of evolution in *On the Origin of Species by Means of Natural Selection* and only a year after his book on the evolution of humans, *The Descent of Man* (1871). Darwin (1872) described the facial expressions, body movements, and postures used to express specific emotions in animals and humans. He argued that emotions reflect evolutionary adaptations to the problems of survival and reproduction.

Like Darwin, today's evolutionary psychologists believe that emotions are the product of evolution (Ermer & others, 2007; Tooby & Cosmides, 2005). Emotions help us solve adaptive problems posed by our environment. They "move" us toward potential resources, and they move us away from potential dangers. Fear prompts us to flee an attacker or evade a threat. Anger moves us to turn and fight a rival. Love propels us to seek out a mate and care for our offspring. Disgust prompts us to avoid a sickening stimulus.

Darwin and Emotion *The Expression of the Emotions in Man and Animals* was a best-seller when it was first published in 1872. It was also the first scientific book to take advantage of the new technology of photography. Charles Darwin was one of the first scientists to systematically study emotional expressions. He hoped to show the continuity of emotional expressions among nonhuman animals and humans—additional evidence for his evolutionary theory.

basic emotions
The most fundamental set of emotion categories, which are biologically innate, evolutionarily determined, and culturally universal.

interpersonal engagement
Emotion dimension reflecting the degree to which emotions involve a relationship with another person or other people.

Obviously, the capacity to feel and be moved by emotion has adaptive value: An organism that is able to quickly respond to rewards or threats is more likely to survive and successfully reproduce.

Darwin (1872) also pointed out that emotional displays serve the important function of informing other organisms about an individual's internal state. When facing an aggressive rival, the snarl of a baboon signals its readiness to fight. A wolf rolling submissively on its back telegraphs its willingness to back down and avoid a fight.

Emotions are also important in situations that go well beyond physical survival. Virtually all human relationships are heavily influenced by emotions. Our emotional experience and expression, as well as our ability to understand the emotions of others, are crucial to the maintenance of social relationships (Reis & others, 2000).

In the next several sections, we'll consider each of the components of emotion in turn, beginning with the component that is most familiar: the subjective experience of emotion.

Table 8.3

The Basic Emotions

Fear	Disgust
Surprise	Happiness
Anger	Sadness

Although there is some disagreement as to exactly which emotions best represent the universal set of basic emotions, most emotion researchers today agree on the six emotions shown above. Other possible candidates are contempt or disdain, pride, and excitement.

The Subjective Experience of Emotion

Most emotion researchers today agree that there are a limited number of **basic emotions** that all humans, in every culture, experience. These basic emotions are thought to be biologically determined, the products of evolution. And what are these basic emotions? As shown in Table 8.3, fear, disgust, surprise, happiness, anger, and sadness are most commonly cited as the basic emotions (Ekman, 1992a; Izard, 2007).

Many psychologists contend that each basic emotion represents a sequence of responses that is innate and hard-wired in the brain (Tooby & Cosmides, 2000). But your emotional experience is not limited to pure forms of each basic emotion. Rather, each basic emotion represents a family of related emotional states (Ekman, 1994a, 1994b). For example, consider the many types of angry feelings, which can range from mild annoyance to bitter resentment or fierce rage.

Further, psychologists recognize that emotional experience can be complex and multifaceted (Cacioppo & Gardner, 1999). People often experience a *blend* of emotions. In more complex situations, people may experience *mixed emotions,* in which very different emotions are experienced simultaneously or in rapid succession.

A common belief is that women are "naturally" more emotional than men. In fact, *both* men and women tend to view women as the more emotional sex (Hess & others, 2000). But are they? We explore this question in the Critical Thinking box, "Are Women *Really* More Emotional Than Men?"

Culture and Emotional Experience

In diverse cultures, psychologists have found general agreement regarding the subjective experience and meaning of different basic emotions (Scherer & Wallbott, 1994). Canadian psychologist James Russell (1991) compared emotion descriptions by people from several different cultures. He found that emotions were most commonly classified according to two dimensions: (1) the degree to which the emotion is *pleasant* or *unpleasant* and (2) the level of *activation,* or arousal, associated with the emotion. For example, joy and contentment are both pleasant emotions, but joy is associated with a higher degree of activation (Feldman Barrett & Russell, 1999).

While these may be the most fundamental dimensions of emotion, cultural variations in classifying emotions do exist (White, 1994). For example, Hazel Rose Markus and Shinobu Kitayama (1991, 1994) found that Japanese subjects classified emotions in terms of not two but three important dimensions. Along with the pleasantness and activation dimensions, they also categorized emotions along a dimension of **interpersonal engagement.** This dimension reflects the idea that some emotions result from your connections and interactions with other people (Kitayama & others, 2000). Japanese participants rated anger and shame as being about the same in terms of unpleasantness and activation, but they rated shame as being much higher than anger on the dimension of interpersonal engagement.

Socially Engaged Emotions in Japan Closeness and interdependence are fostered by Japanese child-rearing practices, and some psychologists believe they also form the basis for such other-focused emotions as *amae,* a central emotion in Japanese culture (Markus & Kitayama, 1991). *Amae* can be defined as the sense of being lovingly cared for and unconditionally accepted by another person. *Amae* can be achieved only within a reciprocal, interdependent relationship with someone else. Thus, *amae* is a prototypical example of a socially engaged emotion—an other-focused emotion that creates and fosters interdependence with significant others (Rothbaum & others, 2007; Yamaguchi & Ariizumi, 2006).

CRITICAL THINKING

Are Women *Really* More Emotional Than Men?

"You never talk about your feelings!!" *she* said in exasperation. "And you never stop talking about yours!!" *he* shot back, frowning. Is this scene familiar?

One of our culture's most pervasive gender stereotypes is that women express their emotions more frequently and intensely than men do. In contrast, men supposedly are calmer and possess greater emotional control (Plant & others, 2000). Women, it's thought, cry easily. *Real* men don't cry at all.

Studies have shown that *both* men and women view women as the more emotional sex (Robinson & Clore, 2002). Women also place a higher value on emotional expressiveness than do men (Shields, 2002).

Women display more emotional awareness than men do (Boden & Berenbaum, 2007). Women are more accurate than men in deciphering the emotional meaning of nonverbal cues, such as facial expressions (Hall & Matsumoto, 2004). And, they tend to be more sensitive and responsive to the emotional exchanges in a relationship, often playing the role of the "emotion specialist." But do such widely held stereotypes reflect actual gender differences in emotional experience?

Consider a study by Ann Kring and Albert Gordon (1998), in which participants separately watched film clips that typically evoke happiness, fear, or sadness. For example, a fear-evoking film clip depicted a man almost falling off the ledge of a tall building. During the film, the participants' facial expressions were secretly videotaped from behind a one-way mirror. Galvanic skin response was also monitored as an index of physiological arousal. *Galvanic skin response* (GSR) measures the skin's electrical conductivity, which changes in response to sweating and increased blood flow. After the film clip, the participants rated the extent to which they experienced different emotions.

Kring and Gordon found that men and women did *not* differ in their self-ratings of the emotions they experienced in response to the film clips. However, the women *were* more emotionally expressive than men. Women displayed more positive facial expressions in response to happy film clips and more negative facial expressions in response to the sad or fearful scenes. In terms of physiological arousal, the sexes did *not* differ in their reactions to the happy or sad films. But when it came to the frightening film clips, the men reacted much more strongly than the women.

In a similar study, electrodes monitored facial muscle activity of male and female participants as they looked at fear-evoking pictures (Thunberg & Dimberg, 2000). Even though men and women rated the pictures as equally unpleasant, the women's facial muscles reacted much more strongly to the fearful images.

These and similar findings suggest that men and women are fairly similar in the *experience* of emotions, but that they do differ in the *expression* of emotions. How can we account for the gender differences in emotional expression?

First, psychologists have consistently found differences in the *types* of emotions expressed by men and women (see Shields, 2002). Analyzing cross-cultural data from 37 countries around the world, Agneta Fischer and her colleagues (2004) found this consistent pattern: Women report experiencing and expressing more sadness, fear, and guilt, while men report experiencing and expressing more anger and hostility.

Fischer and her colleagues (2004) argue that the male role encourages the expression of emotions that emphasize power and assertiveness. These *powerful emotions*—anger, hostility, and contempt—are emotions that confirm the person's autonomy and status. In contrast, the female role encourages the expression of emotions that imply self-blame, vulnerability, and helplessness. These *powerless emotions*—fear, sadness, shame, and guilt—are emotions that help maintain social harmony with others by minimizing conflict and hostility.

For both men and women, the expression of emotions is strongly influenced by *culturally determined display rules,* or societal norms of appropriate behavior in different situations. In many cultures, including the United States, women are allowed a wider range of emotional expressiveness and responsiveness than men. For men, it's considered "unmasculine" to be too open in expressing certain emotions. Crying is especially taboo (Warner & Shields, 2007). Thus, there are strong cultural and gender-role expectations concerning emotional expressiveness and sensitivity.

Like so many stereotypes, the gender stereotypes of emotions are not completely accurate. As psychologists Michael Robinson and Gerald Clore (2002) point out, men and women believe that their emotions differ far more than they actually do. Men and women differ less in their *experience* of emotion than they do in their *expression* of those emotions. However, women *are* the more emotional sex in terms of the ease with which they express their emotions, think about emotions, and recall emotional experiences (Feldman Barrett & others, 2000).

CRITICAL THINKING QUESTIONS

- How are emotionally expressive males generally regarded in your social group? Emotionally expressive females? Does it make you uncomfortable when gender display rules are violated by either sex? Why?
- What kinds of consequences might occur if gender display rules were violated in a business environment? On a sports team? In a classroom?

ZITS

Why would the Japanese emphasize interpersonal engagement as a dimension of emotion? Japan is a collectivistic culture, so a person's identity is seen as interdependent with those of other people, rather than independent, as is characteristic of the more individualistic cultures. Thus, social context is an important part of private emotional experience (Kitayama & Park, 2007).

The Neuroscience of Emotion

Key Theme

- **Emotions are associated with distinct patterns of responses by the sympathetic nervous system and in the brain.**

Key Questions

- **How is the sympathetic nervous system involved in intense emotional responses?**
- **What brain structures are involved in emotional experience, and what neural pathways make up the brain's fear circuit?**
- **How does the evolutionary perspective explain the dual brain pathways for transmitting fear-related information?**

Psychologists have long studied the physiological aspects of emotion. Early research focused on the autonomic nervous system's role in triggering physiological arousal. More recently, brain-imaging techniques have identified specific brain regions involved in emotions. In this section, we'll look at both areas of research.

Emotion and the Sympathetic Nervous System

Hot Heads and Cold Feet

The pounding heart, rapid breathing, trembling hands and feet, and churning stomach that occur when you experience an intense emotion like fear reflect the activation of the sympathetic branch of the *autonomic nervous system*. When you are threatened, the *sympathetic nervous system* triggers the *fight-or-flight response,* a rapidly occurring series of automatic physical reactions. Breathing and heart rate accelerate, and blood pressure surges. You perspire, your mouth goes dry, and the hairs on your skin may stand up, giving you the familiar sensation of goose bumps. Your pupils dilate, allowing you to take in a wider visual field. Blood sugar levels increase, providing a burst of energy. Digestion stops as blood is diverted from the stomach and intestines to the brain and skeletal muscles, sometimes causing the sensations of light-headedness or "butterflies" fluttering in your stomach. The polygraph or "lie detector" measures these physiological reactions associated with emotional arousal.

The sympathetic nervous system is also activated by other intense emotions, such as excitement, passionate love, or extreme joy. If you've ever ridden an exciting roller coaster, self-consciously given a speech in front of your peers, or been reunited with a loved one after a long absence, you've experienced the high levels of physiological arousal that can be produced by other types of emotions. Obviously, not all emotions involve intense physical reactions. And some emotions, such as contentment, are characterized by decreased physical arousal and the slowing of some body processes (Levenson & others, 1990, 1992).

Research has shown that there are differing patterns of physiological arousal for different emotions (Ekman, 2003). In one series of studies, psychologist Robert W. Levenson (1992) found that fear, anger, and sadness are all associated with accelerated heart rate. But comparing anger and fear showed differences that confirm everyday experience. Anger produces greater increases in blood pressure than fear. And while anger produces an increase in skin temperature, fear produces a *decrease* in skin temperature. Perhaps that's why when we are angry, we speak of "getting hot under the collar," and when fearful, we feel clammy and complain of having "cold feet."

Arousal and Intense Emotion: Tears of Joy This Indonesian woman sheds tears of joy at her soldier husband's safe return from a distant war zone. Many intense emotions involve the activation of the sympathetic nervous system. Although emotions like extreme joy, fear, and grief subjectively feel very different, they all involve increases in heart rate, breathing, and blood pressure. From an evolutionary perspective, the physical arousal associated with intense emotion helps gear people up to take action.

Levenson (1992, 2003) believes that these differing patterns of sympathetic nervous system activation are universal, reflecting biological responses to the basic emotions that are hard-wired by evolution into all humans. Supporting this contention, Levenson found that male and female subjects, as well as young and elderly subjects, experience the *same* patterns of autonomic nervous system activity for different basic emotions. These distinctive patterns of emotional physiological arousal were also found in members of a remote culture in western Sumatra, an island in Indonesia (Levenson & others, 1992). Broader surveys of different cultures have also demonstrated that the basic emotions are associated with distinct patterns of autonomic nervous system activity (Levenson, 2003; Scherer & Wallbott, 1994).

amygdala
(uh-MIG-dull-uh) Almond-shaped cluster of neurons in the brain's temporal lobe, involved in memory and emotional responses, especially fear.

The Emotional Brain

Fear and the Amygdala

Sophisticated brain-imaging techniques have led to an explosion of new knowledge about the brain's role in emotion. Of all the emotions, the brain processes involved in *fear* have been most thoroughly studied. Many brain areas are implicated in emotional responses, but the brain structure called the **amygdala** has long been known to be especially important. As described in Chapter 2, the amygdala is an almond-shaped cluster of neurons located deep in the temporal lobe on each side of the brain. The amygdala is part of the *limbic system,* a group of brain structures involved in emotion, memory, and basic motivational drives, such as hunger, thirst, and sex. Neural pathways connect the amygdala with other brain structures.

Several studies have shown that the amygdala is a key brain structure in the emotional response of fear in humans (Davis & Whalen, 2001). For example, brain-imaging techniques have demonstrated that the amygdala activates when you view threatening or fearful faces, or hear people make nonverbal sounds expressing fear (Morris & others, 1999; Öhman & others, 2007). Even when people simply anticipate a threatening stimulus, the amygdala activates as part of the fear circuit in the brain (Phelps & others, 2001).

In rats, amygdala damage disrupts the neural circuits involved in the fear response. For example, rats with a damaged amygdala can't be classically conditioned to acquire a fear response (LeDoux, 2007). In humans, damage to the amygdala also disrupts elements of the fear response. For example, people with amygdala damage lose the ability to distinguish between friendly and threatening faces (Adolphs & others, 1998).

Activating the Amygdala: Direct and Indirect Neural Pathways Let's use an example to show how the amygdala participates in the brain's fear circuit. Imagine that your sister's 8-year-old son sneaks up behind you at a family picnic and pokes you in the back with a long stick. As you quickly wheel around, he shouts, "Look what I found in the woods!" Dangling from the stick is a wriggling, slimy-looking, three-foot-long snake. He tosses the snake into your face, and you let out a yell and jump two feet into the air. As he bursts into hysterical laughter, you quickly realize that the real-looking snake is made of rubber, your nephew is a twit, and your sister is laughing as hard as her son.

Even if you don't know any obnoxious 8-year-old boys, you've probably experienced a sudden fright where you instantly reacted to a threatening stimulus, like a snake, a spider, or an oncoming car. Typically, you respond instinctively, without taking time to consciously or deliberately evaluate the situation.

So how can we respond to potentially dangerous stimuli before we've had time to think about them? Let's stay with our example. When you saw the dangling snake, the visual stimulus was first routed to the *thalamus* (see Figure 8.10 on the next page). As we explained in Chapter 2, all incoming sensory information, with the exception of olfactory sensations, is processed in the thalamus before being relayed to sensory centers in the cerebral cortex.

However, the neuroscientist Joseph LeDoux (1996, 2000) discovered that there are *two* neural pathways for sensory information that project from the thalamus. One leads to the cortex, as previously described, but the other leads directly to the amygdala, bypassing the cortex. When we are faced with a potential threat, sensory information about the threatening stimulus is routed simultaneously along both pathways.

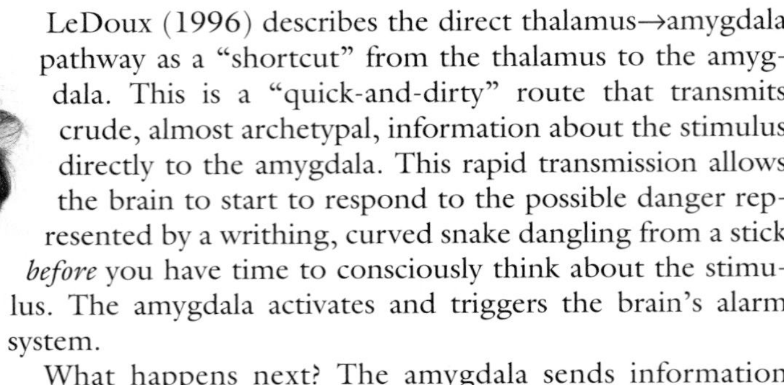

Figure 8.10 Fear Circuits in the Brain When you're faced with a potentially threatening stimulus—like a snake dangling from a stick—information arrives in the thalamus, and is relayed simultaneously along two pathways. Crude, archetypal information rapidly travels the direct route to the amygdala, triggering an almost instantaneous fear response. More detailed information is sent along the pathway to the visual cortex, where the stimulus is interpreted. If the cortex determines that a threat exists, the information is relayed to the amygdala along the longer, slower pathway. The amygdala triggers other brain structures, such as the hypothalamus, which activate the sympathetic nervous system and the endocrine system's release of stress hormones.

Source: Adapted from LeDoux (1994a, b).

LeDoux (1996) describes the direct thalamus→amygdala pathway as a "shortcut" from the thalamus to the amygdala. This is a "quick-and-dirty" route that transmits crude, almost archetypal, information about the stimulus directly to the amygdala. This rapid transmission allows the brain to start to respond to the possible danger represented by a writhing, curved snake dangling from a stick *before* you have time to consciously think about the stimulus. The amygdala activates and triggers the brain's alarm system.

What happens next? The amygdala sends information along neural pathways that project to other brain regions that make up the rest of the brain's fear circuit. One pathway leads to an area of the *hypothalamus,* then on to the *medulla* at the base of the brain. In combination, the hypothalamus and medulla trigger arousal of the sympathetic nervous system. Another pathway projects from the amygdala to a different hypothalamus area that, in concert with the *pituitary gland,* triggers the release of stress hormones (LeDoux, 1995, 2000).

The result? You respond instantly to the threat—"SNAKE!"—by leaping backward, heartbeat and breathing accelerating. But even as you respond to the threat, information is speeding along the other neural pathway that reaches the amygdala by traveling through the cortex. The thalamus sends information to the visual cortex, which creates a detailed and more accurate representation of the visual stimulus. You can also reevaluate the signal that prompted the initial instinctive response. Now you realize that the "snake" is actually just a rubber toy. The cortex sends the "false alarm" message to the amygdala. But note that information traveling the thalamus→cortex→amygdala route takes about twice as long to reach the amygdala as the information traveling along the direct thalamus→amygdala route. Thus, the alarm reaction is already in full swing before signals from the cortex reach the amygdala.

LeDoux believes these dual alarm pathways serve several adaptive functions. The direct thalamus→amygdala pathway rapidly triggers an emotional response to threats that, through evolution, we are biologically prepared to fear, such as snakes, snarling animals, or rapidly moving, looming objects. In contrast, the indirect pathway allows more complex stimuli to be evaluated in the cortex before triggering the amygdala's alarm system. So, for example, the gradually dawning awareness that your job is in jeopardy as your boss starts talking about the need to reduce staff in your department probably has to travel the thalamus→cortex→amygdala pathway before you begin to feel the cold sweat break out on your palms.

In situations of potential danger, it is clearly advantageous to be able to respond quickly. According to LeDoux (1995, 2000), the direct thalamus→amygdala connection represents an adaptive response that has been hard-wired by evolution into the human brain. From the point of view of survival, as LeDoux (1996) remarks, "The time saved by the amygdala in acting on the thalamic interpretation, rather than waiting for the cortical input, may be the difference between life and death."

In support of this evolutionary explanation, Swedish psychologist Arne Öhman and his colleagues (2001b; Schupp & others, 2004) have found that people detect and react more quickly to angry or threatening faces than they do to friendly or neutral faces. Presumably, this reflects the faster processing of threatening stimuli via the direct thalamus→amygdala route (Lundqvist & Öhman, 2005).

FOCUS ON NEUROSCIENCE

Emotions and the Brain

Do Different Emotions Activate Different Brain Areas? The idea that different combinations of brain regions are activated by different emotions received considerable support in a brain-imaging study by neuroscientist Antonio Damasio and his colleagues (2000). In the study, participants were scanned using positron emission tomography (PET) while they recalled emotionally charged memories to generate feelings of sadness, happiness, anger, and fear.

Each of the four PET scans shown here is an averaged composite of all 39 participants in the study. Significant areas of brain activation are indicated in red, while significant areas of deactivation are indicated in purple. Notice that sadness, happiness, anger, and fear each produced a distinct pattern of brain activation and deactivation. These findings confirmed the idea that each emotion involves distinct neural circuits in the brain. Other research has produced similar findings (Dalgleish, 2004; Najib & others, 2004; Phan & others, 2002).

One interesting finding in the Damasio study was that the emotional memory triggered autonomic nervous system activity and physiological arousal *before* the volunteers signaled that they were subjectively "feeling" the target emotion. Areas of the somatosensory cortex, which processes sensory information from the skin, muscles, and internal organs, were also activated. These sensory signals from the body's peripheral nervous system contributed to the overall subjective "feeling" of a particular emotion. Remember Damasio's findings because we'll refer to this study again when we discuss theories of emotion.

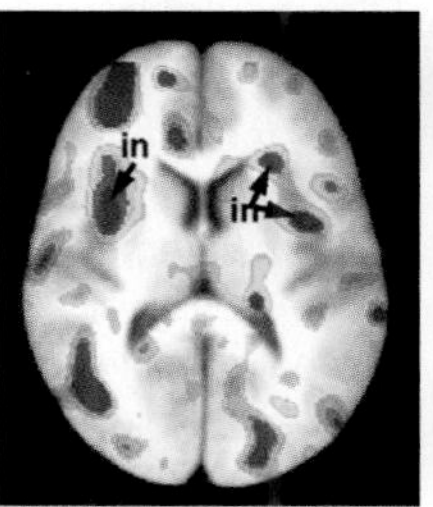

Sadness

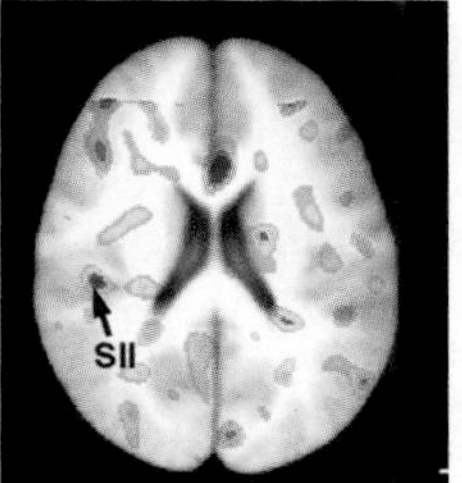

Happiness

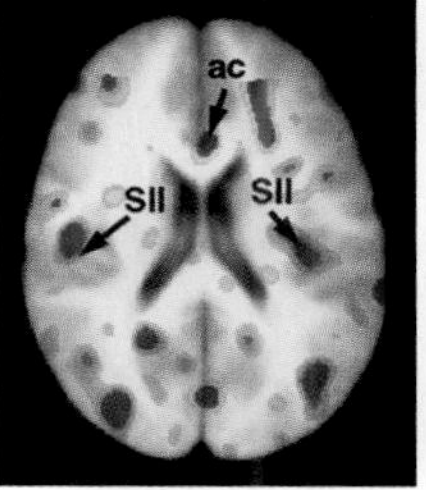

Anger

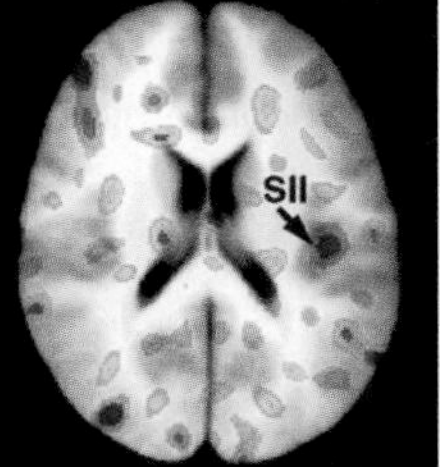

Fear

The Expression of Emotion

Making Faces

Key Theme

- **The behavioral components of emotion include facial expressions and nonverbal behavior.**

Key Questions

- **What evidence supports the idea that facial expressions for basic emotions are universal?**
- **How does culture affect the behavioral expression of emotion?**
- **How can emotional expression be explained in terms of evolutionary theory?**

Every day, we witness the behavioral components of emotions in ourselves and others. We laugh with pleasure, slam a door in frustration, or frown at a clueless remark. But of all the ways that we express and communicate our emotional responses, facial expressions are the most important.

In *The Expression of the Emotions in Man and Animals,* Darwin (1872) argued that human emotional expressions are innate and culturally universal. He also noted the continuity of emotional expression between humans and many other species, citing it as evidence of the common evolutionary ancestry of humans and other animals. But do nonhuman animals actually experience emotions? We explore this question in the Critical Thinking box, "Emotion in Nonhuman Animals: Laughing Rats, Silly Elephants, and Smiling Dolphins?"

CRITICAL THINKING

Emotion in Nonhuman Animals: Laughing Rats, Silly Elephants, and Smiling Dolphins?

Do animals experience emotions? If you've ever frolicked with a playful puppy or shared the contagious contentment of a cat purring in your lap, the answer seems obvious. But before you accept that answer, remember that emotion involves three components: physiological arousal, behavioral expression, and subjective experience. In many animals, fear and other "emotional" responses appear to involve physiological and brain processes that are similar to those involved in human emotional experience. In mammals, it's also easy to observe behavioral responses when an animal is menaced by a predator or the anger in aggressive displays. But what about subjective experience?

Darwin on Animal Emotions

Charles Darwin never doubted that animals experience emotions. In his landmark work *The Expression of the Emotions in Man and Animals,* Darwin (1872) contended that differences in emotional experience between nonhuman animals and humans are a matter of degree, not kind. "The lower animals, like man, manifestly feel pleasure and pain, happiness and misery," he wrote in *The Descent of Man* in 1871. From Darwin's perspective, the capacity to experience emotion is yet another evolved trait that humans share with lower animals (Bekoff, 2007).

Not all psychologists agree with that stance. Staunch behaviorists like Mark Blumberg and his colleagues (2000) argue that there is no need to assume that the behaviors of animals have an emotional or mental component. For example, they contend that the distress cry of infant rats is *not* the expression of an emotional state. Rather, the cries are an "acoustic by-product" of a physiological process, more like a cough or a sneeze than a human cry (Blumberg & Sokoloff, 2001).

One problem in establishing whether animals experience emotion is the difficulty of determining the nature of an animal's subjective experience. Even Darwin (1871) readily acknowledged this problem, writing, "Who can say what cows feel, when they surround and stare intently on a dying or dead companion?"

Foxes in Love? Rather than living in a pack like coyotes or wolves, their evolutionary relatives, red foxes form a monogamous pair bond and often mate for life. They live, play, and hunt together and share in the care of their offspring. It's tempting, but unscientific, to label their bond as "love."

Laughing Rats? Rats are sociable, playful creatures. They emit distinct, high-pitched chirps when they play, anticipate treats, and during positive social interactions. They also chirp when they're tickled by researchers like neuroscientist Jaak Panksepp (2000, 2007a). But when infant rats are separated from their mothers, or when they're cold, they emit a distress cry that is much lower in frequency than the ultrasonic chirps that are associated with pleasant experiences.

Which Is the "True" Smile? Psychologist and emotion researcher Paul Ekman demonstrates the difference between a fake smile *(left)* and the true smile *(right).* If you were able to pick out the true smile, it was because you, like most people, are able to decipher the subtle differences in the facial muscles, especially around the eyes and lips.

Of course, humans are the animals that exhibit the greatest range of facial expressions. Psychologist **Paul Ekman** has studied the facial expression of emotions for more than four decades. Ekman (1980) estimates that the human face is capable of creating more than *7,000* different expressions. This enormous flexibility allows us considerable versatility in expressing emotion in all its subtle variations.

To study facial expressions, Ekman and his colleague Walter Friesen (1978) coded different facial expressions by painstakingly

Anthropomorphism: Happy Dolphins?

Despite the problem of knowing just what an animal is feeling, we often *think* that we do. For example, one reason that dolphins are so appealing is the wide, happy grin they seem to wear. But the dolphin's "smile" is *not* a true facial expression—it's simply the bony curvature of its mouth. If you comment on the friendly, happy appearance of the dolphins frolicking at SeaWorld or another aquarium, you're *projecting* those human emotions onto the dolphins.

You also just committed **anthropomorphism**—you attributed human traits, qualities, or behaviors to a nonhuman animal. The tendency of people to be anthropomorphic is understandable when you consider how extensively most of us were conditioned as children via books, cartoons, and Disney characters to believe that animals are just like people, only with fur or feathers.

Silly Elephants Elephants form tightly knit family groups. When reunited after a long separation, elephants perform an elaborate greeting ceremony—rumbling, trumpeting, flapping their ears, and spinning around as they rush together, exuberantly intertwining their trunks. Even adult elephants play, sometimes with great enthusiasm, which veteran researcher Cynthia Moss (2000) describes as "elephants acting silly." Female elephants are intensely devoted to their offspring, and family members often touch one another with what looks like affection (Bradshaw & others, 2005).

From a scientific perspective, anthropomorphism can hinder progress in understanding animal emotions. By assuming that an animal thinks and feels as we do, we run the risk of distorting or obscuring the reality of the animal's own unique experience (Hauser, 2000).

Instead, we must acknowledge that other animals are not happy or sad in the same way that humans subjectively experience happiness or sadness. As psychologist Mark Hauser (2000) puts it, "Animal minds are wild minds, shaped by a history of environmental pressures. The problem we face is to figure out what kinds of feelings and thoughts animals have, and why they evolved such capacities."

Animals clearly demonstrate diverse emotions—fear, anger, surprise. But to understand how they subjectively *experience* such feelings—and, indeed, whether they do at all—raises questions that cannot be fully answered at this time. Nonetheless, it seems safe to assume that more primitive animals, like fish, turtles, and snakes, probably do not possess a level of self-awareness that would allow them to experience complex emotions like grief, empathy, or altruism (Hauser, 2000). For more sophisticated animals, like dolphins, primates, and elephants, the evidence is more compelling (Bekoff, 2007; Griffin, 2001).

One subjective aspect of the scientific method is how to interpret evidence and data. In the case of the evidence for animal emotions, the scientific debate is far from over. Although the lack of a definitive answer can be frustrating, keep in mind that such scientific debates play an important role in avoiding erroneous conclusions and shaping future research.

CRITICAL THINKING QUESTIONS

- What evidence would lead you to conclude that primates, dolphins, or elephants experience emotions?
- Would you accept different evidence to conclude that a 6-month-old human infant can experience emotions? If so, why?
- Is it possible to be completely free of anthropomorphic tendencies in studying animal emotions?

analyzing the facial muscles involved in producing each expression. In doing so, they precisely classified the facial expressions that characterize the basic emotions of happiness, sadness, surprise, fear, anger, and disgust. When shown photographs of these facial expressions, research participants were able to correctly identify the emotion being displayed (Ekman, 1982, 1992b, 1993).

Ekman concluded that facial expressions for the basic emotions are innate and probably hard-wired in the brain. Further evidence comes from children who are born blind and deaf. Despite their inability to observe or hear others, they express joy, anger, and pleasure using the same expressions as sighted and hearing

anthropomorphism
The attribution of human traits, motives, emotions, or behaviors to nonhuman animals or inanimate objects.

Facial Expressions Are Innate Born deaf and blind, this 7-year-old girl has never observed the facial expressions of those around her. Yet her smile and laughter are unmistakable and identical to those of other children. Facial expressions, especially for basic emotions, seem to be innate rather than learned (Galati & others, 2003).

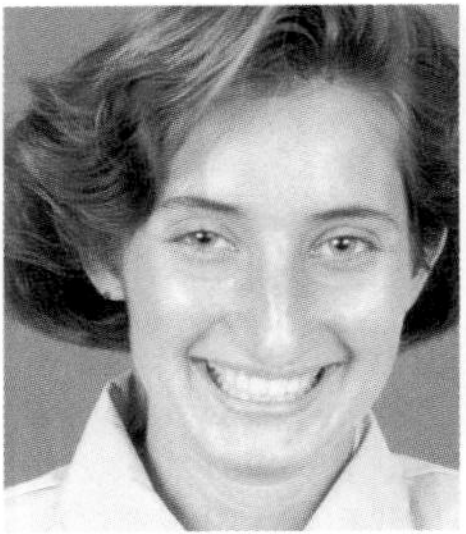
Happiness

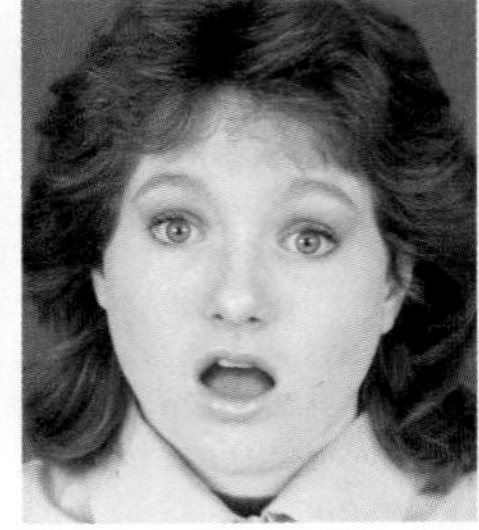
Surprise

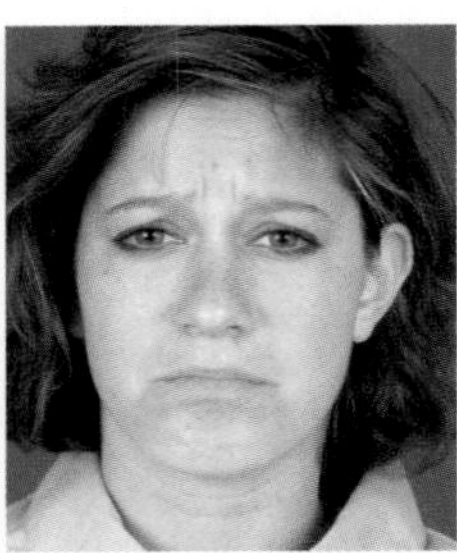
Sadness

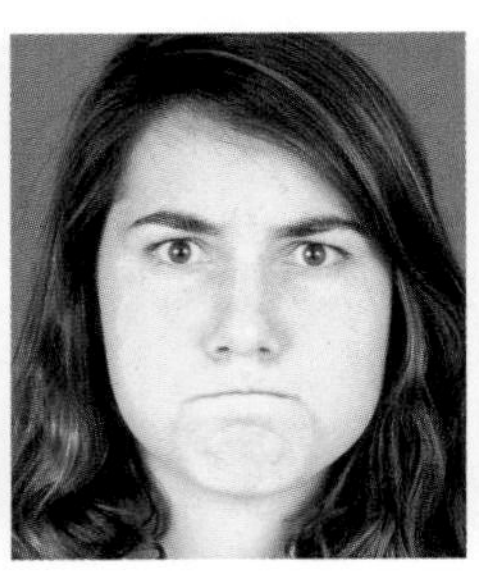
Anger

Disgust

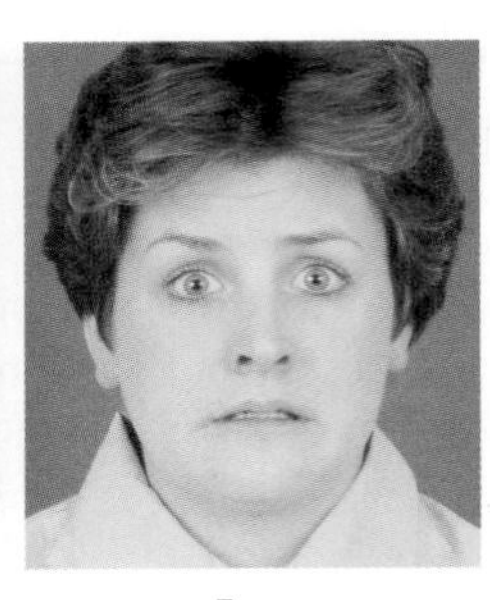
Fear

Basic Emotions and Universal Facial Expressions Paul Ekman and his colleagues have precisely calibrated the muscles used in facial expressions for basic emotions. When photographs like these are shown to people in a wide variety of cultures, they recognize the basic emotions that are being expressed.

children (Eibl-Eibesfeldt, 1973; Goodenough, 1932). Similarly, the spontaneous facial expressions of children and young adults who were born blind do not differ from those of sighted children and adults (Galati & others, 2003, 1997).

Culture and Emotional Expression

Facial expressions for the basic emotions seem to be universal across different cultures (Waller & others, 2008). Ekman (1982) and other researchers showed photographs of facial expressions to people in 21 different countries. Despite their different cultural experiences, all the participants identified the emotions being expressed with a high degree of accuracy (see Ekman, 1998). Even the inhabitants of remote, isolated villages in New Guinea, who had never been exposed to movies or other aspects of Western culture, were able to identify the emotions being expressed. Other research has confirmed and extended Ekman's original findings (see Elfenbein & Ambady, 2002; Frank & Stennett, 2001).

Some specific nonverbal gestures, which are termed *emblems,* vary across cultures. For example, shaking your head means "no" in the United States but "yes" in southern India and Bulgaria. Nodding your head means "yes" in the United States, but in Japan it could mean "maybe" or even "no way!" Nevertheless, some body language seems to be universal (see photos below).

However, in many situations, you adjust your emotional expressions to make them appropriate in that particular social context. For example, even if you are deeply angered by your supervisor's comments at work, you might consciously restrain yourself and maintain a neutral facial expression. How, when, and where we display our emotional expressions are strongly influenced by cultural norms. Cultural differences in the management of facial expressions are called **display rules** (Ekman & others, 1987; Ambady & others, 2006).

Consider a classic experiment in which a hidden camera recorded the facial expressions of Japanese and Americans as they watched films that showed grisly images of surgery, amputations, and so forth (Ekman & others, 1987; Friesen, 1972). When they watched the films alone, the Japanese and American participants displayed virtually identical facial expressions, grimacing with disgust and distaste at the gruesome scenes. But when a scientist was present while the participants watched the films, the Japanese masked their negative facial expressions of disgust or fear with smiles. Why? In

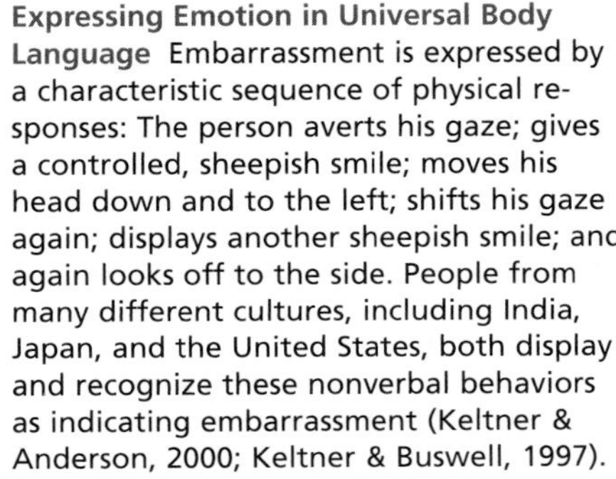
Expressing Emotion in Universal Body Language Embarrassment is expressed by a characteristic sequence of physical responses: The person averts his gaze; gives a controlled, sheepish smile; moves his head down and to the left; shifts his gaze again; displays another sheepish smile; and again looks off to the side. People from many different cultures, including India, Japan, and the United States, both display and recognize these nonverbal behaviors as indicating embarrassment (Keltner & Anderson, 2000; Keltner & Buswell, 1997).

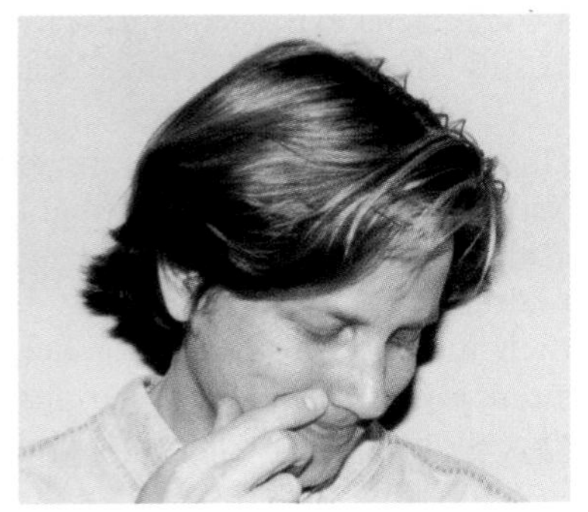

Japan an important display rule is that you should not reveal negative emotions in the presence of an authority figure so as not to offend the higher-status individual.

Display rules can also vary for different groups within a given culture. For example, recall our earlier discussion about gender differences in emotional expression. In many cultures, including the United States, women are allowed a wider range of emotional expressiveness and responsiveness than men. For men, it's considered "unmasculine" to be too open in expressing certain emotions, such as sadness (Fischer & others, 2004; Plant & others, 2004). Crying is especially taboo (Vingerhoets & others, 2000).

So what overall conclusions emerge from the research findings on emotional expressions? First, Paul Ekman and other researchers have amassed considerable evidence that facial expressions for the basic emotions—happiness, sadness, anger, fear, surprise, and disgust—are hard-wired into the brain. They also contend that the basic emotions are biologically determined, the result of evolutionary processes. Second, these emotional expressions serve the adaptive function of communicating internal states to friends and enemies. Like the survival of other social animals, human survival depends on being able to recognize and respond quickly to the emotional state of others. Third, although facial expressions for the basic emotions may be biologically programmed, cultural conditioning, gender-role expectations, and other learning experiences shape how, when, and whether emotional responses are displayed.

display rules
Social and cultural regulations governing emotional expression, especially facial expressions.

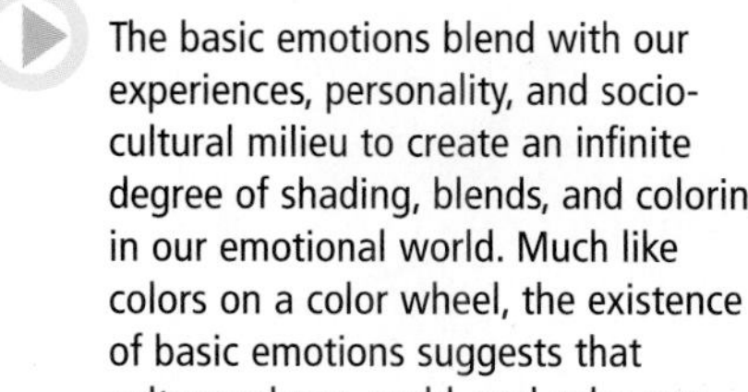
The basic emotions blend with our experiences, personality, and sociocultural milieu to create an infinite degree of shading, blends, and coloring in our emotional world. Much like colors on a color wheel, the existence of basic emotions suggests that cultures shape, mold, and color our emotional lives by using the set of basic emotions as a starting point to create other emotions.

—DAVID MATSUMOTO (2000)

Theories of Emotion

Explaining Emotion

Key Theme

- **Emotion theories emphasize different aspects of emotion, but all have influenced the direction of emotion research.**

Key Questions

- **What are the basic principles and key criticisms of the James–Lange theory of emotion?**
- **How do the facial feedback hypothesis and other contemporary research support aspects of the James–Lange theory?**
- **What are the two-factor theory and the cognitive appraisal theory of emotion, and how do they emphasize cognitive factors in emotion?**

For more than a century, American psychologists have actively debated theories to explain emotion. Like many controversies in psychology, the debate helped shape the direction of psychological research. And, in fact, the earliest psychological theory of emotion, proposed by William James more than a century ago, continues to influence psychological research (Bechara & Naqvi, 2004; Dalgleish, 2004).

In this section, we'll look at the most influential theories of emotion. As you'll see, theories of emotion differ in terms of *which* component of emotion receives the most emphasis—subjective experience, physiological arousal, or expressive behavior.

The James–Lange Theory of Emotion

Do You Run Because You're Afraid? Or Are You Afraid Because You Run?

Imagine that you're walking to your car through the deserted college parking lot late at night. Suddenly, a shadowy figure emerges from behind a parked car. As he starts to move toward you, you walk more quickly. "Hey, what's your hurry?" he calls out, and he picks up his pace.

Common sense says we lose our fortune, are sorry and weep; we meet a bear, are frightened and run; we are insulted by a rival, are angry and strike. The hypothesis here to be defended says that this order of sequence is incorrect, that the one mental state is not immediately induced by the other, that the bodily manifestations must first be interposed between, and that the more rational statement is that we feel sorry because we cry, angry because we strike, afraid because we tremble.

—WILLIAM JAMES (1894)

Your heart starts pounding as you break into a run. Reaching your car, you fumble with the keys, then jump in and lock the doors. Your hands are trembling so badly you can barely get the key into the ignition, but somehow you manage, and you hit the accelerator, zooming out of the parking lot and onto a main street. Still feeling shaky, you ease off the accelerator pedal a bit, wipe your sweaty palms on your jeans, and will yourself to calm down. After several minutes, you breathe a sigh of relief.

In this example, all three emotion components are clearly present. You experienced a subjective feeling that you labeled as "fear." You experienced physical arousal—trembling, sweating, pounding heart, and rapid breathing. And you expressed the fear, both in your facial expression and by bolting into a run. What caused this constellation of effects that you experienced as fear?

The common sense view of emotion would suggest that you (1) recognized a threatening situation and (2) reacted by feeling fearful. This subjective experience of fear (3) activated your sympathetic nervous system and (4) triggered fearful behavior. In one of the first psychological theories of emotion, **William James** (1884) disagreed with this common sense view, proposing a very different explanation of emotion. Danish psychologist Carl Lange proposed a very similar theory at about the same time (see James, 1894; Lange & James, 1922). Thus, this theory, illustrated in Figure 8.11, is known as the **James–Lange theory of emotion.**

Consider our example again. According to the James–Lange theory, your heart didn't pound and you didn't run because you were afraid. Rather, the James–Lange theory holds that you felt afraid *because* your heart pounded and you ran. Feedback from your physiological arousal and from the muscles involved in your behavior caused your subjective feeling of fearfulness. Thus, James believed that emotion follows this sequence: (1) We perceive a stimulus; (2) physiological and behavioral changes occur, which (3) we experience as a particular emotion.

The James–Lange theory stimulated a great deal of research, much of it consisting of attempts to disprove the theory. In 1927, the famous American physiologist **Walter Cannon** challenged the James–Lange theory. First, Cannon pointed out that body reactions are similar for many emotions, yet our subjective experience of various emotions is very different. For example, both fear and rage are accompanied by increased heart rate, but we have no difficulty distinguishing between the two emotions.

Second, Cannon (1927) argued that our emotional reaction to a stimulus is often faster than our physiological reaction. Here's an example to illustrate this

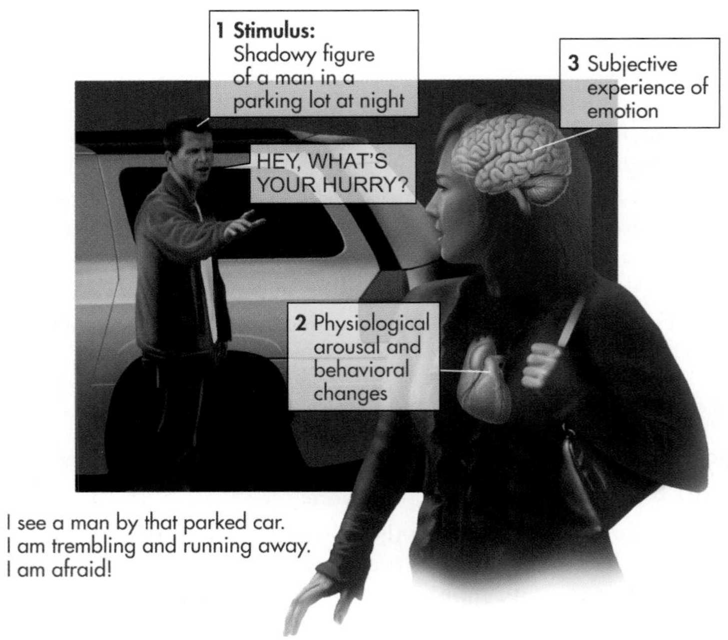

Figure 8.11 The James–Lange Theory of Emotion According to William James, we don't tremble and run because we are afraid, we are afraid because we tremble and run. James believed that body signals trigger emotional experience. These signals include physiological arousal and feedback from the muscles involved in behavior. The James–Lange theory inspired a great deal of research, but only limited aspects of the theory have been supported by research evidence.

point: Sandy's car started to slide out of control on a wet road. She felt fear as the car began to skid, but it was only *after* the car was under control, a few moments later, that her heart began to pound and her hands started to tremble. Cannon correctly noted that it can take several seconds for the physiological changes caused by activation of the sympathetic nervous system to take effect, but the subjective experience of emotion is often virtually instantaneous.

Third, artificially inducing physiological changes does not necessarily produce a related emotional experience. In one early test of the James–Lange theory, Spanish psychologist Gregorio Marañon (1924) injected several subjects with the hormone *epinephrine,* more commonly known as *adrenaline.* Epinephrine activates the sympathetic nervous system. When asked how they felt, the subjects simply reported the physical changes produced by the drug, saying, "My heart is beating very fast." Some reported feeling "as if" they should be feeling an emotion, but they said they did not feel the emotion itself: "I feel *as if* I were afraid."

James (1894) also proposed that if a person were cut off from feeling body changes, he would not experience true emotions. If he felt anything, he would experience only intellectualized, or "cold," emotions. To test this hypothesis, Cannon and his colleagues (1927) disabled the sympathetic nervous system of cats. But the cats still reacted with catlike rage when barking dogs were present: They hissed, growled, and lifted one paw to defend themselves.

What about humans? The sympathetic nervous system operates via the spinal cord. Thus, it made sense to James (1894) that people with spinal cord injuries would experience a decrease in emotional intensity, because they would not be aware of physical arousal or other bodily changes.

Once again, however, research has not supported the James–Lange theory. For example, Dutch psychologist Bob Bermond and his colleagues (1991) found that individuals with spinal cord injuries reported that their experience of fear, anger, grief, sentimentality, and joyfulness had either increased in intensity or was unchanged since their injury. Other researchers have reported similar results (e.g., Chwalisz & others, 1988; Cobos & others, 2004).

James–Lange theory of emotion The theory that emotions arise from the perception of body changes.

"Is that one of the emotions people talk about?"

Evidence Supporting the James–Lange Theory

On the one hand, you'd think that the James–Lange theory of emotion should be nothing more than a historical artifact at this point. Cannon's critique certainly seemed to demolish it. On the other hand, the brilliance of William James is reflected in the fact that researchers keep finding research support for key points in his theory of emotion.

For example, look back at the Focus on Neuroscience on page 351 describing the PET-scan study by Antonio Damasio and his colleagues (2000). It showed that each of the basic emotions produced a distinct pattern of brain activity, a finding that lends support to the James–Lange theory. To generate a particular basic emotion, the participants were asked to recall an emotionally charged memory and then to signal the researcher when they began subjectively "feeling" the target emotion.

The PET scans showed that areas of the brain's *somatosensory cortex,* which processes sensory information from the skin, muscles, and internal organs, were activated during emotional experiences. Interestingly, these internal changes were registered in the somatosensory cortex *before* the participants reported "feeling" the emotion. Along with demonstrating the importance of internal physiological feedback in emotional experience, Damasio's study supports another basic premise of the James–Lange theory: that physiological changes occur *before* we subjectively experience an emotion.

Other contemporary research has supported James's contention that the perception of internal bodily signals is a fundamental ingredient in the subjective experience of emotion (Dalgleish, 2004). For example, in a study by Hugo Critchley and his colleagues (2004), participants who were highly sensitive to their own internal body signals were more likely to experience anxiety and other negative emotions than people who were less sensitive.

Say "Cheese!" Here's a simple test of the facial feedback hypothesis. In a clever study by Fritz Strack and his colleagues (1988), participants who held a pen between their teeth *(left)* thought that cartoons were funnier than participants who held a pen between their lips *(right)*. How does this finding support the facial feedback hypothesis?

Research on the **facial feedback hypothesis** also supports the notion that our bodily responses affect our subjective experience. The facial feedback hypothesis states that expressing a specific emotion, especially facially, causes us to subjectively experience that emotion. Supporting this are studies showing that when people mimic the facial expressions characteristic of a given emotion, such as anger or fear, they tend to report *feeling* the emotion (Duclos & others, 1989; Flack & others, 1999; Schnall & Laird, 2003).

The basic explanation for this phenomenon is that the facial muscles send feedback signals to the brain. In turn, the brain uses this information to activate and regulate emotional experience, intensifying or lessening emotion (Izard, 1990a, 1990b). In line with this explanation, Paul Ekman and Richard Davidson (1993) demonstrated that deliberately creating a "happy" smile produces brain-activity changes similar to those caused by spontaneously producing a happy smile in response to a real event. Collectively, the evidence for the facial feedback hypothesis adds support for aspects of the James–Lange theory.

Cognitive Theories of Emotion

A second theory of emotion, proposed by Stanley Schachter and Jerome Singer, was influential for a short time. Schachter and Singer (1962) agreed with James that physiological arousal is a central element in emotion. But they also agreed with Cannon that physiological arousal is very similar for different emotions. Thus, arousal alone would not produce an emotional response.

Instead, Schachter and Singer proposed that we cognitively label physiological arousal as a given emotion based on our appraisal of a situation. Thus, according to the **two-factor theory of emotion,** illustrated in Figure 8.12, emotion is the result of the *interaction* of physiological arousal and the cognitive label we use to explain our stirred-up state.

Schachter and Singer (1962) tested their theory in a clever, but flawed, experiment. Male volunteers were injected with epinephrine, which produces sympathetic nervous system arousal: accelerated heartbeat, rapid breathing, trembling, and so forth. One group was informed that their symptoms were caused by the injection, but the other group was not given this explanation.

One at a time, the volunteers experienced a situation that was designed to be either irritating or humorous. Schachter and Singer predicted that the subjects who were *informed* that their physical symptoms were caused by the drug injection would be less likely to attribute their symptoms to an emotion caused by the situation. Conversely, the subjects who were *not informed* that their physical symptoms were caused by the drug injection would label their symptoms as an emotion produced by the situation.

facial feedback hypothesis
The view that expressing a specific emotion, especially facially, causes the subjective experience of that emotion.

two-factor theory of emotion
Schachter and Singer's theory that emotion is the interaction of physiological arousal and the cognitive label that we apply to explain the arousal.

cognitive appraisal theory of emotion
The theory that emotional responses are triggered by a cognitive evaluation.

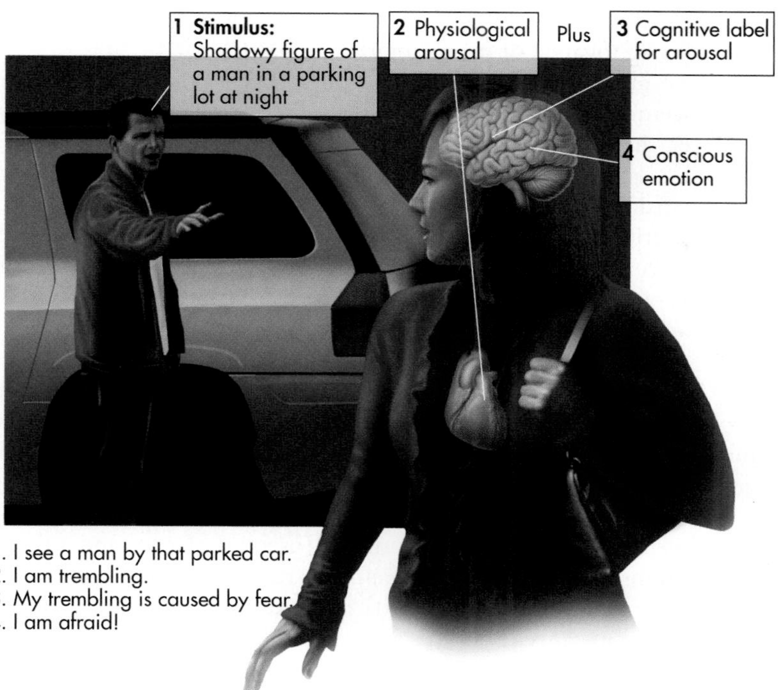

Figure 8.12 The Two-Factor Theory of Emotion According to Stanley Schachter and Jerome Singer, emotional experience requires the interaction of two separate factors: (1) physiological arousal and (2) a cognitive *label* for that arousal.

The results partially supported their predictions. The subjects who were not informed tended to report feeling either happier or angrier than the informed subjects.

Schachter and Singer's theory inspired a flurry of research. The bottom line of those research efforts? The two-factor theory of emotion received little support (Reisenzein, 1983). Nevertheless, Schachter and Singer's theory stimulated a new line of research on the importance of cognition in emotion.

To help illustrate the final theory of emotion that we'll consider, let's go back to the shadowy figure lurking in your college parking lot. Suppose that as the guy called out to you, "Hey, what's your hurry?" you recognized his voice as that of a good friend. Your emotional reaction, of course, would be very different. This simple observation is the basic premise of the **cognitive appraisal theory of emotion.**

Developed by psychologists Craig Smith and Richard Lazarus (1988, 1993), the cognitive appraisal theory of emotion asserts that the most important aspect of an emotional experience is your cognitive interpretation, or *appraisal,* of the situation or stimulus. That is, emotions result from our appraisal of the *personal meaning* of events and experiences. Thus, the same situation might elicit very different emotions in different people (Smith & Kirby, 2000; Smith & others, 2006).

So, in the case of the shadowy figure in the parking lot, your relief that you were not on the verge of being attacked by a mugger could quickly turn to another emotion. If it's a good friend you hadn't seen for a while, your relief might turn to

Appraisal and Emotion: Score! According to cognitive appraisal theory, how you cognitively appraise the personal significance of an event will determine the emotion that you experience. Go to any popular sports bar during a big playoff game and you'll see evidence of this viewpoint. Two friends, each passionately rooting for a different team, will have very different emotional responses to the winning goal—even though the emotion-producing stimulus is exactly the same. Whether a sports fan experiences elation or dismay depends on what the event means to him personally.

pleasure, even joy. If it's someone that you'd prefer to avoid, relief might transform itself into annoyance or even anger.

At first glance, the cognitive appraisal theory and the Schachter–Singer two-factor theory seem very similar. Both theories emphasize the importance of cognitive appraisal. However, the two-factor theory says that emotion results from physiological arousal *plus* a cognitive label. In contrast, some appraisal theorists stressed that cognitive appraisal *is* the essential trigger for an emotional response (Lazarus, 1995).

Some critics of the cognitive appraisal approach objected that emotional reactions to events were virtually instantaneous—too rapid to allow for the process of cognitive appraisal. Instead, Robert Zajonc suggested (1998, 2000), *we feel first and think later.* Today's emotion researchers recognize that emotions can be triggered in *multiple* ways (Forgas, 2008; Scherer & Ellgring, 2007). Complex stimuli—like social situations or personal interactions—must be cognitively appraised before an emotion is generated. And complex emotional responses—like mixed emotions, pride, shame, or guilt—are likely to involve conscious, cognitive processes (Izard, 2007).

On the other hand, some emotional responses are virtually instantaneous, bypassing conscious consideration. As Joseph LeDoux and other neuroscientists have demonstrated, the human brain can respond to biologically significant threats *without* involving conscious cognitive processes (Kihlstrom & others, 2000). So at least in some instances, we do seem to feel first and think later.

>> Closing Thoughts

Psychologists have been interested in the topics of motivation and emotion since the very beginning of psychology as a science. Today, psychologists are acutely aware that all motives reflect the dynamic interaction of biological, psychological, and social factors, including cultural forces. This interaction is perhaps most apparent in the case of human sexuality. Richard's story, told in the chapter Prologue, demonstrates how diverse motives can influence the trajectory of a life, from competing in high school athletics to moving to San Francisco.

Emotions, too, reflect the interaction among biological factors shaped by evolution and personal, cultural, and social factors. As you've read this chapter, we hope you've thought about the multiple factors that influence your own motives and emotional responses in different areas of your life. Finally, in Enhancing Well-Being with Psychology, at the end of the chapter, we'll show you how you can use psychological research to help you achieve *your* goals and aspirations.

ENHANCING WELL-BEING WITH PSYCHOLOGY

Turning Your Goals into Reality

Most people can identify different aspects of their lives they'd like to change. Identifying goals we'd like to achieve is usually easy. Successfully accomplishing these goals is the tricky part. Fortunately, psychological research has identified several strategies and suggestions that can help you get motivated, act, and achieve your goals.

Self-Efficacy: Optimistic Beliefs About Your Capabilities

Your motivation to strive for achievement is closely linked to what you believe about your ability to produce the necessary or desired results in a situation. This is what psychologist Albert Bandura (1997, 2006) calls **self-efficacy**—the degree to which you are convinced of your ability to effectively meet the demands of a particular situation.

Bandura (1997, 2006) has found that if you have an optimistic sense of self-efficacy, you will approach a difficult task as a challenge to be mastered. You will also exert strong motivational effort, persist in the face of obstacles, and look for creative ways to overcome obstacles. If you see yourself as competent and capable, you are more likely to strive for higher personal goals (Bayer & Gollwitzer, 2007; Wood & Bandura, 1991).

People tend to avoid challenging situations or tasks that they *believe* exceed their capabilities (Bandura, 1989a). If self-doubts occur, motivation quickly dwindles because the task is perceived as too difficult and threatening. So how do you build your sense of self-efficacy, especially in situations in which your confidence is shaky?

According to Bandura (1991, 2006), the most effective way to strengthen your sense of self-efficacy is through *mastery experiences*—experiencing success at moderately challenging tasks in which you have to overcome obstacles and persevere. As you tackle a challenging task, you should strive for progressive improvement rather than perfection on your first attempt. Understand that setbacks serve a useful purpose in teaching that success usually requires sustained effort. If you experienced only easy successes, you'd be more likely to become disappointed and discouraged, and to abandon your efforts when you did experience failure (Miceli & Castelfranchi, 2000).

A second strategy is *social modeling,* or *observational learning.* In some situations, the motivation to succeed is present, but you lack the knowledge of exactly how to achieve your goals. In such circumstances, it can be helpful to observe and imitate the behavior of someone who is already competent at the task you want to master (Bandura, 1986, 1990). For example, if you're not certain how to prepare effectively for a test or a class presentation, talk with fellow students who *are* successful in doing this. Ask how they study and what they do when they have difficulty understanding material. Knowing what works is often the critical element in ensuring success.

Implementation Intentions: Turning Goals into Actions

Suppose your sense of self-efficacy is strong, but you still have trouble putting your intentions into action. For example, have you ever made a list of New Year's resolutions and looked back at it six months later? If you're like most people, you'll wonder what went wrong.

How can you bridge the gap between good intentions and effective, goal-directed behavior? German psychologist Peter Gollwitzer (1999) points out that many people have trouble *initiating* the actions required to fulfill their goals and then *persisting* in these behaviors until the goals are achieved. Gollwitzer and his colleagues (2008) have identified some simple yet effective techniques that help people translate their good intentions into actual behavior.

Step 1: Form a goal intention.

This step involves translating vague, general intentions ("I'm going to do my best") into a specific, concrete, and binding goal. Express the specific goal in terms of "I intend to achieve _______ ," filling in the blank with the particular behavior or outcome that you wish to achieve. For example, suppose you made a New Year's resolution to exercise more regularly. Transform that general goal into a much more specific goal intention, such as "I intend to go to aerobics class three times a week." Forming the specific goal intention enhances your sense of personal commitment to the goal, and it also heightens your sense of obligation to realize the goal.

Step 2: Create implementation intentions.

This step involves making a specific plan for turning your good intention into reality. The trick is to specify exactly where, when, and how you will carry out your intended behavior. Mentally link the intended behaviors to specific situational cues, such as saying, "After my psychology class, I will go to the campus athletic center and attend the noon aerobics class in Room 201." By linking the behavior to specific situational cues, you're more likely to initiate the goal behavior when the critical situation is encountered (Oettingen & Gollwitzer, 2001). The ultimate goal

self-efficacy
The degree to which a person is convinced of his or her ability to effectively meet the demands of a particular situation.

of implementation intentions is to create new habits or routines in your life (Aarts & Dijksterhuis, 2000).

As simple as this seems, research has demonstrated that forming specific implementation intentions is very effective (Gollwitzer & Sheeran, 2006; Parks-Stamm & others, 2007). For example, one study involved student volunteers with no enticement for participating in the research, such as money or course credit. Just before the students left for the holidays, they were instructed to write an essay describing how they spent Christmas Eve. The essay had to be written and mailed within two days after Christmas Eve.

Half of the participants were instructed to write out specific implementation intentions describing exactly when and where they would write the report during the critical 48-hour period. They were also instructed to visualize the chosen opportunity and mentally commit themselves to it.

The other half of the participants were not asked to identify a specific time or place, but just instructed to write and mail the report within the 48 hours. The results? Of those in the implementation intention group, 71 percent wrote and mailed the report by the deadline. Only 32 percent of the other group did so (Gollwitzer & Brandstätter, 1997).

Mental Rehearsal: Visualize the Process

The mental images you create in anticipation of a situation can strongly influence your sense of self-efficacy and self-control as well as the effectiveness of your implementation intentions (Gollwitzer, 1999; Ozer & Bandura, 1990). For example, students sometimes undermine their own performance by vividly imagining their worst fears, such as becoming overwhelmed by anxiety during a class presentation or going completely blank during a test. However, the opposite is also possible. Mentally visualizing yourself dealing *effectively* with a situation can enhance your performance (Libby & others, 2007; Conway & others, 2004). Athletes, in particular, are aware of this and mentally rehearse their performance prior to competition.

So strive to control your thoughts in an optimistic way by mentally focusing on your capabilities and a positive outcome, not your limitations and worst fears. The key here is not just imagining a positive outcome. Instead, imagine and mentally rehearse the *process*—the skills you will effectively use and the steps you will take—to achieve the outcome *you* want (Pham & Taylor, 1999). Go for it!

CHAPTER REVIEW: KEY PEOPLE AND TERMS

Walter Cannon, p. 356
Charles Darwin, p. 345
Edward L. Deci, p. 341
Paul Ekman, p. 352
William James, p. 356
Abraham Maslow, p. 340
Richard M. Ryan, p. 341

motivation, p. 319
instinct theories, p. 319
drive theories, p. 320
homeostasis, p. 320
drive, p. 320
incentive theories, p. 321
arousal theory, p. 321
sensation seeking, p. 321
humanistic theories of motivation, p. 321
glucose, p. 323
insulin, p. 323
basal metabolic rate (BMR), p. 323
adipose tissue, p. 323
energy homeostasis, p. 324
ghrelin, p. 324
positive incentive value, p. 325
satiation, p. 325
cholecystokinin (CCK), p. 325
sensory-specific satiety, p. 326
leptin, p. 326
neuropeptide Y (NPY), p. 327
set-point theory, p. 327
settling-point models of weight regulation, p. 327
body mass index (BMI), p. 329
obese, p. 329
cafeteria diet effect, p. 330
leptin resistance, p. 331
weight cycling, p. 331
sexual orientation, p. 335
hierarchy of needs, p. 340
self-actualization, p. 340
self-determination theory (SDT), p. 341
intrinsic motivation, p. 342
extrinsic motivation, p. 342
competence motivation, p. 343
achievement motivation, p. 343
Thematic Apperception Test (TAT), p. 343
emotion, p. 344
emotional intelligence, p. 345
basic emotions, p. 346
interpersonal engagement, p. 346
amygdala, p. 349
anthropomorphism, p. 353
display rules, p. 354
James–Lange theory of emotion, p. 356
facial feedback hypothesis, p. 358
two-factor theory of emotion, p. 358
cognitive appraisal theory of emotion, p. 359
self-efficacy, p. 361

Web Companion Review Activities

You can find additional review activities at **www.worthpublishers.com/discoveringpsych5e.** The *Discovering Psychology* 5th edition Web Companion has self-scoring practice quizzes, flashcards, interactive crossword puzzles, and other activities to help you master the material in this chapter.

CONCEPT MAP

MOTIVATION AND EMOTION

Motivation

Forces that act on or within an organism to imitate or direct behavior

Characterized by:

- Activation
- Persistence
- Intensity

Motivational Concepts and Theories

Instinct theories: Some behaviors are innate and due to evolutionary programming.

Drive theories: Behaviors are motivated by **drives** to maintain **homeostasis.**

Incentive theories: Behaviors are motivated by external rewards.

Arousal theory: People are motivated to maintain optimal levels of arousal.
Sensation seeking: Motivates behaviors involving high levels of arousal.

Humanistic theories: Behaviors are motivated by psychological factors, especially the motive to achieve one's highest potential.

Biological Motivation: Hunger and Eating

Food provides **glucose,** which is regulated by **insulin.** Excess glucose is stored in **adipose tissue.**
Basic metabolic rate (BMR) is the rate at which your body uses energy for vital body functions.
Energy homeostasis helps people maintain their baseline body weight.

Physiological factors correlated with eating:

- Glucose
- Insulin
- **Ghrelin**

Psychological factors that trigger eating:

- Classically conditioned stimuli
- **Positive incentive value**

Satiation signals:

- **Cholecystokinin (CCK)**
- **Sensory-specific satiety**

Chemical signals that regulate body weight:

- **Leptin**
- **Insulin**
- **Neuropeptide Y**
- **Ghrelin**

Explaining long-term weight regulation:

- **Set-point theory**
- **Settling-point models**

Factors contributing to excess weight and obesity:

- Inadequate sleep
- Availability of foods with positive incentive value
- Overeating
- **Cafeteria diet effect**
- Individual differences in BMR
- Sedentary lifestyles
- Genetic susceptibility
- **Leptin resistance**
- **Weight cycling due to frequent dieting**

Human Sexuality

Stages of human sexual response:

- Excitement, plateau, orgasm, resolution

In nonhuman animals, sexual behavior is biologically determined, typically triggered by hormonal changes in the female.

Sexual orientation:

- Not easily categorized
- Causes are unknown
- Develops at an early age and is resistant to change
- Homosexual orientation associated with gender-atypical play in childhood

Motivation

Psychological Needs

Abraham Maslow (1908–1970)
Hierarchy of needs: Motives are arranged in a hierarchy from basic survival needs to self-actualization.

Edward L. Deci (b. 1942) and **Richard Ryan** (b. 1953)
Self-determination theory (SDT)
Stresses importance of:
- Autonomy
- Competence
- Relatedness
- Intrinsic motives versus extrinsic motives

Competence motivation:
- Striving to be capable and exercise control

Achievement motivation:
- Striving to excel and outperform others
- Measured by the **Thematic Apperception Test (TAT)**

Emotion

Components:
- Subjective experience
- Physiological response
- Behavioral or expressive response

Functions of emotions:
- Trigger motivated behavior
- Contribute to rational decision making and purposeful behavior
- Helps solve adaptive problems
- May involve arousal of sympathetic nervous system
- Fear activates the **amygdala**

Theories of Emotion

Cognitive appraisal theory:
Theorists: Craig Smith and Richard Lazarus
- Emotions are triggered by cognitive evaluations of events.

James–Lange theory:
Theorist: William James (1842–1910)
- Emotion results from perception of biological and behavioral responses
- **Facial feedback hypothesis:** Facial expression of emotion creates subjective experience of the emotion

Two-factor theory:
Theorists: Stanley Schachter & Jerome Singer
- Emotion results from applying a cognitive label to feelings of arousal.

Basic emotions:
- Biologically determined and culturally universal
- Include fear, disgust, surprise, happiness, anger, and sadness
- Collectivistic cultures emphasize emotions involving **interpersonal engagement**
- Emotional expression is regulated by **cultural display rules**

Paul Ekman (b. 1934):
- Analyzed facial expressions
- Demonstrated that facial expressions for basic emotions are culturally universal

CHAPTER 9

Lifespan Development

Chapter Outline

Future Plans

PROLOGUE

WE'VE MOVED A COUPLE OF TIMES since we began the first edition of this textbook. Although we know the drill, moving never seems to go smoothly. Despite the best of intentions, the night before the moving van shows up is always a chaotic, frenzied scene. Jumbled piles of assorted, random objects get frantically tossed into boxes as the piercing shrieks of packing tape make the cats race out of the room. "This can all get sorted out later," we reason. This rationalization works well, of course, until "later" actually arrives, and we're confronted by the sea of boxes marked "basement," "files," and "miscellaneous."

Moving is one of those events that forces you to reflect on your past as bits and pieces of memories are unearthed from the corners of closets and drawers, pantry shelves, and storage cabinets. Laura was especially intrigued by a dilapidated cardboard box that held an assortment of books. One small, black book caught her eye. Nearly every page contained notations made in Don's neat handwriting.

"What are all these old books?" she asked.

"The one you're holding is your dad's pilot logbook. The others are his pilot's training manuals," Sandy replied. "I think his skydiving manuals are in there, too."

But it's not just glimpses of our own lives that resurface. Somehow, we've ended up the keepers of our extended families' treasures. Not treasures in the sense of expensive jewelry or antique silver. Treasures like the one that Laura pulled out of one of the many boxes marked "miscellaneous." It was a hand-colored portrait photo of a beautiful young woman with delicate features, blue eyes, dark hair, and a tentative smile.

"Who is this?" Laura asked.

"That's Grandma Fern, when she was about your age. Wasn't she pretty?" Sandy reached into the box and pulled out another treasure, carefully wrapped. A framed black-and-white photo. "Look, here's Grandpa Erv and Grandma Fern's wedding photo."

"How come Grandma isn't wearing a white wedding dress?"

"Well, Grandma Fern and Grandpa Erv got married right after World War II. It was the style then to wear a tailored suit. I don't know when long, white dresses came back into style, but it sure wasn't in the 1940s. Not for working families, anyway. Nobody had extra money, and there were all kinds of shortages. Just think—Fernie was only 19 years old, not much older than you are now!"

"What's this old thing?" Laura asked as she held up a new treasure. The postmark on the crumbling old cardboard mailing tube was gone, but you could still see the

U.S. postage stamp—½¢. Sandy pulled an engraved certificate out of the tube and carefully unrolled it. In ornate, deep blue script, it read:

> *This certifies that* ***Erwin Schmidt*** *has been awarded membership in the '49ers, an organization of young businessmen chosen from among the boy salesmen of Liberty Weekly.*
>
> *He has been selected because of his exceptional sales achievements, outstanding character, splendid personality, and unquestioned loyalty to his duties.*
>
> *It is now his right to wear the gold badge of membership and to enjoy all the privileges of the '49ers.*
>
> *Signed and sealed this* ***10th*** *day of* ***October, 1930.***

"1930," Sandy said, shaking her head in amazement. "Erv would have been only 12 years old. I can't believe he saved this for all those years."

All of us are shaped by the communities in which we grow up. In Fern's case, that community was a tiny farming town in rural Wisconsin in the 1930s. Even though Fern's parents were born in Wisconsin, they still spoke Norwegian at home. In contrast to Fern's childhood spent caring for her younger siblings and roaming the woods and hills, Erv was an only child in the thriving German community of Chicago's Lincoln Square in the 1920s. Fern's stories of chasing chickens to catch and kill for Sunday dinner and jumping across swollen streams each spring on her way to school were hard for her children and grandchildren to believe. But so were Erv's stories of roller-skating down city streets and sleeping on fire escapes or the shores of Lake Michigan on hot summer nights in the city.

We're also profoundly influenced by historical events. Just as the Great Depression defined Fern's and Erv's childhoods, World War II defined their young adult years. Among the treasures we discovered were shoeboxes filled with curling black-and-white snapshots that Erv took of his buddies at the Army Air Force's training camp right before he "shipped out" for the Philippines and New Guinea.

"Mom, what is this thing?" Laura asked, pulling a dangerous-looking tool from a dusty canvas U.S. Army surplus bag. "That's my rock pick," Sandy replied. "Be careful with that—it's pretty sharp. Just think, I used to be able to take that onboard with me when I flew out west to go rock collecting."

"Seriously?" Laura said in disbelief. Of course, Laura doesn't remember a time when people got on planes without having their carry-on luggage searched for potential weapons. "Threat level: Orange" is just an accepted part of daily life for her generation, as bread lines and victory gardens were for her grandparents.

Even at age 18, Laura already had her own boxes of memories from earlier chapters in her life. Legos, Beanie Babies, and Barbies filled a couple of boxes in one corner. Another box held college catalogs, SAT practice tests, programs from high school events, and pictures of friends. And then there were the stacks of T-shirts, commemorating everything from state soccer championships and homecoming games to fund raisers for the Oklahoma Firefighters' Burn Camp.

"You really need to sort through all that stuff and decide what you want to keep," Sandy said.

It's a task that each of us faces: what to keep and why. Why did Erv keep his faded award certificate? Or his gymnastics medals, high school report cards, and eighth-grade autograph book that Sandy found carefully preserved in an old cigar box? Why did Don keep all of his pilot logs, his skydiving manuals, and his father's cufflinks? For that matter, why did Sandy still have her rock pick?

However ordinary or random they may appear to the casual observer who later discovers them, those carefully preserved "treasures" reflect the way you perceive—and remember—your own life story.

"Oh cool! This paperweight is over 100 years old. It says 'To Momma, From Donald, Iowa State Fair, 1908.' Can I have this?"

"Your great-uncle Donald made that for your great-grandmother Gertrude when he was just a little boy. Your dad was named after your great-uncle Donald, which is why that glass paperweight is one of your dad's prized treasures. So you'll have to ask your dad, but I think he was planning to give you that treasure at some point in the future."

>> Introduction: Your Life Story

Key Theme

- **Developmental psychology is the study of how people change over the lifespan.**

Key Questions

- **What are the eight basic stages of the lifespan?**
- **What are some of the key themes in developmental psychology?**

developmental psychology
The branch of psychology that studies how people change over the lifespan.

One way to look at the "big picture" of your life is to think of your life as a story. You, of course, are the main character. Your life story so far has had a distinct plot, occasional subplots, and a cast of supporting characters, including family, friends, and lovers.

Like every other person's life story, yours has been influenced by factors beyond your control. One such factor is the unique combination of genes you inherited from your biological mother and father. Another is the historical era during which you grew up. Your individual development has also been shaped by the cultural, social, and family contexts within which you were raised.

The patterns of your life story, and the life stories of countless other people, are the focus of **developmental psychology**—the study of how people change physically, mentally, and socially throughout the lifespan. Developmental psychologists investigate the influence of biological, environmental, social, cultural, and behavioral factors on development at every age and stage of life.

However, the impact of these factors on individual development is greatly influenced by attitudes, perceptions, and personality characteristics. For example, the adjustment to middle school may be a breeze for one child, but a nightmare for another. So although we are influenced by the events we experience, we also shape the meaning and consequences of those events.

Along with studying common patterns of growth and change, developmental psychologists look at the ways in which people *differ* in their development and life

Continuity and Change over the Lifespan The twin themes of continuity and change throughout the lifespan are evident in the changing nature of relationships. Childhood friendships center on sharing activities, while peer relationships in adolescence emphasize sharing thoughts and feelings. Early adulthood brings the challenge of forming intimate relationships and beginning a family. Close relationships with friends and family continue to contribute to psychological well-being in late adulthood.

stories. As we'll note several times in this chapter, the typical, or "normal," pattern of development can also vary among cultures.

Developmental psychologists often conceptualize the lifespan in terms of basic *stages* of development (see Table 9.1). Traditionally, the stages of the lifespan are defined by age, which implies that we experience relatively sudden, age-related changes as we move from one stage to the next. Indeed, some of life's transitions *are* rather abrupt, such as entering the workforce, becoming a parent, or retiring. And some aspects of development, such as prenatal development and language development, are closely tied to *critical periods,* which are periods during which a child is maximally sensitive to environmental influences.

Still, most of our physical, mental, and social changes occur gradually. As we trace the typical course of human development in this chapter, the theme of *gradually unfolding changes* throughout the ages and stages of life will become more evident.

Another important theme in developmental psychology is the *interaction between heredity and environment.* Traditionally, this was called the *nature–nurture* issue. Although we are born with a specific genetic potential that we inherit from our biological parents, our environment influences how and when that potential is expressed. In turn, our genetic inheritance influences the ways in which we experience and interact with the environment (Diamond, 2009).

Developmental psychology is a broad field, covering a wide range of topics from many different perspectives. Our goal in this chapter is not to try to survey the entire field of lifespan development. Rather, we'll focus on presenting some of the most influential theories in developmental psychology and the key themes that have guided research on each stage of the lifespan. As we do so, we'll describe the typical patterns of development while noting the importance of individual variation.

Table 9.1

Major Stages of the Lifespan

Stage	Age Range
Prenatal	Conception to birth
Infancy and toddlerhood	Birth to 2 years
Early childhood	2 to 6 years
Middle childhood	6 to 12 years
Adolescence	12 to 18 years
Young adulthood	18 to 40 years
Middle adulthood	40 to 65 years
Late adulthood	65 years to death

The Chapters in Your Life Story If you think of your life as an unfolding story, then the major stages of the human lifespan represent the different "chapters" of your life. Each chapter is characterized by fundamentally different physical, cognitive, and social transitions, challenges and opportunities, demands and adjustments. Comparing different life stories reveals many striking similarities in the developmental themes of any given stage. But beyond those similarities, every life story is also characterized by considerable variations in the timing of life events and the pathways that are ultimately followed. In that sense, every life story is unique.

Genetic Contributions to Your Life Story

Key Theme

- **Your genotype consists of the chromosomes inherited from your biological parents, but your phenotype—the actual characteristics you display—results from the interaction of genetics and environmental factors.**

Key Questions

- **What are DNA, chromosomes, and genes?**
- **What role does the environment play in the relationship between genotype and phenotype?**
- **What is epigenetics?**

You began your life as a **zygote,** a single cell no larger than the period at the end of this sentence. Packed in that tiny cell was the unique set of genetic instructions that you inherited from your biological parents. Today, that same set of genetic information is found in the nucleus of nearly every cell of your body.

What form does that genetic data take? The genetic data you inherited from your biological parents is encoded in the chemical structure of the **chromosomes** that are found in the cell nucleus. As depicted in Figure 9.1, each chromosome is a long, threadlike structure composed of twisted parallel strands of **deoxyribonucleic acid,** abbreviated DNA. Put simply, **DNA** stores the inherited information that guides the development of all living organisms.

Each of your chromosomes has thousands of DNA segments called **genes** that are strung like beads along its length. Each gene is a unit of DNA code for making a particular protein molecule. Interestingly, genes actually make up less than 2 percent of human DNA (Human Genome Program, 2008). Determining the functions of the rest of the DNA is an active area of investigation. This DNA was once

zygote
The single cell formed at conception from the union of the egg cell and sperm cell.

chromosome
A long, threadlike structure composed of twisted parallel strands of DNA; found in the cell nucleus.

deoxyribonucleic acid (DNA)
The double-stranded molecule that encodes genetic instructions; the chemical basis of heredity.

gene
A unit of DNA on a chromosome that encodes instructions for making a particular protein molecule; the basic unit of heredity.

genotype
(JEEN-oh-type) The genetic makeup of an individual organism.

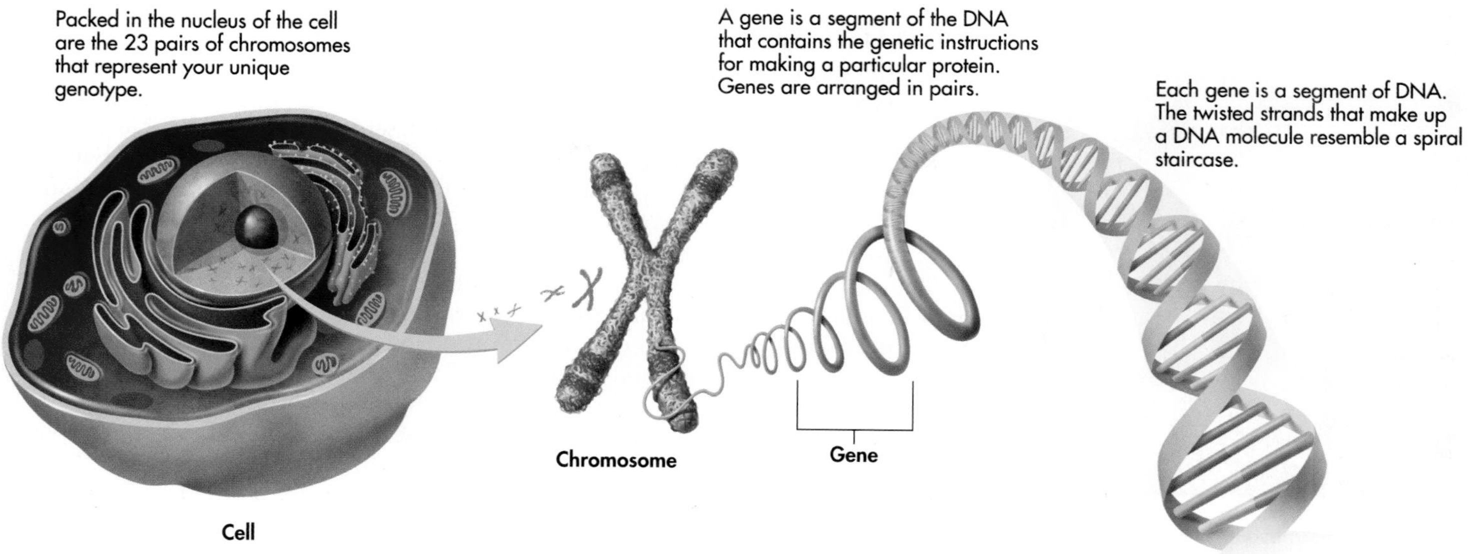

Figure 9.1 Chromosomes, Genes, and DNA Each chromosome contains thousands of genes, and each gene is a unit of DNA instructions. Incredibly fine, the strands of DNA in a single human cell would be more than three inches long if unraveled. If the DNA present in one person were unraveled, it would stretch from Earth to Pluto and back—*twice!*

referred to as "junk DNA," but most researchers today believe that it is involved in regulating gene functioning (Parker & others, 2009; Wray & Babbitt, 2008).

What do genes do? In a nutshell, genes direct the manufacture of proteins. Proteins are used in virtually all of your body's functions—from building cells to manufacturing hormones to regulating brain activity. Your body requires hundreds of thousands of different proteins to function (Henzler-Wildman & Kern, 2007; Marcus, 2004). Each protein is formed by a specific combination of amino acids, and that combination is encoded in a particular gene.

Your Unique Genotype

At fertilization, your biological mother's egg cell and your biological father's sperm cell each contributed 23 chromosomes. This set of 23 chromosome pairs represents your unique **genotype** or genetic makeup. With the exception of the reproductive cells (sperm or eggs), every cell in your body contains a complete, identical copy of your genotype.

Scientists have recently mapped out the *human genome*—the complete set of DNA in the human organism (Human Genome Program, 2008). One surprising discovery was that the complete human genome contains only about 20,000 to 25,000 protein-coding genes, far fewer than previous estimates that put the number as high as 100,000 genes.

Although all humans have the same basic set of genes, these genes can come in different versions, called *alleles.* As a general rule, your genotype contains two copies of each gene—one inherited from each biological parent. These genes may be identical or different. The range of potential alleles varies for individual genes (Baker, 2004). Some genes have just a few different versions, while other genes have 50 or more possible alleles. It is this unique combination of alleles that helps make your genotype—and you—unique.

The best-known, although not the most common, pattern of allele variation is the simple dominant–recessive gene pair. For example, the development of freckles appears to be controlled by a single gene, which can be either dominant or recessive (Zhang & others, 2004). If you inherit a dominant version of the freckles gene from either or both of your biological parents, you'll have the potential to display freckles. But to be freckle-free, you would have to inherit two recessive "no freckles" genes, one from each biological parent.

Unlike freckles, most characteristics involve the interaction of *multiple* genes (Wang & Zhao, 2007). For these characteristics, each gene contributes only a small amount of influence to a particular characteristic.

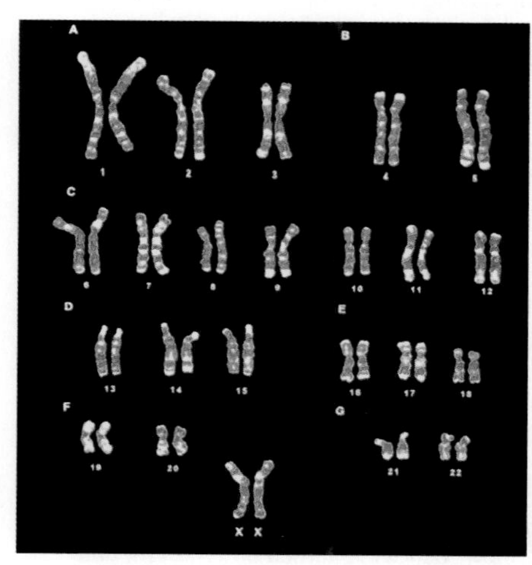

The 23 Pairs of Human Chromosomes Each person's unique genotype is represented in the 23 pairs of chromosomes found in the nucleus of almost all human body cells. This photograph, taken through a microscope, depicts a *karyotype,* which shows one cell's complete set of chromosomes. By convention, the chromosomes are arranged in pairs from largest to smallest, numbered from 1 to 22. The 23rd pair of chromosomes, called the *sex chromosomes,* determines a person's biological sex. The sex chromosomes in this karyotype are XX, indicating a female. A male karyotype would have an XY combination.

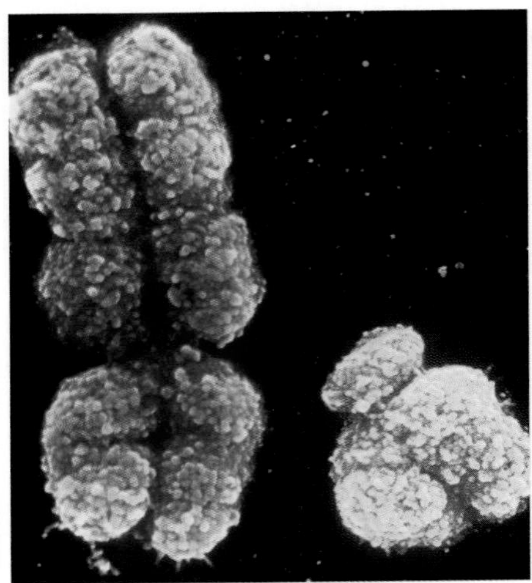

Human Sex Chromosomes: X and Y Biological sex is determined by the 23rd pair of chromosomes, the *sex chromosomes.* While every egg cell has one X chromosome, every sperm cell has either one X or one Y chromosome. Whether a zygote develops into a male or a female depends on whether the egg is fertilized by a sperm cell with a Y chromosome (XY, resulting in a male) or by a sperm cell with an X chromosome (XX, resulting in a female). Notice that the X chromosome (*left*) is larger and has more genes than the Y chromosome (*right*). This confers some protection against certain genetic disorders for females. Why? Because by having two X chromosomes, females are more likely to have a normal allele than a disease-producing allele. If a male has a disease-producing allele on his X chromosome, he is less likely to have a normal allele on his smaller Y chromosome to override it. This is why males are more likely to display various genetic disorders, such as red–green color blindness and hemophilia, which they inherit via the X chromosome contributed by their biological mother.

Most of the genes in each person are dormant. Experience affects which genes are turned on (and off), and when. Thus, the environment participates in sculpting expression of the genome.

ADELE DIAMOND (2009)

phenotype
(FEEN-oh-type) The observable traits or characteristics of an organism as determined by the interaction of genetics and environmental factors.

sex chromosomes
Chromosomes, designated as X or Y, that determine biological sex; the 23rd pair of chromosomes in humans.

From Genotype to Phenotype

While the term *genotype* refers to an organism's unique genetic makeup, the term **phenotype** refers to the characteristics that are actually observed in an organism. In the past, a person's unique genotype was often described as a "genetic blueprint." The blueprint analogy implied that a genotype was a fixed, master plan, like an architectural blueprint. Each person's genetic blueprint was thought to direct and control virtually all aspects of development as it unfolded over the lifespan. But we now know that the genetic blueprint analogy is *not* accurate.

The first problem with the genotype-as-blueprint analogy is that genes don't actually control your physical development or behavior. Rather, your genes direct the synthesis and production of particular proteins. In turn, these proteins are the building blocks of all your body's tissues and functions, which ultimately *do* influence your development and behavior (Marcus, 2004).

Second, environmental factors influence the phenotype you display. For example, even if your genotype contains a copy of the dominant "freckles" gene, you will *not* develop freckles unless the expression of that dominant gene is triggered by a specific environmental factor: sunlight. On the other hand, if you carry two recessive "no freckles" genes, you won't develop freckles no matter how much time you spend in the sunlight.

Here's the important point: *Different genotypes react differently to environmental factors* (Baker, 2004; Rowe, 2003). Thus, psychologists and other scientists often speak of *genetic predispositions* to develop in a particular way (Edwards & Myers, 2007). In other words, people with a particular genetic configuration will be more or less sensitive to particular environmental factors. For example, think of people you know who sunburn easily, such as redheads or people with very fair skin. Their genotype is especially sensitive to the effects of ultraviolet light. One person's freckle factory is another person's light tan—or searing sunburn.

The New Science of Epigenetics

Each of us started life as a single-celled zygote that divided and multiplied. Each new cell contained the exact same set of genetic instructions. Yet some of those cells developed into bones, hair, eyes, joints, lungs, or other specialized tissues. Why, then, are cells so different? How does the single-celled zygote develop into a complex, differentiated organism with kidneys, eyelashes, navels, and kneecaps?

The dramatic differences among the size, shape, and function of cells are due to *which* genes are "expressed" or activated to participate in protein production. Put simply, cells develop differently because different genes are activated at different times. Some genes are active for just a few hours, others for a lifetime. Many genes are *never* expressed. For example, humans carry all of the genes to develop a tail, but we don't develop a tail because those genes are never activated.

What triggers a gene to activate? Gene expression can be triggered by the activity of *other* genes, internal chemical changes, or by external environmental factors, such as sunlight in our earlier freckles example. Thus, gene expression is *flexible,* responsive to both internal and external factors (Panning & Taatjes, 2008; West & others, 2002).

Scientists have only recently begun to understand the processes that guide and determine gene expression. This new field is called **epigenetics**—the study of the mechanisms that control gene expression and its effects on behavior and health (Volkow, 2008). For any given cell, it's the epigenetic "settings" that determine whether it will become a skin cell, a nerve cell, or a heart muscle cell. Thus, epigenetics investigates how gene activity is regulated within a cell, such as identifying the signals that switch genes to "on" or "off."

To help illustrate epigenetic influences, consider identical twins, who develop from a single zygote. Each twin inherits exactly the same set of genes. Yet, as twins develop, differences in physical and psychological characteristics become evident. These differences are due to epigenetic changes—differences in the expression of each twin's genes, *not* to their underlying DNA, which is still identical (Fraga & others, 2005).

The study of epigenetic mechanisms is providing insights into *how* the environment affects gene expression and the phenotype. For example, consider the groundbreaking series of experiments conducted by teams led by Canadian neuroscientist Michael Meaney (2001). He showed that newborn rats that were genetically predisposed to be skittish, nervous, and high-strung would develop into calm, exploratory, and stress-resistant adult rats when raised by genetically unrelated, attentive mother rats. Conversely, newborn rats that were genetically predisposed to be calm and stress-resistant grew up to be nervous, high-strung, and easily stressed out when they were raised by *inattentive*, genetically unrelated mother rats.

The important point is that although the rats' DNA did *not* change, the chemicals that control gene expression *did* change. The rats' upbringing set in motion a cascade of epigenetic changes that changed their brain chemistry and literally "reprogrammed" their behavior (see Hyman, 2009; Sapolsky, 2004). Even more fascinating, the influence of their upbringing extended to the *next* generation: The calm, stress-resistant rats grew up to be attentive mothers themselves.

Interactions among genes, and between the genotype and environmental influences, are two of the critical factors in considering the relationship between genotype and phenotype. Beyond these factors, genes can also *mutate,* or spontaneously change, from one generation to the next. Further, DNA itself can be damaged by environmental factors, such as exposure to ultraviolet light, radiation, or chemical toxins. Just as a typographical error in a complex recipe can ruin a favorite dish, errors in the genetic code can disrupt the production of the correct proteins and lead to birth defects or genetic disorders.

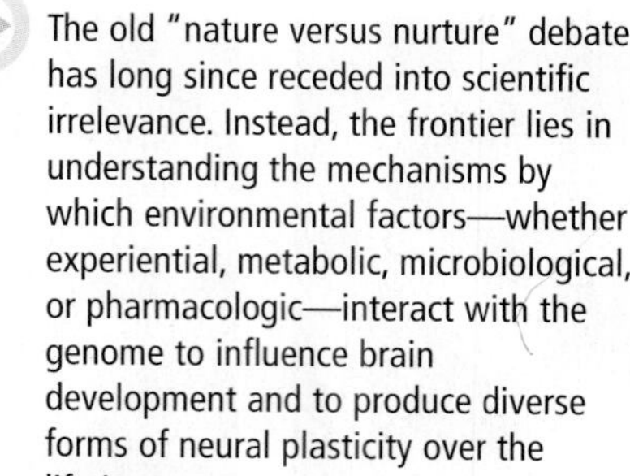

The old "nature versus nurture" debate has long since receded into scientific irrelevance. Instead, the frontier lies in understanding the mechanisms by which environmental factors—whether experiential, metabolic, microbiological, or pharmacologic—interact with the genome to influence brain development and to produce diverse forms of neural plasticity over the lifetime.

STEVEN E. HYMAN (2009)

Prenatal Development

Key Theme

- **During the prenatal stage, the single-celled zygote develops into a full-term fetus.**

Key Questions

- **What are the three stages of prenatal development?**
- **How does the brain develop?**
- **What are teratogens?**

At conception, chromosomes from the biological mother and father combine to form a single cell—the fertilized egg, or *zygote*. Over the relatively brief span of nine months, that single cell develops into the estimated trillion cells that make up a newborn baby. This **prenatal stage** has three distinct phases: the germinal period, the embryonic period, and the fetal period (see photos on page 374).

The Germinal and Embryonic Periods

The **germinal period,** also called the *zygotic period,* represents the first two weeks of prenatal development. During this time, the zygote undergoes rapid cell division before becoming implanted on the wall of the mother's uterus. Some of the zygote's cells will eventually form the structures that house and protect the developing fetus and will provide nourishment from the mother. By the end of the two-week germinal period, the single-celled zygote has developed into a cluster of cells called the *embryo.*

The **embryonic period** begins with week 3 and extends through week 8. During this time of rapid growth and intensive cell differentiation, the organs and major systems of the body form. Genes on the sex chromosomes and hormonal influences also trigger the initial development of the sex organs.

Protectively housed in the fluid-filled *amniotic sac,* the embryo's lifeline is the umbilical cord. Extending from the placenta on the mother's uterine wall to the embryo's abdominal area, the *umbilical cord* delivers nourishment, oxygen, and

epigenetics
Study of the cellular mechanisms that control gene expression and of the ways that gene expression impacts health and behavior

prenatal stage
The stage of development before birth; divided into the germinal, embryonic, and fetal periods.

germinal period
The first two weeks of prenatal development.

embryonic period
The second period of prenatal development, extending from the third week through the eighth week.

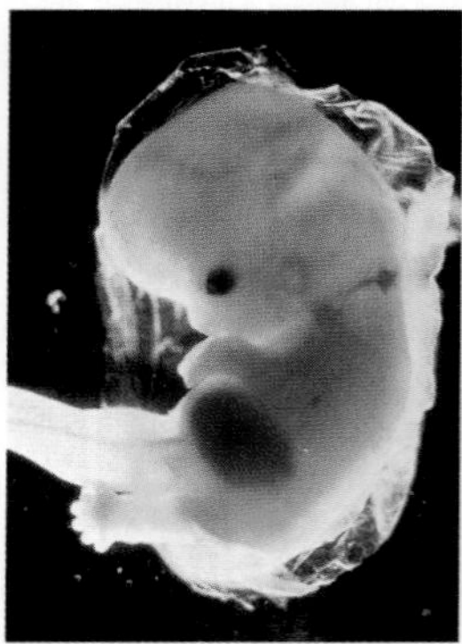

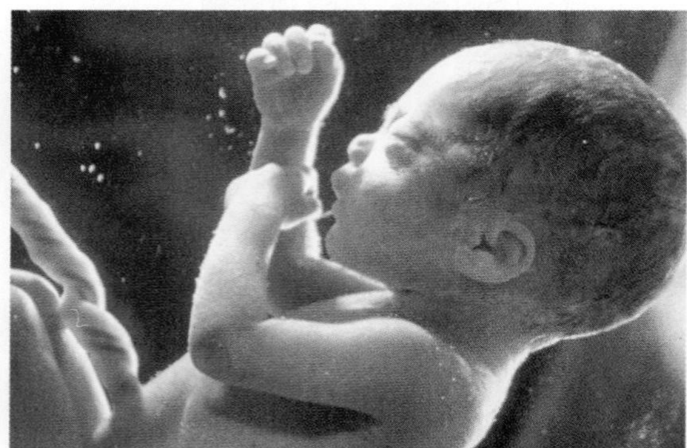

Prenatal Development Although it is less than an inch long, the beginnings of arms, legs, and fingers can already be distinguished in the 7-week-old embryo *(top left)*. The amniotic sac can be clearly seen in this photograph. The fetus at 4 months (*top right*) measures 6 to 10 inches long, and the mother may be able to feel the fetus's movements. Notice the well-formed umbilical cord. Near full term (*bottom*), the 8-month-old fetus gains body fat to help the newborn survive outside the mother's uterus.

water and carries away carbon dioxide and other wastes. The *placenta* is actually a disk-shaped, vascular organ that prevents the mother's blood from directly mingling with that of the developing embryo. Acting as a filter, the placenta prevents many harmful substances that might be present in the mother's blood from reaching the embryo.

The placenta cannot, however, filter out all harmful agents from the mother's blood. Harmful agents or substances that can cause abnormal development or birth defects are called **teratogens.** Generally, the greatest vulnerability to teratogens occurs during the embryonic stage, when major body systems are forming. Known teratogens include:

- Exposure to radiation
- Toxic chemicals and metals, such as mercury, PCBs, and lead
- Viruses and bacteria, such as German measles (rubella), syphilis, genital herpes, and human immunodeficiency virus (HIV)
- Drugs taken by the mother, such as alcohol, cocaine, and heroin

By the end of the embryonic period, the embryo has grown from a cluster of a few hundred cells no bigger than the head of a pin to over an inch in length. Now weighing about an ounce, the embryo looks distinctly human, even though its head accounts for about half its body size.

Prenatal Brain Development

By three weeks after conception, a sheet of primitive neural cells has formed. Just as you might roll a piece of paper to make a tube, this sheet of neural cells curls to form the hollow *neural tube*. The neural tube is lined with stem cells. **Stem cells** are cells that can divide indefinitely, renew themselves, and give rise to a variety of other types of cells. At four weeks, this structure is not much bigger than a grain of salt (MacDonald, 2007).

The neural stem cells divide and multiply, producing other specialized cells that eventually give rise to neurons and glial cells. Gradually, the top of the neural tube thickens into three bulges that will eventually form the three main regions of the brain: the *hindbrain, midbrain,* and *forebrain* (see Figure 9.2). As the neural tube expands, it develops the cavities, called *ventricles*, that are found at the core of the fully developed brain. The ventricles are filled with cerebrospinal fluid, which cushions and provides nutrients for the brain and spinal cord.

During peak periods of brain development, new neurons are being generated at the rate of 250,000 per minute (MacDonald, 2007). The developing brain cells multiply, differentiate, and begin their migration to their final destination. Guided by the fibers of a special type of glial cell, the newly born neurons travel to specific locations (Nadarajah & Parnavelas, 2002). They join with other developing neurons and begin forming the structures of the developing nervous system.

The Fetal Period

The third month heralds the beginning of the **fetal period**—the final and longest stage of prenatal development. The main task during the next seven months is for body systems to grow and reach maturity in preparation for life outside the mother's body. By the end of the third month, the fetus can move its arms, legs, mouth, and head. The fetus becomes capable of reflexive responses, such as fanning its toes if the sole of the foot is stroked and squinting if its eyelids are touched. During the fourth month, the mother experiences *quickening*—she can feel the fetus moving.

The fetal brain is constantly changing, forming as many as 2 million synaptic connections per second. Connections that are used are strengthened, while connections that remain unused are eventually *pruned* or eliminated. By the fifth month, all the brain cells the person will have at birth are present. The fetus now has distinct sleep–wake cycles and periods of activity (Mirmiran & others, 2003). During the sixth month, the fetus's brain activity becomes similar to that of a newborn baby.

teratogens
Harmful agents or substances that can cause malformations or defects in an embryo or fetus.

stem cells
Undifferentiated cells that can divide and give rise to cells that can develop into any one of the body's different cell types.

fetal period
The third and longest period of prenatal development, extending from the ninth week until birth.

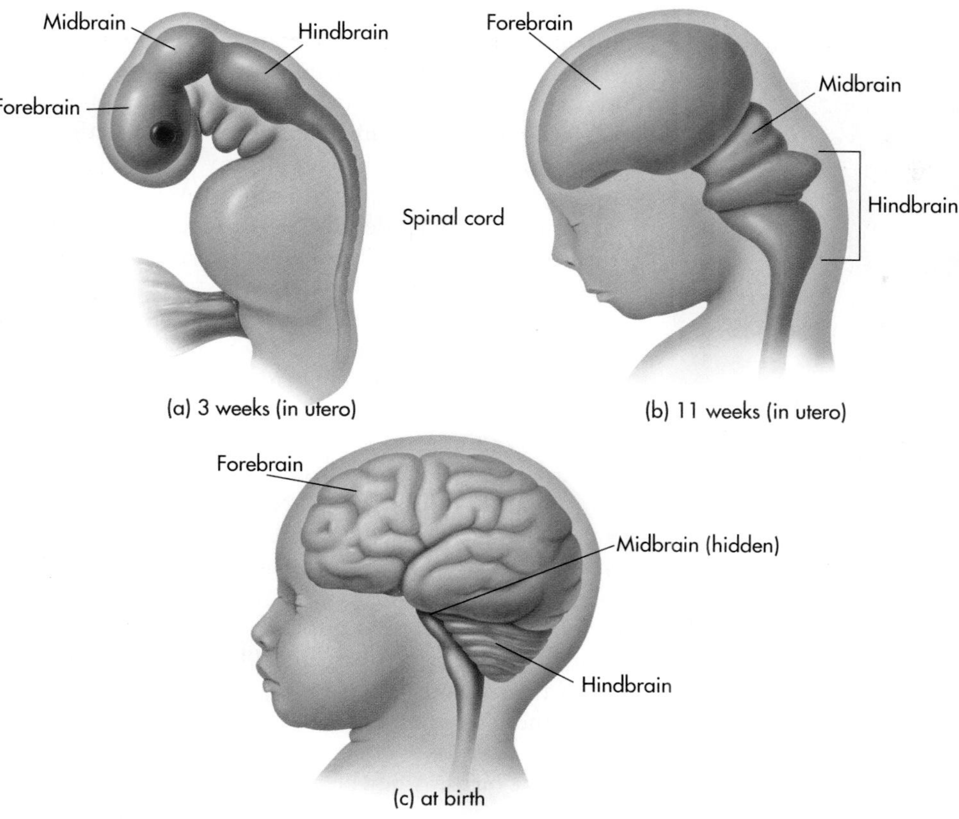

Figure 9.2 The Sequence of Fetal Brain Development The human brain begins as a fluid-filled neural tube at about three weeks after conception. The hindbrain structures are the first to develop, followed by midbrain structures. The forebrain structures develop last, eventually coming to surround and envelop the hindbrain and midbrain structures.

During the final two months of the fetal period, the fetus will double in weight, gaining an additional three to four pounds of body fat. This additional body fat will help the newborn adjust to changing temperatures outside the womb. It also contributes to the newborn's chubby appearance. As birth approaches, growth slows and the fetus's body systems become more active.

At birth, the newborn's brain is only about one-fourth the size of an adult brain, weighing less than a pound. After birth, the neurons grow in size and continue to develop new dendrites and interconnections with other neurons. *Myelin* forms on axons in key areas of the brain, such as those involved in motor control. Axons also grow longer, and the branching at the ends of the axons becomes more dense. But the process of neural development has only begun. The development of dendrites and synapses, as well as the extension of axons, continues throughout the lifespan.

Development During Infancy and Childhood

Key Theme

- **Although physically helpless, newborn infants are equipped with reflexes and sensory capabilities that enhance their chances for survival.**

Key Questions

- **How do the senses and the brain develop after birth?**
- **What roles do temperament and attachment play in social and personality development?**
- **What are the stages of language development?**

The newly born infant enters the world with an impressive array of physical and sensory capabilities. Initially, his behavior is mostly limited to reflexes that enhance his chances for survival. Touching the newborn's cheek triggers the *rooting reflex*—

The Nearsighted Newborn Classic research by psychologist Robert Fantz and his colleagues (1962) showed that the newborn comes into the world very near-sighted, having approximately 20/300 vision. The newborn's ability to detect the contrast of object edges and boundaries is also poorly developed (Stephens & Banks, 1987). As the adjacent image illustrates, even by age 3 months, the infant's world is still pretty fuzzy.

the infant turns toward the source of the touch and opens his mouth. Touching the newborn's lips evokes the *sucking reflex.* If you put a finger on each of the newborn's palms, he will respond with the *grasping reflex*—the baby will grip your fingers so tightly that he can be lifted upright. As motor areas of the infant's brain develop over the first year of life, the rooting, sucking, and grasping reflexes are replaced by voluntary behaviors.

The newborn's senses—vision, hearing, smell, and touch—are keenly attuned to people. In a classic study, Robert Fantz (1961) demonstrated that the image of a human face holds the newborn's gaze longer than do other images. Other researchers have also confirmed the newborn's visual preference for the human face (Farroni & others, 2006; Turati & others, 2002). Newborns only 10 *minutes* old will turn their heads to continue gazing at the image of a human face as it passes in front of them, but they will not visually follow other images (Turati, 2004).

And, newborns quickly learn to differentiate between their mothers and strangers. Within just hours of their birth, newborns display a preference for their mother's voice and face over that of a stranger (Bushnell, 2001). For their part, mothers become keenly attuned to their infant's appearance, smell, and even skin texture (Kaitz & others, 1992). Fathers, too, are able to identify their newborn from a photograph after just minutes of exposure (Bader & Phillips, 2002).

Vision is the least developed sense at birth. A newborn infant is extremely nearsighted, meaning she can see close objects more clearly than distant objects. The optimal viewing distance for the newborn is about 6 to 12 inches, the perfect distance for a nursing baby to focus easily on her mother's face and make eye contact. Nevertheless, the infant's view of the world is pretty fuzzy for the first several months, even for objects that are within close range.

The interaction between adults and infants seems to compensate naturally for the newborn's poor vision. When adults interact with very young infants, they almost always position themselves so that their face is about 8 to 12 inches away from the baby's face. Adults also have a strong natural tendency to exaggerate head movements and facial expressions, such as smiles and frowns, again making it easier for the baby to see them.

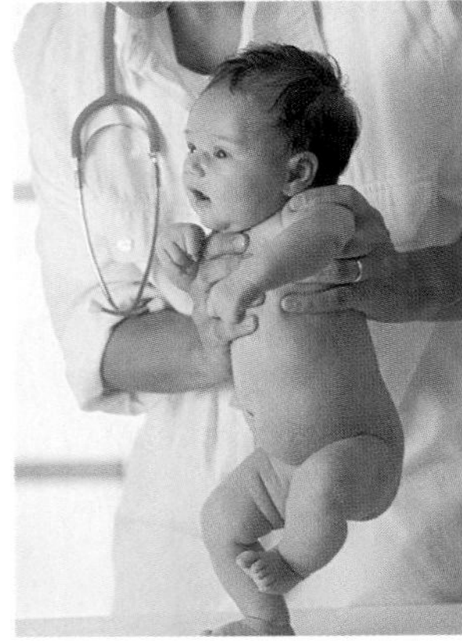

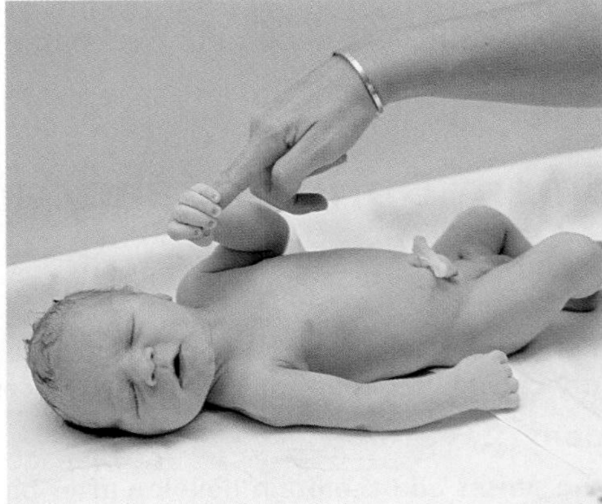

Newborn Reflexes When this 2-week-old baby *(left)* is held upright with her feet touching a flat surface, she displays the *stepping reflex,* moving her legs as if trying to walk. Another reflex that is present at birth is the *grasping reflex* (*right*). The infant's grip is so strong that he can support his own weight. Thought to enhance the newborn's chances for survival, these reflexive responses drop out during the first few months of life as the baby develops voluntary control over movements.

Physical Development

By the time infants begin crawling, at around 7 to 8 months of age, their view of the world, including distant objects, will be as clear as that of their parents. The increasing maturation of the infant's visual system reflects the development of her

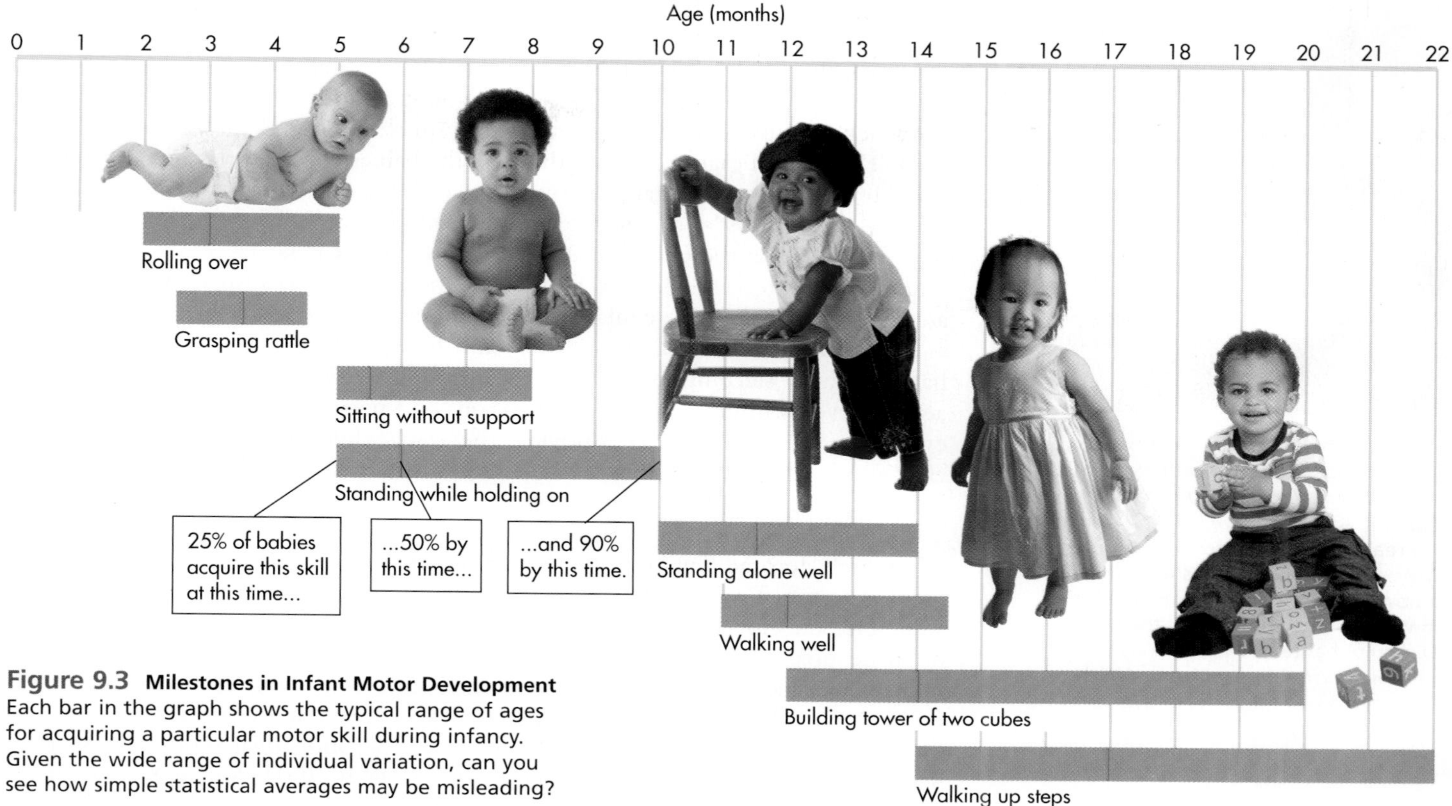

Figure 9.3 Milestones in Infant Motor Development
Each bar in the graph shows the typical range of ages for acquiring a particular motor skill during infancy. Given the wide range of individual variation, can you see how simple statistical averages may be misleading?

brain. At birth, her brain is an impressive 25 percent of its adult weight. In contrast, her birth weight is only about 5 percent of her eventual adult weight. During infancy, her brain will grow to about 75 percent of its adult weight, while her body weight will reach only about 20 percent of her adult weight.

One outward reflection of the infant's developing brain is the attainment of more sophisticated motor skills. Figure 9.3 illustrates the sequence and average ages of motor skill development during infancy. The basic *sequence* of motor skill development is universal, but the *average ages* can be a little deceptive. Infants vary a great deal in the ages at which they master each skill. Although virtually all infants are walking well by 15 months of age, some infants will walk as early as 10 months. Each infant has his own inborn timetable of physical maturation and developmental readiness to master different motor skills.

temperament
Inborn predispositions to consistently behave and react in a certain way.

Social and Personality Development

From birth, forming close social and emotional relationships with caregivers is essential to the infant's physical and psychological well-being. Although physically helpless, the young infant does not play a passive role in forming these relationships. As you'll see in this section, the infant's individual traits play an important role in the development of the relationship between infant and caregiver.

Temperamental Qualities: Babies Are Different!

Infants come into the world with very distinct and consistent behavioral styles. Some babies are consistently calm and easy to soothe. Other babies are fussy, irritable, and hard to comfort. Some babies are active and outgoing; others seem shy and wary of new experiences. Psychologists refer to these inborn predispositions to consistently behave and react in a certain way as an infant's **temperament.**

A temperamental bias can be likened to the basic form of the song of a particular species of bird. The animal's genome constrains the basic architecture of the song but does not determine all of its features; within broad limits, the adult song depends on exposure to the songs of other birds and the opportunity to hear its own vocalizations. A similar principle holds true for the effect of environmental influences on people.

JEROME KAGAN (2004)

Temperamental Patterns Most babies can be categorized into one of three broad temperamental patterns. An "easy" baby is usually easy to soothe, calm, cheerful, and readily adjusts to new situations. "Slow-to-warm-up" babies tend to adapt to new situations and experiences very slowly, but once they adapt, they're fine. "Difficult" babies are more likely to be emotional, irritable, and fussy. Which category do you think the baby shown above fits? Why?

Interest in infant temperament was triggered by a classic longitudinal study launched in the 1950s by psychiatrists Alexander Thomas and Stella Chess. The focus of the study was on how temperamental qualities influence adjustment throughout life. Chess and Thomas rated young infants on a variety of characteristics, such as activity level, mood, regularity in sleeping and eating, and attention span. They found that about two-thirds of the babies could be classified into one of three broad temperamental patterns: *easy, difficult,* and *slow-to-warm-up*. About a third of the infants were characterized as *average* babies because they did not fit neatly into one of these three categories (Thomas & Chess, 1977).

Easy babies readily adapt to new experiences, generally display positive moods and emotions, and have regular sleeping and eating patterns. *Difficult* babies tend to be intensely emotional, are irritable and fussy, and cry a lot. They also tend to have irregular sleeping and eating patterns. *Slow-to-warm-up* babies have a low activity level, withdraw from new situations and people, and adapt to new experiences very gradually. After studying the same children from infancy through childhood, Thomas and Chess (1986) found that these broad patterns of temperamental qualities are remarkably stable.

Other temperamental patterns have been identified. For example, after decades of research, Jerome Kagan (2004; Kagan & Snidman, 2004) has classified temperament in terms of *reactivity. High-reactive* infants react intensely to new experiences, strangers, and novel objects. They tend to be tense, fearful, and inhibited. At the opposite pole are *low-reactive* infants, who tend to be calmer, uninhibited, and bolder. Sociable rather than shy, low-reactive infants are more likely to show interest than fear when exposed to new people, experiences, and objects.

Virtually all temperament researchers agree that individual differences in temperament have a genetic and biological basis (Kagan, 2004; Kagan & Fox, 2006; Rothbart & others, 2000). However, researchers also agree that environmental experiences can modify a child's basic temperament (Pauli-Pott & others, 2004; Rothbart & Putnam, 2002). As Kagan (2004) points out, "Temperament is not destiny. Many experiences will affect high and low reactive infants as they grow up. Parents who encourage a more sociable, bold persona and discourage timidity will help their high reactive children develop a less-inhibited profile."

Because cultural attitudes affect child-rearing practices, infant temperament can also be affected by cultural beliefs. For example, cross-cultural studies of temperament have found that infants in the United States generally displayed more positive emotion than Russian or Asian infants (Gartstein & others, 2003). One explanation is that U.S. parents tend to value and encourage expressions of positive emotions, such as smiling and laughing, in their babies. In contrast, parents in other cultures, including those of Russia and many Asian countries, place a lesser emphasis on the importance of positive emotional expression. Thus, the development of temperamental qualities is yet another example of the complex interaction among genetic and environmental factors.

Mary D. Salter Ainsworth (1913–1999) Although best known for developing the "Strange Situation technique" to measure attachment, Mary D. Salter Ainsworth made many other contributions to developmental psychology. She originated the concept of the *secure base* and was the first researcher in the United States to make extensive, systematic, naturalistic observations of mother–infant interactions in their own homes. Her findings often surprised contemporary psychologists. For example, Ainsworth provided the first evidence demonstrating the importance of the caregiver's responsiveness to the infant's needs (Bretherton & Main, 2000).

Attachment: Forming Emotional Bonds

During the first year of life, the emotional bond that forms between the infant and her caregivers, especially her parents, is called **attachment.** As conceptualized by attachment theorist John Bowlby (1969, 1988) and psychologist **Mary D. Salter Ainsworth** (1979), attachment relationships serve important functions throughout infancy and, indeed, the lifespan. Ideally, the parent or caregiver functions as a *secure base* for the infant, providing a sense of comfort and security—a safe haven from which the infant can explore and learn about the environment. According to attachment theory, an infant's ability to thrive physically and psychologically depends in large part on the quality of attachment (Ainsworth & others, 1978).

In studying attachment, psychologists have typically focused on the infant's bond with the mother, since the mother is often the infant's primary caregiver. Still, it's

CULTURE AND HUMAN BEHAVIOR

Where Does the Baby Sleep?

In most U.S. families, infants sleep in their own beds in a separate room (Willinger & others, 2003). It may surprise you to discover that the United States is very unusual in this respect. In one survey of 100 societies, the United States was the *only* one in which babies slept in separate rooms. Another survey of 136 societies found that in two-thirds of the societies, infants slept in the same beds as their mothers. In the remainder, infants generally slept in the same room as their mothers (Morelli & others, 1992).

Gilda Morelli and her colleagues (1992) compared the sleeping arrangements of several middle-class U.S. families with those of Mayan families in a small town in Guatemala. They found that infants in the Mayan families slept with their mothers until they were 2 or 3, usually until another baby was about to be born. At that point, toddlers moved to the bed of another family member, usually the father or an older sibling. Children continued to sleep with other family members throughout childhood.

Mayan mothers were shocked when the American researchers told them that infants in the United States slept alone and often in a different room from their parents. They believed that the practice was cruel and unnatural and would have negative effects on the infant's development.

When infants and toddlers sleep alone, bedtime marks a separation from their families. To ease the child's transition to sleeping, "putting the baby to bed" often involves lengthy bedtime rituals, including rocking, singing lullabies, or reading stories (Morrell & Steele, 2003). Small children take comforting items, such as a favorite blanket or teddy bear, to bed with them to ease the stressful transition to falling asleep alone. The child may also use his "security blanket" or "cuddly" to comfort himself when he wakes up in the night, as most small children do.

In contrast, the Mayan babies did not take cuddly items to bed, and no special routines marked the transition between wakefulness and sleep. Mayan parents were puzzled by the very idea. Instead, the Mayan babies simply went to bed when their parents did or fell asleep in the middle of the family's social activities.

Morelli and her colleagues (1992) found that the different sleeping customs of the American and Mayan families reflect different cultural values. Some of the American babies slept in the same room as their parents when they were first born, which the parents felt helped foster feelings of closeness and emotional security in the newborns. Nonetheless, most of the American parents moved their babies to a separate room when they felt that the babies were ready to sleep alone, usually by the time they were 3 to 6 months of age. These parents explained their decision by saying that it was time for the baby to learn to be "independent" and "self-reliant."

In contrast, the Mayan parents felt that it was important to develop and encourage the infant's feelings of *interdependence* with other members of the family. Thus, in both Mayan and U.S. families, sleeping arrangements reflect cultural goals for child rearing and cultural values for relations among family members.

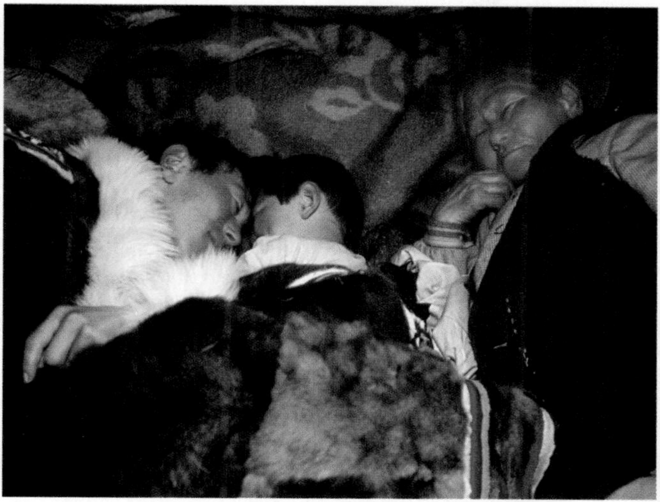

Culture and Co-Sleeping Throughout the world, cultural and ethnic differences influence family decisions about sleeping arrangements for infants and young children (Li & others, 2008; Worthman & Brown, 2007). Among the indigenous Nenets people of Siberia, shown above, *co-sleeping* or *shared sleeping* is common, at least partly for the pragmatic reason of staying warm. Even in the United States, sleeping arrangements vary by racial and ethnic groups. Stephanie Milan and her colleagues (2007) found that Latino and African-American preschoolers were more likely to sleep with a sibling or parent than white preschoolers.

important to note that most fathers are also directly involved with the basic care of their infants and children. In homes where both parents are present, children who are attached to one parent are also usually attached to the other (Furman & Simon, 2004). Infants are also capable of forming attachments to other consistent caregivers in their lives, such as relatives or workers at a day-care center. Thus, an infant can form *multiple* attachments (Field, 1996).

Generally, when parents are consistently warm, responsive, and sensitive to their infant's needs, the infant develops a *secure attachment* to her parents (Goldsmith & Harman, 1994; Koren-Karie & others, 2002). The infant's expectation that her needs will be met by her caregivers is the most essential ingredient to

attachment
The emotional bond that forms between an infant and caregiver(s), especially his or her parents.

CRITICAL THINKING

The Effects of Child Care on Attachment and Development

On average, the infants, toddlers, and preschoolers of working mothers spend 36 hours a week in child care (Leach, 2007; NACCRRA, 2008). Does extensive day care during the first years of life create insecurely attached infants and toddlers? Does it produce negative effects in later childhood? Let's look at the evidence.

Developmental psychologist Jay Belsky (1992, 2001, 2002) sparked considerable controversy when he published studies showing that infants under a year old were more likely to demonstrate insecure attachment if they experienced over 30 hours of day care per week. Based on his research, Belsky contended that children who entered full-time day care before their first birthday were "at risk" to be insecurely attached to their parents. He also claimed that extensive experience with nonmaternal care was linked to aggressive behavior in preschool and kindergarten.

Belsky did not claim that *all* infants in day care were likely to experience insecure attachment. Reviewing the data in Belsky's studies and others, psychologist Alison Clarke-Stewart (1989, 1992) pointed out that the actual difference in attachment was quite small when infants experiencing day care were compared with infants cared for by a parent. The proportion of insecurely attached infants in day care is only slightly higher than the proportion typically found in the general population (Lamb & others, 1992).

In other words, *most* of the children who had started day care in infancy were securely attached, just like most of the children who had not experienced extensive day care during infancy. Similarly, a large, long-term study of the effects of child care on attachment found that spending more hours per week in day care was associated with insecure attachment only in preschoolers who also experienced less sensitive and less responsive maternal care (NICHD, 2006). Preschoolers whose mothers were sensitive and responsive showed no greater likelihood of being insecurely attached, regardless of the number of hours spent in day care.

Individual Attention and Learning Activities High-quality child care centers offer a variety of age-appropriate (and fun!) activities, toys, and experiences that help nurture a child's motor, cognitive, and social skills. Individual attention from consistent caregivers or teachers helps foster the young child's sense of predictability and security in the care setting.

So what about the long-term effects of day care? One study found that third-graders with extensive infant day-care experience were more likely to demonstrate a variety of social and academic problems (Vandell & Corasaniti, 1990). However, these children were not enrolled in high-quality day care. Rather, they experienced average day-care conditions in a state with relatively low standards for day-care centers. But even in this case, it's difficult to assign the

forming a secure attachment to them. And, cross-cultural studies have confirmed that sensitivity to the infant's needs is associated with secure attachment in diverse cultures (Posada & others, 2002, 2004; Vaughn & others, 2007).

In contrast, *insecure attachment* may develop when an infant's parents are neglectful, inconsistent, or insensitive to his moods or behaviors. Insecure attachment seems to reflect an ambivalent or detached emotional relationship between an infant and his parents (Ainsworth, 1979; Isabella & others, 1989).

The Importance of Attachment Secure attachment in infancy forms the basis for emotional bonds in later childhood. At one time, attachment researchers focused only on the relationship between mothers and infants. Today, the importance of the attachment relationship between fathers and children is also recognized (Grossman & others, 2002).

How do researchers measure attachment? The most commonly used procedure, called the *Strange Situation*, was devised by Ainsworth. The Strange Situation is typically used with infants who are between 1 and 2 years old (Ainsworth & others, 1978). In this technique, the baby and his mother are brought into an unfamiliar room with a variety of toys. A few minutes later, a stranger enters the room. The mother stays with the child for a few moments, then departs, leaving the child alone with the stranger. After a few minutes, the mother returns, spends a few minutes in the room, leaves, and returns again. Through a one-way window, observers record the infant's behavior throughout this sequence of separations and reunions.

Psychologists assess attachment by observing the infant's behavior toward his mother during the Strange Situation procedure. When his mother is present, the *securely attached* infant will use her as a "secure base" from which to explore the new environment, periodically returning to her side. He will show distress when his mother leaves the room

Characteristics of High-Quality Child Care

- The setting meets state and local standards and is accredited by a professional organization, such as the National Association for the Education of Young Children.
- Warm, responsive caregivers who encourage children's play and learning.
- Groups of children and adults are consistent over time, helping foster stable, positive relationships. Low staff turnover is essential.
- Groups are small enough to provide the individual attention that very young children need.
- A minimum of two adults care for no more than 8 infants, 12 toddlers, or 20 four- and five-year-olds.
- Caregivers are trained in principles of child development and learning.
- Developmentally appropriate learning materials and toys are available that offer interesting, safe, and achievable activities.

Sources: Eunice Kennedy Shriver National Institute of Child Health and Human Development, 2006; National Association for the Education of Young Children, 2008; National Association of Child Care Resource & Referral Agencies, 2008.

cause of these problems to day care itself. Why? Because developmental problems in the third-graders studied were *also* associated with being raised exclusively by their mothers at home.

Psychologists and other child development researchers agree that the *quality* of child care is a key factor in facilitating secure attachment in early childhood and preventing problems in later childhood (NICHD, 2003a, 2003b). Yet child care is just one aspect of the child's developmental environment. Sensitive parenting and the quality of caregiving in the child's home have been found to have an even greater influence on social, emotional, and cognitive development than the quality of child care (Marshall, 2004; NICHD, 2006).

Many studies have found that children who experience high-quality child care tend to be more sociable, better adjusted, and more academically competent than children who experience poor-quality care (see NICHD, 2006).

For example, Swedish psychologist Bengt-Erik Andersson (1989, 1992) studied children in Sweden who had experienced high-quality day care before age 1. As compared to children who had been cared for by a parent at home or who had started day care later in childhood, children who had started day care in infancy performed better in school and were more socially and emotionally competent.

Clearly, then, day care in itself does not necessarily lead to undesirable outcomes. The critical factor is the *quality* of care (NICHD, 2006). High-quality day care can potentially benefit children, even when it begins in early infancy. In contrast, low-quality care can potentially contribute to social and academic problems in later childhood (Muenchow & Marsland, 2007; Sagi & others, 2002). Unfortunately, high-quality day care is not readily available in many areas of the United States (Pope, 1997).

CRITICAL THINKING QUESTIONS

- Given the positive benefits of high-quality child care, should the availability of affordable, high-quality child care be a national priority?
- Should the American public education system be expanded so that elementary schools are required to offer high-quality child care and preschool to working families in that school district? Why or why not?

and will greet her warmly when she returns. A securely attached baby is easily soothed by his mother (Ainsworth & others, 1978; Lamb & others, 1985).

In contrast, an ***insecurely attached*** infant is less likely to explore the environment, even when her mother is present. In the Strange Situation, insecurely attached infants may appear either very anxious or completely indifferent. Such infants tend to ignore or avoid their mothers when they are present. Some insecurely attached infants become extremely distressed when their mothers leave the room. When insecurely attached infants are reunited with their mothers, they are hard to soothe and may resist their mothers' attempts to comfort them.

The quality of attachment during infancy is associated with a variety of long-term effects (Carlson & others, 2004; Malekpour, 2007). Preschoolers with a history of being securely attached tend to be more prosocial, empathic, and socially competent than are preschoolers with a history of insecure attachment (Collins & Gunnar, 1990; Rydell & others, 2005). In middle childhood, children with a history of secure attachment in infancy are better adjusted and have higher levels of social and cognitive development than do children who were insecurely attached in infancy (Kerns & others, 2007; Kerns & Richardson, 2005; Stams & others, 2002). Adolescents who were securely attached in infancy have fewer problems, do better in school, and have more successful relationships with their peers than do adolescents who were insecurely attached in infancy (Laible, 2007; Sroufe, 1995, 2002; Sweeney, 2007).

Because attachment in infancy seems to be so important, psychologists have extensively investigated the impact of day care on attachment. In the Critical Thinking box above, we take a close look at this issue.

Language Development

Probably no other accomplishment in early life is as astounding as language development. By the time a child reaches 3 years of age, he will have learned approximately 3,000 words and the complex rules of his language.

According to linguist Noam Chomsky, every child is born with a biological predisposition to learn language—*any* language. In effect, children possess a "universal grammar"—a basic understanding of the common principles of language organization. Infants are innately equipped not only to understand language but also to extract grammatical rules from what they hear (Chomsky, 1965). The key task in the development of language is to learn a set of grammatical rules that allow the child to produce an unlimited number of sentences from a limited number of words.

At birth, infants can distinguish among the speech sounds of all the world's languages, no matter what language is spoken in their homes (Werker & Desjardins, 1995; Yoshida & Kiritani, 2006). Infants lose this ability by 10 months of age (Burns & others, 2007; Kuhl & others, 1992). Instead, they can distinguish only among the speech sounds that are present in the language to which they have been exposed. Thus, during the first year of life, infants begin to master the sound structure of their own native language.

Encouraging Language Development: Motherese

Just as infants seem to be biologically programmed to learn language, parents seem to be biologically programmed to encourage language development by the way they speak to infants and toddlers. People in every culture, especially parents, use a style of speech called *motherese,* or *infant-directed speech,* with babies (Bryant & Barrett, 2007; Kuhl & others, 1997).

Motherese is characterized by very distinct pronunciation, a simplified vocabulary, short sentences, high pitch, and exaggerated intonation and expression. Content is restricted to topics that are familiar to the child, and "baby talk" is often used—simplified words such as "go bye-bye" and "night-night." Questions are often asked, encouraging a response from the infant. Research by psychologist Anne Fernald (1985, 1992) has shown that infants prefer infant-directed speech to language spoken in an adult conversational style.

The adult use of infant-directed speech seems to be instinctive. Deaf mothers who use sign language modify their hand gestures when they communicate with infants and toddlers in a way that is very similar to the infant-directed speech of hearing mothers. Furthermore, as infants mature, the speech patterns of parents change to fit the child's developing language abilities (Deckner & others, 2003; Papoušek & others, 1985).

Deaf Babies Babble with Their Hands Deaf babies whose parents use American Sign Language (ASL) babble with their hands, rather than their voices (Petitto & others, 2001; Petitto & Marentette, 1991). Just as hearing babies repeat the same syllables over and over, deaf babies repeat the same simple hand gestures. Hearing babies born to deaf parents who are exposed only to sign language also babble with their hands (Petitto & others, 2004). The hand shapes represent basic components of ASL gestures, much like the syllables that make up the words of spoken language. Here, a baby repeats the sign for "A."

The Cooing and Babbling Stage of Language Development

As with many other aspects of development, the stages of language development appear to be universal. In virtually every culture, infants follow the same sequence of language development and at roughly similar ages (see Figure 9.4).

At about 3 months of age, infants begin to "coo," repeating vowel sounds such as *ahhhhh* or *ooooo,* varying the pitch up or down. At about 5 months of age, infants begin to *babble.* They add consonants to the vowels and string the sounds together in sometimes long-winded productions of babbling, such as *ba-ba-ba-ba, de-de-de-de,* or *ma-ma-ma-ma.*

When infants babble, they are not simply imitating adult speech. Infants all over the world use the *same* sounds when

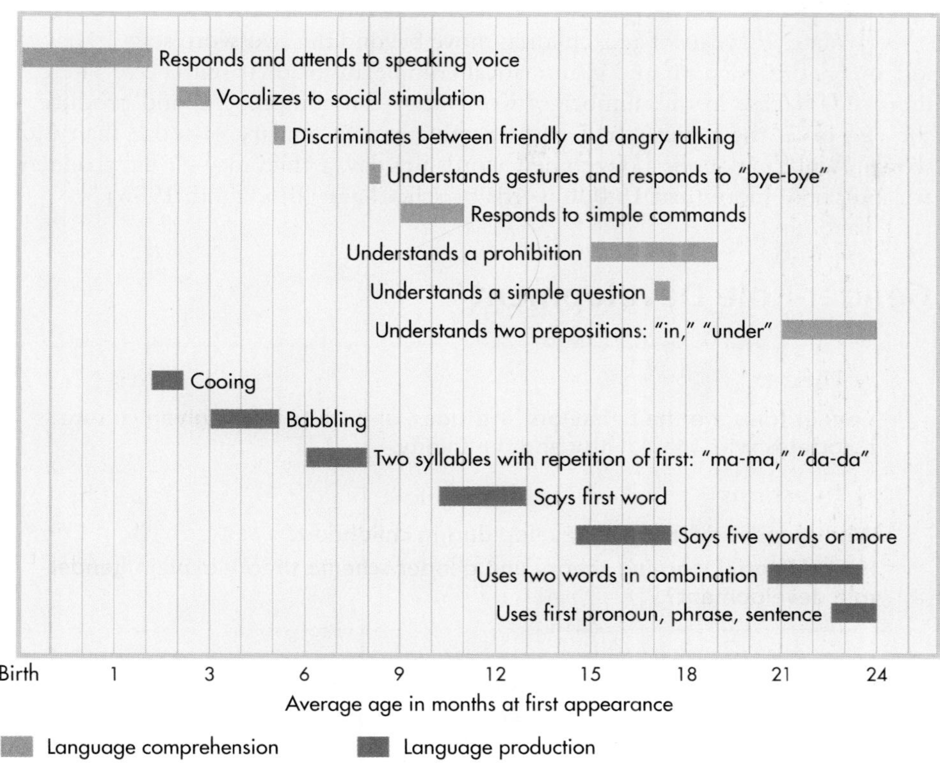

Figure 9.4 Milestones in Language Comprehension and Production Approximate average age ranges for the first appearance of different stages of language development are shown here. Notice that language comprehension occurs much earlier than language production.

Source: Based on Bornstein & Lamb (1992).

they babble, including sounds that do not occur in the language of their parents and other caregivers. At around 9 months of age, babies begin to babble more in the sounds specific to their language. Babbling, then, seems to be a biologically programmed stage of language development (Gentilucci & Dalla Volta, 2007; Petitto & others, 2004).

The One-Word Stage of Language Development

Long before babies become accomplished talkers, they understand much of what is said to them. Before they are a year old, most infants can understand simple commands, such as "Bring Daddy the block," even though they cannot *say* the words *bring, Daddy,* or *block*. This reflects the fact that an infant's **comprehension vocabulary** (the words she understands) is much larger than her **production vocabulary** (the words she can say). Generally, infants acquire comprehension of words more than twice as fast as they learn to speak new words.

Somewhere around their first birthday, infants produce their first real words. First words usually refer to concrete objects or people that are important to the child, such as *mama, daddy,* or *ba-ba* (bottle). First words are also often made up of the syllables that were used in babbling.

During the *one-word stage,* babies use a single word and vocal intonation to stand for an entire sentence. With the proper intonation and context, *baba* can mean "I want my bottle!" "There's my bottle!" or "Where's my bottle?"

The Two-Word Stage of Language Development

Around their second birthday, infants begin putting words together. During the *two-word stage,* infants combine two words to construct a simple "sentence," such as "Mama go," "Where kitty?" and "No potty!" During this stage, the words used are primarily content words—nouns, verbs, and sometimes adjectives or adverbs. Articles (*a, an, the*) and prepositions (*in, under, on*) are omitted. Two-word sentences reflect the first understandings of grammar. Although these utterances include only the most essential words, they basically follow a grammatically correct sequence.

comprehension vocabulary
The words that are understood by an infant or child.

production vocabulary
The words that an infant or child understands and can speak.

gender
The cultural, social, and psychological meanings that are associated with masculinity or femininity.

gender roles
The behaviors, attitudes, and personality traits that are designated as either masculine or feminine in a given culture.

gender identity
A person's psychological sense of being male or female.

At around 2½ years of age, children move beyond the two-word stage. They rapidly increase the length and grammatical complexity of their sentences. There is a dramatic increase in the number of words they can comprehend and produce. By the age of 3, the typical child has a production vocabulary of more than 3,000 words. Acquiring about a dozen new words per day, a child may have a production vocabulary of more than 10,000 words by school age (Bjorklund, 1995).

Gender-Role Development

Key Theme

- **Gender roles are the behaviors, attitudes, and traits that a given culture associates with masculinity and femininity.**

Key Questions

- **What gender differences develop during childhood?**
- **How do social learning theory and gender schema theory explain gender-role development?**

Because the English language is less than precise, we need to clarify a few terms before we begin our discussion of gender-role development. First, we'll use the term **gender** to refer to the cultural and social meanings that are associated with maleness and femaleness. Thus, **gender role** describes the behaviors, attitudes, and personality traits that a given culture designates as either "masculine" or "feminine" (Bailey & Zucker, 1995). Finally, **gender identity** refers to a person's psychological sense of being male or female (Egan & Perry, 2001). When the biological categories of "male" and "female" are being discussed, we'll use the term *sex*.

Color-Coded Video Games Little girls and little boys have a lot in common. Both of these children are clearly absorbed in their Nintendo video games. Nevertheless, the little boy's game is silver, and the little girl's game is pink. Why?

Gender Differences in Childhood Behavior

Batman Versus Barbie

Roughly between the ages of 2 and 3, children can identify themselves and other children as boys or girls, although the details are still a bit fuzzy to them (Zosuls & others, 2006). Preschoolers don't yet understand that sex is determined by physical characteristics. This is not surprising, considering that the biologically defining sex characteristics—the genitals—are hidden from view most of the time. Instead, young children identify the sexes in terms of external attributes, such as hairstyle, clothing, and activities.

A humorous story told by gender researcher Sandra Bem illustrates this point. Bem (1989) describes going along with her preschool son Jeremy's desire to wear barrettes to nursery school. Another little boy at the school repeatedly insisted

BABY BLUES

that Jeremy "must be a girl, because only girls wear barrettes." So, Jeremy attempted to prove that he really was a boy by dropping his pants. The other little boy was not convinced. "Everybody has a penis, only girls wear barrettes," he countered.

From about the age of 18 months to the age of 2 years, sex differences in behavior begin to emerge (Miller & others, 2006). These differences become more pronounced throughout early childhood. Toddler girls play more with soft toys and dolls, and ask for help from adults more than toddler boys do. Toddler boys play more with blocks and transportation toys, such as trucks and wagons. They also play more actively than do girls (see Ruble & others, 2006).

Separate Worlds? In childhood, girls tend to establish close relationships with one or two other girls and to cement their friendships by sharing thoughts and feelings. In contrast, boys tend to play in groups and favor competitive games and team sports. How might such gender differences affect intimate relationships in adolescence and adulthood?

Roughly between the ages of 2 and 3, preschoolers start acquiring gender-role stereotypes for toys, clothing, household objects, games, and work. From the age of about 3 on, there are consistent gender differences in preferred toys and play activities. Boys play more with balls, blocks, and toy vehicles. Girls play more with dolls and domestic toys and engage in more dressing up and art activities. By the age of 3, children have developed a clear preference for toys that are associated with their own sex. This tendency continues throughout childhood (Freeman, 2007).

Children also develop a strong preference for playing with members of their own sex—girls with girls and boys with boys (Egan & Perry, 2001; Fridell & others, 2006). It's not uncommon to hear boys refer to girls as "icky" and girls refer to boys as "mean" or "rough." And, in fact, preschool boys *do* play more roughly than girls, cover more territory, and play in larger groups. Throughout the remainder of childhood, boys and girls play primarily with members of their own sex (Hoffmann & Powlishta, 2001).

According to psychologist Carole Beal (1994), boys and girls almost seem to create separate "social worlds," each with its own style of interaction. They also learn particular ways of interacting that work well with peers of the same sex. For example, boys learn to assert themselves within a group of male friends. Girls tend to establish very close bonds with one or two friends. Girls learn to maintain their close friendships through compromise, conciliation, and verbal conflict resolution. As we'll discuss in Enhancing Well-Being with Psychology at the end of this chapter, these gender differences in styles of social interaction persist into adulthood.

Children are far more rigid than adults in their beliefs in gender-role stereotypes. Children's strong adherence to gender stereotypes may be a necessary step in developing a gender identity (Powlishta, 1995b; Stangor & Ruble, 1987). Boys are far more rigid than girls in their preferences for toys associated with their own sex. Their attitudes about the sexes are also more rigid than are those held by girls. As girls grow older, they become even more flexible in their views of sex-appropriate activities and attributes, but boys become even less flexible (Schmalz & Kerstetter, 2006).

Girls' more flexible attitude toward gender roles may reflect society's greater tolerance of girls who cross gender lines in attire and behavior. A girl who plays with boys, or who plays with boys' toys, may develop the grudging respect of both sexes. But a boy who plays with girls or with girls' toys may be ostracized by both sexes. Girls are often proud to be labeled a "tomboy," but for boys, being called a "sissy" is the ultimate insult (Thorne,

"I don't see liking trucks as a boy thing. I see it as a liking-trucks thing."

1993). One explanation may be that children of both sexes tend to value the male role more highly than the female role.

As we've seen, there are very few significant differences between the sexes in either personality traits or intellectual abilities. Yet in many ways, children's behavior mirrors the gender-role stereotypes that are predominant in our culture.

Are Males More Interested in Sports Than Females? Anyone who's watched a closely matched girls' high school basketball game can attest to the fact that girls can be just as competitive in sports as boys. Contrary to what some people think, there is no evidence to support the notion that girls are inherently less interested in sports than boys. During the middle childhood years, from ages 6 to 10, boys and girls are equally interested in sports (Women's Sports Foundation, 2005). Especially during adolescence, participation in sports enhances the self-esteem of girls (Daniels & Leaper, 2006; Pedersen & Seidman, 2004). Although boys are still provided with more opportunities to participate in sports, girls today receive much more encouragement to compete in sports.

Explaining Gender Roles

Two Contemporary Theories

Many theories have been proposed to explain the differing patterns of male and female behavior in our culture and in other cultures (see Reid & others, 2008). Gender theories have included findings and opinions from anthropology, sociology, neuroscience, medicine, philosophy, political science, economics, and religion. (Let's face it, you probably have a few opinions on the issue yourself.) We won't even attempt to cover the full range of ideas. Instead, we'll describe two of the most influential psychological theories: social learning theory and gender schema theory. In Chapter 10, on personality, we will discuss Freud's ideas on the development of gender roles.

Social Learning Theory

Learning Gender Roles

Based on the principles of learning, **social learning theory of gender-role development** contends that gender roles are learned through *reinforcement, punishment,* and *modeling* (Bussey & Bandura, 2004). According to this theory, from a very young age, children are reinforced or rewarded when they display gender-appropriate behavior and punished when they do not.

How do children acquire their understanding of gender norms? Children are exposed to many sources of information about gender roles, including television, video games, books, films, and observation of same-sex adult role models. Children also learn gender differences through *modeling*: They observe and then imitate the sex-typed behavior of significant adults and older children (Bronstein, 2006; Leaper & Friedman, 2007). By observing and imitating such models—whether it's Mom cooking, Dad fixing things around the house, or a male superhero rescuing a helpless female on television—children come to understand that certain activities and attributes are considered more appropriate for one sex than for the other.

social learning theory of gender-role development
The theory that gender roles are acquired through the basic processes of learning, including reinforcement, punishment, and modeling.

Gender Schema Theory

Constructing Gender Categories

Gender schema theory, developed by **Sandra Bem,** incorporates some aspects of social learning theory (Renk & others, 2006; Martin & others, 2004). However, Bem (1981) approached gender-role development from a more strongly cognitive perspective. In contrast to the relatively passive role played by children in social learning theory, **gender schema theory** contends that children *actively* develop mental categories (or *schemas*) for masculinity and femininity (Martin & Halverson, 1981; Martin & Ruble, 2004). That is, children actively organize information about other people and appropriate behavior, activities, and attributes into gender categories. Saying that "trucks are for boys and dolls are for girls" is an example of a gender schema.

According to gender schema theory, children, like many adults, look at the world through "gender lenses" (Bem, 1987). Gender schemas influence how people pay attention to, perceive, interpret, and remember gender-relevant behavior. Gender schemas also seem to lead children to perceive members of their own sex more favorably than members of the opposite sex (Martin & others, 2002, 2004).

gender schema theory
The theory that gender-role development is influenced by the formation of schemas, or mental representations, of masculinity and femininity.

Like schemas in general (see Chapter 6), children's gender schemas do seem to influence what they notice and remember. For example, in a classic experiment, 5-year-olds were shown pictures of children engaged in activities that violated common gender stereotypes, such as girls playing with trucks and boys playing with dolls (Martin & Halverson, 1981, 1983). A few days later, the 5-year-olds "remembered" that the *boys* had been playing with the trucks and the *girls* with the dolls!

Children also readily assimilate new information into their existing gender schemas (Miller & others, 2006). In another classic study, 4- to 9-year-olds were given boxes of gender-neutral gadgets, such as hole punches (Bradbard & others, 1986). But some gadgets were labeled as "girl toys" and some as "boy toys." The boys played more with the "boy" gadgets, and the girls played more with the "girl" gadgets. A week later, the children easily remembered which gadgets went with each sex. They also remembered more information about the gadgets that were associated with their own sex. Simply labeling the objects as belonging to boys or to girls had powerful consequences for the children's behavior and memory—evidence of the importance of gender schemas in learning and remembering new information.

Children are gender detectives who search for cues about gender—who should or should not engage in a particular activity, who can play with whom, and why girls and boys are different. Cognitive perspectives on gender development assume that children are actively searching for ways to find meaning in and make sense of the social world that surrounds them, and they do so by using the gender cues provided by society to help them interpret what they see and hear.

CAROL LYNN MARTIN AND DIANE RUBLE (2004)

Cognitive Development

Key Theme

- **According to Piaget's theory, children progress through four distinct cognitive stages, and each stage marks a shift in how they think and understand the world.**

Key Questions

- **What are Piaget's four stages of cognitive development?**
- **What are three criticisms of Piaget's theory?**
- **How do Vygotsky's ideas about cognitive development differ from Piaget's theory?**

Just as children advance in motor skill and language development, they also develop increasing sophistication in cognitive processes—thinking, remembering, and processing information. The most influential theory of cognitive development is that of Swiss psychologist **Jean Piaget.** Originally trained as a biologist, Piaget combined a boundless curiosity about the nature of the human mind with a gift for scientific observation (Brainerd, 1996).

Piaget (1952, 1972) believed that children *actively* try to make sense out of their environment rather than passively soaking up information about the world. To Piaget, many of the "cute" things children say actually reflect their sincere attempts to make sense of their world. In fact, Piaget carefully observed his own three children in developing his theory (Fischer & Hencke, 1996).

When Laura was almost 3, Sandy and Laura were investigating the tadpoles in the creek behind our home. "Do you know what tadpoles become when they grow up? They become frogs," Sandy explained. Laura looked very serious. After considering this new bit of information for a few moments, she asked, "Laura grow up to be a frog, too?"

According to Piaget, children progress through four distinct cognitive stages: the sensorimotor stage, from birth to age 2; the preoperational stage, from age 2 to age 7; the concrete operational stage, from age 7 to age 11; and the formal operational stage, which begins during adolescence and continues into adulthood. As a child advances to a new stage, his thinking is *qualitatively different* from that of the previous stage. In other words, each new stage represents a fundamental shift in *how* the child thinks and understands the world.

Piaget saw this progression of cognitive development as a continuous, gradual process. As a child develops and matures, she does not simply acquire more information. Rather, she develops a new understanding of the world in each progressive stage, building on the understandings acquired in the previous stage (Siegler &

Jean Piaget Swiss psychologist Jean Piaget (1896–1980) viewed the child as a little scientist, actively exploring his or her world. Much of Piaget's theory was based on his careful observation of individual children, especially his own children.

Ellis, 1996). As the child *assimilates* new information and experiences, he eventually changes his way of thinking to *accommodate* new knowledge (Miller, 2002).

Piaget believed that these stages were biologically programmed to unfold at their respective ages (Flavell, 1996). He also believed that children in every culture progressed through the same sequence of stages at roughly similar ages. However, Piaget also recognized that hereditary and environmental differences could influence the rate at which a given child progressed through the stages (Fischer & Hencke, 1996; Wadsworth, 1996).

For example, a "bright" child may progress through the stages faster than a child who is less intellectually capable. A child whose environment provides ample and varied opportunities for exploration is likely to progress faster than a child who has limited environmental opportunities. Thus, even though the sequence of stages is universal, there can be individual variation in the rate of cognitive development.

Fuzzy Tastes Different! During the sensorimotor stage, infants and toddlers rely on their basic sensory and motor skills to explore and make sense of the world around them. Piaget believed that infants and toddlers acquire very practical understandings about the world as they touch, feel, taste, push, pull, twist, turn, and manipulate the objects they encounter.

The Sensorimotor Stage

The **sensorimotor stage** extends from birth until about 2 years of age. During this stage, infants acquire knowledge about the world through actions that allow them to directly experience and manipulate objects. Infants discover a wealth of very practical sensory knowledge, such as what objects look like and how they taste, feel, smell, and sound.

Infants in this stage also expand their practical knowledge about motor actions—reaching, grasping, pushing, pulling, and pouring. In the process, they gain a basic understanding of the effects their own actions can produce, such as pushing a button to turn on the television or knocking over a pile of blocks to make them crash and tumble.

At the beginning of the sensorimotor stage, the infant's motto seems to be, "Out of sight, out of mind." An object exists only if she can directly sense it. For example, if a 4-month-old infant knocks a ball underneath the couch and it rolls out of sight, she will not look for it. Piaget interpreted this response to mean that to the infant, the ball no longer exists.

However, by the end of the sensorimotor stage, children acquire a new cognitive understanding, called object permanence. **Object permanence** is the understanding that an object continues to exist even if it can't be seen. Now the infant will actively search for a ball that she has watched roll out of sight. Infants gradually acquire an understanding of object permanence as they gain experience with objects, as their memory abilities improve, and as they develop mental representations of the world, which Piaget called *schemas* (Berthier & others, 2000).

The Preoperational Stage

The **preoperational stage** lasts from roughly age 2 to age 7. In Piaget's theory, the word *operations* refers to logical mental activities. Thus, the "preoperational" stage is a prelogical stage.

FOR BETTER OR WORSE

The hallmark of preoperational thought is the child's capacity to engage in symbolic thought. **Symbolic thought** refers to the ability to use words, images, and symbols to represent the world (DeLoache, 1995). One indication of the expanding capacity for symbolic thought is the child's impressive gains in language during this stage.

The child's increasing capacity for symbolic thought is also apparent in her use of fantasy and imagination while playing (Golomb & Galasso, 1995). A discarded box becomes a spaceship, a house, or a fort, as children imaginatively take on the roles of different characters. In doing so, children imitate (or try to imitate) actions they have mentally symbolized from situations observed days, or even weeks, earlier.

Still, the preoperational child's understanding of symbols remains immature. A 2-year-old shown a picture of a flower, for example, may try to smell it. A young child may be puzzled by the notion that a map symbolizes an actual location—as in the comic above. In short, preoperational children are still actively figuring out the relationship between symbols and the actual objects they represent (DeLoache, 1995).

The thinking of preoperational children often displays **egocentrism.** By *egocentrism,* Piaget did not mean selfishness or conceit. Rather, egocentric children lack the ability to consider events from another person's point of view. Thus, the young child genuinely thinks that Grandma would like a new Beanie Baby or a Spiderman video for her upcoming birthday because that's what *he* wants. Egocentric thought is also operating when the child silently nods his head in answer to Grandpa's question on the telephone.

The preoperational child's thought is also characterized by irreversibility and centration. **Irreversibility** means that the child cannot mentally reverse a sequence of events or logical operations back to the starting point. For example, the child doesn't understand that adding "3 plus 1" and adding "1 plus 3" refer to the same logical operation. **Centration** refers to the tendency to focus, or center, on only one aspect of a situation, usually a perceptual aspect. In doing so, the child ignores other relevant aspects of the situation.

sensorimotor stage
In Piaget's theory, the first stage of cognitive development, from birth to about age 2; the period during which the infant explores the environment and acquires knowledge through sensing and manipulating objects.

object permanence
The understanding that an object continues to exist even when it can no longer be seen.

preoperational stage
In Piaget's theory, the second stage of cognitive development, which lasts from about age 2 to age 7; characterized by increasing use of symbols and prelogical thought processes.

symbolic thought
The ability to use words, images, and symbols to represent the world.

egocentrism
In Piaget's theory, the inability to take another person's perspective or point of view.

irreversibility
In Piaget's theory, the inability to mentally reverse a sequence of events or logical operations.

centration
In Piaget's theory, the tendency to focus, or *center,* on only one aspect of a situation and ignore other important aspects of the situation.

Preoperational Thinking: Manipulating Mental Symbols With a hodgepodge of toys, some fake fruit, a couple of scarves, and a firefighter's helmet, these two are having great fun. The preschool child's increasing capacity for symbolic thought is delightfully reflected in symbolic play and deferred imitation. In *symbolic play,* one object stands for another: A scarf can become a magic cape, a coat, a mask, or a tablecloth. *Deferred imitation* is the capacity to repeat an action observed earlier, such as the action of a checker in a store.

Piaget's Conservation Task Five-year-old Laura compares the liquid in the two short beakers, then watches as Sandy pours the liquid into a tall, narrow beaker. When asked which has more, Laura insists that there is more liquid in the tall beaker. As Piaget's classic task demonstrates, the average 5-year-old doesn't grasp this principle of conservation. Even though Laura repeated this demonstration several times for the photographer, she persisted in her belief that the tall beaker had more liquid. We tried the demonstration again when Laura was almost 7. Now in the concrete operational stage, Laura immediately understood that both beakers held the same amount of liquid—just as Piaget's theory predicts.

The classic demonstration of both irreversibility and centration involves a task devised by Piaget. When Laura was 5, we tried this task with her. First, we showed her two identical glasses, each containing exactly the same amount of liquid. Laura easily recognized the two amounts of liquid as being the same.

Then, while Laura watched intently, we poured the liquid from one of the glasses into a third container that was much taller and narrower than the others. "Which container," we asked, "holds more liquid?" Like any other preoperational child, Laura answered confidently, "The taller one!" Even when we repeated the procedure, reversing the steps over and over again, Laura remained convinced that the taller container held more liquid than did the shorter container.

This classic demonstration illustrates the preoperational child's inability to understand conservation. The principle of **conservation** holds that two equal physical quantities remain equal even if the appearance of one is changed, as long as nothing is added or subtracted (Piaget & Inhelder, 1974). Because of *centration*, the child cannot simultaneously consider the height and the width of the liquid in the container. Instead, the child focuses on only one aspect of the situation, the height of the liquid. And because of *irreversibility*, the child cannot cognitively reverse the series of events, mentally returning the poured liquid to its original container. Thus, she fails to understand that the two amounts of liquid are still the same.

The Concrete Operational Stage

With the beginning of the **concrete operational stage,** at around age 7, children become capable of true logical thought. They are much less egocentric in their thinking, can reverse mental operations, and can focus simultaneously on two aspects of a problem. In short, they understand the principle of conservation. When presented with two rows of pennies, each row equally spaced, concrete operational children understand that the number of pennies in each row remains the same even when the spacing between the pennies in one row is increased.

As the name of this stage implies, thinking and use of logic tend to be limited to concrete reality—to tangible objects and events. Children in the concrete operational stage often have difficulty thinking logically about hypothetical situations or abstract ideas. For example, an 8-year-old will explain the concept of friendship in very tangible terms, such as, "Friendship is when someone plays with me." In effect, the concrete operational child's ability to deal with abstract ideas and hypothetical situations is limited to his or her personal experiences and actual events.

From Concrete Operations to Formal Operations Logical thinking is evident during the concrete operational stage but develops more fully during the formal operational stage. At about the age of 12, the young person becomes capable of applying logical thinking to hypothetical situations and abstract concepts, such as the principles of molecular bonds in this chemistry class. But as is true of each of Piaget's stages, new cognitive abilities emerge gradually. Having a tangible model to manipulate helps these students grasp abstract chemistry concepts.

The Formal Operational Stage

At the beginning of adolescence, children enter the **formal operational stage.** In terms of problem solving, the formal operational adolescent is much more systematic and logical than the concrete operational child.

Formal operational thought reflects the ability to think logically even when dealing with abstract concepts or hypothetical situations (Piaget, 1972; Piaget & Inhelder, 1958). In contrast to the concrete operational child, the formal operational adolescent explains *friendship* by emphasizing more global and abstract characteristics, such as mutual trust, empathy, loyalty, consistency, and shared beliefs (Harter, 1990).

But, like the development of cognitive abilities during infancy and childhood, formal operational thought emerges only gradually. Formal operational thought continues to increase in sophistication throughout adolescence and adulthood. Although an adolescent may deal effectively

Table 9.2

Piaget's Stages of Cognitive Development

Stage	Characteristics of the Stage	Major Change of the Stage
Sensorimotor (0–2 years)	Acquires understanding of object permanence. First understandings of cause-and-effect relationships.	Development proceeds from reflexes to active use of sensory and motor skills to explore the environment.
Preoperational (2–7 years)	Symbolic thought emerges. Language development occurs (2–4 years). Thought and language both tend to be egocentric. Cannot solve conservation problems.	Development proceeds from understanding simple cause-and-effect relationships to prelogical thought processes involving the use of imagination and symbols to represent objects, actions, and situations.
Concrete operations (7–11 years)	Reversibility attained. Can solve conservation problems. Logical thought develops and is applied to concrete problems. Cannot solve complex verbal problems and hypothetical problems.	Development proceeds from prelogical thought to logical solutions to concrete problems.
Formal operations (adolescence through adulthood)	Logically solves all types of problems. Thinks scientifically. Solves complex verbal and hypothetical problems. Is able to think in abstract terms.	Development proceeds from logical solving of concrete problems to logical solving of all classes of problems, including abstract problems.

with abstract ideas in one domain of knowledge, his thinking may not reflect the same degree of sophistication in other areas. Piaget (1973) acknowledged that even among many adults, formal operational thinking is often limited to areas in which they have developed expertise or a special interest.

Table 9.2 summarizes Piaget's stages of cognitive development.

Criticisms of Piaget's Theory

Piaget's theory has inspired hundreds of research studies (Kessen, 1996). Generally, scientific research has supported Piaget's most fundamental idea: that infants, young children, and older children use distinctly different cognitive abilities to construct their understanding of the world. However, other aspects of Piaget's theory have been challenged.

Criticism 1: Piaget underestimated the cognitive abilities of infants and young children. To test for object permanence, Piaget would show the infant an object, cover it with a cloth, and then observe whether the infant tried to reach under the cloth for the object. Obviously, such a response requires the infant to have a certain level of motor skill development. Using this procedure, Piaget found that it wasn't until an infant was about 9 months old that she behaved as if she understood that an object continued to exist after it was hidden. Even at this age, Piaget maintained, an infant's understanding of object permanence was immature and would not be fully developed for another year or so.

But what if the infant "knew" that the object was under the cloth but simply lacked the physical coordination to reach for it? How could you test this hypothesis? Rather than using manual tasks to assess object permanence and other cognitive abilities, psychologist **Renée Baillargeon** has used *visual* tasks. Baillargeon's research is based on the premise that infants, like adults, will look longer at "surprising" events that appear to contradict their understanding of the world.

In this research paradigm, the infant first watches an *expected event*, which is consistent with the understanding that is being tested. Then, the infant is shown an *unexpected event*. If the unexpected event violates the infant's understanding of physical principles, he should be surprised and look longer at the unexpected event than the expected event.

conservation
In Piaget's theory, the understanding that two equal quantities remain equal even though the form or appearance is rearranged, as long as nothing is added or subtracted.

concrete operational stage
In Piaget's theory, the third stage of cognitive development, which lasts from about age 7 to adolescence; characterized by the ability to think logically about concrete objects and situations.

formal operational stage
In Piaget's theory, the fourth stage of cognitive development, which lasts from adolescence through adulthood; characterized by the ability to think logically about abstract principles and hypothetical situations.

As researchers continue to make progress in understanding how infants attain and use their physical knowledge, we come closer to unveiling the complex architecture that makes it possible for them to learn, so very rapidly, about the world around them.

RENÉE BAILLARGEON (2004)

Figure 9.5 Testing Object Permanence in Babies How can you test object permanence in infants who are too young to reach for a hidden object? Three-and-a-half-month-old infants initially watched a possible event: The small carrot passes from one side of the panel to the other without appearing in the window. In the impossible event, the tall carrot does the same. Because the infants are surprised and look longer at the impossible event, Baillargeon and DeVos (1991) concluded that the infants had formed a mental representation of the existence, height, and path of each carrot as it moved behind the panel—the essence of object permanence (Baillargeon, 2004).

Figure 9.5 shows one of Baillargeon's classic tests of object permanence, conducted with Julie DeVos (Baillargeon & DeVos, 1991). If the infant understands that objects continue to exist even when they are hidden, she will be surprised when the tall carrot unexpectedly does *not* appear in the window of the panel.

Using variations of this basic experimental procedure, Baillargeon and her colleagues have shown that infants as young as 2½ months of age display object permanence (Aguiar & Baillargeon, 1999; Luo & others, 2003; Wang & others, 2005). This is more than six months earlier than the age at which Piaget believed infants first showed evidence of object permanence.

Going beyond object permanence, Baillargeon and her colleagues have shown that infants at different ages acquire different expectations about how the physical world operates. They've found that infants develop *event-specific expectations,* rather than general principles (Baillargeon, 2002, 2004).

For example, the two events depicted in Figure 9.6 are similar in that both involve the disappearance of a tall object. However, 4½-month-old infants are surprised by one event—a tall object disappearing behind a short object—and not by the other—a tall object disappearing inside a short container (Hespos & Baillargeon, 2001, 2006). It's not until 7½ months of age that infants react with increased attention to the inside-container event. During infancy, it seems, each event is understood separately.

Piaget's discoveries laid the groundwork for our understanding of cognitive development. However, as developmental psychologists Jeanne Shinskey and Yuko Munakata (2005) observe, today's researchers recognize that "what infants appear to know depends heavily on how they are tested."

Criticism 2: Piaget underestimated the impact of the social and cultural environment on cognitive development. In contrast to Piaget, the Russian psychologist **Lev Vygotsky** believed that cognitive development is strongly influenced by social and cultural factors. Vygotsky formulated his theory of cognitive development at about the same time as Piaget formulated his. However, Vygotsky's writings did not become available in the West until many years after his untimely death from tuberculosis in 1934 (Rowe & Wertsch, 2002; van Geert, 1998).

Vygotsky agreed with Piaget that children may be able to reach a particular cognitive level through their own efforts. However, Vygotsky (1978, 1987) argued that children are able to attain higher levels of cognitive development through the support

4.5 months

Behind Short Container

7.5 months

Inside Short Container

Figure 9.6 Infants Form Event-Specific Expectations About the World Susan Hespos and Renée Baillargeon (2001) found that 4½-month-old infants respond with increased attention when a tall object completely disappears when placed *behind* a shorter object (*left*) but not when a tall object disappears when placed *inside* a short container (*right*). It is not until the age of 7½ months that infants are also surprised by a tall container disappearing inside a short container. According to Baillargeon (2004), such findings demonstrate that infants form *event-specific expectations* about the physical world rather than general principles.

and instruction that they receive from other people. Researchers have confirmed that social interactions, especially with older children and adults, play a significant role in a child's cognitive development (Gopnik, 1996; Wertsch & Tulviste, 1992).

One of Vygotsky's important ideas was his notion of the **zone of proximal development.** This refers to the gap between what children can accomplish on their own and what they can accomplish with the help of others who are more competent (Rowe & Wertsch, 2002). Note that the word *proximal* means "nearby," indicating that the assistance provided goes just slightly beyond the child's current abilities. Such guidance can help "stretch" the child's cognitive abilities to new levels.

Cross-cultural studies have shown that cognitive development is strongly influenced by the skills that are valued and encouraged in a particular environment, such as the ability to weave, hunt, or collaborate with others (Greenfield & others, 2003; Maynard & Greenfield, 2003). Such findings suggest that Piaget's stages are not as universal and culture-free as some researchers had once believed.

Criticism 3: Piaget overestimated the degree to which people achieve formal operational thought processes. Researchers have found that many adults display abstract-hypothetical thinking only in limited areas of knowledge, and that some adults never display formal operational thought processes at all. College students, for example, may not display formal operational thinking when given problems outside their major, as when an English major is presented with a physics problem (DeLisi & Staudt, 1980). Late in his life, Piaget (1972, 1973) suggested that formal operational thinking might not be a universal phenomenon, but instead is the product of an individual's expertise in a specific area.

Rather than distinct stages of cognitive development, some developmental psychologists emphasize the **information-processing model of cognitive development** (Klahr, 1992; Siegler, 1996). This model focuses on the development of fundamental mental processes, like attention, memory, and problem solving (Halford, 2002). In this approach, cognitive development is viewed as a process of continuous change over the lifespan (Courage & Howe, 2002; Craik & Bialystok, 2006). Through life experiences, we continue to acquire new knowledge, including more sophisticated cognitive skills and strategies. In turn, this improves our ability to process, learn, and remember information.

With the exceptions that have been noted, Piaget's observations of the changes in children's cognitive abilities are fundamentally accurate. His description of the distinct cognitive changes that occur during infancy and childhood ranks as one of the most outstanding contributions to developmental psychology (Beilin, 1994).

Lev Vygotsky Russian psychologist Lev Vygotsky was born in 1896, the same year as Piaget. He died in 1934 of tuberculosis. Recent decades have seen a resurgence of interest in Vygotsky's theoretical writings. Vygotsky emphasized the impact of social and cultural factors on cognitive development. According to Vygotsky, cognitive development always takes place within a social and cultural context.

Adolescence

Key Theme

- **Adolescence is the stage that marks the transition from childhood to adulthood.**

Key Questions

- **What factors affect the timing of puberty?**
- **What characterizes adolescent relationships with parents and peers?**
- **What is Erikson's psychosocial theory of lifespan development?**

Adolescence is the transitional stage between late childhood and the beginning of adulthood. Although it can vary by individual and gender, adolescence usually begins around age 11 or 12. It is a transition marked by sweeping physical, social,

zone of proximal development
In Vygotsky's theory of cognitive development, the difference between what children can accomplish on their own and what they can accomplish with the help of others who are more competent.

information-processing model of cognitive development
The model that views cognitive development as a process that is continuous over the lifespan and that studies the development of basic mental processes such as attention, memory, and problem solving.

adolescence
The transitional stage between late childhood and the beginning of adulthood, during which sexual maturity is reached.

puberty
The stage of adolescence in which an individual reaches sexual maturity and becomes physiologically capable of sexual reproduction.

primary sex characteristics
Sexual organs that are directly involved in reproduction, such as the uterus, ovaries, penis, and testicles.

secondary sex characteristics
Sexual characteristics that develop during puberty and are not directly involved in reproduction but differentiate between the sexes, such as male facial hair and female breast development.

adolescent growth spurt
The period of accelerated growth during puberty, involving rapid increases in height and weight.

menarche
(meh-NAR-kee) A female's first menstrual period, which occurs during puberty.

and cognitive changes as the individual moves toward independence and adult responsibilities. Outwardly, the most noticeable changes that occur during adolescence are the physical changes that accompany the development of sexual maturity. We'll begin by considering those changes, then turn to the aspects of social development during adolescence. Following that discussion, we'll consider some of the cognitive changes of adolescence, including identity formation.

Physical and Sexual Development

Nature seems to have a warped sense of humor when it comes to **puberty,** the physical process of attaining sexual maturation and reproductive capacity that begins during the early adolescent years. As you may well remember, physical development during adolescence sometimes proceeds unevenly. Feet and hands get bigger before legs and arms do. The torso typically develops last, so shirts and blouses sometimes don't fit quite right. And the left and right sides of the body can grow at different rates. The resulting lopsided effect can be quite distressing: One ear, foot, testicle, or breast may be noticeably larger than the other. Thankfully, such asymmetries tend to even out by the end of adolescence.

Although nature's game plan for physical change during adolescence may seem haphazard, puberty actually tends to follow a predictable sequence for each sex. These changes are summarized in Table 9.3.

Primary and Secondary Sex Characteristics

The physical changes of puberty fall into two categories. Internally, puberty involves the development of the **primary sex characteristics,** which are the sex organs that are directly involved in reproduction. For example, the female's uterus and the male's testes enlarge in puberty. Externally, development of the **secondary sex characteristics,** which are not directly involved in reproduction, signal increasing sexual maturity. Secondary sex characteristics include changes in height, weight, and body shape; the appearance of body hair and voice changes; and, in girls, breast development.

As you can see in Table 9.3, females are typically about two years ahead of males in terms of physical and sexual maturation. For example, the period of marked acceleration in weight and height gains, called the **adolescent growth spurt,** occurs about two years earlier in females than in males. Much to the chagrin of many sixth- and seventh-grade boys, it's not uncommon for their female classmates to be both heavier and taller than they are.

Girls Get a Head Start These two eighth-graders are the same age! In terms of the progress of sexual and physical maturation, girls are usually about two years ahead of boys.

The statistical averages in Table 9.3 are informative, but—because they are only averages—they cannot convey the normal range of individual variation in the timing of pubertal events (see Ellis, 2004). For example, a female's first menstrual period, termed **menarche,** typically occurs around age 12 or 13, but menarche may take place as early as age 9 or 10 or as late as age 16 or 17. For boys, the testicles typically begin enlarging around age 11 or 12, but the process can begin before age 9 or after age 14. Thus, it's entirely possible for some adolescents to have already completed physical and sexual maturation before their classmates have even begun puberty. Yet they would all be considered well within the normal age range for puberty (Sun & others, 2002).

Less obvious than the outward changes associated with puberty are the sweeping changes occurring in another realm of physical development: the adolescent's brain. We discuss these developments in the Focus on Neuroscience on page 396.

Table 9.3

The Typical Sequence of Puberty

Girls	Average Age	Boys	Average Age
Ovaries increase production of estrogen and progesterone	9	Testes increase production of testosterone	10
Internal sex organs begin to grow larger	9½	External sex organs begin to grow larger	11
Breast development begins	10	Production of sperm and first ejaculation	13
Peak height spurt	12	Peak height spurt	14
Peak muscle and organ growth, including widening of hips	12½	Peak muscle and organ growth, including broadening of shoulders	14½
Menarche (first menstrual period)	12½	Voice lowers	15
First ovulation (release of fertile egg)	13½	Facial hair appears	16

Source: Based on data in Brooks-Gunn & Reiter (1990).

Factors Affecting the Timing of Puberty

Although you might be tempted to think that the onset of puberty is strictly a matter of biological programming, researchers have found that both genetics and environmental factors play a role in the timing of puberty. Genetic evidence includes the observation that girls usually experience menarche at about the same age as their mothers did (Brooks-Gunn & Reiter, 1990; Ersoy & others, 2005). And, not surprisingly, the timing of pubertal changes tends to be closer for identical twins than for nontwin siblings (Mustanski & others, 2004).

"Dad, when will I be old enough to shave?"

Environmental factors, such as nutrition and health, also influence the onset of puberty. Generally, well-nourished and healthy children begin puberty earlier than do children who have experienced serious health problems or inadequate nutrition. As living standards and health care have improved, the average age of puberty has steadily decreased in the United States over the past century.

For example, 150 years ago the average age of menarche in the United States was about 17 years old. Today it is about 12½ years old. The same downward trend is also evident in boys. Compared to the 1960s, boys today are beginning the physical changes of puberty about a year earlier (Herman-Giddens & others, 2001; Irwin, 2005). In recent years, however, the trend toward earlier puberty seems to have slowed (see Parent & others, 2003).

Body size and degree of physical activity are also related to the timing of puberty. In general, stout or heavy children begin puberty earlier than do lean children. Girls who are involved in physically demanding athletic activities, such as gymnastics, figure skating, dancing, and competitive running, can experience delays in menarche of up to two years beyond the average age (Brooks-Gunn, 1988).

Interestingly, the timing of puberty is also influenced by the absence of the biological father in the home environment. Several studies have found that girls raised in homes in which the biological father is absent tend to experience puberty earlier than girls raised in homes with intact families (Bogaert, 2005a; Ellis & Garber, 2000; Hoier, 2003). Researcher Brian Mustanski and his colleagues (2004) found similar results for both sexes in a large-scale study of more than 1,800 pairs of twins. In that study, both boys and girls raised in father-absent homes experienced accelerated physical development.

Other studies have revealed that the quality of family relationships is tied to the timing of puberty. The pattern that emerges is that negative and stressful family environments are associated with an earlier onset of puberty, including earlier

FOCUS ON NEUROSCIENCE

The Adolescent Brain: A Work in Progress

For many adolescents, the teenage years, especially the early ones, seem to seesaw between moments of exhilaration and exasperation. Impressive instances of insightful behavior are counterbalanced by impulsive decisions made with no consideration of the potential risks or consequences. How can erratic adolescent behavior be explained?

For many years, the unpredictable behavior and mood swings of adolescents were explained as being due to "raging hormones." However, researchers have actually found little connection between hormone levels and adolescent behavior. As researcher Ronald Dahl (2003) explains, "High levels of sex hormones are not the cause of emotional problems in adolescents. Many adolescents with peak hormone levels experience no emotional difficulties at all." Rather than raging reproductive hormones, the explanation seems to lie within the adolescent brain.

To track changes in the developing brain, neuroscientists Jay Giedd, Elizabeth Sowell, Paul Thompson, and their colleagues have used magnetic resonance imaging (MRI) since the early 1990s to repeatedly scan the brains of normal kids and teenagers. One striking insight produced by their studies is that the human brain goes through not one but two distinct spurts of brain development—one during prenatal development and one during late childhood just prior to puberty (Giedd & others, 1999; Gogtay & others, 2004a; Lenroot & Giedd, 2006).

Earlier in the chapter, we described how new neurons are produced at an astonishing rate during the first several months of prenatal development—so much so that by the sixth month of prenatal development, there is a vast overabundance of neurons in the fetal brain. During the final months of prenatal development, there is fierce competition among the neurons to make connections and survive. In the neuronal equivalent of "survival of the fittest," those neurons that don't make connections are eliminated. This process is called *pruning.*

During the years of infancy and early childhood, the brain's outer gray matter continues to develop and grow. The tapestry of interconnections between neurons becomes much more intricate as dendrites and axon terminals multiply and branch to extend their reach. White matter also increases as groups of neurons develop *myelin,* the white, fatty covering that insulates some axons, speeding communication between neurons.

Outwardly, these brain changes are reflected in the increasing cognitive and physical capabilities of the child. But in the brain itself, the "use-it-or-lose-it" principle is at work: Unused neuron circuits are being pruned. While it may seem counterintuitive, the loss of unused neurons and neuronal connections actually improves brain functioning by making the remaining neurons more efficient in processing information.

By 6 years of age, the child's brain is about 95 percent of its adult size. This well-documented fact led to the mistaken belief that brain development is essentially complete by late childhood. But the longitudinal MRI studies of normal kids and adolescents revealed something very surprising—a *second* wave of gray matter overproduction just prior to puberty, followed by a second round of neuronal pruning during the teenage years (Sowell & others, 2004).

ZITS

menarche in girls. Why would such factors influence the timing of puberty? Although researchers are trying to pinpoint the exact mechanisms, part of the answer is that stressful family events increase many of the same hormones that are involved in activating puberty. On the other hand, positive family environments are associated with later physical development (see Ellis, 2004; Ellis & Essex, 2007; Romans & others, 2003).

Early Versus Late Maturation

Adolescents tend to be keenly aware of the physical changes they are experiencing as well as of the *timing* of those changes compared with their peer group. Most adolescents are "on time," meaning that the maturational changes are occurring at roughly the same time for them as for others in their peer group.

However, some adolescents are "off time," experiencing maturation noticeably earlier or later than the majority of their peers. For girls, early maturation seems to carry a greater risk for a variety of negative health and psychological outcomes. For

Researchers are still not certain what causes this late childhood surge of cortical gray matter, but they know it is not due to a production of new neurons. Rather, the size, complexity, and connections among neurons all increase. This increase in gray matter peaks at about age 11 for girls and age 12 for boys (Durston & others, 2001).

Pruning Gray Matter from Back to Front

The color-coded series of brain images below shows the course of brain development from ages 5 to 20 (Gogtay & others, 2004). Red indicates more gray matter; blue indicates less gray matter. Courtesy of UCLA neuroscientist Paul Thompson, you can also watch brief time-lapse "movies" of the changing brain at the following web site:
http://www.loni.ucla.edu/~thompson/DEVEL/dynamic.html.

The MRI images reveal that as the brain matures, neuronal connections are pruned and gray matter diminishes in a back-to-front wave. As pruning occurs, the connections that remain are strengthened and reinforced, and the amount of white matter in the brain steadily increases (Giedd, 2009; Sowell & others, 2003).

More specifically, the first brain areas to mature are at the extreme front and back of the brain. These areas are involved with very basic functions, such as processing sensations and movement. The next brain areas to mature are the *parietal lobes,* which are involved in language and spatial skills.

The last brain area to experience pruning and maturity is the *prefrontal cortex.* This is significant because the prefrontal cortex plays a critical role in many advanced or "executive" cognitive functions, such as a person's ability to reason, plan ahead, organize, solve problems, and decide. And when does the prefrontal cortex reach full maturity? According to the MRI studies, not until a person reaches their mid-20s (Gogtay & others, 2004a).

This suggests that an adolescent's occasional impulsive or immature behavior is at least partly a reflection of a brain that still has a long way to go to reach full adult maturity. During adolescence, emotions and impulses can be intense and compelling. But the parts of the brain that are responsible for exercising judgment are still maturing. The result can be behavior that is immature, impulsive, unpredictable—or even risky.

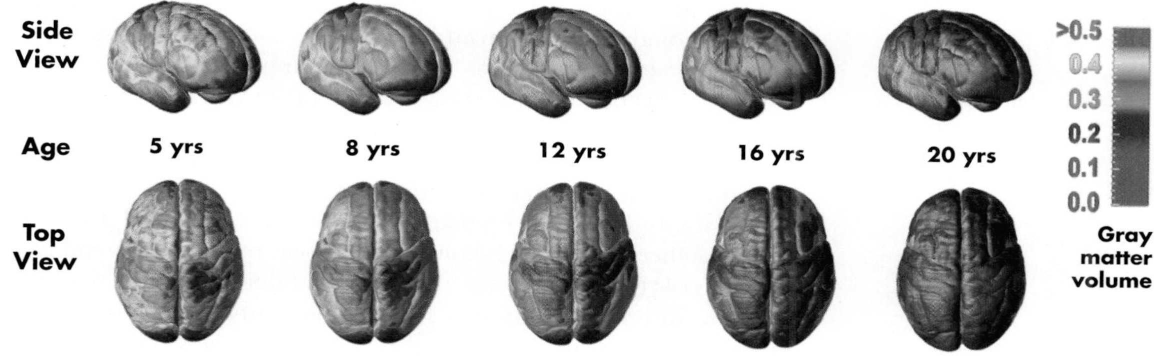

example, early-maturing girls tend to be more likely than late-maturing girls to have negative feelings about their body image and pubertal changes, such as menarche (Ge & others, 2003). Compared to late-maturing girls, early-maturing girls are less likely to have received factual information concerning development. They may also feel embarrassed by unwanted attention from older males (Brooks-Gunn & Reiter, 1990). Early-maturing girls also have higher rates of teenage pregnancy and are at greater risk for unhealthy weight gain later in life (Adair & Gordon-Larsen, 2001; Lien & others, 2006).

Early maturation can be advantageous for boys, but it is also associated with risks. Early-maturing boys tend to be popular with their peers. However, although they are more successful in athletics than late-maturing peers, they are also more susceptible to behaviors that put their health at risk, such as steroid use (McCabe & Ricciardelli, 2004). Early-maturing boys are also more prone to the symptoms of depression, problems at school, and engaging in drug or alcohol use (see Ge & others, 2001, 2003).

Effects of Early Versus Late Maturation As any adult who remembers seventh-grade gym class can attest, the timing of puberty varies widely. Early maturation can have different effects for boys and girls. Early-maturing boys tend to be successful in athletics and popular with their peers, but they are more susceptible to risky behaviors, such as drug, alcohol, or steroid use (McCabe & Ricciardelli, 2004). Early-maturing girls tend to have more negative feelings about the arrival of puberty and body changes, have higher rates of teenage pregnancy, and may be embarrassed or harassed by unwanted attention from older males (Ge & others, 2003; Adair & Gordon-Larsen, 2001).

Social Development

The changes in adolescents' bodies are accompanied by changes in their social interactions, most notably with parents and peers. Contrary to what many people think, parent–adolescent relationships are generally positive. In fact, most teenagers report that they admire their parents and turn to them for advice (Steinberg, 1990, 2001). As a general rule, when parent–child relationships have been good before adolescence, they continue to be relatively smooth during adolescence. Nevertheless, some friction seems to be inevitable as children make the transition to adolescence.

Although parents remain influential throughout adolescence, relationships with friends and peers become increasingly important. Adolescents usually encounter greater diversity among their peers as they make the transitions to middle school and high school. To a much greater degree than during childhood, the adolescent's social network, social context, and community influence his or her values, norms, and expectations (Steinberg & others, 1995).

Parents often worry that peer influences will lead to undesirable behavior. Researchers have found, however, that peer relationships tend to *reinforce* the traits and goals that parents fostered during childhood (Steinberg, 2001). This finding is not as surprising as it might seem. Adolescents tend to form friendships with peers who are similar in age, social class, race, and beliefs about drinking, dating, church attendance, and educational goals.

Friends often exert pressure on one another to study, make good grades, attend college, and engage in prosocial behaviors. So, although peer influence can lead to undesirable behaviors in some instances, peers can also influence one another in positive ways (Berndt, 1992; Mounts & Steinberg, 1995).

Romantic and sexual relationships also become increasingly important throughout the adolescent years. During early and middle adolescence, the physical changes of puberty prime the adolescent's interest in sexuality. One national survey showed

ZITS

identity
A person's definition or description of himself or herself, including the values, beliefs, and ideals that guide the individual's behavior.

that by the age of 12, about one-quarter of adolescents reported having had a "special romantic relationship." By age 15, that percentage increased to 50 percent, and reached 70 percent by the age of 17 (Carver & others, 2003).

Social and cultural factors also influence when, why, and how an adolescent initiates sexual behaviors. The beginning of dating, for example, coincides more strongly with cultural and social expectations and norms, such as when friends begin to date, than with an adolescent's degree of physical maturation (see Collins, 2003).

Far from being trivial, shallow, or transitory, romantic relationships can have a significant impact on the adolescent's psychological and social development (Furman, 2002). In terms of emotional impact, adolescents who are involved in a romantic relationship are more prone to mood swings and, especially when the relationship is a stormy one, depression (Joyner & Udry, 2000). However, by late adolescence, romantic relationships can also lead to overall feelings of enhanced self-worth, feelings of competence, and enhanced relationships with friends and peers (Furman & Shaffer, 2003; Zimmer-Gembeck & Gallaty, 2006).

The physical and social developments we've discussed so far are the more obvious changes associated with the onset of puberty. No less important, however, are the cognitive changes that allow the adolescent to think and reason in new, more complex ways.

Peer Relationships in Adolescence Although parents often worry about the negative impact of peers, peers can also have a positive influence on one another. These teenage volunteers are attending a leadership conference for Drug Free Youth in Town, a national community-based organization that works to prevent substance abuse in children and teens.

Identity Formation: Erikson's Theory of Psychosocial Development

When psychologists talk about a person's **identity,** they are referring to the values, beliefs, and ideals that guide the individual's behavior (Erikson, 1964a; Marcia, 1991). Our sense of personal identity gives us an integrated and continuing sense of self over time. Identity formation is a process that continues throughout the lifespan. As we embrace new and different roles over the course of our lives, we define ourselves in new ways (Erikson & others, 1986; Grotevant, 1992).

For the first time in the lifespan, the adolescent possesses the cognitive skills necessary for dealing with identity issues in a meaningful way (Habermas & Bluck, 2000; Krettenauer, 2005). Beginning in early adolescence, self-definition shifts. Preadolescent children tend to describe themselves in very concrete social and behavioral terms. An 8-year-old might describe himself by saying, "I play with Mark and I like to ride my bike." In contrast, adolescents use more abstract self-descriptions that reflect personal attributes, values, beliefs, and goals (Harter, 1990). Thus, a 14-year-old might say, "I have strong religious beliefs, love animals, and hope to become a veterinarian."

Some aspects of personal identity involve characteristics over which the adolescent really has no control, such as gender, race, ethnic background, and socioeconomic level. In effect, these identity characteristics are fixed and already internalized by the time an individual reaches the adolescent years.

Beyond such fixed characteristics, the adolescent begins to evaluate herself on several different dimensions. Social acceptance by peers, academic and athletic abilities, work abilities, personal appearance, and romantic appeal are some important aspects of self-definition. Another challenge facing the adolescent is to develop an identity that is independent of her parents while retaining a sense of connection to her family. Thus, the adolescent has not one but several self-concepts that she must integrate into a coherent and unified whole to answer the question "Who am I?"

The adolescent's task of achieving an integrated identity is one important aspect of psychoanalyst **Erik Erikson**'s influential theory of psychosocial development. Briefly, Erikson (1968) proposed that each of eight stages of life is associated with a particular psychosocial conflict that can be resolved in either a positive or a negative direction (see Table 9.4). Relationships with others play an important role in determining the outcome of each conflict. According to Erikson, the key psychosocial conflict facing adolescents is *identity versus role confusion.*

Psychoanalyst Erik Erikson Erikson (1902–1994) is shown here with his wife, Joan, in 1988. Erikson's landmark theory of psychosocial development stressed the importance of social and cultural influences on personality throughout the stages of life.

Table 9.4

Erik Erikson's Psychosocial Stages of Development

Life Stage	Psychosocial Conflict	Positive Resolution	Negative Resolution
Infancy (birth to 18 months)	Trust vs. mistrust	Reliance on consistent and warm caregivers produces a sense of predictability and trust in the environment.	Physical and psychological neglect by caregivers leads to fear, anxiety, and mistrust of the environment.
Toddlerhood (18 months to 3 years)	Autonomy vs. doubt	Caregivers encourage independence and self-sufficiency, promoting positive self-esteem.	Overly restrictive caregiving leads to self-doubt in abilities and low self-esteem.
Early childhood (3 to 6 years)	Initiative vs. guilt	The child learns to initiate activities and develops a sense of social responsibility concerning the rights of others; promotes self-confidence.	Parental overcontrol stifles the child's spontaneity, sense of purpose, and social learning; promotes guilt and fear of punishment.
Middle and late childhood (6 to 12 years)	Industry vs. inferiority	Through experiences with parents and "keeping up" with peers, the child develops a sense of pride and competence in schoolwork and home and social activities.	Negative experiences with parents or failure to "keep up" with peers leads to pervasive feelings of inferiority and inadequacy.
Adolescence	Identity vs. role confusion	Through experimentation with different roles, the adolescent develops an integrated and stable self-definition; forms commitments to future adult roles.	An apathetic adolescent or one who experiences pressures and demands from others may feel confusion about his or her identity and role in society.
Young adulthood	Intimacy vs. isolation	By establishing lasting and meaningful relationships, the young adult develops a sense of connectedness and intimacy with others.	Because of fear of rejection or excessive self-preoccupation, the young adult is unable to form close, meaningful relationships and becomes psychologically isolated.
Middle adulthood	Generativity vs. stagnation	Through child rearing, caring for others, productive work, and community involvement, the adult expresses unselfish concern for the welfare of the next generation.	Self-indulgence, self-absorption, and a preoccupation with one's own needs lead to a sense of stagnation, boredom, and a lack of meaningful accomplishments.
Late adulthood	Ego integrity vs. despair	In reviewing his or her life, the older adult experiences a strong sense of self-acceptance and meaningfulness in his or her accomplishments.	In looking back on his or her life, the older adult experiences regret, dissatisfaction, and disappointment about his or her life and accomplishments.

Source: Adapted from Erikson (1964a).

To successfully form an identity, adolescents must not only integrate various dimensions of their personality into a coherent whole but also define the roles that they will adopt within the larger society on becoming an adult (Habermas & Bluck, 2000). To accomplish this, adolescents grapple with a wide variety of issues, such as selecting a potential career and formulating religious, moral, and political beliefs. They must also adopt social roles involving interpersonal relationships, sexuality, and long-term commitments such as marriage and parenthood.

In Erikson's (1968) theory, the adolescent's path to successful identity achievement begins with *role confusion,* which is characterized by little sense of commitment on any of these issues. This period is followed by a *moratorium period,* during which the adolescent experiments with different roles, values, and beliefs. Gradually, by choosing among the alternatives and making commitments, the adolescent arrives at an *integrated identity.*

Psychological research has generally supported Erikson's description of the process of identity formation (Grotevant, 1987; Marcia, 1991). However, it's important to keep in mind that identity continues to evolve over the entire lifespan, not just during the adolescent years (Grotevant, 1992). Adolescents and young adults seem to achieve a stable sense of identity in some areas earlier than in others. Far fewer adolescents and young adults have attained a stable sense of identity in the realm of religious and political beliefs than in the realm of vocational choice.

The Development of Moral Reasoning

An important aspect of cognitive development during adolescence is a change in **moral reasoning**—how an individual thinks about moral decisions. The adolescent's increased capacities to think abstractly, imagine hypothetical situations, and compare ideals to the real world all affect his thinking about moral issues.

moral reasoning
The aspect of cognitive development that has to do with how an individual reasons about moral decisions.

The most influential theory of moral development was proposed by **Lawrence Kohlberg** (1927–1987). Kohlberg's interest in moral development may have been triggered by his experiences as a young adult (see photo on the next page). Kohlberg used hypothetical moral dilemmas to investigate moral reasoning, such as whether a husband should steal a drug he could not afford to cure his dying wife. In Kohlberg's theory (1976, 1984), it is the reasoning people use to justify their answers that is significant. Kohlberg analyzed the responses of children, adolescents, and adults to such hypothetical moral dilemmas. He concluded that there are distinct *stages* of moral development. These stages unfold in an age-related, step-by-step fashion, much like Piaget's stages of cognitive development (Kohlberg, 1981).

"Apparently, he's not ready for stories filled with moral ambiguity."

Kohlberg proposed three distinct *levels* of moral reasoning: preconventional, conventional, and postconventional. Each level is based on the degree to which a person conforms to conventional standards of society. Furthermore, each level has two *stages* that represent different degrees of sophistication in moral reasoning. Table 9.5 describes the characteristics of the moral reasoning associated with each of Kohlberg's levels and stages.

Kohlberg found that the responses of children under the age of 10 reflected *preconventional* moral reasoning based on self-interest—avoiding punishment and maximizing personal gain. Beginning in late childhood and continuing through adolescence and adulthood, responses typically reflected conventional moral reasoning, which emphasizes social roles, rules, and obligations. Thus, the progression from preconventional to conventional moral reasoning is closely associated with age-related cognitive abilities (Kohlberg, 1984; Walker, 1989).

Do people inevitably advance from conventional to postconventional moral reasoning, as Kohlberg once thought? In a 20-year longitudinal study, Kohlberg followed a group of boys from late childhood through early adulthood. Of the 58 subjects in the study, only 8 subjects occasionally displayed stage 5 reasoning, which

Table 9.5

Kohlberg's Levels and Stages of Moral Development

I. Preconventional Level
Moral reasoning is guided by external consequences. No internalization of values or rules.

Stage 1: Punishment and Obedience
"Right" is obeying the rules simply to avoid punishment because others have power over you and can punish you.

Stage 2: Mutual Benefit
"Right" is an even or fair exchange, so that both parties benefit. Moral reasoning guided by a sense of "fair play."

II. Conventional Level
Moral reasoning is guided by conformity to social roles, rules, and expectations that the person has learned and internalized.

Stage 3: Interpersonal Expectations
"Right" is being a "good" person by conforming to social expectations, such as showing concern for others and following rules set by others so as to win their approval.

Stage 4: Law and Order
"Right" is helping maintain social order by doing one's duty, obeying laws simply because they are laws, and showing respect for authorities simply because they are authorities.

III. Postconventional Level
Moral reasoning is guided by internalized legal and moral principles that protect the rights of all members of society.

Stage 5: Legal Principles
"Right" is helping protect the basic rights of all members of society by upholding legalistic principles that promote the values of fairness, justice, equality, and democracy.

Stage 6: Universal Moral Principles
"Right" is determined by self-chosen ethical principles that reflect the person's respect for ideals such as nonviolence, equality, and human dignity. If these moral principles conflict with democratically determined laws, the person's self-chosen moral principles take precedence.

Sources: Based on Kohlberg (1981) and Colby & others (1983).

Lawerence Kohlberg (1927–1987) After graduating from high school in 1945, Kohlberg joined the Merchant Marines. In Europe, he witnessed the aftermath of World War II and met many Holocaust survivors. After finishing his service in the Merchant Marines, Kohlberg helped smuggle Jewish refugees into what was then British-controlled Palestine. He was caught and briefly imprisoned by the British but escaped and eventually made his way back to the United States (Schwartz, 2004). Years later, Kohlberg (1986) wrote, "My experience with illegal immigration into Israel raised all sorts of moral questions, issues which I saw as issues of justice. Was using death or violence right or just for a political end? When is it permissible to be involved with violent means for supposedly just ends?" Kohlberg was to be preoccupied with themes of justice and morality for the rest of his life.

emphasizes respect for legal principles that protect all members of society. *None* of the subjects showed stage 6 reasoning, which reflects self-chosen ethical principles that are universally applied (Colby & others, 1983). Kohlberg and his colleagues eventually dropped stage 6 from the theory, partly because clear-cut expressions of "universal moral principles" were so rare (Gibbs, 2003; Rest, 1983).

Thus, Kohlberg's original belief that the development of abstract thinking in adolescence naturally and invariably leads people to the formation of idealistic moral principles has not been supported. Only a few exceptional people display the philosophical ideals in Kohlberg's highest level of moral reasoning. The normal course of changes in moral reasoning for most people seems to be captured by Kohlberg's first four stages (Colby & Kohlberg, 1984). By adulthood, the predominant form of moral reasoning is conventional moral reasoning, reflecting the importance of social roles and rules.

Kohlberg's theory has been criticized on several grounds (see Krebs & Denton, 2005, 2006). Probably the most important limitation of Kohlberg's theory is that moral *reasoning* doesn't always predict moral *behavior*. People don't necessarily respond to real-life dilemmas as they do to the hypothetical dilemmas that are used to test moral reasoning. Further, people can, and do, respond at different levels to different kinds of moral decisions. As Dennis Krebs and Kathy Denton (2005) point out, people are *flexible* in their real-world moral behavior: The goals that people pursue affect the types of moral judgments they make.

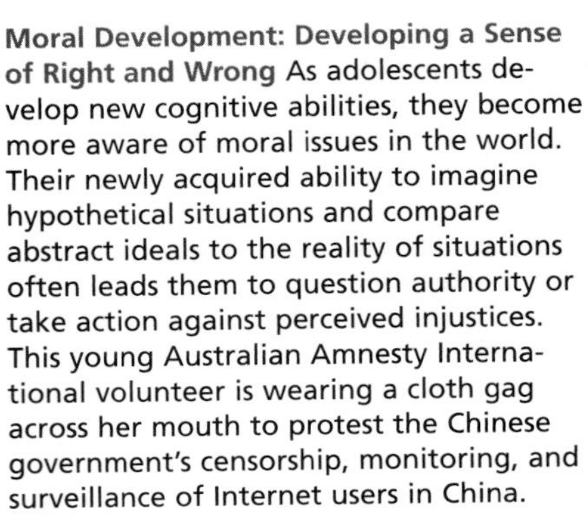

Moral Development: Developing a Sense of Right and Wrong As adolescents develop new cognitive abilities, they become more aware of moral issues in the world. Their newly acquired ability to imagine hypothetical situations and compare abstract ideals to the reality of situations often leads them to question authority or take action against perceived injustices. This young Australian Amnesty International volunteer is wearing a cloth gag across her mouth to protest the Chinese government's censorship, monitoring, and surveillance of Internet users in China.

Gender, Culture, and Moral Reasoning

Other challenges to Kohlberg's theory questioned whether it was as universal as its proponents claimed. Psychologist Carol Gilligan (1982) pointed out that Kohlberg's early research was conducted entirely with male subjects, yet it became the basis for a theory applied to both males *and* females. Gilligan has also noted that in most of Kohlberg's stories, the main actor who faces the moral dilemma to be resolved is a male. When females are present in the stories, they often play a subordinate role. Thus, Gilligan believes that Kohlberg's model reflects a male perspective that may not accurately depict the development of moral reasoning in women.

To Gilligan, Kohlberg's model is based on an *ethic of individual rights and justice,* which is a more common perspective for men. In contrast, Gilligan (1982) developed a model of women's moral development that is based on an *ethic of care and responsibility.* In her studies of women's moral reasoning, Gilligan found that women tend to stress the importance of maintaining interpersonal relationships and responding to the needs of others, rather than focusing primarily on individual rights (Gilligan & Attanucci, 1988).

However, in a meta-analysis of studies on gender differences in moral reasoning, Sara Jaffee and Janet Shibley Hyde (2000) found only slight differences between male and female responses. Instead, the evidence suggested that *both* men and women used a mix of care and justice perspectives. Thus, while disputing Gilligan's idea that men and women had entirely different approaches to moral reasoning, Jaffe and Hyde found empirical support for Gilligan's larger message: that Kohlberg's theory did *not* adequately reflect the way that humans actually experienced moral decision making.

Culture also seems to influence moral reasoning (Haidt & others, 1993; Miller, 2001). Some cross-cultural psychologists argue that Kohlberg's stories and scoring system reflect a Western emphasis on individual rights, harm, and justice that is not shared in many cultures (Shweder & others, 1990a).

For example, Kohlberg's moral stages do not reflect the sense of interdependence and the concern for the overall welfare of the group that is more common in collectivistic cultures. Cross-cultural psychologist Harry Triandis (1994) reports an example of a response that does not fit into Kohlberg's moral scheme. In response to the scenario in which the husband steals the drug to save his wife's life, a man in New Guinea said, "If nobody helped him, I would say that *we* had caused the crime." Thus, there are aspects of moral reasoning in other cultures that do not seem to be reflected in Kohlberg's theory (Haidt, 2007; Shweder & Haidt, 1993).

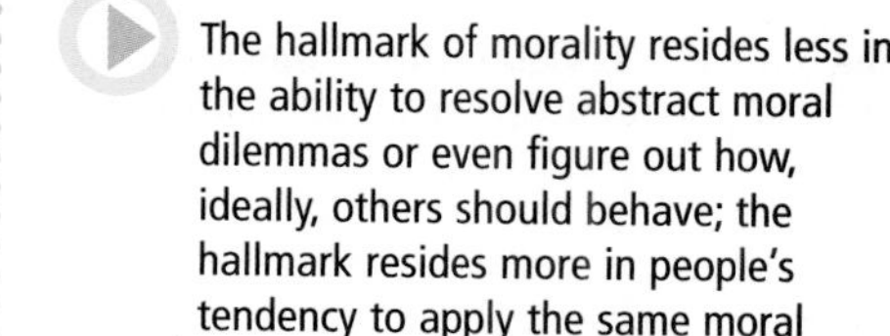

The hallmark of morality resides less in the ability to resolve abstract moral dilemmas or even figure out how, ideally, others should behave; the hallmark resides more in people's tendency to apply the same moral standards to themselves that they apply to others and to function in accordance with them.

DENNIS KREBS AND KATHY DENTON (2006)

"I'm sorry, but I'm morally and politically opposed to hangman."

Adult Development

Key Theme

- **Development during adulthood is marked by physical changes and the adoption of new social roles.**

Key Questions

- **What physical changes take place in adulthood?**
- **What are some general patterns of adult social development?**
- **What characterizes career paths in adulthood?**

You can think of the developmental changes you experienced during infancy, childhood, and adolescence as early chapters in your life story. Those early life chapters helped set the tone and some of the themes for the primary focus of your life

menopause
The natural cessation of menstruation and the end of reproductive capacity in women.

story—adulthood. During the half-century or more that constitutes adulthood, predictable changes continue to occur. Self-definition evolves as people achieve independence and take on new roles and responsibilities. As you'll see in this section, the story of adulthood also reflects the increasing importance of individual variation. Although general patterns of aging exist, our life stories become more distinct and individualized with each passing decade of life (Schaie & Willis, 1996).

Physical Changes

Physical strength typically peaks in *early adulthood,* the 20s and 30s. By *middle adulthood,* roughly from the 40s to the mid-60s, physical strength and endurance gradually decline. Physical and mental reaction times also begin to slow during middle adulthood. During *late adulthood,* from the mid-60s on, physical stamina and reaction time tend to decline further and faster.

Your unique genetic heritage greatly influences the unfolding of certain physical changes during adulthood, such as when your hair begins to thin, lose its color, and turn gray. Such genetically influenced changes can vary significantly from one person to another. For example, **menopause,** the cessation of menstruation that signals the end of reproductive capacity in women, may occur anywhere from the late 30s to the early 50s.

But your destiny is not completely ruled by genetics. Your lifestyle is one key environmental factor that can influence the aging process. Staying mentally and physically active and eating a proper diet can both slow and minimize the degree of physical decline associated with aging.

Another potent environmental force is simply the passage of time. Decades of use and environmental exposure take a toll on the body. Wrinkles begin to appear as we approach the age of 40, largely because of a loss of skin elasticity combined with years of making the same facial expressions. With each decade after age 20, the efficiency of various body organs declines. For example, lung capacity decreases, as does the amount of blood pumped by the heart.

Social Development

In his theory of psychosocial development, Erik Erikson (1982) described the two fundamental themes that dominate adulthood: love and work. According to Erikson (1964b, 1968), the primary psychosocial task of early adulthood is to form a committed, mutually enhancing, intimate relationship with another person. During middle adulthood, the primary psychosocial task becomes one of *generativity*—to contribute to future generations through your children, your career, and other meaningful activities. In this section, we'll consider the themes of love and work by examining adult friendships, marriage, family life, and careers.

Psychosocial Development in Young Adulthood Young adulthood brings many psychological challenges and transitions, not the least of which is choosing a life partner. According to psychoanalyst Erik Erikson (1968), the key psychosocial conflict of young adulthood is intimacy versus isolation. Erikson believed that the ability to establish a meaningful, intimate, and lasting relationship helps set the stage for healthy adult development.

Friends and Lovers in Adulthood

Largely because of competing demands on their time, adults typically have fewer friends than adolescents do. The focus of adult friendships is somewhat different for men and women. Female friends tend to confide in one another about their feelings, problems, and interpersonal relationships. In contrast, male friends typically minimize discussions about relationships or personal feelings or problems. Instead, male friends tend to do things together that they find mutually interesting, such as activities related to sports or hobbies (Grief, 2006; Su & others, 2009).

Beyond friendship, establishing a committed, intimate relationship takes on a new urgency in adulthood. Looking for Mr. or Ms. Right, getting married, and starting a family are the traditional tasks of early adulthood. However, in contrast to their parents, today's young adults are marrying at a later average age. As Figure 9.7 shows, in 1970 the median age for a first marriage was 23 for men and 21 for women. By 2007 those averages had increased to age 28 for men and age 26 for women. Many young adults postpone marriage until their late 20s or early 30s so they can finish their education and become established in a career. And, of course, it is a mistake to assume that the "traditional" family is the norm. There are many Americans who either never marry or don't remarry after they are widowed or divorced. Among adults in the 20 to 34 age range, more than half have never been married. However, by age 55, only about 10 percent of the adult population has never been married (U.S. Census Bureau, 2008a).

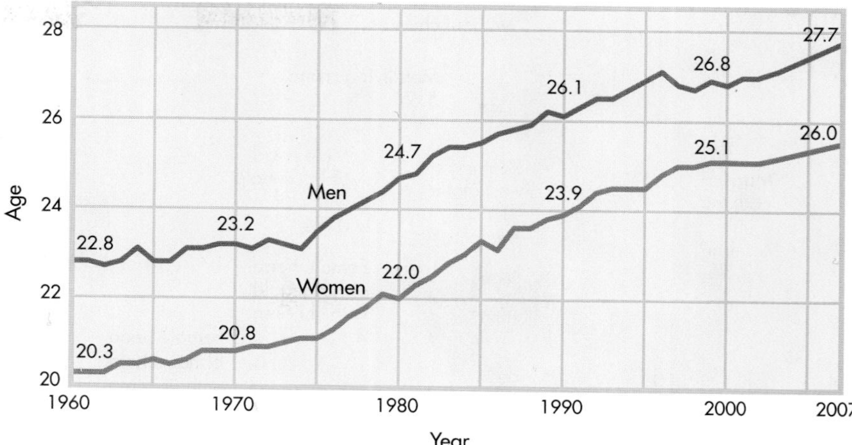

Figure 9.7 The Median Age at First Marriage The average age at first marriage is five years older for young adults today than it was in the 1970s. Part of the explanation for this trend is that more people are postponing marriage in order to complete a college education. Among young adults in the 25 to 34 age range, 26 percent of men and 33 percent of women have earned a bachelor's degree or higher.

Source: U.S. Census Bureau (2008a, 2008b, 2008c).

The Transition to Parenthood: Kids 'R' Us?

Although it is commonly believed that children strengthen the marital bond, marital satisfaction tends to decline after the birth of the first child (Schulz & others, 2006; Twenge & others, 2003). For all the joy that can be derived from watching a child grow and experience the world, the first child's arrival creates a whole new set of responsibilities, pushes, and pulls on the marital relationship.

Without question, parenthood fundamentally alters your identity as an adult. With the birth or adoption of your first child, you take on a commitment to nurture the physical, emotional, social, and intellectual well-being of the next generation. This change in your identity can be a struggle, especially if the transition to parenthood was more of a surprise than a planned event (Grussu & others, 2005).

Parenthood is further complicated by the fact that children are not born speaking fluently so that you can immediately enlighten them about the constraints of adult schedules, deadlines, finances, and physical energy. Instead, you must continually strive to adapt lovingly and patiently to your child's needs while managing all the other priorities in your life.

Not all couples experience a decline in marital satisfaction after the birth of a child. The hassles and headaches of child rearing can be minimized if the marital relationship is warm and positive and if both husband and wife share household and child-care responsibilities (Tsang & others, 2003). It also helps if you're blessed with a child who is born with a good disposition and an easy temperament. When infants are irritable, cry a lot, or are otherwise "difficult," parents find it harder to adjust to their new role (van den Boom & Hoeksma, 1994).

That many couples are marrying at a later age and waiting until their 30s to start a family also seems to be advantageous. Becoming a parent at an older age and waiting longer after marriage to start a family may ease the adjustment to parenthood. Why? Largely because the couple is more mature and the marital relationship is typically more stable.

Although marital satisfaction often declines when people first become parents, it rises again after children leave home (Gorchoff & others, 2008). Successfully launching your children into the adult world represents the attainment of the ultimate parental goal. It also means there is more time to spend in leisure activities with your spouse. Not surprisingly, then, marital satisfaction tends to increase steadily once children are out of the nest and flying on their own.

NON SEQUITUR

Variations in the Paths of Adult Social Development

Up to this point, we've described the "traditional" track of adult social development: finding a mate, getting married, starting and raising a family. However, there is enormous diversity in how the goal of intimacy is realized during adulthood

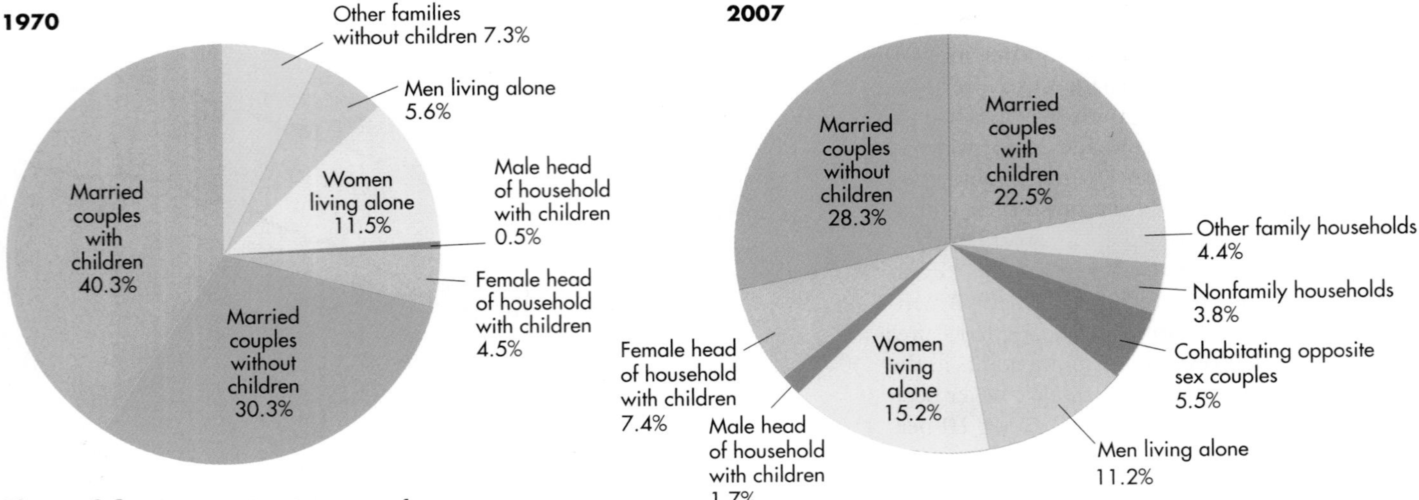

Figure 9.8 The Changing Structure of American Families and Households In a relatively short time, American households have undergone a metamorphosis. Between 1970 and 2007, the number of American households increased from 63 million to 116 million, but the average household size decreased from 3.14 to 2.56 persons. As the living arrangements of American families have become more diversified, the U.S. Census Bureau modified the categories it uses to classify households. Hence, the two pie charts differ slightly. Notice that single-parent family groups have doubled. Today, single mothers or fathers represent 9 percent of all households. In contrast, the number of married couples with children has sharply decreased.

Sources: Kreider, 2008; U.S. Census Bureau, 2008c, 2008d.

(Edwards, 1995b). The nature of intimate relationships and family structures varies widely in the United States (see Figure 9.8).

For example, the number of unmarried couples living together increased dramatically at the end of the twentieth century—to well over 3 million couples. Currently, more than 30 percent of children are being raised by a single parent. Given that more than half of all first marriages end in divorce, the phenomenon of remarrying and starting a "second family" later in life is not unusual. As divorce has become more common, the number of single parents and stepfamilies has also risen. And among married couples, some opt for a "child-free" life together. There are also gay and lesbian couples who, like many married couples, are committed to a long-term, monogamous relationship (Mackey & others, 2004; Solomon & others, 2004).

Such diversity in adult relationships reflects the fact that adult social development does not always follow a predictable pattern. As you travel through adulthood, your life story may include many unanticipated twists in the plot and changes in the cast of characters. Just as the "traditional" family structure has its joys and heartaches, so do other configurations of intimate and family relationships. In the final analysis, *any* relationship that promotes the overall sense of happiness and well-being of the people involved is a successful one.

Careers in Adulthood

People follow a variety of routes in developing careers (Duffy & Sedlacek, 2007; Lachman, 2004). Most people explore different career options, narrow down those options, and tentatively commit to a particular job in a particular field in young adulthood (Super, 1990). However, researchers have found that close to a third of people in their late 20s and early 30s do not just change jobs within a particular field—they completely switch occupational fields (Phillips & Blustein, 1994).

Single-Parent Families Today, more than 30 percent of all children are being raised by a single parent. Many single parents provide their children with a warm, stable, and loving environment. In terms of school achievement and emotional stability, children in stable single-parent households do just as well as children with two parents living in the same home (Dawson, 1991).

Dual-career families have become increasingly common. However, the career tracks of men and women often differ if they have children. Although today's fathers are more actively involved in child rearing than were fathers in previous generations, women still tend to have primary responsibility for child care (Craig, 2006; Wood & Repetti, 2004). Thus, married women with children are much more likely than are single women or childless women to interrupt their careers, leave their jobs, or switch to part-time work because of child-rearing responsibilities.

Do adults, particularly women, experience greater stress because of the conflicting demands of career, marriage, and family? Not necessarily. Generally, multiple roles seem to provide both men and women with a greater potential for increased feelings of self-esteem, happiness, and competence (Cinamon & others, 2007; Gilbert, 1994). The critical factor is not so much the number of roles that people take on but the *quality* of their experiences on the job, in marriage, and as a parent (Barnett & others, 1992; Lee & Phillips, 2006). When experiences in these different roles are positive and satisfying, psychological well-being is enhanced. However, when work is dissatisfying, finding high-quality child care is difficult, and making ends meet is a never-ending struggle, stress can escalate and psychological well-being can plummet—for either sex (Schulz & others, 2004).

Blended Families Approximately 17 percent of all children live in stepfamilies or *blended families,* sharing their home with children from an earlier marriage of their parent or stepparent (U.S. Census Bureau, 2004a). Sometimes, as is the case with this family, the children of the first marriage are much older than the children of the second marriage.

Although the term *blended families* is commonly used, not all stepfamilies agree with its use, pointing out that children in stepfamilies do not lose their identification or emotional attachment to the parent who is not part of the new household (Stepfamily Association of America, 2005).

Late Adulthood and Aging

Key Theme

- **Late adulthood does not necessarily involve a steep decline in physical or cognitive capabilities.**

Key Questions

- **What cognitive changes take place in late adulthood?**
- **What factors influence social development in late adulthood?**

The average life expectancy for men in the United States is about 75 years. For women, the average life expectancy is about 80 years. So the stage of late adulthood can easily last for a decade or longer. Although we experience many physical and sensory changes throughout adulthood, that's not to say that we completely fall apart when we reach our 60s, 70s, or even 80s. Some people in their 90s are healthier and more active than other people who are 20 years younger (Baltes & Mayer, 2001).

In American culture, but certainly not in all cultures, the phrase *old age* is often associated with images of poor health, inactivity, social isolation, and mental and physical incompetence. Are those images accurate? Far from it. The majority of older adults live healthy, active, and self-sufficient lives (Schaie & Willis, 1996).

In fact, the stereotypical image that most elderly people live in nursing homes is a major myth. In Table 9.6, you can see that of *all* American adults aged 65 and over, only 4.5 percent live in nursing homes. It's also interesting to note the downward trend that has occurred over the past decade in the percentages of senior adults who live in nursing homes. Even among those aged 85 and over, fewer than 20 percent live in nursing homes. Some older adults live with relatives, but most live in their own homes (U.S. Census Bureau, 2002).

Although they have more chronic medical conditions, elderly individuals tend to see themselves as relatively healthy, partly because they have fewer acute illnesses, such as colds and flu, than do younger people (National Center for Health Statistics, 2002). Even during the final year of life, the majority of older adults enjoy relatively good health, mental alertness, and self-sufficiency.

The number of older adults in the United States has been gradually increasing over the past several decades. At the beginning of the twentieth century, only about 1 American in 20 was 65 or older; today, 1 of every 8 Americans is. By the year 2030, 1 of 5 Americans will be an older adult (Kinsella & Velkoff, 2001).

Table 9.6

U.S. Population Aged 65 and Older in Nursing Homes by Age: 1990 and 2000

	Percent of Age Group	
Age	**1990**	**2000**
65 years and over	5.1	4.5
65 to 74 years	1.4	1.1
75 to 84 years	6.1	4.7
85 years and over	24.5	18.2

Source: Hetzel & Smith (2001).

Cognitive Changes

During which decade of life do you think people reach their intellectual peak? If you answered the 20s or 30s, you may be surprised by the results of longitudinal studies done by psychologist K. Warner Schaie. Since the 1950s, Schaie and his

"This next one is a hard-rockin', kick-ass, take-no-prisoners tune we wrote about turning sixty."

colleagues have followed some 5,000 people as they have aged to learn what happens to intellectual abilities.

Schaie (1995, 2005) found that general intellectual abilities gradually increase until one's early 40s, then become relatively stable until about age 60. After age 60, a small but steadily increasing percentage of older adults experience slight declines on tests of general intellectual abilities, such as logical reasoning, math skills, word recall, and the ability to mentally manipulate images. But even after age 60, most older adults maintain these previous levels of abilities. A longitudinal study of adults in their 70s, 80s, and 90s found that there were slight but significant declines in memory, perceptual speed, and fluency. However, measures of knowledge, such as vocabulary, remained stable up to age 90 (Singer & others, 2003; Zelinski & Kennison, 2007).

When declines in mental abilities occur during old age, Schaie found, the explanation is often simply a lack of practice or experience with the kinds of tasks used in mental ability tests. Even just a few hours of training on mental skills can improve test scores for most older adults.

Is it possible to minimize declines in mental abilities in old age? In a word, "yes." Consistently, research has found that those who are better educated and engage in physical and mental activities throughout older adulthood show the smallest declines in mental abilities. In contrast, the greatest intellectual declines tend to occur in older adults with unstimulating lifestyles, such as people who live alone, are dissatisfied with their lives, and engage in few activities (see Calero-Garcia & others, 2007; Newson & Kemps, 2005).

Social Development

At one time it was believed that older adults gradually "disengage," or withdraw, from vocational, social, and relationship roles as they face the prospect of their lives ending. But consider Sandy's father, Erv. Even after Erv was well into his 80s, he would join about a dozen other retired men in their 70s and 80s for a monthly poker game and frequent lunches. About once a year, the group took a fishing trip.

activity theory of aging
The psychosocial theory that life satisfaction in late adulthood is highest when people maintain the level of activity they displayed earlier in life.

What Erv and his buddies epitomized is the activity theory of aging. According to the **activity theory of aging,** life satisfaction in late adulthood is highest when you maintain your previous level of activity, either by continuing old activities or by finding new ones (Benyamini & Lomranz, 2004).

Just like younger adults, older adults differ in the level of activity they find personally optimal. Some older adults pursue a busy lifestyle of social activities, travel, college classes, and volunteer work. Other older adults are happier with a quieter

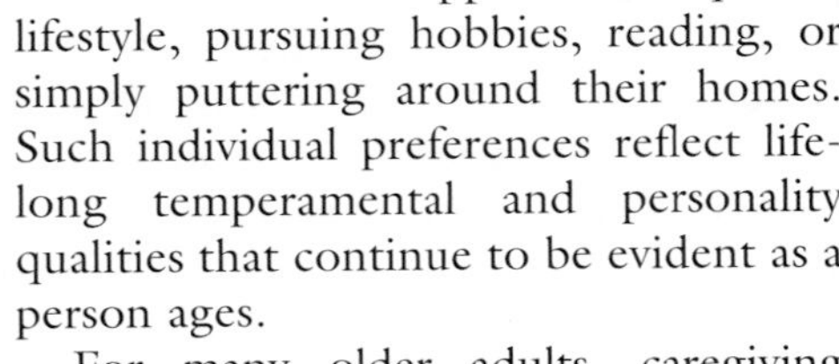

lifestyle, pursuing hobbies, reading, or simply puttering around their homes. Such individual preferences reflect lifelong temperamental and personality qualities that continue to be evident as a person ages.

For many older adults, caregiving responsibilities can persist well into late adulthood. Sandy's mother, Fern, for example, spends a great deal of time helping out with her young grandchildren and caring for some of her older relatives. She's not unusual in that respect. Many older adults who are healthy and active find themselves taking care of other older adults who are sick or have physical limitations.

Japan's Super-Seniors Born in 1906, Japanese educator Dr. Saburo Shochi has completed four international speaking tours over the past four years, lecturing on the importance of early childhood education, especially for developmentally disabled children. He has traveled to countries as far-flung as Senegal, Finland, China, Brazil, and the United States. Shochi was a pioneer in the field of special education in Japan, founding the first school for the disabled in 1954. At the age of 97, Shochi opened a toy-making classroom for children and their parents. Shochi, who turned 102 while on his last world tour, also lectures on healthy aging and the importance of remaining socially engaged and active, whatever your age. There are more than 36,000 centenarians in Japan, which has one of the world's highest life expectancy rates.

Even for an older adult who is not very socially active, it's still important to have at least one confidant. Sometimes the confidant is simply a very close friend. For older men, the confidant is often the spouse. The social support provided by the confidant yields important psychological benefits for the older adult, such as higher morale, better mental health, and better psychological well-being. A confidant can also provide an important buffer for the older adult in coping with stressful events, such as health problems or the deaths of friends or family members.

Along with satisfying social relationships, the prescription for psychological well-being in old age includes achieving what Erik Erikson called *ego integrity*—the feeling that one's life has been meaningful (Erikson & others, 1986). Older adults experience ego integrity when they look back on their lives and feel satisfied with their accomplishments, accepting whatever mistakes or missteps they may have made (Torges & others, 2008).

In contrast, those who are filled with regrets or bitterness about past mistakes, missed opportunities, or bad decisions experience *despair*—a sense of disappointment in life. Often the theme of ego integrity versus despair emerges as older adults engage in a *life review*, thinking about or retelling their life story to others (Bohlmeijer & others, 2007; Staudinger, 2001).

A Lifetime of Experience to Share Like many other senior adults, Edna Warf of Asheville, North Carolina, derives great personal satisfaction from her work as a volunteer helping grade-school students. Contributing to their communities, taking care of others, and helping people both younger and older than themselves are important to many older adults.

The Final Chapter
Dying and Death

Key Theme

- **Attitudes toward dying and death are as diverse in late adulthood as they are throughout the lifespan.**

Key Questions

- **How did Kübler-Ross describe the stages of dying?**
- **What are some individual variations in attitudes toward death and dying?**

It is tempting to view death as the special province of the very old. Of course, death can occur at any point during the lifespan. It's also tempting to assume that older adults have come to a special understanding about death—that they view the prospect of dying with wisdom and serenity. In reality, attitudes toward death in old age show the same diversity that is reflected in other aspects of adult development. Not all older adults are resigned to death, even when poor health has severely restricted their activities (Kastenbaum, 2000, 2005).

As psychologist Robert Kastenbaum (1992) wrote, "Everyone lives in relationship to death at every point in the lifespan." In other words, long before encountering old age, each individual has a personal history of thinking about death. Some people are obsessed with issues of life and death from adolescence or early adulthood onward, while others, even in advanced old age, take more of a one-day-at-a-time approach to living.

In general, anxiety about death tends to peak in middle adulthood, then tends to *decrease* in late adulthood (Wink, 2006). At any age, people respond with a wide variety of emotions when faced with the prospect of imminent death, such as when they are diagnosed with a terminal illness.

Elisabeth Kübler-Ross (1969) interviewed more than 200 terminally ill patients and proposed that the dying go through five stages.

The Last Lecture People vary greatly in how they cope with impending death. At the age of 45, Dr. Randy Pausch, a computer science professor at Carnegie Mellon University, learned that he had pancreatic cancer and was given just a few months to live. Pausch reacted by delivering his now famous "Last Lecture," written in response to the question, "What would you say if you knew you were going to die?" Titled *Really Achieving Your Childhood Dreams,* Pausch's lecture was upbeat, humorous, and inspirational, and has since been viewed by millions on YouTube. Pausch died about ten months after giving his speech.

First, they *deny* that death is imminent, perhaps insisting that their doctors are wrong or denying the seriousness of their illness. Second, they feel and express *anger* that they are dying. Third, they *bargain*—they try to "make a deal" with doctors, relatives, or God, promising to behave in a certain way if only they may be allowed to live. Fourth, they become *depressed*. Finally, they *accept* their fate.

Although Kübler-Ross's research did much to sensitize the public and the medical community to the emotional experience of dying, it now seems clear that dying individuals do *not* necessarily progress through the predictable sequence of stages that she described (Kastenbaum, 2000). Dying is as individual a process as living. People cope with the prospect of dying much as they have coped with other stresses in their lives.

Faced with impending death, some older adults react with passive resignation, others with bitterness and anger. Some people plunge into activity and focus their attention on external matters, such as making funeral arrangements, disposing of their property, or arranging for the care of other family members. And others turn inward, searching for the meaning of their life's story as the close of the final chapter draws near (Kastenbaum, 2000).

But even in dying, our life story doesn't just end. Each of us leaves behind a legacy of memories in the minds of those who survive us. As we live each day, we are building this legacy, through our words, our actions, and the choices we make.

Each of us began life being completely dependent on others for our survival. Over the course of our lifespan, others come to depend on us. It is those people whose lives we have touched in some way, whether for good or for ill, who will remember us. In this sense, the final chapter of our lives will be written not by us, but by those whose life stories have intersected with our own.

>> Closing Thoughts

Traditionally, development in childhood has received the most attention from developmental psychologists. Yet, as we have emphasized throughout this chapter, development is a lifelong process.

Throughout this chapter, you've seen that every life is a unique combination of universal and individualized patterns of development. Although some aspects of development unfold in a predictable fashion, every life story, including yours, is influenced by unexpected events and plot twists. Despite predictable changes, the wonderful thing about the developmental process is that you never *really* know what the next chapter of your life story may hold.

authoritarian parenting style
Parenting style in which parents are demanding and unresponsive toward their children's needs or wishes.

permissive parenting style
Parenting style in which parents are extremely tolerant and not demanding; permissive-indulgent parents are more responsive to their children, whereas permissive-indifferent parents are not.

authoritative parenting style
Parenting style in which parents set clear standards for their children's behavior but are also responsive to their children's needs and wishes.

induction
A discipline technique that combines parental control with explaining why a behavior is prohibited.

ENHANCING WELL-BEING WITH PSYCHOLOGY

Raising Psychologically Healthy Children

Unfortunately, kids don't come with owners' manuals. Maybe that's why if you walk into any bookstore and head for the "parenting" section, you'll see shelves of books offering advice on topics ranging from "how to toilet-train your toddler" to "how to talk to your teenager." We're not going to attempt to cover that range here. However, we will present some basic principles of parenting that have been shown to foster the development of children who are psychologically well-adjusted, competent, and in control of their own behavior.

Basic Parenting Styles and Their Effects on Children

Psychologist Diana Baumrind (1971, 1991, 2005) has described three basic parenting styles: authoritarian, permissive, and authoritative. These parenting styles differ in terms of (1) *parental control* and (2) *parental responsiveness* to the child's needs and wishes.

Parents with an **authoritarian parenting style** are demanding but unresponsive to their children's needs or wishes. Authoritarian parents believe that they should shape and control the child's behavior so that it corresponds to an absolute set of standards. Put simply, they expect children to obey the rules, no questions asked. Rules are made without input from the child, and they are enforced by punishment, often physical.

At the opposite extreme are two **permissive parenting styles** (Maccoby & Martin, 1983). *Permissive-indulgent parents* are responsive, warm, and accepting of their children but impose few rules and rarely punish their children. *Permissive-indifferent parents* are both unresponsive and uncontrolling. Establishing firm rules and consistently enforcing them is simply too much trouble for permissive-indifferent parents. If taken to an extreme, the lack of involvement of permissive-indifferent parenting can amount to child neglect.

The third style is the **authoritative parenting style.** Authoritative parents are warm, responsive, and involved with their children. They set clear standards for mature, age-appropriate behavior and expect their children to be responsive to parental demands. However, authoritative parents also feel a *reciprocal* responsibility to consider their children's reasonable demands and points of view. Thus, there is considerable give-and-take between parent and child. Rules are firm and consistently enforced, but the parents discuss the reasons for the rules with the child (Maccoby & Martin, 1983).

How do these different parenting styles affect young children? Baumrind (1971) found that the children of authoritarian parents are likely to be moody, unhappy, fearful, withdrawn, unspontaneous, and irritable. The children of permissive parents tend to be more cheerful than the children of authoritarian parents, but they are more immature, impulsive, and aggressive. In contrast, the children of authoritative parents are likely to be cheerful, socially competent, energetic, and friendly. They show high levels of self-esteem, self-reliance, and self-control (Buri & others, 1988).

These different parenting styles also affect children's competence, adjustment, and delinquent behavior (Kaufmann & others, 2000; Palmer & Hollin, 2001; Simons and Conger, 2007). Authoritative parenting is associated with higher grades than authoritarian or permissive parenting (Kawamura & others, 2002; Supple and Small, 2006). In one study of several hundred adolescents, this finding was consistent for virtually all adolescents, regardless of ethnic or socioeconomic background (Dornbusch & others, 1987).

Adding to the evidence, psychologist Laurence Steinberg and his colleagues (1995) conducted a three-year longitudinal study involving more than 20,000 U.S. high school students. Steinberg found that authoritative parenting is associated with a broad range of beneficial effects for the adolescent, regardless of socioeconomic or ethnic background. As Steinberg summarized, "Adolescents raised in authoritative homes are better adjusted and more competent, they are confident about their abilities, competent in areas of achievement, and less likely than their peers to get into trouble" (Steinberg & others, 1995).

Why does an authoritative parenting style provide such clear advantages over other parenting styles? First, when children perceive their parents' requests as fair and reasonable, they are more likely to comply with the requests. Second, the children are more likely to *internalize* (or accept as their own) the reasons for behaving in a certain way and thus to achieve greater self-control (Hoffman, 1977, 1994).

In contrast, authoritarian parenting promotes resentment and rebellion (Hoffman, 1977, 1988). Because compliance is based on external control and punishment, the child often learns to avoid the parent rather than independently control his or her own behavior (Gershoff, 2002). Finally, the child with permissive parents may never learn self-control. And because permissive parents have low expectations, the child may well live up to those expectations by failing to strive to fulfill his or her potential (Baumrind, 1971).

How to Be an Authoritative Parent: Some Practical Suggestions

Authoritative parents are high in both responsiveness and control. How can you successfully achieve that balance? Here are several suggestions based on psychological research.

1. Let your children know that you love them.

Attention, hugs, and other demonstrations of physical affection, coupled with a positive attitude toward your child, are some of the most important aspects of parenting, aspects that have enduring effects (Steinberg, 2001). Children who experience warm, positive relationships with their parents are more likely to become happy adults with stable marriages and good relationships with friends (Franz & others, 1991). So the question is simple: Have you hugged your kids today?

ZITS

2. Listen to your children.

Let your children express their opinions, and respect their preferences when it's reasonable to do so. In making rules and decisions, ask for their input and give it genuine consideration. Strive to be fair and flexible, especially on issues that are less than earthshaking, such as which clothes they wear to school.

3. Use induction to teach as you discipline.

The most effective form of discipline is called **induction** because it *induces* understanding in the child. Induction combines controlling a child's behavior with *teaching* (Hoffman, 1977, 1994). Put simply, induction involves consistently explaining (a) the *reason* for prohibiting or performing certain behaviors; (b) the *consequences* of the action for the child; and (c) the *effect* of the child's behavior on others. When parents use induction, the child begins to understand that their actions are not completely arbitrary or unfair. The child is also more likely to internalize the reasoning and apply it in new situations (Kerr & others, 2004; Schulman & Mekler, 1985).

4. Work with your child's temperamental qualities.

Think back to our earlier discussion of temperamental qualities. Be aware of your child's natural temperament and work with it, not against it. If your child is very active, for example, it is unrealistic to expect him to sit quietly during a four-hour plane or bus trip. Knowing that, you can increase the likelihood of positive experiences by planning ahead. Bring coloring books, picture books, or small toys to occupy the young child in a restaurant or at a family gathering. Take frequent "exercise stops" on a long car trip. If your child is unusually sensitive, shy, or "slow-to-warm-up," give her plenty of time to make the transition to new situations and provide lots of preparation so that she knows what to expect.

5. Understand your child's age-related cognitive abilities and limitations.

Some parents make the mistake of assuming that children think in the same way adults do. They may see a toddler or even an infant as purposely "misbehaving," "being naughty," or "rebelling," when the little one is simply doing what 1-year-olds or 3-year-olds do. Your expectations for appropriate behavior should be geared to the child's age and developmental stage (Barclay & Houts, 1995b). Having a thorough understanding of the information in this chapter is a good start. You might also consider taking a developmental psychology or child development class. Or go to your college library and check out some of the developmental psychology texts. By understanding your child's cognitive abilities and limitations at each stage of development, you're less likely to misinterpret behavior or to place inappropriate demands on him.

6. Don't expect perfection, and learn to go with the flow.

Accidents happen. Mistakes occur. Children get cranky or grumpy, especially when they're tired or hungry. Don't get too bent out of shape when your child's behavior is less than perfect. Be patient. Moments of conflict with children are a natural, inevitable, and healthy part of growing up. Look at those moments as part of the process by which a child achieves autonomy and a sense of self.

Finally, effective parenting is an ongoing process in which you, as the parent, should be regularly assessing your impact on your child. It's not always easy to combine responsiveness with control, or flexibility with an appropriate level of firmness. When you make a mistake, admit it not just to yourself, but also to your child. In doing so, you'll teach your child how to behave when she makes a mistake. As you'll discover, children are remarkably forgiving—and also resilient.

CHAPTER REVIEW: KEY PEOPLE AND TERMS

Mary D. Salter Ainsworth, p. 378
Sandra Bem, p. 386
Renée Baillargeon, p. 391
Erik Erikson, p. 399
Lawrence Kohlberg, p. 401
Jean Piaget, p. 387
Lev Vygotsky, p. 392

developmental psychology, p. 369
zygote, p. 370
chromosome, p. 370
deoxyribonucleic acid (DNA), p. 370
gene, p. 370
genotype, p. 370
phenotype, p. 372
sex chromosomes, p. 372
epigenetics, p. 372
prenatal stage, p. 373
germinal period, p. 373
embryonic period, p. 373
teratogens, p. 374
stem cells, p. 374
fetal period, p. 374
temperament, p. 377
attachment, p. 378
comprehension vocabulary, p. 383
production vocabulary, p. 383
gender, p. 384
gender roles, p. 384
gender identity, p. 384
social learning theory of gender-role development, p. 386
gender schema theory, p. 386
sensorimotor stage, p. 388
object permanence, p. 388
preoperational stage, p. 388
symbolic thought, p. 389
egocentrism, p. 389
irreversibility, p. 389
centration, p. 389
conservation, p. 390
concrete operational stage, p. 390
formal operational stage, p. 390
zone of proximal development, p. 393
information-processing model of cognitive development, p. 393
adolescence, p. 393
puberty, p. 394
primary sex characteristics, p. 394
secondary sex characteristics, p. 394
adolescent growth spurt, p. 394
menarche, p. 394
identity, p. 399
moral reasoning, p. 401
menopause, p. 404
activity theory of aging, p. 408
authoritarian parenting style, p. 411
permissive parenting style, p. 411
authoritative parenting style, p. 411
induction, p. 412

Web Companion Review Activities

You can find additional review activities at **www.worthpublishers.com/discoveringpsych5e.** The *Discovering Psychology* 5th edition Web Companion has self-scoring practice quizzes, flashcards, interactive crossword puzzles, and other activities to help you master the material in this chapter.

CONCEPT MAP

LIFESPAN DEVELOPMENT

Developmental Psychology → Study of how people change over the lifespan

Genetic Contributions to Your Life Story

The **genotype** is a person's unique set of inherited genetic information, which is found in every body cell except reproductive cells.

- Genetic information is encoded in **chromosomes,** which are made of **deoxyribonucleic acid (DNA).**
- Each chromosome includes thousands of DNA segments called **genes.**
- **Alleles** are different forms of a particular gene.

The **phenotype** is the collection of characteristics that an organism actually displays and is the result of gene-environment interaction.

- Environmental factors trigger gene expression.
- Different genotypes react differently to environmental factors.
- **Epigenetics** is the study of the factors that control gene expression.
- Most characteristics involve the interaction of multiple genes.

Prenatal Development

Germinal period: Conception to week 2
Single-celled zygote divides and develops into multicellular embryo
Embryonic period: Week 3 to week 8
Major body systems form; period of greatest vulnerability to teratogens; brain development begins
Fetal period: Week 9 to birth
Body systems mature

Development During Infancy and Childhood

Physical development:

- Many reflexes are present at birth.
- Newborn sensory abilities are not fully developed but attuned to caregivers.
- Motor skills develop in a predictable, universal sequence, although ages at which skills are acquired vary.

Language development:
Universal stages include cooing, babbling, the one-word stage, and the two-word stage.
At every stage, **comprehension vocabulary** is larger than **production vocabulary.**

Gender-role development:
Social learning theory is based on the principles of learning; through reinforcement, punishment, and modeling, children learn appropriate behaviors for each gender.
Gender schema theory, developed by **Sandra Lipsitz Bem** (b. 1944): children actively develop mental categories for each gender.

Personality and social development:
Temperament seems to be inborn and biologically based but can be modified by environmental influences; basic temperamental patterns include easy, difficult, slow-to-warm-up.
Attachment refers to the emotional bond between infants and caregivers; **Mary Salter Ainsworth** (1913–1999) devised the Strange Situation to measure attachment.

Cognitive development:
Jean Piaget (1896–1980) proposed that children progress through distinct stages of cognitive development.

- **Renée Baillargeon** (b. 1954) used visual tasks to study **object permanence,** which is acquired through the **sensorimotor stage.**
- **Symbolic thought** is acquired during the **preoperational stage.** Preoperational thought is **egocentric** and characterized by **irreversibility** and **centration.** The preoperational child cannot grasp the principles of **conservation.**
- Children become capable of logical thought during the **concrete operational stage.**
- During the **formal operational stage,** the adolescent can engage in logical mental operations involving abstract concepts.

Lev Vygotsky (1896–1934) stressed the importance of social and cultural influences in cognitive development.

- **Zone of proximal development:** children can progress to higher cognitive levels through the assistance of others who are more competent.

The **information-processing model** of cognitive development emphasizes basic mental processes and stresses that cognitive development is a process of continuous change.

Adolescence

Physical Development:
- Puberty involves the development of **primary** and **secondary sex characteristics,** including **menarche** in girls.
- Girls experience the **adolescent growth spurt** at a younger age than boys.

Erik Erikson (1902–1994) proposed a theory of psychosocial development stressing that every stage of life is marked by a particular psychosocial conflict. **Identity** versus role confusion is associated with adolescence.

Development of moral reasoning:
Lawrence Kohlberg (1927–1987) proposed a theory of moral development in which children progressed from preconventional to conventional and ultimately postconventional moral reasoning.
- Carol Gilligan theorized that males and females reason differently about moral dilemmas, but evidence shows that the moral reasoning of men and women does not differ.

Adult Development

Early and middle adulthood:
Key developmental tasks are forming committed, intimate relationships and **generativity**—which means contributing to future generations through work and family life.
- Marital satisfaction often declines after children are born but often rises after they leave home.
- U.S. families are increasingly diverse, as are career paths today.

Late adulthood and aging:
- Mental abilities begin to decline slightly at around age 60.
- Cognitive decline can be minimized when older adults are better educated, physically healthy, and engage in physical and mental activity.
- **Activity theory of aging:** life satisfaction in late adulthood is highest when people maintain their previous levels of activity.
- Erikson identified ego integrity versus despair as the key psychosocial conflict of old age.

Dying and death
- Elisabeth Kübler-Ross proposed a five-stage model of dying: denial, anger, bargaining, depression, and acceptance.
- Individuals respond in diverse ways to impending death.

CHAPTER 10

Personality

Chapter Outline

The Secret Twin

PROLOGUE

THE TWINS, KENNETH AND JULIAN, were born a few years after the turn of the last century. At first, their parents, Gertrude and Henry, thought they were identical. Both had dark hair and deep brown eyes. Many years later, Kenneth's son, your author Don, would inherit these qualities.

But Gertrude and Henry quickly learned to tell the twins apart. Kenneth was slightly larger than Julian, and, even as infants, their personalities were distinctly different. In the photographs of Kenneth and Julian as children, Julian smiles broadly, almost merrily, his head cocked slightly. But Kenneth always looks straight at the camera, his expression thoughtful, serious, more intense.

We don't know much about Julian's childhood. Kenneth kept Julian's existence a closely guarded secret for more than 50 years. In fact, it was only a few years before his own death that Kenneth revealed that he had once had a twin brother named Julian.

Still, it's possible to get glimpses of Julian's early life from the letters the boys wrote home from summer camp in 1919 and 1920. Kenneth's letters to his mother were affectionate and respectful, telling her about their daily activities and reassuring her that he would look after his twin brother. "I reminded Julian about the boats and I will watch him good," Kenneth wrote in one letter. Julian's letters were equally affectionate, but shorter and filled with misspelled words. Julian's letters also revealed glimpses of his impulsive nature. He repeatedly promised his mother, "I will not go out in the boats alone again."

Julian's impulsive nature was to have a significant impact on his life. When he was 12 years old, Julian darted in front of a car and was seriously injured, sustaining a concussion. In retrospect, Kenneth believed that that was when Julian's problems began. Perhaps it was, because not long after the accident Julian got into serious trouble for the first time: He got caught red-handed stealing money from the "poor box" at church.

Although Kenneth claimed that Julian had always been the smarter twin, Julian fell behind in high school and graduated a year later than Kenneth. After high school, Kenneth left the quiet farming community of Grinnell, Iowa, and moved to Minneapolis. He quickly became self-sufficient, taking a job managing newspaper carriers. Julian stayed in Grinnell and became apprenticed to learn typesetting. Given Julian's propensity for adventure, it's not surprising that he found typesetting monotonous. So in the spring of 1928, Julian quit typesetting. He also decided to leave Iowa and head east to look for more interesting possibilities.

The Twins Julian *(left)* and Kenneth *(right)*, with their father, Henry, when they were about 10 years old. As boys, Kenneth and Julian were inseparable.

He found them in Tennessee. A few months after Julian left Iowa, Henry received word that Julian had been arrested for armed robbery and sentenced to 15 years in a Tennessee state prison. Though Kenneth was only 22 years old, Henry gave him a large sum of money and the family car and sent him to try to get Julian released.

Kenneth's conversation with the judge in Knoxville was the first of many times that he would deal with the judicial system on someone else's behalf. After much negotiation, the judge agreed: If Julian promised to leave Tennessee and never return, and Kenneth paid the cash "fines," Julian would be released from prison.

When Julian walked through the prison gates the next morning, Kenneth stood waiting with a fresh suit of clothes. "Mother and Father want you to come back to Grinnell," he told Julian. But Julian would not hear of it, saying that instead he wanted to go to California to seek his fortune.

"I can't let you do that, Julian," Kenneth said, looking hard at his twin brother.

"You can't stop me, brother," Julian responded, with a cocky smile. Reluctantly, Kenneth kept just enough money to buy himself a train ticket back to Iowa. He gave Julian the rest of the money and the family car.

Julian got as far as Phoenix, Arizona, before he met his destiny. In broad daylight, he robbed a drugstore at gunpoint. As he backed out of the store, a policeman spotted him. A gun battle followed, and Julian was shot twice. Somehow he managed to escape and holed up in a hotel room. Alone and untended, Julian died two days later from the bullet wounds. Once again, Kenneth was sent to retrieve his twin brother.

On a bitterly cold November morning in 1928, Julian's immediate family laid him to rest in the family plot in Grinnell. On the one hand, Kenneth felt largely responsible for Julian's misguided life. "I should have tried harder to help Julian," Kenneth later reflected. On the other hand, Julian had disgraced the family. From the day Julian was buried, the family never spoke of him again, not even in private.

Kenneth took it upon himself to atone for the failings of his twin brother. In the fall of 1929, Kenneth entered law school in Tennessee—the same state from which he had secured Julian's release from prison. Three years later, at the height of the Great Depression, Kenneth established himself as a lawyer in Sioux City, Iowa, where he would practice law for more than 50 years.

As an attorney, Kenneth Hockenbury was known for his integrity, his intensity in the courtroom, and his willingness to take cases regardless of the client's ability to pay. "Someone must defend the poor," he said repeatedly. In lieu of money, he often accepted labor from a working man or produce from farmers.

Almost sixty years after Julian's death, Kenneth died. But unlike the sparse gathering that had attended Julian's burial, scores of people came to pay their last respects to Kenneth Hockenbury. "Your father helped me so much," stranger after stranger told Don at Kenneth's funeral. Without question, Kenneth had devoted his life to helping others.

Why did Kenneth and Julian turn out so differently? Two boys, born on the same day into the same middle-class family. Kenneth the conscientious, serious one; Julian the laughing boy with mischief in his eyes. How can we explain the fundamental differences in their personalities?

No doubt your family, too, is made up of people with very different personalities. By the end of this chapter, you'll have a much greater appreciation for how psychologists explain such personality differences.

>> Introduction: What Is Personality?

Key Theme

- **Personality is defined as an individual's unique and relatively consistent patterns of thinking, feeling, and behaving.**

Key Question

- **What are the four major theoretical perspectives on personality?**

personality
An individual's unique and relatively consistent patterns of thinking, feeling, and behaving.

personality theory
A theory that attempts to describe and explain similarities and differences in people's patterns of thinking, feeling, and behaving.

That you already have an intuitive understanding of the word *personality* is easy to demonstrate. Just from reading this chapter's Prologue, you could easily describe different aspects of Kenneth's and Julian's personalities. Indeed, we frequently toss around the word *personality* in everyday conversations. "He's very competent, but he has an abrasive personality." "She's got such a delightful personality, you can't help liking her."

Your intuitive understanding of personality is probably very similar to the way that psychologists define the concept. **Personality** is defined as an individual's unique and relatively consistent patterns of thinking, feeling, and behaving. A **personality theory** is an attempt to describe and explain how people are similar, how they are different, and why every individual is unique. In short, a personality theory ambitiously tries to explain the *whole person*. At the outset, it's important to stress that no single theory can adequately explain *all* of the aspects of human personality. Every personality theory has its unique strengths and limitations.

Personality theories often reflect the work of a single individual or of a few closely associated individuals. Thus, it's not surprising that many personality theories bear the distinct personal stamp of their creators to a much greater degree than do other kinds of psychological theories. Consequently, we've tried to let the personality theorists speak for themselves. Throughout this chapter, you'll encounter carefully chosen quotations from the theorists' own writings. These quotations will give you brief glimpses into the minds of some of the most influential thinkers in psychology.

There are many personality theories, but they can be roughly grouped under four basic perspectives: the psychoanalytic, humanistic, social cognitive, and trait perspectives. In a nutshell, here's what each perspective emphasizes:

- The *psychoanalytic perspective* emphasizes the importance of unconscious processes and the influence of early childhood experience.
- The *humanistic perspective* represents an optimistic look at human nature, emphasizing the self and the fulfillment of a person's unique potential.
- The *social cognitive perspective* emphasizes learning and conscious cognitive processes, including the importance of beliefs about the self, goal setting, and self-regulation.
- The *trait perspective* emphasizes the description and measurement of specific personality differences among individuals.

After looking at some of the major personality theories that reflect each perspective, we'll consider a closely related topic—how personality is measured and evaluated. And yes, we'll talk about the famous inkblots. But for the inkblots to make sense, we need to trace the evolution of modern personality theories. We'll begin with the tale of a bearded, cigar-smoking gentleman from Vienna of whom you just may have heard—Sigmund Freud.

Explaining Personality Some people are outgoing, expressive, and fun-loving, like this happy family. Other people consistently display the opposite qualities. Are such personality differences due to early childhood experiences? Genetics? Social environment? Personality theories attempt to account for the individual differences that make each one of us unique.

psychoanalysis
Sigmund Freud's theory of personality, which emphasizes unconscious determinants of behavior, sexual and aggressive instinctual drives, and the enduring effects of early childhood experiences on later personality development.

The Psychoanalytic Perspective on Personality

Key Theme

- **Freud's psychoanalysis stresses the importance of unconscious forces, sexual and aggressive instincts, and early childhood experience.**

Key Questions

- **What were the key influences on Sigmund Freud's thinking?**
- **How are unconscious influences revealed?**
- **What are the three basic structures of personality, and what are the defense mechanisms?**

Sigmund Freud, one of the most influential figures of the twentieth century, was the founder of psychoanalysis. **Psychoanalysis** is a theory of personality that stresses the influence of unconscious mental processes, the importance of sexual and aggressive instincts, and the enduring effects of early childhood experience on personality. Because so many of Freud's ideas have become part of our common culture, it is difficult to imagine just how radical he seemed to his contemporaries. The following biographical sketch highlights some of the important influences that shaped Freud's ideas and theory.

Freud the Outsider Sigmund Freud (1856–1939) is shown with his wife, Martha, and youngest child, Anna, at their Vienna home in 1898. Freud always considered himself to be an outsider. First, he was a Jew at a time when anti-Semitism was strong in Europe. Second, Freud's belief that expressions of sexuality are reflected in the behavior of infants and young children was controversial and shocking to his contemporaries. To some degree, however, Freud enjoyed his role as the isolated scientist—it served him well in trying to set himself, and his ideas on personality, apart from other researchers (Gay, 2006).

The Life of Sigmund Freud

Sigmund Freud was born in 1856 in what is today Pribor, Czech Republic. When he was 4 years old, his family moved to Vienna, where he lived until the last year of his life. Sigmund was the firstborn child of Jacob and Amalie Freud. By the time he was 10 years old, there were six more siblings in the household. Of the seven children, Sigmund was his mother's favorite. As Freud later wrote, "A man who has been the indisputable favorite of his mother keeps for life the feeling of being a conqueror, that confidence of success that often induces real success" (Jones, 1953).

Freud was extremely intelligent and intensely ambitious. He studied medicine, became a physician, and then proved himself to be an outstanding physiological researcher. Early in his career, Freud was among the first investigators of a new drug that had anesthetic and mood-altering properties—cocaine. However, one of Freud's colleagues received credit for the discovery of the anesthetic properties of cocaine, which left Freud bitter. Adding to his disappointment, Freud's enthusiasm for the medical potential of cocaine quickly faded when he recognized that the drug was addictive (Fancher, 1973; Gay, 2006).

Prospects for an academic career in scientific research were very poor, especially for a Jew in Vienna, which was intensely anti-Semitic at that time. So when he married Martha Bernays in 1886, Freud reluctantly gave up physiological research for a private practice in neurology. The income from private practice would be needed: Sigmund and Martha had six children. One of Freud's daughters, Anna Freud, later became an important psychoanalytic theorist.

Influences in the Development of Freud's Ideas

Freud's theory evolved gradually during his first 20 years of private practice. He based his theory on observations of his patients as well as on self-analysis. An early influence on Freud was Joseph Breuer, a highly respected physician. Breuer described to Freud the striking case of a young woman with an array of puzzling psychological and physical symptoms. Breuer found that if he first hypnotized this patient, then asked her to talk freely about a given symptom, forgotten memories of traumatic events emerged. After she freely expressed the pent-up emotions associated with the event, her symptom disappeared. Breuer called this phenomenon *catharsis* (Freud, 1925).

At first, Freud embraced Breuer's technique, but he found that not all of his patients could be hypnotized. Eventually, Freud dropped the use of hypnosis and developed his own technique of **free association** to help his patients uncover forgotten memories. Freud's patients would spontaneously report their uncensored thoughts, mental images, and feelings as they came to mind. From these "free associations," the thread that led to the crucial long-forgotten memories could be unraveled. Breuer and Freud described several of their case studies in their landmark book, *Studies on Hysteria*. Its publication in 1895 marked the beginning of psychoanalysis.

In 1900, Freud published what many consider his most important work, *The Interpretation of Dreams*. By the early 1900s, Freud had developed the basic tenets of his psychoanalytic theory and was no longer the isolated scientist. He was gaining international recognition and developing a following.

In 1904, Freud published what was to become one of his most popular books, *The Psychopathology of Everyday Life*. He described how unconscious thoughts, feelings, and wishes are often reflected in acts of forgetting, inadvertent slips of the tongue, accidents, and errors. By 1909, Freud's influence was also felt in the United States, when he and other psychoanalysts were invited to lecture at Clark University in Massachusetts. For the next 30 years, Freud continued to refine his theory, publishing many books, articles, and lectures.

The last two decades of Freud's life were filled with many personal tragedies. The terrible devastation of World War I weighed heavily on his mind. In 1920, one of his daughters died. In the early 1920s, Freud developed cancer of the jaw, a condition for which he would ultimately undergo more than 30 operations. And during the late 1920s and early 1930s, the Nazis were steadily gaining power in Germany.

Given the climate of the times, it's not surprising that Freud came to focus on humanity's destructive tendencies. For years he had asserted that sexuality was the fundamental human motive, but now he added aggression as a second powerful human instinct. During this period, Freud wrote *Civilization and Its Discontents* (1930), in which he applied his psychoanalytic perspective to civilization as a whole. The central theme of the book is that human nature and civilization are in basic conflict—a conflict that cannot be resolved.

Freud's extreme pessimism was undoubtedly a reflection of the destruction he saw all around him. By 1933, Adolf Hitler had seized power in Germany. Freud's books were banned and publicly burned in Berlin. Five years later, the Nazis marched into Austria, seizing control of Freud's homeland. Although Freud's life was clearly threatened, it was only after his youngest daughter, Anna, had been detained and questioned by the Gestapo that Freud reluctantly agreed to leave Vienna. Under great duress, Freud moved his family to the safety of England. A year later, his cancer returned. In 1939, Freud died in London at the age of 83 (Gay, 2006).

This brief sketch cannot do justice to the richness of Freud's life and the influence of his culture on his ideas. Today, Freud's legacy continues to influence psychology, philosophy, literature, art, and psychotherapy (Merlino & others, 2008; O'Roark, 2007).

Freud the Leader In 1909, Freud visited the United States to lecture on his ideas at Clark University in Massachusetts. A year later, Freud and his many followers founded the International Psychoanalytic Association.

free association
A psychoanalytic technique in which the patient spontaneously reports all thoughts, feelings, and mental images as they come to mind.

unconscious
In Freud's theory, a term used to describe thoughts, feelings, wishes, and drives that are operating below the level of conscious awareness.

Freud the Exile In the spring of 1938, Freud fled Nazi persecution for the safety of London on the eve of World War II. Four of Freud's sisters who remained behind later died in the Nazi extermination camps. He is shown arriving in England, his eldest daughter, Mathilde, at his side. Freud died in London on September 23, 1939.

Freud's Dynamic Theory of Personality

Freud (1940) saw personality and behavior as the result of a constant interplay among conflicting psychological forces. These psychological forces operate at three different levels of awareness: the conscious, the preconscious, and the unconscious. All the thoughts, feelings, and sensations that you're aware of at this particular moment represent the *conscious* level. The *preconscious* contains information that you're not currently aware of but can easily bring to conscious awareness, such as memories of recent events or your street address.

However, the conscious and preconscious are merely the visible tip of the iceberg of the mind. The bulk of this psychological iceberg is made up of the **unconscious,** which lies submerged below the waterline of the preconscious and conscious (see Figure 10.1 on the next page). You're not directly aware

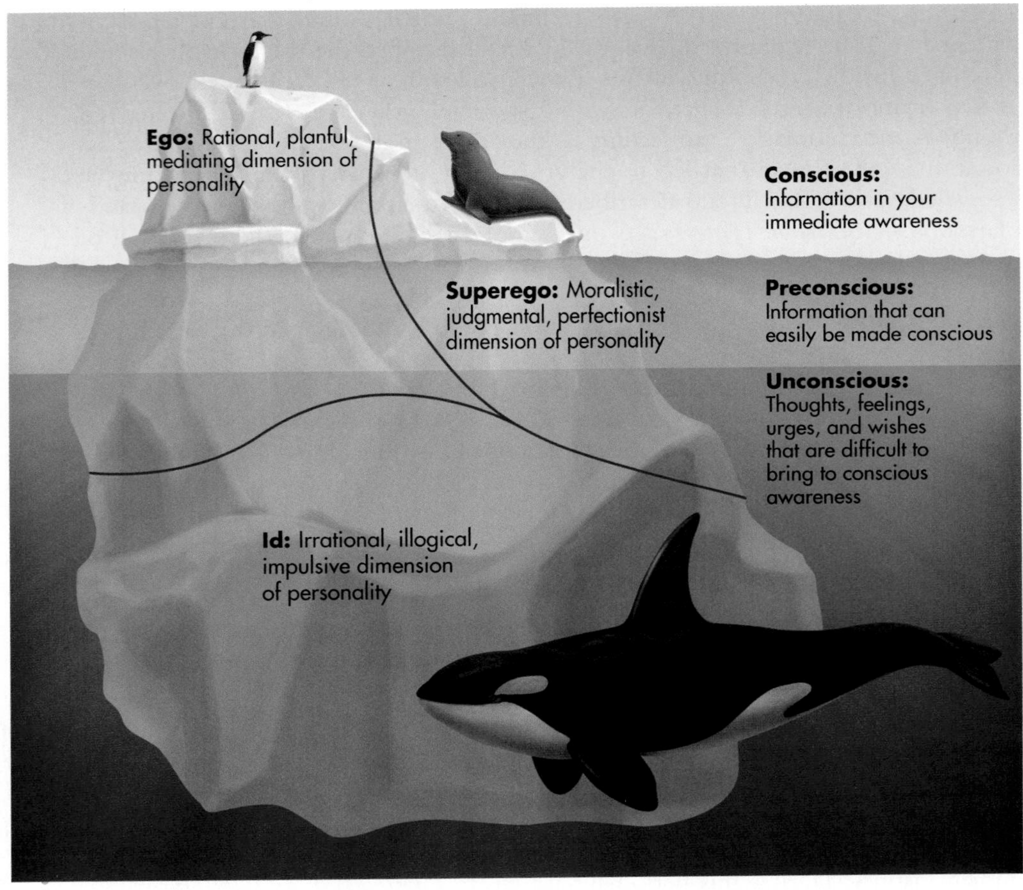

Figure 10.1 Levels of Awareness and the Structure of Personality Freud believed that personality is composed of three psychological processes—the id, the ego, and the superego—that operate at different levels of awareness. If you think of personality as being like an iceberg, the bulk of this psychological iceberg is represented by the irrational, impulsive id, which lies beneath the waterline of consciousness. Unlike the entirely unconscious id, the rational ego and the moralistic superego are at least partially conscious.

of these submerged thoughts, feelings, wishes, and drives, but the unconscious exerts an enormous influence on your conscious thoughts and behavior.

Although it is not directly accessible, Freud (1904) believed that unconscious material often seeps through to the conscious level in distorted, disguised, or symbolic forms. Like a detective searching for clues, Freud carefully analyzed his patients' reports of dreams and free associations for evidence of unconscious wishes, fantasies, and conflicts. Dream analysis was particularly important to Freud. "The interpretation of dreams is the royal road to a knowledge of the unconscious activities of the mind," he wrote in *The Interpretation of Dreams* (1900). Beneath the surface images, or *manifest content,* of a dream lies its *latent content*—the true, hidden, unconscious meaning that is disguised in the dream symbols (see Chapter 4).

Freud (1904, 1933) believed that the unconscious can also be revealed in unintentional actions, such as accidents, mistakes, instances of forgetting, and inadvertent slips of the tongue, which are often referred to as "Freudian slips." According to Freud, many seemingly accidental or unintentional actions are not accidental at all, but are determined by unconscious motives.

Appealing to the Id How would Freud explain the appeal of this billboard? In Freud's theory, the id is ruled by the pleasure principle—the instinctual drive to increase pleasure, reduce tension, and avoid pain. Advertisements like this one, which encourage us to be hedonistic, appeal to the pleasure principle.

The Structure of Personality

According to Freud (1933), each person possesses a certain amount of psychological energy. This psychological energy develops into the three basic structures of personality—the id, the ego, and the superego (see Figure 10.1). Understand that these are *not* separate identities or brain structures. Rather, they are distinct psychological processes.

The **id,** the most primitive part of the personality, is entirely unconscious and present at birth. The id is completely immune to logic, values, morality, danger, and the demands of the external world. It is the original source of psychological energy, parts of which will later evolve into the ego and superego (Freud, 1933, 1940). The id is

cathy® by Cathy Guisewite

rather difficult to describe in words. "We come nearer to the id with images," Freud (1933) wrote, "and call it a chaos, a cauldron of seething excitement."

The id's reservoir of psychological energy is derived from two conflicting instinctual drives: the life instinct and the death instinct. The *life instinct,* which Freud called **Eros,** consists of biological urges that perpetuate the existence of the individual and the species—hunger, thirst, physical comfort, and, most important, sexuality. Freud (1915c) used the word **libido** to refer specifically to sexual energy or motivation. The *death instinct,* which Freud (1940) called **Thanatos,** is destructive energy that is reflected in aggressive, reckless, and life-threatening behaviors, including self-destructive actions.

The id is ruled by the **pleasure principle**—the relentless drive toward immediate satisfaction of the instinctual urges, especially sexual urges (Freud, 1920). Thus, the id strives to increase pleasure, reduce tension, and avoid pain. Even though it operates unconsciously, Freud saw the pleasure principle as the most fundamental human motive.

Equipped only with the id, the newborn infant is completely driven by the pleasure principle. When cold, wet, hungry, or uncomfortable, the newborn wants his needs addressed immediately. As the infant gains experience with the external world, however, he learns that his caretakers can't or won't always immediately satisfy those needs.

Thus, a new dimension of personality develops from part of the id's psychological energy—the **ego.** Partly conscious, the ego represents the organized, rational, and planning dimensions of personality (Freud, 1933). As the mediator between the id's instinctual demands and the restrictions of the outer world, the ego operates on the reality principle. The **reality principle** is the capacity to postpone gratification until the appropriate time or circumstances exist in the external world (Freud, 1940).

As the young child gains experience, she gradually learns acceptable ways to satisfy her desires and instincts, such as waiting her turn rather than pushing another child off a playground swing. Hence, the ego is the pragmatic part of the personality that learns various compromises to reduce the tension of the id's instinctual urges. If the ego can't identify an acceptable compromise to satisfy an instinctual urge, such as a sexual urge, it can *repress* the impulse, or remove it from conscious awareness (Freud, 1915a).

In early childhood, the ego must deal with external parental demands and limitations. Implicit in those demands are the parents' values and morals, their ideas of the right and wrong ways to think, act, and feel. Eventually, the child encounters other advocates of society's values, such as teachers and religious and legal authorities (Freud, 1926). Gradually, these social values move from being externally imposed demands to being *internalized* rules and values.

By about age 5 or 6, the young child has developed an internal, parental voice that is partly conscious—the **superego.** As the internal representation of

id
Latin for *the it*; in Freud's theory, the completely unconscious, irrational component of personality that seeks immediate satisfaction of instinctual urges and drives; ruled by the pleasure principle.

Eros
The self-preservation or life instinct, reflected in the expression of basic biological urges that perpetuate the existence of the individual and the species.

libido
The psychological and emotional energy associated with expressions of sexuality; the sex drive.

Thanatos
The death instinct, reflected in aggressive, destructive, and self-destructive actions.

pleasure principle
The motive to obtain pleasure and avoid tension or discomfort; the most fundamental human motive and the guiding principle of the id.

ego
Latin for *I;* in Freud's theory, the partly conscious rational component of personality that regulates thoughts and behavior and is most in touch with the demands of the external world.

reality principle
The capacity to accommodate external demands by postponing gratification until the appropriate time or circumstances exist.

superego
In Freud's theory the partly conscious, self-evaluative, moralistic component of personality that is formed through the internalization of parental and societal rules.

Establishing the Superego "Don't be mean to your friends" is just one of the many rules and values we learn as children from parents and other authorities. The internalization of such values is what Freud called the superego—the inner voice that is our conscience. When we fail to live up to its moral ideals, the superego imposes feelings of guilt, shame, and inferiority.

Sublimation In Freud's view, creative or productive behaviors represent the rechanneling of sexual energy, or libido—an ego defense mechanism he termed *sublimation*. Freud believed that civilization's greatest achievements are the result of the sublimation of instinctual energy into socially acceptable activities. Later personality theorists criticized Freud's refusal to consider creativity a drive in its own right.

parental and societal values, the superego evaluates the acceptability of behavior and thoughts, then praises or admonishes. Put simply, your superego represents your conscience, issuing demands "like a strict father with a child" (Freud, 1926). It judges your own behavior as right or wrong, good or bad, acceptable or unacceptable. And, should you fail to live up to these morals, the superego can be harshly punitive, imposing feelings of inferiority, guilt, shame, self-doubt, and anxiety. If we apply Freud's terminology to the twins described in the chapter Prologue, Kenneth's superego was clearly stronger than Julian's.

The Ego Defense Mechanisms

Unconscious Self-Deceptions

The ego has a difficult task. It must be strong, flexible, and resourceful to successfully mediate conflicts among the instinctual demands of the id, the moral authority of the superego, and external restrictions. According to Freud (1923), everyone experiences an ongoing daily battle among these three warring personality processes.

When the demands of the id or superego threaten to overwhelm the ego, *anxiety* results (Freud, 1915b). If instinctual id impulses overpower the ego, a person may act impulsively and perhaps destructively. Using Freud's terminology, you could say that Julian's id was out of control when he stole from the church and tried to rob the drugstore. In contrast, if superego demands overwhelm the ego, an individual may suffer from guilt, self-reproach, or even suicidal impulses for failing to live up to the superego's moral standards (Freud, 1936). Using Freudian terminology again, it is probably safe to say that Kenneth's feelings of guilt over Julian were inspired by his superego.

If a realistic solution or compromise is not possible, the ego may temporarily reduce anxiety by *distorting* thoughts or perceptions of reality through processes that Freud called **ego defense mechanisms** (Freud, 1946; Freud, 1915c). By resorting to these largely unconscious self-deceptions, the ego can maintain an integrated sense of self while searching for a more acceptable and realistic solution to a conflict between the id and superego.

The most fundamental ego defense mechanism is **repression** (Freud, 1915a, 1936). To some degree, repression occurs in every ego defense mechanism. In simple terms, repression is unconscious forgetting. Unbeknownst to the person, anxiety-producing thoughts, feelings, or impulses are pushed out of conscious awareness into the unconscious. Common examples include traumatic events, past failures, embarrassments, disappointments, the names of disliked people, episodes of physical pain or illness, and unacceptable urges.

Repression, however, is not an all-or-nothing psychological process. As Freud (1939) explained, "The repressed material retains its impetus to penetrate into consciousness." In other words, if you encounter a situation that is very similar to one you've repressed, bits and pieces of memories of the previous situation may begin to resurface. In such instances, the ego may employ other defense mechanisms that allow the urge or information to remain partially conscious.

This is what occurs with the ego defense mechanism of displacement. **Displacement** occurs when emotional impulses are redirected to a substitute object or person, usually one less threatening or dangerous than the original source of conflict (Freud, 1946). For example, an employee angered by his supervisor's unfair treatment may displace his hostility onto family members when he comes home from work. He consciously experiences anger but directs it toward someone other than its true target, which remains unconscious.

Freud (1930) believed that a special form of displacement, called *sublimation,* is largely responsible for the productive and creative contributions of people and even of whole societies. **Sublimation** involves displacing sexual urges toward "an aim other than, and remote from, that of sexual gratification" (Freud, 1914). In effect, sublimation channels sexual urges into productive, socially acceptable, nonsexual activities.

The major defense mechanisms are summarized in Table 10.1. In Freud's view, the drawback to using any defense mechanism is that maintaining these self-deceptions requires psychological energy. As Freud (1936) pointed out regarding the most basic defense mechanism, repression does not take place "on a single occasion"

"Look, call it denial if you like, but I think what goes on in my personal life is none of my own damn business."

Table 10.1

The Major Ego Defense Mechanisms

Defense	Description	Example
Repression	The complete exclusion from consciousness of anxiety-producing thoughts, feelings, or impulses; most basic defense mechanism.	Three years after being hospitalized for back surgery, a man can remember only vague details about the event.
Displacement	The redirection of emotional impulses toward a substitute person or object, usually one less threatening or dangerous than the original source of conflict.	Angered by a neighbor's hateful comment, a mother spanks her daughter for accidentally spilling her milk.
Sublimation	A form of displacement in which sexual urges are rechanneled into productive, nonsexual activities.	A graduate student works on her thesis 14 hours a day while her husband is on an extended business trip.
Rationalization	Justifying one's actions or feelings with socially acceptable explanations rather than consciously acknowledging one's true motives or desires.	After being rejected by a prestigious university, a student explains that he is glad because he would be happier at a smaller, less competitive college.
Projection	The attribution of one's own unacceptable urges or qualities to others.	A married woman who is sexually attracted to a co-worker accuses him of flirting with her.
Reaction formation	Thinking or behaving in a way that is the extreme opposite of unacceptable urges or impulses.	Threatened by his awakening sexual attraction to girls, an adolescent boy goes out of his way to tease and torment adolescent girls.
Denial	The failure to recognize or acknowledge the existence of anxiety-provoking information.	Despite having multiple drinks every night, a man says he is not an alcoholic because he never drinks before 5 P.M.
Undoing	A form of unconscious repentance that involves neutralizing or atoning for an unacceptable action or thought with a second action or thought.	A woman who gets a tax refund by cheating on her taxes makes a larger-than-usual donation to the church collection on the following Sunday.
Regression	Retreating to a behavior pattern characteristic of an earlier stage of development.	After her parents' bitter divorce, a 10-year-old girl refuses to sleep alone in her room, crawling into bed with her mother.

but rather demands "a continuous expenditure of effort." Such effort depletes psychological energy that is needed to cope effectively with the demands of daily life.

The use of defense mechanisms is very common. Many psychologically healthy people temporarily use ego defense mechanisms to deal with stressful events. When ego defense mechanisms are used in limited areas and on a short-term basis, psychological energy is not seriously depleted. Ideally, we strive to maintain realistic perceptions of the world and our motives, and search for workable solutions to conflicts and problems. Using ego defense mechanisms is often a way of buying time while we consciously or unconsciously wrestle with more realistic solutions for whatever is troubling us. But when defense mechanisms delay or interfere with our use of more constructive coping strategies, they can be counterproductive.

Personality Development

The Psychosexual Stages

Key Theme

- **The psychosexual stages are age-related developmental periods, and each stage represents a different focus of the id's sexual energies.**

Key Questions

- **What are the five psychosexual stages, and what are the core conflicts of each stage?**
- **What is the consequence of fixation?**
- **What role does the Oedipus complex play in personality development?**

According to Freud (1905), people progress through five psychosexual stages of development. The foundations of adult personality are established during the first five years of life, as the child progresses through the *oral*, *anal*, and *phallic*

ego defense mechanisms
Largely unconscious distortions of thoughts or perceptions that act to reduce anxiety.

repression
The unconscious exclusion of anxiety-provoking thoughts, feelings, and memories from conscious awareness; the most fundamental ego defense mechanism.

displacement
The ego defense mechanism that involves unconsciously shifting the target of an emotional urge to a substitute target that is less threatening or dangerous.

sublimation
An ego defense mechanism that involves redirecting sexual urges toward productive, socially acceptable, nonsexual activities; a form of displacement.

psychosexual stages. The *latency stage* occurs during late childhood, and the fifth and final stage, the *genital stage,* begins in adolescence.

Each psychosexual stage represents a different focus of the id's sexual energies. Freud (1940) contended that "sexual life does not begin only at puberty, but starts with clear manifestations after birth." This statement is often misinterpreted. Freud was *not* saying that an infant experiences sexual urges in the same way that an adult does. Instead, Freud believed that the infant or young child expresses primitive sexual urges by seeking sensual pleasure from different areas of the body. Thus, the **psychosexual stages** are age-related developmental periods in which sexual impulses are focused on different bodily zones and are expressed through the activities associated with these areas.

Over the first five years of life, the expression of primitive sexual urges progresses from one bodily zone to another in a distinct order: the mouth, the anus, and the genitals. The first year of life is characterized as the *oral stage.* During this time the infant derives pleasure through the oral activities of sucking, chewing, and biting. During the next two years, pleasure is derived through elimination and acquiring control over elimination—the *anal stage.* In the *phallic stage,* pleasure seeking is focused on the genitals.

"He has a few things to work through, but we're good together."

Fixation

Unresolved Developmental Conflicts

At each psychosexual stage, Freud (1905) believed, the infant or young child is faced with a developmental conflict that must be successfully resolved in order to move on to the next stage. The heart of this conflict is the degree to which parents either frustrate or overindulge the child's expression of pleasurable feelings. Hence, Freud (1940) believed that parental attitudes and the timing of specific child-rearing events, such as weaning or toilet training, leave a lasting influence on personality development.

If frustrated, the child will be left with feelings of unmet needs characteristic of that stage. If overindulged, the child may be reluctant to move on to the next stage. In either case, the result of an unresolved developmental conflict is *fixation* at a particular stage. The person continues to seek pleasure through behaviors that are similar to those associated with that psychosexual stage. For example, the adult who constantly chews gum, smokes, or bites her fingernails may have unresolved oral psychosexual conflicts.

The Oedipus Complex

A Psychosexual Drama

The most critical conflict that the child must successfully resolve for healthy personality and sexual development occurs during the phallic stage (Freud, 1923, 1940). As the child becomes more aware of pleasure derived from the genital area, Freud believed, the child develops a sexual attraction to the opposite-sex parent and hostility toward the same-sex parent. This is the famous **Oedipus complex,** named after the protagonist of a Greek myth. Abandoned at birth, Oedipus does not know the identity of his parents. As an adult, Oedipus unknowingly kills his father and marries his mother.

According to Freud, this attraction to the opposite-sex parent plays out as a sexual drama in the child's mind, a drama with different plot twists for boys and for girls. For boys, the Oedipus complex unfolds as a confrontation with the father for the affections of the mother. The little boy feels hostility and jealousy toward his father, but he realizes that his father is more physically powerful. The boy experiences *castration anxiety,* or the fear that his father will punish him by castrating him (Freud, 1933).

To resolve the Oedipus complex and these anxieties, the little boy ultimately joins forces with his former enemy by resorting to the defense mechanism of **identification.** That is, he imitates and internalizes his father's values, attitudes, and mannerisms.

psychosexual stages
In Freud's theory, age-related developmental periods in which the child's sexual urges are focused on different areas of the body and are expressed through the activities associated with those areas.

Oedipus complex
In Freud's theory, a child's unconscious sexual desire for the opposite-sex parent, usually accompanied by hostile feelings toward the same-sex parent.

identification
In psychoanalytic theory, an ego defense mechanism that involves reducing anxiety by imitating the behavior and characteristics of another person.

There is, however, one strict limitation in identifying with the father. Only the father can enjoy the sexual affections of the mother. This limitation becomes internalized as a taboo against incestuous urges in the boy's developing superego, a taboo that is enforced by the superego's use of guilt and societal restrictions (Freud, 1905, 1923).

Girls also ultimately resolve the Oedipus complex by identifying with the same-sex parent and developing a strong superego taboo against incestuous urges. But the underlying sexual drama in girls follows different themes. The little girl discovers that little boys have a penis and that she does not. She feels a sense of deprivation and loss that Freud termed *penis envy.*

According to Freud (1940), the little girl blames her mother for "sending her into the world so insufficiently equipped." Thus, she develops contempt for and resentment toward her mother. However, in her attempt to take her mother's place with her father, she also *identifies* with her mother. Like the little boy, the little girl internalizes the attributes of the same-sex parent.

Freud's views on female sexuality, particularly the concept of penis envy, are among his most severely criticized ideas. Perhaps recognizing that his explanation of female psychosexual development rested on shaky ground, Freud (1926) admitted, "We know less about the sexual life of little girls than of boys. But we need not feel ashamed of this distinction. After all, the sexual life of adult women is a 'dark continent' for psychology."

Competing with Dad for Mom? According to Freud, the child identifies with the same-sex parent as a way of resolving sexual attraction toward the opposite-sex parent—the Oedipus complex. Freud believed that imitating the same-sex parent also plays an important role in the development of gender identity and, ultimately, of healthy sexual maturity.

The Latency and Genital Stages

Freud felt that because of the intense anxiety associated with the Oedipus complex, the sexual urges of boys and girls become repressed during the *latency stage* in late childhood. Outwardly, children in the latency stage express a strong desire to associate with same-sex peers, a preference that strengthens the child's sexual identity.

The final resolution of the Oedipus complex occurs in adolescence, during the *genital stage*. As incestuous urges start to resurface, they are prohibited by the moral ideals of the superego as well as by societal restrictions. Thus, the person directs sexual urges toward socially acceptable substitutes, who often resemble the person's opposite-sex parent (Freud, 1905).

In Freud's theory, a healthy personality and sense of sexuality result when conflicts are successfully resolved at each stage of psychosexual development (summarized in Table 10.2). Successfully negotiating the conflicts at each psychosexual stage results in the person's capacity to love and in productive living through one's work, child rearing, and other accomplishments.

It often happens that a young man falls in love seriously for the first time with a mature woman, or a girl with an elderly man in a position of authority; this is a clear echo of the [earlier] phase of development that we have been discussing, since these figures are able to re-animate pictures of their mother or father.

SIGMUND FREUD (1905)

Table 10.2

Freud's Psychosexual Stages

Age	Stage	Description
Birth to age 1	Oral	The mouth is the primary focus of pleasurable and gratifying sensations, which the infant achieves via feeding and exploring objects with his mouth.
Ages 1 to 3	Anal	The anus is the primary focus of pleasurable sensations, which the young child derives through developing control over elimination via toilet training.
Ages 3 to 6	Phallic	The genitals are the primary focus of pleasurable sensations, which the child derives through sexual curiosity, masturbation, and sexual attraction to the opposite-sex parent.
Ages 7 to 11	Latency	Sexual impulses become repressed and dormant as the child develops same-sex friendships with peers and focuses on school, sports, and other activities.
Adolescence	Genital	As the adolescent reaches physical sexual maturity, the genitals become the primary focus of pleasurable sensations, which the person seeks to satisfy in heterosexual relationships.

collective unconscious
In Jung's theory, the hypothesized part of the unconscious mind that is inherited from previous generations and that contains universally shared ancestral experiences and ideas.

archetypes
(AR-kuh-types) In Jung's theory, the inherited mental images of universal human instincts, themes, and preoccupations that are the main components of the collective unconscious.

The Neo-Freudians

Freud's Descendants and Dissenters

Key Theme

- **The neo-Freudians followed Freud in stressing the importance of the unconscious and early childhood, but they developed their own personality theories.**

Key Questions

- **How did the neo-Freudians generally depart from Freud's ideas?**
- **What were the key ideas of Jung, Horney, and Adler?**
- **What are three key criticisms of Freud's theory and of the psychoanalytic perspective?**

Freud's ideas were always controversial. But by the early 1900s, he had attracted a number of followers, many of whom went to Vienna to study with him. Although these early followers developed their own personality theories, they still recognized the importance of many of Freud's basic notions, such as the influence of unconscious processes and early childhood experiences. In effect, they kept the foundations that Freud had established but offered new explanations for personality processes. Hence, these theorists are often called *neo-Freudians* (the prefix *neo* means "new"). The neo-Freudians and their theories are considered part of the psychoanalytic perspective on personality.

In general, the neo-Freudians disagreed with Freud on three key points. First, they took issue with Freud's belief that behavior was primarily motivated by sexual urges. Second, they disagreed with Freud's contention that personality is fundamentally determined by early childhood experiences. Instead, the neo-Freudians believed that personality can also be influenced by experiences throughout the lifespan. Third, the neo-Freudian theorists departed from Freud's generally pessimistic view of human nature and society.

In Chapter 9, on lifespan development, we described the psychosocial theory of one famous neo-Freudian, Erik Erikson. In this chapter, we'll look at the basic ideas of three other important neo-Freudians: Carl Jung, Karen Horney, and Alfred Adler.

What we properly call instincts are physiological urges, and are perceived by the senses. But at the same time, they also manifest themselves in fantasies and often reveal their presence only by symbolic images. These manifestations are what I call the archetypes. They are without known origin; and they reproduce themselves in any time or in any part of the world.
CARL JUNG (1964)

Carl Jung

Archetypes and the Collective Unconscious

Born in a small town in Switzerland, **Carl Jung** (1875–1961) was fascinated by the myths, folktales, and religions of his own and other cultures. After studying medicine, Jung was drawn to the relatively new field of psychiatry because he believed it could provide deeper insights into the human mind (Jung, 1963).

Intrigued by Freud's ideas, Jung began a correspondence with him. At their first meeting, the two men were so compatible that they talked for 13 hours nonstop. Freud felt that his young disciple was so promising that he called him his "adopted son" and his "crown prince." It would be Jung, Freud decided, who would succeed him and lead the international psychoanalytic movement. However, Jung was too independent to relish his role as Freud's unquestioning disciple. As Jung continued to put forth his own ideas, his close friendship with Freud ultimately ended in bitterness (Solomon, 2003).

Jung rejected Freud's belief that human behavior is fueled by the instinctual drives of sex and aggression. Instead, Jung believed that people are motivated by a more general psychological energy that pushes them to achieve psychological growth, self-realization, and psychic wholeness and harmony. Jung (1963) also believed that personality continues to develop in significant ways throughout the lifespan.

In studying different cultures, Jung was struck by the universality of many images and themes, which also surfaced in his patients' dreams and preoccupations. These observations led to some of Jung's most intriguing ideas, the notions of the collective unconscious and archetypes.

Jung (1936) believed that the deepest part of the individual psyche is the **collective unconscious,** which is shared by all people and reflects humanity's collective evolutionary history. He described the collective unconscious as containing "the whole spiritual heritage of mankind's evolution, born anew in the brain structure of every individual" (Jung, 1931).

Contained in the collective unconscious are the **archetypes,** the mental images of universal human instincts, themes, and preoccupations (Jung, 1964). Common archetypal themes that are expressed in virtually every culture are the hero, the powerful father, the nurturing mother, the witch, the wise old man, the innocent child, and death and rebirth.

Two important archetypes that Jung (1951) described are the *anima* and the *animus*—the representations of feminine and masculine qualities. Jung believed that every man has a "feminine" side, represented by his anima, and that every woman has a "masculine" side, represented by her animus. To achieve psychological harmony, Jung believed, it is important for men to recognize and accept their feminine aspects and for women to recognize and accept the masculine side of their nature.

Not surprisingly, Jung's concepts of the collective unconscious and shared archetypes have been criticized as being unscientific or mystical. As far as we know, individual experiences cannot be genetically passed down from one generation to the next. Regardless, Jung's ideas make more sense if you think of the collective unconscious as reflecting shared human experiences. The archetypes, then, can be thought of as symbols that represent the common, universal themes of the human life cycle. These universal themes include birth, achieving a sense of self, parenthood, the spiritual search, and death.

Although Jung's theory never became as influential as Freud's, some of his ideas have gained wide acceptance. For example, Jung (1923) was the first to describe two basic personality types: *introverts,* who focus their attention inward, and *extraverts,* who turn their attention and energy toward the outside world. We will encounter these two basic personality dimensions again, when we look at trait theories later in this chapter. Finally, Jung's emphasis on the drive toward psychological growth and self-realization anticipated some of the basic ideas of the humanistic perspective on personality, which we'll look at shortly.

Archetypes in Popular Culture According to Jung, archetypal images are often found in popular myths, novels, and even films. Consider the classic film *The Wizard of Oz.* The motherless child, Dorothy, is on a quest for self-knowledge and selfhood, symbolized by the circular Emerald City. She is accompanied by her symbolic helpers, the Cowardly Lion (seeking courage), the Tin Woodsman (seeking love), and the Scarecrow (seeking wisdom).

The Mandala To Jung (1974), the mandala was the archetypal symbol of the self and psychic wholeness. Mandala images are found in cultures throughout the world. Shown here are a ceremonial buffalo robe of the Plains Indians *(left);* the Bhavacakra, or Buddhist Wheel of Life, from Tibet *(center);* and one of many examples from the Christian tradition, a beautiful rose window in the main portal of the Notre Dame cathedral in Reims, France *(right).*

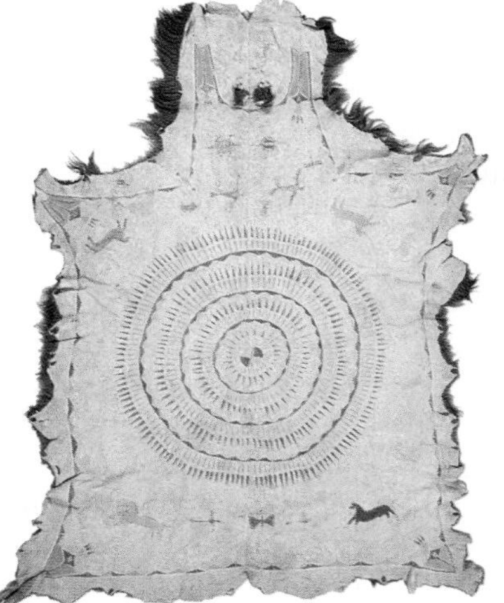

Man, [Freud] postulated, is doomed to suffer or destroy. . . . My own belief is that man has the capacity as well as the desire to develop his potentialities and become a decent human being, and that these deteriorate if his relationship to others and hence to himself is, and continues to be, disturbed. I believe that man can change and go on changing as long as he lives.

KAREN HORNEY (1945)

Karen Horney

Basic Anxiety and "Womb Envy"

Trained as a Freudian psychoanalyst, **Karen Horney** (1885–1952) (pronounced HORN-eye) emigrated from Germany to the United States during the Great Depression in the 1930s. Horney noticed distinct differences between her American and her German patients. While Freud traced psychological problems to sexual conflicts, Horney found that her American patients were much more worried about their jobs and economic problems than their sex lives. Thus, Horney came to stress the importance of cultural and social factors in personality development—matters that Freud had largely ignored (Horney, 1945).

Horney also stressed the importance of social relationships, especially the parent–child relationship, in the development of personality. She believed that disturbances in human relationships, not sexual conflicts, were the cause of psychological problems. Such problems arise from the attempt to deal with *basic anxiety,* which Horney (1945) described as "the feeling a child has of being isolated and helpless in a potentially hostile world."

Horney (1945) described three patterns of behavior that the individual uses to defend against basic anxiety: moving toward, against, or away from other people. Those who move *toward* other people have an excessive need for approval and affection. Those who move *against* others have an excessive need for power, especially power over other people. They are often competitive, critical, and domineering, and they need to feel superior to others. Finally, those who move *away from* other people have an excessive need for independence and self-sufficiency, which often makes them aloof and detached from others.

Horney contended that people with a healthy personality are *flexible* in balancing these different needs, for there are times when each behavior pattern is appropriate. As Horney (1945) wrote, "One should be capable of giving in to others, of fighting, and keeping to oneself. The three can complement each other and make for a harmonious whole." But when one pattern becomes the predominant way of dealing with other people and the world, psychological conflict and problems can result.

Horney also sharply disagreed with Freud's interpretation of female development, especially his notion that women suffer from penis envy. What women envy in men, Horney (1926) claimed, is not their penis, but their superior status in society. In fact, Horney contended that men often suffer *womb envy,* envying women's capacity to bear children. Neatly standing Freud's view of feminine psychology on its head, Horney argued that *men* compensate for their relatively minor role in reproduction by constantly striving to make creative achievements in their work (Gilman, 2001). As Horney (1945) wrote, "Is not the tremendous strength in men of the impulse to creative work in every field precisely due to their feelings of playing a relatively small part in the creation of living beings, which constantly impels them to an overcompensation in achievement?"

Horney shared Jung's belief that people are not doomed to psychological conflict and problems. Also like Jung, Horney believed that the drive to grow psychologically and achieve one's potential is a basic human motive.

Alfred Adler

Feelings of Inferiority and Striving for Superiority

Born in Vienna, **Alfred Adler** (1870–1937) was an extremely sickly child. Yet through determination and hard work, he overcame his physical weaknesses. After studying medicine, he became associated with Freud. But from the beginning of Adler's interest in psychoanalysis, he disagreed with Freud on several issues. In particular, Adler placed much more emphasis on the importance of conscious thought processes and social motives. Eventually, Adler broke away from Freud to establish his own theory of personality.

Adler (1933b) believed that the most fundamental human motive is *striving for superiority*—the desire to improve oneself, master challenges, and move toward self-perfection and self-realization. Striving toward superiority arises from universal *feelings of inferiority* that are experienced during infancy and childhood, when the child is helpless and dependent on others. These feelings motivate people to *compensate* for their real or imagined weaknesses by emphasizing their talents and abilities and by working hard to improve themselves. Hence, Adler (1933a) saw the universal human feelings of inferiority as ultimately constructive and valuable.

However, when people are unable to compensate for specific weaknesses or when their feelings of inferiority are excessive, they can develop an *inferiority complex*—a general sense of inadequacy, weakness, and helplessness. People with an inferiority complex are often unable to strive for mastery and self-improvement.

At the other extreme, people can *overcompensate* for their feelings of inferiority and develop a *superiority complex*. Behaviors caused by a superiority complex might include exaggerating one's accomplishments and importance in an effort to cover up weaknesses and denying the reality of one's limitations (Adler, 1954).

Like Horney, Adler believed that humans were motivated to grow and achieve their personal goals. And, like Horney, Adler emphasized the importance of cultural influences and social relationships (Carlson & others, 2008).

To be a human being means to have inferiority feelings. One recognizes one's own powerlessness in the face of nature. One sees death as the irrefutable consequence of existence. But in the mentally healthy person this inferiority feeling acts as a motive for productivity, as a motive for attempting to overcome obstacles, to maintain oneself in life.

ALFRED ADLER (1933a)

Evaluating Freud and the Psychoanalytic Perspective on Personality

Like it or not, Sigmund Freud's ideas have had a profound and lasting impact on our culture and on our understanding of human nature (see Merlino & others, 2008). Today, opinions on Freud span the entire spectrum. Some see him as a genius who discovered brilliant, lasting insights into human nature. Others contend that Freud was a deeply neurotic, driven man who successfully foisted his twisted personal view of human nature onto an unsuspecting public (Crews, 1984, 1996, 2006).

The truth, as you might suspect, lies somewhere in between. Although Freud has had an enormous impact on psychology and on society, there are several valid criticisms of Freud's theory and, more generally, of the psychoanalytic perspective. We'll discuss three of the most important problems next.

Inadequacy of Evidence

Freud's theory relies wholly on data derived from his relatively small number of patients and from self-analysis. Most of Freud's patients were relatively well-to-do, well-educated members of the middle and upper classes in Vienna at the beginning of the twentieth century. Freud (1916, 1919, 1939) also analyzed the lives of famous historical figures, such as Leonardo da Vinci, and looked to myth, religion, literature, and evolutionary prehistory for confirmation of his ideas. Any way you look at it, this is a small and rather skewed sample from which to draw sweeping generalizations about human nature.

Furthermore, it is impossible to objectively assess Freud's "data." Freud did not take notes during his private therapy sessions. And, of course, when he did report a case in detail, it is still Freud's interpretation of the case that is recorded. For Freud, proof of the validity of his ideas depended on his uncovering similar patterns in different patients. So the critical question is this: Was Freud imposing his own ideas onto his patients, seeing only what he expected to see? Some critics think so (e.g., Grünbaum, 2006, 2007).

A Century of Influence One indicator of Freud's influence is that he appeared on the cover of *Time* magazine four different times—in 1924, just before his death in 1939, in 1993, and again in 1999. The 1999 cover shown here, a caricature of Freud psychoanalyzing Albert Einstein, was a special issue of *Time* commemorating the 100 greatest scientists and thinkers of the twentieth century.

Lack of Testability

Many psychoanalytic concepts are so vague and ambiguous that they are impossible to objectively measure or confirm (Crews, 2006; Grünbaum, 2006). For example, how might you go about proving the existence of the id or the superego? Or how could you operationally define and measure the effects of the pleasure principle, the life instinct, or the Oedipus complex?

> For good or ill, Sigmund Freud, more than any other explorer of the psyche, has shaped the mind of the 20th century. The very fierceness and persistence of his detractors are a wry tribute to the staying power of Freud's ideas.
>
> PETER GAY (1999)

Psychoanalytic "proof" often has a "heads I win, tails you lose" style to it. In other words, psychoanalytic concepts are often impossible to *dis*prove because even seemingly contradictory information can be used to support Freud's theory. For example, if your memory of childhood doesn't jibe with Freud's description of the psychosexual stages or the Oedipus complex, well, that's because you've repressed it. Freud himself was not immune to this form of reasoning (Robinson, 1993). When one of Freud's patients reported dreams that didn't seem to reveal a hidden wish, Freud interpreted the dreams as betraying the patient's hidden wish to disprove Freud's dream theory!

As Freud acknowledged, psychoanalysis is better at explaining *past* behavior than at predicting future behavior (Gay, 1989). Indeed, psychoanalytic interpretations are so flexible that a given behavior can be explained by any number of completely different motives. For example, a man who is extremely affectionate toward his wife might be exhibiting displacement of a repressed incestuous urge (he is displacing his repressed affection for his mother onto his wife), reaction formation (he actually hates his wife intensely, so he compensates by being overly affectionate), or fixation at the oral stage (he is overly dependent on his wife).

> Step by step, we are learning that Freud has been the most overrated figure in the entire history of science and medicine—one who wrought immense harm through the propagation of false etiologies, mistaken diagnoses, and fruitless lines of inquiry.
>
> FREDERICK CREWS (2006)

Nonetheless, several key psychoanalytic ideas *have* been substantiated by empirical research (Cogan & others, 2007; Westen, 1990, 1998). Among these are the ideas that (1) much of mental life is unconscious; (2) early childhood experiences have a critical influence on interpersonal relationships and psychological adjustment; and (3) people differ significantly in the degree to which they are able to regulate their impulses, emotions, and thoughts toward adaptive and socially acceptable ends.

Sexism

Many people feel that Freud's theories reflect a sexist view of women. Because penis envy produces feelings of shame and inferiority, Freud (1925) claimed, women are more vain, masochistic, and jealous than men. He also believed that women are more influenced by their emotions and have a lesser ethical and moral sense than men.

As Horney and other female psychoanalysts have pointed out, Freud's theory uses male psychology as a prototype. Women are essentially viewed as a deviation from the norm of masculinity (Horney, 1926; Thompson, 1950). Perhaps, Horney suggested, psychoanalysis would have evolved an entirely different view of women if it were not dominated by the male point of view.

To Freud's credit, women were quite active in the early psychoanalytic movement. Several female analysts became close colleagues of Freud (Freeman & Strean, 1987; Roazen, 1999, 2000). And, it was Freud's daughter Anna, rather than any of his sons, who followed in his footsteps as an eminent psychoanalyst. Ultimately, Anna Freud became her father's successor as leader of the international psychoanalytic movement.

Anna Freud (1895–1982) Freud's youngest daughter, Anna, became his chief disciple and was herself the founder of a psychoanalytic school. Expanding on her father's theory, she applied psychoanalysis to therapy with children. She is shown here addressing a debate on psychoanalysis at the Sorbonne University in Paris in 1950.

The weaknesses in Freud's theory and in the psychoanalytic approach to personality are not minor problems. All the same, Freud made some extremely significant contributions to modern psychological thinking. Most important, he drew attention to the existence and influence of mental processes that occur outside conscious awareness, an idea that continues to be actively investigated by today's psychological researchers.

The Humanistic Perspective on Personality

Key Theme

- **The humanistic perspective emphasizes free will, self-awareness, and psychological growth.**

Key Questions

- **What role do the self-concept, actualizing tendency, and unconditional positive regard play in Rogers's personality theory?**
- **What are key strengths and weaknesses of the humanistic perspective?**

humanistic psychology
The theoretical viewpoint on personality that generally emphasizes the inherent goodness of people, human potential, self-actualization, the self-concept, and healthy personality development.

By the 1950s, the field of personality was dominated by two completely different perspectives: Freudian psychoanalysis and B. F. Skinner's brand of behaviorism (see Chapter 5). While Freud's theory of personality proposed elaborate and complex internal states, Skinner believed that psychologists should focus on observable behaviors and on the environmental factors that shape and maintain those behaviors (see Rogers & Skinner, 1956). As Skinner (1971) wrote, "A person does not act upon the world, the world acts upon him."

The Emergence of the "Third Force"

Another group of psychologists had a fundamentally different view of human nature. In opposition to both psychoanalysis and behaviorism, they championed a "third force" in psychology, which they called humanistic psychology. **Humanistic psychology** is a view of personality that emphasizes human potential and such uniquely human characteristics as self-awareness and free will (Cain, 2002).

In contrast to Freud's pessimistic view of people as being motivated by unconscious sexual and destructive instincts, the humanistic psychologists saw people as being innately good. Humanistic psychologists also differed from psychoanalytic theorists by their focus on the *healthy* personality rather than on psychologically troubled people.

In contrast to the behaviorist view that human and animal behavior is due largely to environmental reinforcement and punishment, the humanistic psychologists believed that people are motivated by the need to grow psychologically. They also doubted that laboratory research with rats and pigeons accurately reflected the essence of human nature, as the behaviorists claimed. Instead, humanistic psychologists contended that the most important factor in personality is the individual's *conscious, subjective perception of his or her self* (Purkey & Stanley, 2002).

The two most important contributors to the humanistic perspective were Carl Rogers and Abraham Maslow. In Chapter 8, on motivation, we discussed **Abraham Maslow's** famous *hierarchy of needs* and his concept of self-actualization. Like Maslow, Rogers emphasized the tendency of human beings to strive to fulfill their potential and capabilities (Kirschenbaum, 2004; Kirschenbaum & Jourdan, 2005).

At bottom, each person is asking, "Who am I, really? How can I get in touch with this real self, underlying all my surface behavior? How can I become myself?"

CARL ROGERS (1961)

Carl Rogers

On Becoming a Person

Carl Rogers (1902–1987) grew up in a large, close-knit family in Oak Park, Illinois, a suburb of Chicago. His parents were highly religious and instilled a moral and ethical atmosphere in the home, which no doubt influenced Rogers's early decision to become a minister. After studying theology, Rogers decided that the ministry was not for him. Instead, he turned to the study of psychology, ultimately enjoying a long, productive, and distinguished career as a psychotherapist, writer, and university professor.

actualizing tendency
In Rogers's theory, the innate drive to maintain and enhance the human organism.

self-concept
The set of perceptions and beliefs that you hold about yourself.

conditional positive regard
In Rogers's theory, the sense that you will be valued and loved only if you behave in a way that is acceptable to others; conditional love or acceptance.

unconditional positive regard
In Rogers's theory, the sense that you will be valued and loved even if you don't conform to the standards and expectations of others; unconditional love or acceptance.

"To this day, I can hear my mother's voice—harsh, accusing. 'Lost your mittens? You naughty kittens! Then you shall have no pie!'"

Unconditional Positive Regard Rogers contended that healthy personality development is the result of being unconditionally valued and loved as a person (Bozarth, 2007). He advised parents and teachers to control a child's inappropriate behavior without rejecting the child himself. Such a style of discipline teaches acceptable behaviors without diminishing the child's sense of self-worth.

Like Freud, Rogers developed his personality theory from his clinical experiences with his patients. Rogers referred to his patients as "clients" to emphasize their active and voluntary participation in therapy. In marked contrast to Freud, Rogers was continually impressed by his clients' drive to grow and develop their potential.

These observations convinced Rogers that the most basic human motive is the **actualizing tendency**—the innate drive to maintain and enhance the human organism (Bozarth & Wang, 2008). According to Rogers, all other human motives, whether biological or social, are secondary. He compared the actualizing tendency to a child's drive to learn to walk despite early frustration and falls. To get a sense of the vastly different views of Rogers and Freud, read the Critical Thinking box "Freud Versus Rogers on Human Nature."

The Self-Concept

Rogers (1959) was struck by how frequently his clients in therapy said, "I'm not really sure who I am" or "I just don't feel like myself." This observation helped form the cornerstone of Rogers's personality theory: the idea of the self-concept. The **self-concept** is the set of perceptions and beliefs that you have about yourself, including your nature, your personal qualities, and your typical behavior.

According to Rogers (1980), people are motivated to act in accordance with their self-concept. So strong is the need to maintain a consistent self-concept that people will deny or distort experiences that contradict their self-concept.

The self-concept begins evolving early in life. Because they are motivated by the actualizing tendency, infants and young children naturally gravitate toward self-enhancing experiences. But as children develop greater self-awareness, there is an increasing need for positive regard. *Positive regard* is the sense of being loved and valued by other people, especially one's parents (Bozarth, 2007).

Rogers (1959) maintained that most parents provide their children with **conditional positive regard**—the sense that the child is valued and loved only when she behaves in a way that is acceptable to others. The problem with conditional positive regard is that it causes the child to learn to deny or distort her genuine feelings. For example, if little Amy's parents scold and reject her when she expresses angry feelings, her strong need for positive regard will cause her to deny her anger, even when it's justified or appropriate. Eventually, Amy's self-concept will become so distorted that genuine feelings of anger are denied, because they are inconsistent with her self-concept as "a good girl who never gets angry." Because of the fear of losing positive regard, she cuts herself off from her true feelings.

Like Freud, Rogers believed that feelings and experiences could be driven from consciousness by being denied or distorted. But Rogers believed that feelings become denied or distorted not because they are threatening but because they contradict the self-concept. In this case, people are in a state of *incongruence:* Their self-concept conflicts with their actual experience (Rogers, 1959). Such a person is continually defending against genuine feelings and experiences that are inconsistent with his self-concept. As this process continues over time, a person progressively becomes more "out of touch" with his true feelings and his essential self, often experiencing psychological problems as a result.

How is incongruence to be avoided? In the ideal situation, a child experiences a great deal of unconditional positive regard from parents and other authority figures. **Unconditional positive regard** refers to the child's sense of being unconditionally loved and valued, even if she doesn't conform to the standards and expectations of others. In this way, the child's actualizing tendency is allowed its fullest expression. However, Rogers did *not* advocate permissive parenting. He thought that parents were responsible for controlling their children's behavior and for teaching them acceptable standards of behavior. Rogers maintained that parents can discipline their child without undermining the child's sense of self-worth.

For example, parents can disapprove of a child's specific *behavior* without completely rejecting the *child herself.* In effect, the parent's message should be,

CRITICAL THINKING

Freud Versus Rogers on Human Nature

Freud's view of human nature was deeply pessimistic. He believed that the human aggressive instinct was innate, persistent, and pervasive. Were it not for internal superego restraints and external societal restraints, civilization as we know it would collapse: The destructive instincts of humans would be unleashed. As Freud (1930) wrote in *Civilization and Its Discontents:*

> Men are not gentle creatures who want to be loved, and who at the most can defend themselves if they are attacked; they are, on the contrary, creatures among whose instinctual endowments is to be reckoned a powerful share of aggressiveness. As a result, their neighbor is for them not only a potential helper or sexual object, but also someone who tempts them to satisfy their aggressiveness on him, to exploit his capacity for work without compensation, to use him sexually without his consent, to seize his possessions, to humiliate him, to cause him pain, to torture and to kill him. *Man is a wolf to man.* Who, in the face of all his experience of life and of history, will have the courage to dispute this assertion?

In Freud's view, then, the essence of human nature is destructive. Control of these destructive instincts is necessary. Yet societal, cultural, religious, and moral restraints also make people frustrated, neurotic, and unhappy. Why? Because the strivings of the id toward instinctual satisfaction *must* be frustrated if civilization and the human race are to survive. Hence, as the title of Freud's book emphasizes, civilization is inevitably accompanied by human "discontent."

A pretty gloomy picture, isn't it? Yet if you watch the evening news or read the newspaper, you may find it hard to disagree with Freud's negative image of human nature. People *are* often exceedingly cruel and selfish, committing horrifying acts of brutality against strangers and even against loved ones.

However, you might argue that people can also be extraordinarily kind, self-sacrificing, and loving toward others. Freud would agree with this observation. Yet according to his theory, "good" or "moral" behavior does not disprove the essentially destructive nature of people. Instead, he explains good or moral behavior in terms of superego control, sublimation of the instincts, displacement, and so forth.

But is this truly the essence of human nature? Carl Rogers disagreed strongly. "I do not discover man to be well characterized in his basic nature by such terms as *fundamentally hostile, antisocial, destructive, evil,*" Rogers (1957a) wrote. Instead, Rogers believed that people are more accurately described as *"positive, forward-moving, constructive, realistic, trustworthy."*

If this is so, how can Rogers account for the evil and cruelty in the world? Rogers didn't deny that people can behave destructively and cruelly. Yet throughout his life, Rogers insisted that people are innately good. Rogers (1981) explained the existence of evil in this way:

> My experience leads me to believe that it is cultural factors which are the major factor in our evil behaviors. The rough manner of childbirth, the infant's mixed experience with the parents, the constricting, destructive influence of our educational system, the injustice of our distribution of wealth, our cultivated prejudices against individuals who are different—all these elements and many others warp the human organism in directions which are antisocial.

Are People Innately Good . . . or Innately Evil? These volunteers are members of Doctors Without Borders, an international group of medical workers that won the Nobel Peace Prize for its work in helping the victims of violence and disasters all over the world. Here, they carry a wounded survivor of a brutal massacre to safety in a refugee camp. On the one hand, killings motivated by political or ethnic hatred seem to support Freud's contentions about human nature. On the other hand, the selfless behavior of those who help others, often at a considerable cost to themselves, seems to support Rogers's view. Which viewpoint do you think more accurately describes the essence of human nature?

In sharp contrast to Freud, Rogers (1964) said we should *trust* the human organism, because the human who is truly free to choose will naturally gravitate toward behavior that serves to perpetuate the human race and improve society as a whole:

> I dare to believe that when the human being is inwardly free to choose whatever he deeply values, he tends to value those objects, experiences, and goals that will make for his own survival, growth, and development, and for the survival and development of others. . . . The psychologically mature person as I have described him has, I believe, the qualities which would cause him to value those experiences which would make for the survival and enhancement of the human race.

Two great thinkers, two diametrically opposed views of human nature. Now it's your turn to critically evaluate their views.

CRITICAL THINKING QUESTIONS

- Are people inherently driven by aggressive instincts, as Freud claimed? Must the destructive urges of the id be restrained by parents, culture, religion, and society if civilization is to continue? Would an environment in which individuals were unrestrained inevitably lead to an unleashing of destructive instincts?
- Or are people naturally good, as Rogers claimed? If people existed in a truly free and nurturing environment, would they invariably make constructive choices that would benefit both themselves and society as a whole?

"I do not value your behavior right now, but I still love and value *you*." In this way, according to Rogers, the child's essential sense of self-worth can remain intact.

Rogers (1957b) believed that it is through consistent experiences of unconditional positive regard that one becomes a psychologically healthy, fully functioning person. The *fully functioning person* has a flexible, constantly evolving self-concept. She is realistic, open to new experiences, and capable of changing in response to new experiences.

Rather than defending against or distorting her own thoughts or feelings, the person experiences *congruence:* Her sense of self is consistent with her emotions and experiences (Farber, 2007). The actualizing tendency is fully operational, and she makes choices that move her in the direction of greater growth and fulfillment of potential. Rogers (1957b, 1964) believed that the fully functioning person is likely to be creative and spontaneous and to enjoy harmonious relationships with others.

"I am quite aware that out of defensiveness and inner fear individuals can and do behave in ways which are incredibly cruel, horribly destructive, immature, regressive, antisocial, and hurtful. Yet one of the most refreshing and invigorating parts of my experience is to work with such individuals and to discover the strongly positive directional tendencies which exist in them, as in all of us, at the deepest levels."

CARL ROGERS (1961)

Evaluating the Humanistic Perspective on Personality

The humanistic perspective has been criticized on two particular points. First, humanistic theories are hard to validate or test scientifically. Humanistic theories tend to be based on philosophical assumptions or clinical observations rather than on empirical research. For example, concepts like the self-concept, unconditional positive regard, and the actualizing tendency are very difficult to define or measure objectively.

Second, many psychologists believe that humanistic psychology's view of human nature is *too* optimistic. For example, if self-actualization is a universal human motive, why are self-actualized people so hard to find? And, critics claim, humanistic psychologists have minimized the darker, more destructive side of human nature. Can we really account for all the evil in the world by attributing it to a restrictive upbringing or society?

The influence of humanistic psychology has waned since the 1960s and early 1970s (Cain, 2003). Nevertheless, it has made lasting contributions, especially in the realms of psychotherapy, counseling, education, and parenting (Farber, 2007). The humanistic perspective has also promoted the scientific study of such topics as the healthy personality and creativity. Finally, the importance of subjective experience and the self-concept has become widely accepted in different areas of psychology (Sheldon, 2008; Sleeth, 2007).

The Social Cognitive Perspective on Personality

Key Theme

- **The social cognitive perspective stresses conscious thought processes, self-regulation, and the importance of situational influences.**

Key Questions

- **What is the principle of reciprocal determination?**
- **What is the role of self-efficacy beliefs in personality?**
- **What are key strengths and weaknesses of the social cognitive perspective?**

social cognitive theory
Albert Bandura's theory of personality, which emphasizes the importance of observational learning, conscious cognitive processes, social experiences, self-efficacy beliefs, and reciprocal determinism.

reciprocal determinism
A model proposed by psychologist Albert Bandura that explains human functioning and personality as caused by the interaction of behavioral, cognitive, and environmental factors.

self-efficacy
The beliefs that people have about their ability to meet the demands of a specific situation; feelings of self-confidence or self-doubt.

Have you ever noticed how different your behavior and sense of self can be in different situations? Consider this example: You feel pretty confident as you enter your English composition class. After all, you're pulling an A, and your prof nods approvingly every time you participate in the class discussion, which you do frequently. In contrast, your college algebra class is a disaster. You're worried about passing the course, and you feel so shaky about your skills that you're afraid to even ask a question, much less participate in class. Even a casual observer would notice how differently you behave in the two different situations—speaking freely and confidently in one class, staring at your desk in hopes that your instructor won't notice you in the other.

The idea that a person's conscious thought processes in different situations strongly influence his or her actions is one important characteristic of the *social cognitive perspective* on personality (Cervone, 2004). According to the social cognitive perspective, people actively process information from their social experiences. This information influences their goals, expectations, beliefs, and behavior, as well as the specific environments they choose.

The social cognitive perspective differs from psychoanalytic and humanistic perspectives in several ways. First, rather than basing their approach on self-analysis or insights derived from psychotherapy, social cognitive personality theorists rely heavily on experimental findings. Second, the social cognitive perspective emphasizes conscious, self-regulated behavior rather than unconscious mental influences and instinctual drives. And third, as in our English-versus-algebra-class example, the social cognitive approach emphasizes that our sense of self can vary, depending on our thoughts, feelings, and behaviors in a given situation.

The capacity to exercise control over the nature and quality of life is the essence of humanness. Unless people believe they can produce desired results and forestall detrimental ones by their actions, they have little incentive to act or persevere in the face of difficulties.

ALBERT BANDURA (2001)

Albert Bandura and Social Cognitive Theory

Although several contemporary personality theorists have embraced the social cognitive approach to explaining personality, probably the most influential is **Albert Bandura** (b. 1925). We examined Bandura's classic research on *observational learning* in Chapter 5. In Chapter 8, we encountered Bandura's more recent research on self-efficacy. Here, you'll see how Bandura's ideas on both these topics are reflected in his personality theory, called social cognitive theory. **Social cognitive theory** emphasizes the social origins of thoughts and actions but also stresses active cognitive processes and the human capacity for *self*-regulation (Bandura, 2004b, 2006).

As Bandura's early research demonstrated, we learn many behaviors by observing, and then imitating, the behavior of other people. But, as Bandura (1997) has pointed out, we don't merely observe people's actions. We also observe the *consequences* that follow people's actions, the *rules* and *standards* that apply to behavior in specific situations, and the ways in which people *regulate their own behavior*. Thus, environmental influences are important, but conscious, self-generated goals and standards also exert considerable control over thoughts, feelings, and actions (Bandura, 2001).

For example, consider your own goal of getting a college education. No doubt many social and environmental factors influenced your decision. In turn, your conscious decision to attend college determines many aspects of your current behavior, thoughts, and emotions. And your goal of attending college classes determines which environments you choose.

Bandura (1986, 1997) explains human behavior and personality as being caused by the interaction of behavioral, cognitive, and environmental factors. He calls this process **reciprocal determinism** (see Figure 10.2). According to this principle, each factor both influences the other factors and is influenced by the other factors. Thus, in Bandura's view, our environment influences our thoughts and actions, our thoughts influence our actions and the environments we choose, our actions influence our thoughts and the environments we choose, and so on in a circular fashion.

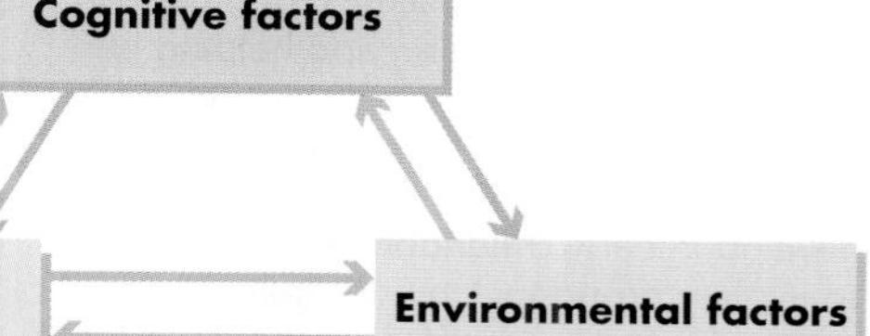

Figure 10.2 Reciprocal Determinism

Source: Bandura (1997).

Beliefs of Self-Efficacy

Anybody Here Know How to Fix a Light Switch?

Collectively, a person's cognitive skills, abilities, and attitudes represent the person's *self-system*. According to Bandura (2001), it is our self-system that guides how we perceive, evaluate, and control our behavior in different situations. Bandura (2004b) has found that the most critical elements influencing the self-system are our beliefs of self-efficacy. **Self-efficacy** refers to the degree to which you are subjectively convinced of your own capabilities and effectiveness in meeting the demands of a particular situation.

The most effective way of developing a strong sense of efficacy is through mastery experiences. Successes build a robust belief in one's efficacy. Failures undermine it. A second way is through social modeling. If people see others like themselves succeed by sustained effort, they come to believe that they, too, have the capacity to do so. Social persuasion is a third way of strengthening people's beliefs in their efficacy. If people are persuaded that they have what it takes to succeed, they exert more effort than if they harbor self-doubts and dwell on personal deficiencies when problems arise.

ALBERT BANDURA (2004b)

For example, your authors, Don and Sandy, are at opposite ends of the spectrum in their beliefs of self-efficacy when it comes to repairs around the house. Don thinks he can fix anything, whether he really can or not. Sandy likes to describe herself as "mechanically challenged." When a light switch broke in our house, it was obvious that Sandy had very little faith in her ability to fix or replace it: She instantly hollered for help. As Don investigated the matter, he casually asked Sandy whether *she* could replace the light switch.

"Me? You must be kidding," Sandy immediately responded. "It would never occur to me to even *try* to replace a light switch."

Bandura would be quick to point out how Sandy's weak belief of self-efficacy about electrical repairs guides her behavior—it would prevent her from even attempting to fix a light switch on her own. When Don reassured Sandy that the directions were right on the light-switch package and that it was a very simple task, Sandy still expressed strong self-doubt about her abilities. "I'd probably blow up the house or burn it down or black out the whole neighborhood," she said.

Albert Bandura would, no doubt, smile at how readily Sandy's remark was an everyday confirmation of his research finding that our beliefs of self-efficacy help shape our imagination of future consequences (Bandura, 1992; Ozer & Bandura, 1990; Sánchez, 2006). In Sandy's case, her weak belief of self-efficacy contributed to her imagination of dire future consequences should she attempt this task.

Bandura's concept of self-efficacy makes it easier to understand why people often fail to perform optimally at certain tasks, even though they possess the necessary skills. Sandy has made presentations in front of hundreds of people, knows how to slab a geode with a diamond saw, can easily navigate Chicago's rush-hour traffic, and once single-handedly landed an eight-pound northern pike. In all these situations, she has strong feelings of self-efficacy. But hand her a package containing a light switch and she's intimidated.

Hence, our self-system is very flexible. How we regard ourselves and our abilities varies depending on the situations or tasks we're facing. In turn, our beliefs influence the tasks we are willing to try and how persistent we'll be in the face of obstacles (Bandura, 1996, 2004b).

With the light switch, Don insisted on proving to Sandy that she was capable of changing it. "Well, maybe if I watched you install one, I might be willing to try it," Sandy finally offered. Sandy's suggestion illustrates how we acquire new behaviors and strengthen our beliefs of self-efficacy in particular situations through observational learning and *mastery experiences* (Bandura, 2001, 2004b). When we perform a task successfully, our sense of self-efficacy becomes stronger. When we fail to deal effectively with a particular task or situation, our sense of self-efficacy is undermined.

From very early in life, children develop feelings of self-efficacy from their experiences in dealing with different tasks and situations, such as athletic, social, and academic activities (Bandura & others, 2003). As Bandura (1992) has pointed out, developing self-efficacy begins in childhood, but it continues as a lifelong process. Each stage of the lifespan presents new challenges. And just for the record, Sandy *did* successfully replace the broken light switch. Now, about that dripping faucet . . .

Self-Efficacy We acquire a strong sense of self-efficacy by meeting challenges and mastering new skills specific to a particular situation. By encouraging and helping her son with his schoolwork, this mother is fostering her son's sense of self-efficacy in this domain. Self-efficacy beliefs begin to develop in early childhood but continue to evolve throughout the lifespan as we encounter new and different challenges.

Evaluating the Social Cognitive Perspective on Personality

A key strength of the social cognitive perspective on personality is its grounding in empirical, laboratory research (Bandura, 2004a). The social cognitive perspective is built on research in learning, cognitive psychology, and social psychology, rather than on clinical impressions. And, unlike vague psychoanalytic and humanistic concepts, the concepts of social cognitive theory are scientifically testable—that is, they can be operationally defined and measured. For example, psychologists can study beliefs of self-efficacy by comparing subjects who are low in self-efficacy in a given situation with subjects who are high in self-efficacy (e.g., Ozer & Bandura, 1990).

Not surprisingly, then, the social cognitive perspective has had a major impact on the study of personality.

However, some psychologists feel that the social cognitive approach to personality applies *best* to laboratory research. In the typical laboratory study, the relationships among a limited number of very specific variables are studied. In everyday life, situations are far more complex, with multiple factors converging to affect behavior and personality. Thus, an argument can be made that clinical data, rather than laboratory data, may be more reflective of human personality.

The social cognitive perspective also ignores unconscious influences, emotions, or conflicts. Some psychologists argue that the social cognitive theory focuses on very limited areas of personality—learning, the effects of situations, and the effects of beliefs about the self. Thus, it seems to lack the richness of psychoanalytic and humanistic theories, which strive to explain the *whole* person, including the unconscious, irrational, and emotional aspects of personality (McAdams & Pals, 2006; Westen, 1990).

Nevertheless, by emphasizing the reciprocal interaction of mental, behavioral, and situational factors, the social cognitive perspective recognizes the complex combination of factors that influence our everyday behavior. By emphasizing the important role of learning, especially observational learning, the social cognitive perspective offers a developmental explanation of human functioning that persists throughout one's lifetime. Finally, by emphasizing the self-regulation of behavior, the social cognitive perspective places most of the responsibility for our behavior—and for the consequences we experience—squarely on our own shoulders.

trait
A relatively stable, enduring predisposition to consistently behave in a certain way.

trait theory
A theory of personality that focuses on identifying, describing, and measuring individual differences in behavioral predispositions.

The Trait Perspective on Personality

Key Theme

- **Trait theories of personality focus on identifying, describing, and measuring individual differences.**

Key Questions

- **What are traits, and how do surface and source traits differ?**
- **What are three influential trait theories, and how might heredity affect personality?**
- **What are key strengths and weaknesses of trait theories of personality?**

Suppose we asked you to describe the personality of a close friend. How would you begin? Would you describe her personality in terms of her unconscious conflicts, the congruence of her self-concept, or her level of self-efficacy? Probably not. Instead, you'd probably generate a list of her personal characteristics, such as "outgoing," "cheerful," and "generous." This rather commonsense approach to personality is shared by the trait theories.

The trait approach to personality is very different from the theories we have encountered thus far. The psychoanalytic, humanistic, and social cognitive theories emphasize the *similarities* among people. They focus on discovering the universal processes of motivation and development that explain human personality (Revelle, 1995, 2007). Although these theories do deal with individual differences, they do so only indirectly. In contrast, the trait approach to personality *focuses primarily on describing individual differences* (Funder, 2001).

Trait theorists view the person as being a unique combination of personality characteristics or attributes, called *traits*. A **trait** is formally defined as a relatively stable, enduring predisposition to behave in a certain way. A **trait theory** of personality, then, is one that focuses on identifying, describing, and measuring individual differences in behavioral predispositions. Think back to our description of the twins, Kenneth and Julian, in the chapter Prologue. You can probably readily identify some

"Oh, God! Here comes little Miss Perky."

surface traits
Personality characteristics or attributes that can easily be inferred from observable behavior.

source traits
The most fundamental dimensions of personality; the broad, basic traits that are hypothesized to be universal and relatively few in number.

of their personality traits. For example, Julian was described as impulsive, cocky, and adventurous, while Kenneth was serious, intense, and responsible.

People possess traits to different degrees. For example, a person might be extremely shy, somewhat shy, or not shy at all. Hence, a trait is typically described in terms of a range from one extreme to its opposite. Most people fall in the middle of the range (average shyness), while fewer people fall at opposite poles (extremely shy or extremely outgoing).

Surface Traits and Source Traits

Most of the terms that we use to describe people are **surface traits**—traits that lie on "the surface" and can be easily inferred from observable behaviors. Examples of surface traits include attributes like "happy," "exuberant," "spacey," and "gloomy." The list of potential surface traits is extremely long. Personality researcher Gordon Allport combed through an English-language dictionary and discovered more than 4,000 words that described specific personality traits (Allport & Odbert, 1936).

Source traits are thought to be more fundamental than surface traits. As the most basic dimension of personality, a source trait can potentially give rise to a vast number of surface traits. Trait theorists believe that there are relatively few source traits. Thus, one goal of trait theorists has been to identify the most basic set of universal source traits that can be used to describe all individual differences (Pervin, 1994).

Two Representative Trait Theories

Raymond Cattell and Hans Eysenck

How many source traits are there? Not surprisingly, trait theorists differ in their answers. Pioneer trait theorist **Raymond Cattell** reduced Allport's list of 4,000 terms to about 171 characteristics by eliminating terms that seemed to be redundant or uncommon (see John, 1990). Cattell collected data on a large sample of people, who were rated on each of the 171 terms. He then used a statistical technique called *factor analysis* to identify the traits that were most closely related to one another. After further research, Cattell eventually reduced his list to 16 key personality factors, which are listed in Table 10.3.

Cattell (1994) believed that these 16 personality factors represent the essential source traits of human personality. To measure these traits, Cattell developed what has become one of the most widely used personality tests, the *Sixteen Personality Factor Questionnaire* (abbreviated *16PF*). We'll discuss the 16PF in more detail later in the chapter.

An even simpler model of universal source traits was proposed by British psychologist **Hans Eysenck** (1916–1997). Eysenck's methods were similar to Cattell's, but his conception of personality includes just three dimensions. The first dimension is *introversion–extraversion*, which is the degree to which a person directs his energies outward toward the environment and other people versus inward toward his inner and self-focused experiences. A person who is high on the dimension of *introversion* might be quiet, solitary, and reserved, avoiding new experiences. A person high on the *extraversion* scale would be outgoing and sociable, enjoying new experiences and stimulating environments.

Eysenck's second major dimension is *neuroticism–emotional stability. Neuroticism* refers to a person's predisposition to become emotionally upset, while *stability* reflects a person's predisposition to be emotionally even. Surface traits associated

Table 10.3

Cattell's 16 Personality Factors

1	Reserved, unsociable	⟷	Outgoing, sociable
2	Less intelligent, concrete	⟷	More intelligent, abstract
3	Affected by feelings	⟷	Emotionally stable
4	Submissive, humble	⟷	Dominant, assertive
5	Serious	⟷	Happy-go-lucky
6	Expedient	⟷	Conscientious
7	Timid	⟷	Venturesome
8	Tough-minded	⟷	Sensitive
9	Trusting	⟷	Suspicious
10	Practical	⟷	Imaginative
11	Forthright	⟷	Shrewd, calculating
12	Self-assured	⟷	Apprehensive
13	Conservative	⟷	Experimenting
14	Group-dependent	⟷	Self-sufficient
15	Undisciplined	⟷	Controlled
16	Relaxed	⟷	Tense

Source: Adapted from Cattell (1973).

Raymond Cattell believed that personality could be described in terms of 16 source traits, or basic personality factors. Each factor represents a dimension that ranges between two extremes.

with neuroticism are anxiety, tension, depression, and guilt. At the opposite end, emotional stability is associated with the surface traits of being calm, relaxed, and even-tempered.

Eysenck believed that by combining these two dimensions people can be classified into four basic types: introverted–neurotic, introverted–stable, extraverted–neurotic, and extraverted–stable. Each basic type is associated with a different combination of surface traits, as shown in Figure 10.3.

In later research, Eysenck identified a third personality dimension, called *psychoticism* (Eysenck, 1990; Eysenck & Eysenck, 1975). A person high on this trait is antisocial, cold, hostile, and unconcerned about others. A person who is low on psychoticism is warm and caring toward others. In the chapter Prologue, Julian might be described as above average on psychoticism, while Kenneth was extremely low on this trait.

Eysenck (1990) believed that individual differences in personality are due to biological differences among people. For example, Eysenck proposed that an introvert's nervous system is more easily aroused than is an extravert's nervous system. Assuming that people tend to seek out an optimal level of arousal (see Chapter 8), extraverts would seek stimulation from their environment more than introverts would. And, because introverts would be more uncomfortable than extraverts in a highly stimulating environment, introverts would be much less likely to seek out stimulation.

Do introverts and extraverts actually prefer different environments? In a clever study, John Campbell and Charles Hawley (1982) found that extraverted students tended to study in a relatively noisy, open area of a college library, where there were ample opportunities for socializing with other students. Introverted students preferred to study in a quiet section of the library, where individual carrels and small tables were separated by tall bookshelves. As Eysenck's theory predicts, the introverts preferred study areas that minimized stimulation, while the extraverts preferred studying in an area that provided stimulation.

Brain-imaging studies provide a different line of evidence to support Eysenck's idea that personality traits reflect biological differences (Canli, 2004, 2006; Canli & others, 2002, 2004; Gusnard, 2005). The Focus on Neuroscience on page 44 describes a pioneering investigation of the association of particular personality traits with distinct patterns of brain activity.

Raymond Cattell (1905–1998) Cattell was a strong advocate of the trait approach to personality. His research led to the development of the Sixteen Personality Factor Questionnaire, one of the most widely used psychological tests for assessing personality.

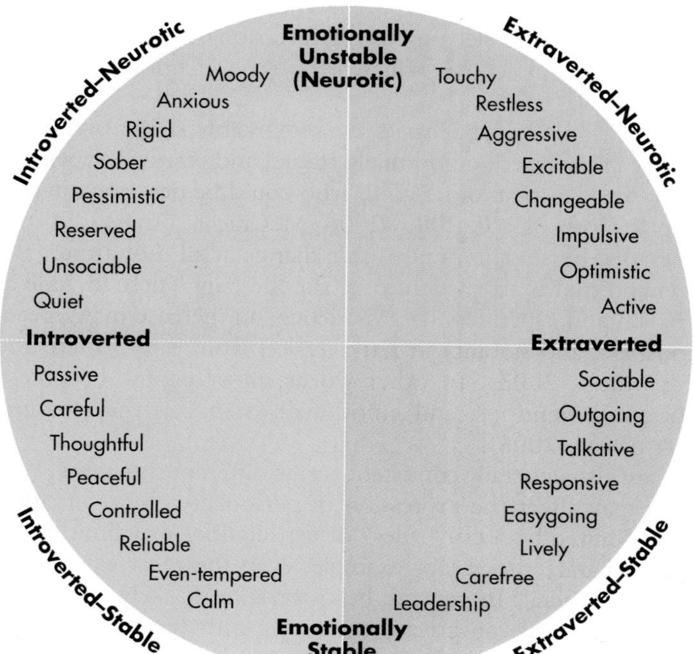

Figure 10.3 Eysenck's Theory of Personality Types Hans Eysenck's representation of the four basic personality types. Each type represents a combination of two basic personality dimensions: extraversion–introversion and neuroticism–emotional stability. Note the different surface traits in each quadrant that are associated with each basic personality type.

Source: Adapted from Eysenck (1982).

Table 10.4

The Five-Factor Model of Personality

Low ⟷	High
Factor 1: Neuroticism	
Calm	Worrying
Even-tempered, unemotional	Temperamental, emotional
Hardy	Affectionate
Factor 2: Extraversion	
Reserved	Affectionate
Loner	Joiner
Quiet	Talkative
Factor 3: Openness to Experience	
Down-to-earth	Imaginative
Conventional, uncreative	Original, creative
Prefer routine	Prefer variety
Factor 4: Agreeableness	
Antagonistic	Acquiescent
Ruthless	Softhearted
Suspicious	Trusting
Factor 5: Conscientiousness	
Lazy	Hardworking
Aimless	Ambitious
Quitting	Persevering

Source: Adapted from McCrae & Costa (1990).

This table shows the five major personality factors, according to Big Five theorists Robert McCrae and Paul Costa, Jr. Listed below each major personality factor are surface traits that are associated with it. Note that each factor represents a dimension or range between two extreme poles. Most people will fall somewhere in the middle between the two opposing poles.

Sixteen Are Too Many, Three Are Too Few

The Five-Factor Model

Many trait theorists felt that Cattell's trait model was too complex and that his 16 personality factors could be reduced to a smaller, more basic set of traits. Yet Eysenck's three-dimensional trait theory seemed too limited, failing to capture other important dimensions of human personality (see Block, 1995).

Today, the consensus among many trait researchers is that the essential building blocks of personality can be described in terms of five basic personality dimensions, which are sometimes called "the Big Five" (Funder, 2001). According to the **five-factor model of personality,** these five dimensions represent the structural organization of personality traits (McCrae & Costa, 1996, 2003).

What are the Big Five? Different trait researchers describe the five basic traits somewhat differently. However, the most commonly accepted five factors are extraversion, neuroticism, agreeableness, conscientiousness, and openness to experience. Table 10.4 summarizes the Big Five traits, as defined by personality theorists Robert McCrae and Paul Costa, Jr. Note that factor 1, neuroticism, and factor 2, extraversion, are essentially the same as Eysenck's first two personality dimensions.

Does the five-factor model describe the universal structure of human personality? According to ongoing research by Robert McCrae and his colleagues (2004, 2005), the answer appears to be yes. In one wide-ranging study, trained observers rated the personality traits of representative individuals in 50 different cultures, including Arab cultures like those in Kuwait and Morocco and African cultures like those in Uganda and Ethiopia (McCrae & others, 2005). With few exceptions, people could be reliably described in terms of the five-factor structure of personality. Other research has shown that people in European, African, Arab, and Asian cultures describe personality using terms that are consistent with the five-factor model (Allik & McCrae, 2004; Rossier & others, 2005). Based on abundant cross-cultural research, trait theorists Jüri Allik and Robert McCrae (2002, 2004) now believe that the Big Five personality traits are basic features of the human species, universal, and probably biologically based.

How can we account for the apparent universality of the five-factor structure? Psychologist David Buss (1991, 1995a) has one intriguing explanation. Buss thinks we should look at the utility of these factors from an evolutionary perspective. He believes that the Big Five traits reflect the personality dimensions that are the most important in the "social landscape" to which humans have had to adapt. Being able to identify who has social power (extraversion), who is likely to share resources (agreeableness), and who is trustworthy (conscientiousness) enhances our likelihood of survival.

Research has shown that traits are remarkably stable over time. A young adult who is very extraverted, emotionally stable, and relatively open to new experiences is likely to grow into an older adult who could be described in much the same way (McCrae & Costa, 1990, 2003, 2006; McCrae & others, 2000). However, this is not to say that personality traits don't change at all. Longitudinal data suggest that some general trends are evident over the lifespan. These include a slight decline in Neuroticism and Openness to Experience, an increase in Agreeableness and Conscientiousness, and stability in Extraversion from early to late adulthood (Terracciano & others, 2005). In other words, most people become more dominant, agreeable, conscientious, and emotionally stable as they mature psychologically (Caspi & others, 2005).

Traits are also generally consistent across different situations. However, situational influences may affect the expression of personality traits. Situations in which your behavior is limited by social "rules" or expectations may limit the expression of your personality characteristics. For example, even the most extraverted person may be subdued at a funeral. In general, behavior is most likely to reflect personality traits in familiar, informal, or private situations with few social rules or expectations (A. H. Buss, 1989, 2001).

five-factor model of personality
A trait theory of personality that identifies extraversion, neuroticism, agreeableness, conscientiousness, and openness to experience as the fundamental building blocks of personality.

FOCUS ON NEUROSCIENCE

Personality Traits and Patterns of Brain Activity

People who rate high on the personality trait of extraversion tend to be upbeat, optimistic, and sociable. They also report experiencing more positive emotions on a daily basis than less extraverted people. In contrast, people who rate high on neuroticism tend to be anxious, worried, and socially insecure. And they report more negative emotions in everyday life than less neurotic people. Could these personality traits also influence how the brain responds to emotional situations?

To investigate this idea, psychologist Turhan Canli and his colleagues (2001) gave 14 healthy female volunteers a personality test to determine their level of extraversion or neuroticism. Then, each woman was placed in a functional magnetic resonance imaging (fMRI) scanner to record her brain's reaction to positive images (e.g., a happy couple, puppies, ice cream, sunsets) or negative images (e.g., angry or crying people, spiders, guns, or a cemetery).

The fMRI showed that the women who scored high on extraversion had greater brain reactivity to positive images than did the women who scored low on extraversion. In image (**a**), red locations show significant positive correlations between extraversion and reactions to positive images. For the extraverted women, brain activity in response to the positive images was most strongly correlated with brain areas associated with emotion, including the frontal cortex and the amygdala.

In contrast, the women who scored high on neuroticism had more brain activation in response to negative images, but in fewer brain areas associated with emotions. In image (**b**), blue locations show significant positive correlations between neuroticism and reactions to negative images. These areas of activation were mostly in the left frontal and temporal cortical areas.

What this study shows is that specific personality traits are associated with individual differences in the brain's reaction to emotional stimuli. According to researcher John Gabrieli (2001), "Depending on personality traits, people's brains seem to amplify some aspects of experience over others. All of the participants in this study saw very positive and very negative scenes, but people's brain reactions were very different. One group saw the cup as being very full while the other group saw it as very empty."

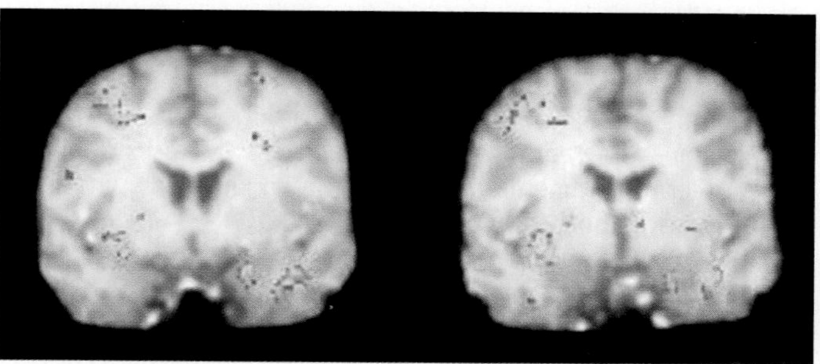

(a) Extraversion correlating with brain reactivity to positive pictures

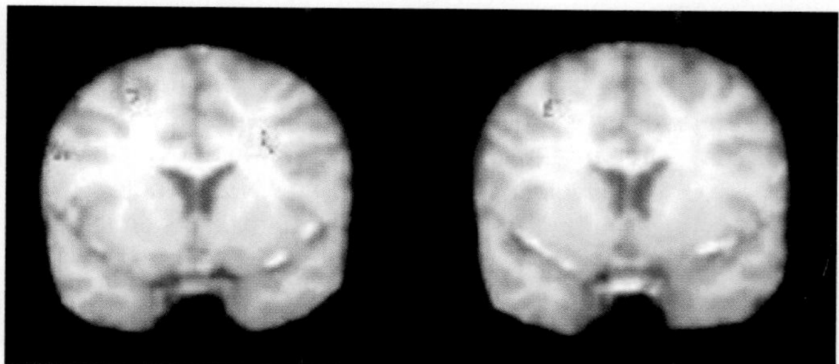

(b) Neuroticism correlating with brain reactivity to negative pictures

Keep in mind, however, that human behavior is the result of a complex *interaction* between traits and situations (Mischel, 2004). People *do* respond, sometimes dramatically, to the demands of a particular situation. But the situations that people choose, and the characteristic way in which they respond to similar situations, are likely to be consistent with their individual personality dispositions (Mischel & Shoda, 1995; Mischel & others, 2002).

Personality Traits and Behavioral Genetics

Just a Chip off the Old Block?

Do personality traits run in families? Are personality traits determined by genetics? Many trait theorists, such as Raymond Cattell and Hans Eysenck, believed that traits are at least partially genetic in origin. For example, our daughter, Laura, has always been outgoing and sociable, traits that she shares with both her parents. But is she outgoing because she inherited that trait from us? Or is she outgoing because we modeled and reinforced outgoing behavior? Is it even possible to sort out the relative influence that genetics and environmental experiences have on personality traits?

The Continuity of Traits over the Lifespan Kenneth's conscientiousness was a trait that was evident throughout his life. Because he was too old to join the military when the United States entered World War II, Kenneth volunteered his legal expertise to the American Red Cross, providing them with legal services for the western half of the United States.

IN FOCUS

Explaining Those Amazing Identical-Twin Similarities

As part of the ongoing *Minnesota Study of Twins Reared Apart* at the University of Minnesota, researchers David Lykken, Thomas Bouchard, and other psychologists have been studying a very unusual group of people: over 100 pairs of identical and fraternal twins who were separated at birth or in early childhood and raised in different homes. Shortly after the study began in 1980, the researchers were struck by some of the amazing similarities between identical twins (Lykken & others, 1992). Despite having been separated for most of their lives, many twins had similar personality traits, occupations, hobbies, and habits.

One of the most famous cases is that of the "Jim twins," who had been separated for close to 40 years. Like many of the other reunited twins, the two Jims had similar heights, postures, and voice and speech patterns. More strikingly, both Jims had married and divorced women named Linda, and then married women named Betty. One Jim named his son James Allan, while the other Jim named his son James Alan. Both Jims bit their nails, chain-smoked Salems, and enjoyed working in their basement workshops. And both Jims had vacationed at the same Florida beach, driving there in the same model Chevrolet (Lykken & others, 1992).

Granted, such similarities could simply be due to coincidence. Linda, Betty, James, and Alan are not exactly rare names in the United States. And literally thousands of people buy the same model car every year, just as thousands of people vacation in Florida. Besides, if you look closely at any two people of the same age, sex, and culture, there are bound to be similarities. It's probably a safe bet, for example, to say that most college students enjoy eating pizza and often wear jeans and T-shirts.

But it's difficult to dismiss as mere coincidences all the striking similarities between identical twins in the Minnesota study. Lykken and his colleagues (1992) have pointed out numerous quirky similarities that occurred in the identical twins they studied but did not occur in the fraternal-twin pairs. For example, in the entire sample of twins, there were only two subjects who had been married five times; two subjects who habitually wore seven rings; and two who left love notes around the house for their wives. In each case, the two were identical twins. And only two subjects independently (and correctly) diagnosed a problem with researcher Bouchard's car—a faulty wheel bearing. Again, the two were members of an identical-twin pair. While Lykken and his colleagues acknowledge that some identical-twin similarities are probably due to coincidence, such as the Jim twins marrying women with the same first names, others are probably genetically influenced.

So does this mean that there's a gene for getting married five times or wearing seven rings? Not exactly. Although some physical characteristics and diseases are influenced by a single gene, complex psychological characteristics, such as your personality, are influenced by a large number of genes acting in combination (Caspi & others, 2005; Marcus, 2004). Unlike fraternal twins and regular siblings, identical twins share the same specific *configuration* of interacting genes. Lykken and his colleagues suggest that many complex psychological traits, including the strikingly similar idiosyncrasies of identical twins, may result from a unique configuration of interacting genes.

Lykken and his colleagues call certain traits *emergenic traits* because they appear (or *emerge*) only out of a unique configuration of many interacting genes. Although they are genetically influenced, emergenic traits do not run in families. To illustrate the idea of emergenic traits, consider the couple of average intelligence who give birth to an extraordinarily gifted child. By all predictions, this couple's offspring should have normal, average intelligence. But because of the unique configuration of the child's genes acting in combination, extraordinary giftedness emerges (Lykken, 2006; Lykken & others, 1992).

David Lykken compares emergenic traits to a winning poker hand. All the members of the family are drawing from the same "deck," or pool of genes. But one member may come up with the special configuration of cards that produces a royal flush—the unique combination of genes that produces a Shakespeare, an Einstein, or a Beethoven. History is filled with cases of people with exceptional talents and abilities in varied fields who grew up in average families.

Finally, it's important to point out that there were many differences, as well as similarities, between the identical twins in the Minnesota study. For example, one twin was prone to depression, while the other was not; one twin was an alcoholic, while the other did not drink. So, even with identical twins, it must be remembered that personality is only *partly* determined by genetics.

Heredity or Environment? Along with sharing common genes, many identical twins share common interests and talents—like concert pianists Alvin (*left*) and Alan Chow. As students at the University of Maryland, they graduated with identical straight-A averages—and shared the stage as co-valedictorians. Both studied piano at Juilliard, and today they are both music professors with active performance schedules. In addition to performing solo, they frequently perform together in recital. However, the Chow twins were reared together, so it would be difficult to determine the relative importance of environmental and genetic influences on their talents and career paths.

The field of **behavioral genetics** studies the effects of genes and heredity on behavior. Most behavioral genetics studies on humans involve measuring similarities and differences among members of a large group of people who are genetically related to different degrees. The basic research strategy is to compare the degree of difference among subjects to their degree of genetic relatedness. If a trait is genetically influenced, then the more closely two people are genetically related, the more you would expect them to be similar on that trait (see Chapter 7).

Such studies may involve comparisons between identical twins and fraternal twins or comparisons between twins reared apart and identical twins reared together (see the In Focus box, "Explaining Those Amazing Identical-Twin Similarities"). Adoption studies, in which adopted children are compared to their biological and adoptive relatives, are also used in behavioral genetics.

Evidence gathered from twin studies and adoption studies shows that certain personality traits *are* substantially influenced by genetics (see Caspi & others, 2005). The evidence for genetic influence is particularly strong for extraversion and neuroticism, two of the Big Five personality traits (Plomin & others, 1994, 2001; Weiss & others, 2008). Twin studies have also found that openness to experience, conscientiousness, and agreeableness are also influenced by genetics, although to a lesser extent (Bouchard, 2004; Harris & others, 2007).

So is personality completely determined by genetics? Not at all. As behavioral geneticists Robert Plomin and Essi Colledge (2001) explain, "Individual differences in complex psychological traits are due at least as much to environmental influences as they are to genetic influences. Behavioral genetics research provides the best available evidence for the importance of the environment." In other words, the influence of environmental factors on personality traits is at least equal to the influence of genetic factors (Rowe, 2003). Some additional evidence that underscores this point is that identical twins are most alike in early life. As the twins grow up, leave home, and encounter different experiences and environments, their personalities become more different (Bouchard, 2004; McCartney & others, 1990).

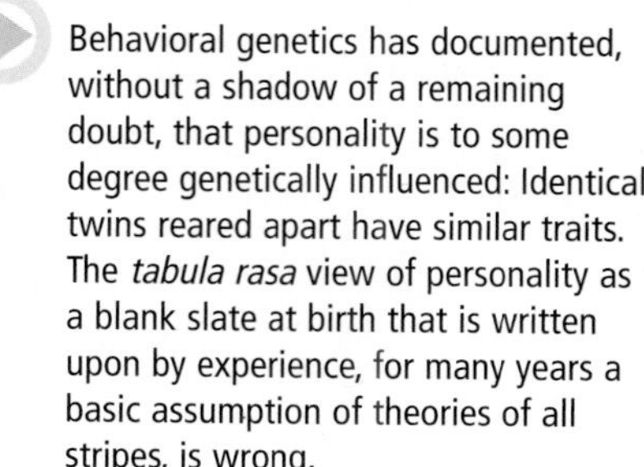

Behavioral genetics has documented, without a shadow of a remaining doubt, that personality is to some degree genetically influenced: Identical twins reared apart have similar traits. The *tabula rasa* view of personality as a blank slate at birth that is written upon by experience, for many years a basic assumption of theories of all stripes, is wrong.

DAVID C. FUNDER (2001)

Genes confer dispositions, not destinies.

DANIELLE DICK & RICHARD ROSE (2002)

behavioral genetics
An interdisciplinary field that studies the effects of genes and heredity on behavior.

Evaluating the Trait Perspective on Personality

Although psychologists continue to disagree on how many basic traits exist, they do generally agree that people can be described and compared in terms of basic personality traits. But like the other personality theories, the trait approach has its weaknesses (Block, 1995).

One criticism is that trait theories don't really explain human personality (Pervin, 1994). Instead, they simply label general predispositions to behave in a certain way. Second, trait theorists don't attempt to explain how or why individual differences develop. After all, saying that trait differences are due partly to genetics and partly to environmental influences doesn't say much.

A third criticism is that trait approaches generally fail to address other important personality issues, such as the basic motives that drive human personality, the role of unconscious mental processes, how beliefs about the self influence personality, or how psychological change and growth occur (McAdams, 1992). Conspicuously absent are the grand conclusions about the essence of human nature that characterize the psychoanalytic and humanistic theories. So, although trait theories are useful in describing individual differences and predicting behavior, there are limitations to their usefulness.

As you've seen, each of the major perspectives on personality has contributed to our understanding of human personality. The four perspectives are summarized in Table 10.5.

Our discussion of personality would not be complete without a description of how personality is formally evaluated and measured. In the next section, we'll briefly survey the tests that are used in personality assessment.

Why Are Siblings So Different? Although two children may grow up in the same home, they experience the home environment in very different ways. Even an event that affects the entire family, such as divorce, unemployment, or a family move, may be experienced quite differently by each child in the family (Dunn & Plomin, 1990). Children are also influenced by varied experiences outside the home, such as their relationships with teachers, classmates, and friends. Illness and accidents are other nonshared environmental influences. Of course, sibling relationships are themselves a potential source of influence on personality development.

Table 10.5

The Major Personality Perspectives

Perspective	Key Theorists	Key Themes and Ideas
Psychoanalytic	Sigmund Freud	Influence of unconscious psychological processes; importance of sexual and aggressive instincts; lasting effects of early childhood experiences
	Carl Jung	The collective unconscious, archetypes, and psychological wholeness
	Karen Horney	Importance of parent–child relationship; defending against basic anxiety; womb envy
	Alfred Adler	Striving for superiority, compensating for feelings of inferiority
Humanistic	Carl Rogers	Emphasis on the self-concept, psychological growth, free will, and inherent goodness
	Abraham Maslow	Behavior as motivated by hierarchy of needs and striving for self-actualization
Social cognitive	Albert Bandura	Reciprocal interaction of behavioral, cognitive, and environmental factors; emphasis on conscious thoughts, self-efficacy beliefs, self-regulation, and goal setting
Trait	Raymond Cattell	Emphasis on measuring and describing individual differences; 16 source traits of personality
	Hans Eysenck	Three basic dimensions of personality: introversion–extraversion, neuroticism–emotional stability, and psychoticism
	Robert McCrae, Paul Costa, Jr.	Five-factor model, five basic dimensions of personality: neuroticism, extraversion, openness to experience, agreeableness, and conscientiousness

Assessing Personality

Psychological Tests

Key Theme

- **Tests to measure and evaluate personality fall into two basic categories: projective tests and self-report inventories.**

Key Questions

- **What are the most widely used personality tests, and how are they administered and interpreted?**
- **What are the strengths and weaknesses of projective tests and self-report inventories?**

When we discussed intelligence tests in Chapter 7, we described what makes a good psychological test. Beyond intelligence tests, there are literally hundreds of **psychological tests** that can be used to assess abilities, aptitudes, interests, and personality (see Plake & Impara, 2001; Plake & others, 2003). Any psychological test is useful insofar as it achieves two basic goals:

1. It accurately and consistently reflects a person's characteristics on some dimension.
2. It predicts a person's future psychological functioning or behavior.

In this section, we'll look at the very different approaches used in the two basic types of personality tests—projective tests and self-report inventories. After looking at some of the most commonly used tests in each category, we'll evaluate the strengths and weaknesses of each approach.

psychological test
A test that assesses a person's abilities, aptitudes, interests, or personality, on the basis of a systematically obtained sample of behavior.

projective test
A type of personality test that involves a person's interpreting an ambiguous image; used to assess unconscious motives, conflicts, psychological defenses, and personality traits.

Projective Tests

Like Seeing Things in the Clouds

Projective tests developed out of psychoanalytic approaches to personality. In the most commonly used projective tests, a person is presented with a vague image, such as an inkblot or an ambiguous scene, then asked to describe what she "sees" in the

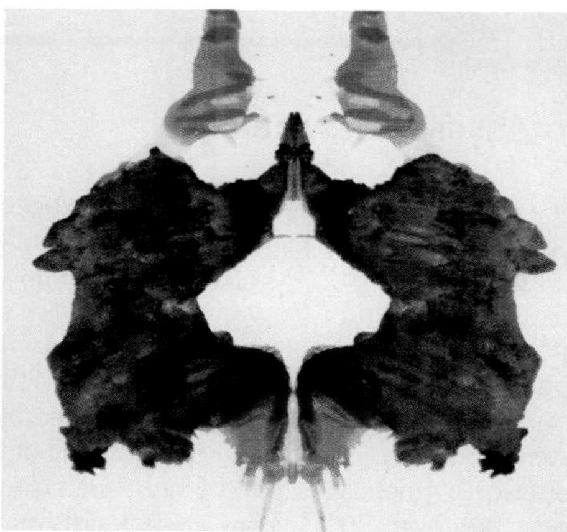

What Do You See in the Inkblot? Intrigued by Freud's and Jung's theories, Swiss psychiatrist Hermann Rorschach (1884–1922) set out to develop a test that would reveal the contents of the unconscious. Rorschach believed that people were more likely to expose their unconscious conflicts, motives, and defenses in their descriptions of the ambiguous inkblots than they would be if the same topics were directly addressed. Rorschach published a series of 10 inkblots with an accompanying manual in a monograph titled *Psychodiagnostics: A Diagnostic Test Based on Perception* in 1921. Because he died the following year, Rorschach never knew how popular his projective test would become. Although the validity of the test is questionable, the Rorschach Inkblot Test is still the icon most synonymous with psychological testing in the popular media.

image. The person's response is thought to be a projection of her unconscious conflicts, motives, psychological defenses, and personality traits. Notice that this idea is related to the defense mechanism of *projection,* which was described in Table 10.1 earlier in the chapter. The first projective test was the famous **Rorschach Inkblot Test,** published by Swiss psychiatrist Hermann Rorschach in 1921 (Hertz, 1992).

The Rorschach test consists of 10 cards, 5 that show black-and-white inkblots and 5 that depict colored inkblots. One card at a time, the person describes whatever he sees in the inkblot. The examiner records the person's responses verbatim and also observes his behavior, gestures, and reactions.

Numerous scoring systems exist for the Rorschach. Interpretation is based on such criteria as whether the person reports seeing animate or inanimate objects, human or animal figures, and movement and whether the person deals with the whole blot or just fragments of it (Exner, 1993; Exner & Erdberg, 2005).

A more structured projective test is the **Thematic Apperception Test,** abbreviated **TAT,** which we discussed in Chapter 8. In the TAT, the person looks at a series of cards, each depicting an ambiguous scene. The person is asked to create a story about the scene, including what the characters are feeling and how the story turns out. The stories are scored for the motives, needs, anxieties, and conflicts of the main character and for how conflicts are resolved (Bellak, 1993; Moretti & Rossini, 2004). As with the Rorschach, interpreting the TAT involves the subjective judgment of the examiner.

Strengths and Limitations of Projective Tests

Although sometimes used in research, projective tests are mainly used in counseling and psychotherapy. According to many clinicians, the primary strength of projective tests is that they provide a wealth of qualitative information about an individual's psychological functioning, information that can be explored further in psychotherapy.

However, there are several drawbacks to projective tests. First, the testing situation or the examiner's behavior can influence a person's responses. Second, the scoring of projective tests is highly subjective, requiring the examiner to make numerous judgments about the person's responses. Consequently, two examiners may test the same individual and arrive at different conclusions. Third, projective tests often fail to produce consistent results. If the same person takes a projective test on two separate occasions, very different results may be found. Finally, projective tests are poor at predicting future behavior.

The bottom line? Despite their widespread use, hundreds of studies of projective tests seriously question their *validity*—that the tests measure what they purport to measure—and their *reliability*—the consistency of test results (Garb & others, 2004; and see Lilienfeld & others, 2000, 2001). Nonetheless, projective tests remain very popular, especially among clinical psychologists (Butcher & Rouse, 1996; Leichtman, 2004).

Rorschach Inkblot Test
A projective test using inkblots, developed by Swiss psychiatrist Hermann Rorschach in 1921.

Thematic Apperception Test (TAT)
A projective personality test that involves creating stories about each of a series of ambiguous scenes.

SCIENCE VERSUS PSEUDOSCIENCE

Graphology: The "Write" Way to Assess Personality?

Does the way that you shape your *d*'s, dot your *i*'s, and cross your *t*'s reveal your true inner nature? That's the basic premise of **graphology,** a pseudoscience that claims that your handwriting reveals your temperament, personality traits, intelligence, and reasoning ability. If that weren't enough, graphologists also claim that they can accurately evaluate a job applicant's honesty, reliability, leadership potential, ability to work with others, and so forth (Beyerstein, 2007; Beyerstein & Beyerstein, 1992).

Handwriting analysis is very popular throughout North America and Europe. In the United States alone, there are over 30 graphology societies, each promoting its own specific methods of analyzing handwriting (Beyerstein, 1996). Many different types of agencies and institutions use graphology. For example, the FBI and the U.S. State Department have consulted graphologists to assess the handwriting of people who mail death threats to government officials (Scanlon & Mauro, 1992).

Graphology is especially popular in the business world. Thousands of American companies, including Sears, U.S. Steel, and Bendix, have used graphology to assist in hiring new employees (Basil, 1991; Taylor & Sackheim, 1988). The use of graphology in hiring and promotions is even more widespread in Europe. According to one estimate, over 80 percent of European companies use graphology in personnel matters (Greasley, 2000; see Simner & Goffin, 2003).

When subjected to scientific evaluation, how does graphology fare? Consider a study by Anthony Edwards and Peter Armitage (1992) that investigated graphologists' ability to distinguish among people in three different groups:

- Successful versus unsuccessful secretaries
- Successful business entrepreneurs versus librarians and bank clerks
- Actors and actresses versus monks and nuns

In designing their study, Edwards and Armitage enlisted the help of leading graphologists and incorporated their suggestions into the study design. The graphologists preapproved the study's format and indicated that they felt it was a fair test of graphology. The graphologists also predicted they would have a high degree of success in discriminating among the people in each group. One graphologist stated that the graphologists would have close to a 100 percent success rate. Remember that prediction.

The three groups—successful/unsuccessful secretaries, entrepreneurs/librarians, and actors/monks—represented a combined total of 170 participants. As requested by the graphologists, all participants indicated their age, sex, and hand preference. Each person also produced 20 lines of spontaneous handwriting on a neutral topic.

Four leading graphologists independently evaluated the handwriting samples. For each group, the graphologists tried to assign each handwriting sample to one category or the other. Two control measures were built into the study: (1) The handwriting samples were also analyzed by four ordinary people with *no* formal training in graphology or psychology; and (2) a *typewritten* transcript of the handwriting samples was evaluated by four psychologists. The psychologists made their evaluations on the basis of the *content* of the transcripts rather than on the handwriting itself.

In the accompanying table, you can see how well the graphologists fared as compared to the untrained evaluators and the psychologists. Clearly, the graphologists fell far short of the nearly perfect accuracy they predicted they would demonstrate. In fact, in one case, the *untrained* assessors actually *outperformed* the graphologists—they were slightly better at identifying successful versus unsuccessful secretaries.

Overall, the completely inexperienced judges achieved a success rate of 59 percent correct. The professional graphologists achieved a slightly better success rate of 65 percent. Obviously, this is not a great difference.

Success Rates by Type of Assessor

Group Assessed	Graphologists	Untrained Assessors	Psychologists
Good/bad secretaries	67%	70%	56%
Entrepreneurs/ librarians	63%	53%	52%
Actors/monks	67%	58%	53%
Overall success rate	65%	59%	54%

Hundreds of other studies have cast similar doubts on the ability of graphology to identify personality characteristics and to predict job performance from handwriting samples (see Dean, 1992; Furnham, 1991; Neter & Ben-Shakhar, 1989). In a global review of the evidence, psychologist Barry Beyerstein (1996) wrote, "Graphologists have unequivocally failed to demonstrate the validity or reliability of their art for predicting work performance, aptitudes, or personality. . . . If graphology cannot legitimately claim to be a scientific means of measuring human talents and leanings, what is it really? In short, it is a pseudoscience."

DILBERT

graphology
A pseudoscience that claims to assess personality, social, and occupational attributes based on a person's distinctive handwriting, doodles, and drawing style.

Self-Report Inventories

Does Anyone Have an Eraser?

Self-report inventories typically use a paper-and-pencil format and take a direct, structured approach to assessing personality. People answer specific questions or rate themselves on various dimensions of behavior or psychological functioning. Often called *objective personality tests,* self-report inventories contain items that have been shown by previous research to differentiate among people on a particular personality characteristic. Unlike projective tests, self-report inventories are objectively scored by comparing a person's answers to standardized norms collected on large groups of people.

The most widely used self-report inventory is the **Minnesota Multiphasic Personality Inventory (MMPI)** (Butcher & Rouse, 1996). First published in the 1940s and revised in the 1980s, the current version is referred to as the *MMPI-2.* The MMPI consists of over 500 statements. The person responds to each statement with "True," "False," or "Cannot say." Topics include social, political, religious, and sexual attitudes; physical and psychological health; interpersonal relationships; and abnormal thoughts and behaviors (Delman & others, 2008; Graham, 1993; McDermut & Zimmerman, 2008). Items similar to those used in the MMPI are shown in Table 10.6.

The MMPI is widely used by clinical psychologists and psychiatrists to assess patients. It is also used to evaluate the mental health of candidates for such occupations as police officers, doctors, nurses, and professional pilots. What keeps people from simply answering items in a way that makes them look psychologically healthy? Like many other self-report inventories, the MMPI has special scales to detect whether a person is answering honestly and consistently (Butcher, 1999; Pope & others, 2006). For example, if someone responds "True" to items such as "I *never* put off until tomorrow what I should do today" and "I *always* pick up after myself," it's probably a safe bet that she is inadvertently or intentionally distorting her other responses.

The MMPI was originally designed to assess mental health and detect psychological symptoms. In contrast, the California Personality Inventory and the Sixteen Personality Factor Questionnaire are personality inventories that were designed to assess normal populations. Of the 462 true–false items on the **California Personality Inventory (CPI),** nearly half are drawn from the MMPI. The CPI provides measures on such characteristics as interpersonal effectiveness, self-control, independence, and empathy. Profiles generated by the CPI are used to predict such things as high school and college grades, delinquency, and job performance (see Crites & Taber, 2002).

The **Sixteen Personality Factor Questionnaire (16PF)** was originally developed by Raymond Cattell and is based on his trait theory. The 16PF uses a forced-choice format in which the person must respond to each item by choosing one of three alternatives. Just as the test's name implies, the results generate a profile on Cattell's 16 personality factors. Each personality factor is represented as a range, with a person's score falling somewhere along the continuum between the two extremes (see Figure 10.4). The 16PF is widely used for career counseling, marital counseling, and evaluating employees and executives (Clark & Blackwell, 2007).

Another widely used personality test is the *Myers-Briggs Type Indicator* (abbreviated *MBTI*). The MBTI was developed by Isabel Briggs Myers and Katharine Cook Briggs (see Gladwell, 2004). Myers and Briggs were intrigued by Carl Jung's personality theory and his proposal that people could be categorized into discrete personality "types." The Myers-Briggs test differs from other self-report tests in that it is designed to assess personality *types* rather than measure personality *traits.*

The notion of personality *types* is fundamentally different from personality *traits.* According to trait theory, people display traits, such as introversion/extraversion, to varying degrees. If you took the 16PF or the CPI, your score would place you somewhere along a continuum from low (very introverted) to high (very extraverted). However, most people would fall in the middle or average range on this trait dimension. But

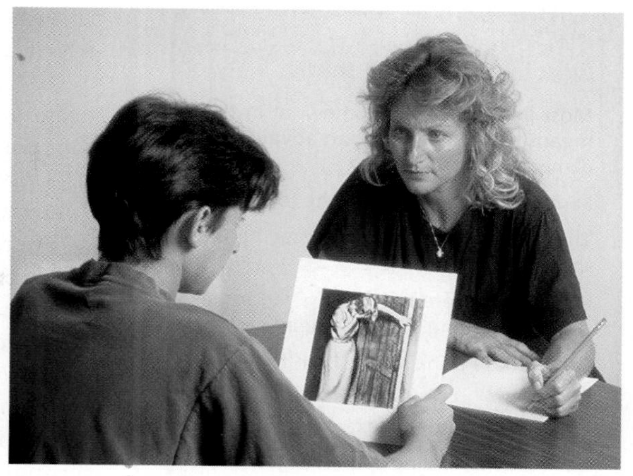

The Thematic Apperception Test Developed by psychologists Christiana Morgan and Henry Murray (1935), the TAT involves creating a story about an ambiguous scene, like the one shown on the card this young man is holding. The person is thought to project his own motives, conflicts, and other personality characteristics into the story he creates. According to Murray (1943), "Before he knows it, he has said things about an invented character that apply to himself, things which he would have been reluctant to confess in response to a direct question."

self-report inventory
A type of psychological test in which a person's responses to standardized questions are compared to established norms.

Minnesota Multiphasic Personality Inventory (MMPI)
A self-report inventory that assesses personality characteristics and psychological disorders; used to assess both normal and disturbed populations.

California Personality Inventory (CPI)
A self-report inventory that assesses personality characteristics in normal populations.

Sixteen Personality Factor Questionnaire (16PF)
A self-report inventory developed by Raymond Cattell that generates a personality profile with ratings on 16 trait dimensions.

Table 10.6

Simulated MMPI-2 Items

Most people will use somewhat unfair means to gain profit or an advantage rather than lose it.

I am often very tense on the job.

The things that run through my head sometimes are horrible.

Sometimes there is a feeling like something is pressing in on my head.

Sometimes I think so fast I can't keep up.

I am worried about sex.

I believe I am being plotted against.

I wish I could do over some of the things I have done.

Source: MMPI-2®.

according to type theory, a person is *either* an extrovert *or* an introvert—that is, one of two distinct categories that don't overlap (Arnau & others, 2003).

The MBTI arrives at personality type by measuring a person's *preferred* way of dealing with information, making decisions, and interacting with others. There are four basic categories of these preferences, which are assumed to be *dichotomies*—that is, opposite pairs. These dichotomies are: *Extraversion/Introversion; Sensing/Intuition; Thinking/Feeling;* and *Perceiving/Judging.*

There are 16 possible combinations of scores on these four dichotomies. Each combination is considered to be a distinct personality type. An individual personality type is described by the initials that correspond to the person's preferences as reflected in his or her MBTI score. For example, an ISFP combination would be a person who is *introverted, sensing, feeling, and perceiving,* while an ESTJ would be a person who is *extroverted, sensing, thinking, and judging.*

Despite the MBTI's widespread use in business, counseling, and career guidance settings, research has pointed to several problems with the MBTI. One problem is *reliability*—people can receive different MBTI results on different test-taking occasions. Equally significant is the problem of *validity.* For example, research does not support the claim of a relationship between MBTI personality types and occupational success (Pittenger, 2005). More troubling is the lack of evidence supporting the existence of 16 distinctly different personality types (Hunsley & others, 2003). Thus, most researchers in the field of psychological testing advise that caution be exercised in interpreting MBTI results, especially in applying them to vocational choices or predictions of occupational success (see Pittenger, 2005).

Strengths and Limitations of Self-Report Inventories

The two most important strengths of self-report inventories are their *standardization* and their *use of established norms* (see Chapter 7). Each person receives the same instructions and responds to the same items. The results of self-report inventories are objectively scored and compared to norms established by previous research. In fact, the MMPI, the CPI, and the 16PF can all be scored by computer.

As a general rule, the reliability and validity of self-report inventories are far greater than those of projective tests. Literally thousands of studies have demonstrated that the MMPI, the CPI, and the 16PF provide accurate, consistent results that can be used to generally predict behavior (Anastasi & Urbina, 1997).

However, self-report inventories also have their weaknesses. First, despite the inclusion of items designed to detect deliberate deception, there is considerable evidence that people can still successfully fake responses and answer in socially desirable ways (Anastasi & Urbina, 1997; Holden, 2008). Second, some people are prone to responding in a set way. They may consistently pick the first alternative or answer

Figure 10.4 The 16PF: Example Questions and Profiles The 16PF, developed by Raymond Cattell, is a self-report inventory that contains 185 items like those shown in part (a). When scored, the 16PF generates a personality profile. In part (b), personality profiles of airline pilots and writers are compared. Cattell (1973) found that pilots are more controlled, more relaxed, more self-assured, and less sensitive than writers.
Source: Cattell & others (1993).

(a)

EXAMPLE QUESTIONS

1. I often like to watch team games.
   a. true
   b. ?
   c. false
2. I prefer friends who are:
   a. quiet
   b. ?
   c. lively
3. Adult is to child as cat is to:
   a. kitten
   b. dog
   c. baby

Note: The person taking the test is instructed to answer "b.?" only when neither a nor c is a better choice for him or her.

(b)

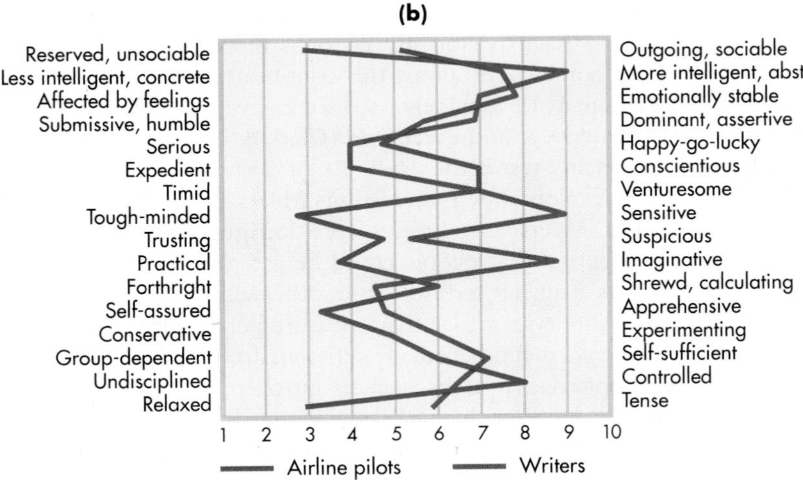

"True" whether the item is true for them or not. And some tests, such as the MMPI and CPI, include hundreds of items. Taking these tests can become quite tedious, and people may lose interest in carefully choosing the most appropriate response.

Third, people are not always accurate judges of their own behavior, attitudes, or attributes. And some people defensively deny their true feelings, needs, and attitudes, even to themselves (Cousineau & Shedler, 2006; Shedler & others, 1993). For example, a person might indicate that she enjoys parties, even though she actually avoids social gatherings whenever possible.

To sum up, personality tests are generally useful strategies that can provide insights about the psychological makeup of people. But no personality test, by itself, is likely to provide a definitive description of a given individual. In practice, psychologists and other mental health professionals usually combine personality test results with behavioral observations and background information, including interviews with family members, co-workers, or other significant people in the person's life.

Finally, people can and often do change over time, especially when their life circumstances undergo a significant change. Hence, projective tests and self-report inventories provide a barometer of personality and psychological functioning only at the time of the test.

possible selves
The aspect of the self-concept that includes images of the selves that you hope, fear, or expect to become in the future.

>> Closing Thoughts

Over the course of this chapter, you've encountered firsthand some of the most influential contributors to modern psychological thought. As you'll see in Chapter 14, the major personality perspectives provide the basis for many forms of psychotherapy. Clearly, the psychoanalytic, humanistic, social cognitive, and trait perspectives each provide a fundamentally different way of conceptualizing personality. That each perspective has strengths and limitations underscores the point that no single perspective can explain all aspects of human personality. Indeed, no one personality theory could explain why Kenneth and Julian were so different. And, given the complex factors involved in human personality, it's doubtful that any single theory ever will capture the essence of human personality in its entirety. Even so, each perspective has made important and lasting contributions to the understanding of human personality.

ENHANCING WELL-BEING WITH PSYCHOLOGY

Possible Selves: Imagine the Possibilities

Some psychologists believe that a person's self-concept is not a singular mental self-image, as Carl Rogers proposed, but a *multifaceted system* of related images and ideas (Hermans, 1996; Markus & Kunda, 1986). This collection of related images about yourself reflects your goals, values, emotions, and relationships (Markus & Cross, 1990; Markus & Wurf, 1987; Unemori & others, 2004).

According to psychologist Hazel Markus and her colleagues, an important aspect of your self-concept has to do with your images of the selves that you *might* become—your **possible selves.** Possible selves are highly personalized, vivid, futuristic images of the self that reflect hopes, fears, and fantasies. As Markus and co-researcher Paula Nurius (1986) wrote, "The possible selves that are hoped for might include the successful self, the creative self, the rich self, the thin self, or the loved and admired self, whereas the dreaded possible selves could be the alone self, the depressed self, the incompetent self, the alcoholic self, the unemployed self, or the bag lady self."

The Influence of Hoped-For and Dreaded Possible Selves

Possible selves are more than just idle daydreams or wishful fantasies. In fact, possible selves influence our behavior in important ways (Markus & Nurius, 1986; Oyserman & others, 1995). We're often not aware of the possible selves that we have incorporated into our self-concepts. Nevertheless, they can serve as powerful forces that either activate or stall our efforts to reach important goals. Your incentive, drive, and motivation are greatly influenced by your possible selves, and so are your decisions and choices about future behavior (Hoyle & Sherrill, 2006; Robinson & others, 2003).

Imagine that you harbor a hoped-for possible self of becoming a professional musician. You would probably practice with greater regularity and intensity than someone who does not hold a vivid mental picture of performing solo at Carnegie Hall or being named Performer of the Year at the American Country Music Awards.

Dreaded possible selves can also influence behavior, whether they are realistic or not. Consider Don's father, Kenneth. Although never wealthy, Kenneth was financially secure throughout his long life. Yet Kenneth had lived through the Great Depression and witnessed firsthand the financial devastation that occurred in the lives of countless people. Kenneth seems to have harbored a dreaded possible self of becoming penniless. When Kenneth died, the family found a $100 bill tucked safely under his mattress.

A positive possible self, even if it is not very realistic, can protect an individual's self-esteem in the face of failure (Markus & Nurius, 1986). A high school girl who thinks she is unpopular with her classmates may console herself with visions of a possible self as a famous scientist who snubs her intellectually inferior classmates at her 10-year class reunion. As Hazel Markus and Paula Nurius (1986) explained:

> Positive possible selves can be exceedingly liberating because they foster hope that the present self is not immutable. At the same time, negative possible selves can be powerfully imprisoning because their [emotional impact] and expectations may stifle attempts to change or develop.

Possible Selves, Self-Efficacy Beliefs, and Motivation

Self-efficacy beliefs are closely connected to the idea of possible selves. Performing virtually any task involves the construction of a possible self that is capable and competent of performing the action required (Ruvolo & Markus, 1992).

Thus, people who vividly imagine possible selves as "successful because of hard work" persist longer and expend more effort on tasks than do people who imagine themselves as "unsuccessful despite hard work" (Ruvolo & Markus, 1992). The motivation to achieve academically increases when your possible selves include a future self who is successful because of academic achievement (Oyserman & others, 1995). To be most effective, possible selves should incorporate concrete strategies for attaining goals. For example, students who visualized themselves taking specific steps to improve their grades—such as doing homework daily or signing up for tutoring—were more successful than students who simply imagined themselves doing better in school (Oyserman & others, 2004).

Applying the Research: Assessing Your Possible Selves

How can you apply these research findings to *your* life? First, it's important to stress again that we're often unaware of how the possible selves we've mentally constructed influence our beliefs, actions, and self-evaluations. Thus, the first step is to consciously assess the role that your possible selves play in your life (Oyserman & others, 1995).

Take a few moments and jot down the "possible selves" that are active in your working self-concept. To help you in this task, write three responses to each of the following questions:

1. Next year, I expect to be . . .
2. Next year, I am afraid that I will be . . .
3. Next year, I want to avoid becoming . . .

After focusing on the short-term future, take these same questions and extend them to 5 years from now or even 10 years from now. Most likely, certain themes and goals will consistently emerge. Now the critical questions:

- How are your possible selves affecting your *current* motivation, goals, feelings, and decisions?
- Are your possible selves even remotely plausible?
- Are they pessimistic and limiting?
- Are they unrealistically optimistic?

Finally, ask yourself honestly: What realistic strategies are you using to try to become like the self that you want to become? To avoid becoming the selves that you dread?

How can you improve the likelihood that you will achieve some of your possible selves? One approach is to link your expectations and hopes to concrete strategies about how to behave to reach your desired possible self (Oyserman & others, 2004).

These questions should help you gain some insight into whether your possible selves are influencing your behavior in productive, constructive ways. If they are not, now is an excellent time to think about replacing or modifying the possible selves that operate most powerfully in your own self-concept. Why is this so important? Because to a large extent, who we become is guided by who we *imagine* we'll become. Just imagine the possibilities of who *you* could become!

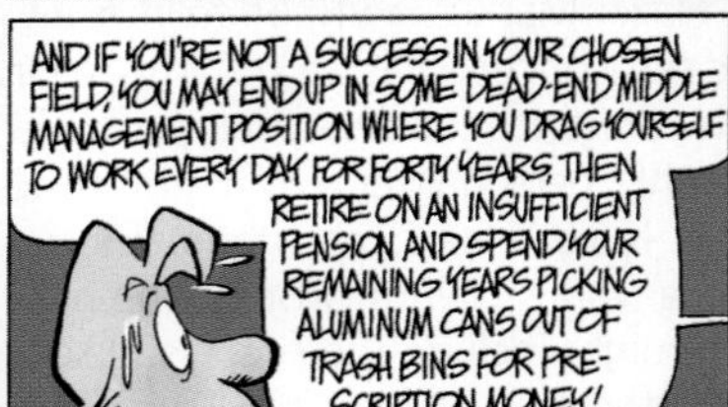

CHAPTER REVIEW: KEY PEOPLE AND TERMS

Alfred Adler, p. 430
Albert Bandura, p. 437
Raymond Cattell, p. 440
Hans Eysenck, p. 440
Sigmund Freud, p. 420
Karen Horney, p. 430
Carl G. Jung, p. 428
Abraham Maslow, p. 433
Carl Rogers, p. 433

personality, p. 419
personality theory, p. 419
psychoanalysis, p. 420
free association, p. 421
unconscious, p. 421
id, p. 422
Eros, p. 423
libido, p. 423
Thanatos, p. 423
pleasure principle, p. 423
ego, p. 423
reality principle, p. 423
superego, p. 423
ego defense mechanisms, p. 424
repression, p. 424
displacement, p. 424
sublimations, p. 424
psychosexual stages, p. 426
Oedipus complex, p. 426
identification, p. 426
collective unconscious, p. 429
archetypes, p. 429
humanistic psychology, p. 433
actualizing tendency, p. 434
self-concept, p. 434
conditional positive regard, p. 434
unconditional positive regard, p. 434
social cognitive theory, p. 437
reciprocal determinism, p. 437
self-efficacy, p. 437
trait, p. 439
trait theory, p. 439
surface traits, p. 440
source traits, p. 440
five-factor model of personality, p. 442
behavioral genetics, p. 445
psychological test, p. 446
projective test, p. 446
Rorschach Inkblot Test, p. 447
Thematic Apperception Test (TAT), p. 447
graphology, p. 448
self-report inventory, p. 449
Minnesota Multiphasic Personality Inventory (MMPI), p. 449
California Personality Inventory (CPI), p. 449
Sixteen Personality Factor Questionnaire (16PF), p. 449
possible selves, p. 451

Web Companion Review Activities

You can find additional review activities at **www.worthpublishers.com/discoveringpsych5e.** The *Discovering Psychology* 5th edition Web Companion has self-scoring practice quizzes, flashcards, interactive crossword puzzles, and other activities to help you master the material in this chapter.

CONCEPT MAP PERSONALITY

Personality

An individual's unique and relatively consistent patterns of thinking, feeling, and behaving

Personality theories explain how people are similar or different in these patterns.

Psychoanalytic Perspective

Psychoanalysis: Theory of personality developed by **Sigmund Freud** (1856–1939) that emphasized:

- Unconscious determinants of behavior and personality
- Innate sexual and aggressive instinctual drives called Eros and Thanatos
- Enduring effects of early childhood experiences on later personality development

Freud contended that personality consists of three conflicting psychological forces:

- The **id** - irrational, impulsive personality dimension ruled by pleasure principle
- The **ego** - rational, mediating personality dimension that operates on reality principle
- The **superego** - moralistic, self-evaluative personality component consisting of internalized parental and societal values and rules

Ego defense mechanisms: Unconscious distortions of reality that temporarily reduce anxiety, including:

- **Repression**
- **Sublimation**
- Projection
- Denial
- Regression
- **Displacement**
- Rationalization
- Reaction formation
- Undoing

Psychosexual stages: Freud's five age-related developmental periods in which sexual impulses are expressed through different bodily zones: oral, anal, phallic, latency, and genital

- During phallic stage, child must resolve Oedipus complex through identification with same-sex parent.
- Fixation at a particular stage may result if the developmental conflicts are not successfully resolved.

The Neo-Freudians:

Carl Jung (1875–1961)

- Emphasized psychological growth and proposed the existence of the collective unconscious and archetypes.

Karen Horney (1885–1952)

- Emphasized role of social relationships in protecting against anxiety.

Alfred Adler (1870–1937)

- Believed most fundamental human motive was to strive for superiority.

Humanistic Perspective

Humanistic psychology emphasizes:

- Inherent goodness of people
- Self-concept, self-awareness, and free will
- Human potential and psychological growth
- Healthy personality development

Carl Rogers (1902–1987) proposed that:

- **Actualizing tendency** is the inborn drive to maintain and enhance the organism
- People are motivated to maintain a consistent **self-concept**
- **Conditional positive regard** by parents leads to incongruence so that self-concept conflicts with experience
- **Unconditional positive regard** by parents leads to congruence

Abraham Maslow (1908–1970) contended that:

- People are motivated by hierarchy of needs
- People strive for self-actualization

Social Cognitive Perspective

Albert Bandura (b. 1925), **social cognitive theory:**
- Active processing of information from social experiences
- Conscious self-generated goals and self-regulation
- Development of a self-system based on a person's skills, abilities, and attitudes

Reciprocal determinism is the interaction of behavioral, cognitive, and environmental factors in the self-regulation of behavior.

Self-efficacy:
- Beliefs in a particular situation influence a person's motivation, behavior, performance, and persistence.

Trait Perspective

Trait theories identify, describe, and measure individual differences in traits.
- **Surface traits** can be inferred from easily observable behaviors.
- **Source traits** are the most basic dimensions of personality.

Raymond Cattell (1905–1998)
- Identified 16 personality factors
- Developed a test to measure the 16 factors

Hans Eysenck (1916–1997)
- Proposed three basic personality dimensions.

Five-factor model of personality identified five source traits:
- Neuroticism
- Extraversion
- Openness to experience
- Agreeableness
- Conscientiousness

Behavioral genetics studies the effects of genes and heredity on behavior and traits.

Assessing Personality

Self-report inventories:
- Use standardized question and answer formats
- Are objectively scored with results compared to established norms
- Include the MMPI, CPI, 16PF, and MBTI

Projective tests:
- Based on psychoanalytic perspective
- Person responds to vague stimulus
- Subjectively scored
- Include **Rorscharch Inkblot Test** and **Thematic Apperception Test**

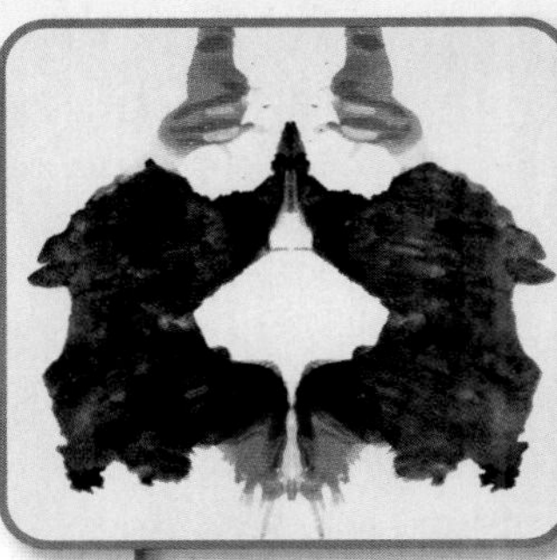

Psychological tests should:
- Be valid and reliable
- Accurately reflect a person's characteristics
- Predict future psychological and behavioral functioning

CHAPTER 11

Social Psychology

Chapter Outline

The "Homeless" Man

PROLOGUE

REMEMBER ERV AND FERN, Sandy's parents, from Chapter 5? A few years ago, Fern and Erv got two free plane tickets when they were bumped from an overbooked flight. They decided to visit a city they had always wanted to see—San Francisco. Even though Fern was excited about the trip, she was also anxious about visiting the earthquake zone. Erv wasn't especially worried about earthquakes, but he was worried about whether his old army buddy could still beat him at penny poker. Mostly, they both wanted to see the famous sights, eat seafood, wander through shops, and explore used bookstores, which was Erv's favorite hobby.

As it turned out, Fern and Erv were both quite taken by the beauty and charm of San Francisco. But they were also disturbed by the number of homeless people they saw on the city streets, sometimes sleeping in the doorways of expensive shops and restaurants. This was especially disturbing to Fern, who has a heart of gold and is known among her family and friends for her willingness to help others, even complete strangers.

On the third morning of their San Francisco visit, Erv and Fern were walking along one of the hilly San Francisco streets near the downtown area. That's when Fern saw a scruffy-looking man in faded jeans sitting on some steps, holding a cup. Something about his facial expression struck Fern as seeming lost, maybe dejected. Surely this was one of San Francisco's less fortunate, Fern thought to herself. Without a moment's hesitation, Fern rummaged through her purse, walked over to the man, and dropped a handful of quarters in his cup.

"Hey, lady! What the hell d'ya think you're doing!?!" the man exclaimed, jumping up.

"Oh, my! Aren't you homeless!?" Fern asked, mortified and turning bright red.

"Lady, this *is* my home," the man snapped, motioning with his thumb to the house behind him. "I live here! And that's my cup of coffee you just ruined!"

Fortunately, the "homeless" man also had a sense of humor. After fishing Fern's quarters out of his coffee and giving them back to her, he chatted with the out-of-towners, enlightening them on the extraordinary cost of San Francisco real estate. As they parted, the not-so-homeless man ended up recommending a couple of his favorite seafood restaurants.

Like Fern, we all try to make sense out of our social environment. As we navigate the world, we constantly make judgments about the traits, motives, and goals of other people. And, like Fern, sometimes we make mistakes!

In this chapter, we will look at how we interpret our social environment, including how we form impressions of other people and explain their behavior. We'll explore how our own behavior, including our willingness to help others, is influenced by the social environment and other people. In the process, we'll come back to Erv and Fern's incident with the "homeless" man to illustrate several important concepts.

>> Introduction: What Is Social Psychology?

Why did Fern think the man on the steps was homeless? How did the "homeless" man initially interpret Fern's efforts to help him? And in contrast to Fern, not everyone who feels compassion toward homeless people acts in accordance with that attitude. Why did Fern do so?

These are the kinds of issues that social psychologists study. **Social psychology** investigates how your thoughts, feelings, and behavior are influenced by the presence of other people and by the social and physical environment. The social situations can include being alone, in the presence of others, or in front of a crowd of onlookers.

Like other psychology specialty areas, social psychology emphasizes certain concepts. For example, one important social psychology concept is that of your *self.* Your **sense of self** involves you as a social being that has been shaped by your interactions with others and by the social environments, including the culture, in which you operate. Thus, your sense of self plays a key role in how you perceive and react to others.

Some social behaviors, such as helping others, are displayed *universally*—that is, they take a consistent form in diverse cultures. When a specific social behavior is universal, social psychologists will often use insights from evolutionary psychology to understand how the behavior is adaptive.

As we discussed in Chapter 1, *evolutionary psychology* is based on the premise that certain psychological processes and behavior patterns evolved over hundreds of thousands of years. Those patterns evolved because in some way they were adaptive, increasing the odds of survival for humans who displayed those qualities. In turn, this survival advantage increased the genetic transmission of those patterns to subsequent generations (see Buss, 2008; Tooby & Cosmides, 2005).

Social psychology research focuses on many different topics. In this chapter, we'll focus on two key research areas in social psychology. We'll start with an area that has been greatly influenced by the experimental methods and findings of *cognitive psychology,* which we discussed in Chapter 7. **Social cognition** refers to how we form impressions of other people, how we interpret the meaning of other people's behavior, and how our behavior is affected by our attitudes (Bodenhausen & others, 2003). As you'll see, sometimes those mental processes are conscious and deliberate but, at other times, they occur automatically and outside of our awareness.

Later in the chapter, we'll look at **social influence,** which focuses on how our behavior is affected by other people and by situational factors. The study of social influence includes such questions as why we conform to group norms, what compels us to obey an authority figure, and under what circumstances people will help a stranger.

Person Perception

Forming Impressions of Other People

Key Theme

- **Person perception refers to the mental processes we use to form judgments about other people.**

Key Questions

- **What four principles are followed in the person perception process?**
- **How do social categorization, implicit personality theories, and physical attractiveness affect person perception?**

Consider the following scenario. You're attending a college in the middle of a big city and commute from your apartment to the campus via the subway. Today you stayed on campus a bit later than usual, so the rush hour is pretty much over. As a seasoned

social psychology
Branch of psychology that studies how a person's thoughts, feelings, and behavior are influenced by the presence of other people and by the social and physical environment.

sense of self
An individual's unique sense of identity that has been influenced by social, cultural, and psychological experiences; your sense of who you are in relation to other people.

social cognition
The mental processes people use to make sense out of their social environment.

social influence
The effects of situational factors and other people on an individual's behavior.

subway rider, you know you're safer when the subway is full of commuters. So as you step off the platform into the subway car, you're feeling just a bit anxious. The car is more than half full. If you want to sit down, you'll have to share a seat with some other passenger. You quickly survey your fellow passengers. In a matter of seconds, you must decide which stranger you'll share your ride home with, elbow to elbow, thigh to thigh. How will you decide?

Even if you've never ridden on a subway, it doesn't matter. You could just as easily imagine choosing a seat on a bus or in a crowded movie theater. What these situations have in common is a task that most of us confront almost every day: On the basis of very limited information, we must quickly draw conclusions about the nature of people who are complete strangers to us. We also have to make some rough predictions as to how those strangers are likely to behave. How do we arrive at these conclusions?

Making Split-Second Decisions About Strangers? Deciding where to sit in a subway car or on a bus involves making rapid evaluations and decisions about people who are complete strangers. What kinds of factors do you notice in forming your first impressions of other people? Do the impressions you form seem to be the result of deliberate or automatic thoughts? Do you think your first impressions are generally accurate?

Person perception refers to the mental processes we use to form judgments and draw conclusions about the characteristics of other people. Person perception is an active, interactive, and subjective process that always occurs in some *interpersonal context* (Smith & Collins, 2009). In the interpersonal context of a subway car, you evaluate people based on minimal interaction.

Initially, you form very rapid *first impressions* based largely on looking at the other people's faces (Macrae & others, 2005; Zebrowitz, 2006). In glancing at another person's face for a mere tenth of a second, you evaluate the other person's attractiveness, likeability, competence, trustworthiness, and aggressiveness (Willis & Todorov, 2006). In addition to glancing at the other person's face, who you decide to sit next to in the subway car is going to be influenced by four key components:

1. the characteristics of the person you are trying to size up;
2. your own self-perception;
3. your goals in the situation; and
4. the specific situation in which the process occurs.

Each component plays a role in some basic principles that guide person perception (see Jones, 1990; Zebrowitz & Montepare, 2006). Let's illustrate those principles using the subway scenario.

Principle 1. Your reactions to others are determined by your perceptions of them, not by who or what they really are. Put simply, you treat others according to how you perceive them to be. So, as you step inside the subway car, you quickly choose not to sit next to the big, burly guy with a scowl on his face. Why? Because *you* perceive Mr. Burly-Surly as potentially threatening. This guy's picture is probably on the FBI's "Ten Most Wanted" list for being an axe murderer, you think. Of course, he could just as easily be a burly florist who's surly because he's getting home late. It doesn't matter. You move past him. Your behavior toward him is determined by your subjective perception of him as potentially threatening.

Principle 2. Your self-perception also influences how you perceive others and how you act on your perceptions. Your decision about where to sit is also influenced by how you perceive your self (Quinn & Macrae, 2005). For example, if you think of yourself as looking a bit intimidating (even though you're really a mild-mannered marketing major), you may choose to sit next to the 20-something text-messaging guy wearing a T-shirt rather than the anxious-looking middle-aged woman who's clutching her purse with both hands.

Principle 3. Your goals in a particular situation determine the amount and kinds of information you collect about others. Your goal in this situation is simple: You want to share a subway seat with someone who will basically leave you alone. Hence, you focus your attention on the characteristics of

person perception
The mental processes we use to form judgments and draw conclusions about the characteristics and motives of other people.

"Goodbye everybody."

other people that seem to be relevant to your goal, ignoring details that are unrelated to it (Hilton, 1998). After all, you're not looking for a date for Saturday night, a plumber, or a chemistry lab partner. If you were, you'd focus on very different aspects of the other people in the situation (Goodwin & others, 2002).

Principle 4. In every situation, you evaluate people partly in terms of how you expect them to act in that situation. Whether you're in a classroom, restaurant, or public restroom, your behavior is governed by **social norms**—the "rules," or expectations, for appropriate behavior in that social situation. Riding a subway is no exception to this principle (Milgram, 1992). For example, you don't sit next to someone else when empty seats are available, you don't try to borrow your seatmate's newspaper, and you avoid eye contact with others.

These "subway rules" aren't posted anywhere, of course. Nevertheless, violating these social norms will draw attention from others and probably make them uneasy. So as you size up your fellow subway passengers, you're partly evaluating their behavior in terms of how people-riding-the-subway-at-night-in-a-big-city should behave.

What these four guiding principles demonstrate is that person perception is not a one-way process in which we objectively survey other people and then logically evaluate their characteristics. Instead, the perceptions we have of others, our self-perceptions and goals, and the specific context all interact. Each component plays a role in the split-second judgments we form of complete strangers.

In the subway example, like other transient situations, it's unlikely that you'll ever be able to verify the accuracy of those first impressions. But in situations that involve long-term relationships with other people, such as in a classroom or at work, we fine-tune our impressions as we acquire additional information about the people we come to know (Smith & Collins, 2009).

Social Categorization

Using Mental Shortcuts in Person Perception

Along with person perception, the subway scenario illustrates our natural tendency to group people into categories. **Social categorization** is the mental process of classifying people into groups on the basis of common characteristics. In many social situations, you're consciously aware of the mental processes you go through in forming impressions of and categorizing other people. Social psychologists use the term **explicit cognition** to refer to deliberate, conscious mental processes involved in perceptions, judgments, decisions, and reasoning.

So how do you socially categorize people who are complete strangers, such as the other passengers in the subway car? To a certain extent, you consciously focus on easily observable features, such as the other person's gender, age, race, clothing, and other physical features (Fiske, 1993; Fiske & Neuberg, 1990; Miron & Branscomben, 2008). So you glance at a person, then socially categorize him as "Asian male, 20-something, backpack next to him on the seat, iPod, reading book, probably a college student."

However, your social perceptions and evaluations are not always completely conscious and deliberate considerations. In many situations, you react to another person with spontaneous and automatic social perceptions, categorizations, and attitudes. At least initially, these automatic evaluations tend to occur *implicitly* or outside of your conscious awareness. Social psychologists use the term **implicit cognition** to describe the mental processes associated with automatic, nonconscious social evaluations (see Krueger & others, 2008; McConnell & others, 2008).

What triggers such automatic, implicit evaluations of other people? People often evaluate others without thinking based on the social category they automatically associate with the other person (see Castelli & others, 2004; McConnell & others, 2008).

social norms
The "rules," or expectations, for appropriate behavior in a particular social situation.

social categorization
The mental process of categorizing people into groups (or *social categories*) on the basis of their shared characteristics.

explicit cognition
Deliberate, conscious mental processes involved in perceptions, judgments, decisions, and reasoning.

implicit cognition
Automatic, nonconscious mental processes that influence perceptions, judgments, decisions, and reasoning.

To illustrate, glance at the margin photo of people crossing a street. Each person in the photo is a unique individual with a unique background and life experiences.

Nevertheless, you probably made several rapid judgments about the people in the photograph. That's because prior experiences and beliefs about different social categories can trigger implicit social reactions ranging from very positive to very negative (Nosek & others, 2007). Without consciously realizing it, your reaction to another person can be swayed by the other person's age, gender, ethnicity, skin tone, physical attractiveness, weight, and clothing. Less obvious social categories that can trigger implicit reactions include sexual orientation as well as political or religious beliefs.

In everyday life, people often assume that certain types of people share certain traits and behaviors. This is referred to as an **implicit personality theory.** Different models exist to explain how implicit personality theories develop and function (e.g., Fiske & others, 2002; Ybarra, 2002). But in general terms, your previous social and cultural experiences influence the cognitive *schemas,* or mental frameworks, you hold about the traits and behaviors associated with different "types" of people. So when you perceive someone to be a particular "type," you assume that the person will display those traits and behaviors (see Uleman & others, 2008).

For example, your choice of a seatmate on the subway might well reflect some of your own implicit personality theories. You might feel comfortable sitting next to the silver-haired man who's reading the *Wall Street Journal,* wearing an expensive suit, and carrying what looks like a leather laptop case. Why? Because these superficial characteristics lead you to assume that he's a particular type of person—a conservative businessman. And on the basis of your implicit personality theory for a "conservative businessman," you conclude that he's probably a "law-abiding citizen" who is not likely to try to pick your pocket or whip out a gun and rob you.

Physical appearance cues play an important role in person perception and social categorization. Particularly influential is the implicit personality theory that most people have for physically attractive people (see Anderson & others, 2008; Langlois & others, 2000). Starting in childhood, we are bombarded with the cultural message that "what is beautiful is good." In myths, fairy tales, cartoons, movies, and games, heroes are handsome, heroines are beautiful, and the evil villains are ugly. As a result of such cultural conditioning, most people have an implicit personality theory that associates physical attractiveness with a wide range of desirable characteristics.

Using Social Categories We often use superficial cues such as clothing and context to assign people to social categories and draw conclusions about their behavior. For example, you might characterize some people in this crowd as belonging to the category of "businessmen" because they are wearing dress shirts and ties—and conclude that they are on their way to work. What other sorts of social categories are evident here?

A Charitable Guy? As a highly successful Wall Street financial adviser, Bernie Madoff managed money for individuals, financial institutions, and numerous charitable foundations, including director Steven Spielberg's Wunderkinder Foundation. A well-known philanthropist, he also gave substantial amounts of his own money to charities. But Bernie Madoff was actually a crook, swindling his clients out of billions of dollars over a period of more than 20 years. In what ways could implicit personality theories help explain how Madoff got away with his crimes for so long?

implicit personality theory
A network of assumptions or beliefs about the relationships among various types of people, traits, and behaviors.

What Is Beautiful Is Good We are culturally conditioned to associate beauty with goodness and evil with ugliness—an implicit personality theory that has been dubbed the "what is beautiful is good" myth. One example of this cultural conditioning is the classic Disney film *Snow White.* In the scene shown, the wicked stepmother is disguised as an old woman, complete with a wart on her nose. She offers the poisoned apple to the innocent and virtuous heroine, Snow White. (The Walt Disney Co.)

For example, good-looking people are perceived as being more intelligent, happier, and better adjusted than other people (Eagly & others, 1991). Are they?

After analyzing dozens of studies, psychologist Alan Feingold (1992) found very *few* personality differences between beautiful people and their plainer counterparts. Physical attractiveness is *not* correlated with intelligence, mental health, or even self-esteem. Overall, attractive people tend to be less lonely, more popular, and less anxious in social situations—all characteristics related to the advantage that their physical attractiveness seems to confer on them in social situations. But as you'll read in the Focus on Neuroscience, there also seems to be a brain-based explanation for the greater social success enjoyed by physically attractive people.

So what general conclusion can we make about the process of person perception? Both deliberate and automatic thought processes influence our impressions, especially our first impressions. To quickly evaluate others, we often rely on easily

FOCUS ON NEUROSCIENCE

Brain Reward When Making Eye Contact with Attractive People

How does physical attractiveness contribute to social success? A study by neuroscientist Knut Kampe and his colleagues (2001) at University College London may offer some insights. In their functional magnetic resonance imaging (fMRI) study, participants were scanned while they looked at color photographs of 40 different faces, some looking directly at the viewer (eye-contact) and some glancing away (non–eye-contact). After the fMRI scanning session, participants rated the attractiveness of the faces they had seen.

The results showed that when we make direct eye contact with a physically attractive person, an area on each side of the brain called the *ventral striatum* is activated (yellow areas in fMRI scan). When the attractive person's eye gaze is shifted away from the viewer, activity in the ventral striatum decreases. What makes this so interesting is that the ventral striatum is a brain area that predicts reward (Bray & O'Doherty, 2007; Schultz & others, 1997). Neural activity in the ventral striatum increases when an unexpected reward, such as food or water, suddenly appears. Conversely, activity in the ventral striatum decreases when an expected reward fails to appear.

As Kampe (2001) explains, "What we've shown is that when we make eye contact with an attractive person, the brain area that predicts reward starts firing. If we see an attractive person but cannot make eye contact with that person, the activity in this region goes down, signaling disappointment. This is the first study to show that the brain's ventral striatum processes rewards in the context of human social interaction."

Other neuroscientists have expanded on Kampe's findings and identified additional brain reward areas that are responsive to facial attractiveness. Of particular note is an area called the *orbital frontal cortex,* which is a region of the *frontal cortex* located just above the orbits (or sockets) of your eyes (Ishai, 2007; O'Doherty & others, 2003). Another region is the *amygdala.* Both the orbital frontal cortex and the amygdala are selectively responsive to the reward value of attractive faces (Winston & others, 2007).

Eye-Contact Face

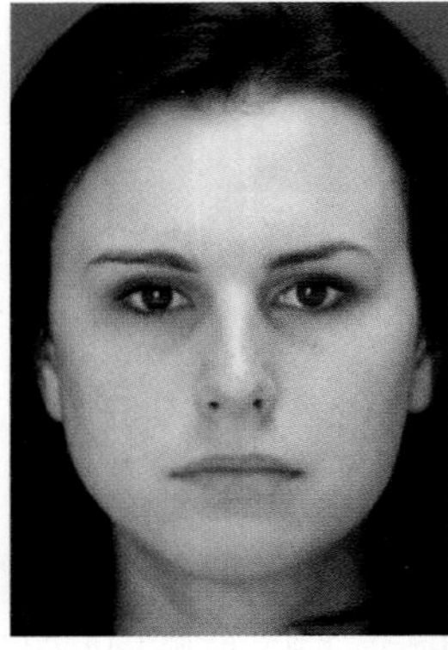

Non–Eye-Contact Face

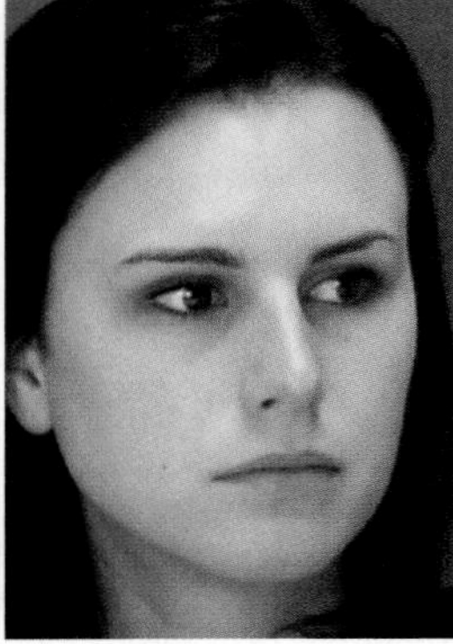

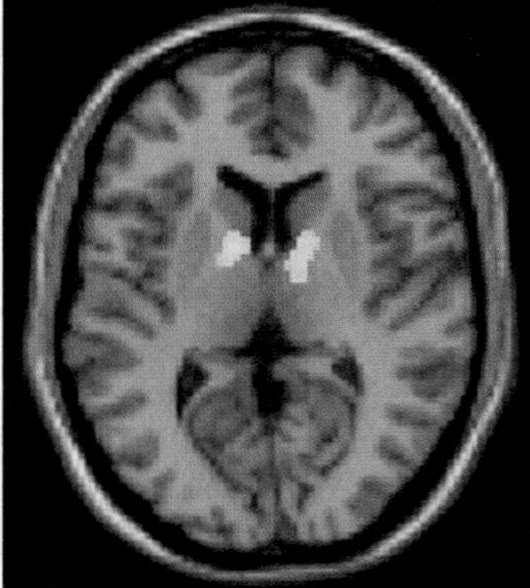

"Facial beauty evokes a widely distributed neural network involving perceptual, decision-making, and reward circuits. [It] may serve as a neural trigger for the pervasive effects of attractiveness in social interactions," writes neuroscientist Anjan Chatterjee and his colleagues (2009). Clearly, then, the social advantages associated with facial attractiveness are reinforced by reward processing in the brain.

observable features, including cues we discern from the other person's face, gender, age, and race. We also use mental shortcuts, such as social categories and implicit personality theories. Whether we react positively or negatively to the particular social category or implicit personality we associate with another person is influenced by our previous social and cultural experiences.

Obviously, there are advantages and disadvantages to this process. On the one hand, relegating someone to a social category on the basis of superficial information ignores that person's unique qualities. In effect, you're jumping to sweeping conclusions about another person on the basis of very limited information. Sometimes these conclusions are wrong, as Fern's was when she categorized the scruffy-looking San Francisco man with a cup in his hand as homeless.

On the other hand, relying on social categories is a natural, adaptive, and efficient cognitive process. Social categories provide us with considerable basic information about other people. Knowing that basic information helps us organize and remember information about others more effectively. And from an evolutionary perspective, the ability to make rapid judgments about strangers is probably an evolved characteristic that conferred survival value in our evolutionary past.

Attribution

Explaining Behavior

Key Theme

- **Attribution refers to the process of explaining your own behavior and the behavior of other people.**

Key Questions

- **What are the fundamental attribution error and the self-serving bias?**
- **How do attributional biases affect our judgments about the causes of behavior?**
- **How does culture affect attributional processes?**

As you're studying in the college library, the activities of two workers catch your attention. The two men are getting ready to lift and move a large file cabinet. "Okay, let's tip it this way and lift it," the first guy says with considerable authority. The second guy sheepishly nods agreement. In unison, they heave and tip the file cabinet. When they do, the top two file drawers fly out, smashing into the first guy's head. As the file cabinet goes crashing to the floor, you bite your lip to keep from laughing and think to yourself, "What a pair of 40-watt bulbs."

Why did you arrive at that conclusion? After all, it's completely possible that the workers are not dimwits. Maybe the lock on the file drawers slipped or broke when they tipped the cabinet. Or maybe someone failed to empty the drawers.

Attribution is the process of inferring the cause of someone's behavior, including your own. Psychologists also use the word *attribution* to refer to the explanation you make for a particular behavior. The attributions you make strongly influence your thoughts and feelings about other people.

If your explanation for the file cabinet incident was that the workers were a couple of clumsy doofuses, you demonstrated a common cognitive bias. The **fundamental attribution error** is the tendency to spontaneously attribute the behavior of others to internal, personal characteristics, while ignoring or underestimating the role of external, situational factors (Ross, 1977). Even though it's entirely possible that situational forces were behind another person's behavior, we tend to automatically assume that the cause is an internal, personal characteristic (Van Boven & others, 1999; Zimbardo, 2007).

attribution
The mental process of inferring the causes of people's behavior, including one's own. Also refers to the explanation made for a particular behavior.

fundamental attribution error
The tendency to attribute the behavior of others to internal, personal characteristics, while ignoring or underestimating the effects of external, situational factors; an attributional bias that is common in individualistic cultures.

blaming the victim
The tendency to blame an innocent victim of misfortune for having somehow caused the problem or for not having taken steps to avoid or prevent it.

hindsight bias
The tendency to overestimate one's ability to have foreseen or predicted the outcome of an event.

just-world hypothesis
The assumption that the world is fair and that therefore people get what they deserve and deserve what they get.

self-serving bias
The tendency to attribute successful outcomes of one's own behavior to internal causes and unsuccessful outcomes to external, situational causes.

Notice, however, that when it comes to explaining our *own* behavior, we tend to be biased in the opposite direction. Rather than internal, personal attributions, we're more likely to explain our own behavior using *external, situational* attributions. He dropped the file cabinet because he's a dimwit; you dropped the file cabinet because there wasn't a good way to get a solid grip on it. Some jerk pulled out in front of your car because she's a reckless, inconsiderate moron; you pulled out in front of her car because an overgrown hedge blocked your view. And so on.

Why the discrepancy in accounting for the behavior of others as compared to our own behavior? Part of the explanation is that we simply have more information about the potential causes of our own behavior than we do about the causes of other people's behavior. When you observe another driver turn directly into the path of your car, that's typically the only information you have on which to judge his or her behavior. But when *you* inadvertently pull in front of another car, you perceive your own behavior in the context of the various situational factors that influenced your action. You're aware of such factors as visual obstacles, road conditions, driving distractions, and so forth. You also know what motivated your behavior and how differently you have behaved in similar situations in the past. Thus, you're much more aware of the extent to which *your* behavior has been influenced by situational factors (Fiske & Taylor, 1991; Jones, 1990).

The fundamental attribution error plays a role in a common explanatory pattern called **blaming the victim.** The innocent victim of a crime, disaster, or serious illness is blamed for having somehow caused the misfortune or for not having taken steps to prevent it. For example, many people blame the poor for their dire straits, the sick for bringing on their illnesses, and battered women and rape survivors for somehow "provoking" their attackers.

The blame the victim explanatory pattern is reinforced by another common cognitive bias. **Hindsight bias** is the tendency, after an event has occurred, to overestimate one's ability to have foreseen or predicted the outcome. In everyday conversations, this is the person who confidently proclaims *after* the event, "I could have told you that would happen" or "I can't believe they couldn't see that coming." In the case of blaming the victim, hindsight bias makes it seem as if the victim should have been able to predict—and prevent—what happened (Goldinger & others, 2003).

Why do people often resort to blaming the victim? People have a strong need to believe that the world is fair—that "we get what we deserve and deserve what we get." Social psychologist Melvin Lerner (1980) calls this the **just-world hypothesis.** Blaming the victim reflects the belief that, because the world is just, the victim must have done something to deserve his or her fate. Collectively, these cognitive biases and explanatory patterns help psychologically insulate us from the uncomfortable thought "It could have just as easily been me" (Alves & Correia, 2008; Ijzerman & Van Prooijen, 2008).

Blaming the Victim Fifteen-year-old Shawn Hornbeck is shown at a press conference, shortly after being reunited with his family. Four years earlier, Shawn had been kidnapped and held captive. When the FBI suspected Shawn's kidnapper in the abduction of another boy, both boys were rescued. As details of Shawn's captivity became public, many people asked why Shawn hadn't tried to escape or call the police while his kidnapper was at work. As it turned out, the kidnapper had abused and terrorized Shawn for months. At one point, he tried to strangle Shawn. When Shawn pleaded for his life, the kidnapper made the boy promise that he would never try to escape. "There wasn't a day when I didn't think that he'd just kill me," Shawn later recalled. Why do people often "blame the victim" after crimes, accidents, or other tragedies?

The Self-Serving Bias

Using Explanations That Meet Our Needs

If you've ever listened to other students react to their grades on an important exam, you've seen the **self-serving bias** in action. When students do well on a test, they tend to congratulate themselves and to attribute their success to how hard they studied, their intelligence, and so forth—all *internal* attributions. But when a student bombs a test, the *external* attributions fly left and right: "They were all trick questions!" "I couldn't concentrate because the guy behind me kept coughing" (Kruger & Gilovich, 2004).

Explaining Misfortune: The Self-Serving Bias Given the self-serving bias, is this bicyclist likely to explain his accident by listing internal factors such as his own carelessness or recklessness? Or is he more likely to blame external factors, such as swerving to miss a spectator or catching his tire in a rut? Just so you know, the fallen rider wearing orange is American Lance Armstrong, who crashed after his handlebars snagged on a plastic bag held by a spectator. Armstrong went on to win the Tour de France.

In a wide range of situations, people tend to credit themselves for their success and to blame their failures on external circumstances (Krusemark & others, 2008; Schlenker & Weigold, 1992). Psychologists explain the self-serving bias as resulting from an attempt to save face and protect self-esteem in the face of failure (Dunning & others, 1995).

Although common in many societies, the self-serving bias is far from universal, as cross-cultural psychologists have discovered (see the Culture and Human Behavior box). The various attributional biases are summarized in Table 11.1 on the next page.

CULTURE AND HUMAN BEHAVIOR

Explaining Failure and Murder: Culture and Attributional Biases

Although the self-serving bias is common in individualistic cultures such as Australia and the United States, it is far from universal. In collectivistic cultures, such as Asian cultures, an opposite attributional bias is often demonstrated (Bond, 1994; Mezulis & others, 2004; Moghaddam & others, 1993). Called the *self-effacing bias* or *modesty bias,* it involves blaming failure on internal, personal factors, while attributing success to external, situational factors.

For example, compared to American students, Japanese and Chinese students are more likely to attribute academic failure to personal factors, such as lack of effort, instead of situational factors (Dornbusch & others, 1996). Thus, a Japanese student who does poorly on an exam is likely to say, "I didn't study hard enough." When Japanese or Chinese students perform poorly in school, they are expected to study harder and longer (Stevenson & Stigler, 1992). In contrast, Japanese and Chinese students tend to attribute academic *success* to *situational* factors. For example, they might say, "The exam was very easy" or "There was very little competition this year" (Stevenson & others, 1986).

Psychologists Hazel Markus and Shinobu Kitayama (1991) believe that the self-effacing bias reflects the emphasis that interdependent cultures place on fitting in with other members of the group. As the Japanese proverb goes, "The nail that sticks up gets pounded down." In collectivistic cultures, self-esteem does not rest on doing better than others in the group. Rather, standing out from the group is likely to produce psychological discomfort and tension.

Cross-cultural differences are also evident with the fundamental attribution error. In general, members of collectivistic cultures are less likely to commit the fundamental attribution error than are members of individualistic cultures (Bond & Smith, 1996; Choi & others, 1999). That is, collectivists are more likely to attribute the causes of another person's behavior to external, situational factors rather than to internal, personal factors—the exact *opposite* of the attributional bias that is demonstrated in individualistic cultures.

To test this idea in a naturally occurring context, psychologists Michael Morris and Kaiping Peng (1994) compared articles reporting the same mass murders in Chinese-language and English-language newspapers. In one case, the murderer was a Chinese graduate student attending a U.S. university. In the other case, the murderer was a U.S. postal worker. Regardless of whether the murderer was American or Chinese, the news accounts were fundamentally different depending on whether the *reporter* was American or Chinese.

The American reporters were more likely to explain the killings by making personal, internal attributions. For example, American reporters emphasized the murderers' personality traits, such as the graduate student's "bad temper" and the postal worker's "history of being mentally unstable."

In contrast, the Chinese reporters emphasized situational factors, such as the fact that the postal worker had recently been fired from his job and the fact that the graduate student had failed to receive an academic award. The Chinese reporters also cited social pressures and problems in U.S. society to account for the actions of the killers.

Clearly, then, how we account for our successes and failures, as well as how we account for the actions of others, is yet another example of how human behavior is influenced by cultural conditioning.

Haughtiness invites ruin; humility receives benefits.

—CHINESE PROVERB

Table 11.1

Common Attributional Biases and Explanatory Patterns

Bias	Description
Fundamental attribution error	We tend to explain the behavior of other people by attributing their behavior to internal, personal characteristics, while underestimating or ignoring the effects of external, situational factors. Pattern is reversed when accounting for our own behavior.
Blaming the victim	We tend to blame the victims of misfortune for causing their own misfortune or for not taking steps to prevent or avoid it. Partly due to the *just-world hypothesis.*
Hindsight bias	After an event has occurred, we tend to overestimate the extent to which we could have foreseen or predicted the outcome.
Self-serving bias	We have a tendency to take credit for our successes by attributing them to internal, personal causes, along with a tendency to distance ourselves from our failures by attributing them to external, situational causes. Self-serving bias is more common in individualistic cultures.
Self-effacing (or modesty) bias	We tend to blame ourselves for our failures, attributing them to internal, personal causes, while downplaying our successes by attributing them to external, situational causes. Self-effacing bias is more common in collectivistic cultures.

The Social Psychology of Attitudes

Key Theme

- **An attitude is a learned tendency to evaluate objects, people, or issues in a particular way.**

Key Questions

- **What are the three components of an attitude?**
- **Under what conditions are attitudes most likely to determine behavior?**
- **What is cognitive dissonance?**

Should high school graduation requirements include a class on basic sex education, birth control methods, and safe sex? Should there be a compulsory military or community service requirement for all young adults? Should there be national health care coverage for all U.S. citizens? Should affordable, high-quality day care centers be a national priority? Should affordable, high-quality elder care centers be a national priority?

On these and many other subjects, you've probably formed an attitude. Psychologists formally define an **attitude** as a learned tendency to evaluate some object, person, or issue in a particular way (Krosnick & others, 2005; Olson & Zanna, 1993; Zimbardo & Leippe, 1991). Attitudes are typically positive or negative, but they can also be *ambivalent,* as when you have mixed feelings about an issue or person (Ajzen, 2001).

As shown in Figure 11.1, attitudes can include three components. First, an attitude may have a *cognitive component:* your thoughts and conclusions about a given topic or object. For example, one of our colleagues, Aaron, is a staunch environmentalist. On more than one occasion, Aaron has said, "In my opinion, cars and trucks need to be much more fuel-efficient so that we can reduce or eliminate air pollution in our cities." Second, an attitude may have an emotional or *affective component,* as when Aaron starts ranting about drivers he sees on the highway: "It makes me furious to see people driving those huge SUVs to work, especially when they don't even have passengers!" Finally, an attitude may have a *behavioral component,* in which attitudes are

attitude
A learned tendency to evaluate some object, person, or issue in a particular way; such evaluations may be positive, negative, or ambivalent.

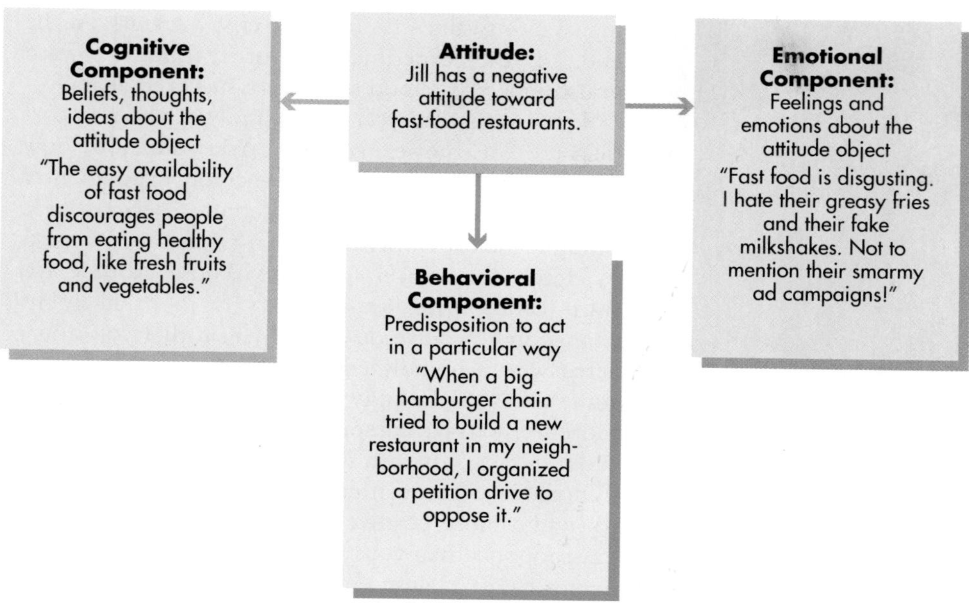

Figure 11.1 The Components of Attitudes An attitude is a positive or negative evaluation of an object, person, or idea. An attitude may have cognitive, emotional, and behavioral components.

reflected in action. In Aaron's case, he bought a hybrid gasoline/electric car that gets 60 miles to the gallon, even in the city. Even so, he frequently rides his bicycle to campus rather than drive.

The Effect of Attitudes on Behavior

Intuitively, you probably assume that your attitudes tend to guide your behavior. But social psychologists have consistently found that people don't always act in accordance with their attitudes. For example, you might disapprove of cheating, yet find yourself peeking at a classmate's exam paper when the opportunity presents itself. Or you might strongly favor a certain political candidate, yet not vote on election day.

When are your attitudes likely to influence or determine your behavior? Social psychologists have found that you're most likely to behave in accordance with your attitudes when:

- You anticipate a favorable outcome or response from others for behaving that way.
- Your attitudes are extreme or are frequently expressed (Ajzen, 2001).
- Your attitudes have been formed through direct experience (Fazio, 1990).
- You are very knowledgeable about the subject (Wood & others, 1995).
- You have a vested interest in the subject and personally stand to gain or lose something on a specific issue (Lehman & Crano, 2002).

Clearly, your attitudes do influence your behavior in many instances. When you feel strongly about an issue, have a personal stake in the issue, and anticipate a positive outcome in a particular situation, your attitudes will influence your behavior. Now, consider the opposite question: Can your behavior influence your attitudes?

Attitudes and Behavior These Greenpeace activists have set up a symbolic wind turbine in front of the Castle Peak coal power station in Hong Kong. They are demonstrating their commitment to renewable energy and their opposition to coal plants in Asia that contribute to global warming. People who hold strong opinions and express them frequently, like these Greenpeace activists, are most likely to behave in accordance with their attitudes.

The Effect of Behavior on Attitudes

Fried Grasshoppers for Lunch?!

Suppose you have volunteered to participate in a psychology experiment. At the lab, a friendly experimenter asks you to indicate your degree of preference for a variety of foods, including fried grasshoppers, which you rank pretty low on the list. During the experiment, the experimenter instructs you to eat some fried grasshoppers. You

Fried Grasshoppers: Tasty or Disgusting? Most Americans do not rate fried grasshoppers as one of their favorite foods. Suppose you agreed to eat a handful of grasshoppers after being asked to do so by a rude, unfriendly experimenter. Do you think your attitude toward fried grasshoppers would improve more than a person who ate grasshoppers after being asked to do so by a friendly, polite experimenter? Why or why not?

manage to swallow three of the crispy critters. At the end of the experiment, your attitudes toward grasshoppers as a food source are surveyed again.

Later in the day, you talk to a friend who also participated in the experiment. You mention how friendly and polite you thought the experimenter was. But your friend had a different experience. He thought the experimenter was an arrogant, rude jerk.

Here's the critical question: Whose attitude toward eating fried grasshoppers is more likely to change in a positive direction? Given that you interacted with a friendly experimenter, most people assume that *your* feelings about fried grasshoppers are more likely to have improved than your friend's attitude. In fact, it is your friend—who encountered the obnoxious experimenter—who is much more likely to hold a more positive attitude toward eating fried grasshoppers than you.

At first glance, this finding seems to go against the grain of common sense. So how can we explain this outcome? The fried grasshoppers story represents the basic design of a classic experiment by social psychologist **Philip Zimbardo** and his colleagues (1965). Zimbardo's experiment and other similar ones underscore the power of cognitive dissonance. **Cognitive dissonance** is an unpleasant state of psychological tension (*dissonance*) that occurs when there's an inconsistency between two thoughts or perceptions (*cognitions*). This state of dissonance is so unpleasant that we are strongly motivated to reduce it (Festinger, 1957, 1962).

Cognitive dissonance commonly occurs in situations in which you become uncomfortably aware that your behavior and your attitudes are in conflict. In these situations, you are simultaneously holding two conflicting cognitions: your original attitude versus the realization your behavior contradicts that attitude. If you can easily rationalize your behavior to make it consistent with your attitude, then any dissonance you might experience can be quickly and easily resolved. But when your behavior *cannot* be easily justified, how can you resolve the contradiction and eliminate the unpleasant state of dissonance? Since you can't go back and change the behavior, *you change your attitude to make it consistent with your behavior.*

Let's take another look at the results of the grasshopper study, this time from the perspective of cognitive dissonance theory. Your attitude toward eating grasshoppers did *not* change, because you could easily rationalize the conflict between your attitude ("Eating grasshoppers is disgusting") and your behavior (eating three grasshoppers). You probably justified your behavior by saying something like, "I ate the grasshoppers because the experimenter was such a nice guy and I wanted to help him out."

However, your friend, who encountered the rude experimenter, can't use that rationalization to explain the contradiction between disliking grasshoppers and voluntarily eating them. Thus, he experiences an uncomfortable state of cognitive dissonance. Since he can't go back and change his behavior, he is left with the only part of the equation that can be changed—his attitude (see Figure 11.2). "You know, eating those grasshoppers wasn't *that* bad," your friend comments. "In fact, they were kind of crunchy." Notice how his change in attitude reduces the dissonance between his previous attitude and his behavior.

Attitude change due to cognitive dissonance is quite common in everyday life. For example, consider the person who impulsively buys a new leather coat that she really can't afford. "It was too good a bargain to pass up," she rationalizes.

Social Psychologist Phil Zimbardo (b. 1933) Zimbardo grew up in an immigrant family in a poor neighborhood in the South Bronx, an experience that sensitized him to the power of situational influences and the destructive nature of stereotypes and prejudice (Zimbardo, 2005, 2007). Much of Zimbardo's research has investigated "the subtle but pervasive power of situations to influence human behavior." Zimbardo's research has ranged from attitude change to shyness, prison reform, and the psychology of evil. As Zimbardo (2000b) observes, "The joy of being a psychologist is that almost everything in life is psychology, or should be, or could be. One can't live mindfully without being enmeshed in the psychological processes that are around us." Later in the chapter, we'll encounter the controversial experiment for which Zimbardo is most famous—the Stanford Prison Experiment.

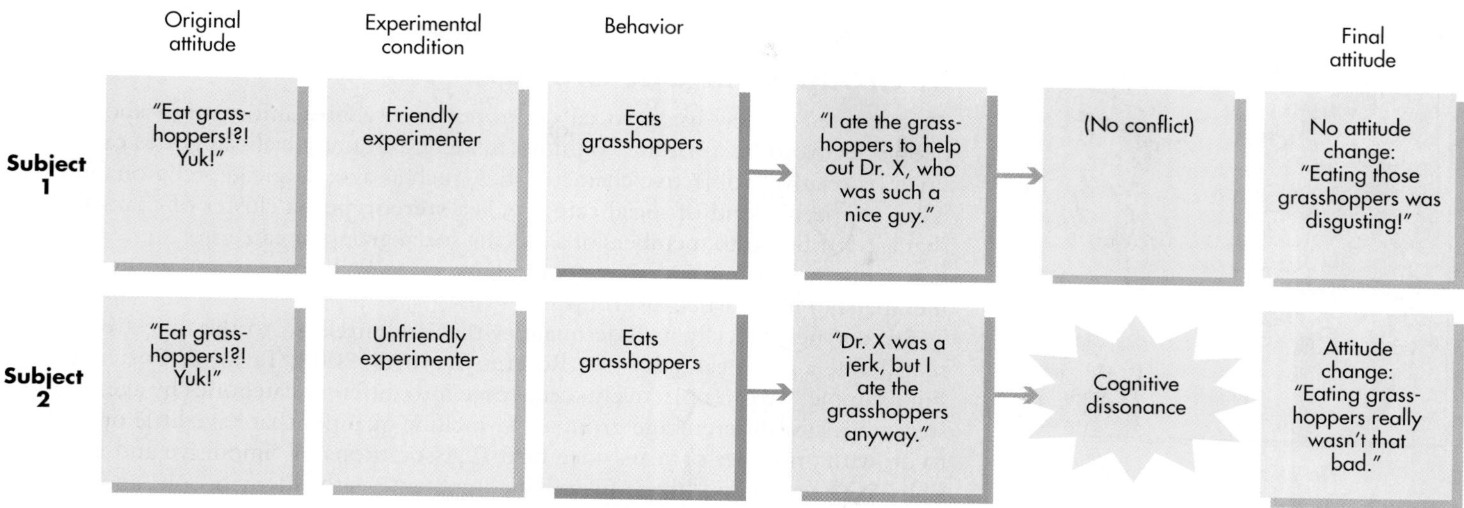

Figure 11.2 How Cognitive Dissonance Leads to Attitude Change When your behavior conflicts with your attitudes, an uncomfortable state of tension is produced. However, if you can rationalize or explain your behavior, the conflict (and the tension) is eliminated or avoided. If you *can't* explain your behavior, you may change your attitude so that it is in harmony with your behavior.

Cognitive dissonance can also change the strength of an attitude to make it consistent with some behavior that has already been performed. For example, people tend to be much more favorably inclined toward a given political candidate *after* they have voted for him or her than just before (Beasley & Joslyn, 2001).

A similar example of cognitive dissonance in action involves choosing between two basically equal alternatives, especially if the decision is important and difficult to undo (Festinger, 1962). Suppose you had to choose between two colleges, two houses, or two cars. Each choice has desirable and undesirable features, creating dissonance. But once you actually make the choice, you immediately bring your attitudes more closely into line with your commitment, reducing cognitive dissonance. In other words, *after* you make the choice, you emphasize the negative features of the choice you've rejected, which is commonly called a "sour grapes" rationalization. You also emphasize the positive features of the choice to which you have committed yourself—a "sweet lemons" rationalization.

Understanding Prejudice

Key Theme

- **Prejudice refers to a negative attitude toward people who belong to a specific social group, while stereotypes are clusters of characteristics that are attributed to people who belong to specific social categories.**

Key Questions

- **What is the function of stereotypes, and how do they relate to prejudice?**
- **What are in-groups and out-groups, and how do they influence social judgments?**
- **What is ethnocentrism?**

In this section, you'll see how person perception, attribution, and attitudes come together in explaining **prejudice**—a negative attitude toward people who belong to a specific social group.

Prejudice is ultimately based on the exaggerated notion that members of other social groups are very different from members of our own social group. So as you read this discussion, it's important for you to keep two well-established points in mind. First, *racial and ethnic groups are far more alike than they are different* (Jones, 1991; Mallett & others, 2008). And second, any differences that may exist *between* members of different racial and ethnic groups are far smaller than differences *among* various members of the same group.

cognitive dissonance
An unpleasant state of psychological tension or arousal (dissonance) that occurs when two thoughts or perceptions (cognitions) are inconsistent; typically results from the awareness that attitudes and behavior are in conflict.

prejudice
A negative attitude toward people who belong to a specific social group.

"The first six are for bullets. This one's for lip balm."

From Stereotypes to Prejudice: In-Groups and Out-Groups

As we noted earlier, using social categories to organize information about other people seems to be a natural cognitive tendency. Many social categories can be defined by relatively objective characteristics, such as age, language, religion, and skin color. A specific kind of social category is a **stereotype**—a cluster of characteristics that are attributed to members of a specific social group or category. Stereotypes are based on the assumption that people have certain characteristics *because* of their membership in a particular group.

Stereotypes typically include qualities that are unrelated to the objective criteria that define a given category (see Rosette & others, 2008; Taylor & Porter, 1994). For example, we can objectively sort people into different categories by age. But our stereotypes for different age groups may include qualities that have little or nothing to do with "number of years since birth." Associations of "impulsive and irresponsible" with teenagers, "forgetful and incompetent" with elderly people, and "boring and conservative" with middle-aged adults are examples of associating unrelated qualities with age groups—that is, stereotyping.

Like our use of other social categories, our tendency to stereotype social groups seems to be a natural cognitive process. Stereotypes simplify social information so that we can sort out, process, and remember information about other people more easily (Macrae & others, 1994). But like other mental shortcuts we've discussed in this chapter, relying on stereotypes can cause problems. Attributing a stereotypic cause for an outcome or event can blind us to the true causes of events (Sanbonmatsu & others, 1994). For example, a parent who assumes that a girl's poor computer skills are due to her gender rather than a lack of instruction might never encourage her to overcome her problem.

Research by psychologist Claude Steele (1997, 2003) has demonstrated another detrimental effect of stereotypes, particularly derogatory stereotypes, which he calls *stereotype threat*. As we discussed in Chapter 7, simply being aware that your social group is associated with a particular stereotype can negatively impact your performance on tests or tasks that measure abilities that are thought to be associated with that stereotype. For example, even mathematically gifted women scored lower on a difficult math test when told that the test tended to produce gender differences than when told that the test did not produce gender differences (Smith & others, 2007; Spencer & others, 1999; also see Cadinu & others, 2005).

Once they are formed, stereotypes are hard to shake. One reason for this is that stereotypes are not always completely false. Sometimes they have a kernel of truth, making them easy to confirm, especially when you see only what you expect to see. Even so, there's a vast difference between a kernel and the cornfield. When stereotypic beliefs become expectations that are applied to *all* members of a given group, stereotypes can be both misleading and damaging (Stangor & Lange, 1994).

Consider the stereotype that men are more assertive than women and that women are more nurturant than men. This stereotype does have evidence to support it, but only in terms of the *average* difference between men and women (see Eagly, 1995b; Hyde, 2005). Thus, it would be inappropriate to automatically apply this stereotype to *every* individual man and woman. Doing so would be an example of prejudice.

Equally important, when confronted by evidence that contradicts a stereotype, people tend to discount that information in a variety of ways (Seta & others, 2003; Seta & Seta, 1993; Weisz & Jones, 1993). For example, suppose you are firmly convinced that all "Zeegs" are dishonest, sly, and untrustworthy. One day you absentmindedly leave your wallet on a store's checkout counter. As you walk into the parking lot, you hear a voice calling, "Hey, you forgot your wallet!" It's a Zeeg running after you and waving your wallet in the air. "I was behind you in line and thought you might need this," the Zeeg smiles, handing you your wallet.

Will this experience change your stereotype of Zeegs as dishonest, sly, and untrustworthy? Probably not. It's more likely that you'll conclude that this individual

Overcoming and Combating Prejudice The self-described "son of a black man from Kenya and a white woman from Kansas," Barack Obama seemed an unlikely presidential candidate. Obama's ability to build a political coalition among people of different racial, ethnic, economic, and age groups led to his winning the White House. In a speech on racial politics in the United States, Obama declared, "I believe deeply that we cannot solve the challenges of our time unless we solve them together—unless we perfect our union by understanding that we may have different stories, but we hold common hopes; that we may not look the same and we may not have come from the same place, but we all want to move in the same direction—towards a better future for our children and our grandchildren."

Zeeg is an *exception* to the stereotype. If you run into more than one honest Zeeg, you may create a mental subgroup for individuals who belong to the larger group but depart from the stereotype in some way (Stangor & Lange, 1994). By creating a subcategory of "honest, hardworking Zeegs," you can still maintain your more general stereotype of Zeegs as dishonest, sly, and untrustworthy.

Creating exceptions allows people to maintain stereotypes in the face of contradictory evidence. Typical of this exception-that-proves-the-rule approach is the person who says, "Hey, I'm not prejudiced! In fact, I've got a couple of good friends who are Zeegs."

Stereotypes are closely related to another tendency in person perception. People have a strong tendency to perceive others in terms of two very basic social categories: "us" and "them." More precisely, the **in-group** ("us") refers to the group or groups to which we belong, and **out-groups** ("them") refer to groups of which we are not a member. In-groups and out-groups aren't necessarily limited to racial, ethnic, or religious boundaries. Virtually any characteristic can be used to make in-group and out-group distinctions: Mac versus PC users, Cubs versus White Sox fans, Northsiders versus Southsiders, math majors versus English majors, and so forth.

The Power of Stereotypes American movies have made the image of the cowboy almost universally recognizable. What kinds of qualities are associated with the stereotype of the cowboy? How might that stereotype be an inaccurate portrayal of a person working on a cattle ranch today?

The Out-Group Homogeneity Effect
They're All the Same to Me

Two important patterns characterize our views of in-groups versus out-groups. First, when we describe the members of our *in-group,* we typically see them as being quite varied, despite having enough features in common to belong to the same group. In other words, we notice the diversity within our own group.

Second, we tend to see members of the *out-group* as much more similar to one another, even in areas that have little to do with the criteria for group membership. This tendency is called the **out-group homogeneity effect.** (The word *homogeneity* means "similarity" or "uniformity.")

For example, what qualities do you associate with the category of "engineering major"? If you're *not* an engineering major, you're likely to see engineering majors as a rather similar crew: male, logical, analytical, conservative, and so forth. However, if you *are* an engineering major, you're much more likely to see your in-group as quite *heterogeneous,* or varied (Park & others, 1992). You might even come up with several subgroups, such as studious engineering majors, party-animal engineering majors, and electrical engineering majors versus chemical engineering majors.

In-Group Bias
We're Tactful—*They're* Sneaky

In-group bias is our tendency to make favorable, positive attributions for behaviors by members of our in-group and unfavorable, negative attributions for behaviors by members of out-groups. We succeeded because we worked hard; they succeeded because they lucked out. We failed because of circumstances beyond our control; they failed because they're stupid and incompetent. We're thrifty; they're stingy. And so on.

One form of in-group bias is called **ethnocentrism**—the belief that one's culture or ethnic group is superior to others. You're engaging in ethnocentrism when you use your culture or ethnic group as the yardstick by which you judge other cultures or ethnic groups. Not surprisingly, ethnocentric thinking contributes to the formation of negative stereotypes about other cultures whose customs differ from our own.

In combination, stereotypes and in-group/out-group bias form the *cognitive* basis for prejudicial attitudes (Hilton & von Hippel, 1996). But, as with many attitudes, prejudice also has a strong *emotional* component. In the case of prejudice, the emotions are intensely negative—hatred, contempt, fear, loathing. *Behaviorally,* prejudice

stereotype
A cluster of characteristics that are associated with all members of a specific social group, often including qualities that are unrelated to the objective criteria that define the group.

in-group
A social group to which one belongs.

out-group
A social group to which one does not belong.

out-group homogeneity effect
The tendency to see members of out-groups as very similar to one another.

in-group bias
The tendency to judge the behavior of in-group members favorably and out-group members unfavorably.

ethnocentrism
The belief that one's own culture or ethnic group is superior to all others and the related tendency to use one's own culture as a standard by which to judge other cultures.

can be displayed in some form of *discrimination*—behaviors ranging from privately sneering at to physically attacking members of an out-group (Duckitt, 2003).

How can we account for the extreme emotions that often characterize prejudice against out-group members? One theory holds that prejudice and intergroup hostility increase when different groups are competing for scarce resources, whether jobs, acreage, oil, water, or political power (see Pratto & Glasford, 2008). Prejudice and intergroup hostility are also likely to increase during times of social change (Brewer, 1994; Staub, 1996).

However, prejudice often exists in the absence of direct competition for resources, changing social conditions, or even contact with members of a particular out-group. What accounts for prejudice in such situations? Research by psychologist Victoria Esses and her colleagues (1993, 2005) has demonstrated that people are often prejudiced against groups that are perceived as threatening important in-group norms and values. For example, a person might be extremely prejudiced against gays and lesbians because he feels that they threaten his in-group's cherished values, such as a strong commitment to traditional sex roles and family structure.

Overcoming Prejudice

Key Theme

- **Prejudice can be overcome when rival groups cooperate to achieve a common goal.**

Key Questions

- **How has this finding been applied in the educational system?**
- **What other conditions are essential to reducing tension between groups?**
- **How can prejudice be overcome at the individual level?**

How can prejudice be combated at the group level? A classic series of studies headed by psychologist **Muzafer Sherif** helped clarify the conditions that produce intergroup conflict *and* harmony. Sherif and his colleagues (1961) studied a group of 11-year-old boys in an unlikely setting for a scientific experiment: a summer camp located at Robbers Cave State Park in Oklahoma.

The Robbers Cave Experiment

Pretending to be camp counselors and staff, the researchers observed the boys' behavior under carefully orchestrated conditions. The boys were randomly assigned to two groups. The groups arrived at camp in separate buses and were headquartered in different areas of the camp. One group of boys dubbed themselves the Eagles, the other the Rattlers. After a week of separation, the researchers arranged for the groups to meet in a series of competitive games. A fierce rivalry quickly developed, demonstrating the ease with which mutually hostile groups could be created.

Creating Conflict Between Groups Psychologist Muzafer Sherif and his colleagues demonstrated how easily hostility and distrust could be created between two groups. Competitive situations, like this tug-of-war, increased tension between the Rattlers and the Eagles.

The rivalry became increasingly bitter. The Eagles burned the Rattlers' flag. In response, the Rattlers trashed the Eagles' cabin. Somewhat alarmed, the researchers tried to diminish the hostility by bringing the two groups together under peaceful circumstances and on an equal basis—having them go to the movies together, eat in the same dining hall, and so forth. But contact alone did not mitigate the hostility. If anything, these situations only served as opportunities for the rival groups to berate and attack each other. For example, when the Rattlers and Eagles ate together in the same dining hall, a massive food fight erupted!

How could harmony between the groups be established? Sherif and his fellow researchers created a series of situations in which the two groups would need to *cooperate to achieve a common goal.* For example, the researchers secretly sabotaged the water supply. Working together, the Eagles and the Rattlers managed to fix it. On another occasion, the researchers sabotaged a truck that was to bring food to the campers. The hungry campers overcame their differences to join forces and restart the truck. After a series of such joint efforts, the rivalry diminished and the groups became good friends (Sherif, 1956; Sherif & others, 1961).

Sherif successfully demonstrated how hostility between groups could be created and, more important, how that hostility could be overcome. However, other researchers questioned whether these results would apply to other intergroup situations. After all, these boys were very homogeneous: white, middle class, Protestant, and carefully selected for being healthy and well-adjusted (Fiske & Ruscher, 1993; Sherif, 1966). In other words, there were no *intrinsic* differences between the Rattlers and the Eagles; there was only the artificial distinction created by the researchers.

The Jigsaw Classroom

Promoting Cooperation

Social psychologist Elliot Aronson (1990, 1992) tried adapting the results of the Robbers Cave experiments to a very different group situation—a newly integrated elementary school. Realizing that mere contact between black and white children was not dissipating tension and prejudice, Aronson reasoned that perhaps the competitive schoolroom atmosphere was partly at fault. Perhaps tension between racial groups might decrease if cooperation replaced competition.

Aronson and his colleagues tried a teaching technique that stressed cooperative, rather than competitive, learning situations (see Aronson, 1990; Aronson & Bridgeman, 1979). Dubbed the *jigsaw classroom technique,* this approach brought together students in small, ethnically diverse groups to work on a mutual project. Like the pieces of a jigsaw puzzle, each student had a unique contribution to make toward the success of the group. Each student became an expert on one aspect of the overall project and had to teach it to the other members of the group. Thus, interdependence and cooperation replaced competition.

Overcoming Group Conflict To decrease hostility between the Rattlers and the Eagles at Robbers Cave, the researchers created situations that required the joint efforts of both groups to achieve a common goal, such as fixing the water supply. These cooperative tasks helped the boys recognize their common interests and become friends.

The results? Children in the jigsaw classrooms benefited. They had higher self-esteem and a greater liking for children in other ethnic groups than did children in traditional classrooms. They also demonstrated a lessening of negative stereotypes and prejudice and a reduction in intergroup hostility (see Aronson, 1987, 1995; Aronson & Bridgeman, 1979). As Aronson (1999) points out, "Cooperation changes our tendency to categorize the out-group from 'those people' to 'us people.'"

Conformity

Following the Crowd

Key Theme

- **Social influence involves the study of how behavior is influenced by other people and by the social environment.**

Key Questions

- **What factors influence the degree to which people will conform?**
- **Why do people conform?**
- **How does culture affect conformity?**

As we noted earlier, *social influence* is the psychological study of how our behavior is influenced by the social environment and other people. For example, if you typically contribute to class discussions, you've probably felt the power of social influence in classes where nobody else said a word. No doubt you found yourself feeling at least slightly uncomfortable every time you ventured a comment or question.

If you changed your behavior to mesh with that of your classmates, you demonstrated conformity. **Conformity** occurs when you adjust your opinions, judgment, or behavior so that it matches other people, or the norms of a social group or situation.

There's no question that all of us conform to group or situational norms to some degree. The more critical issue is *how far* we'll go to adjust our perceptions and opinions so that they're in sync with the majority opinion—an issue that intrigued social psychologist **Solomon Asch.** Asch (1951) posed a straightforward question: Would people still conform to the group if the group opinion was clearly wrong?

Life in society requires consensus as an indispensable condition. But consensus, to be productive, requires that each individual contribute independently out of his experience and insight. When consensus comes under the dominance of conformity, the social process is polluted and the individual at the same time surrenders the powers on which his functioning as a feeling and thinking being depends.

—SOLOMON ASCH (1955)

To study this question experimentally, Asch (1955) chose a simple, objective task with an obvious answer (Figure 11.3). A group of people sat at a table and looked at a series of cards. On one side of each card was a standard line. On the other side were three comparison lines. All each person had to do was publicly indicate which comparison line was the same length as the standard line.

Asch's experiment had a hidden catch. All the people sitting around the table were actually in cahoots with the experimenter, except for one—the real subject. Had you been the real subject in Asch's (1956) experiment, here's what you would have experienced. The first card is shown, and the five people ahead of you respond, one at a time, with the obvious answer: "Line B." Now it's your turn, and you respond the same. The second card is put up. Again, the answer is obvious and the group is unanimous. So far, so good.

Then the third card is shown, and the correct answer is just as obvious: Line C. But the first person confidently says, "Line A." And so does everyone else, one by one. Now it's your turn. To you it's clear that the correct answer is Line C. But the five people ahead of you have already publicly chosen Line A. How do you respond? You hesitate. Do you go with the flow or with what you know?

The real subject was faced with the uncomfortable situation of disagreeing with a unanimous majority on 12 of 18 trials in Asch's experiment. Notice, there was *no* direct pressure to conform—just the implicit, unspoken pressure of answering differently from the rest of the group.

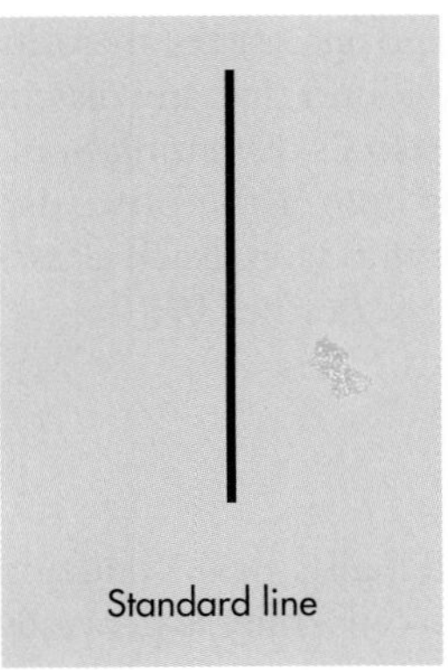

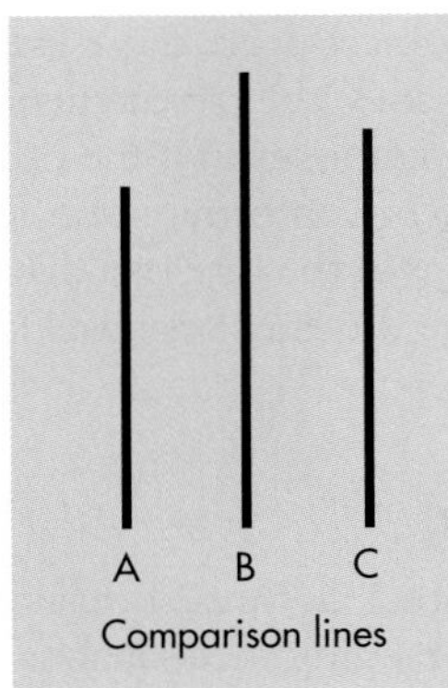

Figure 11.3 The Line Judgment Task Used in the Asch Conformity Studies In Asch's classic studies on conformity, subjects were asked to pick the comparison line that matched the standard line.

Source: Asch (1957).

conformity
Adjusting your opinions, judgments, or behavior so that it matches the opinions, judgments, or behavior of other people, or the norms of a social group or situation.

normative social influence
Behavior that is motivated by the desire to gain social acceptance and approval.

informational social influence
Behavior that is motivated by the desire to be correct.

Over one hundred subjects experienced Asch's experimental dilemma. Not surprisingly, participants differed in their degree of conformity. Nonetheless, the majority of Asch's subjects (76 percent) conformed with the group judgment on at least one of the critical trials. When the data for all subjects were combined, the subjects followed the majority and gave the wrong answer on *37 percent* of the critical trials (Asch, 1955, 1957). In comparison, a control group of subjects who responded alone instead of in a group accurately chose the matching line 99 percent of the time.

Although the majority opinion clearly exerted a strong influence, it's also important to stress the flip side of Asch's results. On almost two-thirds of the trials in which the majority named the wrong line, the subjects stuck to their guns and gave the correct answer, despite being in the minority (see Friend & others, 1990; Hodges & Geyer, 2006).

Factors Influencing Conformity

The basic model of Asch's classic experiment has been used in hundreds of studies exploring the dynamics of conformity (Bond, 2005; Bond & Smith, 1996; Hoffman & others, 2001). Why do we sometimes find ourselves conforming to the larger group? There are two basic reasons.

First is our desire to be liked and accepted by the group, which is referred to as **normative social influence.** If you've ever been ridiculed and rejected for going against the grain of a unanimous group, you've had firsthand experience with the pressure of normative social influence. Second is our desire to be right. When we're uncertain or doubt our own judgment, we may look to the group as a source of accurate information, which is called **informational social influence.**

Asch and other researchers identified several conditions that promote conformity, which are summarized in Table 11.2. But Asch also discovered that conformity *decreased* under certain circumstances. For example, having an ally seemed to counteract

Table 11.2

Factors That Promote Conformity

You're more likely to conform to group norms when:

- You are facing a unanimous group of at least four or five people
- You must give your response in front of the group
- You have not already expressed commitment to a different idea or opinion
- You find the task is ambiguous or difficult
- You doubt your abilities or knowledge in the situation
- You are strongly attracted to a group and want to be a member of it

Sources: Asch (1955); Campbell & Fairey (1989); Deutsch & Gerard (1955); Gerard & others (1968); Tanford & Penrod (1984).

Adolescents and Conformity Conformity to group norms peaks in early adolescence, as the similar hairstyles and clothing of these friends show. Think back to your own adolescence. Do you remember how important it was to you to fit in with other adolescents, especially those in your peer group?

obedience
The performance of a behavior in response to a direct command.

the social influence of the majority. Subjects were more likely to go against the majority view if just one other participant did so. Other researchers have found that any dissent increases resistance to the majority opinion, even if the other person's dissenting opinion is wrong (Allen & Levine, 1969). Conformity also lessens even if the other dissenter's competence is questionable, as in the case of a dissenter who wore thick glasses and complained that he could not see the lines very well (Allen & Levine, 1971).

Culture and Conformity

Do patterns of conformity differ in other cultures? British psychologists Rod Bond and Peter Smith (1996) found in a wide-ranging meta-analysis that conformity is generally higher in collectivistic cultures than in individualistic cultures. Because individualistic cultures tend to emphasize independence, self-expression, and standing out from the crowd, the whole notion of conformity tends to carry a negative connotation.

In collectivistic cultures, however, publicly conforming while privately disagreeing tends to be regarded as socially appropriate tact or sensitivity. Publicly challenging the judgments of others, particularly the judgment of members of one's in-group, would be considered rude, tactless, and insensitive to the feelings of others. Thus, conformity in collectivistic cultures does not seem to carry the same negative connotation that it does in individualistic cultures.

Obedience

Just Following Orders

Key Theme

- **Stanley Milgram conducted a series of controversial studies on obedience, which is behavior performed in direct response to the orders of an authority.**

Key Questions

- **What were the results of Milgram's original obedience experiments?**
- **What experimental factors were shown to increase the level of obedience?**
- **What experimental factors were shown to decrease the level of obedience?**

Stanley Milgram was one of the most creative and influential researchers that social psychology has known (Blass, 2004; Miller, 2009). Sadly, Milgram died of a heart attack at the age of 51. Though Milgram made many contributions to social psychology, he is best known for his experimental investigations of obedience. **Obedience** is the performance of a behavior in response to a direct command. Typically, an authority figure or a person of higher status, such as a teacher or supervisor, gives the command.

Milgram was intrigued by Asch's discovery of how easily people could be swayed by group pressure. But Milgram wanted to investigate behavior that had greater personal significance than simply judging line lengths on a card (Milgram, 1963, 1980). Thus, Milgram posed what he saw as the most critical question: Could a person be pressured by others into committing an immoral act, some action that violated his or her own conscience, such as hurting a stranger? In his efforts to answer that question, Milgram embarked on one of the most systematic and controversial investigations in the history of psychology: to determine how and why people obey the destructive dictates of an authority figure.

Social Psychologist Stanley Milgram (1933–1984) Milgram is best known for his obedience studies, but his creative research skills went far beyond the topic of obedience. To study the power of social norms, for example, Milgram sent his students out into New York City to intrude into waiting lines or ask subway passengers to give up their seats. Milgram often capitalized on the "texture of everyday life" to "examine the way in which the social world impinges on individual action and experience" (Milgram, 1974a).

Milgram's Original Obedience Experiment

Milgram was only 28 years old when he conducted his first obedience experiments. At the time, he was a new faculty member at Yale University in New Haven, Connecticut. He recruited participants through direct-mail solicitations and ads in the local paper. Collectively, Milgram's subjects represented a wide range of occupational and educational backgrounds. Postal workers, high school teachers, white-collar workers, engineers, and laborers participated in the study.

Outwardly, it appeared that two subjects showed up at Yale University to participate in the psychology experiment, but the second subject was actually an accomplice working with Milgram. The role of the experimenter, complete with white lab coat, was played by a high school biology teacher. When both subjects arrived, the experimenter greeted them and gave them a plausible explanation of the study's purpose: to examine the effects of punishment on learning.

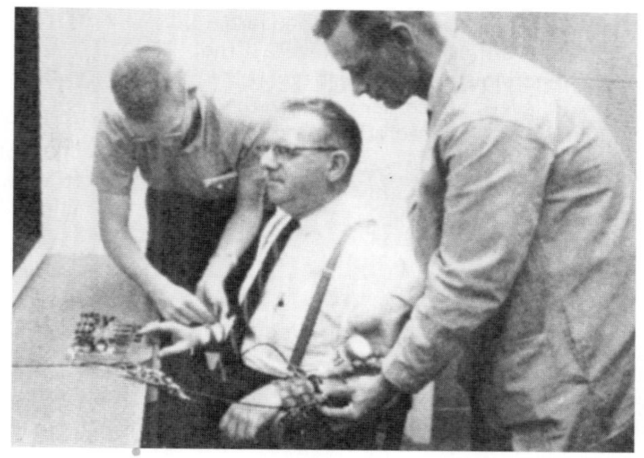

The "Electric Chair" With the help of the real subject, who had been assigned to the role of "teacher," the experimenter straps the "learner" into the electric chair. Unbeknownst to the real subject, the learner was actually a 47-year-old accountant who had been carefully rehearsed for his part in the experimental deception. The experimenter told both subjects, "Although the shocks can be extremely painful, they cause no permanent tissue damage."

Both subjects drew slips of paper to determine who would be the "teacher" and who the "learner." However, the drawing was rigged so that the real subject was always the teacher and the accomplice was always the learner. The learner was actually a mild-mannered, 47-year-old accountant who had been carefully rehearsed for his part in the drama. Assigned to the role of the teacher, the real subject would be responsible for "punishing" the learner's mistakes by administering electric shocks.

Immediately after the drawing, the teacher and learner were taken to another room, where the learner was strapped into an "electric chair." The teacher was then taken to a different room, from which he could hear but not see the learner. Speaking into a microphone, the teacher tested the learner on a simple word-pair memory task. In the other room, the learner pressed one of four switches to indicate with which alternative the word had previously been paired. The learner's response was registered in an answer box positioned on top of the "shock generator" in front of the teacher. Each time the learner answered incorrectly, the teacher was to deliver an electric shock.

Just in case there was any lingering doubt in the teacher's mind about the legitimacy of the shock generator, the *teacher* was given a sample jolt using the switch marked 45 volts. In fact, this sample shock was the only real shock given during the course of the staged experiment.

The first time the learner answered incorrectly, the teacher was to deliver an electric shock at the 15-volt level. With each subsequent error, the teacher was told to progress to the next level on the shock generator. The teacher was also told to announce the voltage level to the learner before delivering the shock.

At predetermined voltage levels, the learner vocalized first his discomfort, then his pain, and, finally, agonized screams. Some of the learner's vocalizations at the different voltage levels are shown in Table 11.3 on the next page. After 330 volts, the learner's script called for him to fall silent. If the teacher protested that he wished to stop or that he was worried about the learner's safety, the experimenter would say, "The experiment requires that you continue" or "You have no other choice, you *must* continue."

According to the script, the experiment would be halted when the teacher–subject refused to obey the experimenter's orders to continue. Alternatively, if the teacher–subject obeyed the experimenter, the experiment would be halted once the teacher had progressed all the way to the maximum shock level of 450 volts.

Either way, after the experiment the teacher was interviewed and it was explained that the learner had not actually received dangerous electric shocks. To underscore this point, a "friendly reconciliation" was arranged between the teacher and the learner, and the true purpose of the study was explained to the subject.

Milgram's "Shock Generator" Machine A young Stanley Milgram sits next to his "shock generator." Milgram went to great lengths to make the shock generator look as authentic as possible. The front panel of the bogus shock generator had been engraved by professional industrial engravers. Whenever the teacher pressed a shock switch, the red light above the switch went on, a buzzing and clicking sound was heard, and the needle on the voltage meter swung to the right. Very convincing details. Do you think you would have been fooled into believing that this was a real shock generator?

This table shows examples of the learner's protests at different voltage levels. If the teacher administered shocks beyond the 330-volt level, the learner's agonized screams were replaced with an ominous silence.

Source: Milgram (1974a).

Table 11.3

The Learner's Schedule of Protests in Milgram's Obedience Experiment

120 volts → Ugh! Hey, *this* really hurts.

150 volts → Ugh!!! Experimenter! That's all. Get me out of here. I told you I had heart trouble. My heart's starting to bother me now. Get me out of here, please. My heart's starting to bother me. I refuse to go on. Let me out.

210 volts → Ugh!! Experimenter! Get me out of here. I've had enough. I *won't* be in the experiment any more.

270 volts → (*Agonized scream.*) Let me out of here. Let me out of here. Let me out of here. Let me out. Do you hear? Let me out of here.

300 volts → (*Agonized scream.*) I absolutely refuse to answer any more. Get me out of here. You can't hold me here. Get me out. Get me out of here.

315 volts → (*Intensely agonized scream.*) I told you I refuse to answer. I'm no longer part of this experiment.

330 volts → (*Intense and prolonged agonized scream.*) Let me out of here. Let me out of here. My heart's bothering me. Let me out, I tell you. (*Hysterically*) Let me out of here. Let me out of here. You have no right to hold me here. Let me out! Let me out! Let me out! Let me out of here! Let me out! Let me out!

The Results of Milgram's Original Experiment

Can you predict how Milgram's subjects behaved? Of the 40 subjects, how many obeyed the experimenter and went to the full 450-volt level? On a more personal level, how do you think *you* would have behaved had you been one of Milgram's subjects?

Milgram himself asked psychiatrists, college students, and middle-class adults to predict how subjects would behave (see Milgram, 1974a). All three groups predicted that *all* of Milgram's subjects would refuse to obey at some point. They predicted that most subjects would refuse at the 150-volt level, the point at which the learner first protested. They also believed that only a few rare individuals would go as far as the 300-volt level. Finally, *none* of those surveyed thought that any of Milgram's subjects would go to the full 450 volts.

As it turned out, they were all wrong. *Two-thirds of Milgram's subjects—26 of the 40—were fully compliant and went to the full 450-volt level.* And of those who defied the experimenter, *not one stopped before the 300-volt level.* Table 11.4 shows the results of Milgram's original obedience study.

Surprised? Milgram himself was stunned by the results, never expecting that the majority of subjects would administer the maximum voltage. Were his results a fluke? Did Milgram inadvertently assemble a sadistic group of New Haven residents who were all too willing to inflict extremely painful, even life-threatening, shocks on a complete stranger?

The answer to both these questions is no. Milgram's obedience study has been repeated many times in the United States and other countries (see Blass, 2000). And, in fact, Milgram (1974a) replicated his own study on numerous occasions, using variations of his basic experimental procedure.

In one replication, for instance, Milgram's subjects were 40 women. Were female subjects any less likely to inflict pain on a stranger? Not at all. The results were identical. Confirming Milgram's results since then, eight other studies also found no sex differences in obedience to an authority figure (see Blass, 2000, 2004; Burger, 2009).

Perhaps Milgram's subjects saw through his elaborate experimental hoax, as some critics have suggested (Orne & Holland, 1968). Was it possible that the subjects did not believe that they were really harming the learner? Again, the answer seems to be no. Milgram's subjects seemed totally convinced that the situation was authentic. And they did not behave in a cold-blooded, unfeeling way. Far from it. As the experiment progressed, many subjects showed signs of extreme tension and conflict.

Table 11.4

The Results of Milgram's Original Study

Shock Level	Switch Labels and Voltage Levels	Number of Subjects Who Refused to Administer a Higher Voltage Level
	Slight Shock	
1	15	
2	30	
3	45	
4	60	
	Moderate Shock	
5	75	
6	90	
7	105	
8	120	
9	135	
10	150	
11	165	
12	180	
	Very Strong Shock	
13	195	
14	210	
15	225	
16	240	
	Intense Shock	
17	255	
18	270	
19	285	
20	300	
	Extreme Intensity Shock	
21	315	5
22	330	
23	345	4
24	360	2
	Danger: Severe Shock	1
25	375	1
26	390	
27	405	1
28	420	
	XXX	
29	435	
30	450	26

Contrary to what psychiatrists, college students, and middle-class adults predicted, the majority of Milgram's subjects did not refuse to obey by the 150-volt level of shock. As this table shows, 14 of Milgram's 40 subjects (35 percent) refused to continue at some point after administering 300 volts to the learner. However, 26 of the 40 subjects (65 percent) remained obedient to the very end, administering the full 450 volts to the learner.

Source: Milgram (1974a).

In describing the reaction of one subject, Milgram (1963) wrote, "I observed a mature and initially poised businessman enter the laboratory smiling and confident. Within 20 minutes he was reduced to a twitching, stuttering wreck, who was rapidly approaching a point of nervous collapse."

Making Sense of Milgram's Findings

Multiple Influences

Milgram, along with other researchers, identified several aspects of the experimental situation that had a strong impact on the subjects (see Blass, 1992, 2000; Milgram, 1965). Here are some of the forces that influenced subjects to continue obeying the experimenter's orders:

- **A previously well-established mental framework to obey.** Having volunteered to participate in a psychology experiment, Milgram's subjects arrived at the lab with the mental expectation that they would obediently follow the directions of the person in charge—the experimenter. They also accepted compensation on their

The Aftereffects of Milgram's Study: Were Subjects Harmed? Milgram's findings were disturbing. But some psychologists found his methods equally upsetting. For example, in one experimental variation, participants were ordered to physically hold the learner's hand on a "shock plate." Thirty percent obeyed. To psychologist Diana Baumrind (1964), it was unethical for Milgram to subject his participants to that level of emotional stress, humiliation, and loss of dignity. But Milgram (1964) countered that he had not set out to create stress in his subjects. It was his unanticipated *results*, not his *methods*, that disturbed people. Who would object to his experiment, he asked, "if everyone had broken off at 'slight shock' or at the first sign of the learner's discomfort?" Concerns were also expressed that participants would experience serious aftereffects from the experiment. However, in a follow-up questionnaire, 84 percent of participants in Milgram's experiment indicated that they were "glad to have taken part in the experiment," and only about 1 percent regretted participating (Milgram, 1974b).

> The individual who is commanded by a legitimate authority ordinarily obeys. Obedience comes easily and often. It is a ubiquitous and indispensable feature of social life.
>
> —STANLEY MILGRAM (1963)

arrival, which may have increased their sense of having made a commitment to cooperate with the experimenter.

- **The situation, or context, in which the obedience occurred.** The subjects were familiar with the basic nature of scientific investigation, believed that scientific research was worthwhile, and were told that the goal of the experiment was to "advance the scientific understanding of learning and memory" (Milgram, 1974a). All these factors predisposed the subjects to trust and respect the experimenter's authority (Darley, 1992). Even when subjects protested, they were polite and respectful. Milgram suggested that subjects were afraid that defying the experimenter's orders would make them appear arrogant, rude, disrespectful, or uncooperative.
- **The gradual, repetitive escalation of the task.** At the beginning of the experiment, the subject administered a very low level of shock—15 volts. Subjects could easily justify using such low levels of electric shock in the service of science. The shocks, like the learner's protests, escalated only gradually. Each additional shock was only 15 volts stronger than the preceding one.
- **The experimenter's behavior and reassurances.** Many subjects asked the experimenter who was responsible for what might happen to the learner. In every case, the teacher was reassured that the *experimenter* was responsible for the learner's well-being. Thus, the subjects could believe that they were not responsible for the consequences of their actions. They could tell themselves that their behavior must be appropriate if the experimenter approved of it.
- **The physical and psychological separation from the learner.** Several "buffers" distanced the subject from the pain that he was inflicting on the learner. First, the learner was in a separate room and not visible. Only his voice could be heard. Second, punishment was depersonalized: The subject simply pushed a switch on the shock generator. Finally, the learner never appealed directly to the teacher to stop shocking him. The learner's pleas were always directed toward the *experimenter*, as in "Experimenter! Get me out of here!" Undoubtedly, this contributed to the subject's sense that the experimenter, rather than the subject, was ultimately in control of the situation, including the teacher's behavior. Similarly, when teachers were told to personally hold the learner's hand down on a "shock plate," obedience dropped to 30 percent. Overall, Milgram demonstrated that the rate of obedience rose or fell depending upon the situational variables the subjects experienced (Zimbardo, 2007).

Conditions That Undermine Obedience

Variations on a Theme

In a lengthy series of experiments, Milgram systematically varied the basic obedience paradigm. To give you some sense of the enormity of Milgram's undertaking, approximately *1,000* subjects, each tested individually, experienced some variation of Milgram's obedience experiment. Thus, Milgram's obedience research represents one of the largest and most integrated research programs in social psychology (Blass, 2000).

By varying his experiments, Milgram identified several conditions that decreased the likelihood of destructive obedience, which are summarized in Figure 11.4. For example, willingness to obey diminished sharply when the buffers that separated the teacher from the learner were lessened or removed, such as when both of them were put in the same room.

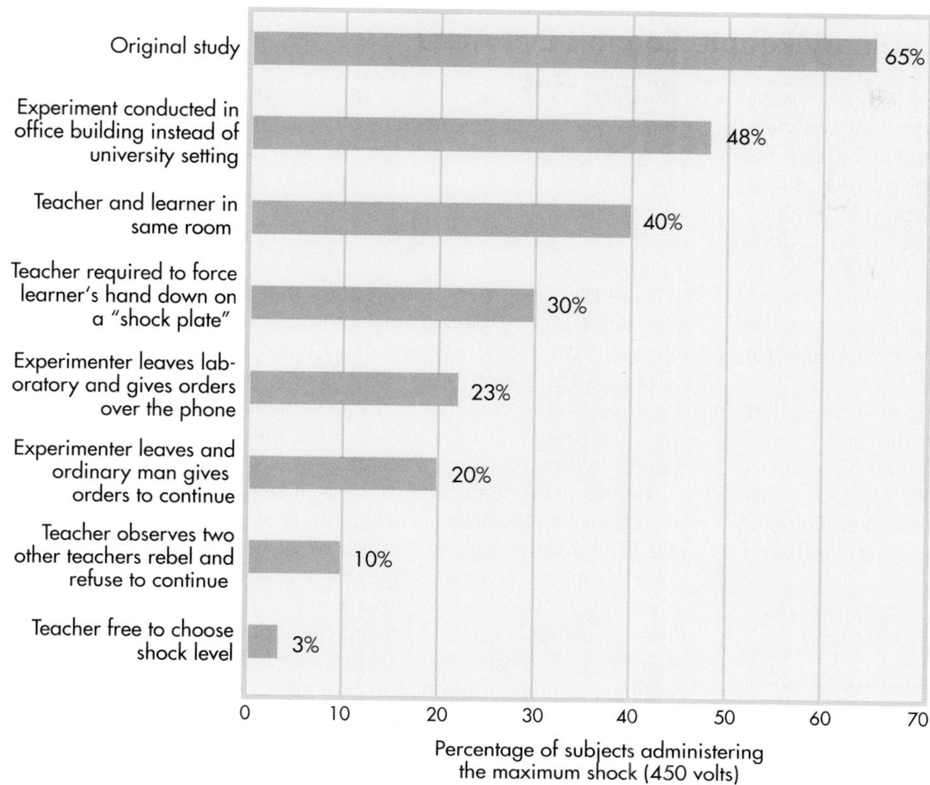

Figure 11.4 Factors That Decrease Destructive Obedience By systematically varying his basic experimental design, Milgram identified several factors that diminish the likelihood of destructive obedience. In this graph, you can see the percentage of subjects who administered the maximum shock in different experimental variations. For example, when Milgram's subjects observed what they thought were two other subjects disobeying the experimenter, the real subjects followed their lead 90 percent of the time and refused to continue.

Source: Adapted from data reported in Milgram (1974a).

If Milgram's findings seem to cast an unfavorable light on human nature, there are two reasons to take heart. First, when teachers were allowed to act as their own authority and freely choose the shock level, 95 percent of them did not venture beyond 150 volts—the first point at which the learner protested. Clearly, Milgram's subjects were not responding to their own aggressive or sadistic impulses, but rather to orders from an authority figure (see Reeder & others, 2008).

Second, Milgram found that people were more likely to muster up the courage to defy an authority when they saw others do so. When Milgram's subjects observed what they thought were two other subjects disobeying the experimenter, the real subjects followed their lead 90 percent of the time and refused to continue. Like the subjects in Asch's experiment, Milgram's subjects were more likely to stand by their convictions when they were not alone in expressing them.

Despite these encouraging notes, the overall results of Milgram's obedience research painted a bleak picture of human nature. And, more than 40 years after the publication of Milgram's research, the moral issues that his findings highlighted are still with us. Should military personnel be prosecuted for obeying orders to commit an immoral or illegal act? Who should be held responsible? We discuss a contemporary instance of destructive obedience in the Critical Thinking box, "Abuse at Abu Ghraib: Why Do Ordinary People Commit Evil Acts?" on the next page.

Asch, Milgram, and the Real World

Implications of the Classic Social Influence Studies

The scientific study of conformity and obedience has produced some important insights. The first is the degree to which our behavior is influenced by situational factors (see Zimbardo, 2007). Being at odds with the majority or with authority figures is very uncomfortable for most people—enough so that our judgment and perceptions can be distorted and we may act in ways that violate our conscience.

CRITICAL THINKING

Abuse at Abu Ghraib: Why Do Ordinary People Commit Evil Acts?

When the first Abu Ghraib photos appeared in 2004, Americans were shocked. The photos graphically depicted Iraqi prisoners being humiliated, abused, and beaten by U.S. military personnel at Abu Ghraib prison. In one photo, an Iraqi prisoner stood naked with feces smeared on his face and body. In another, naked prisoners were piled in a pyramid. Military guard dogs threatened and bit naked prisoners. A hooded prisoner stood on a box with wires dangling from his outstretched arms. Smiling American soldiers, both male and female, posed alongside the corpse of a beaten Iraqi prisoner, giving the thumbs-up sign for the camera.

In the international uproar that followed, U.S. political leaders and Defense Department officials scrambled, damage control at the top of their lists. "A few bad apples" was the official pronouncement—just isolated incidents of overzealous or sadistic soldiers run amok. The few "bad apples" were identified and arrested: nine members of an Army Reserve unit that was based in Cresaptown, Maryland.

Why would ordinary Americans mistreat people like that? How can normal people commit such cruel, immoral acts?

> *Unless we learn the dynamics of "why," we will never be able to counteract the powerful forces that can transform ordinary people into evil perpetrators.*
>
> —PHILIP ZIMBARDO, 2004b

What actually happened at Abu Ghraib?

At its peak population in early 2004, the Abu Ghraib prison complex, some 20 miles west of Baghdad, housed more than 6,000 Iraqi detainees. These were Iraqis who had been detained during the American invasion and occupation of Iraq. The detainees ranged from petty thieves and other criminals to armed insurgents. But also swept up in the detention were many Iraqi civilians who seemed guilty only of being in the wrong place at the wrong time. The prison complex was short of food, water, and basic sanitary facilities, understaffed, and poorly supervised (James, 2008).

There had been numerous reports that prisoners were being mistreated at Abu Ghraib, including official complaints by the International Red Cross. However, most Americans had no knowledge of the prison conditions until late April 2004, when the photographs documenting shocking incidents of abuse were shown on national television and featured in the *New Yorker* magazine (Hersh, 2004a, 2004b).

The worst incidents took place in a particular cell block that was controlled by military intelligence personnel rather than regular Army military police. This cell block held the prisoners who were thought to be most dangerous and who had been identified as potential "terrorists" or "insurgents" (Hersh, 2005). The Army Reserve soldiers assigned to guard these prisoners were told that their role was to assist military intelligence by "loosening up" the prisoners for later interrogation (Taguba, 2004).

Would you have obeyed? "I was instructed by persons in higher rank to 'stand there, hold this leash, look at the camera,'" Lynndie England (2005) said. Among those calling the shots was her then-lover, Corporal Charles Graner, the alleged ringleader who was sentenced to 10 years in prison for his attacks on Iraqi detainees. Graner, England, and one other reservist were convicted of mistreatment and given prison sentences, while the other six reservists made plea deals. No officers were court-martialed or charged with any criminal offense, although some were fined, demoted, or relieved of their command.

What factors contributed to the events that occurred at Abu Ghraib prison?

Multiple elements combined to create the conditions for brutality, including *in-group versus out-group thinking, negative stereotypes, dehumanization,* and *prejudice*. The Iraqi prisoners were of a different culture, ethnic group, and religion than the prison guards, none of whom spoke Arabic. To the American prison guards, the Arab prisoners represented a despised, dangerous, and threatening out-group. Categorizing the prisoners in this way allowed the guards to *dehumanize* the detainees, who were seen as subhuman (Fiske & others, 2004).

Because the detainees were presumed to be potential terrorists, the guards were led to believe that it was their duty to mistreat them in order to help extract useful information. In this way, aggression was transformed from being inexcusable and inhumane into a virtuous act of patriotism (Kelman, 2005). Thinking in this way also helped reduce any *cognitive dissonance* the soldiers might have been experiencing by *justifying* the aggression. "I was doing what I believed my superiors wanted me to do," said Army Reserve Private Lynndie England (2004), a file clerk from West Virginia.

Is what happened at Abu Ghraib similar to what happened in Milgram's studies?

Milgram's controversial studies showed that even ordinary citizens will obey an authority figure and commit acts of destructive obedience. Some of the accused soldiers, like England, did claim that they were "just following orders." The photographs of England with naked prisoners, especially the one in which she was holding a naked male prisoner on a leash, created international outrage and revulsion. But England (2004) testified that her superiors praised the photos and told her, "Hey, you're doing great, keep it up."

But were the guards "just following orders"?

During the investigation and court-martials, soldiers who were called as witnesses for the prosecution testified that no *direct* orders were given to abuse or mistreat any prisoners (Zernike, 2004). However, as a classic and controversial experiment by Stanford University psychologist Philip Zimbardo and his colleagues (1973) showed, *implied* social norms and roles can be just as powerful as explicit orders.

The Stanford Prison Experiment was conducted in 1971 (Haney & others, 1973). Twenty-four male college students were randomly assigned to be either prisoners or prison guards. They played their roles in a makeshift, but realistic, prison that had been set up in the basement of a Stanford University building. All of the participants had been evaluated and judged to be psychologically healthy, well-adjusted individuals.

> *The value of the Stanford Prison Experiment resides in demonstrating the evil that good people can be readily induced into doing to other good people within the context of socially approved roles, rules, and norms . . .*
>
> —PHILIP ZIMBARDO, 2000a

Originally, the experiment was slated to run for two weeks. But after just six days, the situation was spinning out of control. As Zimbardo (2005) recalls, "Within a few days, [those] assigned to the guard role became abusive, red-necked prison guards. Every day the level of hostility, abuse, and degradation of the prisoners became worse and worse. Within 36 hours the first prisoner had an emotional breakdown, crying, screaming, and thinking irrationally." Prisoners who did not have extreme stress reactions became passive and depressed.

While Milgram's experiments showed the effects of *direct authority pressure,* the Stanford Prison Experiment demonstrated the powerful influence of *situational roles* and *conformity to implied social rules and norms.* These influences are especially pronounced in vague or novel situations (Zimbardo, 2007). In confusing or ambiguous situations, *normative social influence* is more likely. When people are not certain what to do, they tend to rely on cues provided by others and to conform their behavior to those in their immediate group (Fiske & others, 2004).

At Abu Ghraib, the accused soldiers received no special training and were ignorant of either international or Army regulations regarding the treatment of civilian detainees or enemy prisoners of war (see James, 2008; Zimbardo, 2007). Lynndie England, for example, was a file clerk, not a prison guard. In the chaotic cell block, the guards apparently took their cues from one another and from the military intelligence personnel who encouraged them to "set the conditions" for interrogation (Hersh, 2005; Taguba, 2004).

Are people helpless to resist destructive obedience in a situation like Abu Ghraib prison?

No. As Milgram demonstrated, *people can and do resist pressure to perform evil actions.* Not all military personnel at Abu Ghraib went along with the pressure to mistreat prisoners (Hersh, 2005; Taguba, 2004). Consider these examples:

- National Guard 1st Lieutenant David Sutton stopped the abuse of a prisoner by other soldiers and immediately reported it to his commanding officer.
- Master-at-Arms William J. Kimbro, a Navy dog handler, adamantly refused to participate in improper interrogations using dogs to intimidate prisoners despite being pressured by the military intelligence personnel (Hersh, 2004b).
- When handed a CD filled with digital photographs depicting prisoners being abused and humiliated, Specialist Joseph M. Darby turned it over to the Army Criminal Investigation Division. It was Darby's conscientious action that finally prompted a formal investigation of the prison.

At the court-martials, army personnel called as prosecution witnesses testified that the abusive treatment shown in the photographs would never be allowed under any stretch of the normal rules for handling inmates in a military prison (Zernike, 2004).

In fact, as General Peter Pace, chairman of the Joint Chiefs of Staff, stated forcefully in a November 2005 press conference, "It is absolutely the responsibility of every U.S. service member, if they see inhumane treatment being conducted, to intervene to stop it. . . . If they are physically present when inhumane treatment is taking place, they have an *obligation* to try to stop it."

Finally, it's important to point out that understanding the factors that contributed to the events at Abu Ghraib does *not* excuse the perpetrators' behavior or absolve them of individual responsibility. And, as Milgram's research shows, the action of even one outspoken dissenter can inspire others to resist unethical or illegal commands from an authority figure.

CRITICAL THINKING QUESTIONS

- How might the fundamental attribution error lead people to blame "a few bad apples" rather than noticing situational factors that contributed to the Abu Ghraib prison abuse?
- Who should be held responsible for the inhumane conditions and abuse that occurred at Abu Ghraib prison?

Accepting Responsibility At her trial, Lynndie England, the file clerk from a small town in West Virginia, apologized for her actions. In an interview after her conviction, England (2005) said that she was still "haunted" by memories of events in the prison. She would always feel guilty, she said, "for doing the wrong thing, posing in pictures when I shouldn't have, degrading [the prisoners] and humiliating them—and not saying anything to anybody else to stop it."

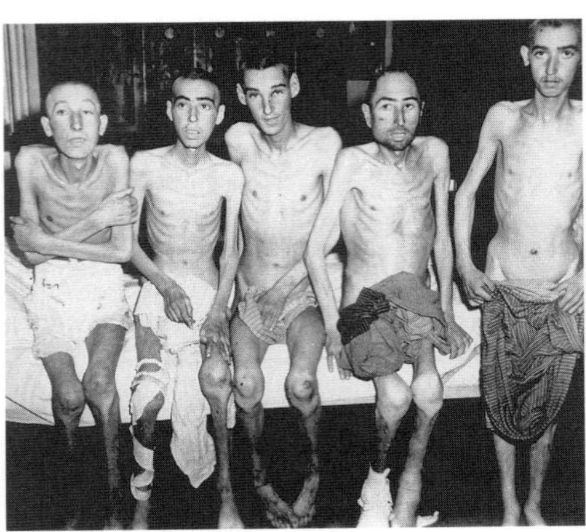

Destructive Obedience and Prejudice Blind obedience to authority combined with ethnic prejudice in Germany during World War II led to the slaughter of millions of Jews in concentration camps. When questioned after the war, Nazi officials and soldiers claimed that they were "just following orders." Over the half-century since the end of World War II, genocide and politically inspired mass killings have occurred in Cambodia, Bosnia, and Rwanda. Today, in the Sudanese Darfur, more than 300,000 people have been killed and thousands more driven from their homes by armed militia groups.

More important, perhaps, is the insight that each of us *does* have the capacity to resist group or authority pressure (Rochat & others, 2000). Because the central findings of these studies are so dramatic, it's easy to overlook the fact that some subjects refused to conform or obey despite considerable social and situational pressure. Consider the response of a subject in one of Milgram's later studies (Milgram, 1974a). A 32-year-old industrial engineer named Jan Rensaleer protested when he was commanded to continue at the 255-volt level:

Experimenter: *It is absolutely essential that you continue.*

Mr. Rensaleer: *Well, I won't—not with the man screaming to get out.*

Experimenter: *You have no other choice.*

Mr. Rensaleer: *I* do *have a choice.* (Incredulous and indignant) *Why don't I have a choice? I came here on my own free will. I thought I could help in a research project. But if I have to hurt somebody to do that, or if I was in his place, too, I wouldn't stay there. I can't continue. I'm very sorry. I think I've gone too far already, probably.*

Like some of the other participants in the obedience and conformity studies, Rensaleer effectively resisted the situational and social pressures that pushed him to obey. So did Sergeant Joseph M. Darby, the young man who turned over the CD with incriminating photos of Abu Ghraib abuse to authorities, triggering the investigation. As Darby later testified, the photos shocked him. "They violated everything that I personally believed in and everything that I had been taught about the rules of war." Another man who took a stand, stopping and then reporting an abusive incident in the prison, was 1st Lieutenant David Sutton. As he put it, "The way I look at it, if I don't do something, I'm just as guilty." Table 11.5 summarizes several strategies that can help people resist the pressure to conform or obey in a destructive, dangerous, or morally questionable situation.

How are such people different from those who conform or obey? Unfortunately, there's no satisfying answer to that question. No specific personality trait consistently predicts conformity or obedience in experimental situations such as those Asch and Milgram created (see Blass, 1991, 2000; Burger, 1992, 2009). In other words, the social influences that Asch and Milgram created in their experimental situations can be compelling even to people who are normally quite independent.

Finally, we need to emphasize that conformity and obedience are not completely bad in and of themselves. Quite the contrary. Conformity and obedience are necessary for an orderly society, which is why such behaviors were instilled in all of us as children. The critical issue is not so much whether people conform or obey, because we all do so every day of our lives. Rather, the critical issue is whether the norms we conform to, or the orders we obey, reflect values that respect the rights, well-being, and dignity of others.

Table 11.5

Resisting an Authority's Unacceptable Orders

- Verify your own discomfort by asking yourself, "Is this something I would do if I were controlling the situation?"
- Express your discomfort. It can be as simple as saying, "I'm really not comfortable with this."
- Resist even slightly objectionable commands so that the situation doesn't escalate into increasingly immoral or destructive obedience.
- If you realize you've already done something unacceptable, stop at that point rather than continuing to comply.
- Find or create an excuse to get out of the situation and validate your concerns with someone who is not involved with the situation.
- Question the legitimacy of the authority. Most authorities have legitimacy only in specific situations. If authorities are out of their legitimate context, they have no more authority in the situation than you.
- If it is a group situation, find an ally who also feels uncomfortable with the authority's orders. Two people expressing dissent in harmony can effectively resist conforming to the group's actions.

Sources: Milgram, 1963, 1974a; Asch, 1956, 1957; Haney & others, 1973; Zimbardo, 2000, 2004, 2007; Blass, 1991, 2004; American Psychological Association, 2005.

Helping Behavior

Coming to the Aid of Strangers

Key Theme

- **Prosocial behavior describes any behavior that helps another person, including altruistic acts.**

Key Questions

- **What factors increase the likelihood that people will help a stranger?**
- **What factors decrease the likelihood that people will help a stranger?**
- **How can the lack of bystander response in the Genovese murder case be explained in light of psychological research on helping behavior?**

It was about 3:20 A.M. on Friday, March 13, 1964, when 28-year-old Kitty Genovese returned home from her job managing a bar. Like other residents in her middle-class New York City neighborhood, she parked her car at an adjacent railroad station. Her apartment entrance was only 100 feet away.

As she got out of her car, she noticed a man at the end of the parking lot. When the man moved in her direction, she began walking toward a nearby police call box, which was under a streetlight in front of a bookstore. On the opposite side of the street was a 10-story apartment building. As she neared the streetlight, the man grabbed her and she screamed. Across the street, lights went on in the apartment building. "Oh, my God! He stabbed me! Please help me! Please help me!" she screamed.

"Let that girl alone!" a man yelled from one of the upper apartment windows. The attacker looked up, then walked off, leaving Kitty on the ground, bleeding. The street became quiet. Minutes passed. One by one, lights went off. Struggling to her feet, Kitty made her way toward her apartment. As she rounded the corner of the building moments later, her assailant returned, stabbing her again. "I'm dying! I'm dying!" she screamed.

Again, lights went on. Windows opened and people looked out. This time, the assailant got into his car and drove off. It was now 3:35 A.M. Fifteen minutes had passed since Kitty's first screams for help. A New York City bus passed by. Staggering, then crawling, Kitty moved toward the entrance of her apartment. She never made it. Her attacker returned, searching the apartment entrance doors. At the second apartment entrance, he found her, slumped at the foot of the steps. This time, he stabbed her to death.

It was 3:50 A.M. when someone first called the police. The police took just two minutes to arrive at the scene. About half an hour later, an ambulance carried Kitty Genovese's body away. Only then did people come out of their apartments to talk to the police.

Over the next two weeks, police investigators learned that a total of 38 people had witnessed Kitty's murder—a murder that involved three separate attacks over a period of about 30 minutes. Why didn't anyone try to help her? Or call the police when she first screamed for help?

Kitty Genovese (1935–1964) Known as Kitty by her friends, Genovese had grown up in Brooklyn. As a young woman, she managed a sports bar in Queens, shown here.

The Murder Scene At the end of the sidewalk you can see the railroad station where Genovese parked her car. Along the sidewalk are entrances to shops as well as stairways leading to apartments above the shops. After Genovese staggered to the entrance of her apartment, her attacker returned and stabbed her to death. Later investigations suggested that there may have been fewer than 38 witnesses' stories, and that some of those witnesses could not have seen the attacks from their windows (Manning & others, 2007, 2008). Nevertheless, the essential story is true: Many people heard Genovese's screams, yet no one stepped forward to help (Brock, 2008).

Prosocial Behavior in Action Everyday life is filled with countless acts of prosocial behavior. Many people volunteer their time and energy to help others. In Modesto, California, Doug Lilly volunteers for "Meals on Wheels." Along with delivering meals to about 65 elderly residents each week, Lilly also checks to make sure they are safe and healthy.

When the *New York Times* interviewed various experts, they seemed baffled, although one expert said it was a "typical" reaction (Mohr, 1964). If there was a common theme in their explanations, it seemed to be "apathy." The occurrence was simply representative of the alienation and depersonalization of life in a big city, people said (see Rosenthal, 1964a, 1964b).

Not everyone bought this pat explanation. In the first place, it wasn't true. As social psychologists **Bibb Latané** and **John Darley** (1970) later pointed out in their landmark book, *The Unresponsive Bystander: Why Doesn't He Help?*:

> People often help others, even at great personal risk to themselves. For every "apathy" story, one of outright heroism could be cited. . . . It is a mistake to get trapped by the wave of publicity and discussion surrounding incidents in which help was not forthcoming into believing that help never comes. People sometimes help and sometimes don't. What determines when help will be given?

That's the critical question, of course. When do people help others? And *why* do people help others?

When we help another person with no expectation of personal benefit, we're displaying **altruism** (Batson & others, 2008). An altruistic act is fundamentally selfless—the individual is motivated purely by the desire to help someone in need. Everyday life is filled with little acts of altruistic kindness, such as Fern giving the "homeless" man a handful of quarters or the stranger who thoughtfully holds a door open for you as you juggle an armful of packages.

Altruistic actions fall under the broader heading of **prosocial behavior,** which describes any behavior that helps another person, whatever the underlying motive. Note that prosocial behaviors are not necessarily altruistic. Sometimes we help others out of guilt. And, sometimes we help others in order to gain something, such as recognition, rewards, increased self-esteem, or having the favor returned (Dovidio & others, 2006).

Factors That Increase the Likelihood of Bystanders Helping

Kitty Genovese's death triggered hundreds of investigations into the conditions under which people will help others (Dovidio, 1984; Dovidio & others, 2006). Those studies began in the 1960s with the pioneering efforts of Latané and Darley, who conducted a series of ingenious experiments in which people appeared to need help. Often, these studies were conducted using locations in and around New York City as a kind of open-air laboratory.

Coming to the Aid of a Stranger Everyday life is filled with examples of people who come to the aid of a stranger in distress, like this sign posted at the corner of Toronto's Queen and Palmerston streets. Without knowing any details beyond those written on the sign, can you identify factors that might have contributed to the helping behavior of the bystanders in this situation?

Other researchers joined the effort to understand what factors influence a person's decision to help another (see Dovidio & others, 2006). Some of the most significant factors that have been found to increase the likelihood of helping behavior are noted below.

- **The "feel good, do good" effect.** People who feel good, successful, happy, or fortunate are more likely to help others (see Forgas & others, 2008; Salovey & others, 1991). Those good feelings can be due to virtually any positive event, such as receiving a gift, succeeding at a task, listening to pleasant music, finding a small amount of money, or even just enjoying a warm, sunny day.
- **Feeling guilty.** We tend to be more helpful when we're feeling guilty. For example, after telling a lie or inadvertently causing an accident, people were more likely to help others (Basil & others, 2006; Baumeister & others, 1994).

Even guilt induced by surviving the 9/11 terrorist attacks spurred helping behavior in many people during the aftermath (Wayment, 2004).

- **Seeing others who are willing to help.** Whether it's donating blood, helping a stranded motorist change a flat tire, or dropping money in the Salvation Army kettle during the holiday season, we're more likely to help if we observe others do the same (Bryan & Test, 1967; Sarason & others, 1991).
- **Perceiving the other person as deserving help.** We're more likely to help people who are in need of help through no fault of their own. For example, people are twice as likely to give some change to a stranger if they believe the stranger's wallet has been stolen than if they believe the stranger has simply spent all his money (Latané & Darley, 1970).
- **Knowing how to help.** Research has confirmed that simply knowing what to do contributes greatly to the decision to help someone else (e.g., Clark & Word, 1974; Huston & others, 1981).
- **A personalized relationship.** When people have any sort of personal relationship with another person, they're more likely to help that person. Even minimal social interaction with each other, such as making eye contact or engaging in small talk, increases the likelihood that one person will help the other (Howard & Crano, 1974; Solomon & others, 1981).

altruism
Helping another person with no expectation of personal reward or benefit.

prosocial behavior
Any behavior that helps another, whether the underlying motive is self-serving or selfless.

bystander effect
A phenomenon in which the greater the number of people present, the less likely each individual is to help someone in distress.

diffusion of responsibility
A phenomenon in which the presence of other people makes it less likely that any individual will help someone in distress because the obligation to intervene is shared among all the onlookers.

Factors That Decrease the Likelihood of Bystanders Helping

It's equally important to consider influences that decrease the likelihood of helping behavior. As we look at some of the key findings, we'll also note how each factor might have played a role in the death of Kitty Genovese.

- **The presence of other people.** People are much more likely to help when they are alone (Latané & Nida, 1981). If other people are present or imagined, helping behavior declines—a phenomenon called the **bystander effect.**

How can we account for this surprising finding? There seem to be two major reasons for the bystander effect. First, the presence of other people creates a **diffusion of responsibility.** The responsibility to intervene is *shared* (or *diffused*) among all the onlookers. Because no one person feels all the pressure to respond, each bystander becomes less likely to help.

Ironically, the sheer number of bystanders seemed to be the most significant factor working against Kitty Genovese. Remember that when she first screamed, a man yelled down, "Let that girl alone!" With that, each observer instantly knew that he or she was not the only one watching the events on the street below. Hence, no single individual felt the full responsibility to help. Instead, there was a diffusion of responsibility among all the bystanders so that each individual's share of responsibility was small indeed.

Second, the bystander effect seems to occur because each of us is motivated to some extent by the desire to behave in a socially acceptable way (*normative social influence*) and to appear correct (*informational social influence*). Thus, we often rely on the reactions of others to help us define a situation and guide our response to it. In the case of Kitty Genovese, the lack of intervention by any of the witnesses may have signaled the others that intervention was not appropriate, wanted, or needed.

- **Being in a big city or a very small town.** Kitty Genovese was attacked late at night in one of the biggest cities in the world, New York. Are people less likely to help strangers in big cities? Researcher Nancy Steblay (1987) has confirmed that this common belief is true—but

The Bystander Effect The couple on the left is obviously trying to ignore the heated argument between the man and woman on the right—even though the man is physically threatening the woman. What factors in this situation make it less likely that bystanders will intervene and try to help a stranger? Do you think you would intervene? Why or why not?

persuasion
The deliberate attempt to influence the attitudes or behavior of another person in a situation in which that person has some freedom of choice.

with a twist. People are less likely to help a stranger in very big cities (300,000 people or more) *or* in very small towns (5,000 people or less). Either extreme—very big or very small—seems to work against helping a stranger.

- **Vague or ambiguous situations.** When situations are ambiguous and people are not certain that help is needed, they're less likely to offer help (Solomon & others, 1978). The ambiguity of the situation may also have worked against Kitty Genovese. The people in the apartment building saw a man and a woman struggling on the street below but had no way of knowing whether the two were acquainted. "We thought it was a lovers' quarrel," some of the witnesses later said (Gansberg, 1964). Researchers have found that people are especially reluctant to intervene when the situation appears to be a domestic dispute or a "lovers' quarrel," because they are not certain that assistance is wanted (Shotland & Straw, 1976).
- **When the personal costs for helping outweigh the benefits.** As a general rule, we tend to weigh the costs as well as the benefits of helping in deciding whether to act. If the potential costs outweigh the benefits, it's less likely that people will help (Dovidio & others, 1991; Hedge & Yousif, 1992). The witnesses in the Genovese case may have felt that the benefits of helping Genovese were outweighed by the potential hassles and danger of becoming involved in the situation.

On a small yet universal scale, the murder of Kitty Genovese dramatically underscores the power of situational and social influences on our behavior. Although social psychological research has provided insights about the factors that influenced the behavior of those who witnessed the Genovese murder, it should not be construed as a justification for the inaction of the bystanders. After all, Kitty Genovese's death probably could have been prevented by a single phone call. If we understand the factors that decrease helping behavior, we can recognize and overcome those obstacles when we encounter someone who needs assistance. If *you* had been Kitty Genovese, how would *you* have hoped other people would react?

>> Closing Thoughts

We began this chapter with a Prologue about Fern trying to help a stranger in a strange city. As it turned out, Fern's social perceptions of the man were inaccurate: He was not a homeless person living on the streets of San Francisco. As simple as this incident was, it underscored a theme that was repeatedly echoed throughout our subsequent discussions of person perception, attribution, and attitudes. Our subjective impressions, whether they are accurate or not, play a pivotal role in how we perceive and think about other people.

A different theme emerged in our later discussions of conformity, obedience, and helping behavior. Social and situational factors, especially the behavior of others in the same situation, can have powerful effects on how we act at a given moment. But like Fern, each of us has the freedom to choose how we respond in a given situation. When we're aware of the social forces that influence us, it can be easier for us to choose wisely.

In the final analysis, we are social animals who often influence one another's thoughts, perceptions, and actions, sometimes in profound ways. In the following Enhancing Well-Being with Psychology section, we'll look at some of the ways that social psychological insights have been applied by professional persuaders—and how you can counteract attempts to persuade you.

ENHANCING WELL-BEING WITH PSYCHOLOGY

The Persuasion Game

Our daughter, Laura, was 3 1/2 years old, happily munching her Cheerios and doodling pictures in the butter on her bread. Don sat across from her at the kitchen table, reading a draft of this chapter. "Don't play with your food, Laura," Don said without looking up.

"Okay, Daddy," she chirped. "Daddy, are you in a happy mood?"

Don paused. "Yes, I'm in a happy mood, Laura," he said thoughtfully. "Are you in a happy mood?"

"Yes, Daddy," Laura replied as she made the banana peel dance around her placemat. "Daddy, will you get me a Mermaid Barbie doll for my birthday?"

Ah, so young and so clever! From very early in life, we learn the basics of **persuasion**—the deliberate attempt to influence the attitudes or behavior of another person in a situation in which that person has some freedom of choice. Clearly, Laura had figured out one basic rule: She's more likely to persuade Mom or Dad when they're in "a happy mood."

Professional persuaders often manipulate people's attitudes and behavior using techniques based on two fundamental social norms: the rule of reciprocity and the rule of commitment (Cody & Seiter, 2001). Here we'll provide you with some practical suggestions to avoid being taken in by persuasion techniques.

The Rule of Reciprocity

The *rule of reciprocity* is a simple but powerful social norm (Cialdini & Trost, 1998). If someone gives you something or does you a favor, you feel obligated to return the favor. So after a classmate lets you copy her lecture notes for the class session you missed, you feel obligated to return a favor when she asks for one.

The "favor" can be almost anything freely given, such as a free soft drink, a free food sample in a grocery store, a free gardening workshop at your local hardware store, a free guide, booklet, planning kit, or trial. The rule of reciprocity is part of the sales strategy used by companies that offer "free" in-home trials of their products. It's also why department stores that sell expensive cosmetics offer "free" makeovers.

Technically, you are under "no obligation" to buy anything. Nonetheless, the tactic often creates an uncomfortable sense of obligation, so you do feel pressured to reciprocate by buying the product (Cialdini, 2000).

One strategy that uses the rule of reciprocity is called the *door-in-the-face technique* (Dillard, 1991; Perloff, 1993; Turner & others, 2007). First, the persuader makes a large request that you're certain to refuse. For example, Joe asks to borrow $500. You figuratively "slam the door in his face" by quickly turning him down. But then Joe, apologetic, appears to back off and makes a much smaller request—to borrow $20. From your perspective, it appears that Joe has made a concession to you and is trying to be reasonable. This puts you in the position of reciprocating with a concession of your own. "Well, I can't lend you $500," you grumble, "but I guess I could lend you 20 bucks." Of course, the persuader's real goal was to persuade you to comply with the second, smaller request.

The rule of reciprocity is also operating in the *that's-not-all technique* (Zimbardo & Leippe, 1991). First, the persuader makes an offer. But before you can accept or reject it, the persuader appears to throw in something extra to make the deal even more attractive to you. So as you're standing there mulling over the price of the more expensive high-definition, flat-panel television, the salesperson says, "Listen, I'm offering you a great price but that's not all I'll do—I'll throw in some top-notch HDMI connector cables at no charge." From your perspective, it appears as though the salesperson has just done you a favor by making a concession you did not ask for. This creates a sense of obligation for you to reciprocate by buying the "better" package.

The Rule of Commitment

Another powerful social norm is the *rule of commitment.* Once you make a public commitment, there is psychological and interpersonal pressure on you to behave consistently with your earlier commitment. The *foot-in-the-door technique* is one strategy that capitalizes on the rule of commitment (Cialdini, 2000; Perloff, 1993). Here's how it works.

First, the persuader makes a small request that you're likely to agree to. For example, she might ask you to wear a lapel pin publicizing a fund-raising drive for a charity (Pratkanis & Aronson, 2001). By agreeing to wear the lapel pin, you've made a *commitment* to the fund-raising effort. At that point, she has gotten her "foot in the door." Later, the persuader asks you to comply with a second, larger request, such as donating money to the charity. Because of your earlier commitment, you feel psychologically pressured to behave consistently by now agreeing to the larger commitment (Gorassini & Olson, 1995).

The rule of commitment is also operating in the *low-ball technique.* First, the persuader gets you to make a commitment by deliberately understating the cost of the product you want. He's thrown you a "low ball," one that is simply too good to turn down. In reality, the persuader has no intention of honoring the artificially low price.

Here's an example of the low-ball technique in action: You've negotiated an excellent price (the "low ball") on a used car and filled out the sales contract. The car salesman shakes your hand and beams, then takes your paperwork into his manager's office for approval. Ten minutes pass—enough time for you to convince yourself that you've made the right decision and solidify your commitment to it.

At that point, the salesman comes back from his manager's office looking dejected. "I'm terribly sorry," the car salesman says. "My manager won't let me sell the car at that price because we'd lose too much money on the deal. I told him I would even take a lower commission, but he won't budge."

Notice what has happened. The attractive low-ball price that originally prompted you to make the commitment has been pulled out from under your feet. What typically happens? Despite the loss of the original inducement to make the purchase—the low-ball price—people often feel compelled to keep their commitment to make the purchase even though it is at a higher price (Cialdini, 2000).

Defending Against Persuasion Techniques

How can you reduce the likelihood that you'll be manipulated into making a decision that may not be in your best interest? Here are three practical suggestions.

1. Sleep on it.

Persuasive transactions typically occur quickly. Part of this is our own doing. We've finally decided to go look at a new laptop, automobile, or whatever, so we're psychologically primed to buy the product. The persuader uses this psychological momentum to help coax you into signing on the dotted line right then and there. It's only later, of course, that you sometimes have second thoughts. So when you think you've got the deal you want, tell the persuader that you always sleep on important decisions before making a final commitment.

The sleep-on-it rule often provides an opportunity to discover whether the persuader is deliberately trying to pressure or manipulate you. If the persuader responds to your sleep-on-it suggestion by saying something like, "This offer is good for today only," then it's likely that he or she is afraid that your commitment to the deal will crumble if you think about it too carefully or look elsewhere.

2. Play devil's advocate.

List all of the reasons why you should *not* buy the product or make a particular commitment (Pratkanis & Aronson, 2001). Arguing *against* the decision will help activate your critical thinking skills. It's also helpful to discuss important decisions with a friend, who might be able to point out disadvantages that you have overlooked.

3. When in doubt, do nothing.

Learn to trust your gut feelings when something doesn't feel quite right. If you feel that you're being psychologically pressured or cornered, you probably are. As a general rule, if you feel any sense of hesitation, lean toward the conservative side and do nothing. If you take the time to think things over, you'll probably be able to identify the source of your reluctance.

CHAPTER REVIEW: KEY PEOPLE AND TERMS

Solomon Asch, p. 474
John M. Darley, p. 486
Bibb Latané, p. 486
Stanley Milgram, p. 476
Muzafer Sherif, p. 472
Philip G. Zimbardo, p. 468

social psychology, p. 458
sense of self, p. 458
social cognition, p. 458
social influence, p. 458
person perception, p. 459
social norms, p. 460
social categorization, p. 460
explicit cognition, p. 460
implicit cognition, p. 460
implicit personality theory, p. 461
attribution, p. 463
fundamental attribution error, p. 463
blaming the victim, p. 464
hindsight bias, p. 464
just-world hypothesis, p. 464
self-serving bias, p. 465
attitude, p. 466
cognitive dissonance, p. 468
prejudice, p. 469
stereotype, p. 470
in-group, p. 471
out-group, p. 471
out-group homogeneity effect, p. 471
in-group bias, p. 471
ethnocentrism, p. 471
conformity, p. 474
normative social influence, p. 475
informational social influence, p. 475
obedience, p. 476
altruism, p. 486
prosocial behavior, p. 486
bystander effect, p. 487
diffusion of responsibility, p. 487
persuasion, p. 489

Web Companion Review Activities

You can find additional review activities at **www.worthpublishers.com/discoveringpsych5e.** The *Discovering Psychology* 5th edition Web Companion has self-scoring practice quizzes, flashcards, interactive crossword puzzles, and other activities to help you master the material in this chapter.

SOCIAL PSYCHOLOGY

Social Psychology

Studies how your thoughts, feelings, and behavior are influenced by the presence of other people and by the social and physical environment.

Social Cognition

Studies how we form impressions of others, how we interpret the meaning of other people's behavior, and how our behavior is affected by our attitudes.

Person Perception

- An active and subjective process that occurs in an interpersonal context
- Is influenced by subjective perceptions, social norms, personal goals, and self-perception

Person perception often involves using mental shortcuts, including:

- Social categorization
- Implicit personality theories

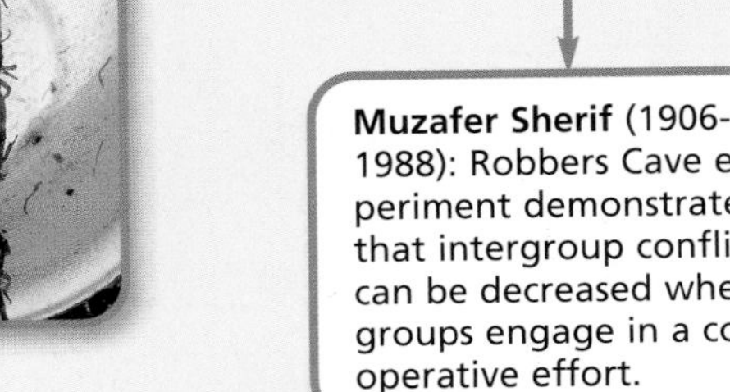

Attribution

Explaining the behavior of others often reflects common cognitive biases and explanatory patterns, including:

- Fundamental attribution error
- Blaming the victim
- Hindsight bias
- Self-serving bias
- Self-effacing bias

Attitudes

- A learned tendency to evaluate an object, person, or issue in a particular way
- Can have cognitive, emotional, and behavioral components
- Although attitudes typically influence behavior, sometimes our behavior influences our attitudes.

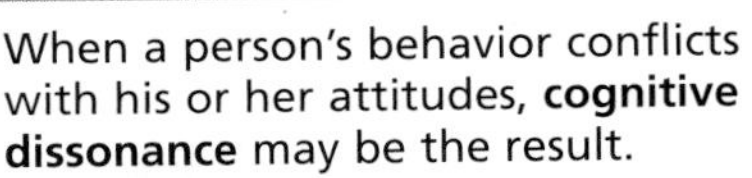

When a person's behavior conflicts with his or her attitudes, **cognitive dissonance** may be the result.

Prejudice

A negative attitude toward people who belong to a specific social group

Stereotypes:

- Form of social categorization in which a cluster of characteristics is attributed to all members of a social group or category
- Stereotypes are fostered by **in-group** and **out-group** thinking, and the **out-group homogeneity** effect
- **In-group bias** occurs when we attribute positive qualities to members of our own group

Muzafer Sherif (1906-1988): Robbers Cave experiment demonstrated that intergroup conflict can be decreased when groups engage in a cooperative effort.

Social Influence

Social psychology research area that investigates how our behavior is affected by situational factors and other people

Conformity

When you adjust your opinions, judgments, or behavior so that it matches other people, or the norms of a social group or situation

Solomon Asch (1907–1996) Conducted pioneering studies of the degree to which people will conform to the majority opinion even when they know it is objectively wrong

Obedience

Performing a behavior in response to a direct command; command is typically given by an authority figure or a person of higher status, such as a teacher or a supervisor.

Stanley Milgram (1933–1984) Conducted landmark series of experiments investigating the conditions under which people will obey—and disobey—the destructive orders of an authority figure

Philip Zimbardo (b. 1933) Conducted Stanford Prison Experiment in which a mock prison was used to study how situational forces and social roles can impact behavior

Helping Behavior

Prosocial behavior: Any behavior that helps others, whether motives are selfless or self-serving

Altruism: Helping behavior with no expectation of personal gain or benefit

Spurred by a tragedy in which multiple bystanders failed to help a young woman who was murdered, **Bibb Latané** (b. 1937) and **John Darley** (b. 1938) conducted the pioneering studies of when people will help a stranger.

Willingness to help a stranger can be undermined by the **bystander effect** and **diffusion of responsibility.**

CHAPTER

12

Stress, Health, and Coping

Katie's Story

PROLOGUE

A **BEAUTIFUL, CRYSTAL-CLEAR NEW YORK** morning. In her high-rise apartment at 1 West Street, our 20-year-old niece Katie was fixing herself some breakfast. From the street below, Katie could hear the muted sound of sirens, but she thought nothing of it. The phone rang. It was Lydia, her roommate, calling from her job in midtown Manhattan. "Katie, you're not going to believe this. A plane hit the World Trade Center. Go up on the roof and take a look!"

Katie hung up the phone and scurried up the fire escape stairwell, joining other residents already gathered on the roof. Down below, sirens were blaring and she could see emergency vehicles, fire engines, and people racing from all directions toward the World Trade Center, just a few blocks away. There was a gaping hole in the north tower. Thick black smoke was billowing out, drifting upward, and filling the sky. She thought she could see the flames. *What a freaky accident.*

After watching for a few minutes, Katie turned to go back downstairs and get ready for her dance class. Then, "Look at that plane!" someone yelled. Seconds later, a massive jet roared overhead and slammed into the World Trade Center's south tower, exploding into a huge fireball.

Katie froze in terror. Then: People screaming. Panic. Pushing and shoving at the stairwell door. *Get back to the apartment.* The television. Live views of the burning towers. Newscaster shouting: "Terrorist attack! New York is being attacked!" The TV went dead. *Don't panic. What am I going to do? Are we being bombed?*

Two thousand miles away. A sunny Colorado morning. Phone ringing. Judy was sound asleep. Ringing. Answer the phone. "Katie? What's wrong? Is someone in your apartment? Calm down, I can't understand. . . ."

"Mom, New York is being attacked! I don't know what to do! What should I do?" Katie sobbed uncontrollably.

Judy flipped on the television. Bizarre scenes of chaos in New York. *Oh my God, Katie's only a few blocks from the World Trade Center.* "Katie, stay in your apartment! Don't. . . ." The phone connection went dead.

Katie dropped the phone. *Worthless. Don't panic.* Lights flickered off, then on. Pounding on the door. "Evacuate the building! Get out!" a man's voice shouted. "Get out now! Use the stairwell!" *Gotta get out of here. Get out.*

Putting on her shoes and pulling a T-shirt over her pajamas, Katie grabbed her cell phone and raced out of her apartment toward the crowded stairwell. On the street was a scene of mass confusion. *Cross the street.* She joined a throng of people gathering in Battery Park. *Breathe. Stay calm.* As the crowd watched the towers burn, people shouted out more news. *Pentagon has been hit. White House is on fire. More planes in the air. President on Air Force One.*

Shaking, she couldn't take her eyes off the burning towers. *What's falling?* Figures falling from the windows of the Trade

Chapter Outline

Center, a hundred stories high. *On fire. That person was on fire. Oh my God, they're jumping out of the buildings! Don't look!* Firefighters, EMT workers, police, media people swarming on the plaza at

the base of the buildings. *This is not real. It's a movie. It's not real.*

Suddenly, unbelievably, the south tower crumbled. Onlookers screaming. *It's collapsing! It's coming down.* A vast ball of smoke formed, mushrooming in the sky. Like everyone else in the park, Katie turned and started running blindly. Behind her, a huge cloud of black smoke, ash, and debris followed, howling down West Street like a tornado.

Running. Cops shouting. "Go north! Don't go back! Get out of here!" *Don't go north. Go toward the ferry.* Choking on the smoke and dust, Katie covered her face with her T-shirt and stumbled down the street, moving toward the harbor. *I'm going to choke . . . can't breathe.* She saw a group of people near the Staten Island Ferry. *Get on the ferry, get out of Manhattan.* Another explosion. Panic. More people running.

Katie is still not certain how, dazed and disoriented, she ended up on a boat—a commuter ferry taking people to Atlantic Highlands, New Jersey. *Stop shaking. I'm safe. Stop shaking.* Covered with soot. Filthy. Standing in her pajamas amid stunned Wall Street workers in their suits and ties. Call anyone. Trying to call people. *Cell phone dead . . . no, please work!* "Here, Miss, use mine, it's working." Call anyone. Crying. *They're dead. Those firemen, the EMT workers on the plaza. They're all dead.* From the boat, she got a call through to her dance teacher, Pam, who lived in New Jersey. Pam would come and get her. She could stay with Pam.

Katie survived, but the next few weeks were difficult ones. Like the other residents of buildings near the World Trade Center, Katie wasn't allowed back into her apartment for many days. She had no money, no clothes, none of her possessions. And the reminders were everywhere. Fire station shrines, signs for the subway stop that didn't exist anymore, photographs of the missing on fences and walls. And the haunting memories—images of people jumping, falling, the faces of the rescue workers, the plane ripping through the building.

Eventually, like millions of other New Yorkers, Katie regained her equilibrium. "Are things back to normal?" Katie asks. "No, things will never be normal again, not in a hundred years. But it's okay. I'm fine. And I'm not going to leave New York. This is where I am, this is where I live, this is where I can dance."

>> Introduction: What Is Stress?

Key Theme

- **When events are perceived as exceeding your ability to cope with them, you experience an unpleasant emotional and physical state called stress.**

Key Questions

- **What is health psychology, and what is the biopsychosocial model?**
- **How do life events, daily hassles, and conflict contribute to stress?**
- **What are some social and cultural sources of stress?**

When you think of the causes of psychological stress, your initial tendency is probably to think of events and issues directly related to yourself, such as school, work, or family pressures. And, indeed, we don't want to minimize those events as stressors. If you're like most of our students, you probably have ample firsthand experience with the stress of juggling the demands of college, work, and family responsibilities. Those pressures represent very real and personal concerns for many of us as we negotiate the challenges of daily life.

stress
A negative emotional state occurring in response to events that are perceived as taxing or exceeding a person's resources or ability to cope.

As the terrorist attacks of September 11, 2001, unfolded, our entire nation was thrown into an extraordinary state of shared psychological stress as we watched, minute by minute, reeling in disbelief. It is impossible, of course, to convey the anguish, grief, and despair experienced by the thousands of people who lost loved ones as a result of the attacks. It is equally impossible to convey the sense of relief that thousands of other people felt when they eventually learned that their loved ones—like our niece Katie—had survived the attack.

But as the days turned into weeks, and then months, the aftereffects of this great national trauma lingered and reverberated, like ripples in a pond. For people who were directly involved, the physical and psychological effects of the attacks and their aftermath lingered for years (Farfel & others, 2008; Stellman & others, 2008). Katie, for example, still has nightmares and occasional waking flashbacks of the towers falling. However, even those Americans who were physically hundreds or thousands of miles away reported high levels of stress after the attacks.

What exactly is *stress*? It's one of those words that is frequently used but is hard to define precisely. Early stress researchers, who mostly studied animals, defined stress in terms of the physiological response to harmful or threatening events (e.g., Selye, 1956). However, people are far more complex than animals in their response to potentially stressful events. Two people may respond very differently to the same potentially stressful event.

Since the 1960s, psychologists have been studying the human response to stress, including the effects of stress on health and how people cope with stressful events. It has become clear that psychological and social factors, as well as biological factors, are involved in the stress experience and its effects.

Today, **stress** is widely defined as a negative emotional state occurring in response to events that are perceived as taxing or exceeding a person's resources or ability to cope. This definition emphasizes the important role played by a person's perception or appraisal of events in the experience of stress. According to **Richard Lazarus,** whether we experience stress depends largely on our *cognitive appraisal* of an event and the resources we have to deal with the event (Lazarus & Folkman, 1984; Miller & others, 2009).

If we think that we have adequate resources to deal with a situation, it will probably create little or no stress in our lives. But if we perceive our resources as being inadequate to deal with a situation we see as threatening, challenging, or even harmful, we'll experience the effects of stress. If our coping efforts are effective, stress will decrease. If they are ineffective, stress will increase. Figure 12.1 on the next page depicts the relationship between stress and appraisal.

"Your mother and I are feeling overwhelmed, so you'll have to bring yourselves up."

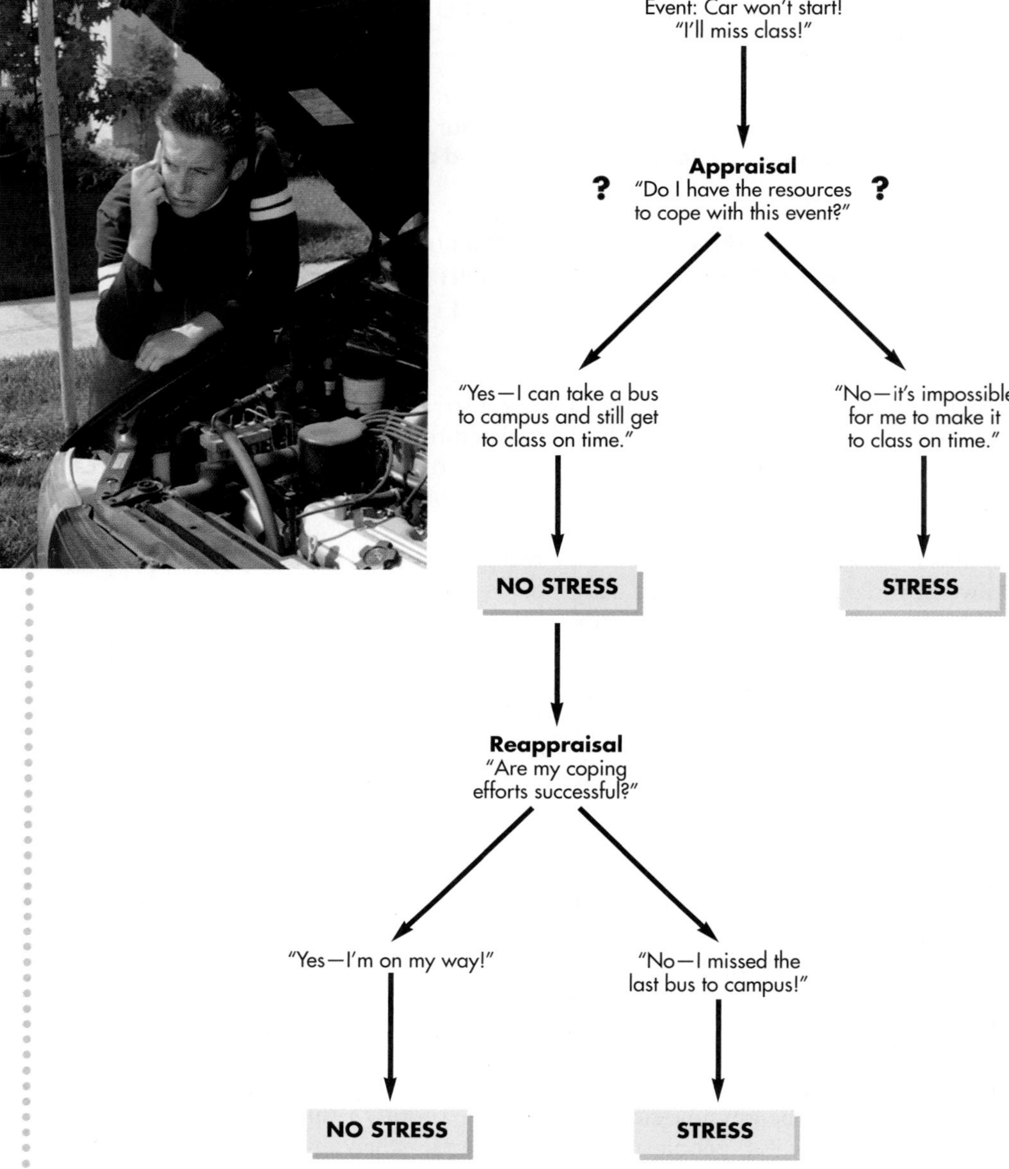

Figure 12.1 Stress and Appraisal According to Richard Lazarus (1999), events are not stressful in and of themselves. Instead, the experience of stress is determined by your subjective response to external events or circumstances. If you believe you have the resources necessary to meet a challenge or solve a problem, you'll experience little or no stress. As we deal with stressful circumstances, we continually appraise our coping responses along the way. If our coping efforts are successful, stress will decrease. If unsuccessful, stress will increase.

The study of stress is a key topic in **health psychology,** one of the most rapidly growing specialty areas in psychology. Health psychology is also sometimes referred to as *behavioral medicine*. Health psychologists are interested in how biological, psychological, and social factors influence health, illness, and treatment. Along with developing strategies to foster emotional and physical well-being, they investigate issues such as the following:

- How to promote health-enhancing behaviors
- How people respond to being ill
- How people respond in the patient–health practitioner relationship
- Why some people don't follow medical advice

health psychology
The branch of psychology that studies how biological, behavioral, and social factors influence health, illness, medical treatment, and health-related behaviors.

biopsychosocial model
The belief that physical health and illness are determined by the complex interaction of biological, psychological, and social factors.

Health psychologists work with many different health care professionals, including physicians, dentists, nurses, social workers, and occupational and physical therapists. In their research and clinical practice, health psychologists are guided by the **biopsychosocial model.** According to this model, health and illness are determined by the complex interaction of biological factors (e.g., genetic predispositions), psychological and behavioral factors (e.g., health beliefs and attitudes, lifestyle, stress), and social conditions (e.g., family relationships, social support, cultural influences) (Miller & others, 2009). Throughout this chapter, we'll look closely at the roles that different biological, psychological, and social factors play in our experience of stress.

stressors
Events or situations that are perceived as harmful, threatening, or challenging.

Sources of Stress

Life is filled with potential **stressors**—events or situations that produce stress. Virtually any event or situation can be a source of stress if you question your ability or resources to deal effectively with it (Lazarus & Folkman, 1984). In this section, we'll survey some of the most important and common sources of stress.

Life Events and Change

Is *Any* Change Stressful?

Early stress researchers Thomas Holmes and Richard Rahe (1967) believed that any change that required you to adjust your behavior and lifestyle would cause stress. In an attempt to measure the amount of stress people experienced, they developed the *Social Readjustment Rating Scale*. The scale included 43 life events that are likely to require some level of adaptation. Each life event was assigned a numerical rating that estimates its relative impact in terms of *life change units*. Sample items from the original Social Readjustment Rating Scale are shown in Table 12.1.

Life event ratings range from 100 life change units for the most stress-producing to 11 life change units for the least stress-producing events. Cross-cultural studies have shown that people in many different cultures tend to rank the magnitude of stressful events in a similar way (McAndrew & others, 1998; Wong & Wong, 2006). Notice that some of the life events are generally considered to be positive events, such as a vacation. According to the life events approach, *any* change, whether positive or negative, is inherently stress-producing.

To measure their level of stress, people simply check off the life events they have experienced in the past year and total the life change units. Holmes and Rahe found that people who had accumulated more than 150 life change units within a year had an increased rate of physical or psychological illness (Holmes & Masuda, 1974; Rahe, 1972).

Despite its initial popularity, several problems with the life events approach have been noted. First, the link between scores on the Social Readjustment Rating Scale and the development of physical and psychological problems is relatively weak. In general, scores on the Social Readjustment Rating Scale are *not* very good predictors of poor physical or mental health. Instead, researchers have found that most people weather major life events without developing serious physical or psychological problems (Coyne & Downey, 1991; Kessler & others, 1985).

Second, the Social Readjustment Rating Scale does not take into account a person's subjective appraisal of an event, response to that event, or ability to cope with the event (Hammen, 2005; Lazarus, 1999). Instead, the number of life change units on the scale is preassigned, reflecting the assumption that a given life event will have the same impact on virtually everyone. But clearly, the stress-producing potential of an event might vary widely from one person to another. For instance, if you are in a marriage that is filled with conflict, tension, and unhappiness, getting divorced (73 life change units) might be significantly less stressful than remaining married.

Third, the life events approach assumes that change in itself, whether good or bad, produces stress. However, researchers have found that negative life events have

Table 12.1

The Social Readjustment Rating Scale: Sample Items

Life Change	Life Event Units
Death of spouse	100
Divorce	73
Marital separation	65
Death of close family member	63
Major personal injury or illness	53
Marriage	50
Fired at work	47
Retirement	45
Pregnancy	40
Change in financial state	38
Death of close friend	37
Change to different line of work	36
Mortgage or loan for major purchase	31
Foreclosure on mortgage or loan	30
Change in work responsibilities	29
Outstanding personal achievement	28
Begin or end school	26
Trouble with boss	23
Change in work hours or conditions	20
Change in residence	20
Change in social activities	18
Change in sleeping habits	16
Vacation	13
Christmas	12
Minor violations of the law	11

Source: Holmes & Rahe (1967).

The Social Readjustment Rating Scale, developed by Thomas Holmes and Richard Rahe (1967), was an early attempt to quantify the amount of stress experienced by people in a wide range of situations. Holmes and Rahe reasoned that any life event that required some sort of adaptation or change would create stress, whether the life event was pleasant or unpleasant.

Major Life Events and Stress
Would the birth of a child or losing your home in a fire both produce damaging levels of stress? According to the life events approach, any event that required you to change or adjust your lifestyle would produce significant stress—whether the event was positive or negative, planned or unexpected. How was the life events approach modified by later research?

greater adverse effects on health, especially when they're unexpected and uncontrollable (Dohrenwend & others, 1993). In contrast, positive or desirable events are much *less* likely to affect your health adversely. Today, most researchers agree that undesirable events are significant sources of stress but that change in itself is not necessarily stressful.

However, the Social Readjustment Rating Scale is still a useful tool for quickly measuring a person's exposure to stressful events. Thus, it continues to be used in stress research (Lynch & others, 2005; Scully & others, 2000). Efforts have also been made to revise and update the scale so that it more fully takes into account the influences of gender, age, marital status, and other characteristics (Hobson & Delunas, 2001).

Daily Hassles

That's Not What I Ordered!

What made you feel "stressed out" in the past week? Chances are it was not a major life event. Instead, it was probably some unexpected but minor annoyance, such as splotching ketchup on your new white T-shirt, misplacing your keys, or getting into an argument with a family member.

Stress researcher Richard Lazarus and his colleagues suspected that such ordinary irritations in daily life might be an important source of stress. To explore this idea, they developed a scale measuring **daily hassles**—everyday occurrences that annoy and upset people (DeLongis & others, 1982; Kanner & others, 1981). The *Daily Hassles Scale* measures the occurrence of everyday annoyances, such as losing something, getting stuck in traffic, and even being inconvenienced by lousy weather. Following the development of the original daily hassles scale, variations of the scale were developed for different groups, including a version for children and one for college students (see Table 12.2).

Table 12.2

Examples of Daily Hassles

Daily Hassles Scale

- Concern about weight
- Concern about health of family member
- Not enough money for housing
- Too many things to do
- Misplacing or losing things
- Too many interruptions
- Don't like current work duties
- Traffic
- Car repairs or transportation problems

College Daily Hassles Scale

- Increased class workload
- Troubling thoughts about your future
- Fight with boyfriend/girlfriend
- Concerns about meeting high standards
- Wasting time
- Computer problems
- Concerns about failing a course
- Concerns about money

Acculturative Daily Hassles for Children

- It bothers me when people force me to be like everyone else.
- Because of the group I'm in, I don't get the grades I deserve.
- I don't feel at home here in the United States.
- People think I'm shy, when I really just have trouble speaking English.
- I think a lot about my group and its culture.

Sources: Adapted from Blankstein & Flett, 1992; Kanner & others, 1981; Ross & others, 1999; Staats & others, 2007; Suarez-Morales & others, 2007.

Arguing that "daily hassles" could be just as stress-inducing as major life events, Richard Lazarus and his colleagues constructed a 117-item Daily Hassles Scale. Later, other researchers developed daily hassles scales for specific groups, such as parents or caregivers. Examples of items from the original Daily Hassles Scale and from scales developed for college students and for immigrant children are shown here.

Psychologist Richard Lazarus (1922–2002)
Lazarus has made several influential contributions to the study of stress and coping. His definition of stress emphasizes the importance of cognitive appraisal in the stress response. He also demonstrated the significance of everyday hassles in producing stress.

Major Life Events, Daily Hassles, and Stress The collapse of the I-35 bridge that carried traffic across the Mississippi River in Minneapolis killed 13 people and injured scores more. Rescuers toiled for weeks to locate the victims and remove debris and submerged vehicles. Beyond the victims and rescue workers, however, thousands of people were affected by the bridge's collapse. Automobile, rail, river, and even bicycle and pedestrian traffic was affected, and thousands of commuters needed to find a new route to downtown Minneapolis. The daily hassles created by major disasters adds to the high level of stress felt by those affected.

Are there gender differences in the frequency of daily hassles? One study measured the daily hassles experienced by married couples (Almeida & Kessler, 1998). The women experienced both more daily hassles and higher levels of psychological stress than their husbands did. For men, the most common sources of daily stress were financial and job-related problems. For women, family demands and interpersonal conflict were the most frequent causes of stress. However, when women *do* experience a stressful day in the workplace, the stress is more likely to spill over into their interactions with their husbands (Schulz & others, 2004). Men, on the other hand, are more likely to simply withdraw.

How important are daily hassles in producing stress? The frequency of daily hassles is linked to both psychological distress and physical symptoms, such as headaches and backaches (Bottos & Dewey, 2004; DeLongis & others, 1988). In fact, the number of daily hassles people experience is a better predictor of physical illness and symptoms than is the number of major life events experienced (Burks & Martin, 1985).

Why do daily hassles take such a toll? One explanation is that such minor stressors are *cumulative* (Repetti, 1993). Each hassle may be relatively unimportant in itself, but after a day filled with minor hassles, the effects add up. People feel drained, grumpy, and stressed out. Daily hassles also contribute to the stress produced by major life events. Any major life change, whether positive or negative, can create a ripple effect, generating a host of new daily hassles (Maybery & others, 2007).

For example, like many other New Yorkers, our niece Katie had to contend with a host of daily hassles after the terrorist attacks. She had no place to live, could not get access to her clothing or other possessions, and was unable to get money from the Red Cross because her roommate's father's name was on the lease. After pleading with the National Guardsmen patrolling the area, Katie and her roommate, Lydia, were allowed to get some of their belongings out of their apartment. They loaded as much as they could into a shopping cart, dragging and pushing the cart some 30 blocks north to a friend's home. Katie had to take a second waitress job to pay for the new, more expensive apartment.

Social and Cultural Sources of Stress

It probably won't come as a shock to you that crowding, crime, unemployment, poverty, inadequate health care, and substandard housing are all social conditions associated with increased stress (Gallo & Matthews, 2003). When people live in an environment that is inherently stressful, they often experience ongoing, or *chronic*, stress (Krantz & McCeney, 2002).

daily hassles
Everyday minor events that annoy and upset people.

In a poverty-stricken neighborhood, people are likely to be exposed to negative life events and to have fewer resources available to cope with those events. Thus, daily hassles are also more common. People in lower socioeconomic groups—who have low incomes, low levels of education, and who are either unemployed or work in low-status occupations—experience more health and economic problems and more incidents of violence than people in higher-status groups (Hatch & Dohrenwend, 2007). Teenagers and young adults report the highest levels of stressful events, especially traumatic, violent, or life-threatening events. Men experience more traumatic events than women. But women are more likely to become upset by the negative events that are experienced by friends and family. We'll return to that aspect of stressful experience later in the chapter.

Given their higher exposure to stressful circumstances, it's not surprising that people in the lowest socioeconomic levels tend to have the highest levels of psychological distress, illness, and death (Mays & others, 2007). They also tend to have higher levels of stress hormones than people in higher-status groups (Cohen & others, 2006).

Interestingly, how someone perceives his or her own social status can influence the physical effects of stress. This was demonstrated in a recent study in which volunteers were exposed to a cold virus. The volunteers who saw themselves as being low on the social status totem pole had higher rates of infection than volunteers who *objectively* matched them on social status measures but did *not* see themselves as being of low status (Cohen & others, 2008).

Racism and discrimination are another important source of chronic stress for many people (Contrada & others, 2000; Ong & others, 2009). In one survey, for example, more than three-quarters of African-American adolescents reported being treated as incompetent or dangerous—or both—because of their race (Sellers & others, 2006). Such subtle instances of racism, called *microaggressions,* take a cumulative toll (Sue & others, 2008). Whether it's subtle or blatant, racism significantly contributes to the chronic stress often experienced by members of minority groups.

Stress can also result when cultures clash. For refugees, immigrants, and their children, adapting to a new culture can be extremely stress-producing (Berry, 2003; Chun & others, 2003; Jamil & others, 2007). The Culture and Human Behavior box, "The Stress of Adapting to a New Culture," describes the factors that influence the degree of stress experienced by people encountering a new culture.

Physical Effects of Stress

The Mind–Body Connection

Key Theme

- **The effects of stress on physical health were demonstrated in research by Walter Cannon and Hans Selye.**

Key Questions

- **What endocrine pathways are involved in the fight-or-flight response and the general adaptation syndrome?**
- **What is psychoneuroimmunology, and how does the immune system interact with the nervous system?**
- **What kinds of stressors affect immune system functioning?**

From headaches to heart attacks, stress contributes to a wide range of disorders, especially when it is long-term, or chronic (Cass, 2006; Krantz & McCeney, 2002). Basically, stress appears to undermine physical well-being in two ways: indirectly and directly (Schneiderman & others, 2005).

acculturative stress
(ah-KUL-chur-uh-tiv) The stress that results from the pressure of adapting to a new culture.

CULTURE AND HUMAN BEHAVIOR

The Stress of Adapting to a New Culture

Refugees, immigrants, and even international students are often unprepared for the dramatically different values, language, food, customs, and climate that await them in their new land. Coping with a new culture can be extremely stress-producing (Johnson & Sandhu, 2007). The process of changing one's values and customs as a result of contact with another culture is referred to as *acculturation*. Thus, the term **acculturative stress** describes the stress that results from the pressure of adapting to a new culture (Berry, 1994, 2003, 2006).

Many factors can influence the degree of acculturative stress that a person experiences. For example, when the new society is one that accepts ethnic and cultural diversity, acculturative stress is reduced (Berry, 2006; Suarez-Morales & others, 2007). The ease of transition is also enhanced when the person has some familiarity with the new language and customs, advanced education, and social support from friends, family members, and cultural associations (Finch & Vega, 2003).

Cross-cultural psychologist John Berry has found that a person's attitudes are important in determining how much acculturative stress is experienced. When people encounter a new cultural environment, they are faced with two fundamental questions: (1) Should I seek positive relations with the dominant society? (2) Is my original cultural identity of value to me, and should I try to maintain it?

The answers to these questions result in one of four possible patterns of acculturation: integration, assimilation, separation, or marginalization (see the diagram). Each pattern represents a different way of coping with the stress of adapting to a new culture (Berry, 1994, 2003).

Integrated individuals continue to value their original cultural customs but also seek to become part of the dominant society. Ideally, the integrated individual feels comfortable in both her culture of origin and the culture of the dominant society, moving easily from one to the other (LaFromboise & others, 1993a). The successfully integrated individual's level of acculturative stress will be low (Ward & Rana-Deuba, 1999).

Assimilated individuals give up their old cultural identity and try to become part of the new society. They may adopt the new clothing, religion, and social values of the new environment and abandon their old customs and language.

Assimilation usually involves a moderate level of stress, partly because it involves a psychological loss—one's previous cultural identity. People who follow this pattern also face the possibility of being rejected either by members of the majority culture or by members of their original culture (LaFromboise & others, 1993a).

Acculturative Stress Adapting to a new culture is a stressful process. However, acculturative stress can be reduced when immigrants learn the language and customs of their newly adopted home. Here, two friends, one from China, one from Cuba, help one another in an English language class in Miami, Florida.

The process of learning new behaviors and suppressing old behaviors can also be moderately stressful.

Individuals who follow the pattern of *separation* maintain their cultural identity and avoid contact with the new culture. They may refuse to learn the new language, live in a neighborhood that is primarily populated by others of the same ethnic background, and socialize only with members of their own ethnic group.

In some instances, such withdrawal from the larger society is self-imposed. However, separation can also be the result of discrimination by the dominant society, as when people of a particular ethnic group are discouraged from fully participating in the dominant society. Not surprisingly, the level of acculturative stress associated with separation is likely to be very high.

Finally, the *marginalized* person lacks cultural and psychological contact with *both* his traditional cultural group and the culture of his new society. By taking the path of marginalization, he has lost the important features of his traditional culture but has not replaced them with a new cultural identity.

Marginalized individuals are likely to experience the greatest degree of acculturative stress, feeling as if they don't really belong anywhere. Essentially, they are stuck in an unresolved conflict between the traditional culture and the new social environment. They are also likely to experience feelings of alienation and a loss of identity (Berry & Kim, 1988; Castillo & others, 2007).

Question 1: Should I seek positive relations with the dominant society?

Question 2: Is my original cultural identity of value to me, and should I try to maintain it?		Yes	No
	Yes	Integration	Separation
	No	Assimilation	Marginalization

Patterns of Adapting to a New Culture According to cross-cultural psychologist John Berry (1994, 2003), there are four basic patterns of adapting to a new culture. Which pattern is followed depends on how the person responds to the two key questions shown.

Figure 12.2 Disrupted Sleep: One Indicator of Stress In the weeks immediately following the 9/11 terrorist attacks, the psychological stress caused by those events was evident in the increased sleep disruptions experienced by millions of Americans. Even years after the attacks, many firefighters, police officers, and other rescue and recovery workers continue to experience insomnia, recurring nightmares, and other sleep problems (Farfel & others, 2008; Stellman & others, 2008).

Percent of American Adults Who Have Had Sleep Problems Prior to and Following September 11

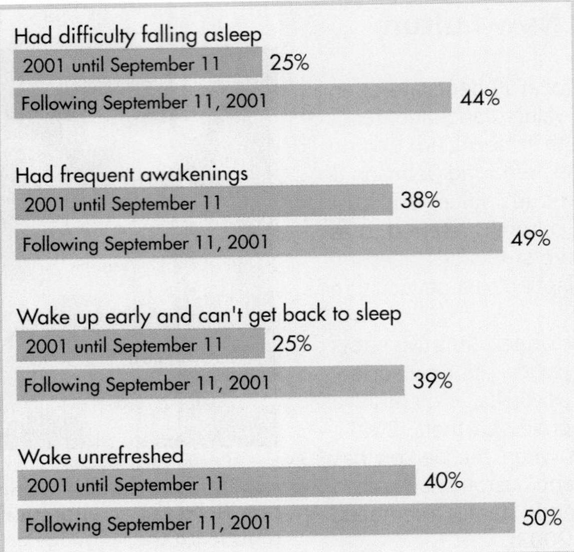

Source: National Sleep Foundation (2002).

First, stress can *indirectly* affect a person's health by prompting behaviors that jeopardize physical well-being, such as not eating or sleeping properly (see Figure 12.2). For example, among residents of Manhattan, there was a sharp rise in substance abuse during the weeks after the September 11 attacks. Almost 30 percent of residents participating in a New York Academy of Medicine survey reported that they had increased their level of alcohol consumption, cigarette smoking, or marijuana use (Vlahov & others, 2002). High levels of stress can also interfere with cognitive abilities, such as attention, concentration, and memory (Mandler, 1993). In turn, such cognitive disruptions can increase the likelihood of accidents and injuries.

Second, stress can *directly* affect physical health by altering body functions, leading to symptoms, illness, or disease (Kiecolt-Glaser & others, 2002). Here's a very common example: When people are under a great deal of stress, their neck and head muscles can contract and tighten, resulting in stress-induced tension headaches. But exactly how do stressful events influence bodily processes, such as muscle contractions?

Stress and the Endocrine System

To explain the connection between stress and health, researchers have focused on how the nervous system, including the brain, interacts with two other important body systems: the endocrine and immune systems. We'll first consider the role of the endocrine system in our response to stressful events and then look at the connections between stress and the immune system.

Walter Cannon

Stress and the Fight-or-Flight Response

Any kind of immediate threat to your well-being is a stress-producing experience that triggers a cascade of changes in your body. As we've noted in previous chapters, this rapidly occurring chain of internal physical reactions is called the **fight-or-flight response.** Collectively, these changes prepare us either to fight or to take flight from an immediate threat.

The fight-or-flight response was first described by American physiologist **Walter Cannon,** one of the earliest contributors to stress research. Cannon (1932) found that the fight-or-flight response involved both the sympathetic nervous system and the endocrine system (see Chapter 2).

With the perception of a threat, the hypothalamus and lower brain structures activate the sympathetic nervous system (see left side of Figure 12.3). The sympathetic nervous system stimulates the adrenal medulla to secrete hormones called **catecholamines,** including *adrenaline* and *noradrenaline.* Circulating through the blood, catecholamines trigger the rapid and intense bodily changes associated with the fight-or-flight response. Once the threat is removed, the high level of bodily arousal subsides gradually, usually within about 20 to 60 minutes.

As a short-term reaction, the fight-or-flight response helps ensure survival by swiftly mobilizing internal physical resources to defensively attack or flee an immediate threat.

Walter B. Cannon (1875–1945) Cannon made many lasting contributions to psychology, including an influential theory of emotion, which we discussed in Chapter 8. During World War I, Cannon's research on the effects of stress and trauma led him to recognize the central role of the adrenal glands in mobilizing the body's resources in response to threatening circumstances—the essence of the *fight-or-flight response.* Cannon also coined the term *homeostasis,* which is the tendency of the body to maintain a steady internal state (see page 320).

Figure 12.3 Endocrine System Pathways in Stress Two different endocrine system pathways are involved in the response to stress (Joëls & Baram, 2009; Lupien & others, 2009). Walter Cannon identified the endocrine pathway shown on the left side of this diagram. This is the pathway involved in the fight-or-flight response to immediate threats. Hans Selye identified the endocrine pathway shown on the right. This second endocrine pathway plays an important role in dealing with prolonged, or chronic, stressors.

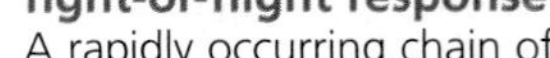

Without question, the fight-or-flight response is very useful if you're suddenly faced with a life-threatening situation, such as a guy pointing a gun at you in a deserted parking lot. However, when exposure to an unavoidable threat is prolonged, the intense arousal of the fight-or-flight response can also become prolonged. Under these conditions, Cannon believed, the fight-or-flight response could prove harmful to physical health.

fight-or-flight response
A rapidly occurring chain of internal physical reactions that prepare people either to fight or take flight from an immediate threat.

catecholamines
(*cat*-eh-COLE-uh-meens) Hormones secreted by the adrenal medulla that cause rapid physiological arousal; include adrenaline and noradrenaline.

general adaptation syndrome
Selye's term for the three-stage progression of physical changes that occur when an organism is exposed to intense and prolonged stress. The three stages are alarm, resistance, and exhaustion.

Hans Selye

Stress and the General Adaptation Syndrome

Cannon's suggestion that prolonged stress could be physically harmful was confirmed by Canadian endocrinologist **Hans Selye.** Most of Selye's pioneering research was done with rats that were exposed to prolonged stressors, such as electric shock, extreme heat or cold, or forced exercise. Regardless of the condition that Selye used to produce prolonged stress, he found the same pattern of physical changes in the rats. First, the adrenal glands became enlarged. Second, stomach ulcers and loss of weight occurred. And third, there was shrinkage of the thymus gland and lymph glands, two key components of the immune system. Selye believed that these distinct physical changes represented the essential effects of stress—the body's response to any demand placed on it.

A Pioneer in Stress Research With his tie off and his feet up, Canadian endocrinologist Hans Selye (1907–1982) looks the very picture of relaxation. Selye's research at the University of Montreal documented the physical effects of exposure to prolonged stress. His popular book *The Stress of Life* (1956) helped make *stress* a household word.

Selye discovered that if the bodily "wear and tear" of the stress-producing event continued, the effects became evident in three progressive stages. He called these stages the **general adaptation syndrome.** During the initial *alarm stage,* intense arousal occurs as the body mobilizes internal physical resources to meet the demands

corticosteroids
(core-tick-oh-STAIR-oydz) Hormones released by the adrenal cortex that play a key role in the body's response to long-term stressors.

immune system
Body system that produces specialized white blood cells that protect the body from viruses, bacteria, and tumor cells.

lymphocytes
(LIMF-oh-sites) Specialized white blood cells that are responsible for immune defenses.

psychoneuroimmunology
An interdisciplinary field that studies the interconnections among psychological processes, nervous and endocrine system functions, and the immune system.

of the stress-producing event. Selye (1976) found that the rapidly occurring changes during the alarm stage result from the release of catecholamines by the adrenal medulla, as Cannon had previously described.

In the *resistance stage,* the body actively tries to resist or adjust to the continuing stressful situation. The intense arousal of the alarm stage diminishes, but physiological arousal remains above normal and resistance to new stressors is impaired.

If the stress-producing event persists, the *exhaustion stage* may occur. In this third stage, the symptoms of the alarm stage reappear, only now irreversibly. As the body's energy reserves become depleted, adaptation begins to break down, leading to exhaustion, physical disorders, and, potentially, death.

Selye (1956, 1976) found that prolonged stress activates a second endocrine pathway (see Figure 12.3) that involves the hypothalamus, the pituitary gland, and the adrenal cortex. In response to a stressor, the hypothalamus signals the pituitary gland to secrete a hormone called *adrenocorticotropic hormone,* abbreviated *ACTH.* In turn, ACTH stimulates the adrenal cortex to release stress-related hormones called **corticosteroids,** the most important of which is *cortisol.*

In the short run, the corticosteroids provide several benefits, helping protect the body against the harm caused by stressors. For example, corticosteroids reduce inflammation of body tissues and enhance muscle tone in the heart and blood vessels. However, unlike the effects of catecholamines, which tend to diminish rather quickly, corticosteroids have long-lasting effects. If a stressor is prolonged, continued high levels of corticosteroids can weaken important body systems, lowering immunity and increasing susceptibility to physical symptoms and illness. There is mounting evidence that chronic stress can lead to increased vulnerability to acute and chronic diseases, including cardiovascular disease, and even to premature aging (Robles & others, 2005; Segerstrom & Miller, 2004). Chronic stress can also lead to depression and other psychological problems (Hammen, 2005).

Selye's pioneering studies are widely regarded as the cornerstone of modern stress research (Cooper & Dewe, 2004). His description of the general adaptation syndrome firmly established some of the critical biological links between stress-producing events and their potential impact on physical health. But as you'll see in the next section, the endocrine system is not the only body system affected by stress: The immune system, too, is part of the mind–body connection.

Figure 12.4 The Immune System Your immune system battles bacteria, viruses, and other foreign invaders that try to set up housekeeping in your body. The specialized white blood cells that fight infection are manufactured in the bone marrow and are stored in the thymus, spleen, and lymph nodes until needed.

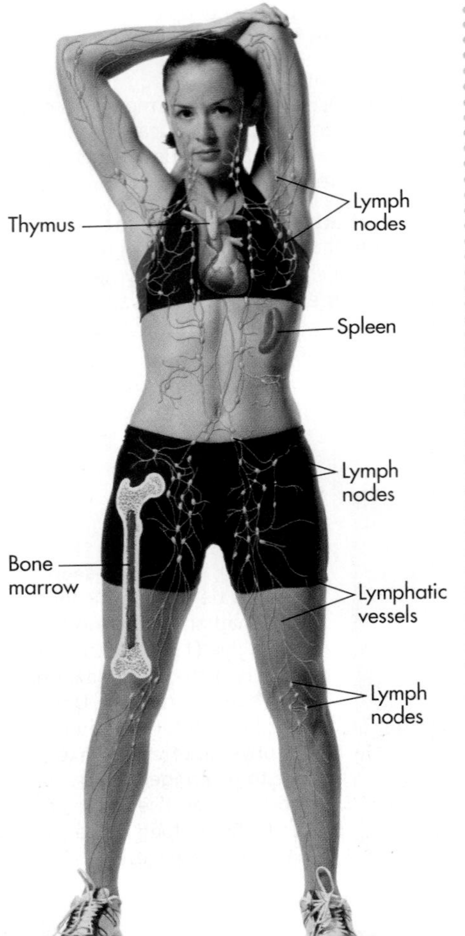

Stress and the Immune System

The **immune system** is your body's surveillance system. It detects and battles foreign invaders, such as bacteria, viruses, and tumor cells. Your immune system comprises several organs, including bone marrow, the spleen, the thymus, and lymph nodes (see Figure 12.4). The most important elements of the immune system are **lymphocytes**—the specialized white blood cells that fight bacteria, viruses, and other foreign invaders. Lymphocytes are initially manufactured in the bone marrow. From the bone marrow, they migrate to other immune system organs, such as the thymus and spleen, where they develop more fully and are stored until needed.

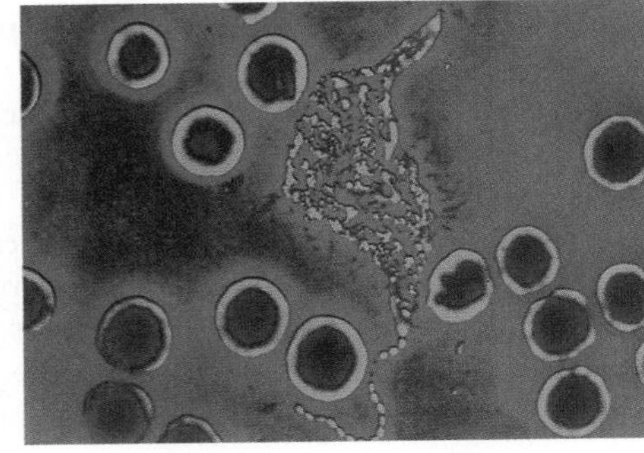

Lymphocytes in Action In this color-enhanced photo, you can see white blood cells, or lymphocytes, attacking and ingesting the beadlike chain of streptococcus bacteria, which can cause diseases such as pneumonia and scarlet fever.

Psychoneuroimmunology

Until the 1970s, the immune system was thought to be completely independent of other body systems, including the nervous and endocrine systems. Thus, most scientists believed that psychological processes could not influence the immune system response.

That notion was challenged in the mid-1970s, when psychologist **Robert Ader** teamed up with immunologist Nicholas Cohen. Ader (1993) recalls, "As a psychologist, I was not aware of the general position of immunology that there were no connections between the brain and the immune system." But Ader and Cohen showed that the immune system response in rats could be classically conditioned (see Chapter 5). After repeatedly pairing flavored water with a drug that suppressed immune system functioning, Ader and Cohen (1975) demonstrated that the flavored water *alone* suppressed the immune system.

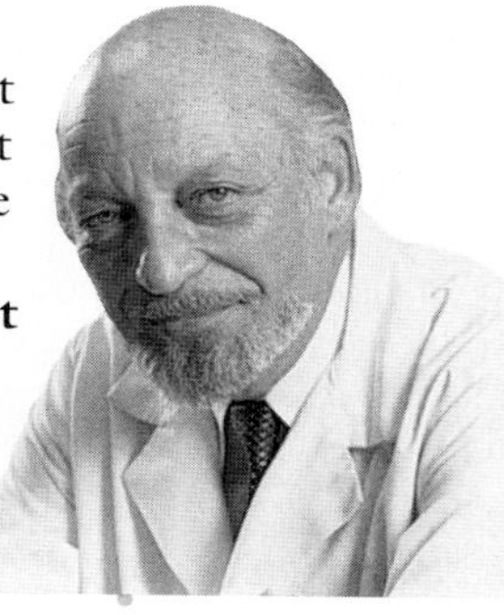

Conditioning the Immune System Psychologist Robert Ader *(left)* teamed with immunologist Nicholas Cohen *(right)* and demonstrated that immune system responses could be classically conditioned. Ader and Cohen's groundbreaking research helped lead to the new field of psychoneuroimmunology—the study of the connections among psychological processes, the nervous system, and the immune system.

Ader and Cohen's research helped establish a new interdisciplinary field called *psychoneuroimmunology*. **Psychoneuroimmunology** is the scientific study of the connections among psychological processes *(psycho-)*, the nervous system *(-neuro-)*, and the immune system *(-immunology)*.

Today, it is known that there are many interconnections among the immune system, the endocrine system, and the nervous system, including the brain (Ader, 2001; Segerstrom & Miller, 2004). First, the central nervous system and the immune system are *directly* linked via sympathetic nervous system fibers, which influence the production and functioning of lymphocytes.

Second, the surfaces of lymphocytes contain receptor sites for neurotransmitters and hormones, including catecholamines and cortisol. Thus, rather than operating independently, the activities of lymphocytes and the immune system are directly influenced by neurotransmitters, hormones, and other chemical messengers from the nervous and endocrine systems.

Third, psychoneuroimmunologists have discovered that lymphocytes themselves *produce* neurotransmitters and hormones. These neurotransmitters and hormones, in turn, influence the nervous and endocrine systems. In other words, there is ongoing interaction and communication among the nervous system, the endocrine system, and the immune system. Each system influences *and* is influenced by the other systems (Kiecolt-Glaser, 2009).

Stressors That Can Influence the Immune System

When researchers began studying how stress affects the immune system, they initially focused on extremely stressful events (see Kiecolt-Glaser & Glaser, 1993). For example, researchers looked at how the immune system was affected by such intense stressors as the reentry and splashdown of returning Skylab astronauts, being forced to stay awake for days, and fasting for a week (Kimzey, 1975; Leach & Rambaut, 1974; Palmblad & others, 1979). Each of these highly stressful events, it turned out, was associated with reduced immune system functioning.

Could immune system functioning also be affected by more common negative life events, such as the death of a spouse, divorce, or marital separation? In a word, yes. Researchers consistently found that the stress caused by the end or disruption of important interpersonal relationships impairs immune function, putting people at greater risk for health problems (Kiecolt-Glaser, 1999; Kiecolt-Glaser & Newton, 2001). And perhaps not surprisingly, chronic stressors that continue for years, such as caring for a family member with Alzheimer's disease, also diminish immune system functioning (Cass, 2006; Robles & others, 2005).

What about the ordinary stressors of life, such as the pressure of exams? Do they affect immune system functioning? Since the 1980s, psychologist **Janice Kiecolt-Glaser** and her husband, immunologist Ronald Glaser, have collected immunological and psychological data from medical students. Several times each academic year, the medical students face three-day examination periods. Kiecolt-Glaser and Glaser have consistently found that even the commonplace stress of exams can adversely affect the immune system (Glaser & Kiecolt-Glaser, 2005; Kiecolt-Glaser & Glaser, 1991, 1993).

Ron Glaser and Janice Kiecolt-Glaser Two of the leading researchers in psychoneuroimmunology are psychologist Janice Kiecolt-Glaser and her husband, immunologist Ron Glaser. Their research has shown that the effectiveness of the immune system can be lowered by many common stressors—from marital arguments to caring for sick relatives (see Glaser & Kiecolt-Glaser, 2005).

FOCUS ON NEUROSCIENCE

The Mysterious Placebo Effect

The *placebo effect* is perhaps one of the most dramatic examples of how the mind influences the body. A *placebo* is an inactive substance with no known effects, like a sugar pill or an injection of sterile water. Placebos are often used in biomedical research to help gauge the effectiveness of an actual medication or treatment. But after being given a placebo, many research participants, including those suffering from pain or diseases, experience benefits from the placebo treatment. How can this be explained?

In Chapter 2, we noted that one possible way that placebos might reduce pain is by activating the brain's own natural painkillers—the *endorphins.* (The endorphins are structurally similar to opiate painkillers, like morphine.) One reason for believing this is that a drug called *naloxone,* which blocks the brain's endorphin response, also blocks the painkilling effects of placebos (Fields & Levine, 1984). Might placebos reduce pain by activating the brain's natural opioid network?

A brain-imaging study by Swedish neuroscientist Predrag Petrovic and his colleagues (2002) tackled this question. In the study, painfully hot metal was placed on the back of each volunteer's hand. Each volunteer was then given an injection of either an actual opioid painkiller or a saline solution placebo. About 30 seconds later, positron emission tomography (PET) was used to scan the participants' brain activity.

Both the volunteers who received the painkilling drug *and* the volunteers who received the placebo treatment reported that the injection provided pain relief. In the two PET scans shown here, you can see that the genuine painkilling drug *(left)* and the placebo *(right)* activated the same brain area, called the *anterior cingulate cortex* (marked by the cross). The anterior cingulate cortex is known to contain many opioid receptors. Interestingly, the level of brain activity was directly correlated with the participants' subjective perception of pain relief. The PET scan on the right shows the brain activity of those participants who had strong placebo responses.

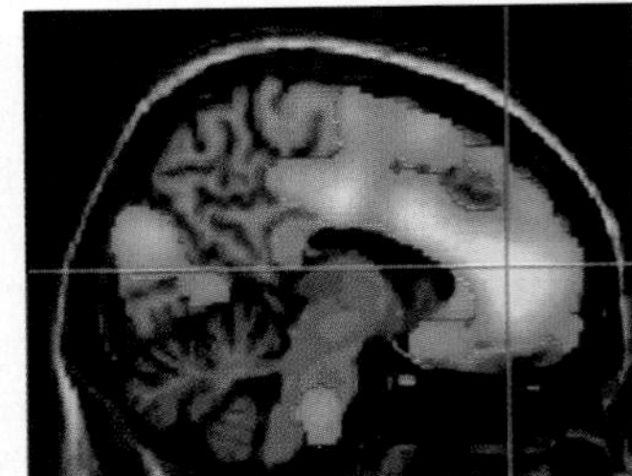

Received opiate painkiller

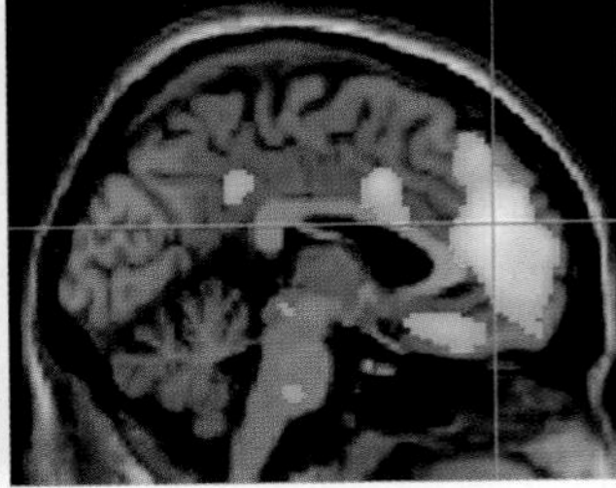

Received placebo

Many questions remain about exactly how placebos work, but the PET scan study by Petrovic and his colleagues (2002) vividly substantiates the biological reality of the placebo effect. In a recent study, Jon-Kar Zubieta and his colleagues (2005) showed that a placebo treatment activated opioid receptors in several brain regions associated with pain. Further, the greater the activation, the higher the level of pain individual volunteers were able to tolerate. As these studies show, cognitive expectations, learned associations, and emotional responses can have a profound effect on the perception of pain. Other studies have shown that placebos produce measurable effects on other types of brain processes, including those of people experiencing Parkinson's disease or major depression (Fuente-Fernández & others, 2001; Leuchter & others, 2002).

What are the practical implications of reduced immune system functioning? One consistent finding is that psychological stress can increase the length of time it takes for a wound to heal. In one study, dental students volunteered to receive two small puncture wounds on the roofs of their mouths (Marucha & others, 1998). To compare the impact of stress on wound healing, the students received the first wound when they were on summer vacation and the second wound three days before their first major exam during the fall term. The results? The wounds inflicted before the major test healed an average of 40 percent more slowly—an extra three days—than the wounds inflicted on the same volunteers during summer vacation. Other studies have shown similar findings (Glaser & Kiecolt-Glaser, 2005).

What about the relationship between stress and infection? In a series of carefully controlled studies, psychologist Sheldon Cohen and his colleagues (1991, 1993, 1998, 2006) demonstrated that people who are experiencing high levels of stress are more susceptible to infection by a cold virus than people who are not under stress (see Figure 12.5).

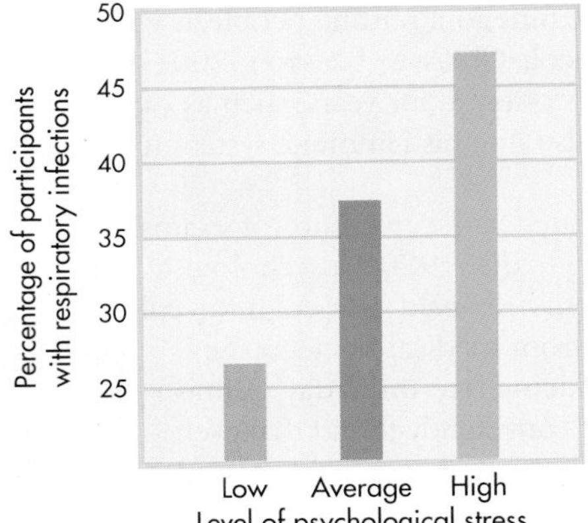

Figure 12.5 Stress and the Common Cold Are you more likely to catch a cold if you're under a great deal of stress? In a classic series of studies, Sheldon Cohen and his colleagues (1991, 1993) measured levels of psychological stress in healthy volunteers, then exposed them to a cold virus. While quarantined in apartments for a week, the participants were monitored for signs of respiratory infection. The results? As shown in the graph, the researchers found an almost perfect relationship between the level of stress and the rate of infection. The higher the volunteers' psychological stress level, the higher the rate of respiratory infection.

Subjects who experienced *chronic* stressors that lasted a month or longer were most likely to develop colds after being exposed to a cold virus. One reason may be that, as Selye showed, chronic stress triggers the secretion of corticosteroids, which influence immune system functioning (Miller & others, 2002). For example, one study showed that stress interfered with the long-term effectiveness of vaccinations against influenza in young adults (Burns & others, 2003). In the short term, stress was associated with a strong immune system response to the flu vaccine. But after five months, the stressed-out young adults were virtually unprotected against the flu. Similarly, women who perceived themselves as being under higher levels of stress had a poorer immune response to the HPV vaccine, developed to protect against cervical cancer (Fang & others, 2008).

Health psychologists have found that a wide variety of stressors are associated with diminished immune system functioning, increasing the risk of health problems and slowing recovery times (see Kiecolt-Glaser, 2009). However, while stress-related decreases in immune system functioning may heighten our susceptibility to health problems, exposure to stressors does not automatically translate into poorer health. Physical health is affected by the interaction of many factors, including heredity, nutrition, health-related habits, and access to medical care. Of course, your level of exposure to bacteria, viruses, and other sources of infection or disease will also influence your likelihood of becoming sick.

Finally, the simple fact is that some people are more vulnerable to the negative effects of stress than others (Gunnar & Quevedo, 2007). Why? As you'll see in the next section, researchers have found that a wide variety of psychological factors can influence people's reactions to stressors.

> How do stressful events and negative emotions influence the immune system, and how big are the effects? This broad question has been intensely interesting to psychoneuroimmunology (PNI) researchers over the last 3 decades, and the consequent discoveries have substantially changed the face of health psychology.
>
> JANICE KIECOLT-GLASER, 2009

Individual Factors That Influence the Response to Stress

Key Theme

- **Psychologists have identified several psychological factors that can modify an individual's response to stress and affect physical health.**

Key Questions

- **How do feelings of control, explanatory style, and negative emotions influence stress and health?**
- **What is Type A behavior, and what role does hostility play in the relationship between Type A behavior and health?**

People vary a great deal in the way they respond to a distressing event, whether it's a parking ticket or a pink slip. In part, individual differences in reacting to stressors result from how people appraise an event and their resources for coping with the event. However, psychologists and other researchers have identified several factors that influence an individual's response to stressful events. In this section, we'll take a look at some of the most important psychological and social factors that seem to affect an individual's response to stress.

Psychological Factors

It's easy to demonstrate the importance of psychological factors in the response to stressors. Sit in any airport waiting room during a busy holiday travel season and observe how differently people react to news of flight cancellations or delays. Some people take the news calmly, while others become enraged and indignant. Psychologists have confirmed what common sense suggests: Psychological processes play a key role in determining the level of stress experienced.

Uncontrollable Events Literally hundreds of thousands of passengers were stranded when more than a thousand planes were grounded in April of 2008 because of a suspected wiring problem. Long lines, chaotic crowds, and uncertainty about when they might be able to fly to their destination contributed to the passengers' frustration. Psychological research has shown that events and situations that are perceived as being beyond your control are especially likely to cause stress (Heth & Somer, 2002). Given that, how might you be able to lessen the stressful impact of such situations?

Personal Control

Who is more likely to experience more stress, a person who has some control over a stressful experience or a person who has no control? Psychological research has consistently shown that having a sense of control over a stressful situation reduces the impact of stressors and decreases feelings of anxiety and depression (Dickerson & Kemeny, 2004; Taylor, Kemeny, & others, 2000). Those who can control a stress-producing event often show no more psychological distress or physical arousal than people who are not exposed to the stressor at all.

Psychologists Judith Rodin and Ellen Langer (1977) demonstrated the importance of a sense of control in a classic series of studies with nursing home residents. One group of residents—the "high-control" group—was given the opportunity to make choices about their daily activities and to exercise control over their environment. In contrast, residents assigned to the "low-control" group had little control over their daily activities. Decisions were made for them by the nursing home staff. Eighteen months later, the high-control residents were more active, alert, sociable, and healthier than the low-control residents. And twice as many of the low-control residents had died (Langer & Rodin, 1976; Rodin & Langer, 1977).

How does a sense of control affect health? If you feel that you can control a stressor by taking steps to minimize or avoid it, you will experience less stress, both subjectively and physiologically (Heth & Somer, 2002; Thompson & Spacapan, 1991). Having a sense of personal control also works to our benefit by enhancing positive emotions, such as self-confidence and feelings of self-efficacy, autonomy, and self-reliance (Taylor, Kemeny, & others, 2000). In contrast, feeling a lack of control over events produces all the hallmarks of the stress response. Levels of catecholamines and corticosteroids increase, and the effectiveness of immune system functioning decreases (see Maier & Watkins, 2000; Rodin, 1986).

However, the perception of personal control in a stressful situation must be *realistic* to be adaptive (Heth & Somer, 2002). Studies of people with chronic diseases, like heart disease and arthritis, have shown that unrealistic perceptions of personal control contribute to stress and poor adjustment (Affleck & others, 1987a; Affleck & others, 1987b).

Further, not everyone benefits from feelings of enhanced personal control. Cross-cultural studies have shown that a sense of control is more highly valued in individualistic, Western cultures than in collectivistic, Eastern cultures. Comparing Japanese and British participants, Darryl O'Connor and Mikiko Shimizu (2002) found that a heightened sense of personal control *was* associated with a lower level of perceived stress—but *only* among the British participants.

Explanatory Style

Optimism Versus Pessimism

We all experience defeat, rejection, or failure at some point in our lives. Yet despite repeated failures, rejections, or defeats, some people persist in their efforts. In contrast, some people give up in the face of failure and setbacks—the essence of *learned helplessness*, which we discussed in Chapter 5. What distinguishes between those who persist and those who give up?

According to psychologist **Martin Seligman** (1990, 1992), how people characteristically explain their failures and defeats makes the difference. People who have an **optimistic explanatory style** tend to use *external, unstable*, and *specific* explanations for negative events. In contrast, people who have a **pessimistic explanatory style** use *internal, stable*, and *global* explanations for negative events. Pessimists are

optimistic explanatory style Accounting for negative events or situations with external, unstable, and specific explanations.

pessimistic explanatory style Accounting for negative events or situations with internal, stable, and global explanations.

also inclined to believe that no amount of personal effort will improve their situation. Not surprisingly, pessimists tend to experience more stress than optimists.

Let's look at these two explanatory styles in action. Optimistic Olive sees an attractive guy at a party and starts across the room to introduce herself and strike up a conversation. As she approaches him, the guy glances at her, then abruptly turns away. Hurt by the obvious snub, Optimistic Olive retreats to the buffet table. Munching on some fried zucchini, she mulls the matter over in her mind. At the same party, Pessimistic Pete sees an attractive female across the room and approaches her. He, too, gets a cold shoulder and retreats to the chips and clam dip. Standing at opposite ends of the buffet table, here is what each of them is thinking:

Optimistic Olive: *What's* his *problem?* (External explanation: The optimist blames other people or external circumstances.)

Pessimistic Pete: *I must have said the wrong thing. She probably saw me stick my elbow in the clam dip before I walked over.* (Internal explanation: The pessimist blames self.)

Optimistic Olive: *I'm really not looking my best tonight. I've just got to get more sleep.* (Unstable, temporary explanation)

Pessimistic Pete: *Let's face it, I'm a pretty boring guy and really not very good-looking.* (Stable, permanent explanation)

Optimistic Olive: *He looks pretty preoccupied. Maybe he's waiting for his girlfriend to arrive. Or his boyfriend! Ha!* (Specific explanation)

Pessimistic Pete: *Women never give me a second look, probably because I dress like a nerd and I never know what to say to them.* (Global, pervasive explanation)

Optimistic Olive: *Whoa! Who's that hunk over there?! Okay, Olive, turn on the charm! Here goes!* (Perseverance after a rejection)

Pessimistic Pete: *Maybe I'll just hold down this corner of the buffet table . . . or go home and soak up some TV.* (Passivity and withdrawal after a rejection)

Most people, of course, are neither as completely optimistic as Olive nor as totally pessimistic as Pete. Instead, they fall somewhere along the spectrum of optimism and pessimism, and their explanatory style may vary somewhat in different situations (Peterson & Bossio, 1993). Even so, a person's characteristic explanatory style, particularly for negative events, is relatively stable across the lifespan (Burns & Seligman, 1989).

Like personal control, explanatory style is related to health consequences (Gillham & others, 2001; Wise & Rosqvist, 2006). One study showed that explanatory style in early adulthood predicted physical health status decades later. On the basis of interviews conducted at age 25, explanatory style was evaluated for a large group of Harvard graduates. At the time of the interviews, all the young men were in excellent physical and mental health. Thirty-five years later, however, those who had an optimistic explanatory style were significantly healthier than those with a pessimistic explanatory style (Peterson & others, 1988; Peterson & Park, 2007).

Other studies have shown that a pessimistic explanatory style is associated with poorer physical health (Bennett & Elliott, 2005; Jackson & others, 2002; Peterson & Bossio, 2001). For example, first-year law school students who had an optimistic, confident, and generally positive outlook experienced fewer negative moods than did pessimistic students (Segerstrom & others, 1998). And, in terms of their immune system measures, the optimistic students had significantly higher levels of lymphocytes, T cells, and helper T cells. Explaining the positive relationship between optimists and good health, Suzanne Segerstrom and her colleagues (2003) suggest that optimists are more inclined to persevere in their efforts to overcome obstacles and challenges. Optimists are also more likely to cope effectively with stressful situations than pessimists, perhaps because they attribute their failures to their coping strategies and adjust them accordingly (Iwanaga & others, 2004).

How Do You Explain Your Setbacks and Failures? Everyone experiences setbacks, rejection, and failure at some point. The way you explain your setbacks has a significant impact on motivation and on mental and physical health. If this California car dealer blames his business failure on temporary and external factors, such as a short-lived downturn in the economy, he may be more likely to try opening a new dealership in the future.

Calvin and Hobbes by Bill Watterson

Chronic Negative Emotions

The Hazards of Being Grouchy

Some people seem to have been born with a sunny, cheerful disposition. But other people almost always seem to be unhappy campers—they frequently experience bad moods and negative emotions (Marshall & others, 1992). Are people who are prone to chronic negative emotions more likely to suffer health problems?

Howard S. Friedman and Stephanie Booth-Kewley (1987, 2003) set out to answer this question. After systematically analyzing more than 100 studies investigating the potential links between personality factors and disease, they concluded that people who are habitually anxious, depressed, angry, or hostile *are* more likely to develop a chronic disease such as arthritis or heart disease.

How might chronic negative emotions predispose people to develop disease? Not surprisingly, tense, angry, and unhappy people experience more stress than do happier people. They also report more frequent and more intense daily hassles than people who are generally in a positive mood (Bolger & Schilling, 1991; Bolger & Zuckerman, 1995). And they react much more intensely, and with far greater distress, to stressful events (Marco & Suls, 1993).

Of course, everyone occasionally experiences bad moods. Are transient negative moods also associated with health risks? One series of studies investigated the relationship between daily mood and immune system functioning (Stone & others, 1987, 1994). For three months, participants recorded their moods every day. On the days on which they experienced negative events and moods, the effectiveness of their immune systems dipped. But their immune systems improved on the days on which they experienced positive events and good moods. And in fact, other studies have found that higher levels of hope and other positive emotions are associated with a decreased likelihood of developing health problems (Richman & others, 2005).

Type A Behavior and Hostility

The concept of Type A behavior originated about 35 years ago, when two cardiologists, Meyer Friedman and Ray Rosenman, noticed that many of their patients shared certain traits. The original formulation of the **Type A behavior pattern** included a cluster of three characteristics: (1) an exaggerated sense of time urgency, often trying to do more and more in less and less time; (2) a general sense of hostility, frequently displaying anger and irritation; and (3) intense ambition and competitiveness. In contrast, people who were more relaxed and laid back were classified as displaying the *Type B behavior pattern* (Hock, 2007; Janisse & Dyck, 1988; Rosenman & Chesney, 1982).

Friedman and Rosenman (1974) interviewed and classified more than 3,000 middle-aged, healthy men as either Type A or Type B. They tracked the health of these men for eight years and found that Type A men were twice as likely to develop heart disease as Type B men. This held true even when the Type A men did not display other known risk factors for heart disease, such as smoking, high blood

Type A behavior pattern
A behavioral and emotional style characterized by a sense of time urgency, hostility, and competitiveness.

pressure, and elevated levels of cholesterol in their blood. The conclusion seemed clear: The Type A behavior pattern was a significant risk factor for heart disease.

Although early results linking the Type A behavior pattern to heart disease were impressive, studies soon began to appear in which Type A behavior did *not* reliably predict the development of heart disease (see Myrtek, 2007; Krantz & McCeney, 2002). These findings led researchers to question whether the different components of the Type A behavior pattern were equally hazardous to health. After all, many people thrive on hard work, especially when they enjoy their jobs. And, high achievers don't necessarily suffer from health problems (Robbins & others, 1991).

When researchers focused on the association between heart disease and each separate component of the Type A behavior pattern—time urgency, hostility, and achievement striving—an important distinction began to emerge (Suls & Bunde, 2005). Feeling a sense of time urgency and being competitive or achievement oriented did *not* seem to be associated with the development of heart disease. Instead, the critical component that emerged as the strongest predictor of cardiac disease was hostility (Cooper & Dewe, 2004; Miller & others, 1996). *Hostility* refers to the tendency to feel anger, annoyance, resentment, and contempt and to hold cynical and negative beliefs about human nature in general. Hostile people are also prone to believing that the disagreeable behavior of others is intentionally directed against them. Thus, hostile people tend to be suspicious, mistrustful, cynical, and pessimistic.

Hostile people are much more likely than other people to develop heart disease, even when other risk factors are taken into account (Niaura & others, 2002). In one study that covered a 25-year span, hostile men were five times as likely to develop heart disease and nearly seven times as likely to die as nonhostile men (Barefoot & others, 1983). The results of this prospective study are shown in Figure 12.6. Subsequent research has found that high hostility levels increase the likelihood of dying from *all* natural causes, including cancer (Miller & others, 1996).

How does hostility predispose people to heart disease and other health problems? First, hostile Type As tend to react more intensely to a stressor than other people do (Lyness, 1993). They experience greater increases in blood pressure, heart rate, and the production of stress-related hormones. Because of their attitudes and behavior, hostile men and women also tend to *create* more stress in their own lives (Suls & Bunde, 2005). They experience more frequent, and more severe, negative life events and daily hassles than other people (Smith, 1992).

In general, the research evidence demonstrating the role of personality factors in the development of stress-related disease is impressive. Nevertheless, it's important to keep this evidence in perspective: Personality characteristics are just *some* of the many factors involved in the overall picture of health and disease. We look at this issue in more detail in the Critical Thinking box on the next page. And, in Enhancing Well-Being with Psychology, at the end of this chapter, we describe some of the steps you can take to help you minimize the effects of stress on your health.

The Type A Behavior Pattern The original formulation of the Type A behavior pattern included hostility, ambition, and a sense of time urgency. Type A people always seem to be in a hurry. They hate wasting time and often try to do two or more things at once. However, later research showed that hostility, anger, and cynicism were far more damaging to physical health than ambition or time urgency (Suls & Bunde, 2005).

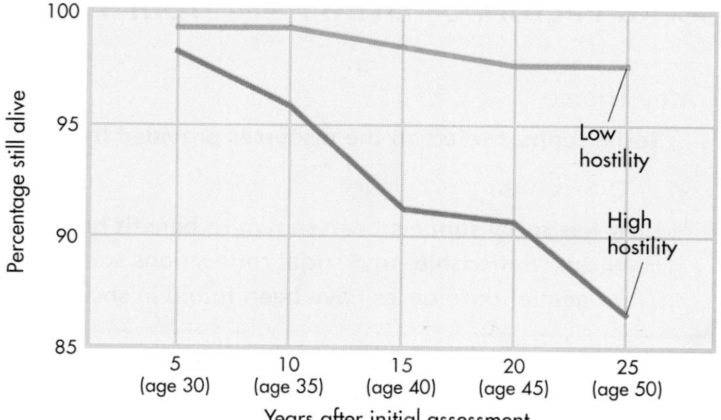

Figure 12.6 Hostility and Mortality Beginning when they were in medical school, more than 250 doctors were monitored for their health status for 25 years. In this prospective study, those who had scored high in hostility in medical school were seven times more likely to die by age 50 than were those who had scored low in hostility.

Source: Based on Barefoot & others (1983), p. 61.

CRITICAL THINKING

Do Personality Factors Cause Disease?

- You overhear a co-worker saying, "I'm not surprised he had a heart attack—the guy is a workaholic!"
- An acquaintance casually remarks, "She's been so depressed since her divorce. No wonder she got cancer."
- A tabloid headline hails, "New Scientific Findings: Use Your Mind to Cure Cancer!"

Statements like these make health psychologists, physicians, and psychoneuroimmunologists extremely uneasy. Why? Throughout this chapter, we've presented scientific evidence that emotional states can affect the functioning of the endocrine system and the immune system. Both systems play a significant role in the development of various physical disorders. We've also shown that personality factors, such as hostility and pessimism, are associated with an increased likelihood of developing poor health. But saying that "emotions affect the immune system" is a far cry from making such claims as "a positive attitude can cure cancer."

Psychologists and other scientists are cautious in the statements they make about the connections between personality and health for several reasons. First, many studies investigating the role of psychological factors in disease are *correlational.* That is, researchers have statistical evidence that two factors happen together so often that the presence of one factor reliably predicts the occurrence of the other. However, correlation does not necessarily indicate causality—it indicates only that two factors occur together. It's completely possible that some third, unidentified factor may have caused the other two factors to occur.

Second, personality factors might indirectly lead to disease via poor health habits. Low control, pessimism, chronic negative emotions, and hostility are each associated with poor health habits (Anton & Miller, 2005; Herbert & Cohen, 1993; Peterson, 2000). In turn, poor health habits are associated with higher rates of illness. That's why psychologists who study the role of personality factors in disease are typically careful to measure and consider the possible influence of the participants' health practices.

Third, it may be that the disease influences a person's emotions, rather than the other way around. After being diagnosed with advanced cancer or heart disease, most people would probably find it difficult to feel cheerful, optimistic, or in control of their lives.

"What do you mean, I have an ulcer? I give ulcers, I don't get them!"

One way researchers try to disentangle the relationship between personality and health is to conduct carefully controlled prospective studies. A *prospective study* starts by assessing an initially healthy group of participants on variables thought to be risk factors, such as certain personality traits. Then the researchers track the health, personal habits, health habits, and other important dimensions of the participants' lives over a period of months, years, or decades. In analyzing the results, researchers can determine the extent to which each risk factor contributed to the health or illness of the participants. Thus, prospective studies provide more compelling evidence than do correlational studies that are based on people who are already in poor health.

CRITICAL THINKING QUESTIONS

- Given that health professionals frequently advise people to change their health-related behaviors to improve physical health, should they also advise people to change their psychological attitudes, traits, and emotions? Why or why not?
- What are the advantages and disadvantages of correlational studies? Prospective studies?

Social Factors: A Little Help from Your Friends

Key Theme

- **Social support refers to the resources provided by other people.**

Key Questions

- **How has social support been shown to benefit health?**
- **How can relationships and social connections sometimes increase stress?**
- **What gender differences have been found in social support and its effects?**

Psychologists have become increasingly aware of the importance that close relationships play in our ability to deal with stressors and, ultimately, in our physical health. Consider the following research evidence:

- After monitoring the health of 2,800 people for seven years, researchers found that people who had no one to talk to about their problems were three times as likely to die after being hospitalized for a heart attack than were those who had at least one person to provide such support (Berkman & others, 1992).
- The health of nearly 7,000 adults was tracked for nine years. Those who had few social connections were twice as likely to die from all causes than were those who had numerous social contacts, even when risk factors such as cigarette smoking, obesity, and elevated cholesterol levels were taken into account (Berkman, 1995; Berkman & Syme, 1979).
- In a study begun in the 1950s, college students rated their parents' level of love and caring. More than 40 years later, 87 percent of those who had rated their parents as being "low" in love and caring had been diagnosed with a serious physical disease. In contrast, only 25 percent of those who had rated their parents as being "high" in love and caring had been diagnosed with a serious physical disease (Russek & Schwartz, 1997; Shaw & others, 2004).

"A Sense of Being Loved by Our Community . . ." Author Philip Simmons had been an English professor for nine years when he learned that he had Lou Gehrig's disease, a fatal neuromuscular condition that usually kills its victims in two to five years. But Simmons beat those odds and lived an incredibly productive life for almost 10 years, in part by learning to ask for—and accept—help from his friends. For several years, some 30 friends and neighbors helped the Simmons family with the routine chores of daily life, such as fixing dinner and chauffeuring kids. Said Philip's wife, Kathryn, "It gives us a sense of being loved by our community."

These are just a few of the hundreds of studies exploring how interpersonal relationships influence our health and ability to tolerate stress (Cohen, 2004; Uchino, 2009). To investigate the role played by personal relationships in stress and health, psychologists measure the level of **social support**—the resources provided by other people in times of need (Hobfoll & Stephens, 1990). Repeatedly, researchers have found that socially isolated people have poorer health and higher death rates than people who have many social contacts or relationships (Southwick & others, 2005; Uchino, 2004, 2009). In fact, social isolation seems to be just as potent a health risk as smoking, high blood cholesterol, obesity, or physical inactivity (Cohen & others, 2000).

Beyond social isolation, researchers have found that the more *diverse* your social network, the more pronounced the health benefits (Cohen & Janicki-Deverts, 2009). That is, prospective studies have shown that the people who live longest are those who have more *different types* of relationships—such as being married; having close relationships with family members, friends, and neighbors; and belonging to social, political, or religious groups (Berkman & Glass, 2000). In fact, researchers have found that people who live in such diverse social networks have:

- greater resistance to upper respiratory infections (Cohen & others, 1997)
- lower incidence of stroke and cardiovascular disease among women in a high-risk group (Rutledge & others, 2004, 2008)
- decreased risk for the recurrence of cancer (Helgeson & others, 1998)
- lower incidence of dementia and cognitive loss in old age (Fratiglioni & others, 2004)

How Social Support Benefits Health

Social support may benefit our health and improve our ability to cope with stressors in several ways (Cohen & others, 2000). First, the social support of friends and relatives can modify our appraisal of a stressor's significance, including the degree to which we perceive it as threatening or harmful. Simply knowing that support and assistance are readily available may make the situation seem less threatening.

Second, the presence of supportive others seems to decrease the intensity of physical reactions to a stressor. Thus, when faced with a painful medical procedure or some other stressful situation, many people find the presence of a supportive friend to be calming.

Third, social support can influence our health by making us less likely to experience negative emotions (Cohen, 2004). Given the well-established link between chronic negative emotions and poor health, a strong social support network can promote positive moods and emotions, enhance self-esteem, and increase feelings of

social support
The resources provided by other people in times of need.

Pets as a Source of Social Support Pets can provide both companionship and social support, especially for people with limited social contacts. Can the social support of pets buffer the negative effects of stress? One study showed that elderly people with pets had fewer doctor visits and reported feeling less stress than elderly people without pets (Siegel, 1990). Other studies have found that the presence of a pet cat or dog can lower blood pressure and lessen the cardiovascular response to acute stress (Allen & others, 2002).

personal control. In contrast, loneliness and depression are unpleasant emotional states that increase levels of stress hormones and adversely affect immune system functioning (Irwin & Miller, 2007).

The flip side of the coin is that relationships with others can also be a significant *source* of stress (McKenry & Price, 2005; Swickert & others, 2002). In fact, negative interactions with other people are often more effective at creating psychological distress than positive interactions are at improving well-being (Lepore, 1993; Rook, 1992). And, although married people tend to be healthier than unmarried people overall, marital conflict has been shown to have adverse effects on physical health, especially for women (Kiecolt-Glaser & Newton, 2001; Liu & Chen, 2006).

Clearly, the quality of interpersonal relationships is an important determinant of whether those relationships help or hinder our ability to cope with stressful events. When other people are perceived as being judgmental, their presence may increase the individual's physical reaction to a stressor. In two clever studies, psychologist Karen Allen and her colleagues (1991, 2002) demonstrated that the presence of a favorite dog or cat was more effective than the presence of a spouse or friend in lowering reactivity to a stressor. Why? Perhaps because the pet was perceived as being nonjudgmental, nonevaluative, and unconditionally supportive. Unfortunately, the same is not always true of friends, family members, and spouses.

Stress may also increase when well-meaning friends or family members offer unwanted or inappropriate social support. The In Focus box offers some suggestions on how to provide helpful social support and avoid inappropriate support behaviors.

Gender Differences in the Effects of Social Support

Women may be particularly vulnerable to some of the problematic aspects of social support, for a couple of reasons. First, women are more likely than men to serve as providers of support, which can be a very stressful role (Ekwall & Hallberg, 2007; Hobfoll & Vaux, 1993). Consider the differences found in one study. When middle-aged male patients were discharged from the hospital after a heart attack, they went home and their wives took care of them. But when middle-aged female heart attack patients were discharged from the hospital, they went home and fell back into the routine of caring for their husbands (Coyne & others, 1990).

Second, women may be more likely to suffer from the *stress contagion effect*, becoming upset about negative life events that happen to other people whom they care about (Belle, 1991). Since women tend to have larger and more intimate social networks than men, they have more opportunities to become distressed by what happens to people who are close to them. And women are more likely than men to be upset about negative events that happen to their relatives and friends.

For example, when Judy was unable to reach her daughter Katie by phone on the morning of September 11, she quickly called two family members for advice and comfort: her mother, Fern, in Chicago, and her sister, your author Sandy, in Tulsa.

The Health Benefits of Companionship This married couple in their 70s are enjoying an afternoon outdoors. Numerous research studies have shown that married people and couples live longer than people who are single, divorced, or widowed (Burman & Margolin, 1992). Because men tend to have fewer close friends than women, they often depend on their spouse or partner for social support.

IN FOCUS

Providing Effective Social Support

A close friend turns to you for help in a time of crisis or personal tragedy. What should you do or say? As we've noted in this chapter, appropriate social support can help people weather crises and can significantly reduce the amount of distress that they feel. Inappropriate support, in contrast, may only make matters worse (Uchino, 2009).

Researchers generally agree that there are three broad categories of social support: emotional, tangible, and informational. Each provides different beneficial functions (Peirce & others, 1996; Taylor & Aspinwall, 1993).

Emotional support includes expressions of concern, empathy, and positive regard. *Tangible support* involves direct assistance, such as providing transportation, lending money, or helping with meals, child care, or household tasks. When people offer helpful suggestions, advice, or possible resources, they are providing *informational support*.

It's possible that all three kinds of social support might be provided by the same person, such as a relative, spouse, or very close friend. More commonly, we turn to different people for different kinds of support (Masters & others, 2007).

Research by psychologist Stevan Hobfoll and his colleagues (1992) has identified several support behaviors that are typically perceived as helpful by people under stress. In a nutshell, you're most likely to be perceived as helpful if you:

- are a good listener and show concern and interest
- ask questions that encourage the person under stress to express his or her feelings and emotions
- express understanding about why the person is upset
- express affection for the person, whether with a warm hug or simply a pat on the arm
- are willing to invest time and attention in helping
- can help the person with practical tasks, such as housework, transportation, or responsibilities at work or school

Just as important is knowing what *not* to do or say. Here are several behaviors that, however well intentioned, are often perceived as unhelpful:

- Giving advice that the person under stress has not requested

- Telling the person, "I know exactly how you feel." It's a mistake to think that you have experienced distress identical to what the other person is experiencing
- Talking about yourself or your own problems
- Minimizing the importance of the person's problem by saying things like, "Hey, don't make such a big deal out of it," "It could be a lot worse," or "Don't worry, everything will turn out okay"
- Joking or acting overly cheerful
- Offering your philosophical or religious interpretation of the stressful event by saying things like, "It's just fate," "It's God's will," or "It's your karma"

Finally, remember that although social support is helpful, it is *not* a substitute for counseling or psychotherapy. If a friend seems overwhelmed by problems or emotions, or is having serious difficulty handling the demands of everyday life, you should encourage him or her to seek professional help. Most college campuses have a counseling center or a health clinic that can provide referrals to qualified mental health workers. Sliding fee schedules, based on ability to pay, are usually available. Thus, you can assure the person that cost need not be an obstacle to getting help—or an additional source of stress!

Of course, there was nothing Sandy or Fern could do to help Katie escape the chaos of lower Manhattan. Like Judy, Sandy and Fern became increasingly upset and worried as they watched the events of the day unfold from hundreds of miles away with no news of Katie's fate. When stressful events strike, women tend to reach out to one another for support and comfort (Taylor & others, 2000b).

In contrast, men are more likely to be distressed only by negative events that happen to their immediate family—their wives and children (Wethington & others, 1987). Men tend to rely heavily on a close relationship with their spouse, placing less importance on relationships with other people. Women, in contrast, are more likely to list close friends along with their spouse as confidants (Ackerman & others, 2007; Shumaker & Hill, 1991). Because men tend to have a much smaller network of intimate others, they may be particularly vulnerable to social isolation, especially if their spouse dies. Thus, it's not surprising that the health benefits of being married are more pronounced for men than for women (Kiecolt-Glaser & Newton, 2001).

Coping

How People Deal with Stress

Key Theme

- **Coping refers to the ways in which we try to change circumstances, or our interpretation of circumstances, to make them less threatening.**

Key Questions

- **What are the two basic forms of coping, and when is each form typically used?**
- **What are some of the most common coping strategies?**
- **How does culture affect coping style?**

Think about some of the stressful periods that have occurred in your life. What kinds of strategies did you use to deal with those distressing events? Which strategies seemed to work best? Did any of the strategies end up working against your ability to reduce the stressor? If you had to deal with the same events again today, would you do anything differently?

Katie survived a terrorist attack on her neighborhood by being resourceful and, as she would be the first to admit, through sheer good luck. But how did she survive the months following? Along with having a good support system—friends, relatives, and a dance teacher who could offer her emotional and tangible help—she used a number of different strategies to cope with the stress that she continued to experience.

Ways of Coping Like the stress response itself, adaptive coping is a dynamic and complex process. Imagine that you had packed up all of your possessions and then found out that the moving van was delayed and wouldn't arrive for another 48 hours. What types of coping strategies might prove most helpful?

Two Ways of Coping

Problem-Focused and Emotion-Focused Coping

The strategies that you use to deal with distressing events are examples of coping. **Coping** refers to the ways in which we try to change circumstances, or our interpretation of circumstances, to make them more favorable and less threatening (Folkman & Lazarus, 1991; Folkman & Moskowitz, 2007; Lazarus, 1999, 2000).

Coping tends to be a dynamic, ongoing process. We may switch our coping strategies as we appraise the changing demands of a stressful situation and our available resources at any given moment. We also evaluate whether our efforts have made a stressful situation better or worse and adjust our coping strategies accordingly (see Cheng, 2003).

When coping is effective, we adapt to the situation and stress is reduced. Unfortunately, coping efforts do not always help us adapt. Maladaptive coping can involve thoughts and behaviors that intensify or prolong distress or that produce self-defeating outcomes (Bolger & Zuckerman, 1995). The rejected lover who continually dwells on her former companion, passing up opportunities to form new relationships and letting her studies slide, is demonstrating maladaptive coping.

Adaptive coping responses serve many functions (Folkman & Moskowitz, 2007; Lazarus, 2000). Most important, adaptive coping involves realistically evaluating the situation and determining what can be done to minimize the impact of the stressor. But adaptive coping also involves dealing with the emotional aspects of the situation. In other words, adaptive coping often includes developing emotional tolerance for negative life events, maintaining self-esteem, and keeping emotions in balance. Finally, adaptive coping efforts are directed toward preserving important relationships during stressful experiences.

Problem-Focused Coping People rely on different coping strategies at different times in dealing with the same stressor. After dealing with the emotional impact of losing their homes to a hurricane, these Florida neighbors engaged in problem-focused coping as they help clear the site before rebuilding.

Psychologists Richard Lazarus and Susan Folkman (1984) described two basic types of coping, each of which serves a different purpose. **Problem-focused coping** is aimed at managing or changing a threatening or harmful stressor. Problem-focused coping strategies tend to be most effective when you can exercise some control over the stressful situation or circumstances (Park & others, 2004). But if you think that nothing can be done to alter a situation, you tend to rely on **emotion-focused coping:** You direct your efforts toward relieving or regulating the emotional impact of the stressful situation. Although emotion-focused coping doesn't change the problem, it can help you feel better about the situation. People are flexible in the coping styles they adopt, often relying on different coping strategies for different stressors (Park & others, 2004).

Although it's virtually inevitable that you'll encounter stressful circumstances, there are coping strategies that can help you minimize their health effects. We suggest several techniques in the Enhancing Well-Being with Psychology section at the end of the chapter.

Problem-Focused Coping Strategies

Changing the Stressor

Problem-focused coping strategies represent actions that have the goal of changing or eliminating the stressor. When people use aggressive or risky efforts to change the situation, they are engaging in *confrontive coping*. Ideally, confrontive coping is direct and assertive without being hostile. When it is hostile or aggressive, confrontive coping may well generate negative emotions in the people being confronted, damaging future relations with them (Folkman & Lazarus, 1991).

In contrast, *planful problem solving* involves efforts to rationally analyze the situation, identify potential solutions, and then implement them. In effect, you take the attitude that the stressor represents a problem to be solved. Once you assume that mental stance, you follow the basic steps of problem solving (see Chapter 7).

Emotion-Focused Coping Strategies

Changing Your Reaction to the Stressor

When the stressor is one over which we can exert little or no control, we often focus on dimensions of the situation that we *can* control—the emotional impact of the stressor on us (Thompson & others, 1994). All the different forms of emotion-focused coping share the goal of reducing or regulating the emotional impact of a stressor.

coping
Behavioral and cognitive responses used to deal with stressors; involves our efforts to change circumstances, or our interpretation of circumstances, to make them more favorable and less threatening.

problem-focused coping
Coping efforts primarily aimed at directly changing or managing a threatening or harmful stressor.

emotion-focused coping
Coping efforts primarily aimed at relieving or regulating the emotional impact of a stressful situation.

When you shift your attention away from the stressor and toward other activities, you're engaging in the emotion-focused coping strategy called *escape–avoidance*. As the name implies, the basic goal is to escape or avoid the stressor and neutralize distressing emotions. Excessive sleeping and the use of drugs and alcohol are maladaptive forms of escape–avoidance, as are escaping into fantasy or wishful thinking. More constructive escape–avoidance strategies include exercising or immersing yourself in your studies, hobbies, or work.

For example, Katie found that returning to her daily dance class was the most helpful thing she did to cope with her feelings. During those two hours, Katie was able to let go of her memories of death and destruction. Doing what she loved, surrounded by people she loved, Katie began to feel whole again.

Because you are focusing your attention on something other than the stressor, escape–avoidance tactics provide emotional relief in the short run. Thus, avoidance strategies can be helpful when you are facing a stressor that is brief and has limited consequences. But avoidance strategies such as wishful thinking tend to be counterproductive when the stressor is a severe or long-lasting one, like a serious or chronic disease (Stanton & Snider, 1993; Vollman & others, 2007). Escape–avoidance strategies are also associated with increased psychological distress in facing other types of stressors, such as adjusting to college (Aspinwall & Taylor, 1992).

In the long run, escape–avoidance tactics are associated with poor adjustment and symptoms of depression and anxiety (Stanton & Snider, 1993). That's not surprising if you think about it. After all, the problem *is* still there. And if the problem is one that needs to be dealt with promptly, such as a pressing medical concern, the delays caused by escape–avoidance strategies can make the stressful situation worse.

Seeking social support is the coping strategy that involves turning to friends, relatives, or other people for emotional, tangible, or informational support. As we discussed earlier in the chapter, having a strong network of social support can help buffer the impact of stressors (Brissette & others, 2002; Finch & Vega, 2003). Confiding in a trusted friend gives you an opportunity to vent your emotions and better understand the stressful situation.

When you acknowledge the stressor but attempt to minimize or eliminate its emotional impact, you're engaging in the coping strategy called *distancing*. Downplaying or joking about the stressful situation is one form of distancing (Abel, 2002). Sometimes people emotionally distance themselves from a stressor by discussing it in a detached, depersonalized, or intellectual way. Among Katie's circle of young friends, distancing was common. They joked about the soot, the dust, and the National Guard troops guarding the subway stations.

In certain high-stress occupations, distancing can help workers cope with painful human problems. Clinical psychologists, social workers, rescue workers, police officers, and medical personnel often use distancing to some degree to help them deal with distressing situations without falling apart emotionally themselves.

Positive Reappraisal: Transcending Tragedy Czech model Petra Nemcova was vacationing with her fiancé, photographer Simon Atlee, at a resort in Thailand when the worst tsunami in modern history struck. Without warning, a giant wave crashed into their bungalow, crushing everything in its path. Swept up in the powerful currents of debris and destruction, Nemcova lost sight of her fiancé in the swirling waters but managed to grab hold of a partly submerged palm tree. Suffering from a shattered pelvis and internal injuries, Nemcova clung to the tree for eight hours before being rescued. Three months later, Atlee's body was found.

After she recovered, Nemcova founded Happy Hearts Fund, an international foundation dedicated to improving the lives of children in areas that have been damaged by natural or other disasters. Happy Hearts has raised tens of millions of dollars and founded schools and clinics in areas hit by natural disasters around the world, including Thailand, Sri Lanka, Pakistan, Cambodia, and Vietnam. Nemcova is shown here at the opening of a kindergarten in an Indonesian village that was devastated by a powerful earthquake.

In contrast to distancing, *denial* is a refusal to acknowledge that the problem even exists. Like escape–avoidance strategies, denial can compound problems in situations that require immediate attention.

Perhaps the most constructive emotion-focused coping strategy is *positive reappraisal*. When we use positive reappraisal, we try not only to minimize the negative emotional aspects of the situation but also to create positive meaning by focusing on personal growth (Folkman, 2009). Even in the midst of deeply disturbing situations, positive reappraisal can help people experience positive emotions and minimize the potential for negative aftereffects (Dasgupta & Sanyal, 2007; Updegraff & others, 2008). For example, Katie noted that in the days following the collapse of the two towers, "It was really beautiful. Everyone was pulling together, New Yorkers were helping each other."

IN FOCUS

Gender Differences in Responding to Stress: "Tend-and-Befriend" or "Fight-or-Flight"?

Physiologically, men and women show the same hormonal and sympathetic nervous system activation that Walter Cannon described as the "fight-or-flight" response to stress (1932). Yet *behaviorally,* the two sexes react very differently.

To illustrate, consider this finding: When men come home after a stressful day at work, they tend to withdraw from their families, wanting to be left alone—an example of the "flight" response (Schulz & others, 2004). After a stressful workday, however, women tend to seek out interactions with their marital partners (Schulz & others, 2004). And, they tend to be more nurturing toward their children, rather than less (Repetti, 1989; Repetti & Wood, 1997).

As we have noted in this chapter, women tend to be much more involved in their social networks than men. And, as compared to men, women are much more likely to seek out and use social support when they are under stress (Glynn & others, 1999). Throughout their lives, women tend to mobilize social support—especially from other women—in times of stress (Taylor & others, 2000b). We saw this pattern in our story about Katie. Just as Katie called her mother, Judy, when her neighborhood came under attack, Judy called her sister, Sandy, and her *own* mother when she feared that her daughter's life was in danger.

Why the gender difference in coping with stress? Health psychologists Shelley Taylor, Laura Klein, and their colleagues (2000, 2002) believe that evolutionary theory offers some insight. According to the evolutionary perspective, the most adaptive response in virtually any situation is one that promotes the survival of both the individual *and* the individual's offspring. Given that premise, neither fighting nor fleeing is likely to have been an adaptive response for females, especially females who were pregnant, nursing, or caring for their offspring. According to Taylor and her colleagues (2000), "Stress responses that enabled the female to simultaneously protect herself and her offspring are likely to have resulted in more surviving offspring." Rather than fighting or fleeing, they argue, women developed a *tend-and-befriend* behavioral response to stress.

What is the "tend-and-befriend" pattern of responding? *Tending* refers to "quieting and caring for offspring and blending into the environment," Taylor and her colleagues (2000) write. That is, rather than confronting or running from the threat, females take cover and protect their young. Evidence supporting this behavior pattern includes studies of nonhuman animals showing that many female animals adopt a "tending" strategy when faced by a threat (Francis & others, 1999; Liu & others, 1997).

The "befriending" side of the equation relates to women's tendency to seek social support during stressful situations. Taylor and her colleagues (2000) describe *befriending* as "the creation of networks of associations that provide resources and protection for the female and her offspring under conditions of stress."

However, both males and females show the same neuroendocrine responses to an acute stressor—the sympathetic nervous system activates, stress hormones pour into the bloodstream, and, as those hormones reach different organs, the body kicks into high gear. So why do women "tend and befriend" rather than "fight or flee," as men do? Taylor points to the effects of another hormone, *oxytocin.* Higher in females than in males, oxytocin is associated with maternal behaviors in all female mammals, including humans. Oxytocin also tends to have a calming effect on both males and females (see Southwick & others, 2005).

Taylor speculates that oxytocin might simultaneously help calm stressed females and promote affiliative behavior. Supporting this speculation is research showing that oxytocin increases affiliative behaviors and reduces stress in many mammals (Carter & DeVries, 1999; Light & others, 2000). For example, one study found that healthy men who received a dose of oxytocin before being subjected to a stressful procedure were less anxious and had lower cortisol levels than men who received a placebo (Heinrichs & others, 2003).

In humans, oxytocin is highest in nursing mothers. Pleasant physical contact, such as hugging, cuddling, and touching, stimulates the release of oxytocin. In combination, all of these oxytocin-related changes seem to help turn down the physiological intensity of the fight-or-flight response for women. And perhaps, Taylor and her colleagues suggest, they also promote the tend-and-befriend response.

"I'm somewhere between O. and K."

Similarly, a study by Barbara Fredrickson and her colleagues (2003) found that some college students "looked for the silver lining" after the September 11 terrorist attacks, reaching out to others and expressing gratitude for the safety of their loved ones. Those who found a positive meaning in the aftermath of the attacks were least likely to develop depressive symptoms and other problems in the follow-

Dancing in Central Park Katie will never forget the events of that September day or the weeks that followed. She still struggles with the occasional nightmare, and certain smells and sounds—smoke, sirens—can trigger feelings of panic and dread. But Katie persevered. After graduating from a college dance conservatory, Katie moved back to New York City, where she is a dancer, choreographer, and producer.

ing weeks. As Fredrickson and her colleagues (2003) observed, "Amidst the emotional turmoil generated by the September 11 terrorist attacks, subtle and fleeting experiences of gratitude, interest, love, and other positive emotions appeared to hold depressive symptoms at bay and fuel postcrisis growth."

Katie, too, was able to creatively transform the meaning of her experience. As part of her application to a college dance conservatory, she choreographed and performed an original dance expressing sadness, fear, hope, and renewal—all the emotions that she experienced on that terrible day. Her ability to express her feelings artistically has helped her come to terms with her memories.

However, it's important to note that there is no single "best" coping strategy. In general, the most effective coping is flexible, meaning that we fine-tune our coping strategies to meet the demands of a particular stressor (Cheng, 2003; Park & others, 2004). And, people often use multiple coping strategies, combining problem-focused and emotion-focused forms of coping. In the initial stages of a stressful experience, we may rely on emotion-focused strategies to help us step back emotionally from a problem. Once we've regained our equilibrium, we may use problem-focused coping strategies to identify potential solutions.

Culture and Coping Strategies

Culture seems to play an important role in the choice of coping strategies. Americans and other members of individualistic cultures tend to emphasize personal autonomy and personal responsibility in dealing with problems. Thus, they are *less* likely to seek social support in stressful situations than are members of collectivistic cultures, such as Asian cultures (Marsella & Dash-Scheuer, 1988). Members of collectivistic cultures tend to be more oriented toward their social group, family, or community and toward seeking help with their problems.

Individualists also tend to emphasize the importance and value of exerting control over their circumstances, especially circumstances that are threatening or stressful (O'Connor & Shimizu, 2002). Thus, they favor problem-focused strategies, such as confrontive coping and planful problem solving. These strategies involve directly changing the situation to achieve a better fit with their wishes or goals (Wong & Wong, 2006).

In collectivistic cultures, however, a greater emphasis is placed on controlling your personal reactions to a stressful situation rather than trying to control the situation itself. This emotion-focused coping style emphasizes gaining control over inner feelings by accepting and accommodating yourself to existing realities (O'Connor & Shimizu, 2002).

For example, the Japanese emphasize accepting difficult situations with maturity, serenity, and flexibility (Gross, 2007). Common sayings in Japan are "The true tolerance is to tolerate the intolerable" and "Flexibility can control rigidity." Along with controlling inner feelings, many Asian cultures also stress the goal of controlling the outward expression of emotions, however distressing the situation (Johnson & others, 1995).

These cultural differences in coping underscore the point that there is no formula for effective coping in all situations. That we use multiple coping strategies throughout almost every stressful situation reflects our efforts to identify what will work best at a given moment in time. To the extent that any coping strategy helps us identify realistic alternatives, manage our emotions, and maintain important relationships, it is adaptive and effective.

Culture and Coping This young boy lost his legs in a devastating earthquake that killed almost 100,000 people in the Sichuan province of southwest China. With his father's encouragement and a new set of artificial legs, he is learning to walk again. Do coping strategies differ across cultures? According to some researchers, people in China, Japan, and other Asian cultures are more likely to rely on emotional coping strategies than people in individualistic cultures (Heppner, 2008; Yeh & others, 2006). Coping strategies that are particularly valued in collectivistic cultures include emotional self-control, gracefully accepting one's fate and making the best of a bad situation, and maintaining harmonious relationships with family members (Heppner, 2008; Yeh & others, 2006).

>> Closing Thoughts

From national tragedies and major life events to the minor hassles and annoyances of daily life, stressors come in all sizes and shapes. Any way you look at it, stress is an unavoidable part of life. Stress that is prolonged or intense can adversely affect both our physical and psychological well-being. Fortunately, most of the time people deal effectively with the stresses in their lives. As Katie's story demonstrates, the effects of even the most intense stressors can be minimized if we cope with them effectively.

Ultimately, the level of stress that we experience is due to a complex interaction of psychological, biological, and social factors. We hope that reading this chapter has given you a better understanding of how stress affects your life and how you can reduce its impact on your physical and psychological well-being. In Enhancing Well-Being with Psychology, we'll suggest some concrete steps you can take to minimize the harmful impact of stress in *your* life.

ENHANCING WELL-BEING WITH PSYCHOLOGY

Minimizing the Effects of Stress

Sometimes stressful situations persist despite our best efforts to resolve them. Knowing that chronic stress can jeopardize your health, what can you do to minimize the adverse impact of stress on your physical well-being? Here are four practical suggestions.

Suggestion 1: Avoid or Minimize the Use of Stimulants

In dealing with stressful situations, people often turn to stimulants to help keep them going, such as coffee or caffeinated energy drinks. If you know someone who smokes, you've probably observed that most smokers react to stress by increasing their smoking (Ng & Jeffery, 2003; Todd, 2004). The problem is that common stimulants like caffeine and nicotine actually work *against* you in coping with stress. They increase the physiological effects of stress by raising heart rate and blood pressure. In effect, users of stimulant drugs are already primed to respond with greater reactivity, exaggerating the physiological consequences of stress (Lovallo & others, 1996; Smith & others, 2001).

The best advice? Avoid stimulant drugs altogether. If that's not possible, make a conscious effort to monitor your use of stimulants, especially when you're under stress. You'll find it easier to deal with stressors when your nervous system is not already in high gear because of caffeine, nicotine, or other stimulants. Minimizing your use of stimulants will also make it easier for you to implement the next suggestion.

Suggestion 2: Exercise Regularly

Numerous studies all point to the same conclusion: Regular exercise, particularly aerobic exercise like walking, swimming, or running, is one of the best ways to reduce the impact of stress (Bass & others, 2002; Ensel & Lin, 2004; Wijndaele & others, 2007). The key word here is *regular.* Try walking briskly for 20 minutes four or five times a week. It will improve your physical health and help you cope with stress. In fact, just about any kind of physical exercise helps buffer the negative effects of stress. (Rapidly right-clicking your computer mouse doesn't count.) Compared to sofa slugs, physically fit people are less physiologically reactive to stressors and produce lower levels of stress hormones (Rejeski & others, 1991, 1992). Psychologically, regular exercise reduces anxiety and depressed feelings and increases self-confidence and self-esteem (Berk, 2007).

Suggestion 3: Get Enough Sleep

With the ongoing push to get more and more done, people often stretch their days by short-changing themselves on sleep. But sleep deprivation just adds to your feelings of stress.

"Without sufficient sleep it is more difficult to concentrate, make careful decisions, and follow instructions," explains researcher Mark Rosekind (2003). "You are more likely to make mistakes or errors, and are more prone to being impatient and lethargic. And, your attention, memory and reaction time are all adversely affected."

The stress–sleep connection also has the potential to become a vicious cycle. School, work, or family-related pressures contribute to reduced or disturbed sleep, leaving you less than adequately rested and making efforts to deal with the situation all the more taxing and distressful (Akerstedt & others, 2002). And inadequate sleep, even for just a few nights, takes a physical toll on the body, leaving us more prone to health problems (Colten & Altevogt, 2006; National Sleep Foundation, 2004).

Fortunately, research indicates that the opposite is also true: Getting adequate sleep promotes resistance and helps buffer the effects of stress (Hamilton & others, 2007; Mohr & others, 2003). For some suggestions to help promote a good night's sleep, see the Enhancing Well-Being with Psychology section at the end of Chapter 4.

Suggestion 4: Practice a Relaxation Technique

You can significantly reduce stress-related symptoms by regularly using any one of a variety of relaxation techniques (Benson, 1993). *Meditation* is one effective stress reduction strategy. As discussed in Chapter 4 (see pp. 163–164), there are many different meditation techniques, but they all involve focusing mental attention, heightening awareness, and quieting internal chatter. Most meditation techniques are practiced while sitting quietly, but others involve movement, such as yoga and walking meditation. Many studies have demonstrated the physical and psychological benefits of meditation (Siegel, 2007; Waelde & others, 2004; Walton & others, 2002). More specifically, meditation has been shown to reduce both the psychological and physiological effects of stress (Dusek & others, 2008; Ludwig & Kabat-Zinn, 2009).

One form of meditation that has been receiving a great deal of attention in psychology is called *mindfulness meditation.* Mindfulness techniques were developed as a Buddhist practice more than two thousand years ago, but modern psychologists and other health practitioners have adapted these practices for use in a secular context (Didonna, 2008).

Definitions of mindfulness are as varied as the practices associated with it. It's important to note, also, that strictly speaking, *mindfulness* refers to an approach to everyday life as well as a formal meditation technique (Shapiro & Carlson, 2009). However, for our purposes, **mindfulness meditation** can be defined as a technique in which practitioners focus *awareness* on *present experience* with *acceptance* (Siegel & others, 2008).

Advocates of mindfulness practice believe that most psychological distress is caused by a person's *reactions* to events and circumstances—their emotions, thoughts, and judgments. As psychologist Mark Williams points out, "We are always explaining the world to ourselves, and we react emotionally to these explanations rather than to the facts.... Thoughts are not facts" (Williams & others, 2007). Mindfulness practice is a way to correct that habitual perspective, clearing and calming the mind in the process. David Ludwig and Jon Kabat-Zinn (2008) explain:

> Mindfulness can be considered a universal human capacity proposed to foster clear thinking and open-heartedness. As such, this form of meditation requires no particular religious or cultural belief system. The goal of mindfulness is to maintain awareness moment by moment, disengaging oneself from strong attachment to beliefs, thoughts, or emotions, thereby developing a greater sense of emotional balance and well-being.

In other words, mindfulness meditation involves paying attention to your ongoing mental experience in a nonjudgmental, nonreactive manner (Ludwig & Kabat-Zinn, 2008). The *Mindfulness of Breathing* technique is a simple mindfulness practice that is often recommended for beginners.

Mindfulness of Breathing

- Find a comfortable place to sit quietly. Assume a sitting posture that is relaxed yet upright and alert. Close your eyes and allow the muscles in your face, neck, and shoulders to slowly relax.
- Focus on your breath as your primary object of attention, feeling the breathing in and breathing out, the rise and fall of your abdomen, the sensation of air moving across your upper lip and in your nostrils, and so forth.
- Whenever some other phenomenon arises in the field of awareness, note it, and then gently bring the mind back to the breathing. As thoughts, feelings, or images arise in your mind, simply note their presence and go back to focusing your attention on the physical sensation of breathing.
- To maintain attention on your breathing, it's sometimes helpful to count your breaths. Inhale gently, exhale, and then speak the word "one" in your mind. Inhale gently, exhale, and mentally speak the word "two." Do the same up until the count of four, and then start over again. Remember, focus on the physical sensation of breathing, such as the feeling of air moving across your nostrils and upper lip, the movement of your chest and abdomen, and so forth.

How long should you meditate? Many meditation teachers advise that you begin with a short, easily attainable goal, such as meditating for five minutes without taking a break. As you become more comfortable in your practice, gradually work your way up to longer periods of time, ideally 20 to 25 minutes.

Sources: Shapiro & Carlson, 2009; Wallace, 2009; Williams & others, 2007.

mindfulness meditation
A technique in which practitioners focus *awareness* on *present experience* with *acceptance.*

CHAPTER REVIEW: KEY PEOPLE AND TERMS

Robert Ader, p. 507
Walter B. Cannon, p. 504
Janice Kiecolt-Glaser, p. 507
Richard Lazarus, p. 497
Martin Seligman, p. 510
Hans Selye, p. 505

stress, p. 497
health psychology, p. 498
biopsychosocial model, p. 498
stressors, p. 499
daily hassles, p. 500
acculturative stress, p. 503
fight-or-flight response, p. 504
catecholamines, p. 504
general adaptation syndrome, p. 505
corticosteroids, p. 506
immune system, p. 506
lymphocytes, p. 506
psychoneuroimmunology, p. 507
optimistic explanatory style, p. 510
pessimistic explanatory style, p. 510
Type A behavior pattern, p. 512
social support, p. 515
coping, p. 518
problem-focused coping, p. 519
emotion-focused coping, p. 519
mindfulness meditation, p. 524

Web Companion Review Activities

You can find additional review activities at **www.worthpublishers.com/discoveringpsych5e.** The *Discovering Psychology* 5th edition Web Companion has self-scoring practice quizzes, flashcards, interactive crossword puzzles, and other activities to help you master the material in this chapter.

CONCEPT MAP

STRESS, HEALTH, AND COPING

Stress

Negative emotional state in response to events appraised as taxing or exceeding a person's resources

Health psychologists:
- Study stress and other factors that influence health, illness, and treatment
- Are guided by the **biopsychosocial model**

Stressors: Events or situations that produce stress

Richard Lazarus (1922-2002)
- Developed cognitive appraisal model of stress
- Established importance of daily hassles

Life events and change:
- Life events approach: Stressors are any events that require adaptation.
- Social Readjustment Rating Scale measures impact of life events.

Social and cultural sources of stress:
- Poverty, low social status, racism, and discrimination can cause chronic stress.
- **Acculturative stress** results from the pressure of adapting to a new culture.

Daily hassles: Minor, everyday events that annoy and upset people

Physical Effects of Stress

Walter Cannon (1871–1945)
- Identified endocrine pathway involved in **flight-or-fight response** to acute stress.
- Noted roles of sympathetic nervous system and release of **catecholamines** by the adrenal medulla.

Hans Selye (1907–1982)
- Identified endocrine pathway in three-stage **general adaptation syndrome** response to prolonged stress.
- Noted roles of hypothalamus, pituitary gland, and release of **corticosteroids** by the adrenal cortex.

Psychoneuroimmunology studies interconnections of psychological processes, nervous and endocrine systems, and immune system.
- **Robert Ader** (b. 1932) demonstrated immune system could be classically conditioned.
- **Janice Kiecolt-Glaser** (b. 1951) showed that everyday stressors affect immune system functioning.

Type A behavior pattern:
- Predicts heart disease
- Hostility is most important health-compromising component

Individual Factors that Influence the Response to Stress

Chronic negative emotions:
- Produce more stress
- Contribute to development of some chronic diseases

Personal control: Impact of stressors reduced when people feel sense of control over situation

Social support:
- Improves health and ability to deal with stressors
- May increase stress when inappropriate
- Women are more likely to provide social support, but also more vulnerable to the stress contagion effect
- Men are less likely to be upset by negative events outside their immediate family

Explanatory style:
- **Optimistic** explanatory style uses external, unstable, specific explanations for negative events.
- **Pessimistic** explanatory style uses internal, stable, global explanations for negative events.

Coping

The ways in which people change circumstances or their interpretations of circumstances to make them more favorable and less threatening

Emotion-focused coping:
- Involves changing emotional reactions to the stressor
- Includes escarpe-avoidance, seeking social support, distancing, denial, and positive reappraisal

Problem-focused coping:
- Attempts to change stressful situation
- Includes confrontive coping and planful problem solving

Culture's effect on coping:
- Individualistic cultures favor problem-focused coping strategies.
- Collectivistic cultures emphasize emotion-focused strategies.

CHAPTER 13

Psychological Disorders

Chapter Outline

PROLOGUE

Behind the Steel Door

ALTHOUGH IT HAPPENED more than 40 years ago, the memories are still vivid in my mind. At the time, I had just turned 13 years old. My dad had gotten very sick and was hospitalized. He nearly died before a diseased kidney was removed, saving his life. Because my junior high (it wasn't called middle school then) was only three blocks from St. Luke's Hospital, I visited him every day after school before going to my paper route.

Lost in my thoughts as I walked through the maze of dim hospital hallways, I took a wrong turn. When I got near the end of the hallway, I realized it was a dead end and started to turn around. That's when her voice pierced the silence, screaming in agony.

"*Help me!* Fire! Fire! Fire! *Please* help me!"

At first I was startled and confused about the direction from which the voice was coming. Then I saw a panic-stricken face against the small wire-reinforced window of a steel door. I ran to the door and tried to open it, but it was locked.

"Help me, *somebody!* Fire! Fire! Fire!" she screamed again.

"I'll get help!" I said loudly through the door, but she didn't seem to see or hear me. My heart racing, I ran back down the dim hallway to a nurses' station.

"There's a woman who needs help! There's a fire!" I excitedly explained to a nurse.

But instead of summoning help, the nurse looked at me with what can only be described as disdain. "Which hallway?" she said flatly, and I pointed in the direction from which I had come. "That's the psychiatric ward down there," she explained. "Those people are crazy."

I stared at her for a moment, feeling confused. *Crazy?* "But she needs help," I finally blurted out.

"That's why she's on the psychiatric ward," the nurse replied calmly. "Which room are you trying to find?"

I didn't answer her. Instead, I walked back down the hallway. I took a deep breath and tried to slow my heart down as I approached the steel door. The woman was still there, talking loudly and pacing. I watched her through the wire-reinforced glass for several seconds. She was completely oblivious to my presence. Then she shouted, "There's fire! I see fire! Fire! Fire! *Fire!*"

She looked like she was in her early 20s. Her face looked gaunt, dirty, her hair stringy and unkempt. I remember the dark circles under her deep-set eyes, her pupils dilated with sheer, raw panic.

"Listen to me, there's *no* fire," I finally said loudly, tapping on the glass, trying to get her attention.

"Help me, *please,*" she sobbed, moving closer to the door.

"My name is Don," I tried to say calmly, tapping on the glass again. "Listen to me, there's no fire."

That's when two attendants came, one male, one female. They spoke to her for several seconds, then stood quietly, waiting for her to respond. When they tried to coax her away from the door, she pushed their hands away. The male attendant glanced at me through the glass and frowned. Gently but firmly, they tried to guide the young woman away from the door. For just an instant, the young woman turned and seemed to look directly into my eyes.

"It's okay, there's *no* fire!" I blurted out, then they led her down the hallway.

Silence. I stood by the steel door, my mind racing. I had never seen someone that confused before. Never. *What was wrong with her? Where did they take her? Did she really see fire? What was going to happen to her?*

When I finally got to my dad's hospital room, we talked the entire time about the young woman. My dad reassured me that the hospital staff would take care of the woman, especially in her extreme state of confusion. As an attorney, my dad knew more about mental disorders than most people. Even so, he wasn't able to answer the most important questions that I wanted answered: What was wrong with the woman? Why was she that way? What could they do to help her?

"If you'd like," my dad finally said, "I can arrange for you to talk to a psychiatrist that I know. He can probably answer your questions better than I can." True to his word, about three weeks later, my dad arranged for me to talk to a psychiatrist named Dr. Starr.

Dr. Starr was perplexed by the locked door. "It's not normally a locked ward," he said. But after asking me a few more questions, he determined that I had been standing at the service entrance at the back of the ward, where the kitchen and housekeeping staff bring in the food and linen carts. "If you go to the actual entrance of the ward," he said, "it's not locked and you can look in and see it's actually quite nice."

He carefully listened as I described the young woman I had seen, nodding several times as I spoke. "She must have just been admitted to the hospital," he said. "There are medications that can help her, but she probably hadn't gotten them yet. Don't worry, I'm sure they'll take good care of her." Years later, I realized that the young woman was probably suffering from *schizophrenia,* a serious mental disorder that is often accompanied by vivid hallucinations that can seem frighteningly real.

In the course of our conversation, Dr. Starr also explained his own training and background. After attending medical school, he had specialized in psychiatry. Because he had had medical training, he was qualified to prescribe medication. Some of his colleagues were clinical psychologists. Although they couldn't write prescriptions or order medical procedures, they were trained in graduate school to use psychotherapy to help people with psychological disorders.

It was right then and there that I decided I wanted to be a clinical psychologist and help people like the confused woman I had seen. Six years later as a college sophomore majoring in psychology, I started working as a technician on the psychiatric unit of a large hospital. For almost seven years I worked at psychiatric facilities, learning enormously from both psychiatrists and clinical psychologists about caring for people with severe mental disorders.

In this chapter, you'll learn about the symptoms that characterize some of the most common psychological disorders, including the disorder experienced by the young woman who saw fire. As you'll see, the symptoms of many psychological disorders are not as outwardly severe as those the young woman was experiencing on that particular day. But whether the psychological symptoms are obvious or not, they can seriously impair a person's ability to function. You'll also learn in this chapter about some of the underlying causes of psychological disorders. As you'll see, biological, psychological, and environmental factors have been implicated as contributing to many psychological disorders.

>> Introduction: Understanding Psychological Disorders

Key Theme

- **Understanding psychological disorders includes considerations of their origins, symptoms, and development, as well as how behavior relates to cultural and social norms.**

Key Questions

- **What is a psychological disorder, and what differentiates abnormal behavior from normal behavior?**
- **What is DSM-IV-TR, and how was it developed?**
- **How prevalent are psychological disorders?**

Does *The Far Side* cartoon on the right make you smile? The cartoon is humorous, but it's actually intended to make some serious points. It reflects several common misconceptions about psychological disorders that we hope will be dispelled by this chapter.

First, there's the belief that "crazy" behavior is very different from "normal" behavior. Granted, sometimes it is, like the behavior of the young woman who was screaming "Fire!" when there was no fire. But as you'll see throughout this chapter, the line that divides "normal" and "crazy" behavior is often not as sharply defined as most people think. In many instances, the difference between normal and abnormal behavior is a matter of degree. For example, as you leave your apartment or house, it's normal to check or even double-check that the door is securely locked. However, if you feel compelled to go back and check the lock 50 times, it would be considered abnormal behavior.

The dividing line between normal and abnormal behavior is also often determined by the social or cultural context in which a particular behavior occurs. For example, among traditional Hindus in India, certain dietary restrictions are followed as part of the mourning process. It would be a serious breach of social norms if an Indian widow ate fish, meat, onions, garlic, or any other "hot" foods within six months of her husband's death. A Catholic widow in the United States would consider such restrictions absurd.

Second, when we encounter people whose behavior strikes us as weird, unpredictable, or baffling, it's easy to simply dismiss them as "just plain nuts," as in *The Far Side* cartoon, or "crazy," as in the nurse's insensitive response in the Prologue. Although convenient, such a response is too simplistic, not to mention unkind. It could also be wrong. Sometimes, unconventional people are labeled as crazy when they're actually just creatively challenging the conventional wisdom with new ideas.

Even if a person's responses are seriously disturbed, labeling that person as "crazy" or "just plain nuts" tells us nothing meaningful. What are the person's specific symptoms? What might be the cause of the symptoms? How did they develop? How long can they be expected to last? And how might the person be helped? The area of psychology and medicine that focuses on these questions is called **psychopathology**—the scientific study of the origins, symptoms, and development of psychological disorders. In this chapter and the next, we'll take a closer look at psychological disorders and their treatment.

The Far Side cartoon reflects a third troubling issue. There is still a strong social stigma attached to suffering from a psychological disorder (Thornicroft, 2006). Because of the social stigma that can be associated with psychological disorders, people are often reluctant to seek the help of mental health professionals (Arboleda-Florez & Sartorius, 2008). People who *are* under the care of a mental health professional often hide the fact, telling only their closest friends—and understandably so. Being labeled "crazy" carries all kinds of implications, most of which reflect negative stereotypes about people with mental illness (Wirth & Bodenhausen, 2009). In the Critical Thinking box "Are People with a Mental Illness as Violent as the Media Portray Them?" we discuss the accuracy of such stereotypes in more detail.

psychopathology
The scientific study of the origins, symptoms, and development of psychological disorders.

CRITICAL THINKING

Are People with a Mental Illness as Violent as the Media Portray Them?

A children's show on public television presented a retelling of the classic novel *Tom Sawyer* by Mark Twain. However, the name of the chief villain had been changed: Twain's "Injun Joe" had been renamed "Crazy Joe." As this example illustrates, writers for television are well aware that it is no longer considered acceptable to portray negative stereotypes of particular racial or ethnic groups, including Native Americans. Unfortunately, it also illustrates that another stigmatized group is still fair game: the mentally ill.

Multiple studies have found that people with a major mental illness belong to one of the most stigmatized groups in modern society (Corrigan & O'Shaughnessy, 2007). In much of the popular media, people with psychological disorders are portrayed in highly negative, stereotyped ways (Gerbner, 1993, 1998). One stereotype is that of the mentally disturbed person as a helpless victim. The other stereotype is that of the mentally disordered person as an evil villain who is unpredictable, dangerous, and violent.

One comprehensive survey found that although 5 percent of "normal" television characters are murderers, 20 percent of "mentally ill" characters are killers (Gerbner, 1998). The same survey found that about 40 percent of normal characters were violent, but 70 percent of characters labeled as mentally ill were violent. This media stereotype reflects and reinforces the widespread belief among Americans that people with mental illness are violent and threatening (Diefenbach & West, 2007). Further reinforcing that belief is selective media reporting that sensationalizes violent acts by people with mental disorders. Clearly, the public perception that people with a mental illness are dangerous contributes to the stigma of mental illness (Fazel & others, 2009).

Are people with mental disorders more violent than other people? One groundbreaking study by psychologist Henry Steadman and his colleagues (1998) monitored the behavior of more than 1,000 former mental patients in the year after they were discharged from psychiatric facilities. For their control group, they also monitored a matched group of people who were not former mental patients but were living in the same neighborhood.

The researchers found that, overall, the former mental patients did *not* have a higher rate of violence than the comparison group. Former mental patients who demonstrated symptoms of substance abuse were the most likely to engage in violent behavior. However, the same was also true of the control group. In other words, substance abuse was associated with more violent behavior in *all* the participants, whether they had a history of mental illness or not. The study also found that the violent behavior that *did* occur was most frequently aimed at friends and family members, not at strangers.

Recent meta-analytic research reviews have confirmed the general finding that substance abuse greatly increases the risk of violent behavior by people who have been diagnosed with a severe mental illness, such as schizophrenia (see Douglas & others, 2009; Fazel & others, 2009). Beyond substance abuse, there is evidence that people with severe mental disorders who are experiencing extreme psychological symptoms, such as bizarre delusional ideas and hallucinated voices, do display a *slightly* higher level of violent and illegal behavior than do "normal" people (Malla & Payne, 2005). However, the person with a mental disorder who is not suffering from such symptoms is no more likely than the average person to be involved in violent or illegal behavior. Other factors, such as living in impoverished neighborhoods and abusing drugs or alcohol, are stronger predictors of violence (Norko & Baranoski, 2005).

Canadian psychologist Kevin Douglas and his colleagues (2009) emphasize that the overall size of the association between psychosis and violence is relatively small. As they point out, "Most violent individuals are not psychotic, and most psychotic individuals are not violent."

Clearly, the incidence of violent behavior among current or former mental patients is exaggerated in media portrayals. In turn, the exaggerated fear of violence from people with a psychological disorder contributes to the stigma of mental illness (Fazel & others, 2009). As one comprehensive review of the research emphasized, "The overall contribution of mental disorders to the total level of violence in society is exceptionally small. In fact, there is very little risk of violence or harm to a stranger from casual contact with an individual who has a mental disorder" (U.S. Department of Health & Human Services, 1999).

CRITICAL THINKING QUESTIONS

- Can you think of any reasons why people with psychological disorders are more likely to be depicted as villains than members of other social groups?
- Can you think of any television shows or movies in which characters with a severe psychological disorder were shown in a sympathetic light? If so, are such depictions more or less common than depictions of people with a mental illness as dangerous or violent?
- What evidence could you cite to challenge the notion that people with psychological disorders are dangerous?

Hollywood Versus Reality In *The Dark Knight,* the Joker takes the image of the insane killer to new heights. As a plot device, the deranged, evil killer on the loose is standard fare in television dramas like *CSI* and film thrillers like the *Halloween* and *Friday the 13th* movies. Such media depictions foster the stereotype that people with a mental illness are evil, threatening, and prone to violence—an image that is *not* supported by psychological research.

What Is a Psychological Disorder?

What exactly are we talking about when we say that someone has a psychological or mental disorder? A **psychological disorder** or **mental disorder** can be defined as a pattern of behavioral or psychological symptoms that causes significant personal distress, impairs the ability to function in one or more important areas of life, or both (DSM-IV-TR, 2000). An important qualification is that the pattern of behavioral or psychological symptoms must represent a serious departure from the prevailing social and cultural norms. Hence, the behavior of a traditional Hindu woman who refuses to eat onions, garlic, or other "hot" foods following the death of her husband is perfectly normal because that norm is part of the Hindu culture.

DSM-IV-TR *The Diagnostic and Statistical Manual of Mental Disorders,* Fourth Edition, was revised in 2000 with updated research. Since then, the lengthy process of assembling DSM-V has begun. It is a collaborative effort involving several mental health organizations, including the American Psychiatric Association and the World Health Organization. One key goal of DSM-V is to incorporate the multidisciplinary research advances in mental health that have occurred worldwide in recent years. DSM-V is scheduled to be published in 2012 (Fink & Taylor, 2008).

What determines whether a given pattern of symptoms or behaviors qualifies as a psychological disorder? Throughout this chapter, you'll notice numerous references to DSM-IV-TR. **DSM-IV-TR** stands for the *Diagnostic and Statistical Manual of Mental Disorders,* Fourth Edition, Text Revision, which was published by the American Psychiatric Association in 2000. (The DSM-IV was published in 1994. The updated "text revision" of DSM-IV was published in 2000 to incorporate new research and information.)

DSM-IV-TR is a book that describes more than 300 specific psychological disorders. It includes the symptoms, the exact criteria that must be met to make a diagnosis, and the typical course for each mental disorder. An example of the diagnostic criteria for one mental disorder is shown in Figure 13.1. DSM-IV-TR provides mental health professionals with both a common language for labeling mental disorders and comprehensive guidelines for diagnosing mental disorders.

The first edition of the *Diagnostic and Statistical Manual* was published in 1952. With each new edition, the number of distinct disorders has progressively increased—from fewer than a hundred in the first edition to more than three times that number in the current version (Horwitz, 2002; Houts, 2002). Some disorders that are relatively well-known today, such as eating disorders, attention-deficit hyperactivity disorder, and

psychological disorder or **mental disorder**
A pattern of behavioral and psychological symptoms that causes significant personal distress, impairs the ability to function in one or more important areas of life, or both.

DSM-IV-TR
Abbreviation for the *Diagnostic and Statistical Manual of Mental Disorders,* Fourth Edition, Text Revision; the book published by the American Psychiatric Association that describes the specific symptoms and diagnostic guidelines for different psychological disorders.

Diagnostic Criteria for 301.7 Antisocial Personality Disorder

A. There is a pervasive pattern of disregard for and violation of the rights of others occurring since age 15 years, as indicated by three (or more) of the following:

(1) failure to conform to social norms with respect to lawful behaviors as indicated by repeatedly performing acts that are grounds for arrest
(2) deceitfulness, as indicated by repeated lying, use of aliases, or conning others for personal profit or pleasure
(3) impulsivity or failure to plan ahead
(4) irritability and aggressiveness, as indicated by repeated physical fights or assaults
(5) reckless disregard for safety of self or others
(6) consistent irresponsibility, as indicated by repeated failure to sustain consistent work behavior or honor financial obligations
(7) lack of remorse, as indicated by being indifferent to or rationalizing having hurt, mistreated, or stolen from another

B. The individual is at least age 18 years.
C. There is evidence of Conduct Disorder with onset before age 15 years.
D. The occurrence of antisocial behavior is not exclusively during the course of Schizophrenia or a Manic Episode.

Figure 13.1 Sample DSM-IV-TR Diagnostic Criteria Each of the more than 250 psychological disorders described in DSM-IV-TR has specific criteria that must be met for a person to be diagnosed with that disorder. Shown left are the DSM-IV-TR criteria for antisocial personality disorder, which is also referred to as *psychopathy, sociopathy,* or *dyssocial personality disorder.* The number 301.7 identifies the specific disorder according to an international code developed by the World Health Organization. The code helps researchers make statistical comparisons of the prevalence of mental disorders in different countries and cultures.

Source: DSM-IV-TR (2000), p. 706.

social phobia, were not added until later editions. And some behavior patterns that were categorized as "disorders" in early editions, such as homosexuality, have been dropped from later editions because they are no longer considered to be psychological disorders.

It's important to understand that DSM-IV-TR was not written by a single person or even a small group of experts. Rather, DSM-IV-TR represents the *consensus* of a wide range of mental health professionals representing many different organizations and perspectives. In developing DSM-IV-TR, teams of mental health professionals conducted extensive reviews of the research findings for each category of mental disorder. More than 1,000 mental health experts, mostly psychiatrists and clinical psychologists, participated in the development of DSM-IV-TR. More than 60 professional organizations, including the American Psychological Association and the Association of Psychological Science, reviewed early drafts of DSM-IV-TR. Despite these efforts, the *Diagnostic and Statistical Manual of Mental Disorders* has many critics (e.g., Achenbach, 2009; Maser & others, 2009). More specifically, DSM-IV-TR has been criticized for:

- including some experiences that are too "normal" to be considered disorders, such as excessive shyness (Langenbucher & Nathan, 2006)
- using arbitrary cutoffs to draw the line between people with and without a particular disorder (Barlow & Durand, 2005)
- gender bias (Caplan & Cosgrove, 2004)
- insufficient sensitivity to cultural diversity (Eriksen & Kress, 2005)

Clinicians and researchers are currently working on the DSM-V, which is scheduled to be published in 2012 (Regier & others, 2009). For now, DSM-IV-TR is still the most comprehensive and authoritative set of guidelines available for diagnosing psychological disorders. Thus, we'll refer to it often in this chapter.

The Prevalence of Psychological Disorders

A 50–50 Chance?

> The mentally ill are not some distinct set of "them" out there who are completely different from "us" sane people. Instead, the vast majority of us have been touched by some form of mental illness at some time in our lives either through personal experience or through the illness of a close loved one.
>
> RONALD C. KESSLER (2003A)

Just how common are psychological disorders? To investigate that question, researcher Ronald C. Kessler and his colleagues (2005a, 2005b) conducted a nationally representative survey of more than 9,000 Americans, ages 18 and older. Called the National Comorbidity Survey Replication (NCS-R), the survey involved more than two years of face-to-face interviews throughout the country. Participants were asked if they had experienced specific symptoms of psychological disorders (a) during the previous 12 months and (b) at any point in their lives. They were also asked about possible risk factors associated with mental disorders, such as substance use.

How Prevalent Are Psychological Disorders? Psychological disorders are far more common than most people think. According to the National Comorbidity Survey Replication (NCS-R), about 1 in 4 American adults has experienced the symptoms of some type of psychological disorder during the previous year. However, most people who experience such symptoms do not receive treatment (Wang & others, 2005).

The NCS-R results reconfirmed many of the findings of previous national surveys, including the finding that psychological disorders are much more prevalent than many people believe (Kessler & others, 2005c). Specifically, the NCS-R found that 1 out of 4 respondents (26 percent) reported experiencing the symptoms of a psychological disorder during the previous year (Kessler & others, 2005b). The NCS-R and other surveys like it also reveal a high degree of *comorbidity*, which means that people diagnosed with one disorder are also frequently diagnosed with another disorder as well.

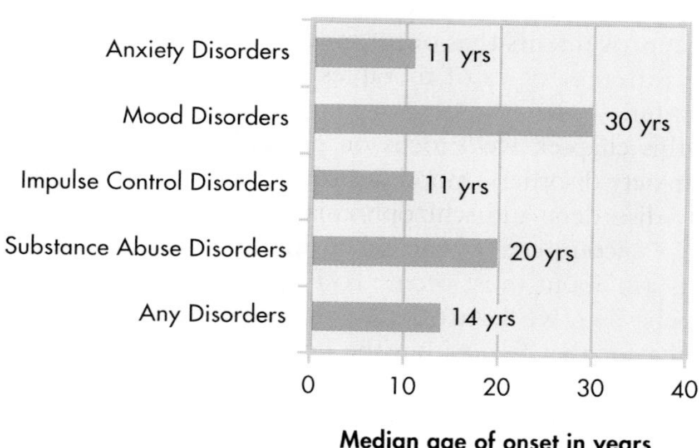

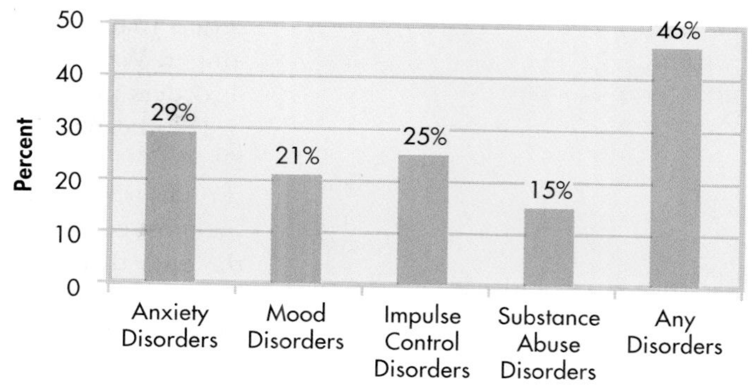

Figure 13.2 Age of Onset and the Lifetime Prevalence of Mental Disorders The left chart shows the median age of onset for common categories of mental disorders in the National Comorbidity Survey Replication (NCS-R). While the onset of anxiety disorders or impulse control disorders tends to occur in the preteen years, the onset of mood disorders typically occurs around age 30, well into young adulthood. The right chart shows the lifetime prevalence for the same mental disorder categories. The NCS-R reconfirmed that the lifetime prevalence of experiencing a mental disorder is almost one out of two.

Figure 13.2 shows the typical age of onset for some of the common mental disorders reported by the NCS-R respondents at any point in their life. As you can see in the left chart, the different categories of mental disorders vary significantly in the median age of onset. Anxiety disorders and impulse control disorders tend to begin at a much earlier age—around age 11— as compared to substance abuse disorders or mood disorders. In the right chart, you can see the lifetime prevalence of the same categories of mental disorders. Like the original National Comorbidity Survey, the NCS-R found that almost one out of two adults (46%) had experienced the symptoms of a psychological disorder at some point thus far in their life.

Although it might initially seem disturbing to think that half of the adult population will experience the symptoms of a mental disorder, lead researcher Ronald C. Kessler helps put these findings into perspective. As Kessler (2003b) points out,

> It wouldn't surprise anyone if I said that 99.9% of the population had been physically ill at some time in their life. Why, then, should it surprise anyone that 50% of the population has been mentally ill at some time in their life? The reason, of course, is that we invest the term 'mentally ill' with excess meaning. A number of common mental illnesses, like adjustment disorders and brief episodes of depression, are usually mild and self-limiting. Many people experience these kinds of disorders at some time in their life.

The NCS-R found that most people with the symptoms of a mental disorder (59 percent) received no treatment during the past year. Of those who did receive some kind of treatment, it was usually provided by a general medical practitioner, psychiatrist, or mental health specialist. Even so, the treatment provided was often inadequate, falling short of established treatment guidelines (Wang & others, 2005).

It seems clear that many people who could benefit from mental health treatment don't receive it. Many factors contribute to this unmet need, including lack of insurance, low income, and living in rural areas where mental health care facilities might not be available. Some people lack awareness about psychological disorders or shun treatment for fear of being stigmatized for seeking help with troubling psychological symptoms.

On the other hand, it also seems clear that most people manage to weather psychological symptoms without becoming completely debilitated and needing professional intervention (Narrow & others, 2002). One explanation for this is that people use a variety of coping strategies—some more effective than others—to manage psychological symptoms.

But it's important to remember that even ineffective strategies can appear to be effective. Why? Because the symptoms of many psychological disorders, especially those involving mild to moderately disruptive symptoms, diminish with the simple passage of time or with improvements in the person's overall situation.

Nevertheless, there are many effective treatments available for psychological disorders that can produce improvements that occur much more quickly and endure longer. We'll look at the different types of therapies used to treat psychological disorders in the next chapter.

For the remainder of this chapter, we'll focus on psychological disorders in six DSM-IV-TR categories: anxiety disorders, mood disorders, eating disorders, personality disorders, dissociative disorders, and schizophrenia. Along with being some of the most common disorders encountered by mental health professionals, they're also the ones that our students ask about most often. To help you distinguish between normal and maladaptive behaviors, we'll start the discussion of each mental disorder category by describing behavior that falls within the normal range of psychological functioning, such as normal feelings of anxiety or normal variations in mood.

Table 13.1 describes other categories of mental disorders contained in DSM-IV-TR. Some of these disorders have been discussed in previous chapters. In the Enhancing Well-Being with Psychology section at the end of this chapter, we'll look at what you can do to help prevent one of the most disturbing consequences of psychological problems—suicide.

Table 13.1

Some Key Diagnostic Categories in DSM-IV-TR

Diagnostic Category	Core Features	Examples of Specific Disorders
Infancy, childhood, or adolescent disorders	Includes a wide range of developmental, behavioral, learning, and communication disorders that are usually first diagnosed in infancy, childhood, or adolescence. Symptoms of a particular disorder may vary depending on a child's age and development level.	**Autistic disorder:** Onset of symptoms prior to age of 3. Characterized by severely impaired social and communication skills, including delayed or a complete lack of language development. Symptoms often include repetitive behaviors, such as body rocking, and abnormal interests, such as intense preoccupation with mechanical toys. **Tourette's disorder:** Onset prior to age of 18. Characterized by motor tics, such as recurring spasmodic movements of the head or arms, and vocal tics, such as recurring and sudden clicking, grunting, or snorting sounds. Sometimes involves uncontrollable utterances of profane or obscene words.
Substance-related disorders (see Chapter 4)	Occurrence of adverse social, behavioral, psychological, and physical effects from seeking or using substances such as alcohol, amphetamines, cocaine, marijuana, hallucinogens, and other drugs.	**Substance abuse:** A recurring pattern of impaired ability to function at work, school, or home due to repeated substance use. **Substance dependence:** A maladaptive pattern of substance use usually resulting in drug tolerance, withdrawal symptoms when the drug is discontinued, and compulsive drug-taking behavior that seriously impairs occupational and social functioning.
Somatoform disorders	Persistent, recurring complaints of bodily (or somatic) symptoms that have no physical or medical basis.	**Body dysmorphic disorder:** Exaggerated concern and preoccupation about minor or imagined defects in appearance. **Hypochondriasis:** Preoccupation with imagined diseases based on the person's misinterpretation of bodily symptoms or functions.
Sexual and gender identity disorders	Difficulty in the expression of normal sexuality, including confusion about gender identity, decreased sexual desire or arousal, difficulty having or in timing of orgasm, pain or discomfort during sex, or the use of inappropriate objects to produce sexual arousal.	**Fetishism:** Recurrent, intense, sexually arousing fantasies, urges, or behaviors, usually involving nonliving objects, such as female undergarments, shoes, boots, or other articles of clothing. **Gender identity disorder:** The strong and persistent desire to be the other sex.
Sleep disorders	Disruptions in the amount, quality, or timing of sleep. Includes difficulty initiating or maintaining sleep, excessive sleepiness, or abnormal behavioral or psychological events during sleep or sleep–wake transitions.	**Narcolepsy:** Recurrent episodes of unintended sleep in inappropriate situations, such as while driving a car or attending a meeting. **Sleep terror disorder:** Repeated episodes of abruptly awakening from sleep, usually beginning with a panicky scream or cry. Intense fear, rapid heartbeat and breathing, sweating, and other signs of autonomic arousal are evident. Also called *night terror* disorder.
Impulse-control disorders	Inability to resist an impulse, urge, or temptation to perform an act that is harmful to the self or others.	**Kleptomania:** The impulse to steal objects not needed for personal use or monetary value. **Pyromania:** The urge to set fires for pleasure, gratification, or relief of tension.

Source: DSM-IV-TR (2000).

Anxiety Disorders

Intense Apprehension and Worry

Key Theme

- **The main symptom of anxiety disorders is intense anxiety that disrupts normal functioning.**

Key Questions

- **How does pathological anxiety differ from normal anxiety?**
- **What characterizes generalized anxiety disorder and panic disorder?**
- **What are the phobias, and how have they been explained?**

Anxiety is a familiar emotion to all of us—that feeling of tension, apprehension, and worry that often hits during personal crises and everyday conflicts. Although it is unpleasant, anxiety is sometimes helpful. Think of anxiety as your personal, internal alarm system that tells you that something is not quite right. When it alerts you to a realistic threat, anxiety is adaptive and normal. For example, anxiety about your grades may motivate you to study harder.

Anxiety has both physical and mental effects. As your internal alarm system, anxiety puts you on *physical alert,* preparing you to defensively "fight" or "flee" potential dangers. Anxiety also puts you on *mental alert,* making you focus your attention squarely on the threatening situation. You become extremely vigilant, scanning the environment for potential threats. When the threat has passed, your alarm system shuts off and you calm down. But even if the problem persists, you can normally put your anxious thoughts aside temporarily and attend to other matters.

In the **anxiety disorders,** however, the anxiety is *maladaptive,* disrupting everyday activities, moods, and thought processes. It's as if you've triggered a faulty car alarm that activates at the slightest touch and has a broken "off" switch.

Three features distinguish normal anxiety from pathological anxiety. First, pathological anxiety is *irrational.* The anxiety is provoked by perceived threats that are exaggerated or nonexistent, and the anxiety response is out of proportion to the actual importance of the situation. Second, pathological anxiety is *uncontrollable.* The person can't shut off the alarm reaction, even when he or she knows it's unrealistic.

And third, pathological anxiety is *disruptive.* It interferes with relationships, job or academic performance, or everyday activities. In short, pathological anxiety is unreasonably intense, frequent, persistent, and disruptive (Beidel & Stipelman, 2007; Woo & Keatinge, 2008).

Anxiety disorders are among the most common of all psychological disorders. According to some estimates, they will affect about 1 in 4 people in the United States during their lifetime (McGregor, 2009; Kessler & others, 2005b). Evidence of disabling anxiety disorders has been found in virtually every culture studied, although symptoms may vary from one cultural group to another (Chentsova-Dutton & Tsai, 2007; Good & Hinton, 2009). Most of the anxiety disorders are much more common in women than men (Barlow & others, 2007).

As a symptom, anxiety occurs in many different psychological disorders. In the anxiety disorders, however, anxiety is the *main* symptom, although it is manifested differently in each of the disorders.

anxiety
An unpleasant emotional state characterized by physical arousal and feelings of tension, apprehension, and worry.

anxiety disorders
A category of psychological disorders in which extreme anxiety is the main diagnostic feature and causes significant disruptions in the person's cognitive, behavioral, or interpersonal functioning.

generalized anxiety disorder (GAD)
An anxiety disorder characterized by excessive, global, and persistent symptoms of anxiety; also called *free-floating anxiety.*

Generalized Anxiety Disorder

Worrying About Anything and Everything

Global, persistent, chronic, and excessive apprehension is the main feature of **generalized anxiety disorder (GAD).** People with this disorder are constantly tense and anxious, and their anxiety is pervasive. They feel anxious about a wide range of life circumstances, sometimes with little or no apparent justification (Craske & Waters, 2005; Sanfelippo, 2006). The more issues about which a person worries excessively, the more likely it is that he or she suffers from generalized anxiety disorder (DSM-IV-TR, 2000).

Normally, anxiety quickly dissipates when a threatening situation is resolved. In generalized anxiety disorder, however, when one source of worry is removed, another quickly moves in to take its place. The anxiety can be attached to virtually any object or to none at all. Because of this, generalized anxiety disorder is sometimes referred to as *free-floating anxiety.*

Explaining Generalized Anxiety Disorder

What causes generalized anxiety disorder? As is true with most psychological disorders, environmental, psychological, and genetic as well as other biological factors are probably involved in GAD (Allen & others, 2008; Heimburg & others, 2004). For example, a brain that is "wired" for anxiety can give a person a head start toward developing GAD in later life, but problematic relationships and stressful experiences can make the possibility more likely. Signs of problematic anxiety can be evident from a very early age, such as in the example of a child with a very shy temperament who consistently feels overwhelming anxiety in new situations or when separated from his parents. Often, but not always, such individuals grow to become adults with anxiety disorders such as GAD (Weems & Silverman, 2008).

Panic Attacks and Panic Disorders

Sudden Episodes of Extreme Anxiety

Generalized anxiety disorder is like the dull ache of a sore tooth—a constant, ongoing sense of uneasiness, distress, and apprehension. In contrast, a **panic attack** is a sudden episode of extreme anxiety that rapidly escalates in intensity. The most common symptoms of a panic attack are a pounding heart, rapid breathing, breathlessness, and a choking sensation. The person may also sweat, tremble, and experience light-headedness, chills, or hot flashes. Accompanying the intense, escalating surge of physical arousal are feelings of terror and the belief that one is about to die, go crazy, or completely lose control. A panic attack typically peaks within 10 minutes of onset and then gradually subsides. Nevertheless, the physical symptoms of a panic attack are so severe and frightening that it's not unusual for people to rush to an emergency room, convinced they are having a heart attack, stroke, or seizure (Beidel & Stipelman, 2007; Craske & Barlow, 2008).

Jeff Tweedy and Panic Disorder Founder of the alternative rock band Wilco, Jeff Tweedy has suffered from severe panic attacks for years. Tweedy (2008) explains the vicious cycle that underlies panic disorder: "You'll have an actual panic attack and for weeks or months after that you'll have a fear of a panic attack that can heighten your anxiety and heighten your stress levels to the point where you end up having another panic attack." After psychological treatment, Tweedy is now better able to manage his symptoms of panic disorder.

Sometimes the first panic attack occurs after a stressful experience, such as an injury or illness, or during a stressful period of life, such as while changing jobs or during a period of marital conflict (Watanabe & others, 2005). In other cases, however, the first panic attack seems to come from nowhere. In a survey of panic disorder patients, 40 percent could not identify any stressful event or negative life experience that might have precipitated the initial panic attack (Shulman & others, 1994).

When panic attacks occur *frequently* and *unexpectedly,* the person is said to be suffering from **panic disorder.** In this disorder, the frequency of panic attacks is highly variable and quite unpredictable. One person may have panic attacks several times a month. Another person may go for months without an attack and then experience panic attacks for several days in a row. Understandably, people with panic disorder are quite apprehensive about when and where the next panic attack will hit (Craske & Waters, 2005; Good & Hinton, 2009).

As a result, some panic disorder sufferers go on to develop **agoraphobia**, a fear of having a panic attack in a place from which escape would be difficult or impossible (Craske & Barlow, 2008). Crowds, stores or elevators, public transportation, standing in lines, and traveling in a car may all be avoided because of the fear of suffering a panic attack and being unable to escape the situation. Consequently, many people with agoraphobia live like prisoners in their own homes.

For example, consider Hahnee, a 45-year-old mother of two school-age children. She can go for days without feeling anxious, but then, without warning, she may suddenly experience an attack of intense anxiety and fearfulness. Her heart begins to pound, she feels as if she can't breathe, and she perspires heavily. On more than one occasion, her children have called an ambulance because Hahnee was convinced she was having a heart attack. As her panic attacks increased in frequency and severity, Hahnee quit her job, fearful that she might have a panic attack at work, and eventually gave up driving because she was afraid that she might have a panic attack in the car. It is becoming harder and harder for Hahnee to force herself to leave her home.

panic attack
A sudden episode of extreme anxiety that rapidly escalates in intensity.

panic disorder
An anxiety disorder in which the person experiences frequent and unexpected panic attacks.

agoraphobia
An anxiety disorder involving the extreme and irrational fear of experiencing a panic attack in a public situation and being unable to escape or get help.

phobia
A persistent and irrational fear of a specific object, situation, or activity.

Explaining Panic Disorder

People with panic disorder are often hypersensitive to the signs of physical arousal (Zvolensky & Smits, 2008). The fluttering heartbeat or momentary dizziness that the average person barely notices signals disaster to the panic-prone. David Barlow and his colleagues (2007) suggested that this oversensitivity to physical arousal is one of three important factors in the development of panic disorder. Their *triple vulnerabilities model* of panic states that a biological predisposition toward anxiety, a low sense of control over potentially life-threatening events, and an oversensitivity to physical sensations combine to make a person vulnerable to panic (Craske & Barlow, 2008).

People with panic disorder may also be victims of their own illogical thinking. According to the *catastrophic cognitions theory*, people with panic disorder are not only oversensitive to physical sensations, they also tend to *catastrophize* the meaning of their experience (Good & Hinton, 2009; Hinton & Hinton, 2009). A few moments of increased heart rate after climbing a flight of stairs is misinterpreted as the warning signs of a heart attack. Such catastrophic misinterpretations simply add to the physiological arousal, creating a vicious circle in which the frightening symptoms intensify. After such occurrences, the person may become even more attuned to the physical changes that could signal the onset of another frightening attack. Ironically, this sensitivity only increases the likelihood that another panic attack will occur.

Syndromes resembling panic disorder have been reported in many cultures(Chentsova-Dutton & Tsai, 2007; Hinton & Hinton, 2009; Li & others, 2007). For example, the Spanish phrase *ataque de nervios* literally means "attack of nerves." It's a disorder reported in many Latin American cultures, in Puerto Rico, and among Latinos in the United States. *Ataque de nervios* has many symptoms in common with panic disorder—heart palpitations, dizziness, and the fear of dying, going crazy, or losing control. However, the person experiencing *ataque de nervios* also becomes hysterical. She may scream, swear, strike out at others, and break things. *Ataque de nervios* typically follows a severe stressor, especially one involving a family member. Funerals, accidents, or family conflicts often trigger such attacks. Because *ataque de nervios* tends to elicit immediate social support from others, it seems to be a culturally shaped, acceptable way to respond to severe stress.

The Phobias

Fear and Loathing

A **phobia** is a persistent and irrational fear of a specific object, situation, or activity. In the general population, *mild* irrational fears that don't significantly interfere with a person's ability to function are very common. Many people are fearful of certain animals, such as dogs or snakes, or are moderately uncomfortable in particular situations, such as flying in a plane or riding in a glass elevator. Nonetheless, many people cope with such fears without being overwhelmed with anxiety. As long as the fear doesn't interfere with their daily functioning, they would not be diagnosed with a psychological disorder.

Table 13.2

Some Unusual Phobias

Amathophobia	Fear of dust
Anemophobia	Fear of wind
Aphephobia	Fear of being touched by another person
Bibliophobia	Fear of books
Catotrophobia	Fear of breaking a mirror
Ergophobia	Fear of work or responsibility
Erythrophobia	Fear of red objects
Gamophobia	Fear of marriage
Hypertrichophobia	Fear of growing excessive amounts of body hair
Levophobia	Fear of things being on the left side of your body
Phobophobia	Fear of acquiring a phobia
Phonophobia	Fear of the sound of your own voice
Triskaidekaphobia	Fear of the number 13

In comparison, people with **specific phobia,** formerly called *simple phobia,* are more than just terrified of a particular object or situation. In some people, encountering the feared situation or object can provoke a full-fledged panic attack. Importantly, the incapacitating terror and anxiety interfere with the person's ability to function in daily life. Even though he knows that his fear is excessive and irrational, the person will go to great lengths to avoid the feared object or situation. Consider the case of Antonio, who has a dog phobia. He works in a pizza parlor, making pizzas and taking orders. He could make more money if he took a job as a delivery person, but he won't even consider it because he is too afraid he might encounter a dog while making deliveries.

About 13 percent of the general population experiences a specific phobia at some time in their lives (Kessler & others, 2005a). More than twice as many women as men suffer from specific phobia. Occasionally, people have unusual phobias, such as the elderly woman that Don knew who was terrified of household cleaning supplies (see Table 13.2). Generally, the objects or situations that produce specific phobias tend to fall into four categories:

- Fear of particular situations, such as flying, driving, tunnels, bridges, elevators, crowds, or enclosed places
- Fear of features of the natural environment, such as heights, water, thunderstorms, or lightning
- Fear of injury or blood, including the fear of injections, needles, and medical or dental procedures
- Fear of animals and insects, such as snakes, spiders, dogs, cats, slugs, or bats

Social Phobia
Fear of Social Situations

A second type of phobia also deserves additional comment—**social phobia.** Also called **social anxiety disorder,** social phobia is one of the most common psychological disorders and is more prevalent among women than men (Altemus, 2006; Kessler & others, 2005b). Social phobia goes well beyond the shyness that everyone sometimes feels at social gatherings. Rather, the person with social phobia is paralyzed by fear of social situations, especially if the situation involves performing even routine behaviors in front of others. Eating a meal in public, making small talk at a party, or using a public restroom can be agonizing for the person with social phobia.

Social Phobia About 1 out of 8 adults in the United States has experienced social phobia at some point in their lives (Kessler & others, 2005a). Social phobia is far more debilitating than everyday shyness. People with social phobia are intensely fearful of being watched or judged by others. Even ordinary activities, such as eating with friends in a shopping mall food court, can cause unbearable anxiety.

The core of social phobia seems to be an irrational fear of being embarrassed, judged, or critically evaluated by others. People with social phobia recognize that their fear is excessive and unreasonable, but they still approach social situations with tremendous anxiety (Hofmann & Otto, 2008). In severe cases, they may even suffer a panic attack in social situations. When the fear of being embarrassed or failing in public significantly interferes with daily life, it qualifies as social phobia (DSM-IV-TR, 2000).

As with panic attacks, cultural influences can add some novel twists to social phobia. Consider the Japanese disorder called *taijin kyofusho*. *Taijin kyofusho* usually affects young Japanese males. It has several features in common with social phobia, including extreme social anxiety and avoidance of social situations. However, the person with *taijin kyofusho* is not worried about being embarrassed in public. Rather, reflecting the cultural emphasis of concern for others, the person with *taijin kyofusho* fears that his appearance or smell, facial expression, or body language will offend, insult, or embarrass other people (Iwamasa, 1997).

specific phobia
An excessive, intense, and irrational fear of a specific object, situation, or activity that is actively avoided or endured with marked anxiety.

social phobia or **social anxiety disorder**
An anxiety disorder involving the extreme and irrational fear of being embarrassed, judged, or scrutinized by others in social situations.

Explaining Phobias

Learning Theories

The development of some phobias can be explained in terms of basic learning principles (Craske & Waters, 2005). *Classical conditioning* may well be involved in the development of a specific phobia that can be traced back to some sort of traumatic event. In Chapter 5, on learning, we saw how psychologist John Watson classically conditioned "Little Albert" to fear a tame lab rat that had been paired with loud noise. Following the conditioning, the infant's fear generalized to other furry objects. In much the same way, our neighbor Michelle has been extremely phobic of dogs ever since she was bitten by a German shepherd when she was 4 years old. In effect, Michelle developed a *conditioned response* (fear) to a *conditioned stimulus* (the German shepherd) that has *generalized* to similar stimuli—any dog.

Operant conditioning can also be involved in the avoidance behavior that characterizes phobias. In Michelle's case, she quickly learned that she could reduce her anxiety and fear by avoiding dogs altogether. To use operant conditioning terms, her *operant response* of avoiding dogs is *negatively reinforced* by the relief from anxiety and fear that she experiences.

Observational learning can also be involved in the development of phobias. Some people learn to be phobic of certain objects or situations by observing the fearful reactions of someone else who acts as a *model* in the situation. The child who observes a parent react with sheer panic to the sight of a spider or mouse may imitate the same behavioral response. People can also develop phobias from observing vivid media accounts of disasters, as when some people become afraid to fly after watching graphic TV coverage of a plane crash.

Yuck! It's hard to suppress a shudder of disgust at the sight of a slug sliming its way across the sidewalk . . . or a cockroach scuttling across the kitchen floor. Are such responses instinctive? Why are people more likely to develop phobias for slugs, maggots, and cockroaches than for mosquitoes or grasshoppers?

We also noted in Chapter 5 that humans seem *biologically prepared* to acquire fears of certain animals or situations, such as snakes or heights, that were survival threats in human evolutionary history (Workman & Reader, 2008). People also seem to be predisposed to develop phobias toward creatures that arouse disgust, like slugs, maggots, or cockroaches (Webb & Davey, 1993). Instinctively, it seems, many people find such creatures repulsive, possibly because they are associated with disease, infection, or filth. Such phobias may reflect a fear of contamination or infection that is also based on human evolutionary history (Cisler & others, 2007).

Post-Traumatic Stress Disorder

Reexperiencing the Trauma

Key Theme

- **Extreme anxiety and intrusive thoughts are symptoms of both post-traumatic stress disorder (PTSD) and obsessive–compulsive disorder (OCD).**

Key Questions

- **What is PTSD, and what causes it?**
- **What is obsessive–compulsive disorder?**
- **What are the most common types of obsessions and compulsions?**

Post-traumatic stress disorder (PTSD) is a long-lasting anxiety disorder that develops in response to an extreme physical or psychological trauma. Extreme traumas are events that produce intense feelings of horror and helplessness, such as a serious physical injury or threat of injury to yourself or to loved ones.

Originally, post-traumatic stress disorder was primarily associated with direct experiences of military combat. Veterans of military conflict in Afghanistan and Iraq, like veterans of earlier wars, have a higher prevalence of PTSD than nonveterans (Fontana & Rosenheck, 2008). However, it's now known that PTSD can *also* develop in survivors of other sorts of extreme traumas, such as natural disasters, physical or sexual assault, random shooting sprees, or terrorist attacks (McNally, 2003). Rescue workers, relief workers, and emergency service personnel can also develop PTSD symptoms (Eriksson & others, 2001). Simply witnessing the injury or death of others can be sufficiently traumatic for PTSD to occur.

In any given year, it's estimated that more than 5 million American adults experience PTSD. There is also a significant gender difference—more than twice as many women as men experience PTSD after exposure to trauma (Olff & others, 2007). Children can also experience the symptoms of PTSD (Kaplow & others, 2006).

Invisible Wounds: PTSD Among Iraqi and Afghanistan Veterans Infantry scout Jesus Bocanegra witnessed firsthand suffering and death in Iraq. After returning, Bocanegra suffered from frequent flashbacks, nightmares, nervousness, and felt emotionally numb. Like Bocanegra, some 300,000 veterans have been diagnosed with PTSD or major depression (Tanielian, 2008). The high rate of PTSD and suicide may be related to unique aspects of the Iraq and Afghanistan conflicts. As Veterans Affairs physician Nancy Seal observes, "The majority of military personnel experience high-intensity guerrilla warfare and the chronic threat of roadside bombs and improvised explosive devices. Some soldiers endure multiple tours of duty, many experience traumatic injury, and more of the wounded survive than ever before" (Seal & others, 2007).

Three core symptoms characterize post-traumatic stress disorder (DSM-IV-TR, 2000). First, the person *frequently recalls the event,* replaying it in her mind. Such recollections are often *intrusive,* meaning that they are unwanted and interfere with normal thoughts. Second, the person avoids *stimuli or situations* that tend to trigger memories of the experience and undergoes a general *numbing of emotional responsiveness.* Third, the person experiences the *increased physical arousal* associated with anxiety. He may be easily startled, experience sleep disturbances, have problems concentrating and remembering, and be prone to irritability or angry outbursts (North & others, 2009).

Post-traumatic stress disorder is somewhat unusual in that the source of the disorder is the traumatic event itself, rather than a cause that lies within the individual. Even well-adjusted and psychologically healthy people may develop PTSD when exposed to an extremely traumatic event (Ozer & others, 2003).

Terrorist attacks, because of their suddenness and intensity, are particularly likely to produce post-traumatic stress disorder in survivors, rescue workers, and observers (Foa & others, 2008; Njenga & others, 2004). For example, four years after the bombing of the Murrah Building in Oklahoma City, more than a third of the survivors suffered from post-traumatic stress disorder. Almost all the survivors had some PTSD symptoms, such as flashbacks, nightmares, intrusive thoughts, and anxiety (North & others, 1999). Similarly, five years after the 9/11 terrorist attacks, more than 11 percent of rescue and recovery workers met formal criteria for PTSD—a rate comparable to that of soldiers returning from active duty in Iraq and Afghanistan (Stellman & others, 2008). Among people who had directly witnessed the attacks, over 16 percent had PTSD symptoms four years after the attacks (Farfel & others, 2008; Jayasinghe & others, 2008).

The Ravages of War: Child Soldiers An estimated quarter-million children serve as unwilling combatants in wars today, most of them kidnapped from their families and forced to serve as soldiers. Child soldiers not only suffer torture and violence, they are also often forced to commit atrocities against others. Not surprisingly, these children suffer from a very high rate of post-traumatic stress disorder (Bayer & others, 2007; Kohrt & others, 2008). One survey of former child soldiers in refugee camps in Uganda found that 97 percent of the children suffered from PTSD symptoms (see Dawson, 2007; Derluyn & others, 2004). Rehabilitation centers have been established throughout Uganda and the Democratic Republic of Congo, where many of these children live, but more assistance is desperately needed (Ursano & Shaw, 2007).

However, it's also important to note that no stressor, no matter how extreme, produces post-traumatic stress disorder in everyone. Why is it that some people develop PTSD while others don't? Several factors influence the likelihood of developing post-traumatic stress disorder. First, people with a personal or family history of psychological disorders are more likely to develop PTSD when exposed to an extreme trauma (Leonardo & Hen, 2005). Second, the magnitude of the trauma plays an important role. More extreme stressors are more likely to produce PTSD. Finally, when people undergo *multiple* traumas, the incidence of PTSD can be quite high.

Obsessive–Compulsive Disorder

Checking It Again . . . and Again

When you leave your home, you probably check to make sure all the doors are locked. You may even double-check just to be on the safe side. But once you're confident that the door is locked, you don't think about it again.

Now imagine you've checked the door *30* times. Yet you're still not quite sure that the door is really locked. You know the feeling is irrational, but you feel compelled to check again and again. Imagine you've *also* had to repeatedly check that the coffeepot was unplugged, that the stove was turned off, and so forth. Finally, imagine that you got only two blocks away from home before you felt compelled to turn back and check *again*—because you still were not certain.

Sound agonizing? This is the psychological world of the person who suffers from one form of obsessive–compulsive disorder. **Obsessive–compulsive disorder (OCD)** is an anxiety disorder in which a person's life is dominated by repetitive thoughts (*obsessions*) and behaviors (*compulsions*).

Obsessions are repeated, intrusive, uncontrollable thoughts or mental images that cause the person great anxiety and distress. Obsessions are not the same as everyday worries. Normal worries typically have some sort of factual basis, even if they're somewhat exaggerated. In contrast, obsessions have little or no basis in reality and are often extremely far-fetched. One common obsession is an irrational fear of dirt, germs, and other forms of contamination. Another common theme is pathological doubt about having accomplished a simple task, such as shutting off appliances (Antony & others, 2007).

post-traumatic stress disorder (PTSD)
An anxiety disorder in which chronic and persistent symptoms of anxiety develop in response to an extreme physical or psychological trauma.

obsessive–compulsive disorder (OCD)
An anxiety disorder in which the symptoms of anxiety are triggered by intrusive, repetitive thoughts and urges to perform certain actions.

obsessions
Repeated, intrusive, and uncontrollable irrational thoughts or mental images that cause extreme anxiety and distress.

compulsions
Repetitive behaviors or mental acts that are performed to prevent or reduce anxiety.

A **compulsion** is a repetitive behavior that a person feels driven to perform. Typically, compulsions are ritual behaviors that must be carried out in a certain pattern or sequence. Compulsions may be *overt physical behaviors*, such as repeatedly washing your hands, checking doors or windows, or entering and reentering a doorway until you walk through exactly in the middle. Or they may be *covert mental behaviors*, such as counting or reciting certain phrases to yourself. But note that the person does not compulsively wash his hands because he enjoys being clean. Rather, he washes his hands because to *not* do so causes extreme anxiety. If the person tries to resist performing the ritual, unbearable tension, anxiety, and distress result (Mathews, 2009).

Obsessions and compulsions tend to fall into a limited number of categories. About three-fourths of obsessive–compulsive patients suffer from multiple obsessions, and slightly more than half report more than one type of compulsion (Rasmussen & Eisen, 1992). The most common obsessions and compulsions are shown in Table 13.3.

Many people with obsessive–compulsive disorder have the irrational belief that failure to perform the ritual action will lead to a catastrophic or disastrous outcome (MacDonald & Davey, 2005). Recent research suggests that many people with OCD, especially those with checking or counting compulsions, are particularly prone to superstitious or "magical" thinking (Einstein & Menzies, 2004). Even though the person knows that his obsessions are irrational or his compulsions absurd, he is unable to resist their force.

People may experience either obsessions or compulsions. More commonly, obsessions and compulsions are *both* present. Often, the obsessions and compulsions are linked in some way. For example, a man who was obsessed with the idea that he might have lost an important document felt compelled to pick up every scrap of paper he saw on the street and in other public places.

Other compulsions bear little logical relationship to the feared consequences. For instance, a woman believed that if she didn't get dressed according to a strict pattern, her husband would die in an automobile accident. In all cases, people with obsessive–compulsive disorder feel that something terrible will happen if the compulsive action is left undone (Mathews, 2009).

Table 13.3

The Most Common Obsessions and Compulsions

Obsession	Description
Contamination	Irrational fear of contamination by dirt, germs, or other toxic substances. Typically accompanied by cleaning or washing compulsion.
Pathological doubt	Feeling of uncertainty about having accomplished a simple task. Recurring fear that you have inadvertently harmed someone or violated a law. Typically accompanied by checking compulsion.
Violent or sexual thoughts	Fear that you have harmed or will harm another person or have engaged or will engage in some sort of unacceptable behavior. May take the form of intrusive mental images or impulses.
Compulsion	**Description**
Washing	Urge to repeatedly wash yourself or clean your surroundings. Cleaning or washing may involve an elaborate, lengthy ritual. Often linked with contamination obsession.
Checking	Checking repeatedly to make sure that a simple task has been accomplished. Typically occurs in association with pathological doubt. Checking rituals may take hours.
Counting	Need to engage in certain behaviors a specific number of times or to count to a certain number before performing some action or task.
Symmetry and precision	Need for objects or actions to be perfectly symmetrical or in an exact order or position. Need to do or undo certain actions in an exact fashion.

Source: Based on Rasmussen & Eisen (1992), Table 1, p. 745.

Interestingly, obsessions and compulsions take a similar shape in different cultures around the world. However, the *content* of the obsessions and compulsions tends to mirror the particular culture's concerns and beliefs. In the United States, compulsive washers are typically preoccupied with obsessional fears of germs and infection. But in rural Nigeria and rural India, compulsive washers are more likely to have obsessional concerns about religious purity (Rapoport, 1989; Rego, 2009).

Explaining Obsessive–Compulsive Disorder

Although the causes of obsessive–compulsive disorder are still being investigated, evidence strongly suggests that biological factors are involved (McGregor, 2009). For example, a deficiency in the neurotransmitters norepinephrine and serotonin has been implicated in obsessive–compulsive disorder. When treated with drugs that increase the availability of these substances in the brain, many OCD patients experience a marked decrease in symptoms.

In addition, obsessive–compulsive disorder has been linked with dysfunction in specific brain areas, such as areas involved in the fight-or-flight response, and the frontal lobes, which play a key role in our ability to think and plan ahead (Anderson & Savage, 2004; Woo & Keatinge, 2008). Another brain area that has been implicated is the *caudate nucleus,* which is involved in regulating movements Guehl & others, 2008; Maia & others, 2009). Dysfunctions in these brain areas might help account for the overwhelming sense of doubt and the lack of control over thoughts and actions that are experienced in obsessive–compulsive disorder.

The anxiety disorders are summarized in Table 13.4.

Howard Hughes and Obsessive–Compulsive Disorder Shown at the controls of his "Spruce Goose" aircraft, Hughes was an extraordinary aviator, engineer, inventor, and film producer and director. But Hughes was also tormented by his obsessive fear of germs, which could be traced back to his childhood. Hughes's mother was constantly fearful that her son would catch polio or be sickened by germs. As an adult, Hughes developed increasingly extreme and bizarre compulsions, such as sitting naked for weeks in "germ free zones" in darkened hotel rooms and wearing tissue boxes on his feet. By the time Hughes died, he was a mentally ill recluse, emaciated, and a drug addict (Bartlett & Steele, 2004; Dittman, 2005).

Table 13.4

The Anxiety Disorders

General Anxiety Disorder (GAD)

- Persistent, chronic, unreasonable worry and anxiety
- General symptoms of anxiety, including persistent physical arousal

Panic Disorder

- Frequent and unexpected panic attacks, with no specific or identifiable trigger

Phobias

- Intense anxiety or panic attack triggered by a specific object or situation
- Persistent avoidance of feared object or situation

Post-Traumatic Stress Disorder (PTSD)

- Anxiety triggered by memories of a traumatic experience

Obsessive–Compulsive Disorder (OCD)

- Anxiety caused by uncontrollable, persistent, recurring thoughts (obsessions), and/or
- Anxiety caused by uncontrollable, persistent urges to perform certain actions (compulsions)

mood disorders
A category of mental disorders in which significant and persistent disruptions in mood or emotions cause impaired cognitive, behavioral, and physical functioning; also called *affective disorders*.

major depression
A mood disorder characterized by extreme and persistent feelings of despondency, worthlessness, and hopelessness, causing impaired emotional, cognitive, behavioral, and physical functioning.

seasonal affective disorder (SAD)
A mood disorder in which episodes of depression typically occur during the fall and winter and subside during the spring and summer

Mood Disorders
Emotions Gone Awry

Key Theme

- **In mood disorders, including major depression and bipolar disorder, disturbed emotions cause psychological distress and impair daily functioning.**

Key Questions

- **What are the symptoms and course of major depression, dysthymic disorder, bipolar disorder, and cyclothymic disorder?**
- **How prevalent are mood disorders?**
- **What factors contribute to the development of mood disorders?**

Let's face it, we all have our ups and downs. When things are going well, we feel cheerful and optimistic. When events take a more negative turn, our mood can sour: We feel miserable and pessimistic. Either way, the intensity and duration of our moods are usually in proportion to the events going on in our lives. That's completely normal.

In mood disorders, however, emotions violate the criteria of normal moods. In quality, intensity, and duration, a person's emotional state does not seem to reflect what's going on in his or her life. A person may feel a pervasive sadness despite the best of circumstances. Or a person may be extremely energetic and overconfident with no apparent justification. These mood changes persist much longer than the normal fluctuations in moods that we all experience.

DSM-IV-TR formally defines a **mood disorder** as a serious, persistent disturbance in a person's emotions that causes psychological discomfort, impairs the ability to function, or both. Mood disorders are also often called *affective disorders*. The word "affect" is synonymous with "emotion" or "feelings". In this section, we'll look at the two most important mood disorders: major depression and bipolar disorder.

Kurt Cobain As leader of the alternative rock band Nirvana, Kurt Cobain seemed to have everything: fame, artistic recognition, wealth, and adulation from both fans and music critics. But Cobain also had a history of troubling episodes of deep depression and had attempted suicide several times. Like other people gripped by depression, Cobain focused on the negative during his dark episodes. This negative outlook was sometimes reflected in his lyrics. Just before the release of *In Utero*, the group's last album, Cobain pulled a song he had written titled "I Hate Myself and I Want to Die." Not long after the release of that album, Cobain committed suicide by shooting himself in the head with a shotgun. In his suicide note, Cobain described himself as a "miserable, self-destructive death rocker."

Major Depression
More Than Ordinary Sadness

The intense psychological pain of **major depression** is hard to convey to those who have never experienced it. In his book *Darkness Visible*, best-selling author William Styron (1990) described his struggle with major depression in this way:

> All sense of hope had vanished, along with the idea of a futurity; my brain, in thrall to its outlaw hormones, had become less an organ of thought than an instrument registering, minute by minute, varying degrees of its own suffering. The mornings themselves were becoming bad now as I wandered about lethargic, following my synthetic sleep, but afternoons were still the worst, beginning at about three o'clock, when I'd feel the horror, like some poisonous fogbank, roll in upon my mind, forcing me into bed. There I would lie for as long as six hours, stuporous and virtually paralyzed, gazing at the ceiling . . .

The Symptoms of Major Depression

The Styron passage gives you a feeling for how the symptoms of depression affect the whole person—emotionally, cognitively, behaviorally, and physically. Take a few minutes to study Figure 13.3, which summarizes the common symptoms of major depression. Depression is also often accompanied by the physical symptoms of anxiety (Klein & others, 2008). Some depressed people experience a sense of physical restlessness or nervousness, demonstrated by fidgeting or aimless pacing.

Suicide is always a potential risk in major depression. Thoughts become globally pessimistic and negative about the self, the world, and the future (Hammen &

Figure 13.3 The Symptoms of Major Depression The experience of major depression can permeate every aspect of life. This figure shows some of the most common emotional, behavioral, cognitive, and physical symptoms of that disorder.

Watkins, 2008). This pervasive negativity and pessimism are often manifested in suicidal thoughts or a preoccupation with death. Rates of completed suicide by those diagnosed with major depression range from 7 to 22 percent (Woo & Keatinge, 2008).

Abnormal sleep patterns are another hallmark of major depression. The amount of time spent in nondreaming, deeply relaxed sleep is greatly reduced or absent (see Chapter 4). Rather than the usual 90-minute cycles of dreaming, the person experiences sporadic REM periods of varying lengths. Spontaneous awakenings occur repeatedly during the night. Very commonly, the depressed person awakens at 3:00 or 4:00 A.M., then cannot get back to sleep, despite feeling exhausted. Less commonly, some depressed people sleep excessively, sometimes as much as 18 hours a day.

To be diagnosed with major depression, a person must display most of the symptoms described for two weeks or longer (DSM-IV-TR, 2000). In many cases, there doesn't seem to be any external reason for the persistent feeling of depression. In other cases, a person's downward emotional spiral has been triggered by a negative life event, stressful situation, or chronic stress (Hammen, 2005; Southwick & others, 2005).

One significant negative event deserves special mention: the death of a loved one. If a family member or close friend dies, it is completely normal to feel despondent and sad for several months as part of the mourning or bereavement process. Even so, most people resume attending to the routine duties of life within a few weeks. Privately, they may still feel a strong sense of loss, but they function adequately, if not optimally. As a general rule, if a person's ability to function after the death of a loved one is still seriously impaired after two months, major depression is suspected (DSM-IV-TR, 2000).

Although major depression can occur at any time, some people experience symptoms that intensify at certain times of the year. For people with **seasonal affective disorder (SAD),** repeated episodes of major depression are as predictable as the changing seasons, especially the onset of autumn and winter when there is the least amount of sunlight. Seasonal affective disorder is more common among women and among people who live in the northern latitudes (Partonen & Pandi-Perumal, 2010).

Sheryl Crow Grammy award-winning singer Sheryl Crow has struggled with depression since she was a young child. Of her chronic depression, she has said, "I grew up in the presence of melancholy, a feeling of loss. . . . It is a shadow for me. It's part of who I am. It is constantly there. I just know how, at this point, to sort of manage it."

dysthymic disorder
(dis-THY-mick) A mood disorder involving chronic, low-grade feelings of depression that produce subjective discomfort but do not seriously impair the ability to function.

Dysthymic Disorder

In contrast to major depression, which significantly impairs a person's ability to function, some people experience a less severe form of depression called *dysthymic disorder*. Briefly, **dysthymic disorder** is chronic, low-grade depression. It's characterized by many of the symptoms of depression, but the symptoms are less intense. Usually, dysthymic disorder develops in response to some stressful event or trauma. Rather than improving over time, however, the negative mood persists indefinitely. Although the person functions adequately, she has a chronic case of "the blues" that can continue for years. The DSM-IV-TR criteria regarding duration of symptoms are a good indicator of the difference between major depression and dysthymic disorder: Major depression requires symptoms to be present for at least two weeks, while dysthymic disorder requires two years.

The Prevalence and Course of Major Depression

Major depression is often called "the common cold" of psychological disorders, and for good reason: It is among the most prevalent psychological disorders. In any given year, about 6 to 7 percent of Americans are affected by major depression (Kessler & others, 2005b). In terms of lifetime prevalence, about 15 percent of Americans will be affected by major depression at some point in their life.

Women are about twice as likely as men to be diagnosed with major depression (Hammen & Watkins, 2008). Why the striking gender difference in the prevalence of major depression? Research by psychologist Susan Nolen-Hoeksema (2001, 2003) suggests that women are more vulnerable to depression because they experience a greater degree of chronic stress in daily life combined with a lesser sense of personal control than men. Women are also more prone to dwell on their problems, adding to the sense of low mastery and chronic strain in their lives. The interaction of these factors creates a vicious circle that intensifies and perpetuates depressed feelings in women (Nolen-Hoeksema, 2010; Nolen-Hoeksema & others, 2007).

Many people who experience major depression try to cope with the symptoms without seeking professional help (Edlund & others, 2008; Kessler & others, 2003). Left untreated, the symptoms of major depression can easily last six months or longer. When not treated, depression may become a recurring mental disorder that becomes progressively more severe. More than half of all people who have been through one episode of major depression can expect a relapse, usually within two years. With each recurrence, the symptoms tend to increase in severity and the time between major depression episodes decreases (Hammen, 2005).

Brain Activity During the Extremes of Bipolar Disorder These PET scans record the brain activity of an individual with bipolar disorder as he cycled rapidly from depression to mania and back to depression over a 10-day period. In the top and bottom PET scans, the blue and green colors clearly show the sharp reduction in overall brain activity that coincided with the episodes of depression. In the center PET scans, the bright red, orange, and yellow colors indicate high levels of activity in diverse brain regions during the intervening episodes of mania.

Source: Lewis Baxter and Michael E. Phelps, UCLA School of Medicine.

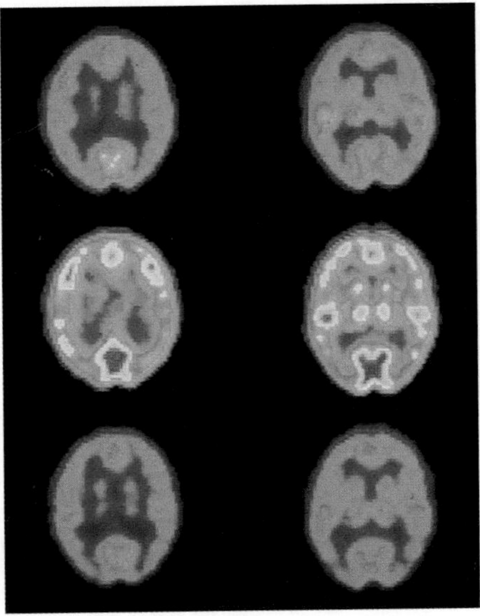

Bipolar Disorder

An Emotional Roller Coaster

Years ago, your author Don worked in the psychiatric ward of a large hospital. As Don arrived for work early one morning and headed for the nurses' station, a tall, overweight young man with black curly hair *zoomed* across the ward and intercepted him.

"Hi! My name's Kelly! What's yours?" he enthusiastically boomed, vigorously shaking hands. But before Don could respond, Kelly had already moved on to new topics. Within the next 90 seconds, Don heard about (1) Kelly's plans to make millions of dollars organizing garage sales for other people; (2) several songs that Kelly had written that were all going to skyrocket to the top of the music charts; (3) Kelly's many inventions; and (4) a variety of movie stars, rock stars, and professional athletes, all of whom were Kelly's close friends.

Kelly spoke so rapidly that his words often got tangled up with each other. His arms and legs looked as if they were about to get tangled up, too—Kelly was in constant motion. His grinning, rapid-fire speech was punctuated with grand, sweeping gestures and exaggerated facial expressions. Before Don could get a word in edgewise, Kelly vigorously shook his hand again and *zoomed* to the other side of the psychiatric ward to intercept another stranger.

The Symptoms of Bipolar Disorder

Kelly displayed classic symptoms of the mental disorder that used to be called *manic depression* and is today called **bipolar disorder.** In contrast to major depression, bipolar disorder almost always involves abnormal moods at *both* ends of the emotional spectrum. In most cases of bipolar disorder, the person experiences extreme mood swings. Episodes of incapacitating depression alternate with shorter periods of extreme euphoria, called **manic episodes.** For most people with bipolar disorder, a manic episode immediately precedes or follows a bout with major depression. However, a small percentage of people with bipolar disorder experience only manic episodes (DSM-IV-TR, 2000).

Manic episodes typically begin suddenly, and symptoms escalate rapidly. During a manic episode, people are uncharacteristically euphoric, expansive, and excited for several days or longer. Although they sleep very little, they have boundless energy. The person's self-esteem is wildly inflated, and he exudes supreme self-confidence. Often, he has grandiose plans for obtaining wealth, power, and fame (Carlson & Meyer, 2006; Miklowitz, 2008). Sometimes the grandiose ideas represent *delusional*, or false, beliefs. Kelly's belief that various celebrities were his close personal friends was delusional.

Kelly's fast-forward speech was loud and virtually impossible to interrupt. During a manic episode, words are spoken so rapidly, they're often slurred as the person tries to keep up with his own thought processes. The manic person feels as if his thoughts are racing along at warp factor 10. Attention is easily distracted by virtually anything, triggering a *flight of ideas,* in which thoughts rapidly and loosely shift from topic to topic.

Not surprisingly, the ability to function during a manic episode is severely impaired. Hospitalization is usually required, partly to protect people from the potential consequences of their inappropriate decisions and behaviors. During manic episodes, people can also run up a mountain of bills, disappear for weeks at a time, become sexually promiscuous, or commit illegal acts. Very commonly, the person becomes agitated or verbally abusive when others question his grandiose claims (Miklowitz & Johnson, 2007).

Some people experience a milder but chronic form of bipolar disorder called cyclothymic disorder. In **cyclothymic disorder,** people experience moderate but frequent mood swings for two years or longer. These mood swings are not severe enough to qualify as either bipolar disorder or major depression. Often, people with cyclothymic disorder are perceived as being extremely moody, unpredictable, and inconsistent.

The Prevalence and Course of Bipolar Disorder

As in Kelly's case, the onset of bipolar disorder typically occurs in the person's early 20s. The extreme mood swings of bipolar disorder tend to start and stop much more abruptly than the mood changes of major depression. And while an episode of major depression can easily last for six months or longer, the manic and depressive episodes of bipolar disorder tend to be much shorter—lasting anywhere from a few days to a couple of months (Bowden, 2005).

Bipolar disorder is far less common than major depression. Unlike major depression, there are no differences between the sexes in the rate at which bipolar disorder occurs. For both men and women, the lifetime risk of developing bipolar disorder is about 1 percent (Miklowitz & Johnson, 2007). Bipolar disorder is rarely diagnosed in childhood. Some evidence suggests that children who display unusually unstable moods are more likely to be diagnosed with bipolar disorder in adulthood (Blader & Carlson, 2008).

In the vast majority of cases, bipolar disorder is a recurring mental disorder (Jones & Tarrier, 2005). A small percentage of people with bipolar disorder display *rapid cycling,* experiencing four or more manic or depressive episodes every year (Marneros & Goodwin, 2005). More commonly, bipolar disorder tends to recur every couple of years. Often, bipolar disorder recurs when the individual stops taking *lithium,* a medication that helps control the disorder.

Carrie Fisher and Bipolar Disorder By age 20, Fisher had become a cultural icon in her role as Princess Leia in George Lucas's *Star Wars* trilogy. By age 24, Fisher was grappling with drug addiction and bipolar disorder. Today, Fisher is a successful actress and writer. Her critically acclaimed one-woman Broadway show, *Wishful Drinking,* is a funny yet bluntly honest memoir of her struggles. During her performance, Fisher displays her photo as it appears in an abnormal psychology textbook. Fisher prefers the older term, *manic-depression*, because, she quips, "It describes what it's like. Bipolar sounds like a gay bear from Alaska." Fisher manages her symptoms with a combination of medication and electroconvulsive therapy, which we discuss in Chapter 14.

bipolar disorder
A mood disorder involving periods of incapacitating depression alternating with periods of extreme euphoria and excitement; formerly called *manic depression.*

manic episode
A sudden, rapidly escalating emotional state characterized by extreme euphoria, excitement, physical energy, and rapid thoughts and speech.

cyclothymic disorder
(si-klo-THY-mick) A mood disorder characterized by moderate but frequent mood swings that are not severe enough to qualify as bipolar disorder.

Explaining Mood Disorders

Multiple factors appear to be involved in the development of mood disorders. First, family, twin, and adoption studies suggest that some people inherit a *genetic predisposition,* or a greater vulnerability, to mood disorders. Researchers have consistently found that both major depression and bipolar disorder tend to run in families (Leonardo & Hen, 2005). And twin studies have shown that major depression has a strong genetic component (Levinson, 2009; Kendler & others, 2006).

A second factor that has been implicated in the development of mood disorders is disruptions in brain chemistry. Since the 1960s, several medications, called *antidepressants,* have been developed to treat major depression. In one way or another, the antidepressants seem to lift the symptoms of depression by increasing the availability of two neurotransmitters, norepinephrine and serotonin, in the brain.

Abnormal levels of another neurotransmitter may also be involved in bipolar disorder. For decades, it's been known that the drug lithium effectively alleviates symptoms of both mania and depression. Apparently, lithium regulates the availability of

CRITICAL THINKING

Does Smoking Cause Depression and Other Psychological Disorders?

Are people with a mental disorder more likely to smoke than other people? Researcher Karen Lasser and her colleagues (2000) assessed smoking rates in American adults with and without psychological disorders. Lasser found that people with mental illness are nearly twice as likely to smoke cigarettes as people with no mental illness. Here are some of the specific findings from Lasser's study:

- Forty-one percent of individuals with a current mental disorder are smokers, as compared to 22 percent of people who have never been diagnosed with a mental disorder.
- People with a mental illness are more likely to be heavy smokers, consuming a pack of cigarettes per day or more.
- People who have been diagnosed with multiple mental disorders have higher rates of smoking and smoke more heavily than people with fewer mental disorders (see the graph on the next page).
- Forty-four percent of all cigarettes smoked in the United States are consumed by people with one or more mental disorders.

What can account for the correlation between smoking and psychological disorders? Subjectively, smokers often report that they experience better attention and concentration, increased energy, lower anxiety, and greater calm after smoking, effects that are probably due to the nicotine in tobacco. So, one possible explanation is that people with a mental illness smoke as a form of self-medication. Notice that this explanation assumes that mental illness *causes* people to smoke.

Nicotine, of course, is a powerful psychoactive drug. It triggers the release of *dopamine* and stimulates key brain structures involved in producing rewarding sensations, including the *thalamus,* the *amygdala,* and the *nucleus accumbens* (Le Foll & Goldberg, 2007; Salokangas & others, 2000; Stein & others, 1998). Nicotine receptors on different neurons also regulate the release of other important neurotransmitters, including *serotonin, acetylcholine, GABA,* and *glutamate* (McGehee & others, 2007; Quattrocki & others, 2000). In other words, nicotine affects multiple brain structures and alters the release of many different neurotransmitters. These same

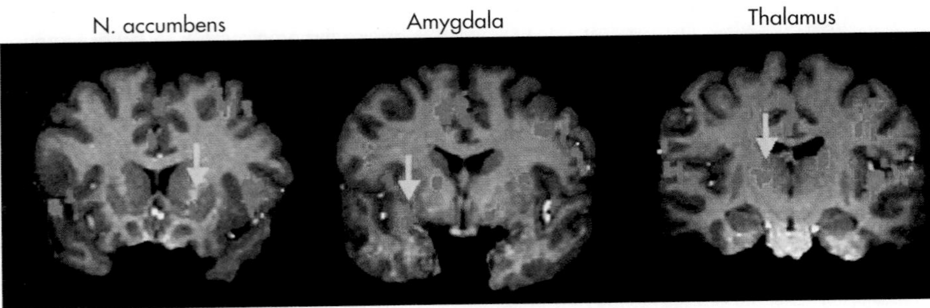

Nicotine's Effects in the Brain After cigarette smokers were injected with up to two milligrams of nicotine, researchers used functional magnetic resonance imaging to track the brain areas activated, which included the *nucleus accumbens,* the *amygdala,* and the *thalamus.* Previous research has shown that these brain structures produce the reinforcing, mood-elevating properties of other abused drugs, including cocaine, amphetamines, and opiates (Stein & others, 1998).

a neurotransmitter called *glutamate*, which acts as an excitatory neurotransmitter in many brain areas (Dixon & Hokin, 1998). By normalizing glutamate levels, lithium helps prevent both the excesses that may cause mania and the deficits that may cause depression.

Stress is also implicated in the development of mood disorders. Major depression is often triggered by traumatic and stressful events (Southwick & others, 2005). Exposure to recent stressful events is one of the best predictors of episodes of major depression. This is especially true for people who have experienced previous episodes of depression and who have a family history of mood disorders. But even in people with no family or personal history of mood disorders, chronic stress can produce major depression (Muscatell & others, 2009).

Finally, recent research has uncovered some intriguing links between cigarette smoking and the development of major depression and other psychological disorders (Munafo & others, 2008; Breslau & others, 2004). We explore the connection between cigarette smoking and mental illness in the Critical Thinking box "Does Smoking Cause Depression and Other Psychological Disorders?"

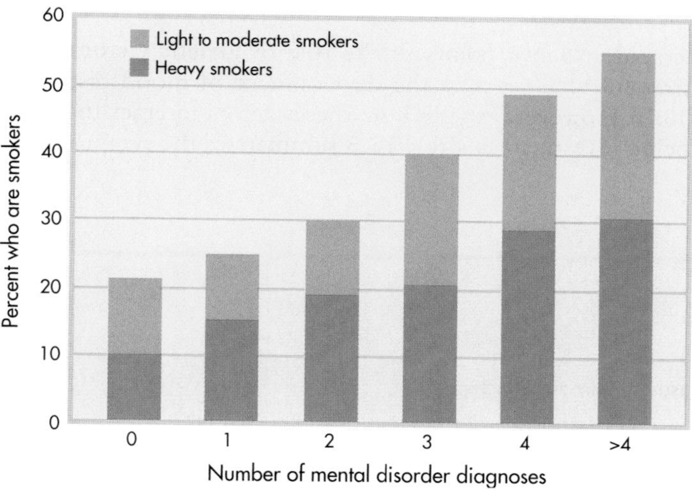

Smoking Rates Compared to the Number of Lifetime Mental Disorder Diagnoses

Source: Lasser & others (2000).

brain areas and neurotransmitters are also directly involved in many different mental disorders.

Although the idea that mental illness causes smoking seems to make sense, some researchers now believe that the arrow of causation points in the *opposite* direction. In the past decade, many studies have suggested that smoking triggers the onset of symptoms in people who are probably already vulnerable to the development of a mental disorder, especially major depression. Consider just a few studies:

- The lifetime prevalence of developing major depression is strongly linked to the number of cigarettes consumed (Breslau & others, 1993, 1998; Kendler, Neale, & others, 1993b). People who smoke a pack of cigarettes or more per day have a 50 percent chance of experiencing major depression, while nonsmokers have about a 17 percent chance.
- Three separate studies focusing on adolescents found that cigarette smoking predicted the onset of depressive symptoms, rather than the other way around (Goodman & Capitman, 2000; Ohayon, 2007; Windle & Windle, 2001; Wu & Anthony, 1999).
- In a study of patients with bipolar disorder, the prevalence and severity of cigarette smoking predicted the severity of psychotic symptoms during manic episodes (Corvin & others, 2001).
- A positive association was found between smoking and the severity of symptoms experienced by people with anxiety disorders (McCabe & others, 2004).
- In a study of people with schizophrenia, 90 percent of the patients had started smoking *before* their illness began (Kelly & McCreadie, 1999). This suggests that in vulnerable people, smoking may precipitate a person's initial schizophrenic episode.

Further research may help disentangle the complex interaction between smoking and mental disorders, but one fact is known: Mentally ill cigarette smokers, like other smokers, are at much greater risk of premature disability and death. So along with the psychological and personal suffering that accompanies almost all psychological disorders, the mentally ill carry the additional burden of consuming nearly half of all the cigarettes smoked in the United States.

CRITICAL THINKING QUESTIONS

- Is the evidence sufficient to conclude that there is a causal relationship between cigarette smoking and the onset of mental illness symptoms? Why or why not?
- Should tobacco companies be required to contribute part of their profits to the cost of mental health treatment and research?

Creativity and Mood Disorders Mood disorders occur more frequently among creative writers and artists than among the general population, leading some researchers to propose a biochemical or genetic link between mood disorders and the artistic temperament (Jamison, 1993). Writer Mark Twain, novelist Ernest Hemingway, and poet Sylvia Plath all suffered from severe bouts of depression throughout their lives. Both Plath and Hemingway committed suicide, as did Hemingway's father, brother, and sister. In 1996, Hemingway's granddaughter, actress Margaux Hemingway, also committed suicide just one day before the 35th anniversary of her famous grandfather's death.

In summary, considerable evidence points to the role of genetic factors, biochemical factors, and stressful life events in the development of mood disorders (Feliciano & Arean, 2007). However, exactly how these factors interact to cause mood disorders is still being investigated. Table 13.5 summarizes the symptoms of mood disorders.

Table 13.5

The Mood Disorders

Major Depression

- Loss of interest or pleasure in almost all activities
- Despondent mood, feelings of emptiness, worthlessness, or excessive guilt
- Preoccupation with death or suicidal thoughts
- Difficulty sleeping or excessive sleeping
- Diminished ability to think, concentrate, or make decisions
- Diminished appetite and significant weight loss

Dysthymic Disorder

- Chronic, low-grade depressed feelings that are not severe enough to qualify as major depression

Seasonal Affective Disorder (SAD)

- Recurring episodes of depression that follow a seasonal pattern, typically occurring in the fall and winter months and subsiding in the spring and summer months

Bipolar Disorder

- One or more manic episodes characterized by euphoria, high energy, grandiose ideas, flight of ideas, inappropriate self-confidence, and decreased need for sleep
- Usually one or more episodes of major depression
- In some cases, may rapidly alternate between symptoms of mania and major depression

Cyclothymic Disorder

- Moderate, recurring mood swings that are not severe enough to qualify as major depression or bipolar disorder

Eating Disorders
Anorexia and Bulimia

Key Theme

- **The most important eating disorders are anorexia nervosa and bulimia, which are psychological disorders characterized by severely disturbed, maladaptive eating behaviors.**

Key Questions

- **What are the symptoms, characteristics, and causes of anorexia nervosa?**
- **What are the symptoms, characteristics, and causes of bulimia nervosa?**

Eating disorders involve serious and maladaptive disturbances in eating behavior. These disturbances can include extreme reduction of food intake, severe bouts of overeating, and obsessive concerns about body shape or weight (American Psychiatric Association, 2000a). The two main types of eating disorders are *anorexia nervosa* and *bulimia nervosa,* which usually begin during adolescence or early adulthood (see Table 13.6). Ninety to 95 percent of the people who experience an eating disorder are female (Thompson & others, 2007). Despite the 10-to-1 gender-difference ratio, the central features of eating disorders are similar for males and females (Andersen, 2002).

Anorexia Nervosa
Life-Threatening Weight Loss

Four key features define **anorexia nervosa.** First, the person refuses to maintain a minimally normal body weight. With a body weight that is 15 percent or more below normal, body mass index can drop to 12 or lower. Second, despite being dangerously underweight, the person with anorexia is intensely afraid of gaining weight or becoming fat. Third, she has a distorted perception about the size of her body. Although emaciated, she looks in the mirror and sees herself as fat or obese. And fourth, she denies the seriousness of her weight loss (American Psychiatric Association, 2000b).

Table 13.6

Eating Disorders

Anorexia Nervosa

- Severe and extreme disturbance in eating habits and calorie intake
- Body weight that is less than 85% of what would be considered normal for the person's age, height, and gender, and refusal to maintain a normal body weight
- Intense fear of gaining weight or becoming fat
- Distorted perceptions about the severity of weight loss and a distorted self-image, such that even an extremely emaciated person may perceive herself as fat
- In females, absence of menstrual cycles

Bulimia Nervosa

- Recurring episodes of binge eating, which is defined as an excessive amount of calories within a two-hour period
- The inability to control or stop the excessive eating behavior
- Recurrent episodes of purging, which is defined as using laxatives, diuretics, self-induced vomiting, or other methods to prevent weight gain

eating disorder
A category of mental disorders characterized by severe disturbances in eating behavior.

anorexia nervosa
An eating disorder characterized by excessive weight loss, an irrational fear of gaining weight, and distorted body self-perception.

Is Anorexia Glamorous? Erika, 26, is a patient at an eating disorders center in Italy. Despite the enormous social pressure on girls and women to be thin, there is nothing glamorous about death by heart or kidney failure. Anorexia also causes loss of hair, muscle, and teeth. Other complications include osteoporosis, loss of reproductive function, chronic fatigue, and physical weakness. Extreme malnutrition produces a fine, soft hair called *lanugo* that may cover the face, chest, arms, and back. Eating disorders are also associated with increased rates of suicide (Crow & others, 2009). For information or help visit the National Eating Disorders Association Web site at www.nationaleatingdisorders.org or call 1-800-931-2237.

The severe malnutrition caused by anorexia disrupts body chemistry in ways that are very similar to those caused by starvation. Basal metabolic rate decreases, as do blood levels of glucose, insulin, and leptin. Other hormonal levels drop, including the level of reproductive hormones. In women, reduced estrogen results in the menstrual cycle stopping. In males, decreased testosterone disrupts sex drive and sexual function (Crosscope-Happel & others, 2000). Because the ability to retain body heat is greatly diminished, people with severe anorexia often develop a soft, fine body hair called *lanugo* (Beumont, 2002).

Bulimia Nervosa

Bingeing and Purging

Like people with anorexia, people with **bulimia nervosa** fear gaining weight. Intense preoccupation and dissatisfaction with their bodies are also apparent. However, people with bulimia stay within a normal weight range or may even be slightly overweight. Another difference is that people with bulimia usually recognize that they have an eating disorder.

People with bulimia nervosa experience extreme periods of binge eating, consuming as many as 50,000 calories on a single binge. Binges typically occur twice a week and are often triggered by negative feelings or hunger. During the binge, the person usually consumes sweet, high-calorie foods that can be swallowed quickly, such as ice cream, cake, and candy. Binges typically occur in secrecy, leaving the person feeling ashamed, guilty, and disgusted by his own behavior. After bingeing, he compensates by purging himself of the excessive food by self-induced vomiting or by misuse of laxatives or enemas. Once he purges, he often feels psychologically relieved. Some people with bulimia don't purge themselves of the excess food. Rather, they use fasting and excessive exercise to keep their body weight within the normal range (American Psychiatric Association, 2000b).

Like anorexia nervosa, bulimia nervosa can take a serious physical toll on the body. Repeated purging disrupts the body's electrolyte balance, leading to muscle cramps, irregular heartbeat, and other cardiac problems, some potentially fatal. Stomach acids from self-induced vomiting erode tooth enamel, causing tooth decay and gum disease. Especially when practiced for long periods of time, frequent vomiting severely damages the gastrointestinal tract as well as the teeth (Powers, 2009).

bulimia nervosa
An eating disorder characterized by binges of extreme overeating followed by self-induced vomiting, misuse of laxatives, or other inappropriate methods to purge the excessive food and prevent weight gain.

Causes of Eating Disorders

A Complex Picture

Both anorexia and bulimia involve decreases in brain activity of the neurotransmitter *serotonin* (Fumeron & others, 2001). Disrupted brain chemistry probably also contributes to the fact that eating disorders frequently co-occur with other psychiatric disorders, such as depression, substance abuse, personality disorders, and anxiety disorders, including obsessive–compulsive disorder (Thompson & others, 2007). While chemical imbalances may cause eating disorders, researchers are also studying whether they can result from them as well (Smolak, 2009).

Family interaction patterns may also contribute to eating disorders. For example, critical comments by parents or siblings about a child's weight, or parental modeling of disordered eating, may increase the odds that an individual develops an eating disorder (Thompson & others, 2007).

Although anorexia and bulimia have been documented for at least 150 years, contemporary Western cultural attitudes toward thinness and dieting probably contribute to the increased incidence of eating disorders today. This seems to be especially true with anorexia, which occurs predominantly in Western or "westernized" countries (Anderson-Fye, 2009; Becker & Fay, 2006; Cafri & others, 2005).

Size 0: An Impossible Cultural Ideal? As average citizens have been getting heavier, top fashion models have been getting thinner. Eating disorders are most prevalent in developed, Western countries where a slender body is the cultural ideal, especially for women and girls. Many psychologists believe that such unrealistic body expectations contribute to eating disorders (Hawkins & others, 2004; Treasure & others, 2008). After the anorexia-related deaths of two famous Brazilian fashion models, France, Germany, and Spain proposed bans on ultra-thin models. Despite periodic outcries, the emaciated, skin-and-bones look continues to be the fashion industry norm.

Personality Disorders

Maladaptive Traits

Key Theme

- **The personality disorders are characterized by inflexible, maladaptive patterns of thoughts, emotions, behavior, and interpersonal functioning.**

Key Questions

- **How do people with a personality disorder differ from people who are psychologically well-adjusted?**
- **What are the three categories of personality disorders?**
- **What behaviors and personality characteristics are associated with the paranoid, antisocial, and borderline personality disorders?**

Like every other person, you have your own unique *personality*—the consistent and enduring patterns of thinking, feeling, and behaving that characterize you as an individual. As we described in Chapter 10, your personality can be described as a specific collection of personality traits. Your *personality traits* are relatively stable predispositions to behave or react in certain ways. In other words, your personality traits reflect different dimensions of your personality.

By definition, personality traits are consistent over time and across situations. But that's not to say that personality traits are etched in stone. Rather, the psychologically well-adjusted person possesses a fair degree of flexibility and adaptiveness. Based on our experiences with others, we are able to modify how we display our personality traits so that we can think, feel, and behave in ways that are more effective.

In contrast, someone with a **personality disorder** has personality traits that are *inflexible* and *maladaptive* across a broad range of situations. Some researchers believe that personality disorders reflect conditions in which "normal" personality traits are taken to an abnormal extreme (Trull & Widiger, 2008; Fowler & others, 2007). However, the behavior of people with personality disorders goes well beyond that of

personality disorder
Inflexible, maladaptive patterns of thoughts, emotions, behavior, and interpersonal functioning that are stable over time and across situations, and deviate from the expectations of the individual's culture.

a normal individual who occasionally experiences a meltdown or who is grumpier, more skeptical, or more careful than most people. By definition, the personality disorders involve pervasive patterns of perceiving, relating to, and thinking about the environment and the self that interfere with long-term functioning. And these maladaptive behaviors are *not* restricted to isolated episodes or specific circumstances.

Usually, personality disorders become evident during adolescence or early adulthood. These maladaptive patterns of emotions, thought processes, and behavior tend to be very stable over time. They also deviate markedly from the social and behavioral expectations of the individual's culture. Personality disorders are evident in about 9 to 15 percent of the general population (Grant & others, 2004; Lenzenweger & others, 2007).

Despite the fact that the maladaptive personality traits consistently cause personal or social turmoil, people with personality disorders may not consider their personality characteristics as being problematic. In other words, they are unable to see that their inflexible style of thinking and behaving is at the root of their personal and social difficulties. Consequently, people with personality disorders often don't seek help because they don't think they have a problem.

Ten distinct personality disorders have been identified. They are categorized into three basic clusters: *odd, eccentric* personality disorders; *dramatic, emotional, erratic* personality disorders; and *anxious, fearful* personality disorders. The key features of each personality disorder are summarized in Table 13.7. In this section, we'll focus our discussion on three of the best-known personality disorders: paranoid personality disorder, antisocial personality disorder, and borderline personality disorder.

Table 13.7

Personality Disorders

Odd, Eccentric Cluster	Dramatic, Emotional, Erratic Cluster	Anxious, Fearful Cluster
Paranoid Personality Disorder • Pervasive but unwarranted distrust and suspiciousness; assumes that other people intend to deceive, exploit, or harm them.	**Antisocial Personality Disorder** • Blatantly disregards or violates the rights of others; impulsive, irresponsible, deceitful, manipulative, and lacks guilt or remorse.	**Avoidant Personality Disorder** • Extreme social inhibition due to feelings of inadequacy, and hypersensitivity to criticism, rejection, or disapproval.
Schizoid Personality Disorder • Pervasive detachment from social relationships; emotionally cold and flat; indifferent to praise or criticism from others.	**Borderline Personality Disorder** • Erratic, unstable relationships, emotions, and self-image; impulsive; desperate efforts to avoid real or imagined abandonment; feelings of emptiness; self-destructive tendencies.	**Dependent Personality Disorder** • Excessive need to be taken care of, leading to submissive, clinging behavior; fears of separation; and the inability to assume responsibility.
Schizotypal Personality Disorder • Odd thoughts, speech, emotional reactions, mannerisms, and appearance; impaired social and interpersonal functioning; often superstitious.	**Histrionic Personality Disorder** • Exaggerated, overly dramatic expression of emotions and attention-seeking behavior that often includes sexually seductive or provocative behaviors.	**Obsessive–Compulsive Personality Disorder** • Rigid preoccupation with orderliness, personal control, rules, or schedules that interferes with completing tasks; unreasonable perfectionism.
	Narcissistic Personality Disorder • Grandiose sense of self-importance; exaggerates abilities and accomplishments; excessive need for admiration; boastful, pretentious.	

Source: Adapted from DSM-IV-TR (2000).

Paranoid Personality Disorder

Pervasive Distrust and Suspiciousness

Doug doesn't trust anyone. He "knows" that strangers, co-workers, and even his family and friends are trying to hurt him. He is convinced that his employer is trying to steal his ideas and treating him unfairly, that the woman he recently began dating is interested only in using him, and that his family members are trying to take advantage of him or humiliate him. Needless to say, other people soon tire of Doug's unfounded suspicions, hostility, and accusations.

Pervasive mistrust and suspiciousness of others are the defining features of the **paranoid personality disorder.** About 3 percent of the general population displays this disorder, which occurs most frequently in men (Oltmanns & Okada, 2006).

Individuals with paranoid personality disorder are constantly on guard. Why? Because they think that other people are out to exploit, harm, or dupe them. For example, when a waitress miscalculated the total on Doug's check, he became furious, assuming she was trying to rip him off. When a neighbor's trash can got tipped over and trash blew into Doug's yard, he was quite angry, convinced that the neighbor had dumped it there on purpose.

People with this personality disorder often misinterpret the innocent comments or actions of others. For example, playful teasing from a co-worker is seen as a deliberate insult, an attack on their character or reputation (Bernstein & Useda, 2007; DSM-IV-TR, 2000). Inappropriate outbursts of anger can occur when the person feels as though he has been wronged by some kind of slight, insult, or injustice—which happens frequently.

People with paranoid personality disorder are distrustful of people who are close to them, even when there is no evidence to support their suspicious beliefs. Not surprisingly, they are very reluctant to form close attachments or confide in others. Doing so, they believe, leaves them vulnerable because the other person could use that information against them. People with this personality disorder also have a strong tendency to blame others for their own shortcomings. They are often harshly critical of what they perceive as the shortcomings of colleagues, friends, or family members. Though they may superficially present themselves as being objective and unemotional, their underlying hostility is evident in sarcastic comments and put-downs. If another person responds in kind, it only confirms their belief that other people are out to attack them.

Pathological jealousy commonly characterizes the intimate relationships of the person with a paranoid personality disorder. Although his spouse or sexual partner may never have given any indication of unfaithfulness, he still suspects and accuses his mate of harboring feelings of infidelity. When his partner is 10 minutes late, makes casual social conversation with other people, or inadvertently rushes out of the house without her wedding ring, the individual with paranoid personality disorder seizes on this behavior as "evidence" of the intent to be unfaithful. The goal of this pathological jealousy is to dominate and maintain complete control of his partner. In doing so, the person thinks he can keep his partner from betraying him and hurting him emotionally.

Unfortunately, there's not a great deal of research on the causes of paranoid personality disorder. Some researchers have hypothesized that childhood abuse or neglect may play a role. Violence, unnecessary litigation, disruptive behavior, and problems in personal relationships are all commonly associated with paranoid personality disorder (Bernstein & Useda, 2007).

Antisocial Personality Disorder

Violating the Rights of Others—Without Guilt or Remorse

Often referred to as a *psychopath* or *sociopath,* the individual with **antisocial personality disorder** has the ability to lie, cheat, steal, and otherwise manipulate and harm other people. And when caught, the person shows little or no remorse for having caused pain, damage, or loss to others (Patrick, 2007). It's as though the person has no conscience or sense of guilt. This pattern of blatantly disregarding and violating the rights of others is the central feature of antisocial personality disorder (DSM-IV-TR, 2000). Researchers have also noted a relative lack of anxiety in these individuals,

paranoid personality disorder
A personality disorder characterized by a pervasive distrust and suspiciousness of the motives of others without sufficient basis.

antisocial personality disorder
A personality disorder characterized by a pervasive pattern of disregarding and violating the rights of others; such individuals are also often referred to as *psychopaths* or *sociopaths.*

An Ordinary Family Man: The Dangers of Antisocial Personality Disorder President of his church council and a very active church member, Dennis Rader had been a Scout leader and worked for the Wichita, Kansas, animal control department. Married for 34 years, Rader had been very involved in the lives of his two children. But Rader was also the sadistic killer who called himself "BTK," which stood for "Bind, torture, kill." In court, Rader shocked even seasoned police officers with his matter-of-fact, emotionless recital of the details of his 10 murders. Like Rader, people with antisocial personality disorder wear a "mask of sanity" (Lynam & Gudonis, 2005). Because they are socially skilled, their crimes often escape detection. Because they lack empathy, they see other people only as objects for their gratification.

especially those most likely to harm others for their own benefit (De Brito & Hodgins, 2009). Approximately 1 to 4 percent of the general population displays the characteristics of antisocial personality disorder, with men far outnumbering women (Grant & others, 2004).

Evidence of this maladaptive personality pattern is often seen in childhood or early adolescence (Hiatt & Dishion, 2008; Lynam & Gudonis, 2005). In many cases, the child has repeated run-ins with the law or school authorities. Behaviors that draw the attention of authorities can include cruelty to animals, attacking or harming adults or other children, theft, setting fires, and destroying property. During childhood and adolescence, this pattern of behavior is typically diagnosed as *conduct disorder*. The habitual failure to conform to social norms and rules often becomes the person's predominant life theme, which continues into adulthood (Patrick, 2007; Myers & others, 1998).

Deceiving and manipulating others for their own personal gain is another hallmark of individuals with antisocial personality disorder. With an uncanny ability to look you directly in the eye and speak with complete confidence and sincerity, they will lie in order to gain money, sex, or whatever their goal may be. When confronted with their actions, they respond with indifference or offer some superficial rationalization to justify their behavior. Often, they are contemptuous about the feelings or rights of others, blaming the victim for his or her stupidity. This quality makes antisocial personality disorder especially difficult to treat because clients often manipulate and lie to their therapists, too (McMurran & Howard, 2009).

Because they are consistently irresponsible, individuals with antisocial personality disorder often fail to hold a job or meet financial obligations. Losing or quitting one job after another, defaulting on loans, and failing to make child support payments are common occurrences. Their past is often checkered with arrests and jail sentences. High rates of alcoholism and other forms of substance abuse are also strongly associated with antisocial personality disorder (Bahlmann & others, 2002; Ladd & Petry, 2003). However, by middle to late adulthood, the antisocial tendencies of such individuals tend to diminish.

Borderline Personality Disorder

Chaos and Emptiness

> Borderline individuals are the psychological equivalent of third-degree burn patients. They simply have no emotional skin. Even the slightest touch or movement can create immense suffering.

This is how Marsha Linehan (2009) describes the chaotic, unstable world of people with **borderline personality disorder.** Borderline personality disorder is characterized by impulsiveness and chronically unstable emotions, relationships, and self-image. Moods and emotions are intense, fluctuating, and extreme, often vastly out of proportion to the triggering incident, and seemingly uncontrollable. The person with borderline personality disorder unpredictably swings from one mood extreme to another. Inappropriate, intense, and often uncontrollable episodes of anger are another hallmark of this disorder (Paris, 2008; Sherry & Whilde, 2008).

borderline personality disorder A personality disorder characterized by instability of interpersonal relationships, self-image, and emotions, and marked impulsivity.

Relationships with others are as chaotic and unstable as the person's moods. The person with borderline personality disorder has a chronic, pervasive sense of emptiness. Above all, she is desperately afraid of abandonment and alternately clings to others and pushes them away. Because her sense of identity is so fragile, she constantly seeks reassurance and self-definition from others. When it is not forthcoming, she may erupt in furious anger or abject despair.

Relationships careen out of control as the person shifts from inappropriately idealizing the newfound lover or friend to viewing them with complete contempt or hostility. She sees herself, and everyone else, as absolutes: ecstatic or miserable, perfect or worthless (South & others, 2008).

The deep despair and inner emptiness that people with BPD experience are outwardly expressed in self-destructive behavior (Linehan & Dexter-Mazza, 2008). "Cutting" or other acts of self-mutilation, threats of suicide, and suicide attempts are common, especially in response to perceived rejection or abandonment. Underscoring the seriousness of borderline personality disorder is a grim statistic: As many as 10 percent of those who meet the BPD criteria eventually commit suicide—a rate that is *50 times* that of the general population (American Psychiatric Association, 2001; Crowell & others, 2009).

Borderline personality disorder is often considered to be the most serious and disabling of the personality disorders. People with this disorder often also suffer from depression, substance abuse, and eating disorders (Mercer & others, 2009; Walter & others, 2009). And because they often lack control over their impulses, self-destructive, impulsive behavior is common, such as gambling, reckless driving, drug abuse, or sexual promiscuity.

Along with being among the most severe of the personality disorders, borderline personality disorder is also the most commonly diagnosed. A recent survey found that BPD was more prevalent than previously thought. Estimates suggest that BPD affects from 1.2 to 6 percent of the population, or possibly some 18 million Americans (Grant & others, 2008). The researchers also found the highest prevalence of borderline personality disorder among women, people in lower income groups, and Native American men, while the lowest incidence was among women of Asian descent.

What Causes Borderline Personality Disorder?

As with the other personality disorders, multiple factors have been implicated. Because people with borderline personality disorder have such intense and chronic fears of abandonment and are terrified of being alone, some researchers believe that a disruption in attachment relationships in early childhood is an important contributing cause (Fonagy & Bateman, 2008; Gunderson & Lyons-Ruth, 2008). Dysfunctional family relationships are common: Many borderline patients report having experienced neglect or physical, sexual, or emotional abuse in childhood (Watson & others, 2006).

A more comprehensive theory, called the *biosocial developmental theory of borderline personality disorder*, has been proposed by psychologist Marsha Linehan (1993; Crowell & others, 2009). According to this view, borderline personality disorder is the outcome of a unique combination of biological, psychological, and environmental factors. Some children are born with a biological temperament that is characterized by extreme emotional sensitivity, a tendency to be impulsive, and the tendency to experience negative emotions. Linehan believes that borderline personality disorder results when such a biologically vulnerable child is raised by caregivers who do not teach him how to control his impulses or help him learn how to understand, regulate, and appropriately express his emotions (Crowell & others, 2009).

In some cases, Linehan believes, parents or caregivers actually shape and reinforce the child's pattern of frequent, intense emotional displays by their own behavior. For example, they may sometimes ignore a child's emotional outbursts and sometimes reinforce them. In Linehan's theory, a history of abuse and neglect may be present but is not a necessary ingredient in the toxic mix that produces borderline personality disorder.

Table 13.8

Dissociative Disorders

Dissociative Amnesia
- Inability to remember important personal information, too extensive to be explained by ordinary forgetfulness

Dissociative Fugue
- Sudden, unexpected travel away from home
- Amnesia
- Confusion about personal identity or assumption of new identity

Dissociative Identity Disorder
- Presence of two or more distinct identities, each with consistent patterns of personality traits and behavior
- Behavior that is controlled by two or more distinct, recurring identities
- Amnesia; frequent memory gaps

The Dissociative Disorders

Fragmentation of the Self

Key Theme

- **In the dissociative disorders, disruptions in awareness, memory, and identity interfere with the ability to function in everyday life.**

Key Questions

- **What is dissociation, and how do normal dissociative experiences differ from the symptoms of dissociative disorders?**
- **What are dissociative amnesia, dissociative fugue, and dissociative identity disorder (DID)?**
- **What is thought to cause DID?**

Despite the many changes you've experienced throughout your lifetime, you have a pretty consistent sense of identity. You're aware of your surroundings and can easily recall memories from the recent and distant past. In other words, a normal personality is one in which *awareness, memory,* and *personal identity* are associated and well-integrated.

In contrast, a **dissociative experience** is one in which a person's awareness, memory, and personal identity become separated or divided. While that may sound weird, dissociative experiences are not inherently pathological. Mild dissociative experiences are quite common and completely normal (Kihlstrom & others, 1994). For example, you become so absorbed in a book or movie that you lose all track of time. Or you're so preoccupied with your thoughts while driving that when you arrive at your destination, you remember next to nothing about the trip. In each of these cases, you've experienced a temporary "break" or "separation" in your memory or awareness—a temporary, mild dissociative experience.

Clearly, then, dissociative experiences are not necessarily abnormal. But in the **dissociative disorders,** the dissociative experiences are much more extreme or more frequent and severely disrupt everyday functioning. Awareness, or recognition of familiar surroundings, may be completely obstructed. Memories of pertinent personal information may be unavailable to consciousness. Identity may be lost, confused, or fragmented (Dell & O'Neil, 2009).

The category of dissociative disorders consists of three basic disorders: *dissociative amnesia, dissociative fugue,* and *dissociative identity disorder,* which was previously called *multiple personality disorder.* Until recently, the dissociative disorders were thought to be extremely rare. How rare? An extensive review conducted in the 1940s uncovered a grand total of 76 reported cases of dissociative disorders since the beginnings of modern medicine in the 1700s (Taylor & Martin, 1944). Although a few more cases were reported during the 1950s and 1960s, the clinical picture changed dramatically in the 1970s when a surge of dissociative disorder diagnoses occurred (Kihlstrom, 2005). Later in this discussion, we'll explore some of the possible reasons as well as the controversy surrounding the "epidemic" of dissociative disorders that began in the 1970s.

Dissociation and Possession A Candomble priestess in Brazil holds a woman who is "possessed" by a Christian saint during a religious ceremony. Such dissociative trance and possession states are common in religions around the world (Krippner, 1994). When dissociative experiences take place within a religious ritual context, they are not considered abnormal. In fact, such experiences may be highly valued (Mulhern, 1991). One study of Brazilian mediums from Candomble or related Christian "spiritistic" religions found that their dissociative experiences were not associated with mental disorders, childhood abuse, or psychological problems (Moreira-Almeida & others, 2008).

Dissociative Amnesia and Fugue

Forgetting and Wandering

Dissociative amnesia refers to the partial or total inability to recall important information that is not due to a medical condition, such as an illness, an injury, or a drug. Usually the person develops amnesia for personal events and information, rather than for general knowledge or skills. That is, the person may not be able to remember his wife's name but does remember how to read and who Martin Luther King, Jr., was. In most cases, dissociative amnesia is a response to stress, trauma, or an extremely distressing situation, such as combat, marital problems, or physical abuse (McLewin & Muller, 2006).

A closely related disorder is dissociative fugue. In **dissociative fugue,** the person outwardly appears completely normal. However, the person has extensive amnesia and is confused about his identity. While in the fugue state, he suddenly and inexplicably travels away from his home, wandering to other cities or even countries. In some cases, people in a fugue state adopt a completely new identity.

Like dissociative amnesia, dissociative fugues are thought to be associated with traumatic events or stressful periods (van der Hart & others, 2006). However, it's unclear as to *how* a fugue state develops, or *why* a person experiences a fugue state rather than other sorts of symptoms, such as simple anxiety or depression. Interestingly, when the person "awakens" from the fugue state, he may remember his past history but have amnesia for what occurred *during* the fugue state (DSM-IV-TR, 2000).

Dissociative Fugue: When Identity Goes "Off Line" Just before a new school year, twenty-three year old teacher Hannah Upp disappeared. Intensive search efforts produced nothing but then Hannah was seen at a Manhattan Apple store and, later, at a Starbucks. Hannah was finally rescued when a Staten Island Ferry crew saw her swimming almost a mile from shore. Hannah had no memories of the events following her disappearance. Although psychologists don't understand what causes dissociative fugue, a rare condition, stressful events are often implicated. "It's as if a whole set of information about one's self, our autobiography, goes off line," says expert Richard Loewenstein. Fortunately, dissociative fugue episodes usually do not reoccur.

Dissociative Identity Disorder

Multiple Personalities

Among the dissociative disorders, none is more fascinating—or controversial—than dissociative identity disorder, formerly known as *multiple personality disorder.* **Dissociative identity disorder (DID)** involves extensive memory disruptions for personal information along with the presence of two or more distinct identities, or "personalities," within a single person.

Typically, each personality has its own name and is experienced as if it has its own personal history and self-image. These alternate personalities, often called *alters* or *alter egos,* may be of widely varying ages and different genders. Alters are not really separate people. Rather, they constitute a "system of mind" (Courtois & Ford, 2009). That is, the alters seem to embody different aspects of the individual's personality that, for some reason, cannot be integrated into the primary personality. The alternate personalities hold memories, emotions, and motives that are not admissible to the individual's conscious mind.

At different times, different alter egos take control of the person's experience, thoughts, and behavior. Typically, the primary personality is unaware of the existence of the alternate personalities. However, the alter egos may have knowledge of each other's existence and share memories (see Kong & others, 2008). Sometimes the experiences of one alter are accessible to another alter but not vice versa.

"Tell me more about these nine separate and distinct personalities."

dissociative experience
A break or disruption in consciousness during which awareness, memory, and personal identity become separated or divided.

dissociative disorders
A category of psychological disorders in which extreme and frequent disruptions of awareness, memory, and personal identity impair the ability to function.

dissociative amnesia
A dissociative disorder involving the partial or total inability to recall important personal information.

dissociative fugue
(fyoog) A dissociative disorder involving sudden and unexpected travel away from home, extensive amnesia, and identity confusion.

dissociative identity disorder (DID)
A dissociative disorder involving extensive memory disruptions along with the presence of two or more distinct identities, or "personalities"; formerly called *multiple personality disorder.*

Herschel Walker and Dissociative Identity Disorder As a professional football player, Walker (2008) was somewhat of an enigma to his teammates because of his diverse pursuits, which ranged from bobsledding to ballet dancing, and because he often referred to himself in the third person. "Herschel played well today," he might say. After retiring from football, Walker began suffering from unexplained violent outbursts, black-outs, and memory loss. Since being diagnosed with dissociative identity disorder, Walker has identified a dozen distinct alters, including "The Warrior" who handled playing football and the pain that went with it, and "The Hero" who made public appearances. With therapy, Walker is learning to manage his disorder and hopes to educate the public about this rare disorder.

Symptoms of amnesia and memory problems are reported in virtually all cases of DID. There are frequent gaps in memory for both recent and childhood experiences. Commonly, those with dissociative identity disorder "lose time" and are unable to recall their behavior or whereabouts during specific time periods. In addition to their memory problems, people with DID typically have numerous psychiatric and physical symptoms, along with a chaotic personal history (Cardena & Gleaves, 2007). Symptoms of major depression, anxiety, post-traumatic stress disorder, substance abuse, sleep disorders, and self-destructive behavior are also very common. Often, the DID patient has been diagnosed with a variety of other psychological disorders before the DID diagnosis is made (Gleaves & others, 2003).

Not all mental health professionals are convinced that dissociative identity disorder is a genuine psychological disorder (Cardena & Gleaves, 2007; Leonard & others, 2005; Piper & Merskey, 2004). For example, a survey by Justine Lalonde and his colleagues (2001) found that fewer than 1 in 7 American and Canadian psychiatrists felt that diagnoses of dissociative disorders were supported by strong scientific evidence. Much of such skepticism is related to the fact that the number of reported cases of DID was extremely low, then suddenly surged in the early 1970s after movies and books about multiple personality disorder were featured in the popular media. As psychologist John Kihlstrom (2005) noted, not only the number of cases but also the number of "alters" showed a dramatic increase. To some psychologists, such findings suggest that DID patients learned "how to behave like a multiple" from media portrayals of sensational cases or by responding to their therapists' suggestions (Gee & others, 2003). On the other hand, DID is not the only psychological disorder for which prevalence rates have increased over time. For example, rates of obsessive–compulsive disorder and PTSD have also increased over the past few decades, primarily because mental health professionals have become more aware of these disorders and more likely to screen for symptoms (Gleaves, 1996). The dissociative disorders are summarized in Table 13.8 on page 560.

Explaining Dissociative Identity Disorder

According to one explanation, dissociative identity disorder represents an extreme form of dissociative coping (Moscowitz & others, 2009). A very high percentage of DID patients report having suffered extreme physical or sexual abuse in childhood—over 90 percent in most surveys (Foote & others, 2006; Sar & others, 2007). According to this explanation, to cope with the trauma, the child "dissociates" himself or herself from it, creating alternate personalities to experience the trauma.

Over time, alternate personalities are created to deal with the memories and emotions associated with intolerably painful experiences. Feelings of anger, rage, fear, and guilt that are too powerful for the child to consciously integrate can be dissociated into these alternate personalities. In effect, dissociation becomes a pathological defense mechanism that the person uses to cope with overwhelming experiences.

Although widely accepted among therapists who work with dissociative identity disorder patients, the dissociative coping theory is difficult to test empirically. One problem is that memories of childhood are notoriously unreliable. Since DID is usually diagnosed in adulthood, it is very difficult, and often impossible, to determine whether the reports of childhood abuse are real or imaginary.

Another problem with the "traumatic memory" explanation of dissociative identity disorder is that just the *opposite* effect occurs to most trauma victims—they are bothered by recurring and intrusive memories of the traumatic event. For example, in a study by Gail Goodman and her colleagues (2003), more than 80 percent of young adults with a documented history of childhood sexual abuse remembered the abuse. Of those who didn't report the abuse, reluctance to disclose the abuse and being too young to remember the abuse seemed to be the most likely explanations. Although the scientific debate about the validity of the dissociative disorders is likely to continue for some time, the dissociative disorders are fundamentally different from the last major category of disorders we'll consider—schizophrenia.

schizophrenia
A psychological disorder in which the ability to function is impaired by severely distorted beliefs, perceptions, and thought processes.

positive symptoms
In schizophrenia, symptoms that reflect excesses or distortions of normal functioning, including delusions, hallucinations, and disorganized thoughts and behavior.

negative symptoms
In schizophrenia, symptoms that reflect defects or deficits in normal functioning, including flat affect, alogia, and avolition.

delusion
A falsely held belief that persists despite compelling contradictory evidence.

Schizophrenia

A Different Reality

Key Theme

- **One of the most serious psychological disorders is schizophrenia, which involves severely distorted beliefs, perceptions, and thought processes.**

Key Questions

- **What are the major symptoms of schizophrenia, and how do positive and negative symptoms differ?**
- **What are the main subtypes of schizophrenia?**
- **What factors have been implicated in the development of schizophrenia?**

Normally, you've got a pretty good grip on reality. You can easily distinguish between external reality and the different kinds of mental states that you routinely experience, such as dreams or daydreams. But as we negotiate life's many twists and turns, the ability to stay firmly anchored in reality is not a given. Rather, we're engaged in an ongoing process of verifying the accuracy of our thoughts, beliefs, and perceptions.

If any mental disorder demonstrates the potential for losing touch with reality, it's schizophrenia. **Schizophrenia** is a psychological disorder that involves severely distorted beliefs, perceptions, and thought processes. During a schizophrenic episode, people lose their grip on reality, like the woman screaming "Fire!" in the chapter Prologue. They become engulfed in an entirely different inner world, one that is often characterized by mental chaos, disorientation, and frustration.

Glimpses of Schizophrenia This drawing was made by a young man hospitalized for schizophrenia. He drew the picture while he was hallucinating and extremely paranoid. The drawing provides glimpses of the distorted perceptions and thoughts that are characteristic of a schizophrenic episode. Notice the smaller face that is superimposed on the larger face, which might represent the hallucinated voices that are often heard in schizophrenic episodes.

Symptoms of Schizophrenia

The characteristic symptoms of schizophrenia can be described in terms of two broad categories: positive and negative symptoms. **Positive symptoms** reflect an excess or distortion of normal functioning. Positive symptoms include (1) *delusions*, or false beliefs; (2) *hallucinations*, or false perceptions; and (3) severely disorganized thought processes, speech, and behavior. In contrast, **negative symptoms** reflect an absence or reduction of normal functions, such as greatly reduced motivation, emotional expressiveness, or speech.

According to DSM-IV-TR, schizophrenia is diagnosed when two or more of these characteristic symptoms are actively present for a month or longer. Usually, schizophrenia also involves a longer personal history, typically six months or more, of odd behaviors, beliefs, perceptual experiences, and other less severe signs of mental disturbance (Malla & Payne, 2005; Torrey, 2006).

People with schizophrenia might hear the roars of Satan or the whispers of children. They might move armies with their thoughts and receive instructions from other worlds. They might feel penetrated by scheming parasites, stalked by enemies, or praised by guardian angels. People with schizophrenia might also speak nonsensically, their language at once intricate and impenetrable. And many would push, or be pushed, to the edge of the social landscape, overcome by solitude.

R. WALTER HEINRICHS, 2005

Positive Symptoms

Delusions, Hallucinations, and Disturbances in Sensation, Thinking, and Speech

A **delusion** is a false belief that persists despite compelling contradictory evidence. Schizophrenic delusions are not simply unconventional or inaccurate beliefs. Rather, they are bizarre and far-fetched notions. The person may believe that secret agents are poisoning his food or that the next-door neighbors are actually aliens from outer space who are trying to transform him into a remote-controlled robot. The delusional person often becomes preoccupied with his erroneous beliefs and ignores any evidence that contradicts them.

Certain themes consistently appear in schizophrenic delusions (Woo & Keatinge, 2008). *Delusions of reference* reflect the person's false conviction that other people's behavior and ordinary events are somehow personally related to her. For example, she is certain that billboards and advertisements are about her or contain cryptic messages

FOCUS ON NEUROSCIENCE

The Hallucinating Brain

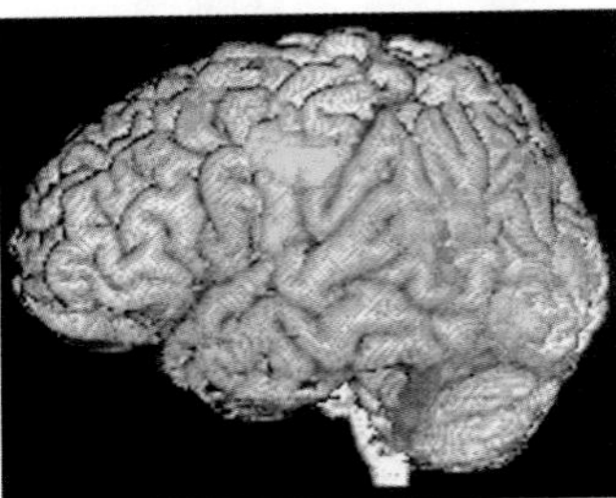

Researcher David Silbersweig and his colleagues (1995) used PET scans to take a "snapshot" of brain activity during schizophrenic hallucinations. The scan shown here was recorded at the exact instant a schizophrenic patient hallucinated disembodied heads yelling orders at him. The bright orange areas reveal activity in the left auditory and visual areas of his brain, but not in the frontal lobe, which normally is involved in organized thought processes.

directed at her. In contrast, *delusions of grandeur* involve the belief that the person is extremely powerful, important, or wealthy. In *delusions of persecution*, the basic theme is that others are plotting against or trying to harm the person or someone close to her. *Delusions of being controlled* involve the belief that outside forces—aliens, the government, or random people, for example—are trying to exert control on the individual.

Schizophrenic delusions are often so convincing that they can provoke inappropriate or bizarre behavior. Delusional thinking may lead to dangerous behaviors, as when a person responds to his delusional ideas by hurting himself or attacking others.

Among the most disturbing experiences in schizophrenia are **hallucinations**, which are false or distorted perceptions—usually voices or visual stimuli—that seem vividly real (see Figure 13.4). The content of hallucinations is often tied to the person's delusional beliefs. For example, if she harbors delusions of grandeur, hallucinated voices may reinforce her grandiose ideas by communicating instructions from God, the devil, or angels. If the person harbors delusions of persecution, hallucinated voices or images may be extremely frightening, threatening, or accusing. The content of hallucinations and delusions may also be influenced by culture and religious beliefs.

CULTURE AND HUMAN BEHAVIOR

Travel Advisory: The Jerusalem Syndrome

Whether it occurs in Baltimore or Beijing, Minneapolis or Moscow, schizophrenia is usually characterized by delusions and hallucinations. However, the *content* of the person's delusions and hallucinations is often influenced by cultural factors, including that culture's dominant religious beliefs. Consider one interesting example: the *Jerusalem syndrome,* which has been described by psychiatrist Yair Bar-El and his colleagues (2000) at Kfar Shaul Mental Health Center in Israel.

Christians, Jews, and Muslims regard the city of Jerusalem as a richly historical and holy city. Annually, about 2 million tourists from around the world visit the city. But for about 100 visitors every year, arriving in the famous holy city triggers a psychotic break that involves religious delusions and hallucinations—the essence of the *Jerusalem syndrome.* About half of these people require psychiatric hospitalization (Fastovsky & others, 2000). The disorder occurs frequently enough that Jerusalem tour guides and hotel personnel are familiar with it and will notify authorities when they spot someone displaying the symptoms.

Identifying with biblical characters is a common feature of the Jerusalem syndrome. As a general rule, Christians tend to believe that they are Jesus Christ, the Virgin Mary, or John the Baptist. In contrast, Jews tend to gravitate toward a Hebrew hero like Moses, Samson, or King David. And Muslims simply tend to say that they're the Mahdi (Messiah).

Usually, the person has a history of serious mental disorders, such as previous episodes of schizophrenia or bipolar disorder. But in about 10 percent of Jerusalem syndrome cases, the person has *no* history of mental disorders. Instead, the person spontaneously experiences a psychotic episode while in Jerusalem.

A Pilgrimage Gone Awry Being in the presence of a historic religious site like the Wailing Wall in Jerusalem is an overwhelming emotional experience for many tourists. In some vulnerable people, such experiences trigger a temporary episode of psychological instability and religious delusions.

For example, a Swiss lawyer was on a three-week group tour of Greece, Israel, and Egypt. Everything was fine until the tour visited Jerusalem. On the first night in Jerusalem, the man became nervous and agitated, withdrew from the group, and became obsessed with becoming clean and pure, taking many showers. Then, using the white hotel linen to make a biblical-style, toga-like gown, he marched to one of Jerusalem's holy sites and delivered a rambling "sermon" about how humanity should adopt a more moral and simple way of life. Fortunately, within a matter of days, the syndrome passed and the man's symptoms abated.

What causes the Jerusalem syndrome? One possible explanation is that the disruptions of travel temporarily influence a person's mental state. According to Bar-El and his colleagues (2000), factors such as time-zone changes, unfamiliar surroundings, and exposure to strangers and foreigners probably contribute to the transient psychological instability. In a vulnerable person, encountering cultural differences in behavior combined with being on a spiritual pilgrimage to one of the world's great holy cities can trigger an acute psychotic episode.

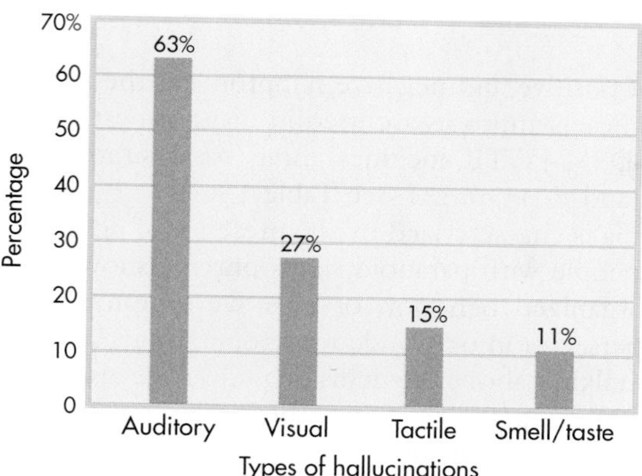

Figure 13.4 Incidence of Different Types of Hallucinations in Schizophrenia Schizophrenia-related hallucinations can occur in any sensory modality. Auditory hallucinations, usually in the form of voices, are the most common type of hallucinations that occur in schizophrenia, followed by visual hallucinations.

Source: Adapted from data in Mueser & others (1990) and Bracha & others (1989).

When a schizophrenic episode is severe, hallucinations can be virtually impossible to distinguish from objective reality. For example, the young woman in the Prologue probably did see vivid but hallucinated images of fire. When schizophrenic symptoms are less severe, the person may recognize that the hallucination is a product of his own mind. As one young man confided to your author Don, "I know the voices aren't real, but I can't make them stop talking to me." As this young man got better, the hallucinated voices did eventually stop.

Other positive symptoms of schizophrenia include disturbances in sensation, thinking, and speech. Visual, auditory, and tactile experiences may seem distorted or unreal. For example, one woman described the sensory distortions in this way:

Young Adulthood and Schizophrenia The onset of schizophrenia typically occurs during the 18-to-25 age range. Amber Main fit that pattern when she started hearing voices during her freshman year of college. She also started believing that hidden cameras were tracking her. Usually an excellent student, her grades plummeted because she couldn't concentrate. In January she was hospitalized. Fortunately, Amber responded well to an antipsychotic medication and was able to return to school. Amber has chosen to openly discuss her illness, even appearing in an MTV documentary. As she explains, "I don't want to hide what I am, or what's a part of me. But I'm not my mental illness, it's just something I have to deal with."

> Looking around the room, I found that things had lost their emotional meaning. They were larger than life, tense, and suspenseful. They were flat, and colored as if in artificial light. I felt my body to be first giant, then minuscule. My arms seemed to be several inches longer than before and did not feel as though they belonged to me. (Anonymous, 1990)

Along with sensory distortions, the person may experience severely disorganized thinking. It becomes enormously difficult to concentrate, remember, and integrate important information while ignoring irrelevant information (Barch, 2005). The person's mind drifts from topic to topic in an unpredictable, illogical manner. Such disorganized thinking is often reflected in the person's speech (Munetz, 2006). Ideas, words, and images are sometimes strung together in ways that seem nonsensical to the listener.

Negative Symptoms

Flat Affect, Alogia, and Avolition

Negative symptoms consist of marked deficits or decreases in behavioral or emotional functioning. One commonly seen negative symptom is referred to as *flat affect,* or *affective flattening.* Regardless of the situation, the person responds in an emotionally "flat" way, showing a dramatic reduction in emotional responsiveness and facial expressions. Speech is slow and monotonous, lacking normal vocal inflections. A closely related negative symptom is *alogia,* or greatly reduced production of speech. In alogia, verbal responses are limited to brief, empty comments.

Finally, *avolition* refers to the inability to initiate or persist in even simple forms of goal-directed behaviors, such as dressing, bathing, or engaging in social activities. Instead, the person seems to be completely apathetic, sometimes sitting still for hours at a time. In combination, the negative symptoms accentuate the isolation of the person with schizophrenia, who may appear uncommunicative and completely disconnected from his or her environment.

hallucination
A false or distorted perception that seems vividly real to the person experiencing it.

Table 13.9

Types of Schizophrenia

Paranoid Type
- Well-organized delusional beliefs reflecting persecutory or grandiose ideas
- Frequent auditory hallucinations, usually voices
- Little or no disorganized behavior, speech, or flat affect

Catatonic Type
- Highly disturbed movements or actions, such as extreme excitement, bizarre postures or grimaces, or being completely immobile
- Echoing of words spoken by others, or imitation of movements of others

Disorganized Type
- Flat or inappropriate emotional expressions
- Severely disorganized speech and behavior
- Fragmented delusional ideas and hallucinations

Undifferentiated Type
- Display of characteristic symptoms of schizophrenia but not in a way that fits the pattern for paranoid, catatonic, or disorganized type

Types of Schizophrenia

Figure 13.5 shows the frequency of positive and negative symptoms at the time of hospitalization for schizophrenia. These symptoms are used in diagnosing the particular subtype of schizophrenia. DSM-IV-TR includes three basic subtypes of schizophrenia: *paranoid, catatonic,* and *disorganized* (see Table 13.9).

The *paranoid type* of schizophrenia is characterized by the presence of delusions, hallucinations, or both. However, people with paranoid schizophrenia show virtually no cognitive impairment, disorganized behavior, or negative symptoms. Instead, well-organized delusions of persecution or grandeur are operating. Auditory hallucinations in the form of voices talking about the delusional ideas are also often evident. Convinced that others are plotting against them, these people react with extreme distrust of others. Or they may assume an air of superiority, confident in the delusional belief that they have "special powers." The paranoid type is the most common type of schizophrenia.

The *catatonic type* of schizophrenia is marked by highly disturbed movements or actions. These may include bizarre postures or grimaces, extremely agitated behavior, complete immobility, the echoing of words just spoken by another person, or imitation of the movements of others. People with this form of schizophrenia will resist direction from others and may also assume rigid postures to resist being moved. Catatonic schizophrenia is often characterized by another unusual symptom, called *waxy flexibility.* Like a wax figure, the person can be "molded" into any position and will hold that position indefinitely. The catatonic type of schizophrenia is very rare.

The prominent features of the *disorganized type* of schizophrenia are extremely disorganized behavior, disorganized speech, and flat affect. Delusions and hallucinations are sometimes present, but they are not well-organized and integrated, like those that characterize paranoid schizophrenia. Instead, people with the disorganized type experience delusions and hallucinations that contain fragmented, shifting themes. Silliness, laughing, and giggling may occur for no apparent reason. In short, the person's behavior is very peculiar. This type of schizophrenia was formerly called *hebephrenic schizophrenia,* and that term is still sometimes used.

Finally, the label *undifferentiated type* is used when an individual displays some combination of positive and negative symptoms that does not clearly fit the criteria for the paranoid, catatonic, or disorganized types.

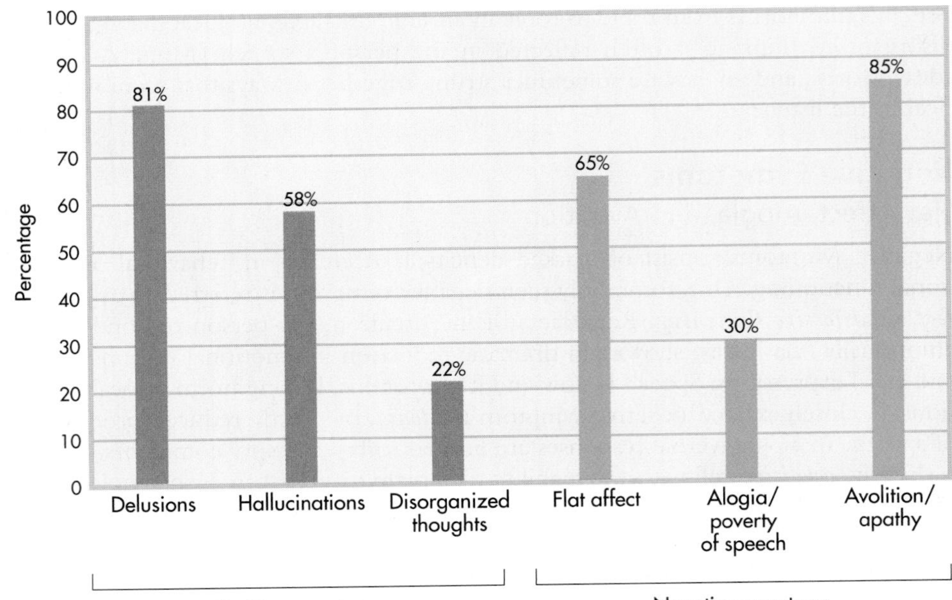

Figure 13.5 Presence of Symptoms in Schizophrenia This graph shows how often specific positive and negative symptoms were present in a study of over 100 individuals at the time they were hospitalized for schizophrenia. Delusions were the most common positive symptom, and avolition, or apathy, was the most common negative symptom.

Source: Based on data reported in Andreasen & Flaum (1991).

The Prevalence and Course of Schizophrenia

Every year, about 200,000 new cases of schizophrenia are diagnosed in the United States, and annually, approximately 1 million Americans are treated for schizophrenia. All told, about 1 percent of the U.S. population will experience at least one episode of schizophrenia at some point in life (Rado & Janicak, 2009). Worldwide, no society or culture is immune to this mental disorder. Most cultures correspond very closely to the 1 percent rate of schizophrenia seen in the United States (Combs & Mueser, 2007).

The onset of schizophrenia typically occurs during young adulthood (Tarrier, 2008; Gourion & others, 2005). However, the course of schizophrenia is marked by enormous individual variability. Even so, a few global generalizations are possible (Malla & Payne, 2005; Walker & others, 2004). The good news is that about one-quarter of those who experience an episode of schizophrenia recover completely and never experience another episode. Another one-quarter experience recurrent episodes of schizophrenia but often with only minimal impairment in the ability to function.

Now the bad news. For the rest of those who have experienced an episode of schizophrenia—about one-half of the total—schizophrenia becomes a chronic mental illness, and the ability to function may be severely impaired. The people in this last category face the prospect of repeated hospitalizations and extended treatment. Thus, chronic schizophrenia places a heavy emotional, financial, and psychological burden on people with the disorder, their families, and society (Combs & Mueser, 2007).

Explaining Schizophrenia

Schizophrenia is an extremely complex disorder. There is enormous individual variability in the onset, symptoms, duration, and recovery from schizophrenia. So it shouldn't come as a surprise that the causes of schizophrenia seem to be equally complex. In this section, we'll survey some of the factors that have been implicated in the development of schizophrenia.

Genetic Factors

Family, Twin, Adoption, and Gene Studies

Studies of families, twins, and adopted individuals have firmly established that genetic factors play a significant role in many cases of schizophrenia. First, family studies have consistently shown that schizophrenia tends to cluster in certain families (Choi & others, 2007; Torrey, 2006). Second, family and twin studies have consistently shown that the more closely related a person is to someone who has schizophrenia, the greater the risk that she will be diagnosed with schizophrenia at some point in her lifetime (see Figure 13.6). Third, adoption studies have consistently shown that if either *biological* parent of an adopted individual had schizophrenia, the adopted individual is at greater risk to develop schizophrenia (Tienari & others, 1994; Wynne & others, 2006). And fourth, by studying families that display a high rate of schizophrenia, researchers have consistently found that the presence of certain genetic variations seems to increase susceptibility to the disorder (Fanous & others, 2005; Williams & others, 2005).

Ironically, some of the best evidence that points to genetic involvement in schizophrenia—the almost 50 percent risk rate for a person whose identical twin has

Figure 13.6 The Risk of Developing Schizophrenia Among Blood Relatives The risk percentages shown here reflect the collective results of about 40 studies investigating the likelihood of developing schizophrenia among blood relatives. As you can see, the greatest risk occurs if you have an identical twin who has schizophrenia (48 percent lifetime risk) or if both of your biological parents have schizophrenia (46 percent lifetime risk). However, environmental factors, as well as genetic ones, are involved in the development of schizophrenia.

Source: Gottesman (1991), p. 96.

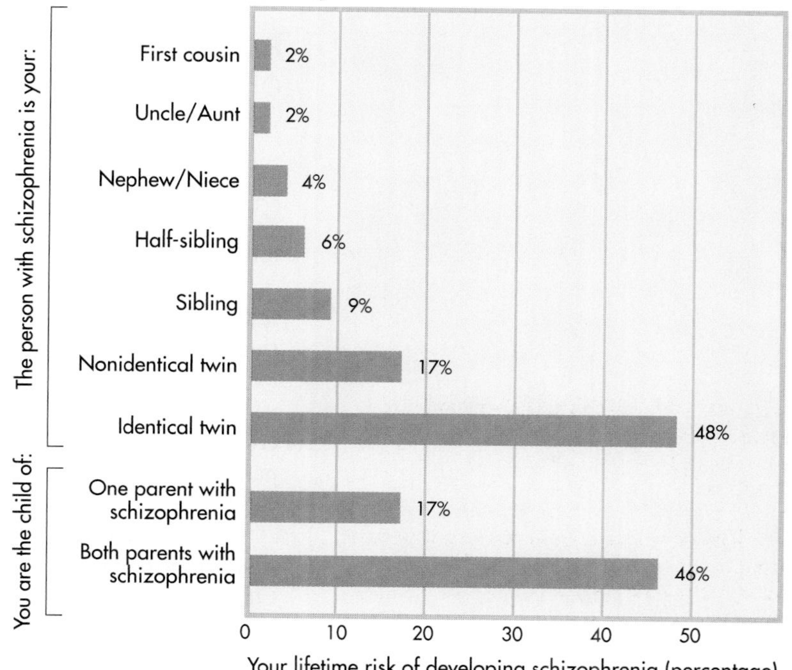

schizophrenia—is the same evidence that underscores the importance of environmental factors (Joseph & Leo, 2006; Torrey, 2006). If schizophrenia were purely a matter of inherited maladaptive genes, then you would expect a risk rate much closer to 100 percent for monozygotic twins. Obviously, nongenetic factors must play a role in explaining why half of identical twins with a schizophrenic twin do *not* develop schizophrenia.

Nevertheless, scientists are getting closer to identifying some of the specific genetic patterns that are associated with an increased risk of developing schizophrenia. New research using sophisticated gene analysis techniques confirms the incredibly complex role that genes play in the development of schizophrenia. Three different research teams compared DNA samples from thousands of people diagnosed with schizophrenia with DNA samples from control groups of people who did *not* have schizophrenia (Shi & others, 2009; Stefansson & others, 2009; Purcell & others, 2009). Some of the people in the control groups had *other* mental or physical disorders, but most were healthy. The researchers were looking for specific genetic variations that were more common in the genomes of people with schizophrenia than in people without schizophrenia.

Collectively, the studies found that schizophrenia was associated with literally *thousands* of common gene variations. Some of the specific variants were quite rare, while others were quite common. Taken individually, none of the gene variants is capable of "causing" schizophrenia. Even in combination, the genetic variants are only associated with an increased *risk* of developing schizophrenia. As yet, no specific pattern of genetic variation can be identified as the genetic "cause" of schizophrenia.

Three particularly interesting results stand out. First, some of the same unique genetic patterns associated with schizophrenia were also found in DNA samples from people with bipolar disorder but were not associated with any other psychological or physical disorder (Purcell & others, 2009). This finding suggests that bipolar disorder and schizophrenia might share some common genetic origins. Second, also implicated were several chromosome locations that are associated with genes that influence brain development, memory, and cognition. Finally, a large number of the gene variants were found to occur on a specific chromosome that is also known to harbor genes involved in the immune response (Shi & others, 2009). Later in this section, we'll discuss some intriguing links between the immune system and schizophrenia.

Paternal Age

Older Fathers and the Risk of Schizophrenia

Despite the fact that family and twin studies point to the role of genetic factors in the risk of developing schizophrenia, no genetic model thus far explains all of the patterns of schizophrenia occurrence within families (Insel & Lehner, 2007; Kendler & Diehl, 1993). Adding to the perplexity is the fact that schizophrenia often occurs in individuals with *no* family history of mental disorders.

One explanation for these anomalies is that for each generation, new cases of schizophrenia arise from genetic mutations carried in the sperm of the biological fathers, especially older fathers. As men age, their sperm cells continue to reproduce by dividing. By the time a male is 20, his sperm cells have undergone about 200 divisions; by the time he is 40, about 660 divisions. As the number of divisions increases over time, the sperm cells accumulate genetic mutations that can then be passed on to that man's offspring. Hence, the theory goes, as paternal age increases, the risk of offspring developing schizophrenia also increases.

Researcher Dolores Malaspina and her colleagues (2001) explored this notion by reviewing data on more than 87,000 people born in Jerusalem from 1964 to 1976. Of this group, 658 people had been diagnosed with schizophrenia by 1998. After controlling for various risk factors, the researchers found that paternal age was a strong and significant predictor of the schizophrenia diagnoses. Specifically, Malaspina and her colleagues (2001) found that:

- Men in the 45-to-49 age group who fathered children were twice as likely to have offspring with schizophrenia as compared to fathers age 25 and under.
- Men in the 50-plus age range were three times more likely to produce offspring with schizophrenia.
- More than one-quarter of the schizophrenia cases could be attributed to the father's age.
- The mother's age appeared to play *no* role in the development of schizophrenia.

Clearly, then, paternal age is a potential risk factor. However, it's important to keep in mind that three-quarters of the cases of schizophrenia in this study were *not* associated with older paternal age.

Environmental Factors

The Viral Infection Theory

One provocative theory is that schizophrenia might be caused by exposure to an influenza virus or other viral infection during prenatal development or shortly after birth. A virus might seem an unlikely cause of a serious mental disorder, but viruses *can* spread to the brain and spinal cord by traveling along nerves. According to this theory, exposure to a viral infection during prenatal development or early infancy affects the developing brain, producing changes that make the individual more vulnerable to schizophrenia later in life.

There is growing evidence to support the viral infection theory. In one compelling study, psychiatrist Alan S. Brown and his colleagues (2004) compared stored blood samples of 64 mothers of people who later developed schizophrenia with a matched set of blood samples from women whose children did not develop schizophrenia. Both sets of blood samples had been collected years earlier during the women's pregnancies. After analyzing the blood samples for the presence of influenza antibodies, Brown and his colleagues (2004) found that women who had been exposed to the flu virus during the first trimester had a sevenfold increased risk of bearing a child who later developed schizophrenia.

Previous studies using maternal recall and the dates of influenza epidemics have demonstrated similar findings: Children whose mothers were exposed to a flu virus during pregnancy, especially during the first or second trimester, show an increased rate of schizophrenia (Carter, 2008; Yudofsky, 2009). A related finding is that schizophrenia occurs more often in people who were born in the winter and spring months, when upper respiratory infections are most common (Torrey, 2006).

Abnormal Brain Structures

Loss of Gray Matter

Researchers have found that about half of the people with schizophrenia show some type of brain structure abnormality. The most consistent finding has been the enlargement of the fluid-filled cavities, called *ventricles,* located deep within the brain (Fraguas & others, 2008). However, researchers are not certain how enlarged ventricles might be related to schizophrenia. Other differences that have been found are a loss of gray matter tissue and lower overall volume of the brain (Cahn & others, 2009). As we discussed in Chapter 2, *gray matter* refers to the glial cells, neuron cell bodies, and unmyelinated axons that make up the quarter-inch-thick cerebral cortex.

To investigate the neurological development of schizophrenia, neuroscientist Paul M. Thompson and his colleagues (2001) undertook a prospective study of brain structure changes in 12 adolescents with early-onset childhood schizophrenia. The six females and six males had all experienced schizophrenic symptoms, including psychotic symptoms, before the age of 12. The intent of the study was to provide a visual picture of the timing, rates, and anatomical distribution of brain structure changes in adolescents with schizophrenia.

Identical Twins but Not Identical Brains David and Steven Elmore are identical twins, but they differ in one important respect—Steven *(right)* has schizophrenia. Behind each is a CAT scan, which reveals that Steven's brain is slightly smaller, with less area devoted to the cortex at the top of the brain. Steven also has larger fluid-filled ventricles, which are circled in red on his brain scan. As researcher Daniel Weinberger (1995) commented, "The part of the cortex that Steven is missing serves as perhaps the most evolved part of the human brain. It performs complicated tasks such as thinking organized thoughts. This might help explain why paranoid delusions and hallucinations are characteristic of schizophrenia."

FOCUS ON NEUROSCIENCE

Schizophrenia: A Wildfire in the Brain

In a five-year prospective study, neuroscientist Paul Thompson and his colleagues (2001) used high-resolution brain scans to map brain structure changes in normal adolescents and adolescents with early-onset schizophrenia. Thompson found marked differences in the brain development of normal teens and teens with schizophrenia. As expected, the healthy teenagers showed a gradual, small loss of gray matter—about 1 percent—over the five-year study. This loss is due to the normal pruning of unused brain connections that takes place during adolescence (see Chapter 9).

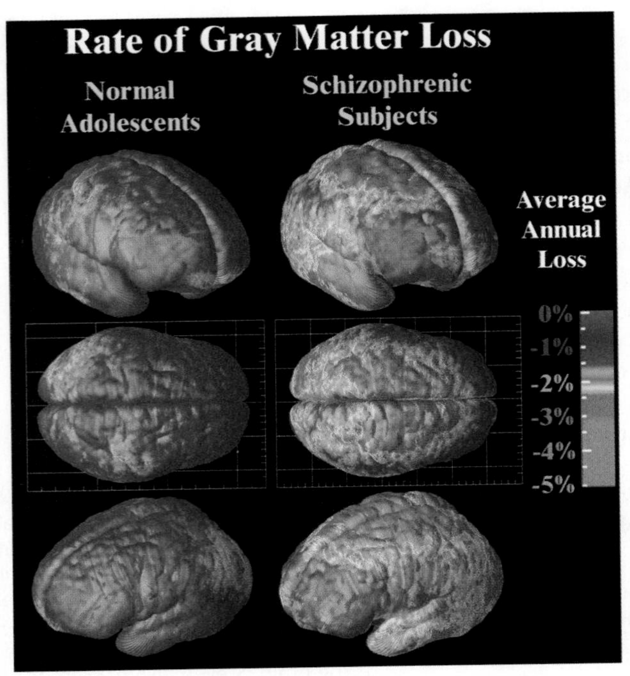

But in sharp contrast to the normal teens, the teenagers with schizophrenia showed a severe loss of gray matter that developed in a specific, wavelike pattern. The loss began in the parietal lobes and, over the five years of the study, progressively spread forward to the temporal and frontal regions. As Thompson (2001) noted, "We were stunned to see a spreading wave of tissue loss that began in a small region of the brain. It moved across the brain like a forest fire, destroying more tissue as the disease progressed."

The brain images show the average rate of gray matter loss over the five-year period. Gray matter loss ranged from about 1 percent (blue) in the normal teens to more than 5 percent (pink) in the schizophrenic teens. One fascinating finding was that the amount of gray matter loss was directly correlated to the teenage patients' clinical symptoms. Psychotic symptoms increased the most in the participants who lost the greatest quantity of gray matter.

Also, the *pattern* of loss mirrored the progression of neurological and cognitive deficits associated with schizophrenia. For example, more rapid gray matter loss in the *temporal lobes* was associated with more severe *positive* symptoms, such as hallucinations and delusions. More rapid loss of gray matter in the *frontal lobes* was strongly correlated with the severity of *negative* symptoms, including flat affect and poverty of speech. When the participants were 18 to 19 years old and the final brain scans were taken, the patterns of gray matter loss were similar to those found in the brains of adult patients with schizophrenia.

Despite the wealth of information generated by Thompson's study, the critical question remains unanswered: What sparks the cerebral forest fire in the schizophrenic brain?

Each of the 12 adolescents was scanned repeatedly with high-resolution MRIs over a five-year period, beginning when the teenagers were about 14. The adolescents were carefully matched with healthy teens of the same gender, age, socioeconomic background, and height. The findings of this important study are featured in the Focus on Neuroscience.

Although there is evidence that brain abnormalities are found in schizophrenia, such findings do not prove that brain abnormalities are the sole cause of schizophrenia. First, some people with schizophrenia do *not* show brain structure abnormalities. Second, the evidence is correlational. Researchers are still investigating whether differences in brain structures and activity are the cause or the consequence of schizophrenia. Third, the kinds of brain abnormalities seen in schizophrenia are also seen in other mental disorders. Rather than specifically causing schizophrenia, it's quite possible that brain abnormalities might contribute to psychological disorders in general.

Abnormal Brain Chemistry

The Dopamine Hypothesis

dopamine hypothesis
The view that schizophrenia is related to, and may be caused by, excessive activity of the neurotransmitter dopamine in the brain.

According to the **dopamine hypothesis,** schizophrenia is related to excessive activity of the neurotransmitter dopamine in the brain. Two pieces of indirect evidence support this notion. First, antipsychotic drugs, such as Haldol, Thorazine, and Stelazine, *reduce or block dopamine activity in the brain.* These drugs reduce schizophrenic symptoms, especially positive symptoms, in many people. Second, drugs that enhance dopamine activity in the brain, such as amphetamines and cocaine, can produce schizophrenia-like symptoms in normal adults or increase symptoms in people who already have schizophrenia.

However, there is also evidence that contradicts the dopamine hypothesis. For example, not all individuals who have schizophrenia experience a reduction of symptoms in response to the antipsychotic drugs that reduce dopamine activity in the brain. And for many patients, these drugs reduce some but not all schizophrenic symptoms. One new theory is that some parts of the brain, such as the limbic system, may have too much dopamine, while other parts of the brain, such as the cortex, may have too little dopamine (Combs & Mueser, 2007). Thus, the connection between dopamine and schizophrenia symptoms remains unclear.

Psychological Factors

Unhealthy Families

Researchers have investigated such factors as dysfunctional parenting, disturbed family communication styles, and critical or guilt-inducing parental styles as possible contributors to schizophrenia (Johnson & others, 2001). However, no single psychological factor seems to emerge consistently as causing schizophrenia. Rather, it seems that those who are genetically predisposed to develop schizophrenia may be more vulnerable to the effects of disturbed family environments (Tienari & Wahlberg, 2008).

Strong support for this view comes from a landmark study conducted by Finnish psychiatrist Pekka Tienari and his colleagues (1987, 1994). In the Finnish Adoptive Family Study of Schizophrenia, researchers followed about 150 adopted individuals whose biological mothers had schizophrenia. As part of their study, the researchers assessed the adoptive family's degree of psychological adjustment, including the mental health of the adoptive parents. The study also included a control group of about 180 adopted individuals whose biological mothers did *not* have schizophrenia.

Tienari and his colleagues (1994, 2006; Wynne & others, 2006) found that adopted children with a schizophrenic biological mother had a much higher rate of schizophrenia than did the children in the control group. However, this was true *only* when the children were raised in a psychologically disturbed adoptive home. As you can see in Figure 13.7, when children with a genetic background of schizophrenia were raised in a psychologically healthy adoptive family, they were *no more likely* than the control-group children to develop schizophrenia.

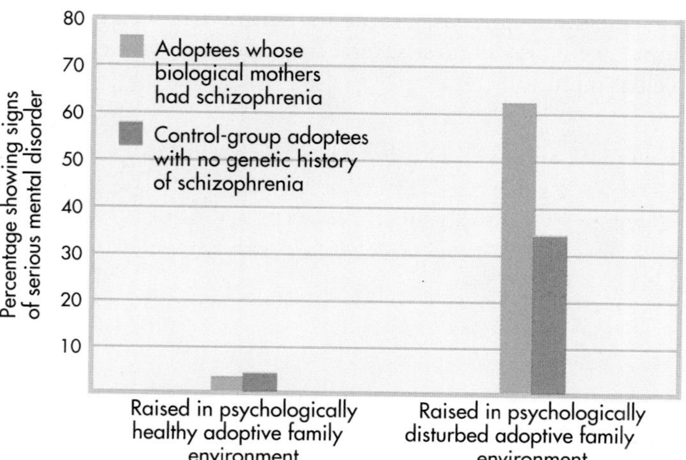

Figure 13.7 The Finnish Adoptive Family Study of Schizophrenia In the Finnish Adoptive Family Study, psychiatrist Pekka Tienari and his colleagues (1994, 2006) tracked the mental health of two groups of adopted individuals: one group with biological mothers who had schizophrenia and a control group whose biological mothers did not have schizophrenia. This graph shows the strong influence of the adoptive family environment on the development of serious mental disorders.

Although adopted children with no genetic history of schizophrenia were less vulnerable to the psychological stresses of a disturbed family environment, they were by no means completely immune to such influences. As Figure 13.7 shows, one-third of the control-group adoptees developed symptoms of a serious psychological disorder if they were raised in a disturbed family environment.

Tienari's study underscores the complex interaction of genetic and environmental factors. Clearly, children who were genetically at risk to develop schizophrenia benefited from being raised in a healthy psychological environment. Put simply, a healthy psychological environment may counteract a person's inherited vulnerability for schizophrenia. Conversely, a psychologically unhealthy family environment can act as a catalyst for the onset of schizophrenia, especially for those individuals with a genetic history of schizophrenia (Tienari & Wahlberg, 2008).

After more than a century of intensive research, schizophrenia remains a baffling disorder. Thus far, no single biological, psychological, or social factor has emerged as the causal agent in schizophrenia. Nevertheless, researchers are expressing greater confidence that the pieces of the schizophrenia puzzle are beginning to form a more coherent picture.

Even if the exact causes of schizophrenia remain elusive, there is still reason for optimism. In the past few years, new antipsychotic drugs have been developed that are much more effective in treating both the positive and negative symptoms of schizophrenia (Sharif & others, 2007). In the next chapter, we'll take a detailed look at the different treatments and therapies for schizophrenia and other psychological disorders.

>> Closing Thoughts

In this chapter, we've looked at the symptoms and causes of several psychological disorders. We've seen that some of the symptoms of psychological disorders represent a sharp break from normal experience. The behavior of the young woman in the Prologue is an example of the severely disrupted functioning characteristic of schizophrenia. In contrast, the symptoms of other psychological disorders, such as the mood disorders, differ from normal experience primarily in their degree, intensity, and duration.

Psychologists are only beginning to understand the causes of many psychological disorders. The broad picture that emerges reflects a familiar theme: Biological, psychological, and social factors all contribute to the development of psychological disorders. In the next chapter, we'll look at how psychological disorders are treated.

In the final section, Enhancing Well-Being with Psychology, we'll explore one of the most serious consequences of psychological problems—suicide. Because people who are contemplating suicide often turn to their friends before they seek help from a mental health professional, we'll also suggest several ways in which you can help a friend who expresses suicidal intentions.

ENHANCING WELL-BEING WITH PSYCHOLOGY

Understanding and Helping to Prevent Suicide

Who Commits Suicide?

Suicide and attempted suicide are all too common. Each year in the United States about 30,000 people take their own lives. For every death by suicide, it's estimated that 25 people have attempted suicide (American Association of Suicidology, 2004). In any given year, some 500,000 people require emergency room treatment as a result of attempted suicide (McCaig & Burt, 2004).

Most people don't realize that close to twice as many Americans die each year from suicide as from homicide. In 2002, suicide was the 11th leading cause of death, while homicide ranked 14th (National Center for Health Statistics, 2004).

Women outnumber men by three to one in the number of suicide attempts. However, men outnumber women by better than four to one in suicide deaths, primarily because men tend to use more lethal methods, such as shooting and hanging (Kochanek & Smith, 2004).

Suicide is the third leading cause of death for young people ages 15 to 24. Over the past four decades, the suicide rate for adolescents and young adults has increased by almost 300 percent (U.S. Public Health Service, 1999). Although this trend has received considerable media attention, the suicide rate of adolescents and young adults is still below that of older adults. In fact, the highest suicide rate consistently occurs in the oldest segments of our population—among those age 75 and above (Kochanek & Smith, 2004).

A notion that is often perpetuated in the popular press is that there is a significant increase in the number of suicides during the winter holidays. This claim is a myth, plain and simple. However, there are consistent seasonal variations in suicide deaths. In the United States, suicide rates are lowest during the winter months and highest in the spring (Romer & others, 2003).

On average, someone commits suicide in the United States every 17 minutes. It is estimated that each suicide affects the lives of at least six other people.

What Risk Factors Are Associated with Suicidal Behavior?

Hundreds of studies have identified psychosocial and environmental factors associated with an increased risk of suicidal behavior (e.g., Brown & others, 2004; Gould & others, 2003; Joiner & others, 2005; Lieb & others, 2005). Some of the factors that increase the risk of suicidal behavior include:

- Feelings of hopelessness and social isolation
- Recent relationship problems or a lack of significant relationships
- Poor coping and problem-solving skills
- Poor impulse control and impaired judgment
- Rigid thinking or irrational beliefs
- A major psychological disorder, especially depression, bipolar disorder, or schizophrenia
- Alcohol or other substance abuse
- Childhood physical or sexual abuse
- Prior self-destructive behavior
- A family history of suicide
- Presence of a firearm in the home

Why Do People Attempt or Commit Suicide?

The suicidal person's view of life has become progressively more pessimistic and negative. At the same time, his view of self-inflicted death as an alternative to life becomes progressively more acceptable and positive (Shneidman, 1998, 2004).

Some people choose suicide to escape the pain of a chronic illness or the slow, agonizing death of a terminal disease. Others commit suicide because of feelings of hopelessness, depression, guilt, rejection, failure, humiliation, or shame (Lester, 1997). The common denominator is that they see suicide as the only escape from their own unbearably painful emotions (Jamison, 2000).

When faced with a dilemma, the average person tends to see a range of possible solutions, accepting the fact that none of the solutions may be ideal. In contrast, the suicidal person's thinking and perceptions have become rigid and constricted. She can see only two ways to solve her problems: a magical resolution or suicide. Because she cannot imagine a realistic way of solving her problems, death seems to be the only logical option (Shneidman, 1998, 2004).

How Can You Help Prevent Suicide?

If someone is truly intent on taking his or her own life, it may be impossible to prevent him or her from doing so. But that does not mean that you can't try to help a friend who is expressing suicidal intentions. People often turn to their friends rather than to mental health professionals. If a friend confides that he or she is feeling hopeless and suicidal, these guidelines may help you help your friend.

It's important to stress, however, that these guidelines are meant only to help you provide "psychological first aid" in a crisis situation. They do *not* qualify you as a suicide prevention expert. Your goal is to help your friend weather the immediate crisis so that he or she can be directed to a mental health professional.

> *So ubiquitous is the impulse to commit suicide that one out of every two Americans has at some time considered, threatened, or actually attempted suicide.*
>
> DAVID LESTER

Guideline 1: Actively listen as the person talks and vents her feelings.

The suicidal person often feels isolated or lonely, with few sources of social support. Let the person talk, and try to genuinely empathize with your friend's feelings. An understanding friend who is willing to take the time to listen patiently without passing judgment may provide just the support the person needs to overcome the immediate suicidal feelings. Hearing themselves talk can also help suicidal individuals identify and better understand their own feelings.

Guideline 2: Don't deny or minimize the person's suicidal intentions.

Brushing aside suicidal statements with platitudes, like "Don't be silly, you've got everything to live for," or clichés, like "Every cloud has a silver lining," is not a helpful response. This is *not* the time to be glib, patronizing, or superficial. Instead, ask your friend if she wants to talk about her feelings. Try to be matter-of-fact and confirm that she is indeed seriously suicidal, rather than simply exaggerating her frustration or disappointment.

How can you confirm that the person is suicidal? Simply ask her, "Are you really thinking about killing yourself?" Talking about specific suicide plans (how, when, and where), giving away valued possessions, and putting her affairs in order are some indications that a person's suicidal intentions are serious.

Guideline 3: Identify other potential solutions.

The suicidal person is operating with psychological blinders that prevent him from seeing alternative courses of action or other ways of looking at his problems. How can you remove those blinders? Simply saying, "Here are some options you may not have thought about" is a good starting point. You might list alternative solutions to the person's problems, helping him to understand that other potential solutions do exist, even though none may be perfect (Shneidman, 1998).

Guideline 4: Ask the person to delay his decision.

Most suicidal people are ambivalent about wanting to die. If your friend did not have mixed feelings about committing suicide, he probably wouldn't be talking to you. If he is still intent on suicide after talking about other alternatives, ask him to *delay* his decision. Even a few days' delay may give the person enough time to psychologically regroup, consider alternatives, or seek help.

Guideline 5: Encourage the person to seek professional help.

If the person is seriously suicidal and may harm herself in the near future, do *not* leave her alone. The most important thing you can do is help to get the person referred to a mental health professional for evaluation and treatment. If you don't feel you can do this alone, find another person to help you.

There are any number of resources you can suggest, including local suicide hotlines or mental health associations, the college counseling service, and the person's family doctor or religious adviser. You can also suggest calling 1-800-SUICIDE (1-800-784-2433), which will connect you with a crisis center in your area.

How to Help a Friend The majority of those who attempt suicide communicate their intentions to friends or family members (Shneidman, 1998). When a friend is despondent and desperate, you can help by listening, expressing your understanding and compassion, and, if necessary, referring him or her to a professional counselor or suicide prevention specialist.

CHAPTER REVIEW: KEY TERMS

psychopathology, p. 531
psychological disorder (mental disorder), p. 533
DSM-IV-TR, p. 533
anxiety, p. 537
anxiety disorders, p. 537
generalized anxiety disorder (GAD), p. 537
panic attack, p. 538
panic disorder, p. 538
agoraphobia, p. 538
phobia, p. 539
specific phobia, p. 540
social phobia (social anxiety disorder), p. 540
post-traumatic stress disorder (PTSD), p. 542
obsessive–compulsive disorder (OCD), p. 543
obsessions, p. 543
compulsions, p. 544
mood disorders, p. 546
major depression, p. 546
seasonal affective disorder (SAD), p. 547
dysthymic disorder, p. 548
bipolar disorder, p. 549
manic episode, p. 549
cyclothymic disorder, p. 549
eating disorder, p. 553
anorexia nervosa, p. 553
bulimia nervosa, p. 554
personality disorder, p. 555
paranoid personality disorder, p. 557
antisocial personality disorder, p. 557
borderline personality disorder, p. 558
dissociative experience, p. 560
dissociative disorders, p. 560
dissociative amnesia, p. 561
dissociative fugue, p. 561
dissociative identity disorder (DID), p. 561
schizophrenia, p. 563
positive symptoms, p. 563
negative symptoms, p. 563
delusion, p. 563
hallucination, p. 564
dopamine hypothesis, p. 570

Web Companion Review Activities

You can find additional review activities at **www.worthpublishers.com/discoveringpsych5e.** The *Discovering Psychology* 5th edition Web Companion has self-scoring practice quizzes, flashcards, interactive crossword puzzles, and other activities to help you master the material in this chapter.

CONCEPT MAP

PSYCHOLOGICAL DISORDERS

Psychological Disorders or Mental Disorders

Patterns of behavioral and psychological symptoms that cause significant personal distress and/or impair person's ability to function

Psychopathology: Scientific study of the origins, symptoms, and development of psychological disorders

Diagnostic and Statistical Manual of Mental Disorders (DSM): Contains information and specific diagnostic criteria for over 300 different psychological disorders

National Comorbidity Survey (NCS-R): Identified lifetime and annual prevalence of mental disorders in general population

Anxiety Disorders

Maladaptive anxiety that disrupts ability to function

Generalized anxiety disorder (GAD): Chronic, global feelings of unreasonable worry and anxiety

Panic disorder: Sudden, unpredictable episodes of **panic attacks**

Phobias:

- Intense, irrational fear and avoidance of an object or situation
- Types include **specific phobia, social phobia (social anxiety disorder),** and **agoraphobia**

Obsessive-compulsive disorder (OCD):

- Chronic, persistent anxiety caused by intrusive repetitive thoughts **(obsessions)**
- Anxiety reduced by performing repetitive behavior or mental act **(compulsion)**

Posttraumatic stress disorder (PTSD):

- Reaction to extreme psychological or physical trauma
- Frequent, intrusive trauma memories
- Avoidance of situations that may trigger recall of trauma event
- Emotional numbness
- Heightened physical arousal and anxiety

Mood Disorders

- Serious, persistent emotional disruptions that cause psychological discomfort and impair ability to function
- Also called *affective disorders*

Bipolar disorder:

- Bouts of **manic episodes** that usually alternate with incapacitating periods of major depression
- Some only experience manic episodes
- Inappropriate euphoria, excitement, flight of ideas, and high energy during mania
- Previously called *manic-depression*

Cyclothymic disorder:

- Frequent, unpredictable mood swings
- Not severe enough to be bipolar disorder or major depression

Major depression:

- Emotional symptoms: despondency, helplessness, worthlessness
- Behavioral symptoms: slowed movements, dejected expressions
- Cognitive symptoms: difficulty thinking, concentrating, and suicidal thoughts
- Physical symptoms: loss of physical and mental energy, appetite and sleep changes

Seasonal affective disorder (SAD):

- Recurring episodes of major depression during fall and winter months
- Associated with reduced sunlight exposure

Dysthymic disorder:

- Chronic, low-grade depressed feelings
- Ability to function not seriously impaired

Eating Disorders

Severe, maladaptive disturbances in eating behavior

Anorexia nervosa:
- Severe restriction of food intake
- Refusal to maintain normal body weight
- Irrational fear of gaining weight
- Distorted self-image and self-perception of body size

Bulimia nervosa:
- Recurring episodes of uncontrollable binge eating
- Recurring episodes of purging food by use of laxatives, self-induced vomiting

Personality Disorders

Personality traits characterized by inflexible, maladaptive patterns of thoughts, emotions, behavior, and interpersonal functioning

Paranoid personality disorder:
- Unjustified pervasive distrust and suspiciousness of motives of others
- Frequent inappropriate outbursts, misinterpretations of events, blaming others
- Pathological jealousy of significant other

Antisocial personality disorder:
- Recurring pattern of blatant lying, cheating, manipulating, and harming others
- No sense of conscience, guilt, or remorse
- Irresponsible and substance abuse common
- Also termed *psychopath* or *sociopath*

Borderline personality disorder:
- Unstable self-image, emotional control, and interpersonal relationships
- Mood swings, impulsiveness, substance abuse, and self-destructive tendencies
- Extreme fear of abandonment

Dissociative Disorders

Extreme **dissociative experiences** that disrupt the normal integration of awareness, memory, and personal identity

Dissociative amnesia: Inability to recall important personal information that is not due to a medical condition, drug, or ordinary forgetfulness

Dissociative fugue:
- Identity confusion combined with sudden, unexplained wandering away from home
- Post-fugue amnesia for event

Dissociative identity disorder (DID):
- Memory disruptions of personal identity combined with presence of two or more distinct identities termed *alters*
- Controversial mental disorder of which many clinicians are skeptical
- Previously called *multiple personality disorder*

Schizophrenia

Severely distorted thought processes, beliefs, and perceptions that impairs functioning

Positive symptoms: Excesses or distortions of normal functioning
- **Delusions:** False beliefs
- **Hallucinations:** false perceptions
- Severely disorganized thoughts, speech, and behavior

Negative symptoms: Deficits in normal functioning
- Flat affect: Emotionally blunted reactions
- Alogia: Greatly reduced speech
- Avolition: Apathy and diminished goal-directed behavior

Types of schizophrenia:
- *Paranoid type:* Delusions of grandeur or persecution, auditory hallucinations, no cognitive impairment
- *Catatonic type:* Disturbed movements, facial expressions, postures
- *Disorganized type:* Severely disorganized behavior and speech, inappropriate emotional expressions
- *Undifferentiated type:* Symptoms do not clearly fit one of first three types

CHAPTER 14

Therapies

"A Clear Sense of Being Heard . . ."

PROLOGUE

HOW WOULD WE DESCRIBE MARCIA? She's an extraordinarily kind, intelligent woman. Her thoughtfulness and sensitivity are tempered by a ready laugh and a good sense of humor. She's happily married, has a good job as a feature writer for a large suburban newspaper, and has two young children, who only occasionally drive her crazy. If Marcia has a flaw, it's that she tends to judge herself much too harshly. She's too quick to blame herself when anything goes wrong.

Juggling a full-time career, marriage, and parenting is a challenge for anyone, but Marcia always makes it look easy. The last time we had dinner at Bill and Marcia's home, the meal featured homegrown vegetables, made-from-scratch bread, and fresh seasonings from the herb pots in the kitchen. Outwardly, Marcia appears to have it all. But a few years ago, she began to experience a pervasive sense of dread and unease—feelings that gradually escalated into a full-scale depression. Marcia describes the onset of her feelings in this way:

> *Physically I began to feel as if I were fraying around the edges. I had a constant sense of anxiety and a recurring sense of being a failure. My daughter, Maggie, was going through a rather difficult stage. Andy was still a baby. I felt worn out. I started worrying constantly about my children. Are they safe? Are they sick? What's going to happen? Are my kids going to get hurt? I knew that I really didn't have any reason to worry that much, but I did. It finally struck me that my worrying and my anxiety and my feelings of being a failure were not going to go away on their own.*

Marcia decided to seek help. She made an appointment with her therapist, a psychiatrist whom Marcia had last seen 10 years earlier, when she had helped Marcia cope with a very difficult time in her life. Marcia summarizes her experience this way:

> *How has therapy helped me? My feelings before a therapy session may vary greatly, depending on the issue under discussion. However, I always find the sessions cathartic and I invariably feel great relief. I feel a sense of being understood by someone who knows me but who is detached from me. I have a clear sense of being heard, as though my therapist has given me a gift of listening and of allowing me to see myself as the worthwhile and capable person I am. It is as though therapy allows me to see more clearly into a mirror that my problems have obscured.*

Over the course of several months, Marcia gradually began to feel better. Today, Marcia is calmer, more confident, and feels much more in control of her emotions and her life. As Marcia's mental health improved, so did her relationships with her children and her husband.

> *Psychotherapy has also helped me communicate more clearly. It has enabled me to become more resilient after some emotional conflict. It has had a preventive effect in*

Chapter Outline

helping me to ignore or manage situations that might under certain circumstances trigger depression, anxiety, or obsessive worry. And it makes me a better parent and marriage partner.

Therapy's negative effects? I'm poorer; it costs money. And therapy poses the risk of becoming an end in itself. Psychotherapy has the attraction of being a safe harbor from the petty assaults of everyday life. There's always the danger of losing sight of the goal of becoming a healthier and more productive person, and becoming stuck in the therapy process.

Marcia's experience with psychotherapy reflects many of the themes we will touch on in this chapter. We'll look at different forms of therapy that psychologists and other mental health professionals use to help people cope with psychological problems. We'll also consider the popularity of self-help groups and how they differ from more structured forms of therapy. Toward the end of the chapter, we'll discuss biomedical approaches to the treatment of psychological disorders. Over the course of the chapter, we'll come back to Marcia's story.

>> Introduction: Psychotherapy and Biomedical Therapy

Key Theme

- **Two forms of therapy are used to treat psychological disorders and personal problems—psychotherapy and the biomedical therapies.**

Key Questions

- **What is psychotherapy, and what is its basic assumption?**
- **What is biomedical therapy, and how does it differ from psychotherapy?**

People seek help from mental health professionals for a variety of reasons. Like Marcia, many people seek help because they are suffering from some form of a *psychological disorder*—troubling thoughts, feelings, or behaviors that cause psychological discomfort or interfere with a person's ability to function.

But not everyone who seeks professional help is suffering from a psychological disorder. Many people seek help in dealing with troubled relationships, such as parent–child conflicts or an unhappy marriage. And sometimes people need help with life's transitions, such as coping with the death of a loved one, dissolving a marriage, or adjusting to retirement.

In this chapter, we'll look at the two broad forms of therapy that mental health professionals use to help people: *psychotherapy* and *biomedical therapy.* **Psychotherapy** refers to the use of psychological techniques to treat emotional, behavioral, and interpersonal problems. While there are many different types of psychotherapy, they all share the assumption that psychological factors play a significant role in a person's troubling feelings, behaviors, or relationships. Table 14.1 summarizes the diverse range of mental health professionals who use psychotherapy techniques to help people.

In contrast to psychotherapy, the **biomedical therapies** involve the use of medication or other medical treatments to treat the symptoms associated with psychological disorders. Drugs that are used to treat psychological or mental disorders are termed *psychotropic medications.* The biomedical therapies are based on the assumption that the symptoms of many psychological disorders involve biological factors, such as abnormal brain chemistry. As we saw in Chapter 13, the involvement of biological factors in many psychological disorders is well documented. Treating psychological disorders with a combination of psychotherapy and biomedical therapy,

Seeking Help People enter psychotherapy for many different reasons. Some people seek to overcome severe psychological disorders, while others want to learn how to cope better with everyday challenges or relationship problems. And, for some people, the goal of therapy is to attain greater self-knowledge or personal fulfillment.

Table 14.1

Who's Who Among Mental Health Professionals

Clinical psychologist	Holds an academic doctorate (Ph.D., Psy.D., or Ed.D.) and is required to be licensed to practice. Assesses and treats mental, emotional, and behavioral disorders. Has expertise in psychological testing and evaluation, diagnosis, psychotherapy, research, and prevention of mental and emotional disorders. May work in private practice, hospitals, or community mental health centers.
Counseling psychologist	Holds an academic doctorate and must be licensed to practice. Assesses and treats mental, emotional, and behavioral problems and disorders, but usually disorders that are of lesser severity.
Psychiatrist	Holds a medical degree (M.D. or D.O.) and is required to be licensed to practice. Has expertise in the diagnosis, treatment, and prevention of mental and emotional disorders. Often has training in psychotherapy. May prescribe medications, electroconvulsive therapy, or other medical procedures.
Psychoanalyst	Usually a psychiatrist or clinical psychologist who has received additional training in the specific techniques of psychoanalysis, the form of psychotherapy originated by Sigmund Freud.
Licensed professional counselor	Holds at least a master's degree in counseling, with extensive supervised training in assessment, counseling, and therapy techniques. May be certified in specialty areas. Most states require licensure or certification.
Psychiatric social worker	Holds a master's degree in social work (M.S.W.). Training includes an internship in a social service agency or mental health center. Most states require certification or licensing. May or may not have training in psychotherapy.
Marriage and family therapist	Usually holds a master's degree, with extensive supervised experience in couple or family therapy. May also have training in individual therapy. Many states require licensing.
Psychiatric nurse	Holds an R.N. degree and has selected psychiatry or mental health nursing as a specialty area. Typically works on a hospital psychiatric unit or in a community mental health center. May or may not have training in psychotherapy.

especially psychotropic medications, has become increasingly common (Hollon & Fawcett, 2007; Thase & Jindal, 2004). Until very recently, only licensed physicians were legally allowed to prescribe psychotropic medications.

However, that tradition may be changing. Since the 1990s, a movement to allow specially trained psychologists to prescribe has achieved some success. It began with the U.S. Department of Defense conducting a successful pilot program in which 10 military psychologists were given intensive training in prescribing psychotropic medications to treat psychological disorders (Ax & others, 2008). The success of the Department of Defense program was one of the factors that persuaded New Mexico lawmakers to enact legislation in 2002 that permitted licensed psychologists to acquire additional training to prescribe psychotropic medications (Dittman, 2003). In 2004, Louisiana became the second state to grant prescription-writing privileges to properly trained psychologists (Holloway, 2004a). Similar legislation is pending in several other states. And, a recent survey of psychology professionals in Canada found that a majority favored extending prescription privileges to Canadian clinical psychologists who were properly trained (St. Pierre & Melnyk, 2004).

However, not all psychologists favor the idea of extending prescription privileges to qualified psychologists (see Heiby & others, 2004; Long, 2005). Some argue that clinical psychologists should focus on what they do best: providing psychological interventions and treatments that help people acquire more effective patterns of thinking and behaving. Others are concerned that the safety and well-being of patients could be at risk if psychologists receive inadequate training to prescribe psychotropic medications (Lavoie & Barone, 2006).

psychotherapy
The treatment of emotional, behavioral, and interpersonal problems through the use of psychological techniques designed to encourage understanding of problems and modify troubling feelings, behaviors, or relationships.

biomedical therapies
The use of medications, electroconvulsive therapy, or other medical treatments to treat the symptoms associated with psychological disorders.

Prescribing Psychologist Elaine LeVine New Mexico psychologist Elaine LeVine (2007) was one of the first psychologists to acquire prescription privileges in the United States. When New Mexico passed the legislation making licensed psychologists eligible for prescription privileges, a key goal was to increase rural access to mental health care. Like other prescribing psychologists, Dr. LeVine uses the therapeutic relationship she builds with patients to help educate and involve them in treatment decisions about the medications she prescribes. As LeVine (2007) explains, "The psychologist's close relationship with the patient, combined with thorough communication with the medical provider, can offer more integrated and thorough care."

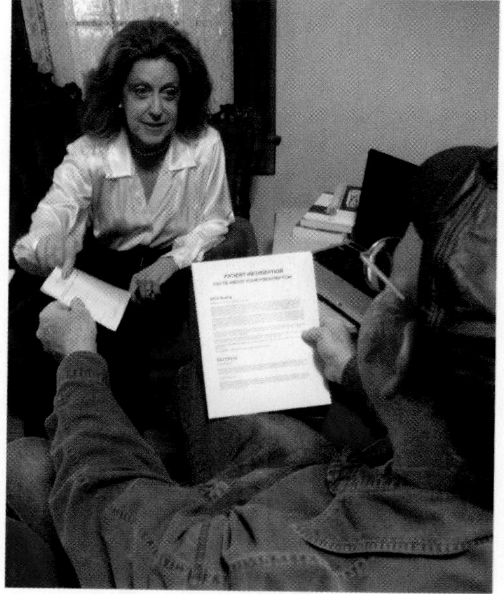

"Look, making you happy is out of the question, but I can give you a compelling narrative for your misery"

We'll begin this chapter by surveying some of the most influential approaches in psychotherapy: psychoanalytic, humanistic, behavioral, and cognitive. Each approach is based on different assumptions about the underlying causes of psychological problems. And each approach uses different strategies to produce beneficial changes in the way a person thinks, feels, and behaves—the ultimate goal of all forms of psychotherapy. After discussing the effectiveness of psychotherapy, we'll look at the most commonly used biomedical treatments for psychological disorders.

Psychoanalytic Therapy

Key Theme

- **Psychoanalysis is a form of therapy developed by Sigmund Freud and is based on his theory of personality.**

Key Questions

- **What are the key assumptions and techniques of psychoanalytic therapy?**
- **How do short-term dynamic therapies differ from psychoanalysis, and what is interpersonal therapy?**

When cartoonists portray a psychotherapy session, they often draw a person lying on a couch and talking while a bearded gentleman sits behind the patient, passively listening. This stereotype reflects some of the key ingredients of traditional **psychoanalysis,** a form of psychotherapy originally developed by **Sigmund Freud** in the early 1900s. Although psychoanalysis was developed a century ago, its assumptions and techniques continue to influence many psychotherapies today (Lerner, 2008; Luborsky & Barrett, 2006).

Sigmund Freud and Psychoanalytic Therapy At the beginning of the twentieth century, Sigmund Freud (1856–1939) developed an influential form of psychotherapy called psychoanalysis. Traditional psychoanalysis is not widely practiced today, partly because it is too lengthy and expensive. However, many of the techniques that Freud pioneered, such as free association, dream analysis, and transference, are still commonly used in different forms of psychotherapy.

Sigmund Freud and Psychoanalysis

As a therapy, traditional psychoanalysis is closely interwoven with Freud's theory of personality. As you may recall from Chapter 10, on personality, Freud stressed that early childhood experiences provided the foundation for later personality development. When early experiences result in unresolved conflicts and frustrated urges, these emotionally charged memories are *repressed,* or pushed out of conscious awareness. Although unconscious, these repressed conflicts continue to influence a person's thoughts and behavior, including the dynamics of his relationships with others.

Psychoanalysis is designed to help unearth unconscious conflicts so the patient attains *insight* as to the real source of her problems. Through the intense relationship that develops between the psychoanalyst and the patient, long-standing psychological conflicts are recognized and reexperienced. If the analytic treatment is successful, the conflicts are resolved.

Freud developed several techniques to coax long-repressed memories, impulses, and conflicts to a patient's consciousness (Liff, 1992). In the famous technique called **free association,** the patient spontaneously reports all her thoughts, mental images, and feelings while lying on a couch. The psychoanalyst usually sits out of view, occasionally asking questions to encourage the flow of associations.

Freud's Famous Couch During psychoanalytic sessions, Freud's patients would lie on the couch. Freud himself sat at the head of the couch, out of the patient's view. Freud believed that this arrangement encouraged the patient's free flow of thoughts, feelings, and images. Although some traditional psychoanalysts still have the patient lie on a couch, many psychoanalysts today favor comfortable chairs on which analyst and patient sit, facing each other.

Blocks in free association, such as a sudden silence or an abrupt change of topic, were thought to be signs of resistance. **Resistance** is the patient's conscious or unconscious attempts to block the process of revealing repressed memories and conflicts (Luborsky & Barrett, 2006). Resistance is a sign that the patient is uncomfortably close to uncovering psychologically threatening material.

Dream interpretation is another important psychoanalytic technique. Because psychological defenses are reduced during sleep, Freud (1911) believed that unconscious conflicts and repressed impulses were expressed symbolically in dream images. Often, the dream images were used to trigger free associations that might shed light on the dream's symbolic meaning.

More directly, the psychoanalyst sometimes makes carefully timed **interpretations,** explanations of the unconscious meaning of the patient's behavior, thoughts, feelings, or dreams. The timing of such interpretations is important. If an interpretation is offered before the patient is psychologically ready to confront an issue, she may reject the interpretation or respond defensively, increasing resistance (Prochaska & Norcross, 2010).

One of the most important processes that occurs in the relationship between the patient and the psychoanalyst is called transference. **Transference** occurs when the patient unconsciously responds to the therapist as though the therapist were a significant person in the patient's life, often a parent. As Freud (1940) explained, "The patient sees in his analyst the return—the reincarnation—of some important figure out of his childhood or past, and consequently transfers on to him the feelings and reactions that undoubtedly applied to this model."

The psychoanalyst encourages transference by purposely remaining as neutral as possible. In other words, the psychoanalyst does not reveal personal feelings, take sides, make judgments, or actively advise the patient. This therapeutic neutrality is designed to produce "optimal frustration" so that the patient transfers and projects unresolved conflicts onto the psychoanalyst (Magnavita, 2008).

As the transference becomes more intense, the patient relives unconscious emotional conflicts that have been repressed since childhood. Only now, these conflicts are being relived and played out in the context of the relationship between the psychoanalyst and the patient.

All of these psychoanalytic techniques are designed to help the patient see how past conflicts influence her current behavior and relationships, including her relationship with the psychoanalyst. Once these kinds of insights are achieved, the psychoanalyst helps the patient work through and resolve long-standing conflicts. As resolutions occur, maladaptive behavior patterns that were previously driven by unconscious conflicts can be replaced with more adaptive emotional and behavioral patterns.

The intensive relationship between the patient and the psychoanalyst takes time to develop. The traditional psychoanalyst sees the patient three times a week or more, often for years (Schwartz, 2003; Zusman & others, 2007). Freud's patients were on the couch six days a week (Liff, 1992). Obviously, traditional psychoanalysis is a slow, expensive process that few people can afford. For those who have the time and the money, traditional psychoanalysis is still available.

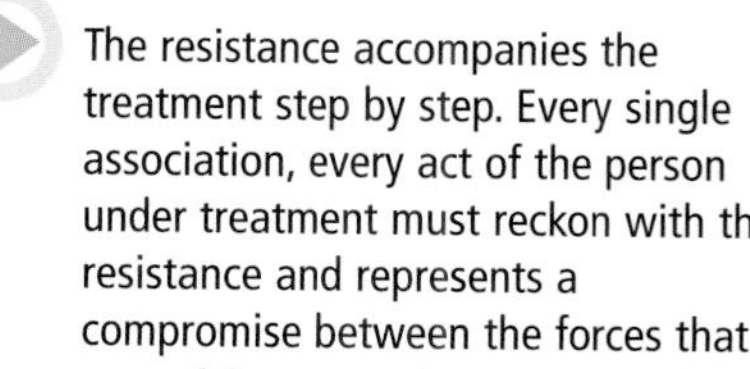

The resistance accompanies the treatment step by step. Every single association, every act of the person under treatment must reckon with the resistance and represents a compromise between the forces that are striving towards recovery and opposing ones.

—SIGMUND FREUD (1912)

psychoanalysis
A type of psychotherapy originated by Sigmund Freud in which free association, dream interpretation, and analysis of resistance and transference are used to explore repressed or unconscious impulses, anxieties, and internal conflicts.

free association
A technique used in psychoanalysis in which the patient spontaneously reports all thoughts, feelings, and mental images as they come to mind, as a way of revealing unconscious thoughts and emotions.

resistance
In psychoanalysis, the patient's unconscious attempts to block the revelation of repressed memories and conflicts.

dream interpretation
A technique used in psychoanalysis in which the content of dreams is analyzed for disguised or symbolic wishes, meanings, and motivations.

interpretation
A technique used in psychoanalysis in which the psychoanalyst offers a carefully timed explanation of the patient's dreams, free associations, or behaviors to facilitate the recognition of unconscious conflicts or motivations.

transference
In psychoanalysis, the process by which emotions and desires originally associated with a significant person in the patient's life, such as a parent, are unconsciously transferred to the psychoanalyst.

BIZZARO

Short-Term Dynamic Therapies

Most people entering psychotherapy today are not seeking the kind of major personality overhaul that traditional psychoanalysis is designed to produce. Instead, people come to therapy expecting help with specific problems. People also expect therapy to provide beneficial changes in a matter of weeks or months, not years.

Many different forms of **short-term dynamic therapies** based on traditional psychoanalytic notions are now available (Gibbons & others, 2008; Levenson, 2003; Rawson, 2005). These short-term dynamic therapies have several features in common. Therapeutic contact lasts for no more than a few months. The patient's problems are quickly assessed at the beginning of therapy. The therapist and patient agree on specific, concrete, and attainable goals. In the actual sessions, most psychodynamic therapists are more directive than are traditional psychoanalysts, actively engaging the patient in a dialogue.

As in traditional psychoanalysis, the therapist uses interpretations to help the patient recognize hidden feelings and transferences that may be occurring in important relationships in her life (Liff, 1992).

One particularly influential short-term psychodynamic therapy is **interpersonal therapy,** abbreviated **IPT.** In contrast to other psychodynamic therapies, interpersonal therapy focuses on *current* relationships and social interactions rather than on past relationships. Originally developed as a brief treatment for depression, interpersonal therapy is based on the assumption that psychological symptoms are caused and maintained by interpersonal problems (Klerman & others, 1984; Weissman & others, 2000).

Interpersonal therapy may be brief or long-term, but it is highly structured (Blanco & others, 2006; Teyber, 2009). In the first phase of treatment, the therapist identifies the interpersonal problem that is causing difficulties. In the interpersonal therapy model, there are four categories of personal problems: unresolved grief, role disputes, role transitions, and interpersonal deficits. *Unresolved grief* refers to problems dealing with the death of significant others, while *role disputes* refer to repetitive conflicts with significant others, such as the person's partner, family members, friends, or co-workers. *Role transitions* include problems involving major life changes, such as going away to college, becoming a parent, getting married or divorced, or retiring. *Interpersonal deficits* refer to absent or faulty social skills that limit the ability to start or maintain healthy relationships with others (Mallinckrodt, 2001). During treatment, the therapist helps the person understand his particular interpersonal problem and develop strategies to resolve it.

IPT is used to treat eating disorders and substance abuse as well as depression. It is also effective in helping people deal with interpersonal problems, such as marital conflict, parenting issues, and conflicts at work (Bleiberg & Markowitz, 2008). In one innovative application, IPT was successfully used to treat symptoms of depression in villagers in Uganda, demonstrating its effectiveness in a non-Western culture (Bolton & others, 2003). Beyond individual psychotherapy, IPT has proved to be valuable in family and group therapy sessions (Woody, 2008; Zimmerman, 2008).

If Sigmund Freud were alive today, would he be upset by these departures from traditional psychoanalysis? Not at all. In fact, Freud himself treated some of his patients using short-term psychodynamic therapy that sometimes lasted for only one lengthy session. Several of Freud's patients completed psychoanalysis in as little as two months (Magnavita, 1993).

Even though traditional, lengthy psychoanalysis is uncommon today, Freud's basic assumptions and techniques continue to be influential. Contemporary research has challenged many of Freud's original ideas. However, modern researchers continue to study the specific factors that seem to influence the effectiveness of basic Freudian techniques, such as dream analysis, interpretation, transference, and the role of insight in reducing psychological symptoms (Glucksman & Kramer, 2004; Luborsky & Barrett, 2006).

short-term dynamic therapies
Type of psychotherapy that is based on psychoanalytic theory but differs in that it is typically time-limited, has specific goals, and involves an active, rather than neutral, role for the therapist.

interpersonal therapy (IPT)
A brief, psychodynamic psychotherapy that focuses on current relationships and is based on the assumption that symptoms are caused and maintained by interpersonal problems.

Humanistic Therapy

client-centered therapy
A type of psychotherapy developed by humanistic psychologist Carl Rogers in which the therapist is nondirective and reflective, and the client directs the focus of each therapy session; also called *person-centered therapy.*

Key Theme

- **The most influential humanistic psychotherapy is client-centered therapy, which was developed by Carl Rogers.**

Key Questions

- **What are the key assumptions of humanistic therapy, including client-centered therapy?**
- **What therapeutic techniques and conditions are important in client-centered therapy?**
- **How do client-centered therapy and psychoanalysis differ?**

The *humanistic perspective* in psychology emphasizes human potential, self-awareness, and freedom of choice (see Chapter 10). Humanistic psychologists contend that the most important factor in personality is the individual's conscious, subjective perception of his or her self. They see people as being innately good and motivated by the need to grow psychologically. If people are raised in a genuinely accepting atmosphere and given freedom to make choices, they will develop healthy self-concepts and strive to fulfill their unique potential as human beings (Kirschenbaum & Jourdan, 2005; Pos & others, 2008).

Carl Rogers (1902–1987) In his classic text, *On Becoming a Person*, Rogers (1961) described how his own thinking changed as he developed client-centered therapy. He wrote, "In my early professional years, I was asking the question: How can I treat, or cure, or change this person? Now I would phrase the question in this way: How can I provide a relationship which this person may use for his own personal growth?"

Carl Rogers and Client-Centered Therapy

The humanistic perspective has exerted a strong influence on psychotherapy (Cain 2002, 2003; Schneider & Krug, 2009). Probably the most influential of the humanistic psychotherapies is **client-centered therapy,** also called *person-centered therapy,* developed by **Carl Rogers.** In naming his therapy, Rogers (1951) deliberately used the word *client* rather than *patient.* He believed that the medical term *patient* implied that people in therapy were "sick" and were seeking treatment from an all-knowing authority figure who could "heal" or "cure" them. Instead of stressing the therapist's expertise or perceptions of the patient, client-centered therapy emphasizes the *client's* subjective perception of himself and his environment (Cain, 2002; Raskin & Rogers, 2005).

Like Freud, Rogers saw the therapeutic relationship as the catalyst that leads to insight and lasting personality change. But Rogers viewed the nature of this relationship very differently from Freud. According to Rogers (1977), the therapist should not exert power by offering carefully timed "interpretations" of the patient's unconscious conflicts. Advocating just the opposite, Rogers believed that

Group Therapy Session with Carl Rogers Rogers filmed many of his therapy sessions as part of an ongoing research program to identify the most helpful aspects of client-centered therapy. Shown on the far right, Rogers contended that human potential would flourish in an atmosphere of genuineness, unconditional positive regard, and empathic understanding.

Client-Centered Therapy The client-centered therapist strives to create a warm, accepting climate that allows the client the freedom to explore troubling issues. The therapist engages in active listening, reflecting both the content and the personal meaning of what the client is saying. In doing so, the therapist helps the client develop a clearer perception and understanding of her own feelings and motives.

the therapist should be *nondirective*. That is, the therapist must not direct the client, make decisions for the client, offer solutions, or pass judgment on the client's thoughts or feelings. Instead, Rogers believed, change in therapy must be chosen and directed by the client (Bozarth & others, 2002). The therapist's role is to create the conditions that allow the client, not the therapist, to direct the focus of therapy.

What are the therapeutic conditions that promote self-awareness, psychological growth, and self-directed change? Rogers (1957c, 1980) believed that three qualities of the therapist are necessary: *genuineness, unconditional positive regard,* and *empathic understanding*. First, *genuineness* means that the therapist honestly and openly shares her thoughts and feelings with the client. By modeling genuineness, the therapist indirectly encourages the client to exercise this capability more fully in himself.

Second, the therapist must value, accept, and care for the client, whatever her problems or behavior. Rogers called this quality *unconditional positive regard* (Bozarth & Wang, 2008). Rogers believed that people develop psychological problems largely because they have consistently experienced only *conditional acceptance*. That is, parents, teachers, and others have communicated this message to the client: "I will accept you only *if* you conform to my expectations." Because acceptance by significant others has been conditional, the person has cut off or denied unacceptable aspects of herself, distorting her self-concept. In turn, these distorted perceptions affect her thoughts and behaviors in unhealthy, unproductive ways.

The therapist who successfully creates a climate of unconditional positive regard fosters the person's natural tendency to move toward self-fulfilling decisions without fear of evaluation or rejection. Rogers (1977) described this important aspect of therapy in this way:

> Unconditional positive regard means that when the therapist is experiencing a positive, acceptant attitude toward whatever the client *is* at that moment, therapeutic movement or change is more likely. It involves the therapist's willingness for the client to be whatever feeling is going on at that moment—confusion, resentment, fear, anger, courage, love, or pride. . . . The therapist prizes the client in a total rather than a conditional way.

Third, the therapist must communicate *empathic understanding* by reflecting the content and personal meaning of the feelings being experienced by the client. In effect, the therapist creates a psychological mirror, reflecting the client's thoughts and feelings as they exist in the client's private inner world. The goal is to help the client explore and clarify his feelings, thoughts, and perceptions. In the process, the client begins to see himself, and his problems, more clearly (Freire, 2007).

Empathic understanding requires the therapist to listen *actively* for the personal meaning beneath the surface of what the client is saying (Watson, 2002). Rogers believed that when the therapeutic atmosphere contains genuineness, unconditional positive regard, and empathic understanding, change is more likely to occur. Such conditions foster feelings of being psychologically safe, accepted, and valued. In this therapeutic atmosphere, change occurs as the person's self-concept and worldview gradually become healthier and less distorted. According to Rogers (1977), "As the client becomes more self-aware, more self-acceptant, less defensive and more open, she finds at last some of the freedom to grow and change in directions natural to the human organism." In effect, the client is moving in the direction of *self-actualization*—the realization of his or her unique potentials and talents.

> An empathic way of being with another person has several facets. It means entering the private perceptual world of the other and becoming thoroughly at home in it. It involves being sensitive, moment by moment, to the changing felt meanings which flow in this other person, to the fear or rage or tenderness or confusion or whatever that he or she is experiencing.
>
> —CARL ROGERS (1980)

A large number of studies have generally supported the importance of genuineness, unconditional positive regard, and empathic understanding (Elliott & others, 2004). Such factors promote trust and self-exploration in therapy. However, these conditions, by themselves, may not be sufficient to help clients change (Cain & Seeman, 2002; Sachse & Elliott, 2002).

Motivational Interviewing: Helping Clients Commit to Change

Like psychoanalysis, client-centered therapy has evolved and adapted to changing times. It continues to have a powerful impact on therapists, teachers, social workers, and counselors (see Cooper & others, 2007). Of particular note has been the development of motivational interviewing (Miller & Rollnick, 2002). *Motivational interviewing (MI)* is designed to help clients overcome the mixed feelings or reluctance they might have about committing to change. Usually lasting only a session or two, MI is more directive than traditional client-centered therapy (Arkowitz & others, 2007; Hettema & others, 2005).

The main goal of MI is to encourage and strengthen the client's self-motivating statements or "change talk." These are expressions of the client's need, desire, and reasons for change. Using client-centered techniques, the therapist responds with empathic understanding and reflective listening, helping the client explore his or her own values and motivations for change. When the client expresses reluctance, the therapist acknowledges the mixed feelings and redirects the emphasis toward change. As Jennifer Hettema and her colleagues (2005) explain:

> The counselor seeks to evoke the client's own motivation, with confidence in the human desire and capacity to grow in positive directions. Instead of implying that "I have what you need," MI communicates, "You have what you need." In this way, MI falls squarely within the humanistic "third force" in the history of psychotherapy.

Along with being influential in individual psychotherapy, the client-centered approach has been applied to marital counseling, parenting, education, business, and even community and international relations (Henderson & others, 2007). Table 14.2 compares some aspects of psychoanalysis and client-centered therapy.

Table 14.2

Comparing Psychodynamic and Humanistic Therapies

Type of Therapy	Founder	Source of Problems	Treatment Techniques	Goals of Therapy
Psychoanalysis	Sigmund Freud	Repressed, unconscious conflicts stemming from early childhood experiences	Free association, analysis of dream content, interpretation, and transference	To recognize, work through, and resolve long-standing conflicts
Client-centered therapy	Carl Rogers	Conditional acceptance that causes the person to develop a distorted self-concept and worldview	Nondirective therapist who displays unconditional positive regard, genuineness, and empathic understanding	To develop self-awareness, self-acceptance, and self-determination

Behavior Therapy

Key Theme

- **Behavior therapy uses learning principles to directly change problem behaviors.**

Key Questions

- **What are the key assumptions of behavior therapy?**
- **What therapeutic techniques are based on classical conditioning, and how are they used to treat psychological disorders and problems?**
- **What therapy treatments are based on operant conditioning, and how are they used to treat psychological disorders and problems?**

Psychoanalysis, client-centered therapy, and other insight-oriented therapies maintain that the road to psychologically healthier behavior is through increased self-understanding of motives and conflicts. As insights are acquired through therapy, problem behaviors and feelings presumably will give way to more adaptive behaviors and emotional reactions.

However, gaining insight into the source of problems does not necessarily result in desirable changes in behavior and emotions. Even though you fully understand *why* you are behaving in counterproductive ways, your maladaptive or self-defeating behaviors may continue. For instance, an adult who is extremely anxious about public speaking may understand that he feels that way because he was raised by a critical and demanding parent. But having this insight into the underlying cause of his anxiety may do little, if anything, to reduce his anxiety or change his avoidance of public speaking.

In sharp contrast to the insight-oriented therapies we discussed in the preceding sections, the goal of **behavior therapy,** also called *behavior modification,* is to modify specific problem behaviors, not to change the entire personality. And, rather than focusing on the past, behavior therapists focus on current behaviors.

Behavior therapists assume that maladaptive behaviors are *learned,* just as adaptive behaviors are. Thus, the basic strategy in behavior therapy involves unlearning maladaptive behaviors and learning more adaptive behaviors in their place. Behavior therapists employ techniques that are based on the learning principles of classical conditioning, operant conditioning, and observational learning to modify the problem behavior.

Behavior Therapy—From Bad Habits to Severe Psychological Disorders Nail biting and cigarette smoking are examples of the kinds of everyday maladaptive behaviors that can be successfully treated with behavior therapy. Behavioral techniques can also be used to treat more severe psychological problems, such as phobias, and to improve functioning in people with severe mental disorders such as schizophrenia and autism.

behavior therapy
A type of psychotherapy that focuses on directly changing maladaptive behavior patterns by using basic learning principles and techniques; also called *behavior modification.*

counterconditioning
A behavior therapy technique based on classical conditioning that involves modifying behavior by conditioning a new response that is incompatible with a previously learned response.

systematic desensitization
A type of behavior therapy in which phobic responses are reduced by pairing relaxation with a series of mental images or real-life situations that the person finds progressively more fear-provoking; based on the principle of counterconditioning.

Techniques Based on Classical Conditioning

Just as Pavlov's dogs learned to salivate to a ringing bell that had become associated with food, learned associations can be at the core of some maladaptive behaviors, including strong negative emotional reactions. In the 1920s, psychologist John Watson demonstrated this phenomenon with his famous "Little Albert" study. In Chapter 5, we described how Watson classically conditioned an infant known as Little Albert to fear a tame lab rat by repeatedly pairing the rat with a loud clanging sound. Over time, Albert's conditioned fear generalized to other furry objects, including a fur coat, cotton, and a Santa Claus mask (Watson & Rayner, 1920).

Mary Cover Jones

The First Behavior Therapist

Watson himself never tried to eliminate Little Albert's fears. But Watson's research inspired one of his students, **Mary Cover Jones,** to explore ways of reversing conditioned fears. With Watson acting as a consultant, Jones (1924a) treated a 3-year-old named Peter who "seemed almost to be Albert grown a bit older." Like Little Albert, Peter was fearful of various furry objects, including a tame rat, a fur coat, cotton, and wool. Because Peter was especially afraid of a tame rabbit, Jones focused on eliminating the rabbit fear. She used a procedure that has come to be known as

counterconditioning—the learning of a new conditioned response that is incompatible with a previously learned response.

Jones's procedure was very simple (Jones, 1924b; Watson, 1924). The caged rabbit was brought into Peter's view but kept far enough away to avoid eliciting fear (the original conditioned response). With the rabbit visible at a tolerable distance, Peter sat in a high chair and happily munched his favorite snack, milk and crackers. Peter's favorite food was used because, presumably, the enjoyment of eating would naturally elicit a positive response (the desired conditioned response). Such a positive response would be incompatible with the negative response of fear.

Every day for almost two months, the rabbit was inched closer and closer to Peter as he ate his milk and crackers. As Peter's tolerance for the rabbit's presence gradually increased, he was eventually able to hold the rabbit in his lap, petting it with one hand while happily eating with his other hand (Jones, 1924a, 1924b). Not only was Peter's fear of the rabbit eliminated, but he also stopped being afraid of other furry objects, including the rat, cotton, and the fur coat (Watson, 1924).

Along with counterconditioning, Jones (1924a) used social imitation, or *observational learning,* techniques to help eliminate Peter's fear of rabbits (Kornfeld, 1989). As part of the treatment, Peter observed other children petting or holding the tame rabbit. Eventually, Peter imitated the actions of the nonfearful children. For her pioneering efforts in the treatment of children's fears, Jones is widely regarded as the first behavior therapist (Gieser, 1993; Rutherford, 2006).

Mary Cover Jones (1896–1987) This photograph, taken around 1919, shows Mary Cover Jones as a college student in her early 20s. Although Jones pioneered the use of behavioral techniques in therapy, she did not consider herself a "behaviorist" and ultimately came to disagree with many of Watson's views. Fifty years after she treated Peter, Jones (1975) wrote, "Now I would be less satisfied to treat the fears of a three-year-old . . . in isolation from him as a tantalizingly complex person with unique potentials for stability and change."

Systematic Desensitization

Mary Cover Jones's pioneering studies in treating children's fears laid the groundwork for the later development of a more standardized procedure to treat phobias and other anxiety disorders. Developed by South African psychiatrist Joseph Wolpe in the 1950s, the procedure is called *systematic desensitization* (Wolpe, 1958, 1982). Based on the same premise as counterconditioning, **systematic desensitization** involves learning a new conditioned response (relaxation) that is incompatible with or inhibits the old conditioned response (fear and anxiety).

Three basic steps are involved in systematic desensitization. First, the patient learns *progressive relaxation,* which involves successively relaxing one muscle group after another until a deep state of relaxation is achieved. Second, the behavior therapist helps the patient construct an *anxiety hierarchy,* which is a list of anxiety-provoking images associated with the feared situation, arranged in a hierarchy from least to most anxiety-producing (see Figure 14.1). The patient also develops an image of a relaxing *control scene,* such as walking on a secluded beach on a sunny day.

Degree of Fear	Imagined Scene
100	Holding mouth open, eyes closed, listening to the sound of the dental drill as a cavity is repaired
95	Holding mouth open in preparation for an oral injection
90	Lying back in dental chair, eyes closed, as dentist examines teeth
85	Lying back in dental chair, mouth open, listening to the sounds of dental equipment as dental technician cleans teeth
80	Lying in dental chair, watching dental technician unwrap sterilized dental tools
75	Being greeted by the dental technician and walking back to dental examination chair
70	Sitting in dentist's waiting room
60	Driving to dentist's office for appointment
50	Looking at the bright yellow reminder postcard on the refrigerator and thinking about dental appointment
40	Listening to a family member talk about her last dental visit
30	Looking at television or magazine advertisements depicting people in a dentist's chair
25	Calling dentist's office to make an appointment
20	Thinking about calling dentist's office to set up an appointment
15	Driving past dentist's office on a workday
10	Driving past dentist's office on a Sunday afternoon

Figure 14.1 A Sample Anxiety Hierarchy Used in Systematic Desensitization As part of systematic desensitization, the therapist helps the client develop an anxiety hierarchy. The sample anxiety hierarchy shown here illustrates the kinds of scenes that might be listed by a person who is phobic of dental treatment (Getka & Glass, 1992). Starting at the bottom of the hierarchy, relaxation is paired with each scene until the client can calmly visualize the image. Only then does he move to the next scene in the hierarchy.

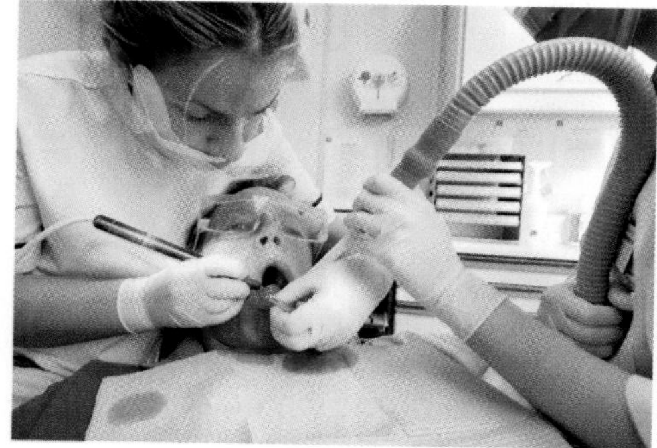

The third step involves the actual process of desensitization. While deeply relaxed, the patient imagines the least threatening scene on the anxiety hierarchy. After he can maintain complete relaxation while imagining this scene, he moves to the next. If the patient begins to feel anxiety or tension, the behavior therapist guides him back to imagining the previous scene or the control scene. If necessary, the therapist helps the patient relax again, using the progressive relaxation technique.

Over several sessions, the patient gradually and systematically works his way up the hierarchy, imagining each scene while maintaining complete relaxation. Very systematically, each imagined scene becomes paired with a conditioned response of relaxation rather than anxiety, and desensitization to the feared situation takes place. Once mastered with mental images, the desensitization procedure may be continued in the actual feared situation. If the technique is successful, the feared situation no longer produces a conditioned response of fear and anxiety. In practice, systematic desensitization is often combined with other techniques, such as *observational learning* (Bandura, 2004b).

Let's consider a clinical example that combines systematic desensitization and observational learning. The client is Michael, a 60-year-old man afraid of flying on airplanes. To overcome this phobia, he's seeing a behavior therapist. The therapist first teaches Michael progressive relaxation so he can induce relaxation in himself. Then, she and Michael move through the anxiety hierarchy they had created. In Michael's case, the hierarchy starts with imagining airplanes flying above high in the sky, then moves on to viewing pictures of airplanes at a distance, then viewing the interior of airplanes, and ultimately actually boarding an airplane and taking a flight. There were other, smaller steps in the hierarchy as well, to make sure Michael could progress from step to step without too much of a "jump."

Michael is able to move through the hierarchy by experiencing relaxation in conjunction with each consecutive stimulus that might have produced anxiety. Because relaxation and anxiety are incompatible, the relaxation essentially "blocks" Michael's anxiety about flying, just as Peter's enjoyment of his milk and cookies blocked his anxiety about the rabbit. Another important aspect of the behavior therapist's treatment of Michael involves observational learning: She shows Michael videos of people calmly boarding and riding on planes. Together, systematic desensitization and observational learning help Michael overcome his phobia, and he is ultimately able to fly with minimal discomfort.

The In Focus box, "Using Virtual Reality to Conquer Phobias," describes the use of computer technology to treat phobias and other anxiety disorders.

Aversive Conditioning

The psychologist John Garcia first demonstrated how taste aversions could be classically conditioned (see Chapter 5). After rats drank a sweet-flavored water, Garcia injected them with a drug that made them ill. The rats developed a strong taste aversion for the sweet-flavored water, avoiding it altogether (Garcia & others, 1966). In much the same way, **aversive conditioning** attempts to create an unpleasant conditioned response to a harmful stimulus, such as cigarette smoking or alcohol consumption. For substance abuse and addiction, taste aversions are commonly induced with the use of nausea-inducing drugs. For example, a medication called *Antabuse* is used in aversion therapy for alcoholism. If a person taking Antabuse consumes any amount of alcohol, he or she will experience extreme nausea (Owen-Howard, 2001). Although aversive conditioning techniques have been applied to a wide variety of problem behaviors (Cain & LeDoux, 2008), mental health professionals are typically very cautious about the use of such techniques, partly because of their potential to harm or produce discomfort for clients (Fisher, 2009; Francis, 2009). In addition, aversive techniques are generally not very effective (Emmelkamp, 2004).

aversive conditioning
A relatively ineffective type of behavior therapy that involves repeatedly pairing an aversive stimulus with the occurrence of undesirable behaviors or thoughts.

IN FOCUS

Using Virtual Reality to Conquer Phobias

Virtual reality (VR) therapy consists of computer-generated scenes that you view wearing goggles and a special motion-sensitive headset. Move your head in any direction and an electromagnetic sensor in the helmet detects the movement, and the computer-generated scene you see changes accordingly. Turning a handgrip lets you move forward or backward to explore your artificial world. You can also use a virtual hand to reach out and touch objects, such as an elevator button or a spider.

VR technology was first used in the treatment of specific phobias, including fear of flying, heights, spiders, and enclosed places (Garcia-Palacios & others, 2002; Rothbaum & others, 2002). In the virtual reality scene, patients are progressively exposed to the feared object or situation. For example, psychologist Ralph Lamson used virtual reality as a form of computer-assisted systematic desensitization to help more than 60 patients conquer their fear of heights. Rather than mental images, the person experiences computer-generated images that seem almost real. Once the helmet is donned, patients begin a 40-minute journey that starts in a café and progresses to a narrow wooden plank that leads to a bridge.

Although computer-generated and cartoonlike, the scenes of being high above the ground on the plank or bridge are real enough to trigger the physiological indicators of anxiety. Lamson encourages the person to stay in the same spot until the anxiety diminishes. Once relaxed, the person continues the VR journey. By the time the person makes the return journey back over the plank, heart rate and blood pressure are close to normal. After virtual reality therapy, over 90 percent of Lamson's patients successfully rode a glass elevator up to the 15th floor.

Once experimental, virtual reality therapy has become an accepted treatment for specific phobias and is now being extended to other anxiety disorders, such as social phobia, panic disorder, and acrophobia (Botella & others, 2007; Parsons & Rizzo, 2008; Powers & Emmelkamp, 2008). One innovative application of VR

therapy is in the treatment of post-traumatic stress disorder (PTSD) in veterans of the wars in Vietnam, Iraq, and Afghanistan (Josman & others, 2006; Reger & Gahm, 2008). Many PTSD patients are unable or unwilling to mentally re-create the traumatic events that caused their disorder, but the vivid sensory details of the "virtual world" encourage the patient to relive the experience in a controlled fashion.

For example, a young woman who suffered from severe PTSD after witnessing and barely escaping the attack on the World Trade Center was finally able to relive the events of the day through controlled, graduated exposure to a virtual reenactment of the events. Similarly, war veterans can be exposed to the sights and sounds of combat in a way that could not be accomplished in the "real world" of a therapist's office or busy downtown street.

VR therapy is easier and less expensive to administer than graduated exposure to the actual feared object or situation. Another advantage is that the availability of VR may make people who are extremely phobic more willing to seek treatment. In one survey of people who were phobic of spiders, more than 80 percent preferred virtual reality treatment over graduated exposure to real spiders (Garcia-Palacios & others, 2001).

Techniques Based on Operant Conditioning

B. F. Skinner's *operant conditioning* model of learning is based on the simple principle that behavior is shaped and maintained by its consequences (see Chapter 5). Behavior therapists have developed several treatment techniques that are derived from operant conditioning. *Shaping* involves reinforcing successive approximations of a desired behavior. Shaping is often used to teach appropriate behaviors to patients who are mentally disabled by autism, mental retardation, or severe mental illness. For example, shaping has been used to increase the attention span of hospitalized patients with severe schizophrenia (Zinbarg & Griffith 2008; Silverstein & others, 2005).

Other operant conditioning techniques involve controlling the consequences that follow behaviors. *Positive* and *negative reinforcement* are used to increase the incidence of desired behaviors. *Extinction,* or the absence of reinforcement, is used to reduce the occurrence of undesired behaviors.

Let's illustrate how operant techniques are used in therapy by describing a behavioral program to treat a 4-year-old girl's sleeping problems (Ronen, 1991). The first step in the treatment program was to identify specific problem behaviors and determine their *baseline rate,* or how often each problem occurred before treatment began (see Figure 14.2 on the next page). After measuring the baseline rate, the therapist could target each problem behavior individually and objectively measure the child's progress.

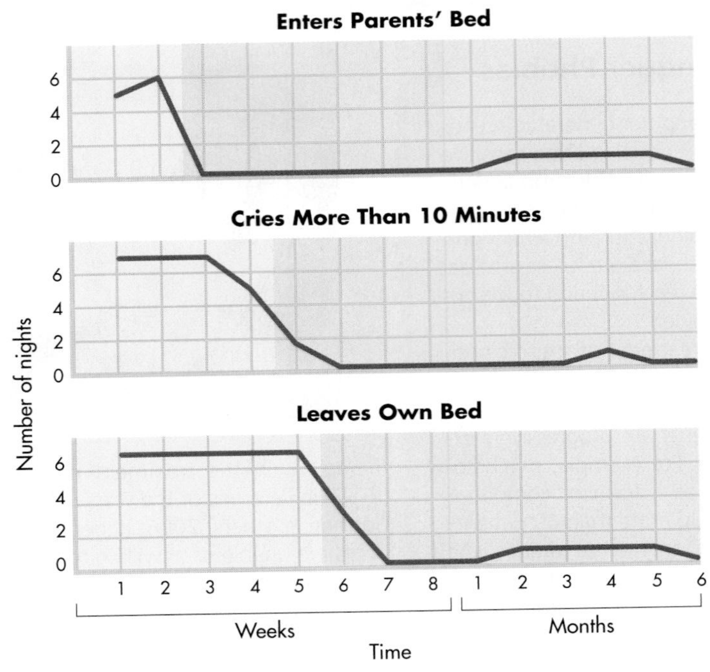

Figure 14.2 The Effect of Operant Conditioning Techniques These graphs depict the changes in three specific sleep-related problem behaviors of a 4-year-old girl over the course of behavioral therapy. The intervention for each problem behavior was introduced separately over several weeks. As you can see, behavior therapy produced a rapid reduction in the rate of each problem behavior. The green area shows the maintenance of desired behavior changes over a six-month follow-up.

Source: Adapted from Ronen (1991).

The parents next identified several very specific behavioral goals for their daughter. These goals included not crying when she was put to bed, not crying if she woke up in the night, not getting into her parents' bed, and staying in her own bed throughout the night.

The parents were taught operant techniques to decrease the undesirable behaviors and increase desirable ones. For example, to *extinguish* the girl's screaming and crying, the parents were taught to ignore the behavior rather than continue to reinforce it with parental attention. In contrast, desirable behaviors were to be *positively reinforced* with abundant praise, encouragement, social attention, and other rewards. Figure 14.2 shows the little girl's progress for three specific problem behaviors.

Operant conditioning techniques have been applied to many different kinds of psychological problems, from habit and weight control to helping autistic children learn to speak and behave more adaptively. Techniques based on operant conditioning have also been successfully used to modify the behavior of people who are severely disabled by retardation or mental disorders (see Zinbarg & Griffith, 2008).

The **token economy** is another example of the use of operant conditioning techniques to modify behavior. A token economy is a system for strengthening desired behaviors through positive reinforcement in a very structured environment. Basically, tokens or points are awarded as positive reinforcers for desirable behaviors and withheld or taken away for undesirable behaviors. The tokens can be exchanged for other reinforcers, such as special privileges.

Token economies have been most successful in controlled environments in which the behavior of the client is under ongoing surveillance or supervision. Thus, token economies have been used in prisons, classrooms, inpatient psychiatric units, and juvenile correction institutions (Ringdahl & Falcomata, 2009; Field & others, 2004). They have been shown to be effective even with severely disturbed patients who have been hospitalized for many years (Paul & Menditto, 1992). Although effective, token economies are difficult to implement, especially in community-based outpatient clinics, so they are not in wide use today (Lieberman, 2000).

A modified version of the token economy has been used with outpatients in treatment programs called *contingency management*. Like the token economy, a contingency management intervention involves carefully specified behaviors that "earn" the individual concrete rewards. Unlike token economies, which cover many behaviors, contingency management strategies are typically more narrowly focused on one or a small number of specific behaviors (Prochaska & Norcross, 2010). Contingency management interventions have proved to be especially effective in the outpatient treatment of people who are dependent on heroin, cocaine, alcohol, or multiple drugs (Lamb & others, 2004; Petry & others, 2004; Stitzer & others, 2007). In some cases, the contingency management intervention significantly reduced substance abuse in patients for whom other forms of treatment had failed.

Table 14.3 summarizes key points about behavior therapy.

token economy
A form of behavior therapy in which the therapeutic environment is structured to reward desired behaviors with tokens or points that may eventually be exchanged for tangible rewards.

cognitive therapies
A group of psychotherapies based on the assumption that psychological problems are due to illogical patterns of thinking; treatment techniques focus on recognizing and altering these unhealthy thinking patterns.

rational-emotive therapy (RET)
A type of cognitive therapy, developed by psychologist Albert Ellis, that focuses on changing the client's irrational beliefs.

Table 14.3

Behavior Therapy

Type of Therapy	Foundation	Source of Problems	Treatment Techniques	Goals of Therapy
Behavior therapy	Based on classical conditioning, operant conditioning, and observational learning	Learned maladaptive behavior patterns	Systematic desensitization, virtual reality, aversive conditioning, reinforcement and extinction, token economy, contingency management interventions, observational learning	To unlearn maladaptive behaviors and replace them with adaptive, appropriate behaviors

Cognitive Therapies

Key Theme

- **Cognitive therapies are based on the assumption that psychological problems are due to maladaptive thinking.**

Key Questions

- **What are rational-emotive therapy and cognitive therapy, and how do they differ?**
- **What is cognitive-behavioral therapy?**

While behavior therapy assumes that faulty learning is at the core of problem behaviors and emotions, the **cognitive therapies** assume that the culprit is *faulty thinking*. The key assumption of the cognitive therapies could be put like this: Most people blame their unhappiness and problems on external events and situations, but the real cause of unhappiness is the way the person *thinks* about the events, not the events themselves. Thus, cognitive therapists zero in on the faulty, irrational patterns of thinking that they believe are causing the psychological problems. Once faulty, irrational patterns of thinking have been identified, the next step is to *change* them to more adaptive, healthy patterns of thinking. In this section, we'll look at how this change is accomplished in two influential forms of cognitive therapy: Ellis's *rational-emotive therapy* (RET) and Beck's *cognitive therapy* (CT).

Albert Ellis and Rational-Emotive Therapy

Shakespeare said it more eloquently, but psychologist **Albert Ellis** has expressed the same sentiment: "You largely feel the way you think." Ellis was trained as both a clinical psychologist and a psychoanalyst. As a practicing psychoanalyst, Ellis became increasingly disappointed with the psychoanalytic approach to solving human problems. Psychoanalysis simply didn't seem to work: His patients would have insight after insight, yet never get any better.

There is nothing either good or bad, but thinking makes it so.

—WILLIAM SHAKESPEARE, *HAMLET*

In the 1950s, Ellis began to take a more active, directive role in his therapy sessions. He developed **rational-emotive therapy,** abbreviated **RET** in the 1950s. RET is based on the assumption that "people are not disturbed by things but rather by their view of things" (Ellis, 1991). The key premise of RET is that people's

Albert Ellis (1913–2007) A colorful and sometimes controversial figure, Albert Ellis developed rational-emotive therapy (RET). Rational-emotive therapy promotes psychologically healthier thought processes by disputing irrational beliefs and replacing them with more rational interpretations of events.

cognitive therapy (CT)
Therapy developed by Aaron T. Beck that focuses on changing the client's unrealistic and maladaptive beliefs.

difficulties are caused by their faulty expectations and irrational beliefs. Rational-emotive therapy focuses on changing the patterns of irrational thinking that are believed to be the primary cause of the client's emotional distress and psychological problems.

Ellis points out that most people mistakenly believe that they become upset and unhappy because of external events. But Ellis (1993) would argue that it's not external events that make people miserable—it's their *interpretation* of those events. It's not David's behavior that's really making Carrie miserable—it's Carrie's *interpretation* of the meaning of David's behavior. In rational-emotive therapy, psychological problems are explained by the "ABC" model, as shown in Figure 14.3. According to this model, when an *Activating event* (**A**) occurs, it is the person's *Beliefs* (**B**) about the event that cause emotional *Consequences* (**C**).

Identifying the core irrational beliefs that underlie personal distress is the first step in rational-emotive therapy. Often, irrational beliefs reflect "musts" and "shoulds" that are absolutes, such as the notion that "I should be competent at everything I do." Other common irrational beliefs are listed in Table 14.4.

The consequences of such thinking are unhealthy negative emotions, like extreme anger, despair, resentment, and feelings of worthlessness. Not only does the person feel miserable, but she also feels that she is unable to control or cope with an upsetting situation. These kinds of irrational cognitive and emotional responses interfere with constructive attempts to change disturbing situations (Ellis & Harper, 1975; O'Donohue & Fisher, 2009). According to RET, the result is self-defeating behaviors, anxiety disorders, depression, and other psychological problems.

The next step in rational-emotive therapy is for the therapist to vigorously *dispute the irrational beliefs*. In doing so, rational-emotive therapists tend to be very direct and even confrontational (Ellis & others, 2009; Haaga & Davison, 1991). Rather than trying to establish a warm, supportive atmosphere, rational-emotive therapists rely on logical persuasion and reason to push the client toward recognizing and surrendering his irrational beliefs (Dryden, 2008). According to Ellis (1991), blunt, harsh language is sometimes needed to push people into helping themselves.

From the client's perspective, rational-emotive therapy requires considerable effort. First, the person must admit her irrational beliefs and accept the fact that those beliefs are irrational and unhealthy, which is not as easy as it sounds. Old mental habits don't always yield easily. Equally challenging, the client must radically change her way of interpreting and responding to stressful events (Dobson & Dobson, 2009; Haaga & Davison, 1991).

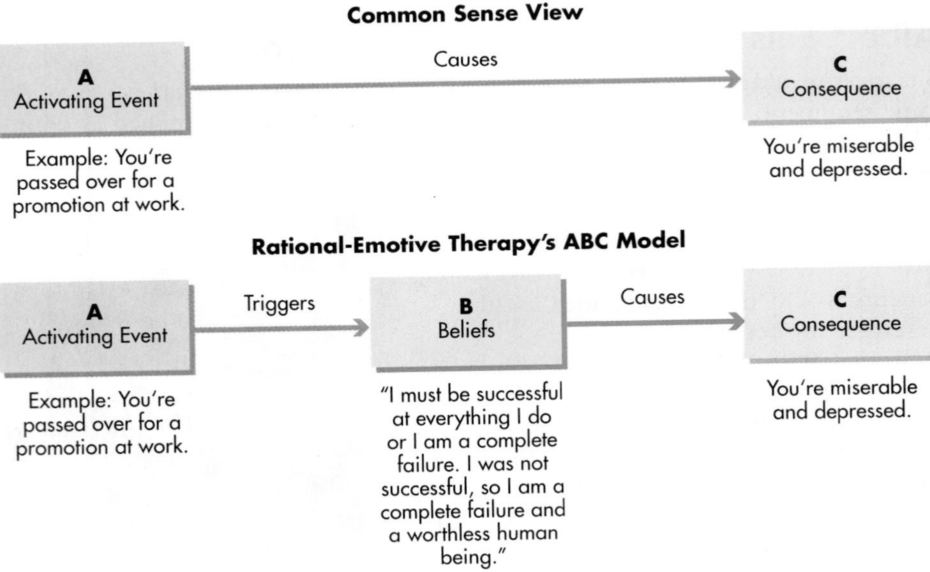

Figure 14.3 The "ABC" Model in Rational-Emotive Therapy Common sense tells us that unhappiness and other unpleasant emotions are caused by unpleasant or disturbing events. This view is shown in the top part of the figure. But Albert Ellis (1993) points out that it is really our *beliefs* about the events, not the events themselves, that make us miserable, as diagrammed in the bottom part of the figure.

Table 14.4

Irrational Beliefs

1.	It is a dire necessity for you to be loved or approved by virtually everyone in your community.
2.	You must be thoroughly competent, adequate, and achieving in all possible respects if you are to consider yourself worthwhile.
3.	Certain people are bad, wicked, or villainous, and they should be severely blamed and punished for their villainy. You should become extremely upset over other people's wrongdoings.
4.	It is awful and catastrophic when things are not the way you would very much like them to be.
5.	Human unhappiness is externally caused, and you have little or no ability to control your bad feelings and emotions.
6.	It is easier to avoid than to face difficulties and responsibilities. Avoiding difficulties whenever possible is more likely to lead to happiness than facing difficulties.
7.	You need to rely on someone stronger than yourself.
8.	Your past history is an all-important determinant of your present behavior. Because something once strongly affected your life, it should indefinitely have a similar effect.
9.	You should become extremely upset over other people's problems.
10.	There is a single perfect solution to all human problems, and it is catastrophic if this perfect solution is not found.

Source: Based on Ellis (1991).

According to rational-emotive therapy, unhappiness and psychological problems can often be traced to people's irrational beliefs. Becoming aware of these irrational beliefs is the first step toward replacing them with more rational alternatives. Some of the most common irrational beliefs are listed here.

The long-term therapeutic goal of RET is to teach clients to recognize and dispute their own irrational beliefs in a wide range of situations. However, responding "rationally" to unpleasant situations does not mean denying your feelings (Dryden 2009, Ellis & Bernard, 1985). Ellis believes that it is perfectly appropriate and rational to feel sad when you are rejected, or regretful when you make a mistake. Appropriate emotions are the consequences of rational beliefs, such as "I would prefer that everyone like me, but that's not likely to happen" or "It would be nice if I never failed at anything, but it's unlikely that I will always succeed in everything I do." Such healthy mental and emotional responses encourage people to work toward constructively changing or coping with difficult situations (Dryden & Branch, 2008; Ellis & Harper, 1975).

Albert Ellis was a colorful figure whose ideas have been extremely influential in psychotherapy (DeAngelis, 2007). Rational-emotive therapy is a popular approach in clinical practice, partly because it is straightforward and simple. It has been shown to be generally effective in the treatment of depression, social phobia, and certain anxiety disorders. Rational-emotive therapy is also useful in helping people overcome self-defeating behaviors, such as an excessive need for approval, extreme shyness, and chronic procrastination (Butler & others, 2006; David & others, 2009).

Aaron Beck and Cognitive Therapy

Like Albert Ellis, psychiatrist **Aaron T. Beck** was initially trained as a psychoanalyst. Beck's development of **cognitive therapy,** abbreviated **CT,** grew out of his research on depression (Beck, 2004; Beck & others, 1979). Seeking to scientifically validate the psychoanalytic assumption that depressed patients "have a need to suffer," Beck began collecting data on the free associations and dreams of his depressed patients. What he found, however, was that his depressed patients did *not* have a need to suffer. In fact, his depressed patients often went to great lengths to avoid being hurt or rejected by others.

Aaron T. Beck (b. 1921) In Aaron Beck's cognitive therapy, clients learn to identify and change their automatic negative thoughts. Originally developed to treat depression, cognitive therapy has also been applied to other psychological problems, such as anxiety disorders, phobias, and eating disorders.

"You only think you're barking at nothing. We're all barking at something."

Instead, Beck discovered that depressed people have an extremely negative view of the past, present, and future (Beck & others, 1979). Rather than realistically evaluating their situation, depressed patients have developed a *negative cognitive bias,* consistently distorting their experiences in a negative way. Their negative perceptions of events and situations are shaped by deep-seated, self-deprecating beliefs, such as "I can't do anything right," "I'm worthless," or "I'm unlovable" (Beck, 1991). Beck's cognitive therapy essentially focuses on correcting the cognitive biases that underlie depression and other psychological disorders (see Table 14.5).

Beck's CT has much in common with Ellis's rational-emotive therapy. Like Ellis, Beck believes that what people think creates their moods and emotions. And like RET, CT involves helping clients identify faulty thinking and replace unhealthy patterns of thinking with healthier ones.

But in contrast with Ellis's emphasis on "irrational" thinking, Beck believes that depression and other psychological problems are caused by *distorted thinking* and *unrealistic beliefs* (Arnkoff & Glass, 1992; Hollon & Beck, 2004). Rather than logically debating the "irrationality" of a client's beliefs, the CT therapist encourages the client to *empirically test the accuracy of his or her assumptions and beliefs* (Hollon & Beck, 2004; Wills, 2009). Let's look at how this occurs in Beck's CT.

The first step in CT is to help the client learn to recognize and monitor the automatic thoughts that occur without conscious effort or control. Whether negative or positive, automatic thoughts can control your mood and shape your emotional and behavioral reactions to events (Ingram & others, 2007). Because their perceptions are shaped by their negative cognitive biases, depressed people usually have automatic thoughts that reflect very negative interpretations of experience. Not surprisingly, the result of such negative automatic thoughts is a deepened sense of depression, hopelessness, and helplessness.

In the second step of CT, the therapist helps the client learn how to *empirically test* the reality of the automatic thoughts that are so upsetting. For example, to test the belief that "I always say the wrong thing," the therapist might assign the person the task of initiating a conversation with three acquaintances and noting how often he actually said the wrong thing.

According to Aaron Beck, depressed people perceive and interpret experience in very negative terms. They are prone to systematic errors in logic, or cognitive biases, which shape their negative interpretation of events. The table shows the most common cognitive biases in depression.

Table 14.5

Cognitive Biases in Depression

Cognitive Bias (Error)	Description	Example
Arbitrary inference	Drawing a negative conclusion when there is little or no evidence to support it.	When Joan calls Jim to cancel their lunch date because she has an important meeting at work, Jim concludes that she is probably going out to lunch with another man.
Selective abstraction	Focusing on a single negative detail taken out of context, ignoring the more important aspects of the situation.	During Jacqueline's annual review, her manager praises her job performance but notes that she could be a little more confident when she deals with customers over the phone. Jacqueline leaves her manager's office thinking that he is on the verge of firing her because of her poor telephone skills.
Overgeneralization	Drawing a sweeping, global conclusion based on an isolated incident and applying that conclusion to other unrelated areas of life.	Tony spills coffee on his final exam. He apologizes to his instructor but can't stop thinking about the incident. He concludes that he is a klutz who will never be able to succeed in a professional career.
Magnification and minimization	Grossly overestimating the impact of negative events and grossly underestimating the impact of positive events so that small, bad events are magnified, but good, large events are minimized.	One week after Emily aces all her midterms, she worries about flunking out of college when she gets a B on an in-class quiz.
Personalization	Taking responsibility, blaming oneself, or applying external events to oneself when there is no basis or evidence for making the connection.	Richard becomes extremely upset when his instructor warns the class about plagiarism. He thinks the instructor's warning was aimed at him, and he concludes that the instructor suspects him of plagiarizing parts of his term paper.

Source: Based on Beck & others (1979), p. 14.

Table 14.6

Comparing Cognitive Therapies

Type of Therapy	Founder	Source of Problems	Treatment Techniques	Goals of Therapy
Rational-emotive therapy (RET)	Albert Ellis	Irrational beliefs	Very directive: Identify, logically dispute, and challenge irrational beliefs	Surrender of irrational beliefs and absolutist demands
Cognitive therapy (CT)	Aaron T. Beck	Unrealistic, distorted perceptions and interpretations of events due to cognitive biases	Directive collaboration: Teach client to monitor automatic thoughts; test accuracy of conclusions; correct distorted thinking and perception	Accurate and realistic perception of self, others, and external events

Initially, the CT therapist acts as a model, showing the client how to evaluate the accuracy of automatic thoughts. By modeling techniques for evaluating the accuracy of automatic thoughts, the therapist hopes to eventually teach the client to do the same on her own. The CT therapist also strives to create a therapeutic climate of *collaboration* that encourages the client to contribute to the evaluation of the logic and accuracy of automatic thoughts (Beck & others, 1979). This approach contrasts with the confrontational approach used by the RET therapist, who directly challenges the client's thoughts and beliefs.

Beck's cognitive therapy has been shown to be effective in treating depression and other psychological disorders, including anxiety disorders, borderline personality disorders, eating disorders, post-traumatic stress disorder, and relationship problems (Dobson & Dobson, 2009; Gaudiano, 2008; G. K. Brown & others, 2004; Hollon & Beck, 2004). Along with effectively treating depression, cognitive therapy may also help *prevent* depression from recurring, especially if clients learn and then use the skills they have learned in therapy. In one recent study, high-risk patients who had experienced several episodes of depression in the past were much less likely to relapse when they continued cognitive therapy after their depression had lifted (Beck & Alford, 2009). Beck's cognitive therapy techniques have even been adapted to help treat psychotic symptoms, such as the delusions and disorganized thought processes that often characterize schizophrenia (Beck & others, 2008; Miles & others, 2007).

Table 14.6 summarizes the key characteristics of Ellis's rational-emotive therapy and Beck's cognitive therapy.

cognitive-behavioral therapy (CBT) Therapy that integrates cognitive and behavioral techniques and that is based on the assumption that thoughts, moods, and behaviors are interrelated.

Cognitive-Behavioral Therapy

Although we've presented cognitive and behavioral therapies in separate sections, it's important to note that cognitive and behavioral techniques are often combined in therapy. **Cognitive-behavioral therapy** (abbreviated **CBT**) refers to a group of psychotherapies that incorporate techniques from *both* approaches. CBT is based on the assumption that cognitions, behaviors, and emotional responses are interrelated (Hollon & Beck, 2004). Thus, changes in thought patterns will affect moods and behaviors, and changes in behaviors will affect thoughts and moods. Along with challenging maladaptive beliefs and substituting more adaptive cognitions, the therapist uses behavior modification, shaping, reinforcement, and modeling to teach problem solving and to change unhealthy behavior patterns.

The hallmark of cognitive-behavioral therapy is its pragmatic approach. Therapists design an integrated treatment plan, utilizing the techniques that are most appropriate for specific problems.

Cognitive-behavioral therapy has been used in the treatment of children, adolescents, and the elderly (Kazdin, 2003; Steele & others, 2008). Studies have shown that cognitive-behavioral therapy is a very effective treatment for many disorders, including depression, eating disorders, substance abuse, and anxiety disorders

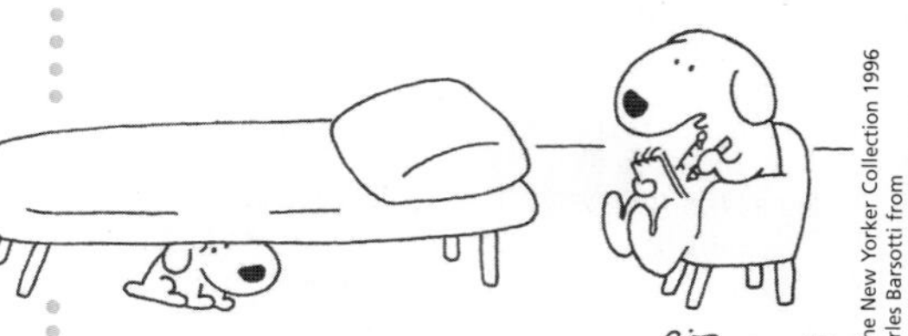

"And what do you think will happen if you do get on the couch?"

group therapy
A form of psychotherapy that involves one or more therapists working simultaneously with a small group of clients.

(Barlow & others, 2007; Craighead & others, 2007; Finney & others, 2007; Wilson & Fairburn, 2007). Cognitive-behavioral therapy can also help decrease the incidence of delusions and hallucinations in patients with schizophrenia and psychotic symptoms (Kopelowicz & others, 2007; Wright & others, 2009). In part, the treatment involves offering patients alternative explanations for their delusions and hallucinations, and teaching them how to test the reality of their mistaken beliefs and perceptions.

Group and Family Therapy

Key Theme

- **Group therapy involves one or more therapists working with several clients simultaneously.**

Key Questions

- **What are some key advantages of group therapy?**
- **What is family therapy, and how do its assumptions and techniques differ from those of individual therapy?**

Individual psychotherapy offers a personal relationship between a client and a therapist, one that is focused on a single client's problems, thoughts, and emotions. But individual psychotherapy has certain limitations. The therapist sees the client in isolation, rather than within the context of the client's interactions with others. Hence, the therapist must rely on the client's interpretation of reality and the client's description of relationships with others. Group and family therapy provides the opportunity to overcome these limitations (Norcross & others, 2005).

Group Therapy

Group therapy involves one or more therapists working with several people simultaneously. Group therapy may be provided by a therapist in private practice or at a community mental health clinic. Often, group therapy is an important part of the treatment program for hospital inpatients. Groups may be as small as 3 or 4 people or as large as 10 or more people (Burlingame & McClendon, 2008).

Virtually any approach—psychodynamic, client-centered, behavioral, or cognitive—can be used in group therapy (Free, 2008; Burlingame & others, 2004). And just about any problem that can be handled individually can be dealt with in group therapy.

Group therapy has a number of advantages over individual psychotherapy. First, group therapy is very cost-effective: A single therapist can work simultaneously with several people. Thus, it is less expensive for the client and less time-consuming for the therapist. Second, rather than relying on a client's self-perceptions about how she relates to other people, the therapist can observe her actual interactions with others. Observing the way clients interact with others in a group may provide unique insights into their personalities and behavior patterns. Sometimes, the group can serve as a microcosm of the client's actual social life (Yalom, 2005; Burlingame & others, 2004).

Third, the support and encouragement provided by the other group members may help a person feel less alone and understand that his or her problems are not unique. For example, a team of family therapists set up group meetings with family members and co-workers of people who had died in the attacks on the World Trade Center (Boss & others, 2003). The therapists' goals included helping the families come to terms with their loss, especially in cases where the bodies of their loved ones had not been recovered. One woman, who had lost dozens of co-workers, some of them close friends, explained the impact of the group sessions in this way:

"So, would anyone in the group care to respond to what Clifford has just shared with us?"

> As I saw the widows dealing with their loss, and believing it a bit more, it helped me to accept it even more. It was easier with sharing together. Strength in numbers. It makes you feel less alone. Out of the thousands of people you bump into, not everyone can understand what you've been through. If I am with any one of the families, I know they will understand what I am going through. We comfort each other. Even a blood sister might not understand as well.

Group therapies in the aftermath of other disasters, including Hurricane Katrina, have provided similar support (Salloum & others, 2009).

Fourth, group members may provide each other with helpful, practical advice for solving common problems and can act as models for successfully overcoming difficulties. Finally, working within a group gives people an opportunity to try out new behaviors in a safe, supportive environment (Yalom, 2005). For instance, someone who is very shy and submissive can practice more assertive behaviors and receive honest feedback from other group members.

Group therapy is typically conducted by a mental health professional. In contrast, *self-help groups* and *support groups* are typically conducted by nonprofessionals. Self-help groups and support groups have become increasingly popular in the United States and can be very helpful. As discussed in the In Focus box, the potential of these groups to promote mental health should not be underestimated.

IN FOCUS

Self-Help Groups: Helping Yourself by Helping Others

Every month our local newspaper publishes a list of more than 300 self-help and support groups that meet in our area. These groups range from the familiar (Alcoholics Anonymous, Tough-Love) to the obscure (Abused by Religion, Cult Awareness Group, Cross-Dressers of Green County), and from the general (Parents of Adolescents, Effective Black Parenting) to the specific (Multiple Sclerosis—Newly Diagnosed). There are also groups for people dealing with life's transitions and crises, such as divorce, retirement, or bereavement.

What this bewildering array of groups have in common is that all of them are organized and led by nonprofessionals. Typically, such groups are made up of members who have a common problem and meet for the purpose of exchanging psychological support. Some groups are focused on psychological growth and change. Other groups have a more practical emphasis, providing information and advice. The groups either are free or charge nominal fees to cover the cost of materials.

Alcoholics Anonymous Many twelve-step self-help groups are modeled after Alcoholics Anonymous. Founded in 1935, today AA has more than 2 million members worldwide. People from all walks of life attend AA meetings, and many credit AA for turning their lives around.

The format of self-help groups varies enormously. Some groups are quite freewheeling, but others are highly structured (McFadden & others, 1992). Meetings may follow a prescribed format, and there may be rules regulating contacts among group members outside the meetings. For example, our friend Marcia attends weekly meetings of a self-help group called Emotions Anonymous. In Marcia's group, each person takes a turn speaking for five minutes. Interruptions are not allowed, and other members simply listen without responding to the speaker's comments.

Many self-help groups follow a 12-step approach, patterned after the famous 12-step program of Alcoholics Anonymous (AA). The 12 steps of AA include themes of admitting that you have a problem, seeking help from a "higher power," confessing your shortcomings, repairing your relationships with others, and helping other people who have the same problem. These 12 steps have been adapted by many different groups to fit their particular problem. Some psychologists criticize the 12-step approach for its emphasis on the idea that people are "powerless" to cope with their problems on their own and must depend on a higher power and on other group members (Kasl, 1992).

Just how helpful are self-help groups? Research has shown that self-help groups can be as effective as therapy provided by a mental health professional, at least for some psychological problems (Christensen & Jacobson, 1994). Given that many people cannot afford professional counseling, self-help groups may be a cost-effective alternative to psychotherapy for some people.

What is not known is *why* self-help groups are effective. Support and encouragement from others are undoubtedly important. So may be the "helper therapy" principle on which all self-help groups are based: People who help other people are themselves helped. But more research is needed to clarify the elements that contribute most to a successful outcome.

Research is also needed to identify the kinds of people and problems that are most likely to benefit from a self-help approach (Christensen & Jacobson, 1994). One study suggests that 12-step attendees who find sponsors and who have a high motivation to change are more likely to stay involved in a program (Kelly & Moos, 2003).

family therapy
A form of psychotherapy that is based on the assumption that the family is a system and that treats the family as a unit.

Family and Couple Therapy

Most forms of psychotherapy tend to see a person's problems—and the solutions to those problems—as primarily originating within the individual himself. **Family therapy** operates on a different premise, focusing on the whole family rather than on an individual. The major goal of family therapy is to alter and improve the ongoing interactions among family members. Typically, family therapy involves many members of the immediate family, including children and adults, and may also include important members of the extended family, such as grandparents or in-laws (Nichols, 2008; Sexton & others, 2004).

A Family Therapy Session Family therapists typically work with all the members of a family at the same time, including young children. The family therapist can then directly observe how family members interact, resolve differences, and exert control over one another. As unhealthy patterns of family interactions are identified, they can often be replaced with new patterns that promote the psychological well-being of the family as a whole.

Family therapy is based on the assumption that the family is a *system*, an interdependent unit, not just a collection of separate individuals. The family is seen as a dynamic structure in which each member plays a unique role. According to this view, every family has certain unspoken "rules" of interaction and communication. Some of these tacit rules revolve around issues such as which family members exercise power and how, who makes decisions, who keeps the peace, and what kinds of alliances members have formed among themselves. As such issues are explored, unhealthy patterns of family interaction can be identified and replaced with new "rules" that promote the psychological health of the family as a unit.

Family therapy is often used to enhance the effectiveness of individual psychotherapy. For example, patients with schizophrenia are less likely to experience relapses when family members are involved in therapy (Prochaska & Norcross, 2010; Kopelowicz & others, 2007; Pitschel-Walz & others, 2001). In many cases, the therapist realizes that the individual client's problems reflect conflict and disturbance in the entire family system (Goldenberg & Goldenberg, 2005; Lebow & Gurman, 1995). For the client to make significant improvements, the family as a whole must become psychologically healthier. Family therapy is also indicated when there is conflict among family members or when younger children are being treated for behavior problems, such as truancy or aggressive behavior (Connell & others, 2007; Kazdin, 1994b).

Many family therapists also provide *marital* or *couple therapy.* The term *couple therapy* is preferred today because such therapy is conducted with any couple in a committed relationship, whether they are married or unmarried, heterosexual or homosexual (Lebow & Gurman, 1995; Sheras & Koch-Sheras, 2006). As is the case with family therapy, there are many different approaches to couple therapy (Lebow, 2008; Sexton & others, 2004). For example, *behavioral couple therapy* is based on the assumption that couples are satisfied when they experience more reinforcement than punishment in their relationship. Thus, it focuses on increasing caring behaviors and teaching couples how to constructively resolve conflicts and problems. In general, most couple therapies have the goal of improving communication, reducing negative communication, and increasing intimacy between the pair.

BIZARRO

Evaluating the Effectiveness of Psychotherapy

Key Themes

- **Decades of research demonstrate that psychotherapy is effective in helping people with psychological disorders.**

Key Questions

- **What are the common factors that contribute to successful outcomes in psychotherapy?**
- **What is eclecticism?**

Let's start with a simple fact: Most people with psychological symptoms do *not* seek help from mental health professionals (Kessler & others, 1994, 2004). This suggests that most people eventually weather their psychological problems without professional intervention. Some people cope with psychological difficulties with the help and support of friends and family. And some people eventually improve simply with the passage of time, a phenomenon called *spontaneous remission* (see Eysenck, 1952, 1994). Does psychotherapy offer significant benefits over just waiting for the possible "spontaneous remission" of symptoms?

The basic strategy for investigating this issue is to compare people who enter psychotherapy with a carefully selected, matched control group of people who do not receive psychotherapy (Freeman & Power, 2007; Nezu & Nezu, 2008). During the past half-century, hundreds of such studies have investigated the effectiveness of the major forms of psychotherapy (Chambless & Ollendick, 2001; Cooper, 2008; Nathan & Gorman, 2007; Orlinsky & others, 2004). To combine and interpret the results of such large numbers of studies, researchers have used a statistical technique called *meta-analysis*. Meta-analysis involves pooling the results of several studies into a single analysis, essentially creating one large study that can reveal overall trends in the data.

"The drug has, however, proved more effective than traditional psychoanalysis."

When meta-analysis is used to summarize studies that compare people who receive psychotherapy treatment to no-treatment controls, researchers consistently arrive at the same conclusion: *Psychotherapy is significantly more effective than no treatment.* On the average, the person who completes psychotherapy treatment is better off than about 80 percent of those in the untreated control group (Cooper, 2008; Lambert & Ogles, 2004).

The benefits of psychotherapy usually become apparent in a relatively short time. As shown in Figure 14.4, approximately 50 percent of people show significant improvement by the eighth weekly session of psychotherapy. By the end of six months of weekly psychotherapy sessions, about 75 percent are significantly improved (Baldwin & others, 2009; Lambert & others, 2001).

The gains that people make as a result of psychotherapy also tend to endure long after the therapy has ended, sometimes for years (Lambert & Ogles, 2004). Even brief forms of psychotherapy tend to produce beneficial and long-lasting changes (Power, 2005).

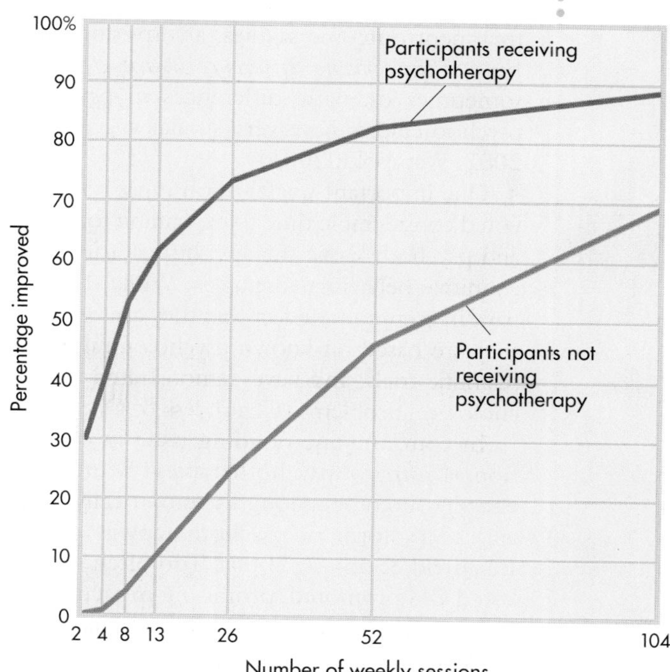

Figure 14.4 Psychotherapy Versus No Treatment This graph depicts the rates of improvement for more than 2,000 people in weekly psychotherapy and for 500 people who did not receive psychotherapy. As you can see, after only eight weekly sessions, better than 50 percent of participants receiving psychotherapy were significantly improved. After the same length of time, only 4 percent of participants not receiving psychotherapy showed "spontaneous remission" of symptoms. Clearly, psychotherapy accelerates both the rate and degree of improvement for those experiencing psychological problems.

Source: Adapted from McNeilly & Howard (1991). Reprinted by permission of Guilford Press.

And, multiple meta-analyses have found that both individual and group therapy are equally effective in producing significant gains in psychological functioning (Burlingame & others, 2004; Cuijpers & others, 2008).

Brain-imaging technologies are providing another line of evidence demonstrating the power of psychotherapy to bring about change (Farmer, 2009). In one study, PET scans were used to measure brain activity before and after 10 weeks of therapy for obsessive–compulsive disorder (Schwartz & others, 1996). The psychotherapy patients who improved showed the same changes in brain function that are associated with effective drug therapy for this disorder (see Chapter 13).

Similarly, as we'll show you later in this chapter, PET scans of patients with depression show changes in brain functioning toward more normal levels after 12 weeks of interpersonal therapy (Martin & others, 2001). In other words, psychotherapy alone produces distinct physiological changes in the brain—changes that are associated with a reduction in symptoms (Arden & Linford, 2009).

Nevertheless, it's important to note that psychotherapy is *not* a miracle cure. While most people experience significant benefits from psychotherapy, not everyone benefits to the same degree. Some people who enter psychotherapy improve only slightly or not at all. Others drop out early, presumably because therapy wasn't working as they had hoped (Barrett & others, 2008). And in some cases, people get worse despite therapeutic intervention (Boisvert & Faust, 2003).

Is One Form of Psychotherapy Superior?

Given that the major types of psychotherapy use different assumptions and techniques, does one type of psychotherapy stand out as more effective than the others? In some cases, one type of psychotherapy *is* more effective than another in treating a particular problem (Barlow, 2008; Beutler, 2002). For example, cognitive therapy and interpersonal therapy are effective in treating depression (Craighead & others, 2007). Cognitive, cognitive-behaviorial, and behavior therapies tend to be more successful than insight-oriented therapies in helping people who are experiencing panic disorder, obsessive–compulsive disorder, and phobias (Chambless & Ollendick, 2001; Craske & Barlow, 2008; Clark & others, 2003; Siev & Chambless, 2007). And, insight-oriented therapies are also less effective than other therapies in the treatment of disorders characterized by severe psychotic symptoms, such as schizophrenia (Mueser & Glynn, 1993).

However, when meta-analysis techniques are used to assess the collective results of treatment outcome studies, a surprising but consistent finding emerges: *In general, there is little or no difference in the effectiveness of different psychotherapies.* Despite sometimes dramatic differences in psychotherapy techniques, all of the standard psychotherapies have very similar success rates (Cooper, 2008; Luborsky & others, 2002; Wampold, 2001).

One important qualification must be made at this point. In this chapter, we've devoted considerable time to explaining four major approaches to therapy: psychoanalytic and psychodynamic therapy; humanistic therapy; behavior therapy; and cognitive and cognitive-behavioral therapies. While distinct, all of these psychotherapy approaches have in common the fact that they are *empirically supported treatments.* In other words, they are based on known psychological principles, have been subjected to controlled scientific trials, and have demonstrated their effectiveness in helping people with psychological problems (Chambless & Ollendick, 2001).

In contrast, one ongoing issue in contemporary psychotherapy is the proliferation of *untested* psychotherapies (Beutler, 2000). The fact that there is little difference in outcome among the empirically supported therapies does *not* mean that any and every form of psychotherapy is equally effective (Herbert & others, 2000; Lilienfeld & others, 2005). Too often, untested therapy techniques are heavily marketed and promoted, promising miraculous cures with little or no empirical research to back up their claims (A. A. Lazarus, 2000; Lilienfeld, 2007).

We examine the empirical evidence for one heavily promoted therapy in the Science Versus Pseudoscience box, "EMDR: Can You Wave Your Fears Away?" on page 604.

What Factors Contribute to Effective Psychotherapy?

How can we explain the fact that different forms of psychotherapy are basically equivalent in producing positive results? One possible explanation is that the factors that are crucial to producing improvement are present in *all* effective therapies. Researchers have identified a number of common factors that are related to a positive therapy outcome (Sparks & others, 2008; Sprenkle & others, 2009).

First and most important is the quality of the *therapeutic relationship* (Cooper, 2008; Safran & others, 2006). When psychotherapy is helpful, the therapist–client relationship is characterized by mutual respect, trust, and hope. Working in a cooperative alliance, both people are actively trying to achieve the same goals.

Second, certain *therapist characteristics* are associated with successful therapy. Helpful therapists have a caring attitude and the ability to listen empathically. They are genuinely committed to their clients' welfare (Aveline, 2005; Strupp, 1996). Regardless of orientation, they tend to be warm, sensitive, and responsive people, and they are perceived as sincere and genuine (Beutler & others, 2004).

Third, *client characteristics* are important (Clarkin & Levy, 2004). If the client is motivated, committed to therapy, and actively involved in the process, a successful outcome is much more likely (Tallman & Bohart, 1999). Emotional and social maturity and the ability to express thoughts and feelings are important. Clients who are optimistic, who expect psychotherapy to help them with their problems, and who don't have a previous history of psychological disorders are more likely to benefit from therapy (Leon & others, 1999). Finally, *external circumstances,* such as a stable living situation and supportive family members, can enhance the effectiveness of therapy.

Therapeutic Sensitivity to Cultural Differences A therapist's sensitivity to a client's cultural values can affect the ability to form a good working relationship and, ultimately, the success of psychotherapy (Thompson & others, 2004). Thus, some clients prefer to see therapists who are from the same ethnic or cultural background, as is the case with the African-American therapist and client shown here. In general, therapists have become more attuned to the important role played by culture in effective psychotherapy.

Effective therapists are also sensitive to the *cultural differences* that may exist between themselves and their clients (Sue & Sue, 2008b; Greene, 2007). As described in the Culture and Human Behavior box on page 606, cultural differences can be a barrier to effective psychotherapy. Increasingly, training in cultural sensitivity and multicultural issues is being incorporated into psychological training programs in the United States (Sammons & Speight, 2008; Utsey & others, 2006).

Notice that none of these factors are specific to any particular brand of psychotherapy. However, this does not mean that differences between psychotherapy techniques are completely irrelevant. Rather, it's important that there be a good

"I utilize the best from Freud, the best from Jung and the best from my Uncle Marty, a very smart fellow."

SCIENCE VERSUS PSEUDOSCIENCE

EMDR: Can You Wave Your Fears Away?

In the late 1980s, a psychology graduate student named Francine Shapiro was walking alone in a park, grappling with some troubling thoughts. According to Shapiro, "I noticed that when a disturbing thought entered my mind, my eyes spontaneously started moving back and forth. At the same time, I noticed that my disturbing thought had shifted from consciousness, and when I brought it back to mind, it no longer bothered me as much" (Shapiro & Forrest, 1997, 2004). Speculating that her back-and-forth eye movements were simulating the rapid eye movements (REM) of dreaming sleep, Shapiro developed a treatment technique in which patients suffering from traumatic memories visually followed her waving finger while simultaneously holding a mental image of disturbing memories, events, or situations.

Ultimately, Shapiro earned her doctorate in psychology by treating 22 patients with post-traumatic stress disorder (PTSD) with her new therapy, which she dubbed **eye movement desensitization reprocessing,** abbreviated **EMDR.** In two published papers, Shapiro (1989a, 1989b) reported that almost all of her patients experienced significant relief from their symptoms after just *one* EMDR therapy session (see also Shapiro, 2007).

This was the beginning of what was to become one of the fastest-growing—and most lucrative—therapeutic techniques of the last 20 years (Herbert & others, 2000). How popular is EMDR? Since Shapiro established her EMDR Institute in 1990, more than 40,000 therapists have been trained in EMDR. Close to a million patients have been treated with the new therapy (EMDR Institute, 2001).

Since its launch, the claims, techniques, and jargon of EMDR have undergone some changes. While originally touted as a one-session treatment for the distress associated with traumatic memories in PTSD (Shapiro, 1989a), EMDR therapy today frequently involves multiple sessions. According to Shapiro (1995), comprehensive EMDR treatment involves eight phases, which combine elements of psychodynamic, behavioral, and cognitive therapies. Along with the eye movements, other forms of "bilateral stimulation" may be used, such as tones in alternating ears or taps on different sides of the body.

Along with post-traumatic stress disorder, EMDR has been used to treat panic disorder and other anxiety disorders, addiction, substance abuse, and sleep disorders. Proponents claim that EMDR is also effective in overcoming depression, phobias, pathological gambling, and self-esteem problems, as well as helping athletes and workers achieve "peak performance" (see EMDR Institute, 2001; Shapiro & Forrest, 2004).

Originally, Shapiro (1989b) contended that the eye movements simulated brain processes during sleep, "releasing" and

Eye Movement Desensitization Reprocessing (EMDR) In EMDR therapy, the client visually follows the therapist's moving finger while mentally focusing on a traumatic memory or vivid mental image of a troubling situation. Supposedly, the rhythmic eye movements help the client to "release" and "integrate" the trauma.

"integrating" traumatic memories. Later, Shapiro (1995) proposed that EMDR facilitates what she calls "Accelerated Information Processing," in which "dysfunctionally stored information can be properly assimilated through a dynamically activated processing system." Supposedly, EMDR "accelerates a natural information processing" that helps heal the nervous system.

Is EMDR "the breakthrough therapy for overcoming anxiety, stress, and trauma," as is claimed on the cover of Shapiro's 1997 book? Does it represent a "paradigm shift" in psychotherapy, as its founder (Shapiro, 1995, 2007) claims? Let's consider the evidence.

Does EMDR Provide Therapeutic Benefits Compared to No Treatment?

Yes. Numerous studies have shown that patients experience relief from symptoms of anxiety after EMDR. In a meta-analysis of dozens of studies examining EMDR, Canadian psychologists Paul Davidson and Kevin Parker (2001) concluded the following: "When outcomes of EMDR treatment are compared with no treatment, and when outcomes are compared with pretreatment status, clients are better off with EMDR treatment than without." Other researchers have also found that patients benefit from EMDR and that EMDR is more effective than no treatment at all (DeBell & Jones, 1997; Goldstein & others, 2000).

Is EMDR More Effective Than Other Standard Therapies?

The alert reader will have noticed that EMDR has many elements in common with other treatment techniques, some of them well established and based on well-documented psychological principles. For example, **exposure therapy** is one technique that has long been recognized as an effective treatment for PTSD and phobias. Exposure therapy is related to systematic desensitization: The person gradually and repeatedly relives the frightening experience under controlled conditions to help him overcome his fear of the dreaded object or situation and establish more adaptive beliefs and cognitions. Using a combination of behavioral and

"match" between the person seeking help and the specific psychotherapy techniques used. One person may be very comfortable with psychodynamic techniques, such as exploring childhood memories and free association. Another person might be more open to behavioral techniques, like systematic desensitization. For therapy to be optimally effective, the individual should feel comfortable with both the therapist and the therapist's approach to therapy.

eclecticism
(eh-KLEK-tuh-*sizz*-um) The pragmatic and integrated use of techniques from different psychotherapies.

Increasingly, such a personalized approach to therapy is being facilitated by the movement of mental health professionals toward **eclecticism**—the pragmatic and integrated use of diverse psychotherapy techniques (Lambert & others, 2004). To-cognitive techniques, exposure therapy has a high rate of success in the treatment of anxiety disorders (Foa & Meadows, 1997).

Is EMDR more effective than exposure therapy or other cognitive-behavioral treatments? No. When Davidson and Parker (2001) compared the effectiveness of EMDR to other exposure treatments, no difference was found. EMDR was no more effective than standard treatments for anxiety disorders, including PTSD. Other researchers have found that EMDR is *less* effective than exposure therapy for PTSD (Taylor & others, 2003).

Are the Eye Movements Necessary?

Several research studies have compared standard EMDR with other treatments that duplicate all aspects of the treatment *except* the eye-movement component. For example, some studies have compared treatment effects between an eye-movement condition (EMDR) and "sham" EMDR, a kind of placebo condition in which the participants fixed their eyes on a bright light that did not move or engaged in finger tapping with alternate hands. All these studies found *no difference* between "real" EMDR and "sham" EMDR (DeBell & Jones, 1997; Feske & Goldstein, 1997; Goldstein & others, 2000). In their meta-analysis, Davidson and Parker (2001) agreed with other researchers: There was *no difference* in outcome between treatments that incorporated eye movements and the "sham" EMDR that did not.

So if you remove the eye movements from the EMDR treatment protocol, what is left? Harvard psychologist Richard McNally (1998), an expert in the treatment of anxiety disorders, puts it succinctly: "What is effective in EMDR is not new, and what is new is not effective." Psychologists Gerald Rosen and Jeffrey Lohr (1997) are more blunt:

> Shapiro took existing elements from cognitive-behavior therapies, added the unnecessary ingredient of finger waving, and then took the technique on the road before science could catch up.

Is EMDR a Pseudoscience?

Some psychologists argue that EMDR is just that—a pseudoscience (Devilly, 2005; Lilienfeld, 1998; Rosen & others, 1999). Psychologist James D. Herbert and his colleagues (2000) note several ways in which EMDR displays the fundamental characteristics of a pseudoscience, which were discussed in Chapter 1:

> EMDR appears to possess the outward form of science but little of its substance. The appearance of science, such as case studies reported in peer reviewed journals, selective publicity of weak tests of effectiveness, [and] scientific-sounding jargon . . . serves to obscure EMDR's lack of scientific substance and have persuaded many of its scientific legitimacy. Although there is little evidence to support the strong claims of EMDR's proponents, this treatment has resulted in a significant financial return.

The case of EMDR highlights an ongoing problem in contemporary psychotherapy. Too often, "revolutionary" new therapies are developed, advertised, and marketed directly to the public—and to therapists—*before* controlled scientific studies of their effectiveness have been conducted (Lazarus, 2000). Many of the untested therapies are ineffective or, as in the case of EMDR, no more effective than established therapies (Lilienfeld & others, 2003; Lohr & others, 2003). Others are downright dangerous, such as the "rebirthing" technique that resulted in the death of a young girl in Colorado in April 2000. Ten-year-old Candace Newmaker suffocated after being wrapped in a blanket, covered with pillows, and restrained by four adult "therapists" who taunted her when she cried, pleaded for air, and repeatedly told them she could not breathe.

Like many pseudosciences, such fringe therapies rely on anecdotes and testimonials to persuade others of their efficacy. Their proponents often resort to vague, scientific-sounding explanations of their mechanisms rather than established—and testable—scientific principles (Lilienfeld, 1998). James Herbert and his colleagues (2000) argue that new therapeutic techniques should be tested *before* they are put into widespread use, not after. The conditions that new therapies should meet are summarized in the table at left.

The Burden of Proof

Psychologist James D. Herbert and his colleagues (2000) argue that before being put into widespread use, new therapies should provide empirically based answers to the following questions:

- Does the treatment work better than no treatment?
- Does the treatment work better than a placebo?
- Does the treatment work better than standard treatments?
- Does the treatment work through the processes that its proponents claim?

Source: Herbert & others (2000).

eye movement desensitization reprocessing (EMDR)
Therapy technique in which the client holds a vivid mental image of a troubling event or situation while rapidly moving his or her eyes back and forth in response to the therapist's waving finger or while the therapist administers some other form of bilateral stimulation, such as sounding tones in alternate ears.

exposure therapy
Behavioral therapy for phobias, panic disorder, post-traumatic stress disorder, or related anxiety disorders in which the person is repeatedly exposed to the disturbing object or situation under controlled conditions.

day, therapists identify themselves as eclectic more often than any other orientation (Norcross, Lambert & Ogles, 2004; Karpiak, & others, 2005). *Eclectic psychotherapists* carefully tailor the therapy approach to the problems and characteristics of the person seeking help. For example, an eclectic therapist might integrate insight-oriented techniques with specific behavioral techniques to help someone suffering from extreme shyness. A related approach is *integrative* psychotherapy. Integrative psychotherapists also use multiple approaches to therapy, but they tend to blend them together rather than choosing different approaches for different clients (Lazarus, 2008; Stricker & Gold, 2008).

CULTURE AND HUMAN BEHAVIOR

Cultural Values and Psychotherapy

The goals and techniques of many established approaches to psychotherapy tend to reflect European and North American cultural values (McGoldrick & others, 2005). In this box, we'll look at how those cultural values can clash with the values of clients from other cultures, diminishing the effectiveness of psychotherapy.

A Focus on the Individual

In Western psychotherapy, the client is usually encouraged to become more assertive, more self-sufficient, and less dependent on others in making decisions. Problems are assumed to have an internal cause and are expected to be solved by the client alone. Therapy emphasizes meeting the client's individual needs, even if those needs conflict with the demands of significant others. In collectivistic cultures, however, the needs of the individual are much more strongly identified with the needs of the group to which he or she belongs (Brewer & Chen, 2007; Pedersen & others, 2008; Sue & Sue, 2008; Triandis, 1996).

For example, traditional Native Americans are less likely than European Americans to believe that personal problems are due to an internal cause within the individual (Garrett, 2008; Sue & others, 1994). Instead, one person's problems may be seen as a problem for the entire community to resolve.

In traditional forms of Native American healing, family members, friends, and other members of the community may be asked to participate in the treatment or healing rituals. One type of therapy, called *network therapy,* is conducted in the person's home and can involve as many as 70 members of the individual's community or tribe (LaFromboise & others, 1993b).

Latino cultures, too, emphasize interdependence over independence. In particular, they stress the value of *familismo*—the importance of the extended family network. Because the sense of family is so central to Latino culture, psychologist Lilian Comas-Diaz (1993) recommends that members of the client's extended family, such as grandparents and in-laws, be actively involved in psychological treatment.

Many collectivistic Asian cultures also emphasize a respect for the needs of others (Lee & Mock, 2005). The Japanese psychotherapy called *Naikan therapy* is a good example of how such cultural values affect the goals of psychotherapy (Reynolds, 1990). According to Naikan therapy, being self-absorbed is the surest path to psychological suffering. Thus, the goal of Naikan therapy is to replace the focus on the self with a sense of gratitude and obligation toward others. Rather than talking about how his own needs were not met by family members, the Naikan client is asked to meditate on how he has failed to meet the needs of others.

The Importance of Insight

Psychodynamic, humanistic, and cognitive therapies all stress the importance of insight or awareness of an individual's thoughts and feelings. But many cultures do *not* emphasize the importance of exploring painful thoughts and feelings in resolving psychological problems. For example, Asian cultures stress that mental health is enhanced by the avoidance of negative thinking. Hence, a depressed or anxious person in China and many other Asian countries would be encouraged to *avoid* focusing on upsetting thoughts (Kim & Park, 2008; Lee, 1997; Sue & others, 1994).

Cultural Values Even after immigrating to the United States, many people maintain strong ties with their cultural heritage. Here, Arab American children attend an Islamic school. Notice that the young female students as well as the teacher are wearing the traditional *chador,* or veil. The traditional beliefs of some cultures, such as the Islamic belief that women should be modest and obedient to their husbands, may conflict with the values inherent in Western psychotherapies.

Intimate Disclosure Between Therapist and Client

Many Western psychotherapies are based on the assumption that the clients will disclose their deepest feelings and most private thoughts to their therapists. But in some cultures, intimate details of one's personal life would never be discussed with a stranger. Asians are taught to disclose intimate details only to very close friends. For example, a young Vietnamese student of ours vowed never to return to see a psychologist she had consulted about her struggles with depression. The counselor, she complained, was too "nosy" and asked too many personal questions. In many cultures, people are far more likely to turn to family members or friends than they are to mental health professionals (Leung & Boehnlein, 2005; Nishio & Bilmes, 1993).

The demands for emotional openness may also clash with cultural values. In Asian cultures, people tend to avoid the public expression of emotions and often express thoughts and feelings nonverbally. Native American cultures tend to value the restraint of emotions rather than the open expression of emotions (Garrett, 2006; LaFromboise & others, 1993b).

Recognizing the need for psychotherapists to become more culturally sensitive, the American Psychological Association has recommended formal training in multicultural awareness for all psychologists (Edwards, 1995a; Fouad & Arredondo, 2007; Hall, 1997). The APA (2003) has also published extensive guidelines for psychologists who provide psychological help to culturally diverse populations. Interested students can download a copy of the APA guidelines at www.apa.org/pi/multiculturalguidelines.pdf

Biomedical Therapies

Key Theme

- **The biomedical therapies are medical treatments for the symptoms of psychological disorders and include medication and electroconvulsive therapy.**

Key Questions

- **What medications are used to treat the symptoms of schizophrenia, anxiety, bipolar disorder, and depression, and how do they achieve their effects?**
- **What is electroconvulsive therapy, and what are its advantages and disadvantages?**

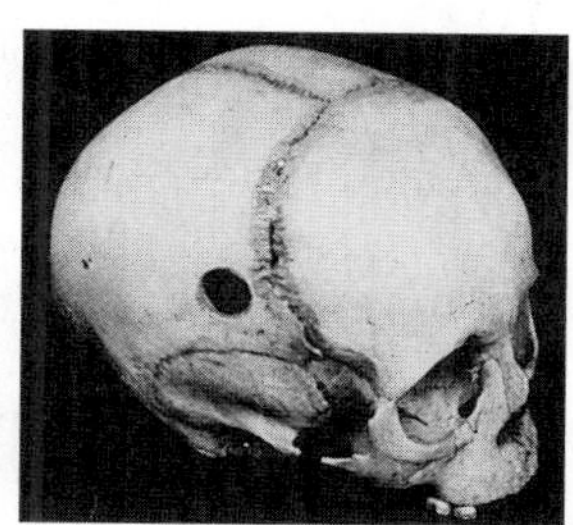

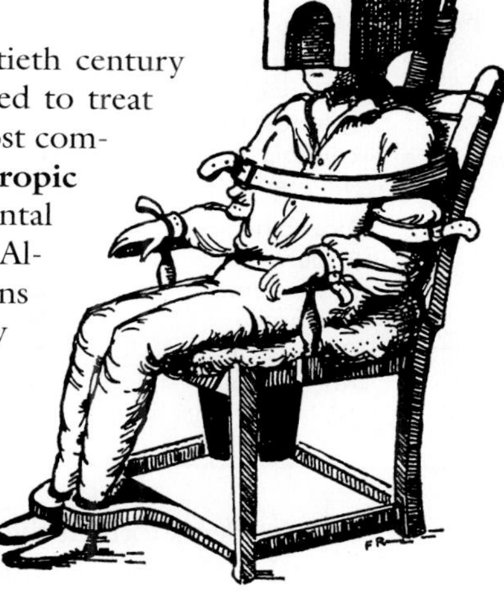

Historical Treatments for Mental Illness *Top left:* Found in Peru, this pre-Columbian skull shows the results of primitive surgery on the brain, called *trephining,* presumably as a treatment to allow evil spirits to leave the body. *Left:* A "tranquilizing chair" was developed in the early 1800s to restrain and sedate unmanageable patients. *Above:* An early treatment apparatus called the "circulating swing" involved spinning patients.

Medical treatments for psychological disorders actually predate modern psychotherapy by hundreds of years. In past centuries, patients were whirled, soothed, drenched, restrained, and isolated—all in an attempt to alleviate symptoms of psychological disorders. Today, such "treatments" seem cruel, inhumane, and useless. Keep in mind, however, that these early treatments were based on the limited medical knowledge of the time. As you'll see in this section, some of the early efforts to treat psychological disorders did eventually evolve into treatments that are widely used today.

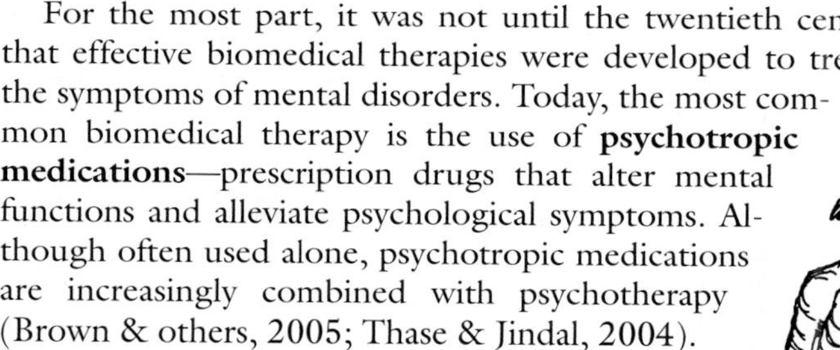

For the most part, it was not until the twentieth century that effective biomedical therapies were developed to treat the symptoms of mental disorders. Today, the most common biomedical therapy is the use of **psychotropic medications**—prescription drugs that alter mental functions and alleviate psychological symptoms. Although often used alone, psychotropic medications are increasingly combined with psychotherapy (Brown & others, 2005; Thase & Jindal, 2004).

Antipsychotic Medications

For more than 2,000 years, traditional practitioners of medicine in India used an herb derived from the snakeroot plant to diminish the psychotic symptoms commonly associated with schizophrenia: hallucinations, delusions, and disordered thought processes (Bhatara & others, 1997). The same plant was used in traditional Japanese medicine to treat anxiety and restlessness (Jilek, 1993). In the 1930s, Indian physicians discovered that the herb was also helpful in the treatment of high blood pressure. They developed a synthetic version of the herb's active ingredient, called *reserpine.*

Reserpine first came to the attention of American researchers as a potential treatment for high blood pressure. But it wasn't until the early 1950s that American researchers became aware of research in India demonstrating the effectiveness of reserpine in treating schizophrenia (Frankenburg, 1994).

It was also during the 1950s that French scientists began investigating the psychoactive properties of another drug, called *chlorpromazine.* Like reserpine, chlorpromazine diminished the psychotic symptoms commonly seen in schizophrenia. Hence, reserpine and chlorpromazine were dubbed **antipsychotic medications.** Because chlorpromazine had fewer side effects than reserpine, it nudged out reserpine as the preferred medication for treating schizophrenia-related symptoms. Since then,

In 2005, psychotropic medications outsold all other categories of medicines in the United States, accounting for $28.7 billion in sales.

—NDC HEALTH, 2005

psychotropic medications (*sy*-ko-TRO-pick) Drugs that alter mental functions, alleviate psychological symptoms, and are used to treat psychological or mental disorders.

antipsychotic medications (*an*-tee-sy-KOT-ick or antī-sī-KOT-ick) Prescription drugs that are used to reduce psychotic symptoms; frequently used in the treatment of schizophrenia; also called *neuroleptics.*

The First Antipsychotic Drug More than 2,000 years ago, ancient Hindu medical texts prescribed the use of an herb derived from *Rauwolfia serpentina,* or snakeroot plant, to treat epilepsy, insomnia, and other ailments. But its primary use was to treat *oonmaad*—a Sanskrit term for an abnormal mental condition that included disruptions in "wisdom, perception, knowledge, character, creativity, conduct, and behavior" (Bhatara & others, 1997). Today it is known that the herb has a high affinity for dopamine receptors in the brain.

chlorpromazine has been better known by its trade name, *Thorazine,* and is still used to treat psychotic symptoms. The antipsychotic drugs are also referred to as *neuroleptic medications* or simply *neuroleptics.*

How do these drugs diminish psychotic symptoms? Reserpine and chlorpromazine act differently on the brain, but both drugs reduce levels of the neurotransmitter called *dopamine.* Since the development of these early drugs, more than 30 other antipsychotic medications have been developed (see Table 14.7). These antipsychotic medications also act on dopamine receptors in the brain (Abi-Dargham, 2004; Laruelle & others, 2003; Richtand & others, 2007).

Table 14.7

Antipsychotic Medications

	Generic Name	Trade Name
Typical Antipsychotics	Chlorpromazine	Thorazine
	Fluphenazine	Prolixin
	Trifluoperazine	Stelazine
	Thioridazine	Mellaril
	Thiothixene	Navane
	Haloperidol	Haldol
Atypical Antipsychotics	Clozapine	Clozaril
	Risperidone	Risperdal
	Olanzapine	Zyprexa
	Sertindole	Serlect
	Quetiapine	Seroquel
	Aripiprazole	Abilify

Source: Adapted from Julien (2008).

The first antipsychotics effectively reduced the *positive symptoms* of schizophrenia—hallucinations, delusions, and disordered thinking (see Chapter 13). This therapeutic effect had a revolutionary impact on the number of people hospitalized for schizophrenia. Until the 1950s, patients with schizophrenia were thought to be incurable. These chronic patients formed the bulk of the population in the "back wards" of psychiatric hospitals. With the introduction of the antipsychotic medications, however, the number of patients in mental hospitals decreased dramatically (see Figure 14.5).

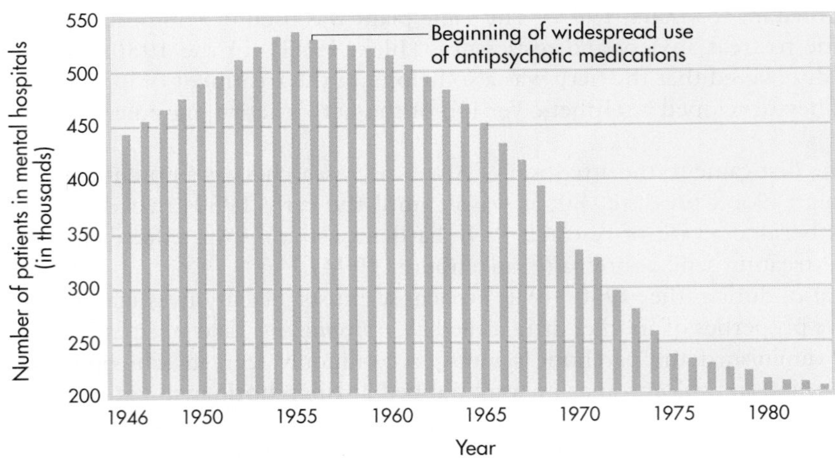

Figure 14.5 Change in the Number of Patients Hospitalized for Mental Disorders, 1946–1983 When the first antipsychotic drugs came into wide use in the late 1950s, the number of people hospitalized for mental disorders began to drop sharply.

Source: Adapted from Julien (2008).

Drawbacks of Antipsychotic Medications

Even though the early antipsychotic drugs allowed thousands of patients to be discharged from hospitals, these drugs had a number of drawbacks. First, they didn't actually *cure* schizophrenia. Psychotic symptoms often returned if a person stopped taking the medication.

Second, the early antipsychotic medications were not very effective in eliminating the *negative symptoms* of schizophrenia—social withdrawal, apathy, and lack of emotional expressiveness. In some cases, the drugs even made negative symptoms worse. Third, the antipsychotics often produced unwanted side effects, such as dry mouth, weight gain, constipation, sleepiness, and poor concentration (Stahl, 2009).

Fourth, the fact that the early antipsychotics *globally* altered brain levels of dopamine turned out to be a double-edged sword. Dopamine pathways in the brain are involved not only in psychotic symptoms but also in normal motor movements. Consequently, the early antipsychotic medications could produce motor-related side effects—muscle tremors, rigid movements, a shuffling gait, and a masklike facial expression. This collection of side effects occurred so commonly that mental hospital staff members sometimes informally referred to it as the "Thorazine shuffle."

Even more disturbing, the long-term use of antipsychotic medications causes a small percentage of people to develop a potentially irreversible motor disorder called *tardive dyskinesia*. Tardive dyskinesia is characterized by severe, uncontrollable facial tics and grimaces, chewing movements, and other involuntary movements of the lips, jaw, and tongue.

Closely tied to the various side effects of the first antipsychotic drugs is a fifth problem: the "revolving door" pattern of hospitalization, discharge, and rehospitalization. Schizophrenic patients, once stabilized by antipsychotic medication, were released from hospitals into the community. But because of the medication's unpleasant side effects, inadequate medical follow-up, or both, many patients eventually stopped taking the medication. When psychotic symptoms returned, the patients were rehospitalized.

The Atypical Antipsychotics

Beginning around 1990, a second generation of antipsychotic drugs began to be introduced. Called **atypical antipsychotic medications,** these drugs affect brain levels of dopamine and *serotonin*. The first atypical antipsychotics were *clozapine* and *risperidone*. More recent atypical antipsychotics include *olanzapine, sertindole,* and *quetiapine*.

The atypical antipsychotics have several advantages over the older antipsychotic drugs (see Barnes & Joyce, 2001; Burton, 2006). First, the new drugs are less likely to cause movement-related side effects. That's because they do not block dopamine receptors in the movement areas of the brain. Instead, they more selectively target dopamine receptors in brain areas associated with psychotic symptoms (Rivas-Vasquez, 2003). The atypical antipsychotics are also much more effective in treating the negative symptoms of schizophrenia—apathy, social withdrawal, and flat emotions (Woo & others, 2009). Some patients who have not responded to the older antipsychotic drugs improve dramatically with the new medications (Turner & Stewart, 2006).

The atypical antipsychotic medications also appear to lessen the incidence of the "revolving door" pattern of hospitalization and rehospitalization. As compared to discharged patients taking the older antipsychotic medications, patients taking risperidone or olanzapine are much less likely to relapse and return to the hospital (Bhanji & others, 2004; Rabinowitz & others, 2001).

Some recently developed antipsychotic medications offer hope for even fewer potential side effects. For example, in 2002, the FDA approved *aripiprazole*, trade name *Abilify*. Rather than merely blocking dopamine receptors, aripiprazole appears to stabilize the availability of dopamine. Depending on the level of dopamine present in the neuronal synapse, the drug either increases or decreases the amount of

atypical antipsychotic medications Newer antipsychotic medications that, in contrast to the early antipsychotic drugs, block dopamine receptors in brain regions associated with psychotic symptoms rather than more globally throughout the brain, resulting in fewer side effects.

Second-Generation Antipsychotics: Are They More Effective? The atypical antipsychotic medications sparked considerable hope for better therapeutic effects, fewer adverse reactions, and greater patient compliance. Although they were less likely to cause movement-related side effects, the second-generation antipsychotics caused some of the same side effects as the first-generation antipsychotics, including weight gain and cardiac problems (Julien, 2008). Equally important, large-scale studies have demonstrated that the newer antipsychotic medications do *not* produce greater improvements than the older traditional antipsychotics. Nonetheless, people who don't benefit from the traditional antipsychotics sometimes improve when they switch to one of the newer atypical antipsychotics (P. Jones & others, 2006; Lieberman & others, 2005; Rosenheck & others, 2006; Swartz & others, 2007).

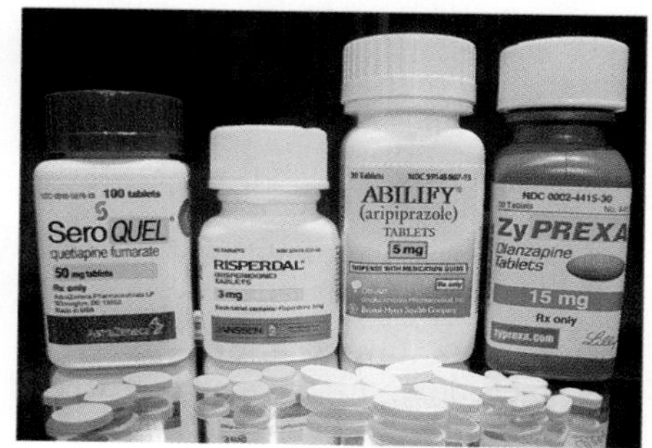

dopamine available. Early clinical trials showed that aripiprazole was as effective as the other atypical antipsychotic medications but had fewer side effects (DeLeon & others, 2004; Rivas-Vasquez, 2003). Adding to the potential of this new medication, Abilify also seems to be effective in the treatment of manic episodes associated with bipolar disorder (Keck & others, 2003; Scherk & others, 2007).

Antianxiety Medications

Anxiety that is intense and persistent can be disabling, interfering with a person's ability to eat, sleep, and function. **Antianxiety medications** are prescribed to help people deal with the problems and symptoms associated with pathological anxiety (see Table 14.8).

The best-known antianxiety drugs are the *benzodiazepines,* which include the trade-name drugs *Valium* and *Xanax.* These antianxiety medications calm jittery feelings, relax the muscles, and promote sleep. They used to go by the name "tranquilizers" because of this effect. They take effect rapidly, usually within an hour or so. In general, the benzodiazepines produce their effects by increasing the level of *GABA,* a neurotransmitter that inhibits the transmission of nerve impulses in the brain and slows brain activity (see Chapter 2).

Taken for a week or two, and in therapeutic doses, the benzodiazepines can effectively reduce anxiety levels. However, the benzodiazepines have several potentially dangerous side effects. First, they can reduce coordination, alertness, and reaction time. Second, their effects can be intensified when they are combined with alcohol and many other drugs, including over-the-counter antihistamines. Such a combination can produce severe drug intoxication, even death.

Third, the benzodiazepines can be physically addictive if taken in large quantities or over a long period of time. If physical dependence occurs, the person must withdraw from the drug gradually, as abrupt withdrawal can produce life-threatening symptoms. Because of their addictive potential, the benzodiazepines are less widely prescribed today.

A newer antianxiety drug with the trade name *Buspar* has fewer side effects. Buspar is not a benzodiazepine, and it does not affect the neurotransmitter GABA. In fact, exactly how Buspar works is unclear, but it is believed to affect brain dopamine and serotonin levels (Davidson & others, 2009). Regardless, Buspar relieves anxiety while allowing the individual to maintain normal alertness. It does not cause the drowsiness, sedation, and cognitive impairment that are associated with the benzodiazepines. And Buspar seems to have a very low risk of dependency and physical addiction.

However, Buspar has one major drawback: It must be taken for two to three *weeks* before anxiety is reduced. While this decreases Buspar's potential for abuse, it also decreases its effectiveness for treating acute anxiety. For immediate, short-term relief from anxiety, the benzodiazepines are still regarded as the most effective medications currently available.

Table 14.8

Antianxiety Medications

	Generic Name	Trade Name
Benzodiazepines	Diazepam	Valium
	Chlordiazepoxide	Librium
	Lorazepam	Ativan
	Triazolam	Halcion
	Alprazolam	Xanax
Non-benzodiazepine	Buspirone	Buspar

Source: Based on Julien (2008).

antianxiety medications
Prescription drugs that are used to alleviate the symptoms of anxiety.

lithium
A naturally occurring substance that is used in the treatment of bipolar disorder.

antidepressant medications
Prescription drugs that are used to reduce the symptoms associated with depression.

Lithium

In Chapter 13, on psychological disorders, we described *bipolar disorder*, previously known as *manic depression*. The medication most commonly used to treat bipolar disorder is **lithium,** a naturally occurring substance. Lithium counteracts both manic and depressive symptoms in bipolar patients. Its effectiveness in treating bipolar disorder has been well established since the 1960s (Preston & others, 2008).

As a treatment for bipolar disorder, lithium can prevent acute manic episodes over the course of a week or two. Once an acute manic episode is under control, the long-term use of lithium can help prevent relapses into either mania or depression. The majority of patients with bipolar disorder respond well to lithium therapy. However, lithium doesn't help everyone. Some people on lithium therapy experience relapses (Nierenberg & others, 2007).

Like all other medications, lithium has potential side effects. If the lithium level is too low, manic symptoms persist. If it is too high, lithium poisoning may occur, with symptoms such as vomiting, muscle weakness, and reduced muscle coordination. Consequently, the patient's lithium blood level must be carefully monitored.

How lithium works was once a complete mystery. Lithium's action was especially puzzling because it prevented mood disturbances at both ends of the emotional spectrum—mania *and* depression. It turns out that lithium affects levels of an excitatory neurotransmitter called *glutamate*, which is found in many areas of the brain. Apparently, lithium stabilizes the availability of glutamate within a narrow, normal range, preventing both abnormal highs and abnormal lows (Dixon & Hokin, 1998; Keck & McElroy, 2009).

Bipolar disorder can also be treated with an anticonvulsant medicine called *Depakote*. Originally used to prevent epileptic seizures, Depakote seems to be especially helpful in treating those who rapidly cycle through bouts of bipolar disorder several times a year. It's also useful for treating bipolar patients who do not respond to lithium (Davis & others, 2005).

Lithium Water Lithium salt, a naturally occurring substance, was used in many over-the-counter medicines before it was discovered to be helpful in the treatment of mania. As this late-nineteenth-century ad shows, small amounts of lithium salt were also added to bottled water. An early version of the soft drink 7-Up included small amounts of lithium (Maxmen & Ward, 1995). Marketed as "lithium soda," the ad campaign claimed that it was the drink that took "the ouch out of the grouch!"

Antidepressant Medications

The **antidepressant medications** counteract the classic symptoms of depression—hopelessness, guilt, dejection, suicidal thoughts, difficulty concentrating, and disruptions in sleep, energy, appetite, and sexual desire. The first generation of antidepressants consists of two classes of drugs, called *tricyclics* and *MAO inhibitors* (see Table 14.9 on the next page). Tricyclics and MAO inhibitors affect multiple neurotransmitter pathways in the brain. Evidence suggests that these medications alleviate depression by increasing the availability of two key brain neurotransmitters, *norepinephrine* and *serotonin*. However, even though brain levels of norepinephrine and serotonin begin to rise within *hours* of taking a tricyclic or MAO inhibitor, it can take up to six *weeks* before depressive symptoms begin to lift (Thase & Denko, 2008).

Tricyclics and MAO inhibitors can be effective in reducing depressive symptoms, but they can also produce numerous side effects (Holsboer, 2009). Tricyclics can cause weight gain, dizziness, dry mouth and eyes, and sedation. And, because tricyclics affect the cardiovascular system, an overdose can be fatal. As for the MAO inhibitors, they can interact with a chemical found in many foods, including cheese, smoked meats, and red wine. Eating these foods while taking an MAO inhibitor can result in dangerously high blood pressure, leading to stroke or even death.

The search for antidepressants with fewer side effects led to the development of the second generation of antidepressants. Second-generation antidepressants include *trazodone* and *bupropion*. Although chemically different from the tricyclics, the second-generation antidepressants were generally no more effective than the first-generation ones, and they turned out to have many of the same side effects.

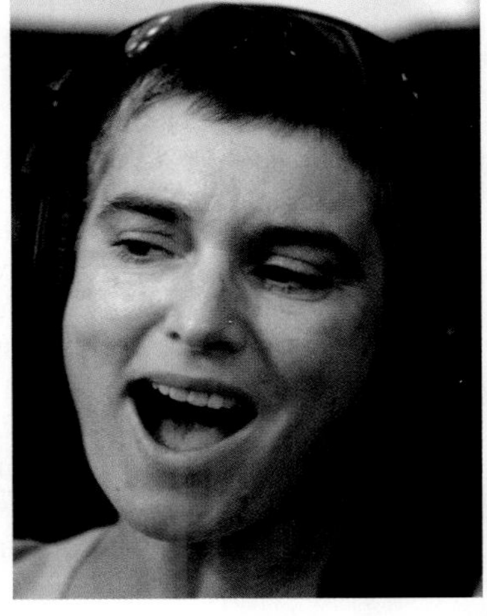

Medication and Mood Disorders: Sinead O'Connor Medication can produce serious side effects and doesn't help everyone who suffers from depression or bipolar disorder. But for some, medication can be a lifesaver. Controversial Irish singer Sinead O'Connor suffered from depression in her twenties, attempted suicide in her early thirties, and was finally diagnosed with bipolar disorder in her late thirties. "The best way I can describe it to you is you're so sad, just terribly sad, that you're like a bucket of water with holes in it. Every pore of you is crying and you don't even understand why or what," O'Connor said. But after she began taking lithium and other medications, her moods and behavior stabilized. "I actually kind of died and got born again as a result of taking the meds and having a chance to, you know, build a life."

selective serotonin reuptake inhibitors (SSRIs)
Class of antidepressant medications that increase the availability of serotonin in the brain and cause fewer side effects than earlier antidepressants; they include Prozac, Paxil, and Zoloft.

Table 14.9
Antidepressant Medications

	Generic Name	Trade Name
First-Generation Antidepressants		
Tricyclic antidepressants	Imipramine Desipramine Amitriptyline	Tofranil Norpramin Elavil
MAO inhibitors	Phenelzine Tranylcypromine	Nardil Parnate
Second-Generation Antidepressants	Trazodone Bupropion	Desyrel Wellbutrin
Selective Serotonin Reuptake Inhibitors (SSRIs)	Fluoxetine Sertraline Paroxetine Fluvoxamine Citalopram Escitalopram	Prozac Zoloft Paxil Luvox Celexa Lexapro
Dual-Action Antidepressants	Nefazodone Mirtazapine	Serzone Remeron
Dual-Reuptake Inhibitors	Venlafaxine Duloxetine	Effexor Cymbalta

Source: Based on Julien (2008).

In 1987, the picture changed dramatically with the introduction of a third group of antidepressants, the **selective serotonin reuptake inhibitors,** abbreviated **SSRIs.** Rather than acting on multiple neurotransmitter pathways, the SSRIs primarily affect the availability of a single neurotransmitter—serotonin. Compared with the earlier antidepressants, the new antidepressants act much more selectively in targeting specific serotonin pathways in the brain. The first SSRI to be released was *fluoxetine,* which is better known by its trade name, *Prozac.* Prozac was quickly followed by its chemical cousins, *Zoloft* and *Paxil.*

Prozac was specifically designed to alleviate depressive symptoms with fewer side effects than earlier antidepressants. It achieved that goal with considerable success. Although no more effective than tricyclics or MAO inhibitors, Prozac and the other SSRI antidepressants tend to produce fewer, and milder, side effects. But no medication is risk-free. Among Prozac's potential side effects are headaches, nervousness, difficulty sleeping, loss of appetite, and sexual dysfunction (Breese & others, 2009). The SSRIs are also helpful in treating anxiety disorders (Davidson & others, 2009).

Because of its overall effectiveness and relatively mild side-effects profile, Prozac quickly became very popular. By the early 1990s, an estimated *1 million prescriptions per month* were being written for Prozac. By the late 1990s, Prozac had become the best-selling antidepressant in the world. Today, Prozac is available in generic form, greatly reducing its cost. But even so, the antidepressants Prozac and Zoloft account for more than $4 billion a year in sales in just the United States (*NOC Health,* 2005).

Since the original SSRIs were released, new antidepressants have been developed, including *Serzone* and *Remeron.* These antidepressants, called *dual-action antidepressants,* also affect serotonin levels, but their mechanism is somewhat different from that of the SSRIs. They are as effective as the SSRIs but have different side effects.

Finally, *Effexor* and *Cymbalta* are two newer antidepressants that are best classified as dual-reuptake inhibitors, affecting levels of both serotonin and norepinephrine. Possibly because of its dual action, Effexor seems to be somewhat more effective than the SSRIs in alleviating the symptoms of depression (see Thase & others, 2008; Nierenberg & others, 2007). However, Effexor's potential side effects include diminished sexual interest and weight gain.

With so many antidepressants available today, which should be prescribed? Certain factors, including previous attempts with antidepressants, possible interactions with other medications, and personal tolerance of side effects, often influence this decision. Currently, medications are typically prescribed on a "trial-and-error" basis—people

The Most Commonly Prescribed Class of Medication: Antidepressants The number of people treated with antidepressant medication more than doubled from 13 million people in 1996 to 27 million people in 2005 (Olfson & Marcus, 2009). With the exception of African-Americans, antidepressant usage increased in virtually every demographic group. But during the same time period, people with depression were less likely to undergo psychotherapy treatment with a psychiatrist, psychologist, or other counselors (Mojtabai & Olfson, 2008). Ironically, although antidepressant usage has increased sharply, new studies suggest that antidepressants may not be as effective as pharmaceutical companies have claimed, especially for cases of mild depression (Kirsch & others, 2008; Turner & others, 2008).

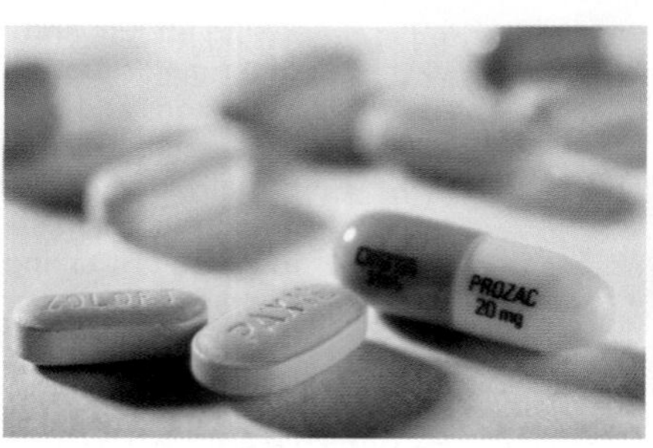

are prescribed different drugs or combinations of drugs in different dosages until they find the regimen that works for them. Thus, patients may need to try multiple medications before finding an effective treatment. Many researchers believe that genetic differences may explain why people respond so differently to antidepressants and other psychotropic medications. The new field of *pharmacogenetics* is the study of how genes influence an individual's response to drugs (Nurnberger, 2009). As this field advances, it may help overcome the trial-and-error nature of prescribing not only antidepressants, but other psychotropic medications as well.

How do antidepressants and psychotherapy compare in their effectiveness? Several large-scale studies have found that both cognitive therapy and interpersonal therapy are just as effective as antidepressant medication in producing remission from depressive symptoms (Imel & others, 2008; Thase & others, 2007). Brain-imaging studies are just beginning to show how such treatments might change brain activity—a topic that we showcase in the Focus on Neuroscience.

FOCUS ON NEUROSCIENCE

Comparing Psychotherapy and Antidepressant Medication

Both antidepressant medication and psychotherapy have been used to treat major depression. As we discussed in Chapter 13, major depression is characterized by a variety of physical symptoms, including changes in brain activity (Abler & others, 2007; Sackeim, 2001; Thase, 2001). Antidepressants are assumed to work their effect by changing brain chemistry and activity. Does psychotherapy have the same effect?

In a recent study, PET scans were done on 24 people with major depression and compared to a matched group of normal control subjects who were *not* depressed (Brody & others, 2001). Compared with the nondepressed adults, the depressed individuals showed increased activity in three areas of the brain: the *prefrontal cortex,* the *caudate nucleus,* and the *thalamus.* The day after the first scan, 10 of the 24 depressed individuals started taking the antidepressant Paxil, an SSRI. The remaining 14 individuals with depression started interpersonal therapy (discussed earlier in this chapter), a psychodynamic therapy that has been shown to be effective in the treatment of depression. Twelve weeks after beginning treatment, the participants' depressive symptoms were measured, and all 24 study participants underwent PET scans again.

Following *either* treatment, patients' depressive symptoms improved. And the PET scans revealed that patients in *both* groups showed a trend toward more normalized brain functioning. Activity declined significantly in brain regions that had shown abnormally high activity before treatment began.

The PET scans shown here depict changes in the prefrontal cortex, one of the regions that showed a significant change toward more normal metabolic levels. Scan **(a)** shows activity levels in the prefrontal cortex before treatment. Scans **(b)** and **(c)** show the metabolic *decrease* in activity following treatment with Paxil **(b)** or interpersonal therapy **(c).** In this comparison, note that **(b)** and **(c)** show the amount of change from the baseline condition, rather than the actual level of metabolic activity.

As these findings emphasize, *both* psychotherapy and antidepressant medication affect brain chemistry and functioning. In another study, both patients who were treated with interpersonal therapy and patients who were treated with the antidepressant Effexor showed improvement and similar changes in brain functioning (Martin & others, 2001). Similarly, later studies have shown that cognitive behavior therapy and antidepressant therapy also produce distinct patterns of brain activity changes in people whose depressive symptoms have improved (Kennedy & others, 2007; Roffman & others, 2005).

Source: Brody & others (2001).

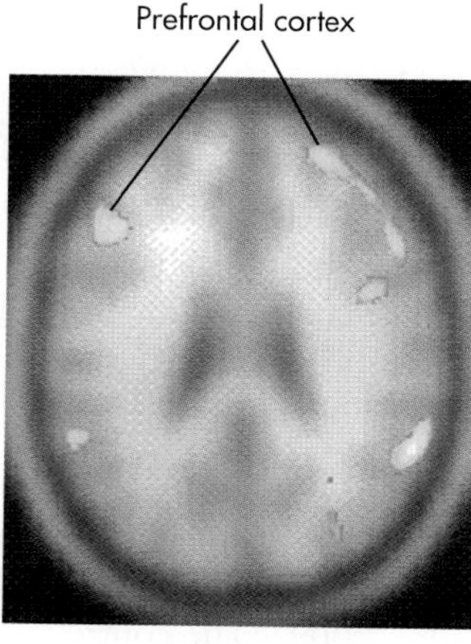

(a)
Baseline—before treatment

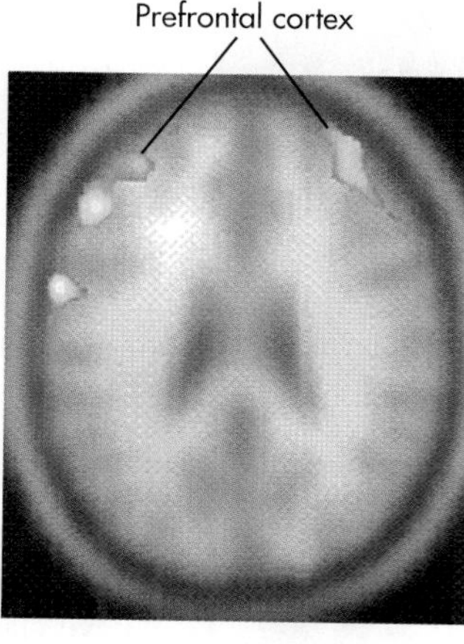

(b)
Decrease in activity after 12 weeks of treatment with Paxil

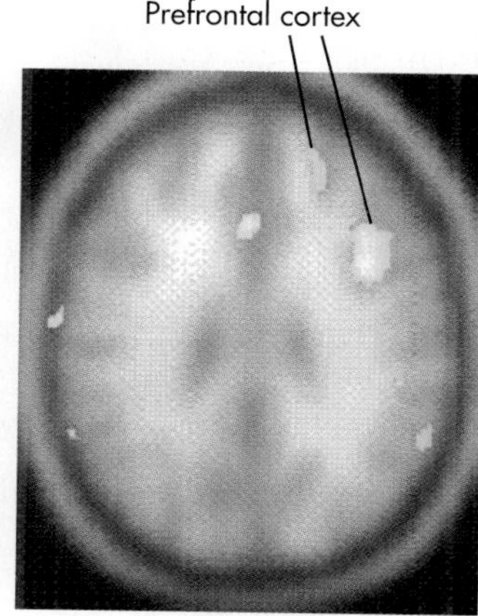

(c)
Decrease in activity after 12 weeks of treatment with interpersonal therapy

electroconvulsive therapy (ECT) A biomedical therapy used primarily in the treatment of depression that involves electrically inducing a brief brain seizure; also called *electroshock therapy.*

Electroconvulsive Therapy

As we have just seen, millions of prescriptions are written for antidepressant medications in the United States every year. In contrast, a much smaller number of patients receive **electroconvulsive therapy,** or **ECT,** as a medical treatment for severe depression. Also known as *electroshock therapy* or *shock therapy,* electroconvulsive therapy involves using a brief burst of electric current to induce a seizure in the brain, much like an epileptic seizure. Although ECT is most commonly used to treat depression, it is occasionally used to treat mania, schizophrenia, and other severe mental disorders (Gazdag & others, 2009).

ECT is a relatively simple and quick medical procedure, usually performed in a hospital. The patient lies on a table. Electrodes are placed on one or both of the patient's temples, and the patient is given a short-term, light anesthetic and muscle-relaxing drugs. To ensure adequate airflow, a breathing tube is sometimes placed in the patient's throat.

While the patient is unconscious, a split-second burst of electricity induces a seizure. The seizure lasts for about a minute. Outwardly, the seizure typically produces mild muscle tremors. After the anesthesia wears off and the patient wakes up, confusion and disorientation may be present for a few hours. Some patients experience a temporary or permanent memory loss for the events leading up to the treatment. To treat major depression, the patient typically receives two to three treatments per week for two to seven weeks, with less frequent follow-up treatments for several additional months (Fink, 2009).

In the short term, ECT is a very effective treatment for severe depression: About 80 percent of depressed patients improve (Glass, 2001; Rasmussen, 2009). ECT also relieves the symptoms of depression very quickly, typically within days. Because of its rapid therapeutic effects, ECT can be a lifesaving procedure for extremely suicidal or severely depressed patients. Such patients may not survive for the several weeks it takes for antidepressant drugs to alleviate symptoms.

Typically, ECT is used only after other forms of treatment, including both psychotherapy and medication, have failed to help the patient, especially when depression is severe. For some people, such as elderly individuals, ECT may be less dangerous than antidepressant drugs. In general, the complication rate from ECT is very low.

Nevertheless, inducing a brain seizure is not a matter to be taken lightly. ECT has potential dangers. Serious cognitive impairments can occur, such as extensive amnesia and disturbances in language and verbal abilities. However, fears that ECT might produce brain damage have not been confirmed by research (Eschweiler, 2007; McDonald & others, 2009).

Electroconvulsive Therapy ECT is used as a treatment for major depression, especially in people who do not respond to antidepressant medications. During an ECT treatment, the person is given a short-acting anesthetic and muscle relaxants. A mild brain seizure, which lasts about a minute, is induced by a brief pulse of electricity. Although ECT can be an effective short-term treatment for people with major depression, the treatment effects tend to be short-lived. About half of the people who undergo ECT experience a relapse of the depression symptoms within a few months (Kellner & others, 2006; Tew & others, 2007).

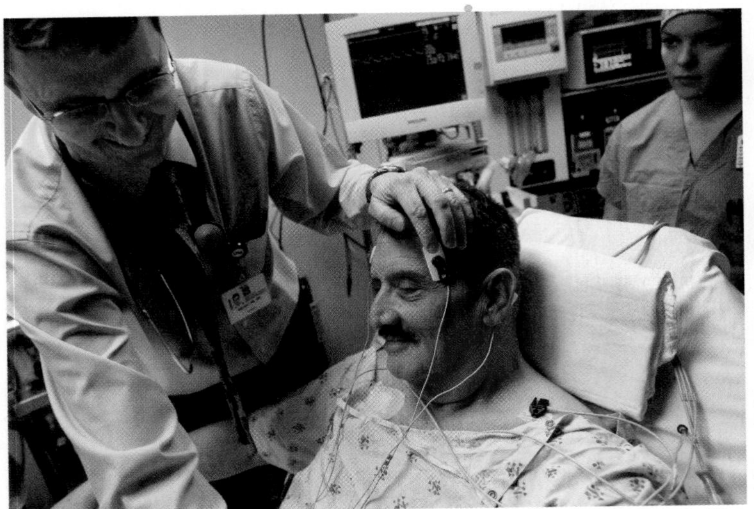

Perhaps ECT's biggest drawback is that its antidepressive effects can be short-lived. Relapses within four months are relatively common (Glass, 2001). About half the patients treated for major depression experience a relapse within six months. Today, patients are often treated with long-term antidepressant medication following ECT, which reduces the relapse rate (Sackeim & others, 2001). In cases of severe, recurrent depression, ECT may also be periodically readministered to prevent the return of depressive symptoms.

At this point, you may be wondering why ECT is not in wider use. The reason is that ECT is the most controversial medical treatment for psychological disorders (Shorter, 2009). Not everyone agrees that ECT is either safe or effective.

Some have been quite outspoken against it, arguing that its safety and effectiveness are not as great as its supporters have claimed (Andre, 2009). The controversy over ECT is tied to its portrayal in popular media over time. The use of ECT declined drastically in the 1960s and 1970s when it was depicted in many popular books and movies, including *One Flew Over the Cuckoo's Nest*, as a brutal treatment with debilitating side effects (Swartz, 2009). Its use has increased greatly since that time, especially in the past decade or two, with ECT now available in most major metropolitan areas in the United States (Shorter, 2009).

How does ECT work? Despite many decades of research, it's still not known exactly why electrically inducing a convulsion relieves the symptoms of depression (Michael, 2009). One theory is that ECT seizures may somehow "reboot" the brain by depleting and then replacing important neurotransmitters (Swartz, 2009).

Some new, experimental treatments suggest that those seizures may not actually be necessary. That is, it may be possible to provide lower levels of electrical current to the brain than traditional ECT delivers and still reduce severe symptoms of depression and other mental illnesses. For example, *transcranial magnetic stimulation (TMS)* involves stimulation of certain regions of the brain with magnetic pulses of various frequencies. Unlike ECT, it requires no anesthetic, induces no seizures, and can be conducted in a private doctor's office rather than a hospital (Rosenberg & Dannon, 2009).

Another experimental treatment, *vagus nerve stimulation (VNS)*, involves the surgical implantation of a device about the size of a pacemaker into the left chest wall. The device provides brief, intermittent electrical stimulation to the left vagus nerve, which runs through the neck and connects to the brain stem (McClintock & others, 2009). Finally, *deep brain stimulation (DBS)* utilizes electrodes surgically implanted in the brain and a battery-powered neurostimulator surgically implanted in the chest. Wires under the skin connect the two implants, and the neurostimulator sends electrical signals to the brain (Fink, 2009; Schlapfer & Bewernick, 2009).

Keep in mind that TMS, VNS, and DBS are still experimental. And like ECT, the specific mechanism by which they may work is not entirely clear. Still, researchers are hopeful that these techniques will provide another viable treatment option for people suffering from severe psychological symptoms (McDonald & others, 2009).

>> Closing Thoughts

As you've seen throughout this chapter, a wide range of therapies are available to help people who are troubled by psychological symptoms and disorders. Like our friend Marcia, whose story we told in the Prologue, many people benefit psychologically from psychotherapy. As the first part of the chapter showed, psychotherapy can help people by providing insight, developing more effective behaviors and coping strategies, and changing thought patterns.

The biomedical therapies, discussed in the second part of the chapter, can also help people with psychological problems. This was also true in Marcia's case, when she reluctantly agreed to try an antidepressant medication. For almost a year, Marcia took a low dose of one of the SSRI antidepressant medications. It helped in the short term, lessening the feelings of depression and anxiety and giving her time to work through various issues in therapy and develop greater psychological resilience. Today, people are increasingly being helped by a combination of psychotherapy and one of the psychotropic medications.

As our discussion of the effectiveness of psychotherapy has shown, characteristics of both the therapist and the client are important to the success of psychotherapy. In the Enhancing Well-Being with Psychology section at the end of this chapter, we describe the attitudes that should be brought to the therapeutic relationship, discuss some general ground rules of psychotherapy, and dispel some common misunderstandings. The Enhancing Well-Being with Psychology section will help you understand the nature of the therapeutic relationship and provide information useful to anyone who may be considering entering psychotherapy.

THE SEVEN DWARFS AFTER THERAPY

ENHANCING WELL-BEING WITH PSYCHOLOGY

What to Expect in Psychotherapy

The cornerstone of psychotherapy is the relationship between the therapist and the person seeking help. But the therapy relationship is different from all other close relationships. On the one hand, the therapist–client relationship is characterized by intimacy and the disclosure of very private, personal experiences. On the other hand, there are distinct boundaries to the therapist–client relationship. To a therapy client, especially one who is undertaking psychotherapy for the first time, the therapy relationship may sometimes seem confusing and contradictory.

The following guidelines should help you understand the special nature of the therapy relationship and develop realistic expectations about the process of psychotherapy.

1. Strengthen your commitment to change.
Therapy is not about maintaining the status quo. It is about making changes in terms of how you think, feel, act, and respond. For many people, the idea of change produces mixed feelings. You can increase the likelihood of achieving your goals in therapy by thinking about the reasons you want to change and reminding yourself of your commitment to change (Hettema & others, 2005).

2. Therapy is a collaborative effort.
Don't expect your therapist to do all the work for you. If you are going to benefit from psychotherapy, you must actively participate in the therapeutic process. Often, therapy requires effort not only during the therapy sessions but also *outside* them. Many therapists assign "homework" to be completed between sessions. You may be asked to keep a diary of your thoughts and behaviors, read assigned material, rehearse skills that you've learned in therapy, and so forth. Such exercises are important components of the overall therapy process.

3. Don't confuse catharsis with change.
In the chapter Prologue, Marcia mentions the cathartic effect of therapy. *Catharsis* refers to the emotional release that people experience from the simple act of talking about their problems. Although it usually produces short-term emotional relief, catharsis in itself does not resolve the problem. Even so, catharsis is an important element of psychotherapy. Discussing emotionally charged issues with a therapist can lessen your sense of psychological tension and urgency and can help you explore the problem more rationally and objectively.

4. Don't confuse insight with change.
Despite what you've seen in the movies, developing insight into the sources or nature of your psychological problems does not magically resolve them. Nor does insight automatically translate into healthier thoughts and behaviors. Instead, insight allows you to look at and understand your problems in a new light. The opportunity for change occurs when your therapist helps you use these insights to redefine past experiences, resolve psychological conflicts, and explore more adaptive forms of behavior. Even with the benefit of insight, it takes effort to change how you think, behave, and react to other people.

5. Don't expect your therapist to make decisions for you.
One of the most common misunderstandings about psychotherapy is that your therapist is going to tell you how to run your life. Not so. Virtually all forms of therapy are designed to increase a person's sense of responsibility, confidence, and mastery in dealing with life's problems. Your therapist won't make your decisions for you, but he or she *will* help you explore your feelings about important decisions—including ambivalence or fear. Some people find this frustrating because they want the therapist to tell them what to do. But if your therapist made decisions for you, it would only foster dependency and undermine your ability to be responsible for your own life.

6. Expect therapy to challenge how you think and act.
As you confront issues that you've never discussed before or even admitted to yourself, you may find therapy very anxiety-provoking. Moments of psychological discomfort are a normal, even expected, part of the therapy process.

Think of therapy as a psychological magnifying glass. Therapy tends to magnify both your strengths and your weaknesses. Such intense self-scrutiny is not always flattering. Examining how you habitually deal with failure and success, conflict and resolution, disappointment and joy can be disturbing. You may become aware of the psychological games you play or of how you use ego defense mechanisms to distort reality. You may have to acknowledge your own immature, maladaptive, or destructive behavior patterns. Although it can be painful, becoming aware that changes are needed is a necessary step toward developing healthier forms of thinking and behavior.

7. Your therapist is not a substitute friend.

Unlike friendship, which is characterized by a mutual give-and take, psychotherapy is focused solely on *you*. Rather than thinking of your therapist as a friend, think of him or her as an expert consultant—someone you've hired to help you deal better with your problems. The fact that your therapist is not socially or personally involved with you allows him or her to respond objectively and honestly. Part of what allows you to trust your therapist and "open up" emotionally is the knowledge that your therapist is ethically and legally bound to safeguard the confidentiality of what you say.

8. Therapeutic intimacy does not include sexual intimacy.

It's very common for clients to have strong feelings of affection, love, and even sexual attraction toward their therapists (Pope & Tabachnick, 1993). After all, the most effective therapists tend to be warm, empathic people who are genuinely caring and supportive (Beutler & others, 2004). However, *it is never ethical or appropriate for a therapist to have any form of sexual contact with a client.* There are *no* exceptions to that statement. Sexual contact between a therapist and a client violates the ethical standards of all mental health professionals.

How often does sexual contact occur? About 7 percent of male and 2 percent of female therapists admit that they have had sexual contact with clients (Davis & others, 1995; Williams, 1992).

Sexual involvement between client and therapist can be enormously damaging (Norris & others, 2003; Pope, 1990). Not only does it destroy the therapist's professional objectivity, but it also destroys the trust the client has invested in the therapist. When a therapist becomes sexually involved with a client, regardless of who initiated the sexual contact, the client is being exploited.

Rather than exploiting a client's feelings of sexual attraction, an ethical therapist will help the client understand and work through such feelings. Therapy should ultimately help you develop closer, more loving relationships with other people—but *not* with your therapist.

9. Don't expect change to happen overnight.

Change occurs in psychotherapy at different rates for different people. How quickly change occurs depends on many factors, such as the seriousness of your problems, the degree to which you are psychologically ready to make needed changes, and the therapist's skill in helping you implement those changes. As a general rule, most people make significant progress in a few months of weekly therapy sessions (McNeilly & Howard, 1991). You can help create the climate for change by choosing a therapist you feel comfortable working with and by genuinely investing yourself in the therapy process.

CHAPTER REVIEW: KEY PEOPLE AND TERMS

Aaron T. Beck, p. 595
Albert Ellis, p. 593
Sigmund Freud, p. 582
Mary Cover Jones, p. 588
Carl Rogers, p. 585

psychotherapy, p. 580
biomedical therapies, p. 580
psychoanalysis, p. 582
free association, p. 582
resistance, p. 583
dream interpretation, p. 583
interpretation, p. 583
transference, p. 583
short-term dynamic therapies, p. 584
interpersonal therapy (IPT), p. 584
client-centered therapy, p. 585
behavior therapy, p. 588
counterconditioning, p. 589
systematic desensitization, p. 589
aversive conditioning, p. 590
token economy, p. 592
cognitive therapies, p. 593
rational-emotive therapy (RET), p. 593
cognitive therapy (CT), p. 595
cognitive-behavioral therapy (CBT), p. 597
group therapy, p. 598
family therapy, p. 600
eye movement desensitization reprocessing (EMDR), p. 604
exposure therapy, p. 604
eclecticism, p. 604
psychotropic medications, p. 607
antipsychotic medications, p. 607
atypical antipsychotic medications, p. 609
antianxiety medications, p. 610
lithium, p. 611
antidepressant medications, p. 611
selective serotonin reuptake inhibitors (SSRIs), p. 612
electroconvulsive therapy (ECT), p. 614

Web Companion Review Activities

You can find additional review activities at **www.worthpublishers.com/discoveringpsych5e.** The *Discovering Psychology* 5th edition Web Companion has self-scoring practice quizzes, flashcards, interactive crossword puzzles, and other activities to help you master the material in this chapter.

CONCEPT MAP

THERAPIES

Psychotherapy

The treatment of emotional, behavioral, and interpersonal problems with psychological techniques

Psychoanalysis

- Developed by **Sigmund Freud** (1856-1939)
- Goal is to unearth repressed conflicts and resolve them in therapy

Techniques and processes include:
- Free association
- Resistance
- Dream interpretation
- Interpretation
- Transference

Short-term dynamic therapies:
- More problem-focused and of shorter duration than traditional psychoanalysis
- Therapists are more directive
- **Interpersonal therapy (IPT)** focuses on current relationships

Behavior Therapy

- Assumes maladaptive behaviors are learned and uses learning principles to directly change problem behaviors
- **Mary Cover Jones** (1896–1987) was first behavior therapist, using **counterconditioning** to extinguish phobic behavior

Classical conditioning principles seen in use of:
- Systematic desensitization
- Aversive conditioning

Operant conditioning techniques:
- Positive and negative reinforcement
- Extinction
- Token economies
- Contingency management interventions

Cognitive Therapies

Assume psychological problems are caused by maladaptive patterns of thinking

Rational-emotive therapy (RET):
- Developed by **Albert Ellis** (1913–2007)
- Involves identifying and challenging core irrational beliefs

Cognitive therapy (CT):
- Developed by **Aaron T. Beck** (b. 1921)
- Involves teaching the client to recognize negative automatic thoughts and cognitive biases

Cognitive-behavioral therapy (CBT) combines cognitive and behavioral techniques.

Humanistic Therapy

Client-centered therapy:
- Developed by **Carl Rogers** (1902–1987)
- Client directs the focus of therapy sessions
- Therapist is genuine, demonstrates unconditional positive regard, and communicates empathic understanding

Group and Family Therapy

- **Group therapy** is cost-effective.
- Therapists can observe clients interacting with other group members.
- Clients benefit from support of other group members.
- Clients can try out new behaviors in a safe environment.
- **Family therapy** assumes the family is an interdependent system.
- Marital or couple therapy seeks to improve communication, problem-solving skills, and intimacy.

Evauating the Effectiveness of Psychotherapy

- Psychotherapy is significantly more effective than no treatment.
- Some therapies are more effective for specific disorders.
- Empirically supported treatments have demonstrated their effectiveness in controlled scientific trials.

Factors that contribute to effective psychotherapy:
- Quality of the therapeutic relationship
- Caring, empathic, responsive therapist
- Motivated, optimistic client
- Supportive family and stable living situation
- Culturally sensitive therapist
- A good match between client and therapy techniques

Most psychotherapists take an *eclectic* approach; **eclecticism** refers to the pragmatic and integrated use of techniques from different psychotherapies.

Biomedical Therapies

Psychotropic medications: Prescription drugs that alter mental functions, alleviate psychological symptoms, and are used to treat psychological or mental disorders

Antipsychotic medications:
- Reserpine
- Chlorpromazine
- Atypical antipsychotics

Lithium treats bipolar disorder.

Antianxiety medications:
- Benzodiazepines
- Buspirone

Antidepressant medications:
- Tricyclics
- MAO inhibitors
- Second-generation antidepressants
- Selective serotonin reuptake inhibitors (SSRIs)
- Dual-action antidepressants
- Dual-uptake inhibitors

Electroconvulsive therapy (ECT): Involves delivering a brief electric shock to the brain

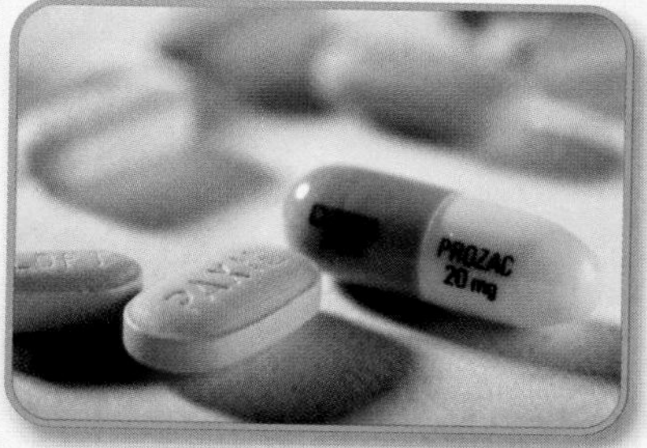

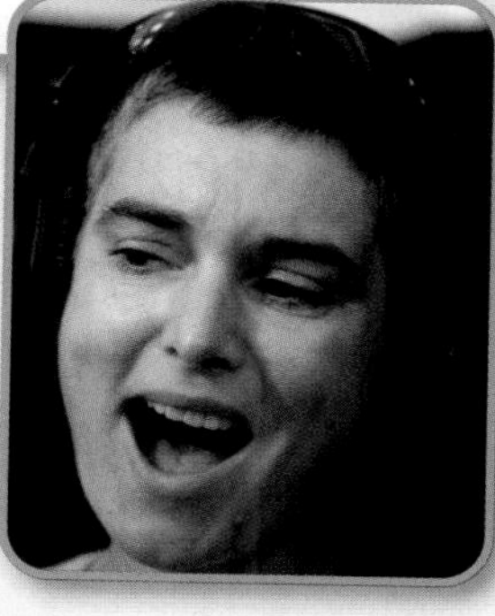

APPENDIX

A

Statistics: Understanding Data

Marie D. Thomas
California State University, San Marcos

Appendix Outline

The Tables Are Turned: A Psychologist Becomes a Research Subject

PROLOGUE

FOR 12 MONTHS I WAS a participant in a research project that was designed to compare the effects of "traditional" and "alternative" diet, exercise, and stress-reduction programs (Riegel & others, 1996). Volunteers who were randomly assigned to the *traditional* program were taught to eat a high-fiber, low-fat diet; do regular aerobic exercise; and practice a progressive muscle relaxation technique. Participants who were randomly assigned to the *alternative* program received instruction in yoga and in a meditation technique, along with a diet based on body type and tastes. I was randomly assigned to the *no-treatment* control group, which was monitored throughout the year for weight and general health but received no diet, exercise, or stress-reduction intervention.

The participants in the study were drawn from a large medical group. Invitations to participate in the study were sent to 15,000 members of the medical group. Out of that initial pool, 124 volunteers were recruited, and about 40 were randomly selected for each group—the *traditional, alternative,* and *no-treatment control groups.* The participants included men and women between the ages of 20 and 56. A total of 88 subjects lasted the full year. The researchers were pleased that so many of us stayed with the project; it isn't easy to get people to commit to a yearlong study!

Data collection began even before participants found out the group to which they had been randomly assigned. We were mailed a thick packet of questionnaires covering a wide range of topics. One questionnaire asked about our current health status, use of prescription and over-the-counter medications, use of vitamins, and visits to both physicians and alternative

health care practitioners. Another questionnaire focused on self-perceptions of health and well-being. Here we rated our mood, energy level, physical symptoms, and health in general. A lifestyle survey requested information about diet (how often did we eat red meat? how many servings of fruits and vegetables did we consume a day?), exercise (how many times per week did we do aerobic exercise?), and behavior (such as cigarette smoking and consumption of alcoholic beverages). The lifestyle survey also assessed psychological variables such as levels of stress and happiness and how well we felt we were coping.

At our first meeting with the researchers, we handed in the questionnaires and were told which of the three groups we had been assigned to. We returned early the next morning to have our blood pressure and weight measured and to have blood drawn for tests of our levels of cholesterol, triglycerides, and glucose. The two intervention groups also received a weekend of training in their respective programs. In addition to daily practice of the techniques they had been taught, people in the *traditional* and *alternative* groups were expected to maintain a "compliance diary"—a daily record of their exercise, diet, and relaxation/meditation activities. The purpose of this diary was to determine whether health outcomes were better for people who practiced the techniques regularly. At first I was disappointed when I was randomly assigned to the control group because I was especially interested in learning the alternative techniques. However, I was relieved later when I found out how much detailed record keeping the intervention groups had to do!

The researchers accumulated even more data over the yearlong period. Every 3 months, our blood pressure and weight were measured. At 6 and 12 months, the researchers performed blood tests and asked us to fill out questionnaires identical to those we'd completed at the beginning of the project.

The study included many variables. The most important independent variable (the variable that the researcher manipulates) was group assignment: *traditional* program, *alternative* program, or *no-treatment* control. The dependent variables (variables that are not directly manipulated by the researcher but that may change in response to manipulations of the independent variable) included weight, blood pressure, cholesterol level, self-perceptions regarding health, and mood. Since the dependent variables were measured several times, the researchers could study changes in them over the course of the year.

This study can help to answer important questions about the kinds of programs that tend to promote health. But the purpose of describing it here is not just to tell you whether the two intervention programs were effective and whether one worked better than the other. In the next couple of sections, I will use this study to help explain how researchers use **statistics** to (1) summarize the data they have collected and (2) draw conclusions about the data. The job of assessing what conclusions can be drawn from the research findings is the domain of *inferential statistics,* which I'll discuss later in this appendix. We'll begin by exploring how research findings can be summarized in ways that are brief yet meaningful and easy to understand. For this, researchers use *descriptive statistics.*

>> Descriptive Statistics

The study of programs to promote health generated a large amount of data. How did the researchers make sense of such a mass of information? How did they summarize it in meaningful ways? The answer lies in descriptive statistics. **Descriptive statistics** do just what their name suggests—they describe data. There are many ways to describe information. This appendix will examine four of the most common: frequency distributions, measures of central tendency, measures of variability, and measures of relationships. Since I don't have access to all the data that the health-promotion researchers gathered, I'll use hypothetical numbers to illustrate these statistical concepts.

statistics
A branch of mathematics used by researchers to organize, summarize, and interpret data.

descriptive statistics
Mathematical methods used to organize and summarize data.

Frequency Distribution

Suppose that at the start of the health-promotion study 30 people in the *traditional* group reported getting the following number of hours of aerobic exercise each week:

2, 5, 0, 1, 2, 2, 7, 0, 6, 2, 3, 1, 4, 5, 2,
1, 1, 3, 2, 1, 0, 4, 2, 3, 0, 1, 2, 3, 4, 1

Even with only 30 cases, it is difficult to make much sense of these data. Researchers need a way to organize such *raw scores* so that the information makes sense at a glance. One way to organize the data is to determine how many participants reported exercising zero hours per week, how many reported exercising one hour, and so on, until all the reported amounts are accounted for. If the data were put into a table, the table would look like Table A.1.

This table is one way of presenting a **frequency distribution**—a summary of how often various scores occur. Categories are set up (in this case, the number of hours of aerobic exercise per week), and occurrences of each category are tallied to give the frequency of each one.

What information can be gathered from this frequency distribution table? We know immediately that most of the participants did aerobic exercise less than three hours per week. The number of hours per week peaked at two and declined steadily thereafter. According to the table, the most diligent exerciser worked out about an hour per day.

Some frequency distribution tables include an extra column that shows the percentage of cases in each category. For example, what percentage of participants reported two hours of aerobic exercise per week? The percentage is calculated by dividing the category frequency (8) by the total number of people (30), which yields about 27 percent.

While a table is good for summarizing data, it is often useful to present a frequency distribution visually, with graphs. One type of graph is the **histogram** (Figure A.1). A histogram is like a bar chart with two special features: The bars are always vertical, and they always touch. Categories (in our example, the number of hours of aerobic exercise per week) are placed on the *x*-axis (horizontal), and the *y*-axis (vertical) shows the frequency of each category. The resulting graph looks something like a city skyline, with buildings of different heights.

Table A.1

A Frequency Distribution Table

Hours of Aerobic Exercise per Week	Frequency
0	4
1	7
2	8
3	4
4	3
5	2
6	1
7	1
	30

A table like this is one way of presenting a frequency distribution. It shows at a glance that most of the people in our hypothetical group of 30 were not zealous exercisers before they began their traditional health-promotion program. Nearly two-thirds of them (19 people) engaged in vigorous exercise for two hours or less each week.

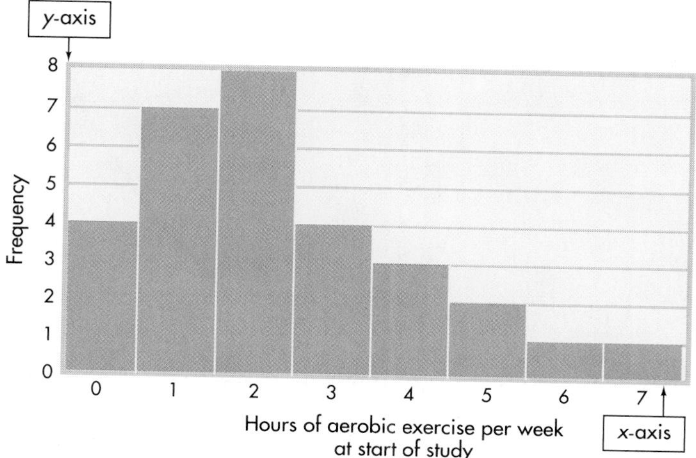

Figure A.1 A Histogram This histogram is another way of presenting the data given in Table A.1. Like the table, the histogram shows that most people do, at best, only a moderate amount of aerobic exercise (two hours or less each week). This is immediately clear from the fact that the highest bars on the chart are on the left, where the hours of exercise are lowest.

frequency distribution
A summary of how often various scores occur in a sample of scores. Score values are arranged in order of magnitude, and the number of times each score occurs is recorded.

histogram
A way of graphically representing a frequency distribution; a type of bar chart that uses vertical bars that touch.

frequency polygon
A way of graphically representing a frequency distribution; frequency is marked above each score category on the graph's horizontal axis, and the marks are connected by straight lines.

skewed distribution
An asymmetrical distribution; more scores occur on one side of the distribution than on the other. In a *positively* skewed distribution, most of the scores are low scores; in a *negatively* skewed distribution, most of the scores are high scores.

symmetrical distribution
A distribution in which scores fall equally on both sides of the graph. The normal curve is an example of a symmetrical distribution.

Another way of graphing the same data is with a **frequency polygon,** shown in Figure A.2. A mark is made above each category at the point representing its frequency. These marks are then connected by straight lines. In our example, the polygon begins before the "0" category and ends at a category of "8," even though both of these categories have no cases in them. This is traditionally done so that the polygon is a closed figure.

Frequency polygons are good for showing the shape of a distribution. The polygon in Figure A.2 looks like a mountain, rising sharply over the first two categories, peaking at 2, and gradually diminishing from there. Such a distribution is asymmetrical, or a **skewed distribution,** meaning that if we drew a line through the middle of the *x*-axis (halfway between 3 and 4 hours), more scores would be piled up on one side of the line than on the other. More specifically, the polygon in Figure A.2 represents a *positively skewed* distribution, indicating that most people had low scores. A *negatively skewed* distribution would have mostly high scores, with fewer scores at the low end of the distribution. For example, if the traditional diet and exercise intervention worked, the 30 participants should, as a group, be exercising more at the end of the study than they had been at the beginning. Perhaps the distribution of hours of aerobic exercise per week at the end of the study would look something like Figure A.3—a distribution with a slight negative skew.

In contrast to skewed distributions, a **symmetrical distribution** is one in which scores fall equally on both halves of the graph. A special case of a symmetrical distribution, the normal curve, is discussed in a later section.

A useful feature of frequency polygons is that more than one distribution can be graphed on the same set of axes. For example, the end-of-study hours of aerobic exercise per week for the *traditional* and *alternative* groups could be compared on a single graph. Doing so would make it possible to see at a glance whether one group was exercising more than the other after a year of their respective programs.

By the way, Figure A.3 is actually a figment of my imagination. According to the diaries kept by the traditional- and alternative-program participants, compliance with the exercise portion of the program decreased over time. This does not necessarily mean that these subjects were exercising *less* at the end of the study than at the beginning, but they certainly did not keep up the program as it was taught to them. Compliance with the prescribed diets was steadier than compliance with exercise; compliance by the alternative group dropped between three months and six months, and then rose steadily over time. There was, however, one major difference between

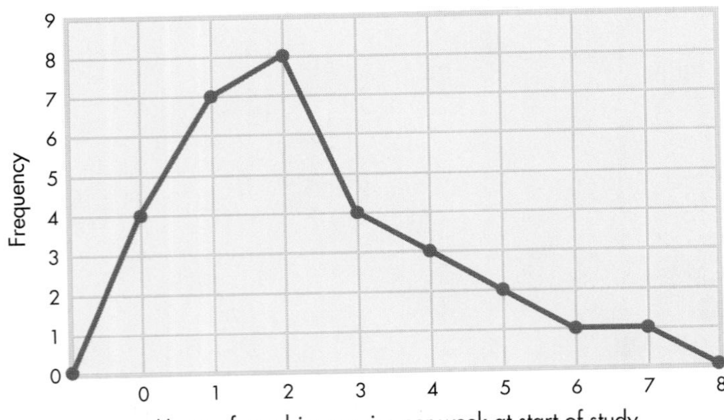

Figure A.2 A Frequency Polygon (Positive Skew) Like Table A.1 and Figure A.1, this frequency polygon shows at a glance that the number of hours of aerobic exercise weekly is not great for most people. The high points come at one and two hours, which doesn't amount to much more than 10 or 15 minutes of exercise daily. An asymmetrical distribution like this one, which includes mostly low scores, is said to be positively skewed.

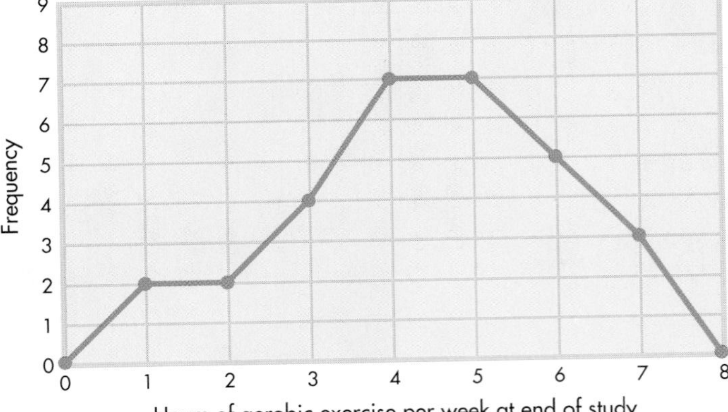

Figure A.3 A Frequency Polygon (Negative Skew) When more scores fall at the high end of a distribution than at the low end, the distribution is said to be negatively skewed. We would expect a negatively skewed distribution if a health-promotion program worked and encouraged more hours of aerobic exercise. The more effective the program, the greater the skew.

the two intervention groups in terms of compliance. Participants in the alternative group were more likely to be meditating at the end of the study than their traditional-group counterparts were to be practicing progressive relaxation.

Measures of Central Tendency

Frequency distributions can be used to organize a set of data and tell us how scores are generally distributed. But researchers often want to put this information into a more compact form. They want to be able to summarize a distribution with a single score that is "typical." To do this, they use a **measure of central tendency.**

The Mode

The **mode** is the easiest measure of central tendency to calculate. The mode is simply the score or category that occurs most frequently in a set of raw scores or in a frequency distribution. The mode in the frequency distribution shown in Table A.1 is 2; more participants reported exercising two hours per week than any other category. In this example, the mode is an accurate representation of central tendency, but this is not always the case. In the distribution 1, 1, 1, 10, 20, 30, the mode is 1, yet half the scores are 10 and above. This type of distortion is the reason measures of central tendency other than the mode are needed.

The Median

Another way of describing central tendency is to determine the **median,** or the score that falls in the middle of a distribution. If the exercise scores were laid out from lowest to highest, they would look like this:

0, 0, 0, 0, 1, 1, 1, 1, 1, 1, 1, 2, 2, 2, 2, 2, 2, 2, 2, 3, 3, 3, 3, 4, 4, 4, 5, 5, 6, 7
↑

What would the middle score be? Since there are 30 scores, look for the point that divides the distribution in half, with 15 scores on each side of this point. The median can be found between the 15th and 16th scores (indicated by the arrow). In this distribution, the answer is easy: A score of 2 is the median as well as the mode.

The Mean

A problem with the mode and the median is that both measures reflect only one score in the distribution. For the mode, the score of importance is the most frequent one; for the median, it is the middle score. A better measure of central tendency is usually one that reflects *all* scores. For this reason, the most commonly used measure of central tendency is the **mean,** or arithmetic average. You have calculated the mean many times. It is computed by summing a set of scores and then dividing by the number of scores that went into the sum. In our example, adding together the exercise distribution scores gives a total of 70; the number of scores is 30, so 70 divided by 30 gives a mean of 2.33.

Formulas are used to express how a statistic is calculated. The formula for the mean is

$$\overline{X} = \frac{\Sigma X}{N}$$

In this formula, each letter and symbol has a specific meaning:

$\overline{X}$ is the symbol for the mean.

Σ is sigma, the Greek letter for capital *S*, and it stands for "sum." (Taking a course in statistics is one way to learn the Greek alphabet!)

X represents the scores in the distribution, so the numerator of the equation says, "Sum up all the scores."

N is the total number of scores in the distribution. Therefore, the formula says, "The mean equals the sum of all the scores divided by the total number of scores."

measure of central tendency
A single number that presents some information about the "center" of a frequency distribution.

mode
The most frequently occurring score in a distribution.

median
The score that divides a frequency distribution exactly in half so that the same number of scores lie on each side of it.

mean
The sum of a set of scores in a distribution divided by the number of scores; the mean is usually the most representative measure of central tendency.

measure of variability
A single number that presents information about the spread of scores in a distribution.

range
A measure of variability; the highest score in a distribution minus the lowest score.

Although the mean is usually the most representative measure of central tendency because each score in a distribution enters into its computation, it is particularly susceptible to the effect of extreme scores. Any unusually high or low score will pull the mean in its direction. Suppose, for example, that in our frequency distribution for aerobic exercise one exercise zealot worked out 70 hours per week. The mean number of aerobic exercise hours would jump from 2.33 to 4.43. This new mean is deceptively high, given that most of the scores in the distribution are 2 and below. Because of just that one extreme score, the mean has become less representative of the distribution. Frequency tables and graphs are important tools for helping us identify extreme scores *before* we start computing statistics.

Measures of Variability

In addition to identifying the central tendency in a distribution, researchers may want to know how much the scores in that distribution differ from one another. Are they grouped closely together or widely spread out? To answer this question, we need some **measure of variability.** Figure A.4 shows two distributions with the same mean but with different variability.

A simple way to measure variability is with the **range,** which is computed by subtracting the lowest score in the distribution from the highest score. Let's say that there are 15 participants in the traditional diet and exercise group and that their weights at the beginning of the study varied from a low of 95 pounds to a high of 155 pounds. The range of weights in this group would be 155 − 95 = 60 pounds.

As a measure of variability, the range provides a limited amount of information because it depends on only the two most extreme scores in a distribution (the highest and lowest scores). A more useful measure of variability would give some idea of the average amount of variation in a distribution. But variation from what? The most common way to measure variability is to determine how far scores in a distribution vary from the distribution's mean. We saw earlier that the mean is usually the best way to represent the "center" of the distribution, so the mean seems like an appropriate reference point.

What if we subtract the mean from each score in a distribution to get a general idea of how far each score is from the center? When the mean is subtracted from a score, the result is a *deviation* from the mean. Scores that are above the mean would have positive deviations, and scores that are below the mean would have negative deviations. To get an average deviation, we would need to sum the deviations and divide by the number of deviations that went into the sum. There is a problem with this procedure, however. If deviations from the mean are added together, the sum will be 0 because the negative and positive deviations will cancel each other out. In fact, the real definition of the mean is "the only point in a distribution where all the scores' deviations from it add up to 0."

We need to somehow "get rid of" the negative deviations. In mathematics, such a problem is solved by squaring. If a negative number is squared, it becomes positive. So instead of simply adding up the deviations and dividing by the number of scores (N), we first square each deviation, then add together the *squared* deviations and divide by N. Finally, we need to compensate for the squaring operation. To do this, we take the square root of the number just calculated. This leaves us with the **standard deviation.** The larger the standard deviation, the more spread out are the scores in a distribution.

Let's look at an example to make this clearer. Table A.2 lists the hypothetical weights of the 15 participants in the traditional group at the beginning of the study. The mean, which is the sum of the weights divided by 15, is calculated to be 124 pounds, as shown at the bottom of the left-hand column. The first step in computing the standard deviation is to subtract the mean from each score, which gives that score's deviation from the mean. These deviations are

Figure A.4 Distributions with Different Variability Two distributions with the same mean can have very different variability, or spread, as shown in these two curves. Notice how one is more spread out than the other; its scores are distributed more widely.

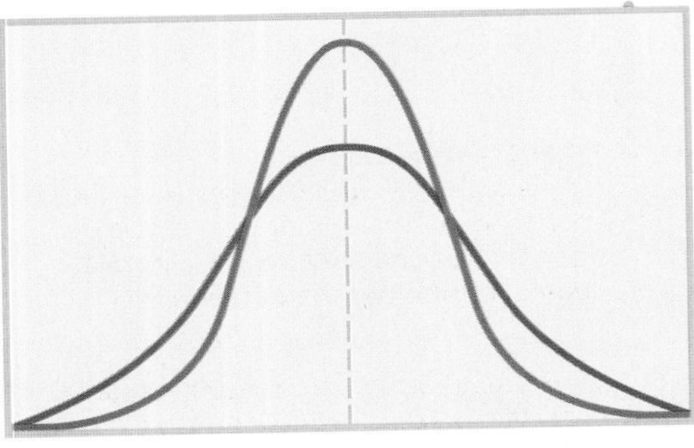

To calculate the standard deviation, you simply add all the scores in a distribution (the left-hand column in this example) and divide by the total number of scores to get the mean. Then you subtract the mean from each score to get a list of deviations from the mean (third column). Next you square each deviation (fourth column), add the squared deviations together, divide by the total number of cases, and take the square root.

Table A.2

Calculating the Standard Deviation

Weight X	Mean $\bar{X}$	Weight − Mean $X - \bar{X}$	(Weight − Mean) Squared $(X - \bar{X})^2$
155	124	31	961
149	124	25	625
142	124	18	324
138	124	14	196
134	124	10	100
131	124	7	49
127	124	3	9
125	124	1	1
120	124	−4	16
115	124	−9	81
112	124	−12	144
110	124	−14	196
105	124	−19	361
102	124	−22	484
95	124	−29	841
Sum (Σ) = 1,860		$\Sigma = 0$	$\Sigma = 4{,}388$
Mean ($\bar{X}$) = 124			

$$SD = \sqrt{\frac{\Sigma(X - \bar{X})^2}{N}} = \sqrt{\frac{4{,}388}{15}} = 17.10$$

listed in the third column of the table. The next step is to square each of the deviations (done in the fourth column), then add the squared deviations (S = 4,388) and divide that total by the number of participants ($N = 15$). Finally, we take the square root to obtain the standard deviation ($SD = 17.10$). The formula for the standard deviation (SD) incorporates these instructions:

$$SD = \sqrt{\frac{\Sigma(X - \bar{X})^2}{N}}$$

Notice that when scores have large deviations from the mean, the *standard deviation* is also large.

z Scores and the Normal Curve

The mean and the standard deviation provide useful descriptive information about an entire set of scores. But researchers can also describe the relative position of any individual score in a distribution. This is done by locating how far away from the mean the score is in terms of standard deviation units. A statistic called a **z score** gives us this information:

$$z = \frac{X - \bar{X}}{SD}$$

This equation says that to compute a z score, we subtract the mean from the score we are interested in (that is, we calculate its deviation from the mean) and divide this quantity by the standard deviation. A positive z score indicates that the score is above the mean, and a negative z score shows that the score is below the mean. The larger the z score, the farther away from the mean the score is.

standard deviation
A measure of variability; expressed as the square root of the sum of the squared deviations around the mean divided by the number of scores in the distribution.

***z* score**
A number, expressed in standard deviation units, that shows a score's deviation from the mean.

standard normal curve or **standard normal distribution**
A symmetrical distribution forming a bell-shaped curve in which the mean, median, and mode are all equal and fall in the exact middle.

Let's take an example from the distribution found in Table A.2. What is the *z* score of a weight of 149 pounds? To find out, you simply subtract the mean from 149 and divide by the standard deviation.

$$z = \frac{149 - 124}{17.10} = 1.46$$

A *z* score of +1.46 tells us that a person weighing 149 pounds falls about one and a half standard deviations above the mean. In contrast, a person weighing 115 pounds has a weight below the mean and would have a negative *z* score. If you calculate this *z* score, you will find it is −.53. This means that a weight of 115 is a little more than one-half a standard deviation below the mean.

Some variables, such as height, weight, and IQ, if graphed for large numbers of people, fall into a characteristic pattern. Figure A.5 shows this pattern, which is called the **standard normal curve** or the **standard normal distribution.** The normal curve is symmetrical (that is, if a line is drawn down its center, one side of the curve is a mirror image of the other side), and the mean, median, and mode fall exactly in the middle. The *x*-axis of Figure A.5 is marked off in standard deviation units, which, conveniently, are also *z* scores. Notice that most of the cases fall between −1 and +1 *SDs*, with the number of cases sharply tapering off at either end. This pattern is the reason the normal curve is often described as "bell shaped."

The great thing about the normal curve is that we know exactly what percentage of the distribution falls between any two points on the curve. Figure A.5 shows the percentages of cases between major standard deviation units. For example, 34.13 percent of the distribution falls between 0 and +1. That means that 84.13 percent of the distribution falls *below* one standard deviation (the 34.13 percent that is between 0 and +1, plus the 50 percent that falls below 0). A person who obtains a *z* score of +1 on some normally distributed variable has scored better than 84 percent of the other people in the distribution. If a variable is normally distributed (that is, if it has the standard bell-shaped pattern), a person's *z* score can tell us exactly where that person stands relative to everyone else in the distribution.

Correlation

So far, the statistical techniques we've looked at focus on one variable at a time, such as hours of aerobic exercise weekly or pounds of weight. Other techniques allow us to look at the relationship, or **correlation,** between two variables. Statistically, the magnitude and direction of the relationship between two variables can be expressed by a single number called a **correlation coefficient**.

To compute a correlation coefficient, we need two sets of measurements from the same individuals or from pairs of people who are similar in some way. To take a

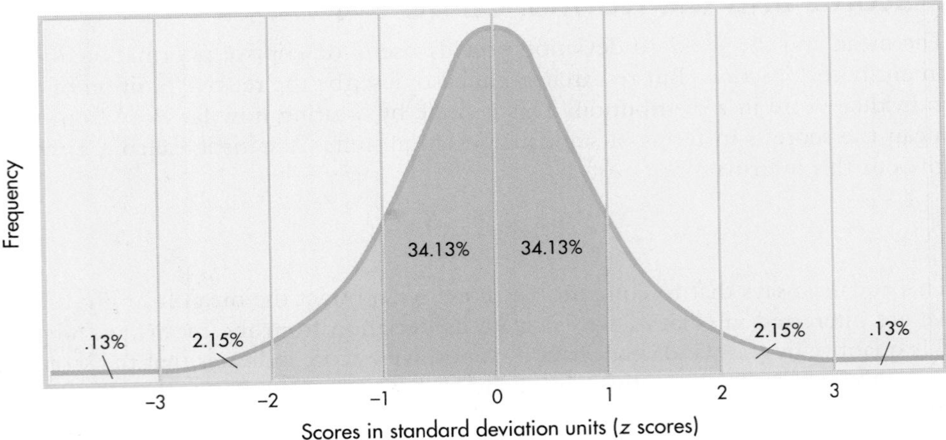

Figure A.5 The Standard Normal Curve
The standard normal curve has several characteristics. Most apparent is its symmetrical bell shape. On such a curve, the mean, the median, and the mode all fall at the same point. But not every curve that is shaped roughly like a bell is a standard normal curve. With a normal curve, specific percentages of the distribution fall within each standard deviation unit from the mean. These percentages are shown on the graph.

simple example, let's determine the correlation between height (we'll call this the *x* variable) and weight (the *y* variable). We start by obtaining height and weight measurements for each individual in a group. The idea is to combine all these measurements into one number that expresses something about the relationship between the two variables, height and weight. However, we are immediately confronted with a problem: The two variables are measured in different ways. Height is measured in inches, and weight is measured in pounds. We need some way to place both variables on a single scale.

Think back to our discussion of the normal curve and *z* scores. What do *z* scores do? They take data of any form and put them into a standard scale. Remember, too, that a high score in a distribution always has a positive *z* score, and a low score in a distribution always has a negative *z* score. To compute a correlation coefficient, the data from both variables of interest can be converted to *z* scores. Therefore, each individual will have two *z* scores: one for height (the *x* variable) and one for weight (the *y* variable).

Then, to compute the correlation coefficient, each person's two *z* scores are multiplied together. All these "cross-products" are added up, and this sum is divided by the number of individuals. In other words, a correlation coefficient is the average (or mean) of the *z*-score cross-products of the two variables being studied:

$$\text{correlation coefficient} = \frac{\sum z_x z_y}{N}$$

A correlation coefficient can range from +1.00 to −1.00. The exact number provides two pieces of information: It tells us about the *magnitude* of the relationship being measured, and it tells us about its *direction.* The magnitude, or degree, of relationship is indicated by the size of the number. A number close to 1 (whether positive or negative) indicates a strong relationship, while a number close to 0 indicates a weak relationship. The sign (+ or −) of the correlation coefficient tells us about the relationship's direction.

A **positive correlation** means that as one variable increases in size, the second variable also increases. For example, height and weight are positively correlated: As height increases, weight tends to increase also. In terms of *z* scores, a positive correlation means that high *z* scores on one variable tend to be multiplied by high *z* scores on the other variable and that low *z* scores on one variable tend to be multiplied by low *z* scores on the other. Remember that just as two positive numbers multiplied together result in a positive number, so two negative numbers multiplied together also result in a positive number. When the cross-products are added together, the sum in both cases is positive.

A **negative correlation,** in contrast, means that two variables are *inversely* related. As one variable increases in size, the other variable decreases. For example, professors like to believe that the more hours students study, the fewer errors they will make on exams. In *z*-score language, high *z* scores (which are positive) on one variable (more

correlation
The relationship between two variables.

correlation coefficient
A numerical indication of the magnitude and direction of the relationship (the correlation) between two variables.

positive correlation
A finding that two factors vary systematically in the same direction, increasing or decreasing in size together.

negative correlation
A finding that two factors vary systematically in opposite directions, one increasing in size as the other decreases.

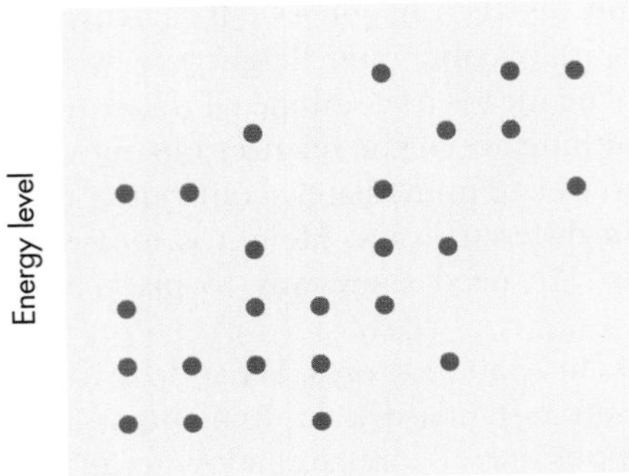

Figure A.6 Scatter Plot of a Positive Correlation A correlation (or the lack of one) can be clearly shown on a scatter diagram. This one shows a moderately strong positive correlation between subjects' compliance with the yoga component of the alternative health-promotion program and their energy level. The positive direction of the correlation is indicated by the upward-sloping pattern of the dots, from bottom left to top right. This means that if one variable is high, the other tends to be high, too, and vice versa. That the strength of the relationship is only moderate is indicated by the fact that the data points (each indicating an individual subject's score) are not all positioned along a straight diagonal line.

hours of study) tend to be multiplied by low *z* scores (which are negative) on the other variable (fewer errors on exams), and vice versa, making negative cross-products. When the cross-products are summed and divided by the number of cases, the result is a negative correlation coefficient.

An easy way to show different correlations is with graphs. Plotting two variables together creates a **scatter diagram** or **scatter plot,** like the ones in Figures A.6, A.7, and A.8. These figures show the relationship between complying with some component of the alternative health-promotion program and some other variable related to health. Although the figures describe relationships actually found in the study, I have made up the specific correlations to illustrate key points.

scatter diagram or **scatter plot** A graph that represents the relationship between two variables.

Figure A.6 shows a moderately strong positive relationship between compliance with the yoga part of the alternative program and a person's energy level. You can see this just by looking at the pattern of the data points. They generally form a line running from lower left to upper right. When calculated, this particular correlation coefficient is +.59, which indicates a correlation roughly in the middle between 0 and +1.00. In other words, people who did more yoga tended to have higher energy levels. The "tended to" part is important. Some people who did not comply well with the yoga routine still had high energy levels, while the reverse was also true. A +1.00 correlation, or a *perfect* positive correlation, would indicate that frequent yoga sessions were *always* accompanied by high levels of energy, and vice versa. What would a scatter diagram of a perfect +1.00 correlation look like? It would be a straight diagonal line starting in the lower left-hand corner of the graph and progressing to the upper right-hand corner.

Several other positive correlations were found in this study. Compliance with the alternative diet was positively associated with increases in energy and positive health

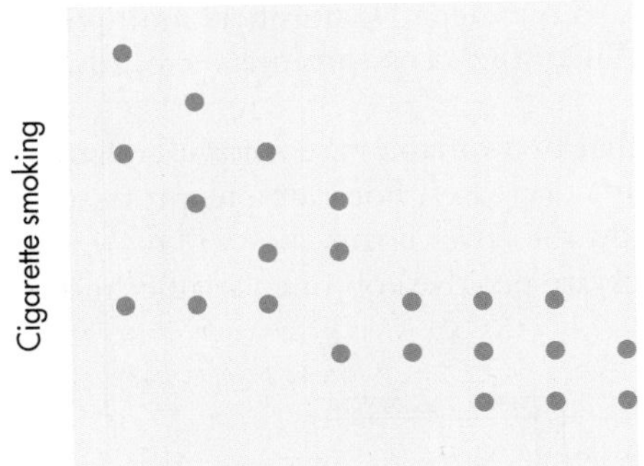

Figure A.7 Scatter Plot of a Negative Correlation In general, people who engage in meditation more often tend to smoke less. This negative correlation is indicated by the downward-sloping pattern of dots, from upper left to lower right. Because these dots are clustered somewhat closer together than those in Figure A.6, we can tell at a glance that the relationship here is somewhat stronger.

Figure A.8 Scatter Plot of No Correlation You may be surprised to learn that in this study, compliance with the aerobic exercise portion of the traditional program was not related to level of coping. This scatter diagram shows that lack of relationship. The points fall randomly, revealing no general direction or trend and thus indicating the absence of a correlation.

perceptions. In addition, following the high-fiber, low-fat traditional diet was associated with a higher level of coping and high vitamin intake.

The study also found some negative correlations. Figure A.7 illustrates a *negative* correlation between compliance with the meditation part of the alternative program and cigarette smoking. This correlation coefficient is −.77. Note that the data points fall in the opposite direction from those in Figure A.6, indicating that as the frequency of meditation increased, cigarette smoking decreased. The pattern of points in Figure A.7 is closer to a straight line than is the pattern of points in Figure A.6. A correlation of −.77 shows a relationship of greater magnitude than does a correlation of +.59. But though −.77 is a relatively high correlation, it is not a perfect relationship. A *perfect* negative relationship would be illustrated by a straight diagonal line starting in the upper left-hand corner of the graph and ending at the lower right-hand corner.

Finally, Figure A.8 shows two variables that are not related to each other. The hypothetical correlation coefficient between compliance with the aerobic exercise part of the traditional program and a person's level of coping is +.03, barely above 0. In the scatter diagram, data points fall randomly, with no general direction to them. From a z-score point of view, when two variables are not related, the cross-products are mixed—that is, some are positive and some are negative. Sometimes high z scores on one variable go with high z scores on the other, and low z scores on one variable go with low z scores on the other. In both cases, positive cross-products result. In other pairs of scores, high z scores on one variable go with low z scores on the other variable (and vice versa), producing negative cross-products. When the cross-products for the two variables are summed, the positive and negative numbers cancel each other out, resulting in a 0 (or close to 0) correlation.

In addition to describing the relationship between two variables, correlation coefficients are useful for another purpose: prediction. If we know a person's score on one of two related variables, we can predict how he or she will perform on the other variable. For example, in a recent issue of a magazine, I found a quiz to rate my risk of heart disease. I assigned myself points depending on my age, HDL ("good") and total cholesterol levels, systolic blood pressure, and other risk factors, such as cigarette smoking and diabetes. My total points (−2) indicated that I had less than a 1 percent risk of developing heart disease in the next five years. How could such a quiz be developed? Each of the factors I rated is correlated to some degree with heart disease. The older you are and the higher your cholesterol and blood pressure, the greater your chance of developing heart disease. Statistical techniques are used to determine the relative importance of each of these factors and to calculate the points that should be assigned to each level of a factor. Combining these factors provides a better prediction than any single factor because none of the individual risk factors correlate perfectly with the development of heart disease.

One thing you cannot conclude from a correlation coefficient is *causality.* In other words, the fact that two variables are highly correlated does not necessarily mean that one variable directly causes the other. Take the meditation and cigarette-smoking correlation. This negative correlation tells us that people in the study who diligently practiced meditation tended to smoke less than those who seldom meditated. Regular meditation may have had a direct effect on the desire to smoke cigarettes, but it is also possible that one or more other variables affected both meditation and smoking. For example, perhaps participation in the study convinced some people that they needed to change their lifestyles completely. Both compliance with the meditation routine and a decreased level of cigarette smoking may have been "caused" by this change in lifestyle. As discussed in Chapter 1, the *experimental method* is the only method that can provide compelling scientific evidence of a cause-and-effect relationship between two or more variables. Can you think of a way to test the hypothesis that regularly practicing meditation causes a reduction in the desire to smoke cigarettes?

inferential statistics
Mathematical methods used to determine how likely it is that a study's outcome is due to chance and whether the outcome can be legitimately generalized to a larger population.

***t*-test**
Test used to establish whether the means of two groups are statistically different from each other.

Inferential Statistics

Let's say that the mean number of physical symptoms (like pain) experienced by the participants in each of the three groups was about the same at the beginning of the health-promotion study. A year later, the number of symptoms had decreased in the two intervention groups but had remained stable in the control group. This may or may not be a meaningful result. We would expect the average number of symptoms to be somewhat different for each of the three groups because each group consisted of different people. And we would expect some fluctuation in level over time, due simply to chance. But are the differences in number of symptoms between the intervention groups and the control group large enough *not* to be due to chance alone? If other researchers conducted the same study with different participants, would they be likely to get the same general pattern of results? To answer such questions, we turn to inferential statistics. **Inferential statistics** guide us in determining what inferences, or conclusions, can legitimately be drawn from a set of research findings.

Depending on the data, different inferential statistics can be used to answer questions such as the ones raised in the preceding paragraph. For example, ***t*-tests** are used to compare the means of two groups. Researchers could use a *t*-test, for instance, to compare average energy level at the end of the study in the traditional and alternative groups. Another *t*-test could compare the average energy level at the beginning and end of the study within the alternative group. If we wanted to compare the means of more than two groups, another technique, *analysis of variance* (often abbreviated as ANOVA), could be used. Each inferential statistic helps us determine how likely a particular finding is to have occurred as a matter of nothing more than chance or random variation. If the inferential statistic indicates that the odds of a particular finding occurring are considerably greater than mere chance, we can conclude that our results are *statistically significant*. In other words, we can conclude with a high degree of confidence that the manipulation of the independent variable, rather than simply chance, is the reason for the results.

To see how this works, let's go back to the normal curve for a moment. Remember that we know exactly what percentage of a normal curve falls between any two *z* scores. If we choose one person at random out of a normal distribution, what is the chance that this person's *z* score is above +2? If you look at Figure A.9 (it's the same as Figure A.5), you will see that 2.28 percent of the curve lies above a *z* score (or standard deviation unit) of +2. Therefore, the chance, or *probability*, that the person we choose will have a *z* score above +2 is .0228 (or 2.28 chances out of 100). That's a pretty small chance. If you study the normal curve, you will see that the majority of cases (95.44 percent of the cases, to be exact) fall between −2 and +2 *SD*s, so in choosing a person at random, that person is not likely to fall above a *z* score of +2.

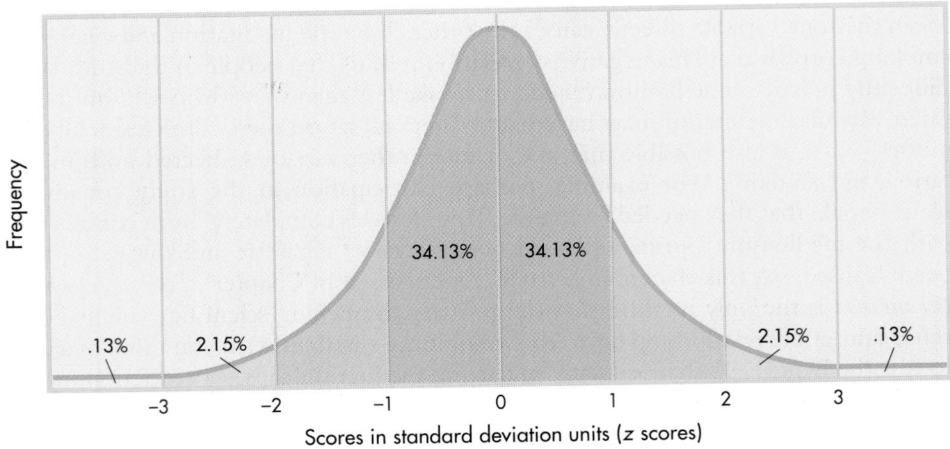

Figure A.9 The Standard Normal Curve

When researchers test for statistical significance, they usually employ statistics other than *z* scores, and they may use distributions that differ in shape from the normal curve. The logic, however, is the same. They compute some kind of inferential statistic that they compare to the appropriate distribution. This comparison tells them the likelihood of obtaining their results if chance alone is operating.

The problem is that no test exists that will tell us for sure whether our intervention or manipulation "worked"; we always have to deal with probabilities, not certainties. Researchers have developed some conventions to guide them in their decisions about whether or not their study results are statistically significant. Generally, when the probability of obtaining a particular result if random factors alone are operating is less than .05 (5 chances out of 100), the results are considered statistically significant. Researchers who want to be even more sure set their probability value at .01 (1 chance out of 100).

Because researchers deal with probabilities, there is a small but real possibility of *erroneously* concluding that study results are significant; this is called a **Type I error**. The results of one study, therefore, should never be completely trusted. For researchers to have greater confidence in a particular effect or result, the study should be repeated, or *replicated*. If the same results are obtained in different studies, then we can be more certain that our conclusions about a particular intervention or effect are correct.

There is a second decision error that can be made—a **Type II error.** This is when a researcher fails to find a significant effect, yet that significant effect really exists. A Type II error results when a study does not have enough *power*; in a sense, the study is not strong enough to find the effect the researcher is looking for. Higher power may be achieved by improving the research design and measuring instruments, or by increasing the number of participants or subjects being studied.

One final point about inferential statistics. Are the researchers interested only in the changes that might have occurred in the small groups of people participating in the health-promotion study, or do they really want to know whether the interventions would be effective for people in general? This question focuses on the difference between a population and a sample. A **population** is a complete set of something—people, nonhuman animals, objects, or events. The researchers who designed this study wanted to know whether the interventions they developed would benefit *all* people (or, more precisely, all people between the ages of 20 and 56). Obviously, they could not conduct a study on this entire population. The best they could do was choose some portion of that population to serve as subjects; in other words, they selected a **sample.** The study was conducted on this sample. The researchers analyzed the sample results, using inferential statistics to make guesses about what they would have found had they studied the entire population. Inferential statistics allow researchers to take the findings they obtain from a sample and apply them to a population.

So what did the health-promotion study find? Did the interventions work? The answer is "yes," sort of. The traditional- and alternative-treatment groups, when combined, improved more than did the no-treatment control group. At the end of the study, participants in the two intervention programs had better self-perceptions regarding health, better mood, more energy, and fewer physical symptoms. Compared with the traditional and the no-treatment groups, the alternative group showed greater improvement in health perceptions and a significant decrease in depression and the use of prescription drugs. Interestingly, participation in the treatment groups did not generally result in changes in health risk, such as lowered blood pressure or decreased weight. The researchers believe that little change occurred because the people who volunteered for the study were basically healthy individuals. The study needs to be replicated with a less healthy sample. In sum, the intervention programs had a greater effect on health perceptions and psychological variables than on physical variables. The researchers concluded that a health-promotion regimen (either traditional or alternative) is helpful. I'm sure other studies will be conducted to explore these issues further!

Type I error
Erroneously concluding that study results are significant.

Type II error
Failing to find a significant effect that does, in fact, exist.

population
A complete set of something—people, nonhuman animals, objects, or events.

sample
A subset of a population.

"It's my fervent hope, Fernbaugh, that these are meaningless statistics."

Endnote

Although I briefly saw other study participants at each three-month data-collection point, I never spoke to anyone. The last measurement session, however, was also a celebration for our yearlong participation in the project. Approximately 30 people attended my session, and participants from each of the three groups were present. After our blood was drawn and our blood pressure and weight readings were taken, we were treated to breakfast. Then one of the principal researchers *debriefed* us: She gave us some background on the study and told us what she hoped to learn. At this point, participants were given the opportunity to talk about how the study had affected their lives. It was fascinating to hear members of the intervention groups describe the changes they had made over the past year. One woman said that a year ago she could never imagine getting up early to meditate, yet now she looks forward to awakening each morning at 4:00 A.M. for her first meditation session. Other people described the modifications they had made in their diet and exercise patterns and how much better they felt. Although I did not experience either of the interventions, I know that simply being a subject in the study made me more conscious of what I ate and how much I exercised. This could have been a confounding factor; that is, it could have inadvertently changed my behavior even though I was in the control group. In fact, my weight decreased and my level of "good" cholesterol increased over the course of the year.

We were not paid for our participation in this study, but we received small gifts as tokens of the researchers' appreciation. In addition, we were all given the option of taking any or all of the intervention training at no cost (and some courses in alternative techniques could be quite expensive). The most important thing for me was the satisfaction of participation—the fact that I had stayed with the study for an entire year and, in a small way, had made a contribution to science.

KEY TERMS

statistics, p. A-2
descriptive statistics, p. A-2
frequency distribution, p. A-3
histogram, p. A-3
frequency polygon, p. A-4
skewed distribution, p. A-4
symmetrical distribution, p. A-4
measure of central tendency, p. A-5
mode, p. A-5
median, p. A-5
mean, p. A-5
measure of variability, p. A-6
range, p. A-6
standard deviation, p. A-6
z score, p. A-7
standard normal curve (standard normal distribution), p. A-8
correlation, p. A-8
correlation coefficient, p. A-8
positive correlation, p. A-9
negative correlation, p. A-9
scatter diagram (scatter plot), p. A-10
inferential statistics, p. A-12
t-test, p. A-12
Type I error, p. A-13
Type II error, p. A-13
population, p. A-13
sample, p. A-13

Web Companion Review Activities

You can find additional review activities at **www.worthpublishers.com/discoveringpsych5e.** The *Discovering Psychology* 5th edition Web Companion has self-scoring practice quizzes, flashcards, interactive crossword puzzles, and other activities to help you master the material in this chapter.

CONCEPT MAP STATISTICS: UNDERSTANDING DATA

Statistics — A branch of mathematics that researchers use to organize and interpret data

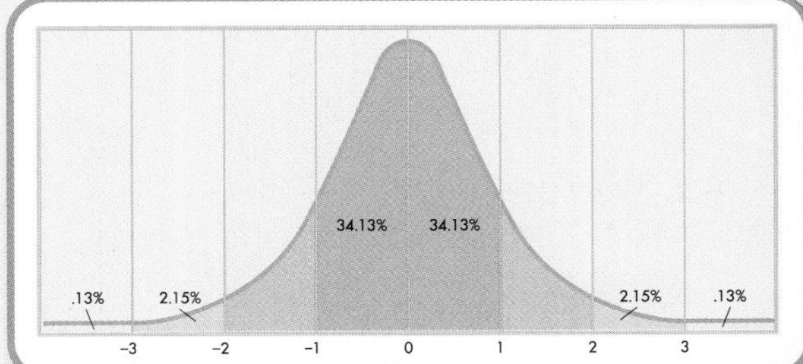

Descriptive Statistics — Summaries of data that make the data meaningful and easy to understand

Frequency distribution:
- Summary of how often various scores occur in a sample of scores
- Can be presented in the form of a table, a **histogram,** or a **frequency polygon**
- Can be **symmetrical distribution** or asymmetrical **(skewed distribution)**
- **Standard normal curve:** A symmetrical distribution forming a bell-shaped curve in which the mean, median, and mode are all equal and fall in the exact middle

Measures of variability show how closely scores in a distribution are grouped.
- **Range:** The highest score minus the lowest score
- **Standard deviation:** The square root of the sum of the squared deviations around the mean divided by the number of scores; eliminates the problem of negative deviations
- ***z* score:** Shows how far away from the mean a score is in terms of standard deviation units

Measures of central tendency of a distribution:
- **Mode:** Most frequent score
- **Median:** Middle score in the distribution
- **Mean:** Arithmetic average of scores; usually the best overall representation of central tendency, but influenced by very high or very low scores

Correlation refers to the relationship between two variables.
- **Positive correlation:** As one variable increases in size, the second variable also increases.
- **Negative correlation:** As one variable increases in size, the second variable decreases.
- A correlational relationship is not necessarily a causal relationship.
- Correlation can be presented visually in a **scatter diagram** or **scatter plot.**

Inferential Statistics
- Used to determine whether a study's outcomes can be generalized to a larger population
- Provide information about whether a study's findings are statistically significant

Population: A complete set of something
Sample: A subset of a population
***t*-test:** Technique used to compare the means of two groups

APPENDIX

B

Industrial/Organizational Psychology

Claudia Cochran-Miller *El Paso Community College*
Marie Waung *University of Michigan, Dearborn*[1]

Appendix Outline

IN THE POPULAR TELEVISION SITCOM *The Office,* Steve Carrell plays Michael Scott, branch office manager of a fictitious paper company. Claiming to be "friend first, boss second," Michael teaches viewers exactly what a manager should *not* say or do. In an episode about sexual harassment, for example, Michael reluctantly announces that he is giving up all non-work-related conversations and jokes, only to immediately lapse into coarse sexual innuendo. It's almost as if he studied the world's worst managers and bought their greatest hits. As a manager, Michael is incompetent, narcissistic, inconsiderate, and blatantly oblivious to any of his deficiencies. His ludicrous approach to problem solving surely leaves experienced managers grinding their teeth. His inappropriate comments and race-based impersonations can send shivers down every human resource manager's spine.

Steve Carrell as Michael Scott in the television sitcom *The Office.*

And this is probably why the show has been so successful. Today's workplace is governed by standards, policies, rules, and laws—all of which Michael flouts on a daily basis. Leading others takes insight, passion, and know-how, none of which Michael possesses. Unfortunately, many managers receive little or no training about assessment, leadership, human relations, human motivation, and the like. Consequently they are often ill-equipped to be effective managers, just like our beloved Michael.

Leadership development has been one of the greatest challenges in the world of industrial and organizational psychology (I/O). This field of psychology also helps build teams, streamline processes, increase job satisfaction, and transform workplace culture, among other objectives. This appendix will introduce you to the many benefits of bringing psychology to the workplace. So, Michael, listen up.

[1]Claudia Cochran-Miller and Marie Waung contributed equally to this appendix.

industrial/organizational (I/O) psychology
The branch of psychology that focuses on the study of human behavior in the workplace.

personnel psychology
A subarea of I/O psychology that focuses on matching people's characteristics to job requirements, accurately measuring job performance, and assessing employee training needs.

organizational behavior
A subarea of I/O psychology that focuses on the workplace culture and its influence on employee behavior.

job analysis
A technique that identifies the major responsibilities of a job, along with the human characteristics needed to fill it.

What Is Industrial/Organizational Psychology?

Industrial/organizational (I/O) psychology is the branch of psychology that focuses on the study of human behavior in the workplace. The "industrial," or "I," side of I/O psychology focuses on measuring human characteristics and matching those characteristics to particular jobs. This process involves applying psychological research findings to personnel functions such as pre-employment testing, placement, training and development, and performance management. This specialty, often called **personnel psychology,** helps companies attract, recruit, select, and train the best employees for the organization.

In contrast, the "organizational," or "O," side focuses on the workplace culture and its influence on employee behavior. Organizational psychology helps companies develop a culture that fulfills organizational goals while addressing employee needs. Organizational psychologists, then, apply psychological findings to areas such as leadership development, team building, motivation, ethics training, and wellness planning. The "O" side of I/O psychology is also called **organizational behavior.**

In their research and work, I/O psychologists generally concentrate on the content areas described below:

1. **Job analysis.** Job analysts must determine the duties of a particular position, as well as the personal characteristics that best match those duties.
2. **Selection and placement.** This area includes the development of assessment techniques to help select job applicants most likely to be successful in a given job or organization.
3. **Training and development.** Psychologists in this field may design customized training programs and evaluate the effectiveness of those programs.
4. **Performance management and evaluation.** Companies are often concerned with ways to improve their performance evaluation systems. Performance management systems include teaching managers how to collect evaluation data, how to avoid evaluation errors, and how to communicate the results.
5. **Organizational development.** The goal of organizational development (OD) is to bring about positive change in an organization, through assessment of the organizational social environment and culture.
6. **Leadership development.** Leadership research strives to identify the traits, behaviors, and skills that great leaders have in common. One goal is matching an organization's mission with the optimal leadership profile.
7. **Team building.** Team membership and successful team design are critical to the needs of today's organizations.
8. **Quality of work life.** Psychologists in this area study the factors that contribute to a productive and healthy workforce, such as perk packages and employee-centered policies.
9. **Ergonomics.** The focus of ergonomics is the design of equipment and the development of work procedures based on human capabilities and limitations. Ergonomics helps employers provide healthier and safer workplaces.

Designing for People One subarea of industrial/organizational psychology is concerned with the human factors involved in the use of workplace procedures and equipment. For example, this factory's procedure for stitching jacket seams requires the sewing machine operator to hold her arms away from her body—an unnatural, painful position. The employer, attentive to ergonomics, installed a pulley system with slings that allow the operator to work with her arms relaxed.

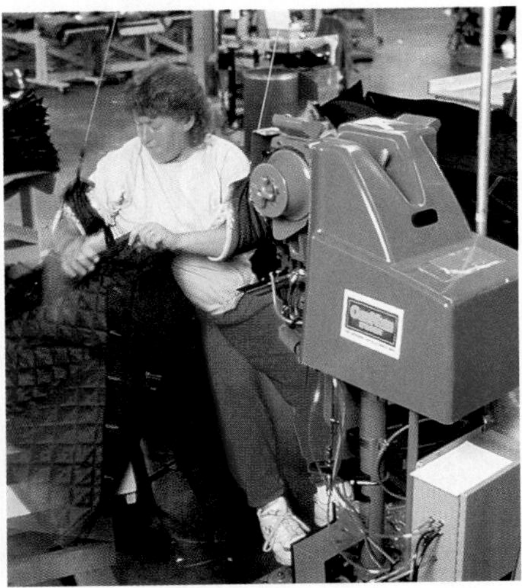

History of I/O Psychology

Although I/O psychology is often misperceived as a new field in psychology, it is actually more than a century old. In Chapter 1, you learned about Wilhelm Wundt, generally credited as the founder of psychology. Wundt's first research assistant, James McKeen Cattell, broke new ground in the field of mental testing (Cattell,

1890), thus influencing the job application process as we know it today. If you've ever taken a personality test, an IQ test, or even a state-mandated academic achievement test, then Cattell's concept of mental testing has affected your life. In 1921, Cattell founded the Psychological Corporation, one of the largest publishers of psychological tests. Today, pre-employment testing has become a basic step for screening job applicants, helping many organizations with their hiring decisions.

Another one of Wundt's students, Hugo Münsterberg, is considered by many to be the father of I/O psychology. His book, *Psychology of Industrial Efficiency* (1913), was the field's first textbook. Here, Münsterberg explained the benefits of matching the job to the worker. He believed that successful matches had multiple benefits, including increased job satisfaction, improved work quality, and higher worker productivity.

Hugo Münsterberg (1863–1916) After earning his Ph.D. in psychology at the University of Leipzig in 1887, Münsterberg established himself as a pioneer in applied psychology, extending his research to business, medical, legal, and educational settings. Invited by William James to teach at Harvard University, Münsterberg taught there until his death.

Industrial (Personnel) Psychology

Three major goals of personnel psychologists are selecting the best applicants for jobs; training employees so that they perform their jobs effectively; and accurately evaluating employee performance. The first step in attaining each of these goals is to perform a job analysis.

Job Analysis

When job descriptions are lacking or inaccurate, employers and employees may experience frustration as tasks are confused and positions are misunderstood or even duplicated. Consequently, I/O psychologists are called upon to conduct job analyses that result in accurate job descriptions, benefiting everyone involved. Outdated or inflated job descriptions may land organizations in legal hot water. More specifically, a job description that indicates more knowledge, skill, or ability than is actually needed to perform well in a job could violate the Americans with Disabilities Act. For example, sewing straight seams may be determined more by one's sense of touch than by perfect vision; thus, if a garment manufacturer required sewing machine operators to have perfect vision, then visually impaired people—some of whom may be able to sew perfect seams—would be excluded unfairly from employment. The Equal Employment Opportunity Commission (EEOC), the Department of Labor (DOL), and the Americans with Disabilities Act (ADA) all endorse job analysis as a precautionary method to avoid legal problems (EEOC, 1999).

Job analysis is a technique that identifies the major responsibilities of a job, along with the human characteristics needed to fill it. Someone performing a job analysis may observe employees at work, interview them, or ask them to complete surveys regarding major job duties and tasks. This information is then used to create or revise job descriptions, such as the example given in Figure B.1 on the next page. Sometimes this information can even be used to restructure an organization.

JOB ANALYST alternate titles: personnel analyst

Collects, analyzes, and prepares occupational information to facilitate personnel, administration, and management functions of organization; consults with management to determine type, scope, and purpose of study. Studies current organizational occupational data and compiles distribution reports, organization and flow charts, and other background information required for study. Observes jobs and interviews workers and supervisory personnel to determine job and worker requirements. Analyzes occupational data, such as physical, mental, and training requirements of jobs and workers, and develops written summaries, such as job descriptions, job specifications, and lines of career movement. Utilizes developed occupational data to evaluate or improve methods and techniques for recruiting, selecting, promoting, evaluating, and training workers, and administration of related personnel programs. May specialize in classifying positions according to regulated guidelines to meet job classification requirements of civil service system, a specialty known as Position Classifier.

Figure B.1 A Sample Job Analysis The job analysis is a crucial tool in personnel psychology. A thorough job analysis can be a necessary step not only for selecting job applicants but also in training employees for specific positions and in evaluating their performance. This job analysis is for the job of job analyst itself.

Source: *Dictionary of Occupational Titles* (1991).

Why should an employer invest in this process? When job analysis is the foundation of recruitment, training, and performance management systems, these systems have a better chance of reducing turnover and improving productivity and morale (Felsberg, 2004).

Job analysis is also important for *designing effective training programs.* In 2007, U.S. organizations spent over $58.5 billion on training programs for their employees ("Training," 2007). I/O psychologists can assist organizations in creating customized and effective training programs that integrate job analysis data with organizational goals. Modern training programs should include collaborative and on-demand methods, such as e-learning, virtual classrooms, and podcasts, so as to maximize training success. "With the younger generation of employees, organizations need to rethink how they deliver learning," explains Karen O'Leonard, analyst and project leader of the "2007 Training Industry Report." "Today the most important trends are toward audio, mobile, and collaborative environments" ("Training," 2007). The best training results are achieved not only through effective delivery methods but also when the training objectives are directly linked to performance measures.

Finally, job analysis is useful in *designing performance appraisal systems.* Job analysis defines and clarifies job competencies so that performance appraisal instruments may be developed and training results can be assessed. This process helps managers make their expectations and ratings clear and easy to understand. As more companies realize the benefits of job analysis, they will call upon I/O psychologists to design customized performance management systems to better track and communicate employee performance.

A Closer Look at Personnel Selection

Whether you are looking for a job or trying to fill a position at your company, it's helpful to understand the personnel selection process. The more you know about how selection decisions are made, the more likely you are to find a job that fits your needs, skills, and interests—and this benefits employers and employees alike.

The goal in personnel selection is to hire only those applicants who will perform the job effectively. There are many selection devices available for the screening process, including psychological tests, work samples, and selection interviews. With so many devices available, each with strengths and weaknesses, personnel psychologists are often called upon to recommend which devices might best be used in a particular selection process. Consequently, they must consider **selection device validity,** the extent to which a selection device is successful in distinguishing between those applicants who will become high performers and those who will not.

Matching Job and Applicant A job analysis helps to pinpoint the qualities a person must have to succeed at a particular job. Not everyone has the special combination of compassion and toughness needed to be an effective physical therapist, for instance.

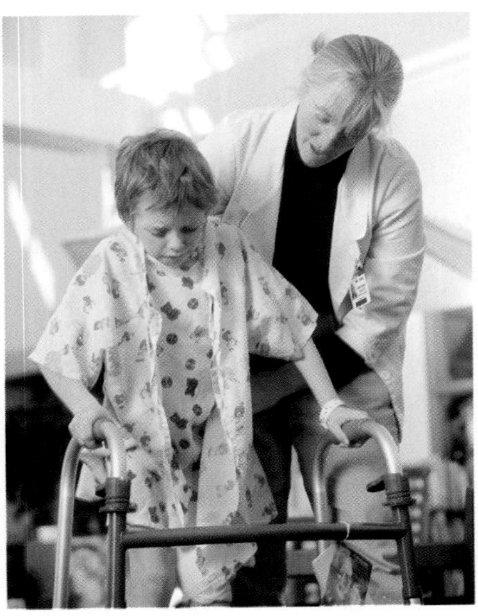

Psychological Tests

Charles Wonderlic, president of the Wonderlic Testing Firm and grandson to the founder, explains why psychological tests are so frequently used in the selection process: "To make better hiring and managing decisions that reduce turnover and improve sales, many store owners add personality profiling tools and other tests to their hiring process because it offers recruiters insight into candidates' traits they may not have even thought to explore" (Wonderlic, 2005). A survey of Fortune 1000 firms ($n = 151$) found that 28 percent of employer respondents use honesty/integrity tests, 22 percent screen for violence potential, and 20 percent screen for personality (Piotrowski & Armstrong, 2006). The survey also reveals that up to a third of employers may soon include online testing as a part of their screening process. Employers want quick, inexpensive, and accurate ways to identify whether applicant qualifications, aptitudes, and personality traits match the position requirements. Common types of psychological tests are integrity/honesty tests, cognitive ability tests, mechanical aptitude tests, motor and sensory ability tests, and personality tests.

Let's first examine the popularity of *integrity tests*, which came about largely because of legislation limiting the use of polygraph tests in the workplace. According to the *2007 National Retail Security Survey* (Hollinger & Adams), employee theft accounted for approximately half of all retail losses, at $19.5 billion—way ahead of the $13.3 billion cost of shoplifting. The hiring of honest employees is definitely in the company's best interest. Unfortunately, integrity tests are plagued with concerns about validity, reliability, fairness, and privacy (Karren & Zacharias, 2007). Some researchers are working diligently to address issues like high rates of false positives, and the ability to "fake" an honest answer (Marcus & others, 2007). Despite these problems, several million integrity tests are administered in the United States every year (Wanek & others, 2003).

Cognitive ability tests measure general intelligence or specific cognitive skills, such as mathematical or verbal ability. The Wonderlic Personnel Test-Revised (WPT-R), was released in January 2007. This 12-minute test of cognitive ability, or general intelligence, has been taken by more than 125 million people since 1937 (Press Release Newswire, 2007). Sample items from two cognitive ability tests are presented in Figure B.2. *Mechanical ability tests* measure mechanical reasoning and may be used to predict job performance for engineering, carpentry, and assembly work. Figure B.3 on the next page presents sample items from the Bennett Test of Mechanical Comprehension. *Motor ability tests* include measures of fine dexterity in fingers and hands, accuracy and speed of arm and hand movements, and eye–hand coordination. *Sensory ability tests* include measures of visual acuity, color vision, and hearing.

selection device validity
The extent to which a personnel selection device is successful in distinguishing between those who will become high performers at a certain job and those who will not.

(a) 1. RESENT/RESERVE — Do these words
1 have similar meanings
2 have contradictory meanings
3 mean neither the same nor opposite
2. Paper sells for 21 cents per pad. What will 4 pads cost?

(b)

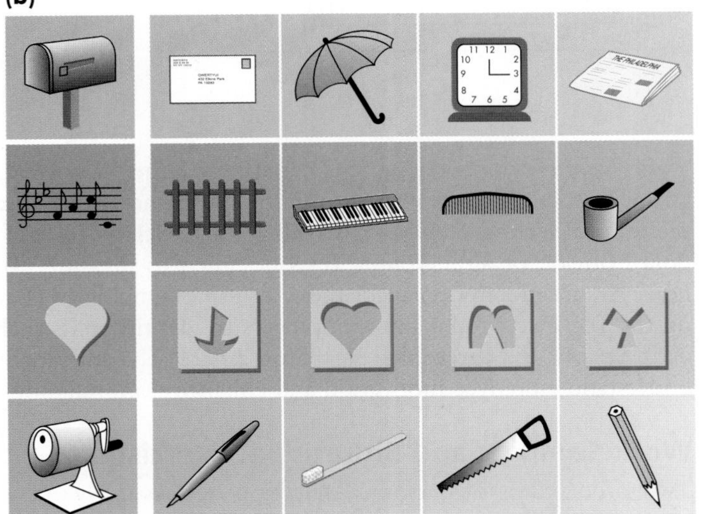

For each item find the picture that goes best with the picture in the first box. Draw a dark line from the upper right corner to the lower left corner in the proper box to show the right answer.

Figure B.2 Sample Items from Two Cognitive Ability Tests Cognitive ability tests can measure either general intelligence or specific cognitive skills, such as mathematical ability. **(a)** These two items are from the Wonderlic Personnel Test, which is designed to assess general cognitive ability. Employers assume that people who cannot answer most questions correctly would not be good candidates for jobs that require general knowledge and reasoning skills. **(b)** The chart is from the Non-Verbal Reasoning Test. It assesses reasoning skills apart from the potentially confounding factor of skill with the English language.

Sources: Corsini (1958); Wonderlic (1998).

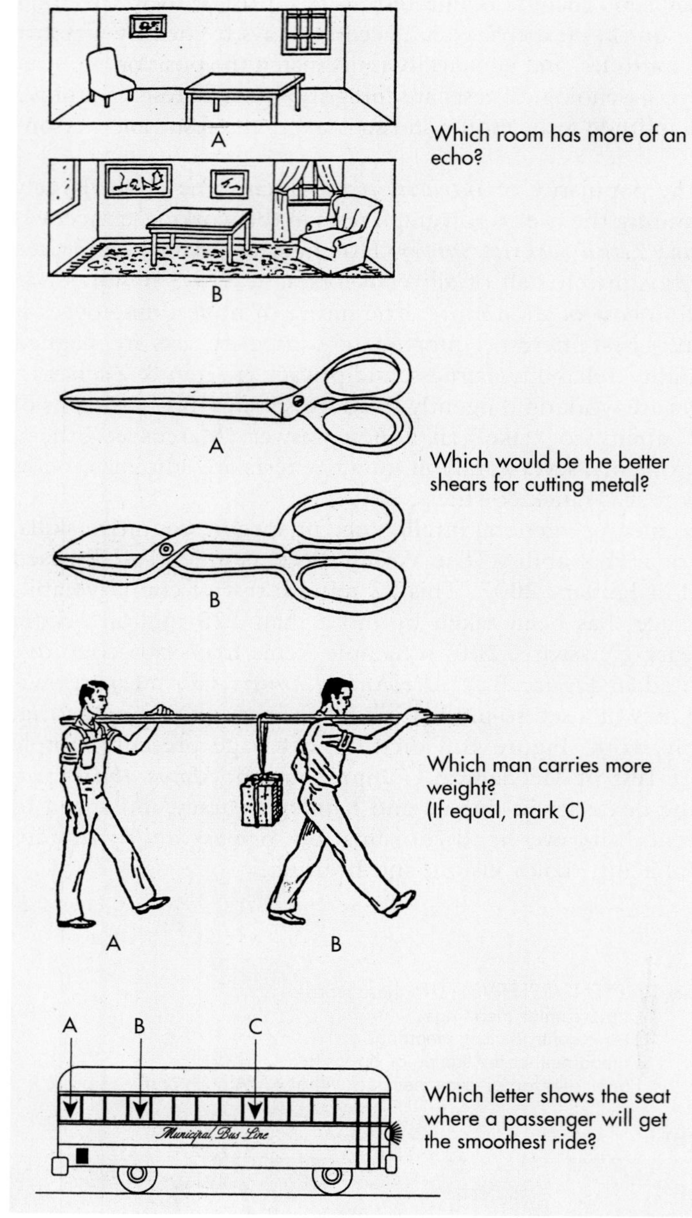

Figure B.3 Sample Items from a Mechanical Ability Test Questions such as these from the Bennett Test of Mechanical Comprehension are designed to assess a person's ability to figure out the physical properties of things. Such a test might be used to predict job performance for carpenters or assembly-line workers.

Source: Bennett (1940).

Personality tests are designed to measure either abnormal or normal personality characteristics. An assessment of abnormal personality characteristics might be appropriate for selecting people for sensitive jobs, such as nuclear power plant operator, police officer, or airline pilot. Tests designed to measure normal personality traits, however, are more popular for the selection of employees (Bates, 2002). Tests based on the Big Five Model allow employers to identify traits such as conscientiousness, extraversion, and agreeableness (Bates, 2002). This information can also be used to understand employee motivation and enhance team building and team placement.

Work Samples and Situational Exercises

Two other kinds of personnel selection devices are work samples and situational exercises. Work samples are typically used for jobs involving the manipulation of objects, while situational exercises are usually used for jobs involving managerial or professional skills. Work samples have been called "high-fidelity simulations" in that they require applicants to complete tasks as if they were on the job (Motowidlo & others, 1997). Recently, companies like Toyota, Quest Diagnostics, and SunTrust Bank have been using interactive job simulations in their selection steps.

At Toyota, applicants must demonstrate their ability to read dials and gauges and spot safety problems in a virtual setting as a part of their "Computer Assembler Audition." Quest Diagnostics is using online video previewing of jobs to educate potential applicants about the typical workday of a phlebotomist. This step helps reduce turnover. Finally, use of an online screening and assessment system allowed SunTrust Bank to shorten the previous two- to four-week pre-employment process down to a single week. Employers are also learning that "Job simulations can reduce the risk of litigation, since these methods are more closely aligned to the job." (Winkler, 2006).

Selection Interviews

Great news! You passed the pre-employment test and have been called in for an interview. Now it's just a matter of sailing through the *objective* interview, right? Wrong! Chances are that the company's interviewing methods are subjective, outdated, and non-research based. The Society for Human Resource Management (SHRM) found that many companies continue to ignore the growing body of research that supports objective selection strategies. In its 2006 survey, SHRM found that as many as 40 percent of responding companies reported continued use of unstructured interviews, sometimes developed "off-the-cuff," as opposed to the structured behavioral interviews recommended by the research. Furthermore, only 24 percent actually used scoring scales to rate the interviewee responses, fostering even greater subjectivity.

In contrast to unstructured interviews, *structured behavioral interviews,* if developed and conducted properly, are adequate predictors of job performance. A structured interview should be based on a job analysis; prepared in advance; standardized for all applicants; and evaluated by a panel of interviewers trained to record and rate the applicant's responses using a numeric rating scale. When these criteria are met, the interview is likely to be an effective selection tool (Krohe, 2006).

Organizational Behavior

Organizational behavior (OB) focuses on how the organization and the social environment in which people work affects their attitudes and behaviors. Job satisfaction is the attitude most thoroughly researched by I/O psychologists, with over 10,000 studies to date. The impact of leadership on attitudes and behaviors is another well-researched OB topic. We will examine both of these topics here.

Job Satisfaction

Lucy and Jane are both engineers who work in the same department of the same company. Lucy is almost always eager to get to work in the morning. She feels that her work is interesting and that she has plenty of opportunities to learn new skills. In contrast, Jane is unhappy because she feels that she doesn't get the recognition she deserves at work. She also complains that the company doesn't give enough vacation time to employees and that it provides inadequate benefits. Jane can't think of many good things about her job. She's even beginning to feel that her job is negatively affecting her personal life.

Fortunately, Lucy is more typical of U.S. workers than Jane is. A recent *International Herald Tribune*/France 24/Harris Interactive survey reported that at least two-thirds of U.S. workers say they are satisfied with the type of work they do and their pay (Harris Interactive, 2007).

discrepancy hypothesis
An approach to explaining job satisfaction that focuses on the discrepancy, if any, between what a person wants from a job and how that person evaluates what is actually experienced at work.

trait approach to leader effectiveness
An approach to determining what makes an effective leader that focuses on the personal characteristics displayed by successful leaders.

Several approaches have been used to explain differences in job satisfaction. An early approach was based on a **discrepancy hypothesis,** which consists of three ideas: (1) that people differ in what they want from a job; (2) that people differ in how they evaluate what they experience at work; and (3) that job satisfaction is based on the difference between what is desired and what is experienced (Lawler, 1973; Locke, 1976). Lucy and Jane, for instance, may not only want different things from their jobs; they may also make different assessments of the same events at work. Although their supervisor may treat them in the same encouraging manner, Lucy may see the boss's encouragement as supportive while Jane may view it as condescending. As a result, one perceives a discrepancy between desires and experiences, whereas the other does not.

Consequent research supported the discrepancy hypothesis. For example, negative discrepancies (getting less than desired) were found to be related to dissatisfaction. Interestingly, positive discrepancies (getting more than desired) were also related to dissatisfaction in some cases (Rice & others, 1989). As an example, you might be dissatisfied with a job because it involves more contact with customers than you wanted or expected.

However, other factors have been identified as contributing to job satisfaction. The 2007 SHRM Job Satisfaction Survey lists compensation, benefits, job security, work–life balance, and communication between employees and senior management as the current top five "very important" job satisfaction aspects for employees (Lockwood, 2007).

Leadership

I/O psychologists have invested extensive energy searching for the formula for a great leader. *Leaders* are those who have the ability to direct groups toward the attainment of organizational goals. There are several classic theories that shaped our early views of leadership. The **trait approach to leader effectiveness,** one of the earliest theories, was based on the idea that great leaders are *born*, not made. This approach assumed that leaders possess certain qualities or characteristics resulting in natural abilities to lead others. Some examples of these "natural-born" leaders included John F. Kennedy, Martin Luther King Jr., and Nelson Mandela. A large number of traits—such as height, physical attractiveness, dominance, resourcefulness, and intelligence—were examined for connections to leader effectiveness. A substantial amount of trait research was initially conducted, much of it showing little connection between personal traits and leader effectiveness (Hollander & Julian, 1969; Stogdill, 1948). Recent trait research continues, with some studies identifying traits, such as emotional intelligence, that can have a positive impact on employee behavior (Rego & others, 2007). Unfortunately, to date, trait researchers still haven't found a comprehensive "leadership recipe."

What Makes a Leader? Nelson Mandela is an extraordinarily charismatic leader. He kept his political organization, the African National Congress, functioning during his 27 years of imprisonment and guided South Africa out of its racist apartheid system with a minimum of violence and turmoil.

Consequently the emphasis turned to another explanation for effective leadership. Could leaders be *made*? Could they be taught "leadership behaviors" that would make them more effective? Researchers exploring the

behavioral theories of leader effectiveness reasoned that the behaviors of effective and ineffective leaders must differ. In 1960, Douglas McGregor published *The Human Side of Enterprise,* in which he outlined Theory X and Theory Y, creating the view that leaders were polarized into those who either cared about the job (X) or cared about the people (Y). Research on these two dimensions found that ineffective managers focused only on one dimension. For example, if your boss cares only about production, then your job satisfaction and morale may decline. In contrast, if your boss is "all heart" but holds no production expectations, your job satisfaction may be high but your productivity low (Bass, 1981; Locke & Schweiger, 1979). A few years after McGregor's book was published, Robert Blake and Jane Mouton expanded upon the theory with their Managerial Grid, claiming it was possible to care about *both* productivity and people. By placing these two variables on a grid, they could plot five primary managerial styles (see Figure B.4). A manager with low ratings in both areas was labeled (1,1) an "Impoverished Manager." In contrast, one scoring highest on both concern for production and concern for people was labeled (9,9) the "Team Leader" (Blake & Mouton, 1985).

Next to evolve were **situational** (or **contingency**) **theories of leadership,** which stated that there was no one "best" way to manage *every* employee. These theories claimed that good leadership skills depend, or are contingent upon, various situational factors, such as the structure of the task and the willingness of the follower. Accordingly, the best leaders will utilize the leadership style most appropriate for the employee and the situation at hand. These theories tended to be complicated, but they did a better job of explaining leader effectiveness than either the trait approach or behavioral theories.

Much of the research on leadership emphasized the impact of leaders on followers, ignoring the fact that followers also influence leaders. In contrast, a modern approach called the **leader–member exchange model** emphasizes two types of relationships that can develop between leaders and employees. Positive leader–member relationships

behavioral theories of leader effectiveness
Theories of leader effectiveness that focus on differences in the behaviors of effective and ineffective leaders.

situational (contingency) theories of leadership
Leadership theories claiming that various situational factors influence a leader's effectiveness.

leader–member exchange model
A model of leadership emphasizing that the quality of the interactions between supervisors and subordinates varies depending on the unique characteristics of both.

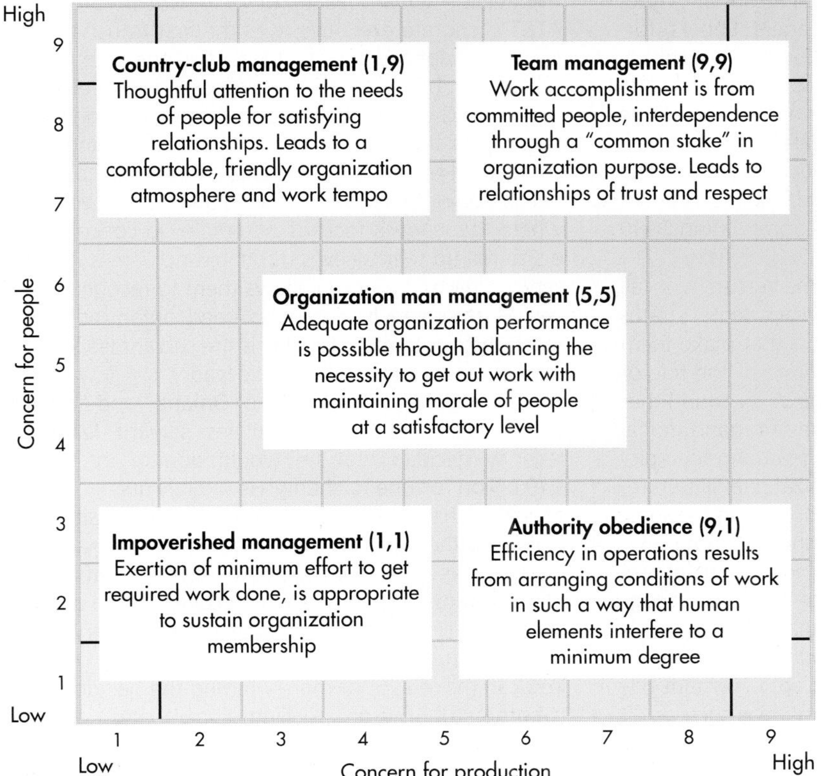

Figure B.4 Robert Blake and Jane Mouton's "Managerial Grid" identifies five different leadership styles. With *concern for production* as the *x*-axis and *concern for the people* as the *y*-axis, managerial styles can be assessed based on whether they rank low or high on these concerns.

What Makes a Leader? At 23 he was worth $1 million, at 24 it was $10 million, by 25 it was over $100 million, and by 30 years of age his board of directors fired him from the company he started. Who is he? Steve Jobs, of course. When he and Steve Wozniak began building computers in his parents' garage, neither one imagined what the future held: the multinational company Apple Inc. *Fortune* credits Jobs with changing the world through computers, phones, music, retailing, and movies. In 2008, *Fortune* chose Jobs as "#1 Most Powerful Business Person" and labeled Apple a "Most Admired Company." Jobs's leadership style wasn't always ideal, as he acknowledges when discussing his past. Fortunately for his many Apple employees, he has learned from his leadership mistakes. Victor Vroom, professor at the Yale School of Management, considers Jobs a transformational leader who "stands for higher order values. . . . [H]e has caused people to do things they might never have done before" (George, 2006).

are characterized by mutual trust, respect, and liking. These relationships have numerous benefits, including higher job satisfaction, goal commitment, improved work climate, and lower turnover rates (Gerstner & Day, 1997). Negative leader–member relationships show a lack of trust, respect, and liking. These relationships lead to decreased job satisfaction and job performance, among other consequences (Gomez & Rosen, 2001). This research shows that effective leaders manage to establish positive relationships by setting high expectations and making an effort to build trust and reciprocal respect.

More recently, leadership research has focused on topics such as transformational versus transactional leadership, charismatic leadership, shared leadership, and servant leadership, which is highlighted in the In Focus box "Servant Leadership: When It's Not All About You." Although they've yet to find the formula for a perfect leader, researchers have shed a bright light on the optimal conditions for leadership development.

IN FOCUS

Servant Leadership: When It's Not All About You

What do Jeffrey Skilling, Bernard Ebbers, and Dennis Kozlowski have in common? They were all entrusted with leadership positions for corporate giants such as Enron, WorldCom, and Tyco. They also failed miserably in their posts as leaders. Ebbers, former CEO of WorldCom, was convicted of fraud and conspiracy and is said to have been personally responsible for the $11 billion loss to WorldCom investors. Formerly CEO of the now-defunct Enron, Jeffrey Skilling is in federal prison after having been found guilty of fraud and insider trading in one of America's most notorious cases of corporate corruption. Kozlowski, too, is in prison, convicted of misappropriating $400 million of his company's funds while he was CEO of Tyco.

All three of these individuals are what some researchers call *narcissistic leaders.* Research on selfish leadership demonstrates that narcissistic leaders display certain behaviors that make them more likely to take self-serving risks, inconsiderate of the role of stewardship placed upon them as leaders. One study found that such CEOs focus on themselves at the expense of organizational awareness (Chatterjee & Hambrick, 2007). By featuring their pictures, their names, and their stories on organizational literature, these CEOs demand all the attention, instead of sharing the spotlight with the hardworking "stagehands" behind the scenes.

If you've ever known a highly narcissistic individual, it was probably not by choice. As employees, we like to receive recognition and at least some acknowledgement that what we do is valued. Selfish leaders are unable to fill our needs because of their own need to have their egos stroked on a constant basis. Their belief system includes self-promoting ideas such as, "I am, by far, the most valuable person in this organization," or "Leadership is a solo endeavor, not a group activity" (Chatterjee & Hambrick, 2007).

Enter the servant leader. In 1970, Robert Greenleaf, a retired AT&T corporate executive, was the first to use the term *servant leader*. He defined a servant leader as one who makes service to others, including one's employees, the foremost leadership objective. Greenleaf believed that servant leaders are successful because of their sincere commitment to helping their followers succeed. They invert the organizational chart, placing employee needs above their own (Zandy, 2007). Employee centeredness, where the leader's focus is on employee concerns, allows leaders to roll up their sleeves during crunch times. Most important, servant leaders' humility allows them to recognize their employees as emerging leaders who need organizational support to reach their potential. Humility is the servant leader's most prominent trait, unlike the narcissistic leader.

Warren Buffet, "The Oracle of Omaha" and richest man in the world (Miller, 2008), exemplifies servant leadership. Buffet recently decided that he would donate the majority of his $40 billion fortune to charity. He did this quietly and strategically, typical of his humble demeanor. His generosity of spirit, little known to the public, is often masked by his financial success. As a leader, he values the development of his staff and colleagues, often acknowledging his own mistakes before announcing their successes. His ethical transparency allows everything to be disclosed. Buffet says, "You don't need to play outside the lines. You can make a lot of money hitting the ball down the middle" (George, 2006). If only Skilling, Ebbers, and Kozlowski had followed his lead.

Workplace Trends and Issues

The Society for Human Resource Management (SHRM, 2007) has identified the top challenges facing companies today:

1. Succession planning (replacement of retiring leaders)
2. Recruitment and selection of talented employees
3. Engaging and retaining talented employees
4. Providing leaders with the skills to be successful
5. Rising health care costs
6. Creating/maintaining a performance-based culture (rewarding exceptional job performance)

To face these challenges, the workplace of the future is expected to become more dynamic, diversified, flexible, and responsive. Organizations and their employees will need to adapt to the ever-changing world of work, complete with resource limitations and technological innovations. Let's examine how some of these challenges are being addressed.

Workforce Diversity: Recruiting and Retaining Diverse Talent

Changing workforce demographics continue to challenge many employers (see the In Focus box "Name, Title, Generation"). Diverse employees have diverse needs, interests, and expectations. Organizations that can best address these issues will be

IN FOCUS

Name, Title, Generation

If you visit MySpace, Facebook, and YouTube as part of your daily routine, you're probably a millennial. If avatar, blog, and Wiki don't sound like Star Wars characters to you, then you're surely a millennial. So what's a millennial? Google it, and you'll find millennials are the Net Generation, born between 1981–1999. Millennials, also called Generation Y, are walking around loaded—with gadgets, that is. They are the most technologically savvy generation, and they have entered the workplace. They're great at multi-tasking, pragmatic thinking, future-looking, team playing, and tech-operating. But they have their faults, too: They wear iPods during meetings, assume everything is public, have narcissistic tendencies, demand immediate praise, and don't like to be criticized, not even constructively (Tyler, 2008).

Generation gaps are challenging employers in many ways. Some employers are seeing as many as four generations of workers walk through their doors. In their book titled *When Generations Collide: Who They Are. Why They Clash. How to Solve the Generational Puzzle at Work* (2002), authors Lynne C. Lancaster and David Stillman discuss the generational issues facing the workplace. Multiple age groups means differing values, goals, and perceptions. In one example, they describe the ways the four generations view the process of feedback:

- Traditionalists (born 1900–1945): No news is good news.
- Baby boomers (born 1946–1964): Once a year, with lots of documentation.

Differing Work Styles Millennials often prefer to work collaboratively and may be most comfortable with the constant interaction that this work environment facilitates.

- Generation Xers (born 1965–1980): Sorry to interrupt, but how am I doing?
- Millennials (born 1981–1999): Feedback whenever I want it at the push of a button . . . and NOW!

Surely, the workplace of the future must embrace all generations, train them to get along, and build complementary teams. Leaders of the future will need to inspire *all* of their employees, from the traditionalists to the millennials alike.

most likely to attract top candidates. Several organizations are creating excellent perk packages to recruit among the diversified field of top candidates. *Fortune's* "100 Best Companies to Work For" (2008) shows more companies are offering telecommuting (84 percent), compressed workweeks (82 percent), on-site gyms (69 percent), job sharing (63 percent), and on-site child care (29 percent), many of which are highly desirable to different populations such as working parents or older workers. Google, *Fortune's* Best Company, doesn't stop there. At Google headquarters in Mountain View, California, employees enjoy an amazing variety of on-site services such as gourmet meals, child care, health care, oil changes, car washes, dry cleaning, massage therapy, gyms, hairstylists, and fitness classes, to name just a few. Often called the Google Campus, this laid-back environment has proved successful in attracting the best candidates in the industry.

Telework and Telecommuting: The Best Retention Tool

The latest estimates show that 33 million Americans hold jobs that could be performed at home by telecommuting (Fisher, 2008). Telecommuting programs offer advantages such as flexible work schedules, more freedom at work, and less time wasted commuting. One study focused on the best practices of several telework organizations, including Intel Corporation, Hewlett-Packard, and Dow Chemical Corporation. These organizations were identified as having model telework programs in place, with recruitment and retention as the primary organizational benefits (Telework Coalition, 2006). More recently, the 2008–2009 WorldatWork Salary Budget Survey (n = 2,288) reported that the number of respondent employers offering telework options to their employees jumped from 30 percent in 2007 to 42 percent in 2008 (WorldatWork, 2008–2009). As with any major change in the workplace, telework poses new challenges to organizations. How does working from home affect performance, workplace relations, and career prospects? A recent meta-analysis asked these and many other questions about the effects of telecommuting (Gajendran & Harrison, 2007). The researchers found telecommuting has predominantly positive effects for both employees and employers, including higher job satisfaction, employee morale and autonomy, and improved supervisor–employee relations. I/O psychologists may guide employers to accept telework as an important solution to many problems.

Telework or Telecommuting: Working at Home As telecommunication technology has become more widespread, so has the number of employees who *telecommute* or work from home. For the self-motivated individual with good communication skills, telecommuting offers the advantages of greater autonomy and flexible time management. On the down side, teleworkers are more likely to work in the evenings and on the weekends (Steward, 2000). Men and women vary in their reasons for telecommuting. Being able to earn money and care for their children at the same time is a motivating factor for many women (Sullivan & Lewis, 2001). The man pictured in this photograph regularly works from home to avoid a long commute. His office uses videoconferencing, instant messaging, and other communications technology to stay connected.

Internet Recruiting: Using the Web to Recruit Top Talent

Internet job-search services, such as monster.com, hotjobs.com, and company Web sites have changed the way in which employees are recruited. In its 2007 survey, the Conference Board, a global business membership and research organization, found that 73 percent of job seekers used the Internet to find information about prospective employers, to post resumes on job boards, and to gain career advice. This surge in Internet job-seeking poses new challenges for employers, such as compliance with new legal requirements for online applicant tracking, or simply how to narrow down the multitude of resume submissions brought on by the ease of resume posting.

Work–Life Balance: Engaging and Retaining Employees with Families

Juggling between the demands of a career and one's family can lead to many conflicts. This struggle, often called *work–family conflict*, results in higher absenteeism, lower morale, and higher turnover in the workplace. Further, results from a meta-analysis reviewing 38 studies found that employee perceptions of family-friendly work culture, along with supportive bosses and spouses, can reduce work–family conflict (Mesmer-Magnus & Viswesvaran, 2006). Therefore, it makes good business sense to help working parents balance the demands of work and family life. Unfortunately, several studies indicate that few U.S. employers have family-friendly policies. A recent *Forbes* survey revealed that the U.S. workplace is not family-oriented when compared to other industrialized countries (*Forbes,* 2007). The *Forbes* survey found that paid maternity and paternity leave, paid sick days, alternative work schedules, and other such family-friendly policies are lacking in many U.S. companies. Research also shows that "Workplace policies for families in the U.S. are weaker than those of *all* high-income countries and even many middle- and low-income countries" (Heymann, 2007). Although many companies are talking the talk by advertising flexible schedules and family-friendliness, for example, few of them are walking the walk and actually building family-friendly environments. More employers must begin to adopt family-friendly policies and build pro-family cultures to attract and retain this large sector of the workforce.

To keep pace with evolving challenges such as the ones described above, I/O psychologists will constantly need to adjust the focus of their research and its applications. In the future, I/O psychologists will continue to have a significant role in and around the workplace. To explore what it's like to be an I/O psychologist, we'll look at the preparation required for the job, and where you might go from there.

Employment Settings, Type of Training, Earnings, and Employment Outlook

Many I/O psychologists belong to Division 14 of the American Psychological Association (APA), the Society for Industrial and Organizational Psychology (SIOP). The division conducts periodic surveys of its members and, as a result, can supply information on topics such as typical work settings, job duties, and salary levels of I/O psychologists.

The employment settings of I/O psychologists are represented in Figure B.5 on the next page. Of the I/O psychologists who belong to SIOP and who responded to the 2006 employment setting survey, 41 percent worked in academic settings (primarily universities and colleges); 22 percent worked as consultants to organizations; 17 percent worked in private organizations; and 9 percent worked for public organizations (Khanna & Medsker, 2007).

Those with bachelor's degrees may find work in fields related to I/O psychology, such as in the administration of training programs or as interviewers. However, a master's (M.A.) or doctorate (Ph.D.) degree is required to work in the field of I/O psychology. Though there are plenty of programs to choose from, with more than 200 master's and doctorate programs available for I/O psychologists in the United States, admission into these programs can be very competitive, especially at the doctoral level.

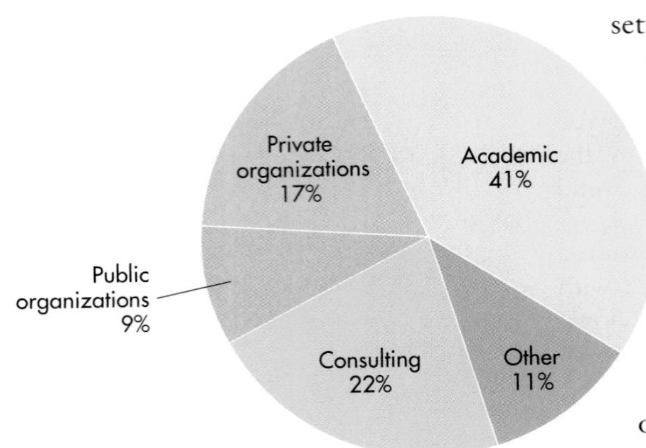

Figure B.5 Work Settings of I/O Psychologists Most I/O psychologists work in institutions of higher education. Forty-one percent of the members of the Society for Industrial and Organizational Psychology work in colleges and universities. Next come I/O psychologists who work as consultants to organizations (22 percent). Another substantial percentage (17 percent) are employed by large private corporations, such as insurance companies and consumer-product manufacturers. Public organizations, such as government agencies, employ half as many I/O psychologists as private organizations do (9 percent versus 17 percent).

Source: Khanna & Medsker (2007).

The majority of SIOP members hold doctorate degrees (87 percent) as opposed to master's degrees (13 percent). When selecting your degree, you must consider the length and requirements of the program. Are you prepared to attend graduate school as a full-time student for five to six years, conduct a detailed research project, and write a dissertation? If your answer to these questions is yes, then a doctorate degree may be for you. This degree qualifies you for I/O psychologist positions at major corporations and research and teaching positions at colleges and universities, and it provides the most credibility to conduct consulting work.

If you would prefer to pursue a degree that allows you to quickly apply your knowledge and skills to the workplace, then a master's degree may be a better fit. Most master's programs require two to three years of graduate course work and the completion of a research project. Having a master's degree allows you to work as an I/O psychologist carrying out I/O duties for private or public organizations, teach at two-year colleges, and take on consulting opportunities.

Finally, a bachelor's degree, attained after four years of undergraduate course work, yields numerous employment opportunities in areas involving I/O psychology. These positions include jobs for personnel, training, and labor-relations specialists. Although these jobs are expected to show faster-than-average job growth through the year 2016, the high number of qualified college graduates and experienced workers will keep these jobs highly competitive (U.S. Bureau of Labor Statistics, 2008).

What's the payoff for all this education and hard work? Salaries for I/O psychologists are dependent upon educational qualifications, industry, and experience. The 2006 salary survey of SIOP members indicated that the median salary for those with doctorate degrees was $98,500; for those with master's degrees, the median salary was $72,000 (Khanna & Medsker, 2007). It also helps to know that the job market for I/O psychologists has remained strong over the years and is projected to have an above-average growth rate (21 percent) through 2016 (Occupational Outlook Handbook, 2008–2009).

If you would like to learn more about career opportunities in I/O psychology, visit some of the Web sites listed in Table B.1.

Table B.1

Below is a list of Web sites that relate to working in the field of industrial/organizational psychology.

www.aomonline.org	Academy of Management
www.dol.gov	U.S. Department of Labor Job Information Site
www.shrm.org	Society for Human Resource Management
www.siop.org	Society for Industrial and Organizational Psychology
www.bls.gov	U.S. Department of Labor, Bureau of Labor Statistics
www.onetcenter.org	Occupational Information Network

APPENDIX REVIEW: KEY TERMS

industrial/organizational (I/O) psychology, p. B-2
personnel psychology, p. B-2
organizational behavior, p. B-2
job analysis, p. B-3
selection device validity, p. B-4
discrepancy hypothesis, p. B-8
trait approach to leader effectiveness, p. B-8
behavioral theories of leader effectiveness, p. B-9
situational (contingency) theories of leadership, p. B-9
leader–member exchange model, p. B-9

Web Companion Review Activities

You can find additional review activities at **www.worthpublishers.com/discoveringpsych5e.** The *Discovering Psychology* 5th edition Web Companion has self-scoring practice quizzes, flashcards, interactive crossword puzzles, and other activities to help you master the material in this chapter.

CONCEPT MAP

INDUSTRIAL/ORGANIZATIONAL PSYCHOLOGY

Industrial/Organizational Psychology

The study of human behavior in the workplace

Personnel Psychology

A sub-area of I/O psychology that focuses on matching people's characteristics to job requirements, accurately measuring job performance, and assessing employee training needs

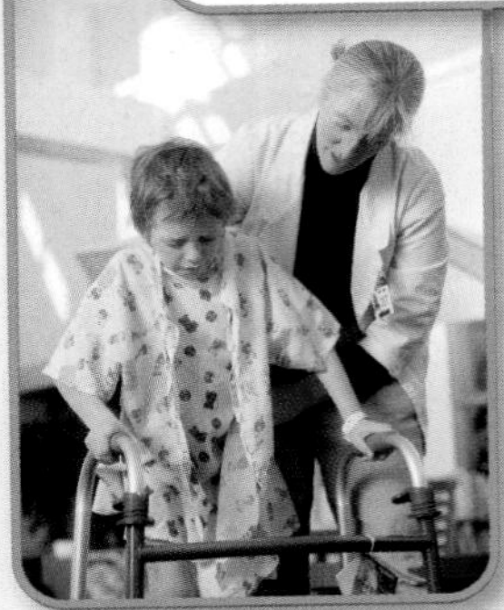

- A **job analysis** helps determine the major responsibilities of a job and the human characteristics needed to fill it.
- **Selection device validity** is the extent to which a device such as an interview or work sample helps distinguish applicants who will become high performers.
- Psychological tests used in the selection process include integrity tests, cognitive ability tests, and personality tests.

Organizational Behavior

A sub-area of I/O psychology that focuses on the workplace culture and its influence on employee behavior

- **Job satisfaction** is studied by examining the discrepancy hypothesis, which looks at the gaps between what a person wants from a job and what that person actually experiences.
- Leadership effectiveness has been studied through the **trait approach, behavioral theories,** and most effectively, through **situational (contingency) theories.** The **leader-member exchange model** is used for describing relationships between leaders and employers.

Careers in I/O Psychology

- A bachelor's degree allows you to work in an I/O-related field.
- A master's or doctorate degree is required to work as an I/O psychologist.
- I/O psychologists may work in academic settings, public institutions, or private corporations.

Workplace Trends and Issues

- Internet recruiting
- Telework and telecommuting
- Work-life balance
- Workforce diversity

APPENDIX C

APA Goals and Outcomes

The APA Task Force intended these Goals and Outcomes to be met as part of a four-year Psychology Major, not as goals for the student embarking on this first course in psychology. However, this document illustrates how well Hockenbury and Hockenbury: *Discovering Psychology,* Fifth Edition sets students on the right path toward achieving these goals.

The Hockenbury and Hockenbury: *Discovering Psychology,* Fifth Edition, media and print supplements package impressively supports the text's efforts to address these Goals and Outcomes.

1.1 Characterize the nature of psychology as a discipline. a. Explain why psychology is a science. b. Identify and explain the primary objectives of psychology: describing, understanding, predicting, and controlling behavior and mental processes. c. Compare and contrast the assumptions and methods of psychology with those of other disciplines. d. Describe the contributions of psychology perspectives to interdisciplinary collaboration.	• (1.1a) Chapter 1 (Introduction and Research Methods) on pp. 2–15 discusses the importance of psychology as a science. • (1.1b) On pp. 16-20 the scientific method is presented, step-by-step. • (1.1c) The Hockenbury & Hockenbury text provides references to other disciplines to help students explore similarities and differences. Chapter 1 includes a discussion of the influence of philosophy and physiology on psychology's development, with a reference on p. 3 to ways in which psychology shares assumptions with other disciplines; p. 10 presents a discussion of disciplines that contribute to neuroscience; Chapter 12 (Stress, Health, and Coping) notes examples of influence or collaboration with the fields of immunology, medicine, and sociology. • (1.1d) Chapter 5 (Learning) provides examples of applications of learning principles to multiple fields; Chapter 12 (Stress, Health, and Coping) gives examples of applications to medicine.
1.2 Demonstrate knowledge and understanding representing appropriate breadth and depth in selected content areas of psychology: a. theory and research representing each of the following four general domains: (1) learning and cognition (2) individual differences, psychometrics, personality, and social processes, including those related to sociocultural and international dimensions (3) biological bases of behavior and mental processes, including physiology, sensation, perception, comparative, motivation, and emotion	• (1.2) For the Fifth Edition of *Discovering Psychology,* the Hockenburys have added 800 new research citations, with over half of those from research no older than 2007. Along with the help of faculty, students, and expert reviewers, the Hockenburys' daily immersion in the field of psychology and contact with others in the field have been instrumental in fully representing the key content areas of psychology, including all areas emphasized in the APA report. An outline locating each of these content areas can be found in the extended table of contents (pp. vii–xix). • (1.2a1) See Chapter 5 (Learning); also the sections "Cognitive Development" on pp. 387–393 and "Cognitive Changes" on pp. 407–409 in Chapter 9 (Lifespan Development).

(4) developmental changes in behavior and mental processes across the life span b. the history of psychology, including the evolution of methods of psychology, its theoretical conflicts, and its sociocultural contexts c. relevant levels of analysis: cellular, individual, group/systems, and culture d. overarching themes, persistent questions, or enduring conflicts in psychology, such as (1) the interaction of heredity and environment (2) variability and continuity of behavior and mental processes within and across species (3) free will versus determinism (4) subjective versus objective perspective (5) the interaction of mind and body e. relevant ethical issues, including a general understanding of the APA Code of Ethics	• (1.2a2) In the section titled "Measuring Intelligence" of Chapter 7 (Thinking, Language, and Intelligence) on pp. 293-298 (especially on pp. 293–297), the text discusses psychometrics and individual differences. Similarly, psychological tests are discussed in Chapter 10 (Personality) on pp. 446–451. • (1.2b) In Chapter 1, see "The Origins of Psychology" on pp. 2–9 and "Contemporary Psychology" on pp. 9–15, especially the discussion of the evolutionary perspective on pp. 12–14. • (1.2c) Throughout Chapter 1 (Introduction and Research Methods), levels of analysis are included in the text narrative; this topic also appears in Chapter 4 (Consciousness and Its Variations), especially on pp. 138–140. • (1.2d1) Along with the Chapter 1 discussion, persistent questions or enduring conflicts in psychology appear in Chapter 7 (Thinking, Language, and Intelligence) on pp. 298–311; in Chapter 9 (Lifespan Development) on pp. 369-370; in an In Focus box titled "Explaining Those Amazing Identical-Twin Similarities" on p. 444; and in the Chapter 13 (Psychological Disorders) discussion of genetic factors in schizophrenia on pp. 567–568. • (1.2d2) Development across the species is part of the Chapter 9 (Lifespan Development) discussion, the Chapter 1 (Introduction and Research Methods) discussion of evolutionary psychology on pp. 12–14, the Chapter 5 (Learning) discussion on animal communication, and the Critical Thinking box titled "Emotion in Nonhuman Animals: Laughing Rats, Silly Elephants, and Smiling Dolphins?" on pp. 352–353. • (1.2d3) Free will is addressed in the Critical Thinking box titled "Is Human Freedom Just an Illusion?" on p. 208; this in-text box also discusses Skinner's determinism as presented in the book *Beyond Freedom and Dignity.* • (1.2d4) Hockenbury & Hockenbury addresses subjective versus objective perspectives in Chapter 4 (Consciousness and Its Variations) on p. 137 and in Chapter 5 (Learning) on pp. 184–185. • (1.2d5) Mind-body interactions are part of the discussion in Chapter 12 (Stress, Health, and Coping), especially on pp. 502–509; the discussion in Chapter 2 (Neuroscience and Behavior) on neuroplasticity, especially on pp. 62-63; and the discussion in Chapter 4 (Consciousness and Its Variations), especially about hypnosis on pp. 159–163 and meditation on pp. 163–164. • (1.2e) See the Chapter 1 (Introduction and Research Methods) section titled "Ethics in Psychological Research" on pp. 33-36, in particular the In Focus box feature titled "Questions About the Use of Animals in Psychological Research" on p. 36; also see the Chapter 11 (Social Psychology) section titled "Obedience" on pp. 476–484, including the in-text Critical Thinking box "Abuse at Abu Ghraib: Why Do Ordinary People Commit Evil Acts?" on pp. 482–483.
1.3 Use the concepts, language, and major theories of the discipline to account for psychological phenomena. a. Describe behavior and mental processes empirically, including operational definitions b. Identify antecedents and consequences of behavior and mental processes c. Interpret behavior and mental processes at an appropriate level of complexity d. Use theories to explain and predict behavior and mental processes e. Integrate theoretical perspectives to produce comprehensive and multi-faceted explanations	• (1.3a) The Hockenburys consistently incorporate the language and concepts of the discipline. The essential concepts and terms within the text appear in bold print, with easy-to-find definitions on the appropriate page side column. (Also, see the Glossary in the back of the text for all the key terms, with definitions and their page references, pp. G-1–G-17.) Concepts and terms related to statistics are presented in Appendix A (Statistics: Understanding Data) on pp. A-1–A-14. Students are provided with a separate Spanish-language glossary on the companion Web page. • (1.3a-c) Hockenbury & Hockenbury maintains accessibility when introducing relevant terms and concepts. For example, see p. 277 where the concept and term "cognition" are introduced and defined in a context students will find understandable as well as meaningful to the study of psychology; or see p. 399 where "identity" is similarly introduced and defined.

Goal	Coverage
	• (1.3d) Founders of the field are discussed in Chapter 1, pp. 4–9 and major perspectives in psychology are presented on pp. 10–14. These perspectives and related theories are linked to behavior and mental processes presented throughout the text. As an example, see Chapter 14 (Therapies) on pp. 580–600, which discusses various therapies based on psychological perspectives and theories. • (1.3e) Throughout the Hockenbury & Hockenbury text, various perspectives are presented as part of discussions on specific topics in psychology. For example, see the Chapter 8 (Motivation and Emotion) section "Theories of Emotion" on pp. 355-360, where explanations of various theories set the stage for students' understanding of behavior linked to emotions. Also, see the Chapter 10 (Personality) section titled "Two Representative Trait Theories" on pp. 440–441.
1.4 Explain major perspectives of psychology (e.g., behavioral, biological, cognitive, evolutionary, humanistic, psychodynamic, and sociocultural). a. Compare and contrast major perspectives b. Describe advantages and limitations of major theoretical perspectives	• (1.4a) All of these perspectives are outlined in the Chapter 1 (Introduction and Research Methods) section titled "Major Perspectives in Psychology" on pp. 10–14. • (1.4ba-b) For specific examples of discussions of various major theoretical perspectives, see pp. 420–446 of Chapter 10 (Personality). In those pages various theoretical perspectives are applied to personality; in those same pages, advantages and limitations of different perspectives when applied to personality are summarized.
2.1 Describe the basic characteristics of the science of psychology.	• (2.1) Chapter 1 (Introduction and Research Methods) on pp. 1–39.
2.2 Explain different research methods used by psychologists. a. Describe how various research designs address different types of questions and hypotheses b. Articulate strengths and limitations of various research designs c. Distinguish the nature of designs that permit causal inferences from those that do not	• (2.2) Chapter 1 sections titled "The Scientific Method," "Descriptive Research Methods," and "The Experimental Method" on pp. 16–32. • (2.2a) The discussion of the different research methods in Chapter 1 includes advantages and disadvantages of each method, as well as presentations of types of questions appropriate for each method. • (2.2c) Hockenbury & Hockenbury distinguishes the nature of designs that permit casual inferences from those that don't throughout the text. For example: see pp. 25–26 in the Chapter 1 section "Correlational Studies," Critical Thinking in-text boxes titled "Do Personality Factors Cause Disease," on p. 514 and "Does Smoking Cause Depression and other Psychological Disorders" on pp. 550–551, and several examples of experimental vs. correlational studies in Chapter 12 (Stress, Health, and Coping).
2.3 Evaluate the appropriateness of conclusions derived from psychological research. a. Interpret basic statistical results b. Distinguish between statistical significance and practical significance c. Describe effect size and confidence intervals d. Evaluate the validity of conclusions presented in research reports	• (2.3a) The interpretation of basic statistical results is addressed in Appendix A (Statistics: Understanding Data) on pp. A-1–A-14; the Chapter 1 sections "Correlational Studies" on pp. 25–26 and "Step 3. Analyze the Data and Draw Conclusions" on pp. 18–19. • (2.3b) To distinguish between statistical significance and practical significance, see p. 18. • (2.2c) This goal is beyond the scope of *Discovering Psychology*. • (2.3d) Hockenbury & Hockenbury addresses the validity of conclusions presented in research reports throughout the text. For examples, see pp. 25–26 for a critique of the Anderson & Dill (2000) experiment, the Critical Thinking in-text boxes titled "Do Personality Factors Cause Disease," on p. 514, "Does Exposure to Media Violence Cause Aggressive Behavior?" on pp. 224–225, and "Does Smoking Cause Depression and other Psychological Disorders?" on pp. 550–551.

2.4 Design and conduct basic studies to address psychological questions using appropriate research methods. a. Locate and use relevant databases, research, and theory to plan, conduct, and interpret results of research studies b. Formulate testable research hypotheses, based on operational definitions of variables c. Select and apply appropriate methods to maximize internal and external validity and reduce the plausibility of alternative explanations d. Collect, analyze, interpret, and report data using appropriate statistical strategies to address different types of research questions and hypotheses e. Recognize that theoretical and sociocultural contexts as well as personal biases may shape research questions, design, data collection, analysis, and interpretation	• (2.4) To help students understand steps of research and the evaluation of conclusions, Chapter 1 (Introduction and Research Methods) provides a step-by-step explanation in the section titled "Steps in the Scientific Method." • (2.4a) In addition to the presentation of research methods in Chapter 1, stated in the previous point, see Appendix A (Statistics: Understanding Data) on pp. A-1–A-14. • (2.4b) Good examples of how to formulate testable research hypotheses based on operational definitions of variables can be found on p. 18 (a photo) and p. 21, where the text describes a pace of life naturalistic observation study. • (2.4d) In addition to coverage in Chapter 1 (Introduction and Research Methods), data is explored in a thorough but student-friendly way in Appendix A (Statistics: Understanding Data) on pp. A-1–A-14. A discussion of test construction principles (standardization, reliability, and validity) appears in Chapter 7 (Thinking, Language, and Intelligence) on pp. 297–298. • (2.4e) As examples, see the Culture and Human Behavior in-text box "What is Cross-Cultural Psychology?" on p. 13 and the Chapter 11 (Social Psychology) discussion of the effects of ethnocentrism, group bias, and prejudice on pp. 469–472.
2.5 Follow the APA Code of Ethics in the treatment of human and nonhuman participants in the design, data collection, interpretation, and reporting of psychological research.	• Hockenbury & Hockenbury repeatedly emphasizes the idea of ethical principles that must be followed in all psychological research. • In addition to addressing ethics issues in the In Focus in-text box titled "Questions About the Use of Animals in Psychological Research" on p. 36, a discussion of the APA code of ethics appears in Chapter 1 (Introduction and Research Methods) on p. 33, highlighting the five key 2002 APA ethics provisions. • At length, Hockenbury & Hockenbury discusses Milgram's experiment on obedience in Chapter 11 (Social Psychology) on pp. 476–481, with a focus on the question of ethics raised in the Critical Thinking in-text box "Abuse at Abu Ghraib: Why Do Ordinary People Commit Evil Acts?" on pp. 482–483.
2.6 Generalize research conclusions appropriately based on the parameters of particular research methods. a. Exercise caution in predicting behavior based on limitations of single studies b. Recognize the limitations of applying normative conclusions to individuals c. Acknowledge that research results may have unanticipated societal consequences d. Recognize that individual differences and sociocultural contexts may influence the applicability of research findings	• (2.6) Various research methods are evaluated in Chapter 1 (Introduction and Research Methods) on pp. 21–32. • (2.6a) The subtitle of a section in Chapter 1 says it all—for the section titled "Case Studies," the subtitle of "Details, Details, Details" has been added. • (2.6b) Hockenbury & Hockenbury reminds students of the need to recognize individual variation among members of any group. For example, see the Culture and Human Behavior in-text box titled "What Is Cross-Cultural Psychology?" on p. 13. • (2.6c) Hockenbury & Hockenbury encourages students to step back and notice the significant societal implications of psychological research. This topic is explored through Chapter 11 (Social Psychology) on pp. 458–490. Another example appears in Chapter 7 (Thinking, Language, and Intelligence) in the section titled "Alfred Binet" on pp. 293–295; this section discusses Binet's intelligence test and its unanticipated later use as a tool for measuring an inborn or permanent level of intelligence, which Binet did not believe he was measuring with his test. • (2.6d) Throughout the chapters, research findings are considered in light of cultural contexts. A list of in-text box features for Culture and Human Behavior appears on pp. xxviii-xxx. In addition, p. xxix presents a complete list of integrated cultural coverage topics and p. xxxi presents a complete list of integrated gender coverage topics within the main narrative of *Discovering Psychology.*

3.1 Use critical thinking effectively. a. Evaluate the quality of information, including differentiating empirical evidence from speculation and the probable from the improbable b. Identify and evaluate the source, context, and credibility of information c. Recognize and defend against common fallacies in thinking d. Avoid being swayed by appeals to emotion or authority e. Evaluate popular media reports of psychological research f. Demonstrate an attitude of critical thinking that includes persistence, open-mindedness, tolerance for ambiguity and intellectual engagement g. Make linkages or connections between diverse facts, theories, and observations	• (3.1) To complement the powerful and student-friendly narrative of the Hockenbury & Hockenbury text are in-text Critical Thinking boxes, which appear throughout *Discovering Psychology*. A list of these critical thinking topics can be found on p. xxviii. • (3.1a) To help students evaluate the quality of information, the narrative approach is complemented with Science Versus Pseudoscience in-text box features. For example, Chapter 1 (Introduction and Research Methods) includes a Science Versus Pseudoscience in-text box titled "What Is a Pseudoscience?" on pp. 22–23. Topics for other Science Versus Pseudoscience in-text boxes can be found on p. xxvii. • (3.1b) To help students evaluate sources, Chapter 1 includes an Enhancing Well-Being with Psychology feature titled "Psychology in the Media: Becoming an Informed Consumer" on pp. 37–38. • (3.1c) See the Critical Thinking in-text boxes titled "The Persistence of Unwarranted Beliefs" on p. 288 and "ESP: Can Perception Occur Without Sensation?" on pp. 116–117. • (3.1e) The evaluation of popular media reports or psychological research is addressed in a Chapter 1 Enhancing Well-Being with Psychology feature titled "Psychology in the Media: Becoming an Informed Consumer" on pp. 37–38 and a Critical Thinking in-text box titled "'His' and 'Her' Brains" on p. 75. • (3.1f) Hockenbury & Hockenbury emphasizes critical thinking attitudes with questions that ask students to actively consider the evidence of different points of view; these questions conclude each Critical Thinking in-text box feature. For example, see the questions that conclude the Critical Thinking boxes titled "Does Exposure to Media Violence *Cause* Aggressive Behavior?" on pp. 224–225 and "The Effects of Child Care on Attachment and Development" on pp. 380–381. • (3.1g) The Hockenburys actively connect diverse elements throughout the text. In the Critical Thinking in-text box "Is Hypnosis a Special State of Consciousness?" students are presented with three competing theories, and observational evidence is interpreted in different ways. See also "Applications of Observational Learning" on pp. 222–223.
3.2 Engage in creative thinking. a. Intentionally pursue unusual approaches to problems b. Recognize and encourage creative thinking and behaviors in others c. Evaluate new ideas with an open but critical mind	• (3.2a–c) Hockenbury & Hockenbury gives students tools for exploring new problem-solving methods; this concept is highlighted in the Chapter 7 (Thinking, Language, and Intelligence) section titled "Enhancing Well-Being with Psychology: A Workshop on Creativity" on pp. 312–313.
3.3 Use reasoning to recognize, develop, defend, and criticize arguments and other persuasive appeals. a. Identify components of arguments (e.g., conclusions, premises/assumptions, gaps, counterarguments) b. Distinguish among assumptions, emotional appeals, speculations, and defensible evidence c. Weigh support for conclusions to determine how well reasons support conclusions d. Identify weak, contradictory, and inappropriate assertions e. Develop sound arguments based on reasoning and evidence	• (3.3c) The Hockenburys' focus in the following Critical Thinking in-text boxes addresses reasoned conclusions: "What Is Critical Thinking?" on p. 17, "Does Exposure to Media Violence *Cause* Aggressive Behavior?" on pp. 224–225, and "The Effects of Child Care on Attachment and Development" on pp. 380–381.
3.4 Approach problems effectively. a. Recognize ill-defined and well-defined problems b. Articulate problems clearly c. Evaluate the quality of solutions and revise as needed d. Generate multiple possible goals and solutions e. Select and carry out the best solution	• (3.4) See Chapter 7 (Thinking, Language, and Intelligence), especially pp. 277–287, in which building blocks of thought as well as problem-solving strategies, obstacles to solving problems, and decision-making strategies are explored.

4.1 Describe major applied areas of psychology (e.g., clinical, counseling, industrial/ organizational, school, health).	• (4.1) Hockenbury & Hockenbury graphically illustrates the variety of specialty areas and employment settings for psychologists in Figure 1.1 on p. 14. Descriptions for these applied areas of psychology are presented in the Chapter 1 (Introduction and Research Methods) section titled "Specialty Areas in Psychology." • Chapter 12 (Stress, Health, and Coping) discusses the work of health psychologists. • Chapter 14 (Therapies) not only addresses the work of psychologists involved in psychotherapy and biomedical therapy, but also presents a table on p. 581 that delineates who's who among mental health professionals. • Hockenbury & Hockenbury also covers I/O psychology in Appendix B (Industrial/Organizational Psychology) on pp. B-1–B-15.
4.2 Identify appropriate applications of psychology in solving problems, such as a. the pursuit and effect of healthy lifestyles b. origin and treatment of abnormal behavior c. psychological tests and measurements d. psychology-based interventions in clinical, counseling, educational, industrial/organizational, community, and other settings and their empirical evaluation	• (4.2a) An application in-text box titled "Minimizing the Effects of Stress" on pp. 523–524 addresses the pursuit of healthy lifestyles. • (4.2b) The origins and treatment of abnormal behavior is covered extensively and in-depth in Chapter 13 (Psychological Disorders) on pp. 531–574 and Chapter 14 (Therapies) on pp. 580–617. • (4.2c) Chapter 7 (Thinking, Language, and Intelligence) presents a section titled "Principles of Test Construction" on p. 297, and Chapter 10 (Personality) presents a section titled "Assessing Personality" on pp. 446–451 to address the issue of psychological tests and measurements. • (4.2d) Chapter 14 (Therapies) provides a discussion of various therapies; a broad range of issues related to the efficacy of psychotherapy is addressed in the section titled "Evaluating the Effectiveness of Psychotherapy" on pp. 601–606.
4.3 Articulate how psychological principles can be used to explain social issues and inform public policy. a. Recognize that sociocultural contexts may influence the application of psychological principles in solving social problems b. Describe how applying psychological principles can facilitate change	• (4.3a) Hockenbury & Hockenbury provides insight to sociocultural contexts that influence the application of applying psychological principles to solving social problems in a Culture and Human Behavior in-text box titled "Cultural Values and Psychotherapy" on p. 606. • (4.3b) In Chapter 11 (Social Psychology), a section titled "Overcoming Prejudice" on pp. 472–474 discusses how psychological principles may be engaged in the facilitation of social change and development of public policy.
4.4 Apply psychological concepts, theories, and research findings as these relate to everyday life.	• Throughout the text, the authors help students apply psychological concepts to everyday life. The Enhancing Well-Being with Psychology in-text box features in every chapter present research-based information in a form that students can use to enhance everyday functioning. The full range of titles for Enhancing Well-Being with Psychology boxes is listed on p. xxxii.
4.5 Recognize that ethically complex situations can develop in the application of psychological principles.	• The Hockenburys openly discuss ethically complex situations that can result from applying psychological research, such as the understanding of the nature/nurture balance, which is introduced on p. 3, or the power of attributions, which is addressed on pp. 463–464.
5.1 Recognize the necessity for ethical behavior in all aspects of the science and practice of psychology.	• Hockenbury & Hockenbury places a focus on ethics in Chapter 1 (Introduction and Research Methods), in particular the section titled "Ethics in Psychological Research" on pp. 33–36 and the In Focus in-text box feature titled "Questions About the Use of Animals in Psychological Research" on p. 36. • Ethics are addressed in discussions of Milgram's experiments on obedience in Chapter 11 (Social Psychology) on pp. 476–484, accompanied by the Critical Thinking in-text box titled "Abuse at Abu Ghraib: Why Do Ordinary People Commit Evil Acts?" on pp. 482–483. As in all other Critical Thinking in-text boxes throughout the text, this one ends with questions that probe and hone students' critical thinking abilities.

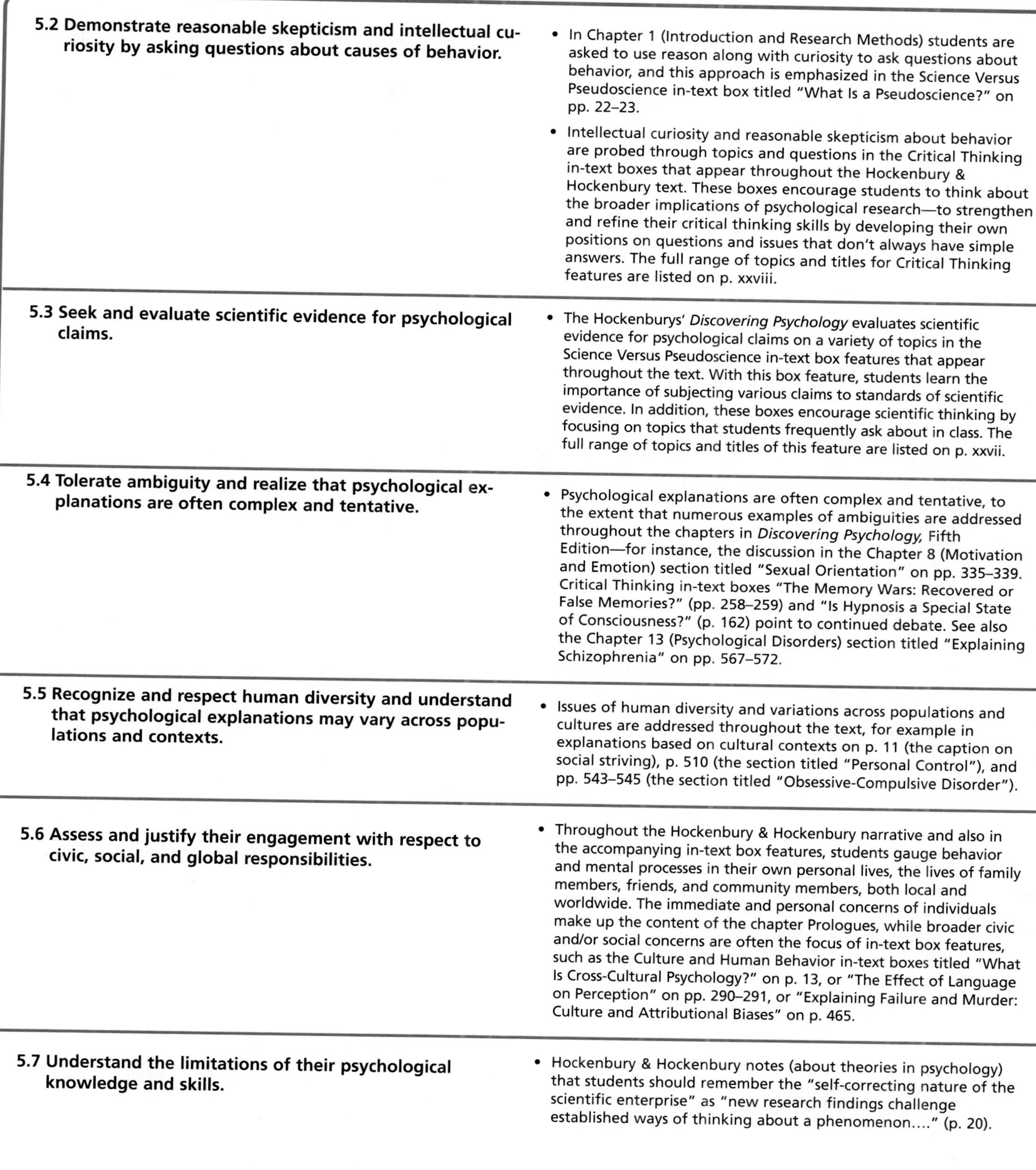

5.2 Demonstrate reasonable skepticism and intellectual curiosity by asking questions about causes of behavior.	• In Chapter 1 (Introduction and Research Methods) students are asked to use reason along with curiosity to ask questions about behavior, and this approach is emphasized in the Science Versus Pseudoscience in-text box titled "What Is a Pseudoscience?" on pp. 22–23. • Intellectual curiosity and reasonable skepticism about behavior are probed through topics and questions in the Critical Thinking in-text boxes that appear throughout the Hockenbury & Hockenbury text. These boxes encourage students to think about the broader implications of psychological research—to strengthen and refine their critical thinking skills by developing their own positions on questions and issues that don't always have simple answers. The full range of topics and titles for Critical Thinking features are listed on p. xxviii.
5.3 Seek and evaluate scientific evidence for psychological claims.	• The Hockenburys' *Discovering Psychology* evaluates scientific evidence for psychological claims on a variety of topics in the Science Versus Pseudoscience in-text box features that appear throughout the text. With this box feature, students learn the importance of subjecting various claims to standards of scientific evidence. In addition, these boxes encourage scientific thinking by focusing on topics that students frequently ask about in class. The full range of topics and titles of this feature are listed on p. xxvii.
5.4 Tolerate ambiguity and realize that psychological explanations are often complex and tentative.	• Psychological explanations are often complex and tentative, to the extent that numerous examples of ambiguities are addressed throughout the chapters in *Discovering Psychology,* Fifth Edition—for instance, the discussion in the Chapter 8 (Motivation and Emotion) section titled "Sexual Orientation" on pp. 335–339. Critical Thinking in-text boxes "The Memory Wars: Recovered or False Memories?" (pp. 258–259) and "Is Hypnosis a Special State of Consciousness?" (p. 162) point to continued debate. See also the Chapter 13 (Psychological Disorders) section titled "Explaining Schizophrenia" on pp. 567–572.
5.5 Recognize and respect human diversity and understand that psychological explanations may vary across populations and contexts.	• Issues of human diversity and variations across populations and cultures are addressed throughout the text, for example in explanations based on cultural contexts on p. 11 (the caption on social striving), p. 510 (the section titled "Personal Control"), and pp. 543–545 (the section titled "Obsessive-Compulsive Disorder").
5.6 Assess and justify their engagement with respect to civic, social, and global responsibilities.	• Throughout the Hockenbury & Hockenbury narrative and also in the accompanying in-text box features, students gauge behavior and mental processes in their own personal lives, the lives of family members, friends, and community members, both local and worldwide. The immediate and personal concerns of individuals make up the content of the chapter Prologues, while broader civic and/or social concerns are often the focus of in-text box features, such as the Culture and Human Behavior in-text boxes titled "What Is Cross-Cultural Psychology?" on p. 13, or "The Effect of Language on Perception" on pp. 290–291, or "Explaining Failure and Murder: Culture and Attributional Biases" on p. 465.
5.7 Understand the limitations of their psychological knowledge and skills.	• Hockenbury & Hockenbury notes (about theories in psychology) that students should remember the "self-correcting nature of the scientific enterprise" as "new research findings challenge established ways of thinking about a phenomenon…." (p. 20).

6.1 Demonstrate information competence at each stage in the following process: a. Formulate a researchable topic that can be supported by database search strategies b. Locate and choose relevant sources from appropriate media, which may include data and perspectives outside traditional psychology and Western boundaries c. Use selected sources after evaluating their suitability based on: • appropriateness, accuracy, quality, and value of the source • potential bias of the source • the relative value of primary versus secondary sources, empirical versus non-empirical sources, and peer-reviewed versus nonpeer-reviewed sources d. Read and accurately summarize the general scientific literature of psychology	• (6.1) On pp. 16–20 of Chapter 1 (Introduction and Research Methods), Hockenbury & Hockenbury outlines the scientific method step by step, from formulating a specific question that can be tested to designing a study to collect relevant data, analyze the data to arrive at conclusions, and report the results. Throughout the text, Hockenbury & Hockenbury discusses research that satisfies the described elements of competence.
6.2 Use appropriate software to produce understandable reports of the psychological literature, methods, and statistical and qualitative analyses in APA or other appropriate style, including graphic representations of data.	• (6.2) Hockenbury & Hockenbury addresses methods in Chapter 1 (Introduction and Research Methods) and provides a helpful discussion of statistical analyses in Appendix A (Statistics: Understanding Data) on pp. A-1–A-14. • On p. 20 of Chapter 1 (Introduction and Research Methods), students learn how to read a journal and report findings with correct citation formatting. • The student Web site includes a link to Diana Hacker's *Research and Documentation,* which provides detailed instruction on finding and documenting sources.
6.3 Use information and technology ethically and responsibly. a. Quote, paraphrase, and cite correctly from a variety of media sources b. Define and avoid plagiarism c. Avoid distorting statistical results d. Honor commercial and intellectual copyrights	• (6.3) When describing studies or referencing ideas, Hockenbury & Hockenbury takes care to demonstrate ethical and responsible use of information; all such material is consistently quoted or cited, allowing students to become familiar with appropriate levels of attribution. • (6.3a) Page 20, Figure 1.2, provides a visual guide to reading a journal reference; the caption links the details of a reference to source citations. • (6.3c) On p. 19, Hockenbury & Hockenbury reviews how meta-analysis is used to reveal overall trends that may not be evident in individual studies. The Chapter 6 (Memory) discussion about memory distortions on pp. 256–258 also serves as a caution.
6.4 Demonstrate these computer skills: a. Use basic word processing, database, email, spreadsheet, and data analysis programs b. Search the World Wide Web for high quality information c. Use proper etiquette and security safeguards when communicating through email	• A companion Web site developed exclusively for the Hockenbury & Hockenbury text allows instructors and students to hone computer skills while reviewing key concepts. See www.worthpublishers.com/discoveringpsych5e.
7.1 Demonstrate effective writing skills in various formats (e.g., essays, correspondence, technical papers, note taking) and for various purposes (e.g., informing, defending, explaining, persuading, arguing, teaching). a. Demonstrate professional writing conventions (e.g., grammar, audience awareness, formality) appropriate to purpose and context b. Use APA style effectively in empirically-based reports, literature reviews, and theoretical papers	• (7.1a–b) The Critical Thinking in-text box features that appear throughout *Discovering Psychology,* Fifth Edition, provide students with opportunities to write responses to thought-provoking questions. Those responses demand critical thinking as well as a command of writing skills. • On p. 20 of Chapter 1 (Introduction and Research Methods), students learn how to read a journal reference (Figure 1.2, "How to Read a Journal Reference") and report findings with correct citation formatting.

7.2 Demonstrate effective oral communication skills in various formats (e.g., group discussion, debate, lecture) and for various purposes (e.g., informing, defending, explaining, persuading, arguing, teaching).	• In addition to writing responses to thought-provoking questions that conclude the Critical Thinking in-text boxes that appear throughout the text, students also have the opportunity to respond to those questions orally in order to explain, persuade, or inform listeners. • The Instructor's Resource Manual, available to all instructors using *Discovering Psychology,* also presents numerous classroom activities that work to develop students' oral communication skills. Suggested activities include role-playing scenarios, presentations, group discussions and exercises, and debates, among other formats. For example, a group decisions and stereotyping activity on page 22 of Chapter 12 in the Instructor's Resource Manual proposes a difficult scenario, then asks students to attempt to gain consensus about it among members of their group.
7.3 Exhibit quantitative literacy. a. Apply basic mathematical concepts and operations to support measurement strategies b. Use relevant probability and statistical analyses to facilitate interpretation of measurements c. Articulate clear and appropriate rationale for choice of information conveyed in charts, tables, figures, and graphs d. Interpret quantitative visual aids accurately, including showing vigilance about misuse or misrepresentation of quantitative information	• (7.3a) Hockenbury & Hockenbury provides Appendix A (Statistics: Understanding Data) on pp. A-1–A-14 to introduce mathematics that researchers use to organize and interpret data. • (7.3b) Appendix A contains graphic presentations of data (from histograms and frequency polygons to standard normal curves and scatter diagrams). This appendix includes "A Frequency Distribution Table" on p. A-3 and a "Calculating the Standard Deviation" table on p. A-7. • (7.3c–d) Appendix A ends with a discussion of inferential statistics in which the author cautions students of the ". . . small but real possibility of *erroneously* concluding that study results are significant." (p. A-13)
7.4 Demonstrate effective interpersonal communication skills. a. Listen accurately and actively b. Use psychological concepts and theory to understand interactions with others c. Identify the impact or potential impact of their behaviors on others d. Articulate ideas thoughtfully and purposefully e. Use appropriately worded questions to improve interpersonal understanding f. Attend to nonverbal behavior and evaluate its meaning in the communications context g. Adapt communication style to accommodate diverse audiences h. Provide constructive feedback to colleagues in oral and written formats	• (7.4b–c) In Chapter 8 (Motivation and Emotion), Hockenbury discusses how people who rate high in emotional intelligence "are able to understand and use their emotions" to help motivate themselves (p. 345). • (7.4d–e) Pages 21–22 point out how articulated ideas and appropriately worded questions are part of naturalistic observation. • (7.4e) The Enhancing Well-Being with Psychology feature throughout the text promotes interpersonal understanding as well as self-understanding that can be articulated. For instance, the Enhancing Well-Being with Psychology feature titled "Using Learning Principles to Improve Self-Control" on pp. 226–227 provides students with strategies that work as short-term and long-term reinforcers to help attain a behavior goal. • (7.4f) Chapter 8 (Motivation and Emotion) includes a section titled "The Expression of Emotion" on pp. 351–355 that focuses on nonverbal behavior communicated by people (universal expressions and cultural expressions) and animals—the latter of which is the topic of a Critical Thinking in-text box titled "Emotion in Nonhuman Animals: Laughing Rats, Silly Elephants, and Smiling Dolphins?" on pp. 352–353.
7.5 Exhibit the ability to collaborate effectively. a. Work with groups to complete projects within reasonable timeframes b. Solicit and integrate diverse viewpoints c. Manage conflicts appropriately and ethically d. Develop relevant workplace skills: mentoring, interviewing, crisis management	• Hockenbury & Hockenbury discusses competence and achievement motivation in Chapter 8 (Motivation and Emotion). • In Appendix B (Industrial/Organizational Psychology) on pp. B-1–B-15, Hockenbury & Hockenbury presents issues and concepts related to collaborative efforts in the workplace. In particular, leadership roles are addressed in the section on Organizational Behavior on pp. B-7–B-10, with an In Focus in-text box feature titled "Servant Leadership: When It's Not All About You" on p. B-10. • For students who hope to affect how people work together, Appendix B offers a detailed exploration about the professions of industrial/organizational (I/O) psychology.

8.1 Interact effectively and sensitively with people from diverse backgrounds and cultural perspectives.	• In *Discovering Psychology,* Fifth Edition, the Hockenburys often and consistently present perspectives based on people's diverse backgrounds and various cultural perspectives, and the topics of Integrated Cultural Coverage are listed on p. xxix. • In addition to the discussions within the text narrative, Hockenbury & Hockenbury focuses on cultural perspectives in the Culture and Human Behavior in-text box feature that accompanies the main text narrative. A listing of the topics of those in-text box features is found on pp. xxviii–xxx. • Gender-related topics and issues are discussed throughout the chapters of *Discovering Psychology*. A listing of topics for Integrated Gender Coverage can be found on p. xxxi.
8.2 Examine the sociocultural and international contexts that influence individual differences.	• Hockenbury & Hockenbury often and consistently presents perspectives based on people's diverse backgrounds and perspectives. The specific topics of Integrated Cultural Coverage are listed on p. xxix. • In addition to the discussions within the text narrative, Hockenbury & Hockenbury focuses on cultural perspectives in the Culture and Human Behavior in-text boxes that accompany the main text narrative. A listing of the topics of those in-text box features is found on pp. xxvii-xxx.
8.3 Explain how individual differences influence beliefs, values, and interactions with others and vice versa.	• Gender-related topics and issues are discussed throughout the chapters of *Discovering Psychology* and a listing of topics for Integrated Gender Coverage can be found on p. xxxi. • Individual differences as they affect human interactions is explored in the Chapter 11 (Social Psychology) Culture and Human Behavior in-text box feature titled "Explaining Failure and Murder: Culture and Attributional Biases" on p. 465 and in discussions within Chapter 8 (Motivation and Emotion) on competence and achievement motivation on pp. 342–344 and culture and emotional expression on p. 346.
8.4 Understand how privilege, power, and oppression may affect prejudice, discrimination, and inequity.	• See "Understanding Prejudice," a section of Chapter 11 (Social Psychology), on pp. 469–472.
8.5 Recognize prejudicial attitudes and discriminatory behaviors that might exist in themselves and others.	• See the section titled "Attribution" on pp. 463–466 and "The Social Psychology of Attitudes" on pp. 466–469, both of which are part of Chapter 11 (Social Psychology).
9.1 Reflect on their experiences and find meaning in them. a. Identify their personal and professional values b. Demonstrate insightful awareness of their feelings, emotions, motives, and attitudes based on psychological principles	• (9.1a) The questions that Hockenbury & Hockenbury poses at the conclusion of each in-text box feature on Critical Thinking invite students to consider how the material reflects on their own lives. For example, personal and professional values are explored as students respond to a concluding question in "'His' and 'Her' Brains?" on p. 75: "Why is the notion that sex differences might be due to brain differences so appealing to many people?" • (9.1b) Insight based on psychological principles is the focus of the concluding questions of the Critical Thinking in-text box feature titled "Freud Versus Rogers on Human Nature" on p. 435: "...are people naturally good, as Rogers claimed? If people existed in a truly free and nurturing environment, would they invariably make constructive choices that would benefit both themselves and society as a whole?"

9.2 Apply psychological principles to promote personal development. a. Demonstrate self-regulation in setting and achieving goals b. Self-assess performance quality accurately c. Incorporate feedback for improved performance d. Purposefully evaluate the quality of one's thinking (metacognition)	• (9.2a–d) The Enhancing Well-Being with Psychology feature at the end of all chapters of *Discovering Psychology,* Fifth Edition, promotes students' opportunities to set goals and perform self-assessment and self-evaluation of their own thinking. In particular, see: "Maximizing Your Brain's Potential" on pp. 81–82 "Strategies to Control Pain" on pp. 129–130 "Stimulus Control Therapy for Insomnia" on p. 178 "Using Learning Principles to Improve Self-Control" on pp. 226–227 "Superpower Memory in Minutes per Day!" on pp. 270–271 "A Workshop on Creativity" on pp. 312–313 "Turning Your Goals Into Reality" on pp. 361–362 "Raising Psychologically Healthy Children" on pp. 411–412 "Possible Selves: Imagine the Possibilities" pp. 451–452 "The Persuasion Game" on pp. 489–490 "Minimizing the Effects of Stress" on pp. 523–524 "Understanding and Helping to Prevent Suicide" on pp. 573–574 • (9.2a) The Enhancing Well-Being with Psychology features "Using Learning Principles to Improve Self-Control" on pp. 226–227 and "Turning Your Goals Into Reality" on pp. 361–362 encourage self-regulation in setting and achieving goals.
9.3 Enact self-management strategies that maximize healthy outcomes.	• See the listed Enhancing Well-Being with Psychology features above, many of which provide self-management strategies that maximize healthy outcomes—in particular, see "Strategies to Control Pain" on pp. 129–130, "Stimulus Control Therapy for Insomnia" on p. 178, "Minimizing the Effects of Stress" on pp. 523–524, and "Understanding and Helping to Prevent Suicide" on pp. 573–574. • See the Chapter 8 (Motivation and Emotion) section titled "Motivational Concepts and Theories" on pp. 319–322. • Also see the Chapter 12 sections "Individual Factors That Influence the Response to Stress" on pp. 509–517 and "Coping" on pp. 518–522.
9.4 Display high standards of personal integrity with others.	• On pp. 378–381 of Chapter 9 (Lifespan Development) Hockenbury & Hockenbury points out research that indicates a long-term outlook for securely attached children: as preschoolers, they tend to be more prosocial, empathetic, and socially competent; as middle schoolers, they have higher levels of development, socially and cognitively; as adolescents, they have fewer problems, do better in school, and have more successful relationships with their peers.
10.1 Apply knowledge of psychology (e.g., decision strategies, life span processes, psychological assessment, types of psychological careers) to formulating career choices.	• The Chapter 1 (Introduction and Research Methods) section titled "Specialty Areas in Psychology" on pp. 14–15 describes the different specialty areas and employment settings. • Appendix B (Industrial/Organization Psychology) on pp. B-1–B-15 explores this field of psychology, along with a variety of careers linked to it.
10.2 Identify the types of academic experience and performance in psychology and the liberal arts that will facilitate entry into the work force, post-baccalaureate education, or both.	• The pie chart in Figure 1.1 on p. 14 points out specialty areas for psychologists who have recently received doctorates and also employment settings.

10.3 Describe preferred career paths based on accurate self-assessment of abilities, achievement, motivation, and work habits.	• Principles outlined in the Enhancing Well-Being with Psychology feature titled "Turning Your Goals Into Reality" on pp. 361–362 help students develop strategies for motivation and achievement.
10.4 Identify and develop skills and experiences relevant to achieving selected career goals.	• As noted above, principles outlined in the Enhancing Well-Being with Psychology feature titled "Turning Your Goals Into Reality" on pp. 361–362 help students develop strategies to achieve goals.
10.5 Demonstrate an understanding of the importance of lifelong learning and personal flexibility to sustain personal and professional development as the nature of work evolves.	• The Hockenburys demonstrate the importance of hard work, learning, flexibility, and creativity throughout the chapters in *Discovering Psychology*. For examples, note the discussion in Chapter 8 (Motivation and Emotion) in the section titled "Motivational Concepts and Theories" on pp. 319–311 and the Enhancing Well-Being with Psychology feature titled "A Workshop on Creativity" on pp. 312–313.

GLOSSARY

A

absolute threshold The smallest possible strength of a stimulus that can be detected half the time (p. 90).

accommodation The process by which the lens changes shape to focus incoming light so that it falls on the retina (p. 94).

acculturative stress (ah-KUL-chur-uh-tiv) The stress that results from the pressure of adapting to a new culture (p. 503.

acetylcholine (uh-*seet*-ull-KO-leen) Neurotransmitter that causes muscle contractions and is involved in learning and memory (p. 52).

achievement motivation The desire to direct one's behavior toward excelling, succeeding, or outperforming others at some task (p. 343).

achievement test A test designed to measure a person's level of knowledge, skill, or accomplishment in a particular area (p. 297).

action potential A brief electrical impulse by which information is transmitted along the axon of a neuron (p. 47).

activation–synthesis model of dreaming The theory that brain activity during sleep produces dream images (*activation*), which are combined by the brain into a dream story (p. 152).

activity theory of aging The psychosocial theory that life satisfaction in late adulthood is highest when people maintain the level of activity they displayed earlier in life (p. 408).

actualizing tendency In Rogers's theory, the innate drive to maintain and enhance the human organism (p. 434).

acupuncture Ancient Chinese medical procedure involving the insertion and manipulation of fine needles into specific locations on the body to alleviate pain and treat illness; modern acupuncture may involve sending electrical current through the needles rather than manipulating them (p. 129).

adipose tissue Body fat that is the main source of stored, or reserve, energy (p. 323).

adolescence The transitional stage between late childhood and the beginning of adulthood, during which sexual maturity is reached (p. 393).

adolescent growth spurt The period of accelerated growth during puberty, involving rapid increases in height and weight (p. 394).

adrenal cortex The outer portion of the adrenal glands (p. 60).

adrenal glands Pair of endocrine glands that are involved in the human stress response (p. 60).

adrenal medulla The inner portion of the adrenal glands; secretes epinephrine and norepinephrine (p. 61).

afterimage A visual experience that occurs after the original source of stimulation is no longer present (p. 100).

agoraphobia An anxiety disorder involving the extreme and irrational fear of experiencing a panic attack in a public situation and being unable to escape or get help (p. 538).

algorithm A problem-solving strategy that involves following a specific rule, procedure, or method that inevitably produces the correct solution (p. 282).

all-or-none law The principle that either a neuron is sufficiently stimulated and an action potential occurs or a neuron is not sufficiently stimulated and an action potential does not occur (p. 49).

alpha brain waves Brain-wave pattern associated with relaxed wakefulness and drowsiness (p. 141).

altruism Helping another person with no expectation of personal reward or benefit (p. 486).

Alzheimer's disease (AD) A progressive disease that destroys the brain's neurons, gradually impairing memory, thinking, language, and other cognitive functions, resulting in the complete inability to care for oneself; the most common cause of *dementia* (p. 268).

amnesia (am-NEE-zha) Severe memory loss (p. 264).

amphetamines (am-FET-uh-meens) A class of stimulant drugs that arouse the central nervous system and suppress appetite (p. 172).

amplitude The intensity or amount of energy of a wave, reflected in the height of the wave; the amplitude of a sound wave determines a sound's loudness (p. 102).

amygdala (uh-MIG-dull-uh) Almond-shaped cluster of neurons in the brain's temporal lobe, involved in memory and emotional responses, especially fear; part of the limbic system (pp. 72, 349).

animal cognition The study of animal learning, memory, thinking, and language; also called *comparative cognition* (p. 293).

anorexia nervosa An eating disorder characterized by excessive weight loss, an irrational fear of gaining weight, and distorted body self-perception (p. 553).

anterograde amnesia Loss of memory caused by the inability to store new memories; forward-acting amnesia (p. 265).

anthropomorphism The attribution of human traits, motives, emotions, or behaviors to nonhuman animals or inanimate objects (p. 353).

antianxiety medications Prescription drugs that are used to alleviate the symptoms of anxiety (p. 610).

antidepressant medications Prescription drugs that are used to reduce the symptoms associated with depression (p. 611).

antipsychotic medications (*an*-tee-sy-KOT-ick or anti-si-KOT-ick) Prescription drugs that are used to reduce psychotic symptoms; frequently used in the treatment of schizophrenia; also called *neuroleptics* (p. 607).

antisocial personality disorder A personality disorder characterized by a pervasive pattern of disregarding and violating the rights of others; such individuals are also often referred to as *psychopaths* or *sociopaths* (p. 557).

anxiety An unpleasant emotional state characterized by physical arousal and feelings of tension, apprehension, and worry (p. 537)

anxiety disorders A category of psychological disorders in which extreme anxiety is the main diagnostic feature and causes significant disruptions in the person's cognitive, behavioral, or interpersonal functioning (p. 537).

aphasia (uh-FAZE-yuh) The partial or complete inability to articulate ideas or understand spoken or written language because of brain injury or damage (p. 73).

aptitude test A test designed to assess a person's capacity to benefit from education or training (p. 297).

archetypes (AR-kuh-types) In Jung's theory, the inherited mental images of universal human instincts, themes, and preoccupations that are the main components of the collective unconscious (p. 429).

arousal theory The view that people are motivated to maintain a level of arousal that is optimal—neither too high nor too low (p. 321).

Asperger's syndrome Behavioral syndrome characterized by varying degrees of difficulty in social and conversational skills but normal-to-above-average intelligence and language development; often accompanied by obsessive preoccupation with particular topics or routines (p. 302).

attachment The emotional bond that forms between an infant and caregiver(s), especially his or her parents (p. 378).

attitude A learned tendency to evaluate some object, person, or issue in a particular way; such evaluations may be positive, negative, or ambivalent (p. 466).

attribution The mental process of inferring the causes of people's behavior, including one's own. Also refers to the explanation made for a particular behavior (p. 463).

atypical antipsychotic medications Newer antipsychotic medications that, in contrast to the early antipsychotic drugs, block dopamine receptors in brain regions associated with psychotic symptoms rather than more globally throughout the brain, resulting in fewer side effects (p. 609).

audition The technical term for the sense of hearing (p. 102).

authoritarian parenting style Parenting style in which parents are demanding and unresponsive toward their children's needs or wishes (p. 411).

authoritative parenting style Parenting style in which parents set clear standards for their children's behavior but are also responsive to their children's needs and wishes (p. 411).

autism Behavioral syndrome associated with differences in brain functioning and sensory responses, and characterized by impaired social interaction, impaired verbal and nonverbal communication skills, repetitive or odd motor behaviors, and highly restricted interests and routines (p. 302).

autonomic nervous system (aw-toe-NOM-ick) Subdivision of the peripheral nervous system that regulates involuntary functions (p. 57).

availability heuristic A strategy in which the likelihood of an event is estimated on the basis of how readily available other instances of the event are in memory (p. 286).

aversive conditioning A relatively ineffective type of behavior therapy that involves repeatedly pairing an aversive stimulus with the occurrence of undesirable behaviors or thoughts (p. 590).

axon The long, fluid-filled tube that carries a neuron's messages to other body areas (p. 46).

axon terminals Branches at the end of the axon that contain tiny pouches, or sacs, called synaptic vesicles (p. 50).

B

barbiturates (barb-ITCH-yer-ets) A category of depressant drugs that reduce anxiety and produce sleepiness (p. 169).

basal metabolic rate (BMR) When the body is at rest, the rate at which it uses energy for vital functions, such as heartbeat and respiration (p. 323).

basic emotions The most fundamental set of emotion categories, which are biologically innate, evolutionarily determined, and culturally universal (p. 346).

basilar membrane (BAZ-uh-ler or BAZE-uh-ler) The membrane within the cochlea of the ear that contains the hair cells (p. 103).

behavior modification The application of learning principles to help people develop more effective or adaptive behaviors (p. 212).

behavior therapy A type of psychotherapy that focuses on directly changing maladaptive behavior patterns by using basic learning principles and techniques; also called *behavior modification* (p. 588).

behavioral genetics An interdisciplinary field that studies the effects of genes and heredity on behavior (p. 445).

behavioral theories of leader effectiveness Theories of leader effectiveness that focus on differences in the behaviors of effective and ineffective leaders (p. B-9).

behaviorism School of psychology and theoretical viewpoint that emphasize the scientific study of observable behaviors, especially as they pertain to the process of learning (pp. 8, 190).

beta brain waves Brain-wave pattern associated with alert wakefulness (p. 141).

binocular cues (by-NOCK-you-ler) Distance or depth cues that require the use of both eyes (p. 120).

biofeedback Technique that involves using auditory or visual feedback to learn to exert voluntary control over involuntary body functions, such as heart rate, blood pressure, blood flow, and muscle tension (p. 129).

biological preparedness In learning theory, the idea that an organism is innately predisposed to form associations between certain stimuli and responses (p. 197).

biological psychology Specialized branch of psychology that studies the relationship between behavior and bodily processes and systems; also called *biopsychology* or *psychobiology* (p. 44).

biomedical therapies The use of medications, electroconvulsive therapy, or other medical treatments to treat the symptoms associated with psychological disorders (p. 580).

biopsychosocial model The belief that physical health and illness are determined by the complex interaction of biological, psychological, and social factors (p. 498).

bipolar cells In the retina, the specialized neurons that connect the rods and cones with the ganglion cells (p. 96).

bipolar disorder A mood disorder involving periods of incapacitating depression alternating with periods of extreme euphoria and excitement; formerly called *manic depression* (p. 549).

blaming the victim The tendency to blame an innocent victim of misfortune for having somehow caused the problem or for not having taken steps to avoid or prevent it (p. 464).

blind spot The point at which the optic nerve leaves the eye, producing a small gap in the field of vision (p. 96).

body mass index (BMI) A numerical scale indicating adult height in relation to weight; calculated as: $(703 \times \text{weight in pounds})/(\text{height in inches})^2$ (p. 329).

borderline personality disorder A personality disorder characterized by instability of interpersonal relationships, self-image, and emotions, and marked impulsivity (p. 558).

bottom-up processing Information processing that emphasizes the importance of the sensory receptors in detecting the basic features of a stimulus in the process of recognizing a whole pattern; analysis that moves from the parts to the whole; also called *data-driven processing* (p. 113).

brainstem A region of the brain made up of the hindbrain and the midbrain (p. 66).

brightness The perceived intensity of a color, which corresponds to the amplitude of the light wave (p. 98).

bulimia nervosa An eating disorder characterized by binges of extreme overeating followed by self-induced vomiting, misuse of laxatives, or other inappropriate methods to purge the excessive food and prevent weight gain (p. 554).

bystander effect A phenomenon in which the greater the number of people present, the less likely each individual is to help someone in distress (p. 487).

C

cafeteria diet effect The tendency to eat more when a wide variety of palatable foods is available (p. 330).

caffeine (kaff-EEN) A stimulant drug found in coffee, tea, cola drinks, chocolate, and many over-the-counter medications (p. 171).

California Personality Inventory (CPI) A self-report inventory that assesses personality characteristics in normal populations (p. 449).

case study An intensive study of a single individual or small group of individuals (p. 22).

cataplexy A sudden loss of voluntary muscle strength and control that is usually triggered by an intense emotion (p. 155).

catecholamines (*cat*-eh-COLE-uh-meens) Hormones secreted by the adrenal medulla that cause rapid physiological arousal; include adrenaline and noradrenaline (p. 504).

cell body Processes nutrients and provides energy for the neuron to function; contains the cell's nucleus; also called the *soma* (p. 46).

central nervous system (CNS) Division of the nervous system that consists of the brain and spinal cord (p. 56).

centration In Piaget's theory, the tendency to focus, or *center*, on only one aspect of a situation and ignore other important aspects of the situation (p. 389).

cerebellum (sare-uh-BELL-um) A large, two-sided hindbrain structure at the back of the brain; responsible for muscle coordination and maintaining posture and equilibrium (p. 67).

cerebral cortex (suh-REE-brull or SARE-uh-brull) The wrinkled outer portion of the forebrain, which contains the most sophisticated brain centers (p. 68).

cerebral hemispheres The nearly symmetrical left and right halves of the cerebral cortex (p. 68).

cholecystokinin (CCK) (kola-sis-tow-KINE-in) Hormone secreted primarily by the small intestine that promotes satiation; also found in the brain (p. 325).

chromosome A long, threadlike structure composed of twisted parallel strands of DNA; found in the cell nucleus (p. 370).

chunking Increasing the amount of information that can be held in short-term memory by grouping related items together into a single unit, or *chunk* (p. 236).

circadian rhythm (ser-KADE-ee-en) A cycle or rhythm that is roughly 24 hours long; the cyclical daily fluctuations in biological and psychological processes (p. 138).

classical conditioning The basic learning process that involves repeatedly pairing a neutral stimulus with a response-producing stimulus until the neutral stimulus elicits the same response (p. 186).

client-centered therapy A type of psychotherapy developed by humanistic psychologist Carl Rogers in which the therapist is nondirective and reflective, and the client directs the focus of each therapy session; also called *person-centered therapy* (p. 585).

clustering Organizing items into related groups during recall from long-term memory (p. 242).

cocaine A stimulant drug derived from the coca tree (p. 174).

cochlea (COCK-lee-uh) The coiled, fluid-filled inner-ear structure that contains the basilar membrane and hair cells (p. 103).

cognition The mental activities involved in acquiring, retaining, and using knowledge (p. 277).

cognitive appraisal theory of emotion The theory that emotional responses are triggered by a cognitive evaluation (p. 359).

cognitive-behavioral therapy (CBT) Therapy that integrates cognitive and behavioral techniques and that is based on the assumption that thoughts, moods, and behaviors are interrelated (p. 597).

cognitive dissonance An unpleasant state of psychological tension or arousal (dissonance) that occurs when two thoughts or perceptions (cognitions) are inconsistent; typically results from the awareness that attitudes and behavior are in conflict (p. 468).

cognitive map Tolman's term for the mental representation of the layout of a familiar environment (p. 214).

cognitive therapies A group of psychotherapies based on the assumption that psychological problems are due to maladaptive patterns of thinking; treatment techniques focus on recognizing and altering these unhealthy thinking patterns (p. 593).

cognitive therapy (CT) A Therapy developed by Aaron T. Beck, that focuses on changing the client's unrealistic and maladaptive beliefs (p. 595).

collective unconscious In Jung's theory, the hypothesized part of the unconscious mind that is inherited from previous generations and that contains universally shared ancestral experiences and ideas (p. 429).

collectivistic cultures Cultures that emphasize the needs and goals of the group over the needs and goals of the individual (p. 13).

color The perceptual experience of different wavelengths of light, involving hue, saturation (purity), and brightness (intensity) (p. 98).

color blindness One of several inherited forms of color deficiency or weakness in which an individual cannot distinguish between certain colors (p. 100).

comparative psychology Branch of psychology that studies the behavior or different animal species (p. 36).

competence motivation The desire to direct one's behavior toward demonstrating competence and exercising control in a situation (p. 343).

comprehension vocabulary The words that are understood by an infant or child (p. 383).

compulsions Repetitive behaviors or mental acts that are performed to prevent or reduce anxiety (p. 544).

concept A mental category of objects or ideas based on properties they share (p. 278).

concrete operational stage In Piaget's theory, the third stage of cognitive development, which lasts from about age 7 to adolescence; characterized by the ability to think logically about concrete objects and situations (p. 390).

conditional positive regard In Rogers's theory, the sense that you will be valued and loved only if you behave in a way that is acceptable to others; conditional love or acceptance (p. 434).

conditioned reinforcer A stimulus or event that has acquired reinforcing value by being associated with a primary reinforcer; also called a *secondary reinforcer* (p. 203).

conditioned response (CR) The learned, reflexive response to a conditioned stimulus (p. 187).

conditioned stimulus (CS) A formerly neutral stimulus that acquires the capacity to elicit a reflexive response (p. 187).

conditioning The process of learning associations between environmental events and behavioral responses (p. 185).

cones The short, thick, pointed sensory receptors of the eye that detect color and are responsible for color vision and visual acuity (p. 95).

conformity Adjusting your opinions, or judgments so that it matches those of other people, or the norms of a social group or situation (p. 474).

consciousness Personal awareness of mental activities, internal sensations, and the external environment (p. 136).

conservation In Piaget's theory, the understanding that two equal quantities remain equal even though the form or appearance is rearranged, as long as nothing is added or subtracted (p. 390).

context effect The tendency to recover information more easily when the retrieval occurs in the same setting as the original learning of the information (p. 246).

continuous reinforcement A schedule of reinforcement in which every occurrence of a particular response is reinforced (p. 210).

control group or control condition In an experiment, the group of participants who are exposed to all experimental conditions, except the independent variable; the group against which changes in the experimental group are compared (p. 30).

coping Behavioral and cognitive responses used to deal with stressors; involves our efforts to change circumstances, or our interpretation of circumstances, to make them more favorable and less threatening (p. 518).

cornea (CORE-nee-uh) A clear membrane covering the visible part of the eye that helps gather and direct incoming light (p. 94).

corpus callosum A thick band of axons that connects the two cerebral hemispheres and acts as a communication link between them (p. 68).

correlation The relationship between two variables (p. A-8).

correlation coefficient A numerical indication of the magnitude and direction of the relationship (the *correlation*) between two variables (pp. 25, A-8).

correlational study A research strategy that allows the precise calculation of how strongly related two factors are to each other (p. 25).

cortical localization The notion that different functions are located or localized in different areas of the brain; also called *localization of function* (pp. 63, 73).

corticosteroids (core-tick-oh-STAIR-oydz) Hormones released by the adrenal cortex that play a key role in the body's response to long-term stressors (p. 506).

counterconditioning A behavior therapy technique based on classical conditioning that involves modifying behavior by conditioning a new response that is incompatible with a previously learned response (p. 589).

creativity A group of cognitive processes used to generate useful, original, and novel ideas or solutions to problems (p. 312).

critical thinking The active process of minimizing preconceptions and biases while evaluating evidence, determining the conclusions that can reasonably be drawn from evidence, and considering alternative explanations for research findings or other phenomena (p. 17).

cross-cultural psychology Branch of psychology that studies the effects of culture on behavior and mental processes (p. 13).

cued recall A test of long-term memory that involves remembering an item of information in response to a retrieval cue (p. 245).

culture The attitudes, values, beliefs, and behaviors shared by a group of people and communicated from one generation to another (p. 13).

cyclothymic disorder (si-klo-THY-mick) A mood disorder characterized by moderate but frequent mood swings that are not severe enough to qualify as bipolar disorder (p. 549).

D

daily hassles Everyday minor events that annoy and upset people (p. 500).

decay theory The view that forgetting is due to normal metabolic processes that occur in the brain over time (p. 250).

decibel (DESS-uh-bell) The unit of measurement for loudness (p. 102).

déjà vu experience A memory illusion characterized by brief but intense feelings or familiarity in a situation that has never been experienced before (p. 251).

delusion A falsely held belief that persists despite compelling contradictory evidence (p. 563).

demand characteristics In a research study, subtle cues or signals expressed by the researcher that communicate the kind of response or behavior that is expected from the participant (p. 28).

dementia Progressive deterioration and impairment of memory, reasoning, and other cognitive functions occurring as the result of a disease or a condition (p. 268).

dendrites Multiple short fibers that extend from the neuron's cell body and receive information from other neurons or from sensory receptor cells (p. 46).

deoxyribonucleic acid (DNA) The double-stranded molecule that encodes genetic instructions; the chemical basis of heredity (p. 370).

dependent variable The factor that is observed and measured for change in an experiment; thought to be influenced by the independent variable; also called the *outcome variable*. (p. 27).

depressants A category of psychoactive drugs that depress or inhibit brain activity (p. 167).

depth perception The use of visual cues to perceive the distance or three-dimensional characteristics of objects (p. 119).

descriptive research methods Scientific procedures that involve systematically observing behavior in order to describe the relationship among behaviors and events (p. 21).

descriptive statistics Mathematical methods used to organize and summarize data (p. A-2).

developmental psychology The branch of psychology that studies how people change over the lifespan (p. 369).

difference threshold The smallest possible difference between two stimuli that can be detected half the time; also called *just noticeable difference* (p. 92).

diffusion of responsibility A phenomenon in which the presence of other people makes it less likely that any individual will help someone in distress because the obligation to intervene is shared among all the onlookers (p. 487).

discrepancy hypothesis An approach to explaining job satisfaction that focuses on the discrepancy, if any, between what a person wants from a job and how that person evaluates what is actually experienced at work (p. B-8).

discriminative stimulus A specific stimulus in the presence of which a particular response is more likely to be reinforced, and in the absence of which a particular response is not reinforced (p. 207).

displacement The ego defense mechanism that involves unconsciously shifting the target of an emotional urge to a substitute target that is less threatening or dangerous (p. 424).

display rules Social and cultural regulations governing emotional expression, especially facial expressions (p. 354).

dissociation The splitting of consciousness into two or more simultaneous streams of mental activity (p. 161).

dissociative amnesia A dissociative disorder involving the partial or total inability to recall important personal information (p. 561).

dissociative anesthetics Class of drugs that reduce sensitivity to pain and produce feelings of detachment and dissociation; includes the club drugs phencyclidine (PCP) and ketamine (p. 177).

dissociative disorders A category of psychological disorders in which extreme and frequent disruptions of awareness, memory, and personal identity impair the ability to function (p. 560).

dissociative experience A break or disruption in consciousness during which awareness, memory, and personal identity become separated or divided (p. 560).

dissociative fugue (fyoog) A dissociative disorder involving sudden and unexpected travel away from home, extensive amnesia, and identity confusion (p. 561).

dissociative identity disorder (DID) A dissociative disorder involving extensive memory disruptions along with the presence of two or more distinct identities, or "personalities"; formerly called *multiple personality disorder* (p. 561).

dopamine (DOPE-uh-meen) Neurotransmitter involved in the regulation of bodily movement, thought processes, and rewarding sensations (p. 52).

dopamine hypothesis The view that schizophrenia is related to, and may be caused by, excessive activity of the neurotransmitter dopamine in the brain (p. 570).

double-blind technique An experimental control in which neither the participants nor the researchers interacting with the participants are aware of the group or condition to which the participants have been assigned (p. 28).

dream An unfolding sequence of thoughts, perceptions, and emotions that typically occurs during REM sleep and is experienced as a series of real-life events (p. 147).

dream interpretation A technique used in psychoanalysis in which the content of dreams is analyzed for disguised or symbolic wishes, meanings, and motivations (p. 583).

drive A need or internal motivational state that activates behavior to reduce the need and restore homeostasis (p. 320).

drive theories The view that behavior is motivated by the desire to reduce internal tension caused by unmet biological needs (p. 320).

drug abuse Recurrent drug use that results in disruptions in academic, social, or occupational functioning or in legal or psychological problems (p. 166).

drug rebound effect Withdrawal symptoms that are the opposite of a physically addictive drug's action (p. 165).

drug tolerance A condition in which increasing amounts of a physically addictive drug are needed to produce the original, desired effect (p. 165).

DSM-IV-TR Abbreviation for the *Diagnostic and Statistical Manual of Mental Disorders,* Fourth Edition, Text Revision; the book published by the American Psychiatric Association that describes the specific symptoms and diagnostic guidelines for different psychological disorders (p. 533).

dyssomnias (dis-SOM-nee-uz) A category of sleep disorders involving disruptions in the amount, quality, or timing of sleep; includes *insomnia, obstructive sleep apnea,* and *narcolepsy* (p. 153).

dysthymic disorder (dis-THY-mick) A mood disorder involving chronic, low-grade feelings of depression that produce subjective discomfort but do not seriously impair the ability to function (p. 548).

E

eardrum A tightly stretched membrane at the end of the ear canal that vibrates when hit by sound waves (p. 102).

eating disorder A category of mental disorders characterized by severe disturbances in eating behavior (p. 553).

eclecticism (eh-KLEK-tuh-*sizz*-um) The pragmatic and integrated use of techniques from different psychotherapies (p. 604).

EEG (electroencephalogram) The graphic record of brain activity produced by an electroencephalograph (p. 140).

ego Latin for *I;* in Freud's theory, the partly conscious rational component of personality that regulates thoughts and behavior and is most in touch with the demands of the external world (p. 423).

ego defense mechanisms Largely unconscious distortions of thoughts or perceptions that act to reduce anxiety (p. 424).

egocentrism In Piaget's theory, the inability to take another person's perspective or point of view (p. 389).

elaborative rehearsal Rehearsal that involves focusing on the meaning of information to help encode and transfer it to long-term memory (p. 239).

electroconvulsive therapy (ECT) A biomedical therapy used primarily in the treatment of depression that involves electrically inducing a brief brain seizure; also called *electroshock therapy* (p. 614).

electroencephalograph (e-lec-tro-en-SEFF-uh-low-graph) An instrument that uses electrodes placed on the scalp to measure and record the brain's electrical activity (p. 140).

embryonic period The second period of prenatal development, extending from the third week through the eighth week (p. 373).

emotion A complex psychological state that involves subjective experience, a physiological response, and a behavioral or expressive response (p. 344).

emotional intelligence The capacity to understand and manage your own emotional experiences and to perceive, comprehend, and respond appropriately to the emotional responses of others (p. 345).

emotion-focused coping Coping efforts primarily aimed at relieving or regulating the emotional impact of a stressful situation (p. 519).

empirical evidence Verifiable evidence that is based upon objective observation, measurement, and/or experimentation (p. 16).

encoding The process of transforming information into a form that can be entered into and retained by the memory system (p. 232).

encoding failure The inability to recall specific information because of insufficient encoding of the information for storage in long-term memory (p. 249).

encoding specificity principle The principle that when the conditions of information retrieval are similar to the conditions of information encoding, retrieval is more likely to be successful (p. 246).

endocrine system (EN-doe-krin) System of glands located throughout the body that secrete hormones into the bloodstream (p. 59).

endorphins (en-DORF-ins) Neurotransmitters that regulate pain perceptions (p. 53).

energy homeostasis The long-term matching of food intake to energy expenditure (p. 324).

epigenetics Study of the cellular mechanisms that control gene expression and of the ways that gene expression impacts health and behavior (p. 372).

episodic memory Category of long-term memory that includes memories of particular events (p. 240).

Eros The self-preservation or life instinct, reflected in the expression of basic biological urges that perpetuate the existence of the individual and the species (p. 423).

ESP (extrasensory perception) Perception of information by some means other than through the normal processes of sensation (p. 116).

ethnocentrism The belief that one's own culture or ethnic group is superior to all others, and the related tendency to use one's own culture as a standard by which to judge other cultures (pp. 13, 471).

evolutionary psychology The application of principles of evolution, including natural selection, to explain psychological processes and phenomena (p. 12).

exemplars Individual instances of a concept or category, held in memory (p. 280).

experimental group or experimental condition In an experiment, the group of participants who are exposed to all experimental conditions, including the independent variable (p. 27).

experimental method A method of investigation used to demonstrate cause-and-effect relationships by purposely manipulating one factor thought to produce change in another factor (p. 27).

explicit cognition Deliberate, conscious mental processes involved in perceptions, judgments, decisions, and reasoning (p. 460).

explicit memory Information or knowledge that can be consciously recollected; also called *declarative memory* (p. 241).

exposure therapy Behavioral therapy for phobias, panic disorder, post-traumatic stress disorder, or related anxiety disorders in which the person is repeatedly exposed to the disturbing object or situation under controlled conditions (p. 604).

extinction (in classical conditioning) The gradual weakening and apparent disappearance of conditioned behavior. In classical conditioning, extinction occurs when the conditioned stimulus is repeatedly presented without the unconditioned stimulus (p. 189).

extinction (in operant conditioning) The gradual weakening and disappearance of conditioned behavior. In operant conditioning, extinction occurs when an emitted behavior is no longer followed by a reinforcer (p. 210).

extraneous variable A factor or variable other than the ones being studied that, if not controlled, could affect the outcome of an experiment; also called a *confounding variable* (p. 27).

extrinsic motivation External factors or influences on behavior, such as rewards, consequences, or social expectations (p. 342).

eye movement desensitization reprocessing (EMDR) Therapy technique in which the client holds a vivid mental image of a troubling event or situation while rapidly moving his or her eyes back and forth in response to the therapist's waving finger or while the therapist administers some other form of bilateral stimulation, such as sounding tones in alternate ears (p. 604).

F

facial feedback hypothesis The view that expressing a specific emotion, especially facially, causes the subjective experience of that emotion (p. 358).

false memory A distorted or fabricated recollection of something that did not actually occur (p. 256).

family therapy A form of psychotherapy that is based on the assumption that the family is a system and that treats the family as a unit (p. 600).

fetal period The third and longest period of prenatal development, extending from the ninth week until birth (p. 374).

fight-or-flight response A rapidly occurring chain of internal physical reactions that prepare people either to fight or take flight from an immediate threat (p. 504).

figure–ground relationship A Gestalt principle of perceptual organization that states that we automatically separate the elements of a perception into the feature that clearly stands out (the figure) and its less distinct background (the ground) (p. 115).

five-factor model of personality A trait theory of personality that identifies extraversion, neuroticism, agreeableness, conscientiousness, and openness to experience as the fundamental building blocks of personality (p. 442).

fixed-interval (FI) schedule A reinforcement schedule in which a reinforcer is delivered for the first response that occurs after a preset time interval has elapsed (p. 211).

fixed-ratio (FR) schedule A reinforcement schedule in which a reinforcer is delivered after a fixed number of responses has occurred (p. 210).

flashbulb memory The recall of very specific images or details surrounding a vivid, rare, or significant personal event; details may or may not be accurate (p. 246).

forebrain The largest and most complex brain region, which contains centers for complex behaviors and mental processes; also called the *cerebrum* (p. 68).

forgetting The inability to recall information that was previously available (p. 248).

formal concept A mental category that is formed by learning the rules or features that define it (p. 279).

formal operational stage In Piaget's theory, the fourth stage of cognitive development, which lasts from adolescence through adulthood; characterized by the ability to think logically about abstract principles and hypothetical situations (p. 390).

fovea (FO-vee-uh) A small area in the center of the retina, composed entirely of cones, where visual information is most sharply focused (p. 95).

free association A technique used in psychoanalysis in which the patient spontaneously reports all thoughts, feelings, and mental images as they come to mind, as a way of revealing unconscious thoughts and emotions (pp. 421, 582).

frequency The rate of vibration, or the number of sound waves per second (p. 102).

frequency distribution A summary of how often various scores occur in a sample of scores. Score values are arranged in order of magnitude, and the number of times each score occurs is recorded (p. A-3).

frequency polygon A way of graphically representing a frequency distribution; frequency is marked above each score category on the graph's horizontal axis, and the marks are connected by straight lines (p. A-4).

frequency theory The view that the basilar membrane vibrates at the same frequency as the sound wave (p. 104).

frontal lobe The largest lobe of each cerebral hemisphere; processes voluntary muscle movements and is involved in thinking, planning, and emotional control (p. 69).

functional fixedness The tendency to view objects as functioning only in their usual or customary way (p. 284).

functional magnetic resonance imaging (fMRI) A noninvasive imaging technique that uses magnetic fields to map brain activity by measuring changes in the brain's blood flow and oxygen levels (p. 34).

functional plasticity The brain's ability to shift functions from damaged to undamaged brain areas (p. 62).

functionalism Early school of psychology that emphasized studying the purpose, or function, of behavior and mental experiences (p. 5).

fundamental attribution error The tendency to attribute the behavior of others to internal, personal characteristics, while ignoring or underestimating the effects of external, situational factors; an attributional bias that is common in individualistic cultures (p. 463).

G

***g* factor** or **general intelligence** The notion of a general intelligence factor that is responsible for a person's overall performance on tests of mental ability (p. 299).

GABA (gamma-aminobutyric acid) Neurotransmitter that usually communicates an inhibitory message (p. 53).

ganglion cells In the retina, the specialized neurons that connect to the bipolar cells; the bundled axons of the ganglion cells form the optic nerve (p. 96).

gate-control theory of pain The theory that pain is a product of both physiological and psychological factors that cause spinal gates to open and relay patterns of intense stimulation to the brain, which perceives them as pain (p. 110).

gender The cultural, social, and psychological meanings that are associated with masculinity or femininity (p. 384).

gender identity A person's psychological sense of being male or female (p. 384).

gender roles The behaviors, attitudes, and personality traits that are designated as either masculine or feminine in a given culture (p. 384).

gender schema theory The theory that gender-role development is influenced by the formation of schemas, or mental representations, of masculinity and femininity (p. 386).

gene A unit of DNA on a chromosome that encodes instructions for making a particular protein molecule; the basic unit of heredity (p. 370).

general adaptation syndrome Selye's term for the three-stage progression of physical changes that occur when an organism is exposed to intense and prolonged stress. The three stages are alarm, resistance, and exhaustion (p. 505).

generalized anxiety disorder (GAD) An anxiety disorder characterized by excessive, global, and persistent symptoms of anxiety; also called *free-floating anxiety* (p. 537).

genotype (JEEN-oh-type) The genetic makeup of an individual organism (p. 371).

germinal period The first two weeks of prenatal development (p. 373).

Gestalt psychology (geh-SHTALT) A school of psychology founded in Germany in the early 1900s that maintained that our sensations are actively processed according to consistent perceptual rules that result in meaningful whole perceptions, or *gestalts* (p. 115).

ghrelin (GRELL-in) Hormone manufactured primarily by the stomach that stimulates appetite and the secretion of growth hormone by the pituitary gland (p. 324).

glial cells (GLEE-ull) Support cells that assist neurons by providing structural support, nutrition, and removal of cell wastes; manufacture myelin (p. 45).

glucose Simple sugar that provides energy and is primarily produced by the conversion of carbohydrates and fats; commonly called *blood sugar* (p. 323).

gonads The endocrine glands that secrete hormones that regulate sexual characteristics and reproductive processes; *ovaries* in females and *testes* in males (p. 61).

graphology A pseudoscience that claims to assess personality, social, and occupational attributes based on a person's distinctive handwriting, doodles, and drawing style (p. 448).

group therapy A form of psychotherapy that involves one or more therapists working simultaneously with a small group of clients (p. 598).

gustation Technical name for the sense of taste (p. 105).

H

hair cells The hairlike sensory receptors for sound, which are embedded in the basilar membrane of the cochlea (p. 103).

hallucination A false or distorted perception that seems vividly real to the person experiencing it (p. 564).

health psychology The branch of psychology that studies how biological, behavioral, and social factors influence health, illness, medical treatment, and health-related behaviors (p. 498).

heritability The percentage of variation within a given population that is due to heredity (p. 305).

heuristic A problem-solving strategy that involves following a general rule of thumb to reduce the number of possible solutions (p. 282).

hidden observer Hilgard's term for the hidden, or dissociated, stream of mental activity that continues during hypnosis (p. 161).

hierarchy of needs Maslow's hierarchical division of motivation into levels that progress from basic physical needs to psychological needs to self-fulfillment needs (p. 340).

higher order conditioning A procedure in which a conditioned stimulus from one learning trial functions as the unconditioned stimulus in a new conditioing trial; the second conditioned stimulus comes to elicit the conditioned response, even though it has never been directly paired with the unconditioned stimulus (p. 188).

hindbrain A region at the base of the brain that contains several structures that regulate basic life functions (p. 66).

hindsight bias The tendency to overestimate one's ability to have foreseen or predicted the outcome of an event (p. 464).

hippocampus A curved forebrain structure that is part of the limbic system and is involved in learning and forming new memories (p. 71).

histogram A way of graphically representing a frequency distribution; a type of bar chart that uses vertical bars that touch (p. A-3).

homeostasis (home-ee-oh-STAY-sis) The idea that the body monitors and maintains internal states, such as body temperature and energy supplies, at relatively constant levels; in general, the tendency to reach or maintain equilibrium (p. 320).

hormones Chemical messengers secreted into the bloodstream primarily by endocrine glands (p. 59).

hue The property of wavelengths of light known as color; different wavelengths correspond to our subjective experience of different colors (p. 98).

humanistic psychology The theoretical viewpoint on personality that generally emphasizes the inherent goodness of people, human potential, self-actualization, the self-concept, and healthy personality development (pp. 9, 433).

humanistic theories of motivation The view that emphasizes the importance of psychological and cognitive factors in motivation, especially the notion that people are motivated to realize their personal potential (p. 321).

hypermnesia (high-perm-NEE-zha) The supposed enhancement of a person's memory for past events through a hypnotic suggestion (p. 160).

hypnagogic hallucinations (hip-na-GAH-jick) Vivid sensory phenomena that occur during the onset of sleep (p. 141).

hypnosis (hip-NO-sis) A cooperative social interaction in which the hypnotized person responds to the hypnotist's suggestions with changes in perception, memory, and behavior (p. 159).

hypocretins A special class of neurotransmitters produced during the daytime to maintain a steady state of wakefulness (p. 156).

hypothalamus (hi-poe-THAL-uh-muss) A peanut-sized forebrain structure that is part of the limbic system and regulates behaviors related to survival, such as eating, drinking, and sexual activity (p. 71).

hypothesis (high-POTH-eh-sis) A tentative statement about the relationship between two or more variables; a testable prediction or question (p. 16).

I

id Latin for *the it;* in Freud's theory, the completely unconscious, irrational component of personality that seeks immediate satisfaction of instinctual urges and drives; ruled by the pleasure principle (p. 422).

identification In psychoanalytic theory, an ego defense mechanism that involves reducing anxiety by imitating the behavior and characteristics of another person (p. 426).

identity A person's definition or description of himself or herself, including the values, beliefs, and ideals that guide the individual's behavior (p. 399).

imagination inflation A memory phenomenon in which vividly imagining an event markedly increases confidence that the event actually occurred (p. 258).

immune system Body system that produces specialized white blood cells that protect the body from viruses, bacteria, and tumor cells (p. 506).

implicit cognition Automatic, nonconscious mental processes that influence perceptions, judgments, and reasoning (p. 460).

implicit memory Information or knowledge that affects behavior or task performance but cannot be consciously recollected; also called *nondeclarative memory* (p. 241).

implicit personality theory A network of assumptions or beliefs about the relationships among various types of people, traits, and behaviors (p. 461).

incentive theories The view that behavior is motivated by the pull of external goals, such as rewards (p. 321).

independent variable The purposely manipulated factor thought to produce change in an experiment; also called the *treatment variable* (p. 27).

individualistic cultures Cultures that emphasize the needs and goals of the individual over the needs and goals of the group (p. 13).

induction A discipline technique that combines parental control with explaining why a behavior is prohibited (p. 412).

industrial/organizational (I/O) psychology The branch of psychology that focuses on the study of human behavior in the workplace (p. B-2).

inferential statistics Mathematical methods used to determine how likely it is that a study's outcome is due to chance and whether the outcome can be legitimately generalized to a larger population (p. A-12).

informational social influence Behavior that is motivated by the desire to be correct (p. 475).

information-processing model of cognitive development The model that views cognitive development as a process that is continuous over the lifespan and that studies the development of basic mental processes such as attention, memory, and problem solving (p. 393).

in-group A social group to which one belongs (p. 471).

in-group bias The tendency to judge the behavior of in-group members favorably and out-group members unfavorably (p. 471).

inhalants Chemical substances that are inhaled to produce an alteration in consciousness (p. 169).

inner ear The part of the ear where sound is transduced into neural impulses; consists of the cochlea and semicircular canals (p. 103).

insight The sudden realization of how a problem can be solved (p. 283).

insomnia A condition in which a person regularly experiences an inability to fall asleep, to stay asleep, or to feel adequately rested by sleep (p. 153).

instinct theories The view that certain human behaviors are innate and due to evolutionary programming (p. 319).

instinctive drift The tendency of an animal to revert to instinctive behaviors that can interfere with the performance of an operantly conditioned response (p. 217).

insulin Hormone produced by the pancreas that regulates blood levels of glucose and signals the hypothalamus, regulating hunger and eating behavior (p. 323).

intelligence The global capacity to think rationally, act purposefully, and deal effectively with the environment (p. 293).

intelligence quotient (IQ) A measure of general intelligence derived by comparing an individual's score with the scores of others in the same age group (p. 294).

interference theory The theory that forgetting is caused by one memory competing with or replacing another (p. 252).

interneuron Type of neuron that communicates information from one neuron to the next (p. 45).

interpersonal engagement Emotion dimension reflecting the degree to which emotions involve a relationship with another person or other people (p. 346).

interpersonal therapy (IPT) A brief, psychodynamic psychotherapy that focuses on current relationships and is based on the assumption that symptoms are caused and maintained by interpersonal problems (p. 584).

interpretation A technique used in psychoanalysis in which the psychoanalyst offers a carefully timed explanation of the patient's dreams, free associations, or behaviors to facilitate the recognition of unconscious conflicts or motivations (p. 583).

intrinsic motivation The desire to engage in tasks that the person finds inherently satisfying and enjoyable, novel, or optimally challenging; the desire to do something for its own sake (p. 342).

intuition Coming to a conclusion or making a judgment without conscious awareness of the thought processes involved (p. 283).

iris (EYE-riss) The colored part of the eye, which is the muscle that controls the size of the pupil (p. 94).

irreversibility In Piaget's theory, the inability to mentally reverse a sequence of events or logical operations (p. 389).

J

James–Lange theory of emotion The theory that emotions arise from the perception of body changes (p. 356).

job analysis A technique that identifies the major responsibilities of a job, along with the human characteristics needed to fill it (p. B-3).

just-world hypothesis The assumption that the world is fair and that therefore people get what they deserve and deserve what they get (p. 464).

K

K complex Single but large high-voltage spike of brain activity that characterizes stage 2 NREM sleep (p. 142).

kinesthetic sense (kin-ess-THET-ick) The technical name for the sense of location and position of body parts in relation to one another (p. 112).

L

language A system for combining arbitrary symbols to produce an infinite number of meaningful statements (p. 287).

latent content In Freud's psychoanalytic theory, the unconscious wishes, thoughts, and urges that are concealed in the manifest content of a dream (p. 151).

latent learning Tolman's term for learning that occurs in the absence of reinforcement but is not behaviorally demonstrated until a reinforcer becomes available (p. 215).

lateralization of function The notion that specific psychological or cognitive functions are processed primarily on one side of the brain (p. 73).

law of effect Learning principle proposed by Thorndike that responses followed by a satisfying effect become strengthened and are more likely to recur in a particular situation, while responses followed by a dissatisfying effect are weakened and less likely to recur in a particular situation (p. 200).

leader–member exchange model A model of leadership emphasizing that the quality of the interactions between supervisors and subordinates varies depending on the unique characteristics of both (p. B-9).

learned helplessness A phenomenon in which exposure to inescapable and uncontrollable aversive events produces passive behavior (p. 216).

learning A process that produces a relatively enduring change in behavior or knowledge as a result of past experience (p. 184).

lens A transparent structure located behind the pupil that actively focuses, or bends, light as it enters the eye (p. 94).

leptin Hormone produced by fat cells that signals the hypothalamus, regulating hunger and eating behavior (p. 326).

leptin resistance A condition in which higher-than-normal blood levels of the hormone leptin do not produce the expected physiological response (p. 331).

libido The psychological and emotional energy associated with expressions of sexuality; the sex drive (p. 423).

limbic system A group of forebrain structures that form a border around the brainstem and are involved in emotion, motivation, learning, and memory (p. 70).

linguistic relativity hypothesis The hypothesis that differences among languages cause differences in the thoughts of their speakers (p. 290).

lithium A naturally occurring substance that is used in the treatment of bipolar disorder (p. 611).

long-term memory The stage of memory that represents the long-term storage of information (p. 233).

long-term potentiation A long-lasting increase in synaptic strength between two neurons (p. 263).

loudness The intensity (or amplitude) of a sound wave, measured in decibels (p. 102).

LSD A synthetic psychedelic drug (p. 174).

lymphocytes (LIMF-oh-sites) Specialized white blood cells that are responsible for immune defenses (p. 506).

M

magnetic resonance imaging (MRI) A noninvasive imaging technique that produces highly detailed images of the body's structures and tissues using electromagnetic signals generated by the body in response to magnetic fields (p. 34).

main effect Any change that can be directly attributed to the independent or treatment variable after controlling for other possible influences (p. 29).

maintenance rehearsal The mental or verbal repetition of information in order to maintain it beyond the usual 20-second duration of short-term memory (p. 236).

major depression A mood disorder characterized by extreme and persistent feelings of despondency, worthlessness, and hopelessness, causing impaired emotional, cognitive, behavioral, and physical functioning (p. 546).

manic episode A sudden, rapidly escalating emotional state characterized by extreme euphoria, excitement, physical energy, and rapid thoughts and speech (p. 549).

manifest content In Freud's psychoanalytic theory, the elements of a dream that are consciously experienced and remembered by the dreamer (p. 151).

marijuana A psychoactive drug derived from the hemp plant (p. 175).

MDMA or ecstasy Synthetic club drug that combines stimulant and mild psychedelic effects (p. 175).

mean The sum of a set of scores in a distribution divided by the number of scores; the mean is usually the most representative measure of central tendency (p. A-5).

measure of central tendency A single number that presents some information about the "center" of a frequency distribution (p. A-5).

measure of variability A single number that presents information about the spread of scores in a distribution (p. A-5).

median The score that divides a frequency distribution exactly in half so that the same number of scores lie on each side of it (p. A-5).

meditation Any one of a number of sustained concentration techniques that focus attention and heighten awareness (p. 163).

medulla (meh-DOOL-uh) A hindbrain structure that controls vital life functions such as breathing and circulation (p. 67).

melatonin (mel-ah-TONE-in) A hormone manufactured by the pineal gland that produces sleepiness (p. 139).

memory The mental processes that enable us to retain and use information over time (p. 232).

memory consolidation The gradual, physical process of converting new long-term memories to stable, enduring long-term memory codes (p. 264).

memory trace or **engram** The brain changes associated with a particular stored memory (p. 261).

menarche (meh-NAR-kee) A female's first menstrual period, which occurs during puberty (p. 394).

menopause The natural cessation of menstruation and the end of reproductive capacity in women (p. 404).

mental age A measurement of intelligence in which an individual's mental level is expressed in terms of the average abilities of a given age group (p. 294).

mental image A mental representation of objects or events that are not physically present (p. 277).

mental retardation Disorder characterized by intellectual function that is significantly below average, usually defined as a measured IQ of 70 or below, and that is caused by brain injury, disease, or a genetic disorder (p. 302).

mental set The tendency to persist in solving problems with solutions that have worked in the past (p. 284).

mere exposure effect The finding that repeated exposure to a stimulus increases a person's preference for that stimulus (p. 91).

mescaline (MESS-kuh-*lin*) A psychedelic drug derived from the peyote cactus (p. 174).

meta-analysis A statistical technique that involves combining and analyzing the results of many research studies on a specific topic in order to identify overall trends (p. 19).

midbrain The middle and smallest brain region, involved in processing auditory and visual sensory information (p. 67).

middle ear The part of the ear that amplifies sound waves; consists of three small bones: the hammer, the anvil, and the stirrup (p. 102).

mindfull meditation A tecnique in which practitioners focus awareness on present experience with acceptance (p. 524).

Minnesota Multiphasic Personality Inventory (MMPI) A self-report inventory that assesses personality characteristics and psychological disorders; used to assess both normal and disturbed populations (p. 449).

mirror neurons A type of neuron that activates both when an action is performed and when the same action is perceived (p. 219).

misinformation effect A memory-distortion phenomenon in which a person's existing memories can be altered if the person is exposed to misleading information (p. 254).

mode The most frequently occurring score in a distribution (p. A-5).

monocular cues (moe-NOCK-you-ler) Distance or depth cues that can be processed by either eye alone (p. 119).

mood congruence An encoding specificity phenomenon in which a given mood tends to evoke memories that are consistent with that mood (p. 246).

mood disorders A category of mental disorders in which significant and persistent disruptions in mood or emotions cause impaired cognitive, behavioral, and physical functioning; also called *affective disorders* (p. 546).

moon illusion A visual illusion involving the misperception that the moon is larger when it is on the horizon than when it is directly overhead (p. 125).

moral reasoning The aspects of cognitive development that has to do with how an individual reasons about matters of wrong and right (p. 401).

motivation The biological, emotional, cognitive, or social forces that activate and direct behavior (p. 319).

motor neuron Type of neuron that signals muscles to relax or contract (p. 45).

Müller-Lyer illusion A famous visual illusion involving the misperception of the identical length of two lines, one with arrows pointed inward, one with arrows pointed outward (p. 124).

myelin sheath (MY-eh-lin) A white, fatty covering wrapped around the axons of some neurons that increases their communication speed (p. 47).

N

narcolepsy (NAR-ko-lep-see) A sleep disorder characterized by excessive daytime sleepiness and brief lapses into sleep throughout the day (p. 155).

natural concept A mental category that is formed as a result of everyday experience (p. 280).

natural experiment A study investigating the effects of a naturally occurring event on the research participants (p. 32).

naturalistic observation The systematic observation and recording of behaviors as they occur in their natural setting (p. 21).

negative correlation A finding that two factors vary systematically in opposite directions, one increasing as the other decreases (pp. 26, A-9).

negative reinforcement A situation in which a response results in the removal of, avoidance of, or escape from a punishing stimulus, increasing the likelihood that the response will be repeated in similar situations (p. 202).

negative symptoms In schizophrenia, symptoms that reflect defects or deficits in normal functioning, including flat affect, alogia, and avolition (p. 563).

neodissociation theory of hypnosis Theory proposed by Ernest Hilgard that explains hypnotic effects as being due to the splitting of consciousness into two simultaneous streams of mental activity, only one of which the hypnotic participant is consciously aware of during hypnosis (p. 161).

nerves Bundles of neuron axons that carry information in the peripheral nervous system (p. 56).

nervous system The primary internal communication network of the body; divided into the central nervous system and the peripheral nervous system (p. 55).

neurogenesis The development of new neurons (p. 62).

neuron Highly specialized cell that communicates information in electrical and chemical form; a nerve cell (p. 45).

neuropeptide Y (NPY) Neurotransmitter found in several brain areas, most notably the hypothalamus, that stimulates eating behavior and reduces metabolism, promoting positive energy balance and weight gain (p. 327).

neuroscience The study of the nervous system, especially the brain (pp. 10, 44).

neurotransmitters Chemical messengers manufactured by a neuron (p. 50).

nicotine A stimulant drug found in tobacco products (p. 172).

nightmare A vivid and frightening or unpleasant anxiety dream that occurs during REM sleep (p. 150).

nociceptors Specialized sensory receptors for pain that are found in the skin, muscles, and internal organs (p. 110).

norepinephrine (nor-ep-in-EF-rin) Neurotransmitter involved in learning, memory, and regulation of sleep; also a hormone manufactured by adrenal glands (p. 52).

normal curve or **normal distribution** A bell-shaped distribution of individual differences in a normal population in which most scores cluster around the average score (p. 297).

normative social influence Behavior that is motivated by the desire to gain social acceptance and approval (p. 475).

NREM sleep Quiet, typically dreamless sleep in which rapid eye movements are absent; divided into four stages; also called *quiet sleep* (p. 141).

O

obedience The performance of a behavior in response to a direct command (p. 476).

obese Condition characterized by excessive body fat and a body mass index equal to or greater than 30.0 (p. 329).

object permanence The understanding that an object continues to exist even when it can no longer be seen (p. 388).

observational learning Learning that occurs through observing the actions of others (p. 218).

obsessions Repeated, intrusive, and uncontrollable irrational thoughts or mental images that cause extreme anxiety and distress (p. 543).

obsessive–compulsive disorder (OCD) An anxiety disorder in which the symptoms of anxiety are triggered by intrusive, repetitive thoughts and urges to perform certain actions (p. 543).

obstructive sleep apnea (OSA) (APP-nee-uh) A sleep disorder in which the person repeatedly stops breathing during sleep (p. 155).

occipital lobe (ock-SIP-it-ull) An area at the back of each cerebral hemisphere that is the primary receiving area for visual information (p. 69).

Oedipus complex In Freud's theory, a child's unconscious sexual desire for the opposite-sex parent, usually accompanied by hostile feelings toward the same-sex parent (p. 426).

olfaction Technical name for the sense of smell (p. 105).

olfactory bulb (ole-FACK-toe-ree) The enlarged ending of the olfactory cortex at the front of the brain where the sensation of smell is registered (p. 106).

operant Skinner's term for an actively emitted (or voluntary) behavior that operates on the environment to produce consequences (p. 200).

operant chamber or Skinner box The experimental apparatus invented by B. F. Skinner to study the relationship between environmental events and active behaviors (p. 209).

operant conditioning The basic learning process that involves changing the probability that a response will be repeated by manipulating the consequences of that response (p. 200).

operational definition A precise description of how the variables in a study will be manipulated or measured (p. 18).

opiates (OH-pee-ets) A category of psychoactive drugs that are chemically similar to morphine and have strong pain-relieving properties (p. 171).

opponent-process theory of color vision The theory that color vision is the product of opposing pairs of color receptors, red–green, blue–yellow, and black–white; when one member of a color pair is stimulated, the other member is inhibited (p. 100).

optic chiasm (KI-az-em) Point in the brain where the optic nerve fibers from each eye meet and partly cross over to the opposite side of the brain (p. 97).

optic disk Area of the retina without rods or cones, where the optic nerve exits the back of the eye (p. 96).

optic nerve The thick nerve that exits from the back of the eye and carries visual information to the visual cortex in the brain (p. 97).

optimistic explanatory style Accounting for negative events or situations with external, unstable, and specific explanations (p. 510).

organizational behavior A subarea of I/O psychology that focuses on the workplace culture and its influence on employee behavior (p. B-2).

outer ear The part of the ear that collects sound waves; consists of the pinna, the ear canal, and the eardrum (p. 102).

out-group A social group to which one does not belong (p. 471).

out-group homogeneity effect The tendency to see members of out-groups as very similar to one another (p. 471).

P

pain The unpleasant sensation of physical discomfort or suffering that can occur in varying degrees of intensity (p. 110).

panic attack A sudden episode of extreme anxiety that rapidly escalates in intensity (p. 538).

panic disorder An anxiety disorder in which the person experiences frequent and unexpected panic attacks (p. 538).

paranoid personality disorder A personality disorder characterized by a pervasive distrust and suspiciousness of the motives of others without sufficient basis (p. 557).

parapsychology The scientific investigation of claims of paranormal phenomena and abilities (p. 116).

parasomnias (pare-uh-SOM-nee-uz) A category of sleep disorders characterized by arousal or activation during sleep or sleep transitions; includes *sleepwalking, sleep terrors, sleepsex, sleep-related eating disorder,* and *REM sleep behavior disorder* (p. 153).

parasympathetic nervous system Branch of the autonomic nervous system that maintains normal bodily functions and conserves the body's physical resources (p. 59).

parietal lobe (puh-RYE-et-ull) An area on each hemisphere of the cerebral cortex located above the temporal lobe that processes somatic sensations (p. 69).

partial reinforcement A situation in which the occurrence of a particular response is only sometimes followed by a reinforcer (p. 210).

partial reinforcement effect The phenomenon in which behaviors that are conditioned using partial reinforcement are more resistant to extinction than behaviors that are conditioned using continuous reinforcement (p. 210).

perception The process of integrating, organizing, and interpreting sensations (p. 89).

perceptual constancy The tendency to perceive objects, especially familiar objects, as constant and unchanging despite changes in sensory input (p. 123).

perceptual illusion The misperception of the true characteristics of an object or an image (p. 124).

perceptual set The tendency to perceive objects or situations from a particular frame of reference (p. 127).

peripheral nervous system (per-IF-er-ull) Division of the nervous system that includes all the nerves lying outside the central nervous system (p. 57).

permissive parenting style Parenting style in which parents are extremely tolerant and not demanding; permissive-indulgent parents are more responsive to their children, whereas permissive-indifferent parents are not (p. 411).

person perception The mental processes we use to form judgments and draw conclusions about the characteristics and motives of other people (p. 459).

personality An individual's unique and relatively consistent patterns of thinking, feeling, and behaving (p. 419).

personality disorder Inflexible, maladaptive patterns of thoughts, emotions, behavior, and interpersonal functioning that are stable over time and across situations, and deviate from the expectations of the individual's culture (p. 555).

personality theory A theory that attempts to describe and explain similarities and differences in people's patterns of thinking, feeling, and behaving (p. 419).

personnel psychology A subarea of I/O psychology that focuses on matching people's characteristics to job requirements, accurately measuring job performance, and assessing employee training needs (p. B-2).

persuasion The deliberate attempts to influence the attitudes or behavior of another person in a situation in which that person has some freedom of choice (p. 489).

pessimistic explanatory style Accounting for negative events or situations with internal, stable, and global explanations (p. 510).

phenotype (FEEN-oh-type) The observable traits or characteristics of an organism as determined by the interaction of genetics and environmental factors (p. 372).

pheromones Chemical signals released by an animal that communicate information and affect the behavior of other animals of the same species (p. 107).

phobia A persistent and irrational fear of a specific object, situation, or activity (p. 539).

phrenology (freh-NOL-uh-gee) A pseudoscientific theory of the brain that claimed that personality characteristics, moral character, and intelligence could be determined by examining the bumps on a person's skull (p. 63).

physical dependence A condition in which a person has physically adapted to a drug so that he or she must take the drug regularly in order to avoid withdrawal symptoms (p. 165).

pitch The relative highness or lowness of a sound, determined by the frequency of a sound wave (p. 102).

pituitary gland (pih-TOO-ih-tare-ee) Endocrine gland attached to the base of the brain that secretes hormones that affect the function of other glands as well as hormones that act directly on physical processes (p. 60).

place theory The view that different frequencies cause larger vibrations at different locations along the basilar membrane (p. 104).

placebo A fake substance, treatment, or procedure that has no known direct effects (p. 27).

placebo effect Any change attributed to a person's beliefs and expectations rather than an actual drug, treatment, or procedure; also called *expectancy effect* (p. 28).

placebo response An individual's psychological and physiological response to what is actually a fake treatment or drug; also called *placebo effect* (p. 194).

pleasure principle The motive to obtain pleasure and avoid tension or discomfort; the most fundamental human motive and the guiding principle of the id (p. 423).

pons A hindbrain structure that connects the medulla to the two sides of the cerebellum; helps coordinate and integrate movements on each side of the body (p. 67).

population A complete set of something—people, nonhuman animals, objects, or events (p. A-13).

positive correlation A finding that two factors vary systematically in the same direction, increasing or decreasing together (pp. 26, A-9).

positive incentive value In eating behavior, the anticipated pleasure of consuming a particular food; in general, the expectation of pleasure or satisfaction in performing a particular behavior (p. 325).

positive psychology The study of positive emotions and psychological states, positive individual traits, and the social institutions that foster positive individuals and communities (p. 11).

positive reinforcement A situation in which a response is followed by the addition of a reinforcing stimulus, increasing the likelihood that the response will be repeated in similar situations (p. 202).

positive symptoms In schizophrenia, symptoms that reflect excesses or distortions of normal functioning, including delusions, hallucinations, and disorganized thoughts and behavior (p. 563).

positron emission tomography (PET scan) An invasive imaging technique that provides color-coded images of brain activity by tracking the brain's use of a radioactively tagged compound, such as glucose, oxygen, or a drug (p. 34).

possible selves The aspect of the self-concept that includes images of the selves that you hope, fear, or expect to become in the future (p. 451).

posthypnotic amnesia The inability to recall specific information because of a hypnotic suggestion (p. 160).

posthypnotic suggestion A suggestion made during hypnosis that the person should carry out a specific instruction following the hypnotic session (p. 160).

post-traumatic stress disorder (PTSD) An anxiety disorder in which chronic and persistent symptoms of anxiety develop in response to an extreme physical or psychological trauma (p. 542).

practice effect Any change in performance that results from mere repetition of a task (p. 28).

prejudice A negative attitude toward people who belong to a specific social group (p. 469).

prenatal stage The stage of development before birth; divided into the germinal, embryonic, and fetal periods (p. 373).

preoperational stage In Piaget's theory, the second stage of cognitive development, which lasts from about age 2 to age 7;

characterized by increasing use of symbols and prelogical thought processes (p. 388).

primary reinforcer A stimulus or event that is naturally or inherently reinforcing for a given species, such as food, water, or other biological necessities (p. 203).

primary sex characteristics Sexual organs that are directly involved in reproduction, such as the uterus, ovaries, penis, and testicles (p. 394).

proactive interference Forgetting in which an old memory interferes with remembering a new memory; forward-acting memory interference (p. 252).

problem solving Thinking and behavior directed toward attaining a goal that is not readily available (p. 281).

problem-focused coping Coping efforts primarily aimed at directly changing or managing a threatening or harmful stressor (p. 519).

procedural memory Category of long-term memory that includes memories of different skills, operations, and actions (p. 240).

production vocabulary The words that an infant or child understands and can speak (p. 383).

projective test A type of personality test that involves a person's interpreting an ambiguous image; used to assess unconscious motives, conflicts, psychological defenses, and personality traits (p. 446).

proprioceptors (pro-pree-oh-SEP-ters) Sensory receptors, located in the muscles and joints, that provide information about body position and movement (p. 112).

prosocial behavior Any behavior that helps another, whether the underlying motive is self-serving or selfless (p. 486).

prospective memory Remembering to do something in the future (p. 250).

prototype The most typical instance of a particular concept (p. 280).

pseudoscience A fake or false science that makes claims based on little or no scientific evidence (p. 22).

psychedelic drugs (*sy*-kuh-DEL-ick) A category of psychoactive drugs that create sensory and perceptual distortions, alter mood, and affect thinking (p. 174).

psychiatry Medical specialty area focused on the diagnosis, treatment, causes, and prevention of mental and behavioral disorders (p. 15).

psychoactive drug A drug that alters consciousness, perception, mood, and behavior (p. 165).

psychoanalysis A type of psychotherapy originated by Sigmund Freud in which free association, dream interpretation, and analysis of resistance and transference are used to explore repressed or unconscious impulses, anxieties, and internal conflicts (pp. 7, 420, 582).

psychological disorder or **mental disorder** A pattern of behavioral and psychological symptoms that causes significant personal distress, impairs the ability to function in one or more important areas of daily life, or both (p. 533).

psychological test A test that assesses a person's abilities, aptitudes, interests, or personality, on the basis of a systematically obtained sample of behavior (p. 446).

psychology The scientific study of behavior and mental processes (p. 3).

psychoneuroimmunology An interdisciplinary field that studies the interconnections among psychological processes, nervous and endocrine system functions, and the immune system (p. 507).

psychopathology The scientific study of the origins, symptoms, and development of psychological disorders (p. 531).

psychosexual stages In Freud's theory, age-related developmental periods in which the child's sexual urges are focused on different areas of the body and are expressed through the activities associated with those areas (p. 426).

psychotherapy The treatment of emotional, behavioral, and interpersonal problems through the use of psychological techniques designed to encourage understanding of problems and modify troubling feelings, behaviors, or relationships (p. 580).

psychotropic medications (*sy*-ko-TRO-pick) Drugs that alter mental functions, alleviate psychological symptoms, and are used to treat psychological or mental disorders (p. 607).

puberty The stage of adolescence in which an individual reaches sexual maturity and becomes physiologically capable of sexual reproduction (p. 394).

punishment The presentation of a stimulus or event following a behavior that acts to decrease the likelihood of the behavior's being repeated (p. 204).

punishment by application A situation in which an operant is followed by the presentation or addition of an aversive stimulus; also called *positive punishment* (p. 204).

punishment by removal A situation in which an operant is followed by the removal or subtraction of a reinforcing stimulus; also called *negative punishment* (p. 205).

pupil The opening in the middle of the iris that changes size to let in different amounts of light (p. 94).

R

random assignment The process of assigning participants to experimental conditions so that all participants have an equal chance of being assigned to any of the conditions or groups in the study (p. 28).

random selection Process in which subjects are selected randomly from a larger group such that every group member has an equal chance of being included in the study (p. 24).

range A measure of variability; the highest score in a distribution minus the lowest score (p. A-5).

rational-emotive therapy (RET) A type of cognitive therapy, developed by psychologist Albert Ellis, that focuses on changing the client's irrational beliefs (p. 593).

reality principle The capacity to accommodate external demands by postponing gratification until the appropriate time or circumstances exist (p. 423).

recall A test of long-term memory that involves retrieving information without the aid of retrieval cues; also called *free recall* (p. 245).

reciprocal determinism A model proposed by psychologist Albert Bandura that explains human functioning and personality as caused by the interaction of behavioral, cognitive, and environmental factors (p. 437).

recognition A test of long-term memory that involves identifying correct information out of several possible choices (p. 245).

reinforcement The occurrence of a stimulus or event following a response that increases the likelihood of that response being repeated (p. 201).

reliability The ability of a test to produce consistent results when administered on repeated occasions under similar conditions (p. 297).

REM rebound A phenomenon in which a person who is deprived of REM sleep greatly increases the amount of time spent in REM sleep at the first opportunity to sleep uninterrupted (p. 146).

REM sleep Type of sleep during which rapid eye movements (REM) and dreaming usually occur and voluntary muscle activity is suppressed; also called *active sleep* or *paradoxical sleep* (p. 141).

REM sleep behavior disorder A sleep disorder characterized by the brain's failure to suppress voluntary actions during REM sleep resluting in the sleeper verbally and physically responding to the dream story (p. 158).

replicate To repeat or duplicate a scientific study in order to increase confidence in the validity of the original findings (p. 19).

representative sample A selected segment that very closely parallels the larger population being studied on relevant characteristics (p. 24).

representativeness heuristic A strategy in which the likelihood of an event is estimated by comparing how similar it is to the prototype of the event (p. 286).

repression Motivated forgetting that occurs unconsciously; a memory that is blocked and unavailable to consciousness (pp. 252, 424).

resistance In psychoanalysis, the patient's unconscious attempts to block the revelation of repressed memories and conflicts (p. 583).

resting potential State in which a neuron is prepared to activate and communicate its message if it receives sufficient stimulation (p. 47).

reticular formation (reh-TICK-you-ler) A network of nerve fibers located in the center of the medulla that helps regulate attention, arousal, and sleep; also called the *reticular activating system* (p. 67).

retina (RET-in-uh) A thin, light-sensitive membrane located at the back of the eye that contains the sensory receptors for vision (p. 95).

retrieval The process of recovering information stored in memory so that we are consciously aware of it (pp. 232, 243).

retrieval cue A clue, prompt, or hint that helps trigger recall of a given piece of information stored in long-term memory (p. 243).

retrieval cue failure The inability to recall long-term memories because of inadequate or missing retrieval cues (p. 243).

retroactive interference Forgetting in which a new memory interferes with remembering an old memory; backward-acting memory interference (p. 252).

retrograde amnesia Loss of memory, especially for episodic information; backward-acting amnesia (p. 264).

reuptake The process by which neurotransmitter molecules detach from a postsynaptic neuron and are reabsorbed by a presynaptic neuron so they can be recycled and used again (p. 50).

rods The long, thin, blunt sensory receptors of the eye that are highly sensitive to light, but not to color, and that are primarily responsible for peripheral vision and night vision (p. 95).

Rorschach Inkblot Test A projective test using inkblots, developed by Swiss psychiatrist Hermann Rorschach in 1921 (p. 447).

S

sample A selected segment of the population used to represent the group that is being studied (p. 24); a subset of a population (p. A-13).

satiation (say-she-AY-shun) In eating behavior, the feeling of fullness and diminished desire to eat that accompanies eating a meal; in general, the sensation of having an appetite or desire fully or excessively satisfied (p. 325).

saturation The property of color that corresponds to the purity of the light wave (p. 98).

scatter diagram or **scatter plot** A graph that represents the relationship between two variables (p. A-10).

schedule of reinforcement The delivery of a reinforcer according to a preset pattern based on the number of responses or the time interval between responses (p. 210).

schema (SKEE-muh) An organized cluster of information about a particular topic (p. 256).

schizophrenia A psychological disorder in which the ability to function is impaired by severely distorted beliefs, perceptions, and thought processes (p. 563).

scientific method A set of assumptions, attitudes, and procedures that guide researchers in creating questions to investigate, in generating evidence, and in drawing conclusions (p. 16).

script A schema for the typical sequence of an everyday event (p. 256).

seasonal affective disorder (SAD) A mood disorder in which episodes of depression typically occur during the fall and winter and subside during the spring and summer (p. 547).

secondary sex characteristics Sexual characteristics that develop during puberty and are not directly involved in reproduction but differentiate between the sexes, such as male facial hair and female breast development (p. 394).

selection device validity The extent to which a personnel selection device is successful in distinguishing between those who will become high performers at a certain job and those who will not (p. B-4).

selective serotonin reuptake inhibitors (SSRIs) Class of antidepressant medications that increase the availability of serotonin in the brain and cause fewer side effects than earlier antidepressants; they include Prozac, Paxil, and Zoloft (p. 612).

self-actualization Defined by Maslow as a person's "full use and exploitation of talents, capacities, and potentialities" (p. 340).

self-concept The set of perceptions and beliefs that you hold about yourself (p. 434).

self-determination theory (SDT) Edward Deci and Richard Ryan's theory that optimal human functioning can occur only if the psychological needs for autonomy, competence, and relatedness are satisfied (p. 341).

self-efficacy The beliefs that people have about their ability to meet the demands of a specific situation; feelings of self-confidence or self-doubt (pp. 361, 437).

self-report inventory A type of psychological test in which a person's responses to standardized questions are compared to established norms (p. 449).

self-serving bias The tendency to attribute successful outcomes of one's own behavior to internal causes and unsuccessful outcomes to external, situational causes (p. 465).

semantic memory Category of long-term memory that includes memories of general knowledge of facts, names, and concepts (p. 240).

semantic network model A model that describes units of information in long-term memory as being organized in a complex network of associations (p. 242).

sensation The process of detecting a physical stimulus, such as light, sound, heat, or pressure (p. 89).

sensation seeking The degree to which an individual is motivated to experience high levels of sensory and physical arousal associated with varied and novel activities (p. 321).

sense of self An individual's unique sense of identity that has been influenced by social, cultural, and psychological experiences; your sense of who you are in relation to other people (p. 458).

sensorimotor stage In Piaget's theory, the first stage of cognitive development, from birth to about age 2; the period during which the infant explores the environment and acquires knowledge through sensing and manipulating objects (p. 386).

sensory adaptation The decline in sensitivity to a constant stimulus (p. 92).

sensory memory The stage of memory that registers information from the environment and holds it for a very brief period of time (p. 233).

sensory neuron Type of neuron that conveys information to the brain from specialized receptor cells in sense organs and internal organs (p. 45).

sensory receptors Specialized cells unique to each sense organ that respond to a particular form of sensory stimulation (p. 89).

sensory-specific satiety (sah-TIE-it-tee) The reduced desire to continue consuming a particular food (p. 326).

serial position effect The tendency to remember items at the beginning and end of a list better than items in the middle (p. 245).

serotonin (ser-ah-TONE-in) Neurotransmitter involved in sensory perceptions, sleep, and emotions (p. 52).

set-point theory Theory that proposes that humans and other animals have a natural or optimal body weight, called the *set-point weight,* that the body defends from becoming higher or lower by regulating feelings of hunger and body metabolism (p. 327).

settling-point models of weight regulation General model of weight regulation suggesting that body weight settles, or stabilizes, around the point at which there is balance between the factors influencing energy intake and energy expenditure (p. 327).

sex chromosomes Chromosomes, designated as X or Y, that determine biological sex; the 23rd pair of chromosomes in humans (p. 371).

sexual orientation The direction of a person's emotional and erotic attraction toward members of the opposite sex, the same sex, or both sexes (pp. 335).

shape constancy The perception of a familiar object as maintaining the same shape regardless of the image produced on the retina (p. 123).

shaping The operant conditioning procedure of selectively reinforcing successively closer approximations of a goal behavior until the goal behavior is displayed (p. 209).

short-term dynamic therapies Type of psychotherapy that is based on psychoanalytic theory but differs in that it is typically time-limited, has specific goals, and involves an active, rather than neutral, role for the therapist (p. 584).

short-term memory The active stage of memory in which information is stored for up to about 20 seconds (p. 233).

situational (contingency) theories of leadership Leadership theories claiming that various situational factors influence a leader's effectiveness (p. B-9).

Sixteen Personality Factor Questionnaire (16PF) A self-report inventory developed by Raymond Cattell that generates a personality profile with ratings on 16 trait dimensions (p. 449).

size constancy The perception of an object as maintaining the same size despite changing images on the retina (p. 123).

skewed distribution An asymmetrical distribution; more scores occur on one side of the distribution than on the other. In a *positively* skewed distribution, most of the scores are low scores; in a *negatively* skewed distribution, most of the scores are high scores (p. A-4).

sleep disorders Serious and consistent sleep disturbances that interfere with daytime functioning and cause subjective distress (p. 153).

sleep paralysis A temporary condition in which a person is unable to move upon awakening in the morning or during the night (p. 144).

sleep-related eating disorder A sleep disorder in which the sleeper will sleepwalk and eat compulsively (p. 158).

sleepsex A sleep disorder involving abnormal sexual behaviors and experiences during sleep; *sexsomnia* (p. 157).

sleep spindles Short bursts of brain activity that characterize stage 2 NREM sleep (p. 142).

sleep terrors A sleep disturbance characterized by an episode of increased physiological arousal, intense fear and panic, frightening hallucinations, and no recall of the episode the next morning; typically occurs during stage 3 or stage 4 NREM sleep; also called *night terrors* (p. 157).

sleep thinking Vague, bland, thoughtlike ruminations about real-life events that typically occur during Non-REM sleep; also called *sleep mentation* (p. 147).

sleepwalking A sleep disturbance characterized by an episode of walking or performing other actions during stage 3 or stage 4 NREM sleep; also called *somnambulism* (p. 157).

social categorization The mental process of categorizing people into groups (or *social categories*) on the basis of their shared characteristics (p. 460).

social cognition The mental processes people use to make sense out of their social environment (p. 458).

social cognitive theory Albert Bandura's theory of personality, which emphasizes the importance of observational learning, conscious cognitive processes, social experiences, self-efficacy beliefs, and reciprocal determinism (p. 437).

social influence The effects of situational factors and other people on an individual's behavior (p. 458).

social learning theory of gender-role development The theory that gender roles are acquired through the basic processes of learning, including reinforcement, punishment, and modeling (p. 386).

social norms The "rules," or expectations, for appropriate behavior in a particular social situation (p. 460).

social phobia or social anxiety disorder An anxiety disorder involving the extreme and irrational fear of being embarrassed, judged, or scrutinized by others in social situations (p. 540).

social psychology Branch of psychology that studies how a person's thoughts, feelings, and behavior are influenced by the presence of other people and by the social and physical environment (p. 458).

social support The resources provided by other people in times of need (p. 575).

somatic nervous system Subdivision of the peripheral nervous system that communicates sensory information to the central nervous system and carries motor messages from the central nervous system to the muscles (p. 57).

source confusion A memory distortion that occurs when the true source of the memory is forgotten (p. 255).

source memory or **source monitoring** Memory for when, where, and how a particular experience or piece of information was acquired (p. 251).

source traits The most fundamental dimensions of personality; the broad, basic traits that are hypothesized to be universal and relatively few in number (p. 440).

specific phobia An excessive, intense, and irrational fear of a specific object, situationm or activity that is actively avoided or endured with marked anxiety (p. 540).

spinal reflexes Simple, automatic behaviors that are processed in the spinal cord (p. 56).

split-brain operation A surgical procedure that involves cutting the corpus callosum (p. 76).

spontaneous recovery The reappearance of a previously extinguished conditioned response after a period of time without exposure to the conditioned stimulus (p. 189).

stage model of memory A model describing memory as consisting of three distinct stages: sensory memory, short-term memory, and long-term memory (p. 232).

standard deviation A measure of variability; expressed as the square root of the sum of the squared deviations around the mean divided by the number of scores in the distribution (p. A-5).

standard normal curve or **standard normal distribution** A symmetrical distribution forming a bell-shaped curve in which the mean, median, and mode are all equal and fall in the exact middle (p. A-8).

standardization The administration of a test to a large, representative sample of people under uniform conditions for the purpose of establishing norms (p. 297).

statistically significant A mathematical indication that research results are not very likely to have occurred by chance (p. 18).

statistics A branch of mathematics used by researchers to organize, summarize, and interpret data (pp. 18, A-2).

stem cells Undifferentiated cells that can divide and give rise to cells that can develop into any one of the body's different cell types (p. 374).

stereotype A cluster of characteristics that are associated with all members of a specific social group, often including qualities that are unrelated to the objective criteria that define the group (p. 470).

stereotype threat A psychological predicament in which fear that you will be evaluated in terms of a negative stereotype about a group to which you belong creates anxiety and self-doubt, lowering performance in a particular domain that is important to you (p. 310).

stimulant-induced psychosis Schizophrenia-like symptoms that can occur as the result of prolonged amphetamine or cocaine use; also called *amphetamine-induced psychosis* or *cocaine-induced psychosis* (p. 174).

stimulants A category of psychoactive drugs that increase brain activity, arouse behavior, and increase mental alertness (p. 171).

stimulus control therapy insomnia treatment involving specific guidelines to create a strict association between the bedroom and rapid sleep onset (p. 178).

stimulus discrimination The occurrence of a learned response to a specific stimulus but not to other, similar stimuli (p. 188).

stimulus generalization The occurrence of a learned response not only to the original stimulus but to other, similar stimuli as well (p. 188).

stimulus threshold The minimum level of stimulation required to activate a particular neuron (p. 47).

storage The process of retaining information in memory so that it can be used at a later time (p. 232).

stress A negative emotional state occurring in response to events that are perceived as taxing or exceeding a person's resources or ability to cope (p. 497).

stressors Events or situations that are perceived as harmful, threatening, or challenging (p. 499).

structural plasticity The brain's ability to change its physical structure in response to learning, active practice, or environmental influences (p. 62).

structuralism Early school of psychology that emphasized studying the most basic components, or structures, of conscious experiences (p. 4).

sublimation In psychoanalytic theory, an ego defense mechanism that involves redirecting sexual urges toward productive, socially acceptable, nonsexual activities; a form of displacement (p. 424).

subliminal perception The detection of stimuli that are below the threshold of conscious awareness; nonconscious perception (p. 91).

substance P A neurotransmitter that is involved in the transmission of pain messages to the brain (p. 110).

substantia nigra (sub-STAN-she-uh NYE-gruh) An area of the midbrain that is involved in motor control and contains a large concentration of dopamine-producing neurons (p. 67).

superego The partly conscious, self-evaluative, moralistic component of personality that is formed through the internalization of parental and societal rules (p. 423).

suppression Motivated forgetting that occurs consciously; a memory that is blocked and unavailable to consciousness (p. 252).

suprachiasmatic nucleus (SCN) (soup-rah-*kye*-az-MAT-ick) A cluster of neurons in the hypothalamus in the brain that governs the timing of circadian rhythms (p. 139).

surface traits Personality characteristics or attributes that can easily be inferred from observable behavior (p. 440).

survey A questionnaire or interview designed to investigate the opinions, behaviors, or characteristics of a particular group (p. 24).

symbolic thought The ability to use words, images, and symbols to represent the world (p. 389).

symmetrical distribution A distribution in which scores fall equally on both sides of the graph. The normal curve is an example of a symmetrical distribution (p. A-4).

sympathetic nervous system Branch of the autonomic nervous system that produces rapid physical arousal in response to perceived emergencies or threats (p. 58).

synapse (SIN-aps) The point of communication between two neurons (p. 49).

synaptic gap (sin-AP-tick) The tiny space between the axon terminal of one neuron and the dendrite of an adjoining neuron (p. 50).

synaptic transmission (sin-AP-tick) The process through which neurotransmitters are released by one neuron, cross the synaptic gap, and affect adjoining neurons (p. 50).

synaptic vesicles (sin-AP-tick VESS-ick-ulls) Tiny pouches or sacs in the axon terminals that contain chemicals called neurotransmitters (p. 50).

systematic desensitization A type of behavior therapy in which phobic responses are reduced by pairing relaxation with a series of mental images or real-life situations that the person finds progressively more fear-provoking; based on the principle of counterconditioning (p. 589).

T

taste aversion A classically conditioned dislike for and avoidance of a particular food that develops when an organism becomes ill after eating the food (p. 196).

taste buds The specialized sensory receptors for taste that are located on the tongue and inside the mouth and throat (p. 108).

temperament Inborn predispositions to consistently behave and react in a certain way (p. 376).

temporal lobe An area on each hemisphere of the cerebral cortex near the temples that is the primary receiving area for auditory information (p. 69).

teratogens Harmful agents or substances that can cause malformations or defects in an embryo or fetus (p. 374).

thalamus (THAL-uh-muss) A forebrain structure that processes sensory information for all senses, except smell, and relays it to the cerebral cortex (p. 71).

Thanatos The death instinct, reflected in aggressive, destructive, and self-destructive actions (p. 423).

Thematic Apperception Test (TAT) A projective personality test that involves creating stories about each of a series of ambiguous scenes (pp. 343, 447).

theory A tentative explanation that tries to integrate and account for the relationship of various findings and observations (p. 20).

thinking The manipulation of mental representations of information in order to draw inferences and conclusions (p. 277).

timbre (TAM-ber) The distinctive quality of a sound, determined by the complexity of the sound wave (p. 102).

tip-of-the-tongue (TOT) experience A memory phenomenon that involves the sensation of knowing that specific information is stored in long-term memory, but being temporarily unable to retrieve it (p. 244).

token economy A form of behavior therapy in which the therapeutic environment is structured to reward desired behaviors with tokens or points that may eventually be exchanged for tangible rewards (p. 592).

top-down processing Information processing that emphasizes the importance of the observer's knowledge, expectations, and other cognitive processes in arriving at meaningful perceptions; analysis that moves from the whole to the parts; also called *conceptually driven processing* (p. 113).

trait A relatively stable, enduring predisposition to consistently behave in a certain way (p. 439).

trait approach to leader effectiveness An approach to determining what makes an effective leader that focuses on the personal characteristics displayed by successful leaders (p. B-8).

trait theory A theory of personality that focuses on identifying, describing, and measuring individual differences in behavioral predispositions (p. 439).

tranquilizers Depressant drugs that relieve anxiety (p. 171).

transduction The process by which a form of physical energy is converted into a coded neural signal that can be processed by the nervous system (p. 89).

transference In psychoanalysis, the process by which emotions and desires originally associated with a significant person in the patient's life, such as a parent, are unconsciously transferred to the psychoanalyst (p. 583).

trial and error A problem-solving strategy that involves attempting different solutions and eliminating those that do not work (p. 281).

triarchic theory of intelligence Robert Sternberg's theory that there are three distinct forms of intelligence: analytic, creative, and practical (p. 301).

trichromatic theory of color vision The theory that the sensation of color results because cones in the retina are especially sensitive to red light (long wavelengths), green light (medium wavelengths), or blue light (short wavelengths) (p. 100).

***t*-test** Test used to establish whether the means of two groups are statistically different from each other (p. A-12).

two-factor theory of emotion Schachter and Singer's theory that emotion is the interaction of physiological arousal and the cognitive label that we apply to explain the arousal (p. 358).

Type I error Erroneously concluding that study results are significant (p. A-13).

Type II error Failing to find a significant effect that does, in fact, exist (p. A-13).

Type A behavior pattern A behavioral and emotional style characterized by a sense of time urgency, hostility, and competitiveness (p. 512).

U

unconditional positive regard In Rogers's theory, the sense that you will be valued and loved even if you don't conform to the standards and expectations of others; unconditional love or acceptance (p. 434).

unconditioned response (UCR) The unlearned, reflexive response that is elicited by an unconditioned stimulus (p. 186).

unconditioned stimulus (UCS) The natural stimulus that reflexively elicits a response without the need for prior learning (p. 186).

unconscious In Freud's theory, a term used to describe thoughts, feelings, wishes, and drives that are operating below the level of conscious awareness (p. 421).

V

validity The ability of a test to measure what it is intended to measure (p. 298).

variable A factor that can vary, or change, in ways that can be observed, measured, and verified (p. 17).

variable-interval (VI) schedule A reinforcement schedule in which a reinforcer is delivered for the first response that occurs after an average time interval, which varies unpredictably from trial to trial (p. 211).

variable-ratio (VR) schedule A reinforcement schedule in which a reinforcer is delivered after an average number of responses, which varies unpredictably from trial to trial (p. 211).

vestibular sense (vess-TIB-you-ler) The technical name for the sense of balance, or equilibrium (p. 112).

W

wavelength The distance from one wave peak to another (p. 93).

Weber's law (VAY-berz) A principle of sensation that holds that the size of the just noticeable difference will vary depending on its relation to the strength of the original stimulus (p. 92).

weight cycling Repeated cycles of dieting, weight loss, and weight regain; also called *yo-yo dieting* (p. 331).

withdrawal symptoms Unpleasant physical reactions, combined with intense drug cravings, that occur when a person abstains from a drug on which he or she is physically dependent (p. 165).

working memory The temporary storage and active, conscious manipulation of information needed for complex cognitive tasks, such as reasoning, learning, and problem solving (p. 238).

Z

***z* score** A number, expressed in standard deviation units, that shows a score's deviation from the mean (p. A-7).

zone of proximal development In Vygotsky's theory of cognitive development, the difference between what children can accomplish on their own and what they can accomplish with the help of others who are more competent (p. 393).

zygote The single cell formed at conception from the union of the egg cell and sperm cell (p. 370).

REFERENCES

Aarts, Henk; & Dijksterhuis, Ap. (2000). Habits as knowledge structures: Automaticity in goal-directed behavior. *Journal of Personality and Social Psychology, 78,* 53–63.

Abad, Vivien C.; & Guilleminault, Christian. (2004). Review of rapid eye movement behavior sleep disorders. *Current Science, 4,* 157–163.

Abel, Millicent H. (2002). Humor, stress, and coping strategies. *Humor, 15,* 365–381.

Abi-Dargham, Anissa. (2004). Do we still believe in the dopamine hypothesis? New data bring new evidence. *International Journal of Neuropsychopharmacology, 7*(Suppl. 1), S1–5.

Abler, Birgit; Erk, Susanne; & Herwig, Uwe. (2007). Anticipation of aversive stimuli activates extended amygdala in unipolar depression. *Journal of Psychiatric Research, 41*(6), 511–522.

Abramov, Israel; & Gordon, James. (1994). Color appearance: On seeing red—or yellow, or green, or blue. *Annual Review of Psychology, 45,* 451–485.

Abrams, Michael. (2002, June). Sight unseen. *Discover, 23,* 54–59.

Abramson, Lyn Y.; Seligman, Martin E. P.; & Teasdale, John D. (1978). Learned helplessness in humans: Critique and reformulation. *Journal of Abnormal Psychology, 87,* 49–74.

Achenback, Thomas M. (2009). Some needed changes in DSM-V: But what about children? *Clinical Psychology: Science and Practice, 16*(1), 50–53.

Ackerman, Joshua M.; Kenrick, Douglas T.; & Schaller, Mark. (2007). Is friendship akin to kinship? *Evolution and Human Behavior, 28*(5), 365–374.

Adair, Linda S.; & Gordon-Larsen, Penny. (2001). Maturational timing and overweight prevalence in US adolescent girls. *American Journal of Public Health, 91,* 642–644.

Ader, Robert. (1993). Conditioned responses. In Bill Moyers & Betty Sue Flowers (Eds.), *Healing and the mind.* New York: Doubleday.

Ader, Robert. (2001). Psychoneuroimmunology. *Current Directions in Psychological Science, 10,* 94–98.

Ader, Robert; & Cohen, Nicholas. (1975). Behaviorally conditioned immunosuppression. *Psychosomatic Medicine, 37,* 333–340.

Adler, Alfred. (1933a/1979). Advantages and disadvantages of the inferiority feeling. In Heinz L. Ansbacher & Rowena R. Ansbacher (Eds.), *Superiority and social interest: A collection of later writings.* New York: Norton.

Adler, Alfred. (1933b/1979). On the origin of the striving for superiority and of social interest. In Heinz L. Ansbacher & Rowena R. Ansbacher (Eds.), *Superiority and social interest: A collection of later writings.* New York: Norton.

Adler, Alfred. (1954). *Understanding human nature.* New York: Fawcett.

Adolphs, Ralph; Tranel, Daniel; & Damasio, Antonio R. (1998). The human amygdala in social judgment. *Nature, 393,* 470–474.

Affleck, Glenn; Tennen, Howard; & Croog, Sydney. (1987a). Causal attribution, perceived control, and recovery from a heart attack. *Journal of Social and Clinical Psychology, 5,* 399–355.

Affleck, Glenn; Tennen, Howard; Pfeiffer, Carol; & Fifield, Judith. (1987b). Appraisals of control and predictability in reacting to a chronic disease. *Journal of Personality and Social Psychology, 53,* 273–279.

Aggarwal, Sunil K.; Carter, Gregory T.; Sullivan, Mark D.; & others. (2009). Medicinal use of cannabis in the United States: Historical perspectives, current trends, and future directions. *Journal of Opioid Management, 5,* 153–168.

Aguiar, Andréa; & Baillargeon, Renée. (1999). 2.5-month-old infants' reasoning about when objects should and should not be occluded. *Cognitive Psychology, 39,* 116–157.

Ahima, Rexford S.; & Osei, Suzette Y. (2004). Leptin and appetite control in lipodystrophy. *Journal of Clinical Endocrinological Metabolism, 89,* 4254–4257.

Aiken, Lewis R. (1997). *Psychological testing and assessment* (9th ed.) Boston: Allyn & Bacon.

Ainslie, George. (1975). Specious reward: A behavioral theory of impulsiveness and impulse control. *Psychological Bulletin, 82,* 463–496.

Ainslie, George. (1992). *Picoeconomics: The strategic interaction of successive motivational states within the person.* Cambridge, England: Cambridge University Press.

Ainsworth, Mary D. Salter. (1979). Attachment as related to mother-infant interaction. In Jay S. Rosenblatt, Robert A. Hinde, Colin Beer, & Marie Busnel (Eds.), *Advances in the study of behavior* (Vol. 9). New York: Academic Press.

Ainsworth, Mary D. Salter; Blehar, Mary C.; Waters, Everett; & Wall, Sally. (1978). *Patterns of attachment: A psychological study of the Strange Situation.* Hillsdale, NJ: Erlbaum.

Ajzen, Icek. (2001). Nature and operations of attitudes. *Annual Review of Psychology, 52*(1), 27–58.

Akerstedt, T.; Knutsson, A.; Westerholm, P.; Theorell, T.; Alfredsson, L.; & Kecklund, G. (2002). Sleep disturbances, work stress and work hours: A cross-sectional study. *Journal of Psychosomatic Research,* 53, 741–748.

Alexander, Charles N.; Robinson, Pat; Orme-Johnson, David W.; & Schneider, Robert H. (1994). The effects of transcendental meditation compared to other methods of relaxation and meditation in reducing risk factors, morbidity, and mortality. *Homeostasis in Health and Disease, 35,* 243–263.

Allen, Daniel N.; Strauss, Gregory P.; Kemtes, Karen A.; & Goldstein, Gerald. (2007). Hemispheric contributions to nonverbal abstract reasoning and problem solving. *Neuropsychology, 21,* 713–720.

Allen, Karen M.; Blascovich, Jim; & Mendes, Wendy B. (2002). Cardiovascular reactivity and the presence of pets, friends, and spouses: The truth about cats and dogs. *Psychosomatic Medicine, 64,* 727–739.

Allen, Karen M.; Blascovich, Jim; Tomaka, Joe; & Kelsey, Robert M. (1991). Presence of human friends and pet dogs as moderators of autonomic responses to stress in women. *Journal of Personality and Social Psychology, 61,* 582–589.

Allen, Laura B.; McHugh, R. Kathryn; & Barlow, David H. (2008). Emotional disorders: A unified protocol. In David H. Barlow (Ed.), *Clinical handbook of psychological disorders* (4th ed., pp. 216–249). New York: Guilford Press.

Allen, Nicola J.; & Barres, Ben A. (2009). Glia—More than just brain glue. *Nature, 457,* 675–677.

Allen, Vernon L.; & Levine, John M. (1969). Consensus and conformity. *Journal of Experimental Social Psychology, 5,* 389–399.

Allen, Vernon L.; & Levine, John M. (1971). Social support and conformity: The role of independent assessment of reality. *Journal of Experimental Social Psychology, 7,* 48–58.

Allik, Jüri; & McCrae, Robert R. (2002). A five-factor theory perspective. In Robert R. McCrae & Jüri Allik (Eds.), *The five-factor model of personality across cultures.* New York: Kluwer Academic/Plenum Press.

Allik, Jüri; & McCrae, Robert R. (2004). Toward a geography of personality traits: Patterns of profiles across 36 cultures. *Journal of Cross-Cultural Psychology, 35,* 13–28.

Allott, Kelly; & Redman, Jennifer. (2007). Are there sex differences associated with the effects of ecstasy/3,4-methylenedioxymethamphetamine (MDMA)? *Neuroscience and Biobehavioral Reviews, 31,* 327–347.

Allport, Gordon W.; & Odbert, Harold S. (1936). Trait-names: A psycho-lexical study. *Psychological Monographs, 47*(211).

Almeida, David M.; & Kessler, Ronald C. (1998). Everyday stressors and gender differences in daily distress. *Journal of Personality and Social Psychology, 75,* 670–680.

Alpers, Georg; & Gerdes, Antje B. M. (2006). Another look at "lookalikes": Can judges match belongings with their owners? *Journal of Individual Differences, 27,* 38–41.

Altemus, Margaret. (2006). Sex differences in depression and anxiety disorders: Potential biological determinants. *Hormones and Behavior, 50*(4), 534–538.

Altmann, Erik M.; & Gray, Wayne D. (2002). Forgetting to remember: The functional relationship of decay and interference. *Psychological Science, 13,* 27–33.

Alves, Hélder; & Correia, Isabel. (2008). On the normativity of expressing the belief in a just world: Empirical evidence. *Social Justice Research, 21,* 106–118.

Alzheimer's Association. (2009). Alzheimer's disease facts and figures. *Alzheimer's & Dementia, 5,* 1–80. Retrieved December 5, 2009, from http://www.alz.org/national/documents/report_alzfactsfigures2009.pdf

Amabile, Teresa. (1996). *Creativity in context.* Boulder, CO: Westview Press.

Amabile, Teresa. (2001). Beyond talent: John Irving and the passionate craft of creativity. *American Psychologist, 56,* 333–336.

Ambady, Nalini; Chiao, Joan Y.; & Chiu, Pearl. (2006). Race and emotion: Insights from a social neuroscience perspective. In John T. Cacioppo, Penny S. Visser, & Cynthia L. Pickett (Eds.), *Social neuroscience: People thinking about thinking people.* Cambridge, MA: MIT Press.

American Association of Suicidology. (2004, December 1). *AAS fact sheets: Suicide in the U.S.* Washington, DC: Author. Retrieved December 5, 2009, from http://www.suicidology.org/web/guest/stats-and-tools/fact-sheets

American Psychiatric Association. (1994). *Diagnostic and statistical manual of mental disorders* (4th ed.). Washington, DC: Author.

American Psychiatric Association. (2000a). *Diagnostic and statistical manual of mental disorders* (4th ed., text revision). Washington, DC: Author.

American Psychiatric Association. (2000b). Practice guidelines for the treatment of patients with eating disorders [Revision]. *American Journal of Psychiatry, 157*(Suppl.).

American Psychiatric Association. (2001). Practice guideline for the treatment of patients with borderline personality disorder. *American Journal of Psychiatry, 158,* 2.

American Psychological Association. (1996). *APA guidelines for ethical conduct in the care and use of animals.* Washington, DC: American Psychological Association Science Directorate. Retrieved December 5, 2009, from http://www.apa.org/science/anguide.html

American Psychological Association. (2002a). Ethical principles of psychologists and code of conduct. *American Psychologist, 57,* 1060–1073. Retrieved December 5, 2009, from http://www.apa.org/ETHICS/code2002.html

American Psychological Association. (2003). Guidelines on multicultural education, training, research, practice, and organizational change for psychologists. *American Psychologist, 58,* 377–402. PDF of guidelines available at www.apa.org/pi/multiculturalguidelines.pdf

American Psychological Association. (2005a). New definition: Hypnosis. Washington, DC: American Psychological Association, Division 30, Society for Psychological Hypnosis. Retrieved December 5, 2009, from http://www.apa.org/divisions/div30/define_hypnosis.html

American Psychological Association. (2005b). Obeying and resisting malevolent orders. Retrieved December 5, 2009, from http://www.psychologymatters.org/milgram.html

American Psychological Association Working Group on Investigation of Memories of Childhood Abuse. (1998). Final conclusions of the American Psychological Association Working Group on Investigation of Memories of Childhood Abuse. *Psychology, Public Policy, and Law, 4,* 933–940.

Anastasi, Anne. (1988). *Psychological testing* (6th ed.). New York: Macmillan.

Anastasi, Anne; & Urbina, Susana. (1997). *Psychological testing* (7th ed.). Upper Saddle River, NJ: Prentice Hall.

Anch, A. Michael; Browman, Carl P.; Mitler, Merrill M.; & Walsh, James K. (1988). *Sleep: A scientific perspective.* Englewood Cliffs, NJ: Prentice Hall.

Andersen, Arnold E. (2002). Rethinking the DSM-IV diagnosis of eating disorders. *Eating Disorders,* 10, 177–180.

Anderson, Craig A.; Berkowitz, Leonard; Donnerstein, Edward; Huesmann, L. Rowell; Johnson, James D.; Linz, Daniel; Malamuth, Neil M.; & Wartella, Ellen. (2003, December). The influence of media violence on youth. *Psychological Science in the Public Interest, 4,* 81–110. Retrieved July 16, 2004, from http://www.psychologicalscience.org/pdf/ pspi/pspi43.pdf

Anderson, Craig A.; & Dill, Karen E. (2000). Video games and aggressive thoughts, feelings, and behavior in the laboratory and in life. *Journal of Personality and Social Psychology, 78,* 772–790.

Anderson, James R.; & Meno, Pauline. (2003). Psychological influences on yawning in children. *Current Psychology Letters: Behaviour, Brain & Cognition, 11*(2), np. Retrieved August 19, 2004, from http://cpl.revues.org/document390.html

Anderson, James R.; Myowa-Yamakoshi, Masako; & Matsuzawa, Tetsuro. (2004). Contagious yawning in chimpanzees. *Proceedings of*

the Royal Society of London: Biology Letters, 271, S468–S470. Retrieved December 6, 2009, from http://rspb.royalsocietypublishing.org/content/271/Suppl_6/S468.full.pdf

Anderson, Karen E.; & Savage, Cary R. (2004). Cognitive and neurobiological findings in obsessive-compulsive disorder. *Psychiatric Clinics of North America, 27,* 37–47.

Anderson, Michael C.; Ochsner, Kevin N.; Kuhl, Brice; Cooper, Jeffrey; Robertson, Elaine; Gabrieli, Susan W.; Glover, Gary H.; & Gabrieli, John D. E. (2004, January 9). Neural systems underlying the suppression of unwanted memories. *Science, 303,* 232–235.

Anderson, Page; Rothbaum, Barbara O.; & Hodges, Larry F. (2003). Virtual reality exposure in the treatment of social anxiety. *Cognitive & Behavioral Practice, 10,* 240–247.

Anderson, Stephanie L.; Adams, Glenn; & Plaut, Victoria C. (2008). The cultural grounding of personal relationship: The importance of attractiveness in everyday life. *Journal of Personality and Social Psychology, 95,* 352–368.

Anderson-Fye, Eileen. (2009). Cross-cultural issues in body image among children and adolescents. In Linda Smolak & J. Kevin Thompson (Eds.), *Body image, eating disorders, and obesity in youth: Assessment, prevention, and treatment* (2nd ed., pp. 113–133). Washington, DC: American Psychological Association.

Andersson, Bengt-Erik. (1989). Effects of day care: A longitudinal study. *Child Development, 60,* 857–866.

Andersson, Bengt-Erik. (1992). Effects of day care on cognitive and socioemotional competence of thirteen-year-old Swedish schoolchildren. *Child Development, 63,* 20–36.

Andre, Linda. (2009). *Doctors of deception: What they don't want you to know about shock treatment.* New Brunswick, NJ: Rutgers University Press.

Andreasen, Nancy C.; & Flaum, Michael. (1991). Schizophrenia: The characteristic symptoms. *Schizophrenia Bulletin, 17,* 27–49.

Andresen, Jensine. (2000). Meditation meets behavioural medicine: The story of experimental research on meditation. *Journal of Consciousness Studies, 7,* 17–73.

Anton, Stephen D.; & Miller, Peter M. (2005). Do negative emotions predict alcohol consumption, saturated fat intake, and physical activity in older adults? *Behavior Modification, 29*(4), 677–688.

Antony, Martin M.; Purdon, Christine; & Summerfeldt, Laura J. (2007). *Psychological treatment of obsessive compulsive disorders: Fundamentals and beyond.* Washington, DC: American Psychological Association.

APA Committee on Animal Research and Ethics (C.A.R.E.). (2008). Washington, DC: American Psychological Association Science Directorate. Retrieved February 23, 2008, from http://www.apa.org/science/anguide.html

Arboleda-Flórez, Julio; & Sartorius, Norman. (2008). *Understanding the stigma of mental illness: Theory and interventions.* Hoboken, NJ: Wiley.

Arden, John B.; & Linford, Lloyd. (2009). *Brain-based therapy with adults: Evidence-based treatment for everyday practice.* Hoboken, NJ: Wiley.

Arendt, Josephine; Stone, Barbara; & Skene, Debra J. (2005). Sleep disruption in jet lag and circadian rhythm-related disorders. In Meir H. Kryger, Thomas Roth, & William C. Dement (Eds.), *Principles and practice of sleep medicine* (4th ed.). Philadelphia: Elsevier Saunders.

Ariely, Dan; & Wertenbroch, Klaus. (2002) Procrastination, deadlines, and performance: Self-control by precommitment. *Psychological Science, 13,* 219–224.

Arkowitz, Hal; Westra, Henny A.; Miller, William R.; & Rollnick, Stephen (Eds.). (2007). *Motivational interviewing in the treatment of psychological problems.* New York: Guilford Press.

Arnau, Randolph C.; Green, Bradley A.; Rosen, David H.; Gleaves, David H.; & Melancon, Janet G. (2003). Are Jungian preferences really categorical? An empirical investigation using taxometric analysis. *Personality and Individual Differences, 34,* 233–251.

Arnett, Jeffrey Jensen; & Cravens, Hamilton. (2006). G. Stanley Hall's *Adolescence:* A centennial reappraisal. *History of Psychology, 9,* 165–171.

Arnkoff, Diane B.; & Glass, Carol R. (1992). Cognitive therapy and psychotherapy integration. In Donald K. Freedheim (Ed.), *History of psychotherapy: A century of change.* Washington, DC: American Psychological Association.

Arnon, Stephen S.; Schechter, Robert; Inglesby, Thomas V.; Henderson, Donald A.; Bartlett, John G.; Ascher, Michael S.; & others. (2001). Botulinum toxin as a biological weapon: Medical and public health management. *Journal of the American Medical Association, 285,* 1059–1070.

Aronson, Elliot. (1987). Teaching students what they think they already know about prejudice and desegregation. In Vivian Parker Makosky (Ed.), *G. Stanley Hall Lecture Series* (Vol. 7). Washington, DC: American Psychological Association.

Aronson, Elliot. (1990). Applying social psychology to desegregation and energy conservation. *Personality and Social Psychology Bulletin, 16,* 118–132.

Aronson, Elliot. (1992). The return of the repressed: Dissonance theory makes a comeback. *Psychological Inquiry, 3,* 303–311.

Aronson, Elliot. (1995). *The social animal* (7th ed). New York: Freeman.

Aronson, Elliot. (1999). The power of self-persuasion. *American Psychologist, 54,* 875–883.

Aronson, Elliot; & Bridgeman, Diane. (1979). Jigsaw groups and the desegregated classroom: In pursuit of common goals. *Personality and Social Psychology Bulletin, 5,* 438–466.

Aronson, Joshua; Fried, Carrie B.; & Good, Catherine. (2002). Reducing the effects of stereotype threat on African American college students by shaping theories of intelligence. *Journal of Experimental Social Psychology, 38,* 113–125.

Aronson, Joshua; Lustina, Michael J.; Good, Catherine; Keough, Kelli; Steele, Claude M.; & Brown, Joseph. (1999). When white men can't do math: Necessary and sufficient factors in stereotype threat. *Journal of Experimental Social Psychology, 35,* 29–46.

Asch, Solomon E. (1951). Effects of group pressure upon the modification and distortion of judgments. In Harold S. Guetzkow (Ed.), *Groups, leadership, and men: Research in human relations. Reports on research sponsored by the Human Relations and Morale Branch of the Office of Naval Research, 1945–1950.* Pittsburgh, PA: Carnegie Press.

Asch, Solomon E. (1955, November). Opinions and social pressure. *Scientific American, 193,* 31–35.

Asch, Solomon E. (1956). Studies of independence and conformity: A minority of one against a unanimous majority. *Psychological Monographs, 70*(9, Whole No. 416).

Asch, Solomon E. (1957). An experimental investigation of group influence. In *Symposium on preventive and social psychiatry.* Washington, DC: U.S. Government Printing Office, Walter Reed Army Institute of Research.

Ashcraft, Mark H. (1994). *Human memory and cognition* (2nd ed.). New York: HarperCollins.

Aspinwall, Lisa G.; & Taylor, Shelley E. (1992). Modeling cognitive adaptation: A longitudinal investigation of the impact of individual differences and coping on college adjustment and performance. *Journal of Personality and Social Psychology, 63,* 989–1003.

Astin, John A. (2004). Mind-body therapies for the management of pain. *Clinical Journal of Pain, 20,* 27–32.

Atkinson, Richard C.; & Shiffrin, Richard M. (1968). Human memory: A proposed system and its control processes. In Kenneth W. Spence & Janet T. Spence (Eds.), *The psychology of learning and motivation: Advances in research and theory* (Vol. 2). New York: Academic Press.

Ator, Nancy A. (2005). Conducting behavioral research: Methodological and laboratory animal welfare issues. In Chana K. Akins, Sangeeta Panicker, & Christopher L. Cunningham (Eds.), *Laboratory animals in research and teaching: Ethics, care, and methods.* Washington, DC: American Psychological Association.

Auld, Frank; Hyman, Marvin; & Rudzinski, Donald. (2005). Theory and strategy of dream interpretation. In Frank Auld, Marvin Hyman, & Donald Rudzinski (Eds.), *Resolution of inner conflict: An introduction to psychoanalytic therapy* (2nd ed.). Washington, DC: American Psychological Association.

Austin, James H. (1998). *Zen and the brain.* Cambridge, MA: MIT Press.

Austin, James H. (2003, Winter). Your self, your brain, and Zen. *Cerebrum, 5,* 47–66.

Aveline, Mark. (2005). The person of the therapist. *Psychotherapy Research, 15*(3), 155–164.

Ax, Robert K.; Bigelow, Brian J.; Harowski, Kathy; Meredith, James M.; Nussbaum, David; & Taylor, Randy R. (2008). Prescriptive authority for psychologists and the public sector: Serving underserved health care consumers. *Psychological Services, 5,* 184–197.

Axelrod, Saul; & Apsche, Jack. (1983). *The effects of punishment on human behavior.* New York: Academic Press.

Baars, Barnard. (2005). Consciousness eclipsed: Jacques Loeb, Ivan P. Pavlov, and the rise of reductionistic biology after 1900. *Consciousness and Cognition, 14,* 219–230.

Baddeley, Alan D. (1992, January 31). Working memory. *Science, 255*(5044), 556–559.

Baddeley, Alan D. (1995). Working memory. In Michael S. Gazzaniga (Ed.), *The cognitive neurosciences.* Cambridge, MA: MIT Press.

Baddeley, Alan D. (2002). Is working memory still working? *European Psychologist, 7,* 85–97.

Baddeley, Alan D. (2007). *Working memory, thought, and action.* New York: Oxford University Press.

Bader, Alan P.; & Phillips, Roger D. (2002). Fathers' recognition of their newborns by visual-facial and olfactory cues. *Psychology of Men and Masculinity, 3,* 79–84.

Baer, John. (1993). *Creativity and divergent thinking: A task-specific approach.* Hillsdale, NJ: Erlbaum.

Baer, Ruth A. (2003). Mindfulness training as a clinical intervention: A conceptual and empirical review. *Clinical Psychology: Science & Practice, 10,* 125–143.

Bahlmann, Miriam; Preuss, Ulrich Wilhelm; & Soyka, Michael. (2002). Chronological relationship between antisocial personality disorder and alcohol dependence. *European Addiction Research, 8,* 195–200.

Bahrami, Bahador; Lavie, Nilli; & Rees, Geraint. (2007). Attentional load modulates response of human primary visual cortex to invisible stimuli. *Current Biology, 17,* 509–513.

Bahrick, Harry P.; & Hall, Lynda K. (1991). Lifetime maintenance of high school mathematics content. *Journal of Experimental Psychology: General, 120,* 20–33.

Bahrick, Harry P.; & Phelps, Elizabeth. (1987). Retention of Spanish vocabulary over eight years. *Journal of Experimental Psychology: Learning, Memory, and Cognition, 13,* 344–349.

Bailey, J. Michael; Bobrow, David; Wolfe, Marilyn; & Mikach, Sarah. (1995). Sexual orientation of adult sons of gay fathers. *Developmental Psychology, 31,* 124–129.

Bailey, J. Michael; Dunne, Michael P.; & Martin, Nicholas G. (2000). Genetic and environmental influences on sexual orientation and its correlates in an Australian twin sample. *Journal of Personality and Social Psychology, 78,* 524–536.

Bailey, J. Michael; & Pillard, Richard C. (1991). A genetic study of male sexual orientation. *Archives of General Psychiatry, 48,* 1089–1096.

Bailey, J. Michael; Pillard, Richard C.; Neale, Michael C.; & Agyei, Yvonne. (1993). Heritable factors influence sexual orientation in women. *Archives of General Psychiatry, 50,* 217–223.

Bailey, J. Michael; & Zucker, Kenneth J. (1995). Childhood sex-typed behavior and sexual orientation: A conceptual analysis and quantitative review. *Developmental Psychology, 31,* 43–55.

Bailey, Marian Breland; & Bailey, Robert E. (1993). "Misbehavior": A case history. *American Psychologist, 48,* 1157–1158.

Bailey, Robert E.; & Gillaspy, J. Arthur, Jr. (2005). Operant psychology goes to the fair: Marian and Keller Breland in the popular press, 1947–1966. *Behavior Analyst, 28,* 143–159.

Baillargeon, Renée. (2002). The acquisition of physical knowledge in infancy: A summary in eight lessons. In Usha Goswami (Ed.), *Handbook of childhood cognitive development.* Oxford, England: Blackwell.

Baillargeon, Renée. (2004). Infants' physical world. *Current Directions in Psychological Science, 13,* 89–94.

Baillargeon, Renée; & De Vos, Julie. (1991). Object permanence in young infants: Further evidence. *Child Development, 62,* 1227–1246.

Baker, Catherine. (2004). *Behavioral genetics: An introduction to how genes and environments interact through development.* New York: American Association for the Advancement of Science.

Baldwin, Scott A.; Berkelion, Arjan; Atkins, David C.; Olsen, Joseph A.; & Nielsen, Stevan L. (2009, April). Rates of change in naturalistic psychotherapy: Contrasting dose-effect and good-enough level models of change. *Journal of Consulting and Clinical Psychology, 77*(2), 203–211.

Ball, Thomas M.; Shapiro, Daniel E.; Monheim, Cynthia J.; & Weydert, Joy A. (2003). A pilot study of the use of guided imagery for the treatment of recurrent abdominal pain in children. *Clinical Pediatrics, 42,* 527–532.

Balsam, Kimberly F.; Beauchaine, Theodore P.; Rothblum, Esther D.; & Solomon, Sondra F. (2008). Three-year follow-up of same-sex couples who had civil unions in Vermont, same-sex couples not in civil unions, and heterosexual married couples. *Developmental Psychology, 44,* 102–116.

Baltes, Paul B.; & Mayer, Karl Ulrich. (2001). *The Berlin aging study: Aging from 70 to 100.* New York: Cambridge University Press.

Bamford, Nigel S.; Zhang, Hui; Joyce, John A.; Scarlis, Christine A.; & others. (2008, April 10). Repeated exposure to methamphetamine causes long-lasting presynaptic corticostriatal depression that is renormalized with drug readministration. *Neuron, 58,* 89–103. Retrieved on December 6, 2009, from: http://www.ncbi.nlm.nih.gov/pmc/articles/PMC2394729/

Bandura, Albert. (1965). Influence of models' reinforcement contingencies on the acquisition of imitative behaviors. *Journal of Personality and Social Psychology, 1,* 589–595.

Bandura, Albert. (1974). Behavior theory and the models of man. *American Psychologist, 29,* 859–869.

Bandura, Albert. (1977). *Social learning theory.* Englewood Cliffs, NJ: Prentice Hall.

Bandura, Albert. (1986). *Social foundations of thought and action: A social cognitive theory.* Englewood Cliffs, NJ: Prentice Hall.

Bandura, Albert. (1989). Human agency in social cognitive theory. *American Psychologist, 44,* 1175–1184.

Bandura, Albert. (1990). Conclusion: Reflections on nonability determinants of competence. In Robert J. Sternberg & John Kolligian, Jr. (Eds.), *Competence considered.* New Haven, CT: Yale University Press.

Bandura, Albert. (1991). Self-regulation of motivation through anticipatory and self-reactive mechanisms. In Richard Dienstbier (Ed.), *Nebraska Symposium on Motivation 1990* (Vol. 38). Lincoln: University of Nebraska Press.

Bandura, Albert. (1992). Exercise of personal agency through the self-efficacy mechanism. In Ralf Schwarzer (Ed.), *Self-efficacy: Thought control of action.* Washington, DC: Hemisphere.

Bandura, Albert. (1996). Failures in self-regulation: Energy depletion or selective disengagement? *Psychological Inquiry, 7,* 20–24.

Bandura, Albert. (1997). *Self-efficacy: The exercise of control.* New York: Freeman.

Bandura, Albert. (2001). Social cognitive theory: An agentic perspective. *Annual Review of Psychology, 52,* 1–26.

Bandura, Albert. (2002). Environmental sustainability by sociocognitive deceleration of population growth. In Peter Schmuck & Wesley P. Schultz (Eds.), *The psychology of sustainable development.* Dordrecht, The Netherlands: Kluwer.

Bandura, Albert. (2004a). Quoted in Population Communications International, "Telling stories, saving lives." Retrieved September 5, 2004, from http://www.population.org/index.shtml

Bandura, Albert. (2004b). Swimming against the mainstream: The early years from chilly tributary to transformative mainstream. *Behaviour Research and Therapy, 42,* 613–630.

Bandura, Albert. (2006). Towards a psychology of human agency. *Perspectives on Psychological Science, 1,* 164–180.

Bandura, Albert; Caprara, Gian Vittorio; Barbaranelli, Claudio; Gerbino, Maria; & Pastorelli, Concetta. (2003). Role of affective self-regulatory efficacy in diverse spheres of psychosocial functioning. *Child Development, 74,* 769–782.

Bandura, Albert; Ross, Dorothea; & Ross, Sheila A. (1963). Imitation of film-mediated aggressive models. *Journal of Abnormal and Social Psychology, 66,* 3–11.

Banich, Marie T. (1998). Integration of information between the cerebral hemispheres. *Current Directions in Psychological Science, 7,* 32–37.

Barch, Deanna M. (2005). The cognitive neuroscience of schizophrenia. *Annual Review of Clinical Psychology, 1,* 321–353.

Barclay, Deborah R.; & Houts, Arthur C. (1995). Parenting skills: A review and developmental analysis of training content. In William O'Donohue & Leonard Krasner (Eds.), *Handbook of psychological skills training: Clinical techniques and applications.* Boston: Allyn & Bacon.

Barefoot, John C.; Dahlstrom, W. Grant; & Williams, Redford B. (1983). Hostility, CHD incidence, and total mortality: A 25-year follow-up study of 255 physicians. *Psychosomatic Medicine, 45,* 59–63.

Bar-El, Yair; Durst, Rimona; Katz, Gregory; Zislin, Josef; Strauss, Ziva & Knobler, Haim Y. (2000). Jerusalem syndrome. *British Journal of Psychiatry, 176,* 86–90.

Barinaga, Marcia. (2003). Buddhism and neuroscience: Studying the well-trained mind. *Science, 302,* 44–46.

Barker, Jamie; & Jones, Marc V. (2005). Using hypnosis to increase self-efficacy: A case study in judo. *Sport and Exercise Psychology, 1,* 36–42.

Barker, Jamie; & Jones, Marc V. (2006). Using hypnosis, technique refinement, and self-modeling to enhance self-efficacy: A case study in cricket. *The Sport Psychologist, 20,* 94–110.

Barlow, David H. (Ed.). (2008). *Clinical handbook of psychological disorders* (4th ed.). New York: Guilford Press.

Barlow, David H.; Allen, Laura B.; & Basden, Shawnee L. (2007). Psychological treatments for panic disorders, phobias, and generalized anxiety disorder. In Peter E. Nathan & Jack M. Gorman (Eds.), *A guide to treatments that work* (3rd ed., pp. 351–394). New York: Oxford University Press.

Barlow, David H.; & Durand, V. Mark. (2005). *Abnormal psychology* (4th ed.). Belmont, CA: Wadsworth.

Barnes, Thomas R. E.; & Joyce, Eileen M. (2001). Antipsychotic drug treatment: Recent advances. *Current Opinion in Psychiatry, 14,* 25–37.

Barnett, Rosalind C.; Marshall, Nancy L.; & Singer, Judith D. (1992). Job experiences over time, multiple roles, and women's mental health: A longitudinal study. *Journal of Personality and Social Psychology, 62,* 634–644.

Barnier, Amanda J.; & McConkey, Kevin M. (1998). Posthypnotic responding away from the hypnotic setting. *Psychological Science, 9,* 256–262.

Barnier, Amanda J.; & McConkey, Kevin M. (1999). Absorption, hypnotizability and context: Non-hypnotic contexts are not all the same. *Contemporary Hypnosis, 16,* 1–8.

Baron-Cohen, Simon. (2000, January 5). Is Asperger's syndrome/high-functioning autism necessarily a disability? Invited submission for Special Millenium Issue of Developmental and Psychopathology. Retrieved September 18, 2008, from http://www.geocities.com/CapitolHill/7138/lobby/disability.htm

Baron-Cohen, Simon. (2005). Enhanced attention to detail and hypersystemizing in autism. Commentary on Elizabeth Milne, John Swettenham, & Ruth Campbell, Motion perception in autism. A review. *Current Psychology of Cognition, 23,* 59–64.

Baron-Cohen, Simon (2007, August 8). Quoted in Emine Saner, "It's not a disease, it's a way of life." *The Guardian.* Retrieved September 15, 2008, from http://www.guardian.co.uk/society/2007/aug/07/health.medicineandhealth

Barrett, Marna S.; Chua, Wee-Jhong; Crits-Christoph, Paul; Gibbons, Mary Beth; & Thompson, Don. (2008, June). Early withdrawal from mental health treatment: Implications for psychotherapy practice. *Psychotherapy: Theory, Research, Practice, Training, 45*(2), 247–267.

Barsh, Gregory S.; Farooqi, L. Sadaf; & O'Rahilly, Stephen. (2000, April 6). Genetics of body-weight regulation. *Nature, 404,* 644–651.

Bartels, Andreas; & Zeki, Semir. (2000, November 27). The neural basis of romantic love. *NeuroReport, 11,* 3829–3834. Retrieved March 1, 2002, from http://www.vislab.ucl.ac.uk/pdf/NeuralBasisOfLove.pdf

Bartlett, Donald L., & Steele, James B. (2004). *Howard Hughes: His life and madness.* New York: Norton.

Bartlett, Frederic C. (1932). *Remembering.* Cambridge, England: Cambridge University Press.

Barzilai, Nir; & Gupta, Gaurav. (1999). Revisiting the role of fat mass in the life extension induced by caloric restriction. *Journal of Gerontology, Series A, 54,* B89–B97.

Basil, Debra Z.; Ridgway, Nancy M.; & Basil, Michael D. (2006). Guilt appeals: The mediating effect of responsibility. *Psychology & Marketing, 23*(12), 1035–1054.

Basil, Robert. (1991). Graphology and personality: "Let the buyer beware." In Kendrick Frazier (Ed.), *The hundredth monkey and other paradigms of the paranormal.* Buffalo, NY: Prometheus Books.

Baskin, Denis G.; Lattemann, Dianne Figlewicz; Seeley, Randy J.; Woods, Stephen C.; Porte, Daniel, Jr.; & Schwartz, Michael W. (1999). Insulin and leptin: Dual adiposity signals to the brain for the regulation of food intake and body weight. *Brain Research, 848,* 114–123.

Bass, Bernard M. (1981). *Stogdill's handbook of leadership.* New York: Free Press.

Bass, Ellen; & Davis, Linda. (1994). *The courage to heal* (3rd ed.). New York: HarperPerennial.

Bass, Martha A.; Enochs, Wendy K.; & DiBrezzo, Ro. (2002). Comparison of two exercise programs on general well-being of college students. *Psychological Reports, 91,* 1195–1201.

Basso, Olga. (2007). Right or wrong? On the difficult relationship between epidemiologists and handedness. *Epidemiology, 18,* 191–193.

Bates, Steve. (2002, February). Personality counts. *HR Magazine, 47,* 28.

Batson, C. Daniel; Ahmad, Nadia; Powell, Adam A.; & Stocks, E. L. (2008). Prosocial motivation. In James Y. Shah & Wendi L. Gardner (Eds.), *Handbook of motivation science.* New York: Guilford Press.

Baum, William; & Heath, Jennifer L. (1992). Behavioral explanations and intentional explanations in psychology. *American Psychologist, 47,* 1312–1317.

Baumeister, Roy F.; & Leary, Mark R. (1995). The need to belong: Desire for interpersonal attachments as a fundamental human motivation. *Psychological Bulletin, 117,* 497–529.

Baumeister, Roy F.; Stillwell, Arlene M.; & Heatherton, Todd F. (1994). Guilt: An interpersonal approach. *Psychological Bulletin, 115,* 243– 267.

Baumrind, Diana. (1964). Some thoughts on ethics of research: After reading Milgram's "Behavioral study of obedience." *American Psychologist, 19,* 421–423.

Baumrind, Diana. (1971). Current patterns of parental authority. *Developmental Psychology Monographs, 4,* 1–103.

Baumrind, Diana. (1991). The influence of parenting style on adolescent competence and substance abuse. *Journal of Early Adolescence, 11,* 56–95.

Baumrind, Diana. (2005). Patterns of parental authority and adolescent autonomy. *New Directions for Child & Adolescent Development, 2005*(108), 61–69.

Baumrind, Diana; Larzelere, Robert E.; & Cowan, Philip A. (2002). Ordinary physical punishment: Is it harmful? Comment on Gershoff (2002). *Psychological Bulletin, 128,* 580–589.

Bausell, R. Barker. (2007). *Snake oil science: The truth about complementary and alternative medicine.* New York: Oxford University Press.

Bayer, Christophe Pierre; Klasen, Fionna; & Adam, Hubertus. (2007). Association of trauma and PTSD symptoms with openness to reconciliation and feelings of revenge among former Ugandan and Congolese child soldiers. *Journal of the American Medical Association, 298,* 555–559.

Bayer, Ute C.; & Gollwitzer, Peter M. (2007). Boosting scholastic test scores by willpower: The role of implementation intentions. *Self and Identity, 6,* 1–19.

Bayley, Peter J.; & Squire, Larry R. (2002). Medial temporal lobe amnesia: Gradual acquisition of factual information by nondeclarative memory. *Journal of Neuroscience, 22,* 5741–5748.

Baylis, Gordon C.; & Driver, Jon. (2001). Shape-coding in IT cells generalizes over contrast and mirror reversal, but not figure-ground reversal. *Nature Neuroscience, 4,* 937–942.

Bayton, James A. (1975). Francis Sumner, Max Meenes, and the training of black psychologists. *American Psychologist,* 185–186.

Beal, Carole R. (1994). *Boys and girls: The development of gender roles.* New York: McGraw-Hill.

Beasley, Ryan K.; & Joslyn, Mark R. (2001). Cognitive dissonance and post-decision attitude change in six presidential elections. *Political Psychology, 22*(3), 521–540.

Beasley, Sandra. (2007). One small step for humankind. *American Scholar, 76,* 1–15.

Beatty, Barbara. (1998). From laws of learning to a science of values: Efficiency and morality in Thorndike's educational psychology. *American Psychologist, 53,* 1145–1152.

Bechara, Antoine; Damasio, Hanna; Tranel, Daniel; & Damasio, Antonio. (1997). Deciding advantageously before knowing the advantageous strategy. *Science, 275,* 1293–1295.

Bechara, Antoine; & Naqvi, Nasir. (2004). Listening to your heart: Interoceptive awareness as a gateway to feeling. *Nature Neuroscience, 7,* 102–103.

Beck, Aaron T. (1991). Cognitive therapy: A 30-year retrospective. *American Psychologist, 46,* 368–375.

Beck, Aaron T. (2004, March). Quoted in Anita Bowles, "Beck in action." *APS Observer, 17*(3), 7–8.

Beck, Aaron T.; & Alford, Brad A. (2009). *Depression: Causes and treatment.* Philadelphia: University of Pennsylvania Press.

Beck, Aaron T; Rector, Neil A.; Stolar, Neal; & Grant, Paul. (2009). *Schizophrenia: Cognitive theory, research, and therapy.* New York: Guilford Press.

Beck, Aaron T.; Rush, A. John; Shaw, Brian F.; & Emery, Gary. (1979). Cognitive therapy of depression. New York: Guilford Press.

Becker, Anne E.; & Fay, Kristen. (2006). Sociocultural issues and eating disorders. In Stephen Wonderlich, James E. Mitchell, Matrina de Zwaan, & Howard Steiger (Eds.), *Annual review of eating disorders* (Pt. 2, pp. 35–64). Oxford, England: Radcliffe Publishing.

Beidel, Deborah C.; & Stipelman, Brooke. (2007). Anxiety disorders. In Michel Hersen, Samuel M. Turner, & Deborah C. Beidel (Eds.), *Adult psychopathology and diagnosis* (5th ed., pp. 349–409). Hoboken, NJ: Wiley.

Beilin, Harry. (1994). Jean Piaget's enduring contribution to developmental psychology. In Ross D. Parke, Peter A. Ornstein, John J. Rieser, & Carolyn Zahn-Waxler (Eds.), *A century of developmental psychology.* Washington, DC: American Psychological Association.

Beilock, Sian L.; Rydell, Robert J.; & McConnell, Allen R. (2007). Stereotype threat and working memory: Mechanisms, alleviation, and spillover. *Journal of Experimental Psychology: General, 136,* 256–276.

Bekoff, Marc. (2007). *The emotional lives of animals.* Novato, CA: New World Library.

Belgrave, Faye Z.; & Allison, Kevin W. (2006). *African American psychology: From Africa to America.* Thousand Oaks, CA: Sage.

Bell, Alan; Weinberg, Martin; & Hammersmith, Sue. (1981). *Sexual preference: Its development in men and women.* Bloomington: Indiana University Press.

Bellak, Leopold. (1993). *The Thematic Apperception Test, the Children's Apperception Test, and the Senior Apperception Technique in clinical use* (5th ed.). Boston: Allyn & Bacon.

Belle, Deborah. (1991). Gender differences in the social moderators of stress. In Alan Monat & Richard S. Lazarus (Eds.), *Stress and coping: An anthology* (3rd ed.). New York: Columbia University Press.

Belsky, Jay. (1992). Consequences of child care for children's development: A deconstructionist view. In Alan Booth (Ed.), *Child care in the 1990s: Trends and consequences.* Hillsdale, NJ: Erlbaum.

Belsky, Jay. (2001). Emanuel Miller Lecture: Developmental risks (still) associated with early child care. *Journal of Child Psychology, Psychiatry and Allied Disciplines, 42,* 845–859.

Belsky, Jay. (2002). Quantity counts: Amount of child care and children's socioemotional development. *Journal of Development & Behavioral Pediatrics, 23,* 167–170.

Bem, Daryl J.; & Honorton, Charles. (1994). Does psi exist? Replicable evidence for an anomalous process of information transfer. *Psychological Bulletin, 115,* 4–18.

Bem, Sandra L. (1981). Gender schema theory: A cognitive account of sex typing. *Psychological Review, 88,* 354–364.

Bem, Sandra L. (1987). Gender schema theory and the romantic tradition. In Philip Shaver & Clyde Hendrick (Eds.), *Sex and gender.* Beverly Hills, CA: Sage.

Bem, Sandra L. (1989). Genital knowledge and gender constancy in preschool children. *Child Development, 60,* 649–662.

Benjamin, Ludy T.; Whitaker, Jodi L.; Ramsey, Russell M.; & Zeve, Daniel R. (2007). John B. Watson's alleged sex research: An appraisal of the evidence. *American Psychologist, 62,* 131–139.

Bennett, David A.; Wilson, Robert S.; Schneider, Julie A.; Evans, D. A.; Mendes de Leon, C. F.; Arnold, S. E; & others. (2003). Education modifies the relation of Alzheimer's disease pathology to level of cognitive function in older persons. *Neurology, 60,* 1909–1915.

Bennett, George K. (1940). *Bennett Test of Mechanical Comprehension.* New York: Psychological Corporation.

Bennett, Kymberley K.; & Elliott, Marta. (2005). Pessimistic explanatory style and cardiac health: What is the relation and the mechanism that links them? *Basic and Applied Social Psychology, 27*(3), 239–248.

Benson, Herbert. (1993). The relaxation response. In Daniel Goleman & Joel Gurin (Eds.), *Mind/body medicine: How to use your mind for better health.* Yonkers, NY: Consumer Reports Books.

Benyamini, Yael; & Lomranz, Jacob. (2004). The relationship of activity restriction and replacement with depressive symptoms among older adults. *Psychology and Aging, 19,* 362–366.

Ben-Zeev, Talia; Fein, Steven; & Inzlicht, Michael. (2005). Arousal and stereotype threat. *Journal of Experimental Social Psychology, 41,* 174–181.

Berk, Michael. (2007). Should we be targeting exercise as a routine mental health intervention? *Acta Neuropsychiatrica, 19*(3), 217–218.

Berkman, Lisa F. (1995). The role of social relations in health promotion. *Psychosomatic Medicine, 57,* 245–254.

Berkman, Lisa F.; & Glass, Thomas. (2000). Social integration, social networks, social support, and health. In Lisa F. Berkman & Ichir Kawachi (Eds.), *Social epidemiology* (pp. 137–173). New York: Oxford University Press.

Berkman, Lisa F.; Leo-Summers, Linda; & Horowitz, Ralph I. (1992). Emotional support and survival after myocardial infarction. *Annals of Internal Medicine, 117,* 1003–1009.

Berkman, Lisa F.; & Syme, S. Leonard. (1979). Social networks, host resistance, and mortality: A nine-year follow-up study of Alameda County residents. *American Journal of Epidemiology, 109,* 186–204.

Berlyne, Daniel E. (1960). *Conflict, arousal, and curiosity.* New York: McGraw-Hill.

Berlyne, Daniel E. (1971). *Aesthetics and psychobiology.* New York: Appleton-Century-Crofts.

Berman, David; & Lyons, William. (2007). The first modern battle for consciousness: J.B. Watson's rejection of mental images. *Journal of Consciousness Studies, 14,* 5–26.

Bermond, Bob; Fasotti, L.; Nieuwenhuyse, B.; & Schuerman, J. (1991). Spinal cord lesions, peripheral feedback and intensities of emotional feelings. *Cognition & Emotion, 5,* 201–220.

Bernard, Luther L. (1924). *Instinct: A study in social psychology.* New York: Holt.

Berndt, Thomas J. (1992). Friendship and friends' influence in adolescence. *Current Directions in Psychological Science, 1,* 156–159.

Bernstein, David P.; & Useda, J. David. (2007). Paranoid personality disorder. In William T. O'Donohue, Katherine A. Fowler, & Scott O. Lilienfeld (Eds.), *Personality disorders: Toward the DSM-V* (pp. 41–62). Thousand Oaks, CA: Sage.

Berry, John W. (1994). Acculturative stress. In Walter J. Lonner & Roy Malpass (Eds.), *Psychology and culture.* Boston: Allyn & Bacon.

Berry, John W. (2003). Conceptual approaches to acculturation. In Kevin M. Chun, Pamela Balls Organista, & Gerardo Marín (Eds.), *Acculturation: Advances in theory, measurement and applied research.* Washington, DC: American Psychological Association.

Berry, John W. (2006). Acculturative stress. In Paul T. P. Wong & C. J. Lilian Wong, *Handbook of multicultural perspectives on stress and coping* (pp. 287–298). Dallas, TX: Spring Publications.

Berry, John W.; & Kim, Uichol. (1988). Acculturation and mental health. In Pierre R. Dasen, John W. Berry, & Norman Sartorius (Eds.), *Health and cross-cultural psychology: Toward applications* (Cross-cultural Research and Methodology Series, Vol. 10). Newbury Park, CA: Sage.

Berry, John W.; & Triandis, Harry C. (2006). Culture. In Kurt Pawlik & Géry d'Ydewalle (Eds.), *Psychological concepts: An international historical perspective.* Hove, England: Psychology Press/Taylor & Francis.

Berson, David M.; Dunn, Felice A.; & Takao, Motoharu. (2002, February 8). Phototransduction by retinal ganglion cells that set the circadian clock. *Science, 295,* 1070–1073.

Berthier, Neil E.; DeBlois, S.; Poirier, Christopher R.; Novak, Melinda A.; & Clifton, Rachel K. (2000). Where's the ball? Two- and three-year-olds reason about unseen events. *Developmental Psychology, 36,* 394–401.

Berthoud, Hans-Rudolf. (2007). Interactions between the "cognitive" and "metabolic" brain in the control of food intake. *Physiology & Behavior, 91,* 486–498.

Beumont, Pierre J. V. (2002). Clinical presentation of anorexia and bulimia nervosa. In Kelly D. Brownell & C. G. Fairburn (Eds.), *Eating disorders and obesity: A comprehensive handbook* (2nd ed.). New York: Guilford Press.

Beutler, Larry E. (2000). Empirically based decision making in clinical practice. *Prevention and Treatment, 3*(article 27). Retrieved from http://journals.apa.org/prevention/volume3/pre0030027a.html

Beutler, Larry E. (2002, February). The dodo bird is extinct. *Clinical Psychology: Science and Practice, 9*(1), 30–34.

Beutler, Larry E.; Malik, Mary; Alimohamed, Shabia; Harwood, T. Mark; Talebi, Hani; Noble, Sharon; & Wong, Eunice. (2004). Therapist variables. In Michael J. Lambert (Ed.), *Bergin and Garfield's handbook of psychotherapy and behavior change* (5th ed.). New York: Wiley.

Beyerstein, Barry L. (1996). Graphology. In Gordon Stein (Ed.), *The encyclopedia of the paranormal.* Amherst, NY: Prometheus Books.

Beyerstein, Barry L. (1999). Whence cometh the myth that we only use 10% of our brains? In Sergio Della Sala (Ed.), *Mind myths: Exploring popular assumptions about the mind and brain.* Chichester, England: Wiley.

Beyerstein, Barry L. (2007). Graphology—A total write-off. In Sergio Della Sala (Ed.), *Tall tales about the mind & brain: Separating fact from fiction* (pp. 233–270). New York: Oxford University Press.

Beyerstein, Barry L.; & Beyerstein, Dale (Eds.). (1992). *The write stuff: Evaluations of graphology—The study of handwriting analysis.* Amherst, NY: Prometheus Books.

Bhanji, Nadeem H.; Chouinard, Guy; & Margolese, Howard C. (2004). A review of compliance, depot intramuscular antipsychotics and the new long-acting injectable atypical antipsychotic risperidone in schizophrenia. *European Neuropsychopharmacology, 14*(2), 87–92.

Bhatara, Vinod S.; Sharma, J. N.; Gupta, Sanjay; & Gupta, Y. K. (1997). *Rauwolfia serpentina:* The first herbal antipsychotic. *American Journal of Psychiatry, 154,* 894.

Bielock, Sian L.; Rydell, Robert J.; & McConnell, Allen R. (2007). Stereotype threat and working memory: Mechanisms, alleviation, and spillover. *Journal of Experimental Psychology: General, 136,* 256–276.

Bihm, Elson M.; & Gillaspy, James A. (2006). Marian Breland Bailey (1920-2001). In *The Encyclopedia of Arkansas History & Culture.* Retrieved from http://www.encyclopediaofarkansas.net on July 15, 2009.

Bilalic, Merim; McLeod, Peter; & Gobet, Fernand. (2008). Inflexibility of experts—Reality or myth? Quantifying the Einstellung effect in chess masters. *Cognitive Psychology, 56,* 73–102.

Binet, Alfred; & Simon, Théodore. (1905). New methods for the diagnosis of the intellectual level of subnormals. *L'Année Psychologique, 11,* 191–244.

Bitterman, M. E. (2006). Classical conditioning since Pavlov. *Review of General Psychology, 10,* 365–376.

Bjork, Daniel W. (1997). *B. F. Skinner: A life.* Washington, DC: American Psychological Association.

Bjorklund, Barbara R. (1995). Language development and cognition. In David F. Bjorklund (Ed.), *Children's thinking: Developmental function and individual differences* (2nd ed.). Pacific Grove, CA: Brooks/Cole.

Blackmore, Susan. (1985). Belief in the paranormal: Probability judgments, illusory control, and the chance baseline shift. *British Journal of Psychology, 76,* 459–468.

Blackmore, Susan. (1998). Lucid dreams. In Kendrick Frazier (Ed.), *Encounters with the paranormal: Science, knowledge, and belief.* Amherst, NY: Prometheus Books.

Blader, Joseph C.; & Carlson, Gabrielle A. (2008). Increased rates of bipolar disorder diagnoses among US child, adolescent, and adult inpatients, 1996–2004. *Biological Psychiatry, 15,* 107–114.

Blair, Irene V. (2002). The malleability of automatic stereotypes and prejudice. *Personality and Social Psychology Review, 6*(3), 242–261.

Blake, Robert R.; & Mouton, Jane S. (1985). *The managerial grid III: The key to leadership excellence.* Houston, TX: Gulf Publishing.

Blanchard, Ray; & Bogaert, Anthony F. (1996). Homosexuality in men and number of older brothers. *American Journal of Psychiatry, 153,* 27–31.

Blanco, Carlos; Clougherty, Kathleen F.; & Lipsitz, W. Joshua. (2006). Homework in Interpersonal Psychotherapy (IPT): Rationale and practice. *Journal of Psychotherapy Integration, 16*(2) [Special issue: Integration of between-session (homework) activities into psychotherapy], 201–218.

Blankstein, Kirk R.; & Flett, Gordon L. (1992). Specificity in the assessment of daily hassles: Hassles, locus of control, and adjustment in college students. *Canadian Journal of Behavioural Science, 24,* 382–398.

Blass, Thomas. (1991). Understanding behavior in the Milgram obedience experiment. *Journal of Personality and Social Psychology, 60,* 398–413.

Blass, Thomas. (1992). The social psychology of Stanley Milgram. In Mark P. Zanna (Ed.), *Advances in experimental social psychology* (Vol. 25). San Diego, CA: Academic Press.

Blass, Thomas. (2000). The Milgram paradigm after 35 years. Some things we now know about obedience to authority. In Thomas Blass (Ed.), *Obedience to authority: Current perspectives on the Milgram paradigm* (pp. 35–59). Mahwah, NJ: Erlbaum.

Blass, Thomas. (2004). *The man who shocked the world: The life and legacy of Stanley Milgram.* New York: Basic Books.

Bleiberg, Kathryn L.; & Markowitz, John C. (2008). Interpersonal psychotherapy for depression. In David H. Barlow (Ed.), *Clinical handbook of psychological disorders: A step-by-step treatment manual* (4th ed.). New York: Guilford Press.

Block, Jack. (1995). A contrarian view of the five-factor approach to personality description. *Psychological Bulletin, 117,* 187–215.

Bloom, Paul. (2006, June 27). Seduced by the flickering lights of the brain. *Seed Magazine.* Retrieved February 22, 2008, from http://seedmagazine.com/news/2006/06/seduced_by_the_flickering_ligh.php

Blumberg, Mark S.; & Sokoloff, Greta. (2001). Do infant rats cry? *Psychological Review, 108,* 83–95.

Blumberg, Mark S.; Sokoloff, Greta; Kirby, Robert F.; & Kent, Kristen J. (2000). Distress vocalizations in infant rats: What's all the fuss about? *Psychological Science, 11,* 78–81.

Blume, Arthur W.; Lostutter, Ty W.; Schmaling, Karen B.; & Marlatt, G. Alan. (2003). Beliefs about drinking behavior predict drinking consequences. *Journal of Psychoactive Drugs, 35,* 395–399.

Blumenthal, Arthur L. (1998). Leipzig, Wilhelm Wundt, and psychology's gilded age. In Gregory A. Kimble & Michael Wertheimer (Eds.), *Portraits of pioneers in psychology* (Vol. 3). Washington, DC: American Psychological Association.

Boden, Matthew T.; & Berenbaum, Howard. (2007). Emotional awareness, gender, and suspiciousness. *Cognition & Emotion, 21,* 268–280.

Bodenhausen, Galen V.; Macrae, C. Neil; & Hugenberg, Kurt. (2003). Social cognition. In Theodore Millon & Melvin J. Lerner (Eds.), *Handbook of psychology: Personality and social psychology, 5,* 257–282. New York: Wiley.

Boduroglu, Ayescan; Minear, Meredith; & Shah, Priti. (2007). Working memory. In Francis T. Durso (Ed.), *Handbook of applied social cognition* (2nd ed.). Chichester, England: Wiley.

Boecker, Henning; Sprenger, Till; Spilker, Mary E.; Henriksen, Gjermund; Koppenhoefer, Marcus; Wagner, Klaus J.; Valet, Michael; Berthele, Achim; & Tolle, Thomas R. (2008). The runner's high: Opioidergic mechanisms in the human brain. *Cerebral Cortex, 18,* 2523–2531.

Bogaert, Anthony F. (2003). Number of older brothers and social orientation: New tests and the attraction/behavior distinction in two national probability samples. *Journal of Personality and Social Psychology, 84,* 644–652.

Bogaert, Anthony F. (2005a). Age at puberty and father absence in a national probability sample. *Journal of Adolescence, 28.* 541–546.

Bogaert, Anthony F. (2005b). Sibling sex ratio and sexual orientation in men and women: New tests in two national probability samples. *Archives of Sexual Behavior, 34,* 111–116.

Bogaert, Anthony F. (2006). Biological versus nonbiological older brothers and men's sexual orientation. *Proceedings of the National Academy of Sciences, 103,* 10771–10774.

Bogaert, Anthony F. (2007). Extreme right-handedness, older brothers, and sexual orientation in men. *Neuropsychology, 21,* 141–148.

Bogaert, Anthony F. (2007, June). Quoted in Michael Abrams, "Born gay?" *Discover,* pp. 58–63, 83.

Bohlmeijer, Ernst; Roemer, Marte; & Cuijpers, Pim. (2007).The effects of reminiscence on psychological well-being in older adults: A meta-analysis. *Aging & Mental Health, 11*(3), 291–300.

Boisvert, Charles M.; & Faust, David. (2003). Leading researchers' consensus on psychotherapy research findings: Implications for the teaching and conduct of psychotherapy. *Professional Psychology: Research and Practice, 34*(5), 508–513.

Bolger, Niall; & Schilling, Elizabeth A. (1991). Personality and problems of everyday life: The role of neuroticism in exposure and reactivity to stress. *Journal of Personality, 59,* 355–386.

Bolger, Niall; & Zuckerman, Adam. (1995). A framework for studying personality in the stress process. *Journal of Personality and Social Psychology, 69,* 890–902.

Bolles, Robert C. (1985). The slaying of Goliath: What happened to reinforcement theory? In Timothy D. Johnston & Alexandra T. Pietrewicz (Eds.), *Issues in the ecological study of learning.* Hillsdale, NJ: Erlbaum.

Bolton, Paul; Bass, Judith; Neugebauer, Richard; Verdeli, Helen; Clougherty, Kathleen F.; Wickramaratne, Priya; & others. (2003). Group interpersonal psychotherapy for depression in rural Uganda: A randomized controlled trial. *Journal of the American Medical Association, 289,* 3117–3124.

Bond, Michael Harris. (1986). *The psychology of the Chinese people.* New York: Oxford University Press.

Bond, Michael Harris. (1994). Continuing encounters with Hong Kong. In Walter J. Lonner & Roy Malpass (Eds.), *Psychology and culture.* Boston: Allyn & Bacon.

Bond, Michael Harris; & Smith, Peter B. (1996). Cross-cultural social and organizational psychology. *Annual Review of Psychology, 47,* 205–235.

Bond, Rod. (2005). Group size and conformity. *Group Processes & Intergroup Relations, 8*(4), 331–354.

Bond, Rod; & Smith, Peter B. (1996). Culture and conformity: A metaanalysis of studies using Asch's (1952b, 1956) line judgment task. *Psychological Bulletin, 119,* 111–137.

Bonnet, Michael H. (2005). Acute sleep deprivation. In Meir H. Kryger, Thomas Roth, & William C. Dement (Eds.), *Principles and practice of sleep medicine* (4th ed.). Philadelphia: Elsevier Saunders.

Bonshtein, Udi; Shaar, Izhar; & Golan, Gabi. (2005). Who wants to control the habit? A multi-dimensional hypnotic model of smoking cessation. *Contemporary Hypnosis, 22,* 193–201.

Borbély, Alexander A; & Achermann, Peter. (2005). Sleep homeostasis and models of sleep regulation. In Meir H. Kryger, Thomas Roth, & William C. Dement (Eds.), *Principles and practice of sleep medicine* (4th ed.). Philadelphia: Elsevier Saunders.

Bornstein, Marc H.; & Lamb, Michael E. (1992). *Development in infancy: An introduction* (3rd ed.). New York: McGraw-Hill.

Bornstein, Marc H.; & Marks, Lawrence E. (1982, January). Color revisionism. *Psychology Today, 16,* 64–73.

Boss, Pauline; Beaulieu, Lorraine; Wieling, Elizabeth; Turner, William; & LaCruz, Shulaika. (2003). Healing loss, ambiguity, and trauma: A community-based intervention with families of union workers missing after the 9/11 attack in New York City. *Journal of Marital and Family Therapy, 29,* 455–467.

Botella, Cristina; García-Palacios, Azucena; Villa, Helena. (2007). Virtual reality exposure in the treatment of panic disorder and agoraphobia: A controlled study. *Clinical Psychology & Psychotherapy, 14*(3), 164–175.

Bottos, Shauna; & Dewey, Deborah. (2004). Perfectionists' appraisal of daily hassles and chronic headache. *Headache: The Journal of Head and Face Pain, 44*(8), 772–779.

Bouchard, Claude. (1997). Genetics of human obesity: Recent results from linkage studies. *Journal of Nutrition, 127,* 1887S–1890S.**Bouchard, Thomas J., Jr.** (2004). Genetic influence on human psychological traits. *Psychological Science, 13,* 148–151.

Bouton, Mark E. (2007). *Learning and behavior: A contemporary synthesis.* Sunderland, MA: Sinauer Associates.

Boxer, Paul; Huesmann, L. Rowell; Bushman, Brad J.; O'Brien, Maureen; & Moceri, Dominic. (2009). The role of violent media preference in cumulative developmental risk for violence and general aggression. *Journal of Youth and Adolescence, 38,* 417–428.

Bowden, Charles L. (2005). Treatment options for bipolar depression. *Journal of Clinical Psychiatry, 66*(Suppl. 1), 3–6.

Bower, Bruce. (1997, March 29). Forbidden flavors: Scientists consider how disgusting tastes can linger surreptitiously in memory. *Science News, 151,* 198–199.

Bowers, Kenneth S.; & Favolden, Peter. (1996). Revisiting a century-old Freudian slip—From suggestion disavowed to the truth repressed. *Psychological Bulletin, 119,* 355–380.

Bowers, Kenneth S.; Regehr, Glenn; Balthazard, Claude; & Parker, Kevin. (1990). Intuition in the context of discovery. *Cognitive Psychology, 22,* 72–110.

Bowlby, John. (1969). *Attachment and loss: Vol. 1. Attachment.* New York: Basic Books.

Bowlby, John. (1988). *A secure base.* New York: Basic Books.

Boyke, Janina; Driemeyer, Joenna; Gaser, Christian; Büchel, Christian; & May, Arne. (2008). Training-induced brain structure changes in the elderly. *The Journal of Neuroscience, 28,* 7031–7035.

Bozarth, Jerold D. (2007). Unconditional positive regard. In Mick Cooper, Maureen O'Hara, Peter F. Schmid, & Gill Wyatt (Eds.), *The handbook of person-centered psychotherapy and counselling.* New York: Palgrave Macmillan.

Bozarth, Jerold D.; & Wang, Chun-Chuan. (2008). The "unitary actualizing tendency" and congruence in client-centered therapy. In Brian E. Levitt (Ed.), *Reflections on human potential: Bridging the person-centered approach and positive psychology.* Ross-on-Wye, England: PCCS Books.

Bozarth, Jerold D.; Zimring, Fred M.; & Tausch, Reinhard. (2002). Client-centered therapy: The evolution of a revolution. In David J. Cain & Julius Seeman (Eds.), *Humanistic psychotherapies: Handbook of research and practice.* Washington, DC: American Psychological Association.

Bracha, H. Stefan; Wolkowitz, Owen M.; Lohr, James B.; Karson, Craig N.; & Bigelow, Llewellyn B. (1989). High prevalence of visual hallucinations in research subjects with chronic schizophrenia. *American Journal of Psychiatry, 146,* 526–528.

Bradbard, Marilyn R.; Martin, Carol L.; Endsley, Richard C.; & Halverson, Charles F. (1986). Influence of sex stereotypes on children's exploration and memory: A competence versus performance distinction. *Developmental Psychology, 22,* 481–486.

Bradshaw, G. A.; Schore, Allan N.; Brown, Janine L.; Poole, Joyce H.; & Moss, Cynthia J. (2005). Elephant breakdown. Social trauma: Early disruption of attachment can affect the physiology, behaviour, and culture of animals and humans over generations. *Nature, 433,* 807.

Braffman, Wayne; & Kirsch, Irving. (1999). Imaginative suggestibility and hypnotizability: An empirical analysis. *Journal of Personality and Social Psychology, 77,* 578–587.

Brain, Marshall. (2008, January 4). "Can your mind control your weight and blood pressure?" Institute for Ethics and Emerging Technologies. Retrieved February 16, 2008, from http://ieet.org/index.php/IEET/more/brain20080103/

Brainerd, Charles J. (1996). Piaget: A centennial celebration. *Psychological Science, 7,* 191–195.

Bransford, John D.; & Stein, Barry S. (1993). *The IDEAL problem solver: A guide for improving thinking, learning, and creativity* (2nd ed.). New York: Freeman.

Braun, Allen R.; Balkin, Thomas J.; Wesensten, Nancy J.; Gwadry, Fuad; Carson, Richard E.; Varga, Mary; & others. (1998, January 2). Dissociated patterns of activity in visual cortices and their projections during human rapid eye movement during sleep. *Science, 279,* 91–95.

Braun, Stephen. (2001, Spring). Ecstasy on trial: Seeking insight by prescription. *Cerebrum, 3,* 10–21.

Bray, Signe; & O'Doherty, John. (2007). Neural coding of reward-prediction error signals during classical conditioning with attractive faces. *Journal of Neurophysiology, 97*(4), 3036–3045.

Bregman, Elsie O. (1934). An attempt to modify the emotional attitude of infants by the conditioned response technique. *Journal of Genetic Psychology, 45,* 169–198.

Breland, Keller; & Breland, Marian. (1961). The misbehavior of organisms. *American Psychologist, 16,* 681–684.

Brennan, Peter A.; & Zufall, Frank. (2006). Pheromonal communication in vertebrates. *Nature, 444,* 308–313.

Brenneis, C. Brooks. (2000). Evaluating the evidence: Can we find authenticated recovered memory? *Psychoanalytic Psychology, 17,* 61–77.

Bresee, Catherine; Gotto, Jennifer; & Rapaport, Mark H. (2009). Treatment of depression. In Alan F. Schatzberg & Charles B. Nemeroff (Eds.), *The American Psychiatric Publishing textbook of psychopharmacology* (4th ed., pp. 1081–1111). Washington, DC: American Psychiatric Publishing.

Breslau, Naomi; Kilbey, M. Marlyne; & Andreski, Patricia. (1993). Nicotine dependence and major depression: New evidence from a prospective investigation. *Archives of General Psychiatry, 50,* 31–35.

Breslau, Naomi; Novak, Scott P.; & Kessler, Ronald C. (2004). Psychiatric disorders and stages of smoking. *Biological Psychiatry, 55,* 69–76.

Breslau, Naomi; Peterson, Edward L.; Schultz, Lonni R.; Chilcoat, Howard D.; & Andreski, Patricia. (1998). Major depression and stages of smoking: A longitudinal investigation. *Archives of General Psychiatry, 55,* 161–166.

Bretherton, Inge; & Main, Mary. (2000). Mary Dinsmore Salter Ainsworth (1913–1999). *American Psychologist, 55,* 1148–1149.

Breuer, Josef; & Freud, Sigmund. (1895/1957). *Studies on hysteria* (James Strachey, Ed. & Trans., in collaboration with Anna Freud). New York: Basic Books.

Brewer, Marilynn B. (1994). The social psychology of prejudice: Getting it all together. In Mark P. Zanna & James M. Olson (Eds.), *The psychology of prejudice: The Ontario Symposium* (Vol. 7). Hillsdale, NJ: Erlbaum.

Brewer, Marilynn B.; & Chen, Ya-Ru. (2007). Where (who) are collectives in collectivism? Toward conceptual clarification of individualism and collectivism. *Psychological Review, 114*(1), 133–151.

Brewer, William F.; & Treyens, James C. (1981). Role of schemata in memory for places. *Cognitive Psychology, 13,* 207–230.

Briere, John; & Conte, Jon. (1993). Self-reported amnesia for abuse in adults molested as children. *Journal of Traumatic Stress, 6*(1), 21–31.

Brissette, Ian; Scheier, Michael F.; & Carver, Charles S. (2002). The role of optimism in social network development, coping, and psychological adjustment during a life transition. *Journal of Personality and Social Psychology, 82,* 102–111.

Brock, Timothy C. (2008). Negligible scholarly impact of 38-witnesses parable. *American Psychologist, 63,* 561–562.

Brody, Arthur L.; Saxena, Sajaya; Stoessel, Paula; Gillies, Laurie; Fairbanks, Lynn A.; Alborzian, Shervin; & others. (2001, July). Regional brain metabolic changes in patients with major depression treated with either paroxetine or interpersonal therapy. *Archives of General Psychiatry, 58,* 631–640.

Bronstein, Phyllis. (2006). The family environment: Where gender role socialization begins. In Judith Worell & Carol D. Goodheart (Eds.), *Handbook of girls' and women's psychological health: Gender and well-being across the lifespan* (pp. 262–271). New York: Oxford University Press.

Brooks-Gunn, Jeanne. (1988). Antecedents and consequences of variations of girls' maturational timing. In Melvin D. Levine & Elizabeth R. McAnarney (Eds.), *Early adolescent transitions.* Lexington, MA: Lexington Books.

Brooks-Gunn, Jeanne; & Reiter, Edward O. (1990). The role of pubertal processes. In S. Shirley Feldman & Glen R. Elliott (Eds.), *At the threshold: The developing adolescent.* Cambridge, MA: Harvard University Press.

Brosnan, Sarah F.; & de Waal, Frans B. M. (2004). Socially learned preferences for differentially rewarded tokens in the brown capuchin monkey (*Cebus apella*). (2004). *Journal of Comparative Psychology, 118,* 133–139.

Brown, Alan S. (2003). A review of the déjà vu experience. *Psychological Bulletin, 129,* 394–413.

Brown, Alan S. (2004). *The déjà vu experience: Essays in cognitive psychology.* New York: Psychology Press.

Brown, Alan S. (2005, January 31). Looking at déjà vu for the first time. *The Scientist, 19*(2), 20–21.

Brown, Alan S.; Begg, Melissa D.; Gravenstein, Stefan; Schaefer, Catherine A.; Wyatt, Richard J.; Bresnahan, Michaeline; Babulas, Vicki P.; & Susser, Ezra S. (2004). Serological evidence of prenatal influenza in the etiology of schizophrenia. *Archives of General Psychiatry, 61,* 774–780.

Brown, Bernard. (1999, April). Optimizing expression of the common human genome for child development. *Current Directions in Psychological Science, 8,* 37–41.

Brown, Culum; Western, Jac; & Braithwaite, Victoria A. (2007). The influence of early experience on, and inheritance of, cerebral lateralization. *Animal Behaviour, 74,* 231–238.

Brown, Gary E.; Davis, Eric; & Johnson, Amanda. (1999). Forced exercise blocks learned helplessness in the cockroach (*Periplaneta americana*). *Psychological Reports, 84,* 155–156.

Brown, Gregory K.; Newman, Cory F.; Charlesworth, Sarah E.; Crits-Christoph, Paul; & Beck, Aaron T. (2004). An open clinical trial of cognitive therapy for borderline personality disorder. *Journal of Personality Disorders, 18,* 257–271.

Brown, Jessica S.; Stellrecht, Nadia E.; & Williams, Foluso M. (2005). A comparison of therapy alone versus therapy and medication in a community clinic. *Journal of Cognitive Psychotherapy, 19*(4), 309–316.

Brown, Lisa M.; Bongar, Bruce; & Cleary, Karin M. (2004). A profile of psychologists' views of critical risk factors for completed suicide in older adults. *Professional Psychology: Research & Practice, 35,* 90–96.

Brown, Roger; & Kulik, James. (1982). Flashbulb memories. In Ulric Neisser (Ed.), *Memory observed: Remembering in natural contexts.* San Francisco: Freeman.

Brown, Ronald T.; Antonuccio, David O.; DuPaul, George J.; Fristad, Mary A.; King, Cheryl A.; Leslie, Laurel K.; McCormick, Gabriele S.; Pelham, William E., Jr.; Piacentini, John C.; & Vitiello, Benedetto. (2008). *Childhood mental health disorders: Evidence base and contextual factors for psychosocial, psychopharmacological, and combined interventions.* Washington, DC: American Psychological Association.

Brüning, Jens C.; Gautam, Dinesh; Burks, Deborah J.; Gillette, Jennifer; Schubert, Markus; Orban, Paul C.; & others. (2000, September 22). Role of brain insulin receptor in control of body weight and reproduction. *Science, 289,* 2122–2125.

Bryan, James H.; & Test, Mary Ann. (1967). Models and helping: Naturalistic studies in aiding behavior. *Journal of Personality and Social Psychology, 6,* 400–407.

Bryant, Gregory A.; & Barrett, H. Clark. (2007) Recognizing intentions in infant-directed speech: Evidence for universals. *Psychological Science, 18,* 746–751.

Buckley, Kerry W. (1982). The selling of a psychologist: John Broadus Watson and the application of behavioral techniques to advertising. *Journal of the History of the Behavioral Sciences, 18,* 207–221.

Buckley, Kerry W. (1989). *Mechanical man: John Broadus Watson and the beginnings of behaviorism.* New York: Guilford Press.

Budney, Alan J.; Roffman, Roger; Stephens, Robert S.; & Walker, Denise. (2007, December). Marijuana dependence and its treatment. *Addiction Science and Clinical Practice, 4,* 4–16.

Burger, Jerry M. (1992). *Desire for control: Personality, social, and clinical perspectives.* New York: Plenum Press.

Burger, Jerry M. (2009). Replicating Milgram: Would people still obey today? *American Psychologist, 64,* 1–11.

Buri, John R.; Louiselle, Peggy A.; Misukanis, Thomas M.; & Mueller, Rebecca A. (1988). Effects of parental authoritarianism and authoritativeness on self-esteem. *Personality and Social Psychology Bulletin, 14,* 271–282.

Burke, Deborah M.; & Shafto, Meredith A. (2004). Aging and language production. *Current Directions in Psychological Science, 13,* 21–24.

Burks, Nancy; & Martin, Barclay. (1985). Everyday problems and life change events: Ongoing versus acute sources of stress. *Journal of Human Stress, 11,* 27–35.

Burlingame, Gary M.; MacKenzie, K. Roy; & Strauss, Bernhard. (2004). Small group treatment: Evidence for effectiveness and mechanisms of change. In Michael J. Lambert (Ed.), *Bergin and Garfield's handbook of psychotherapy and behavior change* (5th ed.). New York: Wiley.

Burlingame, Gary M.; & McClendon, Debra T. (2008). Group therapy. In Jay L. Lebow (Ed.), *Twenty-first century psychotherapies: Contemporary approaches to theory and practice* (pp. 347–388). Hoboken, NJ: Wiley.

Burman, Bonnie; & Margolin, Gayla. (1992). Analysis of the association between marital relationships and health problems: An interactional perspective. *Psychological Bulletin, 112,* 39–63.

Burns, Melanie; & Seligman, Martin E. P. (1989). Explanatory style across the lifespan: Evidence for stability over 52 years. *Journal of Personality and Social Psychology, 56,* 471–477.

Burns, Tracey C.; Yoshida, Katherine A.; Hill, Karen; & Werker, Janet F. (2007). The development of phonetic representation in bilingual and monolingual infants. *Applied Psycholinguistics, 28,* 455–474.

Burns, Victoria E.; Carroll, Douglas; Drayson, Mark; Whitham, Martin; & Ring, Christopher. (2003). Life events, perceived stress and antibody response to influenza vaccination in young, healthy adults. *Journal of Psychosomatic Research, 55,* 569–572.

Burton, Simon. (2006). Symptom domains of schizophrenia: The role of atypical antipsychotic agents. *Journal of Psychopharmacology, 20*(6, Suppl), 6–19.

Bushman, Brad J.; & Anderson, Craig A. (2007). Measuring the effect of violent media on aggression. *American Psychologist, 62,* 253–254.

Bushnell, I. W. R. (2001). Mother's face recognition in newborn infants: Learning and memory. *Infant and Child Development, 10,* 67–74.

Buss, Arnold H. (1989). Personality as traits. *American Psychologist, 44,* 1378–1388.

Buss, Arnold H. (2001). *Psychological dimensions of the self.* Thousand Oaks, CA: Sage.

Buss, David M. (1991). Evolutionary personality psychology. *Annual Review of Psychology, 42,* 459–491.

Buss, David M. (1994). *The evolution of desire: Strategies of human mating.* New York: Basic Books.

Buss, David M. (1995a). Evolutionary psychology: A new paradigm for psychological science. *Psychological Inquiry, 6,* 1–31.

Buss, David M. (1995b). Psychological sex differences: Origins through sexual selection. *American Psychologist, 50,* 164–168.

Buss, David M. (1996). Sexual conflict: Evolutionary insights into feminism and the "Battle of the Sexes." In David M. Buss & Neil M. Malamuth (Eds.), *Sex, power, conflict: Evolutionary and feminist perspectives.* New York: Oxford University Press.

Buss, David M. (Ed.). (2005). *Handbook of evolutionary psychology.* Hoboken, NJ: Wiley.

Buss, David M. (2007a). The evolution of human mating. *Acta Psychologica Sinica, 39*(3) [Special issue: Evolutionary psychology], 502–512.

Buss, David M. (2007b). The evolution of human mating strategies: Consequences for conflict and cooperation. In Steven W. Gangestad & Jeffry A Simpson (Eds.), *The evolution of mind: Fundamental questions and controversies.* New York: Guilford Press.

Buss, David M. (2008). *Evolutionary psychology: The new science of the mind* (3rd ed.). Boston: Pearson.

Buss, David M. (2009). The great struggles of life: Darwin and the emergence of evolutionary psychology. *American Psychologist, 64,* 140–148.

Bussey, Kay; & Bandura, Albert. (2004). Social cognitive theory of gender development and functioning. In Alice H. Eagly, Anne E. Beall, & Robert J. Sternberg (Eds.), *The psychology of gender* (2nd ed.). New York: Guilford Press.

Butcher, James N. (1999). *A beginner's guide to the MMPI-2.* Washington, DC: American Psychological Association.

Butcher, James N.; & Rouse, Steven V. (1996). Personality: Individual differences and clinical assessment. *Annual Review of Psychology, 47,* 87–111.

Butler, Andrew C.; Chapman, Jason E.; Forman, Evan M.; & Beck, Aaron T. (2006, January). The empirical status of cognitive-behavioral therapy: A review of meta-analyses. *Clinical Psychology Review, 26*(1): 17–31.

Butler, Robert A.; & Harlow, Harry F. (1954). Persistence of visual exploration in monkeys. *Journal of Comparative and Physiological Psychology, 47,* 258–263.

Cacioppo, John T.; Berntson, Gary G.; & Nusbaum, Howard C. (2008). Neuroimaging as a new tool in the toolbox of psychological science. *Current Directions in Psychological Science, 17,* 62–67.

Cacioppo, John T.; & Decety, Jean. (2009). What are the brain mechanisms on which psychological processes are based? *Perspectives on Psychological Science, 4,* 10–18.

Cacioppo, John T.; & Gardner, Wendi L. (1999). Emotion. *Annual Review of Psychology, 50,* 191–214.

Cadinu, Mara; Maass, Anne; Rosabianca, Alessandra; & Kiesner, Jeff. (2005). Why do women underperform under stereotype threat? *Psychological Science, 16*(7), 572–578.

Cafri, Guy; Yamamiya, Yuko; Brannick, Michael; & Thompson, J. Kevin. (2005). The influence of sociocultural factors on body image: A meta-analysis. *Clinical Psychology: Science and Practice, 12,* 421–433.

Cahill, Larry. (2006). Why sex matters for neuroscience. *Nature Reviews Neuroscience, 7,* 477–484.

Cahn, Wiepke; Rais, Monica; Stigter, F. Pien; van Haren, Neeltje E.; Caspers, Esther; Hulshoff Pol, Hilleke E.; & others. (2009). Psychosis and brain volume changes during the first five years of schizophrenia. European *Neuropsychopharmacology, 19,* 147–151.

Cain, Christopher K.; & LeDoux, Joseph E. (2008). Brain mechanisms of Pavlovian and instrumental aversive conditioning. In Robert J. Blanchard, D. Caroline Blanchard, Guy Griebel, & David Nutt (Eds.), *Handbook of behavioral neuroscience: Vol. 17. Handbook of anxiety and fear* (pp. 103–124). Amsterdam: Elsevier.

Cain, David J. (2002). Defining characteristics, history, and evolution of humanistic psychotherapies. In David J. Cain & Julius Seeman (Eds.), *Humanistic psychotherapies: Handbook of research and practice.* Washington, DC: American Psychological Association.

Cain, David J. (2003). Advancing humanistic psychology and psychotherapy: Some challenges and proposed solutions. *Journal of Humanistic Psychology, 43,* 10–41.

Cain, David J.; & Seeman, Julius (Eds.). (2002a). *Humanistic psychotherapies: Handbook of research and practice.* Washington, DC: American Psychological Association.

Cain, David J.; & Seeman, Julius. (2002b). Preface. In David J. Cain & Julius Seeman (Eds.), *Humanistic psychotherapies: Handbook of research and practice.* Washington, DC: American Psychological Association.

Calero-García, M. D.; Navarro-González, E.; & Muñoz-Manzano, L. (2007). Influence of level of activity on cognitive performance and cognitive plasticity in elderly persons. *Archives of Gerontology and Geriatrics, 45,* 307–318.

Callahan, Leigh F.; Wiley-Exley, Elizabeth K.; Mielenz, Thelma J.; Brady, Teresa J.; Xiao, Changfu; Currey, Shannon S.; & others. (2009). Use of complementary and alternative medicine among patients with arthritis. *Preventing Chronic Disease,* 6, 1–23. Accessed on October 4, 2009 at: http://www.cdc.gov/pcd/issues/2009/apr/08_0070.htm.

Campbell, Jennifer D.; & Fairey, Patricia J. (1989). Informational and normative routes to conformity: The effect of faction size as a function of norm extremity and attention to the stimulus. *Journal of Personality and Social Psychology, 57,* 457–458.

Campbell, John B.; & Hawley, Charles W. (1982). Study habits and Eysenck's theory of extraversion-introversion. *Journal of Research in Personality, 16,* 139–146.

Campbell, Matthew W.; Carter, J. Devyn; Proctor, Darby; Eisenberg, Michelle L.; & de Waal, Frans B. M. (2009, September 9). Computer animations stimulate contagious yawning in chimpanzees. *Proceedings of the Royal Society, Biological Sciences.* E-Pub: 10.1098/rspb.2009.1087.

Campbell, Scott S. (1997). The basics of biological rhythms. In Mark R. Pressman & William C. Orr (Eds.), *Understanding sleep: The evaluation and treatment of sleep disorders.* Washington, DC: American Psychological Association.

Campfield, L. Arthur; Smith, Francoise J.; Rosenbaum, Michael; & Hirsch, Jules. (1996). Human eating: Evidence for a physiological basis using a modified paradigm. *Neuroscience and Biobehavioral Reviews, 20,* 133–137.

Canli, Turhan. (2004). Functional brain-mapping of extraversion and neuroticism: Learning from individual differences in emotion processing. *Journal of Personality, 72,* 1105–1132.

Canli, Turhan. (2006) *Biology of personality and individual differences.* New York: Guilford Press.

Canli, Turhan; Amin, Zenab; Haas, Brian; Omura, Kazufumi; & Constable, R. Todd. (2004). A double dissociation between mood states and personality traits in the anterior cingulate. *Behavioral Neuroscience, 118,* 897–904.

Canli, Turhan; Sivers, Heidi; Whitfield, Susan L.; Gotlib, Ian H.; & Gabrieli, John D. E. (2002). Amygdala response to happy faces as a function of extraversion. *Science, 296,* 2191.

Canli, Turhan; Zhao, Zuo; Desmond, John E.; Kang, Eunjoo; Gross, James; & Gabrieli, John D. E. (2001). An fMRI study of personality influences on brain reactivity to emotional stimuli. *Behavioral Neuroscience, 115,* 33–42.

Cannon, Walter B. (1927). The James-Lange theory of emotion: A critical examination and an alternative theory. *American Journal of Psychology, 39,* 106–124.

Cannon, Walter B. (1932). *The wisdom of the body.* New York: Norton.

Cannon, Walter B.; Lewis, J. T.; & Britton, S. W. (1927). The dispensability of the sympathetic division of the autonomic nervous system. *Boston Medical and Surgical Journal, 197,* 514.

Canter, Peter H.; & Ernst, Edzard. (2007). *Ginkgo biloba* is not a smart drug: An updated systematic review of randomised clinical trials testing the nootropic effects of *G. biloba* extracts in healthy people. *Human Psychopharmacology: Clinical and Experimental, 22,* 265–278.

Caplan, Paula J.; & Cosgrove, Lisa (Eds.). (2004). *Bias in psychiatric diagnosis.* Lanham, MD: Aronson.

Caporael, Linda R. (2001). Evolutionary psychology: Toward a unifying theory and a hybrid science. *Annual Review of Psychology, 52,* 607–628.

Cardeña, Etzel; & Gleaves, David H. (2007). Dissociative disorders. In Michel Hersen, Samuel M. Turner, & Deborah C. Beidel (Eds.), *Adult psychopathology and diagnosis* (5th ed., pp. 473–503). Hoboken, NJ: Wiley.

Carey, Bendict. (2007). Brainy parrot dies, emotive to the end. *The New York Times.* Retrieved August 20, 2008, from www.nytimes.com/2007/09/11/science/11parrot.html

Carlson, Elizabeth A.; Sroufe, Alan L.; & Egelund, Byron. (2004). The construction of experience: A longitudinal study of representation and behavior. *Child Development, 75,* 66–83.

Carlson, Gabrielle A.; & Meyer, Stephanie E. (2006). Phenomenology and diagnosis of bipolar disorder in children, adolescents, and adults: Complexities and developmental issues. *Development and Psychopathology, 18*(4) [Special issue: Developmental approaches to bipolar disorder], 939–969.

Carlson, Jon; Watts, Richard; & Maniacci, Michael. (2008). *Adlerian therapy: Theory and practice.* Washington, DC: American Psychological Association.

Carretti, Barbara; Borella, Erika; & De Beni, Rossana. (2007). Does strategic memory training improve the working memory performance of younger and older adults? *Experimental Psychology, 54,* 311–320.

Carroll, Marilyn E.; & Overmier, J. Bruce (Eds.). (2001). *Animal research and human health: Advancing human welfare through behavioral science.* Washington, DC: American Psychological Association.

Carroll, Robert Todd. (2003). *The skeptic's dictionary: A collection of strange beliefs, amusing deceptions, and dangerous delusions.* Hoboken, NJ: Wiley.

Carskadon, Mary A.; & Dement, William C. (2005). Normal human sleep: An overview. In Meir H. Kryger, Thomas Roth, & William C. Dement (Eds.), *Principles and practice of sleep medicine* (4th ed.). Philadelphia: Elsevier Saunders.

Carskadon, Mary A.; & Rechtschaffen, Allan. (2005). Monitoring and staging human sleep. In Meir H. Kryger, Thomas Roth, & William C. Dement (Eds.), *Principles and practice of sleep medicine* (4th ed.). Philadelphia: Elsevier Saunders.

Carter, C. Sue; & DeVries, A. Courtney. (1999). Stress and soothing: An endocrine perspective. In Michael Lewis & Douglas Ramsay (Eds.), *Soothing and stress.* Mahwah, NJ: Erlbaum.

Carter, Christopher J. (2008). Schizophrenia susceptibility genes directly implicated in the life cycles of pathogens: Cytomegalovirus, influenza, herpes simplex, rubella, and *toxoplasma gondii.* Schizophrenia Bulletin Advance Access published on June 13, 2008. doi:10.1093/schbul/sbn054

Cartwright, Rosalind. (2004). Sleepwalking violence: A sleep disorder, a legal dilemma, and a psychological challenge. *American Journal of Psychiatry, 161,* 1149–1158.

Cartwright, Rosalind. (2007). Response to M. Pressman: Factors that predispose, prime, and precipitate NREM parasomnias in adults: Clinical and forensic implications. *Sleep Medicine Review, 11,* 5–30.

Carver, Karen; Joyner, Kara; & Udry, J. Richard. (2003). National estimates of adolescent romantic relationships. In Paul Florsheim (Ed.), *Adolescent romantic relations and sexual behavior: Theory, research, and practical implications.* Mahwah, NJ: Erlbaum.

Caspi, Avshalom; Roberts, Brent W.; & Shiner, Rebecca L. (2005). Personality development: Stability and change. *Annual Review of Psychology, 56,* 453–484.

Cass, Hyla. (2006). Stress and the immune system. *Total Health, 27*(6), 24–25.

Castelli, Luigi; Zogmaister, Cristina; Smith, Eliot R.; & Arcuri, Luciano. (2004). On the automatic evaluation of social exemplars. *Journal of Personality and Social Psychology, 86,* 373–387.

Castillo, Linda G.; Conoley, Collie W.; & Brossart, Daniel F. (2007). Construction and validation of the Intragroup marginalization inventory. *Cultural Diversity & Ethnic Minority Psychology, 13*(3), 232–240.

Catania, A. Charles; & Laties, Victor G. (1999). Pavlov and Skinner: Two lives in science (an introduction to B. F. Skinner's "Some responses to the stimulus 'Pavlov' "). *Journal of the Experimental Analysis of Behavior, 72,* 455–461.

Caton, Hiram. (2007). Getting our history right: Six errors about Darwin and his influence. *Evolutionary Psychology, 5,* 52–69.

Cattaneo, Zaira; & Vecchi, Tomaso. (2008). Supramodality effects in visual and haptic spatial processes. *Journal of Experimental Psychology: Learning, Memory, and Cognition, 34,* 631–642.

Cattell, James McKeen. (1890). Mental tests and measurements. *Mind, 15,* 373–381.

Cattell, Raymond B. (1973, July). Personality pinned down. *Psychology Today,* 40–46.

Cattell, Raymond B. (1994). A cross-validation of primary personality structure in the 16 P.F. by two parcelled factor analysis. *Multivariate Experimental Clinical Research, 10*(3), 181–191.

Cattell, Raymond B.; Cattell, A. Karen S.; & Cattell, Heather E. P. (1993). *16 PF questionnaire* (5th ed.). Champaign, IL: Institute for Personality and Ability Testing.

Ceci, Stephen J.; & Loftus, Elizabeth F. (1994). "Memory work": A royal road to false memories? *Applied Cognitive Psychology, 8* [Special issue: Recovery of memories of childhood sexual abuse], 351–364.

Ceci, Stephen J.; & Williams, Wendy M. (2009). Should scientists study race and IQ? Yes: The scientific truth must be pursued. *Nature, 457,* 788–789

Cefalu, William T.; Wang, Zhong Q.; Bell-Farrow, Audrey D.; Collins, Joel; Morgan, Timothy; & Wagner, Janice D. (1997). A study of caloric restriction and cardiovascular aging in cynomolgus monkeys (Macaca fascicularis): A potential model for aging research. *Journal of Gerontology, Series A, 52,* B10–B21.

Centers for Disease Control and Prevention. (2009). BMI: Body mass index for adults. Retrieved December 8, 2009, from http://www.cdc.gov/nccdphp/dnpa/bmi/bmi-adult.htm

Cervone, Daniel. (2004). The architecture of personality. *Psychological Review, 111,* 183–204.

Chambless, Dianne L.; & Ollendick, Thomas H. (2001). Empirically supported psychological interventions: Controversies and evidence. *Annual Review of Psychology, 52,* 685–716.

Chance, Paul. (1999). Thorndike's puzzle boxes and the origins of the experimental analysis of behavior. *Journal of the Experimental Analysis of Behavior, 72,* 433–440.

Chandra, Anita; Martino, Steven C.; Collins, Rebecca L.; Elliott, Marc N.; Berry, Sandra H.; Kanouse, David E.; & Miu, Angela. (2008). Does watching sex on television predict teen pregnancy? Findings from a national longitudinal survey of youth. *Pediatrics, 122,* 1047–1054.

Chandrashekar, Jayaram; Hoon, Mark A.; Ryba, NicholaMays J. P.; & Zuker, Charles S. (2006). The receptors and cells for mammalian taste. *Nature, 444,* 288–294.

Chang, Linda; Wang, Gene-Jack; Volkow, Nora D.; Ernst, Thomas; Telang, Frank; Logan, Jean; & Fowler, Joanna S. (2008). Decreased brain dopamine transporters are related to cognitive deficits in HIV patients with or without cocaine abuse. *NeuroImage, 42,* 869–878.

Chatterjee, Arijit; & Hambrick, Donald C. (2007). It's all about me: Narcissistic chief executive officers and their effects on company strategy and performance. *Administrative Science Quarterly, 52,* 351–386.

Chatterjee, Anjan; Thomas, Amy; Smith, Sabrina E.; & Aguirre, Geoffrey K. (2009). The neural response to facial attractiveness. *Neuropsychology, 23,* 135–143.

Chaudhari, Nirupa; Landin, Ana Marie; & Roper, Stephen D. (2000). A metabotropic glutamate receptor variant functions as a taste receptor. *Nature Neuroscience, 3,* 113–119.

Chen, Eric Y. H.; Wilkins, A. J.; & McKenna, Peter J. (1994). Semantic memory is both impaired and anomalous in schizophrenia. *Psychological Medicine, 24,* 193–202.

Cheney, Dorothy L.; & Seyfarth, Robert M. (1990). *How monkeys see the world.* Chicago: University of Chicago Press.

Cheng, Cecilia. (2003). Cognitive and motivational processs underlying coping flexibility: A dual-process model. *Journal of Personality and Social Psychology, 84,* 425–438.

Chentsova-Dutton, Yulia E.; & Tsai, Jeanne L. (2007). Cultural factors influence the expression of psychopathology. In Scott O. Lilienfeld & William T. O'Donohue (Eds.), *The great ideas of clinical science* (pp. 375–396). New York: Routledge.

Choi, Incheol; Nisbett, Richard E.; & Norenzayen, Ara. (1999). Causal attribution across cultures: Variation and universality. *Psychological Bulletin, 125,* 47–63.

Choi, Kyeong-Sook; Jeon, Hyun Ok; & Lee, Yu-Sang. (2007). Familial association of schizophrenia symptoms retrospectively measured on a lifetime basis. *Psychiatric Genetics, 17*(2), 103–107.

Chomsky, Noam. (1965). *Aspects of a theory of syntax.* Cambridge, MA: MIT Press.

Christensen, Andrew; & Jacobson, Neil S. (1994). Who (or what) can do psychotherapy: The status and challenge of nonprofessional therapies. *Psychological Science, 5,* 8–14.

Chronicle, Edward P.; MacGregor, James N.; & Ormerod, Thomas C. (2004). What makes an insight problem? The roles of heuristics, goal conception, and solution recoding in knowledge-lean problems. *Journal of Experimental Psychology: Learning, Memory, and Cognition, 30,* 14–27.

Chrysikou, Evangelia G. (2006). When shoes become hammers: Goal-derived categorization training enhances problem-solving performance. *Journal of Experimental Psychology: Learning, Memory, and Cognition, 32,* 935–942.

Chua, Hannah Faye; Boland, Julie E.; & Nisbett, Richard E. (2005). Cultural variation in eye movements during scene perception. *Proceedings of the National Academy of Sciences, 102,* 12629–12633.

Chun, Kevin M.; Balls-Organista, Pamela; & Marin, Gerardo (Eds.). (2003). *Acculturation: Advances in theory, measurement and applied research.* Washington, DC: American Psychological Association.

Chwalisz, Kathleen; Diener, Ed; & Gallagher, Dennis. (1988). Autonomic arousal feedback and emotional experience: Evidence from the spinal cord injured. *Journal of Personality and Social Psychology, 54,* 820–828.

Cialdini, Robert B. (2000). *Influence: Science and practice.* Boston: Allyn & Bacon.

Cialdini, Robert B.; & Trost, Melanie R. (1998). Social influence, social norms, conformity, and compliance. In Daniel T. Gilbert, Susan T. Fiske, & Gardner Lindzey (Eds.), *The handbook of social psychology* (4th ed., Vol. 2). New York: McGraw-Hill.

Cinamon, Rachel Gali; Weisel, Amatzia; & Tzuk, Kineret. (2007). Work-family conflict within the family: Crossover effects, perceived parent-child interaction quality, parental self-efficacy, and life role attributions. *Journal of Career Development, 34,* 79–100.

Cisler, Josh M.; Reardon, John M.; & Williams, Nathan L. (2007). Anxiety sensitivity and disgust sensitivity interact to predict contamination fears. *Personality and Individual Differences, 42*(6), 935–946.

Clark, Damon A.; Mitra, Partha P.; & Wang, Samuel S.-H. (2001). Scalable architecture in mammalian brains. *Nature, 411,* 189–193.

Clark, David M.; Ehlers, Anke; McManus, Freda; Hackman, Ann; Fennell, Melanie; Campbell, Helen; Flower, Teresa; Davenport, Clare; & Louis, Beverly. (2003). Cognitive therapy versus fluoxetine in generalized social phobia: A randomized placebo-controlled trial. *Journal of Counseling and Clinical Psychology, 71,* 1058–1067.

Clark, Russell D., III; & Word, Larry E. (1974). Where is the apathetic bystander? Situational characteristics of the emergency. *Journal of Personality and Social Psychology, 29,* 279–287.

Clark, Wendy L.; & Blackwell, Terry L. (2007). 16PF® (5th edition) Personal career development profile: Test review. *Rehabilitation Counseling Bulletin, 50*(4), 247–250.

Clarke-Stewart, K. Alison. (1989). Infant day care: Maligned or malignant? *American Psychologist, 44,* 266–273.

Clarke-Stewart, K. Alison. (1992). Consequences of child care for children's development. In Alan Booth (Ed.), *Child care in the 1990s: Trends and consequences.* Hillsdale, NJ: Erlbaum.

Clarkin, John F.; & Levy, Kenneth N. (2004). The influence of client variables on psychotherapy. In Michael J. Lambert (Ed.), *Bergin and Garfield's handbook of psychotherapy and behavior change* (5th ed.). New York: Wiley.

Cleary, Anne M. (2008). Recognition memory, familiarity, and déjà vu experiences._*Current Directions in Psychological Science, 17,* 353–357.

Cleary, Anne M.; & Specker, Laura E. (2007). Recognition without face identification. *Experimental Psychology: General, 138,* 146–159.

Clifasefi, Seema L.; Garry, Maryanne; & Loftus, Elizabeth. (2007). Setting the record (or video camera) straight on memory: The video camera model of memory and other memory myths. In Della Sala, Sergio (Ed.), *Tall tales about the mind and brain: Separating fact from fiction.* New York: Oxford University Press.

Cloitre, Marylene. (2004). Aristotle revisited: The case of recovered memories. *Clinical Psychology: Science and Practice, 11,* 42–46.

Cobos, Pilar; Sánchez, María; Pérez, Nieves; & Vila, Jaime. (2004). Effects of spinal cord injuries on the subjective component of emotions. *Cognition & Emotion, 18,* 281–287.

Cody, Michael J.; & Seiter, John S. (2001). Compliance principles in retail sales in the United States. In Wihelmina Wosinska, Robert B. Cialdini, Daniel W. Barrett, & Janusz Reykowski (Eds.), *The practice of social influence in multiple cultures.* Mahwah, NJ: Erlbaum.

Coffee, Pete; Rees, Tim; & Haslam, S. Alexander. (2009). Bouncing back from failure: The interactive impact of perceived controllability and stability on self-efficacy beliefs and future task performance. *Journal of Sports Sciences, 27,* 1117–1124.

Cogan, Rosemary; Cochran, Bradley S.; & Velarde, Luis C. (2007). Sexual fantasies, sexual functioning, and hysteria among women: A test of Freud's (1905) hypothesis. *Psychoanalytic Psychology,* 24(4), 697–700.

Cohen, Hal. (2003). Creature comforts: Housing animals in complex environments. *The Scientist, 17*(9), 22–24.

Cohen, Lindsey L. (2002). Reducing infant immunization distress through distraction. *Health Psychology, 21,* 207–211.

Cohen, Sheldon. (2004). Social relationships and health. *American Psychologist, 59,* 676–684.

Cohen, Sheldon; Alper, Cuneyt M.; & Doyle, William J. (2006). Positive emotional style predicts resistance to illness after experimental exposure to rhinovirus or influenza A virus. *Psychosomatic Medicine, 68*(6), 809–815.

Cohen, Sheldon; Alper, Cuneyt M.; Doyle, William J.; Adler, Nancy; Treanor, John J.; & Turner, Ronald B. (2008). Objective and subjective socioeconomic status and susceptibility to the common cold. *Health Psychology, 27,* 268–274.

Cohen, Sheldon; Doyle, William J.; Skoner, David P.; Rabin, Bruce; & Gwaltney, Jack M., Jr. (1997). Social ties and susceptibility to the common cold. *Journal of the American Medical Association, 277,* 1940–1944.

Cohen, Sheldon; Frank, Ellen; Doyle, William J.; Skoner, David P.; Rabin, Bruce; & Gwaltney, Jack M., Jr. (1998). Types of stressors that increase susceptibility to the common cold in healthy adults. *Health Psychology, 17,* 214–223.

Cohen, Sheldon; Gottlieb, Benjamin H.; & Underwood, Lynn G. (2000). Social relationships and health. In Sheldon Cohen, Lynn Underwood, & Benjamin H. Gottlieb (Eds.), *Social support measurement and intervention: A guide for health and social scientists.* New York: Oxford University Press.

Cohen, Sheldon; & Janicki-Deverts, Denise. (2009). Can we improve our physical health by altering our social networks? *Perspectives on Psychological Science, 4,* 375–378.

Cohen, Sheldon; & Lemay, Edward. (2007). Why would social networks be linked to affect and health practices? *Health Psychology, 26,* 410–417.

Cohen, Sheldon; Tyrrell, David A. J.; & Smith, Andrew P. (1991). Psychological stress and susceptibility to the common cold. *New England Journal of Medicine, 325,* 606–612.

Cohen, Sheldon; Tyrrell, David A. J.; & Smith, Andrew P. (1993). Negative life events, perceived stress, negative affect, and susceptibility to the common cold. *Journal of Personality and Social Psychology, 64,* 131–140.

Colangelo, James J. (2007). Recovered memory debate revisited: Practice implications for mental health counselors. *Journal of Mental Health Counseling, 29,* 93–120.

Colby, Anne; & Kohlberg, Lawrence. (1984). Invariant sequence and internal consistency in moral judgment stages. In William M. Kurtines & Jacob L. Gewirtz (Eds.), *Morality, moral behavior, and moral development.* New York: Wiley.

Colby, Anne; Kohlberg, Lawrence; Gibbs, John; & Lieberman, Marcus. (1983). A longitudinal study of moral judgment. *Monographs of the Society for Research in Child Development, 48,* Nos. 1–2, 1–124.

Colicos, Michael A.; Collins, Boyce E.; Sailor, Michael J.; & Goda, Yukiko. (2001). Remodeling of synaptic actin induced by photoconductive stimulation. *Cell, 107,* 605–616.

Collins, Allan M.; & Loftus, Elizabeth F. (1975). A spreading activation theory of semantic processing. *Psychological Review, 82,* 407–428.

Collins, Rebecca L. (2004, September 7). Quoted in "Rand study finds adolescents who watch a lot of TV with sexual content have sex sooner." Retrieved September 8, 2004, from http://www.rand.org/news/press.04/09.07.html

Collins, Rebecca L.; Elliott, Marc N.; Berry, Sandra H.; Kanouse, David E.; Kunkel, Dale; Hunter, Sarah B.; & Miu, Angela. (2004). Watching sex on television predicts adolescent initiation of sexual behavior. *Pediatrics, 114,* 280–289.

Collins, W. Andrew. (2003). More than myth: The developmental significance of romantic relationships during adolescence. *Journal of Research on Adolescence, 13,* 1–24.

Collins, W. Andrew; & Gunnar, Megan. (1990). Social and personality development. *Annual Review of Psychology, 41,* 387–416.

Colten, Harvey R.; & Altevogt, Bruce R. (Eds.). (2006). *Sleep disorders and sleep deprivation: An unmet public health problem.* Washington, DC: Institute of Medicine of the National Academies, National Academies Press.

Comas-Diaz, Lilian. (1993). Hispanic/Latino communities: Psychological implications. In Donald R. Atkinson, George Morten, & Derald Wing Sue (Eds.), *Counseling American minorities: A cross-cultural perspective* (4th ed.). Madison, WI: Brown & Benchmark.

Combs, Dennis R.; & Mueser, Kim T. (2007). Schizophrenia. In Michel Hersen, Samuel M. Turner, & Deborah C. Beidel (Eds.), *Adult psychopathology and diagnosis* (5th ed., pp. 234–285). Hoboken, NJ: Wiley.

The Conference Board. (2007, October 12). Job seekers continue to shift towards the Internet [Press release]. Conference-board.org.

Congressional Public Health Summit. (2000, July 26). Joint statement on the impact of entertainment violence on children. Retrieved December 8, 2009, from http://www.aap.org/advocacy/releases/jstmtevc.htm

Connell, Arin M.; Dishion, Thomas J.; & Yasui, Miwa. (2007). An adaptive approach to family intervention: Linking engagement in family-centered intervention to reductions in adolescent problem behavior. *Journal of Consulting and Clinical Psychology, 75*(4), 568–579.

Contrada, Richard J.; Ashmore, Richard D.; Gary, Melvin L.; Coups, Elliot; Egeth, Jill D.; Sewell, Andrea; & others. (2000). Ethnicity-related sources of stress and their effects on well-being. *Current Directions of Psychological Science, 9,* 136–139.

Conway, Martin A.; Meares, Kevin; & Standart, Sally. (2004). Images and goals. *Memory, 12,* 525–531.

Cook, Travis A. R.; Luczak, Susan E.; Shea, Shoshana H.; Ehlers, Cindy L.; Carr, Lucinda G.; & Wall, Tamara L. (2005). Associations of ALDH2 and ADH1B genotypes with response to alcohol in Asian Americans. *Journal of Studies on Alcohol, 66,* 196–204.

Cooper, Cary L; & Dewe, Philip. (2004). *Stress: A brief history.* Malden, MA: Blackwell.

Cooper, Mick. (2008). *Essential research findings in counseling and psychotherapy.* Thousand Oaks, CA: Sage.

Cooper, Mick; O'Hara, Maureen; Schmid, Peter F.; & Wyatt, Gill (Eds.). (2007). *The handbook of person-centred psychotherapy and counselling.* New York: Palgrave Macmillan.

Cooper, Rosemary. (1994). Normal sleep. In Rosemary Cooper (Ed.), *Sleep.* New York: Chapman & Hall.

Cooper, Rosemary; & Bradbury, Sue. (1994). Techniques in sleep recording. In Rosemary Cooper (Ed.), *Sleep.* New York: Chapman & Hall.

Corballis, Paul M.; Funnell, Margaret G.; & Gazzaniga, Michael S. (2002). Hemispheric asymmetries for simple visual judgments in the split brain. *Neuropsychologia, 40,* 401–410.

Corkin, Suzanne. (1984). Lasting consequences of bilateral medial temporal lobectomy: Clinical course and experimental findings in H.M. *Seminars in Neurology, 4,* 249–259.

Corkin, Suzanne. (2002). What's new with the amnesic patient H.M.? *Nature Reviews Neuroscience, 3,* 153–160.

Corrigan, Patrick W.; & O'Shaughnessy, John R. (2007). Changing mental illness stigma as it exists in the real world. *Australian Psychologist, 42,* 90–97.

Corsini, Raymond J. (1958). *The Nonverbal Reasoning Test: To measure the capacity to reason logically as indicated by solutions to pictoral problems.* Chicago: Pearson Performance Solutions.

Corvin, Aiden; O'Mahony, Ed; O'Regan, Myra; Comerford, Claire; O'Connell; Craddock, Nick; & Gill, Michael. (2001). Cigarette smoking and psychotic symptoms in bipolar affective disorder. *British Journal of Psychiatry, 179,* 35–38.

Courage, Mary L.; & Howe, Mark L. (2002). From infant to child: The dynamics of cognitive change in the second year of life. *Psychological Bulletin, 128,* 250–277.

Courtney, Kelly E.; & Polich, John. (2009). Binge drinking in young adults: Data, definitions, and determinants. *Psychological Bulletin, 135*(1), 142–156.

Courtois, Christine A.; & Ford, Julian D. (Eds.). (2009). *Treating complex traumatic stress disorders: An evidence-based guide.* New York: Guilford Press.

Cousineau, Tara McKee; & Shedler, Jonathan. (2006). Predicting physical health: Implicit mental health measures versus self-report scales. *Journal of Nervous and Mental Disease, 194*(6), 427–432.

Cowan, Nelson. (2001). The magical number 4 in short-term memory: A reconsideration of mental storage capacity. *Behavioral and Brain Sciences, 24,* 87–185.

Cowan, Nelson. (2005). *Working memory capacity: Essays in cognitive psychology.* New York: Psychology Press.

Cowan, Nelson; Chen, Zhijian; & Rouder, Jeffrey N. (2004). Constant capacity in an immediate serial-recall task: A logical sequel to Miller (1956). *Psychological Science, 15,* 634–640.

Cowan, Nelson; Morey, Candice C.; & Chen, Zhijian. (2007). The legend of the magical number seven. In Sergio Della Sala (Ed.), *Tall tales about the mind and brain: Separating fact from fiction.* New York: Oxford University Press.

Coyne, James C.; & Downey, Geraldine. (1991). Social factors and psychopathology: Stress, social support, and coping processes. *Annual Review of Psychology, 42,* 401–425.

Coyne, James C.; Ellard, John H.; & Smith, David A. F. (1990). Social support, interdependence, and the dilemmas of helping. In Barbara R. Sarason, Irwin G. Sarason, & Gregory R. Pierce (Eds.), *Social support: An interactional view.* New York: Wiley.

Craig, Lyn. (2006). Does father care mean fathers share?: A comparison of how mothers and fathers in intact families spend time with children. *Gender & Society, 20*(2), 259–281.

Craighead, W. Edward; Sheets, Erin S.; Brosse, Alisha L.; & Ilardi, Stephen S. (2007). Psychosocial treatments for major depressive disorder. In Peter E. Nathan & James M. Gorman (Eds.), *A guide to treatments that work* (3rd ed., pp. 289–307). New York: Oxford University Press.

Craik, Fergus I. M.; & Bialystok, Ellen. (2006). Cognition through the lifespan: Mechanisms of change. *Trends in Cognitive Sciences, 10,* 131–138.

Craik, Fergus I. M.; Govoni, Richard; Naveh-Benjamin, Moshe; & Anderson, Nicole D. (1996). The effects of divided attention on encoding and retrieval processes in human memory. *Journal of Experimental Psychology: General, 125,* 159–180.

Craske, Michelle G.; & Barlow, David H. (2008). Panic disorder and agoraphobia. In David H. Barlow (Ed.), *Clinical handbook of psychological disorders* (4th ed., pp. 1–64). New York: Guilford Press.

Craske, Michelle G.; & Waters, Allison M. (2005). Panic disorder, phobias, and generalized anxiety disorder. *Annual Review of Clinical Psychology, 1,* 197–225.

Crawford, Mary. (2001). Gender and language. In Rhoda K. Unger (Ed.), *Handbook of the psychology of women and gender.* Hoboken, NJ: Wiley.

Crews, Frederick. (1984/1986). The Freudian way of knowledge. In *Skeptical engagements.* New York: Oxford University Press.

Crews, Frederick. (1996). The verdict on Freud. *Psychological Science, 7,* 63–68.

Crews, Frederick. (2006). The unknown Freud. In Frederick Crews (Ed.), *Follies of the wise: Dissenting essays.* Emeryville, CA: Shoemaker & Hoard.

Critchley, Hugo D.; Wiens, Stefan; Rotshtein, Pia; Ohman, Arne; & Dolan, Raymond J. (2004). Neural systems supporting interoceptive awareness. *Nature Neuroscience, 7,* 189–195.

Crites, John O.; & Taber, Brian J. (2002). Appraising adults' career capabilities: Ability, interest, and personality. In Spencer G. Niles (Ed.), *Adult career development: Concepts, issues and practices* (3rd ed., pp. 120–138). Columbus, OH: National Career Development Association.

Croft, Rodney J.; Klugman, Anthony; Baldeweg, Torsten; & Gruzelier, John H. (2001). Electrophysiological evidence of serotonergic impairment in long-term MDMA ("ecstasy") users. *American Journal of Psychiatry, 158,* 1687–1692.

Croizet, Jean-Claude; & Claire, Theresa. (1998). Extending the concept of stereotype and threat to social class: The intellectual underperformance of students from low socioeconomic backgrounds. *Personality and Social Psychology Bulletin, 24,* 588–654.

Croizet, Jean-Claude; Després, Gérard; Gauzins, Marie-Eve; Huguet, Pascal; Leyens, Jacques-Philippe; & Méot, Alain. (2004). Stereotype threat undermines intellectual performance by triggering a disruptive mental load. *Personality and Social Psychology Bulletin, 30,* 721–731.

Crosscope-Happel, Cindy; Hutchins, David E.; Getz, Hildy G.; & Hayes, Gerald L. (2000). Male anorexia nervosa: A new focus. *Journal of Mental Health Counseling, 22,* 365–370.

Crow, Scott J.; Peterson, Carol B.; Swanson, Sonja A.; Raymond, Nancy C.; Specker, Sheila; Eckert, Elke D.; & Mitchell, James E. (2009, October 15). Increased mortality in bulimia and other eating disorders. *American Journal of Psychiatry.* AJP Epub in Advance. DOI: 10.1176/appi.ajp.2009.09020247

Crowell, Sheila E.; Beauchaine, Theodore P.; & Linehan, Marsha M. (2009). A biosocial developmental model of borderline personality disorder: Elaborating and extending Linehan's theory. *Psychological Bulletin, 135,* 495–510.

Crum, Alia J.; & Langer, Ellen J. (2007). Mind-set matters: Exercise and the placebo effect. *Psychological Science, 18,* 2, 165–171.

Cuijpers, Pim; van Straten, Annemieke; Andersson, Gerhard; & van Oppen, Patricia. (2008). Psychotherapy for depression in adults: A meta-analysis of comparative outcome studies. Journal of Consulting and Clinical Psychology, 76(6), 909–922.

Cummings, David E. (2006). Ghrelin and the short- and long-term regulation of appetite and body weight. *Physiology & Behavior, 89,* 71–84.

Cummings, Donald E.; Weigle, David S.; Frayo, R. Scott; Breen, Patricia A.; Ma, Marina K.; Dellinger, E. Patchen; & Purnell, Jonathan Q. (2002). Plasma ghrelin levels after diet-induced weight loss or gastric bypass surgery. *New England Journal of Medicine, 346,* 1623–1630.

Cunningham, Jacqueline L. (1997). Alfred Binet and the quest for testing higher mental functioning. In Wolfgang G. Bringmann, Helmut E. Lück, Rudolf Miller, & Charles E. Early (Eds.), *A pictorial history of psychology*. Chicago: Quintessence.

Curci, Antonietta; Luminet, Olivier; Finkenauer, Catrin; & Gisle, Lydia. (2001). Flashbulb memories in social groups: A comparative test-retest study of the memory of French President Mitterand's death in a French and a Belgian group. *Memory, 9,* 81–101.

Czeisler, Charles A.; & Dijk, Derk-Jan. (2001). Human circadian physiology and sleep-wake regulation. In Joseph Takahashi, Fred W. Turek, & Robert Y. Moore (Eds.), *Handbook of behavioral neurobiology: Circadian clocks* (Vol. 12). New York: Kluwer/Plenum Press.

Czeisler, Charles A.; Duffy, Jeanne F.; Shanahan, Theresa L.; Brown, Emery N.; Mitchell, Jude F.; Rimmer, David W.; & others. (1999, June 25). Stability, precision, and near-24-hour period of the human circadian pacemaker. *Science, 284,* 2177–2181.

Czienskowski, Uwe; & Giljohann, Stefanie. (2002). Intimacy, concreteness, and the "self-reference effect." *Experimental Psychology, 49,* 73–79.

Dahl, Ronald. (2003, Summer). Beyond raging hormones: The tinderbox in the teenage brain. *Cerebrum, 5*(3), 7–22.

Dalgleish, Tim. (2004). The emotional brain. *Nature Reviews Neuroscience, 5,* 582–589.

Damasio, Antonio R. (1994). *Descartes' error: Emotion, reason, and the human brain.* New York: Putnam.

Damasio, Antonio R. (2004). Emotions and feelings: A neurobiological perspective. In Antony S. R. Manstead, Nico Frijda, & Agneta Fischer (Eds.), *Feelings and emotions: The Amsterdam symposium.* New York: Cambridge University Press.

Damasio, Antonio R.; Grabowski, Thomas J.; Bechara, Antoine; Damasio, Hanna; Ponto, Laura L. B.; Parvizi, Josef; & Hichwa, Richard D. (2000). Subcortical and cortical brain activity during the feeling of self-generated emotions. *Nature Neuroscience, 3,* 1049–1056.

Daniels, E.; & Leaper, C. (2006). A longitudinal investigation of sport participation, peer acceptance, and self-esteem among adolescent girls and boys. *Sex Roles, 55,* 875–880.

Darley, John M. (1992). Social organization for the production of evil [Book review essay]. *Psychological Inquiry, 3,* 199–218.

Darley, John M.; & Shultz, Thomas R. (1990). Moral rules: Their content and acquisition. *Annual Review of Psychology, 41,* 525–556.

Darwin, Charles R. (1859/1998). *On the origin of species by means of natural selection.* New York: Modern Library.

Darwin, Charles R. (1871/1981). *The descent of man, and selection in relation to sex* (Introductions by John T. Bonner and Robert M. May). Princeton, NJ: Princeton University Press.

Darwin, Charles R. (1872/1998). *The expression of the emotions in man and animals* (3rd ed.). New York: Appleton.

Dasgupta, Manisha; & Sanyal, Nilanjana. (2007). Relationship between controllability awareness and cognitive emotion regulation in selected clinical samples: A psychosocial perspective. *Journal of Projective Psychology & Mental Health, 14*(1), 64–75.

Datta, Sublimal; & MacLean, Robert Ross. (2007). Neurobiological mechanisms for the regulation of mammalian sleep–wake behavior: Reinterpretation of historical evidence and inclusion of contemporary cellular and molecular evidence. *Neuroscience and Biobehavioral Reviews, 31,* 775–824.

David, Daniel; Lynn, Steven J.; & Ellis, Albert (Eds.). (2009). *Rational and irrational beliefs: Research, theory, and clinical practice.* New York: Oxford University Press.

Davidson, Jonathan R. T.; Connor, Kathryn M.; & Zhang, Wei. (2009). Treatment of anxiety disorders. In Alan F. Schatzberg & Charles B. Nemeroff (Eds.), *The American Psychiatric Publishing textbook of psychopharmacology* (4th ed., pp. 1171–1199). Washington, DC: American Psychiatric Publishing.

Davidson, Paul R.; & Parker, Kevin C. H. (2001). Eye movement desensitization and reprocessing (EMDR): A meta-analysis. *Journal of Consulting and Clinical Psychology, 69,* 305–316.

Davidson, Richard J. (2002). Toward a biology of positive affect and compassion. In Richard J. Davidson & Anne Harrington (Eds.), *Visions of compassion: Western scientists and Tibetan Buddhists examine human nature.* New York: Oxford University Press.

Davidson, Richard J.; Kabat-Zinn, Jon; Schumacher, Jessica; Rosenkranz, Melissa; Muller, Daniel; Santorelli, Saki F.; & others. (2003). Alterations in brain and immune function produced by mindfulness meditation. *Psychosomatic Medicine, 65,* 564–570.

Davidson, Terry L. (2000). Pavlovian occasion setting: A link between physiological change and appetitive behavior. *Appetite, 35,* 271–272.

Davis, Deborah; & Loftus, Elizabeth F. (2007). Internal and external sources of misinformation in adult witness memory. In Michael P. Toglia, J. Don Read, & R. C. L. Lindsay (Eds.), *The handbook of eyewitness psychology. Vol. I: Memory for events.* Mahwah, NJ: Erlbaum.

Davis, Lori L.; Bartolucci, Al; & Petty, Frederick. (2005). Divalproex in the treatment of bipolar depression: A placebo-controlled study. *Journal of Affective Disorders, 85*(3), 259–266.

Davis, Mary Helen; Drogin, Eric Y.; & Wright, Jesse H. (1995). Therapist-patient sexual intimacy: A guide for the subsequent therapist. *Journal of Psychotherapy Practice and Research, 4,* 140–149.

Davis, Michael; & Whalen, Paul J. (2001). The amygdala: Vigilance and emotion. *Molecular Psychiatry, 6,* 13–14.

Davis, Susan. (2000). Testosterone and sexual desire in women. *Journal of Sex Education and Therapy, 25,* 25–32.

Dawson, Deborah A. (1991). Family structure and children's health and well-being: Data from the 1988 National Health Interview Study on Child Health. *Journal of Marriage and the Family, 53,* 573–584.

Dawson, Jennifer A. (2007). African conceptualisations of posttraumatic stress disorder and the impact of introducing western concepts. *Psychology, Psychiatry, and Mental Health Monographs, 2,* 101–112.

Dawson, Michelle. (2007, August 20–27). Quoted in Sharon Begley, "The puzzle of human ability." *Newsweek.* Retrieved August 20, 2008, from http://www.newsweek.com/id/32250

Dawson, Michelle; Mottron, Laurent; & Gernsbacher, Morton Ann. (2008) Learning in autism. In John H. Byrne & Henry Roediger (Eds.), *Learning and memory: A comprehensive reference: Volume 2. Cognitive psychology.* New York: Elsevier.

Dawson, Michelle; Soulieres, Isabelle; Gernsbacher, Morton Ann; & Mottron, Laurent. (2007). The level and nature of autistic intelligence. *Psychological Science, 18,* 657–659.

De Brito, Stéphane A.; & Hodgins, Sheilagh. (2009). Antisocial personality disorder. In Mary McMurran & Richard Howard (Eds.), *Personality, personality disorder and violence* (pp. 133–153). Chichester, England: Wiley-Blackwell.

de Castro, John M.; Bellisle, France; Dalix, Anne-Marie; & Pearcey, Sharon M. (2000). Palatability and intake relationships in free-living humans: Characterization and independence of influence in North Americans. *Physiology and Behavior, 70,* 343–350.

de Rivera, Joseph. (2000). Understanding persons who repudiate memories recovered in therapy. *Professional Psychology: Research and Practice, 31,* 378–386.

De Vries, Geert J. (2004). Minireview: Sex differences in adult and developing brains: Compensation, compensation, compensation. *Endocrinology, 145,* 1063–1068.

De Vries, J.; Strubbe, J. H.; Wildering, W. C.; Gorter J. A.; & Prins A. J. (1993). Patterns of body temperature during feeding in rats under varying ambient temperatures. *Physiology and Behavior, 53,* 229–235.

Dean, Geoffrey. (1992). The bottom line: Effect size. In Barry Beyerstein & Dale Beyerstein (Eds.), *The write stuff: Evaluations of graphology—The study of handwriting analysis.* Amherst, NY: Prometheus Books.

DeAngelis, Tori. (2007, October). Goodbye to a legend. *Monitor on Psychology, 38,* 38.

DeAngelis, Tori. (2007). Toxic America: A toxic lifestyle? *Monitor on Psychology, 38.*

DeBell, Camille; & Jones, R. Deniece. (1997). As good as it seems? A review of EMDR experimental research. *Professional Psychology: Research and Practice, 28,* 153–163.

Deci, Edward L.; & Ryan, Richard M. (2000). The "what" and "why" of goal pursuits: Human needs and the self-determination of behavior. *Psychological Inquiry, 11,* 227–268.

Deci, Edward L.; & Ryan, Richard M. (2008a). Facilitating optimal motivation and psychological well-being across life's domains. *Canadian Psychology, 49,* 14–23,

Deci, Edward L.; & Ryan, Richard M. (2008b). Self-determination theory: A macrotheory of human motivation, development, and health. *Canadian Psychology/Psychologie canadienne, 49,* 182–185.

Deckner, Deborah F.; Adamson, Lauren B.; & Bakeman, Roger. (2003). Rhythm in mother–infant interactions. *Infancy, 4,* 201–217.

DeGeneres, Ellen. (2005). Quote from interview "The Real Ellen Story—Coming Out Party London." Retrieved February 27, 2005, from http://www.ellen-degeneres.com/

DeKosky, Steven T.; Williamson, Jeff D.; Fitzpatrick, Annette L.; Kronmal, Richard A.; Ives, Diane G.; Saxton, Judith A.; Lopez, Oscar L. & others. (2008, November 19). *Ginkgo biloba* for prevention of dementia: A randomized controlled trial. *Journal of the American Medical Association, 300,* 2253–2262.

DeLeon, Anthony; Patel, Nick C.; & Crismon, M. Lynn. (2004). Aripiprazole: A comprehensive review of its pharmacology, clinical efficacy, and tolerability. *Clinical Therapeutics, 26,* 649–666.

Delgado, Ana R. (2004). Order in Spanish colour words: Evidence against linguistic relativity. *British Journal of Psychology, 95,* 81–90.

DeLisi, Richard; & Staudt, Joanne. (1980). Individual differences in college students' performance on formal operations tasks. *Journal of Applied Developmental Psychology, 1,* 163–174.

Dell, Paul F.; & O'Neil, John Allison (Eds.). (2009). *Dissociation and the dissociative disorders: DSM-V and beyond.* New York: Routledge.

Delman, Howard M.; Robinson, Delbert G.; & Kimmelblatt, Craig A. (2008). General psychiatric symptoms measures. In A. John Rush, Jr., Michael B. First, & Deborah Blacker (Eds.), *Handbook of psychiatric measures* (2nd ed., pp. 61–82). Arlington, VA: American Psychiatric Publishing.

DeLoache, Judy S. (1995). Early symbol understanding and use. In Douglas L. Medin (Ed.), *The psychology of learning and motivation: Advances in research and theory* (Vol. 33). New York: Academic Press.

DeLongis, Anita; Coyne, James C.; Dakof, C.; Folkman, Susan; & Lazarus, Richard S. (1982). Relationship of daily hassles, uplifts, and major life events to health status. *Health Psychology, 1,* 119–136.

DeLongis, Anita; Folkman, Susan; & Lazarus, Richard S. (1988). The impact of stress on health and mood: Psychological and social resources as mediators. *Journal of Personality and Social Psychology, 54,* 486–495.

Derluyn, Ilse; Broekaert, Eric; Schuyten, Gilberte; & De Temmerman, Els. (2004). Post-traumatic stress in former Ugandan child soldiers. *Lancet, 363*(9412), 861–863.

Deutsch, Morton; & Gerard, Harold B. (1955). A study of normative and informational social influence upon individual judgment. *Journal of Abnormal and Social Psychology, 51,* 629–636.

DeValois, Russell L.; & DeValois, Karen K. (1975). Neural coding of color. In Edward C. Carterette & Morton P. Friedman (Eds.), *Handbook of perception* (Vol. 5). New York: Academic Press.

Devanand, D. P.; Michaels-Marston, Kristin S.; Liu, Xinhua; Pelton, Gregory H.; Padilla, Margarita; Marder, Karen; Bell, Karen; Stern, Yaakov; & Mayeux, Richard. (2000). Olfactory deficits in patients with mild cognitive impairment predict Alzheimer's disease at follow-up. *American Journal of Psychiatry, 157,* 1399–1405.

Devane, William A.; Hanus, L.; Breuer, A.; Pertwee, R. G.; Stevenson, L. A.; Griffin, G.; & others. (1992). Isolation and structure of a brain constituent that binds to the cannabinoid receptor. *Science, 258,* 1946–1949.

Devilly, Grant J. (2005). Power therapies and possible threats to the science of psychology and psychiatry. *Australian and New Zealand Journal of Psychiatry, 39*(6), 437–445.

DeVos, George Alphonse. (1992). *Social cohesion and alienation: Minorities in the United States and Japan.* Boulder, CO: Westview Press.

DeVos, George Alphonse; & Wagatsuma, Hiroshi. (1967). *Japan's invisible race: Caste in culture and personality.* Berkeley and Los Angeles: University of California Press.

deWaal, Frans B. M. (1995, March). Bonobo sex and society. *Scientific American, 271,* 82–88.

deWaal, Frans B. M (2007). Bonobos, left and right. *Skeptic, 13*(3), 64–66, 3p; (AN 27214210).

Dewsbury, Donald A. (1998). Celebrating E. L. Thorndike a century after *Animal Intelligence. American Psychologist, 53,* 1121–1124.

Diamond, Adele. (2009). The interplay of biology and the environment broadly defined. *Developmental Psychology, 45,* 1–8.

Diamond, Solomon. (2001). Wundt before Leipzig. In Robert W. Rieber & David K. Robinson (Eds.), *Wilhelm Wundt in history: The making of a scientific psychology.* New York: Kluwer Academic/Plenum Publishers.

Dick, Danielle M.; & Rose, Richard J. (2002). Behavior genetics: What's new? What's next? *Current Directions in Psychological Science, 11,* 70–74.

Dickerson, Sally S.; & Kemeny, Margaret E. (2004). Acute stressors and cortisol responses: A theoretical integration and synthesis of laboratory research. *Psychological Bulletin, 130,* 355–391.

Dickinson, Anthony; & Balleine, Bernard W. (2000). Causal cognition and goal-directed action. In Cecilia Heyes & Ludwig Huber (Eds.), *The evolution of cognition.* Cambridge, MA: MIT Press.

Dictionary of Occupational Titles. (1991). Washington, DC: U.S. Government Printing Office.

Didonna, Fabrizio (Ed.). (2008). *Clinical handbook of mindfulness.* New York: Springer.

Diefenbach, Donald L.; & West, Mark D. (2007). Television and attitudes toward mental health issues: Cultivation analysis and the third-person effect. *Journal of Community Psychology, 35*(2), 181–195.

Dietrich, Arne; & McDaniel, William F. (2004). Endocannabinois and exercise. *British Journal of Sports Medicine, 38,* 536–541.

Dijk, Derk-Jan; & Lockley, Steven W. (2002). Integration of human sleep-wake regulation and circadian rhythmicity. *Journal of Applied Physiology, 92,* 852–862.

Dijksterhuis, Ap; Aarts, Henk; & Smith, Pamela K. (2005). The power of the subliminal: On subliminal persuasion and other potential applications. In Ran R. Hassin, James S. Uleman, & John A. Bargh (Eds.), *The new unconscious.* New York: Oxford University Press.

Dijksterhuis, Ap; & Nordgren, Loran F. (2006). A theory of unconscious thought. *Perspectives on Psychological Science, 1,* 95–109.

Dillard, James Price. (1991). The current status of research on sequential-request compliance techniques. *Personality and Social Psychology Bulletin, 17,* 283–288.

Dillbeck, Michael C.; & Orme-Johnson, David W. (1987). Physiological differences between transcendental meditation and rest. *American Psychologist, 42,* 879–881.

Dinges, David F.; Rogers, Naomi L.; & Baynard, Maurice D. (2005). Chronic sleep deprivation. In Meir H. Kryger, Thomas Roth, & William C. Dement (Eds.), *Principles and practice of sleep medicine* (4th ed.). Philadelphia: Elsevier Saunders.

Dinsmoor, James A. (1992). Setting the record straight: The social views of B. F. Skinner. *American Psychologist, 47,* 1454–1463.

Dinstein, Ilan; Thomas, Cibu; Behrmann, Marlene; & Heeger, David J. (2008). A mirror up to nature. *Current Biology, 18,* R13–R18.

Dittman, Melissa. (2003, February). Psychology's first prescribers. *Monitor on Psychology, 34,* 36–39.

Dittmann, Melissa. (2005, July-August). Fighting phobias: Hughes's germ phobia revealed in psychological autopsy. *Monitor on Psychology, 36,* 102.

Dixon, John F.; & Hokin, Lowell E. (1998, July 7). Lithium acutely inhibits and chronically up-regulates and stabilizes glutamate by presynaptic nerve endings in mouse cerebral cortex. *Proceedings of the National Academy of Sciences, USA, 95,* 8363–8368.

Djordjevic, Jelena; Zatorre, R. J.; Petrides, M.; & Jones-Gotman, M. (2004). The mind's nose: Effects of odor and visual imagery on odor detection. *Psychological Science, 15,* 143–148.

Dobson, Deborah; & Dobson, Keith. (2009). *Evidence-based practice of cognitive-behavioral therapy* New York: Guilford Press.

Dohrenwend, Bruce P.; Raphael, Karen G.; Schwartz, Sharon; Stueve, Ann; & Skodol, Andrew. (1993). The structured event probe and narrative rating method for measuring stressful life events. In Leo Goldberger & Shlomo Breznitz (Eds.), *Handbook of stress: Theoretical and clinical aspects* (2nd ed.). New York: Free Press.

Dolan, Kerry A. (2008, January 28). Andy Grove's last stand. *Forbes, 181,* 71–75.

Domar, Alice D.; Meshay, Irene; Kelliher, Joseph; Alper, Michael; & Powers, R. Douglas. (2009). The impact of acupuncture on in vitro fertilization outcome. *Fertility and Sterility, 91,* 723–726.

Domhoff, G. William. (2003). *The scientific study of dreams: Neural networks, cognitive development, and content analysis.* Washington, DC: American Psychological Association.

Domhoff, G. William. (2004). Why did empirical dream researchers reject Freud? A critique of historical claims by Mark Solms. *Dreaming, 14,* 3–17.

Domhoff, G. William. (2005). The content of dreams: Methodologic and theoretical implications. In Meir H. Kryger, Thomas Roth, & William C. Dement (Eds.), *Principles and practice of sleep medicine* (4th ed.). Philadelphia: Elsevier Saunders.

Domhoff, G. William. (2007). Realistic simulation and bizarreness in dream content: Past findings and suggestions for future research. In Deirdre Barrett & Patrick McNamara (Eds.), *The new science of dreaming: Content, recall, and personality characteristics* (Vol. 2). Westport, CT: Praeger Press.

Dornbusch, Sanford M.; Glasgow, Kristan L.; & Lin, I-Chun. (1996). The social structure of schooling. *Annual Review of Psychology, 47,* 401–429.

Dornbusch, Sanford M.; Ritter, Philip L.; Leiderman, P. Herbert; Roberts, Donald F.; & Fraleigh, Michael J. (1987). The relation of parenting style to adolescent school performance. *Child Development, 58,* 1244–1257.

Douglas, Kevin S.; Gay, Laura S.; & Hart, Stephen D. (2009). Psychosis as a risk factor for violence to others: A meta-analysis. *Psychological Bulletin, 135,* 679–706.

Dovidio, John F. (1984). Helping behavior and altruism: An empirical and conceptual overview. *Advances in Experimental Social Psychology, 17,* 361–427.

Dovidio, John F.; Piliavin, Jane Allyn; Gaertner, Samuel L.; Schroeder, David A.; & Clark, Russell D., III. (1991). The arousal: Cost-reward model and the process of intervention: A review of the evidence. In Margaret S. Clark (Ed.), *Prosocial behavior: Vol. 12. Review of personality and social psychology.* Newbury Park, CA: Sage.

Dovidio, John F.; Piliavin, Jane Allyn; & Schroeder, David A. (2006). *The social psychology of prosocial behavior.* Mahwah, NJ: Erlbaum.

Draganski, Bogdan; Gaser, Christian; Busch, Volker; Schuierer, Gerhard; Bogdahn, Ulrich; & May, Arne. (2004). Neuroplasticity: Changes in grey matter induced by training. *Nature, 427,* 311–312.

Driemeyer, Joenna; Boyke, Janina; Gaser, Christian; Büchel, Christian; & May, Arne. (2008). Changes in gray matter induced by learning—Revisited. *PloS ONE, 3,* e2669.

Drouyer, Elise; Rieux, Camille; Hut, Roelof A.; & Cooper, Howard M. (2007). Responses of suprachiasmatic nucleus neurons to light and dark adaptation: Relative contributions of melanopsin and rod–cone inputs. *The Journal of Neuroscience, 27*(36), 9623–9631.

Drummond, Kelley D.; Bradley, Susan J.; Peterson-Badali, Michele; & Zucker, Kenneth J. (2008). A follow-up study of girls with gender identity disorder. *Developmental Psychology, 44,* 34–45.

Dryden, Windy. (2008). *Rational emotive behaviour therapy: Distinctive features.* New York: Routledge.

Dryden, Windy. (2009). *How to think and intervene like an REBT therapist.* New York: Routledge.

Dryden, Windy; & Branch, Rhena. (2008). *Fundamentals of rational emotive behaviour therapy: A training handbook.* Hoboken, NJ: Wiley.

DSM-IV-TR. (2000). *Diagnostic and statistical manual of mental disorders* (4th ed., text revision). Washington, DC: American Psychiatric Association.

Duckitt, John. (2003). Prejudice and intergroup hostility. In David O. Sears, Leonie Huddy, & Robert Jervis (Eds.), *Oxford handbook of political psychology* (pp. 559–600). New York: Oxford University Press.

Duckworth, Angela L.; Peterson, Christopher; Matthews, Michael D.; & Kelly, Dennis R. (2007). Grit: Perseverance and passion for long-term goals. *Journal of Personality and Social Psychology, 92,* 1087–1101.

Duclos, Sandra E.; Laird, James D.; Schneider, Eric; Sexter, Melissa; Stern, Lisa; & Van Lighten, Lisa. (1989). Emotion-specific effects of facial expressions and postures on emotional experience. *Journal of Personality and Social Psychology, 57,* 100–108.

Dudai, Yadin. (2004). The neurobiology of consolidations, or, How stable is the engram? *Annual Review of Psychology, 55,* 51–86.

Duffy, Ryan D.; & Sedlacek, William E. (2007). The presence of and search for a calling: Connections to career development. *Journal of Vocational Behavior, 70,* 590–601.

Dulac, Catherine; & Torello, A. Thomas. (2003). Molecular detection of pheromone signals in mammals: From genes to behaviour. *Nature Reviews Neuroscience, 4,* 551–562.

Duncker, Karl. (1929/1967). Induced motion. In Willis D. Ellis (Ed.), *Source book of Gestalt psychology.* New York: Humanities Press.

Duncker, Karl. (1945). On problem solving. *Psychological Monographs, 58*(Whole No. 270).

Dunn, Judy; & Plomin, Robert. (1990). *Separate lives: Why siblings are so different.* New York: Basic Books.

Dunning, David; Leuenberger, Ann; & Sherman, David A. (1995). A new look at motivated inference: Are self-serving theories of success a product of motivational forces? *Journal of Personality and Social Psychology, 69,* 58–68.

Duranceaux, Nicole C.E.; Schuckit, Marc A.; Luczak, Susan E.; Eng, Mimy Y.; Carr, Lucinda G.; & Wall, Tamara L. (2008). Ethnic differences in level of response to alcohol between Chinese Americans and Korean Americans. *Journal of Studies on Alcohol and Drugs, 69,* 227–234.

Durston, Sarah; Hulshoff Pol, Hilleke E.; Casey, B.J.; Giedd, Jay N.; Buitelaar, Jan K.; & van Engeland, Herman. (2001). Anatomical MRI of the developing brain: What have we learned? *Journal of the American Academy of Child and Adolescent Psychiatry, 40,* 1012–1020.

Dusek, Jeffrey A.; Out, Hasan H.; Wohlhueter, Ann L.; Bhasin, Manoj; Zerbini, Luiz F.; Joseph, Marie G.; Benson, Herbert; & Libermann, Towia A. (2008). Genomic counter-stress changes induced by the relaxation response. *PLoS ONE, 3,* e2576 (pp. 1–8).

Edlund. Mark J.; Fortney John C.; Reaves, Christina M.; Pyne, Jeffrey M.; & Mittal, Dinesh. (2008). Beliefs about depression and depression treatment among depressed veterans. Medical Care, 46, 581–589.

Eagly, Alice H. (1995). Reflections on the commenters' views. *American Psychologist, 50,* 169–171.

Eagly, Alice H.; Ashmore, Richard. D.; Makhijani, Mona G.; & Longo, Laura C. (1991). What is beautiful is good, but …: A meta-analytic review of research on the physical attractiveness stereotype. *Psychological Bulletin, 110,* 109–128.

Eagly, Alice H.; & Wood, Wendy. (2006). Three ways that data can misinform: Inappropriate partialling, small samples, and anyway, they're not playing our song. *Psychological Inquiry, 17*(2), 131–137.

Eastman, Charmane I.; Gazda Clifford J.; Burgess Helen J.; Crowley, Stephanie J.; & Fogg, Louis F. (2005). Advancing circadian rhythms before eastward flight: A strategy to prevent or reduce jet lag. *Sleep, 28,* 33–44.

Easton, Caroline J.; Mandel, Dolores; & Babuscio, Theresa. (2007). Differences in treatment outcome between male alcohol dependent offenders of domestic violence with and without positive drug screens. *Addictive Behaviors, 32,* 2151–2163.

Ebbinghaus, Hermann. (1885/1987). *Memory: A contribution to experimental psychology* (Henry A. Ruger & Clara E. Bussenius, Trans.). New York: Dover.

Edelson, Meredyth Goldberg. (2006). Are the majority of children with autism mentally retarded? A systematic evaluation of the data. *Focus on Autism and Other Developmental Disabilities, 21,* 66–83.

Edinger, Jack D.; & Means, Melanie K. (2005). Overview of insomnia: Definitions, epidemiology, differential diagnosis, and assessment. In Meir H. Kryger, Thomas Roth, & William C. Dement (Eds.), *Principles and practice of sleep medicine* (4th ed.). Philadelphia: Elsevier Saunders.

Edlund, Mark J.; Fortney, John C.; Reaves, Christina M.; Pyne, Jeffrey M.; & Mittal, Dinesh. (2008). Beliefs about depression and depression treatment among depressed veterans. *Medical Care, 46,* 581–589.

Edwards, Anthony G. P.; & Armitage, Peter. (1992). An experiment to test the discriminating ability of graphologists. *Personality and Individual Differences, 13,* 69–74.

Edwards, David J. A.; Datillio, Frank M.; & Bromley, Dennis B. (2004). Developing evidence-based practice: The role of case-based research. *Professional Psychology: Research and Practice, 35,* 589–597.

Edwards, Randall. (1995a, February). Future demands culturally diverse education. *APA Monitor, 26,* 43.

Edwards, Randall. (1995b, September). Psychologists foster the new definition of family. *APA Monitor, 26,* 38.

Edwards, Thea M.; & Myers, John P. (2007). Environmental exposures and gene regulation in disease etiology. *Environmental Health Perspspectives, 115,* 1264–1270.

EEOC. (1999). Uniform guidelines on employee selection procedures, & testing and assessment: An employer's guide to good hiring practices. U.S. Department of Labor, Employment and Training Administration: Author.

Egan, Susan K.; & Perry, David G. (2001). Gender identity: A multidimensional analysis with implications for psychosocial adjustment. *Developmental Psychology, 37,* 451–463.

Eibl-Eibesfeldt, Irenäus. (1973). The expressive behavior of the deaf-and-blind-born. In M. von Cranach & I. Vine (Eds.), *Social communication and movement.* New York: Academic Press.

Einstein, Danielle; & Menzies, Ross G. (2004). The presence of magical thinking in obsessive compulsive disorder. *Behaviour Research and Therapy, 42,* 539–549.

Eisenberger, Robert; Armeli, Stephen; & Pretz, Jean. (1998). Can the promise of reward increase creativity? *Journal of Personality and Social Psychology, 74,* 704–714.

Eisenberger, Robert; & Cameron, Judy. (1996). Detrimental effects of reward: Reality or myth? *American Psychologist, 51,* 1153–1166.

Ekman, Paul. (1980). *The face of man.* New York: Garland.

Ekman, Paul. (1982). *Emotion in the human face* (2nd ed.). New York: Cambridge University Press.

Ekman, Paul. (1992a). Are there basic emotions? *Psychological Review, 99,* 550–553.

Ekman, Paul. (1992b). Facial expressions of emotion: New findings, new questions. *Psychological Science, 3,* 34–38.

Ekman, Paul. (1993). Facial expression and emotion. *American Psychologist, 48,* 384–392.

Ekman, Paul. (1994a). Are there basic emotions? In Paul Ekman & Richard J. Davidson (Eds.), *The nature of emotion: Fundamental questions.* New York: Oxford University Press.

Ekman, Paul. (1994b). Strong evidence for universals in facial expressions: A reply to Russell's mistaken critique. *Psychological Bulletin, 115,* 268–287.

Ekman, Paul. (1998). Afterword. In Charles Darwin (1872/1998), *The expression of the emotions in man and animals.* New York: Oxford University Press.

Ekman, Paul (2003). *Emotions revealed: Recognizing faces and feelings to improve communication and emotional life.* New York: Henry Holt.

Ekman, Paul; & Davidson, Richard J. (1993). Voluntary smiling changes regional brain activity. *Psychological Science, 4,* 342–345.

Ekman, Paul; & Friesen, Wallace V. (1978). *Facial action coding system: A technique for the measurement of facial movement.* Palo Alto, CA: Consulting Psychologists Press.

Ekman, Paul; Friesen, Wallace V.; O'Sullivan, Maureen; Chan, Anthony; Diacoyanni-Tarlatzis, Irene; Heider, Karl; & others. (1987). Universal and cultural differences in the judgments of facial expressions of emotion. *Journal of Personality and Social Psychology, 53,* 712–717.

Ekwall, Anna Kristensson; & Hallberg, Ingalill Rahm. (2007). The association between caregiving satisfaction, difficulties and coping among older family caregivers. *Journal of Clinical Nursing, 16*(5), 832–844.

Elfenbein, Hillary Anger; & Ambady, Nalini. (2002). On the universality and specificity of emotion recognition: A meta-analysis. *Psychological Bulletin, 128,* 203–235.

Elkins, Gary; Marcus, Joel; & Bates, Jeff. (2006). Intensive hypnotherapy for smoking cessation: A prospective study. *International Journal of Clinical and Experimental Hypnosis, 54,* 303–315.

Ellenbogen, Jeffrey M.; Hu, Peter T.; Payne, Jessica D.; Titone, Debra; & Walker, Matthew P. (2007, May 1). Human relational memory requires time and sleep. *Proceedings of the National Academy of Sciences, 104,* 7723–7728. Retrieved July 21, 2008, from http://www.pnas.org/content/104/18/7723.full.pdf+html

Elliott, Robert; Greenberg, Leslie S.; & Lietaer, Germain. (2004). Research on experiential psychotherapies. In Michael J. Lambert (Ed.), *Handbook of psychotherapy and behavior change* (5th ed.). Hoboken, NJ: Wiley.

Ellis, Albert. (1991). *Reason and emotion in psychotherapy.* New York: Carol.

Ellis, Albert. (1993). Reflections on rational-emotive therapy. *Journal of Consulting and Clinical Psychology, 61,* 199–201.

Ellis, Albert; & Bernard, Michael E. (1985). What is rational-emotive therapy (RET)? In Albert Ellis & Michael E. Bernard (Eds.), *Clinical applications of rational-emotive therapy.* New York: Plenum Press.

Ellis, Albert; & Harper, Robert A. (1975). *A new guide to rational living.* Hollywood, CA: Wilshire Book Company.

Ellis, Bruce J. (2004). Timing of pubertal maturation in girls: An integrated life history approach. *Psychological Bulletin, 130,* 920–958.

Ellis, Bruce J.; & Essex, Marilyn J. (2007). Family environments, adrenarche, and sexual maturation: A longitudinal test of a life history model. *Child Development, 78,* 1799–1817.

Ellis, Bruce J.; & Garber, Judy. (2000). Psychosocial antecedents of variation in girls' pubertal timing: Maternal depression, stepfather presence, and marital and family stress. *Child Development, 71,* 485–501.

EMDR Institute. (2001). Overview and general description of EMDR. Retrieved December 9, 2009, from http://www.emdr.com/studies.htm

Emmelkamp, Paul M. G. (2004). Behavior therapy with adults. In Michael J. Lambert (Ed.), *Bergin and Garfield's handbook of psychotherapy and behavior change* (5th ed.). New York: Wiley.

Empson, Jacob. (2002). *Sleep and dreaming* (3rd ed.). New York: Palgrave/St. Martin's Press.

England, Lynndie. (2004, May 12). Quoted in: "Army private 'ordered to pose.'" *Cable News Network (CNN).* Retrieved May 13, 2004, from http://www.cnn.com/2004/US/05/12/prisoner.abuse.england.ap/index.html.

England, Lynndie. (2005, October 2). Quoted in "Behind the Abu Ghraib photos." *Dateline NBC.* Retrieved November 30, 2005, from http://msnbc.msn.com/id/9532670/

English, Horace B. (1929). Three cases of the "conditioned fear response." *Journal of Abnormal and Social Psychology, 24,* 221–225.

Enriori, Pablo J.; Evans, Anne E.; Sinnayah, Puspha; & Cowley, Michael A. (2006). Leptin resistance and obesity. *Obesity, 14*(Suppl5), 254S–258S.

Ensel, Walter M.; & Lin, Nan. (2004). Physical fitness and the stress process. *Journal of Community Psychology, 32,* 81–101.

Epstein, Leonard H.; Leddy, John J.; & Temple, Jennifer L. (2007). Food reinforcement and eating: A multilevel analysis. *Psychological Bulletin, 133,* 884–906.

Epstein, Mark. (1995). *Thoughts without a thinker: Psychotherapy from a Buddhist perspective.* New York: Basic Books.

Epstein, Russell; & Kanwisher, Nancy. (1998). A cortical representation of the local visual environment. *Nature, 392,* 598–601.

Ericsson, K. Anders; & Kintsch, Walter. (1995). Long-term working memory. *Psychological Review, 102,* 211–245.

Eriksen, Karen; & Kress, Victoria E. (2005). *Beyond the DSM story: Ethical quandaries, challenges, and best practices.* Thousand Oaks, CA: Sage.

Erikson, Erik H. (1964a). *Childhood and society* (Rev. ed.). New York: Norton.

Erikson, Erik H. (1964b). *Insight and responsibility.* New York: Norton.

Erikson, Erik H. (1968). *Identity: Youth and crisis.* New York: Norton.

Erikson, Erik H. (1982). *The life cycle completed: A review.* New York: Norton.

Erikson, Erik H.; Erikson, Joan M.; & Kivnick, Helen Q. (1986). *Vital involvement in old age: The experience of old age in our time.* New York: Norton.

Eriksson, Cynthia B.; Vande Kemp, Hendrika; Gorsuch, Richard; Hoke, Stephen; & Foy, David W. (2001). Trauma exposure and PTSD symptoms in international relief and development personnel. *Journal of Traumatic Stress, 14,* 205–219.

Eriksson, Peter S.; Perfilieva, Ekaterina; Björk-Eriksson, Thomas; Alborn, Ann-Marie; Nordborg, Claes; Peterson, Daniel A.; & Gage, Fred A. (1998). Neurogenesis in the adult hippocampus. *Nature Medicine, 4,* 1313–1317.

Ermer, Elsa; Cosmides, Leda; & Tooby, John. (2007). Functional specialization and the adaptationist program. In Steven W. Gangestad & Jeffry A. Simpson (Eds.), *The evolution of mind: Fundamental questions and controversies.* New York: Guilford Press.

Ersoy, Betul; Balkan, C.; & Gunnay, T. (2005). The factors affecting the relation between the menarcheal age of mother and daughter. *Child: Care, Health and Development, 31,* 303–308.

Eschweiler, Gerhard W.; Vonthein, Reinhard; & Bode, Ruediger. (2007). Clinical efficacy and cognitive side effects of bifrontal versus right unilateral electroconvulsive therapy (ECT): A short-term randomised controlled trial in pharmaco-resistant major depression. *Journal of Affective Disorders, 101*(1–3), 149–157.

Esses, Victoria M.; Haddock, Geoffrey; & Zanna, Mark P. (1993). Values, stereotypes, and emotions as determinants of intergroup attitudes. In Diane M. Mackie & David L. Hamilton (Eds.), *Affect, cognition, and stereotyping: Interactive processes in group perception.* San Diego, CA: Academic Press.

Esses, Victoria M.; Jackson, Lynne M.; & Dovidio, John F. (2005). Instrumental relations among groups: Group competition, conflict, and prejudice. In John F. Dovidio, Peter Glick, & Laurie A. Rudman (Eds.), *On the nature of prejudice: Fifty years after Allport* (pp. 227–243). Malden, MA: Blackwell.

Estes, William K.; & Skinner, B. F. (1941). Some quantitative properties of anxiety. *Journal of Experimental Psychology, 29,* 390–400.

Etscorn, Frank; & Stephens, Ronald. (1973). Establishment of conditioned taste aversions with a 24-hour CS-US interval. *Physiological Psychology, 1,* 251–253.

Eunice Kennedy Shriver National Institute of Child Health and Human Development. (2006). *The NICHD Study of Early Child Care and Youth Development (SECCYD): Findings for children up to age 4 1/2 years* (NIH Publication No. 05-4318). Washington, DC: U.S. Government Printing Office. Retrieved September 18, 2009, from http://www.nichd.nih.gov/publications/pubs/upload/seccyd_051206.pdf

Evans, Gary W.; Bullinger, Monika; & Hygge, Staffan. (1998). Chronic noise exposure and physiological response: A prospective study of children living under environmental stress. *Psychological Science, 9,* 75–77.

Evans, Gary W.; & Hygge, Staffan. (2007). Noise and cognitive performance in children and adults. In Linda M. Luxon & Deepak Prasher (Eds.), *Noise and its effects.* New York: Wiley.

Evans, Rand B. (1991). E. B. Titchener on scientific psychology and technology. In Gregory A. Kimble, Michael Wertheimer, & Charlotte White (Eds.), *Portraits of pioneers in psychology* (Vol. 1). Washington, DC: American Psychological Association.

Evans, Rand B.; & Rilling, Mark. (2000). How the challenge of explaining learning influenced the origins and development of John B. Watson's behaviorism. *American Journal of Psychology, 113,* 275–301.

Everett, Daniel L. (2005). Cultural constraints on grammar and cognition in Pirahã: Another look at the design features of human language. *Current Anthropology, 46,* 621–646.

Everett, Daniel L. (2008, January 19). Quoted in Liz Else & Lucy Middleton, "Interview: Out on a limb over language." *New Scientist,* issue no. 2639, pp. 42–44.

Exner, John E., Jr. (1993). *The Rorschach: A comprehensive system* (3rd ed., Vol. 1). New York: Wiley.

Exner, John E., Jr.; & Erdberg, Philip. (2005). *The Rorschach: A comprehensive system* (3rd ed.). Hoboken, NJ: Wiley.

Eysenck, Hans J. (1952). The effects of psychotherapy: An evaluation. *Journal of Consulting Psychology, 16,* 319–324.

Eysenck, Hans J. (1982). *Personality, genetics, and behavior.* New York: Praeger.

Eysenck, Hans J. (1990). Biological dimensions of personality. In Lawrence A. Pervin (Ed.), *Handbook of personality: Theory and research.* New York: Guilford Press.

Eysenck, Hans J. (1994). The outcome problem in psychotherapy: What have we learned? *Behavior Research and Therapy, 32,* 447–495.

Eysenck, Hans J.; & Eysenck, Sybil B. G. (1975). *Psychoticism as a dimension of personality.* London: Hodder & Stoughton.

Fabiano, Gregory A.; Pelham, William E., Jr.; Karmazin, Karen; Kreher, Joanne; Panahon, Carlos J.; & Carlson, Carl. (2008). A group contingency program to improve the behavior of elementary school students in a cafeteria. *Behavior Modification, 32,* 121–132.

Fan, Hung Y.; Conner, Ross F.; & Villarreal, Luis P. (2007). *AIDS: Science and society* (5th ed.). Sudbury, MA: Jones and Bartlett.

Fan, Yang; Liu, Zhengyan; Weinstein, Philip R.; Fike, John R.; & Liu, Jialing. (2007). Environmental enrichment enhances neurogenesis and improves functional outcome after cranial irradiation. *European Journal of Neuroscience, 25,* 38–46.

Fancher, Raymond E. (1973). *Psychoanalytic psychology: The development of Freud's thought.* New York: Norton.

Fancher, Raymond E. (1996). *Pioneers of psychology* (3rd ed.). New York: Norton.

Fang, Carolyn Y.; Miller, Suzanne M.; Bovberg, Dana; Bergman, Cynthia; Edelson, Mitchell; Rosenblum, Norman G.; Bovey, Betsy A.; Godwin, Andrew K.; Campbell, Donald E.; & Douglas, Steven D. (2008). Perceived stress is associated with impaired T-cell response to HPV-16 in women with cervical dysplasia. *Annals of Behavioral Medicine, 35,* 87–96.

Fanous, Ayman H.; van den Oord, Edwin J.; Riley, Brien P.; Aggen, Steven H.; Neale, Michael C.; O'Neill, F. Anthony; Walsh, Dermot; & Kendler, Kenneth S. (2005). Relationships between a high-risk haplotype in the *DTNBP1* (dysbindin) gene and clinical features of schizophrenia. *American Journal of Psychiatry, 162,* 1824–1832.

Fantz, Robert L. (1961, May). The origin of form perception. *Scientific American, 204,* 66–72.

Fantz, Robert L.; Ordy, J. M.; & Udelf, M. S. (1962). Maturation of pattern vision in infants during the first six months. *Journal of Comparative and Physiological Psychology, 55,* 907–917.

Farber, Barry A. (2007). On the enduring and substantial influence of Carl Rogers' not-quite necessary nor sufficient conditions. *Psychotherapy: Theory, Research, Practice, Training, 44,* 289–294.

Farberman, Rhea K. (1999). What the media needs from news sources. In Lita Linzer Schwartz (Ed.), *Psychology and the media: A second look.* Washington, DC: American Psychological Association.

Farberman, Rhea K. (2003). Strategies for successful interactions with the news media. In Mitchell J. Prinstein & Marcus D. Patterson (Eds.), *The portable mentor: Expert guide to a successful career in psychology.* New York: Kluwer Academic/Plenum Publishers.

Farfel, Mark; DiGrande, Laura; Brackbill, Robert; Prann, Angela; Cone, James; Friedman, Stephen; Walker, Deborah J.; Pezeshki, Grant; Thomas, Pauline; Galea, Sandro; Williamson, David; Frieden, Thomas R.; & Thorpe, Lorne. (2008). An overview of 9/11 experiences and respiratory and mental health conditions among World Trade Center Health Registry enrollees. *Journal of Urban Health, 85,* 880–909.

Farmer, Rosemary L. (2009). *Neuroscience and social work practice: The missing link.* Thousand Oaks, CA: Sage.

Farroni, Teresa; Menon, Enrica; & Johnson, Mark H. (2006). Factors influencing newborns' preference for faces with eye contact. *Journal of Experimental Child Psychology, 95,* 298–308.

Fastovsky, Natasha; Teitelbaum, Alexander; Zislin, Josef; Katz, Gregory; & Durst, Rimona. (2000). The Jerusalem syndrome. *Psychiatric Services, 51,* 1052.

Fazel, Seena; Langstrom, Niklas; Hjern, Anders; Grann, Martin; & Lichtenstein, Paul. (2009). Schizophrenia, substance abuse, and violent crime. *Journal of the American Medical Association, 301,* 2016–2023.

Fazio, Russell H. (1990). Multiple processes by which attitudes guide behavior: The MODE model as an integrative framework. In Mark P. Zanna (Ed.), *Advances in experimental social psychology* (Vol. 23). San Diego, CA: Academic Press.

FDA News. (2007, March 17). FDA requests label change for all sleep disorder drug products (FDA news release P07-45). Retrieved July 14, 2009, from http://www.fda.gov/NewsEvents/Newsroom/PressAnnouncements/2007/ucm108868.htm

Fedulov, Vadim; Rex, Christopher S.; Simmons, Danielle A.; Palmer, Linda; Gall, Christine M.; & Lynch, Gary. (2007). Evidence that long-term potentiation occurs within individual hippocampal synapses during learning. *Journal of Neuroscience, 27,* 8031–8039.

Feingold, Alan. (1992). Good-looking people are not what we think. *Psychological Bulletin, 111*, 304–341.

Feldman Barrett, Lisa; Lane, Richard D.; Sechrest, Lee; & Schwartz, Gary E. (2000). Sex differences in emotional awareness. *Personality and Social Psychology Bulletin, 26,* 1027–1035.

Feldman Barrett, Lisa; & Russell, James A. (1999). The structure of current affect: Controversies and emerging consensus. *Current Directions in Psychological Science, 8*, 10–14.

Feliciano, Leilani; & Areán, Patricia A. (2007). Mood disorders: Depressive disorders. In Michel Hersen, Samuel M. Turner, & Deborah C. Beidel (Eds.), *Adult psychopathology and diagnosis* (5th ed., pp. 286–316). Hoboken, NJ: Wiley.

Felsberg, Eric J. (2004). Conducting job analyses and drafting lawful job descriptions under the Americans with Disabilities Act. *Employment Relations Today, 31*, 91–93.

Ferguson, Christopher J.; & Kilbourn, John. (2009) The public health risks of media violence: A meta-analytic review. *Journal of Pediatrics, 154,* 759–763.

Fernald, Anne. (1985). Four-month-old infants prefer to listen to motherese. *Infant Behavior and Development, 8*, 181–182.

Fernald, Anne. (1992). Human maternal vocalizations to infants as biologically relevant signals: An evolutionary perspective. In Jerome H. Barkow, Leda Cosmides, & John Tooby (Eds.), *The adapted mind: Evolutionary psychology and the generation of culture* (pp. 391–428). New York: Oxford University Press.

Feshbach, Seymour; & Tangney, June. (2008). Television viewing and aggression: Some alternative perspectives. *Perspectives on Psychological Sciences, 3,* 387–389.

Feske, Ulrike; & Goldstein, Alan J. (1997). Eye movement desensitization and reprocessing treatment for panic disorder: A controlled outcome and partial dismantling study. *Journal of Clinical and Consulting Psychology, 65*, 1026–1035.

Festinger, Leon. (1957). *A theory of cognitive dissonance.* Stanford, CA: Stanford University Press.

Festinger, Leon. (1962). Cognitive dissonance. *Scientific American, 207,* 93–99. (Reprinted in *Contemporary psychology: Readings from Scientific American,* 1971, San Francisco: Freeman.)

Field, Clinton E.; Nash, Heather M.; Handwerk, Michael L.; & Friman, Patrick C. (2004). A modification of the token economy for nonresponsive youth in family-style residential care. *Behavior Modification, 28*, 438–457.

Field, Tiffany. (1996). Attachment and separation in young children. *Annual Review of Psychology, 47*, 541–561.

Field, Tiffany. (2009). *Complementary and alternative therapies research.* Washington, D.C.: American Psychological Association.

Field, Tiffany M.; Woodson, Robert; Greenberg, Reena; & Cohen, Debra. (1982). Discrimination and imitation of facial expressions by neonates. *Science, 218*, 179–182.

Fieldhouse, Paul. (1986). *Food and nutrition: Customs and culture.* London: Croom Helm.

Fields, Howard L.; & Levine, Jon D. (1984). Placebo analgesia: A role for endorphins. *Trends in Neuroscience, 7*, 271–273.

Fillingim, Roger B. (2000). *Sex, gender, and pain: Progress in pain research and management* (Vol. 17). Seattle, WA: International Association for the Study of Pain, IASP Press.

Finch, Brian Karl; & Vega, William A. (2003). Acculturation stress, social support, and self-rated health among Latinos in California. *Journal of Immigrant Health, 5*, 109–117.

Fine, Ione. (2002). Quoted in *The man who learnt to see.* BB2 Documentary.

Fine, Ione; Wade, Alex R.; Brewer, Alyssa A.; May, Michael G.; Goodman, Daniel F.; Boynton, Geoffrey M.; Wandell, Brian A.; & MacLeod, Donald I. A. (2003). Long-term deprivation affects visual perception and cortex. *Nature Neuroscience, 6,* 915–916.

Finegold, Leonard; & Flamm, Bruce L. (2006, January 7). Magnet therapy: Extraordinary claims, but no proved benefits. *British Medical Journal, 332*, 4.

Fink, Max. (2009). *Electroconvulsive therapy: A guide for professionals & their patients.* New York: Oxford University Press.

Fink, Max; & Taylor, Michael A. (2008). Issues for DSM-V: The medical diagnostic model. *American Journal of Psychiatry, 165,* 799.

Finney, John W.; Wilbourne, Paula L.; & Moos, Rudolph H. (2007). Psychosocial treatments for substance use disorders. In Peter E. Nathan & Jack M. Gorman (Eds.), *A guide to treatments that work* (3rd ed., pp. 179–202). New York: Oxford University Press.

Finno, Ariel A.; Salazar, Marcos; Frincke, Jessica L.; Pate, William E., II; & Kohout, Jessica. (2006). *Debt, salary, and career data in psychology: What you need to know.* Center for Psychology Workforce Analysis and Research (CPWAR) Presentations. American Psychological Association Research Office. Retrieved March 8, 2008, from http://research.apa.org/presentations.html

Fischer, Agneta H.; Rodriguez-Mosquera, Patricia M.; van Vianen, Annelies E. M.; & Manstead, Antony S. R. (2004). Gender and culture differences in emotion. *Emotion, 4,* 87–94.

Fischer, Benedikt; & Rehm, Jurgen. (2007). Illicit opioid use in the 21st century: Witnessing a paradigm shift? *Addiction, 102,* 499–501.

Fischer, Kurt W.; & Hencke, Rebecca W. (1996). Infants' construction of actions in context: Piaget's contribution to research on early development. *Psychological Science, 7,* 204–210.

Fisher, Anne. (2008). Gas prices too high? Your employer might help. *Fortune Magazine.* Accessed on December 9, 2009 at: http://money.cnn.com/2008/06/02/magazines/fortune/annie_gas.fortune/index.htm

Fisher, Carrie. (2001). In her own words: Carrie Fisher interviewed by Robert Epstein, Ph.D. *Psychology Today, 34,* 36–37.

Fisher, Celia B. (2009). *Decoding the ethics code: A practical guide for psychologists* (2nd ed.). Thousand Oaks, CA: Sage.

Fisher, Celia B.; & Fyrberg, Denise. (1994). Participant partners: College students weigh the costs and benefits of deceptive research. *American Psychologist, 49*, 417–427.

Fisher, Seymour; & Greenberg, Roger. (1996). *Freud scientifically appraised.* New York: Wiley.

Fishman, Joshua A. (1960/1974). A systematization of the Whorfian hypothesis. In John W. Berry & P. R. Dasen (Eds.), *Culture and cognition: Readings in cross-cultural psychology.* London: Methuen.

Fiske, Susan T. (1993). Social cognition and perception. *Annual Review of Psychology, 44*, 155–194.

Fiske, Susan T. (2008). Core social motivations: Views from the couch, consciousness, classroom, computers, and collectives. In James Y. Shah & Wendi L. Gardner (Eds.), *Handbook of motivation science.* New York: Guilford Press.

Fiske, Susan T.; Cuddy, Amy J. C.; Glick, Peter; & Xu, Jun. (2002). A model of (often mixed) stereotype content: Competence and warmth respectively follow from perceived status and competition. *Journal of Personality and Social Psychology, 82*, 878–902.

Fiske, Susan T.; Harris, Lasana T.; & Cuddy, Amy J. C. (2004). Why ordinary people torture enemy prisoners. *Science, 306,* 1482–1483.

Fiske, Susan T.; & Neuberg, Steven L. (1990). A continuum of impression formation, from category-based to individuating processes: Influences of information and motivation on attention and interpretation. In Mark P. Zanna (Ed.), *Advances in experimental social psychology* (Vol. 23). San Diego, CA: Academic Press/Harcourt.

Fiske, Susan T.; & Ruscher, Janet B. (1993). Negative interdependence and prejudice: Whence the affect? In Diane M. Mackie & David L. Hamilton (Eds.), *Affect, cognition, and stereotyping: Interactive processes in group perception.* San Diego, CA: Academic Press.

Fiske, Susan T.; & Taylor, Shelley E. (1991). *Social cognition* (2nd ed.). New York: McGraw-Hill.

Fivush, Robyn; & Nelson, Katherine. (2004). Culture and language in the emergence of autobiographical memory. *Psychological Science, 15,* 573–577.

Flack, William F.; Laird, James D.; & Cavallaro, Lorraine A. (1999). Separate and combined effects of facial expressions and bodily postures on emotional feelings. *European Journal of Social Psychology, 29,* 203–217.

Flaten, Magne Arve; & Blumenthal, Terry D. (1999). Caffeine-associated stimuli elicit conditioned responses: An experimental model of the placebo effect. *Psychopharmacology, 145,* 105–112.

Flavell, John H. (1996). Piaget's legacy. *Psychological Science, 7,* 200–203.

Flavell, Steven W. & Greenberg, Michael E. (2008). Signaling mechanisms linking neuronal activity to gene expression and plasticity of the nervous system. *Annual Review of Neuroscience, 31,* 563–590. Accessed on September 24, 2009 at NIH public access at: http://www.pubmedcentral.nih.gov/picrender.fcgi?artid=2728073&blobtype=pdf

Flor, Herta; Nikolajsen, Lone; & Jensen, Troels Staehelin. (2006). Phantom limb pain: A case of maladaptive CNS plasticity? *Nature Reviews Neuroscience, 7,* 873–881.

Flynn, James R. (1994). IQ gains over time. In Robert J. Sternberg (Ed.), *Encyclopedia of human intelligence.* New York: Macmillan.

Flynn, James R. (1999). Searching for justice: The discovery of IQ gains over time. *American Psychologist, 54,* 5–20.

Flynn, James R. (2007a). Solving the IQ Puzzle. *Scientific American Mind,* 18, 24–31.

Flynn, James R. (2007b). What lies behind g(I) and g(ID). *European Journal of Personality, 21,* 722–724.

Foa, Edna B.; Keane, Terence M.; Friedman, Matthew J.; & Cohen, Judith A. (Eds.). (2008). *Effective treatments for PTSD: Practice guidelines from the International Society for Traumatic Stress Studies* (2nd ed.). New York: Guilford Press.

Foa, Edna B.; & Meadows, Elizabeth A. (1997). Psychosocial treatments for posttraumatic stress disorder: A critical review. *Annual Review of Psychology, 48,* 449–480.

Folkman, Susan. (2009). Questions, answers, issues, and next steps in stress and coping research. *European Psychologist, 14,* 72–77.

Folkman, Susan; & Lazarus, Richard S. (1991). Coping and emotion. In Alan Monat & Richard S. Lazarus (Eds.), *Stress and coping: An anthology* (3rd ed.). New York: Columbia University Press.

Folkman, Susan; & Moskowitz, Judith Tedlie. (2000). Positive affect and the other side of coping. *American Psychologist, 55,* 647–654.

Folkman, Susan; & Moskowitz, Judith Tedlie. (2007). Positive affect and meaning-focused coping during significant psychological stress. In Miles Hewstone, Henk A. W. Schut, John B. F. De Wit, Kees Van Den Bos, & Margaret S. Stroebe (Eds.), *The scope of social psychology: Theory and applications* (pp. 193–208). New York: Psychology Press.

Fonagy, Peter; & Bateman, Anthony. (2008). The development of borderline personality disorder—A mentalizing model. *Journal of Personality Disorders, 22,* 4–21.

Fontana, Alan; & Rosenheck, Robert. (2008). Treatment-seeking veterans of Iraq and Afghanistan: Comparison with veterans of previous wars. *Journal of Nervous and Mental Disease, 196*(7), 513–521.

Foote, Brad; Smolin, Yvette; & Kaplan, Margaret. (2006). Prevalence of dissociative disorders in psychiatric outpatients. *American Journal of Psychiatry, 163*(4), 623–629.

Forbes. (2007). Forbes survey revealed that the U.S. workplace is not family-oriented when compared to other industrialized countries. Retrieved February 15, 2008, from *Forbes,* msn.com.

Forgas, Joseph F. (2008). Affect and cognition. *Perspectives on Psychological Science, 3,* 94–101.

Forgas, Joseph P.; Dunn, Elizabeth; & Granland, Stacey. (2008). Are you being served ...? An unobtrusive experiment of affective influences on helping in a department store. *European Journal of Social Psychology, 38,* 333–342.

Fortune Magazine. (2008). 100 Best companies to work for. Retrieved September 15, 2008, from www.Fortunemagazine.com

Foschi, Renato; & Cicciola, Elisabetta. (2006). Politics and naturalism in the 20th century psychology of Alfred Binet. *History of Psychology, 9,* 267–289.

Fouad, Nadya A.; & Arredondo, Patricia. (2007). Evaluating cultural identity and biases. In Nadya A. Fouad & Patricia Arredondo (Eds.), *Becoming culturally oriented: Practical advice for psychologists and educators* (pp. 15–34). Washington, DC: American Psychological Association.

Fowler, Joanna S.; Volkow, Nora D.; Kassed, Cheryl A.; & Chang, Linda. (2007, April). Imaging the addicted human brain. *Addiction Science and Practice Perspectives, 3,* 4–15.

Fox, Margalit. (2008). *Talking hands: What sign language reveals about the mind.* New York: Simon & Schuster.

Fox, William M. (1982). Why we should abandon Maslow's need hierarchy theory. *Journal of Humanistic Education and Development, 21,* 29–32.

Fraga, Mario F.; Ballestar, Esteban; Paz, Maria F.; Ropero, Santiago; Setien, Fernando; Ballestar, Maria L.; Heine-Suner, Damia; & others. (2005). Epigenetic differences arise during the lifetime of monozygotic twins. *Proceedings of the National Academy of Sciences, 102,* 10413–10414.

Fraguas, David; Reig, Santiago; Desco, Manuel; Rojas-Corrales, Olga; Gibert-Rahola, Juan; Parellada, Mara; Moreno, Dolores; Castro-Fornieles, Josefina; Graell, Montserrat; Baeza, Immaculada; Gonzalez-Pinto, Ana; Otero, Soraya; & Arango, Celso. (2008, April). Oxidative cell damage is related to the enlargement of the lateral ventricles in children and adolescents with first episode schizophrenia. *European Psychiatry, 23*(Suppl. 2), S115–S116.

Fram, Alan. (2007). That's the spirit: One-third of people believe in ghosts—and some report seeing one. *Associated Press Archive,* Record No. D8SGT3CG0. Associated Press, Washington, DC.

Francis, Darlene; Diorio, Josie; Liu, Dong; & Meaney, Michael J. (1999). Nongenomic transmission across generations of maternal behavior and stress responses in the rat. *Science, 286,* 1155–1158.

Francis, Ronald D. (2009). *Ethics for psychologists* (2nd ed.). Chichester, England: Wiley-Blackwell.

Frank, Barney. (1996, February 4). Quoted in Claudia Dreifus, "And then there was Frank." *The New York Times Magazine,* pp. 22–25.

Frank, Mark G.; & Stennett, Janine. (2001). The forced-choice paradigm and the perception of facial expressions of emotion. *Journal of Personality and Social Psychology, 80,* 75–85.

Frank, Michael C.; Everett, Daniel L.; Fedorenko, Evelina; & Gibson, Edward. (2008). Number as a cognitive technology: Evidence from Piraha language and cognition. *Cognition, 108,* 819–824.

Frankenburg, Frances R. (1994). History of the development of antipsychotic medication. *Psychiatric Clinics of North America, 17,* 531–540.

Frankland, Paul W.; & Bontempi, Bruno. (2005). The organization of recent and remote memories. *Nature Reviews Neuroscience, 6,* 119–130.

Franz, Carol E.; McClelland, David C.; & Weinberger, Joel. (1991). Childhood antecedents of conventional social accomplishment in midlife adults: A 36-year prospective study. *Journal of Personality and Social Psychology, 60,* 586–595.

Fratiglioni, Laura; Paillard-Borg, Stephanie; & Winblad, Bengt. (2004). An active and socially integrated lifestyle in late life might protect against dementia. *Lancet Neurology, 3,* 343–353.

Fredrickson, Barbara L.; Tugade, Michele M.; Waugh, Christian E.; & Larkin, Gregory R. (2003). How good are positive motions in crises? A prospective study of resilience and emotions following the terrorist attacks on the United States on September 11, 2001. *Journal of Personality and Social Psychology, 84,* 365–376.

Free, Michael L. (2008). *Cognitive therapy in groups: Guidelines and resources for practice* (2nd ed.). Chichester, England: Wiley.

Freeman, Chris; & Power, Mick. (2007). *Handbook of evidence-based psychotherapies: A guide for research and practice.* Chichester, England: Wiley.

Freeman, Lucy; & Strean, Herbert S. (1987). *Freud and women.* New York: Continuum.

Freeman, Nancy K. (2007). Preschoolers' perceptions of gender appropriate toys and their parents' beliefs about genderized behaviors: Miscommunication, mixed messages, or hidden truths? *Early Childhood Education Journal, 3,* 357–366.

Freidel, Paul; Young, Bruce; & van Hemmen, J. Leo. (2008). Auditory localization of ground-borne vibrations in snakes. *Physical Review Letters, 100,* 048701.

Freire, Elizabeth S. (2007). Empathy. In Mick Cooper, Maureen O'Hara, Peter F Schmid, & Gill Wyatt (Eds.), *The handbook of person-centered psychotherapy and counseling.* New York, NY: Palgrave Macmillan.

Freisthier, Bridget; Merritt, Darcey H.; & Lascala, Elizabeth A. (2006). Understanding the ecology of child maltreatment: A review of the literature and directions for future research. *Child Maltreatment, 11,* 263–280.

Freud, Anna. (1946). *The ego and mechanisms of defence* (Cecil Baines, Trans.). New York: International Universities Press.

Freud, Sigmund. (1900/1974). The interpretation of dreams. In James Strachey (Ed.), *The standard edition of the complete psychological works of Sigmund Freud* (Vols. 4 & 5). London: Hogarth Press.

Freud, Sigmund. (1904/1965). *The psychopathology of everyday life* (Alan Tyson, Trans., & James Strachey, Ed.). New York: Norton.

Freud, Sigmund. (1905/1975). *Three essays on the theory of sexuality* (James Strachey, Ed.). New York: Basic Books.

Freud, Sigmund. (1911/1989). On dreams. In Peter Gay (Ed.), *The Freud reader.* New York: Norton.

Freud, Sigmund. (1912/1958). The dynamics of resistance. *The standard edition of the complete psychological works of Sigmund Freud* (Vol. 12, pp. 97–108). London: Hogarth Press.

Freud, Sigmund. (1914/1948). On narcissism: An introduction. In Joan Riviere (Trans.), *Collected papers: Vol. 4. Papers on metapsychology and applied psychoanalysis.* London: Hogarth Press.

Freud, Sigmund. (1915a/1948). Repression. In Joan Riviere (Trans.), *Collected papers: Vol. 4. Papers on metapsychology and applied psychoanalysis.* London: Hogarth Press.

Freud, Sigmund. (1915b/1959). Analysis, terminable and interminable. In Joan Riviere (Trans.), *Collected papers: Vol. 5. Miscellaneous papers* (2nd ed.). London: Hogarth Press.

Freud, Sigmund. (1915c/1959). Libido theory. In Joan Riviere (Trans.), *Collected papers: Vol. 5. Miscellaneous papers* (2nd ed.). London: Hogarth Press.

Freud, Sigmund. (1916/1964). *Leonardo da Vinci and a memory of his childhood.* (James Strachey, Trans., in collaboration with Anna Freud). New York: Norton.

Freud, Sigmund. (1919/1989). *Totem and taboo: Some points of agreement between the mental lives of savages and neurotics* (James Strachey, Ed. & Trans., with a biographical introduction by Peter Gay). New York: Norton.

Freud, Sigmund. (1920/1961). *Beyond the pleasure principle* (James Strachey, Ed.). New York: Norton.

Freud, Sigmund. (1923/1962). *The ego and the id* (Joan Riviere, Trans., & James Strachey, Ed.). New York: Norton.

Freud, Sigmund. (1925/1989). Some psychical consequences of the anatomical distinction between the sexes. In Peter Gay (Ed.), *The Freud reader.* New York: Norton.

Freud, Sigmund. (1926/1947). *The question of lay analysis: An introduction to psychoanalysis* (Nancy Proctor-Gregg, Trans.). London: Imago.

Freud, Sigmund. (1930/1961). *Civilization and its discontents* (James Strachey, Ed. & Trans.). New York: Norton.

Freud, Sigmund. (1933). *New introductory lectures on psychoanalysis* (W. J. H. Sprott, Trans.). New York: Norton.

Freud, Sigmund. (1936). *The problem of anxiety* (Henry Alden Bunker, Trans.). New York: The Psychoanalytic Quarterly Press and Norton.

Freud, Sigmund. (1939/1967). *Moses and monotheism* (Katherine Jones, Trans.). New York: Vintage Books.

Freud, Sigmund. (1940/1949). *An outline of psychoanalysis* (James Strachey, Trans.). New York: Norton.

Fridell, Sari R.; Owen-Anderson, Allison; Johnson, Laurel L.; Bradley, Susan J.; & Zucker, Kenneth J. (2006). The Playmate and Play Style Preferences Structured Interview: A comparison of children with gender identity disorder and controls. *Archives of Sexual Behavior, 35,* 729–737.

Friedman, Howard S.; & Booth-Kewley, Stephanie. (1987). The "disease-prone personality": A meta-analytic view of the construct. *American Psychologist, 42,* 539–555.

Friedman, Howard S.; Booth-Kewley, Stephanie. (2003). The "disease-prone personality": A meta-analytic view of the construct. In Peter Salovey & Alexander J. Rothman (Eds.), *Social psychology of health* (pp. 305–324). New York: Psychology Press.

Friedman, Jeffrey M. (2000, April 6). Obesity in the new millennium. *Nature, 404,* 632–634.

Friedman, Jeffrey M. (2009). Causes and control of excess body fat. *Nature, 459,* 340–342.

Friedman, Jeffrey M.; & Halaas, Jeffrey L. (1998, October 22). Leptin and the regulation of body weight in mammals. *Nature, 395,* 763–770.

Friedman, Meyer; & Rosenman, Ray H. (1974). *Type A behavior and your heart.* New York: Knopf.

Friend, Ronald; Rafferty, Yvonne; & Bramel, Dana. (1990). A puzzling misinterpretation of the Asch "conformity" study. *European Journal of Social Psychology, 20,* 29–44.

Friesen, Wallace V. (1972). *Cultural differences in facial expressions in a social situation: An experimental test of the concept of display rules.* Unpublished doctoral dissertation, University of California, San Francisco.

Fruth, Barbara; & Hohmann, Gottfried. (2006). Social grease for females? Same-sex genital contacts in wild bonobos. In Volker Sommer & Paul L. Vasey (Eds.), *Homosexual behaviour in animals: An evolutionary perspective.* New York: Cambridge University Press.

Fuente-Fernández, Raúl de la; Ruth, Thomas J.; Sossi, Vesna; Schulzer, Michael; Calne, Donald B.; & Stoessl, A. Jon. (2001, August 10). Expectation and dopamine release: Mechanism of the placebo effect in Parkinson's disease. *Science, 293,* 1164–1166.

Fuller, Patrick M.; Gooley, Joshua J.; & Saper, Clifford B. (2006). Neurobiology of the sleep-wake cycle: Sleep architecture, circadian regulation, and regulatory feedback. *Journal of Biological Rhythms, 21,* 482–493.

Fumeron F.; Betoulle D.; Aubert R.; Herberth, B.; Siest, G.; & Rigaud, D. (2001). Association of a functional 5-HT transporter gene polymorphism with anorexia nervosa and food intake. *Molecular Psychiatry, 6,* 9–10.

Funder, David C. (2001). Personality. *Annual Review of Psychology, 52,* 197–221.

Furman, Wyndol. (2002). The emerging field of adolescent romantic relationships. *Current Directions in Psychological Science, 11,* 177–180.

Furman, Wyndol; & Shaffer, Laura. (2003). National estimates of adolescent romantic relationships. In Paul Florsheim (Ed.), *Adolescent romantic relations and sexual behavior: Theory, research, and practical implications.* Mahwah, NJ: Erlbaum.

Furman, Wyndol; & Simon, Valerie A. (2004). Concordance in attachment states of mind and styles with respect to fathers and mothers. *Developmental Psychology, 40,* 1239–1247.

Furnham, Adam. (2008). *Personality and intelligence at work: Exploring and explaining individual differences at work.* London: Routledge.

Furnham, Adrian. (1991). Write and wrong: The validity of graphological analysis. In Kendrick Frazier (Ed.), *The hundredth monkey and other paradigms of the paranormal.* Buffalo, NY: Prometheus Books.

Fuyuno, Ichiko. (2006). Brain craze. *Nature, 447,* 18–20.

Gable, Shelly L.; & Haidt, Jonathan. (2005). What (and why) is positive psychology? *Review of General Psychology, 9,* 103–110.

Gabrieli, John D. E. (2001, February 4). Quoted in APA news release: *Personality influences the brain's responses to emotional situations more than thought, according to new research.* Retrieved November 9, 2001, from http://www.apa.org/releases/brain.html

Gabrieli, John D. E. (2008, January 30). Quoted in Cathryn M. Delude, "Culture influences brain function, study shows." *MIT Tech Talk, 52*(14), 4.

Gage, Fred H. (2003, September). Brain, repair yourself. *Scientific American,* 46–53.

Gage, Fred H. (2007, August 19). Quoted in Gretchen Reynolds, "Lobes of steel." *The New York Times.* Retrieved October 9, 2007, from http://www.nytimes.com/2007/08/19/sports/playmagazine/0819play-brain.htm

Gage, Fred H.; Kempermann, Gerd; & Song, Hongjun. (2008). *Adult neurogenesis.* Woodbury, NY: Cold Spring Harbor Laboratory Press.

Gajendran, Raji V.; & Harrison, David A. (2007). The good, the bad, and the unknown about telecommuting: Meta-analysis of psychological mediators and individual consequences. *Journal of Applied Psychology, 92,* 1524–1541.

Galanter, Eugene. (1962). Contemporary psychophysics. In Roger Brown, Eugene Galanter, Eckhard H. Hess, & George Mandler (Eds.), *New directions in psychology.* New York: Holt, Rinehart & Winston.

Galati, Dario; Scherer, Klaus B.; & Ricci-Bitti, Pio E. (1997). Voluntary facial expression of emotion: Comparing congenitally blind with normally sighted encoders. *Journal of Personality and Social Psychology, 73,* 1363–1379.

Galati, Dario; Sini, Barbara; Schmidt, Susanne; & Tinti, Carla. (2003). Spontaneous facial expressions in congenitally blind and sighted children aged 8–11. *Journal of Visual Impairment and Blindness, 97,* 418–428.

Galef, Bennett G.; & Whiskin, Elaine E. (1995). Learning socially to eat more of one food than another. *Journal of Comparative Psychology, 109,* 99–101.

Gallese, Vittorio; Fadiga,Luciano; Fogassi, Leonardo; & Rizzolatti, Giacomo. (1996). Action recognition in the premotor cortex. *Brain, 119,* 593–609.

Gallo, Linda C.; & Matthews, Karen A. (2003). Understanding the association between socioeconomic status and physical health: Do negative emotions play a role? *Psychological Bulletin, 129,* 10–51.

Gallup, Andrew C.; & Gallup, Gordon G., Jr. (2007). Yawning as a brain cooling mechanism: Nasal breathing and forehead cooling diminish the incidence of contagious yawning. *Evolutionary Psychology, 5,* 92–101.

Gangestad, Steven W.; Garver-Apgar, Christine E.; Simpson, Jeffry A.; & Cousins, Alita J. (2007). Changes in women's mate preferences across the ovulatory cycle. *Journal of Personality and Social Psychology, 92,* 151–163.

Gangestad, Steven W.; Haselton, Martie G.; & Buss, David M. (2006). Evolutionary foundations of cultural variation: Evoked culture and mate preferences. *Psychological Inquiry, 17,* 75–95.

Gangwisch, James. (2004, November 16). Lack of sleep may lead to excess weight. Paper presented at the North American Association for the Study of Obesity (NAASO) Annual Scientific Meeting, Las Vegas, NV. Summary retrieved December 9, 2009, from http://goliath.ecnext.com/coms2/gi_0199-2785174/Lack-of-Sleep-May-Lead.html.

Ganis, Giorgio; Thompson, William; & Kosslyn, Stephen. (2004). Brain areas underlying visual mental imagery and visual perception: An fMRI study. *Cognitive Brain Research, 20,* 226–241.

Gansberg, Martin. (1964, March 27). 37 who saw murder didn't call the police. *The New York Times,* pp. 1, 38.

Garb, Howard N.; Lilienfeld, Scott O.; & Wood, James M. (2004). Projective techniques and behavioral assessment. In Stephen N. Haynes & Elaine M. Heiby (Eds.), *Comprehensive handbook of psychological assessment: Behavioral assessment* (Vol 3; pp 453–469). Hoboken, NJ: Wiley.

Garcia, John. (1981). Tilting at the paper mills of academe. *American Psychologist, 36,* 149–158.

Garcia, John. (1997). Foreword by Robert C. Bolles: From mathematics to motivation. In Mark E. Bouton & Michael S. Fanselow (Eds.), *Learning, motivation, and cognition: The functional behaviorism of Robert C. Bolles.* Washington, DC: American Psychological Association.

Garcia, John. (2003). Psychology is not an enclave. In Robert J. Sternberg (Ed.), *Psychologists defying the crowd: Stories of those who battled the establishment and won.* Washington, DC: American Psychological Association.

Garcia, John; Ervin, Frank R.; & Koelling, Robert A. (1966). Learning with prolonged delay of reinforcement. *Psychonomic Science, 5,* 121–122.

Garcia, John; & Gustavson, Andrew R. (1997, January). Carl R. Gustavson (1946–1996): Pioneering wildlife psychologist. *APS Observer, 10*(1), 34–35.

Garcia, John; & Koelling, Robert A. (1966). Relation of cue to consequence in avoidance learning. *Psychonomic Science, 4,* 123–124.

Garcia-Palacios, Azucena; Hoffman, Hunter G.; Carlin, Albert; Furness, Thomas A., III; & Botella, Cristina. (2002). Virtual reality in the treatment of spider phobia: A controlled study. *Behavior Research and Therapy, 40,* 983–993.

Garcia-Palacios, Azucena; Hoffman, Hunter G.; See, Sheer Kong; Tsai, Amy; & Botella, Cristina. (2001). Redefining therapeutic success with virtual reality exposure therapy. *CyberPsychology and Behavior, 4,* 341–348.

Gardner, Howard. (1985). *Frames of mind: The theory of multiple intelligences.* New York: Basic Books.

Gardner, Howard. (1993). *Frames of mind: The theory of multiple intelligences* (2nd ed.). New York: Basic Books.

Gardner, Howard. (1995). Cracking open the IQ box. In Steven Fraser (Ed.), *The bell curve wars: Race, intelligence, and the future of America.* New York: Basic Books.

Gardner, Howard. (1998a). Are there additional intelligences? The case for naturalist, spiritual, and existential intelligences. In J. Kane (Ed.), *Education, information, and transformation.* Upper Saddle River, NJ: Prentice Hall.

Gardner, Howard. (1998b, Winter). A multiplicity of intelligences. Scientific American Presents: *Exploring Intelligence, 9,* 18–23.

Gardner, Howard. (2003). Three distinct meanings of intelligence. In Robert Sternberg, Jacques Lautrey, & Todd I. Lubert (Eds.), *Models of intelligence: International perspectives.* Washington, DC: American Psychological Association.

Gardner, Howard; & Taub, James. (1999, Fall). Debating "multiple intelligences." *Cerebrum, 1,* 13–36.

Garnett, Nelson. (2005). Laws, regulations, and guidelines. In Chana K. Akins, Sangeeta Panicker, & Christopher L. Cunningham (Eds.), *Laboratory animals in research and teaching: Ethics, care, and methods.* Washington, DC: American Psychological Association.

Garrett, Michael T. (2006). When Eagle speaks: Counseling Native Americans. In Courtland C. Lee (Ed.), *Multicultural issues in counseling: New approaches to diversity* (3rd. ed., pp. 25–53). Alexandria, VA: American Counseling Association.

Garrett, Michael T. (2008). Native Americans. In Garrett McAuliffe (Ed.), *Culturally alert counseling: A comprehensive introduction* (pp. 220–254). Thousand Oaks, CA: Sage.

Garry, Maryanne; & Gerrie, Matthew P. (2005). When photographs create false memories. *Current Directions in Psychological Science, 14,* 321–325.

Garry, Maryanne; & Hayne, Harlene (Eds.). (2007). *Do justice and let the sky fall: Elizabeth Loftus and her contributions to science, law, and academic freedom.* Mahwah, NJ: Erlbaum.

Garry, Maryanne; & Polaschek, Devon L. L. (2000). Imagination and memory. *Current Directions in Psychological Science, 9,* 6–10.

Garry, Maryanne; Strange, Deryn; Bernstein, Daniel M.; & Kinzett, Toni. (2007). Photographs can distort memory for the news. *Applied Cognitive Psychology, 21,* 995–1004.

Gartstein, Maria A.; Slobodskaya, Helena R.; & Kinsht, Irina A. (2003). Cross-cultural differences in temperament in the first year of life: United States of America (US) and Russia. *International Journal of Behavioral Development, 27,* 316–328.

Gatchel, Robert J.; Peng, Yuan Bo; Peters, Madelon L.; Fuchs, Perry N.; Turk, Dennis N. (2007). The biopsychosocial approach to chronic pain: Scientific advances and future directions. *Psychological Bulletin, 133,* 581–624.

Gaudiano, Brandon A. (2008). Cognitive-behavioural therapies: Achievements and challenges. *Evidence-Based Mental Health, 11,* 5–7.

Gay, Peter (Ed.). (1989). *The Freud reader.* New York: Norton.

Gay, Peter. (1999, March 29). Psychoanalyst: Sigmund Freud. *Time 100 Special Issue: Scientists and Thinkers of the 20th Century, 153*(12), 66–69.

Gay, Peter. (2006). *Freud: A life for our time.* New York: Norton.

Gazdag, Gabor; Mann, Stephan C.; Ungvari, Gabor S.; & Caroff, Stanley N. (2009). Clinical evidence for the efficacy of electroconvulsive therapy in the treatment of catatonia and psychoses. In Conrad M. Swartz (Ed.), *Electroconvulsive and neuromodulation therapies* (pp. 124–148). New York: Cambridge University Press.

Gazzaniga, Michael S. (1995). Consciousness and the cerebral hemispheres. In Michael S. Gazzaniga (Ed.), *The cognitive neurosciences.* Cambridge, MA: MIT Press.

Gazzaniga, Michael S. (2005). Forty-five years of split-brain research and still going strong. *Nature Reviews Neuroscience, 6,* 653–659.

Ge, Xiaojia; Conger, Rand D.; & Elder, Glen H., Jr. (2001). The relation between puberty and psychological stress in adolescent boys. *Journal of Research on Adolescence, 11,* 49–70.

Ge, Xiaojia; Kim, Irene J.; Brody, Gene H.; Conger, Rand D.; Simons, Ronald L.; Gibbons, Frederick X.; & Cutrona, Carolyn E. (2003). It's about timing and change: Pubertal transition effects on symptoms of major depression among African American youths. *Developmental Psychology, 39,* 430–439.

Gear, Robert W.; Miaskowski, Christine; Gordon, N. C.; Paul, S. M.; Heller, P. H.; & Levine, Jon D. (1996). Kappa-opioids produce significantly greater analgesia in women than in men. *Nature Medicine, 2,* 1248–1250.

Gee, Travis; Allen, Kelly; & Powell, Russell A. (2003). Questioning premorbid dissociative symptomatology in dissociative identity disorder: Comment on Gleaves, Hernandez, and Warner (1999). *Professional Psychology: Research and Practice, 34,* 114–116.

Geldard, Frank A. (1972). *The human senses* (2nd ed.). New York: Wiley.

Gelman, Rochel; & Gallistel, C. R. (2004). Language and the origin of numerical concepts. *Science, 306,* 441–443.

Gendolla, Guido H. E. (2000). On the impact of mood on behavior: An integrative theory and a review. *Review of General Psychology, 4,* 378–408.

Gentilucci, Maurizio; & Dalla Volta, Riccardo. (2007). The motor system and the relationships between speech and gesture. *Gesture, 7,* 159–177.

George, Bill. (2006, October 30). The master gives it back. *U.S. News & World Report.*

Gerard, Harold B.; Wilhelmy, Roland A.; & Conolley, Edward S. (1968). Conformity and group size. *Journal of Personality and Social Psychology, 8,* 79–82.

Gerbner, George. (1993). Images that hurt: Mental illness in the mass media. *Journal of the California Alliance for the Mentally Ill, 4*(1), 17–20.

Gerbner, George. (1998). Images of mental illness in the mass media. *Media Development, 2.* Retrieved December 9, 2009, from http://www.waccglobal.org/en/19982-communication-and-disability/885-Images-of-mental-illness-in-the-mass-media—.html

Gernsbacher, Morton Ann. (2004). Language is more than speech: A case study. *Journal of Developmental and Learning Disorders, 8,* 81–98.

Gernsbacher, Morton Ann. (2007a). Neural diversity. *APS Observer, 20*(3), 5, 15.

Gernsbacher, Morton Ann. (2007b). The true meaning of research participation. *APS Observer, 20.*

Gernsbacher, Morton Ann; Sauer, Eve A.; Geye, Heather M.; Schweigert, Emily K.; & Goldsmith, H. Hill. (2008). Infant and toddler oral- and manual-motor skills predict later speech fluency in autism. *Journal of Child Psychology and Psychiatry, 49,* 43–50.

Gerrie, Matthew P.; Garry, Maryanne; & Loftus, Elizabeth F. (2004). False memories. In Neil Brewer & Kip Williams (Eds.), *Psychology and law: An empirical perspective.* New York: Guilford Press.

Gershoff, Elizabeth Thompson. (2002). Corporal punishment by parents and associated child behavior and experiences: A meta-analytic and theoretical review. *Psychological Bulletin, 128,* 539–579.

Gerstner, Charlotte R.; & Day, David V. (1997, December). Meta-analytic review of leader-member exchange theory: Correlates and construct issues. *Journal of Applied Psychology, 82,* 827–844.

Getka, Eric J.; & Glass, Carol R. (1992). Behavioral and cognitive-behavioral approaches to the reduction of dental anxiety. *Behavior Therapy, 23,* 433–448.

Gewirtz, Jonathan C.; & Davis, Michael. (2000). Using Pavlovian higher-order conditioning paradigms to investigate the neural substrates of emotional learning and memory. *Learning & Memory, 7,* 257–266.

Gibbons, Mary Beth Connolly; Crits-Christoph, Paul; & Hearon, Bridget. (2008). The empirical status of psychodynamic therapies. *Annual Review of Clinical Psychology, 4,* 93–108.

Gibbs, John C. (2003). *Moral development and reality: Beyond the theories of Kohlberg and Hoffman.* Thousand Oaks, CA: Sage.

Gibbs, Marie E.; Hutchinson, Dana; & Hertz, Leif. (2008). Astrocytic involvement in learning and memory consolidation. *Neuroscience & Biobehavioral Reviews, 32*(5), 927–944.

Giedd, Jay N. (2009, January/February). The teen brain: Primed to learn, primed to take risks. *Cerebrum.* Retrieved April 13, 2009, from http://www.dana.org/news/cerebrum/detail.aspx?id=19620

Giedd, Jay N.; Blumenthal, Jonathan; Jeffries, Neal O.; Castellanos, F. X.; Liu, Hong; Rapoport, Judith L.; & others. (1999). Brain development during childhood and adolescence: A longitudinal MRI study. *Nature Neuroscience, 2,* 861–863.

Gieser, Marlon T. (1993). The first behavior therapist as I knew her. *Journal of Behavior Therapy and Experimental Psychiatry, 24,* 321–324.

Gigerenzer, Gerd. (2004). Dread risk, September 11, and fatal traffic accidents. *Psychological Sciences, 15,* 286–287.

Gilbert, Lucia Albino. (1994). Current perspectives on dual-career families. *Current Directions in Psychological Science, 3,* 101–105.

Gillham, Jane E.; Shatte, Andrew J.; Reivich, Karen J.; & Seligman, Martin E. P. (2001). Optimism, pessimism, and explanatory style. In Edward C. Chang (Ed.), *Optimism and pessimism: Implications for theory, research, and practice.* Washington, DC: American Psychological Association.

Gilligan, Carol A. (1982). *In a different voice: Psychological theory and women's development.* Cambridge, MA: Harvard University Press.

Gilligan, Carol A.; & Attanucci, Jane. (1988). Two moral orientations: Gender differences and similarities. In Carol A. Gilligan, Janie Victoria Ward, & Jill Maclean Taylor (Eds.), *Mapping the moral domain: A contribution of women's thinking to psychological theory and education.* Cambridge, MA: Harvard University Press.

Gilman, Sander L. (2001). Images in psychiatry: Karen Horney, M.D., 1885–1952. *American Journal of Psychiatry, 158,* 1205.

Gilmore, John H.; Lin, Weili; Prastawa, Marcel W.; Looney, Christopher B.; Vetsa, Sampath K.; Knickmeyer, Rebecca C.; Evans, Dianne D.; Smith, J. Keith; Hamer, Robert M.; Lieberman, Jeffrey A.; & Gerig, Guido. (2007). Regional gray matter growth, sexual dimorphism, and cerebral asymmetry in the neonatal brain. *Journal of Neuroscience, 27,* 1255–1260.

Gilovich, Thomas. (1997, March/April). Some systematic biases of everyday judgment. *Skeptical Inquirer, 21,* 31–35.

Gladwell, Malcolm. (2004, September 20). Annals of psychology: Personality plus. *The New Yorker,* 42–48.

Glaser, Ronald; & Kiecolt-Glaser, Janice K. (2005). Stress-induced immune dysfunction: Implications for health. *Nature Reviews Immunology, 5,* 243–250.

Glass, Richard M. (2001). Electro convulsive therapy: Time to bring it out of the shadows. *Journal of the American Medical Association, 285,* 1346–1348.

Gleaves, David H. (1996). The sociocognitive model of dissociative identity disorder: A reexamination of the evidence. *Psychological Bulletin, 120,* 42–59.

Gleaves, David H.; Hernandez, Elsa; & Warner, Mark S. (2003). The etiology of dissociative identity disorder. Reply to Gee, Allen, and Powell (2003). *Professional Psychology: Research and Practice, 34,* 116–118.

Gleaves, David H.; Smith, Steven M.; Butler, Lisa D.; & Spiegel, David. (2004). False and recovered memories in the laboratory and clinic: A review of experimental and clinical evidence. *Clinical Psychology: Science and Practice, 11,* 3–28.

Gleitman, Henry. (1991). Edward Chace Tolman: A life of scientific and social purpose. In Gregory A. Kimble, Michael Wertheimer, & Charlotte White (Eds.), *Portraits of pioneers in psychology.* Washington, DC: American Psychological Association/Hillsdale, NJ: Erlbaum.

Glucksman, Myron L.; & Kramer, Milton. (2004). Using dreams to assess clinical change during treatment. *Journal of the American Academy of Psychoanalysis and Dynamic Psychiatry, 32,* 345–358.

Glynn, Laura M.; Christenfeld, Nicholas; & Gerin, William. (1999). Gender, social support, and cardiovascular responses to stress. *Psychosomatic Medicine, 61,* 234–242.

Gogtay, Nitin; Giedd, Jay N.; Lusk, Leslie; Hayashi, Kiraless M.; Rapoport, Judith L.; Thompson, Paul M.; & others. (2004, May 25). Dynamic mapping of human cortical development during childhood through early adulthood. *Proceedings of the National Academy of Sciences, 101,* 8174–8179. Retrieved November 30, 2004, from http://www.pnas.org/cgi/reprint/101/21/8174

Gold, Paul E.; Cahill, Larry; & Wenk, Gary L. (2002). Gingko biloba: A cognitive enhancer? *Psychological Science in the Public Interest, 3,* 2–11.

Goldenberg, Herbert; & Goldenberg, Irene. (2005). Family therapy. In Raymond J. Corsini & Danny Wedding (Eds.), *Current psychotherapies* (7th ed., instr. ed., pp. 372–404). Belmont, CA: Thomson Brooks/Cole Publishing.

Goldinger, Stephen D.; Kleider, Heather M.; Azuma, Tamiko; & Beike, Denise R. (2003). "Blame the victim" under memory load. *Psychological Science, 14*(1), 81–85.

Goldsmith, H. Hill; & Harman, Catherine. (1994). Temperament and attachment; individuals and relationships. *Current Directions in Psychological Science, 3,* 53–61.

Goldstein, Alan J.; de Beurs, Edwin; Chambless, Dianne L.; & Wilson, Kimberly A. (2000). EMDR for panic disorder with agoraphobia: Comparison with waiting list and credible attention-placebo control condition. *Journal of Consulting and Clinical Psychology, 68*, 947–956.

Goldstein, Daniel G.; & Gigerenzer, Gerd. (2002). Models of ecological rationality: The recognition heuristic. *Psychological Review, 109*, 75–90.

Goldstein, Jill. (2007, July 31). Quoted in "Sex differences in brains reflect disease risks." *Science Daily.* Retrieved December 4, 2007, from http://www.sciencedaily.com/releases/2007/07/070727183141.htm

Goldstein, Jill M.; Jerram, Matthew; Poldrack, Russell; Anagnoson, Robert; Breiter, Hans C.; Makris, Nikos; Goodman, Julie M.; Tsuang, Ming T.; & Seidman, Larry J. (2005). Sex differences in prefrontal cortical brain activity during fMRI of auditory verbal working memory. *Neuropsychology, 19*, 509–519.

Gollwitzer, Peter M. (1999). Implementation intentions: Strong effects of simple plans. *American Psychologist, 54*, 493–503.

Gollwitzer, Peter M.; & Brandstätter, Veronika. (1997). Implementation intentions and effective goal pursuit. *Journal of Personality and Social Psychology, 73*, 186–199.

Gollwitzer, Peter M.; Parks-Stamm, Elizabeth J.; Jaudas, Alexander; & Sheeran, Paschal. (2008). Flexible tenacity in goal pursuit. In James Y. Shah & Wendi L. Gardner (Eds.), *Handbook of motivation science.* New York: Guilford Press.

Gollwitzer, Peter M.; & Sheeran, Paschal. (2006). Implementation intentions and goal achievement: A meta-analysis of effects and processes. In Mark P. Zanna (Ed.), *Advances in experimental social psychology,* Vol 38. San Diego, CA: Elsevier Academic Press.

Golomb, Claire; & Galasso, Lisa. (1995). Make-believe and reality: Explorations of the imaginary realm. *Developmental Psychology, 31*, 800–810.

Golombok, Susan; & Tasker, Fiona. (1996). Do parents influence the sexual orientation of their children? Findings from a longitudinal study of lesbian families. *Developmental Psychology, 32*, 3–11.

Gomez, C.; & Rosen, B. (2001, December). The leader-member exchange as a link between managerial trust and employee empowerment. *Group & Organization Management, 26*, 512.

Gonzales, Patricia M.; Blanton, Hart; & Williams, Kevin J. (2002). The effects of stereotype threat and double-minority status on the test performance of Latino women. *Personality and Social Psychology Bulletin, 28*, 659–670.

González-Maeso, Javier; Weisstaub, Noelia V.; Zhou, Mingming; Chan, Pokman; Ivic, Lidija; Aug, Roselind; & others. (2007). Hallucinogens recruit specific cortical 5-HT2A receptor-mediated signaling pathways to affect behavior. *Neuron, 53*, 439–452.

Good, Byron J.; & Hinton, David E. (2009). Introduction: Panic disorder in cross-cultural and historical perspective. In David E. Hinton & Byron J. Good (Eds.), *Culture and panic disorder* (pp. 1–28). Stanford, CA: Stanford University Press.

Good, Catherine; Aronson, Joshua; & Harder, Jayne Ann. (2008). Problems in the pipeline: Stereotype threat and women's achievement in high-level math courses. *Journal of Applied Developmental Psychology, 29*, 17–28.

Goodenough, Florence. (1932). The expression of emotion in a blind-deaf child. *Journal of Abnormal Social Psychology, 27*, 328–333.

Goodman, Elizabeth; & Capitman, John. (2000). Depressive symptoms and cigarette smoking among teens. *Pediatrics, 106*, 748–755.

Goodman, Gail S.; Ghetti, Simona; Quas, Jodi A.; Edelstein, Robin S.; Alexander, Kristen Weede; Redlich, Allison D.; Cordon, Ingrid M.; & Jones, David P. H. (2003). A prospective study of memory for child sexual abuse: New findings relevant to the repressed-memory controversy. *Psychological Science, 14*, 113–118.

Goodwin, Stephanie A.; Fiske, Susan T.; Rosen, Lee D.; & Rosenthal, Alisa M. (2002). The eye of the beholder: Romantic goals and impression biases. *Journal of Experimental Social Psychology, 38*(3), 232–241.

Gopnik, Alison. (1996). The post-Piaget era. *Psychological Science, 7*, 221–225.

Gorassini, Donald R.; & Olson, James M. (1995). Does self-perception change explain the foot-in-the-door effect? *Journal of Personality and Social Psychology, 69*, 91–105.

Gorchoff, Sara M.; John, Oliver P.; & Helson, Ravenna. (2008). Contextualizing change in marital satisfaction during middle age: An 18-year longitudinal study. *Psychological Science, 19*, 1194–1200.

Gordon, Peter. (2004, October 15). Numerical cognition without words: Evidence from Amazonia. *Science, 306*, 496–499.

Goswami, Usha. (2006). Neuroscience and education: From research to practice? *Nature Reviews Neuroscience, 7*, 2–7.

Gottesman, Irving I. (1991). *Schizophrenia genesis: The origins of madness.* New York: Freeman.

Gottfredson, Linda S. (1998, Winter). The general intelligence factor. *Scientific American Presents: Exploring Intelligence, 9*, 24–29.

Gould, Elizabeth. (2007). How widespread is adult neurogenesis in mammals? *Nature Reviews Neuroscience, 8*, 481–488.

Gould, Elizabeth; & Gross, Charles G. (2002). Neurogenesis in adult mammals: Some progress and problems. *Journal of Neuroscience, 22*, 619–623.

Gould, Elizabeth; Tanapat, Patima; McEwen, Bruce S.; Flügge, Gabriele; & Fuchs, Eberhard. (1998, March 17). Proliferation of granule cell precursors in the dentate gyrus of adult monkeys is diminished by stress. *Proceedings of the National Academy of Sciences, USA, 95*, 3168–3171.

Gould, Madelyn S.; Greenberg, Ted; Velting, Drew M.; & Shaffer, David. (2003). Youth suicide risk and preventive interventions: A review of the past 10 years. *Journal of the American Academy of Child & Adolescent Psychiatry, 42*, 386–405.

Gould, Stephen Jay. (1993). *The mismeasure of man* (2nd ed.). New York: Norton.

Gourion, David; Goldberger, Celine; & Leroy, Sophie. (2005). Age at onset of schizophrenia: Interaction between brain-derived neurotrophic factor and dopamine D3 receptor gene variants. *Neuroreport: For Rapid Communication of Neuroscience Research, 16*(12), 1407–1410.

Grabe, Shelly; Ward, L. Monique; & Hyde, Janet Shibley. (2008). The role of the media in body image concerns among women: A meta-analysis of experimental and correlational studies. *Psychological Bulletin, 134*, 460–476.

Graham, John R. (1993). *MMPI-2: Assessing personality and psychopathology* (2nd ed.). New York: Oxford University Press.

Graham, William K.; & Balloun, Joe. (1973). An empirical test of Maslow's need hierarchy theory. *Journal of Humanistic Psychology, 13*, 97–108.

Grant, Bridget F.; Chou, S. Patricia; Goldstein, Risë B.; Huang, Boji; Stinson, Frederick S.; Saha, Tulshi D.; Smith, Sharon M.; Dawson, Deborah A.; Pulay, Attila J.; Pickering, Roger P.; & Ruan, W. June. (2008, April). Prevalence, correlates, disability, and comorbidity of DSM-IV borderline personality disorder: Results from the Wave 2 National Epidemiologic Survey on Alcohol and Related Conditions. *Journal of Clinical Psychiatry, 69*(4), 533–545.

Grant, Bridget F.; Hasin, Deborah S.; Stinson, Frederick S.; Dawson, Deborah A.; Chou, S. Patricia; Ruan, W. June; & Pickering, Roger P. (2004). Prevalence, correlates, and disability of personality disorders in the United States: Results from the National Epidemiologic Survey on Alcohol and Related Conditions. *Journal of Clinical Psychiatry, 65,* 948–958.

Greasley, Peter. (2000). Handwriting analysis and personality assessment: The creative use of analogy, symbolism, and metaphor. *European Psychologist, 5,* 44–51.

Green, Joseph P. (1999). Hypnosis, context effects, and the recall of early autobiographical memories. *International Journal of Clinical and Experimental Hypnosis, 47,* 284–300.

Green, Joseph P.; Lynn, Steven Jay; & Montgomery, Guy H. (2006). A meta-analysis of gender, smoking cessation, and hypnosis: A brief communication. *International Journal of Clinical and Experimental Hypnosis, 54,* 224–233.

Green, Richard. (1985). Gender identity in childhood and later sexual orientation: Follow-up of 78 males. *American Journal of Psychiatry, 142,* 339–341.

Green, Richard. (1987). *The "sissy boy syndrome" and the development of homosexuality.* New Haven, CT: Yale University Press.

Greenberg, Daniel L.; & Rubin, David C. (2003). The neuropsychology of autobiographical memory. *Cortex, 39,* 687–728.

Greene, Beverly. (2007). How difference makes a difference. In J. Christopher Muran (Ed.), *Dialogues on difference: Studies of diversity in the therapeutic relationship* (pp. 47–63). Washington, DC: American Psychological Association.

Greenfield, Patricia M. (1997). You can't take it with you: Why ability assessments don't cross cultures. *American Psychologist, 52,* 1115–1124.

Greenfield, Patricia M.; Keller, Heidi; Fuligni, Andrew; & Maynard, Ashley. (2003). Cultural pathways through universal development. *Annual Review of Psychology, 54,* 461–490.

Greenleaf, R. K. (1970/2002). *Servant leadership: A journey into the nature of legitimate power and greatness* (25th anniversary ed.). New York: Paulist Press.

Gregory, Richard L. (1968, November). Visual illusions. *Scientific American, 212,* 66–76.

Gregory, Richard L. (2003). Seeing after blindness. *Nature Neuroscience, 6,* 909–910.

Grief, Geoffrey L. (2006). Male friendships: Implications from research for family therapy. *Family Therapy, 33*(1), 1–15.

Griffin, Donald R. (2001). *Animal minds: Beyond cognition to consciousness* (2nd ed.). Chicago: University of Chicago Press.

Grigg-Damberger, Madeleine; Gozal, David; Marcus, Carole L.; Quan, Stuart F.; Rosen, Carol L.; Chervin, Ronald D.; & others. (2007). Visual scoring of sleep and arousal in infants and children. *Journal of Clinical Sleep Medicine, 3,* 201–240.

Grimes, Tom; Anderson, James A.; & Bergen, Lori. (2008). *Media violence and aggression: Science and ideology.* Los Angeles: Sage.

Grön, Georg; Wunderlich, Arthur P.; Spitzer, Manfred; Tomczak, Reinhard; & Riepe, Matthias W. (2000). Brain activation during human navigation: Gender-different neural networks as substrate of performance. *Nature Neuroscience, 3,* 404–408.

Gross, Charles G. (2000). Neurogenesis in the adult brain: Death of a dogma. *Nature Reviews Neuroscience, 1,* 67–73.

Gross, James J. (2007). The cultural regulation of emotions. In James J. Gross (Ed.), *Handbook of emotion regulation* (pp. 486–503). New York: Guilford Press.

Grossman, Karin; Grossman, Klaus E.; Fremmer-Bombik, Elisabeth; Kindler, Heinz; Scheuerer-Englisch, Hermann; & Zimmermann, Peter. (2002). The uniqueness of the child–father attachment relationship: Fathers' sensitive and challenging play as a pivotal variable in a 16-year longitudinal study. *Social Development, 11,* 307–331.

Grossman, Randi Priluck; & Till, Brian D. (1998). The persistence of classically conditioned brand attitudes. *Journal of Advertising, 27,* 23–31.

Grotevant, Harold D. (1987). Toward a process model of identity formation. *Journal of Adolescent Research, 2,* 203–222.

Grotevant, Harold D. (1992). Assigned and chosen identity components: A process perspective on their integration. In Gerald R. Adams, Thomas P. Gullotta, & Raymond Montemayor (Eds.), *Adolescent identity formation.* Newbury Park, CA: Sage.

Grünbaum, Adolf. (2006). Is Sigmund Freud's psychoanalytic edifice relevant to the 21st century? *Psychoanalytic Psychology, 23,* 257–284.

Grünbaum, Adolf. (2007). The reception of my Freud-critique in the psychoanalytic literature. *Psychoanalytic Psychology, 24,* 545–576.

Grunstein, Ronald. (2005). Continuous positive airway pressure treatment for obstructive sleep apnea-hypopnea syndrome. In Meir H. Kryger, Thomas Roth, & William C. Dement (Eds.), *Principles and practice of sleep medicine* (4th ed.). Philadelphia: Elsevier Saunders.

Grussu, Pietro; Quatraro, Rosa M.; & Nasta, Maria T. (2005). Profile of mood states and parental attitudes in motherhood: Comparing women with planned and unplanned pregnancies. *Birth: Issues in Perinatal Care, 2,* 107–114.

Grutzendler, Jaime; Kasthuri, Narayanan; & Gan, Wen-Biao. (2002). Long-term dendritic spine stability in the adult cortex. *Nature, 420,* 812–816.

Guehl, Dominique; Benazzouz, Abdelhamid; Aouizerate, Bruno; Cuny, Emmanuel; Rotge, Jean-Yves; Rougier, Alain; Tignol, Jean; Bioulac, Bernard; & Burbaud, Pierre. (2008, March). Neuronal correlates of obsessions in the caudate nucleus. *Biological Psychiatry, 63*(6), 557–562.

Gunderson, John G.; & Lyons-Ruth, Karlen. (2008). BPD's interpersonal hypersensitivity phenotype: A gene-environment-developmental model. *Journal of Personality Disorder, 22*(1), 22–41.

Gunnar, Megan; & Quevedo, Karina. (2007). The neurobiology of stress and development. *Annual Review of Psychology, 58,* 145–173.

Gur, Ruben C.; Gunning-Dixon, Faith; Bilker, Warren B.; & Gur, Raquel E. (2002). Sex differences in temporo-limbic and frontal brain volumes of healthy adults. *Cerebral Cortex, 12,* 998–1003.

Gur, Ruben C.; Turetsky, Bruce I.; Matsui, Mie; Yan, Michelle; Bilker, Warren; Hughett, Paul; & Gur, Raquel E. (1999). Sex differences in brain gray and white matter in healthy young adults: Correlations with cognitive performance. *Journal of Neuroscience, 19,* 4065–4072.

Gusnard, Debra A. (2005, December). Being a self: Considerations from functional imaging. *Consciousness and Cognition,* 14(4) [Special issue: The brain and its self], 679–697.

Gustavson, Carl R.; Kelly, Daniel J.; Sweeney, Michael; & Garcia, John. (1976). Prey-lithium aversions: I. Coyotes and wolves. *Behavioral Biology, 17,* 61–72.

Guthrie, Robert V. (2000). Francis Cecil Sumner: The first African American pioneer in psychology. In Gregory A. Kimble & Michael Wertheimer (Eds.), *Portraits of pioneers in psychology* (Vol. 4, pp. 180–193). Washington, DC: American Psychological Association.

Guthrie, Robert V. (2004). *Even the rat was white: A historical view of psychology.* Upper Saddle River, NJ: Pearson Education.

Gyatso, Tenzin. (2003, April 26). The monk in the lab. *The New York Times,* p. A19. Retrieved April 26, 2003, from http://www.nytimes.com/2003/04/26/opinion/26LAMA.html

Haaga, David A. F.; & Davison, Gerald C. (1991). Cognitive change methods. In Frederick H. Kanfer & Arnold P. Goldstein (Eds.), *Helping people change: A textbook of methods* (4th ed.). New York: Pergamon Press.

Habermas, Tilmann; & Bluck, Susan. (2000). Getting a life: The emergence of the life story in adolescence. *Psychological Bulletin, 126,* 748–769.

Haddock, Geoffrey; Zanna, Mark P.; & Esses, Victoria M. (1993). Assessing the structure of prejudicial attitudes: The case of attitudes toward homosexuals. *Journal of Personality and Social Psychology, 65,* 1105–1118.

Haidt, Jonathan. (2007). The new synthesis in moral psychology. *Science, 316,* 998–1002.

Haidt, Jonathan; Koller, Silvia Helena; & Dias, Maria G. (1993). Affect, culture, and morality, or is it wrong to eat your dog? *Journal of Personality and Social Psychology, 65,* 613–628.

Halford, Graeme S. (2002). Information-processing models of cognitive development. In Usha Goswami (Ed.), *Blackwell handbook of childhood cognitive development.* Malden, MA: Blackwell.

Hall, Christine C. Iijima. (1997). Cultural malpractice: The growing obsolescence of psychology with the changing U.S. population. *American Psychologist, 52,* 642–651.

Hall, Judith A.; & Matsumoto, David. (2004). Gender differences in judgments of multiple emotions from facial expressions. *Emotion, 4,* 201–206.

Halliday, Gordon. (1995). Treating nightmares in children. In Charles E. Schaefer (Ed.), *Clinical handbook of sleep disorders in children.* Northvale, NJ: Aronson.

Halpern, Diane F. (2007). The nature and nurture of critical thinking. In Robert J. Sternberg, Henry L. Roediger III, & Diane F. Halpern (Eds.), *Critical thinking in psychology.* New York: Cambridge University Press.

Halpern, Diane F.; Benbow, Camilla P.; Geary, David C.; Gur, Ruben C.; Hyde, Janet Shibley; & Gernsbacher, Morton Ann. (2007). The science of sex differences in science and mathematics. *Psychological Science in the Public Interest, 8,* 1–51.

Halpern, John H.; Sherwood, Andrea R.; Hudson, James I.; Yurgelun-Todd, Deborah; & Pope, Harrison G. (2005). Psychological and cognitive effects of long-term peyote use among Native Americans. *Biological Psychiatry, 58,* 624–631.

Hamilton, Mykol C. (1988). Using masculine generics: Does generic he increase male bias in the user's imagery? *Sex Roles, 19,* 785–799.

Hamilton, Mykol C. (1991, September). Masculine bias in the attribution of personhood: People = male, male = people. *Psychology of Women Quarterly, 15*(3), 393–402.

Hamilton, Nancy A.; Catley, Delwyn; & Karlson, Cynthia. (2007, May). Sleep and the affective response to stress and pain. *Health Psychology, 26*(3), 288–295.

Hammen, Constance. (2005). Stress and depression. *Annual Review of Clinical Psychology, 1,* 293–319.

Hammen, Constance; & Watkins, Edward. (2008). *Depression* (2nd ed.). New York: Psychology Press.

Haney, Craig; Banks, Curtis; & Zimbardo, Philip. (1973). Interpersonal dynamics in a simulated prison. *International Journal of Criminology and Penology, 1,* 69–97.

Harlow, Harry F. (1953a). Learning by Rhesus monkeys on the basis of manipulation-exploration motives. *Science, 117,* 466–467.

Harlow, Harry F. (1953b). Mice, monkeys, men, and motives. *Psychological Review, 60,* 23–32.

Harlow, Harry F. (1953c). Motivation as a factor in new responses. In *Current theory and research in motivation: A symposium.* Lincoln: University of Nebraska Press.

Harris, Ben. (1979). Whatever happened to Little Albert? *American Psychologist, 34,* 151–160.

Harris Interactive. (2007, October 9). Six nation survey finds satisfaction with current job: American workers most likely to feel well-paid and to like their boss. Retrieved from http://www.harrisinteractive.com/news/allnewsbydate.asp?NewsID=1255

Harris, Julie Aitken; Vernon, Philip A.; & Jang, Kerry L. (2007, January). Rated personality and measured intelligence in young twin children. *Personality and Individual Differences, 42*(1), 75–86.

Harter, Susan. (1990). Self and identity development. In S. Shirley Feldman & Glen R. Elliott (Eds.), *At the threshold: The developing adolescent.* Cambridge, MA: Harvard University Press.

Harvey, Megan A.; Sellman, John D.; Porter, Richard J.; & Frampton, Christopher M. (2007). The relationship between non-acute adolescent cannabis use and cognition. *Drug & Alcohol Review, 26,* 309–319.

Harvey, Nigel. (2007, February). Use of heuristics: Insights from forecasting research. *Thinking & Reasoning, 13*(1), 5–24.

Hassin, Ran R.; Ferguson, Melissa, J.; Shidlovski, Daniella; & Gross, Tamar. (2007). Subliminal exposure to national flags affects political thought and behavior. *Proceedings of the National Academy of Sciences, 104,* 19757–19761.

Hatch, Stephani L.; & Dohrenwend, Bruce P. (2007). Distribution of traumatic and other stressful life events by race/ethnicity, gender, SES, and age: A review of the research. *American Journal of Community Psychology, 40,* 313–332.

Hauser, Marc D. (2000). *Wild minds: What animals really think.* New York: Holt.

Hawkins, D. Lynn; Pepler, Debra J.; & Craig, Wendy M. (2001). Naturalistic observations of peer interventions in bullying. *Social Development, 10,* 512–527.

Hawkins, Nicole; Richards, P. Scott; Granley, H. Mac; & Stein, David M. (2004).The impact of exposure to the thin-ideal media image on women. *Eating Disorders: The Journal of Treatment and Prevention, 12,* 35–50

Haydon, Philip G. (2001). Glia: Listening and talking to the synapse. *Nature Reviews Neuroscience, 2,* 185–193.

Heaps, Christopher M.; & Nash, Michael. (2001). Comparing recollective experience in true and false autobiographical memories. *Journal of Experimental Psychology: Learning, Memory, and Cognition, 27,* 920–930.

Hearst, Eliot. (1999). After the puzzle boxes: Thorndike in the 20th century. *Journal of the Experimental Analysis of Behavior, 72,* 441–446.

Hebb, Donald O. (1955). Drives and the C. N. S. (central nervous system). *Psychological Review, 62,* 243–254.

Hedden, Trey; Ketay, Sarah; Aron, Arthur; Markus, Hazel Rose; & Gabrieli, John D. E. (2008). Cultural influences on neural substrates of attentional control. *Psychological Science, 19,* 12–17.

Hedge, Alan; & Yousif, Yousif H. (1992). Effects of urban size, urgency, and cost of helpfulness: A cross-cultural comparison between the United Kingdom and the Sudan. *Journal of Cross-Cultural Psychology, 23,* 107–115.

Heiby, Elaine M.; DeLeon, Patrick H.; & Anderson, Timothy. (2004). A debate on prescription privileges for psychologists. *Professional Psychology: Research and Practice, 35,* 336–344.

Heider, Eleanor Rosch; & Olivier, Donald C. (1972). The structure of the color space in naming and memory for two languages. *Cognitive Psychology, 3,* 337–354.

Heimburg, Richard G.; Turk, Cynthia L.; & Mennin, Douglas S. (2004). *Generalized anxiety disorder: Advances in research and practice.* New York: Guilford Press.

Heine, Steven J.; & Norenzayan, Ara. (2006). Toward a psychological science for a cultural species. *Perspectives on Psychological Science, 1,* 251–269.

Heinrichs, Markus; Baumgartner, Thomas; Kirschbaum, Clemens; & Ehlert, Ulrike. (2003). Social support and oxytocin interact to suppress cortisol and subjective responses to psychosocial stress. *Biological Psychiatry, 54,* 1389–1398.

Heinrichs, R. Walter. (2005). The primacy of cognition in schizophrenia. *American Psychologist, 60,* 229–242.

Helgeson, Vicki S.; Cohen, Sheldon; & Fritz, Heidi L. (1998). Social ties and cancer. In Jimmie C. Holland & William Breitbart (Eds.), *Psycho-oncology* (pp. 99–109). New York: Oxford University Press.

Henderson, Valerie Land; O'Hara, Maureen; Barfield, Gay Leah; & Rogers, Natalie. (2007). Applications beyond the therapeutic context. In Mick Cooper, Maureen O'Hara, Peter F. Schmid, & Gill Wyatt, (Eds.), *The handbook of person-centred psychotherapy and counselling.* New York: Palgrave Macmillan.

Henley, Nancy M. (1989). Molehill or mountain? What we know and don't know about sex bias in language. In Mary Crawford & Margaret Gentry (Eds.), *Gender and thought: Psychological perspectives.* New York: Springer-Verlag.

Henson, Richard J. (2005). What can functional neuroimaging tell the experimental psychologist? *The Quarterly Journal of Experimental Psychology A: Human Experimental Psychology, 58A,* 193–233.

Henzler-Wildman, Katherine; & Kern, Dorthee. (2007). Dynamic personalities of proteins. *Nature, 450,* 964–972.

Heppner, Puncky Paul. (2008). Expanding the conceptualization and measurement of applied problem solving and coping: From stages and dimensions to the almost forgotten cultural context. *American Psychologist, 63,* 805–816.

Herbert, James D.; Lilienfeld, Scott O.; Lohr, Jeffrey M.; Montgomery, Robert W.; O'Donohue, William T.; Rosen, Gerald M.; & Tolin, David F. (2000). Science and pseudoscience in the development of eye movement desensitization and reprocessing: Implications for clinical psychology. *Clinical Psychology Review, 20,* 945–971.

Herbert, Tracy Bennett; & Cohen, Sheldon. (1993). Depression and immunity: A meta-analytic review. *Psychological Bulletin, 113,* 472–486.

Herman, Louis M. (2002). Exploring the cognitive world of the bottlenosed dolphin. In Marc Bekoff, Colin Allen, & Gordon M. Burghardt (Eds.), *The cognitive animal: Empirical and theoretical perspectives on animal cognition.* Cambridge, MA: MIT Press.

Herman, Louis M.; Kuczaj, Stan A., II; & Holder, Mark D. (1993). Responses to anomalous gestural sequences by a language-trained dolphin: Evidence for processing of semantic relations and syntactic information. *Journal of Experimental Psychology: General, 122,* 184–194.

Herman-Giddens, Marcia E.; Wang, Lily; & Koch, Gary. (2001). Secondary sexual characteristics in boys: Estimates from the National Health and Nutrition Examination Survey III, 1988–1994. *Archives of Pediatrics and Adolescent Medicine, 155,* 1022–1028.

Hermans, Hubert J. M. (1996). Voicing the self: From information processing to dialogical interchange. *Psychological Bulletin, 119,* 31–50.

Hersh, Seymour. (2004a, April 30). Torture at Abu Ghraib. *The New Yorker* (Posted online April 30, 2004, print issue of May 10, 2004). Retrieved November 29, 2005, from http://www.newyorker.com/printables/fact/040510fa_fact

Hersh, Seymour. (2004b, May 17). Chain of command. *The New Yorker.* Retrieved December 9, 2009, from http://www.newyorker.com/archive/2004/05/17/040517fa_fact2

Hersh, Seymour. (2005). *Chain of command: The road from 9/11 to Abu Ghraib.* New York: HarperPerennial.

Hertz, Marguerite R. (1992). Rorschach-bound: A 50-year memoir. *Professional Psychology: Research and Practice, 23,* 168–171.

Herzog, Harold A. (2005). Dealing with the controversy of animal research in the classroom and beyond. In Chana K. Akins, Sangeeta Panicker, & Christopher L. Cunningham (Eds.), *Laboratory animals in research and teaching: Ethics, care, and methods.* Washington, DC: American Psychological Association.

Hespos, Susan J.; & Baillargeon, Renée. (2001). Infants' knowledge about occlusion and containment events: A surprising discrepancy. *Psychological Science, 12,* 141–147.

Hespos, Susan J.; & Baillargeon, Renée. (2006). Décalage in infants' knowledge about occlusion and containment events: Converging evidence from action tasks. *Cognition, 99,* B31–B41.

Hess, Ursula; Senecal, Sacha; Kirouac, Gilles; Herrera, Pedro; Philippot, Pierre; & Kleck, Robert E. (2000). Emotional expressivity in men and women: Stereotypes and self-perceptions. *Cognition & Emotion, 14,* 609–642.

Heth, Josephine Todrank; & Somer, Eli. (2002). Characterizing stress tolerance: "Controllability awareness" and its relationship to perceived stress and reported health. *Personality and Individual Differences, 33,* 883–895.

Hettema, Jennifer; Steele, Julie; & Miller, William R. (2005). Motivational interviewing. *Annual Review of Clinical Psychology, 1,* 91–111.

Hetzel, Lisa; & Smith, Annetta. (2001). *The 65 years and over population: Census 2000 brief* (Series C2KBR/01–10). Washington, DC: U.S. Census Bureau. Retrieved February 20, 2002, from http://www.census.gov/prod/2001pubs/c2kbr01–10.pdf

Heyman, Karen. (2003). The enriched environment. *The Scientist, 17*(9), 24–25.

Heymann, Jody. (2007, February). The healthy families act: The importance to Americans' livelihoods, families, and health. Written testimony submitted to the U.S. Senate Committee on Health, Education, Labor, and Pensions. Retrieved September 2009 from http://help.senate.gov/Hearings/2007_02_13/Heymann.pdf.

Hiatt, Kristina D.; & Dishion, Thomas J. (2008). Antisocial personality development. In Theodore P. Beauchaine & Stephen P. Hinshaw (Eds.), *Child and adolescent psychopathology* (pp. 370–404). Hoboken, NJ: Wiley.

Hickok, Gregory; Bellugi, Ursula; & Klima, Edward S. (2001, June). Sign language in the brain. *Scientific American, 184,* 58–65.

Hilgard, Ernest R. (1986a). *Divided consciousness: Multiple controls in human thought and action.* New York: Wiley.

Hilgard, Ernest R. (1986b, January). A study in hypnosis. *Psychology Today, 20,* 23–27.

Hilgard, Ernest R. (1992). Divided consciousness and dissociation. *Consciousness and Cognition, 1,* 16–32.

Hilgard, Ernest R.; Hilgard, Josephine R.; & Barber, Joseph. (1994). *Hypnosis in the relief of pain* (Rev. ed.). New York: Brunner/Mazel.

Hilgard, Ernest R.; & Marquis, D. G. (1940). *Conditioning and learning.* New York: Appleton-Century-Crofts.

Hillman, Charles H.; Erickson, Kirk I.; & Kramer, Arthur F. (2008). Be smart, exercise your heart: Exercise effects on brain and cognition. *Nature Reviews Neuroscience, 9,* 58–65.

Hilton, James L. (1998). Interaction goals and person perception. In John McConnon Darley & Joel Cooper (Eds), *Attribution and social interaction: The legacy of Edward E. Jones.* Washington, DC: American Psychological Association.

Hilton, James L.; & von Hippel, William. (1996). Stereotypes. *Annual Review of Psychology, 47,* 237–271.

Hines, Terence M. (2003). Pseudoscience and the paranormal: A critical examination of the evidence (2nd ed.). Buffalo, NY: Prometheus Books.

Hingson, Ralph; Heeran, Timothy; Zakoc, Ronda C.; Kopstein, Andrea; & Wechsler, Henry. (2002). Magnitude of alcohol-related mortality and morbidity among U.S. college students ages 18–24. *Journal of Studies on Alcohol, 63,* 136–144.

Hinton, Devon E.; & Hinton, Susan D. (2009). Twentieth-century theories of panic in the United States. In Devon E. Hinton & Byron J. Good (Eds.), *Culture and panic disorder* (pp. 113–131). Stanford, CA: Stanford University Press.

Hobfoll, Stevan E.; Lilly, Roy S.; & Jackson, Anita P. (1992). Conservation of social resources and the self. In Hans O. F. Veiel & Urs Baumann (Eds.), *The meaning and measurement of social support.* New York: Hemisphere.

Hobfoll, Stevan E.; & Stephens, Mary Ann Parris. (1990). Social support during extreme stress: Consequences and intervention. In Barbara R. Sarason, Irwin G. Sarason, & Gregory R. Pierce (Eds.), *Social support: An interactional view.* New York: Wiley.

Hobfoll, Stevan E.; & Vaux, Alex. (1993). Social support: Resources and context. In Leo Goldberger & Shlomo Breznitz (Eds.), *Handbook of stress: Theoretical and clinical aspects* (2nd ed.). New York: Free Press.

Hobson, Charles, J.; & Delunas, Linda. (2001). National norms and life-event frequencies for the revised Social Readjustment Rating Scale. *International Journal of Stress Management, 8,* 299–314.

Hobson, Charles J.; Kamen, Joseph; Szostek, Jana; & Nethercut, Carol M. (1998). Stressful life events: A revision and update of the Social Readjustment Rating Scale. *International Journal of Stress Management, 5*(1), 1–23.

Hobson, J. Allan. (1988). *The dreaming brain.* New York: Basic Books.

Hobson, J. Allan. (1995). *Sleep.* New York: Scientific American Library.

Hobson, J. Allan. (1999). *Consciousness.* New York: Scientific American Library.

Hobson, J. Allan. (2001). *The dream drugstore: Chemically altered states of consciousness.* Cambridge, MA: MIT Press.

Hobson, J. Allan. (2004). *Dreaming: An introduction to the science of sleep.* New York: Oxford University Press.

Hobson, J. Allan. (2005, October 27). Sleep is of the brain, by the brain and for the brain. *Nature, 437,* 1254–1264.

Hobson, J. Allan; & McCarley, Robert W. (1977). The brain as a dream state generator: An activation-synthesis hypothesis of the dream process. *American Journal of Psychiatry,134,* 1335–1348.

Hobson, J. Allan; & Stickgold, Robert. (1995).The conscious state paradigm: A neurological approach to waking, sleeping, and dreaming. In Michael S. Gazzaniga (Ed.), *The cognitive neurosciences.* Cambridge, MA: MIT Press.

Hobson, J. Allan; Stickgold, Robert; & Pace-Schott, Edward F. (1998). The neuropsychology of REM sleep dreaming. *NeuroReport, 9*(3), R1–R14.

Hock, Roger R. (2007). Racing against your heart. In Alan Monat, Richard S. Lazarus, & Gretchen Reevy (Eds.), *The Praeger handbook on stress and coping* (Vol. 2, pp. 341–348). Westport, CT: Praeger Publishers/Greenwood.

Hodges, Bert H.; & Geyer, Anne L. (2006). A nonconformist account of the Asch experiments: Values, pragmatics, and moral dilemmas. *Personality and Social Psychology Review, 10*(1), 2–19.

Hodgkinson, Gerard P.; Langan-Fox, Janice; & Sadler-Smith, Eugene. (2008). Intuition: A fundamental bridging construct in the behavioural sciences. *British Journal of Psychology, 99,* 1–27.

Hoffman, John; & Froemke, Susan (Eds.). (2007). *Addiction: Why can't they just stop?* New York: Rodale.

Hoffman, Martin L. (1977). Moral internalization: Current theory and research. In Leonard Berkowitz (Ed.), *Advances in experimental social psychology* (Vol. 10). New York: Academic Press.

Hoffman, Martin L. (1988). Moral development. In Marc H. Bornstein & Michael E. Lamb (Eds.), *Developmental psychology: An advanced textbook.* Hillsdale, NJ: Erlbaum.

Hoffman, Martin L. (1994). Discipline and internalization. *Developmental Psychology, 30,* 26–28.

Hoffmann, Melissa L.; & Powlishta, Kimberly K. (2001, September). Gender segregation in childhood: A test of the interaction style theory. *Journal of Genetic Psychology, 162,*, 298-313.

Hoffstein, Victor. (2005). Snoring and upper airway resistance. In Meir H. Kryger, Thomas Roth, & William C. Dement (Eds.), *Principles and practice of sleep medicine* (4th ed.). Philadelphia: Elsevier Saunders.

Hofmann, Stefan G.; & Otto, Michael W. (2008). *Cognitive behavioral therapy for social anxiety disorder.* New York: Routledge.

Hogan, John D. (2003). G. Stanley Hall: Educator, organizer, and pioneer developmental psychologist. In Gregory A. Kimble & Michael Wertheimer (Eds.), *Portraits of pioneers in psychology* (Vol. 5, pp. 18–36). Washington, DC: American Psychological Association.

Hoier, Sabine. (2003). Father absence and age at menarche: A test of four evolutionary models. *Human Nature, 14,* 209–233.

Holden, Constance. (2003). Future brightening for depression treatments. *Science, 10,* 810–813.

Holden, Ronald R. (2008, January). Underestimating the effects of faking on the validity of self-report personality scales. *Personality and Individual Differences, 44*(1), 311–321.

Hollander, Edwin P.; & Julian, James W. (1969). Contemporary trends in the analysis of the leadership process. *Psychological Bulletin, 71,* 387–397.

Hollinger, Richard C.; & Adams, Amanda. (2007). *2007 National Retail Security Survey.* University of Florida–Gainesville: Author.

Hollon, Steven D.; & Beck, Aaron T. (2004). Behavior therapy with adults. In Michael J. Lambert (Ed.), *Bergin and Garfield's handbook of psychotherapy and behavior change* (5th ed.). New York: Wiley.

Hollon, Steven D.; & Fawcett, Jan. (2007). Combined medication and psychotherapy. In Glen O. Gabbard (Ed.), *Gabbard's treatments of psychiatric disorders* (4th ed., pp. 439–448). Washington, DC: American Psychiatric Publishing.

Holloway, Jennifer Daw. (2004). Louisiana grants psychologists prescriptive authority. *APA Monitor, 35*(6), 20–24.

Holmes, David. (1990). The evidence for repression: An examination of sixty years of research. In Jerome Singer (Ed.), *Repression and dissociation: Implications for personality theory, psychopathology, and health.* Chicago: University of Chicago Press.

Holmes, Thomas H.; & Masuda, Minoru. (1974). Life change and illness susceptibility. In Barbara Snell Dohrenwend & Bruce P. Dohrenwend (Eds.), *Stressful life events: Their nature and effects.* New York: Wiley.

Holmes, Thomas H.; & Rahe, Richard H. (1967). The Social Readjustment Rating Scale. *Journal of Psychosomatic Research, 11,* 213–218.

Holsboer, Florian. (2009). Putative new-generation antidepressants. In Alan F. Schatzberg & Charles B. Nemeroff (Eds.), *The American Psychiatric Publishing textbook of psychopharmacology* (4th ed., pp. 503–529). Washington, DC: American Psychiatric Publishing.

Holyoak, Keith J. (2005). Analogy. In Keith J. Holyoak & Robert G. Morrison (Eds.), *The Cambridge handbook of thinking and reasoning.* New York: Cambridge University Press.

Homer, Bruce D.; Solomon, Todd M.; Moeller, Robert W.; Mascia, Amy; DeRaleau, Lauren; & Halkitis, Perry N. (2008). Methamphetamine abuse and impairment of social functioning: A review of the underlying neurophysiological causes and behavioral implications. *Psychological Bulletin, 134,* 301–310.

Hopkins, William D. (2006). Comparative and familial analysis of handedness in great apes. *Psychological Bulletin, 132,* 538–559.

Hopkins, William D.; & Cantalupo, Claudio. (2005). Individual and setting differences in the hand preferences of chimpanzees (*Pan troglodytes*): A critical analysis and some alternative explanations. *Laterality, 10,* 65–80.

Hopkins, William D.; Russell, Jamie L.; & Cantalupo, Claudio. (2007). Neuroanatomical correlates of handedness for tool use in chimpanzees (*Pan troglodytes*): Implication for theories on the evolution of language. *Psychological Science, 18,* 971–977.

Hopper, Lydia M.; Spiteri, Antoine; Lambeth, Susan P.; Schapiro, Steven J.; Horner, Victoria; & Whiten, Andrew. (2007). Experimental studies of traditions and underlying transmission processes in chimpanzees. *Animal Behaviour, 73,* 1021–1032.

Hoptman, Matthew J.; & Davidson, Richard J. (1994). How and why do the two cerebral hemispheres interact? *Psychological Bulletin, 116,* 195–219.

Horney, Karen. (1926/1967). The flight from womanhood. In Harold Kelman (Ed.), *Feminine psychology.* New York: Norton.

Horney, Karen. (1945/1972). *Our inner conflicts: A constructive theory of neurosis.* New York: Norton.

Horwitz, Allan V. (2002). *Creating mental illness.* Chicago: University of Chicago Press.

Houshmand, Zara; Harringon, Anne; Saron, Clifford; & Davidson, Richard J. (2002). Training the mind: First steps in a cross-cultural collaboration in neuroscientific research. In Richard J. Davidson & Anne Harrington (Eds.), *Visions of compassion: Western scientists and Tibetan Buddhists examine human nature.* New York: Oxford University Press.

Houts, Arthur C. (2002). Discovery, invention, and the expansion of the modern diagnostic and statistical manuals of mental disorders. In Larry E. Beutler & Mary L. Malik (Eds.), *Rethinking the DSM: A psychological perspective.* Washington, DC: American Psychological Association.

Howard, William; & Crano, William D. (1974). Effects of sex, conversation, location, and size of observer group on bystander intervention in a high risk situation. *Sociometry, 37,* 491–507.

Howe, Mark L. (2003). Memories from the cradle. *Current Directions in Psychological Science, 12,* 62–65.

Howell, Michael J.; Schenck, Carlos H.; & Crow, Scott J. (2009). A review of nighttime eating disorders. *Sleep Medicine Reviews, 13,* 23–34.

Hoyle, Rick H.; & Sherrill, Michelle R. (2006, December). Future orientation in the self-system: Possible selves, self-regulation, and behavior. *Journal of Personality, 74*(6), 1673–1696.

Huang, Wei; Kutner, Nancy; & Bliwise, Donald L. (2009). A systematic review of the effects of acupuncture in treating insomnia. *Sleep Medicine Reviews, 13,* 73–104.

Hubel, David H. (1995). *Eye, brain, and vision.* New York: Scientific American Library.

Hubel, David H.; & Wiesel, Torsten N. (2005). *Brain and visual perception: The story of a 25-year collaboration.* New York: Oxford University Press.

Huesmann, L. Rowell; Moise-Titus, Jessica; Podolski, Cheryl-Lynn; & Eron, Leonard D. (2003). Longitudinal relations between children's exposure to TV violence and their aggressive and violent behavior in young adulthood: 1977–1992. *Developmental Psychology, 39,* 201–221.

Huesmann, L. Rowell; & Taylor, Laramie D. (2006). The role of media violence in violent behavior. *Annual Review of Public Health, 27,* 393–415.

Hughes, John R. (2007). A review of sleepwalking (somnambulism): The enigma of neurophysiology and polysomnography with differential diagnosis of complex partial seizures. *Epilepsy & Behavior, 11,* 483–491.

Hull, Clark L. (1943). *Principles of behavior: An introduction to behavior theory.* New York: Appleton-Century-Crofts.

Hull, Clark L. (1952). *A behavior system: An introduction to behavior theory concerning the individual organism.* New Haven, CT: Yale University Press.

Human Genome Project. (2008). *Genomics and its impact on science and society: A primer.* Washington, DC: U.S. Department of Energy, Office of Science. Retrieved October 4, 2008, from http://www.ornl.gov/sci/techresources/Human_Genome/publicat/primer2001/primer11.pdf

Hunsley, John; Lee, Catherine M.; & Wood, James M. (2003). Controversial and questionable assessment techniques. In Scott O. Lilienfeld, Steven Jay Lynn, & Jeffrey M. Lohr (Eds.)., *Science and pseudoscience in clinical psychology.* New York: Guilford Press.

Hunt, Stephen P.; & Mantyh, Patrick W. (2001). The molecular dynamics of pain control. *Nature Reviews Neuroscience, 2,* 83–91.

Huntjens, Rafaele J. C.; Postma, Albert; Peters, Madelon L.; Woertman, Liesbeth; & van der Hart, Onno. (2003). Interidentity amnesia for neutral, episodic information in dissociative identity disorder. *Journal of Abnormal Psychology, 112,* 290–297.

Hurovitz, Craig S.; Dunn, Sarah; Domhoff, G. William; & Fiss, Harry. (1999). The dreams of blind men and women: A replication and extension of previous findings. *Dreaming,* 9, 183–193.

Huston, Ted L.; Ruggiero, Mary; & Conner, Ross. (1981, March). Bystander intervention into crime: A study based on naturally-occurring episodes. *Social Psychology Quarterly, 44*(1), 14–23.

Hyde, Janet Shibley. (2005). The genetics of sexual orientation. In Janet Shibley Hyde (Ed.), *Biological substrates of human sexuality.* Washington, DC: American Psychological Association.

Hyde, Janet Shibley. (2007, October). New directions in the study of gender similarities and differences. *Current Directions in Psychological Science, 16*(5), 259–263.

Hygge, Staffan; Evans, Gary W.; & Bullinger, Monika. (2002). A prospective study of some effects of airport noise on cognitive performance in schoolchildren. *Psychological Science, 13,* 469–474.

Hyman, Ira E., Jr.; & Pentland, Joel. (1996). The role of mental imagery in the creation of false childhood memories. *Journal of Memory & Language, 35,* 101–117.

Hyman, Ray. (1994). Anomaly or artifact? Comments on Bem and Honorton. *Psychological Bulletin, 115,* 19–24.

Hyman, Ray. (2007). Evaluating parapsychological claims. In Robert J. Sternberg, Henry L. Roediger III, & Diane F. Halpern (Eds.), *Critical thinking in psychology.* New York: Cambridge University Press.

Hyman, Steven E. (2005). Neurotransmitters. *Current Biology, 15,* R154–R158.

Hyman, Steven E. (2009). How adversity gets under the skin. *Nature Neuroscience 12,* 241–243.

Iacoboni, Marco. (2008). *Mirroring people: The new science of how we connect with others.* New York: Farrar, Straus and Giroux.

Iacoboni, Marco. (2009). Imitation, empathy, and mirror neurons. *Annual Review of Psychology, 60,* 653–670.

Iacoboni, Marco; & Dapretto, Mirella. (2006). The mirror neuron system and the consequences of its dysfunction. *Nature Reviews Neuroscience, 7,* 942–951.

Iacono, Diego. (2009, July 8). Quoted in Hadley Leggett, "Nun brains show language skills predict future Alzheimer's risk." *Wired* Online Magazine. Accessed on October 29, 2009 at: http://www.wired.com/wiredscience/2009/07/nunstudy/

Iacono, Diego; Markesbery, W. R.; Gross, M.; Pletnikova, Olga; Rudow, Gay; Zandi, P.; & Troncoso, Juan C. (2009). The Nun Study: Clinically silent AD, neuronal hypertrophy, and linguistic skills in early life. *Neurology, 73,* 665–673.

Idler, Ellen L.; & Kasl, Stanislav. (1991). Health perceptions and survival: Do global evaluations of health status really predict mortality? *Journal of Gerontology, 46,* S55–S65.

Ijzerman, Hans; & Van Prooijen, Jan-Willem. (2008, June). Just world and the emotional defense of self. *Social Psychology, 39*(2), 117–120.

Ikeda, Hiroshi. (2001). Buraku students and cultural identity: The case of a Japanese minority. In Nobuo Shimahara, Ivan Z. Holowinsky, & Saundra Tomlinson-Clarke (Eds.), *Ethnicity, race, and nationality in education: A global perspective.* Mahwah, NJ: Erlbaum.

Imel, Zac E.; Malterer, Melanie B.; McKay, Kevin M.; & Wampold, Bruce E. (2008). A meta-analysis of psychotherapy and medication in unipolar depression and dysthymia. *Journal of Affective Disorders, 110,* 197–206.

Ingram, Rick E.; Trenary, Lucy; Odom, Mica; Berry, Leandra; & Nelson, Tyler. (2007). Cognitive, affective and social mechanisms in depression risk: Cognition, hostility, and coping style. *Cognition & Emotion, 21,* 78–94.

Insel, Thomas R.; & Lehner, Thomas. (2007). A new era in psychiatric genetics? *Biological Psychiatry, 61*(9), 1017–1018.

Inui, Akio. (2001). Ghrelin: An orexigenic and somatotrophic signal from the stomach. *Nature Reviews Neuroscience, 2,* 1–9.

Irwin, Charles E., Jr. (2005). Editorial: Pubertal timing: Is there any new news? *Journal of Adolescent Health, 37,* 343–344.

Irwin, Michael R.; & Miller, Andrew H. (2007, May). Depressive disorders and immunity: 20 years of progress and discovery. *Brain, Behavior, and Immunity, 21*(4), 374–383.

Isabella, Russell A.; Belsky, Jay; & von Eye, Alexander. (1989). Origins of infant-mother attachment: An examination of interactional synchrony during the infant's first year. *Developmental Psychology, 25,* 12–21.

Ishai, Alumit. (2007). Sex, beauty and the orbitofrontal cortex. *International Journal of Psychophysiology, 63,* 181–185.

Iversen, Iver H. (1992). Skinner's early research: From reflexology to operant conditioning. *American Psychologist, 47,* 1318–1328.

Iwamasa, Gayle Y. (1997). Asian Americans. In Steven Friedman (Ed.), *Cultural issues in the treatment of anxiety.* New York: Guilford Press.

Iwanaga, Makoto; Yokoyama, Hiroshi; & Seiwa, Hidetoshi. (2004). Coping availability and stress reduction for optimistic and pessimistic individuals. *Personality and Individual Differences, 36,* 11–22.

Izard, Carroll E. (1990a). Facial expressions and the regulation of emotions. *Journal of Personality and Social Psychology, 58,* 487–498.

Izard, Carroll E. (1990b). The substrates and functions of emotion feelings: William James and current emotion theories. *Personality and Social Psychology Bulletin, 16,* 626–635.

Izard, Carroll E. (2007). Basic emotions, natural kinds, emotion schemas, and a new paradigm. *Perspectives on Psychological Science, 2,* 260–280.

Jackson, Benita; Sellers, Robert M.; & Peterson, Christopher. (2002). Pessimistic explanatory style moderates the effect of stress on physical illness. *Personality and Individual Differences, 32,* 567–573.

Jacob, Suma; Kinnunen, Leann H.; Metz, John; Cooper, Malcolm; & McClintock, Martha K. (2001). Sustained human chemosignal unconsciously alters brain function. *NeuroReport, 12,* 2391–2394.

Jacobs, Barry L. (2004). Depression: The brain finally gets into the act. *Current Directions in Psychological Science, 13,* 103–106.

Jaffee, Sara; & Hyde, Janet Shibley. (2000). Gender differences in moral orientation: A meta-analysis. *Psychological Bulletin, 126,* 703–726.

James, Larry C. (2008). *Fixing hell: An Army psychologist confronts Abu Ghraib.* New York: Grand Central Publishing.

James, Lori E.; & Burke, Deborah M. (2000). Phonological priming effects on word retrieval and tip-of-the-tongue experiences in young and older adults. *Journal of Experimental Psychology: Learning, Memory, and Cognition, 26,* 1378–1391.

James, William. (1884). What is an emotion? *Mind, 9,* 188–205.

James, William. (1890). *Principles of psychology.* New York: Holt.

James, William. (1894). The physical basis of emotion. *Psychological Review, 1,* 516–529. (Reprinted in the 1994 Centennial Issue of *Psychological Review, 101,* 205–210)

James, William. (1899/1958). *Talks to teachers.* New York: Norton.

James, William. (1902). *The varieties of religious experience: A study in human nature.* New York: Longmans, Green.

James, William. (1907, March 1). The energies of men. *Science, 25,* No. 635, 321–332. Accessed 9-27-2009 at: http://psychclassics.yorku.ca/James/energies.htm#f1

Jameson, Dorothea; & Hurvich, Leo M. (1989). Essay concerning color constancy. *Annual Review of Psychology, 40,* 1–22.

Jamil, Hikmet; Nassar-McMillan, Sylvia C.; & Lambert, Richard G. (2007, April). Immigration and attendant psychological sequelae: A comparison of three waves of Iraqi immigrants. *American Journal of Orthopsychiatry, 77*(2), 199–205.

Jamison, Kay Redfield. (1993). *Touched with fire: Manic-depressive illness and the artistic temperament.* New York: Free Press.

Jamison, Kay Redfield. (2000). *Night falls fast: Understanding suicide.* New York: Vintage.

Janisse, Michel Pierre; & Dyck, Dennis G. (1988). The Type A behavior pattern and coronary heart disease: Physiological and psychological dimensions. In Michel Pierre Janisse (Ed.), *Individual differences, stress, and health psychology.* New York: Springer-Verlag.

Jara, Elvia; Vila, Javier; & Maldonado, Antonio. (2006). Second-order conditioning of human causal learning. *Learning and Motivation, 37,* 230–246.

Jarvis, Erich D.; Güntürkün, Onur; Bruce, Laura; Csillag, András; Karten, Harvey; & The Avian Brain Nomenclature Consortium. (2005). Avian brains and a new understanding of vertebrate evolution. *Nature Reviews Neuroscience, 6,* 151–159.

Jason, Leonard A.; Pokorny, Steven B.; Sanem, Julia R.; & Adams, Monica L. (2006). Monitoring and decreasing public smoking among youth. *Behavior Modification, 30,* 681–692.

Jayasinghe, Nimali; Giosan, Cezar; Evans, Susan; Spielman, Lisa; & Difede, JoAnn. (2008, November). Anger and posttraumatic stress disorder in disaster relief workers exposed to the September 11, 2001 World Trade Center disaster: One-year follow-up study. *Journal of Nervous and Mental Disease, 196*(11), 844–846.

Jefferson, James W. (1995). Lithium: The present and the future. *Journal of Clinical Psychiatry, 56,* 41–48.

Jenni, Oskar G.; Borbely, Alexander A.; & Achermann, Peter. (2004). Development of the nocturnal sleep electroencephalogram in human infants. *The American Journal of Physiology: Regulatory, Integrative and Comparative Physiology, 286,* R528–R538.

Jilek, Wolfgang G. (1993). Traditional medicine relevant to psychiatry. In Norman Sartorius, Giovanni de Girolamo, Gavin Andrews, G. Allen German, & Leon Eisenberg (Eds.), *Treatment of mental disorders: A review of effectiveness.* Washington, DC: World Health Organization/American Psychiatric Press.

Joëls, Marian; & Baram, Tallie Z. (2009). The neuro-symphony of stress. *Nature Reviews Neuroscience, 10,* 459–466.

John, Elton. (2005, February 7). Quote from interview by Larry King on Cable News Network program "Larry King Live." Retrieved February 26, 2005, from http://transcripts.cnn.com/TRANSCRIPTS/0502/07/lkl.01.html

John, Oliver P. (1990). The "Big Five" factor taxonomy: Dimensions of personality in the natural language and in questionnaires. In Lawrence A. Pervin (Ed.), *Handbook of personality: Theory and research.* New York: Guilford Press.

Johns, Michael; Inzlicht, Michael; & Schmader, Toni. (2008). Stereotype threat and executive resource depletion: Examining the influence of emotion regulation. *Journal of Experimental Psychology: General,137,* 691–705.

Johns, Michael; Schmader, Toni; & Martens, Andy. (2005). Knowing is half the battle: Teaching stereotype threat as a means of improving women's math performance. *Psychological Science, 16,* 175–179.

Johnson, Jeffrey G.; Cohen, Patricia; Kasen, Stephanie; Smailes, Elizabeth M.; & Brook, Judith S. (2001). Association of maladaptive parental behavior with psychiatric disorder among parents and their offspring. *Archives of General Psychiatry, 58,* 453–460.

Johnson, Katrina W.; Anderson, Norman B.; Bastida, Elena; Kramer, B. Josea; Williams, David; & Wong, Morrison. (1995). Panel II: Macrosocial and environmental influences on minority health. *Health Psychology, 14,* 601–612.

Johnson, Laura R.; & Sandhu, Daya Singh. (2007). Isolation, adjustment, and acculturation issues of international students: Intervention strategies for counselors. In Hemla D. Singaravelu & Mark Pope (Eds.), *A handbook for counseling international students in the United States* (pp. 13–35). Alexandria, VA: American Counseling Association.

Johnson, Marcia K.; Hashtroudi, Shahin; & Lindsay, D. Stephen. (1993). Source monitoring. *Psychological Bulletin, 114,* 3–28.

Johnston, Laurance. (2008). Magnetic healing: What's the attraction? Retrieved June 21, 2009, from http://www.healingtherapies.info/magnetic_healing.htm

Joiner, Thomas E.; Brown, Jessica S.; & Wingate, LaRicka R. (2005). The psychology and neurobiology of suicidal behavior. *Annual Review of Psychology, 56,* 287–314.

Jones, Edward E. (1990). *Interpersonal perception.* New York: Freeman.

Jones, Ernest. (1953). *The life and work of Sigmund Freud: Vol. 1. The formative years and the great discoveries: 1856–1900.* New York: Basic Books.

Jones, Gary. (2003). Testing two cognitive theories of insight. *Journal of Experimental Psychology: Learning, Memory, and Cognition, 29,* 1017–1027.

Jones, James M. (1991). Psychological models of race: What have they been and what should they be? In Jacqueline D. Goodchilds (Ed.), *Psychological perspectives on human diversity in America.* Washington, DC: American Psychological Association.

Jones, Mary Cover. (1924a). The elimination of children's fears. *Journal of Experimental Psychology, 7,* 382–390.

Jones, Mary Cover. (1924b). A laboratory study of fear: The case of Peter. Pedagogical Seminary and *Journal of Genetic Psychology, 31,* 308–315.

Jones, Mary Cover. (1975). A 1924 pioneer looks at behavior therapy. *Journal of Behavior Therapy and Experimental Psychiatry, 6,* 181–187.

Jones, Peter B.; Barnes, Thomas R. E.; Davies, Linda; Dunn, Graham; Lloyd, Helen; Hayhurst, Karen P.; & others. (2006). Randomized controlled trial of the effect on quality of life of second- versus first-generation antipsychotic drugs in schizophrenia: Cost utility of the latest antipsychotic drugs in schizophrenia study (CUtLASS 1). *Archives of General Psychiatry, 63,* 1079–1087.

Jones, Steven H.; & Tarrier, Nick. (2005, December). New developments in bipolar disorder. *Clinical Psychology Review, 25*(8) [Special issue: The psychology of bipolar disorder], 1003–1007.

Jones, Warren H.; & Russell, Dan W. (1980). The selective processing of belief-discrepant information. *European Journal of Social Psychology, 10,* 309–312.

Jonides, John; Lewis, Richard L.; Nee, Derek Evan; Lustig, Cindy A.; Berman, Marc G.; & Moore, Katherine Sledge. (2008). The mind and brain of short-term memory. *Annual Review of Psychology, 59,* 193–224.

Jonnes, Jill. (1999). *Hep-cats, narcs, and pipe dreams: A history of America's romance with illegal drugs.* Baltimore: Johns Hopkins University Press.

Jörgens, Silke; Kleiser, Raimund; Indefrey, Peter; & Seitz, Rüdiger. (2007). Handedness and functional MRI-activation patterns in sentence processing. *NeuroReport, 18,* 1339–1343.

Joseph, Jay; & Leo, Jonathan. (2006, Winter). Genetic relatedness and the lifetime risk for being diagnosed with schizophrenia: Gottesman's 1991 figure 10 reconsidered. *Journal of Mind and Behavior, 27*(1), 73–90.

Josman, Naomi; Somer, Eli; & Reisberg, Ayelet. (2006, April). Designing a virtual environment for post-traumatic stress disorder in Israel: A protocol. *CyberPsychology & Behavior, 9*(2) [Special issue: Virtual and physical toys: Open-ended features for non-formal learning], 241–244.

Joyner, Kara; & Udry, J. Richard. (2000). You don't bring me anything but down: Adolescent romance and depression. *Journal of Health and Social Behavior, 41,* 369–391.

Juliano, Laura M.; & Griffiths, Roland R. (2004). A critical review of caffeine withdrawal: Empirical validation of symptoms and signs, incidence, severity, and associated features. *Psychopharmacology, 176,* 1–29.

Julien, Robert M. (2008). *A primer of drug action* (11th ed.). New York: Worth.

Jung, Carl G. (1923/1976). Psychological types. In Joseph Campbell (Ed.), *The portable Jung.* New York: Penguin.

Jung, Carl G. (1931/1976). The structure of the psyche. In Joseph Campbell (Ed.), *The portable Jung.* New York: Penguin.

Jung, Carl G. (1936/1976). The concept of the collective unconscious. In Joseph Campbell (Ed.), *The portable Jung.* New York: Penguin.

Jung, Carl G. (1951/1976). Aion: Phenomenology of the self. In Joseph Campbell (Ed.), *The portable Jung.* New York: Penguin.

Jung, Carl G. (1963). *Memories, dreams, reflections* (Richard and Clara Winston, Trans.). New York: Random House.

Jung, Carl G. (1964). *Man and his symbols.* New York: Dell.

Jung, Carl G. (1974). *Dreams* (R. F. C. Hull, Trans.). New York: MJF Books.

Kaas, Jon H.; & Collins, Christine E. (2001). Evolving ideas of brain evolution. *Nature, 411,* 141–142.

Kagan, Jerome. (2004, Winter). New insights into temperament. *Cerebrum, 6,* 51–66.

Kagan, Jerome. (2008). A trio of concerns. *Perspectives on Psychological Science, 2,* 361–376.

Kagan, Jerome; & Fox, Nathan A. (2006). Biology, culture, and temperamental biases. In Nancy Eisenberg, William Damon, & Richard M. Lerner (Eds.), *Handbook of child psychology, Vol. 3: Social, emotional, and personality development* (pp. 167–225). Hoboken, NJ: Wiley.

Kagan, Jerome; & Snidman, Nancy. (2004). *The long shadow of temperament.* Cambridge, MA: Harvard University Press.

Kahneman, Daniel. (2003). A perspective on judgment and choice: Mapping bounded rationality. *American Psychologist, 58,* 697–720.

Kahneman, Daniel; & Tversky, Amos. (1982). On the psychology of prediction. In Daniel Kahneman, Paul Slovic, & Amos Tversky (Eds.), *Judgment under uncertainty: Heuristics and biases.* New York: Cambridge University Press.

Kaitz, Marsha; Lapidot, Pnina; Bronner, Ruth; & Eidelman, Arthur I. (1992). Parturient women can recognize their infants by touch. *Developmental Psychology, 28,* 35–39.

Kalat, James W. (1985). Taste-aversion learning in ecological perspective. In Timothy D. Johnston & Alexandra T. Pietrewicz (Eds.), *Issues in the ecological study of learning.* Hillsdale, NJ: Erlbaum.

Kalechstein, Ari D.; De La Garza, Richard; Mahoney, James J.; Fantegrossi, William E.; & Newton, Thomas F. (2007). MDMA use and metacognition: A meta-analytic review. *Psychopharmacology, 189,* 531–537.

Kamen, Dean. (2001, December 2). Quoted in John Heilemann, "Reinventing the wheel." *Time Online Edition.* Retrieved February 25, 2005, from http://www.time.com/time/business/article/0,8599,186660-1,00.html

Kamin, Leon J. (1995). The pioneers of IQ testing. In Russell Jacoby & Naomi Glauberman (Eds.), *The bell curve debate: History, documents, opinions.* New York: Times Books.

Kampe, Knut K. W. (2001, October 10). Quoted in *MSNBC Science News,* "When eyes meet, the brain soars." Retrieved February 27, 2002, from http://stacks.msnbc.com/news/641208.asp

Kampe, Knut K. W.; Frith, Chris D.; Dolan, Raymond J.; & Frith, Uta. (2001, October 11). Reward value of attractiveness and gaze. *Nature, 413,* 589.

Kandel, Eric A. (2001). The molecular biology of memory storage: A dialogue between genes and synapses. *Science, 294,* 1030–1038.

Kandel, Eric R. (2006). *In search of memory: The emergence of a new science of mind.* New York: W. W. Norton.

Kanner, Allen D.; Coyne, James C.; Schaefer, Catherine; & Lazarus, Richard S. (1981). Comparison of two modes of stress management: Daily hassles and uplifts versus major life events. *Journal of Behavioral Medicine, 4,* 1–39.

Kanwisher, Nancy. (2001). Faces and places: Of central (and peripheral) interest. *Nature Neuroscience, 4,* 455–456.

Kanwisher, Nancy. (2006). What's in a face? *Science, 311,* 617–618.

Kaplan, Michael S. (2001). Environment complexity stimulates visual cortex neurogenesis: Death of a dogma and a research career. *Trends in Neurosciences, 24,* 617–620.

Kaplan, Steve. (1990). Capturing your creativity. In Michael G. Walraven & Hiram E. Fitzgerald (Eds.), *Annual editions: Psychology: 1990/91.* Guilford, CT: Dushkin.

Kaplow, Julie B.; Saxe, Glenn N.; & Putnam, Frank W. (2006, Winter). The long-term consequences of early childhood trauma: A case study and discussion. *Psychiatry: Interpersonal and Biological Processes, 69*(4), 362–375.

Karren, Ronald J.; & Zacharias, Larry. (2007, June). Integrity tests: Critical issues. *Human Resource Management Review, 17,* 221–234.

Kasl, Charlotte Davis. (1992). *Many roads, one journey: Moving beyond the twelve steps.* New York: HarperPerennial.

Kasser, Tim; & Sharma, Yadika S. (1999). Reproductive freedom, educational equality, and females' preference for resource-acquisition characteristics in mates. *Psychological Science, 10,* 374–377.

Kastenbaum, Robert. (1992). *The psychology of death.* New York: Springer-Verlag.

Kastenbaum, Robert. (2000). Death attitudes and aging in the 21st century. In Adrian Tomer (Ed), *Death attitudes and the older adult: Theories, concepts, and applications. Series in death, dying, and bereavement.* New York: Brunner-Routledge.

Kastenbaum, Robert. (2005). Is death better in utopia? *Illness, Crisis, & Loss, 13*(1), 31–48.

Kaufman, Alan S. (1990). *Assessing adolescent and adult intelligence.* Boston: Allyn & Bacon.

Kaufman, James C.; Grigorenko, Elena L.; & Sternberg, Robert J. (Eds.). (2009). *The essential Sternberg: Essays on intelligence, psychology, and education.* New York: Springer.

Kaufman, Lloyd; Vassiliades, Vassias; & Noble, Richard. (2007). Perceptual distance and the moon illusion. *Spatial Vision, 20,* 155–175.

Kaufmann, Dagmar; Gesten, Ellis; Santa Lucia, Raymond C.; Salcedo, Octavio; Rendina-Gobioff, Gianna; & Gadd, Ray Gadd. (2000). The relationship between parenting style and children's adjustment: The parents' perspective. *Journal of Child and Family Studies, 9,* 231–245.

Kawamura, Kathleen Y.; Frost, Randy O.; & Harmatz, Morton G. (2002). The relationship of perceived parenting styles to perfectionism. *Personality and Individual Differences, 32,* 317–327.

Kay, Paul; & Regier, Terry. (2007). Color naming universals: The case of Berinmo. *Cognition, 102,* 289–298.

Kazdin, Alan E. (2001). *Behavior modification in applied settings* (6th ed.). Belmont, CA: Wadsworth.

Kazdin, Alan E. (2003). Psychotherapy for children and adolescents. *Annual Review of Psychology, 54,* 253–276.

Kazdin, Alan. (2008). *Behavior modification in applied settings.* Long Grove, IL: Waveland Press.

Kazdin, Alan E.; & Benjet, Corina. (2003). Spanking children: Evidence and issues. *Current Directions in Psychological Science, 12,* 99–103.

Keck, Paul E., Jr.; Marcus, Ronald; Tourkodimitris, Stavros; Ali, Mirza; Liebeskind, Amy; Saha, Anutosh; & Ingenito, Gary. (2003). A placebo-controlled, double-blind study of the efficacy and safety of aripiprazole in patients with acute bipolar mania. *American Journal of Psychiatry, 160,* 1651–1658.

Keck, Paul E., Jr.; & McElroy, Susan L. (2009). Treatment of bipolar disorder. In Alan F. Schatzberg & Charles B. Nemeroff (Eds.), *The American Psychiatric Publishing textbook of psychopharmacology* (4th ed., pp. 1113–1133). Washington, DC: American Psychiatric Publishing.

Keel, Pamela A.; Baxter, Mark G.; & Heatherton, Todd F. (2007). A 20-year longitudinal study of body weight, dieting, and eating disorder symptoms. *Journal of Abnormal Psychology, 116,* 422–432.

Keesey, Richard E.; & Hirvonen, Matt D. (1997). Body weight set-points: Determination and adjustment. *Journal of Nutrition, 127,* 1875S–1883S.

Kellner, Charles H.; Knapp, Rebecca G.; Petrides, Georgios; Rummans, Teresa A.; Husain, Mustafa M.; Rasmussen, Keith; & others. (2006). Continuation electroconvulsive therapy vs pharmacotherapy for relapse prevention in major depression: A multisite study from the Consortium for Research in Electroconvulsive Therapy (CORE). *Archives of General Psychiatry, 63,* 1337–1344.

Kelly, Ciara; & McCreadie, Robin. (1999). Smoking habits, current symptoms, and premorbid characteristics of schizophrenic patients in Nithsdale, Scotland. *American Journal of Psychiatry, 156,* 1751–1757.

Kelly, John F.; & Moos, Rudolf. (2003). Dropout from 12-step self-help groups: Prevalence, predictors, and counteracting treatment influences. *Journal of Substance Abuse Treatment, 24,* 241–250.

Kelman, Herbert C. (2005). The policy context of torture: A social-psychological analysis. *International Review of the Red Cross, 87,* 123–134.

Keltner, Dacher; & Anderson, Cameron. (2000). Saving face for Darwin: The functions and uses of embarrassment. *Current Directions in Psychological Science, 9,* 187–192.

Keltner, Dacher; & Buswell, Brenda N. (1997). Embarrassment: Its distinct form and appeasement functions. *Psychological Bulletin, 122,* 250–270.

Kemmer, Susanne. (2007, February/March). Sticking point. *Scientific American Mind,* 64–69.

Kempermann, Gerd; & Gage, Fred H. (1999, May). New nerve cells for the adult brain. *Scientific American, 280,* 48–53.

Kempermann, Gerd; Kuhn, H. Georg; & Gage, Fred H. (1998, May 1). Experience-induced neurogenesis in the senescent dentate gyrus. *Journal of Neuroscience, 18,* 3206–3212.

Kendler, Kenneth S.; Bulik, Cynthia M.; Silberg, Judy; Hettema, John M.; Myers, John; & Prescott, Carol A. (2000). Childhood sexual abuse and adult psychiatric and substance use disorders in women: An epidemiological and Cotwin control analysis. *Archives of General Psychiatry, 57,* 953–959.

Kendler, Kenneth S.; & Diehl, Scott R. (1993). The genetics of schizophrenia: A current genetic-epidemiologic perspective. *Schizophrenia Bulletin, 19,* 261–285.

Kendler, Kenneth S.; Gatz, Margaret; Gardner, Charles O.; & Pedersen, Nancy L. (2006). A Swedish national twin study of lifetime major depression. *American Journal of Psychiatry, 163,* 109–114.

Kendler, Kenneth S.; Neale, Michael C.; MacLean, Charles J.; Heath, A. C.; Eaves, L. J., & Kessler, R. C. (1993). Smoking and major depression: A causal analysis. *Archives of General Psychiatry, 50,* 36–43.

Kennedy, Sidney H.; Konarski, Jakub Z.; Segal, Zindel V.; Lau, Mark A.; Bieling, Peter J.; McIntyre, Roger S.; & Mayberg, Helen S. (2007). Differences in brain glucose metabolism between responders to CBT and venlafaxine in a 16-week randomized controlled trial. *American Journal of Psychiatry, 164,* 778–788.

Kerns, Kathryn A.; Abraham, Michelle M.; & Schlegelmilch, Andrew. (2007). Mother-child attachment in later middle childhood: Assessment approaches and associations with mood and emotion regulation. *Attachment & Human Development, 9,* 33–53.

Kerns, Kathryn A.; & Richardson, Rhonda A. (2005). *Attachment in middle childhood.* New York: Guilford Press.

Kerr, David C. R.; Lopez, Nestor L.; Olson, Sheryl L.; & Sameroff, Arnold J. (2004). Parental discipline and externalizing behavior problems in early childhood: The roles of moral regulation and child gender. *Journal of Abnormal Child Psychology, 32*(4), 369–383.

Kershaw, Trina C.; & Ohlsson, Stellan. (2004). Multiple causes of difficulty in insight: The case of the nine-dot problem. *Journal of Experimental Psychology: Learning, Memory, and Cognition, 30,* 3–13.

Kessen, William. (1996). American psychology just before Piaget. *Psychological Science, 7,* 196–199.

Kessler, Ronald C. (2003a). Epidemiology of women and depression. *Journal of Affective Disorders, 74,* 5–13.

Kessler, Ronald C. (2003b, February). [*In-cites* interview with Dr. Ronald C. Kessler.] *ISI Essential Science Indicators.* Thompson Scientific, Philadelphia. Retrieved January 9, 2005, from http://www.in-cites.com/papers/DrRonaldKessler.html

Kessler, Ronald C.; Berglund, Patricia; Demler, Olga; Jin, Robert; Koretz, Doreen; Merikangas, Kathleen R.; Rush, A. John; Walters, Ellen E.; & Wang, Philip S. (2003, June 18). The epidemiology of major depressive disorder: Results from the National Comorbidity Survey Replication (NCS-R). *Journal of the American Medical Association, 289,* 3095–3105.

Kessler, Ronald C.; Berglund, Patricia; Demler, Olga; Jin, Robert; Merikangas, Kathleen R.; & Walters, Ellen E. (2005a). Lifetime prevalence and age-of-onset distributions of DSM-IV disorders in the National Comorbidity Survey Replication. *Archives of General Psychiatry, 62,* 593–602.

Kessler, Ronald C.; Chiu, Wai Tat; Demler, Olga; & Walters, Ellen E. (2005b). Prevalence, severity, and comorbidity of 12-month DSM-IV disorders in the National Comorbidity Survey Replication. *Archives of General Psychiatry, 62,* 617–627.

Kessler, Ronald C.; Demler, Olga; Frank, Richard G.; Olfson, Mark; Pincus, Harold Alan; Walters, Ellen E.; Wang, Philip; Wells, Kenneth B.; & Zaslavsky, Alan M. (2005c, June 16). Prevalence and treatment of mental disorders, 1990 to 2003. *New England Journal of Medicine, 352,* 2515–2523.

Kessler, Ronald C.; McGonagle, Katherine A.; Zhao, Shanyang; Nelson, Christopher B.; Hughes, Michael; Eshleman, Suzann; & others. (1994). Lifetime and 12-month prevalence of DSM-III-R psychiatric disorders in the United States: Results from the National Comorbidity Survey (NCS). *Archives of General Psychiatry, 51,* 8–19.

Kessler, Ronald C.; Price, Richard H.; & Wortman, Camille B. (1985). Social factors in psychopathology: Stress, social support, and coping processes. *Annual Review of Psychology, 36,* 531–572.

Kessler, Ronald C.; & researchers from the World Health Organization. (2004, June 2). World Mental Health Survey Consortium: Prevalence, severity, and unmet need for treatment of mental disorders in the World Health Organization mental health surveys. *Journal of the American Medical Association, 291,* 2581–2590. Retrieved January 9, 2005, from http://jama.ama-assn.org/cgi/reprint/291/21/2581.pdf

Khanna, Charu; & Medsker, Gina J. (2007). 2006 income and employment survey results for the Society for Industrial and Organizational Psychology. *The Industrial-Organizational Psychologist, 45.*

Kheriaty, Aaron. (2007). The return of the unconscious. *Psychiatric Annals, 37,* 285–287.

Kiecolt-Glaser, Janice K. (1999). Stress, personal relationships, and immune function: Health implications. *Brain, Behavior and Immunity, 13*(1), 61–72.

Kiecolt-Glaser, Janice K. (2009). Psychoneuroimmunology: Psychology's gateway to the biomedical future. *Perspectives on Psychological Science, 4,* 367–369.

Kiecolt-Glaser, Janice K.; & Glaser, Ronald. (1991). Stress and immune function in humans. In Robert Ader, David L. Felten, & Nicholas Cohen (Eds.), *Psychoneuroimmunology.* San Diego, CA: Academic Press.

Kiecolt-Glaser, Janice K.; & Glaser, Ronald. (1993). Mind and immunity. In Daniel Goleman & Joel Gurin (Eds.), *Mind/body medicine: How to use your mind for better health.* Yonkers, NY: Consumer Reports Books.

Kiecolt-Glaser, Janice K.; McGuire, Lynanne; Robles, Theodore, F.; & Glaser, Ronald. (2002). Emotions, morbidity, and mortality: New perspectives from psychoneuroimmunology. *Annual Review of Psychology, 53,* 83–107.

Kiecolt-Glaser, Janice K.; & Newton, Tamara L. (2001). Marriage and health: His and hers. *Psychological Bulletin, 127,* 472–503.

Kiefer, Amy K.; & Sekaquaptewa, Denise. (2007). Implicit stereotypes, gender identification, and math-related outcomes: A prospective study of female college students. *Psychological Science, 18,* 13–18.

Kihlstrom, John F. (2001). Hypnosis and the psychological unconscious. In Howard S. Friedman (Ed.), *Assessment and therapy: Specialty articles from the encyclopedia of mental health.* San Diego, CA: Academic Press.

Kihlstrom, John F. (2004). An unbalanced balancing act: Blocked, recovered, and false memories in the laboratory and clinic. *Clinical Psychology: Science and Practice, 11,* 34–41.

Kihlstrom, John F. (2005). Dissociative disorders. *Annual Review of Clinical Psychology, 1,* 227–253.

Kihlstrom, John F. (2007). Consciousness in hypnosis. In Philip David Zelazo, Morris Moscovitch, & Evan Thompson (Eds.), *The Cambridge handbook of consciousness.* New York: Cambridge University Press.

Kihlstrom, John F.; Dorfman, Jennifer; & Park, Lillian. (2007). Implicit and explicit memory and learning. In Max Velmans & Susan Schneider (Eds.), *The Blackwell companion to consciousness.* Malden, MA: Blackwell.

Kihlstrom, John F.; Glisky, Martha L.; & Angiulo, Michael J. (1994). Dissociative tendencies and dissociative disorders. *Journal of Abnormal Psychology, 103,* 117–124.

Kihlstrom, John F.; Mulvaney, Shelagh; Tobias, Betsy A.; & Tobias, Irene P. (2000). In Eric Eich, John F. Kihlstrom, Gordon H. Bower, Josheph P. Forgas, & Paula M. Niedenthal (Eds.), *Cognition and emotion.* New York: Oxford University Press.

Kim, Bryan S. K.; & Park, Yong S. (2008). East and Southeast Asian Americans. In Garrett McAuliffe (Ed.), *Culturally alert counseling: A comprehensive introduction* (pp. 188–219). Thousand Oaks, CA: Sage.

Kim, Yu Kyeong; Yoon, In-Young; Shin, Yoon-Kyung; Cho, Sang Soo; & Kim, Sang Eun. (2007). Modafinil-induced hippocampal activation in narcolepsy. *Neuroscience Letters, 422,* 91–96.

Kimzey, Stephen L. (1975). The effects of extended spaceflight on hematologic and immunologic systems. *Journal of the American Medical Women's Association, 30,* 218–232.

King, D. Brett; Cox, Michaella; & Wertheimer, Michael. (1998). Karl Duncker: Productive problems with beautiful solutions. In George A. Kimble & Michael Wertheimer (Eds.), *Portraits of pioneers in psychology* (Vol. 3). Washington, DC: American Psychological Association.

King, Laura A. (2008). Personal goals and life dreams: Positive psychology and motivation in daily life. In James Y. Shah & Wendi L. Gardner (Eds.), *Handbook of motivation science.* New York: Guilford Press.

Kinsella, Kevin; & Velkoff, Victoria A. (2001). *An aging world: 2001* (International Population Report, Series P95/01–1). Washington, DC: U.S. Government Printing Office, U.S. Census Bureau.

Kirsch, Irving; & Braffman, Wayne. (2001). Imaginative suggestibility and hypnotizability. *Current Directions in Psychological Science, 10,* 57–61.

Kirsch Irving; Deacon, Brett J.; Huedo-Medina, Tania B.; Scoboria, Alan; Moore, Thomas J.; & Johnson, Blair T. (2008). Initial severity and antidepressant benefits: A meta-analysis of data submitted to the Food and Drug Administration. *PLoS Medicine 5*(2): e45.

Kirsch, Irving; Lynn, Steven Jay; & Vigorito, Michael. (2004). The role of cognition in classical and operant conditioning. *Journal of Clinical Psychology, 60,* 369–392.

Kirsch, Irving; Montgomery, Guy; & Sapirstein, Guy. (1995). Hypnosis as an adjunct to cognitive-behavioral psychotherapy: A meta-analysis. *Journal of Consulting and Clinical Psychology, 63,* 214–220.

Kirschenbaum, Howard. (2004). Carl Rogers's life and work: An assessment on the 100th anniversary of his birth. *Journal of Counseling and Development, 82,* 116–124.

Kirschenbaum, Howard; & Jourdan, April. (2005). The current status of Carl Rogers and the person-centered approach. *Psychotherapy: Theory, Research, Practice, Training, 42,* 37–51.

Kitayama, Shinobu; Markus, Hazel Rose; & Kurokawa, Masaru. (2000). Culture, emotion, and well-being: Good feelings in Japan and the United States. *Cognition & Emotion, 14,* 93–124.

Kitayama, Shinobu; Markus, Hazel Rose; Matsumoto, Hisaya; & Norasakkunkit, Vinai. (1997). Individual and collective processes in the construction of the self: Self-enhancement in the United States and self-criticism in Japan. *Journal of Personality and Social Psychology, 72,* 1245–1267.

Kitayama, Shinobu; & Park, Hyekyung. (2007). Cultural shaping of self, emotion, and well-being: How does it work? *Social and Personality Psychology Compass, 1,* 202–222.

Klahr, David. (1992). Information-processing approaches. In Ross Vasta (Ed.), *Six theories of child development: Revised formulations and current issues.* London: Jessica Kingsley.

Kleider, Heather M.; Pezdek, Kathy; Goldinger, Stephen D.; & Kirk, Alice. (2008). Schema-driven source misattribution errors: Remembering the expected from a witnessed event. *Applied Cognitive Psychology, 22,* 1–20.

Klein, Daniel N.; Torpey, Dana C.; & Bufferd, Sara J. (2008). Depressive disorders. In Theodore P. Beauchaine & Stephen P. Hinshaw (Eds.), *Child and adolescent psychopathology* (pp. 477–509). Hoboken, NJ: Wiley.

Kleinhans, Natalia; Akshoomoff, Natacha; & Dells, Dean C. (2005). Executive functions in autism and Asperger's disorder: Flexibility, fluency, and inhibition. *Developmental Neuropsychology, 27,* 379–401.

Klerman, Gerald L.; Weissman, Myrna M.; Rounsaville, Bruce J.; & Chevron, Eve S. (1984). *Interpersonal psychotherapy of depression.* New York: Basic Books.

Knapp, Samuel; & VandeCreek, Leon. (2000). Received memories of childhood abuse: Is there an underlying professional consensus? *Professional Psychology: Research and Practice, 31,* 365–371.

Knight, Robert T. (2007). Neural networks debunk phrenology. *Science, 316,* 1578–1579.

Knoblich, Gunther; & Öllinger, Michael. (2006, October). The Eureka moment. *Scientific American Mind, 17*(5), 38–43.

Knowles, John B. (1963). Conditioning and the placebo effect: The effects of decaffeinated coffee on simple reaction time in habitual coffee drinkers. *Behavior Research and Therapy, 1,* 151–157.

Kochanek, Kenneth D.; & Smith, Betty L. (2004, February 11). Deaths: Preliminary data for 2002. *National Vital Statistics Reports, 52,* No. 13. Atlanta, GA: Centers for Disease Control, U.S. Department of Health and Human Services. Retrieved January 7, 2005, from http://www.cdc.gov/nchs/data/nvsr/nvsr52/nvsr5213.pdf.

Koenig, Anne M.; & Eagly, Alice H. (2005). Stereotype threat in men on a test of social sensitivity. *Sex Roles, 52,* 489–496.

Koenigs, Michael; & Tranel, Daniel. (2007). Irrational economic decision-making after ventromedial prefrontal damage: Evidence from the Ultimatum Game. *Journal of Neuroscience, 27,* 951–956.

Koffka, Kurt. (1935). *Principles of Gestalt psychology.* New York: Harcourt, Brace.

Kohlberg, Lawrence. (1976). Moral stages and moralization: The cognitive developmental approach. In T. Lickona (Ed.), *Moral development and behavior: Theory, research, and social issues.* New York: Holt, Rinehart & Winston.

Kohlberg, Lawrence. (1981). *The philosophy of moral development: Moral stages and the idea of justice: Vol 1. Essays on moral development.* New York: Harper & Row.

Kohlberg, Lawrence. (1984). *The psychology of moral development.* New York: Harper & Row.

Kohler, Evelyne; Keysers, Christian; Umiltà, M. Allessandra; Fogassi, Leonardo; Gallese, Vittorio; & Rizzolatti, Giacomo. (2002). Hearing sounds, understanding actions: Action representation in mirror neurons. *Science, 297,* 846–848.

Kohn, P. M.; Lafrenier, K.; & Gurevich, M. (1990). The Inventory of College Students' Recent Life Experiences: A decontaminated hassles scale for a special population. *Journal of Behavioral Medicine, 13,* 619–630.

Kohrt, Brandon A.; Jordans, Mark J. D.; Tol, Wietse A.; Speckman, Rebecca A.; Maharjan, Sujen M.; Worthman, Carol M.; & Komproe, Ivan H. (2008). Comparison of mental health between former child soldiers and children never conscripted by armed groups in Nepal. *Journal of the American Medical Association, 300*(6), 691–702.

Kojima, Masayasu; Hosoda, Hiroshi; Date, Yukari; Nakazato, Masamitsu; Matsuo, Hisayuki; & Kangawa, Kenji. (1999). Ghrelin is a growth-hormone-releasing acylated peptide from stomach. *Nature, 402,* 656–660.

Koltko-Rivera, Mark E. (2006). Rediscovering the later version of Maslow's hierarchy of needs: Self-transcendence and opportunities for theory, research, and unification. *Review of General Psychology, 10,* 302–317.

Komatsu, Hidehiko. (2006). The neural mechanisms of perceptual fillingin. *Nature Reviews Neuroscience, 7,* 220–231.

Kong, Lauren L.; Allen, John J. B.; & Glisky, Elizabeth L. (2008). Interidentity memory transfer in dissociative identity disorder. *Journal of Abnormal Psychology, 117,* 686–692.

Koob, George F., & Volkow, Nora D. (2009, August 26). Neurocircuitry of addiction. *Neuropsychopharmacology,* advance online publication, DOI: 10.1038/npp.2009.110.

Kopelman, Peter G. (2000, April 6). Obesity as a medical problem. *Nature, 404,* 635–643.

Kopelowicz, Alex; Liberman, Robert P.; & Zarate, Roberto. (2007). Psychosocial treatments for schizophrenia. In Peter E. Nathan & Jack M. Gorman (Eds.), *A guide to treatments that work* (3rd ed., pp. 243–269). New York: Oxford University Press.

Koplan, Jeffrey P.; & Dietz, William H. (1999, October 27). Caloric imbalance and public health policy. *Journal of the American Medical Association, 282,* 1579–1581.

Koren-Karie, Nina; Oppenheim, David; Dolev, Smadar; Sher, Efrat; & Etzion-Carasso, Ayelet. (2002). Mothers' insightfulness regarding their infants' internal experience: Relations with maternal sensitivity and infant attachment. *Developmental Psychology, 38,* 534–542.

Kornell, Nate. (2008, February). How to study. *British Psychological Society Research Digest Blog.* Retrieved May 15, 2008, from http://bps-research-digest.blogspot.com/2008/02/how-to-study.html

Kornfeld, Alfred D. (1989). Mary Cover Jones and the Peter case: Social learning versus conditioning. *Journal of Anxiety Disorders, 3,* 187–195.

Kosslyn, Stephen M. (2001, May-June). Quoted in Andrew Cocke, "The science behind hypnosis." *BrainWork: The Neuroscience Newsletter, 11,* 7.

Kosslyn, Stephen M.; Ball, Thomas M.; & Reiser, Brian J. (1978). Visual images preserve metric spatial information: Evidence from studies of image scanning. *Journal of Experimental Psychology: Human Perception and Performance, 4,* 47–60.

Kosslyn, Stephen M.; Ganis, Giorgio; & Thompson, William L. (2001). Neural foundations of imagery. *Nature Reviews Neuroscience, 2,* 635–642.

Kosslyn, Stephen M.; & Thompson, William L. (2000). Shared mechanisms in visual imagery and visual perception: Insights from cognitive neuroscience. In Michael S. Gazzaniga (Ed.), *The new cognitive neurosciences* (2nd ed.). Cambridge, MA: MIT Press.

Kosslyn, Stephen M.; Thompson, William L.; Costantini-Ferrando, Maria F.; Alpert, Nathaniel M.; & Spiegel, David. (2000). Hypnotic visual illusion alters color processing in the brain. *American Journal of Psychiatry, 157,* 1279–1284.

Kostic, Bogdan; & Cleary, A. M. (2009). Song recognition without identification: When people cannot "name that tune" but can recognize it as familiar. *Journal of Experimental Psychology: General, 138,* 146–159.

Kramer, Arthur F.; & Erickson, Kirk I. (2007). Capitalizing on cortical plasticity: Influence of physical activity on cognition and brain function. *TRENDS in Cognitive Science, 11,* 342–348.

Krantz, David S.; & McCeney, Melissa K. (2002). Effects of psychological and social factors on organic disease: A critical assessment of research on coronary heart disease. *Annual Review of Psychology, 53,* 341–369.

Krebs, Dennis L.; & Denton, Kathy. (2005). Toward a more pragmatic approach to morality: A critical evaluation of Kohlberg's model. *Psychological Bulletin, 112,* 629–649.

Krebs, Dennis L.; & Denton, Kathy. (2006). Explanatory limitations of cognitive-developmental approaches to morality. *Psychological Bulletin, 113,* 672–675.

Kreider, Rose M. (2008, March 3). *Improvements to demographic household data in the current population survey: 2007.* Washington, DC: U.S. Census Bureau, Housing and Household Economic Statistics Division.

Kreshel, Peggy J. (1990). John B. Watson at J. Walter Thompson: The legitimation of "science" in advertising. *Journal of Advertising, 19,* 49–59.

Krettenauer, Tobias. (2005). The role of epistemic cognition in adolescent identity formation: Further evidence. *Journal of Youth and Adolescence, 34*(3), 185–198.

Kring, Ann M.; & Gordon, Albert H. (1998). Sex differences in emotion: Expression, experience, and physiology. *Journal of Personality and Social Psychology, 74,* 686–703.

Krippner, Stanley. (1994). Cross-cultural treatment perspectives of dissociative disorders. In Steven Jay Lynn & Judith W. Rhue (Eds.), *Dissociation: Clinical and theoretical perspectives.* New York: Guilford Press.

Krohe, James. (2006). Are workplace tests worth taking? Only if you do them right—which you probably don't. *Across the Board,* 16–23.

Krosnick, Jon A.; Betz, Andrew L.; Jussim, Lee J.; & Lynn, Ann R. (1992). Subliminal conditioning of attitudes. *Personality and Social Psychology Bulletin, 18,* 152–162.

Krosnick, Jon A.; Judd, Charles M.; & Wittenbrink, Bernd. (2005). The measurement of attitudes. In Dolores Albarracín, Blair T. Johnson, & Mark P. Zanna (Eds.), *The handbook of attitudes* (pp. 21–76). Mahwah, NJ: Erlbaum.

Krueger, Joachim I.; DiDonato, Theresa E.; & Krueger, Joachim I. (2008, March). Social categorization and the perception of groups and group differences. *Social and Personality Psychology Compass, 2*(2), 733–750.

Kruger, Justin; & Gilovich, Thomas. (2004). Actions, intentions, and self-assessment: The road to self-enhancement is paved with good intentions. *Personality and Social Psychology Bulletin, 30*(3), 328–329.

Krusemark, Elizabeth A.; Campbell, W. Keith; & Clementz, Brett A. (2008, July). Attributions, deception, and event related potentials: An investigation of the self-serving bias. *Psychophysiology, 45*(4), 511–515.

Kübler-Ross, Elisabeth. (1969). *On death and dying.* New York: Macmillan.

Kucian, Karin; Loenneker, Thomas; Dietrich, Thomas; Martin, Ernst; & Von Aster, Michael. (2005). *Psychology Science, 47,* 112–131.

Kufahl, Peter; Li, Zhu; Risinger, Robert; Rainey, Charles; Piacentine, Linda; Wu, Gaohong; Bloom, Alan; Yang, Zheng; & Li, Shi-Jiang. (2008). Expectation modulates human brain responses to acute cocaine: A functional magnetic resonance imaging study. *Biological Psychiatry, 63,* 222–230.

Kuhl, Brice A.; Dudukovic, Nicole M.; Kahn, Itamar; & Wagner, Anthony D. (2007). Decreased demands on cognitive control reveal the neural processing benefits of forgetting. *Nature Neuroscience, 10,* 908–914.

Kuhl, Patricia K.; Andruski, Jean E.; Chistovich, Inna A.; Chistovich, Ludmilla A.; Kozhevnikova, Elena V.; Ryskina, Viktoria L.; & others. (1997, August 1). Cross-language analysis of phonetic units in language addressed to infants. *Science, 277,* 684–686.

Kuhl, Patricia K.; Williams, Karen A.; Lacerda, Francisco; Stevens, Kenneth N.; & Lindblom, Bjorn. (1992, January 31). Linguistic experience alters phonetic perception in infants by 6 months of age. *Science, 255,* 606–608.

Kuhn, Cynthia M.; & Wilson, Wilkie A. (2001, Spring). Ecstasy on trial: Our dangerous love affair with ecstasy. *Cerebrum, 3,* 22–33.

Kunoh, Hiroshi; & Takaoki, Eiji. (1994). *3-D planet: The world as seen through stereograms.* San Francisco: Cadence Books.

Kurson, Robert. (2007). Crashing through. New York: Random House.

Kuttner, Leora; & Catchpole, Rosalind E. H. (2007). Developmental considerations: Hypnosis with children. In William C. Wester II & Laurence I. Sugarman (Eds.), *Therapeutic hypnosis with children and adolescents.* Norwalk, CT: Crown House.

Lachman, Margie E. (2004). Development in midlife. *Annual Review of Psychology, 55,* 305–331.

Ladd, George T.; & Petry, Nancy M. (2003). Antisocial personality in treatment-seeking cocaine abusers: Psychosocial functioning and HIV risk. *Journal of Substance Abuse Treatment, 24,* 323–330.

LaFromboise, Teresa D.; Coleman, Hardin L. K.; & Gerton, Jennifer. (1993a). Psychological impact of biculturalism: Evidence and theory. *Psychological Bulletin, 114,* 395–412.

LaFromboise, Teresa D.; Trimble, Joseph E.; & Mohatt, Gerald V. (1993b). Counseling intervention and American Indian tradition: An integrative approach. In Donald R. Atkinson, George Morten, & Derald Wing Sue (Eds.), *Counseling American minorities: A cross-cultural perspective* (4th ed.). Madison, WI: Brown & Benchmark.

Lahav, Amir; Saltzman, Elliot; & Schlaug, Gottfried. (2007). Action representation of sound: Audiomotor recognition network while listening to newly acquired actions. *Journal of Neuroscience, 27,* 308–314.

Laible, Deborah. (2007). Attachment with parents and peers in late adolescence: Links with emotional competence and social behavior. *Personality and Individual Differences, 43,* 1185–1197.

Lalonde, Justine K.; Hudson, James I.; Gigante, Robin A.; & Pope, Harrison G. (2001). Canadian and American psychiatrists' attitudes toward dissociative disorders diagnoses. *Canadian Journal of Psychiatry, 46,* 407–412.

Lamb, Michael E.; Sternberg, Kathleen J.; & Prodromidis, Margardita. (1992). Nonmaternal care and the security of infant-mother attachment: A reanalysis of the data. *Infant Behavior and Development, 15,* 71–83.

Lamb, Michael E.; Thompson, Ross A.; Gardner, William; & Charnov, Eric L. (1985). *Infant–mother attachment: The origins and developmental significance of individual differences in Strange Situation behavior.* Hillsdale, NJ: Erlbaum.

Lamb, Richard J.; Kirby, Kimberly C.; Morral, Andrew; Galbicka, Gregory; & Iguchi, Martin Y. (2004). Improving contingency management programs for addiction. *Addictive Behaviors, 29,* 507–523.

Lambert, Michael J.; Garfield, Sol L.; & Bergin, Allen E. (2004). Overview, trends, and future issues. In Michael J. Lambert (Ed.), *Bergin and Garfield's handbook of psychotherapy and behavior change* (5th ed.). New York: Wiley.

Lambert, Michael J.; Hansen, Nathan B.; & Finch, Arthur E. (2001). Patient-focused research: Using patient outcome data to enhance treatment effects. *Journal of Consulting and Clinical Psychology, 69,* 159–172.

Lambert, Michael J.; & Ogles, Benjamin M. (2004). The efficacy and effectiveness of psychotherapy. In Michael J. Lambert (Ed.), *Bergin and Garfield's handbook of psychotherapy and behavior change* (5th ed.). New York: Wiley.

Lampinen, James M.; Copeland, Susann M.; & Neuschatz, Jeffrey S. (2001). Recollections of things schematic: Room schemas revisited. *Journal of Experimental Psychology: Learning, Memory, and Cognition, 27,* 1211–1222.

Lampinen, James M.; Faries, Jeremiah M.; Neuschatz, Jeffrey S.; & Toglia, Michael P. (2000). Recollections of things schematic: The influence of scripts on recollective experience. *Applied Cognitive Psychology, 14,* 543–554.

Lampinen, James M.; Meier, Christopher R.; & Arnal, Jack D. (2005). Compelling untruths: Content borrowing and vivid false memories. *Journal of Experimental Psychology: Learning, Memory, and Cognition, 31,* 954–963.

Lancaster, Lynne C.; & Stillman, David. (2002). *When generations collide: Who they are. Why they clash. How to solve the generational puzzle at work.* New York: HarperCollins.

Lander, Hans Jürgen. (1997). Hermann Ebbinghaus. In Wolfgang G. Bringmann, Helmut E. Lück, Rudolf Miller, & Charles E. Early (Eds.), *A pictorial history of psychology.* Chicago: Quintessence.

Landolt, Hans-Peter. (2008). Sleep homeostasis: A role for adenosine in humans? *Biochemical Pharmacology, 75,* 2070–2079.

Lange, Carl G.; & James, William. (1922). *The emotions* (I. A. Haupt, Trans.). Baltimore: Williams & Wilkins.

Langenbucher, James; & Nathan, Peter E. (2006). Diagnosis and classification. In Michel Hersen & Jay C. Thomas (Eds.), *Comprehensive handbook of personality and psychopathology* (Vol. 2, pp. 3–20). Hoboken, NJ: Wiley.

Langer, Ellen; & Rodin, Judith. (1976). The effects of choice and enhanced personal responsibility for the aged: A field experiment in an institutional setting. *Journal of Personality and Social Psychology, 34,* 191–198.

Langlois, Judith H.; Kalakanis, Lisa; Rubenstein, Adam J.; Larson, Andrea; Hallam, Monica; & Smoot, Monica. (2000). Maxims or myths of beauty? A meta-analytic and theoretical review. *Psychological Bulletin, 126,* 390–423.

Långström, Niklas; Rahman, Qazi; Carlström, Eva; & Lichtenstein, Paul. (2008). Genetic and environmental effects on same-sex sexual behavior: A population study of twins in Sweden. *Archives of Sexual Behavior.* Retrieved September 2009 from http://www.springerlink.com/content/2263646523551487/?p=5310511181974ce6b6abe4ac49752533=4

Laruelle, Marc; Kegeles, Lawrence S.; & Abi-Dargham, Anissa. (2003). Glutamate, dopamine, and schizophrenia: From pathophysiology to treatment. *Annals of the New York Academy of Sciences, 1003,* 138–158.

Lashley, Karl S. (1929). *Brain mechanisms and intelligence.* Chicago: University of Chicago Press.

Lashley, Karl S. (1950). In search of the engram. *Symposia of the Society for Experimental Biology, 4,* 454–482.

Lasser, Karen; Boyd, J. Wesley; Woolhandler, Steffie; Himmelstein, David U.; McCormick, Danny; & Bor, David H. . (2000). Smoking and mental illness: A population-based prevalence study. *Journal of the American Medical Association, 284,* 2606–2610.

Latané, Bibb; & Darley, John M. (1970). *The unresponsive bystander: Why doesn't he help?* New York: Appleton-Century-Crofts.

Latané, Bibb; & Nida, Steve A. (1981). Ten years of research on group size and helping. *Psychological Bulletin, 89,* 308–324.

Latané, Bibb; Williams, Kipling; & Harkins, Stephen. (1979). Many hands make light the work: The causes and consequences of social loafing. *Journal of Personality and Social Psychology, 37,* 822–832.

Laviolette, Steven R.; & van der Kooy, Derek. (2004). The neurobiology of nicotine addiction: Bridging the gap from molecules to behaviour. *Nature Reviews Neuroscience, 5,* 55–65.

Lavoie, Kim L.; & Barone, Silvana. (2006). Prescription privileges for psychologists: A comprehensive review and critical analysis of current issues and controversies. *CNS Drugs, 20*(1), 51–66.

Lawler, Edward E., III. (1973). *Motivation in work organizations.* Pacific Grove, CA: Brooks/Cole.

Lazarus, Arnold A. (2000). Will reason prevail? From classic psychoanalysis to New Age therapy. *American Journal of Psychotherapy, 54,* 152–155.

Lazarus, Arnold A. (2008). Technical eclecticism and multimodal therapy. In Jay L. Lebow (Ed.), *Twenty-first century psychotherapies: Contemporary approaches to theory and practice* (pp. 424–452). Hoboken, NJ: Wiley.

Lazarus, Richard S. (1995). Vexing research problems inherent in cognitive-mediational theories of emotion—and some solutions. *Psychological Inquiry, 6,* 183–197.

Lazarus, Richard S. (1999). *Stress and emotion: A new synthesis.* New York: Springer.

Lazarus, Richard S. (2000). Toward better research on stress and coping. *American Psychologist, 55,* 556–773.

Lazarus, Richard S.; & Folkman, Susan. (1984). *Stress, appraisal, and coping.* New York: Springer.

Lazarus, Richard S.; & Smith, Craig A. (1988). Knowledge and appraisal in the cognition-emotion relationship. *Cognition & Emotion, 2,* 281–300.

Le Foll, Bernard; & Goldberg, Steven R. (2007). Targeting the dopamine D-sub-3 receptor for treatment of nicotine dependence. In Tony P. George (Ed.), *Medication treatments for nicotine dependence* (pp. 199–212). Boca Raton, FL: CRC Press.

Le Foll, David; Rascle, Olivier; & Higgins, N. C. (2008). Attributional feedback-induced changes in functional and dysfunctional attributions, expectations of success, hopefulness, and short-term persistence in a novel sport. *Psychology of Sport and Exercise, 9,* 77–101.

Leach, Carolyn S.; & Rambaut, Paul C. (1974). Biochemical responses of the Skylab crewmen. *Proceedings of the Skylab Life Sciences Symposium, 2,* 427–454.

Leach, Penelope. (2007). Child care and child development. Results from the NICHD Study of Early Child Care and Youth Development. *Journal of Child Psychology & Psychiatry, 48*(9), 959.

Leaper, Campbell; & Bigler, Rebecca S. (2004). Gendered language and sexist thought. *Monographs of the Society for Research in Child Development, 69,* 128–142.

Leaper, Campbell; & Friedman, Carly Kay. (2007). The socialization of gender. In Joan E. Grusec & Paul D. Hastings (Eds.), *Handbook of socialization: Theory and research.* New York: Guilford Press.

Leary, Mark R.; & Cox, Cody B. (2008). Belongingness motivation: A mainspring of social action. In James Y. Shah & Wendi L. Gardner (Eds.), *Handbook of motivation science.* New York: Guilford Press.

LeBlanc, Jacques. (2000). Nutritional implications of cephalic phase thermogenic responses. *Appetite, 34,* 214–216.

Lebow, Jay L. (2008). Couple and family therapy. In Jay L. Lebow (Ed.), *Twenty-first century psychotherapies: Contemporary approaches to theory and practice* (pp. 307–346). Hoboken, NJ: Wiley.

Lebow, Jay L.; & Gurman, Alan S. (1995). Research assessing couple and family therapy. *Annual Review of Psychology, 46,* 27–57.

LeDoux, Joseph E. (1994a, June). Emotion, memory, and the brain. *Scientific American, 270,* 50–57.

LeDoux, Joseph E. (1994b). Memory versus emotional memory in the brain. In Paul Ekman & Richard J. Davisdon (Eds.), *The nature of emotion: Fundamental questions.* New York: Oxford University Press.

LeDoux, Joseph E. (1995). Emotion: Clues from the brain. *Annual Review of Psychology, 46,* 209–235.

LeDoux, Joseph E. (1996). *The emotional brain: The mysterious underpinnings of emotional life.* New York: Simon & Schuster.

LeDoux, Joseph E. (2000). Emotion circuits in the brain. *Annual Review of Neuroscience, 23,* 155–184.

LeDoux, Joseph E. (2007). The amygdala. *Current Biology, 17,* R868–R874.

Lee, Evelyn (Ed.). (1997). *Working with Asian Americans: A guide for clinicians.* New York: Guilford Press.

Lee, Evelyn; & Mock, Matthew R. (2005). Asian families: An overview. In Monica McGoldrick, Joe Giordano, & Nydia Garcia-Petro (Eds.), *Ethnicity & family therapy* (3rd ed., pp. 269–289). New York: Guilford Press.

Lee, Jo Ann; & Phillips, Stephen J. (2006). Work and family: Can you have it all? *Psychologist-Manager Journal, 9*(1), 41–75.

Lehman, Barbara J.; & Crano, William D. (2002). The pervasive effects of vested interest on attitude-criterion consistency in political judgment. *Journal of Experimental Psychology, 38,* 101–112.

Lehrer, Jonah. (2006, February/March). The reinvention of the self. *Seed.* Retrieved February 2008, from http://www.seedmagazine.com/news/2006/02/the_reinvention_of_the_self.php

Leichtman, Martin. (2004). Projective tests: The nature of the task. In Mark J. Hilsenroth & Daniel L. Segal (Eds.), *Comprehensive handbook of psychological assessment, Vol. 2: Personality assessment* (pp. 297–314). Hoboken, NJ: Wiley.

Leichtman, Michelle D.; & Ceci, Stephen J. (1995). The effects of stereotypes and suggestions on preschoolers' reports. *Developmental Psychology, 31,* 568–578.

Lenroot, Rhoshel K.; & Giedd, Jay N. (2006). Brain development in children and adolescents: Insights from anatomical magnetic resonance imaging. *Neuroscience & Biobehavioral Reviews, 30*(6), 718–729.

Lenzenweger, Mark F.; Lane, Michael C.; Loranger, Armand W.; & Kessler, Ronald C. (2007, September 15). DSM-IV personality disorders in the National Comorbidity Survey Replication. *Biological Psychiatry, 62*(6), 553–564.

Leon, Scott C.; Kopta, S. Mark; Howard, Kenneth I.; & Lutz, Wolfgang. (1999). Predicting patients' responses to psychotherapy: Are some more predictable than others? *Journal of Consulting and Clinical Psychology, 67,* 698–704.

Leonard, David; Brann, Susan; & Tiller, John. (2005, October). Dissociative disorders: Pathways to diagnosis, clinician attitudes and their impact. *Australian and New Zealand Journal of Psychiatry, 39*(10), 940–946.

Leonardo, E. D.; & Hen, René. (2005). Genetics of affective and anxiety disorders. *Annual Review of Clinical Psychology, 57,* 117–137.

Lepore, Stephen J. (1993). Social conflict, social support, and psychological distress: Evidence of cross-domain buffering effects. *Journal of Personality and Social Psychology, 63,* 857–867.

Lerner, Howard D. (2008). Psychodynamic perspectives. In Michael Hersen & Alan M. Gross (Eds.), Handbook of clinical psychology: Vol. 1. Adults (pp. 127–160). Hoboken, NJ: Wiley.

Lerner, Melvin J. (1980). *The belief in a just world: A fundamental delusion.* New York: Plenum Press.

Lester, David. (1997). *Making sense of suicide: An in-depth look at why people kill themselves.* Philadelphia: Charles Press.

Lester, Gregory W. (2000, November/December). Why bad beliefs don't die. *Skeptical Inquirer, 24,* 40–43.

Leuchter, Andrew F.; Cook, Ian A.; Witte, Elise A.; Morgan, Melinda; & Abrams, Michelle. (2002). Changes in brain function of depressed subjects during treatment with placebo. *American Journal of Psychiatry, 159,* 122–129.

Leung, Paul K.; & Boehnlein, James K. (2005). Vietnamese families. In Monica McGoldrick, Joseph Giordano, & Nydia Garcia-Petro (Eds.), *Ethnicity & family therapy* (3rd ed., pp. 363–373). New York: Guilford Press.

LeVay, Simon. (2007). A difference in hypothalamic structure between heterosexual and homosexual men. In Gillian Einstein (Ed.), *Sex and the brain.* Cambridge, MA: MIT Press.

Levenson, Hanna. (2003). Time-limited dynamic psychotherapy: An integrationist perspective. *Journal of Psychotherapy Integration, 13,* 300–333.

Levenson, Robert W. (1992). Autonomic nervous system differences among emotions. *Psychological Science, 3,* 23–27.

Levenson, Robert W. (2003). Blood, sweat, and fears: The autonomic architecture of emotion. In Paul Ekman, Joseph Campos, Richard J. Davidson, & Frans B. M. de Waal (Eds.), *Emotions inside out: 130 years after Darwin's: The expression of the emotions in man and animals. Annals of the New York of Sciences: Vol. 1000.* New York: New York University Press.

Levenson, Robert W.; Ekman, Paul; & Friesen, Wallace V. (1990). Voluntary facial action generates emotion-specific autonomic nervous system activity. *Psychophysiology, 27,* 363–384.

Levenson, Robert W.; Ekman, Paul; Heider, Karl; & Friesen, Wallace V. (1992). Emotion and autonomic nervous system activity in the Minangkabau of west Sumatra. *Journal of Personality and Social Psychology, 62,* 972–988.

Levin, Ross; & Nielsen, Tore A. (2007). Disturbed dreaming, posttraumatic stress disorder, and affect distress: A review and neurocognitive model. *Psychological Bulletin, 133,* 482–528.

LeVine, Elaine S. (2007). Experiences from the frontline: Prescribing in New Mexico. *Psychological Services, 4,* 59–71.

Levine, Robert V. (1997). *A geography of time: The temporal misadventures of a social psychologist, or how every culture keeps time just a little bit differently.* New York: Basic Books.

Levine, Robert V.; & Norenzayan, Ara. (1999). The pace of life in 31 countries. *Journal of Cross-Cultural Psychology, 30,* 178–205.

Levinson, Douglas F. (2009). Genetics of major depression. In Ian H. Gotlib & Constance L. Hammen (Eds.), *Handbook of depression* (2nd ed., pp. 165–186). New York: Guilford Press.

Levy, Becca. (1996). Improving memory in old age through implicit self-stereotyping. *Journal of Personality and Social Psychology, 71,* 1092–1107.

Levy, Benjamin L.; & Anderson, Michael C. (2002). Inhibitory processes and the control of memory retrieval. *Trends in Cognitive Science, 6,* 299–305.

Lewontin, Richard. (1970, March). Race and intelligence. *Bulletin of the Atomic Scientists,* 2–8.

Li, Jin. (2005). Mind or virtue: Western and Chinese beliefs about learning. *Current Directions in Psychological Science, 14,* 190–194.

Li, Shenghui; Jin, Xingming; Yan, Chonghuai; Wu, Shenghu; Jiang, Fan; & Shen, Xiaoming. (2008). Bed- and room-sharing in Chinese school-aged children: Prevalence and association with sleep behaviors. *Sleep Medicine, 9,* 555–563.

Li, Susan Tinsley; Jenkins, Sandra; & Sundsmo, Alecia. (2007). Impact of race and ethnicity. In Michel Hersen, Samuel M. Turner, & Deborah C. Beidel (Eds.), *Adult psychopathology and diagnosis* (5th ed., pp. 101–121). Hoboken, NJ: Wiley.

Li, Ting-Kai; Volkow, Nora D.; Baler, Ruben D.; & Egli, Mark. (2007). The biological bases of nicotine and alcohol co-addiction. *Biological Psychiatry, 61,* 1–3.

Li, Wen; Luxenberg, Erin; Parrish, Todd; & Gottfried, Jay A. (2006). Learning to smell the roses: Experience-dependent neural plasticity in human piriform and orbitofrontal cortices. *Neuron, 21,* 1097–1108.

Li, Wen; Moallem, Isabel; Paller, Ken A.; & Gottfried, Jay A. (2007). Subliminal smells can guide social preferences. *Psychological Science, 18,* 1044–1049.

Libby, Lisa K.; Shaeffer, Eric M.; Eibach, Richard P.; & Slemmer, Jonathan. (2007). Picture yourself at the polls: Visual perception in mental imagery affects self-perception and behavior. *Psychological Science, 18,* 199–203.

Lieb, Roselind; Bronisch, Thomas; Höfler, Michael; Schreier, Andrea; & Wittchen, Hans-Ulrich. (2005). Maternal suicidality and risk of suicidality in offspring: Findings from a community study. *American Journal of Psychiatry, 162,* 1665–1671.

Lieberman, Jeffrey A.; Stroup, T. Scott; McEvoy, Joseph P.; Swartz, Marvin S.; Rosenheck, Robert A.; & CATIE Study Investigators. (2005). Effectiveness of antipsychotic drugs in patients with chronic schizophrenia. *New England Journal of Medicine, 353,* 1209–1223.

Lieberman, Matthew D. (2000). Intuition: A social cognitive neuroscience approach. *Psychological Bulletin, 126,* 109–137.

Lieberman, Robert Paul. (2000). The token economy. *American Journal of Psychiatry, 157,* 1398.

Lien, Lars; Dalgard, Florence; & Heyerdahl, Sonja. (2006). The relationship between age of menarche and mental distress in Norwegian adolescent girls and girls from different immigrant groups in Norway: Results from an urban city cross-sectional survey. *Social Science & Medicine, 63*(2), 285–295.

Liff, Zanvel A. (1992). Psychoanalysis and dynamic techniques. In Donald K. Freedheim (Ed.), *History of psychotherapy: A century of change.* Washington, DC: American Psychological Association.

Light, Kathleen C.; Smith, Tara E.; Johns, Josephine M.; Brownley, Kimberly A.; Hofheimer, Julie A.; & Amico, Janet. (2000). Oxytocin responsivity in mothers of infants: A preliminary study of relationships with blood pressure during laboratory stress and normal ambulatory activity. *Health Psychology, 19,* 560–567.

Lilienfeld, Scott O. (1998, Fall). Pseudoscience in contemporary clinical psychology: What it is and what we can do about it. *Clinical Psychologist, 51,* 3–9.

Lilienfeld, Scott O. (2007). Psychological treatments that cause harm. *Perspectives on Psychological Science, 2*(1), 53–69.

Lilienfeld, Scott O.; Fowler, Katherine A.; & Lohr, Jeffrey M. (2005). Pseudoscience, nonscience, and nonsense in clinical psychology: Dangers and remedies. In Rogers H. Wright & Nicholas A. Cummings (Eds.), *Destructive trends in mental health: The well-intentioned path to harm* (pp. 187–218). New York: Routledge.

Lilienfeld, Scott O.; Lynn, Steven Jay; & Lohr, Jeffrey M. (Eds.). (2003). *Science and pseudoscience in clinical psychology.* New York: Guilford Press.

Lilienfeld, Scott O.; Wood, James M.; & Garb, Howard N. (2000). The scientific status of projective techniques. *Psychological Science in the Public Interest, 1,* 27–66.

Lilienfeld, Scott O.; Wood, James M.; & Garb, Howard N. (2001). What's wrong with this picture? *Scientific American, 284,* 80–87.

Lindberg, Eva; Berne, Christian; Elmasry, Ahmed; Hedner, Jan; & Janson, Christer. (2006). CPAP treatment of a population-based sample: What are the benefits and the treatment compliance? *Sleep Medicine, 7,* 553–560.

Lindsay, D. Stephen; Hagen, Lisa; Read, J. Don; Wade, Kimberley A.; & Garry, Maryanne. (2004a). True photographs and false memories. *Psychological Science, 15,* 149–154.

Lindsay, D. Stephen; & Read, J. Don. (1994). Psychotherapy and memories of childhood and sexual abuse: A cognitive perspective. *Applied Cognitive Psychology 8,* 281–338.

Lindsay, D. Stephen; Wade, Kimberley A.; Hunter, Michael A.; & Read, J. Don. (2004b). Adults' memories of childhood: Affect, knowing, and remembering. *Memory, 12,* 27–43.

Lindsey, Delwin T.; & Brown, Angela M. (2004). Commentary: Sunlight and "blue": The prevalence of poor lexical color discrimination within the "grue" range. *Psychological Science, 15,* 291–294.

Linehan, Marsha M. (1993). *Cognitive-behavioral treatment of borderline personality disorder.* New York: Guilford Press.

Linehan, Marsha M. (2009, May 2). Radical compassion: Translating Zen into psychotherapy. Presented at Meditation and Psychotherapy: Cultivating Compassion and Wisdom, Boston, MA.

Linehan, Marsha M.; & Dexter-Mazza, Elizabeth T. (2008). Dialectical behavior therapy for borderline personality disorder. In David H. Barlow (Ed.), *Clinical handbook of psychological disorders* (4th ed., pp. 365–420). New York: Guilford Press.

Little, Karley Y.; Krolewski, David M.; Zhang, Lian; & Cassin, Bader J. (2003). Loss of striatal vesicular monoamine transporter protein (VMAT2) in human cocaine users. *American Journal of Psychiatry, 160,* 47– 55.

Liu, Dong; Diorio, Josie; Tannenbaum, Beth; Caldji, Christian; Francis, Darlene; Freedman, Alison; & others. (1997). Maternal care, hippocampal glucocorticoid receptors, and hypothalamic-pituitary-adrenal responses to stress. *Science, 277,* 1659–1662.

Liu, Ruth X.; & Chen, Zeng-Yin. (2006, June). The effects of marital conflict and marital disruption on depressive affect: A comparison between women in and out of poverty. *Social Science Quarterly, 87*(2), 250–271.

Livianos-Aldana, Lorenzo; Rojo-Moreno, Luis; & Sierra-San-Miguel, Pilar. (2007). F. J. Gall and the phrenological movement. *American Journal of Psychiatry, 164,* 414.

Livingstone, Margaret; & Hubel, David. (1988, May 6). Segregation of form, color, movement and depth: Anatomy, physiology, and perception. *Science, 240,* 740–749.

Lledo, Pierre-Marie; Alonso, Mariana; & Grubb, Matthew S. (2006). Adult neurogenesis and functional plasticity in neuronal circuits. *Nature Reviews Neuroscience, 7,* 179–193.

LoBue, Vanessa; & DeLoache, Judy S. (2008). Detecting the snake in the grass: Attention to fear-relevant stimuli by adults and young children. *Psychological Science, 19,* 284–289.

Lockard, Robert B. (1971). Reflections on the fall of comparative psychology: Is there a message for us all? *American Psychologist, 26,* 168–179.

Locke, Edwin A. (1976). The nature and causes of job satisfaction. In M. D. Dunnette (Ed.), *Handbook of industrial and organizational psychology* (pp. 1297–1349). Chicago: Rand McNally.

Locke, E. A., & Schweiger, D. M. (1979). Participation in decision-making: One more look. *Research in Organizational Behavior, 1,* 265–339.

Lockhart, Robert S.; & Craik, Fergus I. M. (1990). Levels of processing: A retrospective commentary on a framework for memory research. *Canadian Journal of Psychology, 44*(1), 87–112.

Lockwood, Nancy R. (2007, July). Planning for retention. (Future Focus) Survey about job satisfaction of human resource professionals and nonhuman resource employees. *HR Magazine, 52.*

Loewenstein, George F.; Weber, Elke U.; Hsee, Christopher K.; & Welch, Ned. (2001). Risk as feelings. *Psychological Bulletin, 127,* 267–286.

Loftus, Elizabeth F. (1996). *Eyewitness testimony* (Rev. ed.). Cambridge, MA: Harvard University Press.

Loftus, Elizabeth F. (2001). Imagining the past. *The Psychologist, 14,* 584–587.

Loftus, Elizabeth F. (2002). Memory faults and fixes. *Issues in Science and Technology, 18*(4), 41–50.

Loftus, Elizabeth F. (2003). Our changeable memories: Legal and practical implications. *Nature Reviews Neuroscience, 4,* 231–234.

Loftus, Elizabeth F. (2004, 18 December). Dispatch from the (un)civil memory wars. *The Lancet, 364*(Suppl. 1), s20–s21.

Loftus, Elizabeth F. (2007). Memory distortions: Problems solved and unsolved. In Maryanne Garry & Harlene Hayne (Eds.), *Do justice and let the sky fall: Elizabeth Loftus and her contributions to science, law, and academic freedom.* Mahwah, NJ: Erlbaum.

Loftus, Elizabeth F.; & Cahill, Larry. (2007). Memory distortion: From misinformation to rich false memory. In James S. Nairne (Ed.), *The foundation of remembering: Essays in honor of Henry L. Roediger, III.* New York: Psychology Press.

Loftus, Elizabeth F.; & Davis, Deborah. (2006). Recovered memories. *Annual Review of Clinical Psychology, 2,* 469–498.

Loftus, Elizabeth F.; Donders, Karen; Hoffman, Hunter G.; & Schooler, Jonathan W. (1989). Creating new memories that are quickly accessed and confidently held. *Memory & Cognition, 17,* 607–616.

Loftus, Elizabeth F.; Garry, Maryanne; Brown, Scott W.; & Rader, Marcella. (1994). Near-natal memories, past-life memories, and other memory myths. *American Journal of Clinical Hypnosis, 36,* 176–179.

Loftus, Elizabeth F.; & Ketcham, Katherine. (1991). *Witness for the defense: The accused, the eyewitness, and the expert who puts memory on trial.* New York: St. Martin's Press.

Loftus, Elizabeth F.; & Ketcham, Katherine. (1994). *The myth of repressed memory: False memories and allegations of sexual abuse.* New York: St. Martin's Press.

Loftus, Elizabeth F.; & Palmer, J. C. (1974). Reconstruction of automobile destruction: An example of the interaction between language and memory. *Journal of Verbal Learning and Verbal Behavior, 13,* 585–589.

Loftus, Elizabeth F.; & Pickrell, Jacqueline E. (1995). The formation of false memories. *Psychiatric Annals, 25,* 720–725.

Lohr, Jeffrey M.; Hooke, Wayne; Gist, Richard; & Tolin, David F. (2003). Novel and controversial treatments for trauma-related stress disorders. In Scott O. Lilienfeld, Steven Jay Lynn, & Jeffrey M. Lohr (Eds.), *Science and pseudoscience in clinical psychology.* New York: Guilford Press.

LoLordo, Vincent M. (2001). Learned helplessness and depression. In Marilyn E. Carroll & J. Bruce Overmier (Eds.), *Animal research and human health: Advancing human welfare through behavioral science.* Washington, DC: American Psychological Association.

Long, James E., Jr. (2005). Power to prescribe: The debate over prescription privileges for psychologists and the legal issues implicated. *Law & Psychology Review, 29,* 243–260.

Longstreth, W. T., Jr.; Koepsell, Thomas D.; Ton, Thang G.; Hendrickson, Audrey F.; & van Belle, Gerald. (2007). The epidemiology of narcolepsy. *Sleep, 30,* 13–26.

Lord, Charles G.; Ross, Lee; & Lepper, Mark R. (1979). Biased assimilation and attitude polarization: The effects of prior theories on subsequently considered evidence. *Journal of Personality and Social Psychology, 37,* 2098–2109.

Lovallo, William R.; al'Absi, Mustafa; Pincomb, Gwen A.; Everson, Susan A.; Sung, Bong Hee; Passey, Richard B.; & Wilson, Michael F. (1996). Caffeine and behavioral stress effects on blood pressure in borderline hypertensive Caucasian men. *Health Psychology, 15,* 11–17.

Lu, Ying; Sweitzer, Sarah M.; Laurito, Charles E.; & Yeomans, David C. (2004). Differential opioid inhibition of C- and A delta-fiber mediated thermonociception after stimulation of the nucleus raphe magnus. *Anesthesia & Analgesia, 98,* 414–419.

Lubbadeh, Jens. (2005, June). Same brain for speech and sign. *Scientific American Mind, 16*(2), 86–87.

Luborsky, Lester; & Barrett, Marna S. (2006). The history and empirical status of key psychoanalytic concepts. *Annual Review of Clinical Psychology, 2,* 69–78.

Luborsky, Lester; Rosenthal, Robert; Diguer, Louis; Andrusyna, Tomasz P.; Berman, Jeffrey S.; Levitt, Jill T.; Seligman, David A.; & Krause, Elizabeth D. (2002). The dodo bird verdict is alive and well—mostly. *Clinical Psychology: Science and Practice, 9,* 2–12.

Luders, Eileen; Narr, Katherine L.; Thompson, Paul M.; Rex, David E.; Jancke, Lutz; Steinmetz, Helmuth; & Toga, Arthur W. (2004). Gender differences in cortical complexity. *Nature Neuroscience, 7,* 799–800.

Ludwig, David S.; & Kabat-Zinn, Jon. (2008). Mindfulness in medicine. *Journal of the American Medical Association, 300,* 1350–1352.

Lundqvist, Daniel; & Öhman, Arne. (2005). Caught by the evil eye: Nonconscious information processing, emotion, and attention to facial stimuli. In Lisa Feldman Barrett, Paula M. Niedenthal, & Piotr Winkielman (Eds.), *Emotion and consciousness.* New York: Guilford Press.

Luo, Yuyan; Baillargeon, Renée; Brueckner, Laura; & Munakata, Yuko. (2003). Reasoning about a hidden object after a delay: Evidence for robust representations in 5-month-old infants. *Cognition, 88,* B23–B32.

Lupien, Sonia J.; McEwen, Bruce S.; Gunnar, Megan R.; & Heim, Christine. (2009). Effects of stress throughout the lifespan on the brain, behavior, and cognition. *Nature Reviews Neuroscience, 10,* 434–445.

Lüthje, Lars; & Andreas, Stefan. (2008). Obstructive sleep apnea and coronary artery disease. *Sleep Medicine Reviews, 12,* 19–31.

Lutz, Antoine; Greischar, Lawrence L.; Rawlings, Nancy B.; Richard, Matthieu; & Davidson, Richard J. (2004, November 16). Long-term meditators self-induce high-amplitude gamma synchrony during mental practice. *Proceedings of the National Academy of Sciences, 101,* 16369–16373.

Lykken, David T. (2006, June). The mechanism of emergenesis. *Genes, Brain & Behavior, 5*(4), 306–310.

Lykken, David T.; McGue, Matthew; Tellegen, Auke; & Bouchard, Thomas J., Jr. (1992). Emergenesis: Genetic traits that may not run in families. *American Psychologist, 47,* 1565–1577.

Lyn, Heidi; Greenfield, Patricia; & Savage-Rumbaugh, Sue. (2006). The development of representational play in chimpanzees and bonobos: Evolutionary implications, pretense, and the role of interspecies communication. *Cognitive Development, 21,* 199–213.

Lynam, Donald R.; & Gudonis, Lauren. (2005). The development of psychopathy. *Annual Review of Clinical Psychology, 1,* 381–407.

Lynch, Denis J.; McGrady, Angele; Alvarez, Elizabeth; & Forman, Justin. (2005). Recent life changes and medical utilization in an academic family practice. *Journal of Nervous and Mental Disease, 193,* 633–635.

Lyness, Scott A. (1993). Predictors of differences between Type A and B individuals in heart rate and blood pressure reactivity. *Psychological Bulletin, 114,* 266–295.

Lynn, Steven Jay; & Kirsch, Irving. (2006). *Essentials of clinical hypnosis: An evidence-based approach.* Washington, DC: American Psychological Association.

Lynn, Steven Jay; Lock, Timothy; Loftus, Elizabeth F.; Krackow, Elisa; & Lilienfeld, Scott O. (2003). The remembrance of things past: Problematic memory recovery techniques in psychotherapy. In Scott O. Lilienfeld, Steven Jay Lynn, & Jeffrey M. Lohr (Eds.), *Science and pseudoscience in clinical psychology.* New York: Guilford Press.

Lynn, Steven Jay; Lock, Timothy G.; Myers, Bryan; & Payne, David G. (1997). Recalling the unrecallable: Should hypnosis be used to recover memories in psychotherapy? *Current Directions in Psychological Science, 6,* 79–83.

Lytton, William W. (2008). Computer modeling of epilepsy. *Nature Reviews Neuroscience, 9,* 626–637.

Maccoby, Eleanor E.; & Martin, John A. (1983). Socialization in the context of the family: Parent-child interaction. In Paul H. Mussen (Ed.), *Handbook of child psychology: Vol. 4. Socialization, personality, and social development.* New York: Wiley.

MacDonald, Ann. (2007). Prenatal development. In Floyd E. Bloom, M. Flint Beal, & David J. Kupfer (Eds.), *The Dana guide to brain health.* Washington, DC: Dana Press.

MacDonald, Benie; & Davey, Graham C. L. (2005). Inflated responsibility and perseverative checking: The effect of negative mood. *Journal of Abnormal Psychology, 114,* 176–182.

Macht, Michael. (2008). How emotions affect eating: A five-way model. *Appetite, 50,* 1–11.

Mackey, Richard A.; Diemer, Matthew A.; & O'Brien, Bernard A. (2004). Relational factors in understanding satisfaction in the lasting relationships of same-sex and heterosexual couples. *Journal of Homosexuality, 47*(1), 111–136.

Macrae, C. Neil; Milne, Alan B.; & Bodenhausen, Galen V. (1994). Stereotypes as energy-saving devices: A peek inside the cognitive toolbox. *Journal of Personality and Social Psychology, 66,* 37–47.

Macrae, C. Neil; Quinn, Kimberly A.; Mason, Malia F.; & Quadflieg, Susanne. (2005). Understanding others: The face and person construal. *Journal of Personality and Social Psychology, 89,* 686–695.

Madsen, Matias Vested; Gøtzsche, Peter C.; & Hróbjartsson, Asbjørn. (2009, January 27). Acupuncture treatment for pain: Systematic review of randomised clinical trials with acupuncture, placebo acupuncture, and no acupuncture groups. *British Medical Journal, 338,* a3115. Retrieved July 12, 2009, from http://www.bmj.com/cgi/reprint/338/jan27_2/a3115.pdf

Magnavita, Jeffrey J. (1993). The evolution of short-term dynamic psychotherapy: Treatment of the future? *Professional Psychology: Research and Practice, 24,* 360–365.

Magnavita, Jeffrey J. (2008). Psychoanalytic psychotherapy. In Jay L. Lebow (Ed.), *Twenty-first century psychotherapies: Contemporary approaches to theory and practice* (pp. 206–236). Hoboken, NJ: Wiley.

Maguire, Eleanor A.; Gadian, David G.; Johnsrude, Ingrid S.; Good, Catriona D.; Ashburner, John; Frackowiak, Richard S. J.; & Frith, Christopher D. (2000). Navigation-related structural change in the hippocampi of taxi drivers. *Proceedings of the National Academy of Sciences, USA, 97,* 4398–4403.

Maguire, Eleanor A.; Woollett, Katherine; & Spiers, Hugo J. (2006). London taxi drivers and bus drivers: A structural MRI and neuropsychological analysis. *Hippocampus, 16,* 1091–1101.

Mahowald, Mark W. (2005). Other parasomnias. In Meir H. Kryger, Thomas Roth, & William C. Dement (Eds.), *Principles and practice of sleep medicine* (4th ed.). Philadelphia: Elsevier Saunders.

Mahowald, Mark W.; & Bornemann, Michael A. Cramer. (2005). Sleep Arousals. In Meir H. Kryger, Thomas Roth, & William C. Dement (Eds.), *Principles and practice of sleep medicine* (4th ed.). Philadelphia: Elsevier Saunders.

Mahowald, Mark W.; & Schenck, Carlos H. (2005, October 27). Insights from studying human sleep disorders. *Nature, 437,* 1279–1285.

Maia, Tiago V.; Cooney, Rebecca E; & Peterson, Bradley S. (2009). The neural bases of obsessive-compulsive disorder in children and adults. *Development and Psychopathology, 20*(4), 1251–1283.

Maier, Andrea; Vickers, Zata; & Inman, J. Jeffrey (2007). Sensory-specific satiety, its crossovers, and subsequent choice of potato chip flavors. *Appetite, 49,* 419–428.

Maier, Steven F.; Seligman, Martin E.; & Solomon, Richard L. (1969). Pavlovian fear conditioning and learned helplessness: Effects of escape and avoidance behavior of (a) the CS=UCS contingency, and (b) the independence of the UCS and voluntary responding. In Byron A. Campbell & Russell M. Church (Eds.), *Punishment and aversive behavior.* New York: Appleton-Century-Crofts.

Maier, Steven F.; & Watkins, Linda R. (2000). The neurobiology of stressor controllability. In Jane E. Gillham (Ed.), *The science of optimism and hope: Research essays in honor of Martin E. P. Seligman.* Philadelphia: Templeton Foundation Press.

Majid, Asifa; Bowerman, Melissa; Kita, Sotaro; Haun, Daniel B. M.; & Levinson, Stephen C. (2004). Can language restructure cognition? The case for space. *Trends in Cognitive Sciences, 8,* 108–114.

Major, Geneviève C.; Doucet, Eric; & Trayhurn, Paul. (2007). Clinical significance of adaptive thermogenesis. *International Journal of Obesity, 31,* 204–212.

Malaspina, Dolores; Harlap, Susan; Fennig, Shmuel; Heiman, Dov; Nahon, Daniella; Feldman, Dina; & Susser, Ezra. (2001). Advancing paternal age and the risk of schizophrenia. *Archives of General Psychiatry, 58,* 361–367.

Malekpour, Mokhtar. (2007). Effects of attachment on early and later development. *British Journal of Developmental Disabilities, 53,* 81–95.

Malenka, Robert C. (2003). The long-term potential of LTP. *Nature Reviews Neuroscience, 4,* 923–926.

Malla, Ashok; & Payne, Jennifer. (2005). First-episode psychosis: Psychopathology, quality of life, and functional outcome. *Schizophrenia Bulletin, 31,* 650–671.

Mallett, Robyn K.; Wilson, Timothy D.; & Gilbert, Daniel T. (2008, February). Expect the unexpected: Failure to anticipate similarities leads to an intergroup forecasting error. *Journal of Personality and Social Psychology, 94*(2), 265–277.

Mallinckrodt, Brent. (2001). Interpersonal processes, attachment, and development of social competencies in individual and group psychotherapy. In Barbara R. Sarason & Steve Duck (Eds.), *Personal relationships: Implications for clinical and community psychology.* Chichester, England: Wiley.

Mandler, George. (1993). Thought, memory, and learning: Effects of emotional stress. In Leo Goldberger & Shlomo Breznitz (Eds.), *Handbook of stress: Theoretical and clinical aspects* (2nd ed.). New York: Free Press.

Mann, J. John; Waternaux, Christine; Haas, Gretchen L.; & Malone, Kevin M. (1999). Toward a clinical model of suicidal behavior in psychiatric patients. *American Journal of Psychiatry, 156,* 181–189.

Manning, Rachel; Levine, Mark; & Collin, Alan. (2007). The Kitty Genovese murder and the social psychology of helping: The parable of the 38 witnesses. *American Psychologist, 62,* 555–562.

Manning, Rachel; Levine, Mark; & Collin, Alan. (2008). The legacy of the 38 witnesses and the importance of getting it right. *American Psychologist, 63,* 562–563.

Maple, Terry. (2006, November). Tales of an animal psychologist. *APS Observer, 19,* 11–13.

Maple, Terry. (2007). Toward a science of welfare for animals in the zoo. *Journal of Applied Animal Welfare Science, 10,* 63–70.

Marañon, Gregorio. (1924). Contribution à l'étude de l'action émotive de l'adrenaline. *Revue Francaise d'Endocrinologie, 2,* 301–325.

Marcelino, A. S.; Adam, A. S.; Couronne, T.; Köster, E. P; & Sieffermann, J. M. (2001). Internal and external determinants of eating initiation in humans. *Appetite, 36,* 9–14.

Marcia, James E. (1991). Identity and self-development. In R. M. Lerner, A. C. Petersen, & Jeanne Brooks-Gunn (Eds.), *Encyclopedia of adolescence* (Vol. 1). New York: Garland.

Marco, Christine A.; & Suls, Jerry. (1993). Daily stress and the trajectory of mood: Spillover, response assimilation, contrast, and chronic negative affectivity. *Journal of Personality and Social Psychology, 64,* 1053–1063.

Marcus, Gary. (2004). *The birth of the mind: How a tiny number of genes creates the complexities of human thought.* New York: Basic Books.

Marcus, Bernd; Lee, Kibeom; & Ashton, Michael C. (2007). Personality dimensions explaining relationships between integrity tests and counterproductive behavior: Big Five, or one in addition? *Personnel Psychology, 60,* 1–34.

Markman, Arthur B.; & Gentner, Dedre. (2001). Thinking. *Annual Review of Psychology, 52,* 223–247.

Markus, Hazel Rose; & Cross, Susan. (1990). The interpersonal self. In Lawrence A. Pervin (Ed.), *Handbook of personality: Theory and research.* New York: Guilford Press.

Markus, Hazel Rose; & Kitayama, Shinobu. (1991). Culture and the self: Implications for cognition, emotion, and motivation. *Psychological Review, 98,* 224–253.

Markus, Hazel Rose; & Kitayama, Shinobu. (1994). The cultural construction of self and emotion: Implications for social behavior. In Shinobu Kitayama & Hazel Rose Markus (Eds.), *Emotion and culture: Empirical studies of mutual influence.* Washington, DC: American Psychological Association.

Markus, Hazel Rose; & Kitayama, Shinobu. (1998). The cultural psychology of personality. *Journal of Cross-Cultural Psychology, 29,* 63–87.

Markus, Hazel Rose; & Kunda, Ziva. (1986). Stability and malleability of the self-concept. *Journal of Personality and Social Psychology, 51,* 858–866.

Markus, Hazel Rose; & Nurius, Paula. (1986). Possible selves. *American Psychologist, 41,* 954–969.

Markus, Hazel Rose; Uchida, Yukiko; Omoregie, Heather; Townsend, Sarah S. M.; & Kitayama, Shinobu. (2006). Going for the gold: Models of agency in Japanese and American contexts. *Psychological Science, 17,* 103–112.

Markus, Hazel Rose; & Wurf, Elissa. (1987). The dynamic self-concept: A social psychological perspective. *Annual Review of Psychology, 38,* 299–337.

Marler, Peter. (1967). Animal communication symbols. *Science, 35,* 63–78.

Marmie, William R.; & Healy, Alice F. (2004). Memory for common objects: Brief intentional study is sufficient to overcome poor recall of US coin features. *Applied Cognitive Psychology, 18,* 445–453.

Marneros, Andreas; & Goodwin, Frederick (Eds.). (2005). *Bipolar disorders: Mixed states, rapid cycling, and atypical forms.* Cambridge, England: Cambridge University Press.

Marsella, Anthony J.; & Dash-Scheuer, Alice. (1988). Coping, culture, and healthy human development: A research and conceptual overview. In Pierre R. Dasen, John W. Berry, & Norman Sartorius (Eds.), *Health and cross-cultural psychology: Toward applications* (Vol. 10, Cross-cultural Research and Methodology Series). Newbury Park, CA: Sage.

Marshall, Grant N.; Wortman, Camille B.; Kusulas, Jeffrey W.; Hervig, Linda K.; & Vickers, Ross R., Jr. (1992). Distinguishing optimism from pessimism: Relations to fundamental dimensions of mood and personality. *Journal of Personality and Social Psychology, 62,* 1067–1074.

Marshall, Lisa; & Born, Jan. (2007). The contribution of sleep to hippocampus-dependent memory consolidation. *Trends in Cognitive Sciences, 11,* 442–450.

Marshall, Nancy L. (2004). The quality of early child care and children's development. *Current Directions in Psychological Science, 13,* 165–168.

Martin, Alex. (2007). The representation of object concepts in the brain. *Annual Review of Psychology, 58,* 25–45.

Martin, Bruce. (1998, May). Coincidences: Remarkable or random? *Skeptical Inquirer, 22,* 23–28.

Martin, Carol Lynn; & Halverson, Charles F., Jr. (1981). A schematic processing model of sex typing and stereotyping in children. *Child Development, 52,* 1119–1134.

Martin, Carol Lynn; & Halverson, Charles F., Jr. (1983). The effects of sex-typing schemas on young children's memory. *Child Development, 54,* 563–574.

Martin, Carol Lynn; & Ruble, Diane N. (2004). Children's search for gender cues: Cognitive perspectives on gender development. *Psychological Science, 13,* 67–70.

Martin, Carol Lynn; Ruble, Diane N.; & Szkrybalo, Joel. (2002). Cognitive theories of early gender development. *Psychological Bulletin, 128,* 903–933.

Martin, Carol Lynn; Ruble, Diane N.; & Szkrybalo, Joel. (2004). Recognizing the centrality of gender identity and stereotype knowledge in gender development and moving toward theoretical integration: Reply to Bandura and Bussey. *Psychological Bulletin, 130,* 702–710.

Martin, Laura. (1986). "Eskimo words for snow": A case study in the genesis and decay of an anthropological example. *American Anthropologist, 88,* 418–423.

Martin, Rod A. (2007). *The psychology of humor: An integrative approach.* Amsterdam: Elsevier.

Martin, Stephen D.; Martin, Elizabeth; Santoch, S. Rai; Richardson, Mark A.; & Royall, Robert. (2001). Brain blood flow changes in depressed patients treated with interpersonal psychotherapy or venlafaxine hydrochloride. *Archives of General Psychiatry, 58,* 641–648.

Martinez-Salazar, Gloria Maria; Faintuch, Salomao; & Lang, Elvira V. (2008). Adjunctive hypnotic management of acute pain in invasive medical interventions. In Joseph F. Audette & Allison Bailey (Eds.), *Integrative pain medicine: The science and practice of complementary and alternative medicine in pain management.* Totowa, NJ: Humana Press.

Marucha, Phillip T.; Kiecolt-Glaser, Janice K.; & Favagehi, Mehrdad. (1998). Mucosal wound healing is impaired by examination stress. *Psychosomatic Medicine, 60,* 362–365.

Maser, Jack D.; Norman, Sonya B.; Zisook, Sidney; Everall, Ian P.; Stein, Murray B.; Schettler, Pamela J.; & Judd, Lewis L. (2009, February 17). Psychiatric nosology is ready for a paradigm shift in DSM-V. *Clinical Psychology: Science and Practice, 16*(1) 24–40.

Masland, Richard H. (2001). The fundamental plan of the retina. *Nature Neuroscience, 4,* 877–886.

Masliah, Eliezer. (2008). Neuropathology: Alzheimer's in real time. *Nature, 451,* 638–639.

Maslow, Abraham H. (1943). A theory of human motivation. *Psychological Review, 50,* 370–396.

Maslow, Abraham H. (1954). *Motivation and personality.* New York: Harper.

Maslow, Abraham H. (1968). *Toward a psychology of being* (2nd ed.). Princeton, NJ: Van Nostrand.

Maslow, Abraham H. (1970). *Motivation and personality* (2nd ed.). New York: Harper & Row.

Masters, Kevin S.; Stillman, Alexandra M.; & Spielmans, Glen I. (2007, February). Specificity of social support for back pain patients: Do patients care who provides what? *Journal of Behavioral Medicine, 30*(1), 11–20.

Masters, William H.; & Johnson, Virginia E. (1966). *Human sexual response.* Boston: Little, Brown.

Masters, William H.; Johnson, Virginia E.; & Kolodny, Robert C. (1995). *Human sexuality* (5th ed.). New York: HarperCollins.

Matarazzo, Joseph D. (1981). Obituary: David Wechsler (1896–1981). *American Psychologist, 36,* 1542–1543.

Mathews, Carol A. (2009). In Martin M. Antony & Murray B. Stein (Eds.), *Oxford handbook of anxiety and related disorders* (pp. 56–64). New York: Oxford University Press.

Matson, Claire A.; Reid, Dana F.; Cannon, Todd A.; & Ritter, Robert C. (2000). Cholecystokinin and leptin act synergistically to reduce body weight. *American Journal of Physiology, 278,* R882–R890.

Matson, Johnny L.; & LoVullo, Santino V. (2008). A review of behavioral treatments for self-injurious behaviors of persons with autism spectrum disorders. *Behavior Modification, 32,* 61–70.

Matson, Johnny L.; Matson, Michael L.; & Rivet, Tessa T. (2007). Social-skills treatments for children with autism-spectrum disorders: An overview. *Behavior Modification, 31,* 682–707.

Matsumoto, David. (2000). *Culture and psychology: People around the world* (2nd ed.). Belmont, CA: Wadsworth/Thomson Learning.

Matsumoto, David; & Juang, Linda. (2008). *Culture and psychology* (4th ed.). Wadsworth: Belmont, CA.

Matsumoto, David; & Yoo, Seung Hee. (2006). Toward a new generation of cross-cultural research. *Perspectives on Psychological Science, 1,* 234–250.

Maxmen, Jerrold S.; & Ward, Nicholas G. (1995). *Essential psychopathology and its treatment* (2nd ed.). New York: Norton.

May, Mike. (2002a, June). Quoted in Michael Abrams, "Sight unseen." *Discover, 23,* 54–59.

May, Mike. (2002b, September 26). Quoted in British Broadcasting Corporation (BBC) transcript, September 26, 2002. *LiveChat: The man who learned to see.* Retrieved August 2, 2004, from http://www.bbc.co.uk/ouch/wyp/mikemayqa.shtml

May, Mike. (2004). Quoted in Sendero Group, "Mike's journal." Retrieved August 2, 2004, from http://www.senderogroup.com/mikejournal.htm

Maybery, D. J.; Neale, Jason; Arentz, Alex; & Jones-Ellis, Jenny. (2007, June). The Negative Event Scale: Measuring frequency and intensity of adult hassles. *Anxiety, Stress & Coping, 20*(2), 163–176.

Mayer, John D.; Salovey, Peter; & Caruso, David R. (2004). Emotional intelligence: Theory, findings, and intelligence. *Psychological Inquiry, 15,* 197–215.

Mayer, John D.; Salovey, Peter; & Caruso, David R. (2008). Emotional intelligence: New ability or eclectic traits? *American Psychologist, 63,* 503–517.

Maynard, Ashley E.; & Greenfield, Patricia M. (2003). Implicit cognitive development in cultural tools and children: Lessons from Maya Mexico. *Cognitive Development, 18,* 489–510.

Mayor, Tracy. (2008, April 2). Asperger's and IT: Dark secret or open secret? *Computerworld.* Retrieved August 30, 2008, from http:www.computerworld.com/action/article.do?command=viewArticleBasic&articleId=9072119

Mays, Vickie M.; Cochran, Susan D.; & Barnes, Namdi W. (2007). Race, race-based discrimination, and health outcomes among African Americans. *Annual Review of Psychology, 58,* 201–225.

Mazzoni, Giuliana; & Lynn, Steven Jay. (2007). Using hypnosis in eyewitness memory: Past and current issues. In Michael P. Toglia, J. Don Read, David F. Ross, & Lindsay, R. C. L. (Eds.), *The handbook of eyewitness psychology, Vol. I: Memory for events.* Mahwah, NJ: Erlbaum.

Mazzoni, Giuliana; & Scoboria, Alan. (2007). False memories. In Francis T. Durso (Ed.), *Handbook of applied social cognition. Second edition.* Chichester, England: Wiley.

McAdams, Dan P. (1992). The five-factor model in personality: A critical appraisal. *Journal of Personality, 60,* 329–362.

McAdams, Dan P.; & Pals, Jennifer L. (2006). A new Big Five: Fundamental principles for an integrative science of personality. *American Psychologist, 61,* 204–217.

McAndrew, Francis T.; Akande, Adebowale; Turner, Saskia; & Sharma, Yadika. (1998). A cross-cultural ranking of stressful life events in Germany, India, South Africa, and the United States. *Journal of Cross-Cultural Psychology, 29,* 717–727.

McCabe, Marita P.; & Ricciardelli, Lina A. (2004). A longitudinal study of pubertal timing and extreme body change behaviors among adolescent boys and girls. *Adolescence, 39,* 145–166.

McCabe, Randi E.; Chudzik, Susan M.; Antony, Martin M.; Young, Lisa; Swinson, Richard P.; & Zolvensky, Michael J. (2004). Smoking behaviors across anxiety disorders. *Anxiety Disorders, 18,* 7–18.

McCaig, Linda F.; & Burt, Catharine W. (2004, March 18). National Hospital Ambulatory Medical Care Survey: 2002 emergency department summary. *Advance Data from Vital and Health Statistics.* No. 340. Hyattsville, MD: National Center for Health Statistics. Retrieved January 6, 2005, from http://www.cdc.gov/nchs/data/ad/ad340.pdf

McCarley, Robert W. (2007). Neurobiology of REM and NREM sleep. *Sleep Medicine, 8,* 302–330.

McCarthy, Margaret M. (2007). GABA receptors make teens resistant to input. *Nature Neuroscience, 10,* 397–399.

McCartney, Kathleen; Harris, Monica J.; & Bernieri, Frank. (1990). Growing up and growing apart: A developmental meta-analysis of twin studies. *Psychological Bulletin, 107,* 226–237.

McClelland, David C. (1961). *The achieving society.* Princeton, NJ: Van Nostrand.

McClelland, David C. (1975). *Power: The inner experience.* New York: Irvington.

McClelland, David C. (1976). *The achieving society* (2nd ed.). Oxford, England: Irvington.

McClelland, David C. (1985a). How motives, skills, and values determine what people do. *American Psychologist, 40,* 812–825.

McClelland, David C. (1985b). *Human motivation.* Glenview, IL: Scott, Foresman.

McClelland, David C. (1987). Characteristics of successful entrepreneurs. *Journal of Creative Behavior, 21,* 219–233.

McClelland, David C. (1989). Motivational factors in health and disease. *American Psychologist, 44,* 675–683.

McClelland, David C.; Atkinson, John W.; Clark, Russell A.; & Lowell, Edgar L. (1953). *The achievement motive.* New York: Appleton-Century-Crofts.

McClelland, David C.; & Winter, David G. (1971). *Motivating economic achievement.* New York: Free Press.

McClintock, Martha K. (1971). Menstrual synchrony and suppression. *Nature, 229,* 244–245.

McClintock, Martha K. (1992, October). Quoted in John Easton, "Sex, rats, and videotapes: From the outside in." *The University of Chicago Magazine, 85*(1), 32–36.

McClintock, Martha K. (2001, July 25). Quoted in Marcella S. Kreiter, "Neurology: Brain smells out signals." *MedServ Medical News.* Retrieved November 8, 2001, from http://www.medserv.no/article/php?sid=666

McClintock, Shawn M.; Trevino, Kenneth; & Husain, Mustafa M. (2009). Vagus nerve stimulation: Indications, efficacy, and methods. In Conrad M. Swartz (Ed.), *Electroconvulsive and neuromodulation therapies* (pp. 543–555). New York: Cambridge University Press.

McConnell, Allen R.; Rydell, Robert J.; Strain, Laura M.; & Mackie, Diane M. (2008). Forming implicit and explicit attitudes toward individuals: Social group association cues. *Journal of Personality and Social Psychology, 94,* 792–807.

McCoy, Bob. (2000). *Quack!: Tales of medical fraud from the Museum of Questionable Medical Devices.* Santa Monica, CA: Santa Monica Press.

McCoy, Robert. (1996). Phrenology. In Gordon Stein (Ed.), *The encyclopedia of the paranormal.* Amherst, NY: Prometheus Books.

McCrae, Robert R.; & Costa, Paul T., Jr. (1990). *Personality in adulthood.* New York: Guilford Press.

McCrae, Robert R.; & Costa, Paul T., Jr. (1996). Toward a new generation of personality theories: Theoretical contexts for the five-factor model. In Jerry S. Wiggins (Ed.), *The five-factor model of personality: Theoretical perspectives.* New York: Guilford Press.

McCrae, Robert R.; & Costa, Paul T., Jr. (2003). *Personality in adulthood: A five-factor theory perspective* (2nd ed.). New York: Guilford Press.

McCrae, Robert R.; & Costa, Paul T., Jr. (2006). Cross-cultural perspectives on adult personality trait development. In David K. Mroczek & Todd D. Little (Eds.), *Handbook of personality development.* Mahwah, NJ: Erlbaum.

McCrae, Robert R.; Costa, Paul T., Jr.; Martin, Thomas A.; Oryol, Valery E.; Rukavishnikov, Alexey A.; Senin, Ivan G.; Hrebícková, Martina; & Urbánek, Tomás. (2004). Consensual validation of personality traits across cultures. *Journal of Research in Personality, 38,* 179–201.

McCrae, Robert R.; Costa, Paul T., Jr.; Ostendorf, Fritz; Angleitner, Alois; Hrebícková, Martina; Avia, Maria D.; & others. (2000). Nature over nurture: Temperament, personality, and life span development. *Journal of Personality and Social Psychology, 78,* 173–186.

McCrae, Robert R.; Terracciano, Antonio; & Members of the Personality Profiles of Cultures Project. (2005). Universal features of personality traits from the observer's perspective: Data from 50 cultures. *Journal of Personality and Social Psychology, 88,* 547–561.

McDermut, Wilson; & Zimmerman, Mark. (2008). Personality disorders, personality traits, and defense mechanisms measures. In A. John Rush, Jr., Michael B. First, & Deborah Blacker (Eds.), *Handbook of psychiatric measures* (2nd ed., pp. 687–729). Arlington, VA: American Psychiatric Publishing.

McDonald, William M.; Meeks, Thomas W.; McCall, W. Vaughan; & Zorumski, Charles F. (2009). Electroconvulsive therapy. In Alan F. Schatzberg & Charles B. Nemeroff (Eds.), *The American Psychiatric Publishing textbook of psychopharmacology* (4th ed., pp. 861–899). Washington, DC: American Psychiatric Publishing.

McDougall, William. (1908). *Introduction to social psychology.* London: Methuen.

McFadden, Lisa; Seidman, Edward; & Rappaport, Julian. (1992). A comparison of espoused theories of self- and mutual help: Implications for mental health professionals. *Professional Psychology: Research and Practice, 23,* 515–520.

McGaugh, James L. (2000, January 14). Memory: A century of consolidation. *Science, 287,* 248–251.

McGaugh, James L. (2004). The amygdala modulates the consolidation of memories of emotionally arousing experiences. *Annual Review of Neuroscience, 27,* 1–28.

McGehee, Daniel S.; Iacoviello, Michael; & Mitchum, Robert. (2007). Cellular and synaptic effects of nicotine. In Tony P. George (Ed.), *Medication treatments for nicotine dependence* (pp. 25–38). Boca Raton, FL: CRC Press.

McGoldrick, Monica; Giordano, Joseph; & Garcia-Preto, Nydia. (2005). Overview: Ethnicity and family therapy. In Monica McGoldrick, Joseph Giordano, & Nydia Garcia-Preto (Eds.), *Ethnicity & family therapy* (3rd ed., pp. 1–40). New York: Guilford Press.

McGregor, Jacqueline C. (2009). Anxiety disorders. In Robert E. Rakel & Edward T. Bope (Eds.), *Conn's current therapy 2009* (pp. 1111–1115). Philadelphia: Saunders Elsevier.

McGue, Matt; Bouchard, Thomas J., Jr.; Iacono, William G.; & Lykken, David T. (1993). Behavioral genetics of cognitive ability: A lifespan perspective. In Robert Plomin & Gerald E. McClearn (Eds.), *Nature, nurture, and psychology.* Washington, DC: American Psychological Association.

McKean, Keith Joseph. (1994). Academic helplessness: Applying learned helplessness theory to undergraduates who give up when faced with academic setbacks. *College Student Journal, 28,* 456–462.

McKenry, Patrick C., & Price, Sharon J. (Eds.) (2005). *Families and change: Coping with stressful events and transitions.* Thousand Oaks, CA: Sage.

McLewin, Lise A.; & Muller, Robert T. (2006, September-October). Childhood trauma, imaginary companions, and the development of pathological dissociation. *Aggression and Violent Behavior, 11*(5), 531–545.

McMurran, Mary & Howard, Richard. (2009). Personality, personality disorder and violence: Implications for future research and practice. In Mary McMurran & Richard Howard (Eds.), *Personality, personality disorder and violence* (pp. 299–311). West Sussex, England: Wiley-Blackwell.

McNab, Fiona; & Klingberg, Torkel. (2008). Prefrontal cortex and basal ganglia access in working memory. *Nature Neuroscience, 11,* 103–107.

McNally, Richard J. (1998, September 14). Quoted in Judy Foreman, "New therapy for trauma is doubted." *The Boston Globe Online.* Retrieved October 10, 2001, from http://www.globe.com/globe/search/stories/health/healthsense/091498.htm

McNally, Richard J. (2003). Progress and controversy in the study of posttraumatic stress disorder. *Annual Review of Psychology, 54,* 229–252.

McNally, Richard J. (2004) The science and folklore of traumatic amnesia. *Clinical Psychology: Science and Practice, 11,* 29–33.

McNally, Richard J. (2007). Dispelling confusion about traumatic dissociative amnesia. *Mayo Clinic Proceedings, 82,* 1083–1087.

McNeilly, Cheryl L.; & Howard, Kenneth I. (1991). The effects of psychotherapy: A reevaluation based on dosage. *Psychotherapy Research, 1,* 74–78.

Meaney, Michael J. (2001). Maternal care, gene expression, and the transmission of individual differences in stress reactivity across generations. *Annual Review of Neuroscience, 24,* 1161–1192.

Medina, Jorge H.; Bekinschtein, Pedro; Cammarota, Martin; & Izquierdo, Iván. (2008. Do memories consolidate to persist or do they persist to consolidate? *Behavioural Brain Research, 192,* 61–69.

Melanson, Kathleen J.; Smith, Françoise J.; Campfield, L. Arthur; & others. (1999). Blood glucose patterns and appetite in time-blinded humans: Carbohydrate versus fat. *American Journal of Physiology, 277,* R337–R345.

Melton, Lisa. (2005, December 17). Use it, don't lose it. *New Scientist, 188,* 32–35.

Meltzoff, Andrew N. (2007). 'Like me': A framework for social cognition. *Developmental Science, 10,* 126-134.

Meltzoff, Andrew N.; & Moore, M. Keith. (1977). Imitation of facial and manual gestures by human neonates. *Science, 198,* 75–78.

Meltzoff, Andrew N.; & Moore, M. Keith. (1983). Newborn infants imitate adult facial gestures. *Child Development, 54,* 702–709.

Meltzoff, Andrew N.; & Moore, M. Keith. (1989). Imitation in newborn infants: Exploring the range of gestures imitated and the underlying mechanisms. *Developmental Psychology, 25,* 954–962.

Melzack, Ronald; & Wall, Patrick D. (1965). Pain mechanisms: A new theory. *Science, 150,* 971–980.

Melzack, Ronald; & Wall, Patrick D. (1996). *The challenge of pain* (2nd ed.). Harmondworth, England: Penguin.

Menaker, Michael. (2003, January 10). Perspectives: Circadian photoreception. *Science, 299,* 213–214.

Menand, Louis. (2001). *The Metaphysical Club: A story of ideas in America.* New York: Farrar, Straus, & Giroux.

Mercer, Deanna; Douglass, Alan B.; & Links, Paul S. (2009, April). Meta-analyses of mood stabilizers, antidepressants and antipsychotics in the treatment of borderline personality disorder: Effectiveness for depression and anger symptoms. *Journal of Personality Disorders, 23*(2), 156–174.

Merckelbach, Harald; Arntz, Arnoud; Arrindell, Willem A.; & De Jong, Peter J. (1992). Pathways to spider phobia. *Behavior Research and Therapy, 30,* 543–546.

Merlino, Joseph P.; Jacobs, Marily S.; Kaplan, Judy Ann; & Moritz, Lynne K. (Eds.). (2008). *Freud at 150: 21st-century essays on a man of genius.* Lanham, MD: Jason Aronson.

Mervis, Carolyn B.; & Rosch, Eleanor. (1981). Categorization of natural objects. *Annual Review of Psychology, 32,* 89–115.

Mesmer-Magnus, Jessica R.; & Viswesvaran, Chockalingam. (2006). How family-friendly work environments affect work-family conflict: A meta-analytic examination. *Journal of Labor Research, 27,* 555–574.

Metcalfe, Janet; & Mischel, Walter. (1999). A hot/cool-system analysis of delay of gratification: Dynamics of willpower. *Psychological Review, 106,* 3–19.

Meyer-Luehmann, Melanie; Spires-Jones, Tara L.; Prada, Claudia; Garcia-Alloza, Monica; de Calignon, Alix; Rozkalne, Anete; Koenigsknecht-Talboo, Jessica; Holtzman, David M.; Bacskai, Brian J.; & Hyman, Bradley T. (2008). Rapid appearance and local toxicity of amyloid-plaques in a mouse model of Alzheimer's disease. *Nature, 451,* 720–724.

Mezulis, Amy H.; Abramson, Lyn Y.; & Hyde, Janet S. (2004, September). Is there a universal positivity bias in attributions? A meta-analytic review of individual, developmental, and cultural differences in the self-serving attributional bias. *Psychological Bulletin, 130*(5), 711–747.

Miceli, Maria; & Castelfranchi, Cristiano. (2000). Nature and mechanisms of loss of motivation. *Review of General Psychology, 4,* 238–263.

Michael, Nikolaus. (2009). Hypothesized mechanisms and sites of action of electroconvulsive therapy. In Conrad M. Swartz (Ed.), *Electroconvulsive and neuromodulation therapies* (pp. 75–93). New York: Cambridge University Press.

Michael, Robert T.; Gagnon, John H.; Laumann, Edward O.; & Kolata, Gina. (1994). *Sex in America: A definitive survey.* New York: Warner Books.

Mikalsen, Anita; Bertelsen, Bård; & Flaten, Magne Arve. (2001). Effects of caffeine, caffeine-associated stimuli, and caffeine-related information on physiological and psychological arousal. *Psychopharmacology, 157,* 373–380.

Miklowitz, David J. (2008). Bipolar disorder. In David H. Barlow (Ed.), *Clinical handbook of psychological disorders* (4th ed., pp. 421–462). New York: Guilford Press.

Miklowitz, David J.; & Johnson, Sheri L. (2007). Bipolar disorder. In Michel Hersen, Samuel M. Turner, & Deborah C. Beidel (Eds.), *Adult psychopathology and diagnosis* (5th ed., pp. 317–348). Hoboken, NJ: Wiley.

Milan, Stephanie; Snow, Stephanie; & Belay, Sophia. (2007). The context of preschool children's sleep: Racial/ethnic differences in sleep locations, routines, and concerns. *Journal of Family Psychology, 21*(1), 20–28.

Milar, Katharine S. (2000). The first generation of women psychologists and the psychology of women. *American Psychologist, 55,* 616–619.

Miles, Helen; Peters, Emmanuelle; & Kuipers, Elizabeth. (2007, January). Service-user satisfaction with CBT for psychosis. *Behavioural and Cognitive Psychotherapy, 35*(1), 109–116.

Milgram, Stanley. (1963). Behavioral study of obedience. *Journal of Abnormal Psychology, 67,* 371–378.

Milgram, Stanley. (1964). Issues in the study of obedience: A reply to Baumrind. *American Psychologist, 19,* 848–852.

Milgram, Stanley. (1965/1992). Some conditions of obedience and disobedience to authority. In John Sabini & Maury Silver (Eds.), *The individual in a social world: Essays and experiments* (2nd ed.). New York: McGraw-Hill.

Milgram, Stanley. (1974a). *Obedience to authority: An experimental view.* New York: Harper & Row.

Milgram, Stanley. (1974b, June). Interview by Carol Tavris: The frozen world of the familiar stranger: An interview with Stanley Milgram. *Psychology Today,* 71–80.

Milgram, Stanley. (1980). Interview by Richard I. Evans. In Richard I. Evans (Ed.), *The making of social psychology: Discussions with creative contributors.* New York: Gardner Press.

Milgram, Stanley. (1992). On maintaining social norms: A field experiment in the subway. In John Sabini & Maury Silver (Eds.), *The individual in a social world: Essays and experiments* (2nd ed.). New York: McGraw-Hill.

Miller, Arthur G. (2009). Reflections on "Replicating Milgram" (Burger, 2009). *American Psychologist, 64,* 20–27.

Miller, Cindy Faith; Trautner, Hanns Martin; & Ruble, Diane N. (2006). The role of gender stereotypes in children's preferences and behavior. In Lawrence Balter & Catherine S. Tamis-LeMonda (Eds.), *Child psychology: A handbook of contemporary issues* (2nd ed.). New York: Psychology Press.

Miller, George A. (1956/1994). The magical number seven, plus or minus two: Some limits on our capacity for processing information [Special centennial issue]. *Psychological Review, 101,* 343–352.

Miller, Gregory E.; Chen, Edith; & Cole, Steve W. (2009). Health psychology: Developing biologically plausible models linking the social world and physical health. *Annual Review of Psychology, 60,* 501–524.

Miller, Gregory E.; Cohen, Sheldon; & Ritchey, A. Kim. (2002). Chronic psychological stress and the regulation of pro-inflammatory cytokines: A glucocorticoid-resistance model. *Health Psychology, 21,* 531–541.

Miller, Joan G. (2001). Culture and moral development. In David Matsumoto (Ed.), *The handbook of culture and psychology.* New York: Oxford University Press.

Miller, Matthew. (2008). The world's richest people: Gates no longer world's richest man. Retrieved December 7, 2009, from http://www.forbes.com/2008/03/05/buffett-worlds-richest-cx_mm_0229buffetrichest.html

Miller, Patricia H. (2002). *Theories of developmental psychology* (4th ed.). New York: Worth Publishers.

Miller, Todd Q.; Smith, Timothy W.; Turner, Charles W.; Guijarro, Margarita L.; & Hallet, Amanda J. (1996). A meta-analytic review of research on hostility and physical health. *Psychological Bulletin, 119,* 322–348.

Miller, William R.; & Rollnick, Stephen. (2002). *Motivational interviewing: Preparing people for change* (2nd ed.). New York: Guilford Press.

Miller-Jones, Dalton. (1989). Culture and testing. *American Psychologist, 44,* 360–366.

Milner, Brenda. (1954). Intellectual function of the temporal lobes. *Psychological Bulletin, 51,* 42–62.

Milner, Brenda. (1970). Memory and the medial temporal regions of the brain. In Karl H. Pribram & Donald E. Broadbent (Eds.), *Biology of memory.* New York: Academic Press.

Milton, Julie; & Wiseman, Richard. (1999). Does psi exist? Lack of replication of an anomalous process of information transfer. *Psychological Bulletin, 125,* 387–391.

Milton, Julie; & Wiseman, Richard. (2001). Does psi exist? Reply to Storm and Ertel (2001). *Psychological Bulletin, 127,* 434–438.

Minda, John Paul; & Smith, J. David. (2001). Prototypes in category learning: The effects of category size, category structure, and stimulus complexity. *Journal of Experimental Psychology: Learning, Memory, and Cognition, 27,* 775–799.

Mindell, Jodi A. (1997). Children and sleep. In Mark R. Pressman & William C. Orr (Eds.), *Understanding sleep: The evaluation and treatment of sleep disorders.* Washington, DC: American Psychological Association.

Mindell, Jodi A.; & Barrett, Kristen M. (2002). Nightmares and anxiety in elementary-aged children: Is there a relationship? *Child: Care, Health and Development, 28,* 317–322.

Mineka, Susan; & Nugent, Kathleen. (1995). Mood-congruent memory biases in anxiety and depression. In Daniel L. Schacter (Ed.), *Memory distortion: How minds, brains, and societies reconstruct the past.* Cambridge, MA: Harvard University Press.

Mirmiran, Majid; Maas, Yolanda G. H.; & Ariagno, Ronald L. (2003). Development of fetal and neonatal sleep and circadian rhythms. *Sleep Medicine Reviews, 7,* 321–334.

Miron, Anca M.; & Branscomben, Nyla R. (2008). Social categorization, standards of justice, and collective guilt. In Arie Nadler, Thomas E. Malloy, & Jeffrey D. Fisher (Eds.), *The social psychology of intergroup reconciliation* (pp. 77–96). New York: Oxford University Press.

Mischel, Walter. (1966). Theory and research on the antecedents of self-imposed delay of reward. *Progress in Experimental Personality Research, 3,* 85–132.

Mischel, Walter. (1996). From good intentions to willpower. In Peter M. Gollwitzer & John A. Bargh (Eds.), *The psychology of action: Linking cognition and motivation to behavior.* New York: Guilford Press.

Mischel, Walter. (2004). Toward an integrative science of the person. *Annual Review of Psychology, 55,* 1–22.

Mischel, Walter; & Shoda, Yuichi. (1995). A cognitive-affective system theory of personality: Reconceptualizing situations, dispositions, dynamics, and invariance in personality structure. *Psychological Review, 102,* 246–268.

Mischel, Walter; Shoda, Yuichi; & Mendoza-Denton, Rodolfo. (2002). Situation-behavor profiles as a locus of consistency in personality. *Current Directions in Psychological Science, 11,* 50–54.

Mischel, Walter; Shoda, Yuichi; & Rodriguez, Monica L. (1989, May 26). Delay of gratification in children. *Science, 244,* 933–938.

Mistlberger, Ralph E.; & Rusak, Benjamin. (2005). Circadian rhythms in mammals: Formal properties and environmental influences. In Meir H. Kryger, Thomas Roth, & William C. Dement (Eds.), *Principles and practice of sleep medicine* (4th ed.). Philadelphia: Elsevier Saunders.

Mistlberger, Ralph E.; & Skene, Debra J. (2005). Nonphotic entrainment in humans? *Journal of Biological Rhythms, 20,* 339–352.

Mitchell, Laura A.; & MacDonald, Raymond A. R. (2006). An experimental investigation of the effects of preferred and relaxing music listening on pain perception. *Journal of Music Therapy, 43,* 295–316.

Miyamoto, Yuri; Nisbett, Richard E.; & Masuda, Takahiko. (2006). Culture and the physical environment: Holistic versus analytic affordances. *Psychological Science, 17,* 113–119.

Moeller-Saxone, Kristen. (2008). Cigarette smoking and interest in quitting among consumers at a psychiatric disability rehabilitation and support service in Victoria. *Australia and New Zealand Journal of Public Health, 32*(5), 479–481.

Moffet, Howard H. (2006, July 7). How might acupuncture work? A systematic review of physiologic rationales from clinical trials. *BMC Complementary and Alternative Medicine, 6.* Retrieved July 12, 2009, from http://www.biomedcentral.com/content/pdf/1472-6882-6-25.pdf

Moffet, Howard H. (2009). Sham acupuncture may be as efficacious as true acupuncture: A systematic review of clinical trials. *The Journal of Alternative and Complementary Medicine, 15,* 213–216

Moghaddam, Fathali M. (2002). *The individual and society: A cultural integration.* New York: Worth Publishers.

Moghaddam, Fathali M.; Taylor, Donald M.; & Wright, Stephen C. (1993). *Social psychology in cross-cultural perspective.* New York: Freeman.

Mogil, Jeffrey S.; Wilson, Sonya G.; Chesler, Elissa J.; Rankin, A. L.; Nemmani, K. V.; Lariviere, W. R.; & others. (2003, April 15). The melanocortin-1 receptor gene mediates female-specific mechanisms of analgesia in mice and humans. *Proceedings of the National Academy of Sciences, 100,* 4867–4872.

Mohr, Charles. (1964, March 28). Apathy is puzzle in Queens killing: Behavioral specialists hard put to explain witnesses' failure to call police. *The New York Times,* pp. 21, 40.

Mohr, David; Vedantham, Kumar; Neylan, Thomas; Metzler, Thomas J.; Best, Suzanne; & Marmar, Charles R. (2003). The mediating effects of sleep in the relationship between traumatic stress and health symptoms in urban police officers. *Psychosomatic Medicine, 65,* 485–489.

Mombaerts, Peter. (2004). Genes and ligands for odorant, vomeronasal, and taste receptors. *Nature Reviews Neuroscience, 5,* 263–278.

Montgomery, Catharine; & Fisk, John E. (2008). Ecstasy-related deficits in the updating component of executive processes. *Human Psychopharmacology, 23,* 495–511.

Montgomery, Catharine; Fisk, John E.; Wareing, Michelle; & Murphy, Philip. (2007). Self reported sleep quality and cognitive performance in ecstasy users. *Human Psychopharmacology: Clinical and Experimental, 22,* 537–548.

Moore, David W. (2005, June 15). Three in four Americans believe in paranormal. Gallup News Service. Retrieved February 22, 2008, from http://www.gallup.com/poll/16915/Three-Four-Americans-Believe-Paranormal.aspx

Moore, Jay. (2005a). Some historical and conceptual background to the development of B. F. Skinner's "radical behaviorism"—Part 1. *Journal of Mind and Behavior, 26,* 65–94.

Moore, Jay. (2005b). Some historical and conceptual background to the development of B. F. Skinner's "radical behaviorism"—Part 3. *Journal of Mind and Behavior, 26,* 137–160.

Moore, Joseph E. (1942). Some psychological aspects of yawning. *Journal of General Psychology, 27,* 289–294.

Moore, Robert Y. (2007). Suprachiasmatic nucleus in sleep–wake regulation. *Sleep Medicine, 8,* 27–33.

Moreira-Almeida, Alexander; Neto, Francisco Lotufo; & Cardeña, Etzel. (2008). Comparison of brazilian spiritist mediumship and dissociative identity disorder. *Journal of Nervous Mental Disorders, 196*(5), 420–424.

Morelli, Gilda A.; Rogoff, Barbara; Oppenheim, David; & Goldsmith, Denise. (1992). Cultural variation in infants' sleeping arrangements: Questions of independence. *Developmental Psychology, 28,* 604–613.

Moretti, Robert J.; & Rossini, Edward D. (2004). The Thematic Apperception Test (TAT). In Mark J. Hilsenroth & Daniel L. Segal (Eds.), *Comprehensive handbook of psychological assessment, Vol. 2: Personality assessment.* Hoboken, NJ: Wiley.

Morgan, Christiana; & Murray, Henry A. (1935). A method of investigating fantasies: The Thematic Apperception Test. *Archives of Neurology and Psychiatry, 4,* 310–329.

Morgan, William P. (2002). Hypnosis in sport and exercise psychology. In J. L. Van Raalte & B. W. Brewer (Eds.), *Exploring sport and exercise psychology.* Washington, DC: American Psychological Association.

Morin, Charles M.; Bootzin, Richard R.; Buysse, Daniel J.; Edinger, Jack D.; Espie, Colin A.; & Lichstein, Kenneth L. (2006). Psychological and behavioral treatment of insomnia: Update of the recent evidence (1998–2004). *Sleep, 29,* 1398–1414.

Morling, Beth; & Kitayama, Shinobu. (2008). Culture and motivation. In James Y. Shah & Wendi L. Gardner (Eds.), *Handbook of motivation science.* New York: Guilford Press.

Morrell, Julian; & Steele, Howard. (2003). The role of attachment security, temperament, maternal perception, and care-giving behavior in persistent infant sleeping problems. *Infant Mental Health Journal, 24,* 447–468.

Morris, John A.; Jordan, Cynthia L.; & Breedlove, S. Marc. (2004). Sexual differentiation of the vertebrate nervous system. *Nature Neuroscience, 7,* 1034–1039.

Morris, John S.; Scott, Sophie K.; & Dolan, Raymond J. (1999). Saying it with feeling: Neural responses to emotional vocalizations. *Neuropsychologia, 37,* 1155–1163.

Morris, Michael W.; & Peng, Kaiping. (1994). Culture and cause: American and Chinese attributions for social and physical events. *Journal of Personality and Social Psychology, 67,* 949–971.

Morrison, Adrian R. (2003). The brain on night shift. *Cerebrum, 5,* 23–36.

Morrison, Christopher D. (2008). Leptin resistance and the response to positive energy balance. *Physiology & Behavior, 94,* 660–663.

Moskowitz, Andrew; Schafer, Ingo; & Dorahy, Martin Justin. (2009). *Psychosis, trauma, and dissociation.* New York: Wiley.

Moss, Cynthia. (2000). *Elephant memories: Thirteen years in the life of an elephant family.* Chicago: University of Chicago Press.

Motowidlo, Stephan J.; Borman, Walter C.; & Schmit, Mark J. (1997). A theory of individual differences in task and contextual performance. *Human Performance, 10,* 71–83.

Motowidlo, Stephan J., Hanson, Mary A.; & Crafts, Jennifer L. (1997). Low-fidelity simulations. In D. L. Whetzel & G. R. Wheaton (Eds.), *Applied measurement methods in industrial psychology* (pp. 241–260). Palo Alto, CA: Consulting Psychologists Press.

Mottron, Laurent. (2006, February 20). Quoted in André Picard, "The postie and the prof dispute perceptions of autism." *Globe and Mail.* Retrieved February 20, 2006, from http://www.theglobeandmail.com/servlet/story/RTGAM.20060220.wxautism0220/BNStory/specialScienceandHealth/home

Mottron, Laurent. (2008, February 25). Quoted in David Wolman, "The truth about autism: Scientists reconsider what they *think* they know." *Wired Magazine: 16.03.* Retrieved March 2, 2008, from http://www.wired.com/ print/medtech/health/magaine/16-03/ff_autism

Mounts, Nina S.; & Steinberg, Laurence. (1995). An ecological analysis of peer influence on adolescent grade point average and drug use. *Developmental Psychology, 31,* 915–922.

Moyer, Christopher A.; Rounds, James.; & Hannum, James W. (2004). A meta-analysis of massage therapy research. *Psychological Bulletin, 130,* 3–18.

Mueller, Shane T.; Seymour, Travis L.; Kieras, David E.; & Meyer, David E. (2003). Theoretical implications of articulatory duration, phonological similarity, and phonological complexity in verbal working memory. *Journal of Experimental Psychology: Learning, Memory, and Cognition, 29,* 1353–1380.

Muenchow, Susan; & Marsland, Katherine W. (2007). Beyond baby steps: Promoting the growth and development of U.S. child-care policy. In J. Lawrence Aber, Sandra J. Bishop-Josef, Stephanie M. Jones, Kathryn Taaffe McLearn, & Deborah A. Phillips (Eds.), *Child development and social policy: Knowledge for action* (pp. 97–112). Washington, DC: American Psychological Association.

Mueser, Kim T.; Bellack, Alan S.; & Brady, E. U. (1990). Hallucinations in schizophrenia. *Acta Psychiatrica Scandinavica, 82,* 26–29.

Mueser, Kim T.; & Glynn, Shirley M. (1993). Efficacy of psychotherapy for schizophrenia. In Thomas R. Giles (Ed.), *Handbook of effective psychotherapy.* New York: Plenum Press.

Mulhern, Sherrill. (1991). Embodied alternative identities: Bearing witness to a world that might have been. *Psychiatric Clinics of North America, 14,* 769–786.

Munafo, Marcus R.; Hitsman, Brian; Rende, Richard; Metcalfe, Chris; & Niaura, Raymond. (2008, January). Effects of progression to cigarette smoking on depressed mood in adolescents: Evidence from the National Longitudinal Study of Adolescent Health. *Addiction, 103*(1), 162–171.

Munetz, Mark R. (2006, August). Review of schizophrenic speech: Making sense of bathroots and ponds that fall in doorways. *Psychiatric Services, 57*(8), 1222.

Munsey, Christopher. (2007a, September). A psychologist and a soldier. *Monitor on Psychology, 38,* 47–48.

Munsey, Christopher. (2007b, September). Transforming military mental health. *Monitor on Psychology, 38,* 38–41.

Munsey, Christopher. (2007c, September). Helping and healing. *Monitor on Psychology, 38,* 42–46.

Munsey, Christopher (2008b, February). Prescriptive authority in the states. *Monitor on Psychology, 39,* 60.

Munsey, Christopher. (2008, February). Dateline: Iraq. *Monitor on Psychology, 39,* 14.

Münsterberg, Hugo. (1913). *Psychology and industrial efficiency.* Boston: Houghton Mifflin.

Murray, Henry A. (1938). *Explorations in personality.* New York: Oxford University Press.

Murray, Henry A. (1943). *Thematic Apperception Test manual.* Cambridge, MA: Harvard University Press.

Murray, John B. (1995). Evidence for acupuncture's analgesic effectiveness and proposals for the physiological mechanisms involved. *Journal of Psychology, 129,* 443–461.

Murray, John P. (2008). Media violence: The effects are both real and strong. *American Behavioral Scientist, 51,* 1212–1230.

Muscatell, Keeley A.; Slavich, George M.; Monroe, Scott M.; & Gotlib, Ian H. (2009). Stressful life events, chronic difficulties, and the symptoms of clinical depression. *Journal of Nervous and Mental Disease, 197,* 154–160.

Mustanski, Brian S.; Chivers, Meredith L.; & Bailey, J. Michael. (2002). A critical review of recent biological research on human sexual orientation. *Annual Review of Sex Research, 13,* 89–140.

Mustanski, Brian S.; Viken, Richard J.; Kaprio, Jaakko; Pulkkinen, Lea; & Rose, Richard J. (2004). Genetic and environmental influences on pubertal development: Longitudinal data from Finnish twins at ages 11 and 14. *Developmental Psychology, 40,* 1188–1198.

Musto, David F. (1991, July). Opium, cocaine and marijuana in American history. *Scientific American, 265,* 40–47.

Muzur, Amir; Pace-Schott, Edward F.; & Hobson, J. Allan. (2002). The prefrontal cortex in sleep. *Trends in Cognitive Sciences, 6,* 475–481.

Myers, Isabel Briggs; McCaulley, Mary H.; Quenk, Naomi L.; & Hammer, Allen L. (1998). *Manual: A guide to the development and use of the Myers-Briggs Type Indicator* (3rd ed.). Palo Alto, CA: Consulting Psychologist Press.

Myers, Mark G.; Steward, David G.; & Brown, Sandra A. (1998). Progression from conduct disorder to antisocial personality disorder following treatment for adolescent substance abuse. *American Journal of Psychiatry, 155,* 479–485.

Myrtek, Michael. (2007). Type A behavior and hostility as independent risk factors for coronary heart disease. In Jochen Jordan, Benjamin Bardé, & Andreas Michael Zeiher (Eds.), *Contributions toward evidence-based psychocardiology: A systematic review of the literature* (pp. 159–183). Washington, DC: American Psychological Association.

Nadarajah, Bagirathy; & Parnavelas, John G. (2002) Modes of neuronal migration in the developing cerebral cortex. *Nature Reviews Neuroscience, 3,* 423-432.

Nader, Karim; & Wang, Szu-Han. (2006). Fading in. *Learning & Memory, 13,* 530–535.

Nairne, James S. (2002). Remembering over the short-term: The case against the standard model. *Annual Review of Psychology, 53,* 53–81.

Najib, Arif; Lorberbaum, Jeffrey P.; Kose, Samet; Bohning, Daryl E.; & George, Mark S. (2004). Regional brain activity in women grieving a romantic relationship breakup. *American Journal of Psychiatry, 161,* 2245–2256.

Najjar, Muhammad. (2007). Zolpidem and amnestic sleep related eating disorder. *Journal of Clinical Sleep Medicine, 3,* 637–638.

Nakazato, Masamitsu; Murakami, Noboru; Date, Yukari; Kojima, Masayasu; Matsuo, Hisayuki; Kangawa, Kenji; & Matsukura, Shigeru. (2001, January 11). A role for ghrelin in the central regulation of feeding. *Nature, 409,* 194–198.

Narrow, William E.; Rae, Donald S.; Robins, Lee N.; & Regier, Darrel A. (2002). Revised prevalence estimates of mental disorders in the United States: Using a clinical significance criterion to reconcile 2 surveys' estimates. *Archives of General Psychiatry, 59,* 115–123.

Nash, Michael R. (2001, July). The truth and the hype of hypnosis. *Scientific American, 285,* 46–49, 52–55.

Nathan, Peter E.; & Gorman, Jack M. (Eds.). (2007). *A guide to treatments that work* (3rd ed.). New York: Oxford University Press.

National Association for the Education of Young Children. (2009). *Developmentally appropriate practice in early childhood programs serving children from birth through age 8.* Washington, DC: Author. Retrieved December 8, 2009, from http://www.naeyc.org/files/naeyc/file/positions/PSDAP.pdf

National Association of Child Care Resource & Referral Agencies. (2008, May). *Is this the right place for my child? 38 research-based indicators of high-quality child care.* Arlington, VA: Author. Retrieved September 18, 2009, from http://www.naccrra.org/docs/parent/38_QueBrochure-highqual.pdf

National Cancer Institute. (2008). *Acupuncture: Health professional version.* Retrieved July 12, 2009, from http://www.cancer.gov/cancertopics/pdq/cam/acupuncture/healthprofessional

National Center for Complementary and Alternative Medicine. (2004). Research report: Questions and answers about using magnets to treat pain. Retrieved June 21, 2009, from http://nccam.nih.gov/health/magnet/magnet.pdf

National Center for Complementary and Alternative Medicine. (2007, December). *Backgrounder: Acupuncture: An introduction* (NCCAM Publication No. D404). Bethesda, Maryland: National Institutes of Health. Retrieved July 12, 2009, from http://nccam.nih.gov/health/acupuncture/D404_BKG.pdf

National Center for Complementary and Alternative Medicine. (2009). *Get the facts: Magnets for pain.* Retrieved June 21, 2009, from http://nccam.nih.gov/health/magnet/D408_GTF.pdf

National Center for Health Statistics. (2000c). *Prevalence of sedentary leisure-time behavior among adults in the United States.* Centers for Disease Control and Prevention, National Center for Health Statistics, Health E-Stats. Retrieved May 25, 2001, from http://www.cdc.gov/nchs/products/pubs/pubd/hestats/3and4/sedentary.htm

National Center for Health Statistics. (2002a). *Health, United States, 2002, with chartbook on trends in the health of Americans* (DHHS Publication No. [PHS] 2002–1232). Hyattsville, MD: U.S. Department of Health and Human Services, Centers for Disease Control and Prevention, National Center for Health Statistics. Retrieved January 3, 2003, from http://www.cdc.gov/nchs/data/hus/hus02.pdf

National Center for Health Statistics. (2004). *Health, United States, 2004: With chartbook on trends in the health of Americans.* Hyattsville, MD. Retrieved January 6, 2005, from http://www.cdc.gov/nchs/data/hus/hus04.pdf

National Highway Traffic Safety Administration. (2003, March). *National survey of distracted and drowsy driving attitudes and behavior: 2002: Volume 1.* Washington, DC: National Highway Traffic Safety Administration. Retrieved February 13, 2005, from http://www.nhtsa.dot.gov/people/injury/drowsydriving1/distracted03/ DISTRFINFINRPt-8mar04.pdf

National Science Board. (2008). *Science and engineering indicators: 2008.* (Vol. 1). (NSB 08-01) & 2 (NSB 08-01A). Arlington, VA: National Science Foundation.

National Sleep Foundation. (2000). *Adolescent sleep needs and patterns: Research report and resource guide.* Washington, DC: Author. Retrieved February 12, 2005, from http://www.sleepfoundation.org/publications/sleepandteensreport1.pdf

National Sleep Foundation. (2004a, March). *2004 Sleep in America Poll: Final report.* Washington, DC: Author. Retrieved August 20, 2004, from http://www.sleepfoundation.org/polls/2004SleepPollFinalReport.pdf

National Sleep Foundation. (2004c). *Got caffeine? Try our caffeine calculator.* Washington, DC: Author. Retrieved August 20, 2004, from http://www.sleepfoundation.org/caffeine.cfm

National Sleep Foundation. (2005, March 29). *2005 Sleep in America Poll: Sleep habits of American adults.* Washington, DC: Author. Retrieved July 21, 2008, from http://www.sleepfoundation.org

National Sleep Foundation. (2006, March 27). *2006 Sleep in America Poll: America's adolescents are not getting the sleep they need.* Washington, DC: Author. Retrieved July 21, 2008, from http://www.sleepfoundation.org

National Sleep Foundation. (2007, March 6). *2007 Sleep in America Poll: Stressed-out American women have no time for sleep.* Washington, DC: Author. Retrieved July 21, 2008, from http://www.sleepfoundation.org

National Standard Monographs. (2009). Magnet therapy. Retrieved July 9, 2009, from http://www.naturalstandard.com/naturalstandard/demos/patient-magnet.asp

National Standard Research Collaboration. (2008, March 1). MedlinePlus: Drugs and supplements: Ginkgo (Ginkgo biloba L.). Retrieved September 4, 2008, from www.nlm.nih.gov/medlineplus/druginfo/natural/patient-ginkgo.html

National Television Violence Study (Vol. 1). (1996). Thousand Oaks, CA: Sage.

National Television Violence Study (Vol. 2). (1997). Thousand Oaks, CA: Sage.

National Television Violence Study (Vol. 3). (1998). Thousand Oaks, CA: Sage.

Nave, Klaus-Armin; & Trapp, Bruce D. (2008). Axon-glial signalling and the glial support of axon function. *Annual Review of Neuroscience, 31,* 535–561.

NDCHealth. (2005). U.S. pharmaceutical industry data: Excerpts from *2005 Pharma Insight.* Retrieved December 18, 2005, from www.ndchealth.com/press_center/uspharmaindustrydata/NDCHealth_2005PharmaInsight_excerptsfinal.ppt

Nederkoorn, Chantal; Smulders, Fren T.Y.; & Jansen, Anita. (2000). Cephalic phase responses, craving and food intake in normal subjects. *Appetite, 35,* 45–55.

Neher, Andrew. (1991). Maslow's theory of motivation: A critique. *Journal of Humanistic Psychology, 31,* 89–112.

Neisser, Ulric (Chair); **Boodoo, Gwyneth; Bouchard, Thomas J., Jr.; Boykin, A. Wade; Brody, Nathan; Ceci, Stephen J.; & others.** (1996). Intelligence: Knowns and unknowns. *American Psychologist, 51,* 77–101.

Nelson, Elliot C.; Heath, Andrew C.; Madden, Pamela A. F.; Cooper, M. Lynne; Dinwiddie, Stephen H.; Bucholz, Kathleen K.; Glowinski, Anne; McLaughlin, Tara; Dunne, Michael P.; Statham, Dixie J.; & Martin, Nicholas G. (2002). Association between self-reported childhood sexual abuse and adverse psychosocial outcomes: Results from a twin study. *Archives of General Psychiatry, 59,* 139–145.

Nelson, Katherine; & Fivush, Robyn. (2004). The emergence of autobiographical memory: A social cultural developmental theory. *Psychological Review, 111,* 486–511.

Nelson, Marcia Z. (2001). *Come and sit: A week inside meditation centers.* Woodstock, VT: Skylight Paths.

Nelson, Toben F.; Naimi, Timothy S.; Brewer, Robert D.; & Wechsler, Henry. (2005). The state sets the rate: The relationship of college binge drinking to state binge drinking rates and selected state alcohol control policies. *American Journal of Public Health, 95,* 441–446.

Nestler, Eric J.; & Malenka, Robert C. (2004, March). The addicted brain. *Scientific American, 290,* 78–85.

Nestoriuc, Yvonne; & Martin, Alexandra. (2007). Efficacy of biofeedback for migraine: A meta-analysis. *Pain, 128,* 111–127.

Neter, Efrat; & Ben-Shakhar, Gershon. (1989). The predictive validity of graphological inferences: A meta-analytic approach. *Personality and Individual Differences, 10,* 737–745.

Newberg, Andrew B.; & Iversen, Jeremy. (2003). The neural basis of the complex mental task of meditation: Neurotransmitter and neurochemical considerations. *Medical Hypotheses, 61,* 282–291.

Newson, Rachel S.; & Kemps, Eva B. (2005). General lifestyle activities as a predictor of current cognition and cognitive change in older adults: A cross-sectional and longitudinal examination. *Journals of Gerontology, Series B: Psychological Sciences and Social Sciences, 60,* P113–P120.

Nezu, Arthur M.; & Nezu, Christine M. (Eds.). (2008). *Evidence-based outcome research: A practical guide to conducting randomized controlled trials for psychosocial interventions.* New York: Oxford University Press.

Ng, Debbie M.; & Jeffery, Robert W. (2003). Relationships between perceived stress and health behaviors in a sample of working adults. *Health Psychology, 22,* 638–642.

Niaura, Raymond; Todaro, John F.; Stroud, Laura; Spiro, Avron; Ward, Kenneth D.; & Weiss, Scott. (2002). Hostility, the metabolic syndrome, and incident coronary heart disease. *Health Psychology, 21,* 588–593.

Niccols, Alison. (2007). Fetal alcohol syndrome and the developing socioemotional brain. *Brain and Cognition, 65,* 135–142.

NICHD Early Child Care Research Network. (2003a). Does quality of child care affect child outcomes at age 4 1/2? *Developmental Psychology, 39,* 451–469.

NICHD Early Child Care Research Network. (2003b). Families matter—even for kids in child care. *Journal of Developmental & Behavioral Pediatrics, 24,* 58–62.

NICHD. (2006). The NICHD Study of Early Child Care and Youth Development (SECCYD): Findings for children up to Age 4 1/2 years. Eunice Kennedy Shriver National Institute of Child Health and Human Development, NIH Publication No. 05-4318. Washington, DC: U.S. Government Printing Office.

Nichols, Michael P. (2008). *Family therapy: Concepts and methods* (8th ed.). Boston: Allyn & Bacon.

Nickerson, Raymond S.; & Adams, Marilyn J. (1982). Long-term memory for a common object. In Ulric Neisser (Ed.), *Memory observed: Remembering in natural contexts.* San Francisco: Freeman.

Nielsen, Tore A.; & Stenstrom, Philippe. (2005, October 27). What are the memory sources of dreaming? *Nature, 437,* 1286–1289.

Nielsen, Tore A.; Stenstrom, Philippe; & Levin, Ross. (2006). Nightmare frequency as a function of age, gender, and September 11, 2001: Findings from an Internet questionnaire. *Dreaming, 16,* 145–158.

Nielsen, Tore A.; & Zadra, Antonio. (2005). Nightmares and other common dream disturbances. In Meir H. Kryger, Thomas Roth, & William C. Dement (Eds.), *Principles and practice of sleep medicine* (4th ed.). Philadelphia: Elsevier Saunders.

Nierenberg, Andrew A.; Ostacher, Michael J.; Delgado, Pedro L.; Sachs, Gary S.; Gelenberg, Alan J.; Rosenbaum, Jerrold F.; & Fava, Maurizio. (2007). Antidepressant and antimanic medications. In Glen O. Gabbard (Ed.), *Gabbard's treatments of psychiatric disorders* (4th ed., pp. 385–407). Washington, DC: American Psychiatric Publishing.

Nisbett, Richard E.; & Masuda, Takahiko. (2003). Culture and point of view. *Proceedings of the National Academy of Sciences, 100,* 11163–11170.

Nishio, Kazumi; & Bilmes, Murray. (1993). Psychotherapy with Southeast Asian American clients. In Donald R. Atkinson, George Morten, & Derald Wing Sue (Eds.), *Counseling American minorities: A cross-cultural perspective* (4th ed.). Madison, WI: Brown & Benchmark.

Nithianantharajah, Jess; & Hannan, Anthony J. (2006). Enriched environments, experience-dependent plasticity, and disorders of the nervous system. *Nature Reviews Neuroscience, 7,* 697–709.

Njenga, Frank G.; Nicholls, P. J.; Nyamai, Caroline; Kigamwa, Pius; & Davidson, Jonathan R. T. (2004). Post-traumatic stress after terrorist attack: Psychological reactions following the U.S. embassy bombing in Nairobi: Naturalistic study. *British Journal of Psychiatry, 185,* 328–333.

Noble, Meredith; Tregear, Stephen J.; Treadwell, Jonathan R.; & Schoelles, Karen. (2008). Long-term opioid therapy for chronic noncancer pain: A systematic review and meta-analysis of efficacy and safety. *Journal of Pain and Symptom Management, 35,* 214–228.

Nocon, Agnes; Wittchen, Hans-Ulrich; Pfister, Hildegard; Zimmermann, Petra; & Lieb, Roselind. (2006). Dependence symptoms in young cannabis users? A prospective epidemiological study. *Journal of Psychiatric Research, 40,* 394–403.

Nofzinger, Eric A. (2005b). Neuroimaging and sleep medicine. *Sleep Medicine Review, 9,* 157–172.

Nofzinger, Eric A. (2006). Neuroimaging of sleep and sleep disorders. *Current Neurology and Neuroscience Reports, 6,* 149–155.

Nolen-Hoeksema, Susan. (2001). Gender differences in depression. *Current Directions in Psychological Science, 10,* 173–176.

Nolen-Hoeksema, Susan. (2003). *Women who think too much: How to break free of over-thinking and reclaim your life.* New York: Henry Holt.

Nolen-Hoeksema, Susan. (2010). Women conquering depression: How to gain control of eating, drinking, and overthinking and embrace a healthier life. New York: Holt Paperbacks.

Nolen-Hoeksema, Susan; Stice, Eric; & Wade, Emily. (2007, February). Reciprocal relations between rumination and bulimic, substance abuse, and depressive symptoms in female adolescents. *Journal of Abnormal Psychology, 116*(1), 198–207.

Norcross, John C.; Karpiak, Christie P.; & Santoro, Shannon O. (2005). Clinical psychologists across the years: The division of clinical psychology from 1960 to 2003. *Journal of Clinical Psychology, 61,* 1467–1483.

Norenzayan, Ara; & Heine, Steven J. (2005). Psychological universals: What are they and how can we know? *Psychological Bulletin, 131,* 763–784.

Norko, Michael; & Baranoski, Madelon V. (2005, January). The state of contemporary risk assessment research. *Canadian Journal of Psychiatry, 50*(1), 18–26.

Norris, Donna M.; Gutheil, Thomas G.; & Strasburger, Larry H. (2003, April). This couldn't happen to me: Boundary problems and sexual misconduct in the psychotherapy relationship. *Psychiatric Services, 54*(4), 517–522.

Norris, Joan E.; & Tindale, Joseph A. (1994). *Among generations: The cycle of adult relationships.* New York: Freeman.

North, Carol S.; Nixon, Sara Jo.; Shariat, Sheryll; Mallonee, Sue; McMillen, J. Curtis; Spitznagel, Edward L.; & Smith, Elizabeth M. (1999). The psychiatric impact of the Oklahoma City bombing on survivors of the direct blast. *Journal of the American Medical Association, 282,* 755–762.

North, Carol S.; Suris, Alina M.; Davis, Miriam; & Smith, Rebecca P. (2009). Toward validation of the diagnosis of posttraumatic stress disorder. *American Journal of Psychiatry, 166,* 34–41.

Nosek, Brian A.; Smyth, Frederick. L.; Hansen, Jeffery J.; Devos, Thierry; Lindner, Nichole M.; Ranganath, Kate A.; & others. (2007). Pervasiveness and correlates of implicit attitudes and stereotypes. *European Review of Social Psychology, 18,* 36–88. Retrieved September 28, 2009, from http://projectimplicit.net/nosek/stimuli/

Nosofsky, Robert M.; & Zaki, Safa R. (2002). Exemplar and prototype models revisited: Response strategies, selective attention, and stimulus generalization. *Journal of Experimental Psychology: Learning, Memory, and Cognition, 28,* 924–940.

Novick, Laura R.; & Bassok, Miriam. (2005). Problem solving. In Keith J. Holyoak & Robert G. Morrison (Eds.), *The Cambridge handbook of thinking and reasoning.* New York: Cambridge University Press.

Numbers in the news. (2006, March). *Policy & Practice of Public Human Services, 64*(1), 34.

Nurnberger, John I. (2009, June). New hope for pharmacogenetic testing. *American Journal of Psychiatry, 166*(6), 635–638.

O'Connor, Akira R.; & Moulin, Christopher J. A. (2006). Normal patterns of déjà experience in a healthy, blind male: Challenging optical pathway delay theory. *Brain and Cognition, 62,* 246–249.

O'Connor, Daryl B.; & Shimizu, Mikiko. (2002). Sense of personal control, stress and coping style: A cross-cultural study. *Stress and Health, 18,* 173–183.

O'Craven, Kathleen M.; & Kanwisher, Nancy. (2000). Mental imagery of faces and places activates corresponding stimulus-specific brain regions. *Journal of Cognitive Neuroscience, 12,* 1013–1023.

O'Doherty, J.; Winston, Joel S.; Critchley, H.; Perrett, D.; Burt, D. M.; & Dolan, R. J. (2003). Beauty in a smile: The role of medial orbitofrontal cortex in facial attractiveness. *Neuropsychologia, 41,* 147–155.

O'Donohue, William T.; & Fisher, Jane E. (2009). *Cognitive behavior therapy: Applying empirically supported techniques in your practice* (2nd ed.). Hoboken, NJ: Wiley.

O'Kane, Gail; Kensinger, Elizabeth A.; & Corkin, Suzanne. (2004). Evidence for semantic learning in profound amnesia: An investigation with patient H.M. *Hippocampus, 14,* 417–425.

O'Roark, Ann M. (2007). The best of consulting psychology 1900–2000: Insider perspectives. *Consulting Psychology Journal: Practice and Research, 59,* 189–202.

Oberman, Lindsay M.; & Ramachandran, Vilayanur S. (2007). The simulating social mind: The role of the mirror neuron system and simulation in the social and communicative deficits of autism spectrum disorders. *Psychological Bulletin, 133,* 310–327.

Occupational Outlook Handbook. (2008–2009). Psychologists. Retrieved September 23, 2008, from http://www.bls.gov/oco/ocos056.htm#outlook

Oettingen, Gabriele; & Gollwitzer, Peter M. (2001). Goal setting and goal striving. In A. Tesser & N. Schwarz (Vol. Eds.) & M. Hewstone & M. Brewer (Series Eds.), *The Blackwell handbook in social psychology: Vol l. Intraindividual processes.* Oxford, England: Blackwell.

Ogbu, John U. (1986). The consequences of the American caste system. In Ulric Neisser (Ed.), *The school achievement of minority children: New perspectives.* Hillsdale, NJ: Erlbaum.

Ogbu, John U. (2008). Minority status, oppositional culture, and schooling: Sociocultural, political, and historical studies in education. New York: Routledge.

Ogden, Cynthia L.; Carroll, Margaret D.; Curtin, Lester R.; McDowell, Margaret A.; Tabak, Carolyn J; & Flegal, Katherine M. (2006). Prevalence of overweight and obesity in the United States, 1999–2004. *Journal of the American Medical Association, 295,* 1549–1555.

Ogden, Cynthia L.; Carroll, Margaret D.; McDowell, Margaret A.; & Flegal, Katherine M. (2007). Obesity among adults in the United States—No change since 2003–2004. *NCHS data brief no 1.* Hyattsville, MD: National Center for Health Statistics. Retrieved June 9, 2008, from http://www.cdc.gov/nchs/data/databriefs/db01.pdf

Ogden, Jenni A.; & Corkin, Suzanne. (1991). Memories of H. M. In Wickliffe C. Abraham, Michael Corballis, & K. Geoffrey White (Eds.), *Memory mechanisms: A tribute to G. V. Goddard.* Hillsdale, NJ: Erlbaum.

Ohayon, Maurice M. (2007, April–June). Epidemiology of depression and its treatment in the general population. *Journal of Psychiatric Research, 41*(3–4), 207–213.

Ohayon, Maurice M.; Carskadon, Mary A.; Guilleminault, Christian; & Vitiello, Michael V. (2004). Meta-analysis of quantitative sleep parameters from childhood to old age in healthy individuals: Developing normative sleep values across the human lifespan. *Sleep,* 27, 1255–1273.

Öhman, Arne; Carlsson, Katrina; & Lundqvist, Daniel. (2007). On the unconscious subcortical origin of human fear. *Physiology & Behavior, 92,* 180–185.

Öhman, Arne; Lundqvist, Daniel; & Esteves, Francisco. (2001b). The face in the crowd revisited: A threat advantage with schematic stimuli. *Journal of Personality and Social Psychology, 80,* 381–396.

Öhman, Arne; & Mineka, Susan. (2001). Fear, phobias, and preparedness: Toward an evolved module of fear and fear learning. *Psychological Review, 108,* 483–522.

Öhman, Arne; & Mineka, Susan. (2003). The malicious serpent: Snakes as a prototypical stimulus for an evolved module of fear. *Current Directions in Psychological Science, 12,* 5–9.

Ohno, Kousaku; & Sakurai, Takeshi. (2008). Orexin neuronal circuitry: Role in the regulation of sleep and wakefulness. *Frontiers in Neuroendocrinology, 29,* 70–87.

Olff, Miranda; Langeland, Willie; & Draijer, Nel. (2007, March). Gender differences in posttraumatic stress disorder. *Psychological Bulletin, 133*(2), 183–204.

Ollinger, Michael; Jones, Gary; & Knoblich, Günther. (2008). Investigating the effect of mental set on insight problem solving. *Experimental Psychology, 55,* 269–282.

Olson, James M.; & Zanna, Mark P. (1993). Attitudes and attitude change. *Annual Review of Psychology, 44,* 117–154.

Olson, Michael A.; & Fazio, Russell H. (2001). Implicit attitude formation through classical conditioning. *Psychological Science, 12,* 413–417.

Olsson, Andreas; & Phelps, Elizabeth A. (2007). Social learning of fear. *Nature Neuroscience, 10,* 1095–1102.

Olszweski, Pawel K.; Schiöth, Helgi B.; & Levine, Allen S. (2008). Ghrelin in the CNS: From hunger to a rewarding and memorable meal? *Brain Research Reviews, 58,* 160–170.

Oltmanns, Thomas F.; & Okada, Mayumi. (2006). Paranoia. In Jane E. Fisher & William T. O'Donohue (Eds.), *Practitioner's guide to evidence-based psychotherapy* (pp. 503–513). New York: Springer Science + Business Media.

Olton, David S. (1992). Tolman's cognitive analysis: Predecessors of current approaches in psychology. *Journal of Experimental Psychology: General, 121,* 427–428.

Ong, Anthony D.; Fuller-Rowell, Thomas; & Burrow, Anthony L. (2009). Racial discrimination and the stress process. *Journal of Personality and Social Psychology, 96,* 1259–1271.

Onishi, Norimitsu. (2009, January 15). Japan's outcasts still wait for acceptance. *The New York Times.* Retrieved March 16, 2009, from http://www.nytimes.com/2009/01/16/world/asia/16outcasts.html

Orlinsky, David E.; Ronnestad, Michael Hedge; & Willutzki, Ulrike. (2004). Fifty years of psychotherapy process-outcome research: Continuity and change. In Michael J. Lambert (Ed.), *Bergin and Garfield's handbook of psychotherapy and behavior change* (5th ed.). New York: Wiley.

Orne, Martin T.; & Holland, Charles H. (1968). On the ecological validity of laboratory deceptions. *International Journal of Psychiatry, 6,* 282–293.

Osborne, Jason W. (2007). Linking stereotype threat and anxiety. *Educational Psychology, 27,* 135–154.

Owen-Howard, M. (2001). Pharmacological aversion treatment of alcohol dependence. I. Production and prediction of conditioned alcohol aversion. *American Journal of Drug and Alcohol Abuse, 27,* 561–585.

Oyserman, Daphna; Bybee, Deborah; Terry, Kathy; & Hart-Johnson, Tamera. (2004). Possible selves as roadmaps. *Journal of Research in Personality, 38,* 130–149.

Oyserman, Daphna; Grant, Larry; & Ager, Joel. (1995). A socially contextualized model of African American identity: Possible selves and school persistence. *Journal of Personality and Social Psychology, 69,* 1216–1232.

Ozer, Elizabeth M.; & Bandura, Albert. (1990). Mechanisms governing empowerment effects: A self-efficacy analysis. *Journal of Personality and Social Psychology, 58,* 472–486.

Ozer, Emily J.; Best, Suzanne R.; Lipsey, Tami L.; & Weiss, Daniel S. (2003). Predictors of posttraumatic stress disorder and symptoms in adults: A meta-analysis. *Psychological Bulletin, 129,* 52–73.

Pace-Schott, Edward F. (2005). The neurobiology of dreaming. In Meir H. Kryger, Thomas Roth, & William C. Dement (Eds.), *Principles and practice of sleep medicine* (4th ed.). Philadelphia: Elsevier Saunders.

Packard, Erica. (2007, September). A closer look at Division 22: A growing field meets the challenges of war. *Monitor on Psychology, 39,* 54–55.

Padian, Kevin. (2008, February 7). Darwin's enduring legacy. *Nature, 451,* 632–634.

Pagel, James F. (2003). Non-dreamers. *Sleep Medicine, 4,* 235–241.

Pagel, Mark. (2009). Natural selection 150 years on. *Nature, 457,* 808–811.

Paivio, Allan. (1986). *Mental representations: A dual coding approach.* New York: Oxford University Press.

Paivio, Allan. (1995). Imagery and memory. In Michael S. Gazzaniga (Ed.), *The cognitive neurosciences.* Cambridge, MA: MIT Press.

Palm, Kathleen M.; & Gibson, Pamela. (1998). Recovered memories of childhood sexual abuse: Clinicians' practices and beliefs. *Professional Psychology: Research and Practice, 29,* 257–261.

Palmblad, Jan; Petrini, Bjorn; Wasserman, Jerzy; & Akerstedt, Torbjorn. (1979). Lymphocyte and granulocyte reactions during sleep deprivation. *Psychosomatic Medicine, 41,* 273–278.

Palmer, Emma J.; & Hollin, Clive R. (2001). Sociomoral reasoning, perceptions of parenting and self-reported delinquency in adolescents. *Applied Cognitive Psychology, 15,* 85–100.

Palmer, John. (2003a). ESP in the ganzfeld: Analysis of a debate. *Journal of Consciousness Studies, 10,* 51–58.

Palmer, Stephen E. (2002). Perceptual grouping: It's later than you think. *Current Directions in Psychological Science, 11,* 101–106.

Panksepp, Jaak. (2000). The riddle of laughter: Neural and psychoevolutionary underpinnings of joy. *Psychological Science, 9,* 183–186.

Panksepp, Jaak. (2007a). Neuroevolutionary sources of laughter and social joy: Modeling primal human laughter in laboratory rats. *Behavioural Brain Research,182,* 231–244.

Panning, Barbara; & Taatjes, Dylan J. (2008). Transcriptional regulation: It takes a village. *Molecular Cell, 5,* 622–629.

Papa, Michael J.; Singhal, Arvind; Law, Sweety; Pant, Saumya; Sood, Suruchi; Rogers, Everett M.; & Shefner-Rogers, Corinne. (2000). Entertainment, education and social change: An analysis of parasocial interaction, social learning, collective efficacy, and paradoxical communication. *Journal of Communication, 50,* 31–55.

Papini, Mauricio R. (2002). Pattern and process in the evolution of learning. *Psychological Review, 109,* 186–201.P

Papousek, Mechthild; Papousek, Hanus; & Bornstein, Marc H. (1985). The naturalistic vocal environment of young infants: On the significance of homogeneity and variability in parental speech. In Tiffany M. Field & N. Fox (Eds.), *Social perception in infants.* Norwood, NJ: Ablex.

Parent, Anne-Simone; Teilmann, Grete; Juul, Anders; Skakkebaek, Niels E.; Toppari, Jorma; & Bourguignon, Jean-Pierre. (2003). The timing of normal puberty and the age limits of sexual precocity: Variations around the world, secular trends, and changes after migration. *Endocrine Reviews, 24,* 668–693.

Paris, Joel. (2008). The treatment of borderline personality disorder: Implications of research on diagnosis, etiology, and outcome. *Annual Review of Clinical Psychology, 5,* 277–290.

Parish, Amy R.; & de Waal, Frans B. M. (2000). The other "closest living relative": How bonobos (*Pan paniscus*) challenge traditional assumptions about females, dominance, intra- and intersexual interactions, and hominid evolution. In Dori LeCroy & Peter Moller, (Eds), *Evolutionary perspectives on human reproductive behavior. Annals of the New York Academy of Sciences, vol. 907.* New York: New York Academy of Sciences.

Park, Bernadette; Ryan, Carey S.; & Judd, Charles M. (1992). Role of meaningful subgroups in explaining differences in perceived variability for in-groups and out-groups. *Journal of Personality and Social Psychology, 63*(4), 553–567.

Park, Crystal L.; Armeli, Stephen; & Tennen, Howard. (2004). Appraisal-coping goodness of fit: A daily Internet study. *Personality and Social Psychology Bulletin, 30,* 558–569.

Parker, Andrew J. (2007). Binocular depth perception and the cerebral cortex. *Nature Reviews Neuroscience, 8,* 379–391.

Parker, Stephen C. J.; Hansen, Loren; Abaan, Hatice Ozel; Tullius, Thomas D.; & Margulies, Elliott H. (2009). Local DNA topography correlates with functional noncoding regions of the human genome. *Science, 324,* 389–392.

Parks-Stamm, Elizabeth J.; Gollwitzer, Peter M.; & Oettingen, Gabriele. (2007). Action control by implementation intentions: Effective cue detection and efficient response initiation. *Social Cognition, 25,* 248–266.

Parsons, Dee. (2007, February 21). World of magnets: Magnetic bracelets therapy: Natural pain relief magnet products for arthritis, back pain treatments, fibromyalgia treatment. Retrieved June 22, 2009, from http://www.worldofmagnets.co.uk/

Parsons, Thomas D.; & Rizzo, Albert A. (2008). Affective outcomes of virtual reality exposure therapy for anxiety and specific phobias: A meta-analysis. *Journal of Behavior Therapy and Experimental Psychiatry, 39,* 250–261.

Partonen, Timo; & Pandi-Perumal, S. R. (2010). *Seasonal affective disorder: Practice and research.* New York: Oxford University Press.

Pascual-Leone, Alvaro; Amedi, Amir; Fregni, Felipe; & Merabet, Lotfi B. (2005). The plastic human cortex. *Annual Review of Neuroscience, 28,* 377–401.

Patapoutian, Ardem; Peier, Andrea M.; Story, Gina M.: & Viswanath, Veena. (2003). ThermoTRP channels and beyond: Mechanisms of temperature sensation. *Nature Reviews Neuroscience, 4,* 529–539.

Patrick, Christopher J. (2007). Antisocial personality disorder and psychopathy. In William T. O'Donohue, Kevin A. Fowler, & Scott O. Lilienfeld (Eds.), *Personality Disorders: Toward the DSM-V* (pp. 109–166). Thousand Oaks, CA: Sage.

Patterson, Charlotte J. (2006). Children of gay and lesbian parents. *Current Directions in Psychological Science, 15,* 241–244.

Patterson, Charlotte J. (2008). Sexual orientation across the life span: Introduction to the special section. *Developmental Psychology, 44,* 1–4.

Paul, Diane B.; & Blumenthal, Arthur L. (1989). On the trail of Little Albert. *The Psychological Record, 39,* 547–553.

Paul, Gordon L.; & Menditto, Anthony A. (1992). Effectiveness of inpatient treatment programs for mentally ill adults in public psychiatric facilities. *Applied and Preventive Psychology, 1,* 41–63.

Pauli-Pott, Ursula; Mertesacker, Bettina; & Beckman, Dieter. (2004). Predicting the development of infant emotionality from maternal characteristics. *Development and Psychopathology, 16,* 19–42.

Pavlov, Ivan. (1904/1965). On conditioned reflexes. In Richard J. Herrnstein & Edwin G. Boring (Eds.), *A source book in the history of psychology.* Cambridge, MA: Harvard University Press.

Pavlov, Ivan. (1927/1960). *Conditioned reflexes: An investigation of the physiological activity of the cerebral cortex* (G. V. Anrep, Trans.). New York: Dover Books. Retrieved May 25, 2001, from http://psychclassics.yorku.ca/Pavlov/index.htm

Pavlov, Ivan. (1928). *Lectures on conditioned reflexes.* New York: International Publishers.

Payne, Christina; & Jaffe, Klaus. (2005). Self seeks like: Many humans choose dog pets following rules used for assortative mating. *Journal of Ethology, 23,* 15–18.

Payton, Jack R. (1992, May 16). The sad legacy of Japan's outcasts. *Chicago Tribune*, Sect. 1, p. 21.

Pedersen, Paul B.; Crethar, Hugh C.; & Carlson, Jon. (2008). Defining inclusive cultural empathy. In Paul B. Pedersen, Hugh C. Crethar, & Jon Carlson (Eds.), *Inclusive cultural empathy: Making relationships central in counseling and psychotherapy* (pp. 41–44). Washington, D.C.: American Psychological Association.

Pedersen, Sara; & Seidman, Edward. (2004). Team sports achievement and self-esteem development among urban adolescent girls. *Psychology of Women Quarterly, 28,* 412–422.

Peirce, Robert S.; Frone, Michael R.; Russell, Marcia; & Cooper, M. Lynne. (1996). Financial stress, social support, and alcohol involvement: A longitudinal test of the buffering hypothesis in a general population study. *Health Psychology, 15,* 38–47.

Peissig, Jessie J.; & Tarr, Michael J. (2007). Visual object recognition: Do we know more now than we did 20 years ago? *Annual Review of Psychology, 58,* 75–96.

Pendergrast, Mark. (1996). *Victims of memory: Sex abuse accusations and shattered lives* (2nd ed.). Hinesburg, VT: Upper Access.

Pepperberg, Irene M. (1993). Cognition and communication in an African gray parrot (*Psittacus erithacus*): Studies on a nonhuman, nonprimate, nonmammalian subject. In Herbert L. Roitblat, Louis M. Herman, & Paul E. Nachtigall (Eds.), *Language and communication: Comparative perspectives.* Hillsdale, NJ: Erlbaum.

Pepperberg, Irene M. (2000). *The Alex studies: Cognitive and communicative abilities of gray parrots.* Cambridge, MA: Harvard University Press.

Pepperberg, Irene M. (2007). Grey parrots do not always "parrot": The roles of imitation and phonological awareness in the creation of new labels from existing vocalizations. *Language Sciences, 29,* 1–13.

Pereira, Ana C.; Huddleston, Dan H.; Brickman, Adam M.; Sosunov, Alexander A.; Hene, Rene; McKhann, Guy M.; Sloan, Richard; Gage, Fred H.; Brown, Truman R.; & Small, Scott A. (2007). An *in vivo* correlate of exercise-induced neurogenesis in the adult dentate gyrus. *Proceedings of the National Academy of Sciences, 104,* 5638–5643.

Perlis, Michael L.; Smith, Michael T.; & Pigeon, Wilfred R. (2005). Etiology and pathophysiology of insomnia. In Meir H. Kryger, Thomas Roth, & William C. Dement (Eds.), *Principles and practice of sleep medicine* (4th ed.). Philadelphia: Elsevier Saunders.

Perloff, Richard M. (1993). *The dynamics of persuasion.* Hillsdale, NJ: Erlbaum.

Pert, Candace B.; & Snyder, Solomon H. (1973). Opiate receptor: Demonstration in the nervous tissue. *Science, 179,* 1011–1014.

Pervin, Lawrence A. (1994). A critical analysis of current trait theory. *Psychological Inquiry, 5,* 103–113.

Pesant, Nicholas; & Zadra, Antonio. (2004). Working with dreams in therapy: What do we know and what should we do? *Clinical Psychology Review, 24,* 489–512.

Petersen, Ronald C. (2002). *Mayo Clinic on Alzheimer's disease.* Rochester, MN: Mayo Clinic Press.

Peterson, Christopher. (2000). Optimistic explanatory style and health. In Jane E. Gillham (Ed.), *The science of optimism and hope: Research essays in honor of Martin E. P. Seligman.* Philadelphia: Templeton Foundation Press.

Peterson, Christopher. (2006). *A primer in positive psychology.* New York: Oxford University Press.

Peterson, Christopher; & Bossio, Lisa M. (1993). Healthy attitudes: Optimism, hope, and control. In Daniel Goleman & Joel Gurin (Eds.), *Mind/ body medicine: How to use your mind for better health.* Yonkers, NY: Consumer Reports Books.

Peterson, Christopher; & Bossio, Lisa M. (2001). Optimism and physical well-being. In Edward C. Chang (Ed.), *Optimism and pessimism: Implications for theory, research, and practice.* Washington, DC: American Psychological Association.

Peterson, Christopher; & Park, Nansook (2007). Explanatory style and emotion regulation. In James J. Gross (Ed.), *Handbook of emotion regulation.* New York: Guilford Press.

Peterson, Christopher; Seligman, Martin E. P.; & Vaillant, George E. (1988). Pessimistic explanatory style as a risk factor for physical illness: A thirty-five-year longitudinal study. *Journal of Personality and Social Psychology, 55,* 23–27.

Peterson, Lloyd R.; & Peterson, Margaret J. (1959). Short-term retention of individual items. *Journal of Experimental Psychology, 58,* 193–198.

Petitto, Laura Ann; Holowka, Siobhan; Sergio, Lauren E.; Levy, Bronna; & Ostry, David J. (2004). Baby hands that move to the rhythm of language: Hearing babies acquiring sign languages babble silently on the hands. *Cognition, 93,* 43–73.

Petitto, Laura Ann; Holowka, Siobhan; Sergio, Lauren E.; & Ostry, David. (2001). Language rhythms in baby hand movements. *Nature, 413,* 35–36.

Petitto, Laura Ann; & Marentette, Paula F. (1991). Babbling in the manual mode: Evidence for the ontogeny of language. *Science, 251,* 1493–1496.

Petrovic, Predrag; Kalso, Eija; Petersson, Karl Magnus; & Ingvar, Martin. (2002, March 1). Placebo and opioid analgesia—Imaging a shared neuronal network. *Science, 295,* 1737–1740.

Petry, Nancy M.; Tedford, Jacqueline; Austin, Mark; Nich, Charla; Carroll, Kathleen M.; & Rounsaville, Bruce J. (2004). Prize reinforcement contingency management for treating cocaine users: How low can we go, and with whom? *Addiction, 99,* 349–360.

Pfaffenberger, Angela. (2007). Different conceptualizations of optimal development. *Journal of Humanistic Psychology, 47,* 474–496.

Pham, Lien B.; & Taylor, Shelley E. (1999). From thought to action: Effects of process- versus outcome-based mental simulations on performance. *Personality and Social Psychology Bulletin, 25,* 250–260.

Phan, K. Luan; Wager, Tor; Taylor, Stephan F.; & Liberzon, Israel. (2002). Functional neuroanatomy of emotion: A meta-analysis of emotion activation studies in PET and fMRI. *NeuroImage, 16,* 331–348.

Phelps, Elizabeth A. (2006). Emotion and cognition: Insights from studies of the human amygdala. *Annual Review of Psychology, 57,* 27–53.

Phelps, Elizabeth A.; O'Connor, Kevin J.; Gatenby, J. Christopher; Gore, John C.; Grillon, Christian; & Davis, Michael. (2001). Activation of the left amygdala to a cognitive representation of fear. *Nature Neuroscience, 4,* 237–441.

Phillips, Susan D.; & Blustein, David L. (1994). Readiness for career choices: Planning, exploring, and deciding. *The Career Development Quarterly, 43,* 63–75.

Piaget, Jean. (1952). *The origins of intelligence in children* (Margaret Cook, Trans.). New York: International Universities Press.

Piaget, Jean. (1972). Intellectual evolution from adolescence to adulthood. *Human Development, 15,* 1–12.

Piaget, Jean. (1973). The stages of cognitive development: Interview with Richard I. Evans. In Richard I. Evans (Ed.), *Jean Piaget: The man and his ideas.* New York: Dutton.

Piaget, Jean; & Inhelder, Bärbel. (1958). *The growth of logical thinking from childhood to adolescence: An essay on the construction of formal operational structures* (Anne Parsons & Stanley Milgram, Trans.). New York: Basic Books.

Piaget, Jean; & Inhelder, Bärbel. (1974). *The child's construction of quantities: Conservation and atomism.* London: Routledge & Kegan Paul.

Pica, Pierre; Lemer, Cathy; Izard, Veronique; & Dehaene, Stanislas. (2004, October 15). Exact and approximate arithmetic in an Amazonian indigene group. *Science, 306,* 499–503.

Piliavin, Jane Allyn. (2008). Long-term benefits of habitual helping: Doing well by doing good. In Brandon A Sullivan, Mark Snyder, & John L. Sullivan (Eds.), *Cooperation: The political psychology of effective human interaction.* Malden, MA: Blackwell.

Pillemer, David B. (1998). *Momentous events, vivid memories.* Cambridge, MA: Harvard University Press.

Pinel, John P. J.; Assanand, Sunaina; & Lehman, Darrin R. (2000). Hunger, eating, and ill health. *American Psychologist, 55,* 1105–1116.

Pinker, Steven. (1994). *The language instinct: How the mind creates language.* New York: Morrow.

Pinker, Steven. (1995). Introduction: Language. In Michael S. Gazzaniga (Ed.), *The cognitive neurosciences.* Cambridge, MA: MIT Press.

Piomelli, Daniele. (2003). The molecular logic of endocannabinoid signalling. *Nature Reviews Neuroscience, 4,* 873–884.

Piotrowski, C.; & Armstrong, T. (2006). Current recruitment and selection practices: A national survey of Fortune 1000 firms. *North American Journal of Psychology, 8,* 489–496.

Piper, August; & Merskey, Harold. (2004, September). The persistence of folly: A critical examination of dissociative identity disorder. Part I. The excesses of an improbable concept. *Canadian Journal of Psychiatry, 49*(9), 592–600.

Pitschel-Walz, Gabi; Leucht, Stefan; Bauml, Josef; Kissling, Werner; & Engel, Rolf. (2001). The effect of family interventions on relapse and rehospitalization in schizophrenia—A meta-analysis. *Schizophrenia Bulletin, 27,* 73–92.

Pittenger, David J. (2005). Cautionary comments regarding the Myers-Briggs Type Indicator. *Consulting Psychology Journal: Practice and Research, 57,* 210–221.

Plake, Barbara S.; & Impara, James C. (2001). *The mental measurements yearbook* (14th ed.). Lincoln: Buros Institute of Mental Measurements/University of Nebraska Press.

Plake, Barbara S., Impara, James C.; & Spies, Robert A. (Eds.). (2003). *The fifteenth mental measurements yearbook.* Lincoln: Buros Institute of Mental Measurements/University of Nebraska Press.

Plant, E. Ashby; Hyde, Janet Shibley; Keltner, Dacher; & Devine, Patricia G. (2000). The gender stereotyping of emotions. *Psychology of Women Quarterly, 24,* 81–92.

Plant, E. Ashby; Kling, Kristen C.; & Smith, Ginny L. (2004). The influence of gender and social role on the interpretation of facial expressions. *Sex Roles, 51,* 187–196.

Plassmann, Hilke; O'Doherty, John; Shiv, Baba; & Rangel, Antonio. (2008). Marketing actions can modulate neural representations of experienced pleasantness. *Proceedings of the National Academy of Sciences, 105,* 1050–1054.

Platek, Steven M.; Critton, Samuel R.; Meyers, Thomas E.; & Gallup, Gordon G., Jr. (2003). Contagious yawning: The role of self-awareness and mental state attribution. *Cognitive Brain Research, 17,* 223–227.

Platek, Steven M.; Mohamed, Feroze B.; & Gallup, Gordon G., Jr. (2005). Contagious yawning and the brain. *Cognitive Brain Research, 23,* 448–452.

Plomin, Robert. (2003). General cognitive ability. In Robert Plomin, John C. DeFries, & Peter McGuffin (Eds.), *Behavioral genetics in the postgenomic era.* Washington, DC: American Psychological Association.

Plomin, Robert; & Colledge, Essi. (2001). Genetics and psychology: Beyond heritability. *European Psychologist, 6,* 229–240.

Plomin, Robert; DeFries, John C.; McClearn, Gerald E.; & McGuffin, Peter. (2001*). Behavioral genetics* (4th ed.). New York: Worth.

Plomin, Robert; Owen, Michael J.; & McGuffin, Peter. (1994, June 17). The genetic basis of complex human behaviors. *Science, 264,* 1733–1739.

Plomin, Robert; & Spinath, Frank M. (2004). Intelligence: Genetics, genes, and genomics. *Journal of Personality and Social Psychology, 86,* 112–129.

Polk, Thad A.; & Newell, Allen. (1995). Deduction as verbal reasoning. *Psychological Review, 102,* 533–566.

Pollick, Amy. (2007, November). Institutional review boards (IRBs): Navigating the maze. *Observer, 20,* 16–21.

Pope, Kenneth S. (1990). Therapist–patient sexual involvement: A review of the research. *Clinical Psychology Review, 10,* 477–490.

Pope, Kenneth S.; Butcher, James N.; & Seelen, Joyce. (2006). Joyce assessing malingering and other aspects of credibility. In Kenneth S. Pope, James N. Butcher, & Joyce Seelen (Eds.), *The MMPI, MMPI-2, & MMPI-A in court: A practical guide for expert witnesses and attorneys* (3rd. ed., pp. 129–160); Washington, DC: American Psychological Association.

Pope, Kenneth S.; & Tabachnick, Barbara G. (1993). Therapists' anger, hate, fear, and sexual feelings: National survey of therapist responses, client characteristics, critical events, formal complaints, and training. *Professional Psychology: Research and Practice, 24,* 142–152.

Pope, Victoria. (1997, August 4). Day-care dangers. *U.S. News & World Report, 123,* 30–37.

Porkka-Heiskanen, Tarja; Strecker, Robert E.; Thakkar, Mahesh; Bjørkum, Alvhild A.; Greene, Robert W.; & McCarley, Robert W. (1997, May 23). Adenosine: A mediator of the sleep-inducing effects of prolonged wakefulness. *Science, 276,* 1265–1268.

Porter, Jess; Craven, Brent; Khan, Rehan M.; Chang, Shao-Ju; Kang, Irene; Judkewitz, Benjamin; Volpe, Jason; Settles, Gary; & Sobel, Noam. (2007). Mechanisms of scent-tracking in humans. *Nature Neuroscience, 10,* 27–29.

Portrat, Sophie; Barrouillet, Pierre; & Camos, Valérie. (2008). Time-related decay or interference-based forgetting in working memory? *Journal of Experimental Psychology: Learning, Memory, and Cognition, 34,* 1561–1564.

Pos, Alberta E.; Greenberg, Leslie S.; & Elliott, Robert. (2008). Experiential therapy. In Jay L. Lebow (Ed.), *Twenty-first century psychotherapies: Contemporary approaches to theory and practice* (pp. 80–122). Hoboken, NJ: Wiley.

Posada, German; Carbonell, Olga A.; Alzate, Gloria; & Plata, Sandra J. (2004). Through Colombian lenses: Ethnographic and conventional analyses of maternal care and their associations with secure base behavior. *Developmental Psychology, 40,* 508–518.

Posada, German; Jacobs, Amanda; Richmond, Melissa K.; Carbonell, Olga A.; Alzate, Gloria; Bustamonte, Maria R.; & Quiceno, Julio. (2002). Maternal caregiving and infant security in two cultures. *Developmental Psychology, 38,* 67–78.

Power, A. Kathryn. (2005). Achieving the promise through workforce transformation: A view from the Center for Mental Health Services. *Administration and Policy in Mental Health, 32,* 489–495.

Powers, Mark B.; & Emmelkamp, Paul M. G. (2008). Virtual reality exposure therapy for anxiety disorders: A meta-analysis. *Journal of Anxiety Disorders, 22,* 561–569.

Powers, Pauline M. (2009). Bulimia nervosa. In Robert E. Rakel & Edward T. Bope (Eds.), *Conn's current therapy 2009* (pp. 1115–1117). Philadelphia: Saunders Elsevier.

Powers, Theodore A. (2005). Working with the clock ticking. In Lise Motherwell & Joseph J. Shay (Eds.), *Complex dilemmas in group therapy: Pathways to resolution* (pp. 231–241). New York: Brunner-Routledge.

Powlishta, Kimberly K. (1995). Intergroup processes in childhood: Social categorization and sex role development. *Developmental Psychology, 31,* 781–788.

Pratkanis, Anthony R.; & Aronson, Elliot. (2001). *Age of propaganda: The everyday use and abuse of persuasion* (Rev. ed.). New York: Freeman.

Pratto, Felicia; & Glasford, Demis E. (2008). Ethnocentrism and the value of a human life. *Journal of Personality and Social Psychology, 95,* 1411–1428.

Premack, David. (2007). Human and animal cognition: Continuity and discontinuity. *Proceedings of the National Academy of Sciences, 104,* 13861–13867.

Press Release Newswire, PRweb.com. (2007, January). Wonderlic announces release of revised Wonderlic Personnel Test (WPT-R): Update incorporates the latest advances in test development and scoring, accurately measuring intelligence and predicting success on the job. Libertyville, IL: Wonderlic.

Pressman, Mark R. (2007). Disorders of arousal from sleep and violent behavior: The role of physical contact and proximity. *Sleep, 30,* 1039–1047.

Preston, John D.; O'Neal, John H.; & Talaga, Mary C. (2008). *Handbook of clinical psychopharmacology for therapists* (5th ed.). Oakland, CA: New Harbinger.

Preti, George; Cutler, Winnifred B.; Garcia, C. R.; Huggins, G. R.; & Lawley, H. J. (1986). Human axillary secretions influence women's menstrual cycles: The role of donor extract of females. *Hormones and Behavior, 20,* 474–482.

Previde, Emanuela Prato; & Poli, Marco D. (1996). Social learning in the golden hamster (*Mesocricetus auratus*). *Journal of Comparative Psychology, 110,* 203–208.

Price, Michael. (2008, February). Division 55's drive for RxP. *Monitor on Psychology, 39,* 58–59.

Prinzmetal, William. (1995). Visual feature integration in a world of objects. *Current Directions in Psychological Science, 4,* 90–94.

Prochaska, James O.; & Norcross, John C. (2010). *Systems of psychotherapy* (7th ed.). Belmont, CA: Brooks/Cole.

Provine, Robert R. (1989). Faces as releasers of contagious yawning: An approach to face detection using normal human subjects. *Bulletin of the Psychonomic Society, 27,* 211–214.

Pullum, Geoffrey K. (1991). *The great Eskimo vocabulary hoax and other irreverent essays on the study of language.* Chicago: University of Chicago Press.

Purcell, Shaun M.; Wray, Naomi R.; Stone, Jennifer L.; Visscher, Peter M.; O'Donovan, Michael C.; Sullivan, Patrick F.; & Sklar, Pamela. (2009). Common polygenic variation contributes to risk of schizophrenia and bipolar disorder. *Nature, 460,* 748–752.

Purkey, William Watson; & Stanley, Paula Helen. (2002). The self in psychotherapy. In David J. Cain & Julius Seeman (Eds.), *Humanistic psychotherapies: Handbook of research and practice.* Washington, DC: American Psychological Association.

Quattrocki, Elizabeth; Baird, Adigail; & Yurgelun-Todd, Deborah. (2000). Biological aspects of the link between smoking and depression. *Harvard Review of Psychiatry, 8,* 99–110.

Quinn, Kimberly A.; & Macrae, C. Neil. (2005). Categorizing others: The dynamics of person construal. *Journal of Personality and Social Psychology, 88,* 467–479.

Rabinowitz, Jonathan; Lichtenberg, Pesach; Kaplan, Zeev; Mark, Mordechai; Nahon, Danielle; & Davidson, Michael. (2001). Rehospitalization rates of chronically ill schizophrenic patients discharged on a regimen of risperidone, olanzipine, or conventional antipsychotics. *American Journal of Psychiatry, 158,* 266–269.

Rachlin, Howard. (1974). Self-control. *Behaviorism, 2,* 94–107.

Rachlin, Howard. (1995). The value of temporal patterns in behavior. *Current Directions in Psychological Science, 4,* 188–192.

Rachlin, Howard. (2000). *The science of self-control.* Cambridge, MA: Harvard University Press.

Racine, Eric; Bar-Ilan, Ofek; & Illes, Judy. (2005). fMRI in the public eye. *Nature Reviews Neuroscience, 6*(2), 159–164.

Rado, Jeffrey; & Janicak, Philip G. (2009). Schizophrenia. In Robert E. Rakel & Edward T. Bope (Eds.), *Conn's current therapy 2009* (pp. 1128–1131). Philadelphia: Saunders Elsevier.

Rahe, Richard H. (1972). Subjects' recent life changes and their near-future illness reports. *Annals of Clinical Research, 4,* 250–265.

Raichle, Katherine A.; Hanley, Marisol; Jensen, Mark P.; & Cardenas, Diana D. (2007). Cognitions, coping, and social environment predict adjustment to pain in spinal cord injury. *Journal of Pain, 8,* 718–729.

Raisman, Geoffrey. (2004). The idea that scandalized brain science. *Cerebrum, 6,* 21–34.

Raj, John Dilip; Nelson, John Abraham; & Rao, K. S. P. (2006). A study on the effects of some reinforcers to improve performance of employees in a retail industry. *Behavior Modification, 30,* 848–866.

Ramachandran, Vilayanur S. (1992a, May). Blind spots. *Scientific American, 266,* 86–91.

Ramachandran, Vilayanur S. (1992b). Filling in gaps in perception: Part 1. *Current Directions in Psychological Science, 1,* 199–205.

Ramachandran, Vilayanur S.; & Rogers-Ramachandran, Diane. (2007, April/May). Paradoxical perceptions. *Scientific American Mind, 2,* 18–20.

Rapoport, Judith L. (1989). *The boy who couldn't stop washing: The experience and treatment of obsessive-compulsive disorder.* New York: Dutton.

Rasch, Bjorn; & Born, Jan. (2008). Reactivation and consolidation of memory during sleep. *Current Directions in Psychological Science, 17,* 188–192.

Raskin, Nathaniel J.; & Rogers, Carl R. (2005). Person-centered therapy. In Raymond J. Corsini & Danny Wedding (Eds.), *Current psychotherapies* (7th ed., instr. ed., pp. 130–165). Belmont, CA: Thomson Brooks/Cole Publishing.

Rasmussen, Keith G. (2009). Evidence for electroconvulsive therapy efficacy in mood disorders. In Conrad M. Swartz (Ed.), *Electroconvulsive and neuromodulation therapies* (pp. 109–123). New York: Cambridge University Press.

Rasmussen, Steven A.; & Eisen, Jane L. (1992). The epidemiology and clinical features of obsessive-compulsive disorder. *Psychiatric Clinics of North America, 15,* 743–758.

Ravussin, Eric; & Danforth, Elliot, Jr. (1999, January 8). Beyond sloth—Physical activity and weight gain. *Science, 283*, 184–185.

Rawson, Nancy E. (2006). Olfactory loss in aging. *Science of Aging Knowledge Environment, 5*, pe6.

Rawson, Penny. (2005). *A handbook of short-term psychodynamic psychotherapy.* Karnac Books.

Raynor, Hollie A.; & Epstein, Leonard H. (2001). Dietary variety, energy regulation, and obesity. *Psychological Bulletin, 127*, 325–341.

Reader, Simon M.; Kendal, Jeremy R.; & Laland, Kevin N. (2003). Social learning of foraging sites and escape routes in wild Trinidadian guppies. *Animal Behaviour, 66*, 729–739.

Recanzone, Gregg H.; & Sutter, Mitchell L. (2008). The biological basis of audition. *Annual Review of Psychology, 59*, 119–142.

Redline, Susan. (2005). Genetics of obstructive sleep apnea. In Meir H. Kryger, Thomas Roth, & William C. Dement (Eds.), *Principles and practice of sleep medicine* (4th ed.). Philadelphia: Elsevier Saunders.

Reeder, Glenn D.; Monroe, Andrew E.; & Pryor, John B. (2008). Impressions of Milgram's obedient teachers. Situational cues inform inferences about motives and traits. *Journal of Personality and Social Psychology, 95*, 1–17.

Refinetti, Roberto. (2000). *Circadian physiology.* Boca Raton, FL: CRC Press.

Reger, Greg M.; & Gahm, Gregory A. (2008). Virtual reality exposure therapy for active duty soldiers. *Journal of Clinical Psychology, 64*, 940–946.

Regier, Darrel; Narrow, Wiliam E.; Kuhl, Emily A.; & Kupfer, David J. (2009). The conceptual development of DSM-V. *American Journal of Psychiatry, 166*, 645–650.

Rego, Arménio; Sousa, Filipa; Pina e Cunha, Miguel; Correia, Anabela; & Saur-Amaral, Irina. (2007). Leader self-reported emotional intelligence and perceived employee creativity: An exploratory study. *Creativity & Innovation Management, 16*, 250–264.

Rego, Simon A. (2009). Culture and anxiety disorders. In Sussie Eshun & Regan A. R. Gurung (Eds.), *Culture and mental health: Sociocultural influences, theory, and practice* (pp. 197–220). West Sussex, England: Wiley-Blackwell.

Reid, Pamela Trotman; Cooper, Shauna M.; & Banks, Kira Hudson. (2008). Girls to women: Developmental theory, research, and issues. In Florence L. Denmark & Michele A. Paludi (Eds.). *Psychology of women: A handbook of issues and theories* (2nd ed.). Westport, CT: Praeger Publishers/Greenwood Publishing Group.

Reis, Harry T.; Collins, W. Andrew; & Berscheid, Ellen. (2000). The relationship context of human behavior and development. *Psychological Bulletin, 126*, 844–872.

Reisenzein, Rainer. (1983). The Schachter theory of emotion: Two decades later. *Psychological Bulletin, 94*, 239–264.

Reissig, Chad J.; Strain, Eric C.; & Griffiths, Roland R. (2009). Caffeinated energy drinks—A growing problem. *Drug and Alcohol Dependence, 99*, 1–10.

Rejeski, W. Jack; Gregg, Edward; Thompson, Amy; & Berry, Michael. (1991). The effects of varying doses of acute aerobic exercise on psychophysiological stress responses in highly trained cyclists. *Journal of Sport and Exercise Psychology, 13*, 188–199.

Rejeski, W. Jack; Thompson, Amy; Brubaker, Peter H.; & Miller, Henry S. (1992). Acute exercise: Buffering psychosocial responses in women. *Health Psychology, 11*, 355–362.

Reneman, Liesbeth; Booij, Jan; de Bruin, Kora; Reitsma, Johannes B.; deWolff, Frederik A.; Gunning, W. Boudewijn; den Heeten, Gerard J.; & van den Brink, Wim. (2001). Effects of dose, sex, and long-term abstention from use on toxic effects of MDMA (ecstasy) on brain serotonin neurons. *Lancet, 358*, 1864–1869.

Reneman, Liesbeth; Lavalaye, Jules; Schmand, Ben; deWolff, Frederik A.; van den Brink, Wim; den Heeten, Gerard J.; & Booji, Jan. (2001b). Cortical serotonin transporter density and verbal memory in individuals who stopped using 3,4-methylenedioxymethamphetamine (MDMA or "ecstasy"). *Archives of General Psychiatry, 58*, 901–906.

Reneman, Liesbeth; Schilt, T.; & de Win, Maartje M. (2006). Memory function and serotonin transporter promoter gene polymorphism in ecstasy (MDMA) users. *Journal of Psychopharmacology, 20*, 389–399.

Renk, Kimberly; Donnelly, Reesa; McKinney, Cliff; & Agliata, Allison Kanter. (2006). The development of gender identity: Timetables and influences. In Kam-Shing Yip (Ed.), *Psychology of gender identity: An international perspective.* Hauppauge, NY: Nova Science Publishers.

Repetti, Rena L. (1989). Effects of daily workload on subsequent behavior during marital interaction: The roles of withdrawal and spouse support. *Journal of Personality and Social Psychology, 57*, 651–659.

Repetti, Rena L. (1993). Short-term effects of occupational stressors on daily mood and health complaints. *Health Psychology, 12*, 125–131.

Repetti, Rena L.; & Wood, Jenifer. (1997). The effects of daily stress at work on mothers' interactions with preschoolers. *Journal of Family Psychology, 11*, 90–108.

Rescorla, Robert A. (1968). Probability of shock in the presence and absence of CS in fear conditioning. *Journal of Comparative and Physiological Psychology, 66*, 1–5.

Rescorla, Robert A. (1980). Pavlovian second-order conditioning: Studies in associative learning. Hillsdale, NJ: Erlbaum.

Rescorla, Robert A. (1988). Pavlovian conditioning: It's not what you think it is. *American Psychologist, 43*, 151–160.

Rescorla, Robert A. (1997). Quoted in James E. Freeman, "Pavlov in the classroom: An interview with Robert A. Rescorla." *Teaching of Psychology, 24*, 283–286.

Rescorla, Robert A. (2001). Retraining of extinguished Pavlovian stimuli. *Journal of Experimental Psychology: Animal Behavior Processes, 27*, 115–124.

Rest, James R. (1983). Morality. In Paul H. Mussen, John H. Flavell, & Ellen M. Markman (Eds.), *Handbook of child psychology* (4th ed., Vol. 3). New York: Wiley.

Rétey, J. V.; Adam, M.; Honegger, E.; Khatami, R.; Luhmann, U. F. O.; Jung, H. H.; Berger, W.; & Landolt, H.-P. (2005). A functional genetic variation of adenosine deaminase affects the duration and intensity of deep sleep in humans. *Proceedings of the National Academy of Sciences, 102*, 15676–15681.

Revelle, William. (1995). Personality processes. *Annual Review of Psychology, 46*, 295–328.

Revelle, William. (2007). Experimental approaches to the study of personality. In Richard W. Robins, R. Chris Fraley, & Robert F. Krueger (Eds.), *Handbook of research methods in personality psychology* (pp. 37-61). New York: Guilford Press.

Reynolds, David K. (1990). *A thousand waves: A sensible life-style for sensitive people.* New York: Morrow.

Ricaurte, George A.; & McCann, Una D. (2001). Assessing long-term effects of MDMA (ecstasy). *Lancet, 358*, 1831–1832.

Riccio, David C.; Millin, Paula M.; & Gisquet-Verrier, Pascale. (2003). Retrograde amnesia: Forgetting back. *Current Directions in Psychological Science, 12*, 41–44.

Rice, Robert W.; McFarlin, Dean B.; & Bennett, Debbie E. (1989). Standards of comparison and job satisfaction. *Journal of Applied Psychology, 74* (4), 591–598.

Richardson, Robert D. (2006). *William James: In the maelstrom of American modernism.* Boston: Houghton Mifflin.

Richman, Laura Smart; Kubzansky, Laura; Masello, Joanna; Kawachi, Ichiro; Choo, Peter; & Bauer, Mark. (2005). Positive emotion and health: Going beyond the negative. *Health Psychology, 24,* 422–429.

Richtand, Neil M.; Welge, Jeffrey A.; & Logue, Aaron D. (2007, August). Dopamine and serotonin receptor binding and antipsychotic efficacy. *Neuropsychopharmacology, 32*(8), 1715–1726.

Riegel, B.; Simon, D.; Bickel, S. R.; Clopton, P.; Gocka, I.; & Weaver, J. (1998). Teaching Ayurvedic and western health promotion strategies to healthy adults. *American Journal of Health Promotion, 12*(4): 258-61.

Riegel, B.; Simon D.; Weaver, J.; Carlson, B.; Clapton, P.; & Gocka, I. (1996). *Ayurvedic medicine demonstration project* (1R21 RR09726–01). Bethesda, MD: Report submitted to the National Institutes of Health, Institute for Alternative Medicine.

Rieger, Gerulf; Chivers, Meredith L.; & Bailey, J. Michael. (2005). Sexual arousal patterns of bisexual men. *Psychological Science, 16,* 579–584.

Rieger, Gerulf; Linsenmeier, Joan A. W.; & Gygax, Lorenz. (2008, January). Sexual orientation and childhood gender nonconformity: Evidence from home videos. *Developmental Psychology, 44*(1), 46–58.

Riggio, Heidi; & Halpern, Diane F. (2006). Understanding human thought: Educating students as critical thinkers. In William Buskist & Stephen F. Davis (Eds.), *Handbook of the teaching of psychology.* Malden, MA: Blackwell.

Riley, J. R.; Greggers, U.; Smith, A. D.; Reynolds, D. R.; & Menzel, R. (2005). The flight paths of honeybees recruited by the waggle dance. *Nature, 435,* 205–207.

Rilling, Mark. (2000). John Watson's paradoxical struggle to explain Freud. *American Psychologist, 55,* 301–312.

Ringdahl, Joel E.; & Falcomata, Terry S. (2009). Applied behavior analysis and the treatment of childhood psychopathology and developmental disabilities. In Johnny L. Matson, Frank Andrasik, & Michael L. Matson (Eds.), *Treating childhood psychopathology and developmental disabilities* (pp. 29–54). New York: Springer.

Risen, Jane; & Gilovich, Thomas. (2007). Informal logical fallacies. In Robert J. Sternberg, Henry Roediger III, & Diane F. Halpern (Eds), *Critical thinking in psychology.* New York: Cambridge University Press.

Rivas-Vasquez, Rafael A. (2003). Aripiprazole: A novel antipsychotic with dopamine stabilizing properties. *Professional Psychology: Research and Practice, 34,* 108–111.

Rivers, Ian; Poteat, V. Paul; & Noret, Nathalie. (2008). Victimization, social support, and psychosocial functioning among children of same-sex and opposite-sex couples in the United Kingdom. *Developmental Psychology, 44,* 127–134.

Rizzolatti, Giacomo. (2005). The mirror neuron system and imitation. In Susan Hurley & Nick Chater (Eds.), *Perspectives on imitation from neuroscience to social science. Vol. 1: Mechanisms of imitation and imitation in animals.* Boston: MIT Press.

Rizzolatti, Giacomo; & Craighero, Laila. (2004). The mirror-neuron system. *Annual Review of Neuroscience, 27,* 169–192.

Rizzolatti, Giacomo; Fogassi, Leonardo; & Gallese, Vittorio. (2006, November). Mirrors in the mind. *Scientific American, 295,* 54–61.

Rizzolatti, Giacomo; & Sinigaglia, Corrado. (2008). *Mirrors in the brain: How our minds share actions and emotions* (Frances Anderson, Trans.). New York: Oxford University Press.

Roazen, Paul. (1999). *Freud: Political and social thought.* Piscataway, NJ: Transaction.

Roazen, Paul. (2000). *The historiography of psychoanalysis.* Piscataway, NJ: Transaction.

Robb, Drew. (2004). Screening for speedier selection software can eliminate unqualified applicants, leaving recruiters with fewer worthless resumes. *HR Magazine.*

Robbins, Ann S.; Spence, Janet T.; & Clark, Heather. (1991). Psychological determinants of health and performance: The tangled web of desirable and undesirable characteristics. *Journal of Personality and Social Psychology, 61,* 755–765.

Robbins, Steven B.; Lauver, Kristy; Le, Huy; Davis, Daniel; Langley, Ronelle; & Carlstrom, Aaron. (2004). Do psychosocial and study skill factors predict college outcomes? A meta-analysis. *Psychological Bulletin, 130,* 261–288.

Roberts, Amy; & Nelson, Gareth. (2005, June 18). Quoted in Bijal Trevedi, "Autistic and proud of it." *New Scientist,* issue 2504, p. 36.

Robinson, Barbara S.; Davis, Kathleen L.; & Meara, Naomi M. (2003). Motivational attributes of occupational possible selves for low-income rural women. *Journal of Counseling Psychology, 50,* 156–164.

Robinson, John P.; & Godbey, Geoffrey. (1998, February). No sex, please ... we're college students. *American Demographics, 20*(2), 18–23.

Robinson, Michael D.; & Clore, Gerald L. (2002). Belief and feeling: Evidence for an accessibility model of emotional self-report. *Psychological Bulletin, 128,* 934–960.

Robinson, Paul. (1993). *Freud and his critics.* Berkeley: University of California Press.

Robles, Theodore K.; Glaser, Ronald; & Kiecolt-Glaser, Janice K. (2005). Out of balance: A new look at chronic stress, depression, and immunity. *Psychological Science, 14,* 111–115.

Rochat, François; Maggioni, Olivier; & Modigliani, Andre. (2000). Captain Paul Grueninger: The chief of police who saved Jewish refugees by refusing to do his duty. In Thomas Blass (Ed.), *Obedience to authority: Current perspectives on the Milgram paradigm.* Mahwah, NJ: Erlbaum.

Rock, Irvin. (1995). *Perception.* New York: Scientific American Library.

Rodin, Judith. (1986, September 19). Aging and health: Effects of the sense of control. *Science, 233,* 1271–1275.

Rodin, Judith; & Langer, Ellen. (1977). Long-term effects of a control-relevant intervention with the institutionalized aged. *Journal of Personality and Social Psychology, 35,* 897–902.

Roehrs, Timothy; & Roth, Thomas. (2008). Caffeine: Sleep and daytime sleepiness. *Sleep Medicine Reviews, 12*(2), 153–162.

Roenneberg, Till; Wirz-Justice, Anna; & Merrow, Martha. (2003). Life between clocks: Daily temporal patterns of human chronotypes. *Journal of Biological Rhythms, 18,* 80–90.

Roffman, Joshua L.; Marci, Carl D.; Glick, Debra M.; Dougherty, Darin D.; & Rauch, Scott L. (2005). Neuroimaging and the functional neuroanatomy of psychotherapy. *Psychological Medicine, 35,* 1385–1398.

Rogers, Carl R. (1951). *Client-centered psychotherapy.* Boston: Houghton-Mifflin.

Rogers, Carl R. (1957a/1989). A note on "The Nature of Man." In Howard Kirschenbaum & Valerie Land Henderson (Eds.), *The Carl Rogers reader.* Boston: Houghton Mifflin.

Rogers, Carl R. (1957b/1989). A therapist's view of the good life: The fully functioning person. In Howard Kirschenbaum & Valerie Land Henderson (Eds.), *The Carl Rogers reader.* Boston: Houghton Mifflin.

Rogers, Carl R. (1957c). The necessary and sufficient conditions of therapeutic personality change. *Journal of Consulting Psychology, 21,* 95–103.

Rogers, Carl R. (1959). A theory of therapy, personality, and interpersonal relationships, as developed in the client-centered framework. In S. Koch (Ed.), *Psychology: A study of a science: Vol. 3. Formulations of the person and the social context.* New York: McGraw-Hill.

Rogers, Carl R. (1961). *On becoming a person.* Boston: Houghton Mifflin.

Rogers, Carl R. (1964/1989). Toward a modern approach to values: The valuing process in the mature person. In Howard Kirschenbaum & Valerie Land Henderson (Eds.), *The Carl Rogers reader.* Boston: Houghton Mifflin.

Rogers, Carl R. (1977). *Carl Rogers on personal power: Inner strength and its revolutionary impact.* New York: Delacorte Press.

Rogers, Carl R. (1980). *A way of being.* Boston: Houghton Mifflin.

Rogers, Carl R. (1981/1989). Notes on Rollo May. In Howard Kirschenbaum & Valerie Land Henderson (Eds.), *Carl Rogers: Dialogues.* Boston: Houghton Mifflin.

Rogers, Carl R.; & Skinner, B. F. (1956, November 30). Some issues concerning the control of human behavior: A symposium. *Science, 124,* 1057–1066.

Rohrer, Doug; & Taylor, Kelli. (2006). The effects of overlearning and distributed practice on the retention of mathematics knowledge. *Applied Cognitive Psychology, 20,* 1209–1224.

Roisman, Glenn I.; Clausell, Eric; & Holland, Ashley. (2008, January). Adult romantic relationships as contexts of human development: A multimethod comparison of same-sex couples with opposite-sex dating, engaged, and married dyads. *Developmental Psychology, 44*(1), 91–101.

Romans, Sarah E.; Martin, M.; Gendall, K.; & Herbison, G. P. (2003). Age of menarche: The role of some psychosocial factors. *Psychological Medicine, 33,* 933–939.

Romer, Daniel; Jamieson, Patrick; Holtschlag, Nancy J.; Mebrathu, Hermon; & Jamieson, Kathleen Hall. (2003). Suicide and the media. Philadelphia: Annenberg Public Policy Center of the University of Pennsylvania. Retrieved January 7, 2005, from http://www.annenbergpublicpolicycenter.org/07adolescentrisk/suicide/dec14%20suicide%20report.htm

Ronen, Tammie. (1991). Intervention package for treating sleep disorders in a four-year-old girl. *Journal of Behavior Therapy and Experimental Psychiatry, 22,* 141–148.

Rook, Karen S. (1992). Detrimental aspects of social relationships: Taking stock of an emerging literature. In Hans O. F. Veiel & Urs Baumann (Eds.), *The meaning and measurement of social support.* New York: Hemisphere.

Rosch, Eleanor H. (1973). Natural categories. *Cognitive Psychology, 4,* 328–350.

Rosch, Eleanor H. (1978). Principles of categorization. In Eleanor H. Rosch & Barbara B. Lloyd (Eds.), *Cognition and categorization.* Hillsdale, NJ: Erlbaum.

Rosch, Eleanor H. (1987). Linguistic relativity. *Et Cetera, 44,* 254–279.

Rosch, Eleanor H.; & Mervis, Carolyn B. (1975). Family resemblances: Studies in the internal structure of categories. *Cognitive Psychology, 7,* 573–605.

Rose, Jed E.; Behm, Frederique M.; Westman, Eric C.; Mathew, Roy J.; London, Edythe D.; Hawk, Thomas C.; Turkington, Timothy G.; & Coleman, R. Edward. (2003). PET studies of the influences of nicotine on neural systems in cigarette smokers. *American Journal of Psychiatry, 160,* 323–333.

Rose, Steven. (2009). Should scientists study race and IQ? NO: Science and society do not benefit. *Nature, 457,* 786–788.

Rosekind, Mark. (2003, April 8). Quoted in National Sleep Foundation press release, "Sleep is important when stress and anxiety increase, says the National Sleep Foundation." Washington, DC. Retrieved January 4, 2005, from http://www.sleepfoundation.org/PressArchives/stress.cfm

Rosen, Gerald M.; & Lohr, Jeffrey. (1997, January/February). Can eye movements cure mental ailments? *NCAHF Newsletter.* Retrieved October 15, 2001, from http://www.pseudoscience.org/rosen-and-lohr.htm

Rosen, Gerald M.; McNally, Richard J.; & Lilienfeld, Scott O. (1999). Eye movement magic: Eye movement desensitization and reprocessing a decade later. *Skeptic, 7*(4), 66–69.

Rosenbaum, David A.; Carlson, Richard A.; & Gilmore, Rick O. (2001). Acquisition of intellectual and perceptual-motor skills. *Annual Review of Psychology, 52,* 453–470.

Rosenberg, Oded; & Dannon, Pinhas N. (2009). Transcranial magnetic stimulation. In Conrad M. Swartz (Ed.), *Electroconvulsive and neuromodulation therapies* (pp. 527–542). New York: Cambridge University Press.

Rosenheck, Robert A.; Leslie, Douglas L.; Sindelar, Jody; & CATIE Study Investigators. (2006). Cost-effectiveness of second-generation antipsychotics and perphenazine in a randomized trial of treatment for chronic schizophrenia. *American Journal of Psychiatry,* 163, 2080–2089.

Rosenkranz, Melissa A. (2007). Substance P at the nexus of mind and body in chronic inflammation and affective disorders. *Psychological Bulletin, 133,* 1007–1037.

Rosenman, Ray H.; & Chesney, Margaret A. (1982). Stress, Type A behavior, and coronary disease. In Leo Goldberger & Shlomo Breznitz (Eds.), *Handbook of stress: Theoretical and clinical aspects.* New York: Free Press.

Rosenthal, Abraham M. (1964a, May 3). Study of the sickness called apathy. *The New York Times Magazine,* Sect. VI, pp. 24, 66, 69–72.

Rosenzweig, Mark; Krech, David; Bennett, Edward L.; & Diamond, Marian. (1962). Effects of environmental complexity on brain chemistry and anatomy: A replication and extension. *Journal of Comparative and Physiological Psychology, 55,* 429–437.

Rosenzweig, Saul. (1997). Freud's only visit to America. In Wolfgang G. Bringmann, Helmut E. Lück, Rudolf Miller, & Charles E. Early (Eds.), *A pictorial history of psychology.* Chicago: Quintessence.

Rosette, Ashleigh Shelby; Leonardelli, Geoffrey J.; & Phillips, Katherine W. (2008, July). The white standard: Racial bias in leader categorization. *Journal of Applied Psychology, 93*(4), 758–777.

Ross, Barbara. (1991). William James: Spoiled child of American psychology. In Gregory A. Kimble, Michael Wertheimer, & Charlotte White (Eds.), *Portraits of pioneers in psychology.* Washington, DC: American Psychological Association.

Ross, Lee. (1977). The intuitive psychologist and his shortcomings: Distortions in the attribution process. In Leonard Berkowitz (Ed.), *Advances in experimental social psychology* (Vol. 10). New York: Academic Press.

Ross, Lee; & Anderson, Craig A. (1982). Shortcomings in the attribution process: On the origins and maintenance of erroneous social assessments. In Daniel Kahneman, Paul Slovic, & Amos Tversky (Eds.), *Judgment under uncertainty: Heuristics and biases.* New York: Cambridge University Press.

Ross, Shannon E.; Niebling, Bradley C.; & Heckert, Teresa M. (1999). Sources of stress among college students. *College Student Journal, 33,* 312–317.

Rossier, Jerome; Dahourou, Donatien; & McCrae, Robert R. (2005). Structural and mean level analyses of the five-factor model and locus of control: Further evidence from Africa. *Journal of Cross-Cultural Psychology, 36,* 227–246.

Rothbart, Mary K.; Ahadi, Stephan A.; & Evans, David E. (2000). Temperament and personality: Origins and outcomes. *Journal of Personality and Social Psychology, 78,* 122–135.

Rothbart, Mary K.; & Putnam, Samuel P. (2002). Temperament and socialization. In Lea Pulkkinen & Avshalom Caspi (Eds.), *Paths to successful development: Personality in the life course.* New York: Cambridge University Press.

Rothbaum, Barbara O.; Hodges, Larry; Anderson, Page L.; Price, Larry; & Smith, Samantha. (2002). Twelve-month follow-up of virtual reality and standard exposure therapy for the fear of flying. *Journal of Consulting and Clinical Psychology, 70,* 428–432.

Rothbaum, Fred; Kakinuma, Miki; Nagaoka, Rika; & Azuma, Hiroshi. (2007). Attachment and AMAE: Parent-child closeness in the United States and Japan. *Journal of Cross-Cultural Psychology, 38,* 465–486.

Rouder, Jeffrey N.; Morey, Richard D.; Cowan, Nelson; Zwilling, Christopher E.; Morey, Candice C.; & Pratte, Michael S. (2008). An assessment of fixed-capacity models of visual working memory. *Proceedings of the National Academy of Sciences, USA, 105,* 5975–5979.

Rowe, David C. (2003). Assessing genotype-environment interactions and correlations in the postgenomic era. In Robert Plomin, John C. DeFries, Ian W. Craig, & Peter McGuffin (Eds.), *Behavioral genetics in the postgenomic era.* Washington, DC: American Psychological Association.

Rowe, Shawn M.; & Wertsch, James V. (2002). Vygotsky's model of cognitive development. In Usha Gowsami (Ed.), *Blackwell handbook of childhood cognitive development.* Malden, MA: Blackwell.

Roy, Michael M.; & Christenfeld, Nicholas J. S. (2004). Do dogs resemble their owners? *Psychological Science, 15,* 361–363.

Rozin, Paul. (1996). The socio-cultural context of eating and food choice. In H. L. Meiselman & H. J. H. MacFie (Eds.), *Food choice, acceptance and consumption.* London: Blackie Academic and Professional.

Rozin, Paul. (2006). About 17 (+/-2) potential principles about links between the innate mind and culture: Preadaptation, predispositions, preferences, pathways, and domains. In Peter Carruthers, Laurence Stephen, & Stephen Stich (Eds.), *The innate mind Volume 2: Culture and cognition.* New York: Oxford University Press.

Rozin, Paul. (2007). Food and eating. In Shinobu Kitayama & Dov Cohen (Eds.), *Handbook of cultural psychology.* New York: Guilford Press.

Rubin, Edgar. (1921/2001). Readings in perception. In Steven Yantis (Ed.), *Visual perception: Essential readings.* Philadelphia: Psychology Press.

Rubin, Nava. (2001). Figure and ground in the brain. *Nature Neuroscience, 4,* 857–858.

Ruble, Diane N.; Martin, Carol Lynn; & Berenbaum, Sheri A. (2006). Gender development. In Nancy Eisenberg, William Damon, & Richard M. Lerner (Eds), *Handbook of child psychology: Vol. 3, Social, emotional, and personality development* (6th ed.). Hoboken, NJ: Wiley.

Runco, Mark A. (2007). *Creativity: Theories and themes: Research, development, and practice.* San Diego, CA: Elsevier Academic Press.

Ruscio, John. (1998, November/December). The perils of post-hockery. *Skeptical Inquirer, 22,* 44–48.

Russek, Linda G.; & Schwartz, Gary E. (1997). Perceptions of parental caring predict health status in midlife: A 35-year follow-up to the Harvard Mastery of Stress Study. *Psychosomatic Medicine, 59,* 144–149.

Russell, James A. (1991). Culture and the categorization of emotions. *Psychological Bulletin, 110,* 426–450.

Russon, Anne E.; & Galdikas, Birute M. F. (1995). Constraints on great apes' imitation: Model and action selectivity in rehabilitant orangutan (*Pongo pygmaeus*) imitation. *Journal of Comparative Psychology, 109,* 5–17.

Rutherford, Alexandra. (2000). Radical behaviorism and psychology's public: B. F. Skinner in the popular press, 1934–1990. *History of Psychology, 3,* 371–395.

Rutherford, Alexandra. (2003). B. F. Skinner's technology of behavior in American life: From consumer culture to counterculture. *Journal of the History of the Behavioral Sciences, 39,* 1–23.

Rutherford, Alexandra. (2006). Mother of behavior therapy and beyond: Mary Cover Jones and the study of the "whole child." In Donald A. Dewsbury, Lucy T. Benjamin, & Michael Wertheimer (Eds.), *Portraits of pioneers in psychology* (Vol. VI, pp. 189–204). Washington, DC: American Psychological Association.

Rutledge, Thomas; Linke, Sarah E.; Olson, Marian B.; Francis, Jennifer; Johnson, B. Delia; Bittner, Vera; York, Kaki; McClure, Candace; Kelsey, Sheryl F.; Reis, Steven E.; Cornell, Carol E.; Vaccarino, Viola; Sheps, David S.; Shaw, Leslee J.; Krantz, David S.; Parashar, Susmita; & Merz, C. Noel Bairey. (2008). Social networks and incident stroke among women with suspected myocardial ischemia. *Psychosomatic Medicine, 70,* 282–287.

Rutledge, Thomas; Reis, Steven E.; Olson, Marian; Owens, Jane; Kelsey, Sheryl F.; Pepine, Carl J.; Mankad, Sunil; Rogers, William J.; Merz, Noel Bairey; Sopko, George; Cornell, Carol E.; Sharaf, Barry; & Matthews, Karen A. (2004). Social networks are associated with lower mortality rates among women with suspected coronary disease: The National Heart, Lung, and Blood Institute–sponsored Women's Ischemia Syndrome Evaluation Study. *Psychosomatic Medicine, 66,* 882–888.

Rutter, Michael. (1997). Nature-nurture integration: The example of antisocial behavior. *American Psychologist, 52,* 390–398.

Rutter, Michael. (2008). Proceeding from observed correlation to causal interference: The use of natural experiments. *Perspectives on Psychological Science, 2,* 377–396.

Ruvolo, Ann Patrice; & Markus, Hazel Rose. (1992). Possible selves and performance: The power of self-relevant imagery. *Social Cognition, 10,* 95–124.

Ryan, Richard M.; & Deci, Edward L. (2000). Self-determination theory and the facilitation of intrinsic motivation, social development, and well-being. *American Psychologist, 55,* 68–78.

Ryan, Richard M.; & Deci, Edward L. (2001). On happiness and human potentials: A review of research on hedonic and eudaimonic well-being. *Annual Review of Psychology, 52,* 141–166.

Ryan, Richard M.; & La Guardia, Jennifer G. (2000). What is being optimized over development? A self-determination theory and basic psychological needs. In Sara Honn Qualls & Norman Abeles (Eds.), *Psychology and the aging revolution: How we adapt to longer life.* Washington, DC: American Psychological Association.

Rydell, Ann-Margaret; Bohlin, Gunilla; & Thorell, Lisa B. (2005). Representations of attachment to parents and shyness as predictors of children's relationships with teachers and peer competence in preschool. *Attachment & Human Development, 7,* 187–204.

Sacchi, Dario L. M.; Agnoli, Franca; & Loftus, Elizabeth F. (2007). Changing history: Doctored photographs affect memory for past public events. *Applied Cognitive Psychology, 21,* 1005–1022.

Sachse, Rainer; & Elliott, Robert. (2002). Process–outcome research on humanistic therapy variables. In David J. Cain & Julius Seeman (Eds.), *Humanistic psychotherapies: Handbook of research and practice.* Washington, DC: American Psychological Association.

Sackeim, Harold A. (2001). Functional brain circuits in major depression and remission. *Archives of General Psychiatry, 58,* 649–650.

Sackeim, Harold A.; Haskett, Roger F.; Mulsant, Benoit H.; Thase, Michael E.; Mann, J. John; Pettinati, Helen M.; & others. (2001). Continuation psychotherapy in the prevention of relapse following electroconvulsive therapy: A randomized controlled trial. *Journal of the American Medical Association, 285,* 1299–1307.

Sadoski, Mark. (2005). A dual coding view of vocabulary learning. *Reading & Writing Quarterly, 21,* 221–238.

Safer, Adam B.; & Grace, Michael S. (2004). Infrared imaging in vipers: Differential responses of crotaline and viperine snakes to paired thermal targets. *Behavioural Brain Research, 154,* 55–61.

Safran, Jeremy D.; Muran, J. Christopher; & Rothman, Michael. (2006). The therapeutic alliance: Cultivating and negotiating the therapeutic relationship. In William O'Donohue, Nicholas A. Cummings, & Janet L. Cummings (Eds.), *Clinical strategies for becoming a master psychotherapist* (pp. 37–54). Amsterdam: Elsevier.

Sagi, Abraham; Koren-Karie, Nina; Gini, Motti; Ziv, Yair; & Joels, Tirtsa. (2002). Shedding further light on the effects of various types and quality of early child care on infant–mother attachment relationship: The Haifa Study of Early Child Care. *Child Development, 73,* 1166–1186.

Sahay, Amar; & Hen, Rene. (2007). Adult hippocampal neurogenesis in depression. *Nature Neuroscience, 10,* 1110–1115.

Sakheim, David K.; & Devine, Susan E. (Eds.). (1992). *Out of darkness: Exploring satanism and ritual abuse.* New York: Lexington Books.

Salloum, Alison; Garside, Laura W.; Irwin, C. Louis; Anderson, Adrian D.; & Francois, Anita H. (2009). Grief and trauma group therapy for children after Hurricane Katrina. *Social Work With Groups, 32*(1), 64–79.

Salokangas, Raimo K. R.; Vilkman, Harry; Ilonen, Tuula; Taiminen, Tero; Bergman, Jörgen; Haaparanta, Merja; Solin, Olof; Alanen, Anu; Syvälahti, Erkka; & Hietala, Jarmo. (2000). High levels of dopamine activity in the basal ganglia of cigarette smokers. *American Journal of Psychiatry, 157,* 632–634.

Salovey, Peter; Mayer, John D.; & Rosenhan, David L. (1991). Mood and helping: Mood as a motivator of helping and helping as a regulator of mood. In Margaret S. Clark (Ed.), *Prosocial behavior: Vol. 12. Review of personality and social psychology.* Newbury Park, CA: Sage.

SAMHSA. (2007). Substance Abuse and Mental Health Services Administration: *Results from the 2006 National Survey on Drug Use and Health: National findings* (Office of Applied Studies, NSDUH Series H-32, DHHS Publication No. SMA 07-4293). Rockville, MD.

Sammons, Cynthia C; & Speight, Suzette L. (2008). A qualitative investigation of changes in graduate students associated with multicultural counseling courses. *The Counseling Psychologist, 36*(6), 814–838.

Sanbonmatsu, David M.; Akimoto, Sharon A.; & Gibson, Bryan D. (1994). Stereotype-based blocking in social explanation. *Personality and Social Psychology Bulletin, 20,* 71–81.

Sánchez, José Carlos. (2006, September). Efectos de la presentación del mensaje para realizar conductas saludables: El papel de la autoeficacia y de la motivación cognitiva. Effects of message framing to perform health behaviors: The role of self-efficacy and the cognitive motivation. *International Journal of Clinical and Health Psychology, 6*(3), 613–630.

Sandler, Wendy; Meir, Irit; Padden, Carol; & Aronoff, Mark. (2005). The emergence of grammar in a new sign language. *Proceedings of the National Academy of Sciences, 102,* 2661–2665.

Sanfelippo, Augustin J. (2006). *Panic disorders: New research.* Hauppauge, NY: Nova Biomedical Books.

Sanofi-Aventis. (2008, January). *Ambien CR: Highlights of prescribing information* (Document: AMBCR-JAN08a-F-A). Bridgewater, NJ: Sanofi-Aventis. Retrieved July 14, 2009, from http://products.sanofi-aventis.us/ambien_cr/ambiencr.pdf

Sansone, Randy A. (2008). Zopidem, somnambulism, and nocturnal eating. *General Hospital Psychiatry, 30,* 90–91.

Saper, Clifford B.; Scammell, Thomas E.; & Lu, Jun. (2005, October 27). Hypothalamic regulation of sleep and circadian rhythms. *Nature, 437,* 1257–1263.

Sapolsky, Robert M. (2004). Mothering style and methylation. *Nature Neuroscience, 7,* 791–792.

Sar, Vedat; Koyuncu, Ahmet; & Ozturk, Erdinc. (2007, January–February). Dissociative disorders in the psychiatric emergency ward. *General Hospital Psychiatry, 29*(1), 45–50.

Sarason, Irwin G.; Sarason, Barbara R.; Pierce, Gregory R.; Shearin, Edward N.; & Sayers, Merlin H. (1991). A social learning approach to increasing blood donations. *Journal of Applied Social Psychology, 21,* 896–918.

Saul, Stephanie. (2007a, March 14). F.D.A. warns of odd effects of sleeping pills. Retrieved July 14, 2009, from http://www.nytimes.com/2007/03/14/business/15drugcnd.html

Saul, Stephanie. (2007b, March 15). F.D.A. warns of sleeping pills' strange effects. Retrieved July 14, 2009, from http://www.nytimes.com/2007/03/15/business/15drug.ready.html

Saults, J. Scott; & Cowan, Nelson. (2007). A central capacity limit to the simultaneous storage of visual and auditory arrays in working memory. *Journal of Experimental Psychology: General, 136,* 663–684.

Savage, Joanne; & Yancey, Christina. (2008). The effects of media violence exposure on criminal aggression: A meta-analysis. *Criminal Justice and Behavior, 35,* 722–791.

Savage, Seddon R. (2005). Critical issues in pain and addiction. *Pain Management Rounds, 2,* 1–6.

Savage-Rumbaugh, E. Sue; & Lewin, Roger. (1994, September). Ape at the brink. *Discover, 15,* 91–98.

Savic, Ivanka; & Lindström, Per. (2008). PET and MRI show differences in cerebral asymmetry and functional connectivity between homo- and heterosexual subjects. *Proceedings of the National Academy of Sciences, 105,* 9403–9408.

Savin-Williams, Ritch C. (2006). Who's gay? Does it matter? *Current Directions in Psychological Science, 15,* 40–44.

Savin-Williams, Ritch C. (2008). Then and now: Recruitment, definition, diversity, and positive attributes of same-sex populations. *Developmental Psychology, 44,* 135–138.

Sawyer, Thomas F. (2000). Francis Cecil Sumner: His views and influence on African American higher education. *History of Psychology, 3,* 122–141.

Scanlon, Matthew; & Mauro, James. (1992, November/December). The lowdown on handwriting analysis: Is it for real? *Psychology Today, 25,* 46–53.

Schachter, Stanley; & Singer, Jerome E. (1962). Cognitive, social, and physiological determinants of emotional state. *Psychological Review, 69*, 379–399.

Schacter, Daniel L. (1995, April). Memory wars. *Scientific American, 272*, 135–139.

Schacter, Daniel L. (2001). *The seven sins of memory: How the mind forgets and remembers.* Boston: Houghton Mifflin.

Schacter, Daniel L.; Norman, Kenneth A.; & Koutstaal, Wilma. (1998). The cognitive neuroscience of constructive memory. *Annual Review of Psychology, 49*, 289–318.

Schaie, K. Warner. (1995). *Intellectual development in adulthood: The Seattle Longitudinal Study.* New York: Cambridge University Press.

Schaie, K. Warner. (2005). *Developmental influences on adult intelligence: The Seattle longitudinal study.* New York: Oxford University Press.

Schaie, K. Warner; & Willis, Sherry L. (1986). Can decline in adult intellectual functioning be reversed? *Developmental Psychology, 22,* 223–232.

Schaie, K. Warner; & Willis, Sherry L. (1996). *Adult development and aging* (4th ed.). New York: HarperCollins.

Schattschneider, Doris. (1990). *Visions of symmetry: Notebooks, periodic drawings, and related work of M. C. Escher* (p. 169, notes on p. 301). New York: Freeman.

Schatzman, Morton; & Fenwick, Peter. (1994). Dreams and dreaming. In Rosemary Cooper (Ed.), *Sleep.* New York: Chapman & Hall.

Schenck, Carlos H. (2007). *Sleep: The mysteries, the problems, and the solutions.* New York: Penguin.

Schenck, Carlos H.; Arnulf, Isabelle; & Mahowald, Mark W. (2007). Sleep and sex: What can go wrong? A review of the literature on sleep related disorders and abnormal sexual behaviors and experiences. *Sleep, 30*, 683–702.

Schenck, Carlos H.; & Mahowald, Mark W. (2002). REM sleep behavior disorder: Clinical, developmental, and neuroscience perspectives 16 years after its formal identification in SLEEP. *Sleep, 25*, 120–138.

Scherer, Klaus R.; & Ellgring, Heiner. (2007). Multimodal expression of emotion: Affect programs or componential appraisal patterns? *Emotion, 7,* 158–171.

Scherer, Klaus R.; & Wallbott, Harald G. (1994). Evidence for universality and cultural variation of differential emotion response patterning. *Journal of Personality and Social Psychology, 66*, 310–328.

Scherk, Harold; Pajonk, Frank Gerald; & Leucht, Stefan. (2007, April). Second-generation antipsychotic agents in the treatment of acute mania: A systematic review and meta-analysis of randomized controlled trials. *Archives of General Psychiatry, 64*(4), 442–455.

Schilt, Thelma; de Win, Maartje M. L.; Koeter, Maarten; Jager, Gerry; Korf, Dirk J.; van den Brink, Wim; & Schmand, Ben. (2007). Cognition in novice ecstasy users with minimal exposure to other drugs: A prospective cohort study. *Archives of General Psychiatry, 64,* 728–736.

Schläpfer, Thomas E.; & Bewernick, Bettina H. (2009). Deep brain stimulation: Methods, indications, locations, and efficacy. In Conrad M. Swartz (Ed.), *Electroconvulsive and neuromodulation therapies* (pp. 556–572). New York: Cambridge University Press.

Schlenker, Barry R.; & Weigold, Michael F. (1992). Interpersonal processes involving impression regulation and management. *Annual Review of Psychology, 43*, 133–168.

Schlitz, Marilyn; Wiseman, Richard; & Watt, Caroline. (2006). Of two minds: Sceptic-proponent collaboration within parapsychology. *British Journal of Psychology,* 97, 313–322.

Schmader, Toni; & Johns, Michael. (2003) Converging evidence that stereotype threat reduces working memory capacity. *Journal of Personality and Social Psychology, 85,* 440–452.

Schmader, Toni; Johns, Michael; & Forbes, Chad. (2008). An integrated process model of stereotype threat effects on performance. *Psychological Review, 115,* 236–256.

Schmalz, Dorothy L.; & Kerstetter, Deborah L. (2006). Girlie girls and manly men: Children's stigma consciousness of gender in sports and physical activities. *Journal of Leisure Research, 38,* 536–557.

Schmitt, David P. (2006). Cultural influences on human mating strategies: Evolutionary theories, mechanisms, and explanations of change. *Psychological Inquiry, 17,* 116–117.

Schnall, Simone; & Laird, James D. (2003). Keep smiling: Enduring effects of facial expressions and postures on emotional experience and memory. *Cognition & Emotion, 17,* 787–797.

Schneider, Kirk J.; & Krug, Orah. T. (2009). *Existential-humanistic therapy.* Washington, DC: American Psychological Association.

Schneiderman, Neil; Ironson, Gail; & Siegel, Scott D. (2005). Stress and health: Psychological, behavioral, and biological determinants. *Annual Review of Clinical Psychology, 1,* 607–628.

Scholz, Joachim; & Woolf, Clifford J. (2002). Can we conquer pain? *Nature Neuroscience, 5*(Suppl.), 1062–1067.

Schooler, Jonathan W. (2001). Discovering memories of abuse in the light of meta-awareness. *Journal of Aggression, Maltreatment, & Trauma, 42,* 105–136.

Schrater, Paul; Knill, David C.; & Simoncelli, Eero P. (2001). Perceiving visual expansion without optic flow. *Nature, 410*, 616–619.

Schroth, Marvin L.; & McCormack, William A. (2000) Current problems and resolutions—Sensation seeking and need for achievement among study-abroad students. *The Journal of Social Psychology, 140,* 533.

Schulman, Michael; & Mekler, Eva. (1985). *Bringing up a moral child: A new approach for teaching your child to be kind, just, and responsible.* Reading, MA: Addison-Wesley.

Schultz, Wolfram; Dayan, Peter; & Montague, P. Read. (1997, March 14). A neural substrate of prediction and reward. *Science, 275*, 1593–1599.

Schulz, Marc S.; Cowan, Philip A.; Cowan, Carolyn Pape; & Brennan, Robert T. (2004). Coming home upset: Gender, marital satisfaction, and the daily spillover of workday experience into couple interactions. *Journal of Family Psychology, 18,* 250–263.

Schulz, Marc S.; Cowan, Carolyn Pape; & Cowan, Philip A. (2006). Promoting healthy beginnings: A randomized controlled trial of a preventive intervention to preserve marital quality during the transition to parenthood. *Journal of Consulting & Clinical Psychology, 74*(1), 20–31.

Schupp, Harald T.; Öhman, Arne; Junghöfer, Markus; Weike, Almut I.; Stockburger, Jessica; & Hamm, Alfons O. (2004). The facilitated processing of threatening faces: An ERP analysis. *Emotion, 4,* 189–200.

Schwab, Richard J.; Kuna, Samuel T.; & Remmers, John E. (2005). Anatomy and physiology of upper airway obstruction. In Meir H. Kryger, Thomas Roth, & William C. Dement (Eds.), *Principles and practice of sleep medicine* (4th ed.). Philadelphia: Elsevier Saunders.

Schwartz, Bennett L. (1999). Sparkling at the end of the tongue: The etiology of tip-of-the-tongue phenomenology. *Psychonomic Bulletin and Review, 6,* 379–393.

Schwartz, Bennett L. (2002). *Tip-of-the-tongue states: Phenomenology, mechanism, and lexical retrieval.* Mahwah, NJ: Erlbaum.

Schwartz, Charlotte. (2003). A brief discussion on frequency of sessions and its impact upon psychoanalytic treatment. *Psychoanalytic Review, 90,* 179–191.

Schwartz, Earl. (2004, Summer/Fall). Why some ask why: Kohlberg and Milgram. *Judaism, 53,* 230–240.

Schwartz, Jeffrey M.; Stoessel, Paula W.; & Phelps, Michael E. (1996). Systematic changes in cerebral glucose metabolic rate after successful behavior modification treatment of obsessive–compulsive disorder. *Archives of General Psychiatry, 53,* 109–117.

Schwartz, Michael W.; Woods, Stephen C.; Porte, Daniel, Jr.; Seeley, Randy J.; & Baskin, Denis G. (2000, April 6). Central nervous system control of food intake. *Nature, 404,* 661–671.

Scoville, William Beecher; & Milner, Brenda. (1957). Loss of recent memory after bilateral hippocampal lesions. *Journal of Neurology, Neurosurgery, and Psychiatry, 20,* 11–21.

Scully, Judith A.; Tosi, Henry; & Banning, Kevin. (2000). Life event checklists: Revisiting the Social Readjustment Rating Scale after 30 years. *Educational and Psychological Measurement, 60,* 864–876.

Segal, Zindel V.; Williams, J. Mark G.; & Teasdale, John D. (2002). *Mindfulness-based cognitive therapy for depression: A new approach to preventing relapse.* New York: Guilford Press.

Segall, Marshall H. (1994). A cross-cultural research contribution to unraveling the nativist/empiricist controversy. In Walter J. Lonner & Roy Malpass (Eds.), *Psychology and culture.* Boston: Allyn & Bacon.

Segall, Marshall H.; Campbell, Donald T.; & Herskovits, Melville J. (1963). Cultural differences in the perception of geometric illusions. *Science, 193,* 769–771.

Segall, Marshall H.; Campbell, Donald T.; & Herskovits, Melville J. (1966). *The influence of culture on visual perception.* Indianapolis, IN: Bobbs-Merrill.

Segerdahl, Pär; Fields, William; & Savage-Rumbaugh, Sue. (2006). *Kanzi's primal language: The cultural initiation of primates into language.* New York: Palgrave Macmillan.

Segerstrom, Suzanne C.; Castañeda, Jay O.; & Spencer, Theresa E. (2003). Optimism effects on cellular immunity: Testing the affective and persistence models. *Personality and Individual Differences, 35,* 1615–1624.

Segerstrom, Suzanne C.; & Miller, Gregory E. (2004). Psychological stress and the human immune system: A meta-analytic study of 30 years of inquiry. *Psychological Bulletin, 130,* 601–630.

Segerstrom, Suzanne C.; Taylor, Shelley E.; Kemeny, Margaret E.; & Fahey, John L. (1998). Optimism is associated with mood, coping, and immune change in response to stress. *Journal of Personality and Social Psychology, 74,* 1646–1655.

Self, David W. (2005). Neural basis of substance abuse and dependence. In Benjamin J. Sadock & Virginia A. Sadock (Eds.), *Comprehensive textbook of psychiatry* (8th ed.). Baltimore: Lippincott, Williams, & Wilkins.

Seligman, Martin E. P. (1970). On the generality of the laws of learning. *Psychological Review, 77,* 406–418.

Seligman, Martin E. P. (1971). Phobias and preparedness. *Behavior Therapy, 2,* 307–320.

Seligman, Martin E. P. (1990). *Learned optimism.* New York: Knopf.

Seligman, Martin E. P. (1992). *Helplessness: On development, depression, and death.* New York: Freeman.

Seligman, Martin E. P.; & Csikszentmihalyi, Mihaly. (2000). Positive psychology: An introduction. *American Psychologist, 55,* 5–14.

Seligman, Martin E. P.; & Maier, Steven F. (1967). Failure to escape traumatic shock. *Journal of Experimental Psychology, 37B,* 1–21.

Seligman, Martin E. P.; Rashid, Tayyab; & Parks, Acacia C. (2006). Positive psychotherapy. *American Psychologist, 61,* 774–788.

Seligman, Martin E. P.; Steen, Tracy A.; Park, Nansook; & Peterson, Christopher. (2005). Positive psychology progress: Empirical validation of interventions. *American Psychologist, 60,* 410–421.

Sellers, Robert M.; Copeland-Linder, Nikeea; Martin, Pamela P.; & Lewis, R. L'Heureux. (2006). Racial identity matters: The relationship between racial discrimination and psychological functioning in African American adolescents. *Journal of Research on Adolescence, 16,* 187–216.

Selye, Hans. (1956). *The stress of life.* New York: McGraw-Hill.

Selye, Hans. (1976). *The stress of life* (Rev. ed.). New York: McGraw-Hill.

Senghas, Ann; Kita, Sotaro; & Özyürek, Asli. (2004, September 17). Children creating core properties of language: Evidence from an emerging sign language in Nicaragua. *Science, 305,* 1779–1782.

Senko, Corwin; Durik, Amanda M.; & Harackiewicz, Judith M. (2008). Historical perspectives and new directions in achievement goal theory: Understanding the effects of mastery and performance-approach. In James Y. Shah & Wendi L. Gardner (Eds.), *Handbook of motivation science.* New York: Guilford Press.

Seta, John J.; & Seta, Catherine E. (1993). Stereotypes and the generation of compensatory and noncompensatory expectancies of group members. *Personality and Social Psychology Bulletin, 19,* 722–731.

Seta, John J.; Seta, Catherine E.; & McElroy, Todd. (2003, February). Attributional biases in the service of stereotype maintenance: A schema-maintenance through compensation analysis. *Personality and Social Psychology Bulletin, 29*(2), 151–163.

Sexton, Thomas L.; Alexander, James F.; & Mease, Alyson Leigh. (2004). Levels of evidence for the models and mechanisms of therapeutic change in family and couple therapy. In Michael J. Lambert (Ed.), *Bergin and Garfield's handbook of psychotherapy and behavior change* (5th ed.). New York: Wiley.

Shapiro, Francine. (1989a). Efficacy of the eye movement desensitization procedure in the treatment of traumatic memories. *Journal of Traumatic Stress, 2,* 199–223.

Shapiro, Francine. (1989b). Eye movement desensitization: A new treatment for post-traumatic stress disorder. *Journal of Behavior Therapy and Experimental Psychiatry, 20,* 211–217.

Shapiro, Francine. (1995). *Eye movement desensitization and reprocessing: Basic principles, protocols, and procedures.* New York: Guilford Press.

Shapiro, Francine. (2007). EMDR and case conceptualization from an adaptive information processing perspective. In Francine Shapiro, Florence W. Kaslow, & Louise Maxfield (Eds.), *Handbook of EMDR and family therapy processes* (pp. 3–34). Hoboken, NJ: Wiley.

Shapiro, Francine; & Forrest, Margot Silk. (2004). *EMDR: The breakthrough therapy for overcoming anxiety, stress, and trauma.* New York: Basic Books.

Shapiro, Shauna L.; & Carlson, Linda E. (2009). *The art and science of mindfulness: Integrating mindfulness into psychology and the helping professions.* Washington, DC: American Psychological Association.

Sharman, Stefanie J.; Garry, Maryanne; & Beuke, Carl J. (2004). Imagination or exposure causes imagination inflation. *American Journal of Psychology, 117,* 157–168.

Shavinina, Larisa V. (2001). Beyond IQ: A new perspective on the psychological assessment of intellectual abilities. *New Ideas in Psychology, 19,* 27–47.

Shaw, Benjamin A.; Krause, Neal; Chatters, Linda M.; & Ingersoll-Dayton, Berit. (2004). Emotional support from parents early in life, aging, and health. *Psychology of Aging, 19,* 4–12.

Shaywitz, Bennett A.; Shaywitz, Sally E.; & Gore, J. C. (1995, February 16). Sex differences in the functional organization of the brain for language. *Nature, 373*, 607–615.

Shedler, Jonathan; Mayman, Martin; & Manis, Melvin. (1993). The illusion of mental health. *American Psychologist, 48*, 1117–1131.

Sheldon, Kennon M. (2008). The interface of motivation science and personology: Self-concordance, quality motivation, and multilevel personality integration. In James Y. Shah & Wendi L. Gardner (Eds.), *Handbook of motivation science.* New York: Guilford Press.

Sheldon, Kennon M.; Elliot, Andrew J.; Kim, Youngmee; & Kasser, Tim. (2001). What is satisfying about satisfying events? Testing 10 candidate psychological needs. *Journal of Personality and Social Psychology, 80*, 325–339.

Shepard, Roger N. (1990). *Mind sights: Original visual illusions, ambiguities, and other anomalies, with a commentary on the play of mind in perception and art.* New York: Freeman.

Shepherd, Gordon M. (2004). Unsolved mystery: The human sense of smell: Are we better than we think? *PloS Biology, 2*, 0572–0575.

Shepherd, Gordon M. (2006). Smell images and the flavour system in the human brain. *Nature, 444*, 316–321.

Shepherd, Jonathan. (2007). Preventing alcohol-related violence: A public health approach. *Criminal Behaviour & Mental Health, 17*, 250–264.

Sheras, Peter L.; & Koch-Sheras, Phyllis R. (2006). Redefining couple: Shifting the paradigm. In Peter L. Sheras & Phyllis R. Koch-Sheras, *Couple power therapy: Building commitment, cooperation, communication, and community in relationships* (pp. 19–39). Washington, DC: American Psychological Association.

Sherif, Muzafer. (1956, November). Experiments in group conflict. *Scientific American, 195*, 33–47.

Sherif, Muzafer. (1966). *In common predicament: Social psychology of intergroup conflict and cooperation.* Boston: Houghton Mifflin.

Sherif, Muzafer; Harvey, O. J.; White, B. Jack; Hood, William R.; & Sherif, Carolyn W. (1961/1988). *The Robbers Cave experiment: Intergroup conflict and cooperation.* Middletown, CT: Wesleyan University Press.

Shermer, Michael. (2002). *Why people believe weird things: Pseudoscience, superstition, and other confusions of our time.* New York: Henry Holt.

Sherry, Alissa; & Whilde, Margaret R. (2008). Borderline personality disorder. In Michel Hersen & Johan Rosqvist (Eds.), *Handbook of psychological assessment, case conceptualization and treatment, Volume 1, Adults.* Hoboken, NJ: Wiley

Shevell, Steven K.; & Kingdom, Frederick A. A. (2008). Color in complex scenes. *Annual Review of Psychology, 5*, 143–166.

Shi, Jianxin; Levinson, Douglas F.; Duan, Jubao; Sanders, Alan R.; Zheng, Yonglan; Pe'er, Itsik; Dudbridge, Frank; Holmans, Peter A.; Whittemore, Alice S.; Mowry, Bryan J.; Olincy, Ann; Amin, Farooq; Cloninger, C. Robert; & others. (2009). Common variants on chromosome 6p22.1 are associated with schizophrenia. *Nature, 460*, 753–757.

Shields, Stephanie A. (2002*). Speaking from the heart: Gender and the social meaning of emotion.* Cambridge, England: Cambridge University Press.

Shiffrin, Richard M.; & Atkinson, Richard C. (1969). Storage and retrieval processes in long-term memory. *Psychological Review, 76*(2), 179–193.

Shih, Margaret; Pittinsky, Todd L.; & Ambady, Nalini. (1999). Stereotype susceptibility: Identity salience and shifts in quantitative performance. *Psychological Science, 10*, 80–83.

Shih, Margaret; Pittinsky, Todd L.; & Trahan, Amy. (2006). Domain-specific effects of stereotypes on performance. *Self and Identity, 5*, 1–14.

Shinskey, Jeanne L.; & Munakata, Yuko. (2005). Familiarity breeds searching: Infants reverse their novelty preferences when reaching for hidden objects. *Psychological Science, 16*, 596–600.

Shneidman, Edwin S. (1998). *The suicidal mind.* New York: Oxford University Press.

Shneidman, Edwin S. (2004). *Autopsy of a suicidal mind.* New York: Oxford University Press.

Shorter, Edward. (2009). History of electroconvulsive therapy. In Conrad M. Swartz (Ed.), *Electroconvulsive and neuromodulation therapies* (pp. 167–179). New York: Cambridge University Press.

Shotland, R. Lance; & Straw, Margret K. (1976). Bystander response to an assault: When a man attacks a woman. *Journal of Personality and Social Psychology, 34*, 990–999.

SHRM. (2006, November). Finding and keeping the right talent—A strategic view: One of HR's top imperatives today is finding and retaining the right talent through strategic human resource initiatives, policies, and practices. SHRM Survey-2006. Alexandria, VA: Author.

SHRM. (2007, December). Strategic research on human capital challenges: Executive summary. Alexandria, VA: Author.

Shulman, Ian D.; Cox, Brian J.; Swinson, Richard P.; Kuch, Klaus; & Reichman, Jaak T. (1994). Precipitating events, locations and reactions associated with initial unexpected panic attacks. *Behavior Research and Therapy, 32*, 17–20.

Shumaker, Sally A.; & Hill, D. Robin. (1991). Gender differences in social support and physical health. *Health Psychology, 10*, 102–111.

Shweder, Richard A.; & Haidt, Jonathan. (1993). The future of moral psychology: Truth, intuition, and the pluralist way. *Psychological Science, 4*, 360–365.

Shweder, Richard A.; Mahapatra, Manamohan; & Miller, Joan G. (1990). Culture and moral development. In Jerome Kagan & Sharon Lamb (Eds.), *The emergence of morality in young children.* Chicago: University of Chicago Press.

Siegal, Michael. (2004, September 17). Signposts to the essence of language. *Science, 305*, 1720–1721.

Siegel, Daniel J. (2007). *The mindful brain: Reflection and attunement in the cultivation of well-being.* New York: Norton.

Siegel, Judith M. (1990). Stressful life events and use of physician services among the elderly. *Journal of Personality and Social Psychology, 58*, 1081–1086.

Siegel, Ronald D.; Gormer, Christopher K.; & Olendzki, Andrew. (2008). Mindfulness: What is it? Where does it come from? In Fabrizio Didonna (Ed.), *Clinical handbook of mindfulness.* New York: Springer.

Siegler, Robert S. (1992). The other Alfred Binet. *Developmental Psychology, 28*, 179–190.

Siegler, Robert S. (1996). *Emerging minds: The process of change in children's thinking.* New York: Oxford University Press.

Siegler, Robert S.; & Ellis, Shari. (1996). Piaget on childhood. *Psychological Science, 7*, 211–215.

Siev, Jedidiah; & Chambless, Dianne L. (2007, August). Specificity of treatment effects: Cognitive therapy and relaxation for generalized anxiety and panic disorders. *Journal of Consulting and Clinical Psychology, 75*(4), 513–522.

Sigman, Marian; Spence, Sarah J.; & Wang, A. Ting. (2006). Autism from developmental and neuropsychological perspectives. *Annual Review of Clinical Psychology, 2*(3), 327–355.

Signorielli, Nancy. (2005). *Violence in the media: A reference handbook.* Santa Barbara, CA: ABC-Clio.

Silber Michael H.; Krahn, Lois E.; Olson, Eric J.; & Pankratz, V. Shane. (2002). The epidemiology of narcolepsy in Olmsted County, Minnesota: A population-based study. *Sleep, 25,* 197–202.

Silbersweig, David A.; Stern, Emily; & Frackowaik, R. S. J. (1995, November 9). A functional neuroanatomy of hallucinations in schizophrenia. *Nature, 387,* 176–184.

Silva, Chrisopher; Bridges, K. Robert; & Metzger, Mitchell. (2005). Personality, expectancy, and hypnotizability. *Personality and Individual Differences, 39,* 131–142.

Silverstein, Steven M.; Hatashita-Wong, Michi; & Solak, Beth Anne. (2005, June). Effectiveness of a two-phase cognitive rehabilitation intervention for severely impaired schizophrenia patients. *Psychological Medicine, 35*(6), 829–837.

Simner, Marvin L.; & Goffin, Richard D. (2003, December). A position statement by the International Graphonomics Society on the use of graphology in personnel selection testing. *International Journal of Testing, 3*(4), 353–364.

Simons, Christopher T.; & Noble, Ann C. (2003). Challenges for the sensory sciences from the food and wine industries. *Nature Reviews Neuroscience, 4,* 599–605.

Simons, Daniel J.; Hannula, Deborah E.; Warren, David E.; & Day, Steven W. (2007). Behavioral, neuroimaging, and neuropsychological approaches to implicit perception. In Philip David Zelazo, Morris Moscovitch, & Evan Thompson (Eds.), *The Cambridge handbook of consciousness.* New York: Cambridge University Press.

Simons, Leslie Gordon; & Conger, Rand D. (2007). Linking mother–father differences in parenting to a typology of family parenting styles and adolescent outcomes. *Journal of Family Issues, 28*(2), 212–241.

Singer, Tania; Verhaeghen, Paul; Ghisletta, Paolo; Lindenberger, Ulman; & Baltes, Paul. (2003). The fate of cognition in very old age: Six-year longitudinal findings in the Berlin Aging Study (BASE). *Psychology and Aging, 18,* 318–331.

Singhal, Arvind; Cody, Michael J.; Rogers, Everett M.; & Sabido, Miguel (Eds.). (2004). *Entertainment-education and social change: History, research, and practice.* Mahwah, NJ: Erlbaum.

Skinner, B. F. (1938). *The behavior of organisms: An experimental analysis.* New York: Appleton-Century-Crofts.

Skinner, B. F. (1948a/1976). *Walden two.* Englewood Cliffs, NJ: Prentice Hall.

Skinner, B. F. (1948b/1992). Superstition in the pigeon. *Journal of Experimental Psychology: General, 121,* 273–274.

Skinner, B. F. (1953). *Science and human behavior.* New York: Macmillan.

Skinner, B. F. (1956). A case history in scientific method. *American Psychologist, 11,* 221–233.

Skinner, B. F. (1961, November). Teaching machines. *Scientific American, 205,* 90–102.

Skinner, B. F. (1966). Some responses to the stimulus "Pavlov." *Conditional Reflex, 1,* 74–78. (Reprinted in 1999 in the *Journal of the Experimental Analysis of Behavior, 72,* 463–465.)

Skinner, B. F. (1967). B. F. Skinner . . . an autobiography. In E. G. Boring & G. Lindzey (Eds.), *A history of psychology in autobiography* (Vol. 5). New York: Appleton-Century-Crofts.

Skinner, B. F. (1971). *Beyond freedom and dignity.* New York: Bantam Books.

Skinner, B. F. (1974). *About behaviorism.* New York: Knopf.

Skinner, B. F. (1979). *The shaping of a behaviorist.* New York: Knopf.

Slabbert, J. M.; & Rasa, O. Anne E. (1997). Observational learning of an acquired maternal behaviour pattern by working dog pups: An alternative training method? *Applied Animal Behavior Science, 53,* 309–316.

Slack, Gordy. (2007, November 12). Source of human empathy found in the brain. *New Scientist,* issue 2629, p. 12.

Sleeth, Daniel B. (2007). The self system: Toward a new understanding of the whole person (Part 3). *The Humanistic Psychologist, 35,* 45–66.

Slotnick, Scott D.; & Schacter, David L. (2007). *The cognitive neuroscience of memory and consciousness.* In Philip David Zelazo, Morris Moscovitch, & Evan Thompson (Eds.), *The Cambridge handbook of consciousness.* New York: Cambridge University Press.

Smith, Andrew W.; Whitney, Helen; Thomas, Marie; Perry, Kate; & Brockman, Pip. (1997). Effects of caffeine and noise on mood, performance and cardiovascular functioning. *Human Psychopharmacology: Clinical and Experimental, 12,* 27–33.

Smith, Barry D.; Cranford, David; & Green, Lee. (2001). Hostility and caffeine: Cardiovascular effects during stress and recovery. *Personality & Individual Differences, 30,* 1125–1137.

Smith, Craig A.; David, Bieke; & Kirby, Leslie D. (2006). Emotion-eliciting appraisals of social situations. In Joseph P. Forgas (Ed.), *Affect in social thinking and behavior.* New York: Psychology Press.

Smith, Craig A.; & Kirby, Leslie D. (2000). Consequences require antecedents: Toward a process model of emotion elicitation. In Joseph P. Forgas (Ed), *Feeling and thinking: The role of affect in social cognition.* New York: Cambridge University Press.

Smith, Craig A.; & Lazarus, Richard. (1993). Appraisal components, core relational themes, and the emotions. *Cognition & Emotion, 7,* 233–269.

Smith, David E.; & Seymour, Richard B. (1994). LSD: History and toxicity. *Psychiatric Annals, 24,* 145–147.

Smith, Eliot R.; & Collins, Elizabeth C. (2009). Contextualizing person perception: Distributed social cognition. *Psychological Review, 116,* 343–364.

Smith, Gerard P.; & Gibbs, James. (1998). The satiating effects of cholecystokinin and bombesin-like peptides. In Gerard P. Smith (Ed.), *Satiation: From gut to brain.* New York: Oxford University Press.

Smith, Gregory T.; Spillane, Nichea S.; & Annus, Agnes M. (2006). Implications of an emerging integration of universal and culturally specific psychologies. *Perspectives on Psychological Science, 1,* 211–233.

Smith, Jessi L.; Sansone, Carol; & White, Paul H. (2007, February). The stereotyped task engagement process: The role of interest and achievement motivation. *Journal of Educational Psychology, 99*(1), 99–114.

Smith, Pamela K.; Dijksterhuis, Ap; & Chaiken, Shelly. (2008). Subliminal exposure to faces and racial attitudes: Exposure to whites makes whites like blacks less. *Journal of Experimental Social Psychology, 44,* 50–64.

Smith, Timothy W. (1992). Hostility and health: Current status of a psychosomatic hypothesis. *Health Psychology, 11,* 139–150.

Smolak, Linda. (2009). Risk factors in the development of body image, eating problems, and obesity. In Linda Smolak & J. Kevin Thompson (Eds.), *Body image, eating disorders, and obesity in youth: Assessment, prevention, and treatment* (2nd ed., pp. 135–155). Washington, DC: American Psychological Association.

Smuts, Barbara. (1996). Male aggression against women: An evolutionary perspective. In David M. Buss & Neil M. Malumuth (Eds.), *Sex, power, conflict: Evolutionary and feminist perspectives.* New York: Oxford University Press.

Snyder, C. R.; & Lopez, Shane J. (Eds.). (2005). *Handbook of positive psychology.* New York: Oxford University Press.

Snyder, Rebecca J.; Zhang, An J.; Zhang, Zhi H.; Li, Guang H.; Tian, Yu Z.; Huang, Xiang M.; Luo, Lan; Bloomsmith, Mollie A.; Forthman, Debra L.; & Maple, Terry L. (2003). Behavioral and developmental consequences of early rearing experience for captive giant pandas (*Alluropoda melanoleuca*). *Journal of Comparative Psychology, 117,* 235–245.

Snyder, Solomon H. (1984). Drug and neurotransmitter receptors in the brain. *Science, 224,* 22–31.

Society for Industrial and Organizational Psychology. (2006). Member survey employment setting. Retrieved September 15, 2008, from Questar: http://www.siop.org/userfiles/image/2006membersurvey/2006%20Employment%20Setting1.pdf

Solomon, Henry; Solomon, Linda Zener; Arnone, Maria M.; Maur, Bonnie J.; Reda, Rosina M.; & Roth, Esther O. (1981). Anonymity and helping. *Journal of Social Psychology, 113,* 37–43.

Solomon, Hester McFarland. (2003). Freud and Jung: An incomplete encounter. *Journal of Analytical Psychology, 48,* 553–569.

Solomon, Linda Zener; Solomon, Henry; & Stone, Ronald. (1978). Helping as a function of number of bystanders and ambiguity of emergency. *Personality and Social Psychology Bulletin, 4,* 318–321.

Solomon, Paul R.; Adams, Felicity; Silver, Amanda; Zimmer, Jill; & DeVeaux, Richard. (2002). Ginkgo for memory enhancement: A randomized controlled trial. *Journal of the American Medical Association, 288,* 835–840.

Solomon, Sondra E.; Rothblum, Esther D.; & Balsam, Kimberly F. (2004). Pioneers in partnership: Lesbian and gay male couples in civil unions compared with those not in civil unions and married heterosexual siblings. *Journal of Family Psychology, 18,* 275–286.

Son, Lisa K. (2004). Spacing one's study: Evidence for a metacognitive control strategy. *Journal of Experimental Psychology: Learning, Memory, and Cognition, 30,* 601–604.

Sood, Suruchi; SenGupta, Manisha; Mishra, Pius Raj; & Jacoby, Caroline. (2004). "Come gather around together": An examination of radio listening groups in Fulbari, Nepal. *Gazette: The International Journal for Communication Studies, 66,* 63–86.

South, Susan C.; Turkheimer, Eric; & Oltmanns, Thomas F. (2008). Personality disorder symptoms and marital functioning. *Journal of Consulting and Clinical Psychology, 76,* 769–780.

Southwick, Steven M.; Vythilingam, Meena; & Charney, Dennis S. (2005). The psychobiology of depression and resilience to stress: Implications for prevention and treatment. *Annual Review of Clinical Psychology, 1,* 255–291.

Sowell, Elizabeth R.; Peterson, Bradley S.; Thompson, Paul M.; Welcome, Suzanne E.; Henkenius, Amy L.; & Toga, Arthur W. (2003). Mapping cortical change across the human life span. *Nature Neuroscience, 6,* 309–315.

Sowell, Elizabeth R.; Thompson, Paul M.; Leonard, Christiana M.; Welcome, Suzanne E.; Kan, Eric; & Toga, Arthur W. (2004, September 22). Longitudinal mapping of cortical thickness and brain growth in normal children. *Journal of Neuroscience, 24,* 8223–8231.

Spangler, William D. (1992). Validity of questionnaire and TAT measures of need for achievement: Two meta-analyses. *Psychological Bulletin, 112,* 140–154.

Spanos, Nicholas P. (1987–1988, Winter). Past-life hypnotic regression: A critical view. *Skeptical Inquirer, 12,* 174–180.

Spanos, Nicholas P. (1991). A sociocognitive approach to hypnosis. In Steven Jay Lynn & Judith W. Rhue (Eds.), *Theories of hypnosis: Current models and perspectives.* New York: Guilford Press.

Spanos, Nicholas P. (1994). Multiple identity enactments and multiple personality disorder: A sociocognitive perspective. *Psychological Bulletin, 116,* 143–165.

Spanos, Nicholas P.; Barber, T. X.; & Lang, Gerald. (2005). Cognition and self-control: Cognitive control of painful sensory input. *Integrative Physiological & Behavioral Science, 40,* 119–128.

Spanos, Nicholas P.; McNulty, Stacey A.; DuBreuil, Susan C.; & Pires, Martha. (1995). The frequency and correlates of sleep paralysis in a university sample. *Journal of Research in Personality, 29,* 285–305.

Sparks, Jacqueline A.; Duncan, Barry L.; & Miller, Scott D. (2008). Common factors in psychotherapy. In Jay L. Lebow (Ed.), *Twenty-first century psychotherapies: Contemporary approaches to theory and practice* (pp. 453–497). Hoboken, NJ: Wiley.

Spearman, Charles E. (1904). "General intelligence" objectively determined and measured. *American Journal of Psychology, 15,* 201–293.

Spencer, Natasha A.; McClintock, Martha K.; Sellergren, Sarah A.; Bullivant, Susan; Jacob, Suma; & Mennella, Julie A. (2004). Social chemosignals from breastfeeding women increase sexual motivation. *Hormones and Behavior, 46,* 362–370.

Spencer, Steven J.; Steele, Claude M.; & Quinn, Diane M. (1999). Stereotype threat and women's math performance. *Journal of Experimental Social Psychology, 35,* 1–28.

Sperling, George. (1960). The information available in brief visual presentations. *Psychological Monographs, 74*(Whole No. 48).

Sperry, Roger W. (1982). Some effects of disconnecting the cerebral hemispheres. *Science, 217,* 1223–1226.

Spiegel, Alix. (Writer). (2008, January 3). Hotel maids challenge the placebo effect [Radio broadcast episode]. *Morning Edition.* Washington, DC: National Public Radio. Retrieved February 22, 2008, from http://www.npr.org/templates/story/story.php?storyId=17792517

Spiegel, Karine; Tasali, Esra; Penev, Plamen; & Van Cauter, Eve. (2004). Sleep curtailment in healthy young men is associated with decreased leptin levels, elevated ghrelin levels, and increased hunger and appetite. *Annals of Internal Medicine, 141,* 846–850.

Spillmann, Lothar; Otte, Tobias; Hamburger, Kai; & Magnussen, Svein. (2006). Perceptual filling-in from the edge of the blind spot. *Vision Research, 46,* 4252–4257.

Sprenkle, Douglas H.; Davis, Sean D.; & Lebow, Jay L. (2009). Common factors in couple and family therapy: The overlooked foundation for effective practice. New York: Guilford Press.

Springer, Sally P.; & Deutsch, Georg. (2001). *Left brain, right brain. Perspectives from cognitive neuroscience* (5th ed.). New York: W. H. Freeman/Worth Publishers.

Squire, Larry R.; Schmolck, Heike; & Buffalo, Elizabeth A. (2001). Memory distortions develop over time: A reply to Horn. *Psychological Science, 12,* 182.

Sroufe, L. Alan. (1995, September). Quoted in Beth Azar, "The bond between mother and child." *APA Monitor, 26*(9), 28.

Sroufe, L. Alan. (2002). From infant autonomy to promotion of adolescent autonomy: Prospective, longitudinal data on the role of parents in development. In John G. Borkowski & Sharon Landesman Ramey (Eds.), *Parenting and the child's world: Influences on academic, intellectual, and social-emotional development.* Mahwah, NJ: Erlbaum.

Staats, Sara; Cosmar, David; & Kaffenberger, Joshua. (2007). Sources of happiness and stress for college students: A replication and comparison over 20 years. *Psychological Reports, 10,* 685–696.

Stahl, Stephen M. (2009). *Stahl's illustrated antipsychotics.* New York: Cambridge University Press.

Stams, Geert-Jan J. M.; Juffer, Femmie; & Van Ijzendorn, Marinus H. (2002). Maternal sensitivity, infant attachment, and temperament in early childhood predict adjustment in middle childhood: The case of adopted children and their biologically unrelated parents. *Developmental Psychology, 38,* 806–821.

Stangor, Charles; & Lange, James E. (1994). Mental representations of social groups: Advances in understanding stereotypes and stereotyping. In Mark P. Zanna (Ed.), *Advances in experimental social psychology* (Vol. 26). San Diego, CA: Academic Press.

Stangor, Charles; & Ruble, Diane N. (1987). Development of gender role knowledge and gender constancy. In Lynn S. Liben & Margaret L. Signorella (Eds.), *Children's gender schemata* (New Directions for Child Development Series, No. 38). San Francisco: Jossey-Bass.

Stanley, Scott M.; Amato, Paul R.; Johnson, Christine A.; & Markman, Howard J. (2006). Premarital education, marital quality, and marital stability: Findings from a large, random household survey. *Journal of Family Psychology, 20,* 117–126.

Stanton, Annette L.; & Snider, Pamela R. (1993). Coping with a breast cancer diagnosis: A prospective study. *Health Psychology, 12,* 16–23.

Staub, Ervin. (1996). Cultural-societal roots of violence: The examples of genocidal violence and of contemporary youth violence in the United States. *American Psychologist, 51,* 117–132.

Staudinger, Ursula. (2001). Life-reflection: A social-cognitive analysis of life review. *Review of General Psychology, 5,* 148–160.

Steadman, Henry J.; Mulvey, Edward P.; Monahan, John; Robbins, Pamela Clark; Appelbaum, Paul S.; Grisso, Thomas; & others. (1998). Violence by people discharged from acute psychiatric inpatient facilities and by others in the same neighborhoods. *Archives of General Psychiatry, 55,* 393–401.

Steblay, Nancy Mehrkens. (1987). Helping behavior in urban and rural environments: A meta-analysis. *Psychological Bulletin, 102,* 346–356.

Steel, Piers. (2007). The nature of procrastination: A meta-analytic and theoretical review of quintessential self-regulatory failure. *Psychological Bulletin, 133,* 65–94.

Steele, Claude M. (1997). A threat in the air: How stereotypes shape intellectual identity and performance. *American Psychologist, 52,* 613–629.

Steele, Claude M. (2003). Through the back door to theory. *Psychological Inquiry, 14,* 314–317.

Steele, Claude M.; & Aronson, Joshua. (1995). Stereotype threat and the intellectual performance of African Americans. *Journal of Personality and Social Psychology, 69,* 797–811.

Steele, Jennifer R.; Reisz, Leah.; Williams, Amanda.; & Kawakami, Kerry. (2007). Women in mathematics: Examining the hidden barriers that gender stereotypes can impose. In Ronald J. Burke & Mary C. Mattis (Eds.), *Women and minorities in science, technology, engineering and mathematics: Upping the numbers.* London: Edward Elgar.

Steele, Ric G.; Elkin, T. David; & Roberts, Michael C. (Eds.). (2008). *Handbook of evidence-based therapies for children and adolescents: Bridging science and practice.* New York: Springer.

Stefansson, Hrein; Ophoff, Roei A.; Steinberg, Stacy; Andreassen, Ole A.; Cichon, Sven; Rujescu, Dan; Werge, Thomas; Pietiläinen, Olli P.; Mors, Ole; Mortensen, Preben B.; Sigurdsson, Engilbert; Gustafsson, Omar; Nyegaard, Mette; Tuulio-Henriksson, Annamari; Ingason, Andres; Hansen, Thomas; & others. (2009). Common variants conferring risk of schizophrenia. *Nature, 460,* 744–747.

Stein, Elliot A.; Pankiewicz, John; Harsch, Harold H.; Cho, Jung-Ki; Fuller, Scott A.; Hoffmann, Raymond G.; & others. (1998). Nicotine-induced limbic cortical activation in the human brain: A functional MRI study. *American Journal of Psychiatry, 155,* 1009–1015.

Steinberg, Laurence. (1990). Autonomy, conflict, and harmony in the family relationship. In S. Shirley Feldman & Glen R. Elliott (Eds.), *At the threshold: The developing adolescent.* Cambridge, MA: Harvard University Press.

Steinberg, Laurence. (2001). We know some things: Parent–adolescent relationships in retrospect and prospect. *Journal of Research on Adolescence, 11,* 1–19.

Steinberg, Laurence; Darling, Nancy E.; Fletcher, Anne C.; Brown, B. Bradford; & Dornbusch, Sanford M. (1995). Authoritative parenting and adolescent adjustment: An ecological journey. In Phyllis Moen, Glen H. Elder, Jr., & Kurt Luscher (Eds.), *Examining lives in context: Perspectives on the ecology of human development.* Washington, DC: American Psychological Association.

Stellmann, Jeanne Mager; Smith, Rebecca P.; Katz, Craig L.; Sharma, Vansh; Charney, Dennis S.; Herbert, Robin; Moline, Jacqueline; Luft, Benjamin J.; Markowitz, Steven; Udasin, Iris; Harrison, Denise; Baron, Sherry; Landrigan, Philip J.; Levin, Stephen M.; & Southwick, Steven. (2008). Enduring mental health morbidity and social function impairment in World Trade Center rescue, recovery, and cleanup workers: The psychological dimension of an environmental health disaster. *Environmental Health Perspectives, 116,* 1248–1253.

Stephens, Benjamin R.; & Banks, Martin S. (1987) Contrast discrimination in human infants. *Journal of Experimental Psychology: Human Perception and Performance, 13,* 558–565.

Stern, Kathleen; & McClintock, Martha K. (1998, March 12). Regulation of ovulation by human hormones. *Nature, 392,* 177.

Stern, Peter. (2001). Sweet dreams are made of this. *Science, 294,* 1047.

Stern, Yaakov; Alexander, Gene E.; & Prohovnik, Isak. (1992). Inverse relationship between education and parietotemporal perfusion deficit in Alzheimer's disease. *Annals of Neurology, 32,* 371–377.

Stern, Yaakov; Gurland, B.; & Tatemichi, T. K. (1994, April 6). Influence of education and occupation on the incidence of Alzheimer's disease. *Journal of the American Medical Association, 271*(13), 1004–1007.

Sternberg, Robert J. (1986). *Intelligence applied: Understanding and increasing your intellectual skills.* San Diego, CA: Harcourt Brace Jovanovich.

Sternberg, Robert J. (1988). A three-facet model of creativity. In Robert J. Sternberg (Ed.), *The nature of creativity.* New York: Cambridge University Press.

Sternberg, Robert J. (1990). *Metaphors of mind: Conceptions of the nature of intelligence.* New York: Cambridge University Press.

Sternberg, Robert J. (1995). For whom the bell curve tolls: A review of the bell curve. *Psychological Science, 6,* 257–261.

Sternberg, Robert J. (1997). The concept of intelligence and its role in lifelong learning and success. *American Psychologist, 52,* 1030–1037.

Sternberg, Robert J. (2008). Applying psychological theories to educational practice. *American Educational Research Journal, 45,* 150–165.

Sternberg, Robert J. (2009). It all started with those darn IQ tests: Half a career spent defying the crowd. In James C. Kaufman, Elena L. Grigorenko, & Robert J. Sternberg (Eds.), *The essential Sternberg: Essays on intelligence, psychology, and education.* New York: Springer.

Stevens, Gwendolyn; & Gardner, Sheldon. (1982). *The women of psychology: Vol. I. Pioneers and innovators.* Cambridge, MA: Schenkman.

Stevenson, Harold L.; & Stigler, James. (1992). *The learning gap: Why our schools are failing and what we can learn from Japanese and Chinese education.* New York: Summit Books.

Stevenson, Harold W.; & Lee, Shin-Ying. (1990). Contexts of achievement: A study of American, Chinese, and Japanese children. *Monographs of the Society for Research in Child Development, 55* (Serial No. 221, Nos. 1–2).

Stevenson, Harold W.; Lee, Shin-Ying; & Stigler, James W. (1986). Mathematics achievements of Chinese, Japanese, and American children. *Science, 236,* 693–698.

Steward, Barbara. (2000). Changing times: The meaning, measurement and use of time in teleworking. *Time & Society, 9,* 57–74.

Stewart, V. Mary. (1973). Tests of the "carpentered world" hypothesis by race and environment. *International Journal of Psychology, 8,* 12–34.

Stewart-Williams, Steve; & Podd, John. (2004). The placebo effect: Dissolving the expectancy versus conditioning debate. *Psychological Bulletin, 130,* 324–340.

Stickgold, Robert. (2005, October 27). Sleep-dependent memory consolidation. *Nature, 437,* 1272–1278.

Stickgold, Robert; & Walker, Matthew P. (2007). Sleep-dependent memory consolidation and reconsolidation. *Sleep Medicine, 8,* 331–343.

Stipek, Deborah. (1998). Differences between Americans and Chinese in the circumstances evoking pride, shame, and guilt. *Journal of Cross-Cultural Psychology, 29,* 616–629.

Stitzer, Maxine L.; Peirce, Jessica; & Petry, Nancy M. (2007, August). Abstinence-based incentives in methadone maintenance: Interaction with intake stimulant test results. *Experimental and Clinical Psychopharmacology, 15*(4), 344–350.

Stogdill, Ralph M. (1948). Personal factors associated with leadership: A survey of the literature. *Journal of Psychology, 25,* 35–71.

Stone, Arthur A.; Cox, Donald S.; Valdimarsdottir, Heiddis; Jandorf, Lina; & Neale, John M. (1987). Evidence that secretory IgA antibody is associated with daily mood. *Journal of Personality and Social Psychology, 52,* 988–993.

Stone, Arthur A.; Neale, John M.; Cox, Donald S.; Napoli, Anthony; Valdimarsdottir, Heiddis; & Kennedy-Moore, Eileen. (1994). Daily events are associated with a secretory immune response to an oral antigen in men. *Health Psychology, 13,* 440–446.

Storm, Lance; & Ertel, Suitbert. (2001). Does psi exist? Comments on Milton and Wiseman's (1999) meta-analysis of Ganzfeld research. *Psychological Bulletin, 127,* 424–435.

St-Pierre, Edouard S.; & Melnyk, William T. (2004). The prescription privilege debate in Canada: The voices of today's and tomorrow's psychologists. *Canadian Psychology, 45,* 284–292.

Strack, Fritz; Martin, Leonard L.; & Stepper, Sabine. (1988). Inhibiting and facilitating conditions of the human smile: A non-obtrusive test of the facial-feedback hypothesis. *Journal of Personality and Social Psychology, 54,* 768–777.

Strahan, Erin J.; Spencer, Steven J.; & Zanna, Mark P. (2005). Subliminal priming and persuasion: How motivation affects the activation of goals and the persuasiveness of messages. In Frank R. Kardes, Paul M. Herr, & Jacques Nantel (Eds.), *Applying social cognition to consumer-focused strategy.* Mahwah, NJ: Erlbaum.

Streitberger, Konrad; Ezzo, Jeanette; & Schneider, Antonius. (2006). Acupuncture for nausea and vomiting: An update of clinical and experimental studies. *Autonomic Neuroscience: Basic and Clinical, 129,* 107–117.

Stricker, George; & Gold, Jerold. (2008). Integrative therapy. In Jay L. Lebow (Ed.), *Twenty-first century psychotherapies: Contemporary approaches to theory and practice* (pp. 389–423). Hoboken, NJ: Wiley.

Strickland, Bonnie R. (1995). Research on sexual orientation and human development: A commentary. *Developmental Psychology, 31,* 137–140.

Strubbe, Jan H.; & Woods, Stephen C. (2004). The timing of meals. *Psychological Review, 111,* 128–141.

Strupp, Hans H. (1996). The tripartite model and the Consumer Reports study. *American Psychologist, 51,* 1017–1024.

Stuart, Richard B.; & Davis, Barbara. (1972). *Slim chance in a fat world.* Champaign, IL: Research Press.

Styron, William. (1990). *Darkness visible: A memoir of madness.* New York: Vintage.

Suarez-Morales, Lourdes; Dillon, Frank R.; & Szapocznik, Jose. (2007). Validation of the Acculturative Stress Inventory for Children. *Cultural Diversity and Ethnic Minority Psychology, 13,* 216–224.

Subiaul, Francys; Cantlon, Jessica F; Holloway, Ralph L.; & Terrace, Herbert S. (2004). Cognitive imitation in rhesus macaques. *Science, 305,* 407–410.

Substance Abuse and Mental Health Services Administration. (2002). *The National Household Survey on Drug Abuse report.* Retrieved November 2, 2002, from http://www.samhsa.gov/oas/nhsda/2klnhsda/vol1/highlights.htm

Substance Abuse and Mental Health Services Administration. (2008). *Results from the 2007 National Survey on Drug Use and Health: National findings* (Office of Applied Studies, NSDUH Series H-34, DHHS Publication No. SMA 08-4343). Rockville, MD.

Sue, David; & Sue, Diane M. (2008). *Foundations of counseling and psychotherapy: Evidence-based practices for a diverse society.* Hoboken, NJ: Wiley.

Sue, Derald Wing; Capodilupo, Christina M.; & Holder, Aisha M. B. (2008). Racial microaggressions in the life experience of black Americans. *Professional Psychology: Research and Practice, 39,* 329–336.

Sue, Diane W.; & Sue, David. (2008). *Counseling the culturally diverse: Theory and practice* (5th ed.). Hoboken, NJ: Wiley.

Sue, Stanley; Zane, Nolan; & Young, Kathleen. (1994). Research on psychotherapy with culturally diverse populations. In Allen E. Bergin & Sol L. Garfield (Eds.), *Handbook of psychotherapy and behavior change* (4th ed.). New York: Wiley.

Sullivan, Cathy & Lewis, Suzan. (2001). Home-based telework, gender, and the synchronization of work and family: Perspectives of teleworkers and their co-residents. *Gender, Work & Organization, 8,* 123–145.

Suls, Jerry; & Bunde, James. (2005). Anger, anxiety, and depression as risk factors for cardiovascular disease: The problems and implications of overlapping affective dispositions. *Psychological Bulletin, 131,* 260–300.

Sun, Shumei S.; Schubert, Christine M.; Chumlea, William Cameron; Roche, Alex F.; Kulin, Howard E.; Lee, Peter A.; & others. (2002). National estimates of the timing of sexual maturation and racial differences among US children. *Pediatrics, 110,* 911–919.

Super, Donald E. (1990). Career and life development. In Duane Brown, Linda Brooks, & Associates (Eds.), *Career choice and development: Applying contemporary theories to practice.* San Francisco: Jossey-Bass.

Supple, Andrew J.; & Small, Stephen A. (2006). The influence of parental support, knowledge, and authoritative parenting on Hmong and European American adolescent development. *Journal of Family Issues, 27*(9), 1214–1232.

Swaisgood, Ronald R. (2007). Current status and future directions of applied behavioral research for animal welfare and conservation. *Applied Animal Behaviour Science, 102*, 139–162.

Swan, Daniel C.; & Big Bow, Harding. (1995, Fall). Symbols of faith and belief—Art of the Native American Church. *Gilcrease Journal, 3*, 22–43.

Swartz, Conrad M. (2009). Preface. In Conrad M. Swartz (Ed.), *Electroconvulsive and neuromodulation therapies* (pp. xvii–xxx). New York: Cambridge University Press.

Swartz, Marvin S.; Perkins, Diana O.; Stroup, T. Scott; Davis, Sonia M.; & CATIE Study Investigators. (2007). Effects of antipsychotic medications on psychosocial functioning in patients with chronic schizophrenia: Findings from the NIMH CATIE study. *American Journal of Psychiatry, 164*, 428–436.

Sweeney, Gladys M. (2007). Why childhood attachment matters: Implications for personal happiness, families, and public policy. In A. Scott Loveless & Thomas B. Holman (Eds.), *The family in the new millennium: World voices supporting the "natural" clan, Vol. 1: The place of family in human society* (pp. 332–346). Westport, CT: Praeger/Greenwood.

Swickert, Rhonda J.; Rosentreter, Christina J.; Hittner, James B.; & Mushrush, Jane E. (2002). Extraversion, social support processes, and stress. *Personality and Individual Differences, 32*, 877–891.

Taguba, Antonio M. (2004). Article 15-6. Investigation of the 800th military police brigade. Retrieved December 8, 2005, from http://www.npr.org/iraq/2004/prison_abuse_report.pdf

Taheri, Shahrad; Lin, Ling; Austin, Diane; Young, Terry; & Mignot, Emmanuel. (2004, December). Short sleep duration is associated with reduced leptin, elevated ghrelin, and increased body mass index. *PloS Medicine, 1*(3), e62, 001–008. Retrieved December 8, 2009, from http://www.plosmedicine.org/article/info%3Adoi%2F10.1371%2Fjournal.pmed.0010062

Takeuchi, Tomoka; Fukuda, Kazuhiko; Sasaki, Yuka; Inugami, Maki; & Murphy, Timothy I. (2002). Factors related to the occurrence of isolated sleep paralysis elicited during a multi-phasic sleep-wake schedule. *Sleep, 25*, 89–96.

Talarico, Jennifer M.; & Rubin, David C. (2003). Confidence, not consistency, characterizes flashbulb memories. *Psychological Science, 14*, 455–461.

Talarico, Jennifer M.; & Rubin, David C. (2007). Flashbulb memories are special after all; in phenomenology, not accuracy [sic]. *Applied Cognitive Psychology, 21*, 557–578.

Talbot, Margaret. (2008, May 12). Birdbrain: The woman behind the world's chattiest parrots. *The New Yorker*, 64–75.

Tallman, Karen; & Bohart, Arthur C. (1999). The client as a common factor: Clients as self-healers. In Mark A. Hubble, Barry L. Duncan, & Scott D. Miller (Eds.), *The heart and soul of change: What works in therapy.* Washington, DC: American Psychological Association.

Tanaka-Matsumi, Junko; & Draguns, Juris G. (1997). Culture and psychopathology. In John W. Berry, Marshall H. Segall, & Cigdem Kagitçibasi (Eds.), *Handbook of cross-cultural psychology: Vol. 3. Social behavior and applications.* Boston: Allyn & Bacon.

Tanford, Sarah; & Penrod, Steven. (1984). Social influence model: A formal integration of research on majority and minority influence processes. *Psychological Bulletin, 95*, 189–225.

Tarrier, Nicholas. (2008). Schizophrenia and other psychotic disorders. In David H. Barlow (Ed.), *Clinical handbook of psychological disorders* (4th ed., pp. 463–491). New York: Guilford Press.

Tart, Charles T. (1994). *Living the mindful life: A handbook for living in the present moment.* Boston: Shambhala.

Taylor, Donald M.; & Porter, Lana E. (1994). A multicultural view of stereotyping. In Walter J. Lonner & Roy Malpass (Eds.), *Psychology and culture.* Boston: Allyn & Bacon.

Taylor, Humphrey. (2003, February 26). *The Harris poll #11: The religious and other beliefs of Americans 2003.* Rochester, NY: Harris Interactive. Retrieved January 2, 2005, from http://www.harrisinteractive.com/harrispoll/index.asp?PID=359

Taylor, Shelley E.; & Aspinwall, Lisa G. (1993). Coping with chronic illness. In Leo Goldberger & Shlomo Breznitz (Eds.), *Handbook of stress: Theoretical and clinical aspects* (2nd ed.). New York: Free Press.

Taylor, Shelley E.; Klein, Laura Cousino; Lewis, Brian P.; Gruenewald, Tara L.; Gurung, Regan A.; & Updegraff, John A. (2000b). Biobehavioral responses to stress in females: Tend-and-befriend, not fight-or-flight. *Psychological Review, 107*, 411–429.

Taylor, Shelley E.; Lewis, Brian P.; Gruenewald, Tara L.; Gurung, Regan A. R.; Updegraff, John A.; & Klein, Laura Cousino. (2002). Sex differences in biobehavioral response to threat: Reply to Geary and Flinn (2002). *Psychological Review, 109*, 751–753.

Taylor, Steven; Thordarson, Dana S.; Maxfield, Louise; Fedoroff, Ingrid C.; Lovell, Karina; & Ogrodniczuk, John. (2003). Comparative efficacy, speed, and adverse effects of three PTSD treatments: Exposure therapy, EMDR, and relaxation training. *Journal of Consulting and Clinical Psychology, 71*, 330–338.

Taylor, Susan M.; & Sackheim, Kathryn K. (1988). Graphology. *Personnel Administrator, 33*, 71–76.

Taylor, W. S.; & Martin, M. F. (1944). Multiple personality. *Journal of Abnormal and Social Psychology, 39*, 281–300.

Telework Coalition. (2006, March). *Benchmarking study. Best practices for large-scale implementation in public and private sector organizations.* Washington, DC: Author.

Templeton, Jennifer J. (1998). Learning from others' mistakes: A paradox revisited. *Animal Behaviour, 55*, 79–85.

Terman, Lewis M. (1916). *Measurement of intelligence.* Boston: Houghton Mifflin.

Terman, Lewis M. (1926). *Genetic studies of genius* (2nd ed., Vol. I). Stanford, CA: Stanford University Press.

Terman, Lewis M.; & Oden, Melita H. (1947). *Genetic studies of genius: Vol. IV. The gifted child grows up: Twenty-five years' follow-up of a superior group.* Stanford, CA: Stanford University Press.

Terman, Lewis M.; & Oden, Melita H. (1959). *Genetic studies of genius: Vol. V. The gifted at mid-life: Thirty-five years' follow-up of the superior child.* Stanford, CA: Stanford University Press.

Terracciano, Antonio; McCrae, Robert R.; Brant, Larry J.; & Costa, Paul T., Jr. (2005). Hierarchical linear modeling analyses of the NEO-PI-R Scales in the Baltimore Longitudinal Study of Aging. (2005). *Psychology and Aging, 20*, 493–506.

Terrace, Herbert S. (1985). In the beginning was the "name." *American Psychologist, 40*, 1011–1028.

Tew, James D.; Mulsant, Benoit H.; Haskett, Roger F.; Prudic, Joan; Begley, Amy E.; & Sackeim, Harold A. (2007). Relapse during continuation pharmacotherapy after acute response to ECT: A comparison of usual care versus protocolized treatment. *Annals of Clinical Psychiatry*, 19, 1–4.

Teyber, Edward. (2009). *Interpersonal process in therapy: An integrative model* (6th ed.) Pacific Grove, CA: Thomson Brooks/Cole.

Thanos, Panayotis K.; Michaelides, Michael; Piyis, Yiannis K.; Wang, Gene-Jack; & Volkow, Nora D. (2008). Food restriction markedly increases dopamine D2 receptor (D2R) in a rat model of obesity as assessed with in-vivo mPET imaging ([11C]Raclopride) and in-vitro ([3H]spiperone) autoradiography. *Synapse, 62,* 50–61.

Thase, Michael E. (2001). Neuroimaging profiles and the differential therapies of depression. *Archives of General Psychiatry, 58,* 651–653.

Thase, Michael E.; & Denko, Timothey. (2008). Pharmacotherapy of mood disorders. *Annual Review of Clinical Psychology, 4,* 53–91.

Thase, Michael E.; Friedman, Edward S.; Biggs, Melanie M.; Wisniewski, Stephen R.; Trivedi, Madhukar H.; Luther, James F.; Fava, Maurizio; Nierenberg, Andrew A.; McGrath, Patrick J.; Warden, Diane; Niederehe, George; Hollon, Steven D.; & Rush, A. John. (2007). Cognitive therapy versus medication in augmentation and switch strategies as second-step treatments: A STAR*D report. *American Journal of Psychiatry, 164,* 739–752.

Thase, Michael E.; & Jindal, Ripu D. (2004). Combining psychotherapy and psychopharmacology for treatment of mental disorders. In Michael J. Lambert (Ed.), *Bergin and Garfield's handbook of psychotherapy and behavior change* (5th ed.). New York: Wiley.

Thayer, Amanda; & Lynn, Steven Jay. (2006). Guided imagery and recovered memory therapy: Considerations and cautions. *Journal of Forensic Psychology Practice, 6,* 63–73.

Thomas, Alexander; & Chess, Stella. (1977). *Temperament and development.* New York: Brunner/Mazel.

Thomas, Alexander; & Chess, Stella. (1986). The New York Longitudinal Study: From infancy to early adult life. In Robert Plomin & Judith Dunn (Eds.), *The study of temperament: Changes, continuities, and challenges.* Hillsdale, NJ: Erlbaum.

Thomas, Ayanna K.; Bulevich, John B.; & Loftus, Elizabeth F. (2003). Exploring the role of repetition and sensory elaboration in the imagination inflation effect. *Memory & Cognition, 31,* 630–640.

Thompson, Clara. (1950/1973). Some effects of the derogatory attitude toward female sexuality. In Jean Baker Miller (Ed.), *Psychoanalysis and women.* Baltimore: Penguin Books.

Thompson, J. Kevin; Roehrig, Megan; & Kinder, Bill N. (2007). Eating disorders. In Michel Hersen, Samuel M. Turner, & Deborah C. Beidel (Eds.), *Adult psychopathology and diagnosis* (5th ed., pp. 571–600). Hoboken, NJ: Wiley.

Thompson, Paul. (2001, September 25). Quoted in "UCLA Researchers map how schizophrenia engulfs teen brains." University of California–Los Angeles press release. Retrieved March 6, 2005, from http://www.loni.ucla.edu/~thompson/MEDIA/PNAS/Pressrelease.html

Thompson, Paul M.; Hayashi, Kiralee M.; Simon, Sara L.; Geaga, Jennifer A.; Hong, Michael S.; Sui, Yihong; Lee, Jessica Y.; Toga, Arthur W.; Ling, Walter; & London, Edythe D. (2004). Structural abnormalities in the brains of human subjects who use methamphetamine. *Journal of Neuroscience, 24,* 6028–6036.

Thompson, Paul M.; Hayashi, Kiralee M.; de Zubicaray, Greig; Janke, Andrew L.; Rose, Stephen E.; Semple, James; Herman, David; Hong, Michael S.; Dittmer, Stephanie S.; Doddrell, David M.; & Toga, Arthur W. (2003). Dynamics of gray matter loss in Alzheimer's disease. *Journal of Neuroscience, 23,* 994–1005. Retrieved July 10, 2004, from http://www.loni.ucla.edu/~thompson/PDF/ADwave.pdf

Thompson, Paul M.; Vidal, Christine; Gledd, Jay N.; Gochman, Peter; Blumenthal, Jonathan; Nicolson, Robert; & others. (2001). Mapping adolescent brain change reveals dynamic wave of accelerated gray matter loss in very early-onset schizophrenia. *Proceedings of the National Academy of Sciences, USA, 98,* 11650–11655.

Thompson, Richard F. (1994). Behaviorism and neuroscience. *Psychological Review, 101,* 259–265.

Thompson, Richard F. (2005). In search of memory traces. *Annual Review of Psychology, 56,* 1–23.

Thompson, Robin; Emmorey, Karen; & Gollan, Tamar H. (2005). "Tip of the fingers" experiences by deaf signers. *Psychological Science, 16,* 856–860.

Thompson, Suzanne C.; Nanni, Christopher; & Levine, Alexandra. (1994). Primary versus secondary and central versus consequence-related control in HIV-positive men. *Journal of Personality and Social Psychology, 67,* 540–547.

Thompson, Suzanne C.; & Spacapan, Shirlynn. (1991). Perceptions of control in vulnerable populations. *Journal of Social Issues, 47,* 1–21.

Thompson, Vetta L. Sanders; Bazile, Anita; & Akbar, Maysa. (2004). African Americans' perceptions of psychotherapy and psychotherapists. *Professional Psychology: Research and Practice, 35,* 19–26.

Thorndike, Edward L. (1898). Animal intelligence: An experimental study of the associative processes in animals. *Psychological Review Monograph Supplement, 2*(Serial No. 8).

Thorndike, Robert L. (1991). Edward L. Thorndike: A professional and personal appreciation. In Gregory A. Kimble, Michael Wertheimer, & Charlotte L. White (Eds.), *Portraits of pioneers in psychology.* Washington, DC: American Psychological Association.

Thorne, Barrie. (1993). *Gender play: Girls and boys in school.* New Brunswick, NJ: Rutgers University Press.

Thornhill, Randy. (2007). The evolution of women's estrus, extended sexuality, and concealed ovulation, and their implications for human sexuality research. In Steven W. Gangestad & Jeffry A. Simpson (Eds.). *The evolution of mind: Fundamental questions and controversies.* New York, NY: Guilford Press.

Thornicroft, Graham. (2006). *Shunned: Discrimination against people with mental illness.* New York: Oxford University Press.

Thorpy, Michael J. (2005a). Classification of sleep disorders. In Meir H. Kryger, Thomas Roth, & William C. Dement (Eds.), *Principles and practice of sleep medicine* (4th ed.). Philadelphia: Elsevier Saunders.

Thorpy, Michael. (2007). Therapeutic advances in narcolepsy. *Sleep Medicine, 8,* 427–440.

Thunberg, Monika; & Dimberg, Ulf. (2000). Gender differences in facial reactions to fear-relevant stimuli. *Journal of Nonverbal Behavior, 24,* 45–51.

Thurstone, Louis L. (1937). *Primary mental abilities.* Chicago: University of Chicago Press.

Tienari, Pekka; Sorri, Anneli; Lahti, Ilpo; Naarala, Mikko; Wahlberg, Karl-Erik; Moring, Juha; & others. (1987). Genetic and psychosocial factors in schizophrenia: The Finnish Adoptive Family Study. *Schizophrenia Bulletin, 13,* 477–484.

Tienari, Pekka; & Wahlberg, Karl-Erik. (2008). Family environment and psychosis. In Craig Morgan, Kwame McKenzie, & Paul Fearon (Eds.), *Society and psychosis.* New York: Cambridge University Press.

Tienari, Pekka; Wahlberg, Karl-Erik; & Wynne, Lyman C. (2006, Winter). Finnish Adoption Study of Schizophrenia: Implications for family interventions. *Families, Systems, & Health, 24*(4), 442–451.

Tienari, Pekka; Wynne, Lyman C.; Moring, Juha; Lahti, Ilpo; Naarala, Mikko; Sorri, Anneli; & others. (1994). The Finnish Adoptive Family Study of Schizophrenia: Implications for family research. *British Journal of Psychiatry, 164*(Suppl.), 20–26.

Tobler, Irene. (2005). Phylogeny of sleep regulation. In Meir H. Kryger, Thomas Roth, & William C. Dement (Eds.), *Principles and practice of sleep medicine* (4th ed.). Philadelphia: Elsevier Saunders.

Todd, James T.; & Morris, Edward K. (1992). Case histories in the great power of steady misrepresentation. *American Psychologist, 47,* 1441–1453.

Todd, Michael. (2004). Daily processes in stress and smoking: Effects of negative events, nicotine dependence, and gender. *Psychology of Addictive Behaviors, 18,* 31–39.

Toga, Arthur W.; & Thompson, Paul M. (2003). Mapping brain asymmetry. *Nature Reviews Neuroscience, 4,* 37–48.

Tolman, Edward C. (1932). *Purposive behavior in animals and men.* New York: Appleton-Century-Crofts.

Tolman, Edward C. (1948). Cognitive maps in rats and men. *Psychological Review,* 55, 189–208.

Tolman, Edward C.; & Honzik, Charles H. (1930a). "Insight" in rats. University of California, Berkeley, *Publications in Psychology, 4,* 215–232.

Tolman, Edward C.; & Honzik, Charles H. (1930b). Introduction and removal of reward, and maze performance in rats. University of California, Berkeley, *Publications in Psychology, 4,* 257–275.

Tolman, Edward C.; Ritchie, B. F.; & Kalish, D. (1946/1992). Studies in spatial learning. I. Orientation and the short-cut. *Journal of Experimental Psychology: General, 121,* 429–434.

Tomasi, Dardo; Goldstein, Rita Z.; Telang, Frank; Maloney, Thomas; Alia-Klein, Nelly; Caparelli, Elisabeth C.; & Volkow, Nora D. (2007a). Thalamo-cortical dysfunction in cocaine abusers: Implications in attention and perception. *Psychiatry Research: Neuroimaging, 155*(3), 189–201.

Tomasi, Dardo; Goldstein, Rita Z.; Telang, Frank; Maloney, Thomas; Alia-Klein, Nelly; Caparelli, Elisabeth C.; & Volkow, Nora D. (2007b). Widespread disruption in brain activation patterns to a working memory task during cocaine abstinence. *Brain Research, 1171,* 83–92.

Tooby, John; & Cosmides, Leda. (2000). Evolutionary psychology and the emotions. In Michael Lewis & Jeanette M. Haviland-Jones (Eds.), *Handbook of emotions* (2nd ed.). New York: Guilford Press.

Tooby, John; & Cosmides, Leda. (2005) Conceptual foundations of evolutionary psychology. In David M. Buss (Ed.), *Handbook of evolutionary psychology.* Hoboken: NJ: Wiley.

Torges, Cynthia M.; Stewart, Abigail J.; & Nolen-Hoeksema, Susan. (2008). Regret resolution, aging, and adapting to loss. *Psychology and Aging, 23,* 169–180.

Torrey, E. Fuller. (2006). *Surviving schizophrenia: A manual for families, patients, and providers.* New York: Harper Paperbacks.

Toth, Karen; & King, Bryan Y. (2008). Asperger's syndrome: Diagnosis and treatment. *American Journal of Psychiatry, 165,* 958–963.

Trachtenberg, Joshua T.; Chen, Brian E.; Knott, Graham W.; Feng, Guoping; Sanes, Joshua R.; Welker, Egbert; & others. (2002). Long-term in vivo imaging of experience-dependent synaptic plasticity in adult cortex. *Nature, 420,* 788–794.

2007 Training Industry Report. (2007, November/December). *Training, 44,* 8-24.

Treffert, Darold A.; & Wallace, Gregory L. (2003). Islands of genius. *Scientific American, vv,* 14–23.

Triandis, Harry C. (1994). *Culture and social behavior.* New York: McGraw-Hill.

Triandis, Harry C. (1996). The psychological measurement of cultural syndromes. *American Psychologist, 51,* 407–415.

Triandis, Harry C. (2005). Issues in individualism and collectivism. In Richard M. Sorrentino, Dov Cohen, James M. Olson, & Mark P. Zanna (Eds.), *Cultural and social behavior: The Ontario Symposium, vol. 10.* Mahwah, NJ: Erlbaum.

Trivedi, Bijal. (2005, June 18). Autistic and proud of it. *New Scientist,* issue 2504, p. 36.

Trope, Yaacov; & Fishbach, Ayelet. (2000). Counteractive self-control in overcoming temptation. *Journal of Personality and Social Psychology, 79,* 493–506.

Trull, Timothy J.; & Widiger, Thomas A. (2008). Geology 102: More thoughts on a shift to a dimensional model of personality disorders. *Social and Personality Psychology Compass, 2,* 949–967.

Tsang, Laura Lo Wa; Harvey, Carol D. H.; Duncan, Karen A.; & Sommer, Reena. (2003). The effects of children, dual earner status, sex role traditionalism, and marital structure on marital happiness over time. *Journal of Family and Economic Issues, 24,* 5–26.

Tsao, Doris. (2006a). A dedicated system for processing faces. *Science, 314,* 72–73.

Tsao, Doris; Freiwald, Winrich A.; Tootell, Roger B. H.; & Livingstone, Margaret S. (2006b). A cortical region consisting entirely of face-selective cells. *Science, 311,* 670–674.

Tschöp, Matthias; Smiley; David L.; & Heiman, Mark L. (2000, October 19). Ghrelin induces adiposity in rodents. *Nature, 407,* 908–913.

Tulving, Endel. (1983). *Elements of episodic memory.* Oxford, England: Clarendon Press/Oxford University Press.

Tulving, Endel. (1985). How many memory systems are there? *American Psychologist, 40,* 385–398.

Tulving, Endel. (2002). Episodic memory: From mind to brain. *Annual Review of Psychology, 53,* 1–25.

Tulving, Endel. (2007). Are there 256 different kinds of memory? In James S. Nairne (Ed.), *The foundations of remembering: Essays in honor of Henry L. Roediger, III.* New York: Psychology Press.

Turati, Chiara. (2004). Why faces are not special to newborns: An alternative account of the face preference. *Current Directions in Psychological Science, 13,* 5–8.

Turati, Chiara; Simion, Francesca; Milani, Idanna; & Umiltà, Carlo. (2002). Newborns' preference for faces: What is crucial? *Developmental Psychology, 38,* 875–882.

Turk, Dennis C.; & Winter, Frits. (2006). *The pain survival guide: How to reclaim your life.* Washington, DC: American Psychological Association.

Turkheimer, Eric; Haley, Andreana; Waldron, Mary; D'Onofrio, Brian; & Gottesman, Irving I. (2003). Socioeconomic status modifies heritability of IQ in young children. *Psychological Science, 14,* 623–628.

Turner, Martin S.; & Stewart, Duncan W. (2006, November). Review of the evidence for the long-term efficacy of atypical antipsychotic agents in the treatment of patients with schizophrenia and related psychoses. *Journal of Psychopharmacology, 20*(6, Suppl.), 20–37.

Turner, Monique Mitchell; Tamborini, Ron; Limon, M. Sean; & Zuckerman-Hyman, Cynthia. (2007, September). The moderators and mediators of door-in-the-face requests: Is it a negotiation or a helping experience? *Communication Monographs, 74*(3), 333–356.

Turner, Patricia J.; & Gervai, Judit. (1995). A multidimensional study of gender typing in preschool children and their parents: Personality, attitudes, preferences, behavior, and cultural differences. *Developmental Psychology, 31,* 759–772.

Tversky, Amos. (1972). Elimination by aspects: A theory of choice. *Psychological Review, 80,* 281–299.

Tversky, Amos; & Kahneman, Daniel. (1982). Judgment under uncertainty: Heuristics and biases. In Daniel Kahneman, Paul Slovic, & Amos Tversky (Eds.), *Judgment under uncertainty: Heuristics and biases.* New York: Cambridge University Press.

Tweney, Ryan D. (1997). Edward Bradford Titchener (1867–1927). In Wolfgang G. Bringmann, Helmut E. Lück, Rudolf Miller, & Charles E. Early (Eds.), *A pictorial history of psychology.* Chicago: Quintessence.

Twenge, Jean M.; Campbell, W. Keith; & Foster, Craig A. (2003). Parenthood and marital satisfaction: A meta-analytic review. *Journal of Marriage and Family, 65,* 574–583.

Tyler, Kathryn. (2008, January). Generation gaps: Millennials may be out of touch with workplace behavior. *HR Magazine, 53.*

U.S. Bureau of Labor Statistics. (2000). *Occupational outlook handbook.* Washington, DC: U.S. Department of Labor.

U.S. Bureau of Labor Statistics. (2008). Human resources, training, and labor relations managers and specialists profile. *Occupational outlook handbook.* www.bls.gov/OCO

U.S. Census Bureau. (2002). *Statistical abstract of the United States: 2001* (121st ed.). Washington, DC: U.S. Government Printing Office.

U.S. Census Bureau. (2004). Facts for features: Special edition: Unmarried and single Americans week. Retrieved November 30, 2004, from http://www.census.gov/PressRelease/www/releases/archives/|factsforfeaturesspecialeditions/002265.html

U.S. Census Bureau. (2004a). *America's families and living arrangements: 2003.* Annual Social and Economic Supplement: 2003 Current Population Survey, Current Population Reports, Series P20-553. Retrieved November 20, 2004, from http://www.census.gov/population/socdemo/hh-fam/tabMS-2.pdf

U.S. Census Bureau. (2008a). 2007 American Community Survey 1-year estimates: Marital status. Retrieved November 4, 2008, from http://factfinder.census.gov/

U.S. Census Bureau. (2008b). 2007 American Community Survey 1-year estimates: Ranking table R1204: Median age at first marriage for men. Retrieved November 4, 2008, from http://factfinder.census.gov/

U.S. Census Bureau. (2008c). 2007 American Community Survey 1-year estimates: Ranking table R1205: Median age at first marriage for women. Retrieved November 4, 2008, from http://factfinder.census.gov/

U.S. Census Bureau. (2008d). 2007 American Community Survey 1-year estimates: Table S1501: Educational attainment. Retrieved November 4, 2008, from http://factfinder.census.gov/

U.S. Department of Health and Human Services. (1999). *Mental health: A report of the surgeon general.* Rockville, MD: U.S. Department of Health and Human Services, Center for Mental Health Services, National Institute of Mental Health. Retrieved February 22, 2000, from http://www.nimh.nih.gov/-mhsgrpt/home.html

U.S. Public Health Service. (1999). *The surgeon general's call to action to prevent suicide.* Washington, DC: U.S. Government Printing Office. Retrieved October 30, 2001, from http://www.surgeongeneral.gov/library/calltoaction/calltoaction.pdf

Uchino, Bert N. (2004). *Social support and physical health.* New Haven, CT: Yale University Press.

Uchino, Bert N. (2009). Understanding the links between social support and physical health: A life-span perspective with emphasis on the separation of perceived and received support. *Perspectives on Psychological Science, 4,* 246–255.

Uleman, James S.; Saribay, S. Adil; & Gonzalez, Celia M. (2008). Spontaneous inferences, implicit impressions, and implicit theories. *Annual Review of Psychology, 59,* 329–360.

Ulett, George A.; & Han, Songping. (2002). *The biology of acupuncture.* St. Louis, MO: Warren H. Green.

Ulett, George A.; Han, Songping; & Han, Ji-sheng. (1998). Electroacupuncture: Mechanisms and clinical application. *Biological Psychiatry, 44,* 129–138.

Umiltà, M. Alessandra; Kohler, Evelayne; Gallese, Vittorio; Fogassi, Leonardo; Fadiga, Luciano; Keysers, Christian; & Rizzolatti, Giacomo. (2001). I know what you are doing: A neurophysiological study. *Neuron, 31,* 155–165.

Unemori, Patrick; Omoregie, Heather; & Markus, Hazel Rose. (2004, October–December). Self-portraits: Possible selves in European-American, Chilean, Japanese and Japanese-American cultural contexts. *Self and Identity, 3*(4), 321–328.

Updegraff, John A.; Silver, Roxane Cohen; & Holman, E. Alison (2008). Searching for and finding meaning in collective trauma: Results from a national longitudinal study of the 9/11 terrorist attacks. *Journal of Personality and Social Psychology, 95,* 709–722.

Ursano, Robert J.; & Shaw, Jon A. (2007). Children of war and opportunities for peace. *Journal of the American Medical Association, 298,* 567–568.

Utsey, Shawn O.; Grange, Christina; & Allyne, Renee. (2006). Guidelines for evaluating the racial and cultural environment of graduate training programs in professional psychology. In Medonna G. Constantine & Derald Wing Sue (Eds.), *Addressing racism: Facilitating cultural competence in mental health and educational settings* (pp. 213–232). Hoboken, NJ: Wiley.

Van Boven, Leaf; Kamada, Akiko; & Gilovich, Thomas. (1999). The perceiver as perceived: Everyday intuitions about the correspondence bias. *Journal of Personality and Social Psychology, 77,* 1188–1199.

Van Cauter, Eve. (2005). Endocrine physiology. In Meir H. Kryger, Thomas Roth, & William C. Dement (Eds.), *Principles and practice of sleep medicine* (4th ed.). Philadelphia: Elsevier Saunders.

van den Boom, Dymphna C.; & Hoeksma, Jan B. (1994). The effect of infant irritability on mother-infant interaction: A growth-curve analysis. *Developmental Psychology, 30,* 581–590.

van der Hart, Onno; Nijenhuis, Ellert R. S.; & Steele, Kathy. (2006). *The haunted self: Structural dissociation and the treatment of chronic traumatization.* New York: Norton.

van der Helm, Peter A. (2000). Simplicity versus likelihood in visual perception: From surprisals to precisals. *Psychological Bulletin, 126,* 770–800.

van Geert, Paul. (1998). A dynamic systems model of basic developmental mechanisms: Piaget, Vygotsky, and beyond. *Psychological Review, 105,* 634– 677.

van Heck, Guus L.; & den Oudsten, Brenda L. (2008). Emotional intelligence: Relationships to stress, health, and well-being. In Ad Vingerhoets, Ivan Nyklicek, & Johan Denollet (Eds.), *Emotion regulation: Conceptual and clinical issues.* New York: Springer Science + Business Media.

van Praag, Henriette. (2005, September 20). Quoted in "Exercise may reverse mental decline brought on by aging." Society for Neurosciences news release. Retrieved September 27, 1995, from http//apu.sfn.org/content/AboutSFN1/NewsReleases/pr_091405.html

van Praag, Henriette; Kempermann, Gerd; & Gage, Fred H. (2000). Neural consequences of environmental enrichment. *Nature Reviews Neuroscience, 1,* 191–198.

van Praag, Henriette; Schinder, Alejandro F.; Christie, Brian R.; Toni, Nicolas; Palmer, Theo D.; & Gage, Fred H. (2002, February 28). Functional neurogenesis in the adult hippocampus. *Nature, 415,* 1030–1034.

van Praag, Henriette; Shubert, Tiffany; Zhao, Chunmei; & Gage, Fred H. (2005). Exercise enhances learning and hippocampal neurogenesis in aged mice. *Journal of Neuroscience, 25,* 8680–8685.

van Wyhe, John. (2000). *The history of phrenology on the Web.* Retrieved January 17, 2000, from http://www.jmvanwyhe.freeserve.co.uk/

Vandell, Deborah Lowe; & Corasaniti, Mary Ann. (1990). Child care and the family: Complex contributors to child development. In Kathleen McCartney (Ed.), *Child care and maternal employment: A social ecology approach* (New Directions for Child Development Series, No. 49). San Francisco: Jossey-Bass.

Vartanian, Lenny R.; Herman, C. Peter; & Polivy, Janet. (2007). Consumption stereotypes and impression management: How you are what you eat. *Appetite, 48,* 265–277.

Vaughn, Bradley V.; & D'Cruz, O'Neill F. (2005). Cardinal manifestations of sleep disorders. In Meir H. Kryger, Thomas Roth, & William C. Dement (Eds.), *Principles and practice of sleep medicine* (4th ed.). Philadelphia: Elsevier Saunders.

Vaughn, Brian E.; Coppola, Gabrielle; & Verissimo, Manuela. (2007). The quality of maternal secure-base scripts predicts children's secure-base behavior in three sociocultural groups. *International Journal of Behavioral Development, 31,* 65–76.

Vilain, Eric J. N. (2008). Genetics of sexual development and differentiation. In David L. Rowland & Luca Incrocci (Eds.), *Handbook of sexual and gender identity disorders.* Hoboken, NJ: Wiley.

Viney, Wayne; & Burlingame-Lee, Laura. (2003). Margaret Floy-Washburn: A quest for the harmonies in the context of a rigorous scientific framework. In Gregory A. Kimble & Michael Wertheimer (Eds.), *Portraits of pioneers in psychology. Vol. V.* Washington, DC: American Psychological Association.

Vingerhoets, Ad J. J. M.; Cornelius, Randolph R.; Van Heck, Guus L.; & Becht, Marleen C. (2000). Adult crying: A model and review of the literature. *Review of General Psychology, 4,* 354–377.

Vlahov, David; Galea, Sandro; Resnick, Heidi; Shern, Jennifer; Boscarino, Joseph A.; Bucuvalas, Michael; & others. (2002). Increased use of cigarettes, alcohol, and marijuana among Manhattan, New York, residents after the September 11 terrorist attacks. *American Journal of Epidemiology, 155,* 988–996.

Volkow, Nora D. (2008). Epigenetics: The promise of a new science. *NIDA Notes, 21*(5). Washington, DC: U.S. Department of Health and Human Services.

Volkow, Nora D.; Chang, Linda; Wang, Gene-Jack; Fowler, Joanna S.; Ding, Yu-Sin; Sedler, Mark; Logan, Jean; Franceschi, Dinko; Gatley, John; Hitzemann, Robert; Gifford, Andrew; Wong, Christopher; & Pappas, Naomi. (2001a). Low level of brain dopamine D2 receptors in methamphetamine abusers: Association with metabolism in the orbitofrontal cortex. *American Journal of Psychiatry, 158,* 2015–2021.

Volkow, Nora D.; Chang, Linda; Wang, Gene-Jack; Fowler, Joanna S.; Franceschi, Dinko; Sedler, Mark J.; Gatley, S. John; Hitzemann, Robert; Ding, Yu-Shin; Wong, Christopher; & Logan, Jean. (2001b). Higher cortical and lower subcortical metabolism in detoxified methamphetamine abusers. *American Journal of Psychiatry, 158,* 383–389.

Volkow, Nora D.; Fowler, Joanna S.; Wang, Gene-Jack; Baler, Ruben D.; & Telang, Frank. (2009). Imaging dopamine's role in drug abuse and addiction. *Neuropharmacology, 56*(Suppl. 1), 3–8.

Volkow, Nora D.; Fowler, Joanna S.; Wang, Gene-Jack; Swanson, James M.; & Telang, Frank. (2007). Dopamine in drug abuse and addiction: Results of imaging studies and treatment implications. *Archives of Neurology, 64,* 1575–1579.

Volkow, Nora D.; Wang, Gene-Jack; Fowler, Joanna S.; Logan, Jean; Gatley, Samuel J.; Gifford, Andrew; Hitzemann, Robert; Ding, Yu-Shin; & Pappas, Naomi. (1999). Prediction of reinforcing responses to psychostimulants in humans by brain dopamine D2 receptor levels. *American Journal of Psychiatry, 156,* 1440–1443.

Volkow, Nora D.; Wang, Gene-Jack; Telang, Frank; Fowler, Joanna S.; Logan, Jean; Childress, Anna-Rose; Jayne, Millard; Ma, Yeming; & Wong, Christopher. (2006). Cocaine cues and dopamine in dorsal striatum: Mechanism of craving in cocaine addiction. *Journal of Neuroscience, 26,* 6583–6588.

Volkow, Nora D.; & Wise, Roy A. (2005). How can drug addiction help us understand obesity? *Nature Neuroscience, 8,* 555–560.

Vollman, Michael W.; LaMontagne, Lynda L.; & Hepworth, Joseph T. (2007, March–April). Coping with depressive symptoms in adults living with heart failure. *Journal of Cardiovascular Nursing, 22*(2), 125–130.

Voorspoels, Wouter; Vanpaemel, Wolf; & Storms, Gert. (2008). Exemplars and prototypes in natural language concepts: A typicality-based evaluation. *Psychonomic Bulletin & Review, 15,* 630–637.

Vul, Edward; Harris, Christine; Winkielman, Piotr; & Pashler, Harold. (2009) Puzzlingly high correlations in fMRI studies of emotion, personality, and social cognition (the paper formerly known as Voodoo Correlations in Social Neuroscience). *Perspectives on Psychological Science, 4,* 274–290.

Vygotsky, Lev S. (1978). *Mind in society: The development of higher psychological processes.* Cambridge, MA: Harvard University Press.

Vygotsky, Lev S. (1987). *Thinking and speech* (Norris Minick, Trans.). New York: Plenum Press.

Wackerman, Jiri; Pütz, Peter; & Allefeld, Carsten. (2008). Ganzfeld-induced hallucinatory experience, its phenomenology and cerebral electrophysiology. *Cortex, 44,* 1364–1378.

Wade, Nicholas J.; Sakurai, Kenzo; & Gyoba, Jiro. (2007). Whither Wundt? *Perception, 36,* 163–166.

Wadsworth, Barry J. (1996). *Piaget's theory of cognitive and affective development: Foundations of constructivism* (5th ed.). White Plains, NY: Longman.

Waelde, Lynn C.; Thompson, Larry; & Gallagher-Thompson, Dolores. (2004). A pilot study of a yoga and meditation intervention for dementia caregiver stress. *Journal of Clinical Psychology, 60,* 677–687.

Wagstaff, Graham F. (1999). Hypnosis. In Sergio Della Sala (Ed.), *Mind myths: Exploring popular assumptions about the mind and brain.* Chichester, England: Wiley.

Wagstaff, Graham; & Cole, Jon. (2005). Levels of explanation and the concept of a hypnotic state. *Contemporary Hypnosis, 22,* 14–17.

Wahba, Mahmoud A.; & Bridwell, Lawrence G. (1976). Maslow reconsidered: A review of research on the need hierarchy theory. *Organizational Behavior and Human Decision Processes, 15,* 212–240.

Wainwright, Jennifer L.; & Patterson, Charlotte J. (2008). Peer relations among adolescents with female same-sex parents. *Developmental Psychology, 44,* 117–126.

Wald, George. (1964). The receptors of human color vision. *Science, 145,* 1007–1017.

Walker, Elaine; Kestler, Lisa; Bollini, Annie; & Hochman, Karen M. (2004). Schizophrenia: Etiology and course. *Annual Review of Psychology, 55,* 401–430.

Walker, Lawrence J. (1989). A longitudinal study of moral reasoning. *Child Development, 60,* 157–166.

Walker, Matthew P. (2005). A new model of sleep and the time course of memory formation. *Behavioral and Brain Sciences, 28,* 51–104.

Walker, Matthew P. (2008, March 23). Interview: *KCBS In Depth: Sleep.* Retrieved July 21, 2008, from www.kcbs.com/episode_download.php?contentType=36&contentId=1685669

Walker, Matthew P.; & Stickgold, Robert. (2006). Sleep, memory, and plasticity. *Annual Review of Psychology, 57,* 139–166.

Wallace, B. Alan. (2009). *Mind in the balance: Meditation in science, Buddhism, and Christianity.* New York: Columbia University.

Waller, Bridget M.; Cray, James J., Jr.; & Burrows, Anne M. (2008). Selection for universal facial emotion *Emotion, 8,* 435–439.

Walter, Marc; Gunderson, John G.; Zanarini, Mary C.; Grilo, Carlos M.; Morey, Leslie C.; Stout, Robert L.; Skodol, Andrew E.; Yen, Shirley; McGlashan, Thomas H.; & Sanislow, Charles A. (2009). New onsets of substance use disorders in borderline personality disorder over 7 years of follow-ups: Findings from the Collaborative Longitudinal Personality Disorders Study. *Addiction, 104,* 97–103.

Walton, Gregory M.; & Cohen, Geoffrey L. (2003). Stereotype lift. *Journal of Experimental Social Psychology, 39,* 456–467.

Walton, Gregory M.; & Spencer, Scott J. (2009). Latent ability: Grades and test scores systematically underestimate the intellectual ability of negatively stereotyped students. *Psychological Science, 20,* 1132–1139.

Walton, Kenneth G.; Schneider, Robert H.; Nidich, Sanford I.; Salerno, John W.; Nordstrom, Cheryl K.; & Merz, C. Noel Bairey. (2002). Psychosocial stress and cardiovascular disease, part 2: Effectiveness of the Transcendental Meditation program in treatment and prevention. *Behavioral Medicine, 28,* 106–123.

Wampold, Bruce E. (2001). *The great psychotherapy debate: Models, methods, and findings.* Mahwah, NJ: Erlbaum.

Wanek, James E.; Sackett, Paul R.; & Ones, Deniz S. (2003). Towards an understanding of integrity test similarities and differences: An item-level analysis of seven tests. *Personnel Psychology, 56,* 873–894.

Wang, Gene-Jack; Volkow, Nora D.; Logan, Jean; Pappas, Naomi R.; Wong, Christopher T.; Zhu, W.; Netusil, Noelwah; & Fowler, Joanna S. (2001). Brain dopamine and obesity. *Lancet, 357,* 354–357.

Wang, Gene-Jack; Volkow, Nora D.; Thanos, Panayotis K.; & Fowler, Joanna S. (2004). Similarity between obesity and drug addiction as assessed by neurofunctional imaging: A concept review. *Journal of Addictive Diseases, 23,* 39–53.

Wang, Philip S.; Lane, Michael; Olfson, Mark; Pincus, Harold A.; Wells, Kenneth B.; & Kessler, Ronald C. (2005). Twelve-month use of mental health services in the United States: Results from the National Comorbidity Survey Replication. *Archives of General Psychiatry, 62,* 629–640.

Wang, Qi. (2001). Culture effects on adults' earliest childhood recollection and self-description: Implications for the relation between memory and the self. *Journal of Personality and Social Psychology, 81,* 220–223.

Wang, Qi. (2006). Earliest recollections of self and others in European American and Taiwanese young adults. *Psychological Science, 17,* 708–714.

Wang, Qi. (2007). "Remember when you got the big, big bulldozer?" Mother-child reminiscing over time and across cultures. *Social Cognition, 25,* 455–471.

Wang, Qi. (2008). Being American, being Asian: The bicultural self and autobiographical memory in Asian Americans. *Cognition, 107,* 743–751.

Wang, Shuang; & Zhao, Hongyu. (2007). Sample size needed to detect gene-gene interactions using linkage analysis. *Annals of Human Genetics, 71,* 828–842.

Wang, Su-hua; Baillargeon, Renée; & Paterson, Sarah. (2005). Detecting continuity violations in infancy: A new account and new evidence from covering and tube events. *Cognition, 95,* 129–173.

Ward, Colleen; & Rana-Deuba, Arzu. (1999). Acculturation and adaptation revisited. *Journal of Cross-Cultural Psychology, 30*(4), 422–442.

Wargo, Eric. (2008). The many lives of superstition. *APS Observer, 21,* 18–24.

Warner, Leah R.; & Shields, Stephanie A. (2007). The perception of crying in women and men: Angry tears, sad tears, and the "right way" to cry. In Ursula Hess & Pierre Philippot (Eds.), *Group dynamics and emotional expression.* New York: Cambridge University Press.

Wasserman, Edward A.; & Zentall, Thomas R. (2006). *Comparative cognition: Experimental explorations of animal intelligence.* New York: Oxford University Press.

Watanabe, Akira; Nakao, Kazuhisa; & Tokuyama, Madoka. (2005, April). Prediction of first episode of panic attack among white-collar workers. *Psychiatry and Clinical Neurosciences, 59*(2), 119–126.

Watson, Jeanne C. (2002). Re-visioning empathy. In David J. Cain & Julius Seeman (Eds.), *Humanistic psychotherapies: Handbook of research and practice.* Washington, DC: American Psychological Association.

Watson, John B. (1913). Psychology as the behaviorist views it. *Psychological Review, 20,* 158–177.

Watson, John B. (1916). The place of the conditioned-reflex in psychology. *Psychological Review, 23,* 89–116.

Watson, John B. (1919). A schematic outline of the emotions. *Psychological Review, 26,* 165–196.

Watson, John B. (1924/1970). *Behaviorism.* New York: Norton.

Watson, John B. (1930). *Behaviorism* (Rev. ed.). Chicago: University of Chicago Press.

Watson, John B.; & Rayner, Rosalie. (1920/2000). Conditioned emotional reactions. *Journal of Experimental Psychology, 3,* 1–14. (Reprinted March 2000: *American Psychologist, 55*[3], 313–317)

Watson, Stuart; Chilton, Roy; & Fairchild, Helen. (2006). Association between childhood trauma and dissociation among patients with borderline personality disorder. *Australian and New Zealand Journal of Psychiatry, 40*(5), 478–481.

Wayment, Heidi A. (2004). It could have been me: Vicarious victims and disaster-focused distress. *Personality and Social Psychology Bulletin, 30*(4), 515–528.

Weaver, Terri E.; & George, Charles F. P. (2005). Cognition and performance in patients with obstructive sleep apnea. In Meir H. Kryger, Thomas Roth, & William C. Dement (Eds.), *Principles and practice of sleep medicine* (4th ed.). Philadelphia: Elsevier Saunders.

Webb, Katie; & Davey, Graham C. L. (1993). Disgust sensitivity and fear of animals: Effect of exposure to violent or revulsive material. *Anxiety, Coping and Stress, 5,* 329–335.

Wechsler, David. (1944). *The measurement of adult intelligence* (3rd ed.). Baltimore: Williams & Wilkins.

Wechsler, David. (1977). *Manual for the Wechsler Intelligence Scale for Children* (Rev.). New York: Psychological Corporation.

Wechsler, Henry; Lee, Jae Eun; Kuo, Meichun; Seibring, Mark; Nelson, Toben F.; & Lee, Hang. (2002). Trends in college binge drinking during a period of increased prevention efforts: Findings for 4 Harvard School of Public Health College Alcohol Study Surveys: 1993–2001. *Journal of American College Health, 50,* 203–217.

Weems, Carl; & Silverman, Wendy. (2008). Anxiety disorders. In Theodore P. Beauchaine & Stephen P. Hinshaw (Eds.), *Child and adolescent psychopathology* (pp. 447–476). Hoboken, NJ: Wiley.

Weinberger, Daniel R. (1995, June). Quoted in Joel L. Swerdlow, "Quiet miracles of the brain." *National Geographic, 187,* 2–41.

Weindruch, Richard. (1996). Caloric restriction and aging. *Scientific American, 274,* 46–52.

Weiner, Bernard. (1985). An attributional theory of achievement motivation and emotion. *Psychological Review, 92,* 548–573.

Weinstein, Lissa N.; Schwartz, David G.; & Arkin, Arthur M. (1991). Qualitative aspects of sleep mentation. In Steven J. Ellman & John S. Antrobus (Eds.), *The mind in sleep: Psychology and psychophysiology* (2nd ed.). New York: Wiley.

Weintraub, Michael I.; Wolfe, Gil I.; Barohn, Richard A.; Cole, Steven P.; Parry, Gareth J.; Hayat, Ghazala; & others. (2003). Static magnetic field therapy for symptomatic diabetic neuropathy: A randomized, double-blind, placebo-controlled trial. *Archives of Physical Medicine and Rehabilitation, 84,* 736–746.

Weisberg, Robert W. (1988). Problem solving and creativity. In Robert J. Sternberg (Ed.), *The nature of creativity.* New York: Cambridge University Press.

Weisberg, Robert W. (1993). *Creativity: Beyond the myth of genius.* New York: Freeman.

Weiss, Alexander; Bates, Timothy C.; & Luciano, Michelle. (2008, March). Happiness is a personal(ity) thing: The genetics of personality and well-being in a representative sample. *Psychological Science, 19*(3), 205–210.

Weissman, Daniel H.; & Banich, Marie T. (2000). The cerebral hemispheres cooperate to perform complex but not simple tasks. *Neuropsychology, 14,* 41–59.

Weissman, Myrna M.; Markowitz, John C.; & Klerman, Gerald L. (2000). *Comprehensive guide to interpersonal psychotherapy.* New York: Basic Books.

Weisz, Carolyn; & Jones, Edward E. (1993). Expectancy disconfirmation and dispositional inference: Latent strength of target-based and category-based expectancies. *Personality and Social Psychology Bulletin, 19,* 563–573.

Welles-Nystrom, Barbara. (2005). Co-sleeping as a window in Swedish culture: Considerations of gender and health care. *Scandinavian Journal of Caring Sciences, 19,* 354–360.

Wells, Gary L.; & Loftus, Elizabeth F. (2003). Eyewitness memory for people and events. In Alan M. Goldstein (Ed.), *Handbook of psychology: Vol. 11. Forensic psychology* (pp. 149–160). New York: Wiley.

Werker, Janet; & Desjardins, Renee. (1995). Listening to speech in the 1st year of life: Experiential influences on phoneme production. *Current Directions in Psychological Science, 4,* 76–81.

Werner, John S.; Pinna, Baingio; & Spillman, Lothar. (2007, March). Illusory color and the brain. *Scientific American, 296,* 90–95.

Wertheimer, Max. (1912/1965). Experimentelle Studien über das Sehen von Bewegung. *Zeitschrift für Psychologie, 61,* 162–163, 221–227. (Portions of original publication translated and reprinted in Richard J. Herrnstein & Edwin G. Boring [Eds.], *A source book in the history of psychology* [Don Cantor, Trans.]. Cambridge, MA: Harvard University Press)

Wertsch, James V.; & Tulviste, Peeter. (1992). L. S. Vygotsky and contemporary developmental psychology. *Developmental Psychology, 28,* 548–557.

West, Anne E.; Griffith, Eric C.; & Greenberg, Michael E. (2002). Regulation of transcription factors by neuronal activity. *Nature Reviews Neuroscience, 3,* 921–931.

Westen, Drew. (1990). Psychoanalytic approaches to personality. In Lawrence A. Pervin (Ed.), *Handbook of personality: Theory and research.* New York: Guilford Press.

Westen, Drew. (1998). The scientific legacy of Sigmund Freud: Toward a psychodynamically informed psychological science. *Psychological Bulletin, 124,* 333–371.

Westen, Drew; Weinberger, Joel; & Bradley, Rebekah. (2007). Motivation, decision making, and consciousness: From psychodynamics to subliminal priming and emotional constraint satisfaction. In Philip David Zelazo, Morris Moscovitch, & Evan Thompson (Eds.), *The Cambridge handbook of consciousness.* New York: Cambridge University Press.

Wester, William C., II. (2007). Hypnotic treatment of habit disorders. In William C. Wester II & Laurence I. Sugarman, (Eds), *Therapeutic hypnosis with children and adolescents.* Norwalk, CT: Crown House.

Wethington, Elaine; McLeod, Jane D.; & Kessler, Ronald C. (1987). The importance of life events for explaining sex differences in psychological distress. In Rosalind C. Barnett, Lois Biener, & Grace K. Baruch (Eds.), *Gender and stress.* New York: Free Press.

Wheeler, Mark E.; Petersen, Steven E.; & Buckner, Randy L. (2000). Memory's echo: Vivid remembering reactivates sensory-specific cortex. *Proceedings of the National Academy of Sciences, USA, 97,* 11125–11129.

White, Geoffrey M. (1994). Affecting culture: Emotion and morality in everyday life. In Shinobu Kitayama & Hazel Rose Markus (Eds.), *Emotion and culture: Empirical studies of mutual influence.* Washington, DC: American Psychological Association.

White, Robert W. (1959). Motivation reconsidered: The concepts of competence. *Psychological Review, 66,* 297–333.

Whiten, Andrew. (2009). The identification and differentiation of culture in chimpanzees and other animals: From natural history to diffusion experiments. In Kevin N. Leland & Bennett G. Galef (Eds.), *The question of animal culture.* Cambridge, MA: Harvard University Press.

Whiten, Andrew; Spiteri, Antoine; Horner, Victoria; Bonnie, Kristin E.; Lambeth, Susan P.; Schapiro, Steven J.; & de Waal, Frans B. M. (2007). Transmission of multiple traditions within and between chimpanzee groups. *Current Biology,* 17, 1038–1043.

Whorf, Benjamin L. (1956). Science and linguistics. In J. B. Carroll (Ed.), *Language, thought, and reality: Selected papers of Benjamin Lee Whorf.* Cambridge, MA: MIT Press.

Wijndaele, Katrien; Matton, Lynn; & Duvigneaud, Nathalie. (2007, July). Association between leisure time physical activity and stress, social support and coping: A cluster-analytical approach. *Psychology of Sport and Exercise, 8*(4), 425–440.

Wilcoxon, Hardy C.; Dragoin, William B.; & Kral, Paul A. (1971). Illness-induced aversions in rat and quail: Relative salience of visual and gustatory cues. *Science, 171,* 826–828.

Wilder, David A.; Chen, Liyu; Atwell, Julie; Pritchard, Josh; & Weinstein, Phillip. (2006). Brief functional analyses and treatment of tantrums associated with transitions in preschool children. *Journal of Applied Behavior Analysis, 39,* 103–107.

Wester, William C. III, & Sugarman, Laurence I. (Eds). (2007). *Therapeutic hypnosis with children and adolescents.* Norwalk, CT: Crown House.

Williams, Mark; Teasdale, John; Segal, Zindel; & Kabat-Zinn, Jon. (2007). *The mindful way through depression: Freeing yourself from chronic unhappiness.* New York: Guilford Press.

Williams, Martin H. (1992). Exploitation and inference: Mapping the damage from therapist-patient sexual involvement. *American Psychologist, 47,* 412–421.

Williams, Nigel M.; O'Donovan, Michael C.; & Owen, Michael J. (2005). Is the dysbindin *(DTNBP1)* a susceptibility gene for schizophrenia? *Schizophrenia Bulletin, 31,* 800–805.

Willinger, Marian; Ko, Chia-Wen; Hoffman, Howard J.; Kessler, Ronald C.; & Corwin, Michael J. (2003). Trends in infant bed sharing in the United States, 1993–2000: The National Infant Sleep Position Study. *Archives of Pediatrics and Adolescent Medicine, 157,* 43–49.

Willis, Janine; & Todorov, Alexander. (2005). First impressions: Making up your mind after a 100-ms exposure to a face. *Psychological Science, 17,* 592–598.

Willis, Sherry L.; Tennstedt, Sharon L.; Marsiske, Michael; Ball, Karlene; Elias, Jeffrey; Koepke, Kathy Mann; Rebok, George W.; Unversagt, Frederick W.; Stoddard, Anne W.; & Wright, Elizabeth. (2006). Long-term effects of cognitive training on everyday functional outcomes in older adults. *Journal of the American Medical Association, 296,* 2805–2814.

Wills, Frank. (2009). *Beck's cognitive therapy: Distinctive features.* New York: Routledge.

Wilson, G. Terence; & Fairburn, Christopher G. (2007). Treatments for eating disorders. In Peter E. Nathan & Jack M. Gorman (Eds.), *A guide to treatments that work* (3rd ed., pp. 579–609). New York: Oxford University Press.

Wilson, Timothy D.; & Dunn, Elizabeth W. (2004). Self-knowledge: Its limits, value, and potential for improvement. *Annual Review of Psychology, 55,* 493–518.

Windholz, George. (1990). Pavlov and the Pavlovians in the laboratory. *Journal of the History of the Behavioral Sciences, 26,* 64–73.

Windle, Michael; & Windle, Rebecca C. (2001). Depressive symptoms and cigarette smoking among middle adolescents: Prospective associations and intrapersonal and interpersonal influences. *Journal of Consulting and Clinical Psychology, 69,* 215–226.

Winemiller, Mark H.; Billow, Robert G.; Laskowski, Edward R.; & Harmsen, W. Scott. (2005, September). Effect of magnetic vs shammagnetic insoles on nonspecific foot pain in the workplace: A randomized, double-blind, placebo-controlled trial. *Mayo Clinic Proceedings, 80,* 1138–1145.

Wink, Paul. (2006). Who is afraid of death? Religion, spirituality, and death anxiety. *Journal of Religion Spirituality and Aging, 18,* 93–110.

Winkelman, John W. (2006). Sleep-related eating disorder and night eating syndrome: Sleep disorders, eating disorders, or both? *Sleep, 29,* 876–877.

Winkler, Connie. (2006, September). Job tryouts go virtual: Online job simulations provide sophisticated candidate assessments. *HR Magazine, 51.*

Winston, Joel S.; O'Doherty, John; Kilner, James M.; Perrett, David I.; & Dolan, Raymond J. (2007). Brain systems for assessing facial attractiveness. *Neuropsychologia, 45,* 195–206.

Wirth, James H; & Bodenhausen, Galen V. (2009). The role of gender in mental-illness stigma: A national experiment. *Psychological Science, 20*(2), 169–173.

Wise, Deborah; & Rosqvist, Johan. (2006). Explanatory style and well-being. In Jay C. Thomas, Daniel L. Segal, & Michel Hersen (Eds.), *Comprehensive handbook of personality and psychopathology. Vol. 1: Personality and everyday functioning* (pp. 285–305). Hoboken, NJ: Wiley.

Wixted, John T. (2004). The psychology and neuroscience of forgetting. *Annual Review of Psychology, 55,* 235–269.

Woerle, Sandra; Roeber, Jim; & Landen, Michael G. (2007). Prevalence of alcohol dependence among excessive drinkers in New Mexico. *Alcoholism: Clinical and Experimental Research, 31,* 293–298.

Wohlschläger, Andreas; & Wohlschläger, Astrid. (1998). Mental and manual rotation. *Journal of Experimental Psychology: Human Perception and Performance, 24,* 397–412.

Wolman, David. (2005, November 5). The secrets of human handedness. *New Scientist,* issue 2524, p. 36.

Wolpe, Joseph. (1958). *Psychotherapy by reciprocal inhibition.* Stanford, CA: Stanford University Press.

Wolpe, Joseph. (1982). *The practice of behavior therapy.* New York: Pergamon Press.

Women's Sports Foundation. (2005). Title IX: Questions and answers. Retrieved March 1, 2005, from http://www.womenssportsfoundation.org/ Issues-And-Research/ Title-IX/What-is-Title-IX.aspx

Wonderlic, Charles. (2005). Pre-employment testing and employee selection. Retrieved December 7, 2009, from furninfo.com

Wonderlic, E. F. (1998). *Wonderlic personnel test manual.* Libertyville, IL: Wonderlic.

Wong, Paul T. P.; & Wong, Lilian C. J. (Eds.). (2006). *Handbook of multicultural perspectives on stress and coping.* New York: Springer.

Woo, Stephanie M.; & Keatinge, Carolyn. (2008). *Diagnosis and treatment of mental disorders across the lifespan.* Hoboken, NJ: Wiley.

Woo, Tsung-Ung W.; Canuso, Carla M.; Wojcik, Joanne D.; Brunette, Mary F.; & Green, Alan I. (2009). Treatment of schizophrenia. In Alan F. Schatzberg & Charles B. Nemeroff (Eds.), *The American Psychiatric Publishing textbook of psychopharmacology* (4th ed.), pp. 1135–1169. Washington, DC: American Psychiatric Publishing.

Wood, Jeffrey J.; & Repetti, Rena L. (2004). What gets Dad involved? A longitudinal study of change in parental child caregiving involvement. *Journal of Family Psychology, 18,* 237–249.

Wood, Robert; & Bandura, Albert. (1991). Social cognitive theory of organizational management. In Richard M. Steers & Lyman W. Porter (Eds.), *Motivation and work behavior.* New York: McGraw-Hill.

Wood, Wendy; Rhodes, Nancy; & Bick, Michael. (1995). Working knowledge and attitude strength: An information processing analysis. In Richard E. Petty & Jon A. Krosnick (Eds.), *Attitude strength: Antecedents and consequences.* Hillsdale, NJ: Erlbaum.

Woods, Stephen C.; Schwartz, Michael W.; Baskin, Denis G.; & Seeley, Randy J. (2000). Food intake and the regulation of body weight. *Annual Review of Psychology, 51,* 255–277.

Woodworth, Robert S. (1918). *Dynamic psychology.* New York: Columbia University Press.

Woodworth, Robert S. (1921). *Psychology: A study of mental life.* New York: Holt.

Woody, Robert Henley. (2008). The evolution and modern practice of interpersonal process family therapy, *American Journal of Family Therapy, 36,* 99–106.

Workman, Lance; & Reader, Will. (2008). *Evolutionary psychology: An introduction.* New York: Cambridge University Press.

World Health Organization. (2001, February 6). *Nutrition data banks: Global database on obesity and body mass index (BMI) in adults.* Retrieved May 25, 2001, from http://www.who.int/nut/dbbmi.htm

World Health Organization. (2009). Global strategy on diet, physical activity, and health. Retrieved May 19, 2009, from http://www.who.int/dietphysicalactivity/publications/facts/obesity/en/

WorldatWork. (2008–2009). WorldatWork survey finds telework on the rise in the U.S., Canada: Analysis of employee retention practices shows some cross-border differences. Retrieved December 7, 2009, from http://www.worldatwork.org/waw/adimLink?id=28062

Worthman, Carol M.; & Brown, Ryan A. (2007). Companionable sleep: Social regulation of sleep and cosleeping in Egyptian families. *Journal of Family Psychology, 21,* 124–135.

Wray, Gregory A., & Babbitt, Courtney C. (2009). Enhancing gene regulation. *Science, 321,* 1300–1301.

Wright, Jesse H.; Turkington, Douglas; Kingdon, David G.; & Basco, Monica Ramirez. (2009). *Cognitive-behavior therapy for severe*

mental illness: An illustrated guide. Washington, DC: American Psychiatric Publishing.

Wu, Li-Tzy; & Anthony, James C. (1999). Tobacco smoking and depressed mood in late childhood and early adolescence. *American Journal of Public Health, 89,* 1837–1840.

Wundt, Wilhelm. (1874/2001). *Grundz_uge der physiologischen Psychologie* [Principles of physiological psychology], 5th ed. Leipzig, Germany: Engelmann. (English version published by Macmillan, New York, 1904)

Wyatt, Tristram D. (2009). Fifty years of pheromones. *Nature, 457,* 262–263.

Wynne, Lyman C.; Tienari, Pekka; & Nieminen, P. (2006, December). Genotype-environment interaction in the schizophrenia spectrum: Genetic liability and global family ratings in the Finnish adoption study. *Family Process, 45*(4), 419–434.

Yalom, Irvin D. (2005). *The theory and practice of group psychotherapy* (5th ed.). New York: Basic Books.

Yamaguchi, Susumu; & Ariizumi, Yukari. (2006). Close interpersonal relationships among Japanese: Amae as distinguished from attachment and dependence. In Uichol Kim, Kuo-Shu Yang, & Kwang-Kuo Hwang (Eds.), *Indigenous and cultural psychology: Understanding people in context*. New York: Springer Science + Business Media.

Yarnell, Phillip R.; & Lynch, Steve. (1970, April 25). Retrograde memory immediately after concussion. *Lancet, 1,* 863–865.

Ybarra, Oscar. (2002). Naive causal understanding of valenced behaviors and its implications for social information processing. *Psychological Bulletin, 128,* 421–441.

Yeung, Nai Chi Jonathan; & von Hippel, Courtney. (2008). *Accident Analysis and Prevention, 40,* 667–674.

Yoo, Seung-Schik; Gujar, Ninad; Hu, Peter; Jolesz, Ferenc A.; & Walker, Matthew P. (2007). The human emotional brain without sleep: A prefrontal-amygdala disconnect. *Current Biology, 17,* 877–878.

Yoshida, Keiko; & Kiritani, Shigeru. (2006). Developmental changes in perception of speech sounds. *Japanese Psychological Review, 49,* 215–225.

Yoshizaki, Kazuhito; Weissman, Daniel H.; & Banich, Marie T. (2007). A hemispheric division of labor aids mental rotation. *Neuropsychology, 21,* 326–336.

Young, Michael W. (2000, March). The tick-tock of the biological clock. *Scientific American, 282*(3), 64–71.

Yudofsky, Stuart C. (2009). Contracting schizophrenia: Lessons from the influenza epidemic of 1918–1919. *Journal of the American Medical Association, 301*(3), 324–326.

Zajonc, Robert B. (1998). Emotions. In Daniel T. Gilbert, Susan T. Fiske, & Gardner Lindzey (Eds.), *Handbook of social psychology* (4th ed.). New York: McGraw-Hill.

Zajonc, Robert B. (2000). Feeling and thinking: Closing the debate over the independence of affect. In Joseph F. Forgas (Ed), *Feeling and thinking: The role of affect in social cognition*. New York: Cambridge University Press.

Zajonc, Robert B. (2001). Mere exposure: A gateway to the subliminal. *Current Directions in Psychological Science, 10,* 224–228.

Zandstra, Elizabeth H.; de Graaf, Cees; & van Trijp, Hans C. M. (2000). Effects of variety and repeated in-home consumption on product acceptance. *Appetite, 35,* 113–119.

Zandy, Amy. (2007, July/August). If you want to lead, learn to serve. *Debt Cubed*. Retrieved September 15, 2008, from http://www.debt3online.com/?page=article&article_id=189

Zebrowitz, Leslie A. (2006). Finally, faces find favor. *Social Cognition, 24,* 657–701.

Zebrowitz, Leslie A.; & Montepare, Joann M. (2005). Appearance DOES matter. *Science, 308,* 1565–1566.

Zebrowitz, Leslie A.; & Montepare, Joann M. (2006). The ecological approach to person perception: Evolutionary roots and contemporary offshoots. In Mark Schaller, Jeffry A. Simpson, & Douglas T. Kenrick (Eds.), *Evolution and social psychology* (pp. 81–113). Madison, CT: Psychosocial Press.

Zeidner, Moshe; Roberts, Richard D.; & Matthews, Gerald. (2008). The science of emotional intelligence: Current consensus and controversies. *European Psychologist, 13,* 64–78.

Zeki, Semir. (2001). Localization and globalization in conscious vision. *Annual Review of Neuroscience, 24,* 57–86.

Zelinski, Elizabeth M.; & Kennison, Robert F. (2007). Not your parents' test scores: Cohort reduces psychometric aging effects. *Psychology and Aging, 22*(3), 546–557.

Zeman, Adam. (2005). Tales from the temporal lobes. *New England Journal of Medicine, 352,* 119–121.

Zentall, Thomas R. (2003). Imitation by animals: How do they do it? *Current Directions in Psychological Science, 12,* 91–95.

Zernicke, Kate. (2004, August 7). At abuse hearing, no testimony that G.I.'s acted on orders. *The New York Times*. Retrieved August 7, 2004, from http://www.nytimes.com/2004/08/07/international/middleeast/07abuse.html

Zhang, Xue-Jun; He, Ping-Ping; Liang, Yan-Hua; Yang, Sen; Yuan, Wen-Tao; Xu, Shie-Jie; & Huang, Wei. (2004). A gene for freckles maps to chromosome 4q32-q34. *Journal of Investigative Dermatology, 122,* 286–290.

Zimbardo, Philip G. (2000a). Prologue: Reflections on the Stanford Prison Experiment: Genesis, transformations, consequences. In Thomas Blass (Ed.), *Obedience to authority: Current perspectives on the Milgram paradigm*. Mahwah, NJ: Erlbaum.

Zimbardo, Philip G. (2000b, September/October). Quoted in Christina Maslach, "Emperor of the edge." *Psychology Today*. Retrieved September 29, 2008, from http://www.psychologytoday.com/articles/pto-20000901-000032.html

Zimbardo, Philip G. (2004a). A situationist perspective on the psychology of evil: Understanding how good people are transformed into perpetrators. In Arthur G. Miller (Ed.), *The social psychology of good and evil*. New York: Guilford Press.

Zimbardo, Philip G. (2004b, May 9). Power turns good soldiers into "bad apples." *Boston Globe*. Retrieved December 5, 2005, from http://www.boston.com/news/globe/editorial_opinion/oped/articles/2004/05/09/power_turns_good_soldiers_into_bad_apples.html

Zimbardo, Philip G. (2005, January 19). You can't be a sweet cucumber in a vinegar barrel: A talk with Philip Zimbardo. *Edge: The Third Culture*. Retrieved October 8, 2005, from http://www.edge.org/3rd_culture/zimbardo05_index.html

Zimbardo, Philip. (2007). *The Lucifer effect: Understanding how good people turn evil*. New York: Random House.

Zimbardo, Philip G.; Banks, W. Curtis; Haney, Craig; & Jaffe, David. (1973, April 8). The mind is a formidable jailer: A Pirandellian prison. *The New York Times Magazine,* pp. 38ff.

Zimbardo, Philip G.; & Leippe, Michael R. (1991). *The psychology of attitude change and social influence*. New York: McGraw-Hill.

Zimbardo, Philip G.; Weisenberg, Matisyohu; Firestone, Ira; & Levy, Burton. (1965). Communicator effectiveness in producing public conformity and private attitude change. *Journal of Personality, 33,* 233–256.

Zimmer-Gembeck, Melanie J.; & Gallaty, Karen J. (2006). Hanging out or hanging in?: Young females' socioemotional functioning and the changing motives for dating and romance. In Alexandra Columbus (Ed.), *Advances in psychology research* (pp. 87–112). Hauppauge, NY: Nova Science Publishers.

Zimmerman, Isaiah M. (2008). Interpersonal group psychotherapy. In George Max Saiger, Sy Rubenfeld, & Mary D. Dluhy (Eds.), *Windows into today's group therapy: The National Group Psychotherapy Institute of the Washington School of Psychiatry.* New York: Routledge/Taylor & Francis Group.

Zinbarg, Richard E.; & Griffith, James W. (2008). Behavior therapy. In Jay L. Lebow (Ed), *Twenty-first century psychotherapies: Contemporary approaches to theory and practice.* Hoboken, NJ: Wiley.

Zohar, Dov; Tzischinsky, Orna; Epstein, Rachel; & Lavie, Peretz. (2005). The effects of sleep loss on medical residents' emotional reactions to work events: A cognitive-energy model. *Sleep, 28*, 47–54.

Zola-Morgan, Stuart. (1995). Localization of brain function: The legacy of Franz Joseph Gall (1758–1828). *Annual Review of Neuroscience, 18*, 359–383.

Zosuls, Kristina M.; Ruble, Diane N.; Tamis-LeMonda, Catherine S.; Bornstein, Marc H.; Greulich, Faith K.; & Shrout, Patrick E. (2009). The acquisition of gender labels in infancy: Implications for gender-typed play. *Developmental Psychology, 45,* 688–701.

Zubieta, Jon-Kar; Bueller, Joshua A.; Jackson, Lisa R.; Scott, David J.; Xu, Yanjun; Koeppe, Robert A.; Nichols, Thomas E.; & Stohler, Christian S. (2005). Placebo effects mediated by endogenous opioid activity on opioid receptors. *Journal of Neuroscience, 25,* 7754–7762.

Zucker, Kenneth J.; & Cohen-Kettenis, Peggy T. (2008). Gender identity disorder in children and adolescents. In David L. Rowland & Luca Incrocci (Eds.), *Handbook of sexual and gender identity disorders.* Hoboken, NJ: Wiley.

Zuckerman, Marvin. (1979). *Sensation seeking: Beyond the optimal level of arousal.* Hillsdale, NJ: Erlbaum.

Zuckerman, Marvin. (2007). Sensation seeking and risky behavior. Washington, DC: American Psychological Association.

Zusman, Jose Alberto; Cheniaux, Elie; & de Freitas, Sergio (2007). Psychoanalysis and change: Between curiosity and faith. *International Journal of Psychoanalysis, 88,* 113–125.

Zusne, Leonard; & Jones, Warren H. (1989). *Anomalistic psychology: A study of magical thinking* (2nd ed.). Hillsdale, NJ: Erlbaum.

Zvolensky, Michael J.; & Smits, Jasper A. J. (Eds.). (2008). *Anxiety in health behaviors and physical illness.* New York: Springer.

ILLUSTRATION CREDITS

CHAPTER 1

xlvi Reuters/Christian Hartmann **2** AP Photo/Fabian Bimmer **3** *(top)* Ted Spiegel/Corbis; *(bottom)* Blend Images/Alamy **4** *(top)* Corbis; *(bottom)* Archives of the History of American Psychology, The University of Akron **5** *(top)* Corbis; *(bottom)* Vintage Images/Alamy **6** Corbis **7** *(left)* Wellesley College Archives; *(center)* Archives of the History of American Psychology, The University of Akron; *(right)* Courtesy of the Moorland-Spingarn Research Center, Howard University Archives; *(bottom)* Clark University **8** *(left)* Culver Pictures; *(center)* Underwood & Underwood/Corbis; *(right)* Archives of the History of American Psychology, The University of Akron **9** *(left)* Special Collections, Donald C. Davidson Library/University of California, Santa Barbara; *(right)* Courtesy of Robert D. Farber University Archives at Brandeis University **10** *(top)* Dr. Lu Fan/courtesy Dr. Karyn Frick; *(bottom)* AP Photo/Lenny Ignelzi **11** Wolfgang Kaehler/Corbis **12** *(left)* Corbis/Keren Su; *(right)* Steve Prezant/Corbis **13** Figaro Magahn/Photo Researchers **15** *(top)* Phil Soheili/soheili.eu; *(bottom)* Voisin/Photo Researchers **17** ©The New Yorker Collection 2007 Roz Chast from cartoonbank.com. All rights reserved. **18** Alissa Rosenhaft **19** *(top)* Photofusion Picture Library/Alamy; *(bottom)* APS OBSERVER by APS. Copyright 2008 by Association for Psychological Science. Reproduced with permission of Association for Psychological Science in the format Textbook via Copyright Clearance Center. **20** Copyright ©2009 by the American Psychological Association. Reproduced with permission. **21** Image State/Alamy **22** The Granger Collection, New York **24** ©The New Yorker Collection 2009 Joe Dator from cartoonbank.com. All rights reserved **26** *(top)* Joel Wintermantle/Alamy; *(left)* Paul Almasy/Corbis; *(right)* Jeremy Horner/Corbis **28** Joe Raedle/Getty Images **30** Tim Pannell/Corbis **32** Flonline digitale Bildagentur GmbH/Alamy **33** From the film *Obedience*, distributed by the New York University Film Library **34** Dr. Marcus E. Raichle, Professor of Radiology & Neurology/Washington University School of Medicine **35** *(bottom)* Hippocampus, Vol. 16, 2006, p. 1097. Reprinted with permission of Wiley-Liss, Inc., a subsidiary of John Wiley & Sons, Inc.; *(top)* Reprinted from Current Biology, Vol. 17, Ryu Soojin, Mahler Julia, Acampora Dario, Holzschuh Jochen, Erhardt Simone, Omodei Daniela, Simeone Antonio and Driever Wolfgang, Orthopedia Homeodomain Protein Is Essential for Diencephalic Dopaminergic Neuron Development, p, 8. With permission from Elsevier. **36** Courtesy of Zoo Atlanta **38** Courtesy Psychological Science Journal

CHAPTER 2

42 Nice One Productions/Corbis **44** Panorama Media/Almay **45** Ellisman and Bushong/National Center for Microscopy and Imaging Research **46** Stephen Waxman, Hank Morgan/Photo Researchers **47** Courtesy Tim Murphy and Gil Wier, The University of British Columbia **52** Andreas Rentz/Getty Images **53** Reuters/Corbis **54** *(top)* Tim McGuire/Taxi/Getty Images; *(bottom)* From Cerebral Cortex doi:10.1093/cercor/bhn013,"The Runner's High: Opiodergic Mechanisms in the Human Brain," Boecker, Henning, figure 4, p9. By permission of Oxford University Press. **56** *(top)* PhotoAlto/Frederic Cirou/Getty Images; *(bottom)* Biophoto Associates/Science Source/Photo Researchers **59** Frank Siteman/Stock Boston **60** *(left)* Radius Images/Jupiterimages; *(right)* Image Source/Jupiterimages **61** Stockbyte/Alamy **62** Geoff Tompkinson/SPL/Photo Researchers **63** *(top)* Mary Evans Picture Library/The Image Works; *(bottom)* M. James Nichols & William T. Newsome (1999, December 2). "The neurobiology of cognition." *Nature*, vol. 402, no. 6761 **64** *(top)* Zeta RF/Alamy; *(bottom)* Courtesy of Dr. Arne May, *Nature, 427,* 311–312 (22 January 2004), Neuroplasticity: Changes in grey matter induced by training, Bogdan Draganski, Christian Gaser, Volker Busch, Gerhard Schuierer, Ulrich Boddahn & Arne May **65** *(top)* Martin Schoeller/Corbis Outline; *(bottom)* Photo courtesy Fred H. Gage, The Salk Institute, San Diego **66** Jupiterimages/Photos.com/Alamy **68** *(left to right)* Tracy Kahn/Corbis; DLILLC/Corbis; Photodisc/Punchstock; Grove Pashley/Corbis/Jupiterimages **69** Martin M. Rotker **72** Courtesy of Terence Williams, University of Iowa **73** *(both)* National Library of Medicine Collection **74** *(both)* Courtesy of Dr. William D. Hopkins **75** ©1995 Newsweek, Inc. All rights reserved. Reprinted with permission. Photo by Douglas Levere **76** Courtesy California Institute of Technology **77** Dan McCoy/Rainbow **78** EMEK.net Studios **80** Bryn Alan **81** Courtesy of Dr. Elizabeth Gould/Princeton University **82** Getty Images

CHAPTER 3

86 LWA/Getty Images **88** *(both)* Florence Low **89** Rich Reid/Getty Images **90** JGI/Blend Images/Getty Images **93** John Downer/Planet Earth Pictures **94** Ian M. Butterfield/Alamy **95** Omikron/Science Photo Library **97** Image Source Black/Alamy **99** *Nature Neuroscience*, [2003] Vol 6, No. 9, 915–916. Page 916, Figure 3. "Long term deprivation affects visual perception and cortex." Authors: Ione Fine, Alex R. Wade, Alyssa Brewer, Michael G. May, Daniel F. Goodman, Geoffrey M. Boynton, Brian A. Wandell, & Donald I. A. MacLeod (2003). **100** *(both)* Sue Cunningham Photographic/Alamy **103** G. Brederg/Photo Researchers **104** By permission of Dave Coverly and Creators Syndicate, Inc. **105** *(top)* bickwinkel/Alamy; *(bottom)* Photographed by Krijn van Noordwijk. Supplied courtesy of Lloyd's of London by permission of Ilja Gort. **106** Lennart Nilsson/Bonnier Alba AB/Behold Man; Little, Brown & Company **107** Claire Dubois/Jupiterimages **108** *(top)* Courtesy Noam Sobel; *(bottom)* Whitemann/zefa/Corbis **109** Fox Searchlight/Photofest **111** Photonica **112** BananaStock/Jupiterimages **113** Courtesy of the Authors **114** *(top)* James Warwick/Getty Images; *(bottom)* Courtesy of Trey Hedden/McGovern Institute, MIT **115** *(top)* Bettmann/Corbis; *(bottom)* Fabio Colombini/Animals Animals **116** Dr. Elmar R. Gruber **118** *(top, left)* PhotoDisc; *(top, right)* Dan Chung/Reuters/Corbis; *(bottom, left)* Richard Broadwell/Alamy; *(bottom, right)* Andre Jenny/Alamy **119** *(top)* ©Dan Piraro. Reprinted with special permission of King Features Syndicate; *(bottom)* Julie Houck/Stock Boston **120** *(left)* Mike Caldwell/Tony Stone/Getty Images; *(center)* Superstock; *(right)* Steve McGurry/Magnum Photos **121** Hiroshi Kunoh. Originally published in *3-D Planet*, Cadence Books, San Francisco. Reprinted by permission. **122** *(top)* Florence Low; *(bottom)* Gustoimages/Photo Researchers **123** Joel Meyerowitz **124** Sol Mednick **125** Shay Stevens Photography **126** From Mind Sights by Shepard. ©1990 by Roger N. Shepard. Used with permission of W. H. Freeman and Company. **127** Robert Estall Photo Agency/Alamy **128** *(top)* Courtesy of Goldenpalace.com; *(bottom)* Alyson Aliano **129** Gaetan Bally/Keystone/Corbis **130** Simon Weir/Alamy

CHAPTER 4

134 Pornchai Kittiwongsakul/AFP/Getty Images **136** Phoenix Police Department, Public Records **137** *(top)* moodboard/Corbis; *(bottom)* Alamy **138** Vincent Oliver/Getty Images **139** *(top)* Image Source/Punchstock; *(bottom)* Kieran Doherty/Reuters/Corbis **140** Garo/Phanie/Photo Researchers **141** by Jim Davis copyright 1989 PAWS INC. reprinted with permission from Universal Press Syndicate **142** *(all)* Ted Spagna/Photo Researchers **143** *(top, left)* AP Photo/Vincent Yu; *(top, right)* AP Photo/Douglas Engle; *(bottom, left)* Newscom; *(bottom, right)* AP Photo/Nam Y. Huh **144** AP Photo/Kathy Willens **145** David Lassman/Syracuse Newspapers/The Image Works **146** Reprinted from Yoo, Seung-Schik; Gujar, Ninad; Hu, Peter; Jolesz, Ferenc A.; & Walker, Matthew P. (2007). The human emotional brain without sleep: A prefrontal-amygdala disconnect. *Current Biology, 17*, 877–878. Copyright 2007, with permission from Elsevier. **147** Robert Landau/Corbis **148** Courtesy of Dr. Allen R. Braun, Language Section, National Institute on Deafness and other Communication Disorders, NIH**149** *(top)* ©The New Yorker Collection 2006

Robert Mankoff from cartoonbank.com All rights reserved.; *(bottom)* Bizarro (new) ©Dan Piraro. King Features Syndicate **150** ©The New Yorker Collection Charles Saxon from CartoonBank.com. All rights reserved. **151** AKG/Photo Researchers **152** *(top)* Courtesy of J. Allan Hobson; *(bottom)* Corbis **153** Snodgrass/Photonica **154** ©The New Yorker Collection 2008 Roz Chast from cartoonbank.com. All rights reserved. **155** Rob and Ann Simpson/Visuals Unlimited **156** Joel Deutsch/Slim Films **157** Carol and Mike Werner/Phototake **158** Creative Ventures Unlimited **159** Kyoko Hamada **160** Courtesy of the late Ernest Hilgard, Photo News and Publications Service, Stanford University **161** Juame Gual/age footstock **162** Courtesy of Stephen Kosslyn, Ph.D. and William L. Thompson, Dept. of Psychology, Harvard University **163** David Sutherland/Getty Images **164** R. Davidson/W. M. Keck Laboratory for Functional Brain Imaging and Behavior, University of Wisconsin **165** ©The New Yorker Collection 2008 Mike Twohy from cartoonbank.com. All rights reserved. **166** Reprinted with permission from the American Journal of Psychiatry, Copyright 2002. American Psychiatric Association. Goldstein, Rita Z. & Volkow, Nora D. (2002). Drug addiction and its underlying neurobiological basis: Neuroimaging evidence for the involvement of the frontal cortex. *American Journal of Psychiatry, 159,* 1642–1652. **167** *(top)* Bruce Yuan-Yue Bi/Lonely Planet Images; *(bottom)* AP Photo/Dima Gavrysh, File **168** Jake Schoellkopf/AP Photos **169** Bob Daemmrich/Stock Boston **170** *(top)* Carl De Souza/AFP/Getty Images; *(bottom)* Bettmann/Corbis **171** James Braund/Lonely Planet Images **172** ©The New Yorker Collection 1993 Mort Gerberg from cartoonbank.com All rights reserved. **173** *(top)* The Granger Collection; *(bottom)* Thompson, Paul M.; Hayashi, Kiralee M.; Simon, Sara L.; Lonkon, Edyth D., et al. (2004) Structural abnormalities in the brains of human subjects who use methamphetamine. *Journal of Neuroscience, 24,* 6028–6036. **174** Kal Muller/Woodfin Camp & Associates **175** Jim Wilson/*The New York Times*/Redux **176** *(top)* Arclight/Alamy; *(bottom)* Dr. Liesbeth Reneman, Academisch Medisch Centrum, Universiteit van Amsterdam, Amsterdam, Netherlands **177** Jeff Scheid/Getty Images **178** ©The New Yorker Collection 2006 Barbara Smaller from cartoonbank.com. All rights reserved.

CHAPTER 5

182 Deborah Waters - 35mm/Alamy **185** *(top)* Rick D'Elia/Corbis; *(bottom)* Stock Montage **185** Sovfoto **187** Bizzaro cartoon, Copyright 12/30/02 Kings Features Syndicate **188** *(top)* Banana Stock/Jupiterimages; *(bottom)* ©The New Yorker Collection Roz Chast from cartoonbank.com. All rights reserved. **190** Archives of the History of American Psychology, The University of Akron **191** Archives of the History of American Psychology, The University of Akron **192** *(right)* Gaslight Advertising Archives; *(left)* Duke University, Special Collections Library **193** *(top)* Courtesy of the Authors; *(bottom)* ©1998 CATHY GUISEWITE distributed by Universal Press Syndicate **194** David Bishop/FoodPix/Jupiterimages **195** Courtesy of Dr. Robert Rescorla **196** Darren Bennett/Animals Animals **197** Courtesy John Garcia **198** *(top)* face to face Bildagentur GmbH/Alamy; *(bottom)* Mike Kemp/Rubberball Images/Jupiterimages **199** Stuart Ellins, California State University **200** *(top)* Courtesy of Columbia University; *(bottom)* Yale University Library **201** Bettmann/Corbis **203** *(top)* Non Sequitur ©2008 Wiley Miller. Distributed by Universal Press Syndicate. Reprinted with permission. All rights reserved; *(bottom, left)* Duomo/Corbis; *(bottom, right)* Kay Nietfeld/epa/Corbis **205** Jupiterimages/Banana Stock/Alamy **206** *(top)* AP Photo/Chris Dorst; *(bottom)* ©Baby Blues Partnership. Reprinted with special permission of King Features Syndicate **208** *(top)* Reprinted through the courtesy of the Editors of TIME Magazine ©2008 Time Inc.; *(bottom)* copyright 1996 Washington Post Writers Group **209** *(top)* Time & Life Pictures/Getty Images; *(bottom)* Courtesy of the Authors **210** AP Photo/Gene J. Puskar **212** Jim Bourg/Reuters **213** Archives of the History of American Psychology, The University of Akron **215** *(top)* ©The New Yorker Collection 1994 Sam Gross from cartoonbank.com. All rights reserved; *(bottom)* Courtesy of The Positive Psychology Center **216** Bob Thomas/Stone/Getty Images **217** *(right)* Robert E. Bailey; *(left)* Courtesy of Dr. J. Arthur Gillaspy **219** Lahav, Amir; Saltzman, Elliot; & Schlaug, Gottfried. (2007, January 10). Action representation of sound: Adiomotor recognition network while listening to newly acquired actions. *Journal of Neuroscience, 27,* No. 2, 308–314. Fig. 3 **220** *(top)* Courtesy of Albert Bandura; *(bottom)* Courtesy Albert Bandura, Stanford University **221** Lewis J Houghton/www.lewspics.com **222** THE CW/courtesy Everett Collection **223** Courtesy of Population Communications International/Wencai Audio Video **225** Bill Watterson ©1995 Distributed by Universal Press Syndicate **226** Bizarro (new) ©Dan Piraro. King Features Syndicate

CHAPTER 6

230 Jean Michel Foujols/Getty Images **232** Ariel Skelley/Corbis **233** Wernher Krutein/The Gamma-Liaison Network **234** Courtesy of George Sperling **235** Travis Morisse/The Hutchinson News **237** ©The New Yorker Collection 2007 by Charles Barsotti from cartoonbank.com. All rights reserved. **239** ©The New Yorker Collection 1983 Ed Fisher from cartoonbank.com. All rights reserved. **240** Doug Menuez/Photodisc/Getty Images **241** Dean Conger/Corbis **244** Michael Newman/Photo Edit **245** AP Photo/Mark Baker **246** Courtesy of the Authors **247** AP Photo/The Chapel Hill News, Grant Halverson **248** Bettmann/Corbis **252** Non Sequitur ©2002 Wiley Miller. Distributed by Universal Press Syndicate **253** ©1994 G. B.Trudeau. Universal Press Syndicate **254** Reuters/Corbis **255** *(top)* Courtesy of Elizabeth Loftus; *(bottom, left)* Stuart Franklin/Magnum Photos; *(bottom, right)* Stuart Franklin/Magnum Photos and courtesy of Elizabeth Loftus and Dario Sacchi **256** Brewer, W. F., and Treyens, J. C. (1981). "Role of Schemata in memory for place." *Cognitive Psychology, 23,* Figure 1, pp. 207–230. **257** Michael Newman/Photo Edit **260** ©The New Yorker Collection 1990 Jack Ziegler from cartoonbank.com. All rights reserved. **261** *(top)* Archives of the History of American Psychology, The University of Akron; *(bottom)* APS OBSERVER by APS. ©2008 by Association for Psychological Science. Reproduced with permission of Association for Psychological Science in the format Textbook via Copyright Clearance Center. **262** Courtesy of Mark E. Wheeler, Randy L. Buckner, and Steven E. Petersen **263** Karen Kuehn **264** *(top)* Michael Colicos, UCSD; *(bottom)* Jonathan Daniel/Allsport **265** *(top)* Copyright ©2009 by Suzanne Corkin, reprinted with permission of The Wylie Agency LLC; *(bottom)* Courtesy of Suzanne Corkin **266** *(left)* Bettmann/Corbis; *(center)* Franco Origlia/Getty Images; *(right)* Bettmann/Corbis **268** *(left)* Dr. Paul Thompson, UCLA; *(right)* National Geographic Image Collection/Maggie Steber **269** Karen Kasmauski/Corbis **271** Non Sequitur ©2004 Wiley Miller. Distributed by Universal Press Syndicate. Reprinted with permission. All rights reserved.

CHAPTER 7

274 Sven Torfinn/PANOS **276** Photo courtesy of Arkansas.com **277** Jim Sugar/Corbis **279** Courtesy of Kathleen O'Craven, Rotman Research Institute **280** *(left)* B. G. Thomso/Photo Researchers; *(center)* Frans Lanting/Corbis; *(right)* Peter Guttman/Corbis **281** *(top)* Dan Piraro. Reprinted with special permission of King Features Syndicate; *(bottom)* Bigshots/Getty Images **282** ©The New Yorker Collection 2006 Christopher Weyant from cartoonbank.com. All rights reserved. **283** *(top)* ©The New Yorker Collection 2005 Drew Dernavich from cartoonbank.com. All rights reserved; *(bottom)* ©The New Yorker Collection 2006 Sam Gross from cartoonbank.com. All rights reserved. **285** ©The New Yorker Collection 1983 Leo Cullum from cartoonbank.com. All rights reserved. **286** Dan Joyce/Corbis **288** ©2002, Sidney Harris **289** *(top)* John Birdsall/age footstock; *(bottom, left)* Oswaldo Rivas/Reuters/Corbis; *(bottom, right)* Sign Language Research Lab, University of Haifa. **291** ©Edward Gibson, MIT Brain and Cognitive Sciences **292** *(top)* Gallo Images/Corbis; *(bottom)* www.GreatApeTrust.org **293** ©Arlene Levin-Rowe **294** Archives of the History of American Psychology/The University of Akron **295** *(top)* Archives of the History of American Psychology/The University of Akron; *(bottom)* News Service, Stanford University **296** *(top)* Archives of the History of American Psychology/The University of Akron; *(bottom)* David Young-Wolff/Photo Edit **299** *(both)* Archives of the History of American Psychology, The University of Akron **300** *(top)* Jay Gardner ©2004; *(bottom, left)* John Blaustein/The Gamma-Liaison Network; *(bottom, center)* Clive Brunskill/Getty Images; *(bottom, right)* Eliseo Fernandez/Reuters/Corbis **301** Courtesy Robert Sternberg/Tufts University **302** Standard Parallel, Sets A–E. Copyright ©1998 by NCS Pearson, Inc. Reproduced with permission. All rights reserved. **303** Tyrel Featherston/Ottawa Citizen. Republished by permission. **304** ©The New Yorker Collection 2001 David Sipress from cartoonbank.com. All rights reserved. **305** Digital Vision/Alamy **307** Patrick Frilet/Hemis/Corbis **309** Masaru Goto/Global Compassion.com **310** Commercial Eye/Getty Images **311** Linda A. Cicero/Stanford News Service **312** ©The New Yorker Collection 1998 Leo Cullum from cartoonbank.com. All rights reserved. **313** Wesley Bocxe/The Image Works

CHAPTER 8

316 Reuters/Ian Waldie **319** ©The New Yorker Collection 2002 Barbra Smaller from cartoonbank.com. All rights reserved. **320** Sharon King Grimm **321** Alden Pellett/The Image Works **322** Harlow Primate Laboratory, University of Wisconsin **323** Robert Harding **325** Corbis **326** *(top)* Richard

Eskite Photography, Inc./Jupiterimages; *(bottom)* Remi Banali/Liaison **327** PhotosIndia.com LLC/Alamy **328** Layne Kennedy/Corbis **329** Geech 2/24 ©2001 Jerry Bittle. Distributed by United Feature Syndicate. **331** Courtesy of Dr. Gene-Jack Wang, Brookhaven National Laboratory **332** TIME Magazine ©2009 Time Inc. Reprinted by permission. **333** Frans Lanting/Minden Pictures **334** *(left)* LWA/Dann Tardif/Blend Images/Corbis; *(right)* A. Bartels and S. Zeki, University College London. Originally published in *NeuroReport*, "Neural Basis of Romantic Love," vol. 11, no. 17, pages 3829–3834 (2000) **335** *(left)* Reuters/Catherine Benson; *(right)* Hubert Boesl/dpa/Corbis **336** ©Dan Piraro. Reprinted with special permission of King Features Syndicate **337** AP Photo/Ron Edmonds **338** Angela Jimenez/Getty Images **339** ©The New Yorker Collection 1993 Roz Chast from cartoonbank.com. All rights reserved. **341** Courtesy of Brandeis University **342** ©The New Yorker Collection 2002 Roz Chast from cartoonbank.com. All rights reserved. **343** Courtesy Siemens Foundation **344** *(top)* Reuters/Ian Waldie; *(bottom)* Blend Images/Jupiterimages **345** *(top)* RNT Productions/Corbis; *(bottom)* Charles Darwin, *The Expression of the Emotions in Man and Animals,* Definitive Edition. Paul Ekman (Ed.). New York: Oxford University Press, 1998. **346** amana images inc./Alamy **347** ©Zits Partnership. Reprinted with permission of King Features Syndicate. **348** Crack Palinggi/Reuters/Corbis **349** ©Dan Piraro. Reprinted with special permission of King Features Syndicate **350** *(left)* Westend61/Punchstock; *(right)* PhotoSpin, Inc./Alamy **351** Courtesy of Antonio R. Damasio, Department of Neurology and PET Imaging Center, University of Iowa College of Medicine **352** *(left)* Michael Dick/Animals Animals; *(right)* Alan & Sandy Carey; *(bottom)* Louis Schakel/Michael Kausman/The New York Times Pictures **353** *(top)* Art Wolfe/Photo Researchers; *(bottom)* From Eibl-Eibesfeldt, I. (1970). Ethology: The Biology of Behavior. New York: Holt. Photo courtesy of I. Eibl-Eibesfeldt **354** *(top)* From Matsumoto, D., & Ekman, P. (1989) *Japanese and Caucasian Facial Expressions of Emotion.* JACFEE. Photographs courtesy of Paul Ekman; *(bottom)* Courtesy of Dacher Keltner, Deptartment of Psychology, University of California, Berkeley **356** Corbis **357** ©The New Yorker Collection 2006 Charles Barsotti from cartoonbank.com. All rights reserved. **358** Joel Gordon **359** Corbis Super RF/Alamy **361** ©The New Yorker Collection 1995 Roz Chast from cartoonbank.com. All rights reserved. **362** Jim Davis 9/9/1989 ©GARFIELD 1989 Paws, Inc. Universal Press Syndicate

CHAPTER 9

366 Compassionate Eye Foundation/Ivan Hunter **368** *(all)* Courtesy of Sandy Hockenbury **369** *(top, left)* Comstock Images/Jupiterimages; *(top, right)* Randy Faris/Corbis; *(bottom, left)* Ariel Skelly/Masterfile; *(bottom, right)* John Henley/Corbis **371** Science Photo Library/Photo Researchers **372** Biophoto Associates/Photo Researchers **374** *(all)* Petit Format/Nestle/Science Source/Photo Researchers **376** *(top)* Photographs copyright of Anthony Young from First Glances by Davida Y. Teller, *Journal of Investigative Ophthalmology and Visual Science,* Vol. 38, 1997, pp. 2183–2203; *(bottom, left & right)* Picture Partner/Alamy **377** *(left to right)* Bubbles Photolibrary/Alamy; Image Source/Getty Images; Brand X Pictures/Punchstock; Katie Moss/Jupiterimages; Jupiterimages/BananaStock/Alamy **378** *(top)* Jordan Reeder/Jupiterimages; *(bottom)* Robert Marvin **379** Maria Stenzel/NGS **380** *(top)* Cindy Charles/Photo Edit; *(bottom)* Corbis Premium RF/Alamy **382** Romilly Lockyer/The Image Bank **384** *(top)* Jack Sullivan/Alamy; *(bottom)* 4/5/00 ©2000 Baby Blues partnership. King Features Syndicate **385** *(left)* Brand X Pictures/Jupiterimages; *(right)* Workbook Stock/Jupiterimages; *(bottom)* ©The New Yorker Collection 2008 Liza Donnelly from cartoonbank.com. All rights reserved. **386** Larry Dale Gordon/Getty Images **388** *(top)* Bill Anderson/Photo Researchers; *(bottom)* David Young-Wolff/Photo Edit **389** *(top)* 7/14/94 ©Lynn Johnston Prod. Universal Press Syndicate; *(bottom)* Laura Dwight **390** *(top)* Bill Armstrong; *(bottom)* Jon Feingersh/Jupiterimages **391** Courtesy of Renee Baillargeon, University of Illinois at Urbana-Champaign **393** Sovfoto/Eastfoto **394** Ellen Senisi/The Image Works **395** ©The New Yorker Collection 1995 MIchael Crawford from cartoonbank.com. All rights reserved. **396** ©Zits Partnership. Reprinted with special permission of King Features Syndicate **397** Image courtesy of Paul Thompson, Kiralee Hayashi, Arthur Toga, UCLA/Nitin Gogtay, Jay Giedd, Judy Rapoport/NIMH **398** *(top)* Courtesy of the Authors; *(bottom)* 12/26/00 ©Zits Partnership. King Features Syndicate **399** *(top)* Jeff Greenberg/The Image Works; *(bottom)* Sarah Putnam/The Picture Cube/Index Stock **401** ©The New Yorker Collection 2003 William Haefeli from cartoonbank.com. All rights reserved. **402** *(top)* Lee Lockwood/Time & Life Pictures/Getty Images *(bottom)* Reuters/Will Burgess **403** ©The New Yorker Collection 2004 Danny Shanahan from cartoonbank.com. All rights reserved. **404** Corbis/Jupiterimages **405** 4/30/98 ©1998 Willey Miller. Distributed The Washington Post Writers Group **406** Hill Street Studios/Jupiterimages **407** Kayte M. Deioma/Photo Edit **408** *(top)* ©The New Yorker Collection 2004 David Sipress from cartoonbank.com. All rights reserved; *(bottom)* Kyodo News **409** *(top)* Owen Franken/Corbis; *(bottom)* SHNS photo by Pam Panchak/Pittsburgh Post-Gazette **410** ©Lynn Johnston Productions, Inc. Distributed by United Press Syndicate **412** ©Zits Partnership. Reprinted with special permission of King Features Syndicate

CHAPTER 10

416 Tom Stewart/Corbis **418** Courtesy of Don Hockenbury **419** Tracy Kahn/Corbis **420** Mary Evans/Sigmund Freud Copyrights/Photo Researchers **421** *(top)* Culver Pictures; *(bottom)* Corbis **422** Bill Aron/Photo Edit **423** *(top)* Cathy Guisewite 4/18/95 ©Universal Press Syndicate; *(bottom)* Michael Newman/Photo Edit **424** Tom Stewart/Corbis **426** ©The New Yorker Collection 1995 Tom Cheney from cartoonbank.com. All rights reserved. **427** Lon C. Diehl/Photo Edit **428** Karsh/Woodfin Camp & Associates **429** *(top)* Photofest; *(left)* Courtesy of Dept. of Library Services, American Museum of Natural History. Photo by P. Hollembeak.; *(center)* Courtesy Dharma Publishing; *(right)* Paul Almasy/Corbis **430** Corbis **431** *(top)* Corbis; *(bottom)* Reprinted through the courtesy of the Editors of TIME Magazine ©1999 Time Inc. **432** Corbis **433** Courtesy of Carl Rogers Memorial Library **434** *(top)* ©The New Yorker Collection 1994 Dan Reilly from cartoonbank.com. All rights reserved; *(bottom)* Bill Aron/Photo Edit **435** Jean Michel Turpin/The Gamma-Liaison Network **437** Courtesy of Albert Bandura **438** Myrleen Ferguson Cate/Photo Edit **439** ©The New Yorker Collection 2005 Lee Lorenz from cartoonbank.com. All rights reserved. **441** Courtesy of Mary Cattell **443** *(top)* Courtesy of Dr. Turhan Canali, Stanford University; *(bottom)* Courtesy of Don Hockenbury **444** photo by Jim Bailey/courtesy of Alan and Alvin Chow **445** Myrleen Ferguson Cate/Photo Edit **447** *(left)* Spencer Grant/Photo Edit; *(right)* The Granger Collection, New York **448** 8/15/01 © 2001 United Features Syndicate **449** Lewis J. Merrim/Photo Researchers **452** By Jeremy Scorr and Jim Borgman ©2001 Zits Partnership. King Features Syndicate

CHAPTER 11

456 Digital Vision/Getty Images **459** Janine Wiedel/drr.net **460** ©The New Yorker Collection 2004 Robert Leighton from cartoonbank.com. All rights reserved. **461** *(top)* Robert Brenner\Photo Edit; *(bottom)* Ruby Washington/*The New York Times*/Redux **462** *(top)* Photofest; *(bottom)* Knut Kampe, University College London **464** AP Photo/Tom Gannam, File **465** Reuters/Corbis **467** Samantha Sin/AFP/Getty Images **468** *(top)* Bernard Napthine/Lonely Planet Images; *(bottom)* Courtesy of Zimbardo Collection/©Nila Winter **470** *(top)* ©The New Yorker Collection 2006 Matthew Diffee from cartoonbank.com. All rights reserved; *(bottom)* Reuters/Tim Shaffer **471** Dean Dunson/Corbis **472** 3/19 ©2003 Wiley Miller Distributed By Universal Press Syndicate **473** *(both)* From Sherif, Muzafer; Harvey, O. J.; White, B. Jack; Hood, William R.; & Sherif, Carolyn W. (1961/1988). *The Robbers Cave Experiment: Intergroup Conflict and Cooperation.* Middletown, CT: Wesleyan University Press. **474** Courtesy of The Solomon Asch Center for Study of Ethnopolitical Conflict **475** Kevin Dodge/Corbis **476** Courtesy of CUNY Graduate School and University Center **477** *(top)* From the film *Obedience,* distributed by the New York University Film Library; *(bottom)* Courtesy of Alexandra Milgram **480** From the film *Obedience,* distributed by the New York University Film Library **483** AP Photo/LM Otero **484** *(left)* USHMM, courtesy of Tibor Vince; *(right)* AP Photo/Nasser Nasser, File **485** *(top)* Daily News Pix; *bottom)* Edward Hausner/The New York Times Pictures/Redux **486** *(top)* AP Photo/Al Golub; *(bottom)* Miles Storey **487** Michael Newman/Photo Edit **490** 2/22 ©1999 Bill Amend. Universal Press Syndicate

CHAPTER 12

492 AP Photo/Norfolk Daily News, Darin Epperly **496** *(top)* AP Photo/Carmen Tylor; *(middle)* AP Photo/Paul Hawthorne; *(bottom)* AP Photo/Ed Bailey **497** ©The New Yorker Collection 1999 David Sipress from cartoonbank.com. All rights reserved. **498** Myrleen Ferguson Cate/Photo Edit **500** *(top)* Redlink Production/Corbis; *(bottom)* Courtesy University of California, Berkeley **501** *(left)* AP Photo/Pioneer Press/Scott Takushi; *(right)* ©The New Yorker Collection 2007 Jason Patterson from cartoonbank.com. All rights reserved. **503** Joe Raedle/Getty Images

504 *(top)* AP Photo/Tina Fineberg; *(bottom)* Edgar Fahs Smith Collection, University of Pennsylvania Library **505** *(top)* Custom Medical Stock Photo/Alamy; *(bottom)* ©1974 John Olson/*People* Weekly **506** *(left)* Rubber-Ball/Alamy; *(right)* Omikron/Science Source/Photo Researchers **507** *(top, left)* Courtesy of Robert Ader, photo by James Montanus, University of Rochester; *(top, right)* Courtesy of Nicholas Cohen, University of Rochester; *(bottom)* Courtesy of Janice Kiecolt-Glaser, Ohio State University College of Medicine **508** *Science, 295,* 1737–1740. Petrovic, Predrag; Kalso, Eija; Petersson, Karl M.; and Ingvar, Martin. Placebo and opioid analgesia—Imaging shared neuronal network. **510** Reuters/John Gress **511** *(top)* ©The New Yorker Collection 1990 Roz Chast from cartoonbank.com. All rights reserved.; *(bottom)* AP Photo/Damian Dovarganes **512** 5/11 by Bill Watterson ©1993 Watterson. Distributed by Universal Press Syndicate **513** Steve Prezant/Corbis **514** ©The New Yorker Collection 2000 Joseph Farris from cartoonbank.com. All rights reserved. **515** Dan Habib/Corbis **516** *(top)* Joe Carini/The Image Works; *(bottom)* John Henley/Jupiterimages **517** Andrew Hobbs/Getty Images **518** David Young-Wolff/Photo Edit **519** AP Photo **520** AP Photo/Purwowiyoto **521** ©The New Yorker Collection 2002 Edward Koren from cartoonbank.com. All rights reserved. **522** *(top)* Joshua Griffler; *(bottom)* Imaginechina via AP Images **523** ©The New Yorker Collection 2005 John Jonik from cartoonbank.com. All rights reserved.

CHAPTER 13

528 Ian Hooton/Photo Researchers **531** Gary Larson ©1996 Farworks Inc., Distributed by Creators Syndicate **532** Warner Bros./Courtesy Everett Collection **533** Reprinted with permission from *Diagnostic and Statistical Manual of Mental Disorders,* Fourth Edition, Text Revision. Copyright ©2000 by the American Psychiatric Association. **534** Glowimages/Getty Images **537** ©The New Yorker Collection 2001 Roz Chast from the cartoonbank.com. All rights reserved. **538** Joe Kohen/WireImage for New York Post/Getty Images **539** ©The New Yorker Collection 2004 Roz Chast from cartoonbank.com. All rights reserved. **540** Rob Walls/Alamy **541** *(left)* John Kaprielian/Photo Researchers; *(right)* Punchstock **542** Chris Hondros/Getty Images **543** *(top)* Andy Sewell/Getty Images; *(bottom)* Reprinted from *Health* Magazine **545** Getty Images **546** Frank Micelotta/Getty Images **547** *(top)* Image Source/SuperStock; *(bottom)* Reuters/Brendan McDermid **548** ©1996, American Medical Association from Archives of General Psychiatry, February 1996, Vol. 53. Courtesy of Jeffrey M. Schwartz. **549** Sara Krulwich/*The New York Times*/Redux **550** *(top)* Jeff Greenberg/Photo Edit; *(bottom)* Courtesy of Dr. Elliot A. Stein, Dept. of Psychiatry, Medical College of Wisconsin **552** *(left)* Corbis; *(center)* Corbis; *(right)* Robert Capa/Magnum Photos **554** Annette Schreyer/laif/Redux **555** AP Photo/Charles Sykes **557** ©The New Yorker Collection 1995 Tom Cheney from cartoonbank.com. All rights reserved. **558** AP Photo/Bo Rader, Pool **560** K. McGlynn/The Image Works **561** *(top)* Nicole Bengiveno/*The New York Times*; *(bottom)* John Caldwell **562** AP Photo/John Amis **563** Courtesy of Mental Health Clinical Research Center, University of Iowa **564** *(top)* Courtesy of David Silbersweig, M.D., Emily Stern, M.D., Cornell Medical Center; *(bottom)* A. Ramey/Photo Edit **565** AP Photo/The Daily Press, Dave Bowman **569** Joe McNally/Getty Images **570** Courtesy of Dr. Paul Thompson, Dept. of Neurology, UCLA Lab of Neuro-Imaging & Brain Mapping Division **574** Somos/Veer/Getty Images

CHAPTER 14

578 ©John Birdsall **580** Don Bayley/istockphoto **581** Photo by R. Dylan Thompson **582** *(top)* ©The New Yorker Collection 2007 Robert Mankoff from cartoonbank.com. All rights reserved; *(bottom)* Bettmann/Corbis **583** AP Photo **584** ©Dan Piraro 11/7/1995 distributed by Universal Press Syndicate **585** *(top)* Roger Ressmeyer/Corbis; *(bottom)* Michael Rougier, LIFE Magazine Inc. **586** David Buffington/Getty Images **587** Schulz © UFS Inc. **588** AJ Photo/Photo Researchers **589** *(top)* Larson/Watson Papers, Archives of the History of American Psychology, The University of Akron; *(bottom)* David White/Alamy **591** Hiroko Masuike/*The New York Times*/Redux **593** Photo courtesy of Albert Ellis Institute **595** Photo courtesy of Beck Institute for Cognitive Therapy and Research **596** ©The New Yorker Collection 1996 Leo Cullum from cartoonbank.com. All rights reserved. **597** ©The New Yorker Collection 1996 Charles Barsotti from cartoonbank.com. All rights reserved. **598** ©The New Yorker Collection 2005 Tom Cheney from cartoonbank.com. All rights reserved. **599** Larry Mulvehill/Photo Researchers **600** *(top)* Bruce Ayres/Getty Images; *(bottom)* ©Dan Piraro 1/17/03 distributed by Universal Press Syndicate **601** ©The New Yorker Collection 2008 Paul Noth from cartoonbank.com. All rights reserved. **603** *(top)* Spencer Grant/Photo Edit; *(bottom)* ©The New Yorker Collection 1999 Sidney Harris from cartoonbank.com. All rights reserved. **604** Worth Publishers **606** Steve Liss/The Gamma-Liaison Network **607** *(top, left)* The Granger Collection; *(bottom, left)* Corbis; *(right)* Culver Pictures **608** blickwinkel/Alamy **609** Creative Ventures Unlimited **610** ©The New Yorker Collection 2007 Mick Stevens from cartoonbank.com. All rights reserved. **611** *(top)* Corbis; *(bottom)* AP Photo/Richard Drew **612** Jonathan Nourok/Stone/Getty Images **613** Courtesy of Arthur Brody, M.D., UCLA **614** Ethan Hyman/*Raleigh News & Observer*/Newscom **615** ©The New Yorker Collection 1991 Mike Twohy from cartoonbank.com. All rights reserved. **616** Non Sequitur ©2004 Wiley Miller. Distributed By Universal Press Syndicate. Reprinted with permission. All rights reserved.

APPENDIX A

A-2 ©Dan Piraro. Reprinted with special permission of King Features Syndicate **A-9** ©The New Yorker Collection 1994 Lew Cullum from cartoonbank.com. All rights reserved. **A-14** ©The New Yorker Collection 1989 Leo Cullum from cartoonbank.com. All rights reserved.

APPENDIX B

B-1 NBC/Photofest **B-2** Ralf Finn-Hestoft/CORBIS SABA **B-3** Science Source/Photo Researchers **B-4** Tom Stewart/Corbis **B-7** By permission of John Deering and Creators Syndicate, Inc. **B-8** REUTERS/Jeff Christensen **B-10** AP Photo/Paul Sakuma **B-11** Getty Images/Image Source **B-12** AP Photo/Stanley Leary

NAME INDEX

SUBJECT INDEX